TUTT

Po
Japanese Dictionary

Japanese-English
English-Japanese

Samuel E. Martin

Revised and Updated by
Sayaka Khan & Fred Perry

TUTTLE Publishing

Tokyo | Rutland, Vermont | Singapore

Published by Tuttle Publishing, an imprint of Periplus Editions (HK) L

www.tuttlepublishing.com

ISBN 978-4-8053-1513-2

Distributed by:

North America, Latin America, and Europe
Tuttle Publishing
364 Innovation Drive, North Clarendon,
VT 05759-9436 USA.
Tel: 1 (802) 773-8930; Fax: 1 (802) 773-6993
info@tuttlepublishing.com
www.tuttlepublishing.com

Asia Pacific
Berkeley Books Pte. Ltd.
3 Kallang Sector #04-01
Singapore 349278
Tel: (65) 6741-2178
Fax: (65) 6741-2179
inquiries@periplus.com.sg
www.tuttlepublishing.com

Japan
Tuttle Publishing
Yaekari Building,
3rd Floor, 5-4-12 Osaki,
Shinagawa-ku,
Tokyo 141-0032
Tel: (81) 3 5437-0171
Fax: (81) 3 5437-0755
sales@tuttle.co.jp
www.tuttle.co.jp

27 26 25 24 23 11 10 9 8 7 2303MP
Printed in Singapore

CONTENTS

Samuel E. Martin is the author of numerous books and papers on Japanese and Korean, including the definitive *A Reference Grammar of Japanese* and *A Reference Grammar of Korean*.

Sayaka Khan has a BSC (Biology, 2000) from Waseda University. She has worked as a translator and interpreter for companies in various industries, such as patent offices, science think tank, pharmaceutical firm, film production, game company, etc. She has established a translation corporation with her husband, Afaque Khan.

Fred Perry has a BA (History, 1956) from Yale University as well as an MBA from St Sophia University, Tokyo (1984). He arrived in Japan in 1956, and continues to live there today. He has worked as a market researcher and consultant. Traveling throughout Japan as part of his job has provided the opportunity to learn about the local dialects spoken in different parts of the country.

PART I
JAPANESE – ENGLISH

A

ā **1.** *adv* ああ like that, that way **2.** *interj* ああ oh; yes **3.** *interj* ああ hello (*on encountering someone*)
á *interj* あっ oh!
abakimásu, abaku *v* 暴きます, 暴く discloses
abara-ya *n* あばら屋 hovel
abaremásu, abareru *v* 暴れます, 暴れる rages, storms, rampages
abare-mono *n* 暴れ者 ruffian, roughneck, wild person
abékku *n* アベック young unmarried couple
abekobe *n* あべこべ upside down
abimásu, abiru *v* 浴びます, 浴びる bathes oneself in; douses, showers
abisemásu, abiseru *v* 浴びせます, 浴びせる pours on, showers
abuku *n* あぶく bubble; abuku-zéni *n* あぶく銭 easy money
abunaí *adj* 危ない dangerous (= **kiken (na)** 危険(な)), Watch out!
abunakkashii *adj* 危なっかしい is insecure, unsteady
abunōmaru *adj* アブノーマル abnormal
abura *n* 油 oil, grease
abura *n* 脂 fat (= **shibō** 脂肪)
aburá(a)ge *n* 油揚げ deep-fried bean curd
aburakkói *adj* 油っこい oily, greasy
aburakkói *adj* 脂っこい fatty
aburimásu, abúru *v* 炙ります, 炙る grills
āchi(-gata) *n* アーチ(形) arch (= **yumi-gata** 弓形)
ācherii *n* アーチェリー archery
achí-kochi *adv* あちこち here and there (= **achíra-kóchira** あちらこちら)
achira *pron* あちら **1.** that one (of two) over there, the other one (over there) **2.** over there, yonder **3.** he/him, she/her, they/them
achira-gawa *n* あちら側 that (his/her/their) side, other side
ada *adj* あだ meaningless
ada *n* 仇 [BOOKISH] disservice, foe: **~ o uchimásu** 仇を討ちます avenges, revenges
adana *n* あだ名 nickname
adaputā *n* アダプター (electrical) adapter
adéyaka *adj* 艶やか gorgeous, fascinatingly elegant
adobáisu *n* アドバイス advice
adokenai *adj* あどけない innocent, childlike; adokenai kao *n* あどけない顔 an innocent face
adoresu *n* アドレス address: **mēru-~** メールアドレス e-mail address
adoribu *n* アドリブ ad-lib
aegimásu, aégu *v* 喘ぎます, 喘ぐ gasps, pants (for breath)
aemásu, aéru *v* 和えます, 和える dresses (vegetables, etc.)
aenai *adj* 敢えない tragic, sad:

aénaku mo 敢えなくも tragically enough
áete *v* 敢えて: **áete … (shimásu)** 敢えて…(します) dares (*to do*)
afuremásu, afuréru *v* 溢れます, 溢れる overflows
Afurika *n* アフリカ Africa; Afurika-jin *n* アフリカ人 an African
afutā-sābisu *n* アフターサービス service (*maintenance and repair*), servicing
agakimásu, agaku *v* 足掻きます, 足掻く struggles
agaméru *v* 崇める worships, adores, respects: **kami o ~** 神を崇めます worships [adores] God
agarí *n, adj* 上がり finishing, (*resulting*) finish
agarimásu, agaru *v* 上がります, 上がる **1.** goes up, rises **2.** feels self-conscious, nervous; gets stage fright
agari-guchi, agari-kuchi *n* 上り口 the entrance
...-ágari (no) *adj* …上がり(の) fresh from …, right after …: **yami ~ no hitó** 病み上がりの人 a person just out of sickbed
age-ashi *n* 揚げ足 fault finding
ageku *n* 挙句 negative outcome; ageku no hate 挙句の果て in the end
agemásu, agerú *v* **1.** あげます, あげる gives **2. ...-te agerú** ...てあげる does someone's favor
agemásu, agerú *v* 上げます, 上げる raises up
agemásu, agerú *v* 揚げます, 揚げる fries; raises
ago *n* あご・顎 jaw, chin; ago-hige *n* あごひげ beard, goatee, (chin-) whiskers
agura *n* あぐら sitting cross-legged
áhen *n* アヘン・阿片 opium
ahiru *n* アヒル duck (*tame*)
aho, ahō *n* あほ(う)・阿呆 fool
ái *n* 愛 love (= **aijō** 愛情)
ái *n* 藍 Japanese indigo plant; ái zome *n* 藍染め Japanese indigo dye
aibikí *n* 逢引 secret rendezvous
aibō *n* 相棒 partner
áibu *n* 愛撫 caress
aichaku *n* 愛着 affection
aida *n, prep, adv* 間 interval, space, between; while
aidagara *n* 間柄 relationship (*between people*)
aidéa *n* アイデア idea
aidoku *n* 愛読 reading with pleasure
áidoru *n* アイドル idol
aigo *n* 愛護 [BOOKISH] protection
ai-hanshimásu, ai-hansuru *v* 相反します, 相反する conflicts
aiirenai *adj* 相容れない exclusive, incompatible, irreconcilable
ai-jin *n* 愛人 mistress
aijō *n* 愛情 affection, love (= **ai** 愛)
aikawarazu *adv* 相変わらず as usual/ever/always: **~ génki desu** 相変わらず元気です stays well (as always)
aikí-dō *n* 合気道 aikido, an art of weaponless defense
áiko *n* あいこ(**o-aikó** おあいこ) tie (*in sports, games*), stalemate

aikō-ka *n* 愛好家 lover (*devotee of ...*)
aikoku-shin *n* 愛国心 patriotism
aikotoba *n* 合い言葉 password, shibboleth [INFORMAL talk]
aikyō *n* 愛嬌[愛敬] charm, attractiveness: **~ ga arimásu** 愛嬌[愛敬]があります is nice, attractive, charming
aima *n* 合間 spare time
aimai (na) *adj* 曖昧(な) vague
aimasu, áu *v* 会います, 会う: **... ni ~** ...に会います meets; sees (a person)
aimasu, áu *v* 合います, 合う: **... ni ~** ...に合います matches with: **kuchi ni ~** 口に合います suits one's taste; **(...ni) ma ni ~** (...に) 間に合います is in time (for ...)
...-aimasu, -au/-áu ...合います, 合う [VERB INFINITIVE +] (*to*) each other
ainiku *adv* あいにく unfortunately
ainiku (na) *adj* あいにく(な) regrettable
ainoko *n* あいの子 person of mixed race [IN NEGATIVE SENSE]
ainorí *n* 相乗り ride together
ainote *n* あいの手 short interlude
airashii *adj* 愛らしい lovely, sweet
airon *n* アイロン iron(ing)
Airurándo *n* アイルランド Ireland
áisatsu *n* 挨拶, [HONORIFIC] **go-~** ご挨拶 greeting: **(...) ni ~ shimásu** (...)に挨拶します greets
ai-shimásu, ai-súru *v* 愛します, 愛する (= **ai-su** 愛す) loves
aishō *n* 愛称 nickname
aishō *n* 相性 compatibility, congeniality: **~ ga/no íi** 相性が/のいい congenial, compatible
aisó, aisō *n* あいそ(う)・愛想 **1. aisó (aisō) ga/no íi** あいそ(う)[愛想]が/のいい is amiable, sociable, agreeable **2. o-aiso, o-aisō** お愛想 (*restaurant*) bill, check; incense
aisu... *prefix* アイス... iced...; aisu-kōhii *n* アイスコーヒー iced coffee; aisu-kuriimu *n* アイスクリーム ice cream; aisu-tii *n* アイスティー iced tea
aite *n* 相手 (**o-aite** お相手) the other fellow; companion, partner; adversary, opponent
aitō *n* 哀悼 condolence: mourning: **fukai ~** 深い哀悼 deep mourning
aitsu *pron* あいつ that guy, that creep; aitsú-ra *pron* あいつら those damn ones
aitsúide *adv* 相次いで one after another
aitii (IT) *n* IT(アイティー) information technology (*computer*)
āiu *adj* ああいう ... that kind/sort of ... (= **anna** あんな, **āyū** ああゆう)
aiuchí *n* 相打ち hitting/killing each other at the same time: **~ ni narimásu** 相打ちになります hits/kills each other at the same time
aiúeo *n* あいうえお the Japanese syllabary
áizu *n* 合図 signal, sign

aizúchi *n* 相槌 give responses: **~ o uchimásu** 相槌を打ちます gives responses to make the conversation go smoothly
ají *n* 味 taste; flavor, seasoning: **~ ga shimásu** 味がします it tastes (has flavor); **~ ga usuidesu** 味が薄いです is bland: **~ o oboemásu** 味を覚えます acquires a taste for
áji *n* アジ・鯵 horse mackerel, saurel
Ájia *n* アジア Asia; **Ajiá-jin** *n* アジア人 an Asian
ajike-nái *adj* 味気ない insipid, flavorless, flat
ajiwaimásu, ajiwáu *v* 味わいます, 味わう tastes it
áka *n* 赤 red (*color*); **aka-bō** *n* 赤帽 redcap, porter; **áka-chan** *n* 赤ちゃん・あかちゃん baby; **aká-gai** *n* 赤貝 ark shell, blood(y) clam; **akai** *adj* 赤い red; **aka-jí** *n* 赤字 red letters, deficit figures: **~ ni narimásu** 赤字になります goes/gets in the red; **aka-mi** *n* 赤身 lean (meat/fish); unfatty (red) tuna; **aka-shíngo** *n* 赤信号 red light (*signal*)
aká *n* あか・垢 dirt, grime
akádemii *n* アカデミー academy
akademíkku *n* アカデミック academic
aka-gane *n* あかがね・銅 copper
áka-no-tanin *n* 赤の他人 complete stranger [IN NEGATIVE SENSE]
akaramemásu, akarameru *v* 赤らめます, 赤らめる blushes
akarasama (na/ni) *adj*, *adv* あからさま(な/に) frank(ly), plain(ly), open(ly) [IN NEGATIVE SENSE]
akari *n* 明かり light, lamp
akarui *adj* 明るい bright, light, clear, gay, cheerful
akarumi *n* 明るみ a light place; the (open/bright) light: **~ ni demásu** 明るみに出ます surfaces, is brought to light
akéba *v* 開けば (if it comes open)
ākēdo *n* アーケード arcade, roofed passageway, shopping arcade
akegata *n*, *adv* 明け方 daybreak, dawn
akemáshite o-medetō (gozaimásu [HONORIFIC]**)** *interj* 明けましておめでとう(ございます) Happy New Year!
akemásu, akeru *v* 開けます, 開ける opens it
akemásu, akeru *v* 空けます, 空ける leaves empty, vacates
akemásu, akeru *v* 明けます, 明ける it opens up, (the day/year) begins
áki *n* 秋 autumn, fall; **aki-same** *n* 秋雨 autumn rain
akí- *prefix* 空き empty, vacant; **aki-bako** *n* 空き箱 empty box; **aki-beya** *n* 空き部屋 empty room; **aki-kan** *n* 空き缶 empty can; **aki-shitsu** *n* 空き室 empty room/office; **aki-ya** *n* 空き家 vacant/empty house; **aki-su** *n* あき巣狙い・空き巣 sneak thief
akimásu, akíru *v* 飽きます, 飽きる wearies (*gets tired*) of; gets enough of

akimásu̲, aku *v* 開きます, 開く opens, comes open; it comes unbuttoned/unzipped/unlocked

akimásu, aku *v* 空きます, 空く gets empty/vacant

akinaimásu̲, akinau *v* 商います, 商う blushes

akíndo *n* 商人 merchant

akíraka *adj* 明らか clear (*evident*): **~ ni shimásu̲** 明らかにします makes it public, reveals, explains

akirame *n* 諦め resignation, acceptance: **~ ga warui** 諦めが悪い not knowing when to give up

akiramemásu̲, akiraméru *v* 諦めます, 諦める: **… o ~** …を諦めます gives up (*on*), resigns oneself to

akiremásu̲, akireru *v* 呆れます, 呆れる gets amazed; gets disgusted

akkan *n* 圧巻 overwhelming

akke-nái *adj* あっけない not long enough: **akkenaku makeru** あっけなく負ける is beaten too easily

akke ni toraremásu̲ (torareru) *v* 呆気に取られます(取られる) is stunned

akkerakán (to) *adv* あっけらかん(と) looks unconcerned

akogaremásu̲, akogaréru *v* 憧れます, 憧れる adores, admires; longs for, yearns for

akogi (ná) *adj* あこぎ(な) cruel and heartless

áku *n* 悪 an evil; **aku-fū** *n* 悪風 bad custom, bad practice, a vice; **aku-heki** *n* 悪癖 [BOOKISH] bad habit; **aku-hō** *n* 悪法 bad law; **aku-hyō** *n* 悪評 criticism (*unfavorable*); **áku-i** *n* 悪意 ill will, malice; **aku-jōken** *n* 悪条件 bad/unfavorable/adverse condition; **aku-júnkan** *n* 悪循環 vicious circle; **áku-ma** *n* 悪魔 devil, evil spirit, Satan; **áku-mu** *n* 悪夢 nightmare: **~ ni chigai arimasen** 悪夢に違いありません must be a nightmare; **aku-nin** *n* 悪人 an evil person; **aku-ratsu (na)** *adj* 悪辣(な) unscrupulous, foul, nasty, mean; **aku-sei** *n* 悪政 [BOOKISH] bad government; **aku-sen** *n* 悪銭 [BOOKISH] ill-gotten gains; **aku-shumí** *n* 悪趣味 bad/poor taste; **aku-toku** *n* 悪徳 (a) vice: **~-gyōsha** 悪徳業者 dishonest business person; **aku-zei** *n* 悪税 [BOOKISH] unreasonable tax

akú *n* アク・灰汁 scum, lye: **~ o torimásu̲** 灰汁を取ります removes the scum

akuaríumu *n* アクアリウム aquarium

akurobátto *n* アクロバット acrobat, acrobatics

akúryoku *n* 握力 grip (of hand)

áku̲seku *adv* あくせく laboriously, (working) hard, drudging (away)

áku̲sento *n* アクセント accent

áku̲seru *n* アクセル gas pedal, accelerator

áku̲sesari(i) *n* アクセサリ(ー) accessory

ákushon *n* アクション action; **akushon-eiga** *n* アクション映画 an action film

áku̲shu *n* 握手 handshake

áku̲ta *n* 芥 dirt, rubbish

amá *n* 尼 nun
áma *n* 海女 woman sea diver, a pearl diver
ama-... *prefix* 雨 rain; **amá-do** *n* 雨戸 rain shutters; **ama-gasa** *n* 雨傘 umbrella (= **kasa** 傘)
amá(chuá) *n* アマ(チュア) amateur
amaemásu, amaéru *v* 甘えます, 甘える presumes on someone's good-will, acts like a baby
amanógawa *n* あまのがわ・天の川 the Milky Way
amai *adj* 甘い sweet; lenient, permissive
amaku mimásu (míru) *v* 甘くみます(みる) kids oneself about ..., underestimates
amari *n* 余り remainder, surplus, leftover
amari *adv* あまり [+ NEGATIVE verb] not very, not much, not many (= **anmari** あんまり)
amarimásu, amáru *v* 余ります, 余る is left over, remains, is in excess, is too much/many
amarí(ni) *adv* あまり(に) too, too much, very
amayakashimásu, amayakásu *v* 甘やかします, 甘やかす pampers, babies
amé *n* アメ・飴 candy
áme *n* 雨 rain: **~ ga furimásu** 雨が降ります it rains
amḗba *n* アメーバ amoeba
Amerika *n* アメリカ America, U.S.(A.); **Amerika-jin** *n* アメリカ人 an American
amí *n* 網 net; **amí-do** *n* 網戸 screen door
amimásu, ámu *v* 編みます, 編む knits, braids
amí-mono *n* 編み物 knitting, knitted goods
ā́mondo *n* アーモンド almond
án *n* 案 **1.** proposal, suggestion, idea **2.** plan
án *n* あん・餡 bean jam/paste; **án-ko** *n* あんこ・餡子 bean jam/paste
aná *n* 穴 hole; slot; **ana-go** *n* アナゴ conger eel; **ana-guma** *n* アナグマ・穴熊 badger
anáta *pron* あなた you; **anatá-tachi, anatá-gáta** *pron* あなた達, あなた方 you (all); **anáta(-tachi) no** *pron* あなた(達)の your(s)
anaúnsā *n* アナウンサー announcer
andārain *n* アンダーライン underline
andāshátsu *n* アンダーシャツ undershirt
andon *n* 行灯 traditional paper-covered night-light
anadorimásu, anadoru *v* 侮ります, 侮る not think much of: **imamade ... o anadotte imáshita** いままで…を侮っていました hadn't used to think much of ...
ándo *n* 安堵 relief
áne *n* 姉 older sister (= **(o-)nḗ-san** (お)姉さん)
ángai *adv* 案外 **1.** unexpectedly (much) **2.** contrary to expectations; **ángai (na)** *adj* 案外(な) unexpected

angō *n* 暗号 secret code
anguru *n* アングル angle (= **kakudo** 角度), viewpoint
áni *n* 兄 elder brother (= **(o-)nii´-san** (お)兄さん)
anime, animēshon *n* アニメ,アニメーション animation, animaed cartoon
anji *n* 暗示 a hint; jiko-anji *n* 自己暗示 autosuggestion
ánkā *n* アンカー anchor
ankēto *n* アンケート questionnaire
ankí *n* 暗記 memorizing: ~ **shite** 暗記して by/from memory
ankōru *n* アンコール encore
anma *n* 按摩 masseur/masseuse
an-man *n* アンマン steamed bun stuffed with bean jam
anmari *adv* あんまり too much, overly; [+ NEGATIVE] not (very) much
anna... *adj* あんな… that kind of…: ~ **ni** あんなに to that extent
annái *n* 案内, [HONORIFIC] **go-~** ご案内 guidance, information; annai-jó *n* 案内所 information booth/desk; annái-nin *n* 案内人 guide (*person*), usher; annái-shó *n* 案内書 guide(book)
anó *adj* あの that (over there; *known to you and me*); anó-hito *pron* あの人 he/him, she/her; anó-ko *pron* あの子 she/her, he/him; ano-yo *n* あの世 the next world, another world
ano, anō *interj* あの, あのう (*with nervous diffidence*) well, uh …
ano né *interj* あのね (*mostly children or female*) well, listen, you know
anpáia *n* アンパイア umpire
anpán *n* アンパン sweet roll with bean jam inside
anpéa *n* アンペア ampere
anpo *n* 安保 security
anpu *n* アンプ amplifier
anpuru *n* アンプル ampule
anraku *n* 安楽 comfort; anraku (na) *adj* 安楽(な) comfortable, easy; anraku shi *n* 安楽死 mercy killing, euthanasia
ansei *n* 安静 rest: ~ **ni shimásu** 安静にします keeps/lies quiet
anshín *n* 安心 peace of mind; relief; security; confidence, trust
anshitsu *n* 暗室 darkroom
anshō *n* 暗唱 recitation from memory
antei *n* 安定 stability
antena *n* アンテナ antenna, aerial
ánzan *n* 安産 safe delivery, easy delivery; anzan kigan *n* 安産祈願 wishing someone a safe delivery
anzán *n* 暗算 mental calculation
anzen (na) *adj* 安全(な) safe (*harm-proof*); anzén-pin *n* 安全ピン safety pin
anzimásu, anjiru (anzuru) *v* 案じます, 案じる(案ずる) worries, concerns
anzu *n* アンズ・杏 apricot
áo *n* 青 blue, green (color); aói *adj* 青い blue, green, pale; ao-mi *n* 青味 blueness; ao-nísai *n* 青二才 immature [IN NEGATIVE SENSE];

ao-shíngō *n* 青信号 green light (*signal*); ao-suji *n* 青筋 vein: **~ o tateru** 青筋を立てる bursts a blood vessel; ao-yagi *n* 青柳 budding willow

aogimásu, aógu *v* 扇ぎます, 扇ぐ fans; fans oneself

aogimásu, aógu *v* 仰ぎます, 仰ぐ looks up at/to; respects (= **miageru** 見上げる)

aomuké *n* 仰向け facing upward

aorimásu, aóru *v* 煽ります, 煽る fans; stirs up, incites

ao-zamemásu, aozameru *v* 青ざめます, 青ざめる pales, is pale

apā´to *n* アパート apartment (*house*)

appaku *n* 圧迫 pressure; oppression, suppression

appáre *adj*, *interj* あっぱれ Bravo!: **~ na taido** あっぱれな態度 admirable attitude

áppu *n* アップ raising, up; appu-dē´to *n* アップデート update; appu-gurē´do *n* アップグレード upgrade; appu-rō´do *n* アップロード upload

apurō´chi *n* アプローチ approach

ára *interj* あら (*female*) oh!! (*shows surprise, amazement*): **árámā** あらまあ (*female*) Oh, dear!

ará *n* あら・粗 fault; ará sagashi *n* あら捜し nitpicking; ara-suji *n* あらすじ summary, outline, synopsis

Arabia, Árabu *n* アラビア, アラブ Arabia; Arabia-go *n* アラビア語 Arabic; Arabia-jin, Arabú-jin *n* アラビア人, アラブ人 an Arab

araemásu, araeru *v* 洗えます, 洗える can wash

araí *adj* 荒い rough, coarse; ara-ryōji *n* 荒療治 take drastic measures (*steps*)

araí *adj* 粗い rough, not smooth, coarse

araimásu, arau *v* 洗います, 洗う washes

arakajime *adv* あらかじめ in advance (= **maemotte** 前もって)

arare *n* **1.** あられ・霰 hail: **~ ga furimásu** あられ[霰]が降ります it hails (= **hyō´** ひょう[雹]) **2.** あられ rice-cracker cubes (*tidbits*)

árashi *n* 嵐 storm

arashimásu, arásu *v* 荒らします, 荒らす devastates, damages, ruins

arasoí *n* 争い controversy, contention, struggle; argument, dispute, quarrel; strife, disturbance

arasoimásu, arasóu *v* 争います, 争う struggles/contends for; argues, quarrels

aratamarimásu, aratamáru *v* 改まります, 改まる to be changed, to be replaced by something new

aratamemásu, arataméru *v* 改めます, 改める changes, alters, corrects

aratámete *adv* 改めて newly, anew; again

arawaremásu, arawaréru *v* 現れます, 現れる appears, shows up, comes out

arawashimásu, arawásu *v* 現します・現す shows, reveals

arawashimásu, arawásu *v* 表します・表す expresses (= **hyōgen shimás<u>u</u>** 表現します)

arawashimás<u>u</u>, arawásu *v* 著します, 著す publishes, writes

arayúru *adj* あらゆる all, every (= **subete no** すべての)

aré *pron* あれ that one (*over there; known to you and me*); **aré-ra** *pron* あれら those, they/them

aré *interj* あれ! Dear! (*surprise*)

aremás<u>u</u>, areru *v* 荒れます, 荒れる goes to ruin, falls to waste, gets dilapidated; gets rough/wild; rages

aremoyō (no) *adj* 荒れ模様(の) stormy, inclement

arérugii *n* アレルギー allergy: **kafun-~** 花粉アレルギー hay fever (= **kafunshō** 花粉症)

arí *n* アリ・蟻 ant

ariári (to) *adv* ありあり(と) vividly

ariawase *n* ありあわせ on hand

aribai *n* アリバイ alibi

arifúreta *adj* ありふれた very common, commonplace

arigachi *adj* ありがち common, typical [IN NEGATIVE SENSE]

arigatai *adj* ありがたい appreciated, welcome; grateful: **~ meiwaku** ありがた迷惑 unwanted favor, misplaced favor

arígatō (gozaimás<u>u</u> [HONORIFIC]**)** ありがとう(ございます) Thank you (very much)

árika *n* 在り処 whereabouts

arikitari *adj* ありきたり commonplace, so typical [IN NEGATIVE SENSE]

arimás<u>u</u>, aru *v* あります, ある there is, we've got; it is (located)

ari-sama *n* ありさま condition, state; scene, sight

ari-sō´(na) *adj* ありそう(な) likely; **~´mo nái** ありそうもない unlikely

aritē´ni-iu (to) *v* ありていに言う(と) frankly speaking [INFORMAL]

áritoarayúru *adj* ありとあらゆる every single, all kinds/sorts of

arittake *n* ありったけ utmost [INFORMAL]

arō´ *v* あろう [LITERARY] = **áru darō´** あるだろう = **áru deshō** あるでしょう (probably is)

áru ... *adj* ある certain ..., some ...; **áru-hi** ある日 *n* one/certain day

arubáito *n* アルバイト side job, sideline, part-time job

arufabétto *n* アルファベット alphabet

árugamama *n* あるがまま as is, for what it is: **~ (ni) uketorimás<u>u</u>** あるがまま(に)受け取ります takes things as they are

arúi-wa *conj* 或いは or else; maybe, possibly

arukimás<u>u</u>, arúku *v* 歩きます, 歩く walks

arukōru *n* アルコール alcohol

aruminíum *n* アルミニウム aluminum

ása *n, adv* 朝 morning; **ása-ban (ni)** *n, adv* 朝晩(に) morning and night/evening; **asa-yake** *n* 朝焼け a red glow in the morning sky; **asa-góhan** *n* 朝ご飯 breakfast; **ása-hi** *n* 朝日 morning sun, rising sun

asái *adj* 浅い shallow; **asá-haka (na)** *adj* 浅はか(な) shallow; **asa-se** *n* 浅瀬 shallows

Asakusa *n* 浅草 Asakusa

asátsuki *n* アサツキ・浅葱 scallion, green onion; chives

asátte *n, adv* あさって・明後日 the day after tomorrow

áse *n* 汗 sweat: **~ ga demásu** 汗が出ます, **~ o kakimásu** 汗をかきます sweats; **hiya-~** 冷や汗 cold sweat

Asean *n* アセアン ASEAN

asemásu, aséru *v* 褪せます, 褪せる fades

aserimásu, aséru *v* 焦ります, 焦る feels rushed/pressed

áshi *n* アシ・葦 reed

ashí *n* 足 foot, 脚 leg; **ashi-áto** *n* 足跡 footprint; **ashi-de mátoi** *n* 足手まとい a drag (*on*): **shusse no ~** 出世の足手まとい a drag on one's career; **ashí-kubi** *n* 足首 ankle; **ashi-móto** *n* 足もと・足元 step, gait: **~ ni ki o tsukéte** 足元に気を付けて Watch your step!

ashi-dome saremásu (sareru) *v* 足止めされます(される) is strained, is stuck

ashi-ga-demásu (deru) *v* 足が出ます(出る) runs over the budget

ashí-o-araimásu (arau) *v* 足を洗います(洗う) washes one's hands of cuts one's ties with

ashí-o-nobashimásu (nobasu) *v* 足を伸ばします(伸ばす) goes a little farther

ashirai *n* あしらい treatment, hospitality, service, arrangement

ashiraimásu, ashiráu *v* あしらいます, あしらう handles, manages, deals with; receives (a guest)

ashísutanto *n* アシスタント assistant (= **joshu** 助手)

ashita *n, adv* あした・明日 tomorrow

asobi 遊び *n* fun, amusement; a game, play; a visit; **asobi hanbun (de)** *adv* 遊び半分(で) half-seriously

asobimásu, asobu *v* 遊びます, 遊ぶ has fun, plays; visits

asoko, asuko *pron* あそこ, あすこ (that place) over there; that place (*known to you and me*)

assári *adj, adv* あっさり simple/simply, plain(ly); easy/easily; frank(ly), without apparent difficulty

assén *n* あっせん・斡旋 **1.** mediation; good offices, help (= **sewá** 世話): **2.** recommendation (= **suisen** 推薦)

asshō *n* 圧勝 an overwhelming win

asshuku *n* 圧縮 compression

asu *n, adv* あす・明日 tomorrow (= **ashita** あした・明日)

asufáruto *n* アスファルト asphalt

asupara(gásu) *n* アスパラ(ガス) asparagus

asupirin *n* アスピリン aspirin

asurechikku-kúrabu *n* アスレチッククラブ athletic club

āsu-sen *n* アース線 ground wire

asutarísuku *n* アスタリスク asterisk (such as "＊") (= **hoshi-jírushi** 星印)
asutorinzen *n* アストリンゼン astringent
ataemásu, ataeru *v* 与えます, 与える gives, provides, grants
átafuta *n* あたふた fluster; frenzied hurry
ataisuru *v, adj* 値する deserves, deserved
átakamo *adv* あたかも as if
atákku *n* アタック attack, strenuous effort
atama *n* 頭 head; **atama-dékkachi (no)** *adj* 頭でっかち(の) [INFORMAL] [IN NEGATIVE SENSE] top-heavy, too many chiefs, not enough Indians, an armchair theorist; **atama-kín** *n* 頭金 down payment, up-front money; deposit
atama-ni-kimásu (kuru) *v* 頭にきます(くる) gets mad at, be angry with
atama-o-kakaemásu (kakaeru) *v* 頭を抱えます(抱える) tears one's hair (out), holds one's head in one's hands
atama-o-tsukaimásu (tsukau) *v* 頭を使います(使う) uses one's head/mind
atarashíi *adj* 新しい new; fresh
ataráshiku *adv* 新しく newly, anew, freshly
atarazu-sawarazu *adj, adv* 当たらずさわらず innocuous: **~ no henji** 当たらずさわらずの返事 give a harmless answer
atari 当たり **1.** *n* a hit **2.** *adj* good luck, lucky; **atari-yaku** *n* 当たり役 is a hit in the role; **atari-kuji** *n* 当たりくじ winning number
átari *n* 辺り neighborhood: **kono ~ de/wa** この辺りで/は around here
atarichirashimásu, atarichirasu *v* 当たり散らします, 当たり散らす takes out one's spite on everybody
ataridokoro-ga-warui *adj* 当たり所が悪い hitting in a vital spot
atarimae (no) *adj* 当たり前(の) natural, reasonable, proper; suitable, sensible
atarimásu, ataru *v* 当たります, 当たる hits, faces; applies; is correct
atashi *pron* あたし (*mostly children or female*) I/me (= **wata(ku)shi** わた(く)し・私)
atasshu-kḗsu *n* アタッシュケース attache case, briefcase
atatakái *adj* 暖かい warm (*air temperature*)
atatakái *adj* 温かい warm (*liquid, heart, etc.*)
atatamarimásu, atatamáru *v* 暖まります, 暖まる warms up
atatamarimásu, atatamáru *v* 温まります, 温まる warms up
atatamemásu, atataméru *v* 温めます, 温める warms it up, heats
atchi *pron* [INFORMAL] あっち, [FORMAL] **achira** あちら (*the other one, over there*)
ate 当て **1.** *n* reliance, trust **2.** *n* anticipation, expectation (= **kitai**

期待) **3.** goal, object (= **moku-teki** 目的) **4.** *n* clue, trace (= **tegákari** 手掛かり)

...-ate (nó) *suffix, adj* ...宛て(の) addressed to ...; **ate-na** *n* 宛(て)名 address

ate-hamarimásu, ate-hamáru *v* 当てはまります, 当てはまる fits, conforms

ate-hamemásu, ate-haméru *v* 当てはめます, 当てはめる applies, conforms, adapts, fits it (*to*): **... ni ate-hámete** ...に当てはめて in conformity/accordance with ...

atekosuri *n* 当てこすり a snide remark

atemásu, ateru *v* 当てます, 当てる guesses; hits; sets aside, designates; touches; addresses

ā'tisuto *n* アーティスト/アーチスト artist (= **geijutsu-ka** 芸術家)

áto (de/ni) *prep, adv* 後(で/に) after(wards), later (= **nochi ni** 後に): **áto no ...** 後の...the remaining ...; **ato-máwashi** *n* 後回し leaving something until later: ~ **ni shimásu** 後回しにします postpones, leaves something until later; **ató-aji** *n* 後味 aftertaste: ~ **ga warui** 後味が悪い leaves a bad aftertaste; **ato-kátazuke** *n* 後片付け cleanup; **áto-no-matsurí** *n* 後の祭(り) The damage is done; **ato-módori** *n* 後戻り retreat, back tracking; **ato-saki** *n* 後先 consequence; **ato-shímatsu** *n* 後始末 settling, putting in order, cleaning up after

áto *n* 跡 mark, track, trace; scar; footprint; **ató-tsugi** *n* あとつぎ・跡継ぎ successor

ā'to *n* アート art

atorakushon *n* アトラクション attraction, side entertainment

atorie *n* アトリエ studio, workshop, atelier

atsuatsu (no) *adj* アツアツ(の) lovey-dovey

atsuatsu (no) *adj* 熱々(の) piping hot

atsubottai *adj* 厚ぼったい thick

atsui *adj* 厚い thick; **atsu-zoko** *n* 厚底 heavy-bottom (*things*), ~ **nabe** 厚底なべ heavy-bottomed saucepan

atsúi *adj* 暑い hot (*air temperature*)

atsúi *adj* 熱い hot

atsukamashii *adj* 厚かましい impudent

atsukaimásu, atsukau *v* 扱います, 扱う deals with

atsumarimásu, atsumáru *v* 集まります, 集まる meets, assembles; it accumulates

atsumemásu, atsuméru *v* 集めます, 集める collects, gathers, accumulates

atsúryoku *n* 圧力 pressure

atsusa *n* 厚さ thickness

átsusa *n* 暑さ heat, warmth (*air temperature*)

átsusa *n* 熱さ heat, warmth (= **netsu** 熱)

attakái *adj* 暖かい warm (= **atatakái** 暖かい)

attakái *adj* 温かい warm (= **atata-kái** 温かい)
at(a)tamemásu̱, at(a)taméru *v* 温めます, 温める warms it up, heats
atto-hō´mu (na) *adj* アットホーム(な) homelike, homely
atto-mā´ku *n* アットマーク a mark (such as "@")
attō-shimásu̱ (suru) *v* 圧倒します(する) overwhelms
attō-teki na *adj* 圧倒的な overwhelming
áuto *n* アウト out (*baseball*); **auto-putto** アウトプット output; **auto-rain** アウトライン outline
awa *n* 泡 bubble; foam
áwa *n* アワ・粟 millet
áwabi *n* アワビ・鮑 abalone
áware (na) *adj* 哀れ(な) pity, pitiful
awase *n* 袷・あわせ lined garment
awasemásu̱, awaséru *v* 合わせます, 合わせる puts together, combines, joins
awatadashii *adj* 慌ただしい hurried, flustered, confused
awatemásu̱, awateru *v* 慌てます, 慌てる gets flustered/confused
awate-mono *n* 慌て者 a person easily flustered; a scatterbrain (= **awatenbō** あわてん坊)
ayabumimásu̱, ayabumu *v* 危ぶみます, 危ぶむ doubts
ayafuya (na) *adj* あやふや(な) indecisive
ayamari *n* 誤り error, mistake
ayamari *n* 謝り apology
ayamarimásu̱, ayamáru *v* 誤ります, 誤る errs, makes a mistake
ayamarimásu̱, ayamáru *v* 謝ります, 謝る apologizes
ayashii *adj* 怪しい questionable, suspicious, shady; uncertain; unreliable; weird
ayashimásu, ayasu *v* あやします, あやす lulls: **akanbō o ayashite nekashitsukemáshita** 赤ん坊をあやして寝かしつけました lulled a baby to sleep
ayatóri *n* あやとり cat's cradle
ayatsurimásu̱, ayatsúru *v* 操ります, 操る manipulates
ayauku *adv* 危うく (*something undesirable*) about to happen or likely to happen.
āyū *adj* ああゆう ... that kind/sort of ... (= **āiu** ああいう, **anna** あんな)
áyu *n* アユ・鮎 (= **ái** アイ・鮎) sweetfish, river trout
aza *n* 痣 bruise
azakeri *n* あざけり・嘲り mockery
azakerimásu̱, azakeru *v* あざけり・嘲ります, あざける・嘲る mocks, scorns
azárashi *n* アザラシ・海豹 seal (*animal*)
azawarai *n* あざ[嘲]笑い mockery, sneer, scornful laugh
azawaraimásu̱, azawarau *v* あざ[嘲]笑います, あざ[嘲]笑う mocks, sneers
azáyaka (na) *adj* 鮮やか(な) bright, vivid
azen-to-shimásu̱ (-suru) *v* あ然とします is dumbfounded

azukarimásu, azukáru *v* 預かります, 預かる takes in trust, keeps, holds
azukemásu, azukéru *v* 預けます, 預ける gives in trust, entrusts, checks, deposits
azuki *n* アズキ・小豆 red beans

B

...-ba *conj* …ば [EMPHATIC] (if) indeed: **... nára(ba)** …なら(ば) if; **... dáttara(ba)** …だったら(ば); **...-káttara(ba)** …かったら(ば) if/when it is (or was); **...-tára(ba)** …たら(ば) if/when it does (or did)
ba *n* 場 **1.** place (*for something*) (= **basho** 場所) **2.** occasion, time **3.** scene
bā´ *n* バー bar (*for drinking*)
baai, bawai *n* 場合 situation, case, circumstance, occasion: **... no baai/bawai** … の場合 if
baba-shatsu *n* ばばシャツ long sleeved thermal undershirt for female
bābékyū *n* バーベキュー barbecue
bachí *n* 罰 retribution, punishment (= **batsu** 罰)
ba-chígai (na/no) *adj* 場違い(な/の) **1.** out of place **2.** not from the right/best place
bā´gen *n* バーゲン bargain sale
bái *n* 倍 double; bai-ritsu *n* 倍率 magnification, magnifying power
...-bai *suffix* …倍 …times, …-fold
bai-... *prefix* 売… selling; bái-bai *n* 売買 buying and selling; bai-shun *n* 売春 prostitution; bai-ten *n* 売店 booth, kiosk, stand (*selling things*)
Báiburu *n* バイブル Bible (= **seisho** 聖書)
báidoku *n* 梅毒 [BOOKISH] syphilis
baikin *n* ばい菌 germ
báikingu *n* バイキング smorgasbord
báiku *n* バイク motorbike
baindā *n* バインダー binder
baiorin *n* バイオリン violin
baio-tekunórojii *n* バイオテクノロジー biotechnology
baipasu *n* バイパス bypass
bairíngaru *n* バイリンガル bilingual
baishō´-kin *n* 賠償金 indemnity, reparation
baiyā *n* バイヤー buyer (*professional*)
baji *n* バッジ badge
báka *n* ばか・バカ・馬鹿 fool, idiot; báka na *adj* ばかな foolish, stupid; baka-bakashíi, baka-rashíi *adj* ばかばかしい absurd, foolish; baka-bánashi *n* ばか話 nonsense; idle talk; hot air, bull (= **muda-bánashi** 無駄話); báka-me *adj* ばかめ damn (fool) idiot
...bákari, ...bákkari, ... bákkashi *suffix* …ばかり, …ばっかり, …ばっかし only, just (= **dake** だけ): **bákari de/ja naku ...mo ...** …ばかりで/じゃなく…も not only …, but also

bakazu-o-fumimásu (fumu) *v* 場数を踏みます(踏む) gets a lot of practical experience
bakégaku *n* 化学・化け学 chemistry (= **kágaku** 化学)
bake-móno *n* 化け物 monster, ghost
baken *n* 馬券 betting ticket
baketsu *n* バケツ bucket
bakkin *n* 罰金 fine, penalty
bákku *n* バック back; bakku-áppu *n* バックアップ backup, support; bakku-mírā *n* バックミラー rearview mirror
bákku, baggu *n* バック, バッグ bag
bakuchi *n* 博打 gambling
bakudai (na) *adj* ばくだい(な) immense, vast, huge, enormous
bakudan *n* 爆弾 bomb
bákufu *n* 幕府 (*the time of*) the shogunate
bakugeki *n* 爆撃 bombing
bakuhatsu *n* 爆発 explosion, bursting
bakuteria *n* バクテリア bacteria
bakuzen (to) *adv* 漠然(と) vaguely, obscurely
bámen *n* 場面 scene (= **shiin** シーン)
ban *n* 晩 [BOOKISH] evening, night; **kon-~** 今晩 tonight; **mai-~** 毎晩 every night; ban-góhan, ban-meshi *n* 晩ご飯,晩飯 evening meal (*dinner/supper*) (= **yūshoku** 夕食)
bán *n* 番 guard, watch; ban-ken *n* 番犬 watchdog
...-ban *suffix* . . . 番 number; ban-chi *n* 番地 address (*house number*); ban-gō´ *n* 番号 number (*assigned*); ...-banmé (no) *suffix, adj* ...番目(の) [numeral] -th; ...-ban-sen *suffix* ... 番線 track number ... (*train station*)
bānā *n* バーナー burner
bánana *n* バナナ banana
ban-cha *n* 番茶 coarse green tea
bando *n* バンド **1.** strap, band (*watch, etc.*); belt **2.** band (*music*)
bane (-jíkake) *n* ばね(仕掛け) spring (*device*)
ban-gasa *n* 番傘 oilpaper umbrella
bangumi *n* 番組 program (*TV, etc.*)
Bánkoku *n* バンコク Bangkok
bánkoku *n* 万国 **1.** international **2.** all the world; bánkoku-hakubútsu-kan, banpaku *n* 万国博物館, 万博 international exposition
bánira *n* バニラ vanilla
bannō *n* 万能 versatility, ability to do anything
bansō *n* 伴奏 musical accompaniment
bansōko, bansōkō *n* 絆創膏 adhesive plaster/tape
banzái *interj* 万歳 hurray!
bara *n* バラ・薔薇 rose (*flower*)
bára (de) *adv* ばら(で) loose, separately
barabara (ní) *adv* ばらばら(に) scattered, in pieces
baransu *n* バランス balance: **~ o torimásu** バランスをとります redress the balance
barashimásu, barásu *v* ばらします, ばらす **1.** exposes (*a secret*) **2.** takes it apart, disassembles **3.** kills, shoots (*to death*)
bárē *n* バレエ ballet

barē(bō´ru) *n* バレー(ボール) volleyball
baremásu, baréru *v* [INFORMAL] ばれます, ばれる surfaces, is disclosed, is discovered
barentáindē *n* バレンタインデー Valentine's Day
bareriina *n* バレリーナ ballerina
barikan *n* バリカン clippers (*barber's*)
bariki *n* 馬力 horsepower
baromē´tā *n* バロメーター barometer
barukónii *n* バルコニー balcony
basho *n* 場所 place
bassári *adv* ばっさり fast and furious, without hesitation
basshi *n* 抜歯 pulling out a tooth/ teeth
basshimásu, bassuru *v* 罰します, 罰する punishes
básu *n* バス bus; **basu-téi** *n* バス停 bus stop; **basu-rū´mu** *n* bathroom (= **furo** 風呂); **basu-tsuki** バス付き with bath
basue *n* 場末 suburb (*outskirts*)
basukétto *n* バスケット basket
basukétto bō´ru *n* バスケットボール basketball, basketball game
básuto *n* バスト bust
bátā *n* バター butter
batafurai *n* バタフライ butterfly (*swimming*)
batán (to) *adv* ばたん(と) with a bang, with a thud
bāten(dā) *n* バーテン(ダー) bartender
batomínton *n* バトミントン badminton
baton *n* バトン baton
baton tatchi *n* バトンタッチ passing the torch, having someone take over
bátsu *n* ばつ cross (= X "*wrong*")
bátsu *n* 罰 retribution, punishment
batta *n* バッタ grasshopper
báttā *n* バッター batter (*baseball*)
battári *adv* ばったり unexpectedly
battén *n* ばってん X ("*wrong*"), a black mark
batterii *n* バッテリー battery
battingu *n* バッティング batting (*baseball*)
bátto *n* バット bat (*baseball*)
baundo *n* バウンド bound
bawai, baai *n* 場合 situation, case, circumstance, occasion
bázā *n* バザー bazaar
bebiishíttā *n* ベビー・シッター baby sitter
béddo, bétto *n* ベッド,ベット bed (*Western*)
beddo-táun *n* ベット・タウン bedroom community, suburb
Bei *n* 米 America(*n*): **nich-~** 日米 Japan and America; **ō-~** 欧米 Europe and America; **Béi-koku** *n* 米国 America (= **Amerika** アメリカ); **Bei-koku-jin** *n* 米国人 American (= **Amerika-jin** アメリカ人)
beiju *n* 米寿 (*auspicious, happy event*) eighty-eighth birthday
beikingu-páudā *n* ベイキング・パウダー baking powder
... béki *suffix* ...べき: **...-suru ~**

desu するべきです should do, ought to do [BOOKISH]
bekkan *n* 別館 annex (*building*)
bekkyo *n* 別居 separate living
bē´kon *n* ベーコン bacon
bén *n* 弁 valve
bén *n* 便 **1.** convenience (**= béngi** 便宜) **2.** feces; bén-jo *n* 便所 toilet; bén-ki *n* 便器 bedpan; bén-pi *n* 便秘 constipation
...-bén *suffix* …遍 = **…-hén, ...-pén** 遍 (*counts times or occasions*)
bénchi *n* ベンチ bench
béngi *n* 便宜 convenience, accommodation: **~ o hakarimásu** 便宜を図ります does someone a favor
bengóshi *n* 弁護士 lawyer
béni *n* 紅 rouge
benkai *n* 弁解 [BOOKISH] justification (**= iiwake** 言い訳)
benkyō *n* 勉強 study, (*mental*) work; cutting a price
bénri (na) *adj* 便利(な) handy, convenient
benri-ya *n* 便利屋 handyman (*or his shop*)
benron *n* 弁論 [BOOKISH] debate, speech, rhetoric; benron-taikai *n* 弁論大会 speech contest
benshō *n* 弁償 compensation
bentō *n* 弁当 box lunch
berabō (ni) *adv* べらぼう(に) astonishingly, considerably: **~ ni takai** べらぼうに高い extremely expensive
beranda *n* ベランダ veranda
béru *n* ベル bell, doorbell
Berurín *n* ベルリン Berlin
beruto *n* ベルト belt; anzen-béruto *n* 安全ベルト safety belt
bessō´ *n* 別荘 villa, vacation house
bēsu *n* ベース **1.** base, basis **2.** base (*baseball*) **3. = bēsu gitā** ベースギター bass guitar
bēsu áppu *n* ベースアップ upping/raising the base pay; a pay raise
bēsubōru *n* ベースボール baseball
bésuto *n* ベスト best; besuto-tén *n* ベストテン best ten; besuto-serā´ *n* ベストセラー best seller
beteran *n* ベテラン veteran, expert
betsu (na/no) *adj* 別(な/の) separate, special, particular; **…wa ~ to shite** … は別として apart/aside from …, except for …; betsu-betsu (na/no) *adj* 別々(な/の) separate, individual; betsu-ryō´kin *n* 別料金 extra (*charge*), separate bill
betsu (ni) *adv* 別(に) **1.** [+ NEGATIVE] not particularly **2. … tó wa ~ ni (shite)** とは別に(して) quite apart/separately from …
bia-hō´ru *n* ビアホール beer hall
bifuteki *n* ビフテキ = **biifu sutēki** ビーフステーキ beefsteak
bíichi *n* ビーチ beach
bíiru *n* ビール beer
bíjin *n* 美人 beautiful woman, a beauty
bíjinesu *n* ビジネス business; bíjinesu-hoteru *n* ビジネスホテル economy hotel; bíjinesu-man *n* ビジネスマン businessperson

bijón *n* ビジョン vision: **~ o hakkiri sasemásu** ビジョンをはっきりさせます clarifies one's vision
bíjutsu *n* 美術 art; **bijútsú-kan** 美術館 *n* art museum (*art gallery*)
bikkúri-shimásu (-suru) *v* びっくりします(する) gets startled, gets a surprise (**= odorokimásu** 驚きます)
bimyō (na) *adj* 微妙(な) delicate, subtle, fine, nice
bín *n* 瓶 bottle; jar
...'-bin *suffix* 便 flight (number) ...
bínbō (na) *adj* 貧乏(な) poor (*needy*)
biní(i)ru *n* ビニ(ー)ル vinyl, polyvinyl; plastic; **bini(i)rú-bukuro** *n* ビニ(ー)ル袋 plastic bag
binkan (na) *adj* 敏感(な) sensitive
binsen *n* 便箋 (letter-)writing paper, stationery
bínta *n* びんた slapping (*a person's face*)
birá *n* びら leaflet, handbill, pamphlet
bíri (no) *adj* びり(の) the last, the tail end, the rear
birōdo *n* ビロード velvet
bíru *n* ビル building
Bíruma *n* ビルマ Burma (Myanmar)
bisai (na) *adj* 微細(な) minute, detailed, fine
bishonure *n* びしょ濡れ soddenness, sopping wet
bisshíri *adv* びっしり cramped
bisshóri *adv* びっしょり completely soaked: **ase ~** 汗びっしょり is all sweaty
bisukétto *n* ビスケット crackers
bitámin *n* ビタミン vitamin(s); **bitámin-zai** *n* ビタミン剤 vitamin pills
bitoku *n* 美徳 virtue
bíwa *n* ビワ・枇杷 loquat (*fruit*)
biya-hō'ru *n* ビヤホール beer hall
biyō'in *n* 美容院 beauty parlor
bíza *n* ビザ visa (**= sashō** 査証)
bō *n* 棒 pole (*rod*); stick, club; **tetsu-bō** *n* 鉄棒 (*iron*) bar
bóchi *n* 墓地 cemetery, graveyard
bōchō shimásu (suru) *v* 膨脹します(する) swells, expands
bōchū'zai *n* 防虫剤 insecticide; mothballs
bōdai (na) *adj* 膨大(な) enormous, gigantic, massive
bōdō *n* 暴動 riot
bōei *n* 防衛 defense (**= bōgyo** 防御)
Bōei-shō *n* 防衛省 Ministry of Defense (DA)
bōeki *n* 貿易 commerce, trade; **bōeki-shōsha/gaisha** *n* 貿易商社/会社 trader, trading company
bōenkyō *n* 望遠鏡 telescope
bōfū *n* 暴風 storm, gale, hurricane
bōfú-zai *n* 防腐剤 antiseptic (*substance*), preservative
bōhan-béru *n* 防犯ベル burglar alarm
bōhatéi *n* 防波堤 breakwater
bōi-furéndo *n* ボーイフレンド boyfriend (**= káre(-shi)** 彼(氏))
boikótto *n* ボイコット boycott
boin *n* 拇印 thumbprint
boin *n* 母音 vowel

boin *n* ボイン (*slang*) big bust
bóirā *n* ボイラー boiler
bōisukáuto *n* ボーイスカウト boy scout
bōkaru *n* ボーカル vocalist
bokashimásu, bokásu *v* ぼかします, ぼかす: **hanashí o ~** 話をぼかします beats around the bush, is noncommittal
bōken *n* 冒険 adventure
bóki *n* 簿記 bookkeeping
bō-kire, bōkkíre *n* 棒きれ, 棒っきれ pole (*rod*); stick, club (= **bō** 棒)
bokkusu *n* ボックス; denwa-bókkusu *n* 電話ボックス phone booth
bókoku *n* 母国 mother country, homeland
bóku *pron* 僕 (*male*) I/me; bóku-ra, bóku-táchi *pron* 僕ら, 僕たち we/us
bokuchiku *n* 牧畜 stockbreeding
bokujō *n* 牧場 ranch
bókushi *n* 牧師 (*Christian*) minister, pastor; Reverend
bókushingu *n* ボクシング boxing
bon *n* 盆 (**o-bon** お盆) tray
Bón *n* 盆 (**O-bón** お盆) Bon Festival (*Buddhist All Saints Day*)
...-bon *suffix* …本 book, volume, text
...´-bon (...´-hon, ...´-pon) *suffix* …本 (*counts long objects*)
bō´nasu *n* ボーナス (*wage*) bonus
bonchí *n* 盆地 (*geographical*) basin
bōnén-kai *n* 忘年会 year-end party
bonnétto *n* ボンネット (car-)hood, bonnet
bonsai *n* 盆栽 dwarf trees (in pots)
bon'yári-shimásu (suru) *v* ぼんやりします(する) is absent-minded, daydreams
bonyū *n* 母乳 breast milk
bora *n* ボラ gray mullet
borántia *n* ボランティア volunteer
boraremásu, boraréru *v* ぼられます, ぼられる [INFORMAL] gets overcharged (*ripped off*)
bōrei *n* 亡霊 Japanese ghost (*commonly lacks legs and feet*)
borimásu, bóru *v* ぼります, ぼる overcharges
bōringu *n* ボーリング bowling
bóro *n* ぼろ rag
bōru *n* ボール ball
bōru-gami *n* ボール紙 cardboard
bōru-pen *n* ボールペン ballpoint pen
boruto *n* ボルト bolt (*of nut and bolt*); volt
bō´ryoku *n* 暴力 violence (*brute force*); bōryoku-dan *n* 暴力団 mob, gangbanger
boryūmu *n* ボリューム volume
bō-san *n* 坊さん (**obō-sán** お坊さん) Buddhist monk (= **bō´zu** 坊主)
bósei *n* 母性 maternity
bōseki *n* 紡績 [BOOKISH] spinning
bōshi *n* 帽子 hat
boshikátei *n* 母子家庭 family without a father: **~ de sodachimásu** 母子家庭で育ちます grows up without a father.
boshū *n* 募集 recruitment
bōsōzoku *n* 暴走族 motorcycle gang
bōsui (no) *adj* 防水(の) waterproof
bótan *n* ボタン button

bótchan *n* 坊ちゃん (little) boy, (your) son (= **bō´ya** 坊や)
bō´to *n* ボート boat
bōtō *n* 冒頭 opening, at [in] the beginning
bōtoku *n* 冒とく sacrilege, violence: **kami e no ~** 神への冒とく blasphemy
bótsubotsu *adv* ぼつぼつ **1.** *adv* (= **sórosoro** そろそろ) little by little, gradually; (leave) before long **2.** *n* (*with*) dots, spots, bumps
bōtto-shimásu (-suru) *v* ボーっとします (する) stupefies: **bōtto shita atama** ボーっとした頭 vacant mind
bottō-shimásu (-suru) *v* 没頭します devotes oneself: **shigoto ni ~** 仕事に没頭します buries oneself in one's work
boyakimásu, boyáku *v* ぼやきます, ぼやく grumbles, complains
bōzen *adj* 茫然 stunned: **~ to shita kao** 茫然とした顔 dazed-looking
bōzu *n* 坊主 Buddhist monk or priest; **bōzu-atama** *n* 坊主頭 shaven head
bú *n* 部 **1.** (*suffix* **…´-bu** …部) part, division, section; **bú-bun** *n* 部分 part, portion; **bu-chō** *n* 部長 department/division/section head, manager, chief (*in the office*); **bu-hín** *n* 部品 parts **2.** (*performance*) **yóru-no-bú** 夜の部 evening performance
…´-bu *suffix* **1.** …分 (1-9) percent **2.** …部 copies (*of a book*); **ichí-bu** 一部 one copy
buai *n* 歩合 commission; **buai-sei** 歩合制 commission system
bu-áisō (na) *adj* 無愛想(な) curt, unsociable, blunt, brusque
buatsuí *adj* 分厚い thick
buchimásu, butsu *v* ぶちます, ぶつ hits
bu-chō´hō *n* 不調法 a gaffe, a blunder; **bu-chō´hō (na)** *adj* 不調法(な) awkward, clumsy, impolite
Budda *n* 仏陀 Buddha
budō *n* ブドウ・葡萄 grapes
búdō *n* 武道 martial arts
budō-shu *n* ブドウ酒 wine
bu-énryo (na) *adj* 不遠慮(な) frank, unreserved, pushy, rude
búffe *n* ビュッフェ buffet
būingu *n* ブーイング booing
buji (ni) *adv* 無事(に) safely (*without incident*)
bujoku *n* 侮辱 insult(ing)
bújutsu *n* 武術 martial arts
búki *n* 武器 weapon, arms
bu-kimi (na) *adj* 不気味(な) ghasty, eerie: **~ na shizukesa** 不気味な静けさ eerie silence
bu-kíryō (na) *adj* 不器量(な) homely, ugly
bu-kíyō (na) *adj* 不器用(な) clumsy
bukká *n* 物価 commodity prices
bukkirábō (na) *adj* ぶっきらぼう(な) blunt, brusque, curt
bukku *n* ブック book; **bukku-fea** *n* ブックフェア book fair
Búkkyō *n* 仏教 Buddhism
bū´mu *n* ブーム boom (*fad*)
bún *n* 文 sentence, text; **bun-bō-gu**

n 文房具, **bunpō´-gu** 文房具 stationery supplies; bún-gaku *n* 文学 literature; bún-go *n* 文語 literary language/word; bún-ka *n* 文化 culture, civilization; bun-ko (-bon) *n* 文庫(本) pocketbook; bun-mei *n* 文明 civilization; bun-pō *n* 文法 grammar; bún-shō *n* 文章 (written) sentence

bún-... *prefix* 分... part, portion, share; state, status; bun-ben *n* 分娩 childbirth delivery; bun-dóki *n* 分度器 protractor; bun-jō *n* 分譲 sale in lots, lotting out: **~man-shon** 分譲マンション condominium; bun-kai *n* 分解 breakup (*material*); bun-katsu *n* 分割 dividing, splitting; bun-pu *n* 分布 distribution; bun-retsu *n* 分裂 breakup (*countries, human relationship*); bun-rui *n* 分類 classification; bun-seki *n* 分析 analysis; bun-tan *n* 分担 (taking) partial charge; allotment, share: **~ shimásu** 分担します takes partial charge of, shares in; pays/does one's share

...-bun *suffix* ...分 numeral -th; yon-bun no ichí 4分の1 one-fourth

búppō *n* 仏法 the teachings of Buddhism

búrabura *adv* ぶらぶら idly dangling, idling, hang around: **ashi o ~ sasemásu** 足をぶらぶらさせます swings one's leg (*back and forth*)

buraindo *n* ブラインド sunblind, window shade

burá(jā) *n* ブラ(ジャー) bra(ssiere)

Burajiru *n* ブラジル Brazil

burakku-bókkusu *n* ブラックボックス black box

burakku-kō´hii *n* ブラックコーヒー black coffee

burakku-rísuto *n* ブラックリスト black list

burakku-yū´moa *n* ブラックユーモア black humor

buránch *n* ブランチ brunch

burandē *n* ブランデー brandy

burando *n* ブランド brand

buránketto *n* ブランケット blanket

buránko *n* ブランコ a swing (*in a park, etc.*)

burári (to) *v* ぶらり(と) drop by

burasagarimásu, burasagaru *v* ぶら下がります, ぶら下がる hangs (down)

burasagemásu, burasageru *v* ぶら下げます, ぶら下げる hangs (down), suspends

búrashi *n* ブラシ brush; ha-burashi *n* 歯ブラシ toothbrush

buratsukimásu, buratsuku *v* ぶらつきます, ぶらつく hangs around, wonders, strolls around

buraun-kán *n* ブラウン管 TV tube

buráusu *n* ブラウス blouse

burauza *n* ブラウザ browser (*computer*)

buréi *n* 無礼 discourtesy; buréi na *adj* 無礼な impolite, rude

burēkā *n* ブレーカー circuit breaker (box)

burē´ki *n* ブレーキ (*car*) brake
buréźā *n* ブレザー blazer: **seifuku no** ~ 制服のブレザー blazer uniform
buríifu *n* ブリーフ brief(s)
buriifu-kē´su *n* ブリーフケース briefcase
buríjji *n* ブリッジ bridge (*card game*)
buriki *n* ブリキ tin
burō´chi *n* ブローチ brooch
burōdobando n ブロードバンド broadband (*computer*)
burogu *n* ブログ blog, weblog
burōkā *n* ブローカー agent, broker
burókkori(i) *n* ブロッコリ(ー) broccoli
buronzu *n* ブロンズ bronze
burū *adj* ブルー feeling blue
burudóggu *n* ブルドッグ bulldog
burudō´zā *n* ブルドーザー bull-dozer (*machine*)
burujoa *n* ブルジョア bourgeois
burūsu *n* ブルース blues (*music*)
bu-sáhō *n* 無[不]作法 a social gaffe, a faux pas; bu-sáhō na *adj* 無[不]作法な rude, blunt
bu-sata *n* 無沙汰 neglecting to write/visit (= **go-busata** ご無沙汰)
búshi *n* 武士 Japanese warrior, samurai
bushí-dō *n* 武士道 Bushido, the way of the samurai
búsho *n* 部署 department (*in the office*)
bushō (na) *adj* 無[不]精(な) lazy; slovenly; bushō-mono *n* 無精者 sluggard, sloven person
búshu *n* 部首 radical (*Chinese character*): **~-kensaku** 部首検索 index by radical
...-búsoku *n* ...不足 shortage: **ne-~** 寝不足 not enough sleep
busshitsu *n* 物質 matter, substance; busshitsu-teki (na) *adj* 物質的(な) material
busshoku *n* 物色 looking around for
bussō´(na) *adj* 物騒(な) troubled, unsafe, dangerous
búsu *n* ぶす ugly female
butá *n* ブタ・豚 pig; buta-niku *n* 豚肉 pork
bútai *n* 舞台 stage
bútai *n* 部隊 detachment of troops, unit, outfit
butchō-zura *n* 仏頂面 a sullen face
bútikku *n* ブティック boutique
Butsu *n* 仏 Buddha (= **budda** 仏陀); butsu-dan *n* 仏壇 household altar (*Buddhist*); Butsu-zō *n* 仏像 Buddha (*statue*)
būtsu *n* ブーツ boot
bútsubutsu iimásu (iu) *v* ぶつぶつ言います(言う) complains (*muttering, grumbling*)
butsukarimásu, butsukaru *v* ぶつかります, ぶつかる collides with, runs into
butsukemásu, butsukeru *v* ぶつけます, ぶつける hits
bútsuri, butsurígaku *n* 物理,物理学 physics; butsurigákú-sha *n* 物理学者 physicist
buttai *n* 物体 thing, matter, object, body, material body

buttobashimásu, buttobasu *v* [INFORMAL] ぶっ飛ばします, ぶっ飛ばす beats up, burns up

buttōshi (de) *adv* [INFORMAL] ぶっ通し(で) without a break: **~ de hatarakimásu** ぶっ通しで働きます works without a break

buttsuke-honban (de) *adv* ぶっつけ本番(で) without rehearsal

buttsuzuke (de) *adv* [INFORMAL] ぶっ続け(で) without a break, continuously

búzā *n* ブザー buzzer

byákudan *n* ビャクダン・白壇 sandalwood

byō´ *n* 秒 a second (*of time*); **byō´-yomi** *n* 秒読み countdown

byō´... *prefix* 病... sickness, patients; **byō-in** *n* 病院 hospital; clinic, health service: **kyūkyū-~** 救急病院 emergency hospital; **byō-ki (no)** *adj* 病気(の) sick, ill; sickness, illness: **~-gachi (na)** 病気がち(な) sickly, unhealthy; **byō-nin** *n* 病人 an invalid, a patient; **byō-reki** *n* 病歴 medical history

byō´ *n* 鋲 a tack; a thumbtack (= **gabyō** 画鋲)

byōbu *n* 屏風 screen (*folding*)

byōdō (na) *adj* 平等(な) equal

byōsha *n* 描写 depiction, description: **~ ga umai** 描写が上手い is good at describing

C

cha *n* 茶 (**o-chá** お茶) tea, green tea; **cha-dái** *n* 茶代 (**o-chadái** お茶代) ① tea charges (*in café, etc.*) ② tip (*money*); **cha-gará** *n* 茶殻 tea leaves; **cha-iro (no)** *adj* 茶色(の) brown; **cha-no-má** *n* 茶の間 (**o-cha-no-má** お茶の間) (*Japanese style*) living room: **o-cha-no-má de onajimi** お茶の間でお馴染み familiar to TV viewers; **cha-nomi-tómodachi** *n* 茶飲み友達 coffee-drinking companion, crony; **cha-saji** *n* 茶匙 teaspoon; **cha-wán** *n* 茶碗 (**o-cháwan** お茶碗) ① rice bowl ② tea cup (*for tea ceremony*); **cha-wán-mushi** *n* 茶碗むし steamed egg hotchpotch in a teacup (*made from broth and egg*)

...cha *suffix* ...ちゃ = **...-téwa** ...ては (doing/being, if one does/be)

cháchi (na) *adj* [INFORMAL] ちゃち(な) petty, flimsy, cheap

chā´han *n* チャーハン・炒飯 (*Chinese*) fried rice

cháimu *n* チャイム chime

chairudo-shíito *n* チャイルドシート child seat

chāji *n* チャージ charge

chákku *n* チャック zipper

chakashimásu, chakasu *v* [INFORMAL] ちゃかします, ちゃかす mimes, makes fun of, ridicules

... cháku *suffix* …着 arriving at (TIME/PLACE)

chakkarishite-(i)másu ((i)ru) *v* [INFORMAL] ちゃっかりして(い)ます((い)る) is nimble, adroit, shrewd and calculating

chakkō *n* 着工 starting

chakuchaku (to) *adv* 着々(と) steadily

chakuchí *n* 着地 landing on

chakufukú *n* 着服 [BOOKISH] embezzlement, misappropriation

chakugán *n* 着眼 [BOOKISH] attention; chakugán-ten 着眼点 viewpoint

chakujítsu (na) *adj* 着実(な) steady, constant

chakunan *n* 嫡男 [BOOKISH] heir, eldest son

chakurikú *n* 着陸 (*from sky or wide water area*) landing, touching ground

chakushi *n* 嫡子 [BOOKISH] heir

chakushoku *n* 着色 coloring, stain, color

chákushu *v* 着手 [BOOKISH] begin, start

chakusō *n* 着想 [BOOKISH] conception, idea, inspiration

chakusúi *n* 着水 landing on water, splashing down

chā´mingu *n* チャーミング charming, attractive

...(-) chan *suffix* …ちゃん (*mostly attached to children's or girls' names.* [INFORMAL])

chanbará *n* ちゃんばら sword battle (*historical period drama*)

chánchara okashíi *adj* ちゃんちゃらおかしい [INFORMAL] laughable, absurd, fiddle-dee-dee

chánnerú *n* チャンネル channel (TV)

chánpion *n* チャンピオン champion

chánpon *n* ちゃんぽん alternating, skipping back and forth, mixing one's drinks/foods

chánsu *n* チャンス chance

chantó *adv* ちゃんと safe(ly) (*without incident*), firmly, securely; chantó shita *adj* ちゃんとした proper, secure

chárachara shita *adj* ちゃらちゃらした [INFORMAL] showy [IN NEGATIVE SENSE]

charanporán (na) *adj* [INFORMAL] ちゃらんぽらん(な) irresponsible, sloppy, halfway, unreliable [IN NEGATIVE SENSE]

charénji *n* チャレンジ challenge

charinkó *n* チャリンコ [INFORMAL] bicycle

cháritii *n* チャリティー charity

charumerá *n* チャルメラ noodle vendor's flute

chāshū *n* チャーシュー (*Chinese*) roast pork; chāshū-men *n* チャーシュー麵 Chinese noodles with sliced roast pork

chātā *n* チャーター charter; chātā-bin *n* チャーター便 chartered flight, charter service

chatto *n* チャット chatting, chat (*Internet*)
chékku *n* チェック **1.** *v* check **2.** *n* check (*bank*) (= **kogitte** 小切手) **3.** *n* check (*pattern*)
chekku-áuto *n* チェックアウト check-out
chekkú-in *n* チェックイン check-in
chē´n *n* チェーン chain, snow chain
chéro *n* チェロ cello
chi *n* 血 blood: **~ ga demás<u>u</u>** 血が出ます bleeds; chi-bashítta *adj* 血走った bloodshot; chi-daraké *adj* 血だらけ bloody; chi-namagusái *adj* 血生臭い bloody; chi-no-ke ga nái *adj* 血の気がない pale
chi *n* 地 ground, earth, land: **~ ni ashi o tsukemás<u>u</u>** 地に足をつけます grounds oneself; chi-chū´ *n* 地中 underground; chi-hei-sén *n* 地平線 horizon (*on land*); chi-hō´, chí-iki *n* 地方 area, region, province, district; chí-ka *n* 地下 underground: **~shitsu** 地下室 basement: **~tetsu** 地下鉄 subway; chi-kakú *n* 地殻 (*geology*) the earth's crust; chí-ku *n* 地区 section, sector (*area*); chi-shitsú *n* 地質 the geology (*of a place*); chi-sō *n* 地層 (*geology*) stratum; chi-tai *n* 地帯 zone: **anzen-~** 安全地帯 safety zone; chí-zu *n* 地図 map
chián *n* 治安 law and order, security, public order
chiaríidā *n* チアリーダー cheer-leader
Chibetto *n* チベット Tibet
chíbi *n* ちび [INFORMAL] midget; chibi-kko *n* ちびっ子 (tiny) tot
chibirimás<u>u</u>, chibiru *v* ちびります, ちびる [INFORMAL] wets one's pants, wets oneself
chíbu *n* 恥部 **1.** private parts, pubic area **2.** source of embarrassment
chíbusa *n* 乳房 (woman's) breasts
ch<u>i</u>chi (oya) *n* 父(親) father
ch<u>i</u>chi *n* 乳 **1.** mother's milk **2.** breasts and nipples; chi(chi)-bánare *n* 乳離れ is weaned
chidorí-ashi *n* 千鳥足 swaying gait, a reeling movement
chié *n* 知恵 wisdom; chié-okure (no) *n, adj* 知恵遅れ(の) mentally retarded
chién *n* 遅延 [BOOKISH] delay
chífusu *n* チフス typhus (*fever*), typhoid (*fever*)
chigaí 違い *n* difference, discrepancy
chigaimás<u>u</u>, chigau *v* 違います, 違う is different; is wrong; is not like that
chigirimás<u>u</u>, chigiru *v* 千切ります, 千切る tears into pieces
chigúhagú (na) *adj* ちぐはぐ(な), ill-assorted, mismatched, is all mixed up: **~ na kaiwa** ちぐはぐな会話 talking at cross-purposes
chihō (-shō´) *n* 痴呆(症) dementia
chíi *n* 地位 rank, position, status
chíifu *n* チーフ chief
chíimu *n* チーム team; chiimuwāku *n* チームワーク teamwork

chiisái, chíisa na *adj* 小さい, 小さな little, small
chíitā *n* チーター cheetah
chiizu *n* チーズ cheese
chiji *n* 知事 governor
chijimárimásu, chijimaru *v* 縮まります, 縮まる shrinks, shortens
chijimemásu, chijimeru *v* 縮めます, 縮める shortens (it)
chijimimásu, chijimu *v* 縮みます, 縮む (it) shrinks
chijín *n* 知人 [BOOKISH] acquaintance
chijiremásu, chijireru *v* 縮れます, 縮れる becomes curly
chijoku *n* 恥辱 disgrace, shame
chiká goro *n, adv* 近頃 lately, recently
chikaí *n* 誓い vow, pledge, oath
chikái *adj* 近い near, close by: ~ **uchí ni** 近いうちに in the near future
chikaimásu, chikáu *v* 誓います, 誓う swears, vows, pledges
chíkaku *adj, adv* 近く **1.** close **2.** near-by **3.** shortly
chikakú *n* 知覚 perception
chiká-michi *n* 近道 short cut
chikán *n* 痴漢 (*sexual*) molester, groper
chikará *n* 力 power, strength; ability; effort (= **o-chi-kara** お力); influence
chika-yorimásu, chika-yoru 近寄ります, 近寄る approaches, draws/comes near
chika-zukemásu, chika-zukéru *v* 近付けます, 近付ける lets one approach, brings close; associates (*keeps company*) with; can approach it
chika-zukimásu, chika-zúku *v* 近付きます, 近付く (= **chika-yorimásu, chika-yoru** 近寄ります, 近寄る)
chíketto *n* チケット ticket
chikén *n* 知見 knowledge, learning, information
chíkin *n* チキン chicken
chikokú *n* 遅刻 lateness
chíkubi *n* 乳首 nipple, teat
chíkuchiku-shimásu (suru) *v* ちくちくします(する) pricks, prickles, tickles
chikuón-ki *n* 畜音機 phonograph
chikúrimásu, chikuru *v* チクります, チクる tells, snitches on
chikusekí *n* 蓄積 accumulation, store
chikushō, chikishō 畜生, ちきしょう **1.** *interj* Damn! (*curse*) **2.** *n* beast(s)
chikuwá *n* チクワ broiled fish cake
chikyū´ *n* 地球 the Earth; **chikyū´-gi** *n* 地球儀 globe
chímachima *adv* ちまちま small and neatly arranged: ~ **to kurashimásu** ちまちまと暮らします lives frugally
chimatá *n* 巷 public: ~ **no uwasa dewa…** 巷のうわさでは… People say that…
chiméikizu *n* 致命傷 vital wound, fatal injury
chiméiteki (na) *adj* 致命的(な) fatal, capital, mortal, deadly

chimitsú *adj* 緻密 close, minute, elaborate: **~ na keikaku** 緻密な計画 careful planning
chinatsu *n* 鎮圧 suppression
chinbotsu *n* 沈没 sinking
chínchin *n* ちんちん (**o-chínchin** おちんちん) penis [*baby, informal talk*]
chinden *n* 沈殿 deposition, precipitation: **~ shimásu** 沈殿します is deposited, settles down
chíngin *n* 賃金 wage
chinjutsú *n* 陳述 statement, parol
chinka *n* 沈下 sinkage, subsidence
chínmi *n* 珍味 delicacy
chinmokú *n* 沈黙 silence: **~ shimásu** 沈黙します stops talking
chínō *n* 知能 intelligence; chinō-shisū *n* 知能指数 intelligence quotient
chinomígo *n* 乳飲み子 an infant, nursling: **~ (o) kakaete** 乳飲み子(を)抱えて with a baby/babies
chinpánjii *n* チンパンジー chimpanzee
chínpira *n* ちんぴら・チンピラ a punk; hoodlum; juvenile delinquent
chinretsu *n* 陳列 exhibition, display
chinseizai *n* 鎮静剤 sedative, tranquilizer
chinshaku *n* 賃借 letting and hiring, rental
chíntai *n* 賃貸 lease, rental, rented apartment
chíppu *n* チップ tip (*money*)
chírachira hikarimásu (hikaru) *v* チラチラ光ります(光る) glimmers
chírachira suru mono *n* チラチラするもの fluff stuff
chirári-to-mimásu (miru) *v* ちらりと見ます(見る) glances
chira(ka)shimásu, chira(ka)su *v* 散ら(か)します, 散ら(か)す scatters, strews
chirashí *n* チラシ leaflet
chirashí-zushi *n* ちらし寿司[鮨] sushi rice covered with fish tidbits
chiratsuki *n* ちらつき flicker: **gamen no ~** 画面のちらつき screen that flickers
chirí *n* 塵 dust (*on ground, floor, etc.*); chirí-tóri *n* ちり[塵]取り dustpan
chíri *n* 地理 the geography, the lay of the land; chirí-gaku *n* 地理学 (*the study/science of*) geography; chiri-jō (no) *adj* 地理上(の) geographical
chiri-gamí, chiri-kami, chiri-shi *n* ちり紙 tissues (*Kleenex*) (**= tisshu (pēpā)** ティッシュ(ペーパー))
chirimásu, chiru *v* 散ります, 散る disperses, scatters, falls about
chiryō *n* 治療 treatment (*medical*)
chísei *n* 知性 intellect, mind, intelligence, mentality
chiséi *n* 治世 reign
chishiteki (na) *adj* 致死的(な) death-dealing
chisetsú *n* 稚拙 childish
chíshiki *n* 知識 knowledge; chishiki-jin *n* 知識人 intellectual(s)

Chishimá *n* 千島, **~-réttō** 千島列島 the Kurile Islands
chishíryō *n* 致死量 overdose
chísso *n* チッソ・窒素 nitrogen
chissokú *n* 窒息 suffocation
chisui *n* 治水 flood control
chitchái *adj* ちっちゃい [INFORMAL] little
chiteki (na) *adj* 知的(な) intelligent, intellectual (= **chiseiteki (na)** 知性的(な))
chitsu *n* 膣 vagina
chítsujo *n* 秩序 order, discipline, system
chittó-mo *adv* ちっとも [+ NEGATIVE verb] [INFORMAL] not a bit, not in the least: **~ ki ni narimasen** ちっとも気になりません not care a bit
chō *n* 腸 intestines
chō´ *n* チョウ・蝶 butterfly; chō-músubi *n* 蝶結び bow (*of a ribbon*); chō-nékutai *n* 蝶ネクタイ bow tie
(...-)chō´ *suffix* (...)丁 block (*or block area*) of a city: **(...-) chō-mé** (...)丁目 (...-th) block (*of city*)
(...-) chō´ *suffix* (...)長 head, chief, leader
(...-) chō´ *suffix* (...)兆 trillion
chóbo *n* ちょぼ a dot
chōbó *n* 帳簿 (*account*) book
chōchín *n* 提灯 lantern
chō´chō *n* 町長 town mayor
chōdai-shimásu (suru) *v* ちょうだい[頂戴]します(する) I (humbly) receive/accept
...chōdái *interj* ...ちょうだい [INFORMAL] **1.** Please **2.** Give me...
chōdo *adv* ちょうど exactly, just
chōgō *n* 調合 preparation
chō´hō (na) *adj* 重宝(な) useful, convenient, valued; **~ garimásu** 重宝がります values, cherishes, makes full use of
chō´ji *n* 丁子 cloves
chō´jo *n* 長女 eldest daughter
chojō´ *n* 頂上 top, summit, peak
chō´ka *n* 超過 [BOOKISH] excess
chōkán *n* 長官 chief (*head*)
chō´ki *n* 長期 long period, long range
chokín *n* 貯金 deposit, savings; chokin-bako *n* 貯金箱 saving box
chokkán *n* 直感 intuition
chokkí *n* チョッキ vest
chōkoku *n* 彫刻 carving, engraving
choko(rē´to) *n* チョコ(レート) chocolate
chō´ku *n* チョーク chalk
chokuryū´ *n* 直流 DC, direct current
chokusén *n* 直線 straight line
chokusetsu *adj, adv* 直接 direct(ly)
chō-kyóri *n* 長距離 long distance
chō´mi *n* 調味 seasoning (*food*); chōmí-ryō *n* 調味料 spice
chō´nán *n* 長男 eldest son
chónbo *n* ちょんぼ・チョンボ a booboo, a goof, a blunder
chōryū *n* 潮流 current, tide; trend
chō´sa *n* 調査 examination, inquiry, investigation, research, survey
chosáku-ken *n* 著作権 copyright

chōséi *n* 調整 adjustment
chōsén *n* 挑戦 challenge; **chōsén-sha** *n* 挑戦者 challenger
Chō´sén *n* 朝鮮 → **Kita Chōsén, Kankoku**
chōsetsú *n* 調節 → **chōséi**
chósha *n* 著者 writer, author
chōshí *n* 調子 tune; condition; trend; **~ ga demásu** 調子が出ます gets into the swing of things: **~ ga ii/warui** 調子がいい/悪い is in good/bad condition
chósho *n* 著書 one's book
chō´sho *n* 長所 strong point, advantage, merit
chōshokú *n* 朝食 morning meal, breakfast (= **asa-gohan** 朝ご飯)
chōshu *n* 聴取 listening in; **chōshu-sha** *n* 聴取者 (*radio*) listener
chōshū *n* 聴衆 audience
chōshū *n* 徴収 [BOOKISH] collection (*of taxes, etc.*), levying
chosúi-chi *n* 貯水池 reservoir
chō´ten *n* 頂点 climax, peak, high-point
chō-tsúgai *n* 蝶つがい hinge
chótto *adv* ちょっと just a little; just a minute; somewhat
chottóshitá *adj* … ちょっとした… **1.** slight, trivial **2.** quite a …, a decent/respectable …: **~ toraburu** ちょっとしたトラブル queer
chōwá *n* 調和 harmony, agreement
chū *n* 注 annotation, note
chū *adj* 中 middle; medium; **chū´-bu** *n* 中部 middle (*part*); **chū-gákkō** *n* 中学校 middle school (*junior high school*); **chū-gáku-sei** *n* 中学生 junior high school student; **chū-gatá (no)** *n* 中型(の) medium-size (*model*); **chū-gén** *n* 中元 mid-summer gift; **chū-jíen** *n* 中耳炎 middle ear infection; **chū-jún** *n* 中旬 the middle of (*month*); **chū-kán** *n* 中間 middle: **~-shiken** 中間試験 intermediate exam, **~-kan-rishoku** 中間管理職 mid-level executive, middle management; **chū-nen** *n* 中年 middle age, **~ (no)** 中年(の) middle-aged (*person*); **chū´-sa** *n* 中佐 lieutenant colonel, (*navy*) commander; **chū´-sei** *n* 中世 medieval times, the Middle Ages; **chū-shōkígyō** *n* 中小企業 medium-sized and small companies; **Chū´-tō** *n* 中東 the Middle East; **chū-toró** *n* 中とろ・中トロ medium-fat (pink) tuna
...-chū *suffix* 中 **1. ... chū (ni)** ...中(に) during, while, within (*time*) **2. ... chū (no)** ...中(の) in course …of, under (*doing*); **kōji-chū** *n* 工事中 under construction
chū´bu *n* チューブ tube
chū´cho *n* ちゅうちょ・躊躇 [BOOKISH] hesitation
chū´doku *n* 中毒 addiction, poisoning; **shoku-chū´doku** 食中毒 food poisoning
Chū´goku *n* 中国 China; **Chūgokú-jin** *n* 中国人 a Chinese; **Chūgoku-go** *n* 中国語 Chinese (*language*)
Chūgoku-chíhō *n* 中国地方 the Chugoku area of Japan

chū'i *n* 注意 attention; note, notice, reminder: ~ **shimásu** 注意します ① pays attention ② is careful of ③ advises, warns; **chūi-bukái** *adj* 注意深い careful
chūingámu *n* チューインガム chewing gum
chūjitsu (na) *adj* 忠実(な) faithful
chū'ka *n, adj* 中華 Chinese..., Chinese food; **chū'ka-gai** *n* 中華街 Chinatown; **chū'ka-ryō'ri(-ten)** *n* 中華料理(店) Chinese cooking (restaurant)
chūkái *n* 仲介 mediation; **chūkái-gyōsha** *n* 仲介業者 broker, intermediary agent
chūko (no) *adj* 中古(の) second-hand; **chūkó-sha** *n* 中古車 used car
chūkokú *n* 忠告 advice
chūmoku *n* 注目 attention, notice
chūmon *n* 注文 an order (of goods)
chūō' *n* 中央 the center; **chūō no** *adj* 中央の central; **Chūō-sen** *n* 中央線 the (JR) Chuo Line
chūritsú *n* 中立 neutral(ity)
chūséi *n* 忠誠 loyalty, fidelity, allegiance
chūséi *adj* 中性 neutral
chūsén *n* 抽選 lottery, drawing
chūshá *n* 駐車 parking; **chūsha-jō** *n* 駐車場 parking lot/garage; **chū-sha-kinshi** *n* 駐車禁止 No Parking
chūshá *n* 注射 injection: **yobō-~** 予防注射 preventive injection, immunization; **chūshá-ki** *n* 注射器 syringe (*for injections*)
chūshí *n* 中止 suspension (*abeyance*)
chūshín *n* 中心 center, heart, middle; **chūshín no** *adj* 中心の central; **chūshín-chi** *n* 中心地 central area
chūshō *n* 中傷 slander
chūshokú *n* 昼食 lunch (= **hiru-góhan** 昼ご飯, **ranchi** ランチ)
chūshō-teki (na) *adj* 抽象的(な) abstract
chūsū (shinkei) *n* 中枢(神経) nerve center
chūsúi-ki *n* 注水器 douche, syringe (*for water*)
chūto (de) *adv* 中途(で) on the way, halfway
chūyō *n* 中庸 [BOOKISH] moderation: ~ **o emásu** 中庸を得ます exercises moderation
chūzái *n*, 駐在 residence, presence; **chūzái-in** *n* 駐在員 resident officer; **chūzái-táishi** *n* 駐在大使 ambassador
chūzetsu *n* 中絶 abortion: **~-shujutsu o ukemásu** 中絶手術を受けます undergoes an abortion

D

... da *suffix* …だ: **... -ta** た

... dá *v* …だ = **... désu** …です is; it is

daben *n* 駄弁 idle talk: **~ o rōshi-másu** 駄弁をろうします talks rubbish, talks nonsense: **~ka** 駄弁家 long-winded speaker

daberimásu, dabéru *v* だべります, だべる shoots the breeze/bull, chews the fat (*idly talks*)

dabingu *n* ダビング dubbing

daboku-shō *n* 打撲傷 bruise

dabudabu (no) *adj* だぶだぶ(の) baggy, loose, full, voluminous: **~ no fuku** だぶだぶの服 voluminous dress

daburimásu, dabúru *v* ダブります, ダブる gets doubled, overlaps, repeats, is repeated (by mistake)

dáburu *n* ダブル **1. = ~-rū´mu** ダブルルーム a double (*room*) **2.** double(-size) drink **3.** double-breasted suit **4. ~-su** ダブルス (*tennis*) doubles; **daburu-béddo** *n* ダブルベッド double bed

dachin *n* 駄賃 reward, tip

dada *n* 駄々 fretful: **dadakko** 駄々っ子 fretful/unreasonable/spoiled child

dadappiroi *adj* だだっ広い rambling, too spacious

daeki *n* 唾液 [BOOKISH] saliva

daen *n* 楕円 ellipse, oval

dága *conj* だが [BOOKISH] but (= **shikashi** しかし)

dageki *n* 打撃 blow, shock

daha *n* 打破 defeat

dái- *prefix* 第 [+ number] number …; (= **…-banmé**…番目) [numeral] -th; (*separate word except when attached to a single-unit numeral*); **dái-go** *adj* 第五 number five; (= **go-banmé** 五番目) fifth; **dái-ichi** *adj* 第一 number one; (= **ichi-banmé** 一番目) first: **dái-ichi no** 第一の (the) first; **dái-ichi ni** 第一に first (of all); **Dái-ni-ji Sekai-taisen** 第二次世界大戦 World War II; **dái-san** *adj* 第三 number three; (= **sanbanmé** 三番目) third: **~-sha** 第三者 third party

dái *n* 題 **1.** title (= **daimei** 題名) **2.** topic, theme (= **daimokú** 題目)

dai 代 **1.** *n* (**o-dai** お代) charge (*fee*), bill: **o-~ wa itadakimasen** お代はいただきません Compliments of the house.: **takushii-~** タクシー代 taxi fare **2.** [numeral] **-dai** …age, generation: **nijū´-~** 20代 twenties; **ni-dai(me)** 2代目 The Second, junior (*family*)

... dai *suffix* …だい [INFORMAL] (= **... désu ka** …ですか [FORMAL]): **dáre/nán dai** 誰/何だい who/what is it?

dai *n* 台 stand, (*low*) table

...´-dai *suffix* …台 (*counts mounted machines, vehicles*)

daibā *n* ダイバー diver
daiben *n* 大便 defecation, bowel movement, feces
daiben *n* 代弁 speaking for another
daibingu *n* ダイビング dive
daibu *adv* 大分 quite, very, much
dai-búbun *n* 大部分 most, the majority
daibutsu *n* 大仏 giant statue of Buddha
daidái *n* ダイダイ・橙 bitter orange; daidái-iro *n* 橙色 (*color*) orange
dáidai *adj, adv* 代々 generation after generation, for generations
daidokoro *n* 台所 kitchen
daietto *n* ダイエット diet
daifuku (mochi) *n* 大福(もち) soft rice cake stuffed with sweet bean jam
daigaku *n* 大学 college, university; daigakú-in *n* 大学院 graduate school: **~ín-sei** 大学院生 graduate student
daigiin *n* 代議員 deputy
daigishi *n* 代議士 Diet member
daigomi *n* 醍醐味 relish, whole point
daihitsu *n* 代筆 ghost-writing
daihon *n* 台本 script (= **kyakuhon** 脚本)
daihyō *n* 代表 representative; daihyō-sha *n* 代表者 a representative (*person*)
daiji *n* 大事 a matter of importance; **~ o torimásu̱** 大事をとります plays it safe: **(o-)karada o (o-)~ ni shi̱te kudasái** (お)体を(お)大事にして下さい take good care of yourself; daijí (na) *adj* 大事(な) important, precious
dáijin *n* 大臣 minister (*cabinet*)
dai-jō'bu *adj* 大丈夫 OK, all right; safe (and sound); no need to worry, no problem: **~ desu̱** 大丈夫です It's all right.
dáikichi *n* 大吉 very good luck, excellent luck
daikin *n* 代金 the price/charge, the bill: **~ hi̱kikae (de)** 代金引換え(で) **(= daibiki (de)** 代引き(で)**)** C.O.D., collect (on delivery)
daikō *n* 代行 acting as agent; daikō'-sha *n* 代行者 agent
daikō *n* 代講 substitute class/teacher
daikoku-bashira *n* 大黒柱 pillar, breadwinner
daikon *n* 大根 giant white radish; daikon-óroshi *n* 大根おろし grated radish
dáiku *n* 大工 carpenter
daikyū *n* 代休 compensation day, substitute holiday
daiméishi *n* 代名詞 pronoun
daimoku *n* 題目 topic (= **dái** 題)
daimyō' *n* 大名 feudal lord
dainamaito *n* ダイナマイト dynamite
dainashi *n* 台無し ruin, spoil
dainingu-kitchin (DK) *n* ダイニングキッチン (DK) a combined dining room-kitchen, an eat-in kitchen

daininġu-rūmu *n* ダイニングルーム dining room
daí (no) ... *adj* 大(の) ..., **dai-...** 大... big, great; dai-kirai (na) *adj* 大嫌い(な) loathing, aversion; dái-suki (na) *adj* 大好き(な) favorite, greatly liked; dai-tasū *n* 大多数 large number; majority
dairi *n* 代理 commission, agent, agency; dairi-bo *n* 代理母 surrogate mother; dairí-nin *n* 代理人 agent; dairí-ten *n* 代理店 agency
daishi *n* 台紙 mount, board (art)
dai-shō *n* 大小 size
dai-shō *n* 代償 price, compensation, reparation
dái-sū *n* 代数 algebra, literal arithmetic
daitai *adv* 大体 in general, on the whole, approximately, almost
daitán (na) *adj* 大胆(な) bold
daitōryō *n* 大統領 president (*of a nation*)
dáiya *n* **1.** ダイヤ schedule (*train*) **2.** (= **daiyamóndo**) ダイヤ(モンド) diamond
daiyaku *n* 代役 substitute, alternate
daiyaru *n* ダイヤル dial
daiyō *n* 代用 substitution
daiza *n* 台座 pedestal, seat
daizai *n* 題材 material, subject matter: **kankyō-hogo o ~ ni shita eiga** 環境保護を題材にした映画 film on ecology
dáizu *n* 大豆・ダイズ soy beans
dajare *n* 駄洒落 pun, equivoque
...´-daka ...高 **1.** quantity, volume; sum **2.** higher by ...: **hyakuén-daka** 百円高 100 yen up
dákara (sa) *conj* だから(さ) and so; therefore; that's why
... daké *suffix* ...だけ only, just: ... **(-ta) ~ de** ...(た)だけで just from (*having done it*)
dakemásu, dakeru *v* 抱けます, 抱ける can hug, can hold in the arms
dakimásu, daku *v* 抱きます, 抱く holds in the arms
dakyō *n* 妥協 compromise
damarimásu, damáru *v* 黙ります, 黙る is/becomes silent; shuts up
damashimásu, damásu *v* 騙します, 騙す deceives, cheats
damé (na) *adj* 駄目(な) no good, no use, won't; bad, broken, malfunctioning; don't!; **~ ni shimásu** 駄目にします ruins it, spoils it
dámu *n* ダム dam
dán *n* 段 **1.** step(s); grade, order **2.** (*page*) column; scene, act **3.** (**...dán** ... 段) case, event; dan-chō no omoi *n* 断腸の思い heartbreaking grief; dan-dán *adv* 段々 gradually; dan-kai *n* 段階 grade, rank, stage (*of a process*); dan-raku *n* 段落 paragraph; dan-tei *n* 断定 decision, conclusion
dan *n* 団 group, party, team; danchi *n* 団地 housing development; dan-chō *n* 団長 leader, head; dango *n* 団子 dumpling; dan-tai *n* 団体 organization, group
dan *n* 壇 platform
dan *n* conversation, talk; dan-shō

n 談笑 chatting; **dan-wa** *n* 談話 [BOOKISH] conversation: **~-shitsu** 談話室 common room
dan-... *prefix* 男... male; **dán-jo** *n* 男女 male and female: **~-kyōgaku** 男女共学 coeducation; **dan-kon** *n* 男根 penis; **dan-sei** *n* 男性 male; **dán-shi** *n* 男子 boy: **~-gakusei/seito** 男子学生/生徒 schoolboy; **dan-shō** *n* 男娼 male prostitute; **dan-shoku** *n* 男色 male homosexual love
danatsu *n* 弾圧 suppression
danbō *n* 暖房 heating (*of room, house*); **danbō-sō´chi** *n* 暖房装置 heating device, radiator
dangan *n* 弾丸 [BOOKISH] bullet
dani *n* ダニ mite, tick
danna *n* 旦那 **1.** my husband **2. ~-san/-sama** 旦那さん/様 (*your/someone else's*) husband **3.** master (*of a shop, etc.*)
danpingu *n* ダンピング dumping
danryoku *n* 弾力 elastic force
danshoku *n* 暖色 warm color(s)
dansu *n* ダンス dance
dan'yaku *n* 弾薬 ammunition, powder and ball
daradara (to) *adj* だらだら(と) lengthy: **~ (to) sugoshimásu** だらだら(と)過ごします slobs about
daraku *n* 堕落 corruption
darari-to *adv* だらりと loosely, lollingly
darashinai *adj* だらしない slovenly, loose
dáre *pron* 誰 who: **~ no** 誰の whose; **~ dé mo** 誰でも anybody (at all), everybody; **dáre ka** *pron* 誰か somebody, someone; **dáre mo** *adv* 誰も (not) anybody; [+ NEGATIVE verb] nobody
...darō´ *suffix* ...だろう probably, probably (it) is; I think; don't you think? (= **...deshō´**...でしょう)
dasai *adj* ださい tasteless, insipid, bland
dasei *n* 惰性 inertia, (*force of*) habit
dasha *n* 打者 a batter/hitter
dashí *n* だし soup stock, broth: **~ no moto** だしの素 instant bouillon
dashimásu, dásu *v* 出します, 出す puts out; serves (*food/drink*); produces; pays, spends; mails; begins
dashimono *v* 出し物 play, attraction, show
dashin *n* 打診 (*medical examination by*) percussion, tapping; sounding a person out
dashinuke (ni) *adv* 出し抜け(に) abruptly
dashinukimásu, dashinuku *v* 出し抜きます, 出し抜く outwits, gets the better of
dasoku *n* 蛇足 icing on the cake
dassen *n* 脱線 derailment
dasshí-men *n* 脱脂綿 absorbent cotton
dasshí-nyū *n* 脱脂乳 skim milk
dasshū´-zai *n* 脱臭剤 deodorant (*personal*) (= **deodoranto** デオドラント)
dassō *n* 脱走 escape, desertion

dā´su *n* ダース dozen: **ichi-~** 1ダース one dozen
datai *n* 堕胎 abortion
datō *n* 打倒 overthrow, defeat
datō *adj* 妥当 appropriate, reasonable
datsuraku *n* 脱落 omission, dropout
datsuryoku *n* 脱力 faintness, lassitude
...dátta *v* …だった was; it was (= **…déshita** … でした)
dattai *n* 脱退 withdrawal
...dáttara *conj* …だったら if/when it is (or was)
...dáttari (shimásu/desu) *suffix* …だったり(します/です) being representatively/sometimes/alternately …: **dáttari…ja nákattari** …だったり…じゃなかったり (is) off and on, sometimes is and sometimes isn't
dátte *conj* だって but; however, even so, though (= **démo** でも)
...dátte *suffix* …だって even being …; … or something (= **…démo** … でも)
de *n* 出 **1.** a person's origins (*family, birthplace, school*); (… **no ~** …の出) born in/of …, a graduate of … **2.** (out)flow: **mizu no ~ ga íi** 水の出がいい/悪い has good/bad water pressure **3.** emergence, appearance
...de particle …で **...-te** …て
...dé *suffix* …で (*happening*) at, in, on; with, by (*means of*), through
...dé *conj* …で is/was and; being, its being; with (its being) [COPULA GERUND]
...de arimásu *v* …であります = **… désu** …です is; it is
...de gozaimashō´ *v* … でございましょう = **… deshō´** …でしょう probably is; I think it is (, sir/ma'am)
...de gozaimásu *v* …でございます [DEFERENTIAL] = **…desu** … です is; it is (sir/ma'am)
...de imásu *v* …でいます stays/keeps (*goes on*) being
...de orimásu *v* …でおります [DEFERENTIAL/HUMBLE] (*I/we*) stay/keep (*go on*) being
deaikeisaito *n* 出会い系サイト dating service website, meet-a-mate site, online dating website (*Internet*)
de-aimásu, de-áu *v* 出会います, 出会う: **… ni de-aimásu** …に出会います encounters, meets, happens to see/meet, runs/bumps into
déguchi *n* 出口 exit, outlet
deiríguchi *n* 出入り口 gate(way), doorway
dekakemásu, dekakeru *v* 出掛けます, 出掛ける starts off/out, goes out, departs
dekiai *n* 溺愛 blind love
dekiai (no) *adj* 出来合い(の) ready-made
dekígoto *n* 出来事 happening, accident
dekimásu, dekíru *v* 出来ます, 出来る can (*do*), is possible, produced, done, finished, through, ready

dekí-mónó, o-déki *n* できもの, おでき swelling, sore, boil, pimple

dekíru-dake *adv* できるだけ as much as possible

dek(k)ai *adj* で(っ)かい [INFORMAL] big (= **ōkii** 大きい)

dékki *n* デッキ deck

dekoboko (no) *adj* でこぼこ(の) **1.** bump(y), rough (*road, etc.*) **2.** uneven(ness), imbalance

déma *n* デマ false rumor

demae *n* 出前 catering, food delivered to order, restaurant delivery (*service/person*)

demásu̱, déru *v* 出ます, 出る goes/comes out, emerges, appears; is served; leaves, starts

démo *conj* でも but, however, even so, though

démo *n* デモ demonstration

... démo *suffix* ...でも even/also (*being*) ..., even if it be; ...or something: **gaka ~ sakka ~ arimasen.** 画家でも作家でもありません is neither a painter nor a writer

demokurashii *n* デモクラシー democracy

de-mukaemásu̱, de-mukaéru *v* 出迎えます, 出迎える meets, greets, welcomes

denbu *n* 臀部 [BOOKISH] buttock, hips (*medical*)

denbun *n* 伝聞 hearsay

denbun *n* 電文 telegram, telegraphic message

dénchi *n* 電池 battery

denchō *n* 電柱 telephone/light pole

dendō *n* 伝道 conduction; **dendō-sha** *n* 伝道者 a missionary

déndō *n* 電動 electric operation, electric-powered; **déndō-isu** *n* 電動椅子 electric-powered wheelchair

dengon *n* 伝言 message (= **messēji** メッセージ)

denki *n* 伝記 biography

dénki *n* 電気 electricity, power; lights; **denki̱-su̱tándo** *n* 電気スタンド desk/floor lamp; **denki̱-yō´hin** *n* 電気用品 electrical appliances; **denki̱-kónro** *n* 電気コンロ hot plate; **denki̱-sōjíki** *n* 電気掃除機 vacuum cleaner; **denki-ya (san)** *n* 電気屋(さん) electrician

denmāku *n* デンマーク Denmark

dénpa *n* 電波 electric wave, radiowave

denpō *n* 電報 telegram, telegraph

denpun *n* でんぷん starch (*for cooking*); **denpún-shitsu (no)** *n (adj)* でんぷん質(の) starch(y)

denpyō *n* 伝票 check (*restaurant bill*)

denrai *n* 伝来 [BOOKISH] introduction, import: **senzo ~ (no)** 先祖伝来(の) descendant, patrimonial

denrei *n* 伝令 [BOOKISH] orderly, herald

dénryoku *n* 電力 electric power; **denryoku-gáisha** *n* 電力会社 power company

denryū *n* 電流 electric current

densen *n* 電線 electric wire, power line

densen *n* 伝染 contagion; **densen-byō** *n* 伝染病 contagious/infectious/disease, epidemic

densetsu *n* 伝説 tradition (*legend*): ~ **no otoko** 伝説の男 legendary man

dénsha *n* 電車 (*electric*) train, streetcar

dénshi (no) *adj* 電子(の) electron(ic); **denshi-manē** *n* 電子マネー electronic money, cyberbuck (*Internet*); **denshi-shoseki** *n* 電子書籍 digital book, e-book, electronic book (*Internet*)

dentatsu *n* 伝達 conveyance, transmission

dentō *n* 電灯 lamp, light, flashlight

dentō *n* 伝統 tradition; **dentō-teki (na)** *adj* 伝統的(な) traditional

denwa *n* 電話 telephone (call): ~ **ni demásu** 電話に出ます answers the phone; ~ **o kakemásu/shimásu** 電話をかけます/します makes a phone call; **denwa-bángō** *n* 電話番号 telephone number; **denwa-kōkánshu** *n* 電話交換手 telephone operator; **denwa-sen** *n* 電話線 phone line, telephone wire(s)

deodoranto *n* デオドラント deodorant

depāto *n* デパート department store

déppa *n* 出っ歯 protruding tooth, bucktooth

deshí *n* 弟子 apprentice, disciple

... déshita *v* …でした **1.** was; it was **2. ...-masén** ~ …ませんでした didn't

... deshō *v* …でしょう probably, probably (it) is; I think; don't you think?

... desu, dá *v* …です, だ is, has been (and still is), will be; it is

dē'ta *n* データ data

detarame *n* でたらめ nonsense; **detarame na** *adj* でたらめな irresponsible, unreliable

detchiagemásu, detchiagéru *v* でっちあげます, でっちあげる fake

dē'to *n* デート date (*time; engagement*)

dé wa *conj* では well then; in that case; and so; and now (= **ja** じゃ)

... dé wa *suffix* では (*with*) its being, it is and; if it be: ~ **arimasén (~ nái)** …ではありません(ではない) = **ja arimasén (ja nái)** じゃありません(じゃない) it is not

dezáin *n* デザイン design

dezáinā *n* デザイナー designer

dezā'to *n* デザート dessert

dii-kē' *n* ディーケー (= **DK**)

dainingu-kítchin ダイニングキッチン

disukáunto *n* ディスカウント discount

do *n* 度 degree; moderation; ~ **o sugoshimásu/koshimásu** 度を過ごします/越します goes too far, goes to excess

do-... *prefix* ど… exactly, really; **do-mannaka** *n* ど真ん中 dead center; do-konjō *n* ど根性 a lot of guts

...-dó *suffix* …度 **1.** times (*occasions*) **2.** degrees

dō´ *adj* どう how, why; (*in*) what (*way*); **Dō´-shimáshita ka.** どうしましたか. What happened? What did you do?; **Dō´-itashimashite.** どういたしまして. You're welcome.

dō´ *n* 銅 copper (= **aka-gane** あかがね・銅); dō´-ka *n* 銅貨 coin (*brass or copper*); dō-sei (no) *adj* 銅製(の) made of copper

dō´ *n* 胴 torso (= **dōtai** 胴体)

dō´-... *prefix* 同… the same …; dō-gaku *n* 同額 a like amount, the same amount (of money); dō-gyō *n* 同業 same trade: **~-sha** 同業者 professional brother/brethren; dō-hō *n* 同胞 brother(s)/sister(s) with same mother, fellow countryman/countrymen; dō-itsu (no) *adj* 同一(の) same; dō´-ji *n* 同時 ① **~ (no)** 同時(の) simultaneous ② **… to ~ ni** …と同時に at the same time as …; while …, on the other hand ③ at a (single) time, at one time; dō-jidai (ni) *adv* 同時代(に) (*in*) the same age/era; dō´-jidai (no) *adj* 同時代(の) contemporaneous, same generation; dō-jō *n* 同情 sympathy, compassion; dō-ka *n* 同化 elaboration, assimilation; dō-kan *n* 同感 same sentiment, empathy; dō´-ki *n* 同期 the same period; dō´-kí (-sei) *n* 同期(生) classmates who joined the school in the same year (= **dō-kyū´-sei** 同級生), employees who joined the company in the same year; dō-koku-jin *n* 同国人 fellow countryman/countrymen; dō-kyū´-sei *n* 同級生 classmate; dō-ryō *n* 同僚 colleague; dō-sei (no) *adj* 同性(の) person of the same sex; dō-sei (no) *adj* 同姓(の) having the same name; dō-shitsú *n* 同室 same room: **~-sha** 同室者 roommate; dō-zai (no) *adj* 同罪(の) being equally guilty: **dōzai-sha** 同罪者 fellow sinners

dóa *n* ドア door; doa-nobu *n* ドアノブ door knob

doai *n* 度合い degree, level, rate

do-bin *n* 土瓶 teapot

dobu *n* どぶ・溝 gutter

dōbutsu *n* 動物 animal; dōbutsú-en *n* 動物園 zoo

dóchira *pron* どちら which one (*of the two*) = **dotchi** どっち; [DEFERENTIAL] where (= **dóko** どこ), who (= **dáre** 誰); dóchira dé mo *adv* どちらでも either one of the two; [+ NEGATIVE verb] neither one of the two; dóchira ka *adj, adv* どちらか one of the two; dochira mo *adv* どちらも ① [+ NEGATIVE verb] neither one ② both; dóchira sama *n* どちら様 [DEFERENTIAL] who (are you)

dō dé mo *adv* どうでも anyhow (at all)

dōfū shimásu (suru) *v* 同封します(する) encloses (*in envelope*)

dogeza *n* 土下座 kneeling on the ground: ~ **shite ayamarimásu** 土下座して謝ります falls on one's knees to ask for pardon
dōgi *n* 道義 moral principle
dogitsui *adj* どぎつい [INFORMAL] gaudy; dogitsui hyōgen *n* どぎつい表現 shocking expression
dōgú *n* 道具 tool; dōgú-bako *n* 道具箱 tool box
dohyō *n* 土俵 sumo-wrestling ring: ~ **ni agarimásu** 土俵に上がります steps onto the sumo ring
dōi *n* 同意 agreement, approval
dōin *n* 動員 mobilization, recruitment
dóitsu *pron* どいつ which damn one
Dóitsu *n* ドイツ Germany; Doitsu-go *n* ドイツ語 German language; Doitsú-jin *n* ドイツ人 a German
dṓiu ... *adj* どういう… what kind/sort of…
doji *n* どじ goof (= **hema** へま) boob
dō-jimásu, dō-jíru *v* 動じます, 動じる gets agitated, upset
dō-jinai = (…-témo) dō-jimasén (…ても)動じません (is unfazed (by))
dojō *n* ドジョウ loach, mudfish
dojō *n* 土壌 [BOOKISH] soil borne: **yutaka na** ~ 豊かな土壌 rich soil
dṓjō *n* 道場 martial arts hall
dṓka *interj* どうか please: ~ **onegai desukara** どうかお願いですから for God's [*Christ's, Heaven's, Pete's*] sake
... dṓka *suffix* …どうか **... ka ~** …かどうか (whether …) or not, ~ **shite imasu** どうかしています something wrong with, crazy, mad
dōkan *n* 導管 pipe, duct
dóki *n* 土器 earthenware
dōki *n* 動機 motivation, motive
dōki *n* 動悸 beat, pulse: ~ **ga shimásu** 動悸がします palpitates
dókidoki shimásu (suru) *v* どきどきします(する) one's heart throbs (beats, flutters)
dokimásu, doku *v* 退きます, 退く gets out of the way
dókku *n* ドック dock
dóko *pron* どこ where, what part/place; dóko-dé-mo *adv* どこでも anywhere (at all); dóko-doko *pron* どこどこ somewhere or other, such-and-such a place (= **dóko-soko** どこそこ); dóko ka *n, adv* どこか somewhere; dóko made *adv* どこまで where to; how far; doko mo *adv* どこも [+ NEGATIVE verb/adj] nowhere; dóko-soko *pron* どこそこ somewhere or other (= **dóko-doko** どこどこ)
dōkoku *n* 慟哭 [BOOKISH] crying out with grief
...-dókoroka *adv* …どころか = **sore-~** それどころか rather, on the contrary
dokú *n* 毒 (= **dokú-butsu** 毒物) poison; doku-késhí *n* 毒消し antidote
dokudan *n* 独断 dogma; dokudan-jō *n* 独壇場 [BOOKISH] monopoly

dokudoku nagaremásu (nagareru) *v* どくどく流れます(流れる) gurgles
dokudokushii *adj* 毒々しい gaudy, virulent
dokugaku *n* 独学 self-study
dokuhaku *n* 独白 monologue
dokuritsu *n* 独立 independence; **~ shite imásu** 独立しています standing on one's own two feet, being independent; **~shita …** 独立した… independent
dokuryoku (de) *adj* 独力(で) by oneself
dokusái-sha *n* 独裁者 dictator, absolute ruler
dókusha *n* 読者 reader (*person*)
dokushin *n* 独身 single, unmarried, bachelor; **dokushin-sha** *n* 独身者 single
dokusho *n* 読書 reading books
dokusō *n* 独走 leaving all the other runners far behind
dokusō *n* 独奏 solo performance
dokusō-sei *n* 独創性 originality: **~ ni kakeru/toboshii** 独創性に欠ける/乏しい unoriginal
dokutoku (no/na) *adj* 独特(の/な) characteristic, peculiar, unique
dō´kutsu *n* 洞窟 cave
dokuzetsu *n* 毒舌 a barbed/spiteful tongue; **dokuzetsu-ka** *n* 毒舌家 person with a poisonous/sharp tongue
dokyumentarii dorama *n* ドキュメンタリー・ドラマ infotainment (*documentary film*)
…´-dómo …共 (*makes humble plurals*): **watakushi-~** わたくし[私]ども we/us
domein-mei (nēmu) *n* ドメイン名(ネーム) domain-name (*Internet*)
dō´mo どうも **1.** *interj* thank you **2.** *interj* excuse me **3.** *adj* somehow, vaguely
dōmō (na) *adj* 獰猛(な) fierce, savage
domorimásu, domoru *v* どもります, どもる stammers, stutters
dón どん・ドン boom, bam (*sound*)
…-don *n* …丼 **donburi** どんぶり[丼]
donarimásu, donáru *v* 怒鳴ります, 怒鳴る shouts, yells
dónata *pron* どなた [DEFERENTIAL] who (= **dáre** 誰)
donburi *n* どんぶり・丼 large rice bowl
donburi-mono, don-mono *n* 丼もの a bowl of rice with some kind of topping
dóndon *adv* どんどん one right after another, in large numbers
do-nichi *n* 土日 Saturday and Sunday
dō´ni ka *adv* どうにか somehow
Donmai *interj* ドンマイ Don't worry., Never mind.
dónna *adj* … どんな… what kind of…: **~ ni** どんなに to what extent, how much
dóno … *adj* どの… which … (*of more than two*)
dono-gurai/kurai *adv* どの位 how many/much/far/long

dónsu *n* どんす・緞子 damask
donyori (to shita) *adj* どんより(とした) dull, gray, somber: **~ to shita me** どんよりとした目 dull eyes
dorafuto *n* ドラフト draft
doraggu *n* ドラッグ drug
doraggu sutoa *n* ドラッグストア drugstore
doraibā *n* ドライバー driver
doraibu *n* ドライブ drive; **doraibu-surū** *n* ドライブスルー drive-through (*restaurant*)
dorai-kuríiníngu *n* ドライクリーニング dry cleaning
dorái (na) *adj* ドライ(な) dry; modern, sophisticated, unsentimental
doraiyā *n* ドライヤー dryer, drier
dōrákú *n* 道楽 **1.** dissipation **2. (o-dōrakú** お道楽) pastime, hobby
dóre *pron* どれ which one (*of more than two*): **~ ka** どれか some/any one of them; **~ dé mo** どれでも whichever/any of them; **~ mo** どれも (not) any of them; **~-gurai/kurai** どれ位 how many/much/far/long
dorei *n* 奴隷 slave
dóresu *n* ドレス dress, frock
dōrí *n* 道理 reason (*what is sensible*)
...-dōrí …通り avenue; just as (*according with*): **jikan-~ (ni)** 時間通り(に) on time …
dóriru *n* ドリル drill (*tool; practice*)
doró *n* 泥 mud; muck (*filth, dirt*); **doro-dárake/mamire (no)** *adj* 泥だらけ/まみれ(の) muddy
dō´ro *n* 道路 road; **dōro-hyō´shiki** 道路標識 road sign
dorobō *n* 泥棒 thief, robber, burglar
dóru *n* ドル dollar; **dóru-bako** *n* ドル箱 cash cow, gold mine, moneymaker
dóryoku *n* 努力 effort
dō´sa *n* 動作 (body) movements, gestures
dosamawari *n* どさまわり road show: **~ o shimásu̲** どさ回りをします goes on the road, goes on a tour
dō´san *n* 動産 [BOOKISH] movable property
dōsei *n* 同棲 living together (*for unmarried couple*)
dosha *n* 土砂 earth and sand; **dosha-buri** *n* 土砂降り torrential downpour
dōshi *n* 動詞 verb
...dō´shi *suffix* …同士: **otoko-~ no yakusoku** 男同士の約束 promise between man and man
dō´shi *n* 同志 fellow …, comrade
dōshin̲ *n* 童心 juvenile mind
dō´-shi̲te *adv* どうして why; how: **~ mo** どうしても one way or another, some how or other
dosō *n* 土葬 burial under the earth
dōsō´-kai *n* 同窓会 alumni association; class reunion
dossari *adv* どっさり all of a heap: **~ aru shigoto** どっさりある仕事 a pile of work
dotabata *adv* どたばた noisily:

~-kigeki どたばた喜劇 slapstick comedy
dotanba (de) *adv* 土壇場(で) (*at*) the last moment
dótchi *pron* どっち = **dóchira** どちら which one (*of the two*)
dote *n* 土手 dike
dōtei *n* 童貞 virgin (*male*)
dōtoku *n* 道徳 morals, morality; dōtoku-teki (na) *adj* 道徳的(な) moral
dótto *adv* どっと suddenly, with a rush: **~-waraimás<u>u</u>** どっと笑います everybody laughs
dōwa *n* 童話 fairy tale
doyagai *n* どや街 skid row
doyashimás<u>u</u>, doyasu *v* どやします, どやす chews out
dōyō (no) *adj* 同様(の) the same
dōyō *n* 動揺 [BOOKISH] agitation, unrest
Doyō´(bi) *n* 土曜(日) Saturday
doyomeki *n* どよめき clamor, hubbub
doyomekimásu, doyomaku *v* どよめきます, どよめく rings, (*a crowd of people*) makes a ruckus
dō´yū ("iu") ... *adj* どうゆう(いう)... what kind/sort of... (= **dónna ...** どんな ...)
dō´zo *interj* どうぞ **1.** please **2.** here it is
dy... j...
dz... z...

E

é *n* 絵 picture, painting, drawing; e-hágaki *n* 絵葉書 picture postcard
e *n* 柄 handle
e (-sá) *n* え(さ)・餌 bait
e *interj* えっ eh?, what?
ē *interj* ええ yes
... e particle ...へ to (*a place*); [replaces **... ni** ...に *before* **... no ...** ...の...] to (*a person*)
ea-kon *n* エアコン air conditioning/conditioner
eamēru *n* エアメール airmail
earain *n* エアライン airline
earobíkusu *n* エアロビクス aerobics
eatāminaru *n* エアターミナル air terminal: **~-basu** エアターミナルバス air terminal bus
eba-míruku *n* エバミルク evaporated milk
ebi *n* エビ・海老 shrimp: **kurumá-~** 車エビ prawn; **isé-~** 伊勢エビ lobster; **shibá-~** 芝エビ tiny shrimp
ē-bii-shíi *n* エービーシー・ABC alphabet (ABC)
echikétto *n* エチケット etiquette
eda *n* 枝 branch
efutiipii (FTP) *n* FTP・エフティーピー File Transfer Protocol, FTP (*computer*)
egakimás<u>u</u>, egáku *v* 描きます, 描く draws (a picture)

egao *n* 笑顔 smiling face
egetsunái *adj* えげつない [INFORMAL] gross, nasty [IN NEGATIVE SENSE]
ei-... *prefix* 英. . . **1.** English **2.** great; ei-bun *n* 英文 English text; eiei-jiten *n* 英英辞典 English-English dictionary; Ei-go *n* 英語 English (*language*); ei-kaiwa *n* 英会話 English conversation; ei-ki *n* 英気 vigor, energy; Ei-koku *n* 英国 Great Britain, the United Kingdom (U.K.) = **Igirisu** イギリス England; ei-wa *n, adj* 英和 English-Japanese: **~-jíten** 英和辞典 English-Japanese dictionary; ei-yaku *n* 英訳 English translation; ei-yū *n* 英雄 hero, heroine
eieiō *interj* エイエイおう Hip, hip, hurrah!
eien (no) *adj* 永遠(の) eternal, permanent; eien ni *adv* 永遠に eternally, permanently
eíga *n* 映画 movie, film; eigá-kan *n* 映画館 movie theater; eiga-sutā *n* 映画スター movie star
eiga *n* 栄華 prosperity
eigō *n* 永劫 [BOOKISH] eon: **mirai-~** 未来永劫 for eternity
eigyō *n* 営業 (*running a*) business; eigyō-jíkan *n* 営業時間 business hours, operating hours
eikan *n* 栄冠 crown, laurel
eiki *n* 鋭気 spirit
eikō *n* 栄光 glory, honor
eikyō *n* 影響 influence; **~ o ukemásu** 影響を受けます receives an influence
eikyū (ni) *adv* 永久(に) eternally, permanently, forever
eisei *n* 衛生 hygiene, health, sanitation; eisei-teki (na) *adj* 衛生的(な) sanitary
eisei *n* 衛星 satellite; eisei chūkei *n* 衛星中継 satellite transmission
éito, ē′to *n* エイト/エート eight; 8-oared racing boat
eiyō *n* 栄養 nutrition, nourishment
eizō *n* 映像 picture, image
eizoku *n* 永続 lasting for a long time, permanence
éizu *n* エイズ AIDS
éki *n* 駅 railroad station; eki-ben 駅弁 box lunches sold at railroad stations; eki-chō *n* 駅長 station-master
ekisu *n* エキス extract
ekitai *n* 液体 liquid
ekkusu-sen *n* エックス[X]線 X-ray (= **rentogen** レントゲン)
ékubo *n* えくぼ dimple
emásu, éru *v* 得ます, 得る [BOOKISH] gets; can do
én *n* 円 circle (= **maru** 丸): **~ taku** 円卓 round table; en-kei *n* 円形 circle; en-shū *n* 円周 circumference: **~-ritsu** 円周率 circle ratio, pi
én *n* 円, **...′-en** ..円 yen (¥): **en-daka (/-yasu)** 円高(/安) high (/low) value of the yen
enchaku *n* 延着 delayed arrival
enbō *n* 遠望 distant view
enchō *n* 延長 extension; enchō-kō′do 延長コード extension cord

endan *n* 縁談 marriage proposal
endan *n* 演壇 lecture platform
éndō, éndō-mame *n* エンドウ, エンドウ豆 peas
enen (to) *adv* 延々(と) endlessly: **~ to hanashimásu** 延々と話します goes on and on about
enérúgii *n* エネルギー energy
enérugísshu (na) *adj* エネルギッシュ(な) energetic
engan *n* 沿岸 the coast
engawa *n* 縁側 (*wooden*) veranda, porch (*in traditional Japanese house*)
engei *n* 園芸 gardening
engeki *n* 演劇 drama, play; **engeki-jin** *n* 演劇人 theater people
engi *n* 縁起 **1.** omen, luck **2.** (*historical*) origin; **~ ga/no yoi** 縁起が/の良い is of good omen
éngi *n* 演技 performance; acting; **engí-sha** *n* 演技者 performer
engo *n* 援護 support
engun *n* 援軍 rescue forces, support arms, reinforcement
engumi *n* 縁組み marriage, match
énjin *n* エンジン engine (*of automobile*)
enjínia *n* エンジニア engineer, specialist
enjimasu, enjiru *v* 演じます, 演じる plays, acts, performs
énjo *n* 援助 support (*aid*), backing
enjói *n* エンジョイ enjoyment
enjuku *n* 円熟 [BOOKISH] fully maturing
enka *n* 演歌 sad and melancholic Japanese songs (*ballad*)
enkai *n* 宴会 party, banquet: **~ o hirakimásu** 宴会を開きます holds a party
enkaku *n* 沿革 [BOOKISH] history
enkaku *n* 遠隔 [BOOKISH] remoteness; **enkaku-sōsa** *n* 遠隔操作 remote handling
enkei *n* 遠景 [BOOKISH] distant landscape
enki *n* 延期 postponement
enkinkan *n* 遠近感 perspective
enkyori *n* 遠距離 long distance; **enkyori-ren'ai** *n* 遠距離恋愛 long-distance love affair
enma-daiō *n* エンマ(大王) the (great) King of Hell/the Buddhist Hades, Yama
enmaku *n* 煙幕 smoke screen
enman (na) *adj* 円満(な) satisfactory
enmei *n* 延命 life extension; **enmei-chiryō** *n* 延命治療 life-sustaining treatment
enmoku *n* 演目 program
enmusubi *n* 縁結び matchmaking: **~ no kami** 縁結びの神 the god of marriage
énnichi *n* 縁日 a temple fair (*festival*)
ennō *n* 延納 [BOOKISH] delayed payment
enokí-dake/take *n* エノキダケ・榎茸 straw mushrooms
enpitsu *n* 鉛筆 pencil; **enpitsu-kezuri** *n* 鉛筆削り pencil sharpener
enro *n* 遠路 from a long distance: **~ harubaru** 遠路はるばる all the way

enryo *n* 遠慮 (**go-enryo** ご遠慮 [HONORIFIC]) reticence, social reserve, shyness; **Go-~ náku.** ご遠慮なく. Don't be shy/reticent.; **~ shite okimásu** 遠慮しておきます takes a rain check, declines for now
enshi *n* 遠視 farsightedness (*presbyopia*)
enshutsu *n* 演出 production, staging (*play, movie*)
énso *n* 塩素 chlorine
ensō *n* 演奏 performance (*musical instrument*); **ensō'-kai** *n* 演奏会 concert
ensoku *n* 遠足 picnic, outing
entai *n* 延滞 arrear (*overdues*); **entai-ryōkin** *n* 延滞料金 deferred premium
entātei(n)mento *n* エンターテイ(ン)メント entertainment
enten *n* 炎天 [BOOKISH] scorching sun/weather: **~-ka de** 炎天下で under a blazing sun
entotsu *n* 煙突 chimney, smoke-stack
enzetsu *n* 演説 speech (*public*)
épuron *n* エプロン apron
erā *n* エラー error; **erā-messēji** *n* エラーメッセージ error message
erabimásu, erábu *v* 選びます, 選ぶ chooses, selects, elects
erái *adj* 偉い **1.** great, grand, superior (*person*) **2.** terrible, awful (= **hidoi** ひどい・酷い)
erebē'tā *n* エレベーター elevator
ereganto (na) *adj* エレガント(な) elegant (= **yūga (na)** 優雅(な))
erí *n* えり・襟 collar (*of closing/clothes*): **~ o tadashimásu** 襟を正します straightens oneself
éro-hon *n* エロ本 [INFORMAL] pornography book
ese-... *adj* えせ… pseudo-…
essē *n* エッセー essay
esu-efu *n* SF science fiction
esukarē'tā *n* エスカレーター escalator
etai-no-shirenai *adj* 得体の知れない strange, as deep as a well
étchi (na) *adj* エッチ(な) dirty-minded: **~ na hanashí** エッチな話 a dirty (*an off-color*) story
éte-shite *adv* 得てして usually
ē-to *interj* えーと/ええと well now, uh, let me see

F

fáiawōru *n* ファイアウォール firewall (*Internet security*)
fáibā *n* ファイバー fiber
fáibu *n* ファイブ five
fáindā *n* ファインダー finder
fáiringu *n* ファイリング filing
fáiru *n* ファイル file
fáito *n* ファイト fight
fákkusu *n* ファックス fax, facsimile (= **fakushimiri** ファクシミリ)

fán *n* ファン fan (*enthusiast*); **ya-kyū-~** 野球ファン baseball fan; fan-kurabu *n* ファンクラブ fan club

fánkushon *n* ファンクション function

fánshii *n* ファンシー fancy

fántajii *n* ファンタジー fantasy

fáshisuto *n* ファシスト fascist

fásshon *n* ファッション fashion

fásunā *n* ファスナー fastener, zipper

fāsuto-fūdo *n* ファーストフード fast food

fāsuto-nēmu *n* ファーストネーム first name

fáuru *n* ファウル foul

feisu bukku *n* フェイスブック Facebook (*Internet*)

fiibā *n* フィーバー fever

Firípin *n* フィリピン Philippines

fírumu, fuirumu *n* フィルム, フイルム film

fírutā *n* フィルター filter

fisshingu *n* フィッシング phishing (*fraud*)

fō *n* フォー, **fóa** フォア four

fō′ku *n* フォーク fork

fu *n* フ・麩 pieces of dried wheat gluten

fu- *prefix* 不 un-, non-; fu-an (na) *adj* 不安(な) uneasy, anxious; fú-ben (na) *adj* 不便(な) inconvenient, unhandy; fu-dō′toku *n* 不道徳 immorality; fugō′kaku *n* 不合格 failure; fu-kánō (na) *adj* 不可能(な) impossible; fu̲-kai (na) *adj* 不快(な) unpleasant, displeasing, displeased (= **fu-yúkai (na)** 不愉快(な)); fu̲-kéiki *n* 不景気 depression, recession, hard times; fu̲-kísóku (na) *adj* 不規則(な) irregular; fu-kō′ *n* 不幸 misfortune; fu-kō′hei (na) *adj* 不公平(な) unfair; fu-kyō *n* 不況 business slump, depression; fú-jiyū (na) *adj* 不自由(な) inconvenient, restricted; needy; weak: **okane ni ~ shinai** お金に不自由しない has no shortage of money; fu-man(zoku) *n* 不満(足) discontent; fu-mei (no) *adj* 不明(の) unknown, obscure: **yukue ~ (no)** 行方不明(の) disappearance, missing; fú-ri (na) *adj* 不利(な) unfavorable, adverse; fu-rin *n* 不倫 adultery; fu-ryō (no) *adj* 不良(の) bad, no good, inferior; fu-senmei (na) *adj* 不鮮明(な) obscure, unclear; fu̲-shin *n* 不審 doubt, suspicion; fu-shi (no) *adj* 不死(の) immortal(ity); fu̲-shízen (na) *adj* 不自然(な) unnatural; fu̲-shō′ji *n* 不祥事 scandal: **~ o okoshimásu̲** 不祥事を起こします disgraces; fu̲-soku *n* 不足 shortage, insufficiency, deficiency, scarcity, lack; fu̲-tegiwa *n* 不手際 blunder, mismanagement; fu̲-tei (no) *adj* 不定(の) unfixed, uncertain, indefinite, undecided: **~-ki (no)** 不定期(の) irregular; fu̲-tei (na) *adj* 不貞(な) unchaste, unfaithful (to her husband); fu̲-teki (na) *adj* 不敵(な) bold, lawless: **daitan-futeki**

(na) 大胆不敵(な) fearless; fu-tekinin (na) *adj* 不適任(な) unfit: **futekinin-sha** 不適任者 misfit; fu-tekisetsu (na) *adj* 不適切(な) irrelevance, inappropriate; fu-tekitō (na) *adj* 不適当(な) inadequate, unsuitable; fu-tettei (na) *adj* 不徹底(な) not thorough, imperfect, halfway; fu-tokui (na/no) *adj* 不得意(な/の) poor/weak at; fu-tokutei (no) *adj* 不特定(の) indefinite; fu-tō (na) *adj* 不当(な) unfair, unjustified: ; fu-tōshiki *n* 不等式 inequality; fu-tōitsu *n* 不統一 lacking of unity, disunity; fu-tōkō *n* 不登校 nonattendance at school, truancy; fu-tsuriai *n* 不釣合い imbalance; fu-un (na) *adj* 不運(な) unfortunate; fu-yō (no) *adj* 不要(の) unnecessary, unneeded; fu-yō (no) *adj* 不用(の) useless, disused; fu-yúkai (na) *adj* 不愉快(な) un--pleasant, displeasing, displeased; fu-zai *n* 不在 absence: **~-tōhyō** 不在投票 absentee vote

fú *n, suffix* 府, **…´-fu** … 府 an urban prefecture: **Kyōto-fu** 京都府 Kyoto Prefecture

fū´ *n* 封 sealing: **… no ~ o shimásu** …の封をします seals a letter

fúbo *n* 父母 father and mother, one's parents (= **ryōshin** 両親)

fúbuki *n* 吹雪 snowstorm

fuchí *n* 縁 edge, rim, frame

fuda *n* 札 label, tag, card, check

fúdan *adv* 普段 usually, ordinarily, always; fúdan (no) *adj* 普段(の) usual, everyday, ordinary; fudán-gí *n* 普段着 everyday clothes

fude *n* 筆 writing/painting brush; fude-bako *n* 筆箱 pencil box/case

fudō (no) *adj* 不動(の) [BOOKISH] steadfast: **~ no chii ni imásu** 不動の地位にいます is in an impregnable position

fudō´san *n* 不動産 real estate

fuemásu, fuéru *v* 増えます, 増える multiplies; grows in quantity/number, gets bigger, swells, increases, expands

fū´fu *n* 夫婦 husband and wife, Mr. and Mrs., (*married*) couple: **fūfu-tomo(domo)** 夫婦共(々) both husband and wife

fúgú *n* フグ・河豚 blowfish, puffer

fú-gú *n* (*discriminatory term*) 不具 cripple

fui (ni) *adv* 不意(に) suddenly

fuji *n* フジ・藤 wisteria

fujin *n* 婦人 lady, woman (**go-fujin** ご婦人 [HONORIFIC])

fujin *n* 夫人 wife: **-fujin** -夫人 Mrs. …

Fuji (-san) *n* 富士(山) Mount Fuji, Fujiyama

fujo *n* 婦女 [BOOKISH] lady, woman (= **fujin** 婦人): **fujo-bōkō** 婦女暴行 sexual assault

fujo *n* 扶助 aid, support: **fujo-kin** 扶助金 benefits

fuká *n* フカ big shark (*used in western Japan*) (→ **same** サメ・鮫)

fukái *adj* 深い deep: **fukáku** 深く deeply
fukása *n* 深さ depth
fukashimásu, fukásu *v* 蒸かします, 蒸かす steams (*food*)
fukashimásu, fukásu *v* 吹かします, 吹かす smokes: **énjin o ~** エンジンを吹かします, 吹かす races the engine
fukashimásu, fukásu *v* 更かします, 更かす sits up late: **yó o ~** 夜を更かします, 更かす stays up late
fuké *v* ふけ dandruff
fū́kei *n* 風景 scenery, landscape; fūkei-ga *n* 風景画 landscape painting(s)/picture(s)
fukemásu, fukéru *v* 更けます, 更ける gets late: **yo ga ~** 夜が更けます, 更ける (*the night*) grows late
fukemásu, fukéru *v* 老けます, 老ける gets old, ages
fuketsu (na) *adj* 不潔(な) unclean, dirty, filthy
fuki *n* フキ・蕗 bog rhubarb
fukimásu, fuku *v* 拭きます, 拭く wipes
fukimásu, fúku *v* 葺きます, 葺く thatches (a roof), tiles roof: **... no yáne o ~** ...の屋根を葺きます covers with a roof, roofs: **kawara de ~** 瓦で葺きます tiles a roof: **káya/kusá/wára de ~** 茅/草/藁で葺きます thatches
fukimásu, fúku *v* 吹きます, 吹く blows
fukín *n* 布きん napkin, towel, cloth, washcloth, dishcloth
fukín *n* 付近 vicinity
fukkakemásu, fukkakéru *v* ふっかけます, ふっかける overcharges
fukú *n* 服 clothes, suit, dress uniform
fuku *n* 福 happiness; fuku-biki *n* 福引 lottery; raffle; fuku no kami *n* 福の神 god of wealth
fuku- *prefix* 副- vice-, assistant-; fuku-kaichō *n* 副会長 vice chairman/chairperson; fuku-shachō *n* 副社長 vice-president (*of a company*); fukú-sayō *n* 副作用 side-effect, after-effect
fuku- *n* 複 double; fuku-sei *n* 複製 replica, reproduction, reprint; fuku-sha *n* 複写 reproduction, copy; fuku-sū *n* 複数 plural
fukugō-go *n* 複合語 compound (*word*)
fukumemásu, fukuméru *v* 含めます, 含める includes, adds
fukumimásu, fukúmu *v* 含みます, 含む holds in the mouth; contains; implies; bears/keeps in mind
fukuramashimásu, fukuramásu *v* 膨らまします, 膨らます bulges, inflates
fukurami *v* 膨らみ bulge
fukuramimásu, fukuramu *v* 膨らみます, 膨らむ swells up, bulges
fukuremásu, fukureru *v* 膨れます, 膨れる swells up; pouts, sulks
fukuró *n* 袋 bag, sack
fukúrō *n* フクロウ・梟 owl
fukushi *n* 副詞 adverb
fukúshi *n* 福祉 welfare; fukushi-shí-

setsu *n* 福祉施設 welfare facility
fukushū *n* 復習 review (*study*)
fukushū *n* 復讐 revenge, vengeance
fukushū shimásu (suru) *v* 復習します(する) reviews (*study*)
fukushū shimásu (suru) *v* 復讐します(する) takes revenge, revenges
fukusō *n* 服装 dress, attirement, clothes, costume
fukuzatsu (na) *adj* 複雑(な) complicated: **~ na shinkyō** 複雑な心境 mixed feelings: **~ na tachiba** 複雑な立場 complicated situation
fukyū *n* 普及 diffusion, popularization: **pasokon no ~ (ga susunde)** パソコンの普及(が進んで) (*with*) the increase of computer users
fumemásu, fumeru *v* 踏めます, 踏める can tread
fū'mí *n* 風味 flavor: **~ o tamochimásu** 風味を保ちます keeps/preserves a flavor; **~ no aru ryōri** 風味のある料理 savory dish
fumi-komimásu, fumi-kómu *v* 踏み込みます, 踏み込む **1.** steps into/on **2.** trespasses (*on*); raids
fumimásu, fumu *v* 踏みます, 踏む steps on, treads
fumotó *n* 麓 foot (*of a mountain*)
fún *n* 糞 feces, dung
...'-fun *suffix* …分 minute(s)
funá-... *prefix* 船. . . ship, vessel; funá-bin *n* 船便 sea mail; funá-nori *n* 船乗り sailor, crew (*member*); funá-yoi *n* 船酔い seasick(ness)
funbari *n* 踏ん張り effort: **mō hito ~** もうひと踏ん張り one last effort; **~ ga kikimasen** 踏ん張りがききません can't hold on
funbetsu *n* 分別 discretion, sense: **~ ga tsukimásu** 分別がつきます cuts a tooth
fundoshi *n* ふんどし・褌 loincloth, breechcloth: **hito no ~ de sumō o torimásu** 人のふんどしで相撲を取ります rides on someone's back
fúne *n* 船[舟] boat, ship
fungai *n* 憤慨 [BOOKISH] indignation, resentment
fun'íki *n* 雰囲気 atmosphere (*of a place*), mood, aura, air: **~-zukuri** 雰囲気作り creating atmosphere
funka *n* 噴火 eruption: **~-kō** 噴火口 crater
funmatsu *n* 粉末 powder: **~ ni shimásu** 粉末にします makes into powder, pulverizes
funpatsu *n* 奮発 putting a lot of effort, spoiling oneself
funshitsu *n* 紛失 loss: **~-todoke o dashimásu** 紛失届けを出します reports a missing item
funsō *n* 扮装 disguise: **~ shimásu** 扮装します is costumed, makes up
funsō *n* 紛争 conflict, dispute; funsō-chiiki *n* 紛争地域 disputed area, conflict-affected region
funsui *n* 噴水 fountain
funtō *n* 奮闘 struggle
funuke *n* 腑抜け coward: **~-mono** 腑抜け者 cowardly man
furafura *adv* ふらふら staggers, reels: **~-kan** ふらふら感 wooziness

furai-pan *n* フライパン frying pan

furamenko *n* フラメンコ flamenco: **~ dansu** フラメンコダンス flamenco dance

Furansu *n* フランス France; Furansu-go *n* フランス語 French (*language*); Furansú-jin *n* フランス人 a French

furari (to) *adv* ふらり(と) aimlessly: **~ tachiyorimásu** ふらりと立ち寄ります drops in

furasuko *n* フラスコ flask

furatsukimásu *v* ふらつきます staggers, sways

furemásu, fureru *v* 触れます, 触れる touches (= **sawarimásu** 触ります) **1.** contacts with; touches upon **2.** mentions, refers to

furemásu, fureru *v* 振れます, 振れる can wave it, can shake it

fureraremásu, furerareru *v* 触れられます, 触れられる can touch

furí *v* 振り manner, pretense, air

furí *v* 降り the rain/snow, the downpour

furi-gana *n* ふりがな・フリガナ readings marked (*for Chinese characters*)

furi-kae *n* 振(り)替(え) transfer (*of funds*); furikae-yókin *n* 振替預金 transfer deposit; furikae-kyūjitsu *n* 振替休日 compensating/substitute holiday

furi-kaemásu, furi-kaeru *v* 振(り)替えます, 振(り)替える transfers it

furi-kaerimásu, furi-kaéru *v* 振り返ります, 振り返る looks back

furi-kake *n* ふりかけ flavor sprinkles (*to top rice*)

furi-kakemásu, furi-kakéru *v* 振り掛けます, 振り掛ける sprinkles it

furimásu, furu *v* 振ります, 振る **1.** waves, shakes, swings **2.** wags it **3.** gives someone the ax

furimásu, fúru *v* 降ります, 降る falls, it precipitates (*rains, snows*)

furi-mukimásu, furi-múku *v* 振り向きます, 振り向く looks back

fūrin *n* 風鈴 wind-chimes

furisodé *n* 振り袖 long-sleeved kimono

furo *n* 風呂 (**o-fúro** お風呂) bath: **~ ni hairimásu** 風呂に入ります takes a bath; furo-bá *n* 風呂場 bathroom

furonto *n* フロント front desk; furonto-garasu *n* フロントガラス automobile windshield

furō´-sha *n* 浮浪者 vagabond, vagrant, tramp, homeless person

furuemásu, furueru *v* 震えます, 震える it shakes

furui *n* ふるい sieve, sifter

furúi *adj* 古い old (*not new*), stale (*not fresh*); secondhand, used

furumai *n* 振る舞い behavior (*deportment*): **furumaimásu** 振る舞います behaves

furui(okoshi)masu, furui(okosu), furu-u *v* 奮い(起こし)ます, 奮い(起こす), 奮う summons: **yūki o furuiokoshite/furutte...** ...勇気を奮い起こして/奮って ...with gathering up of one's courage

furū'to *n* フルート flute
furūtsu *n* フルーツ fruit: **~kakuteru** フルーツカクテル fruit cocktail
fū'ryū (na) *adj* 風流(な) elegant
fusá *n* 房 bunch (*cluster*)
fusagarimásu, fusagaru *v* 塞がります, 塞がる gets blocked (off), clogged/stopped up, gets occupied, booked up, engaged
fusagimásu, fusagu *v* 塞ぎます, 塞ぐ stops up, closes, blocks
fusái *n* 夫妻 Mr. and Mrs.; husband and wife (= **fūfu** 夫婦)
fusawashíi *adj* 相応しい suitable, worthy; becoming: **fusawáshiku** 相応しく suitably
fusegimásu, fuségu *v* 防ぎます, 防ぐ prevents; defends, protects
fusemásu, fuséru *v* 伏せます, 伏せる covers (up), conceals; lays it face down: **mi o fuséru** 身を伏せます gets down, crouches (*so as not to be seen*): **fuse-ji** 伏せ字 turned letter(s), unprintable word(s)
fūsen *n* 風船 balloon: **kami-~** 紙風船 paper balloon; fūsen-gámu *n* 風船ガム bubble gum
fushí *n* 節 joint; gnarl, knot, knob; tune, air; point (*in a statement*); fushi-me *n* 節目 turning point
fushigi (na) *adj* 不思議(な) weird, strange, mysterious; wonderful; suspicious, odd, funny, uncanny
fushin *n* 普請 building (*construction*), repairs
fu-shínsetsu (na) *adj* 不親切(な) unkind
fushō *n* 負傷 injury
fusso *n* フッ素 fluorine
fusumá *n* 襖 opaque sliding panel/door
futa *n* 蓋 lid, cover; flap (*of envelope, etc.*)
futa-... *adj* 二... two: **futá-ban** 二晩 two nights: **futá-kumi** 二組 two pairs (*of*)
futago *n* 双子 twins
futamatá (no) *adj* 二又[叉](の) forked, bifurcate(d): **futamata-sokétto** 二又[叉]ソケット two-way socked, double plug
futarí *n* 二人・ふたり (**o-futari** お二人) two persons
futa-sén *n* 二千・2,000, two thousand (= **ni-sén** 二千・2,000)
futatsú *n* 二つ・2つ・ふたつ two (*pieces, small objects*) (= **ní-ko** 二個); two years old (= **ní-sai** 二歳[才])
futatsú-mi(t)tsu *n* 二つ三つ two or three
futebuteshii *adj* ふてぶてしい impudent, audacious
futekusareta *adj* ふてくされた pouty: **futekusaremásu** ふてくされます has the sulks, gets sulky
futene *n* ふて寝 going to bed in a huff, staying in bed sulking
futo *adv* ふと unexpectedly; by chance, suddenly: **~ ki ga tsukimásu** ふと気がつきます comes to a sudden realization
futō *n* 埠頭 pier, wharf, quay
fūtō *n* 封筒 envelope: **henshin-yō ~**

返信用封筒 return-mail envelope

futodoki (na) *adj* 不届き(な) outrageous: **~ na okonai** 不届きな行い outrageous conduct

futō-fukutsu (na/no) *adj* 不撓不屈(な/の) indomitable, stubborn, unyielding: **~ no seishin** 不撓不屈の精神 indomitable spirit

futói *adj* 太い fat, plump, thick (and round)

futoji *n* 太字 boldface

futokoro *n* 懐 bosom, finance: **~ ga atatakai** 懐が暖かい has a heavy purse: **~ ga fukai** 懐が深い is magnanimous, has deep insight, has depth

futomomo *n* 太腿 thigh

futon *n* 布団(**o-futón** お布団) padded quilt, futon: **~ o hoshimásu** 布団を干します airs out futons

futorimásu, futóru *v* 太ります, 太る gets fat: **futótte imásu** 太っています is fat

futsū *adj, adv* 普通 ordinar(il)y, usual(ly), regular(ly), typical(ly), normal(ly): **~-dénsha** 普通電車 local (= *non-express*) train

futsū *n* 不通 disconnect

futsubun *n* 仏文 French sentence, French literature

futsufutsu (to) *adv* ふつふつ(と) gradually; **yūki ga ~ waku** 勇気がふつふつと沸く gets courage gradually

futsuka *n* 二日・2日・ふつか **1.** 2nd day (of month) **2.** two days: **~-kan** 二日間 for two days

futsū-yókin *n* 普通預金 (*ordinary*) savings account

futten *n* 沸点 boiling point

futtō *n* 沸騰 boiling

futto bōru *n* フットボール American football

futto wāku *n* フットワーク footwork: **~ ga karui** フットワークが軽い light on one's feet

fuyashimásu, fuyásu *v* 増やします, 増やす increases it/them

fuyō *n* 扶養 support, keeping; **fuyō-kazoku** *n* 扶養家族 dependent family/relatives; **fuyō-teate** *n* 扶養手当 family allowance

fuyú *n* 冬 winter: ~ 冬ご; **fuyu-yásumi** *n* 冬休み winter break/vacation

fuzakemásu, fuzakeru *v* ふざけます, ふざける fool around, kid around

fuzei *n* 風情 taste, appearance, look: **~ no aru keshiki/nagame** 風情のある景色/眺め scenic view

fuzoku *n* 付属・附属 attachment, belonging, accessory; **fuzokú-hin** *n* 付属品 attachments, accessories

fuzoroi *n* 不揃い irregularity

G

ga *n* ガ・蛾 moth

ga *n* 我 oneself, ego, atman: **~ o tōshimásu (tōsu)** 我を通します has one's own way: **~ o orimásu** 我を折ります gives yield

...ga …が *particle*: marks subject (who does, what is), but marks also object of: **... ga arimásu** …があります (has what): **... ga irimásu** …が要ります (needs/wants what): **... ga wakarimásu** …が分かります (understands what): **... ga dekimásu** …が出来ます (can do what)

... ga *conj* …が but (= **shikashi** しかし)

...´-ga *suffix* …画 painting, picture

gabugabu *adv* ガブガブ gulping down

gabyō *n* 画鋲 thumbtack

gachō *n* ガチョウ・鵞鳥 goose

gādeningu *n* ガーデニング gardening

gādoman *n* ガードマン guard

gādorēru *n* ガードレール guardrail

gādoru *n* ガードル girdle

gāgā *adv* ガーガー quack, croak: **~ iu oto** ガーガーいう音 rasping sound

gágaku *n* 雅楽 [BOOKISH] music traditional to the imperial court

gái *n* 害 damage, harm, injury

gai-... *prefix* 外… external, foreign: **gai(kokú)-jin** 外国人;

...´-gai …外 outside (*of*): **sen-mon-~ (no)** 専門外(の) unprofessional; **gái-bu** *n* 外部 the outside, the exterior; **gai-jin** *n* 外人 = **gaikokú-jin** 外国人 foreigner; **gai-ken** *n* 外見 appearance; **gai-kō** *n* 外交 diplomacy, diplomatic relations: **~ kan** 外交官 diplomat(ic) officer; **gai-koku** *n* 外国 foreign countries: **~-go** 外国語 foreign language(s); **~-jin** 外国人 foreigner; **gai-sen** *n* 外線 outside line/extension (*phone*); **gai-shoku** *n* 外食 eating out; **gai-tō** *n* 外套 coat, overcoat; **gai-sha** *n* 外車 foreign car; **gai-yō** *n* 外洋 high sea

...-gai *suffix* …貝 (*name of*) shell: **hotate-gai** ホタテガイ・帆立貝 scallop

gáido *n* ガイド guide

gáidoku *n* 害毒 [BOOKISH] evil, harm, bad influence on society

gaikan *n* 概観 survey, bird's-eye view

gaikotsu *n* 骸骨 skeleton

gaikyō *n* 概況 [BOOKISH] overall condition

Gaimú-shō *n* 外務省 Ministry of Foreign Affairs of Japan (MOFA)

gáinen *n* 概念 concept

gairo *n* 街路 broad street(s) in the town

gáisan *n* 概算 approximate calculation: **~-chi** 概算値 estimated figure

...-gáisha *n* …会社 = **kaisha** 会社 company

gaisha *n* 該者 = **hi-gaisha** 被害者 victim

gaitame *n* 外為 = **gaikoku-kawase** 外国為替 foreign currency operations

gaitō *n* 街頭 the street, the wayside

gaiyō *n* 概要 outline, summary

gaka *n* 画家 painter, artist

...-gákari …係 attendant (*in charge*)

gake *n* 崖 cliff

gakí *n* 餓鬼 [BOOKISH] hungry/begging ghost; ガキ・がき・餓鬼 brat: **~-daishō** がき大将 bully, little turk

gakka *n* 学科 subject (*school*): **~-shiken** 学科試験 examinations in academic subjects

gakkai *n* 学会 scholarly society, association

gakkári shimásu (suru) *v* がっかりします(する) is disappointed, discouraged

gakki *n* 学期 term (*of school*); semester

gakki *n* 楽器 musical instrument

gakkō *n* 学校 school

gakkyū *n* 学級 class/grade in school

gaku *n* 学 learning, study, science: **...´-gaku** …学 …-ology

gáku *n* 額 amount, sum

gakubu *n* 学部 department

gaku-buchi *n* 額縁 frame (*of picture*)

gakuchō *n* 学長 president of a school (*college/university*)

gakudan *n* 楽団 band (*of musicians*)

gakudō *n* 学童 school child(ren): **~-hoiku** 学童保育 after-school care for children

gakuen *n* 学園 academy

gakufu *n* 楽譜 musical score

gakugei *n* 学芸 liberal arts

gakugyo *n* 学業 schoolwork, academic work

gakuha *n* 学派 school of thought

gakuhi *n* 学費 academic fees

gákui *n* 学位 academic degree

gakúmon *n* 学問 knowledge, learning, education

gakunen *n* 学年 school year

gakureki *n* 学歴 educational background

gakuryoku *n* 学力 academic ability

gakusei *n* 学生 student: **~-fuku** 学生服 school uniform: **~-shō** 学生証 student identification card

gakusha *n* 学者 scholar

gákushi *n* 学士 bachelor's degree: **~-rónbun** 学士論文 senior essay

gakushū *n* 学習 study, learning

gakushū´-sha *n* 学習者 the student of a subject (*in general*): **Eigo-~** 英語学習者 the student of English

gamaguchi *n* がま口 purse, wallet, pocketbook (= **saifu** 財布)

gáman *n* 我慢 patience, perseverance; **~ dekimasén (dekinai)** 我慢できません(できない) cannot stand it; **~-zuyói** 我慢強い is patient, persevering hard(er)

gamen *n* 画面 screen (*of TV, computer, etc.*)
gámu *n* ガム (chewing) gum
gán *n* がん・癌 cancer, carcinoma
gāna *n* ガーナ Ghana
ganbarimásu, ganbáru *n, interj* 頑張ります, 頑張る stands firm, bears up, hangs in there; tries hard
gani-mata (no) *adj* がに股(の) bowlegged
ganjitsu, gantan *n* 元日, 元旦 New Year's day, first day of the year
gánko (na) *adj* 頑固(な) stubborn
gánnen *n* 元年 the first year of an era; Year One
gánrai *adv* 元来 originally, primarily
gánsho *n* 願書 application
gantan *n* 元旦 = **ganjitsu** 元日 (New Year's day, first day of the year)
gan'yaku *n* 丸薬 pill (= **jōzai** 錠剤)
gappei *n* 合併 merger, combination, union
gáragara がらがら・ガラガラ **1.** *n* rattle **2.** *adj* rattling: ~ **narimásu** がらがら鳴ります it rattles
garakuta *n* がらくた junk
garasu *n* ガラス glass (*substance*)
garasú-bin *n* ガラス瓶 glass jar/bottle
gárē'ji *n* ガレージ garage
gári *n* ガリ pickled ginger slices
gāru-furéndo *n* ガールフレンド girlfriend (= **kánojo** 彼女)
gasorin *n* ガソリン gasoline: ~**-sutándo** ガソリンスタンド gas(oline)/service station
gassō *n* 合奏 concert: ~ **shimásu** 合奏します plays in a concert
gásu *n* ガス (*natural*) gas; **gasú-gáisha** *n* ガス会社 gas company; **gasú-kónro** *n* ガスこんろ (*gas*) hot plate; **gasú-rénji** *n* ガスレンジ gas range
...-gata …型 type, model; size
...gáta …方 [HONORIFIC PLURAL] esteemed (*persons*)
gā'tā *n* ガーター garter
gátagata shimásu (suru) *v* がたがたします(する) clatters, rattles
gatchi *n* 合致 accordance: ~ **shimásu** 合致します matches
gatchiri-shita *adj* がっちりした well-built
...-gatsu …月 (*name of*) month of the year
gatten *n* 合点 consent, assent, understanding
-gawa *n* 側 side, **mukō-gawa** 向こう側 the other side
gāze *n* ガーゼ gauze
gazō *n* 画像 image
gé *n* 下 = **ge-kan** 下巻 last volume (*of a set of 2 or 3*)
gedoku-zai *n* 解毒剤 antidote
gehín (na) *adj* 下品(な) vulgar: ~ **na kotoba** 下品な言葉 vulgar language
géi *n* 芸 arts, accomplishments; tricks, stunts
géi *n* ゲイ gay: ~**-bā** ゲイバー gay bar
geigō *n* 迎合 assent: ~ **shimásu**

迎合します panders to one's feelings/opinions/wishes
geijutsu *n* 芸術 art(s); geijutsu-ka *n* 芸術家 artist
geinō *n* 芸能 performance arts, public entertainments; geinō´-jin *n* 芸能人 entertainer(s)
geisha *n* 芸者 geisha
gejun *n* 下旬 late part/end of a month (last 1/3 of the month)
geka *n* 外科 surgery (*as a medical specialty*); geká-i *n* 外科医 surgeon
ge-kan *n* 下巻 last volume (*of a set of 2 or 3*)
géki *n* 劇 play, drama
gékido *n* 激怒 furious anger
geki-ga *n* 劇画 graphic novel
gekijō *n* 劇場 theater
gekiron *n* 激論 violent controversy
gekkei *n* 月経 menstruation (= **seiri** 生理): **~ ga hajimarimásu** 月経が始まります one's period begins
gekkyū *n* 月給 monthly salary
geko *n* 下戸 non-drinker
gekokujō *n* 下克上 forcible displacement of a superior by one's inferior
gē´mu *n* ゲーム game
gén *n* 弦 string; gen-gakki *n* 弦楽器 string instrument(s)
gén(-) ... *prefix* 現 … present (*time*), current; gen-ba *n* 現場 site; gén-dai *n* 現代 the present: **~ (no)** 現代(の) modern, up-to-date; gen-jitsu *n* 現実 actuality, reality; **~-teki (na)** 現実的(な) realistic; gen-jō *n* 現状 the present conditions/state, status quo; gen-jū´sho *n* 現住所 current address; gen-kín *n* 現金 ready money; gen-kōhan (no) *adj* 現行犯(の) red-handed: **~ de tsukamarimásu** 現行犯で捕まります is caught red handed; gén-zai *n*, *adv* 現在 the present (*time*); at present, now
géndo *n* 限度 limit: **saidai/saikō-~** 最大/最高限度 the maximum/highest (degree)
géngo *n* 言語 language: **~-gaku** 言語学 linguistics
gengō *n* 元号 era name
gen'in *n* 原因 cause, origin, root: **~ to kekka** 原因と結果 cause and effect
genjū (na) *adj* 厳重(な) strict: **~ keibi** 厳重な警備 very strict guard
génkan *n* 玄関 entrance (hall), porch
génki *n* 元気(**o-génki** お元気) energy, vigor, pep: **~ (na)** 元気(な) healthy, well, cheerful, vigorous: **O-genki desu ka.** お元気ですか. How are you?
genko *n* 拳固, **genkotsu** 拳骨 fist
genkō *n* 言行 sayings and doings
genkō *n* 原稿 manuscript: **~ o shiagemásu** 原稿を仕上げます finishes one's article
genkoku *n* 原告 suitor, accuser
genkyū shimásu (suru) *v* 言及します(する) [BOOKISH] refers to …, mentions … (= **(… ni) furemásu** (… に)触れます)

génmai *n* 玄米 unpolished rice; genmai-cha *n* 玄米茶 Genmaicha, brown rice tea
genmitsu (na) *adj* 厳密(な) strict
genryō´ *n* 原料 (*raw*) materials, basic ingredient
gensaku *n* 原作 the original (*writing*)
gensan (no) *adj* 原産(の) (*plants and animals*) native to: **~-chi** 原産地 place of origin
génshi *n* 原子 atom; genshi-bákudan *n* 原子爆弾 atomic bomb
génshi (no) *adj* 原始(の) primitive
genshō *n* 現象 phenomenon
genshō *n* 減少 decrease
gensoku *n* 原則 a basic principle, a rule: **~ to shi̲te** 原則として as a (*general*) rule
gentei *n* 限定 limitation
genzō shimásu (suru) *v* 現像します(する) develops (*film*)
geppu *n* 月賦 monthly install-ments/payments: **~-barai** 月賦払い monthly payments
géppu *n* げっぷ belch, burp
geragera waraimásu̲ (warau) *v* げらげら[ゲラゲラ] 笑います(笑う) laughs with great guffaws
geretsu *adj* 下劣 rude, abusive, mean
geri *n* 下痢 diarrhea
geshi *n* 夏至 summer solstice
geshu̲ku *n* 下宿 lodgings, room (and board); geshuku-ya *n* 下宿屋 rooming/boarding house
gés-súi-kin *n* 月水金 Monday-Wednesday-Friday

gesui *n* 下水 sewage; (*kitchen*) drain; gesui-dō *n* 下水道 sewage system
getá *n* 下駄 wooden clogs (*shoes*)
...-getsu *suffix* ...月 month
getsumatsu *n* 月末 the end of a month
getsumen *n* 月面 surface of the moon
Getsuyō´(bi) *n* 月曜(日) Monday
gettō *n* ゲットー ghetto(s)
gezai *n* 下剤 laxative
gi-... *prefix* 偽... pseudo- ...; gi-shō *n* 偽証 false testimony; gi-zen *n* 偽善 hypocrisy
gi-... *prefix* 義 = **giri (no)** 義理の ...-in-law; gí-bo *n* 義母 = **girí no haha** 義理の母 mother-in-law; gí-fu *n* 義父 = **girí no chichi** 義理の父 father-in-law; gi-kei *n* 義兄 = **girí no ani** 義理の兄 elder brother-in-law; gi-mai *n* 義妹 = **girí no imōto** 義理の妹 young sister-in-law; gi-tei *n* 義弟 = **girí no otōto** 義理の弟 young brother-in-law
gífu̲to *n* ギフト gift
giin *n* 議員 member of parliament: **Kokkai-~** 国会議員 member of a national legislature
giji-dō *n* 議事堂: **kokkai ~** 国会議事堂 Diet building
gíjutsu *n* 技術 technique; giju̲tu-sha *n* 技術者 technician, engineer
gíkai *n* 議会 parliament, assembly, congress; (*the Japanese*) Diet (= **kokkai** 国会)

rubber band; gomú-naga(gutsu) *n* ゴム長(靴) rubber boots

gondora *n* ゴンドラ gondola(s)

gonge *n* 権化 incarnation, embodiment

gongodōdan (na) *adj* 言語道断(な) egregious

gongu *n* ゴング gong: **~ o narashimasu** ゴングを鳴らします sounds a gong

goraku *n* 娯楽 entertainment, recreation, amusement; goraku-shisetsu *n* 娯楽施設 amusement facility

goran *v* ご覧: **~ ni narimásu** ご覧になります [HONORIFIC] (you) see; **~ kudasai** ご覧下さい Please look/see. → **mimasu** 見ます

gōri *n* 合理 accordance with reason: **~-teki (na)** 合理的(な) rational, reasonable, sensible; gōri-ka *n* 合理化 rationalization (*making it reasonable*); streamlining

gorin *n* 五輪 Olympics

gorira *n* ゴリラ gorilla

... góro (ni) *suffix, adv* ...ごろ[頃](に) (*at*) about (*a time*)

goro-ne *n* ごろ寝 lying dozing, sacking out

orotsuki *n* ごろつき cheap oodlum(s)

ru *n* ゴール goal (*sports*): ~ **ipā** ゴールキーパー goalkeeper

den-uíiku/wíiku *n* ゴールデンウーク/ウィーク Golden Week days (29 April – 5 May)

n ゴルファー golfer

górufu *n* ゴルフ golf; gorufu-jō *n* ゴルフ場 golf course

gōryū *n* 合流 merger, confluence: **"Gōryū chū'ī"** "合流注意" Lanes Merge (Ahead), Merge (Lanes); gōryū-ten *n* 合流点 confluence

gó-sai *n* 五歳 five years old (= **itsutsu** 五つ)

gōsain *n* ゴーサイン go sign, green light

go-sén *n* 五千・5,000 five thousand

... -gō'sha *suffix* ...号車 train car number ...

go-shín *n* 護身 self-defense: **~-jutyu** 護身術 art of self-defense

gósho *n* 御所 imperial palace (*in Kyoto*)

gotaku *n* ごたく cant: **~ o narabemásu** ごたくを並べます talks a load of garbage

gotamaze *n* ごたまぜ jumble

gōtō *n* 強盗 robber; robbery

... gótoku (ni) *suffix, adv* ...ごとく(に) [LITERARY] = **... yō' (ni)** ...よう(に) like

... góto (ni) *suffix, adv* ...ごと(に) every ..., each ...: **koto áru ~ (ni)** ことあるごと(に) every chance one gets

gō'u *n* 豪雨 heavy rain, (*torrential*) downpour: **shūchū-~** 集中豪雨 local downpour, local heavy rain

gozá *n* ござ (*thin floor mat*) straw mat

gozaimásu *v* ございます [DEFERENTIAL] = **arimásu** あります there is, we've got; it is (located)

gikochinái *adj* ぎこちない awkward, clumsy

gimon *n* 疑問 question, doubt; gimón-fu *n* 疑問符 question mark

gímu *n* 義務 duty, obligation; gimu-kyō'iku *n* 義務教育 compulsory education

gín *n* 銀 silver; gin-iro (no) *adj* 銀色(の) silver (*color*); gín-ka *n* 銀貨 silver coin

Gínga *n* 銀河 the Milky Way

ginjō *n* 吟醸 produce from the use of selected ingredient(s): **~-shu** 吟醸酒 quality sake brewed from the finest rice

ginkō *n* 銀行 bank; ginkō'-in *n* 銀行員 bank clerk

ginmi *n* 吟味 investigation

ginnán *n* ギンナン・銀杏 gingko nuts

ginshō *n* 吟唱 intonation

ginyūshijin *n* 吟遊詩人 minstrel

girei *n* 儀礼 courtesy

girí *n* 義理(**o-gíri** お義理) obligation, sense of obligation, honor: **girí no ...** 義理の... ...-in-law: **girí no ane** 義理の姉 elder sister-in-law

Gírish(i)a *n* ギリシャ・ギリシア Greece; Girish(i)a-go ギリシャ・ギリシア語 Greek (*language*); Girish(i)a-jin ギリシャ人・ギリシア人 Greek (*people*)

gíron *n* 議論 discussion

giryo *n* 技量 skills, abilities

gisei *n* 犠牲 a sacrifice: **... o ~ ni shimásu** ...を犠牲にします makes a sacrifice/scapegoat of ...; **~ ni narimásu** 犠牲になります falls a victim, is sacrificed; giséi-sha *n* 犠牲者 victim

gíshi *n* 技師 engineer

gíshiki *n* 儀式 ceremony, ritual

gítā *n* ギター guitar

gítcho (no) *adj* (*discriminatory term*) ぎっちょ(の) left-handed (*person*) (= **hidari-kiki (no)** 左利き(の))

giwaku *n* 疑惑 doubt, suspicion

gizō *n* 偽造 forgery

gó *n* 碁 the board game Go (= **ígo** 囲碁): **go-ban** 碁盤 a Go board

gó *n* 五・5 five; go-ban *n* 五番 number five; go-banmé (no) *adj* 五番目(の) fifth; go-dai *n* 五台 five machines/vehicles; go-dó *n* 五度 five times (= **go-kai** 五回); gó-do *n* 五度 five degrees; gó-hiki *n* 五匹 five (*fishes/bugs, small animals*); go-hon *n* 五本 five (*pencils/bottles, long things*); go-kái *n* 五回 five times; go-kai *n* 五階 five floors/stories; fifth floor; gó-ko *n* 五個 five (*pieces, small objects*); go-mai *n* 五枚 five sheets (*flat things*); go-nen *n* 五年 the year 5: **~-kan** 五年間 (*for*) five years; go-nín *n* 五人 five people; gó-satsu *n* 五冊 five copies (*books, magazines*); go-tō *n* 五頭 five (*horses/oxen, large animals*); gó-wa *n* 五羽 five (*birds, rabbits*)

go-... *prefix* ご・御... honorific (personalizing) *prefix* (*cf.* **o-** お

・御); go-chisō *n* ごちそう・ご馳走 treat (*of food*); **gochisō-sama (deshita).** ごちそうさま(でした). Thank you for the treat (the reply is **o-sómatsu-sama (deshita).** お粗末さま(でした).); go-fujō *n* ご不浄・御不浄 [HONORIFIC] toilet, rest room, lavatory (= **tóire** トイレ); go-jibun *n* ご自分 you, yourself [HONORIFIC]; go-kazoku *n* ご家族 (*your/someone else's*) family [HONORIFIC] → **kázoku** 家族; go-kigen *n* ご機嫌 mood, feeling: ~ **ikága desu ka** ご機嫌いかがですか. How are you (feeling)?: ~ **yō´** ごきげんよう. Good-bye./Hello. [HONORIFIC] → **kigen** 機嫌; go-mottomo *interj* ごもっとも You're absolutely right.; go-ón *n* ご恩 (*your/someone else's*) kindness, my obligation to you [HONORIFIC] → **ón** 恩; go-riyaku *n* ご利益 divine help/grace; go-ryō´shin *n* ご両親 (*your/someone else's*) parents [HONORIFIC] → ryō´shin 両親; go-shínsetsu *n* ご親切 (*your/someone else's*) kindness [HONORIFIC] : ~ **ni dōmo arigatō (gozaimásu)** ご親切にどうもありがとう(ございます) Thank you very much for your kindness. → **shínsetsu** 親切; go-shújin *n* ご主人 (*your/someone else's*) husband [HONORIFIC] → **shújin** 主人; go-téinei (na) *adj* ご丁寧(な) polite; careful [HONORIFIC]: ~ **na henshin arigatō gozaimásu** ご丁寧な返信ありがとうございます Thank you for your polite reply. → **téinei** 丁寧; go-tsugō *n* ご都合 convenience [HONORIFIC]: **itsu ga ~ yoroshiidesuka** いつがご都合よろしいですか When is it convenient for you? → **tsugō** 都合; go-yō´ *n* ご用 (*your/someone else's*) business [HONORIFIC] → **yō´** 用; gó-zen *n* ご膳 low meal table, dining tray; meal [HONORIFIC]; go-zónji *v* ご存知: ~ **désu ka?** ご存知ですか? Do you know? [HONORIFIC] (= **shitte(i)másuka?** 知って(い)ますか?); **zónji(age) masén** 存知(あげ)ません don't know [HONORIFIC] (= **shirimasén** 知りません)

go-... *prefix* ご・誤… wrong; go-hō *n* 誤報 false report; go-shín *n* 誤診 wrong diagnosis; go-kai *n* 誤解 misunderstanding

go-... *prefix* 語... language; word(s); go-chō *n* 語調 tone of talk, intonation; gó-gaku *n* 語学 (*foreign*) language learning; gó-i *n* 語彙 vocabulary (*item*)

-go *suffix* 後 after, later, since: **sono-go** その後 after that, since then

...-go *suffix* …語 (*name of*) language; word(s): **Nihon-go** 日本語 the Japanese (*language*)

-gō *suffix* 号: (*magazine issues*) **…-gatsugō** …月号; (*train numbers*) **…-gō´sha** 号車; (*room numbers*) **…-gōshitsu** …号室

go-busata *n* ご無沙汰 failure to keep in touch: ~ **shite orimásu** ご無沙汰しております I have been neglectful (*in keeping in touch with you*).

gochagocha (shita) *adj* ごちゃごちゃ(した) messy, jumble

gochamaze *adj* ごちゃ混ぜ jumble

góchō *n* 伍長 (*army*) corporal

gōdō *n* 合同 combination, union, fusion; congruence

gofuku *n* 呉服 yard/dry goods; (*traditional Japanese clothing*) kimono: **~-ya** 呉服屋 dry goods store; kimono shop

Gó-gatsu *n* 五月・5月 May

gógo *n* 午後 afternoon, p.m.

góhan *n* ご飯 (*cooked*) rice; meal, dinner (= **shokuji** 食事); food

go-hyakú *n* 五百・500 five hundred

gō´i *n* 合意 agreement

gōin (na) *adj* 強引(な) forcible, highhanded: ~ **ni** 強引に forcibly, highhandedly

go-ishi *n* 碁石 a Go stone (piece)

go-jū´ *n* 五十・fifty 50

go-jū´on *n* 五十音 the Japanese *kana* syllabary

gō´ka (na) *adj* 豪華(な) luxurious, deluxe: ~ **na shokuji** 豪華な食事 delicious cuisine

gōkai (na) *adj* 豪快(な) dynamic: ~ **na nomippuri** 豪快な飲みっぷり dynamic way of drinking (alcohol)

gō´ka-kenran *adj* 豪華絢爛 absolutely gorgeous: ~ **ni iwaimásu** 豪華絢爛に祝います celebrates with pomp and splendor

gōkaku *n* 合格 passing (*an exam*)

gōkan *n* 強姦 rape

gōkei *n* 合計 total (*sum*)

goke (-san) *n* 後家(さん) widow

gokiburi *n* ゴキブリ cockroach

góku *adv* 極 very, exceedingly

gōkyū *n* 号泣 crying bitterly, crying out

goma *n* ゴマ・胡麻 sesame (*seeds*): ~ **o surimásu** ゴマをすります grinds sesame; flatters; goma-súri *n* ごますり flattery

gomakashimásu, gomakásu *v* ごまかします, ごまかす deceives, cheats, misrepresents; **tsurisen o** ~ 釣り銭をごまかします shortchanges

go-mán *n* 五万・50,000 fifty thousand

gōman (na) *adj* 傲慢(な) haughty, arrogant

gomen *interj* ごめん: ~ **nasái.** ごめんなさい. Excuse me. (= **sumimásen** すみません); ~ **kudasái.** ごめん下さい. ① Hello, anybody home? ② Excuse me for interrupting.

gomí *n* ゴミ trash, rubbish, garbage, house refuse, (*house*) gomí-bako *n* ゴミ箱 trash b… garbage can, dustbin; gom… *n* ゴミ袋 garbage bag

gomoku-nárabe *n* 五目並… (a simplified version … board game *Go*)

gómu *n* ゴム rubber

gózen *n* 午前 morning, a.m

gu *n* 具 ingredients, fillings

gu *n* 愚 stupidity: **~ no kotchō** 愚の骨頂 ultimate silliness

guai *n* 具合 condition, shape, feelings (*of health*): **~ ga warúi** 具合が悪い is out of order, is not working properly, is not feeling good/right, is upset

guchi *n* 愚痴 complaint, gripe

...-guchi *suffix* …口: **mado-~** window, wicket: **deiri-~** 出入り口 doorway, gateway

gugen (ka) *n* 具現(化) realization

gū´gū *adv* グーグー snoring (away), Zzz

gūhatsu teki (na/ni) *adj*, *adv* 偶発的(な/に) accidental(ly)

guigui (to) *adv* グイグイ(と) strongly: **~ to nomimásu/guinomi shimásu̱** グイグイと飲みます/グイ飲みします gulps down a drink

gui(t)to *adv* グイ(ッ)と with a jerk

gún *n* 軍 army, troops; **gun-jin** *n* 軍人 soldier, military person; **gun-kan** *n* 軍艦 warship; **gun-puku** *n* 軍服 military uniform; **gún-sō** *n* 軍曹 sergeant

gún *n* 郡 county

gū-no-ne mo demasen (denai) *v* ぐうの音も出ません(出ない) is unable to argue against

gunshū *n* 群衆 crowd

gúrabu *n* グラブ → **gúrōbu** グローブ

gurafu *n* グラフ graph

... gúrai *suffix* …位・ぐらい about (*an amount*; *the same extent as*); at least

gúramu *suffix n* グラム gram(s)

gúrasu *n* グラス glass (*container*)

gura(u)ndo *n* グラ(ウ)ンド playground

gurē´ (no) *adj* グレー(の) gray

gurēpufurū´tsu *n* グレープフルーツ grapefruit

guríin (no) *adj* グリーン(の) green: **~-sha** グリーン車 the Green Car (*first-class seats*)

gúrōbu *n* グローブ (*baseball, boxing*) glove (= **gúrabu** グラブ)

guruguru (to) *adv* ぐるぐる(と) round and round

gurukōsu *n* グルコース glucose

gurume *n* グルメ gourmet

gurū´pu *n* グループ group

gusaku *n* 愚策 stupid/idiotic plan

gusari-to sashimásu̱ (sasu) *v* グサリと刺します(刺す) stabs

gussúri *adv* ぐっすり (*sleeping*) soundly

gutai-rei *n* 具体例 specific example

gutai-teki (na) *adj* 具体的(な) concrete, substantial, tangible, material

gūtara (mono) *n* ぐうたら(者) lazybones, drone

gút(-to) *adv* グッ(と) with a jerk/gulp, suddenly

gūwa *n* 寓話 allegory, fable

gūzen (no) *adj* 偶然(の) accidental, fortuitous: **~ ni** 偶然に by chance, accidentally

gūzō *n* 偶像 idol

gúzu *n* ぐず dullard
gúzuguzu iimásu (iu/yū) *v* ぐずぐず言います(言う) complains, grumbles
gúzuguzu shimásu (suru) *v* ぐずぐずします(する) delays, dawdles
gyaku (no/ni) *adj, adv* 逆(の/に) opposite, contrary, backwards
gyakutai shimásu (suru) *v* 虐待します(する) mistreats
gyáppu *n* ギャップ gap
gyo- *prefix* 御 → **go-** ご・御
gyō´ *n* 行 line (*of words*); line of the *kana* chart: **sá-~** さ行 the sa-shi-su-se-so (さしすせそ): **gyōkan** 行間 line space
gyō´ *n* 業 line of work (= **shokúgyō** 職業)
gyōchū *n* ギョウチュウ・ぎょう虫 pinworm
gyófu *n* 漁夫 fisherman
gyōgi *n* 行儀 behavior, manners
gyógyō *n* 漁業 fishing (*business*)
gyōgyōshii *adj* 仰々しい pompous
gyō´jí *n* 行事 ceremony, event
gyōkai *n* 業界 industry, world: **~-yōgo** 業界用語 industry jargon
gyōketsu *n* 凝結 condensation
gyōko *n* 凝固 coagulation
gyomin *n* 漁民 fisherperson
gyōmu *n* 業務 business, work: **~-jikan** 業務時間 business hours
gyoro-me *n* ぎょろ目 goggling eyes
gyorori to niramimasu (niramu) *v* ぎょろりと睨みます[にらみます](睨む[にらむ]) goggles, glares
gyorui *n* 魚類 fishes
gyōsei *n* 行政 administration (*of government*)
gyōseki *n* 業績 achievements: **~ o agemásu** 業績を上げます improves performance
gyosha *n* 御者 coachman
gyotto shimasu (suru) *v* ぎょっとします(する) is startled
gyōza *n* ギョウザ・餃子 crescent-shaped dumpling stuffed with ground pork, etc.
gyūgyū *adj* ぎゅうぎゅう詰め jam-packed: **~zume no densha** ぎゅうぎゅう詰めの電車 jam-packed train
gyūniku *n* 牛肉 beef
gyūnyū *n* 牛乳 (cow's) milk

H

ha *n* 葉 leaf (= **happa** 葉っぱ): **ochi-ba** 落ち葉 fallen leave(s)
há *n* 歯 tooth; **ha-búrashi** *n* 歯ブラシ tooth brush; **há-guki** *n* 歯茎 gum (*teethridge*); **há-isha** *n* 歯医者 dentist; **ha-ita** *n* 歯痛 toothache (= **shitsū** 歯痛)
há *n* 刃 edge (*of knife*), blade (*of razor*)
ha *interj* は [DEFERENTIAL] yes

hā *interj* はあ **1.** aha **2.** phew
haba *n* 幅 width
habakari-nágara ... *interj* はばかりながら …I beg your pardon, but …
habamemásu, habaméru *v* 阻めます, 阻める can prevent/thwart
habamimásu, habámu *v* 阻みます, 阻む prevents, thwarts
habatsu *n* 派閥 faction, clique
hā´bu *n* ハーブ herb(s)
habukimásu, habúku *v* 省きます, 省く cuts out, reduces, saves, eliminates, omits
hachi *n* ハチ・蜂 bee (= **mitsú-bachi** 蜜蜂); hachi-mitsu *n* ハチミツ・蜂蜜 honey
hachí *n* 鉢 bowl, basin, pot, rice bucket/tub; hachí-mono *n* 鉢物 potted plant
hachí *n* 八・8 eight; hachí-dó *n* 八度 eight times (= **hachi-kái, hak-kái** 八回, **hap-pen** 八編); hachí-do *n* 八度 eight degrees; hachi-hon, háp-pon *n* 八本 eight (*pencils/bottles, long objects*); hachi-ko, hák-ko *n* 八個 eight pieces (*small objects*) (= **yáttsu** 八つ); hachí-mai *n* 八枚 eight sheets (*flat things*); hachí-wa, háp-pa *n* 八羽 eight (*birds, rabbits*)
Hachí-gatsu *n* 八月 August
hachi-mán *n* 八万・80,000 eighty thousand
hachūrui *n* ハ虫類・爬虫類 reptile
háda *n* 肌 skin: **~-iro** 肌色 flesh color
hadaka (no) *adj* 裸・はだか(の) naked: **~ no ō-sama** 裸の王様 naked king
hadashi *n* 裸足 barefoot
hadé (na) *adj* 派手(な) gaudy, showy, flashy, bright, loud (*color*)
hādowéa *n* ハードウェア (*computer*) hardware: **~ to sofutowea** ハードウェアとソフトウェア hardware and software
hae *n* ハエ・蝿 (house)fly
haemásu, haéru *v* 生えます, 生える (*tooth, hair, mold, …*) grows
hagaki *n* はがき・葉書 postcard
hagane *n* ハガネ・鋼 steel
hagashimásu, hagasu *v* 剥がします, 剥がす peels off, tears off
háge *n* 禿 bald spot, baldness
hagemashimásu, hagemásu *v* 励まします 励ます encourages
hagemásu, hagéru *v* 剥げます, 剥げる it peels off
hagemásu, hagéru *v* 禿[はげ]ます, 禿げる・はげる gets/goes bald
hagemimásu, hagému *v* 励みます, 励む works hard
hageshíi *adj* 激しい violent, severe, fierce, acute
hagimásu, hágu *v* 剥ぎます, 剥ぐ peels it off
hagó-íta *n* 羽子板 battledore
ha-gúruma *n* 歯車 cog (*wheel*), gear
háha, haha-oya *n* 母, 母親 mother (= **okā´-san** お母さん)
hahen *n* 破片 broken piece(s): **garasu no ~** ガラスの破片 broken pieces of glass

hai *n* 灰 ashes; hai-zara *n* 灰皿 ash tray
hai *n* 肺 lungs; hai-byō *n* 肺病 tuberculosis, TB (= **kekkaku** 結核); hai-en *n* 肺炎 pneumonia; hai-gan *n* 肺がん lung cancer
hái *interj* **1.** はい yes (= **ē** ええ (*mostly female*)) **2.** here you are!
...´-hai *suffix* …杯 cupful(s), bowlful(s)
haiboku *n* 敗北 defeat, loss
haibōru *n* ハイボール highball
haibun *n* 配分 distribution
haichi *n* 配置 layout, allocation, location, placement, setup
haifu *n* 配布 distribution, circulation
haigo *n* 背後 rear, backside
haigō *n* 配合 composition; **~-zai** 配合剤 compounding agent
haigūsha *n* 配偶者 spouse
haigyō *n* 廃業 closure of an operation, end of a business
haihiiru *n* ハイヒール high-heeled shoes
hai-iro (no) *adj* 灰色(の) gray: **~ no sora** 灰色の空 gray sky
haijin *n* 俳人 *haiku* poet
haijin *n* 廃人 cripple, wreck
háijo *n* 排除 removal, elimination, exclusion
haikan *n* 配管 piping
haikan *n* 廃刊 publication discontinuation
haikan *n* 拝観 admission: **~ shimásu** 拝観します [HUMBLE] has the honor of seeing; haikan-ryō *n* 拝観料 admission fee
haikara (na) *adj* ハイカラ(な) fashionable, high-class
haikei *n* 背景 background, BG
háikei *n* 拝啓 [BOOKISH] Dear Sir/Madam (*in a letter*)
haiken *n* 拝見: **~ shimásu** 拝見します [HUMBLE] I/We (will) look at/see (= **mimasu** 見ます)
haiki *n* 排気 exhaust; haiki-gásu *n* 排気ガス exhaust (*fumes*); haikí-sen *n* 排気扇 exhaust fan
haiki *n* 廃棄 disposal, abolition, rejection: **~ shimásu** 廃棄します scraps, **~-butsu** 廃棄物, waste(s)
háikingu *n* ハイキング hike, hiking
háiku *n* 俳句 *haiku* (short (17-syllable) poem)
haikyo *n* 廃墟 ruin
haikyū *n* 配給 rationing
haimásu, háu *v* 這います, 這う crawls
hairemásu, hairéru *v* 入れます, 入れる can enter
hairimásu, háiru *v* 入ります, 入る enters; **háitte imásu** 入っています is inside
hairyo *n* 配慮 consideration: **go-~ (itadaki) arigatō-gozaimasu** ご配慮(いただき)ありがとうございます Thank you all for your help and support.
haishaku-shimásu (suru) *v* 拝借します(する) [HUMBLE] (I) borrow (= **karimasu** 借ります)
haishi *n* 廃止 abolition
haishinkōi *n* 背信行為 treachery
haisui *n* 排水 drainage; haisui-ponpu *n* 排水ポンプ drainage pump

haita *n* 排他 exclusion; **haita-teki (na)** *adj* 排他的(な) exclusive

haitatsu *n* 配達 delivery

haitōkin *n* 配当金 dividends, annuity: **~ o uketorimásu** 配当金を受け取ります gets an annuity

háiyā *n* ハイヤー limousine for hire

haiyū *n* 俳優 actor (= **yaku-sha** 役者), actress (= **joyū** 女優)

haji(-kko) *n* 端っこ edge, end

hají *n* 恥 shame: embarrassment: **~ o kakimásu** 恥をかきます disgraces/embarrasses oneself

hajikemásu, hajikéru *v* はじけます, はじける it pops, snaps

hajikí *n* はじき marbles

hajikimásu, hajíku *v* はじきます, はじく snaps it, repels it

hajimari *v* 始まり beginning, start

hajimarimásu, hajimaru *v* 始まります, 始まる it begins (*starts*)

hajimásu, hajiru *v* 恥ます, 恥じる feels shame, feels embarrassed

hajime *n* 初め the beginning; in the beginning: **~ no** 初めの the first …; **~ wa** 初めは at first

Hajimemáshite. *interj* 初めまして How do you do? (*on being introduced*)

hajimemásu, hajimeru *v* 始めます, 始める begins (*starts*) it

hajimeraremásu, hajimerareru *v* 始められます, 始められる can begin it

hajímete *adv* はじめて・初めて for the first time

haká *n* 墓 grave (*tomb*): **~-mairi** 墓参り visiting someone's grave;

haka-bá *n* 墓場 graveyard, cemetery

hakadorimásu, hakaréru *v* はかどります, はかどる makes good progress: **shigoto ga ~** 仕事がはかどります gets ahead with one's work

hakai *n* 破壊 destruction, demolition

hakaku (no) *adj* 破格(の) unprecedented: **~ no nedan** 破格の値段 rock-bottom price, bargain price

hakama *n* 袴 traditional Japanese skirtlike trousers for male

hakanái *adj* 儚い fleeting, transitory

hakaraimásu, hakarau *v* 計らいます, 計らう arranges

hakaremásu, hakaréru *v* 測れます, 測れる can measure

hakaremásu, hakaréru *v* 量れます, 量れる can weigh

hakarí *n* 秤 (*weighting/weight*) scales

hakarigóto *n* 謀 plot, trick, scheme

hakarimásu, hakáru *v* 測ります, 測る measures

hakarimásu, hakáru *v* 量ります, 量る weighs

hakarimásu, hakáru *v* 図ります[謀ります], 図[謀]る plans, designs; plots

hákase *n* 博士 doctor (Ph.D.) (= **hakushi** 博士): **~-rónbun** 博士論文 doctoral dissertation

haké *n* 刷毛 brush

haké *n* 捌け drainage, draining ~ **ga íi désu** 捌けがいいです it drains/sells well

haké-kuchi/-guchi *n* 捌け口 outlet (*for water/emotion/goods*)

hakemásu, hakeru *v* 履けます, 履ける can wear (*footwear, pants, skirt, socks*)

hakemásu, hakéru *v* 捌けます, 捌ける it drains off; it sells (well)

hakemásu, hakéru *v* 吐けます, 吐ける can vomit/spill out

hakemásu, hakéru *v* 掃けます, 掃ける can sweep

haken *n* 派遣 dispatch: **jinzai-~-gaisha** 人材派遣会社 temporary-employment agency

háki *n* 覇気 ambition (*energetic spirit*): **~ ga arimásu** 覇気があります is full of spirit

hakihaki (to) *adj* はきはき(と) lively, briskly: **~ to henji o shimásu** はきはきと返事をします answers clearly and crisply

haki-ké *n* 吐き気 nausea: **~ ga shimásu** 吐き気がします, **~ o moyōshimásu** 吐き気を催します feels nauseated/queasy

hakimásu, haku *v* 履きます, 履く wears (*on feet or legs*), puts/slips on (*shoes, socks, pants*)

hakimásu, háku *v* 吐きます, 吐く **1.** vomits **2.** spits out

hakimásu, háku *v* 掃きます, 掃く sweeps

hakimono *n* 履物 footwear

hakka *n* ハッカ peppermint

hakkā *n* ハッカー hacker, hack (*computer*)

hak-kái, hachi-kái *n* 八回 eight times

hakken *n* 発見 discovery

hakketsu-byō *n* 白血病 leukemia

hakkí *n* 発揮 exertion

hakkíri *adv* はっきり plainly, clearly, distinctly, exactly: **~ (to) shimásu** はっきり(と)します becomes clear

hák-ko, hachi-kó *n* 八個 eight pieces (*small objects*) (= **yáttsu** 八つ)

hakkō *n* 発行 publication: **hakkōsha** 発行者 publisher

hakkō *n* 発光 light emission

hakkō *n* 発酵 ferment

hakkutsu *n* 発掘 exhumation: **~ shimásu** 発掘します digs up, excavates

hakkyō *n* 発狂 derangement: **~ shimásu** 発狂します becomes insane

hako *n* 箱 box, case, chest, container

hakobimásu, hakobu *v* 運びます, 運ぶ carries, conveys

haku-... *prefix* 白... white; **haku-chō** *n* ハクチョウ・白鳥 swan; **háku-i** *n* 白衣 white coat: **~ no tenshi** 白衣の天使 nurse, angel (*not to literally mean, "angel in white"*); **haku-jin** *n* 白人 Caucasian; **hakú-mai** *n* 白米 polished rice; **haku-shi** *n* 白紙 blank sheet of paper: **~ ni modoshimásu** 白紙に戻します withdraws, takes back; **haku-sho** *n* 白書 white paper

...-haku *suffix* ...泊, **...-paku** ...泊 (*counts nights of lodging*)

hakuai *n* 博愛 humanitarianism: **~-shugi** 博愛主義 philanthropy

hakubútsu-kan *n* 博物館 museum

hakuchūmu *n* 白昼夢 daydreaming: **~ o mimásu** 白昼夢を見ます is spaced out

hakugai *n* 迫害 persecution: **~ o ukemásu** 迫害を受けます suffers from persecution

hakujaku (na) *adj* 薄弱(な) weak, tenuous: **ishi-~** 意志薄弱 weak will: **~ na konkyo** 薄弱な根拠 poor reason

hákujō *n* 白状 confession

hakujō (na) *adj* 薄情(な) [BOOKISH] unfeeling, heartless, cruel: **~ hito** 薄情な人 heartless person

hakurai (no) *adj* 舶来(の) imported; hakurai-hin *n* 舶来品 imported goods

hakurán-kai *n* 博覧会 exhibition, exposition

hakuryoku *n* 迫力 punch, power: **~ ga arimásu** 迫力があります is powerful

hakusái *n* ハクサイ・白菜 Chinese cabbage

hakushi *n* 博士 doctor (Ph.D.) (= **hakase** 博士): **~-katei** 博士課程 doctoral course

hákushu *n* 拍手 clapping

hamá *n* 浜 beach: **~-be** 浜辺 beach, seashore

hamachi *n* ハマチ・魚 young yellowtail

hamáguri *n* ハマグリ・蛤 clam

hamé *n* はめ plight, fix (*one gets into*)

hamemásu, hameru *v* はめます, はめる wears (on fingers, hands (*ring, gloves, etc.*))

hame(ra)remásu, hame(ra)reru *v* はめ(ら)れます, はめ(ら)れる can wear (*on fingers, hands*)

hametsu *n* 破滅 ruin

hamidashimásu, hamidasu *v* はみ出します, はみ出す protrudes, runs off the edge, sticks out, goes over

há-mono *n* 刃物 cutlery, knives

hámu *n* ハム ham: **~-éggu** ハムエッグ ham and eggs; **~-sándo** ハムサンド ham sandwich

hán *n* 半 half (= **hanbún** 半分): **han-...** 半 ... half a ...; **...-hán** ... 半 and a half

hán *n* 判 a "chop" = a seal (*to stamp name*) (= **hankó** 判こ)

hana *n* 鼻 nose; trunk (*of elephant*); hana-ji *n* 鼻血 nosebleed: hana-mizú *n* 鼻水 snivel, nasal mucus: **~ ga demásu** 鼻水が出ます has a runny nose

hana *n* はな nasal mucus, snivel (= **hana-mizú** 鼻水): **~ o kamimásu** はなをかみます blows one's nose

haná *n* 花 flower; flower arrangement; hana-mí *n* 花見 cherry blossom viewing: **~ o shimásu** 花見をします goes to see the cherry blossom; haná-tába *n* 花束 bouquet; hana-wa *n* 花輪 wreath (*of flower*); haná-ya *n* 花屋 florist, flower shop

hána *n* はな・端 beginning, outset; edge

hána-bi *n* 花火 fireworks: **~-taikai**

花火大会 big exhibition of fireworks
haná-fuda *n* 花札 (*the game of*) flower cards
hanágata *n* 花形 a star (*in a theatrical production*): **~-senshu** 花形選手 star player
hanahada *adv* はなはだ extremely
haná-michi *n* 花道 the runway to the stage (in Kabuki)
hana-múko *n* 花婿 bridegroom
hanao *n* 鼻緒 thong (on *geta*)
hanaremásu, hanaréru *v* 離れます, 離れる separates, becomes distant, leaves
hanasemásu, hanaséru *v* 話せます, 話せる can speak
hanashí *n* 話 talk, story, tale, speech, conversation; something to talk about: **~ o shimásu** 話をします talks, speaks
hanashi-ái *n* 話し合い conference, discussion, negotiation
hanashi-aimásu, hanashi-áu *v* 話し合います, 話し合う talk together, discuss, confer, negotiate
hanashi-ka *n* 噺家 (a comic) storyteller (= **rakugo-ka** 落語家)
hanashimásu, hanásu *v* 話します, 話す speaks, talks
hanashimásu, hanásu *v* 放します, 放す release, lets loose, lets go, sets free
hanashimásu, hanásu *v* 離します, 離す separates (*something*) from, parts with; detaches, disconnects
hanáyaka (na) *adj* 華やか(な) colorful, showy, gorgeous, glorious, bright
haná-yome *n* 花嫁 bride
hanbā´gā *n* ハンバーガー a hamburger
hanbai *n* 販売 sale; **hanbái-ki** *n* 販売機 vending machine; **hanbái-daka** *n* 販売高 sales volume; **hanbai-in** *n* 販売員 salesperson; **hanbai-nin** *n* 販売人 seller, dealer; **hanbái-ten** *n* 販売店 sales outlet; **hanbai-sokushin** *n* 販売促進 sales promotion (= **hansoku** 販促); **hanbai-kakaku** *n* 販売価格 selling price
hanbei (no) *adj* 反米(の) anti-American
hanbún *n* 半分 half
hándán *n* 判断 judgment
handō *n* 反動 reaction, repercussion; **handō-teki (na)** *adj* 反動的(な) reactionary; **handō-shugisha** *n* 反動主義者 reactionary
handobággu, handobákku *n* ハンドバッグ, ハンドバック handbag, pocketbook
handoru *n* ハンドル steering wheel; handle
hane *n* 羽 feather
hane *n* 羽根 wing; shuttlecock
hanei *n* 反映 reflection
hanei *n* 繁栄 prosperity
hanemásu, hanéru *v* 跳ねます, 跳ねる jumps, splashes
hanga *n* 版画 woodblock print
hángā *n* ハンガー hanger
hangaku *n* 半額 half price
hangyaku *n* 反逆 rebellion; han-

gyákú-sha *n* 反逆者 rebel
hanhan *n* 半々 half-and-half
hán'i *n* 範囲 scope, range, limits: **(… no) ~-gai/-nai** (…の)範囲外/内 beyond/within the limits (of …)
hanigo *n* 反意語 antonym
hanikamimásu, hanikámu *v* はにかみます, はにかむ acts shy, is bashful: **hanikami-ya** はにかみ屋 shy
hánji *n* 判事 judge
hánjō *n* 繁盛 prosperity: **shōbai-~** 商売繁盛 flourishing business, boom of business
hánkachi *n* ハンカチ handkerchief
hankagai *n* 繁華街 downtown area, shopping and amusement districts
hankan *n* 反感 antipathy: **~ o kaimásu** 反感を買います provokes one's antipathy
hankei *n* 半径 radius
hanketsu *n* 判決 judgment: **~ o kudashimásu** 判決を下します adjudges, gives sentence
hankó *n* はんこ・判子 a "chop" (*signature seal, name stamp*) (= **han** 判, **in** 印, **inkan** 印鑑)
hankō *n* 反抗 opposition, resistance: **… ni ~ shimásu** …に反抗します opposes, resists (= **hanpatsu** 反発)
hankō *n* 犯行 crime, perpetration: **~-genba** 犯行現場 scene of a crime: **~-seimei** 犯行声明 criminal declaration
hankyō *n* 反響 echo: **~-on** 反響音 acoustic echo
hankyōran *n* 半狂乱 frantic, partial insanity: **~ ni narimásu** 半狂乱になります becomes frantic
hankyū *n* 半休 half day off: **~ o torimásu** 半休を取ります takes a half day off
hankyū *n* 半球 hemisphere
hánmā *n* ハンマー hammer
hanmei *n* 判明 coming-out
hanmen *n* 反面 on the other hand: **~-kyōshi** 反面教師 person who serves as an example of how not to be
hanmen (no) *adj* 半面(の) half-faced
han-nichí *n* 半日 half a day, a half-day
hannichi (no) *adj* 反日(の) anti-Japanese
hánnin *n* 犯人 a criminal, culprit
hannō *n* 反応 reaction, response
hanpa *n* 半端 half: **~-mono** 半端物 oddments → **chūto ~ (na)** 中途半端(な)
hanpatsu *n* 反発 **1.** repelling **2.** repulsion **3.** resistance (= **hankō** 反抗)
hanpén *n* ハンペン・はんぺん boiled fish cake
hanran *n* 反乱 revolt: **~ o okosu** 反乱を起こす revolts, rebels
hanran *n* 氾濫 overflowing
hanrei *n* 凡例 explanatory notes (*on how to use a reference work*)
hanryo *n* 伴侶 companion: **shōgai no ~** 生涯の伴侶 spouse (*literally, "lifetime companion"*)

hánsa (na) *adj* 煩瑣(な) troublesome, complicated

hansei *n* 反省 reflection, thinking-over

hansen (no) *adj* 反戦(の) antiwar: **~-katsudō** 反戦活動 antiwar activity

hansha *n* 反射 reflection

hánshi *n* 半紙 rice paper (*stationery*)

han-shimásu (-súru) *v* 反します(する) is contrary (*to*), goes against, opposes: **... ni hánshite** ...に反して contrary to, against, in contrast with

hanshō (no) *n* 半焼(の) partial loss by fire (= **han'yake (no)** 半焼け(の))

hanshū *n* 半周 semicircle

hansoku *n* 反則 (*sports*) foul play

hansoku *n* 販促 sales promotion: **~-tsūru** 販促ツール sales promotion tool (= **hanbai-sokushin** 販売促進)

hantai *n* 反対 opposite, contrary, reverse (= **gyaku** 逆): **~-gawa** 反対側 opposite side; **~-go** 反対語 antonym; **~ ni** 反対に vice versa

hantén *n* 半纏 *happi* coat (= **happi** はっぴ・法被)

hantō *n* 半島, **...-hántō** ...半島 peninsula: **Izu-hántō** 伊豆半島 Izu Peninsula

han-toshí *n* 半年 half a year

han-tsukí *n* 半月 half a month

han'yake (no) *adj* 半焼け(の) **1.** medium-rare (*meat*), half-done **2.** partial loss by fire

hanzai *n* 犯罪 crime: **~ o okashimásu** 犯罪を犯します commits a crime

hanzatsu (na) *adj* 煩雑(な) troublesome, complicated

hanzubon *n* 半ズボン short-pants

haori *n* 羽織 traditional Japanese coat

hap- *n* 八・8 eight; **hap-pén** *n* 八遍 eight times (= **hachí-kai** 八回, **hachí-do** 八度); **háp-pa, hachí-wa** *n* 八羽 eight (*birds, rabbits*); **hap-pikí** *n* 八匹 eight (*fishes/bugs, small animals*); **háp-pon, hachi-hon** *n* 八本 eight (*pencils/bottles, long objects*); **háp-pun** *n* 八分 eight minutes

happa *n* 葉っぱ leaf (= **ha** 葉)

happi *n* 法被 *happi* coat

hap-pyakú *n* 八百・800 eight hundred

happyō *n* 発表 announcement, publication; (*research*) paper

hā́pu *n* ハープ harp (*Western*)

hará *n* 腹 **1.** belly, stomach: **~ ga herimásu** 腹が減ります gets hungry; **~ ga itamimásu** 腹が痛みます one's stomach aches **2.** mind, heart: **~ ga tachimásu** 腹が立ちます, **~ o tatemásu** 腹を立てます gets angry; **~ ga futói** 腹が太い is big-hearted; **~ ga kurói** 腹が黒い black-hearted; **... no hará o yomimásu** ...の腹を読みます reads the mind of ...

hára, hárappa *n* 原, 原っぱ field

haradatashíi *adj* 腹立たしい aggravating, vexatious

haraemásu, haraéru *v* 払えます, 払える **1.** can pay **2.** can brush aside, can shake out

harahara *adv* はらはら heart goes pit-a-pat: **~ shimásu** はらはらします gets anxious, is scared; **~ sasemásu** はらはらさせます scares

haraimásu, haráu *v* 払います, 払う **1.** pays **2.** brushes aside, shakes out

harai-modoshi *n* 払い戻し a refund

harai-modoshimásu, harai-modósu *v* 払い戻します, 払い戻す refunds

hará-maki *n* 腹巻き stomach band

haremásu, hareru *v* 腫れます, 腫れる swells up

haremásu, hareru *v* 貼れます, 貼れる can paste

haremásu, hareru *v* 張れます; 張れる can spread/stretch it

haremásu, haréru *v* 晴れます, 晴れる (*weather*) clears up: **hárete imásu** 晴れています is clear/fair/sunny

hare-mono *n* 腫れ物 swelling, boil (*on skin*)

haretsu *n* 破裂 bursting: **~ shimásu** 破裂します bursts

hári *n* 針 needle, pin; needlework; hand (*of clock*); a staple (*of stapler*); hari-gane *n* 針金 wire; hari-shígoto *n* 針仕事 needlework (*of all types*)

hári *n* 鍼 acupuncture

harimásu, haru *v* 貼ります, 貼る sticks on, pastes

harimásu, haru *v* 張ります, 張る spreads/stretches it

háru *n* 春 spring (*season*); haru-yásumi *n* 春休み spring break/vacation

harubaru *adv* はるばる all the way

háruka (ni) *adv* 遥か(に) far (off); long ago; by far; háruka na *adj* 遥か(な) distant, far

haru-maki *n* 春巻 Chinese egg rolls, spring rolls

hasamarimásu, hasamáru *v* 挟まります, 挟まる gets caught (*in*) between, becomes sandwiched (*in*) between

hasamemásu, hasaméru *v* 挟めます, 挟める can insert (put between)

hasamí *n* はさみ・鋏 scissors, clippers

hasamí *n* はさみ・螯 pincer(s), claw (*of crab*)

hasamimásu, hasámu *v* 挟みます, 挟む inserts, puts between: **háshi de ~** 箸で挟みます picks it up with chopsticks

hasan *n* 破産 bankruptcy

hashi *n* 端 edge, end; hashi-kko *n* 端っこ edge, end

hashí *n* 橋 bridge

háshi *n* 箸 chopsticks: **~ o tsukaimásu** 箸を使います uses chopsticks; hashí-óki *n* 箸置き chopstick rest

hashigo *n* 梯子 ladder, stairs: **~-zake** はしご酒 bar hopping; **~-dan** 梯子段 wooden stairs

hashika *n* はしか measles

hashira *n* 柱 pillar, post: **ikka no ~** 一家の柱 pillar of the family

hashiremásu, hashiréru *v* 走れます, 走れる can run

hashirimásu, hashíru *v* 走ります, 走る runs

hashitanai *adj* はしたない in bad taste, shameful: **~-kuchi** はしたない口 vulgar language

hason *n* 破損 damage

hassan *n* 発散 emanation, transpiration: **sutoresu ~** ストレス発散 stress release

hás-satsu *n* 八冊 eight copies (*books, magazines*)

hassei *n* 発生 outbreak, occurrence, origin, birth, growth

has-sén *n* 八千・8,000 eight thousand

hassha *n* 発車 departure

hasshin *n* 発進 (*vehicle etc.*) starts: **kuruma o ~ sasemásu** 車を発進させます moves the car

hasshin *n* 発信 transmission: **~ shimásu** 発信します sends, transmits

hasshin *n* 発疹 (*skin*) rash

hasu *n* ハス・蓮 lotus: **~ no hana** ハスの花 lotus bloom

hasu (no) *n* 斜(の) oblique, slanting: **~ ni** 斜に・はすに obliquely (= **naname (ni)** 斜(に))

hata *n* 端 **1.** the side: **(… no) ~ de** (…の)端で off to the side (*of*) **2.** the outside; **~ kara** 端から from the outside, to an outsider

hatá *n* 旗 flag

hatá *n* 機 loom

hátachi *n* 二十歳 20 years old

hatake *n* 畑 field (*dry*): **~ o tagayashimásu** 畑を耕します cultivates one's patch

hatakimásu, hatáku *v* はたきます, はたく slaps, beats; dusts (= **tatakimásu** 叩きます)

hatan *n* 破綻 bankruptcy, failure, collapse

hatarakemásu, hatarakeru *v* 働けます, 働ける can work

hataraki *n* 働き work(ing), activity, operation, function; achievement; ability

hatarakimásu, hataraku *v* 働きます, 働く works, labors; commits (*a crime*)

hataraki-mono *n* 働き者 hard worker

hatasemásu, hataséru *v* 果たせます, 果たせる can accomplish

hatashimásu, hatásu *v* 果たします, 果たす accomplishes: **yakusoku o ~** 約束を果たします fulfills a promise

háto *n* ハト・鳩 pigeon, dove

hato-ba *n* 波止場 pier, wharf, quay (= **futō** 埠頭)

hatsu (no) *adj* 初(の) first

hatsuan *n* 発案 design idea

hatsubai *n* 発売 sale, release; hatsubai-bi *n* 発売日 sale date, release date

hatsudén-ki *n* 発電機 generator

hatsudō'-ki *n* 発動機 motor

hatsuiku *n* 発育 growth: **~ ga yoi/ii** 発育が良い/いい is well grown

hatsuka *n* 二十日 20 days; 20th of the month: **~-mé** 二十日目 the 20th day
hatsukoi *n* 初恋 first love
hatsumei *n* 発明 invention
hatsuon *n* 発音 pronunciation
hattatsu *n* 発達 development
hatte imásu (iru) *v* 張っています(いる) is tense, taut
hátte imásu (iru) *v* 這っています(いる) is crawling
hatten *n* 発展 development, expansion, growth; **hatten-tojō´koku** *n* 発展途上国 developing nation
hát-tō *n* 八頭 eight (*horses/oxen, large animals*)
hatto (shite) *adv* はっと(して) with a sudden start (*of surprise*)
Háwai *n* ハワイ Hawaii
hayái *adj* 速い fast, quick
hayái *adj* 早い early, soon
háyaku *adv* 速く(*so as to be*) fast
háyaku *adv* 早く(*so as to be*) early, soon: **~-tomo** 早くとも at the earliest
hayamé ni *adv* 早めに early (*in good time*)
hayarimásu, hayáru *v* 流行ります, 流行る gets popular, comes into fashion, spreads; (*disease*) spreads rapidly, is fast-spreading
hayari (no) *adj* 流行り(の) fashionable, popular
háyasa *n* 速さ speed
hayashi ráisu *n* ハヤシライス beef hash over rice
hayashí *n* 林 grove
hayashí *n* 囃し (**o-hayashi** お囃し) Japanese instrument accompaniment
hayashimásu, hayásu *v* 生やします, 生やす grows it (*hair, teeth*); lets it grow (*sprout*)
hayashimásu, hayásu *v* 囃します, 囃す (*musically*) accompanies
囃す (*musically*) accompanies
háze *n* ハゼ・沙魚 goby (*fish*)
hazenoki *n* ハゼノキ・櫨の木・黄櫨 sumac, Japanese wax tree (*plant*)
... hazu désu *v* …はずです presumably; ought to, should
... hazu ga/wa arimasén (nái) *v* … はずが/はありません(ない) there is no reason to expect/think that …
hazukashíi *adj* 恥ずかしい ashamed; embarrassed, shy; shameful, disgraceful
hazumi 弾み *n* impetus, momentum; impulse; chance
hazumimásu, hazumu *v* 弾みます, 弾む bounces (back)
hazuremásu, hazureru *v* 外れます, 外れる gets disconnected, comes off; misses, fails
hazushimásu, hazusu *v* 外します, 外す disconnects, takes off, undoes, unfastens; misses: **séki o ~** 席を外します leaves one's seat
hé *n* 屁 flatulence, fart: **~ o hirimásu/shimásu** 屁をひります/します flatulates, farts
hē *interj* へえ oh, really, wow
hébi *n* ヘビ・蛇 snake

hechima *n* ヘチマ・糸瓜 sponge gourd, luffa (loofah)

hedatarimásu, hedatáru *v* 隔たります, 隔たる is distant, is estranged

hedatemásu, hedatéru *v* 隔てます, 隔てる estranges them, separates them, gets them apart

heddoráito *n* ヘッドライト headlight(s)

hédo *n* 反吐 vomit

hei *n* 塀 wall, fence

hei *n* 兵 soldier (= **heishi** 兵士); hei-eki *n* 兵役 military service: ~ **ni tsukimásu** 兵役につきます serves in the army; hei-ki *n* 兵器 weapon, arms; hei-ryoku *n* 兵力 military force; héi-sha *n* 兵舎 barracks; hei-shi *n* 兵士 soldier (= **hei** 兵); hei-tai *n* 兵隊 soldier (boy), rank

heibon (na) *adj* 平凡(な) commonplace, conventional, ordinary

heichi *n* 平地 flat land; (= **heiya** 平野) plain

heijitsu *n* 平日 weekday

heijō (ni) *adv* 平常(に) usually, ordinarily, generally

heijō-shin *n* one's senses/mind: ~ **o tamochimásu** 平常心を保ちます keeps one's cool/calm

heika *n* 陛下 majesty, Your Majesty.

heikai *n* 閉会 closing a meeting: **~-shiki** 閉会式 closing ceremony

heikin *n* 平均 average, on the average: ~ **nenrei** 平均年令 average age; ~ **jumyō** 平均寿命 average life span (*lifetime*); **~-ten** 平均点 average score

heiki (na) *adj* 平気(な) calm, composed, cool, unperturbed, unfazed: ~ **de** 平気で calmly

heikō *n* 平行 parallel, parallelism: **~-sen o tadorimásu** 平行線をたどります fails to reach an agreement, remains as far apart as ever

heikō-shimásu (suru) *v* 閉口します(する) is annoyed, is overwhelmed, gets stuck

heimen *n* 平面 flat surface: **~-zu** 平面図 two-dimensional diagram

heimin *n* 平民 common person: **~-kaikyū** 平民階級 common people

heisa *n* 閉鎖 closing: **kōjō-~** 工場閉鎖 factory closure

heiten *n* 閉店 closing a store

heiwa *n* 平和 peace; ~ **ni narimásu** 平和になります becomes peace; ~ **na kuni** 平和な国 peaceful nation; haiwa na *adj* 平和な peaceful

heiya *n* 平野 plain (*flat land*)

heizen (to) *adv* 平然(と) without embarrassment: ~ **to shiteimásu** 平然としています remains unruffled

hekichi *n* 僻地 remote area (= **henpi na tochi** 辺ぴな土地)

hekieki-shimásu (suru) *v* 辟易します(する) is disgusted

hekiga *n* 壁画 wall painting

hekomimásu, hekomu *v* へこみます, へこむ gets hollow, depressed,

dents: ~ **imásu** へこんでいます is dented, depressed
héma *n* へま [INFORMAL] bungle, mess, goof: ~ **(o) shimásu** へま(を)します goofs up
hemásu, héru *v* 経ます, 経る passes (by), elapses
... hen *suffix* …辺 vicinity, nearby, neighborhood (= **chikaku** 近く)
...-hén *suffix* …遍 (*counts times*) (= **do** 度, **kai** 回)
hen'átsu-ki *n* 変圧器 voltage converter, transformer
henjí *n* 返事 answer, reply, response: ~ **(o) shimásu** 返事(を)します answers, replies, responds
hénka *n* 変化 change: **... ni ~ shimásu** …に変化します it changes into …
henkaku *n* 変革 innovative changes
henkan *n* 変換 conversion: **~-ki** 変換器 converter; **~-kíi** 変換キー the *kana*-to-*kanji* conversion key (*on a Japanese computer*)
henkan *n* 返還 return: **Hoppō ryōdo ~** 北方領土返還 return of Russian-held northern territories
henken *n* 偏見 prejudice
henkin *n* 返金 refund ([*note*] tax refund = **kanpu** 還付)
hén (na) *adj* 変(な) strange, odd, peculiar, funny, queer
enpi (na) *adj* 辺ぴ(な) odd, off the beaten path: ~ **na tochi** 辺ぴな土地 odd parts, places that are off the beaten track (= **hekichi** 僻地)
henryū'-ki *n* 変流器 converter (*AC-DC*)
hensei *n* 編成 organization
henshin *n* 返信 reply, return mail
henshin *n* 変身 transformation
henshū *n* 編集 editing; **henshū-chō** *n* 編集長 editor in chief; **henshū-sha** *n* 編集者 editor
hensoku-rébā *n* 変速レバー gear-shift
hentō *n* 返答 [BOOKISH] = **henjí** 返事
herashimásu, herasu *v* 減らします, 減らす decreases it, cuts it down, shortens, lessens, curtails
heri *n* 減り a decrease
herí *n* 縁 border, edge, rim
herikoputā *n* ヘリコプター helicopter
herikudarimásu, herikudaru *v* へりくだります, へりくだる is modest, abases oneself: **herikudatta taido** へりくだった態度 modest attitude
herikutsu *n* 屁理屈 sophistry, quiddity (*using clever arguments to support something that is not true*): **~ o iimásu** 屁理屈を言います quibbles
herimásu, heru *v* 減ります, 減る decreases, dwindles, goes down
heripōto *n* ヘリポート heliport
heroin *n* ヘロイン heroin
herumetto *n* ヘルメット helmet
herunia *n* ヘルニア hernia
hérupā *n* ヘルパー helper

hérupesu *n* ヘルペス herpes
hérupu *n* ヘルプ help: **~-kinō** ヘルプ機能 (*computer*) help function
heso *n* へそ navel, bellybutton
hesokuri *n* へそくり・ヘソクリ pin money tucked away, pin money hidden away: **~ ga arimásu** ヘソクリがあります has some pin money tucked away
hetá (na) *adj* 下手(な); unskillful, inept, clumsy, poor, bad, inexpert: **~ o suru to** へたをすると if you are unlucky, if you are not careful: **~ no yokozuki** 下手の横好き dabster, likes to but not very good at
hetakuso (na) *adj* 下手くそ(な) → **hetá (na)** 下手(な)
hetarikomimásu, hetarikomu *v* へたり込みます, へたり込む collapses, sinks down: **jimen ni ~** 地面にへたり込みます slumps on the ground
hetoheto *adj* へとへと is dead, is beaten: **~ ni tsukaremásu** へとへとに疲れます is fagged out, is dead tired
heyá *n* 部屋 room
hi *n* 日 day; **hí-bi** *n* 日々 every day: **~ no seikatsu** 日々の生活 daily life; **hí-goto (ni)** *adv* 日毎(に) day by day; **hi-nichi** *n* 日にち (*fixed*) day; number of days; **hi-zuke** *n* 日付 date (*of month*)
hi *n* 日 (**ohi-sama** お日様) sun (= **taiyō** 太陽): **~ no hikari** 日の光 sunshine (= **níkkō** 日光); **hi-atari** *n* 日当たり exposure to the sun, sunniness; **hi-gása** *n* 日傘 parasol (*umbrella*); **hi-gure** *n* 日暮れ sunset (*time*); the dark; **hi-kage** *n* 日陰 shadow (*from sunlight*); **hi-nata** *n* 日なた sunshine: **~-bókko** 日なたぼっこ sunbathing, basking (*in the sun*); **hi-no-de** *n* 日の出 sunrise; **hi-no-iri** *n* 日の入り sunset; **hi-yake** *n* 日焼け sunburn; **hi-yoke** *n* 日よけ sunshade, blind, awning; **hi-yori** *n* 日和 weather (conditions); **hi-yorimi** *n* 日和見 waiting policy: **~-seisaku** 日和見政策 wait-and-see policy
hí *n* 火 fire; **hí-bachi** *n* 火鉢 *hibachi*, charcoal brazier: **~ ni atarimásu** 火鉢に当たります warm oneself at a *hibachi*/charcoal brazier; **hí-bana** *n* 火花 spark; **hí-bashi** *n* 火箸 tongs (*for fire*)
...´-hi *suffix* …費 expense
hibí *n* ひび crack (*fine*): **~ ga dekimásu** ひびができます crazes
hibikí 響き *n* echo
hibikimásu, hibíku *v* 響きます, 響く echoes, resounds
Hibiya *n* 日比谷 Hibiya: **Hibiya-Kō´en** 日比谷公園 Hibiya Park
hibō *n* 誹謗 [BOOKISH] slander; **hibō-chūshō** 誹謗中傷 mental abuse
hichíriki *n* ひちりき an oboe-like reed instrument (in *gagaku*)
hidari *n* 左 left: **~-dónari** 左隣り next (door) on the left; **~-kiki/-giki (no)** 左利き(の) left-handed (*person*); **~-máwari (ni)** 左回り(に) counterclockwise

hidari-gawa *n* 左側 left side
hidói *adj* ひどい severe, terrible, unreasonable, vicious, bitter, awful: **~-kao** ひどい顔 face like a dropped pie
hídoku *adv* ひどく hard, cruelly, terribly: **~ obiemásu** ひどく脅[怯え]ます has one's heart in one's mouth
hiemásu, hiéru *v* 冷えます, 冷える gets cold
hífu *n* 皮膚 skin
higái *n* 被害 damage, injury, casualty: **~-chi** 被害地 stricken area; **~-sha** 被害者 victim (= **gaisha** 該者)
higashí *n* 東 east: **~-guchi** 東口 the east exit/entrance; **~-yori (no kaze)** 東寄り(の風) easterly (*wind*); **~-káigan** 東海岸 east coast
hige *n* ひげ・髭 beard; mustache (= **kuchí-hige** 口ひげ); **~ o sorimásu** ひげを剃ります shaves
hige *n* ひげ・ヒゲ whiskers
hígeki *n* 悲劇 tragedy
híhan *n* 批判 judgment, criticism; **hihán-sha** *n* 批判者 critic, judge; **híhan-teki (na)** *adj* 批判的(な) critical
hihyō *n* 批評 criticism, review; **hihyō-ka** *n* 批評家 critic, reviewer
híiki *n* ひいき illegitimate favor, patronage: **~ shimásu** ひいきします shows preference/partiality
híitā *n* ヒーター heater
hijí *n* 肘 elbow: **~ o harimásu** 肘を張ります bends out one's elbows: **~-kake isu** 肘掛け椅子 armchair
hijō *n* 非常 emergency: **~-burē ki** 非常ブレーキ emergency brake; **~-guchi** 非常口 emergency exit; **~ no ba(w)ai** 非常の場合 in (the) event of emergency; **hijō na** *adj* 非常(な) unusual, extreme; **hijō ni** *adv* 非常(に) extremely
hikaemásu, hikaeru *v* 控えます, 控える refrains, withholds
hikaemé (na) *adj* 控え目(な) modest
hikaku *n* 比較 comparison; **hikaku-teki (ni)** *adv* 比較的(に) relatively, comparatively
hikan *n* 悲観 pessimism; **hikan-teki (na)** *adj* 悲観的(な) pessimistic
hikaremásu, hikareru *v* 引かれます, 引かれる gets pulled (out), gets drawn/dragged/tugged/subtracted
hikaremásu, hikareru *v* 轢かれます, 轢かれる gets run over: **torákku ni ~** トラックに轢かれます gets run over by a truck
hikaremásu, hikareru *v* 挽かれます, 挽かれる gets sawed
hikaremásu, hikareru *v* 弾かれます, 弾かれる gets played
hikaremásu, hikareru *v* ひかれます, ひかれる gets ground
hikaremásu, hikareru *v* 惹かれます, 惹かれる get attracted (*to*)
hikaremásu, hikareru *v* 光れます, 光れる can glow/shine
hikari-kēburu *n* 光ケーブル optical cable (*Internet*)

hikarimásu, hikáru *v* 光ります, 光る it shines, glows
hikemásu, hikeru *v* 引けます, 引ける can pull
hiketsu *n* 秘訣 [BOOKISH] secret, formula: **seikō é no ~** 成功への秘訣 key to success
...-hiki (-ppiki) …匹 (*counts small animals, fish, insects (bugs)*)
hiki-age *n* 引き上げ refloating; rise/hike (*in price, wage, fee*)
hiki-age *n* 引き揚げ evacuation, repatriation; salvage
hiki-agemásu, hiki-agéru *v* 引き上げます, 引き上げる pulls up; refloats; raises (*price, wage, fee*)
hiki-agemásu, hiki-agéru *v* 引き揚げます, 引き揚げる withdraws, leaves; evacuates, gets repatriated
hikiagé-sha *n* 引(き)揚げ者 evacuee, repatriate
hikidashi *n* 引き出し drawer
hikidashimásu, hikidasu *v* 引き出します, 引き出す pulls/draws out; withdraws
hiki-fune *n* 引き(曳き)船[舟] tugboat
hikigane *n* 引き金 trigger
hiki-haraimásu, hiki-haráu *v* 引き払います, 引き払う checks out (*of hotel*)
hikiimásu, hikiíru *v* 率います, 率いる leads, commands
hiki-kaemásu, hiki-káéru *v* 引き換えます, 引き換える exchanges, converts
hiki-kaeshimásu, hiki-káésu *v* 引き返します, 引き返す turns back, returns
hikimásu, hiku *v* 引きます, 引く pulls (*out*); draws; drags, tugs; catches; attracts; deducts; looks up a word (*in dictionary*)
hikimásu, hiku *v* 轢きます, 轢く runs over (*a person*)
hikimásu, hiku *v* 挽きます, 挽く saws
hikimásu, hiku *v* 弾きます, 弾く plays (*a stringed instrument*)
hikimásu, hiku *v* 挽きます, 挽く grinds (*into powder*)
hikimásu, hiku *v* 退きます, 退く retires
hikinige *n* ひき[轢き]逃げ hit and run
hiki-torimásu, hiki-tóru 引き取ります, 引き取る **1.** leaves, withdraws, retires **2.** takes over, looks after, receives **3. íki o ~** 息を引き取ります takes/draws one's last breath, dies
hiki-tsugimásu, hiki-tsúgu *v* 引き継ぎます, 引き継ぐ takes over, succeeds (*in a projection*)
hiki-ukemásu, hiki-ukéru *v* 引き受けます, 引き受ける undertakes, takes charge of, takes responsibility for; guarantees: **tegata o ~** 手形を引き受けます accepts a bill (*of payment*)
hiki-wakemásu, hiki-wakeru 引き分けます, 引き分ける *v* draws apart; plays to a draw: **hikiwake** *n* 引き分け tie, draw

hiki-zan *n* 引き算 subtraction
hiki-zurimásu, hiki-zuru *v* 引きずります, 引きずる drags
hik-kakimásu, hik-káku *v* 引っ掻きます, 引っ掻く scratches it
hikki *n* 筆記 writing down; hikki-tai *n* 筆記体 running hand, script; hikki-yōgu *n* 筆記用具 writing instrument
hikkoshi 引っ越し *n* moving (*house*); hikkoshi-ya *n* 引っ越し屋 (house) mover; hikkoshi-torákku *n* 引っ越しトラック mover's van
hikkoshimásu, hikkósu *v* 引っ越します, 引っ越す moves (*house*)
hikkuri-kaerimásu, hikkuri-káeru *v* 引っくり返ります, 引っくり返る it tips (over); it upsets
hikkuri-kaeshimásu, hikkuri-káesu *v* 引っくり返します, 引っくり返す upsets (*overturns*) it
hikō *n* 飛行 flying (*a plane*); hikō-jō *n* 飛行場 airport (= **kūkō** 空港); hikō'-ki *n* 飛行機 airplane: ~ **ni norimásu** 飛行機に乗ります gets on a plane; hikō-yoi *n* 飛行酔い airsick(ness)
hi-kō'shiki (no) *adj* 非公式(の) unofficial, informal: ~ **kaigi** 非公式の会議 informal conference
hikúi *adj* 低い low, short
hikyō' (na) *adj* 卑怯(な) cowardly
hima *n* 暇 time; leisure, spare time; leave; dismissal (*of servant*): ~**-tsubushi** 暇つぶし killing time; hima na *adj* 暇(な) at leisure, unoccupied, not busy; slow (*business*)
híme *n* 姫 (**ohíme-sama** (お)姫様) princess
himei *n* 悲鳴 a scream: ~ **o agemásu** 悲鳴を上げます screams out
himitsu (no) *adj* 秘密(の) secret, mystery
himo *n* ひも string, cord, tape, strap, ribbon
hin *n* 品 elegance, refinement, dignity: ~ **ga arimásu** 品があります has class
hinagata *n* ひな形 form; pattern; shape
hina-mátsuri *n* ひな祭(り) the Dolls Festival (3 March)
hínan *n* 非難 blame, reproach
hínan *n* 避難 taking refuge; hinán-sha *n* 避難者 refugee
hina-níngyō *n* ひな人形 (*festival*) dolls
hinerimásu, hinéru *v* 捻ります, 捻る twists; turns
hiniku *n* 皮肉 sarcasm: ~ **o iimásu** 皮肉を言います makes sarcastic remarks; hiniku na *adj* 皮肉(な) sarcastic, cynical
hinin *n* 避妊 contraception; hinín-gu *n* 避妊具 contraceptive (*device*); hinín-yaku *n* 避妊薬 contraceptive drug/pill
hinkon *n* 貧困 poverty; hinkon na *adj* 貧困(な) needy
hinmín-kutsu/-gai *n* 貧民窟/街 slum
hinoki butai *n* 檜舞台 stage of a major (*first-class, leading*) theater

hinshi *n* 品詞 part of speech
hinshi *n* 瀕死 moribundity, near death
hinshitsu *n* 品質 quality: **~ o hoshō-shimásu** 品質を保証します guarantees the quality
hinshuku-o-kaimásu (kau) *v* ひんしゅくを買います(買う) invites frowns of disgust, is frowned upon
hínto *n* ヒント hint, reminder
hipparimásu, hippáru *v* 引っ張ります, 引っ張る pulls, drags, tugs (*at*), takes, brings
hira-ayamari *n* 平謝り humble apology: **~ ni ayamarimásu** 平謝りに謝ります makes a humble apology
hiragáná *n* ひらがな・平仮名 hiragana (*the roundish Japanese letters*)
hiraki 開き *n* open and dried fish: **sanma no ~** サンマの開き open and dried saury
hirakí-do *n* 開き戸 hinged door
hirakimásu, hiráku *v* 開きます, 開く opens up; has/holds (*a party*)
hirame *n* ヒラメ・平目 flounder
hiramekimásu, hirameku *v* ひらめきます, ひらめく comes to one in a flash
hiraoyogi *n* 平泳ぎ breast-stroke
hira (shain) *n* 平(社員) rank-and-file employee
hiratai *adj* 平たい flat (= **tiara na** 平らな): **~-hana** 平たい鼻 flat nose
hirataku *adv* 平たく flat: **~ iu to/ieba** 平たく言うと/言えば put simply
hire *n* ヒレ・鰭 fin
hire *n* ヒレ fillet (*of pork, etc.*)
hirefushimásu, hirefusu *v* ひれ伏します, ひれ伏す grovels, falls on one's face
hirei *n* 比例 proportion
hirimásu, híru *v* ひります, ひる discharges (*excretes*) from the body: **hé o ~** 屁をひります flatulates, farts
híró-bá *n* 広場 a square, a place, (*public*) an open space
hiroemásu, hiroeru *v* 拾えます, 拾える can pick it up
hirogarimásu, hirogaru *v* 広がります, 広がる it spreads, widens
hirogemásu, hirogeru *v* 広げます, 広げる spreads/widens it
hirói *adj* 広い wide, broad; big (*room, etc.*)
hiroimásu, hirou *v* 拾います, 拾う picks it up
hiroku *adv* 広く wide, widely
hiromarimásu, hiromáru *v* 広まります, 広まる it spreads, gets diffused
hiromemásu, hiroméru *v* 広めます, 広める spreads/diffuses it
hírosa *n* 広さ width
Hiroshima *n* 広島 Hiroshima
hírō *n* 披露 presentation; **hirō´-en** *n* 披露宴 reception, wedding banquet (*engagement, wedding, etc.*); **hirō´-kai** *n* 披露会 reception (*engagement, wedding, etc.*)

hirú *n* 昼 daytime, noon: **~ kara** 昼から after noon; **~ no bú** 昼の部 matinee; hiru-góhan *n* 昼ご飯 noon meal, lunch (= **hirumeshi** 昼飯); hiru-má *n* 昼間 daytime; hiru-ne *n* 昼寝 nap; hiru-súgi *n* 昼過ぎ afternoon

híru *n* ヒル・蛭 leech

hisashi-buri (ni) *adv* 久しぶり(に) after a long time (*of absence*)

hishaku *n* 柄杓 scoop, ladle

hishó *n* 秘書 secretary (*private*)

hi´ssha *n* 筆者 the writer/author (= **chosha** 著者)

hisúi *n* ヒスイ・翡翠 jade

hitai *n* 額 forehead, brow

hitashi-mono *n* 浸し物 (**o-hitáshi** お浸し) boiled vegetables (*usually greens*) served cold with seasoning

hitchaku *n* 必着 must-reach: **ni-gatsu muika ~** 2月6日必着 due NLT (*not later than*) February 6

hitei *n* 否定 denial

hito *n* 人, **… hitó** …人 person, man, fellow, people; someone, somebody; hitó-bito *n* 人々 people (*in general*); hito-gara *n* 人柄 character, personality; hito-góroshi *n* 人殺し murder; hitó-tachi *n* 人達 people

hito-... *prefix* 一… one, a; hito-ánshin *n* ひと安心 a relief (*from worry*) → **anshín** 安心; hitó-ban *n* 一晩 one night; hito-gomi *n* ひとごみ・人込み crowd; hitó-hako *n* 一箱 one boxful; hitó-iki *n* 一息 a breath: **~ de** 一息で with a gulp: **~ iremásu/tsukimásu** 一息入れます/つきます catches one's breath; hitó-kátamari *n* ひと固まり・一塊 one lump/loaf; hitó-kire *n* 一切れ (one) piece (*a cut*); hitó-koto *n* 一言 a word: **~ de iuto** 一言で言うと put simply; hitó-kuchi *n* 一口 one mouthful; one bite; one drink, sip: **~ ni iuto** 一口に言うと in a word; hitó-kumi *n* 一組 a set (*collection*); hitó-maki *n* 一巻き one (*roll, bolt of cloth*); hitó-mori *n* 一盛り scoop (*one scoopful*); hitó-nemuri *n* 一眠り a nap; hitó-oyogi *n* ひと泳ぎ a swim; hitó-ri *n* 一人 one person; (**~ de** ひとりで・独りで) alone; **~-mónó** 独り者 single (*unmarried*) person; hitó-saji *n* 一匙 one spoonful; hito-shibai *n* 一芝居 playing a trick, acting; hito-shigoto *n* 一仕事 bout of work; hito-suji *n* 一筋 shaft; **~-nawa dewa ikimasen** 一筋縄ではいきません is not an easy job; hitó-tsu *n* ひとつ・一つ one (= **ík-ko** 一個): one year old (= **ís-sai** 一歳); one and the same; hitó-yama *n* 一山 one heap/bunch

hitómazu (wa) *adv* ひとまず(は) for a while; for the time being

hitori-de ni *adv* ひとりでに spontaneously, automatically, by/of itself

hitori-goto *n* 独り言 talking to oneself: **~ o iimásu** 独り言を言います says to oneself

hitosashiyubi *n* 人差し指 forefinger, index finger
hitoshíi *adj* 等しい equal, identical, similar
hitsugi *n* 棺 coffin
hitsuji *n* ヒツジ・羊 sheep
hitsujuhin *n* 必需品 necessity: **seikatsu-~** 生活必需品 daily necessities, commodities
hitsuyō *n* 必要 necessity, need: **... suru ~ ga arimásu** . . . する必要があります needs to...: **... ga ~ desu** . . . が必要です needs...; **hitsuyō na** 必要な *adj* necessary, essential
hitteki *n* 匹敵 comparison
híttó *n* ヒット a hit (*baseball*); **híttó-kyoku** *n* ヒット曲 hit song
híya *n* 冷や cold water
hiya-múgi *n* 冷や麦・ひやむぎ chilled wheat-flour noodles (*cf.* **sō´men** そうめん)
hiyashimásu, hiyásu *v* 冷やします, 冷やす cools it off, refrigerates, chills: **atama o ~** 頭を冷やします cools one's head
hiya-yákko *n* 冷ややっこ cooled bean curd
híyō *n* 費用 cost, expense: **~ ga kakarimásu** 費用がかかります costs
hiyowa *adj* ひ弱 weak: **~ na kodomo** ひ弱な子供 frail child
hiza *n* 膝 knee, lap
hizamazukimásu, hizamazuku *v* ひざまずきます, ひざまずく falls on one's knees, kneels down
hizume *n* 蹄 hoof
hó *n* 帆 sail
hō *interj* ほお? oh?
hō *n* 法 law (= **hōritsu** 法律); rule; method
hō *n* ほお・頬 cheek (= **hoho** ほほ・頬, **hoppéta** ほっぺた)
... hō´ *n* ...方 alternative, the one (*of two*) that ...: **~ ga íi desu** ...方がいいです ... is better
hōbi *n* 褒美 (**go-hō´bi** ご褒美 [HONORIFIC]) prize, reward
hóbo *adj* ほぼ nearly; roughly
hō´bō n, *adv* 方々 everywhere, all over, every which way
hōchi *n* 放置 neglect: **~-jitensha** 放置自転車 illegally-parked bicycle
hóchikisu *n* ホチキス stapler
hochō *n* 歩調 pace: **~ o awasemásu** 歩調を合わせます keeps step
hōchō *n* 包丁 knife (*big*); butcher knife; cleaver
hochōki *n* 補聴器 hearing aids: **~ o tsukemásu** 補聴器をつけます wears a hearing aid
hōdan *n* 砲弾 bombshell
...-hōdai *suffix* 放題 can...as much as: **tabe-~** 食べ放題 all-you-can-eat: **nomi-~** 飲み放題 all-you-can-drink: **shitai-~** したい放題 does whatever one feel like doing
hōden *n* 放電 electric(al) discharge
(...) hodo *suffix* (...)程・ほど extent; limits; moderation; approximate time; about (*as much*

as), (not) so much as; the more … the more

hodō *n* 歩道 walk(way), pavement, sidewalk: **~-kyō** 歩道橋 crossover bridge

hōdō *n* 報道 news report

hodokemásu, hodokéru *v* 解けます, 解ける comes loose, comes undone

hodokimásu, hodóku *v* 解きます, 解く undoes, unties

hodokóshi *v* 施し charity: **~ o ukemásu** 施しを受けます accepts charity

hoemásu, hoéru *v* 吠えます, 吠える (dog) barks

hoeraremásu, hoeraréru *v* 吠えられます, 吠えられる can bark; is barked

hō´fu (na) *adj* 豊富(な) rich: **~ na keiken** 豊富な経験 abundant experience

hō´gai (na) *adj* 法外(な) exorbitant, inordinate, excessive, unreasonable, steep: **~ na kingaku/nedan** 法外な金額/値段 unreasonable price

hōgaku *n* 方角 direction, one's bearings

hōgaku *n* 邦楽 Japanese music

hō´gaku (-bu) *n* 法学(部) (*science/ study of*) law; School of Law

hōgan *n* 包含 inclusion, comprehension

hōgan *n* 砲丸 cannonball

hógaraka (na) *adj* 朗らか(な) bright, sunny; cheerful

hogei *n* 捕鯨 whaling

hōgén *n* 方言 dialect

hógo *n* 保護 protection; **hogo-sha** *n* 保護者 guardian

hoguremásu, hoguréru *v* 解れます, 解れる it loosens

hoho *n* ほほ・頬 cheek (= **hō** ほお・頬, **hoppéta** ほっぺた)

hōhō *n* 方法 method, process

hohoemashii *adj* 微笑ましい heartwarming, pleasant

hohoemí *n* 微笑み smile

hohoemimásu, hohoému *v* 微笑みます, 微笑む smiles

hoikú-en *n* 保育園 nursery school, pre-kindergarten

hōji *n* 法事 mass (*Buddhist*), Buddhist memorial service: **~ o okonaimásu** 法事を行います holds a Buddhist service (*for the dead*)

hōjin *n* 法人 corporation; **hōjin-zei** *n* 法人税 corporation tax

hójo *n* 補助 help, assistance; **hojo-kin** *n* 補助金 grant: **~-seido** 補助金制度 bounty system

hoka *n* ほか・外・他 other, in addition to, other than (= **ta** 他): **~ no** 他の other, another

hoken *n* 保険 insurance: **… ni ~ o kakemásu** …に保険をかけます insures; **kenkō-hoken** *n* 健康保険 health insurance

hoken *n* 保健 healthcare, preservation of health: **sekai-~-kikō** 世界保健機関 World Health Organization

hōken *n* 封建 feudal(ism): **~-jídai**

封建時代 feudal period
hoketsu *n* 補欠 substitute, alternate: **~-sha-meibo** 補欠者名簿 waiting list
hō´ki *n* 放棄 abandonment
hō´ki *n* 箒 broom: **~ de hakimásu** 箒で掃きます sweeps with a broom; **hōkí-boshi** *n* 箒星 comet
Hokkáidō *n* 北海道 Hokkaido
hókkē *n* ホッケー hockey
hókku *n* ホック hook (*snap*): **~ de tomemásu** ホックでとめます hooks up
Hokkyoku *n* 北極 North Pole, Arctic; **Hokkyoku-guma** *n* ホッキョクグマ・北極グマ polar bear, white bear (= **shiro-kuma** 白熊); **Hokkyoku-sei** *n* 北極星 North Star
hōkō *n* 方向 direction
hōkoku *n* 報告 report; **hōkoku-sho** *n* 報告書 report, statement
hokora *n* 祠 small shrine
hokorashii *adj* 誇らしい is proud
hokoremásu, hokoréru *v* 誇れます, 誇れる can brag
hokori *n* 埃 dust (*in the air*): **~ o haraimásu** 埃を払います brushes dust off
hokorí 誇り *n* pride, boast
hokorimásu, hokóru *v* 誇ります, 誇る brags about/of
hokōsha *n* 歩行者 pedestrian: **~-tengoku** 歩行者天国 areas of streets temporarily closed to vehicular traffic, pedestrian mall
hoku-... *prefix* 北… north (= **kita no...** 北の…); **Hoku-Bei** *n* 北米 = **Kita-Ámerika** 北アメリカ North America; **hóku-bu** *n* 北部 the north, the northern part; **hóku-i** *n* 北緯 north latitude; **Hoku-ō** *n* 北欧 Northern Europe; **hoku-sei** *n* 北西 northwest; **hoku-tō** *n* 北東 northeast; **hoku-yō** *n* 北洋 northern sea
hokuro *n* 黒子 mole (*on skin*)
hokosoemimásu, hokusoemu *v* ほくそ笑みます, ほくそ笑む chuckles, snickers to oneself
hokyō *n* 補強 reinforcement, corroboration
hokyū *n* 補給 supply
hōkyū *n* 俸給 pay, wages, salary
homé *n* 褒め praise: **~ ni azukari-masu** お褒めにあずかります is praised [HONORIFIC]
home-kótoba *n* 褒め言葉 compliment, word of praise
homemásu, homéru *v* 褒めます, 褒める praises, admires
hōmén *n* 方面, **...-hō´men** …方面 direction, quarter, district
hómo (no) *adj* ホモ(の) homosexual, gay
hōmon *n* 訪問 visit, call on
homosapiensu *n* ホモサピエンス Homo sapiens
hō´mu *n* ホーム **1.** platform (*at station*) **2.** home
hōmu-dórama *n* ホームドラマ soap opera
hōmuresu *n* ホームレス homeless
hōmushikku *n* ホームシック homesick: **~ ni narimásu/kakarimásu**

ホームシックになります/かかります gets homesick

Hōmu-shō *n* 法務省 Ministry of Justice

hōmu-sutei *n* ホームステイ home stay

hón *n* 本 book; hón-bako *n* 本箱 bookcase; hón-dana *n* 本棚 bookshelf; hón-ya *n* 本屋 bookshop

hon-... *prefix* 本… main; chief; this; the; the present; real; hon-ba *n* 本場 original place, area of production, real thing: ~ **no nihon ryōri** 本場の日本料理 authentic Japanese food; hon-ban *n* 本番 real part, real thing; hón-bu *n* 本部 central office, headquarters (= **hón-sha** 本社); hon-dai *n* 本題 main issue; hon-dō *n* 本道 the main route; hon-mono *n* 本物 the real thing: ~ **no aji** 本物の味 authentic flavor: ~ **no daiyamondo** 本物のダイヤモンド real diamond; hon-ne *n* 本音 true (*inner*) feeling, real intention (= **hon-shin** 本心); hon-nin *n* 本人 (*the person*) himself/herself/myself, principal; hón-rai *n* 本来 originally, from the start; hon-ron *n* 本論 main discussion, main issue: ~ **ni hairimásu** 本論に入ります get down to business; hón-seki *n* 本籍 permanent residence; hon-shin *n* 本心 true (*inner*) feeling, real intention; hon-ten *n* 本店 head office, main store

...´-hon (...´-pon, ...´-bon) *suffix* …本 (*counts long objects*)

hónbun *n* 本分 one's duty

honé *n* 骨 bone: ~ **o orimásu** 骨を折ります takes (great) pains, goes to much trouble; hone-gúmi *n* 骨組み framework; hone-órí *n* 骨折り(**o-honeori** お骨折り [HONORIFIC]) effort

hongoshi-o-iremásu (ireru) *v* 本腰を入れます (入れる) gets down to seriously

honki (no/de) *adj, adv* 本気(の/で) serious(ly), (*in*) earnest: **... o ~ ni shimásu** …を本気にします takes it seriously

Hónkón *n* ホンコン・香港 Hong Kong

honmei *n* 本命 the favorite

honmō *n* 本望 (*one's*) heart's desire, one's long-cherished desire: ~ **o togemásu** 本望を遂げます realizes one's heart's desire

honno ... *adj* ほんの …just a (*little*), only a, a mere/slight …: ~ **sukoshi/chotto** ほんの少し/ちょっと … just a little; just a minute

honō´ *n* 炎 flame

honomekashí *n* 仄めかし a hint

honomekashimásu, honomekásu *v* 仄めかします, 仄めかす hints

Honóruru *n* ホノルル Honolulu

hon-ryō *n* 本領 one's element/sphere: ~ **o hakki shimásu** 本領を発揮します show oneself at one's best

Hónshū *n* 本州 Honshū

hontō (no), honto (no) *adj* 本当(の),

ほんと(の) true, real, genuine: **~ no koto** 本当の事 truth; **~ ni** 本当に really, truly, indeed, absolutely

hon'yaku *n* 翻訳 translation; hon'yákụ´-sha(ka) 翻訳者(家) translator

hoppéta *n* ほっぺた cheek (= **hō, hoho** ほお・ほほ・頬)

hoppō *n* 北方 the north

hóra *n* ホラ・法螺 **1.** trumpet-shell (= **horá-gai** 法螺貝) **2.** exaggeration, bragging, bull (= **uso** 嘘): **~ o fụkimásụ** ほらを吹きます brags, talks big

hóra *interj* ほら! Look!, Here!, There!, You see!

horā *n* ホラー horror; horā-eiga *n* ホラー映画 horror movie/film

hora-ana *n* 洞穴 cave

horá-gai *n* 法螺貝 trumpet-shell

hōrei *n* 法令 law, act

horemásụ, horeru *v* 惚れます, 惚れる falls in love, loses one's heart to : **... ni hore(komi)másụ** ...に惚れ(込み)ます falls in love (*with*)

horemásụ, horéru 掘れます, 掘れる can dig

hōrénsō *n* ホウレンソウ・ほうれん草 spinach

horí *n* 掘 ditch, moat; hori-wari *n* 掘(り)割り canal

horidashi-mono *n* 掘り出し物 a bargain, a real find, lucky find: **~ o sagashimásụ** 掘り出し物を探します searches for bargains

horimásụ, hóru *v* 掘ります, 掘る digs, carves; excavates

horimásụ, hóru *v* 彫ります, 彫る carves

horí-mónó *n* 彫物 a carving, tattoo

hōritsu *n* 法律 law (*legal system*); hōritsu-ka *n* 法律家 jurist

hōrō *n* 放浪 wandering

horobimásụ, horobíru *v* 滅びます, 滅びる perishes

horoboshimásụ, horobósu *v* 滅ぼします, 滅ぼす destroys

hōrókú *n* 焙烙 earthenware pan

hórun *n* ホルン horn (*music*)

hōsaku *n* 方策 measures, policy

hōsaku *n* 豊作 abundant/rich harvest

hōseki *n* 宝石 jewel, gem; hōseki-shō *n* 宝石商 jeweler, gem dealer

hosemásụ, hoséru *v* 干せます, 干せる can dry it

hōshanō *n* 放射能 radioactivity

hōshasen *n* 放射線 (nuclear) radiation

hoshi *n* 星 star; hoshi-jírushi *n* 星印 star (*symbol*), asterisk (*); hoshi-uranai *n* 星占い astrology

hōshi *n* 奉仕 service; hōshi-katsudō *n* 奉仕活動 voluntary service, voluntary activity

hōshi *n* 胞子 spore(s)

hoshigarImásụ, hoshigáru *v* 欲しがります, 欲しがる wants it

hoshíi *v* 欲しい is desired/desirable; desires, wants, would like, wishes

hoshimásụ, hósu *v* 干します, 干す dries it; airs it

hōshin *n* 方針 policy, course (*of action*), aim (*direction*)
hōshin *n* 疱疹 (*medical*) herpes
hōshin *n* 放心 absent-mindedness: **~ jōtai** 放心状態 is lost in abstraction
hóshi (ta) *adj* 干し(た) dried; hoshimono *n* 干(し)物 drying washed clothes, dried clothes
hoshō *n* 保証 guarantee, warranty: **~´-sho** 保証書 letter of guarantee
hoshō *n* 補償 compensating; hoshō´-kin 補償金 compensation (*money*), indemnity
hōshoku *n* 飽食 full feeding: **~ no jidai** 飽食の時代 age of plenty
hōshoku *n* 宝飾 jewelry: **~-hin** 宝飾品 jewelry items
hóshu *n* 保守 maintenance, upkeep; hoshu-ha *n* 保守派 conservative wing; hoshu-teki (na) *adj* 保守的(な) conservative: **~ kangae** 保守的な考え conservative thinking/view
hóshu *n* 捕手 catcher
hōshū *n* 報酬 reward
hōshutsu *n* 放出 emission
hōsō *n* 放送 broadcasting
hōsō *n* 包装 packing, wrapping; hōsō´-butsu *n* 包装物 package, packet; hōsō´-shi *n* 包装紙 package, wrapper
hosói *adj* 細い slender; narrow; thin
hōsoku *n* 法則 rule(s), law(s)
hosomichi *n* 細道 lane, path, narrow road
hosonagái *adj* 細長い long and slender/narrow
hossa *n* 発作 attack, seizure: **shinzō-~** 心臓発作 heart attack
hō´su *n* ホース hose
hósu̲tesu *n* ホステス hostess
hósu̲to *n* ホスト host
hōtai *n* 包帯 bandage
hotaru *n* ホタル・蛍 lightning bug, firefly: **~-no-hikari** ① ホタルの光 gleam of fireflies ② 「ほたるの光」 "Auld Lang Syne"
hotaté-gai *n* ホタテガイ・帆立貝 scallop(s)
hōtei *n* 法廷 law court
hōteishiki *n* 方程式 equation
hōten *n* 法典 code law
hóteru *n* ホテル hotel: **ichiryū-~** 一流ホテル first-class hotel
hōtō *n* 放蕩 [BOOKISH] debauchery
hotobashiru *v* ほとばしる gushes: **~-kanjō** ほとばしる感情 outpouring of emotion
Hotoke(-sámá) *n* 仏(様) Buddha (= **budda** 仏陀)
hotóndo *adv* ほとんど almost (*all*), nearly; almost all the time; [+ NEGATIVE verb] hardly (*ever*), seldom
hottan *n* 発端 beginning, onset
hotte/hōtte oku *v* ほって/放っておく leaves alone, lets alone
hotto doggu *n* ホットドッグ hot dog
hotto kēki *n* ホットケーキ pancake
hótto (na) *adj* ホット(な) hot: **~ wadai** ホットな話題 hot topic

hotto purēto *n* ホットプレート hot plate
hotto rain *n* ホットライン hotline
hóttó-shimásu (-suru) *v* ほっとします(する) breathes a sigh of relief
hōwa *n* 飽和 saturation, impregnation; **hōwa-jōtai** *n* 飽和状態 saturated state
hoyō *n* 保養 rest, recuperation: **me no** ~ 目の保養 feast for the eyes
hu... ふ…・フ… → **fu...**
hyakka-jíten *n* 百科事典 encyclopedia
hyakká-ten *n* 百貨店 department store (= **depāto** デパート)
hyákkanichi *n* 百か日 a memorial service 100 days after the death
hyakú *n* 百・100 hundred; **hyakú-do** *n* 百度 ① a hundred times (= **hyak-kái** 百回) ② a hundred degrees; **hyakú-doru** *n* 百ドル a hundred dollars: **~-satsu** 百ドル札 a hundred-dollar bill; **hyaku en-dama** *n* 百円玉 hundred yen coin; **hyaku-mán** *n* 百万・1,000,000 one million; **hyakú-nen** *n* 百年 100 years; a century (= **~-kan** 百年間); **hyakushō** *n* 百姓 farmer
hyappatsu-hyakuchū *n* 百発百中 hitting the mark ten times out of ten
hyō *n* 表 table, schedule, list
hyō´ *n* ヒョウ・豹 leopard
hyō´ *n* ひょう・雹 hail (= **arare** あられ・霰)
hyō *n* 票 vote: ~ **o tōjiru** 票を投じる votes, casts a vote
hyōban *n* 評判 reputation, fame: ~ **no** 評判の famous, popular: ~ **ga warui** 評判が悪い have a bad reputation
hyōdai *n* 表題・標題 title (*of book, article, e-mail...*)
hyō´ga *n* 氷河 glacier: **~-ki** 氷河期 ice age: **shūshoku ~-ki** 就職氷河期 hard times for college-graduate job seekers
hyōgén *n* 表現 expression (words)
hyōgo *n* 標語 slogan; motto
Hyō´go *n* 兵庫 Hyogo
hyōgu-ya *n* 表具屋 paper-hanger/-repairer, picture-framer
hyōhen *n* 豹変 sudden change
hyōhyō to *adv* ひょうひょうと aloof from the world: ~ **shite imásu** ひょうひょうとしています is free as the wind
hyōjō´ *n* 表情 expression (*on face*): **~´ o yawaragemásu** 表情を和らげます softens one's expression
hyōjun *n* 標準 standard; **hyōjun-go** *n* 標準語 standard Japanese (*language*)
hyō´ka *n* 評価 grade, opinion, appraisal: **hito no ~ o kinishi-masen** 人の評価を気にしません does not worry about what others think of
hyōkín (na) *adj* ひょうきん(な) funny, comical
hyokkori *adv* ひょっこり accidentally, by chance: ~ **arawaremásu** ひょっこり現れます appears unexpectedly

hyokohyoko *adv* ひょこひょこ lightly
hyōmén *n* 表面 surface: **~-chōr-yoku** 表面張力 surface tension
hyōri *n* 表裏 two faces: **~-ittai** 表裏一体 two sides of the same coin: **~-no-aru...** 表裏のある... two-faced
hyōron *n* 評論 criticism, comment (ary); **hyōron-ka** *n* 評論家 critic, commentator, reviewer
hyōryū *n* 漂流 drift
hyōshi′ *n* 表紙 cover (*book, magazine, etc.*)
hyōshiki *n* 標識 sign, mark(er): **kōtsū-~** 交通標識 traffic sign; **dōro-~** 道路標識 road sign
hyōshō *n* 表彰 official commendation: **~-jō** 表彰状 certificate of commendation: **~-shiki** 表彰式 awarding ceremony
hyōtán *n* 瓢箪 gourd: **~ kara koma** 瓢箪から駒 produces an unexpected dividend
hyōten *n* 評点 evaluation score, grade
hyōten *n* 氷点 freezing point
hyótto-shite *adv* ひょっとして by any chance, maybe, possibly, could be
hyō′zan *n* 氷山 iceberg: **~ no ikkaku** 氷山の一角 tip of the iceberg
hyū′zu *n* ヒューズ fuse

I

i *n* 胃 = **i-búkuro** 胃袋 stomach; **i-búkuro** *n* 胃袋 [BOOKISH] stomach; **i-chō** *n* 胃腸 [BOOKISH] stomach and intestines; **i-gan** *n* 胃癌 (*medical*) stomach cancer; **i-káiyō** *n* 胃潰瘍 (*medical*) (*gastric*) ulcer
i-... *prefix* 医... medicine, medical, doctoring; **í-gaku** *n* 医学 medicine, medical science/studies: **igaku-sei** 医学生 medical student; **i-sha** *n* 医者 doctor, physician
...-i *suffix* ...医 doctor, (= **senmón-i** 専門医) medical specialist
...-i *suffix* ... 位 rank, grade
ian *n* 慰安 consolation, comfort; recreation
ibarimásu, ibáru *v* 威張ります, 威張る is/acts arrogant, haughty; swaggers
ibikí *n* いびき snoring
ibo *n* 異母 different mother: **~-kyōdai** 異母兄弟 half brother(s): **~-shimai** 異母姉妹 half sister(s)
ibuningu-doresu *n* イブニングドレス evening dress
ibushimásu, ibusu *v* いぶします, いぶす smokes, fumigates, fumes
ibutsu *n* 異物 exogenous material, foreign body
ibutsu *n* 遺物 relics, artifact

icha *v* [INFORMAL] いちゃ = **ité wa** いては

ichí *n* 一・1 one: ~ **ka bachi ka** 一か八か all or nothing; ichí-ban (no) *adj* 一番(の) number one; first; ichí-banme (no) *adj* 一番目(の) first; ichí-bu *n* 一部 a part, portion; a copy (*of a book*); ichí-byō *n* 一秒 a second (*1/60 minute*); ichí-dai *n* 一台 one (*machine*, *vehicle*); ichi-danraku *n* 一段落 one stage; ichi-dó *n* 一度 one time (= **ik-kái** 一回, **íp-pen** 一遍); ichí-do *n* 一度 one degree; ichi-en *n* 一円 one yen; ichí-go *n* 一語 one word; ichí-ji *n* 一時 ① one o'clock ② ~ **(no)** 一時(の) at one-time, once, temporary; ichi-jitsú *n* 一日 one day; someday (= **aru hi** ある日, **ichi-nichí** 一日); ichí-mai *n* 一枚 a sheet; one sheet (*flat things*); ichí-mei *n* 一名 [BOOKISH] one person (= **hitóri** 一人); ichí-nen *n* 一年 the year 1; one year (= **~-kan** 一年間): **~-sei** 一年生 first-year student, freshman; ichi-nichí *n* 一日 one day; ichí-wa *n* 一羽 one (*bird*, *rabbit*); ichí-wari *n* 一割 ten percent

íchi *n* 位置 position, location, situation

íchi(bá) *n* 市(場) market, marketplace

ichi-ban *n* 一番 most: ~ **íi/warui** 一番いい/悪い best/worst

ichibu-shijū *n* 一部始終 all the details: ~ **o katarimásu** 一部始終を語ります tells the whole story

ichidō *n* 一同 all (*who are concerned/present*)

Ichi-gatsú *n* 一月・1月 January (= **Shōgatsú** 正月)

ichigo *n* いちご・イチゴ・苺 strawberry

ichigo-ichie *n* 一期一会 one in a lifetime

ichii *n* いちい・イチイ yew

ichi-ichi *adv* いちいち one by one, one after another, each time

ichi-in *n* 一員 a member

ichi-in *n* 一因 a cause

ichíjiku *n* イチジク・無花果 fig: **~-no-ki** いちじくの木 fig tree

ichijirushíi *adj* 著しい [BOOKISH] conspicuous, prominent, remarkable, striking

ichiji-teki (na) *adj* 一時的(な) temporary

ichi-mán *n* 一万・10,000 ten thousand

ichi-mi *n* 一味 accomplice: **tōzokudan no ~** 盗賊団の一味 member(s) of a robber band

ichiō *adv* 一応・いちおう as far as it goes, to some extent, just in case, tentatively

ichi-rei *n* 一例 an example

ichiryū (no) *adj* 一流(の) first-rate, topflight, elite: ~ **kashu** 一流の歌手 superb singer

ichō *n* イチョウ・銀杏 gingko (*tree*)

idai (na) *adj* 偉大(な) great: ~ **hito/jinbutsu** 偉大な人(物) great person

iden *n* 遺伝 heredity; iden-shi *n* 遺伝子 gene
ideorogii *n* イデオロギー ideology
í(do) *n* 井(戸) a well
ído *n* 緯度 latitude
ie *interj* いえ (= **iie** いいえ) no
ié *n* 家 a house, a home
ie-dé *n* 家出 running away from home; iede-nin *n* 家出人 a runaway
iemásu̲, ieru *v* 言えます, 言える can say/tell
iemásu̲, iéru *v* 癒えます, 癒える heals
Ierō-pēji *n* イエローページ Yellow Pages
Iesu (Kirisuto) *n* イエス (キリスト) Jesus Christ
íga *n* 衣餓 clothes moth
ígai (na) *adj* 意外(な) unexpected; ígai ni *adv* 意外(に) unexpectedly
(...) ígai *suffix* (…)以外 outside (of …), except (*for*) …
igen *n* 威厳 dignity: **~ o tamochimásu̲** 威厳を保ちます keep one's dignity
ígi *n* 意義 [BOOKISH] significance, sense, meaning: **~ no aru shigoto** 意義のある仕事 meaningful work
ígi *n* 異議 [BOOKISH] objection
Igirisu *n* イギリス England (= **Eikoku** 英国): **~-jin** イギリス人 an English person
ígo *n* 囲碁 the board game *Go* (= **gó** 碁)
(...) ígo *suffix* (…)以後 afterward, from … on (= (…) **ikō** (…)以降)
igokochi *n* 居心地 feeling of staying: **~ ga ii** 居心地がいい feels comfortable while staying
iguana *n* イグアナ iguana
igyō *n* 偉業 great achievement: **~ o nashitogemásu̲** 偉業を成し遂げます accomplishes a great achievement
ihan *n* 違反 violation, offense: **kōtsū-~** 交通違反 traffic violation
ii *adj* いい good; OK, right, correct (= **yoi** 良い): [NEGATIVE] **yóku arimasén** 良くありません; [PAST] **yókatta desu̲** 良かったです; ii-hi̲to *n* いい人 ① a good person ② sweetheart, lover
ii-arawashimásu̲, ii-arawásu *v* 言い表(わ)します, 言い表(わ)す expresses, puts into words
iie *interj* いいえ no
ii-kaemasu̲, ii-kaéru *v* 言い換えます, 言い換える rephrases, puts/says it another way
ii-kagen *adj* **1.** いい加減 rather, pretty, moderate **2. ~ na** いい加減(な) random, perfunctory, halfhearted, haphazard
ii-kata *n* 言い方 way of saying/telling/putting it, expression
iimásu̲, iu/yū *v* 言います, 言う(ゆう) says, tells; expresses
íin *n* 委員 committee member(s); iín-kai *n* 委員会 committee
ii-tai *v* 言いたい wants to say: **~ kotó** 言いたいこと[事] what one wants to say; **~ hō´dai** 言いたい放題 says whatever one wants/feels

ii-tsukemásu, ii-tsukéru *v* 言い付けます, 言い付ける commands, orders; tells on, tattles on

ii-wake *n* 言い訳 explanation, excuse: **~ o shinaidekudasai.** 言い訳をしないで下さい Please don't give an excuse.

ijí *n* 意地 temper, disposition: **~-waru** 意地悪 ill-tempered, mean(-spirited)

íji *n* 維持 maintenance, upkeep, support

ijí-hi *n* 維持費 upkeep (*expense*)

ijime いじめ *n* teasing, torment

ijimek-ko *n* いじめっ子 bully

ijimemásu, ijimeru *v* いじめます, いじめる teases, torments

ijō *n* 異状/異常 something unusual/wrong (*the matter*), abnormality: **~-kishō** 異常気象 abnormal climate

(...) íjō n, *suffix* (…)以上 above, over, upwards of; the above; that's it! (*end of message/speech*) = thank you (*for your attention*)

ijū *n* 移住 emigration, immigration; **ijū-sha** *n* 移住者 emigrant, immigrant (= **imin** 移民)

ika *n* イカ cuttlefish, squid

(...) íka *n, suffix* (…)以下 below (…), less than …: **~ no tōri desu** 以下の通りです as (*described*) below, as follows

ikada *n* 筏 raft

ikága *adv* いかが how (about it)? [DEFERENTIAL] (= **dō´** どう): **chōshi wa ~ desuka?** 調子はいかがですか? How's it going?

ikagawashíi *adj* いかがわしい suspicious, questionable, shady: **~ uwasa** いかがわしい噂 suspicious rumors

ika-hodo *adj* いかほど how many? (= **íkura** いく[幾]ら); how ...? (= **dono-gurai (-kurai)** どの位)

ikan *n* 遺憾 regret

ikaremásu, ikareru *v* 行かれます, 行かれる **1.** can go **2.** [PASSIVE] have them go (*to one's distress*); [HONORIFIC] goes (= **irasshaimásu** いらっしゃいます)

ikari *n* 錨 anchor

ikarí *n* 怒り anger: **~ o shizume-másu** 怒りを静めます calms the anger

ikasemásu, ikaseru *v* 行かせます, 行かせる sends (*a person*); lets (*a person*) go

ikashimásu, ikásu *v* 生かします, 生かす **1.** lets/makes it live, brings life to, enlivens; keeps it alive; revives **2.** makes the most of, makes good use of

iké *n* 池 pond

ikébana *n* 生け花 [活花] flower arrangement

ikemasén, ikenai *v* いけません, いけない **1.** it won't do; you mustn't; don't **2.** (*that's*) too

ikemásu, ikéru *v* 生[活]けます, 生[活]ける arranges (flowers)

íken *n* 意見 opinion, idea: **go-~** ご意見 (*your/someone else's*) opinion [HONORIFIC]

íken *n* 違憲 constitutional violation

iki (na) *adj* 粋(な) smart, stylish

íki *n* 息 breath: **~ o shimásu** 息をします breathes; iki-gire *n* 息切れ shortness of breath: **hashitta ato ni ~ ga shimásu** 走った後に息切れがします gets out of breath after running; iki-gurushii *adj* 息苦しい stuffy

...-iki (no) *suffix* …行き(の) bound for …

ikidōrí *n* 憤り indignation, resentment

ikidōrimásu, ikidō´ru *v* 憤ります, 憤る gets indignant, resents

ikigai *n* 生き甲斐 something to live for: **~ o kanjimásu** 生き甲斐を感じます feels one's life is worth living, feels alive

ikimásu, iku *v* 行きます, 行く goes

ikimásu, ikíru *v* 生きます, 生きる lives

ikímono *n* 生き物 living thing(s), animal(s), creature(s)

ikiói *n* 勢い energy: **~ yóku** 勢いよく energetically

ikisatsu *n* いきさつ details, circumstances, complexities; complications

iki-yasúi *adj* 行きやすい accessible, easy to get to

iki-zumarimásu, iki-zumáru *v* 行き詰まります, 行き詰まる gets bogged down

ik-kai *n* 一階 one floor/story; first floor, ground floor

ik-kái (no) *n, adj* 一回(の) one time, once (= **ichi-dó** 一度)

ikkansei *n* 一貫性 consistency: **hanashi ni ~ ga arimásu** 話に一貫性があります has consistency in one's talk

ík-ken *n* 一軒 one house/building (*counter for buildings*)

ík-ken *n* 一件 one case/matter

ík-ki ni *adv* 一気に with a gulp, with a dash, with a burst

ík-ko *n* 一個 one (*piece, small object*) (= **hitótsu** ひとつ・一つ)

ik-ko *n* 一戸 a house, a household

ik-kō *n* 一考 consideration

ik-kō (ni)... *adv* 一向(に)... [+ NEGATIVE] not at all, never: **~ ni kamaimasen** 一向に構いません I don't mind at all.

ik-kyoku *n* 一曲 a piece of music, a song, a tune

ik-kyoku *n* 一局 a game ((i)go (*the board game* **Go**) *and/or* shōgi (*Japanese chess*))

ik-kyū *n* 一級 first class

ikō *n* 意向 one's mind, inclination, intention; one's views

(...) íkō *suffix* (…)以降 afterward, from … on (= (…) **ígo** (…)以後)

ikoi *n* 憩い rest and relaxation: **~ no ba(sho)** 憩いの場(所) recreation area

ikoku *n* 異国 foreign countries; ikoku-jōcho (no) *adj* 異国情緒(の) exotic

ikon *n* 遺恨 grudge

ikotsu *n* 遺骨 remains (*of person*)

íku-... *prefix* いく・幾 ... = **nán-...** 何... how many ...

ikudōon (ni) *adv* 異口同音(に) unanimously

ikuji *n* 育児 child care: **~-kyūka** 育児休暇 child-care leave

ikuji-nashi *n* 意気地なし coward, chicken: **ikuji (no/ga) nai** 意気地(の/が)ない is a coward, cowardly

ikura *n* イクラ salmon roe (*caviar*)

íkura *n* いくら how much: **~ ka** いくらか some, a little; **~ mo** いくらも ever so much, [+ NEGATIVE] not very much; **~ de mo** いくらでも a lot, as much as you like

ikusa *n* 戦 war (= **sensō** 戦争)

ikusei *n* 育成 training, nuture, cultivation

íkutsu *n* いくつ how many; how old; **~-ka** いくつか several, a number of; **~ mo** いくつも ever so many, [+ NEGATIVE] not very many; **~ de mo** いくつでも as many as you like

ímá *n* 居間 living room (*Western-style*)

íma *n* 今 now, this time: **~ wa** 今は at present; **~ no tokoró wa** 今のところは for the time being, so far; **~ goro wa** 今ごろは about this time; ima-máde *adv* 今まで until now, up to the present (time); íma-ni *adv* 今に before long, soon, by and by, presently: **~-ni mo** 今にも at any moment; ima-sara *adv* 今さら at this point

ima-da ni *adv* 未だに still (= **mada** まだ)

imásu, iru *v* います, いる is, stays

imásu, íru *v* 射ます, 射る shoots

imē'ji *n* イメージ (*psychological/social*) image (= **gazō** 画像)

iimēru *n* Eメール e-mail (= **mēru** メール)

ími *n* 意味 meaning: **... to iu ~ desu** ...という意味です, **... o ~ shimásu** ...を意味します it means ...

imin *n* 移民 immigrant(s)/emigrant(s)

imó *n* イモ・芋 yam; potato

imó *n* いも dork, country bumpkin (= **inaka-mono** 田舎者)

imōtó *n* 妹 younger sister: **~-san** 妹さん (your) younger sister

inabíkari *n* 稲光 lightning

inada *n* イナダ baby yellowtail

(...) ínai *suffix* (...)以内 within

inaka *n* 田舎 country(side); one's home area (*hometown*): **~ no** 田舎の rural; **~-mono** 田舎者 country bumpkin (= **imó** いも)

inarí-zushi *n* いなり鮨[寿司] sushi in a bag of *aburage* (fried bean-curd) (= **o-inari san** お稲荷さん)

inázuma *n* イナズマ・稲妻 lightning

inbō *n* 陰謀 dark plot(s), intrigue(s)

(...-)ínchi *suffix* (...)インチ inch(es)

inchiki (na) *adj* いんちき(な) fake, fraud(ulent): **~ shōbai** いんちきな商売 fraud business

inchō *n* 院長 hospital head/director

Indian *n* インディアン (*American*) Indian, native American
Indo *n* インド India; **Indó-jin** *n* インド人 Indian (*from India*)
Indonéshia *n* インドネシア Indonesia; **Indoneshia-go** *n* インドネシア語 Indonesian (*language*); **Indoneshiá-jin** *n* インドネシア人 an Indonesian
íne *n* 稲 rice plant
inemúri-shimásu (suru) *v* 居眠りします(する) dozes off
infomēshon *n* インフォメーション information
infure *n* インフレ inflation
infuruénza *n* インフルエンザ flu, influenza
íngen, ingénmame *n* インゲン・いんげん, インゲンマメ・いんげん豆 kidney beans, French beans
ín(kan) *n* 印(鑑) seal, stamp (= **hán** 判, **hankó** 判子)
inkei *n* 陰茎 penis
inki (na) *adj* 陰気(な) gloomy, glum
ínku, ínki *n* インク, インキ ink
ínku-jetto *n* インクジェット ink jet: ~ **purintā** インクジェットプリンター inkjet printer
ínochi *n* 命 one's life (= **séimei** 生命)
inorí *n* 祈り prayer
inorimásu, inóru *v* 祈ります, 祈る prays; wishes for, hopes for
inpo *n* インポ sexual impotence
inreki *n* 陰暦 lunar calendar
inryoku *n* 引力 attractive force, gravity
inryō-sui *n* 飲料水 drinking water (= **inyō-sui** 飲用水)
insatsu *n* 印刷 printing: ~**-butsu** 印刷物 printed matter
inshi *n* 印紙 revenue stamp
inshō *n* 印象 impression; **inshō-teki (na)** *adj* 印象的(な) impressive
inshoku *n* 飲食 drinking and eating; **inshoku-ten** *n* 飲食店 restaurant(s) (= **resutoran** レストラン)
inshu *n* 飲酒 drinking: ~**-unten** 飲酒運転 driving after drinking
insutanto *n* インスタント instant: ~ **kōhii** インスタントコーヒー instant coffee
insutorakutā *n* インストラクター instructor
insutōru *n* インストール installation (*on computer*)
intabyū *n* インタビュー interview: ~**-kiji** インタビュー記事 interview article
intāchenji *n* インターチェンジ highway interchange(s)
intāhon *n* インターホン intercom
intai *n* 引退 retirement
intān *n* インターン intern
intānashonaru *n* インターナショナル international
intānetto *n* インターネット Internet; **intānetto-kafe** *n* インターネットカフェ Internet cafe; **intānetto-tsūhan** *n* インターネット通販 online shopping, Internet shopping
intān-shippu *n* インターンシップ internship

Interi *n* インテリ intellectual; highbrow
interia *n* インテリア interior (*accessory*)
inú *n* イヌ・犬 dog
in'yō *n* 引用 quoting, quotation
inyō-sui *n* 飲用水 drinking water (= **inryō-sui** 飲料水)
inzei *n* 印税 royalties (*from one's book*(*s*))
ippai *n* いっぱい fully, full of; many, much, lots (= **takusan** たくさん): **~ (no)** いっぱい(の) full, filled
-ippai *suffix* いっぱい whole, entire: **konshu-~** 今週いっぱい all this week, whole week
íp-pai *n* 一杯 a cupful, a glassful; a drink
ip-paku *n* 一泊 one night's lodging/stay
ippan (no) *adj* 一般(の) general, overall; ippan-teki (na/ni) *adj, adv* 一般的(な/に) general, in general
ip-pén *n* 一遍 one time (= **ichi-dó** 一度, **ik-kái** 一回)
ip-pi̥kí *n* 一匹 one (*fish/bug, small animal*)
ippin-ryō'ri *n* 一品料理 à la carte dishes
ippō' *n* 一方 **1.** one side **2. mō ~ (de wa)** もう一方(では) the other side, on the other hand; but, meanwhile; ippō-tsū'kō *n* 一方通行 one-way (*traffic, argument*)
íp-pon *n* 一本 one (*pencil/bottle, long thing*), a point
íp-pun *n* 一分 one minute
irai *n* 依頼 request; dependence, reliance; trust, commission
(...) írai *suffix, conj* (...)以来 (ever) since...
iraremásu̥, irareru *v* いられます, いられる can stay/be
irasshaimásu̥, irasshyáru *v* いらっしゃいます, いらっしゃる [HONORIFIC] **1.** comes (= **kimásu** 来ます) **2.** goes (= **ikimásu** 行きます) **3.** stays, is (= **imásu** います) **4.** *interj* = **irasshaimáse** いらっしゃいませ (Welcome!)
irásu̥to *n* イラスト illustration
iremásu̥, ireru *v* 入れます, 入れる puts in, lets in, admits; includes: **denwa o ~** 電話を入れます puts in a call; ire-ba *n* 入れ歯 false teeth; ire-mono *n* 入れ物 container; ire-zumi *n* 入れ墨・刺青 tattoo (= **tatū** タトゥー)
iremásu̥, iréru *v* 炒れます, 炒れる can roast
iremásu̥, iréru *v* 射れます, 射れる can shoot (arrow)
iriguchi, iriku̥chi *n* 入口 entrance
irimásu̥, iru *v* 要ります, 要る is necessary; needs, wants
irimásu̥, íru *v* 炒ります, 炒る roasts
iri-támago *n* 炒り卵 scrambled eggs
iri-yō (na) *adj* 入り用(な) needed (= **nyūyō (na)** 入用(な))
iró *n* 色 color; sex; iro-ai *n* 色合い tone (*coloring*); iró-gami *n* 色紙 colored paper
i ró (yo) *v* いろ(よ) [IMPERATIVE] (stay!)

iroiro (no/na) *adj* いろいろ(の/な) various

ironna ... *adj* いろんな… various

iroppói *adj* 色っぽい erotic

isé-ebi *n* 伊勢エビ[海老] lobster

isei *n* 異性 (*person of*) the opposite sex: **~ no yūjin** 異性の友人 friend(s) of the opposite sex

isei (ga/no) ii *adj* 威勢(が/の)いい spirited, buckish

iseki *n* 遺跡 remains

iseki *n* 移籍 transfer

isharyō *n* 慰謝料 compensation/damages for mental suffering: **~ o motomemásu̱** 慰謝料を求めます asks for compensation

ishí *n* 石 stone, rock

íshi *n* 意志 will, intention

íshi̱ki *n* 意識 consciousness: **~ o ushinaimásu** 意識を失います loses consciousness, passes out

íshindenshin (de) *adv* 以心伝心(で) (by) telepathy

ísho *n* 遺書 will

íshō *n* 衣装 costume

íshoku *n* 移植 transplantation: **shinzō-~** 心臓移植 cardiac transplant

ishokujū *n* 衣食住 food, clothing and shelter

isogashíi *adj* 忙しい busy: **shigoto ga ~** 仕事が忙しい is busy at work

isogí *n* 急ぎ haste; **~ no** *adj* 急ぎの hasty, hurried, urgent

isogimásu̱, isógu *v* 急ぎます, 急ぐ hurries, rushes

isōrō *n* 居候 freeloader

íssái *adj, adv* 一切 all, everything, without exception

ís-sai *n* 一歳 one year old (= **hi̱tótsu** 一つ)

issakú- *prefix* 一昨-: **~-ban/-ya** 一昨晩/夜 night before last (= **ototoí no ban/yoru** 一昨日の晩/夜); **~-jitsu** 一昨日 day before yesterday (= **ototói** 一昨日)

is-satsú *n* 一冊 one book (*magazine*)

ís-sei *n* 一世 **1.** first generation: **nikkei-~** 日系一世 first-generation Japanese immigrants **2.** … the First: **Erizabesu-~** エリザベス一世 Elizabeth I **3.** one generation: **~ ichidai (no)** 一世一代(の) once in a lifetime

is-sei (ni) *adv* 一斉(に) all together

is-seki-nichō *n* 一石二鳥

is-sén *n* 一千・1,000 one thousand (= **sén** 千)

issetsú *n* 一節 passage (*of text*)

isshō *n* 一生 one's whole life

ís-shō *n* 一升 1.8 liters: **~´-bin** 一升瓶 a 1.8-liter bottle (*of saké*)

isshō-kénmei (ni) *adv* 一生懸命(に) desperately; very hard

issho (ni) *adv* 一緒(に) together

ís-shu *n* 一種 a kind, a sort

isshun *n* 一瞬 a moment: **~ no dekigoto** 一瞬の出来事 moment event/happening

isso *adv* いっそ rather, preferably

issō *adv* 一層 all the more…, still/much more …

issō *n* 一掃 sweep, cleanup

isu *n* いす・イス・椅子 chair
Isuraeru *n* イスラエル Israel; Isuraeru-jin *n* イスラエル人 Israeli
Isuramu-kyō *n* イスラム教 Islam (= **kaikyō** 回教); Isuramu-kyōto *n* イスラム教徒 Muslim, Moslem
íta *n* 板 board, plank; ita-choko *n* 板チョコ chocolate bar
itachi *n* イタチ weasel: **itachi-~** イタチごっこ vicious circle
itadaki *n* 頂 peak, summit (= **chōjō´** 頂上)
itadakimásu, itadaku *v* いただきます, いただく (*I/we humbly*) receive, eat, drink
itade *n* 痛手 damage: **~ o ukemásu** 痛手を受けます gets damage(s)
itái *adj* 痛い painful, hurting, sore
itamae *n* 板前 chef (*of Japanese food*)
itamemásu, itaméru *v* 痛めます, 痛める hurts, injures
itamemásu, itaméru *v* 傷めます, 傷める damages, spoils it
itamemásu, itaméru *v* 炒めます, 炒める (pan-)fries, sautés: **itame-mono** 炒め物 stir-fry
itamimásu, itámu *v* 痛みます, 痛む it aches
itamimásu, itámu *v* 傷みます, 傷む it spoils, rots
itamiwake *n* 痛み[傷み]分け draw caused by injuries in Sumo match
itarimásu, itáru *v* 至ります, 至る arrives (*at*), reaches (*to*), goes/comes (*to*)
Itaria *n* イタリア Italy; Itaria-go *n* イタリア語 Italian (*language*); Itariá-jin *n* イタリア人 an Italian
itashimásu, itásu *v* 致します, 致す [HUMBLE/DEFERENTIAL] do(es) (= **shimásu** します)
itatte *adv* 至って extremely
itazura *n* いたずら mischief, prank: **~-denwa** いたずら電話 prank call; itazurá-kko *n* いたずらっ子 naughty child
itazura ni *adv* いたずらに in vain, for nothing: **~ toki o sugoshimásu** いたずらに時を過ごします spends one's time in idleness
itchi *n* 一致 agreement, consensus
ite *n* 射手 archer
íto *n* 糸 thread, yarn, string: **tako-~** 凧糸 kite string; itó-maki *n* 糸巻き spool; reel
íto *n* 意図 intention, plan, purpose; ito-teki ni *adv* 意図的に on purpose
itóko *n* いとこ・従兄弟・従姉妹 cousin: **(o-)~-san** (お)いとこさん (*your/someone else's*) cousin
itomá *n* 暇 **1.** leave-taking, farewell **2.** free time (= **hima** 暇); leave of absence
itoshíi *adj* 愛しい dear (*beloved*)
ítsu *n, adv* いつ when
ítsu dé mo *adv* いつでも any time (*at all*)
itsu-goro *n* いつ頃 about when
itsuká *n* 五日 five days; fifth day (*of month*)
ítsu-ka *adv* いつか sometime
ítsu kara *adv* いつから since when, how long

itsukushimi *n* 慈しみ tender love (= **jiai** 慈愛): **itsukushi mimásu** 慈しみます loves tenderly

ítsu made *adv* いつまで until when, how long

ítsu made mo *adv* いつまでも forever

ítsu made ni *adv* いつまでに by when

ítsu-mo *adv* いつも always, usually: ~ **no** いつもの usual

ítsu-no-ma-ni (ka) *adv* いつの間]に(か) before one knows it

itsútsu *n* 五つ five pieces (*small objects*) (= **gó-ko** 五個); five years old (= **gó-sai** 五歳)

itsuwári *n* 偽り falsehood, lie (= **uso** 嘘)

ittai ... *adv* 一体 … on earth, … ever … !: ~ **dōshitan desuka?** 一体どうしたんですか? What on earth happened

ittai-ka *n* 一体化 unification

ittei (no) *adj* 一定(の) fixed, settled, definite

Itte(i)rasshái *interj* いって(い)らっしゃい, **Itte(i)rassháimáse** [HONORIFIC] いって(い)らしゃいませ Good-bye! (*said to those departing home*)

Itte kimásu, Itte mairimásu *interj* 行ってきます/参ります. Good-bye! (*said to those staying home*)

it-tō´(no) *n, adj* 一等(の) first, first class: **~seki/-sha** 一等席/車 first-class seat/car

ít-tō *n* 一頭 one (*horse/ox, large animal*)

it-tsui *n* 一対 a pair

iwá *n* 岩 rock, crag

íwa ba *conj* いわば so to speak

iwái *n* 祝い celebration → **iwai-másu** 祝います

iwaimásu, iwáu *v* 祝います, 祝う celebrates

iwashi *n* イワシ・鰯 sardine

iwáyúru *adj* いわゆる so-called, what is known as

iya *interj* いや (*usually male*) no, nope

iyá (na) *adj* 嫌(な) unpleasant; disagreeable; disgusting, nasty

iya-garimásu, iya-gáru *v* 嫌がります, 嫌がる dislikes, hates

íyaringu *n* イヤリング earring

iyashii *adj* 卑しい lowly, vulgar

iyó-iyo *adv* いよいよ **1.** at last, finally **2.** more and more **3.** surely

iza *adv* いざ when it comes to (actually do so): ~ **to iu toki** いざという時 in a pinch, in the worst case

(...) ízen *suffix* (…)以前 before, up until …, ago

izumi *n* 泉 fountain, spring

izure *adv* いずれ some other time; someday: ~ **mata chikaiuchini oaishimashō** いずれまた近いうちにお会いしましょう Let's meet up again sometime soon.

J

ja *interj, adv* [INFORMAL] じゃ, **jā´** じゃあ well, well then; in that case; (well) now (= **déwa** では)

...ja *suffix* [INFORMAL] …じゃ = **…dé wa** …では

ja *n* 蛇 snake

jaaku (na) *adj* [BOOKISH] 邪悪(な) evil

jabu *n* ジャブ jab

jagā *n* ジャガー jaguar

jagaimo *n* じゃがいも・ジャガイモ (*Irish*) potato

jaguchi *n* 蛇口 faucet, tap

jajauma *n* じゃじゃ馬 shrew

jāji *n* ジャージ jersey

jakétto *n* ジャケット jacket

jakén (na/ni) *adj, adv* 邪険(な/に) blunt(ly)

jakkan (no) *adj* 若干(の) some (*amount of*), several

jakku *n* ジャック jack

jakō *n* ジャコウ・麝香 civet, musk: **~-jika** ジャコウジカ musk deer: **~-neko** ジャコウネコ musk cat

jakuhai (mono) *n* [BOOKISH] 若輩(者) young and inexperienced person

jakunen-sha *n* [BOOKISH] 若年者 the young, a youth (= **wakamono** 若者)

jakusha *n* 弱者 the weak (*person*)

jaku̲ten *n* 弱点 weak point

jama *n* 邪魔 disturbance, hindrance, obstacle: **~ (na)** 邪魔(な) intrusive, bothersome; **~ ni narimásu̲** 邪魔になります, **~ o shimásu̲** 邪魔をします gets in the way, becomes a bother

Jamaika *n* ジャマイカ Jamaica

jámu *n* ジャム jam (*to eat*)

...ja nákereba *suffix, v* [INFORMAL] …じゃなければ unless it be: **~ narimasén** …じゃなければなりません must (*has to*) be

...ja náku̲(te) *suffix, v* [INFORMAL] …じゃなく(て) (it) is not and/but; without being

...ja náku̲te mo *suffix, v* [INFORMAL] …じゃなくても even if it not be: **~ íi desu** …じゃなくてもいいです it need not be

...ja náku̲te wa *suffix, v* [INFORMAL] じゃなくては, **…ja nákya** …じゃなきゃ not being, without being; unless it be: **ja nákya ikemasén** …じゃなくては(じゃなきゃ)いけません it must (*has to*) be

jānarisuto *n* ジャーナリスト journalist

jānaru *n* ジャーナル journal

janbo *n* ジャンボ jumbo: **~ jetto-ki** ジャンボジェット機 jumbo jet aircraft

jánguru *n* ジャングル jungle: **~-jímu** ジャングルジム jungle gym

janku-fūdo *n* ジャンクフード junk food

jánpā *n* ジャンパー windbreaker (*jacket*)

jánpu *n* ジャンプ jump

janru *n* ジャンル genre
jarajara *adj* ジャラジャラ jangling sound
jara-shimásu, jara-su *v* じゃらします, じゃらす plays with: **(ko)neko o ~** (子)猫をじゃらします plays with a kitten/cat
jari *n* 砂利 gravel, pebbles
Jawa *n* ジャワ Java
jazu *n* ジャズ jazz
Jei āru, Jē āru *n* ジェイアール, ジェーアール, JR (*Japan Railway*)
jettó-ki *n* ジェット機 jet (*plane*)
ji *n* 痔 hemorrhoids
jí *n* 字 = **moji** 文字 a letter (*symbol*): **kanji** 漢字 a Chinese character
jí *n* 地 land, ground; texture; fabric
ji-... *prefix* 自… self; one's own; ji-bun *n* 自分 oneself; myself; alone; **~ de** 自分で by oneself, in person; **~ no** 自分の (*one's*) own; **go-~** ご自分 yourself; jí-ga *n* 自我 ego; jí-ko *n* 自己 (one)self; ji-sei *n* 自制 self-control; ji-shin *n* 自信 self-confidence/-assurance: **~ o mótte ... (shimásu)** 自信を持って…(します) (*does it*) with confidence; ji-taku *n* 自宅 one's home/residence
...-ji *suffix* …時 o'clock: **roku-~** 6時 six o'clock
...-ji *suffix* …寺 temple (*name*): **Kinkaku-ji** 金閣寺
jiai *n* [BOOKISH] 慈愛 tender love (= **itsukushimi** 慈しみ)
jibikí *n* 字引き dictionary (= **jísho** 辞書)
jíbun *n* 時分 time
jidai *n* 時代 age, period, era, time, **...-jídai** …時代 period: **Edo-~** 江戸時代 the Edo period
jídō *n* 児童 child (*elementary school student*) (= **seito** 生徒)
jidō *n* 自動 automatic; jidō-doa *n* 自動ドア auto(matic) door; jidō-hanbaiki *n* 自動販売機 vending machine; jidō´-sha *n* 自動車 automobile (= **kuruma** 車)
Jiei-tai *n* 自衛隊 the Self-Defense Forces
jigoku´ *n* 地獄 hell
jígyō *n* 事業 enterprise, business, undertaking
jii *n* 自慰 masturbation (= **onanii** オナニー)
jii-pan *n* ジーパン blue jeans
jijitsu *n* 事実 fact, truth
jijō *n* 事情 circumstances; conditions: **~ o nomikomimásu** 事情を飲み込みます understands the situation
jikan *n* 時間 time; hour(s): **~ ga kakarimásu** 時間がかかります it takes time; **~-dō´ri (no/ni)** 時間通り(の/に) on time
...-jikan *suffix* …時間 time; hour(s): **eigyō-~** 営業時間 business hours; **kinmu-~** 勤務時間 working hours
jikan-hyō *n* 時間表 timetable, schedule
jíka ni *adv* 直に directly; personally
jíken *n* 事件 happening, incident,

event, affair, case: **~ o kaiketsu-shimásu̲** 事件を解決します solves a case/cases

jíki *n* 時期 time; season: **~-shōsō** 時期尚早 prematurity

jíki *n* 時機 opportune time, opportunity, chance: **~ o machimásu̲** 時機を待ちます waits for a chance

jíki *n* 磁器 porcelain → **tō´ki** 陶器

jíki (no) *n* 磁気(の) magnetic

jiki (ni) *adv* 直(に) soon; immediately

jikka *n* 実家 one's parent's home

jikken *n* 実験 experiment: **kagaku (no) ~** 化学(の)実験 chemical experiment

jikkō *n* 実行 performance; practice; realization, running: **puroguramu o ~ shimásu̲** プログラムを実行します runs a program

jíko *n* 事故 accident

jíkoku *n* 時刻 time (*specified*)

jikoku-hyō *n* 時刻表 time schedule, timetable: **densha no ~** 電車の時刻表 railway timetable

jikú *n* 軸 axis, axle: **chi-jiku** 地軸 earth axis; **jiten-jiku** 自転軸 (*planet's*) rotational axis

jiman *n* 自慢 pride, boast

jímen *n* 地面 ground (*surface*)

jimí (na) *adj* 地味(な) plain, sober

jimu *n* 事務 business, office work; jimu-sho *n* 事務所 office

jímu *n* ジム gym(nasium)

...´-jín *suffix* ...人 person

jínbutsu *n* 人物 personage

jindō *n* 人道 **1.** humanity **2.** walkway, pedestrian path

jingū´ *n* 神宮 (*large*) Shinto shrine

jinin *n* 人員 personnel

jínja *n* 神社 Shinto shrine

jínji *n* 人事 personnel/human affairs; jinji-ka *n* 人事課 personnel (*section*)

jínjō *adj* 尋常 [BOOKISH] usual, normal (= **futsū** 普通): **~-denai** 尋常でない unusual, abnormal

jinken *n* 人権 human rights

jinkō *n* 人口 population

jinkō (no) *adj* 人工(の) artificial

jinríkí-sha *n* 人力車 ricksha

jínrui *n* 人類 human beings, the human race

jinsei *n* 人生 (*one's*) life

jinshu *n* 人種 race (*peoples*): **~ sabetsu** 人種差別 racial discrimination: **~ no rutsubo** 人種のるつぼ melting pot

ji-nushi *n* 地主 landowner

jinzō *n* 腎臓 kidneys

jinzō (no) *adj* 人造(の) artificial, imitation, false (*man-made*)

jíppā *n* ジッパー zipper

jira-shimásu̲, jira-su *v* じらします, じらす irritates someone, tantalizes, teases

jírojiro mimásu̲ (míru) *v* じろじろ見ます(見る) stares at

jísa *n* 時差 difference in time: **~-boke** 時差ぼけ jet lag; **~-shu̲kkin** 時差出勤 staggered work hours

jisan shimásu̲ (suru) *v* 持参します(する) brings along, takes along

jisatsu *n* 自殺 suicide: **~-ganbō** 自殺願望 desire of suicide
jisei *n* 時勢 (*the trend of*) the times
jisei *n* 時世 the times
jísetsu *n* 時節 season; (*appropriate*) time, occasion, opportunity
jíshaku *n* 磁石 magnet
jishin *n* 地震 earthquake
jishin *n* 磁針 magnetic needle: **hōi-~** 方位磁針 compass
-jishin *n* 自身 oneself; myself (= **jibun-~** 自分自身): **kare-~** 彼自身 himself
jísho *n* 辞書 dictionary
jishoku *n* 辞職 resignation (*from a position*)
jisoku *n* 時速 (*per hour*) speed
jissai *n*, *adv* 実際 actual conditions, reality; in practice; in fact, really
ji-súberi *n* 地滑り landslide
jítai *n* 事態 situation, state of affairs
jítai *n*, *adv* 自体 **1.** the thing itself **2.** originally
jítai *n* 辞退 non-acceptance, refusal
jitchi *n* 実地 actuality, (*putting to*) practice: **~ (no) keiken o tsumimásu** 実地(の)経験を積みます gets on-the-job experience(s)
jiten *n* 辞典 dictionary (= **jísho** 辞書): **kokugo-~** 国語辞典 Japanese dictionary: **eiwa-~** 英和辞典, **einichi-~** 英日辞典 English-Japanese dictionary
jiten *n* 事典 dictionary, subject book: **hyakka-~** 百科事典 encyclopedia
jitén-sha, jidén-sha *n* 自転車 bicycle: **jitensha-ya** 自転車屋 bicycle shop/dealer
jitsú *n* 実 truth: **~ ni** 実に truly, really, indeed; **~ no** 実の true, real; **jitsu-butsu** *n* 実物 the real thing; the actual person; **jitsu-ryoku** *n* 実力 (real) strength, ability, proficiency; force, power; **jitsu-yō** *n* 実用 practical use/application, utility
jitsugyō *n* 実業 business, enterprise: **~-ka** 実業家 businessperson, businessman
jitto *adv* じっと intently, steadily, fixedly (*staring*); quietly, patiently
jiyū´ *n* 自由 freedom, liberty: **~ (na)** 自由(な) free; fluent, at ease; **~ ni** 自由に freely; fluently; **~-gyō** 自由業 freelancing, freelance work; **~-seki** 自由席 unreserved seat
jizen *n* 慈善 charity
jō´ *n* 錠 **1.** (= **jō-mae** 錠前) lock **2.** (= **jōzai** 錠剤) pill
jō *adj*, *n* 上 **1.** (= **jōtō (na)** 上等(な)) deluxe **2.** (= **~-kan** 上巻) first volume (*of a set of 2 or 3*)
...´-jō *suffix* ...畳 (*counts room sizes by tatami mat*): **hachí-~ (ma)** 八畳(間) eight *tatami* mats (room)
...´-jō *suffix* ...城 castle (*name*): **Osaka-jō** 大阪城 the Osaka-jō castle
jōbu (na) *adj* 丈夫(な) sturdy, firm, healthy; safe (= **daijōbu** 大丈夫)
jochō *n* 助長 promotion, furtherance

jochū *n* 女中 maid-servant
jōdán *n* 冗談 joke: ~ **hanbun (ni)** 冗談半分(に) half in jest
jōei *n* 上映 showing (*movie*)
jōen *n* 上演 performance
jo-gákusei, joshi gákusei *n* 女学生, 女子学生 female student
jōge *n* 上下 top and bottom, high and row, up and down
jōgi *n* 定規 ruler (*to measure with*)
jogingu *n* ジョギング jog(ging)
jō´go *n* 漏斗 funnel
jōhín (na) *adj* 上品(な) elegant, refined
jōhō *n* 情報 information
jō-kan *n* 上巻 first volume (*of a set of 2 or 3*)
jōkén *n* 条件 condition, term, stipulation, provision
jō´ki *n* 蒸気 steam, vapor
jokki *n* ジョッキ jug, (*beer*) mug
jōkyaku *n* 乗客 passenger
jōkyō *n* 状況・情況 situation, circumstances, state of affairs
jo-kyō´ju *n* 助教授 assistant professor
jōkyū *n* 上級 high class, upper class: ~ **kōsu** 上級コース advanced course
jō-mae *n* 錠前 lock (= **kagi** 鍵)
jomei *n* [BOOKISH] 除名 excision, excommunication
jomei *n* 助命 sparing the life/lives (= **kyūmei** 救命): ~**-katsudō** 助命活動 rescue work
jōmén *n* 上面 top (*top side*)
jōmuin *n* 乗務員 crew: **kyakushitsu** ~ 客室乗務員 (*airplane*) flight attendant
jōnetsu-teki (na) *adj* 情熱的(な) passionate
joō´ *n* 女王 queen
jōriku *n* 上陸 disembarking, landing
jorō´ *n* 女郎 whore, prostitute
jōryū (no) *adj* 上流(の) classy, upper; upstream
jōryū´-sui *n* 蒸留水 distilled water
josei *n* 女性 woman, female: ~**-go** 女性語 women's language (*terms*) (= **onna kotoba** 女言葉)
joseki *n* 除籍 removal from register, expulsion (*from a school/university*)
joseikin *n* 助成金 grant
josetsu *n* 除雪 removing the snow
jōsha *n* 乗車 getting into a car, getting on a train/bus, boarding; **jōshá-ken** *n* 乗車券 passenger ticket
joshi *n* 助詞 particle (*auxiliary word*)
jóshi *n* 女子 girl, woman: ~**-dáisei** 女子大生 woman college student; ~**-kō´sei** 女子高生 female (*senior*) high school student
jōshiki *n* 常識 common sense
joshō *n* 序章 introduction section (*book*)
joshu *n* 助手 helper, assistant
josō *n* 助走 running up
josō *n* 除草 weeding
josō *n* 女装 drag: ~ **shimásu** 女装します is in drag
josō *n* 序奏 (*music*) introduction
jōsúi-chi *n* 浄水池 reservoir

jotai *n* 除隊 discharge
jōtai *n* 状態 condition, situation, state, circumstances
jōtō (no) *adj* 上等(の) the best, first-rate, deluxe
joya *n* 除夜 New Year's Eve: **~ no kane** 除夜の鐘 the bells on New Year's Eve
jōyaku *n* 条約 treaty, agreement
jōyō *n* 常用 common use: **~-kanji** 常用漢字 Chinese characters in common use
jōyō´-sha *n* 乗用車 passenger car
jōyō´-sha *n* 常用者 addict
joyū *n* 女優 actress
jōzai *n* 錠剤 pill, tablet
jōzō-sho *n* 醸造所 brewery
jōzú (na) *adj* 上手(な) skilled, clever, good at
jū´ *n* 銃 gun: **~-sei** 銃声 gunshot(s)
jū´ *n* 十・10 ten; jū-bai *n* 十倍 ten times, tenfold; jū-banmé (no) *adj* 十番目(の) tenth; jū´-do *n* 十度 ten times (= **júk-kai** 十回); ten degrees; jū-en-dama *n* 十円玉 ten-yen coin; jū´-ji *n* 十時・10時 ten o'clock; jū-má *n* 十万・100,000 a hundred thousand; jū-nána *n* 十七・17 seventeen; jū-óku *n* 十億・10億 a thousand million; (*U.S.*) a billion; jū-shi *n* 十四・14 fourteen (= **jū-yon** 十四); jū-yok-ka *n* 十四日 14 days; 14th day (*of month*); jū-yon *n* 十四・14 fourteen (= **jū-shi** 十四); **~-nin** *n* 十四人 14 people
...-jū *suffix* ...じゅう・中 throughout the (*entire*)...: **ichi-nen-~** 一年中 throughout the year: **sekai-~** 世界中 all over the world
jūatsu *n* 重圧 pressure
jūbako *n* 重箱 nested boxes; picnic boxes: **~ no sumi o tsutsukimásu** 重箱の隅をつつきます split hairs, nitpicks
jūbún (na) *adj* 十分[充分](な) enough, sufficient
jūdai (na) *adj* 重大(な) serious (*heavy, grave*); important: **~-ji** 重大事 a matter of importance
jū´dō *n* 柔道 judo, jujitsu (*an art of weaponless defense*)
Jū-gatsú *n* 十月・10月 October
jūgeki *n* 銃撃 gunfight
jūgun *n* 従軍 serving in an army
júgyō *n* 授業 class instruction, classroom teaching; **~ o okonaimásu** 授業を行います teaches (*class*): **~ o ukemásu** 授業を受けます attends a class
jūgyō *n* 従業 employment; jūgyō´-in *n* 従業員 employee
jūi *n* 獣医 veterinarian
Jū-ichi-gatsu *n* 十一月・11月 November
jū´ji *n* 十字 a cross (*symbol*); jūji-ka *n* 十字架 a cross (*wooden*); jūjí-ro *n* 十字路 crossroad(s)
jū´ji *n* 従事 engaging in (*an activity*)
jūkinzoku *n* 重金属 heavy metal
jūketsu *n* 充血 congestion: **me ga ~ shimásu** 目が充血します gets red eyes

juk-kai *n* 十階 ten floors/stories; tenth floor
júk-kai *n* 十回 ten times (= **jū´-do** 十度)
júk-ko *n* 十個 ten (*pieces, small objects*)
júku *n* 塾 a cram/tutoring school; juku-kō(shi) *n* 塾講(師) tutor(s) in a tutoring school
jukudoku *n* 熟読 reading thoroughly
jukugo *n* 熟語 idiomatic expression
jukukō, jukkō *n* 熟考 serious thought (= **jukuryo** 熟慮)
jukunen *n* 熟年 mature age
jukuryo *n* 熟慮 serious thought
jukushimásu, jukúsú *v* 熟します, 熟す ripens, gets ripe
jukusui *n* 熟睡 sound sleep
jukutatsu *n* 熟達 mastery
Júkyō *n* 儒教 Confucianism
jukyū *n* 需給 supply and demand
jūmin *n* 住民 resident: ~ **hyō** 住民票 residence certificate
jun *n* 順 order: **jun(ban) ni** 順(番)に in order
jún (na) *adj* 純(な) pure
junban *n* 順番 (*place in*) order, turn
júnbi *n* 準備 preparation(s), ar-- rangements
junchō (na) *adj* 順調(な) smooth(-ly going)
Jū-ni-gatsú *n* 十二月・12月 December
jun-jimásu, jun-jiru *v* [BOOKISH] 準じます, 準じる applies correspondingly (*to*); is made to accord (*with*)
júnjo *n* 順序 order, sequence
junkan *n* 循環 circulation; cycle
jun-kyō´ju *n* 準教授 associate professor
júnsa *n* 巡査 policeman, patrolman (= **omawari-san** お巡りさん)
junshō *n* 準将 brigadier-general
junsui (na) *adj* 純粋(な) pure: ~ **na kokoro** 純粋な心 pure heart
jūō *n* 縦横 vertical and horizontal; jūō-mujin (ni) *adv* 縦横無尽(に) freely
júp-pa *n* 十羽 ten (*birds*)
júp-pon *n* 十本 ten (*pencils/bottles, long things*)
júp-pun *n* 十分 10 minutes
jū´rai (wa) *adv* 従来(は) traditionally, up to now, hitherto, previously
jūryō´ *n* 重量 weight: **~-age** 重量挙げ weight-lifting
juryō´-shō *n* 受領証 receipt
jū´sho *n* 住所 residence, address
jushō *n* 受賞 winning an award; jushō´-sha *n* 受賞者 winner, awardee
jus-sai *n* 十歳 ten years old (= **tō** とお・十)
jus-satsu *n* 十冊 ten copies (*books, magazines*)
jū´su *n* ジュース juice: **orenji** ~ オレンジジュース orange juice
jūtai *n* 渋滞 congestion: **~-jō´kyō** 渋滞状況 congested (*traffic*): ~ **shite imásu** 渋滞しています is congested (*backed up*)
jūtaku *n* 住宅 residence, house
jū´tan *n* じゅうたん・絨毯 rug, carpet (= **kā´pétto** カーペット)

jut-tō *n* 十頭 ten (*horses/oxen, large animals*)
juwá-ki *n* 受話器 (*telephone*) receiver
júyo *n* 授与 awarding, conferring
jūyō (na) *adj* 重要(な) important
juzú *n* 数珠 beads: **~ tsunagi ni narimásu** 数珠つな[繋]ぎになります is chained together

K

ka *n* カ・蚊 mosquito: **~-tori senkō** 蚊取り線香 mosquito coil; **ka-ya** *n* 蚊帳・かや mosquito net: **ka-ya no soto** 蚊帳の外 out of scheme
ka *n* 可 pass: (*grade*) **yū, ryō, ~, fuka** 優、良、可、不可 Excellent, Good, Poor, Failing
ká *n* 課, **…´-ka** …課 section, division; lesson: **Jinji-~** 人事課 Human Resources Division: **dai ik-~** 第1課 Lesson 1
ká *n* 科 **1.** family (*biological taxonomy*) **2.** department: (*university*) **Eibun-~** 英文科 Department of English Language & Literature; (*hospital*), **Nai-~** 内科 internal medicine
ka-... *prefix* 仮… temporary (*tentative*)
... ka *conj* …か or; (*the question*) whether
...-ka *suffix* …化 …-ization: **~ shimásu** …化します …-izes
kaba *n* カバ・河馬 hippopotamus
kabā *n* カバー cover, covering: **bukku-~** ブックカバー book cover: **kabā-~** カバーレター covering letter (= **sōfu-jō** 送付状)
kabaimásu, kabau *v* 庇います, 庇う protects, defends
kaban *n* かばん・カバン・鞄 briefcase, bag
kabayaki *n* 蒲焼き broiled eel
kabe *n* 壁 wall: **~-gami** 壁紙 wallpaper
kabi *n* カビ mold, mildew
kabin *n* 花瓶・かびん flower vase
kabocha *n* カボチャ pumpkin
kabu *n* 株 stock (*in a company*): **kabushiki-shijō** 株式市場 stock market
kā´bu *n* カーブ curve (*road*)
kabuki *n* 歌舞伎 a traditional style of Japanese theater: **~-za** 歌舞伎座 the Kabuki theater (*building*)
kabu(ra) *n* カブ(ラ)・蕪 a turnip
kaburimásu, kabúru *v* 被ります, 被る wears on head; puts on
kabushiki-gáisha *n* 株式会社 joint-stock corporation
káchi *n* 価値 value: **~ ga arimásu** 価値があります is worth
kachí *n* 勝ち victory, win
kachimásu, kátsu *v* 勝ちます, 勝つ wins

ka-chō *n* 課長 section manager
kadai *n* [BOOKISH] 課題 **1.** problem, difficult matter (= **mondai** 問題) **2.** assignment, homework, task **3.** subject, theme
kádan *n* 花壇 flower bed
kádan *n* 下段 [BOOKISH] lower stand
kádan *n* [BOOKISH] 果断 [BOOKISH] decisiveness: **~ na kōi** 果断な行為 decisive action
kādigan *n* カーディガン cardigan
kádo *n* 角 (*outside*) corner, street corner
kádo *n* [BOOKISH] 過度 excessiveness: **~ no undō** 過度の運動 extreme exercise
kadō *n* [BOOKISH] 稼動 [BOOKISH] operating
kadō *n* 華道 flower arrangement: **~-kyōshitsu** 華道教室 flower arrangement class(es)
kādo *n* カード card: **messēji-~** メッセージカード message card
kaede *n* カエデ・楓 maple
kaemásu, kaeru *v* 変えます, 変える changes it
kaemásu, kaeru *v* 換え[替え]ます, 換える[替える] exchanges, replaces
kaerí *n* 帰り (the) return
kaerimásu, káeru *v* 帰ります, 帰る goes home, goes back, returns, leaves
kaeru *n* カエル・蛙 frog: **hiki-gaeru** ヒキガエル toad
kaeshimásu, káesu *v* 返します, 返す returns it
káette *adv* 却って contrary to expectations
kafún *n* 花粉 pollen: **~-shō** 花粉症 hay fever
káfusu *n* カフス cuff: **~-botan** カフスボタン cuff links
kagai *n* 課外 extracurricular: **~-katsudō** 課外活動 extracurricular activity
kágaku *n* 科学 = **sáiensu** サイエンス science: **~-teki (na)** 科学的(な) scientific; **kagáku-sha** *n* 科学者 scientist
kágaku *n* 化学 = **bake-gaku** 化け学・化学 chemistry: **~-séihin** 化学製品 chemicals, **~-yakuhin** 化学薬品 pharmaceuticals; **kagáku-sha** *n* 化学者 chemist
kagamí *n* 鏡 mirror: **te-~** 手鏡 hand mirror
kagamimásu, kagamu *v* 屈みます, 屈む bends over
kagayakimásu, kagayáku *v* 輝きます, 輝く shines, gleams, glitters
káge *n* 影 shadow: **hito-~** 人影 shadow of a person, human figure: **~-bō´shi** 影法師 shadow (*of a person*)
káge *n* 陰 shade: **ko-~** 木陰 shade of trees
kágeki *n* 歌劇 opera
kageki (na) *adj* 過激(な) excessive, extreme, radical
kagen *n* 加減 **1.** (*state of*) one's health (= **guai** 具合): **o-~ (wa) ikaga desuka?** お加減(は)いか

がですか? (*to sick person*) How are you feeling?, How is your (*health*) condition? **2.** allowance for (= **tekagen** 手加減) **3.** degree, extent (= **teido** 程度): **yu-~** 湯加減 hot water temperature: **oyu-~ wa ikaga desuka?** お湯加減はいかがですか? How is the water temperature? (*for the bath water, the water to wash customer's hair in a beauty salon, etc.*) **4.** adjustment, moderation (= **chōsei** 調整) (→ **ii-kagen** いい加減)

...-ká-getsu *suffix* …か月・ヶ月・カ月・箇月 (*counts months*): **ik-~ (kan)** 1か月(間) (*for*) one month

kagí *n* 鉤 hook: **~-tsume** 鉤つめ claw: **~-kakko** かぎ括弧 Japanese quotation marks (「」)

kagí *n* カギ・鍵 key: **(… no) ~ ga kakarimásu** (…の)鍵がかかります it locks, **(… no) ~ o kakemásu** (…の)鍵をかけます locks it;

kagi-ana *n* 鍵穴 keyhole

kagimásu, kagu *v* か嗅ぎます, 嗅ぐ smells it

kágiri *n* 限り limit

kagirimásu, kagíru *v* 限ります, 限る limits (*delimits*) it: **… ni ~** …に限ります there is nothing like (*so good as, better than*) …

kago *n* かご・籠 basket, (*bird*) cage: **tori-~** 鳥かご birdcage

kágu *n* 家具 furniture: **~-tsuki (no) apāto** 家具付き(の)アパート furnished apartment(s); kagú-ya *n* 家具屋 furniture store

kágura *n* 神楽 Shinto music and dances

kái *n* カイ・貝 shellfish

... kai? *interj* …かい? [INFORMAL] = **desu ka?** ですか? [FORMAL] (yes-or-no question)

...-kai *suffix* …階 (*counts floors/ stories*)

...-kái *suffix* …回 (*counts times/ occasions*)

...-kai *suffix* …会 society, association, club; social gathering, party, meeting: **(o-)tanjō´bi-~** (お)誕生日会 birthday party: **nomi-~** 飲み会 drinking party: **en-~** 宴会 party, banquet

...-kai *suffix* …海 (*name of*) sea: **Nihon-~** 日本海 Japan Sea

kaibatsu *n* 海抜 above sea level

kaibō *n* [BOOKISH] 解剖 autopsy: **~-gaku** 解剖学 anatomy

kaibutsu *n* 怪物 monster

kaichō *n* 会長 chairperson

kaichū (no) *adj* 懐中(の) pocket(able): **~-déntō** 懐中電灯 flashlight

kaichū (de/no) *adv, adj* 海中(で/の) in the sea, under the sea

kaichū *n* 回虫 (intestinal) worms

kaidan *n* 階段 stairs, stairway

kaidan *n* 会談 [BOOKISH] (*official*) meeting: **shunō-~** 首脳会談 summit

kaidan *n* 怪談 ghost story, scary story

kaidame *n* 買いだめ hoarding: **~ shimásu** 買いだめします hoards

kaido *n* 会堂 an auditorium
kaidō *n* 街道 main road/avenue
kaien *n* 開演 starting a performance: **~-chū** 開演中 during the performance; **~-jíkan** 開演時間 curtain time
kaifuku *n* 回復 recovery, recuperation
káiga *n* 絵画 painting, picture
káigai *n* 海外 overseas, abroad: **~-ryokō** 海外旅行 overseas travel
kaigan *n* 海岸 seashore, coast, beach: **~-sen** 海岸線 shoreline, coastline
kai-gara *n* 貝殻 shell (*of shellfish*)
káigi *n* 会議 meeting, conference [FORMAL] (= **míitingu** ミーティング): **~-chū** 会議中 in conference, in a meeting; **~-shitsu** 会議室 conference room
káigun *n* 海軍 navy: **~-kichi** 海軍基地 navy base
kaigyō *n* 開業 [BOOKISH] opening a business: **~ shimásu** 開業します opens a business
kaihatsu *n* 開発 [BOOKISH] development; kenkyū-kaihatsu *n* 研究開発 research and development, R&D
kaiheitai *n* 海兵隊 marines, Marine Corps
kaihi *n* 会費 membership fee, dues: **nen-~** 年会費 annual membership fee
kaihō *n* 解放 [BOOKISH] liberation
kaihō *n* 開放 [BOOKISH] open: **~ shimásu** 開放します opens, leaves open (*windows, doors, etc.*)
kaíi *adj* かいい [INFORMAL] = **kayúi** かゆい・痒い (itchy)
kai-in *n* 会員 member: **~-sei (no)** 会員制(の) membership system, members-only
kaijō *n* 開場 [BOOKISH] opening (*of place/event*); **~-jíkan** 開場時間 opening time; **~´-shiki** 開場式 opening ceremony
kaijō *n* 会場 hall
kaijō (de/no) *adv, adj* 海上(で/の) on the sea (*surface*)
kaijū *n* 怪獣 monster: **~-eiga** 怪獣映画 monster film
kaika *n* 開花 flowering
kaika *n* 階下 downstairs
kaikaku *n* 改革 [BOOKISH] reformation, reinvention
kaikan *n* 会館 public hall, building
kaikan *n* 開館 [BOOKISH] opening (*a hall*)
kaikan *n* 快感 [BOOKISH] pleasure, pleasant feeling: **~ o ajiwaimásu/oboemásu** 快感を味わいます/覚えます feels pleasure
kaikei *n* 会計 **1. o-~** お会計 accounts; bill, check (= **o-kanjō** お勘定) **2.** accountant (= **~-gákari** 会計係, **~-shi** 会計士)
kaiken *n* 会見 [BOOKISH] interview: **kisha-~** 記者会見 press conference
kaiketsu *n* 解決 [BOOKISH] solution, settlement
kaiki *n* 回帰 [BOOKISH] revolution, recurrence, retouring: **kita-~-sen** 北回帰線 the Tropic of Cancer:

minami-~-sen 南回帰線 the Tropic of Capricorn
kaíko *n* 解雇 [BOOKISH] dismissal (*from employment*), discharge
káiko *n* 蚕 silkworm
kaikyaku *n* 開脚 legs spread (*exercise*)
kaikyo *n* 快挙 remarkable/wonderful achievement: **~ o nashitoge-másu** 快挙を成し遂げます has great accomplishments
kaikyō *n* 海峡 strait(s)
kaikyō *n* 回教 Islam (= **Isuramu-kyō** イスラム教)
kaikyū *n* 階級 class, rank: **chūryū-~** 中流階級 the middle class
kaimásu, kau *v* 買います, 買う buys
kaimásu, káu *v* 飼います, 飼う raises, keeps (*pets, farm animals, etc.*)
kaimen *n* 海綿 sponge
kai-mono *n* 買い物 shopping
kaioki *n* 買い置き **1.** things bought in for the future, hoarded things **2.** hoarding
kaiō-sei *n* 海王星 Neptune
kairaku *n* 快楽 pleasure
kairi *n* [BOOKISH] 解離 disaggregation, dissociation
kairi *n* 海里 nautical mile
kairyō *n* [BOOKISH] 改良 improvement, modification
kairyū *n* 海流 ocean current
kaisai *n* 開催 [BOOKISH] holding, opening (*an event*)
kaisan shimásu (suru) *v* 解散します (する) breaks up, disperses
kaisatsu *n* 改札 ticket examining/punching/collecting: **~-guchi** 改札口 (ticket) wicket
kaisei *n* 改正 [BOOKISH] revision
kaisei *n* 快晴 clear and fine weather
kaiseki (ryōri) *n* 懐石(料理) an assortment of elegant ceremonial-type Japanese foods, Japanese foods in season
kaisetsu *n* 解説 explanation, comment; **nyū´su ~** ニュース解説 news commentary; **kaisétsu-sha** *n* 解説者 commentator
kaisha *n* 会社 company, business concern; "the office" (= **kígyō** 企業): **~-in** 会社員 company employee (= **sha-in** 社員, **sara-rii-man** サラリーマン)
káishaku *n* 解釈 [BOOKISH] interpretation, explanation, exposition
kaisho *n* 楷書 block-style letter (*of Japanese*): **~-tai** 楷書体 printed style/square of writing Chinese characters
kaisō *n* 海藻・海草 seaweed
kaisō *n* 回送 **1.** forwarding (*mail matter, letter, etc.*) **2.** deadhead (*an empty car, etc.*): **~-sha** 回送車 a car out of service, an off-duty taxi; **~-ressha** 回送列車 deadhead train
kaisō *n* 回想: recollection; **kaisō shiin** *n* 回想シーン retrospective scene
kaisū *n* 回数 the number of times; **kaisū´-ken** *n* 回数券 ticket book (*for commuting*), coupon ticket
kaisui *n* 海水 seawater; **kaisui-yoku**

n 海水浴 sea bathing: **~-yoku o shimásu** 海水浴をします has a bath in the sea

kai-te *n* 買い手 buyer

kaitei *n* 改訂 revision (*of documents, books, etc.*): **~-ban** 改訂版 revised version

kaitei *n* 海底 bottom of the sea

kaiteki (na) *adj* 快適(な) comfortable, peasant

kaiten *n* 回転 revolution, rotation

kaiten *n* 開店 opening a shop (*for the first time or for the day*)

kaitō *n* 解答 answer

kaitō *n* 回答 reply

kai-torimásu, kai-tóru *v* 買い取ります, 買い取る buys up

kaiun *n* 開運 fortune, good-luck

kaiwa *n* 会話 conversation

kaizen *n* 改善 improvement

kaizoku *n* 海賊 pirate: **~-ban** 海賊版 pirated edition

káji *n* 火事 a fire (*accidental*): **Káji da!** 火事だ! Fire!

káji *n* 舵 helm: **~ o torimásu** 舵をとります takes the helm, steers

káji *n* 家事 housework: **~-tetsudai** 家事手伝い housework helper

kájiki *n* カジキ swordfish

kajirimásu, kajíru *v* かじります, かじる gnaws, nibbles

kajō *n* 過剰 glut, surplus, excess: **~ (no)** 過剰(の) superfluous, surplus: **~-hannō** 過剰反応 overreaction, overresponse

kakaemásu, kakaéru *v* 抱えます, 抱える **1.** holds in one's arms/under one's arm: **atama o ~** 頭を抱えます tears one's hair out **2.** keeps, retains, has; employs: **takusan no shain o kakaete imásu** たくさんの社員を抱えています has a lot of employees **3.** has family to support/take care of (*sick person(s), child(ren), etc.*): **byōnin o ka-kaete imásu** 病人を抱えています has a sick person in one's family **4.** has a problem/problems: **shakkin o kakaete imásu** 借金を抱えています has debts

kakaku *n* 価格 price: **~-kyōsō** 価格競争 price competition

kakan (ni) *adv* 果敢(に) boldly, decisively: **~ ni tatakaimásu** 果敢に戦います fights with valor

kákari *n* 係 = **~-in** 係員 attendant (*in charge*)

kakarimásu, kakáru *v* 掛かります, 掛かる **1.** it hangs **2.** it takes, requires **3.** it weighs **4.** it begins, (*engine*) starts

kakarimásu, kakáru *v* 架かります, 架かる is built

kakashi *n* カカシ・案山子 scarecrow

kakato *n* 踵 heel: **~ no takai kutsu** 踵の高い靴 high-heeled shoes

kake *n* 欠け lacking, a lack, wane: **tsuki no michi-~** 月の満ち欠け wax and wane of the moon

kaké *n* 掛け credit: **~ de kaimásu** 掛けで買います buys on credit

kake-búton *n* 掛け布団 overquilt, top quilt

kakegoe *n* 掛け声 shout of encouragement: **~ o kakemásu** 掛け声をかけます shouts encouragement
kaké (goto) *n* 賭け(事) gambling; a bet
kakehiki *n* 駆け引き tactics, bargaining: **~ ga umai** 駆け引きが上手い is good at bargaining
kakei *n* 家計 household budget: **~-bo** 家計簿 housekeeping book
kakei *n* 家系 one's family line: **~-zu** 家系図 a family tree (= **keizu** 系図)
kakéji *n* 掛け字 = **kaké-jiku** 掛け軸, scroll (*hanging*)
kakemásu, kakéru *v* 掛けます, 掛ける hangs it; multiplies; begins it: **... ni denwa o ~** ...に電話を掛けます telephones; **énjin o ~** エンジンを掛けます starts (*engine*)
kakemásu, kakéru *v* 欠けます, かける・欠ける lacks it, needs
kakemásu, kakéru *v* 賭けます, 賭ける bets
kakemásu, kakéru *v* 駆けます, ・駆ける runs, gallops (*human, animal*)
kaké-mono *n* 掛け物 scroll (*hanging*) (= **kaké-jiku** 掛け軸)
kakera *n* カケラ・欠片 fragment
kákete *v* **... ni ~** ...にかけて (*extending*) through, with respect to, as regards
kake-uri *v* 掛け売り credit sales (= **uri-kake** 売り掛け)
kaké-ya *n* 賭け屋 bookie
kaké-zan *n* 掛け算 multiplication
kaki *n* カキ・柿 (*fruits*) persimmon
káki *n* カキ・牡蠣 oyster
káki *n* 下記 the following: **~ no tōri** 下記の通り as follows, as below
káki *n* 花器 flower vase
káki *n* 夏期 summer (*period/term*): **~-kyūkā** 夏季休暇 summer holiday: **~-orinpikku** 夏季オリンピック Olympic Summer Games
kaki *n* 火気 [BOOKISH] fire, flame: **Kaki-genkin** 火気厳禁 No Fire, Flammables
kakiage *n* かき揚げ a tangle of tidbits fried as *tenpura*, fritters
kaki-atsumemásu, kaki-atsuméru *v* かき集めます, かき集める rakes (*them up*)
kaki-iremásu, kaki-iréru *v* 書き入れます, 書き入れる fills in (*information*)
kaki-kaemásu, kaki-kaéru *v* 書き換えます, 書き換える rewrites
kaki-kata *n* 書き方 way of writing; spelling
kakimásu, káku *v* 欠きます, 欠く it lacks, it is lacking/wanting
kakimásu, káku *v* 書きます, 書く writes
kakimásu, káku *v* 描きます, 描く paints, draws: **e o ~** 絵を描きます draws a picture (= **egakimásu** 描きます)
kakimásu, káku *v* 掻きます, 掻く scratches: **senaka o ~** 背中を掻きます scratches one's back
kaki-mawashimásu, kaki-mawasu *v* かき回します, かき回す stirs

kaki-naoshimásu, kaki-naósu *v* 書き直します, 書き直す rewrites
kakíne *n* かき根・垣根 fence
kakitome (yūbin) *n* 書留(郵便) registered mail
kakitori *n* 書き取り dictation
kakki *n* 活気 liveliness, activity
kakko *n* 括弧 parenthesis, square bracket, brace
kakkō *n* **1.** 格好 shape, form, appearance: **~ ga íi** 格好がいい = **~ ii** かっこいい shapely, cool, stylish **2. ~ (na/no)** 格好(な/の) suitable, moderate, reasonable (*price*)
kákkō *n* カッコウ cuckoo
káko *n* 過去 the past; kako-kei *n* 過去形 the past tense; kako-kanryō *n* 過去完了 the past perfect: **~ kanryō-kei** 過去完了形 the past perfect tense
kakō *n* 加工 [BOOKISH] processing (*industrially treating*)
kakō *n* 下降 [BOOKISH] descent
kakō *n* 河口 estuary
kakō *n* 火口 crater (= **kurētā** クレーター)
kakō´-gan *n* 花崗岩 granite
kakoku *n* [BOOKISH] 過酷 too severe, harsh: **~ na kankyō** 過酷な環境 harsh environment: **~ na rōdō-jōken** 過酷な労働条件 harsh working conditions
...-kákoku *suffix* …か国・ヶ国・カ国 (*counts countries*)
kakomi *n* 囲み an enclosure, a box: **~-kiji** 囲み記事 column, boxed article(s) (= **koramu** コラム)
kakomimásu, kakomu *v* 囲みます, 囲む surrounds (= **tori-kakomimásu** 取り囲みます)
kakon *n* 禍根 the source of trouble, the root of evil: **~ o tachimásu** 禍根を断ちます removes the root of an evil
káku *n* 角 corner: **san-kaku(kei)/san-kakkei** 三角(形) triangle; **shikakú(kei)/shikakkei** 四角(形) square
káku (do) *n* 角(度) angle: **chok-~** 直角 right angle; **ei~** 鋭角 acute angle
káku *n* 核 core, heart, stone: **chū-~** 中核 (*central*) core; kaku-heiki *n* 核兵器 nuclear weapon; káku (no) *n* 核(の) nucleus, nuclear
káku(-) *prefix* 各… each, every; kakú-eki *n* 各駅 every station: **~-téisha/ressha** 各駅停車/列車 local train (*which stops at every station*); kaku-ron *n* 各論 each detail: **~ ni hairimásu** 各論に入ります gets down into specifics;
...káku *suffix* . . . 覚 sense (*five senses*): **shi-~** 視覚 sense of sight: **chō-~** 聴覚 sense of hearing: **mi-~** 味覚 sense of taste: **shū-~** 嗅覚 sense of smell: **shok-~** 触覚 sense of touch
kakū (no) *adj* 架空(の) imaginary: **~ no sekai** 架空の世界 imaginary world: **~ no jinbutsu** 架空の人物 fictional character
kakudai *n* 拡大 enlargement

kakudan (ni/no) *adv, adj* 格段(に/の) remarkably, remarkable

kakugen *n* 格言 maxim, wise saying

kákugo *n* 覚悟 resolution, resignation, premeditation: **~ shimásu̲** 覚悟します, **~ o kimemásu̲** 覚悟を決めます is resolved (*to do*), is prepared for, is resigned to

kakuheki *n* 隔壁 [BOOKISH] division wall, partition

kakuho *n* 確保 [BOOKISH] securement, saving: **seki no ~** 席の確保 grabbing a seat

kakujitsu *n* 確実 certainly; **~ (na)** 確実(な) certain, reliable, authentic (= **tashi̲ka na** 確かな)

kakumaimasu̲, kakumau *v* [BOOKISH] 匿います, 匿う harbors, shelters: **hannin o ~** 犯人を匿います harbors a criminal

kakumaku *n* 角膜 cornea

kakumaku *n* 隔膜 diaphragm

kakumei *n* 革命 [BOOKISH] revolution (*political, etc.*)

kakunin *n* 確認 confirmation

kakuran *n* かく乱 [BOOKISH] disturbance

kakurega *n* 隠れ家 asylum, shelter, refuge

kakuremásu, kakuréru *v* 隠れます, 隠れる hides: **kakurenbo, kakurenbō** かくれんぼ, 隠れん坊 hide-and-seek

kakuri *n* 隔離 [BOOKISH] isolation; **kakuri-byō´tō´** 隔離病棟 isolation ward

kakuritsu *n* 確立 establishment

kakuritsu *n* 確率 probability

kakusei *n* 覚醒 [BOOKISH] awakening, emergence; **kakusei-zai** *n* 覚醒剤 stimulant drug

kaku̲séi-ki *n* 拡声器 loudspeaker

kaku̲shimásu̲, kakúsú *v* 隠します, 隠す hides (*something*)

kaku̲shin *n* 核心 core, heart (= **káku** 核): **~ ni furemásu** 核心に触れます touches the core of…

kaku̲tei *n* 確定 determination, ~, settlement; **kakutei-shinkoku** 確定申告 final income tax return

kákuteru *n* カクテル cocktail: **~-pātii** カクテルパーティ cocktail party

kakutō *n* 格闘 fight; **kakutō-gi** *n* 格闘技 martial art

kakutō *n* 確答 [BOOKISH] definite answer

kaku̲toku *n* [BOOKISH] 獲得 [BOOKISH] acquisition, gain

kakuyasu *n* 格安 bargain, discount: **~-kōkūken** 格安航空券 discounted airline ticket

kakuzai *n* 角材 block of wood

kakuzuke *n* [BOOKISH] 格付け rating, grading

kakyū (no) *adj* 下級(の) low-class: **kakyūsei** 下級生 underclassman

kamá *n* かま・窯 oven, kiln

kamá *n* かま・釜 (*Japanese style*) kettle, iron pot, cauldron, boiler: **onaji ~ no meshi o taberu** 同じ釜の飯を食べる eats from the same bowl → **kamameshi** 釜飯

káma *n* 鎌 sickle
kamaboko *n* かまぼこ・カマボコ steamed fish cake
kamachí *n* 框 frame, rail
kamado *n* かまど (*Japanese traditional*) kitchen range, stove; oven; furnace
kamaimasén, kamawánai *v* 構いません, 構わない it makes no difference; never mind; not to bother, it's o.k.
kamakiri *n* カマキリ praying mantis
kamameshi *n* 釜飯 (*cooked*) rice (*with chicken, crab, or shrimp*) served in a clay pot
kamasú *v* カマス barracuda, saury-pike
kamé *n* 瓶 jar (*with large mouth*)
káme *n* カメ・亀 tortoise, turtle
kamei *n* 仮名 an assumed name; a temporary/tentative name
kamei *n* 加盟 affiliation
kamei *n* 家名 family name
kamen *n* 仮面 mask
kámera *n* カメラ camera: **dejitaru-~** デジタルカメラ digital camera: **bideo-~** ビデオカメラ video camera
kamí *n* 紙 paper; kami-básami *n* 紙ばさみ file folder; file; paperclip; kami-búkuro *n* 紙袋 paper bag; kami-hikōki *n* 紙飛行機 paper airplane; kami-kúzu *n* 紙くず wastepaper
kámi *n* 神 **1.** God, gods (= **kámi-sama** 神様) **2.** divinity (= **shinsei** 神性); kami-dana *n* 神棚 household altar (*Shinto*); kámi-sama *n* 神様 God, gods, Dear Lord
kamimásu, kamu *v* かみます, かむ blows (one's nose)
kamimásu, kámu *v* 噛みます, 噛む chews, bites: **(fūsen) gamu o ~** (風船)ガムを噛みます chews (*bubble*) gum: **shita o kamisō na kotoba** 舌をかみそうな言葉 a jawbreaker
kaminári *n* かみなり・カミナリ・雷 thunder, thunderstorm: **~ ga narimásu** 雷が鳴ります it thunders
kamí (no ke) *n* 髪(の毛) hair (*on head*): **~ (no ke) o araimásu** 髪(の毛)を洗います shampoos
kami-san *n* かみさん [INFORMAL] my wife
kamisóri *n* 剃刀 razor: **~ no ha** 剃刀の刃 razor blade
kami-tsukimásu, kami-tsuku *v* 噛みつきます, 噛みつく bites
kámo *n* カモ・鴨 wild duck
kámo *n* かも・カモ dupe, sucker
kamoku *n* 科目 subject, course (*in school*): **hisshū-~** 必修科目 required course/subject
kamome *n* カモメ・鴎 seagull
... kámo (shiremasén/shirenai) *suffix, v* …かも(しれません/しれない) = maybe …, perhaps …
kán *n* 缶 can → **kan-zúmé (no ...)** 缶詰(の…); kan-biiru 缶ビール canned beer: kan-kírí 缶切り can opener
kán *n* 燗 heating rice wine: **~ o tsukemásu/shimásu** 燗をつけます/します warms the saké

kán *n* 管 tube, pipe, duct: **suidō-~** 水道管 water pipe: **kek-~** 血管 blood vessel

kán *n* 巻 volume (*books, tapes*): **(dai) ik-~** (第)一巻 vol. 1

...´-kan *suffix* ...間 for the interval of; between

...´-kan *suffix* ...感 feeling, sense: **dai-rok-~** 第六感 sixth sense: **shok-~** 触感 tactile (*sensation*): **shok-~** 食感 food texture

kana *n* かな kana (*Japanese syllabic writing*) → **furi-gana** ふりがな・フリガナ

...ka na/ne *interj* ...かな/かね I wonder/whether (= **deshō ka** でしょうか)

Kánada *n* カナダ Canada; **Kanadá-jin** *n* カナダ人 a Canadian

kánai *n* 家内 **1.** my wife **2.** one's family: **~-anzen** 家内安全 well-being/safety of one's family: **~-kōgyō** 家内工業 cottage industry

kanaimás<u>u</u>, kanáu *v* 適います, 適う accords/agrees (*with*): **dōri ni ~** 道理にかないます it stands to reason; **mokuteki ni ~** 目的にかないます it serves the purpose

kanaimás<u>u</u>, kanáu *v* 敵います, 敵う is a match (*for*), matches, is equal (*to*): **aité ni kanaimasén** 相手に敵いません is no match for the opponent

kanaimás<u>u</u>, kanáu *v* 叶います, 叶う (= **dekimásu** できます) is accomplished, attained, realized, achieved: **nozomi ga ~** 望みが叶います a desire is realized (*fulfilled*): **yume ga ~** 夢が叶います a dream comes true

kanamono *n* 金物 hardware: **~-ya** 金物屋 hardware store

kanarazu *adv* 必ず for sure; necessity; inevitably

kánari *adv* かなり fairly, rather

kanaria *n* カナリア canary

kanashii *adj* 悲しい sad

kanashimi *n* 悲しみ sadness

kanashimimásu, kanashimu *v* 悲しみます, 悲しむ to be sad

kanazuchi *n* かなづち・カナヅチ・金槌 **1.** hammer **2.** a person who cannot swim

kanban *n* 看板 **1.** signboard, sign **2.** (*diner, pub*) closing time; kanban-musume *n* 看板娘 beautiful lady who attracts consumers/customers; kanban-yakusha *n* 看板役者 star actor

kanbasu *n* カンバス canvas

kanbatsu *n* かんばつ・干ばつ drought (= **hideri** ひでり・日照り)

kanben (na) *n, adj* 簡便(な) convenience, convenient, simple and easy

kanben shitekudasai *interj* 勘弁して下さい Please give me a break

kanbi *n* 完備 full equipment

kanbi (na) *adj* 甘美(な) sweet, luscious, dulcet: **~ kajitsu** 甘美な果実 sweet fruit: **~ merodii** 甘美なメロディー dulcet melody

kanbu *n* 患部 [BOOKISH] diseased part, affected area

kanbu *n* 幹部 [BOOKISH] executive
kanbun *n* 漢文 Chinese classics
kanbutsu *n* 乾物 dry food
kanbō *n* 感冒 [BOOKISH] common cold: **ryūkōsei-~** 流行性感冒 influenza (= **infuruénza** インフルエンザ)
kanbō *n* 官房 [BOOKISH] Secretariat
kanbō *n* 監房 [BOOKISH] ward, jail cell
kanbojia *n* カンボジア Cambodia; Kanbojia-go *n* カンボジア語 Cambodian (*language*); Kanbojia-jin *n* カンボジア人 a Cambodian
kanboku *n* 潅[灌]木 bush
kanbotsu *n* 陥没 [BOOKISH] subsidence, cave-in, sinking
kanbyō *n* 看病 nursing
kanchi *n* 感知 appreciation, sense
kanchi *n* 完治 [BOOKISH] complete cure
kanchō *n* 浣腸 enema
kánchō *n* 艦長 captain (*of warship*)
kánchō *n* 官庁 government office
kanchō *n* 干潮 ebb, low tide
kandai (na) *adj* 寛大(な) generous, lenient: **~ na hito** 寛大な人 broad-minded person: **~ na kokoro** 寛大な心 generous heart, big heart
kandán-kei *n* 寒暖計 (*room*) thermometer
kandō *n* 感動 (strong) emotion, (deep) feeling
kane *n* 金 **1.** money **2.** metal (= **kinzoku** 金属)
kane *n* 鐘 large bell (*of church, temple, etc.*): **joya no ~** 除夜の鐘 the bells on New Year's Eve
... ka ne *interj* …かね (mostly male. INFORMAL) = **... ka ne/na** …かね/かな (I wonder/whether)
kane-bako *n* 金箱 **1.** cashbox, money box (= **zeni-bako** 銭箱) **2.** patron, gold mine, money-maker, cash cow
kanemásu, kanéru *v* 兼ねます, 兼ねる combines, unites; dually/concurrently serves as
kanemóchí (no) *adj* 金持ち(の) rich (*wealthy*)
kan'en *n* 肝炎 hepatitis
kāneshon *n* カーネーション carnation(s): **haha-no-hi ni okuru ~** 母の日に贈るカーネーション carnations gifted for Mother's Day
kanetsu *n* 加熱 heat, heating; kanetsu-ki *n* 加熱器 heater
kangáe 考え *n* thought, idea, opinion
kangaemásu, kangáeru *v* 考えます, 考える thinks, considers
kangei *n* 歓迎 welcome (= **kantai** 歓待); kangei-kai *n* 歓迎会 reception (*welcome party*)
kangeki *n* 感激 (*strong*) emotion (*feeling*) (= **kandō** 感動)
kango *n* 漢語 Chinese word/vocabulary (*in Japanese*)
kángo *n* 看護 nursing (*a patient*); kangó-shi *n* 看護師 a nurse
kani *n* カニ・蟹 crab
kānibaru *n* カーニバル carnival
kanja *n* 患者 (*medical*) patient

kanji *n* 漢字 a Chinese character (*symbol*), kanji

kanji *n* 感じ feeling (= **kankaku** 感覚): **konna-~ (de/no)** こんな感じ(で/の) like this: **sonna/anna-~ (de/no)** そんな/あんな感じ(で/の) like that

kan-jimásu, kan-jiru *v* 感じます, 感じる feels

kanjō *n* 感情 emotion

kanjō *n* 環状 [BOOKISH] loop (*shape*): **~ (no)** 環状(の) ring-shaped, circular; **~-sen** 環状線 loop/belt line

kanjō´ *n* 勘定 bill, check, account; **kanjō-gákari** 勘定係 cashier

kankaku *n* 感覚 sense, sensibility, feeling, sensation

kankaku *n* 間隔 space, interval (*of time, space*)

kankei *n* 関係 connection, relationship, interest, concern, relevance: **… no ~-sha** …の関係者 the people/ authorities concerned with …, the … people

kánki *n* 換気 ventilation: **~-sen** 換気扇 ventilator

kankō *n* 観光 sightseeing, tour: **~-básu** 観光バス sightseeing bus; **~-réssha** 観光列車 sightseeing train; **kankō´-kyaku** *n* 観光客 tourist, sightseer

Kánkoku *n* 韓国 South Korea; **Kankoku-go** *n* 韓国語 Korean (*language*); **Kankokú-jin** *n* 韓国人 a Korean

kankyaku *n* 観客 audience, spectator

kankyō *n* 環境 environment: **~-osen** 環境汚染 environmental pollution; **~-hogo** 環境保護 environmental protection

Kankyō-shō *n* 環境省 Ministry of the Environment (MOE)

kanmatsu *n* 巻末 end of a book

kanmi *n* 甘味 sweetness: **~-ryō** 甘味料 sweetening

kanna *n* かんな・カンナ plane (*tool*)

kannai (de/ni) *adv* 管内(で/に) within the jurisdiction

kannai (de/ni) *adv* 館内(で/に) inside the building: **~-tsuā** 館内ツアー guided tour of the building

kannen *n* 観念 **1.** idea (*Platonism*) **2.** concept, conception **3.** giving up **4.** meditation (*Buddhism*)

kannin *n* 堪忍 [BOOKISH] patience: **~ shitekudasai** 堪忍して下さい Please forgive me.: **~-bukuro no o ga kireru** 堪忍袋の緒が切れる runs out of patience

kanningu *n* カンニング (*during examination, test, etc.*) cheating; **kanningu-pēpā** *n* カンニングペーパー crib note

kannō *n* 完納 [BOOKISH] full payment

kannō *n* 感応 [BOOKISH] response, participation

kannō teki (na) *adj* 官能的(な) sensual, erotic

kannúki *n* かんぬき bolt (*of door*)

kánnushi *n* 神主 priest (*Shinto*)

káno-jo *pron* 彼女 she/her; girlfriend, mistress
kanō (na) *adj* 可能(な) possible: **~-sei** 可能性 possibility
kanpa *n* カンパ fund-raising campaign
kanpai *n* 乾杯 a toast, "bottoms up": **Kanpai!** 乾杯 Cheers!
kanpai *n* 完敗 complete defeat
kanpán *n* 甲板 deck (*of ship*)
kanpan *n* 乾パン hardtack
kanpeki (na) *n, adj* 完璧(な) perfection, perfect
kanpi *n* 官費 government expense, government expenditure
kanpō *n* 官報 gazette
kanpō (yaku) *n* 漢方(薬) Chinese medicine
kanpu *n* 還付 refund: **~-kin** 還付金 tax refund
kanpū *n* 寒風 cold wind
kanpū *n* 完封 shut-out: **~-jiai** 完封試合 shutout game
kanpuku *n* 感服 admiration (= **kanshin** 感心, **kantan** 感嘆)
kanpyō´ *n* カンピョウ dried gourd strips, dried ground shavings
kanrán-seki *n* 観覧席 grandstand (*seats*)
kanren *n* 関連 relevance (= **kankei** 関係): **(… ni) ~ shimásu** (…に)関連します is relevant (*to*), is connected (*with*)
kánri *n* 管理 control (= **kontorōru** コントロール); **kanri-nin** *n* 管理人 custodian, janitor, manager, landlord (*rental manager*); **kanri-sha** *n* 管理者 administrator
kanroku *n* 貫禄 presence (= **igen** 威厳): **~ ga arimásu** 貫禄があります has a presence
kansai-chihō *n* 関西地方 the Kansai area of Japan (*Kyoto, Osaka, Kobe, Nara, Shiga, Hyogo, Wakayama prefecture etc.*)
kansatsu *n* 観察 [BOOKISH] observation, watching; **kansatsú-sha** *n* 観察者 observer
kansatsu *n* 監察 [BOOKISH] inspection; **kansatsú-kan** *n* 監察官 inspector
kansatsu *n* 鑑札 [BOOKISH] license (tag): **inú no ~** 犬の鑑札 a dog(-license) tag
kansei *n* 完成 completion, perfection
kansetsu *n* 関節 joint (*of two bones*): **(shu)shi-~** (手)指関節 knuckle: **~-en** 関節炎 arthritis
kansetsu (no) *adj* 間接(の) indirect; **kansetsu(-teki) ni** *adj* 間接(的)に indirectly
kánsha *n* 感謝 thanks, gratitude; **kansha-sai** *n* 感謝祭 Thanksgiving
kan-shimásu (-súru) *v* 関します relates (*to*), concerns, is connected (*with*): **… ni kánshite** …に関して concerning, as regards, with respect to …
kanshin *n* 関心 concern, interest (= **kyōmi** 興味): **~ ga arimásu** 関心があります is interested in
kanshin *n* 感心 admiration
kanshō *n* 干渉 interference,

meddling: **~ shinai de kudasai** 干渉しないで下さい Please stay away from me., Please stay out of it.
kanshō *n* 鑑賞 [BOOKISH] appreciation (*art, work, music*)
kanshō *n* 観賞 [BOOKISH] admiration, enjoyment: **~-shokubutsu** 観賞植物 ornamental plant
kansoku *n* 観測 observation; opinion (= **íken** 意見): **hoshi no ~** 星の観測 observation of the stars
kansō *n* 感想 impression: **dokusho ~-bun** 読書感想文 book report (*at school*)
kansō *n* 乾燥 dryness; **kansō-ki** *n* 乾燥機 dryer (*washing machine*)
kansōgei-kai *n* 歓送迎会 welcome and farewell party
kantai *n* 歓待 [BOOKISH] welcome (= **kangei** 歓迎)
kantan *n* 感嘆 [BOOKISH] admiration (= **kanshin** 感心, **kanpuku** 感服)
kantan (na) *adj* 簡単(な) easy, simple, brief
kantei *n* 鑑定 [BOOKISH] judgment
kantei *n* 官邸 [BOOKISH] official residence: **shushō-~** 首相官邸 official residence of the prime minister
kantō-chihō *n* 関東地方 the Kantō area of Japan (*Tokyō, Chiba, Saitama, Kanagawa, Ibaraki, Tochigi, Gunma, Yamanashi prefecture*) → **shutó-ken** 首都圏
kantoku *n* 監督 supervision; supervisor, superintendent, overseer, manager, director; **eiga-kantoku** *n* 映画監督 film director
kantō´shi *n* 間投詞 interjection
kanzei *n* 関税 customs duty (*tariff*)
kanzen *n* 完全 perfection, completeness: **~ ni** 完全に completely
kanzō *n* 肝臓 liver
kan-zúmé (no ...) *adj* 缶詰(の…) **1.** canned (*food*), can, tin **2.** confine oneself: **hoteru ni ~ ni natte kiji o kakimásu** ホテルに缶詰になって記事を書きます confines oneself to a hotel room to write articles
kao *n* 顔 face; looks, a look: **… (no) ~ o shite imásu …** (の)顔をしています has/wears an expression of …; **kao-iro** *n* 顔色 complexion
kaomoji *n* 顔文字 Emoticon
kaori *n* 香(り) fragrance, incense (= **kō´** 香): **kōsui no ~** 香水の香り fragrance of perfume
kā´pétto *n* カーペット carpet
kappa *n* かっぱ・カッパ・河童 water imp
kapparaimásu, kapparáu *v* かっぱらいます, かっぱらう [INFORMAL] swipes, steals, shoplifts
kappatsu (na) *adj* 活発(な) active, lively
kappō *n* 割烹 [BOOKISH] Japanese restaurant, Japanese cuisine: **~-gi** 割烹着 Japanese-style apron
káppu *n* カップ a cup (*with handle*): **magu-~** マグカップ mug

káppuru *n* カップル a couple (*of lovers*)
kápuseru *n* カプセル capsule: **~-hoteru** カプセルホテル capsule hotel
kara *n* 殻 shell, crust: **monuke no ~** もぬけのから[殻] completely empty (= **karappo (no)** 空っぽ(の))
kara (no) *adj* から[空](の) empty: **karappo (no)** から[空]っぽ(の) completely empty
... kará *prep, conj* …から **1.** from…, since… (*time, space*): **... kara, ... máde** …から…まで from … to … **2.** because…
kárā *n* カラー collar (= **eri** 襟)
kárā *n* カラー color (= **iro** 色)
karada *n* 体・身体 body; one's health: **~ ni ki o tsukete kudasai** (身)体に気をつけて下さい Please take care of yourself.
karái *adj* 辛い **1.** spicy, hot, peppery, pungent **2.** salty
karakaimásu, karakáu *v* からかいます, からかう teases, pokes fun at
kara-kása *n* 唐傘 (*oil-paper*) umbrella
karaoke *n* カラオケ karaoke
karashi *n* カラシ・芥子 mustard
kárasu *n* カラス・烏 crow
karate *n* カラテ・空手 karate (*weaponless self-defense*): **~-gí** 空手着 karate outfit/suit
káre *pron* 彼 he/him; **káre-ra** *pron* 彼ら they/them
káre *n* 彼 boyfriend (*lover*) (= **kare-shi** 彼氏)
karē *n* カレー curry: **~-ráisu** カレーライス rice with curry
kárei *n* カレイ flatfish, turbot
karemásu, kareru *v* 枯れます, 枯れる withers: **karete imásu** 枯れています is withered
karemásu, kareru *v* 刈れます, 刈れる can mow/cut
karéndā *n* カレンダー calendar
káre-shi *n* 彼氏 boyfriend (*lover*) (= **káre** 彼)
kari (no) *adj* 仮(の) temporary, tentative: **~-zumai** 仮住まい temporary residence
kári 狩り *n* hunting: **~ o shimásu** 狩りをします hunts
kari 借り *n* borrowing: **~ ga arimásu** 借りがあります I owe you.; **karí-chin** *n* 借り賃 rent (*charge*); **kari-te** *n* 借り手 the borrower/renter, the lessee, the tenant
karimásu, karu *v* 刈ります, 刈る mows, cuts
karimásu, kariru *v* 借ります, 借りる borrows/rents it (from …)
karō *n* 過労 overfatigue: **~-shi** 過労死 death from overwork
kāru *n* カール curl
karui *adj* 軽い light (*of weight*)
karuishi *n* 軽石 pumice
Karukatta *n* カルカッタ Calcutta (Kolkata)
kása *n* 傘・かさ umbrella: **~-date** 傘立て umbrella stand
kása *n* 笠 bamboo hat; (*mushroom*) cap

kasá *n* 嵩 bulk
kasabarimásu̲, kasabaru *v* かさばります, かさばる is bulky, takes up much space
kasai *n* 火災 fire (*accidental*) (= **káji** 火事): **~-kéihō** 火災警報 fire alarm, **~-hōchi̲ki** 火災報知器 fire alarm (*device*), fire bell
kasanarimásu̲, kasanaru *v* 重なります, 重なる they pile up
kasanemásu̲, kasaneru *v* 重ねます, 重ねる piles them up, puts one on top of another
kase *n* かせ shackles: **te-~** 手かせ handcuffs: **~ o hazushimásu̲** かせを外します unshackles
kasegimásu̲, kaségu *v* 稼ぎます, 稼ぐ earns, works for (*money*)
kasei *n* 火星 Mars; kaséi-jin *n* 火星人 a Martian
kaséi-fu *n* 家政婦 housekeeper, hired maid
kaseki *n* 化石 fossil(s)
kasen *n* 下線 underline: **~ o hi̲kimásu̲** 下線を引きます draws an underline
kasen *n* 化繊 [BOOKISH] synthetic fiber
kasetto (tēpu) *n* カセット(テープ) cassette (tape)
káshi *n* 歌詞 lyrics
káshi *n* 菓子 cakes, sweets, pastry; kashí-ya *n* 菓子屋 candy store, confectioner
kashi̲kiri-básu *n* 貸し切りバス chartered bus
kashi̲kói *adj* 賢い wise
kashi̲komarimáshi̲ta かしこまりました. I understand and will comply (*with your request*). [HONORIFIC]
kashí-ma *n* 貸間 rooms for rent; rented/rental room(s)
kashimásu̲, kasu *v* 貸します, 貸す lends; rents (*it out to*)
kashirá *n* 頭 head; chief, leader
... káshira *interj* …かしら (*mostly female*) I wonder/whether
kashi̲-te *n* 貸し手 the lender/ lessor, the landlord
kashitsu *n* 過失 mistakes, errors, faults: **~-sekinin** 過失責任 negligence liability
kashi-ya *n* 貸家 house for rent; rented/rental house
...-kásho *suffix* …か所・箇所・個所 (*counter for places, installations, institutions*)
kashoku-shō *n* 過食症 bulimia nervosa
kashu *n* 歌手 singer: **~-kashu** 流行歌手 pop singer
kasō *n* 仮装 disguise: **~-pātii** 仮装パーティ costume party: **~-ishō** 仮装衣装 costume
kasō *n* 火葬 cremation
kasō *n* 仮想 [BOOKISH] virtual, imaginary: **~-kūkan** 仮想空間 virtual space
kasō *n* 下層 [BOOKISH] lower layer: **~-kaikyū** 下層階級 lower class society
kasoku̲ *n* 加速 acceleration; kasoku-pédaru 加速ペダル gas pedal
kāsoru *n* カーソル cursor (*on the*

computer screen, etc.)

kásu *n* かす[滓] **1.** sediment, dregs, grounds: **kōhii-~** コーヒーかす coffee grounds **2.** waste, scum, trash, rags, scrap, junk (= **kúzu** くず[屑]): **moe-~** 燃えかす cinders: **ningen/seken no ~** 人間/世間のかす the scum of the earth **3.** particles: **tabe-~** 食べかす food particles

kásu *n* かす[糟・粕] lees

kásuka (na/ni) *adj, adv* かすか(な/に)・微か(な/に) faint(ly), dim(ly), slight(ly)

kasumemásu, kasumeru *v* 掠めます, 掠める skims, grazes

kasume-torimásu, kasume-toru *v* 掠め取ります, 掠め取る skims off; robs (*it of* ...), cheats (*one out of* ...) (= **kasumemásu** 掠めます)

kasumi *n* かすみ・霞 haze, mist

kasumimásu, kasumu *v* 霞みます, 霞む gets dim, hazy, misty

kasurimásu, kasuru *v* かすります, かする grazes

kasutera *n* カステラ Japanese sponge cake, Castella

kata *n* 型 **1.** form, shape, size, mold, pattern: **~ ni hamemásu** 型にはめます stereotypes: **ō-gata** 大型 large-size **2.** type, model: **ketsueki-~** 血液型 blood type

káta *n* 肩 shoulder(s); **kata-gaki** *n* 肩書き (*business/position*) title

...-kata *suffix* ...方 manner of doing, way: **yari-~** やり方 method, process (= **hōhō** 方法): **kangae-~** 考え方 one's way of thinking, one's point of view

... katá *n* ...方 (**o-kata** お方) (*honored*) person: **anata-gata** あなた方 you people

kata-... *prefix* 片... one (*of a pair*) (= **katáhō** 片方): **~-ashi** 片足 one leg/foot: **~-gawa** 片側 one side; **katá-hō** *n* 片方, **katáppō** 片っぽう, **katáppo** 片っぽ one of a pair; the other one (*of a pair*); **kata-koto** *n* 片言 imperfect language, limited language; **kata-michi** *n* 片道 one-way: **~ kíppu** 片道切符 one way ticket

katachi *n* 形 form, shape

katadoru *adj* かたど[象・模]る imitated, copied, modeled, symbolized (= **shōchō** 象徴)

... katá-gata *suffix* ...方々 (*honored*) persons (= **... katá-tachi** ...方達)

katagi (na) *adj* 堅気(な) respectable, steady, honest

katai *adj* 固い hard; tight; strong; firm; strong; strict

katai *adj* 硬い hard, stiff; stilted upright

katai *adj* 堅い hard; solid; sound; reliable; serious; formal

katákána *n* カタカナ・片かな・片仮名 katakana (*the squarish Japanese letters*)

katamari *n* 固まり・塊 a lump, a clot, a mass; a loaf (*of bread*)

katamarimásu, katamaru *v* 固まります, 固まる it hardens, congeals, clots, (*mud*) cakes

katamemásu, katameru *v* 固めます, 固める hardens it, congeals it; strengthens it
katamuki *n* 傾き slant; inclination, tendency
katamukimásu, katamúku *v* 傾きます, 傾く leans (*to one side*), slants
kataná *n* 刀 sword
katáppo *n* 片っぽ one of a pair; the other one (*of a pair*)
katarimásu *v* 語ります, **kataru** 語る relates, tells
... katá-tachi *n* …方達 (*honored*) persons
katáwa *n* 片輪 (*discriminatory term*) cripple
kata-yorimásu, kata-yóru *v* 片寄り[偏り]ます, 片寄る[偏る] leans (*to one side*); is partial (*to*)
kata-zukemásu, kata-zukéru *v* 片付けます, 片付ける puts in order, straightens up, tidies, cleans up
kata-zukimásu, kata-zúku *v* 片付きます, 片付く it gets tidy (put in order)
katei *n* 仮定 hypothesis, supposition
katei *n* 課程 process (*course, stage*)
katei *n* 家庭 home, household; **katei-yō′gu/yō′hin** *n* 家庭用具/用品 home appliances
katemásu, katéru *v* 勝てます, 勝てる can win
kā′ten *n* カーテン curtain, drapes: **~-róddo** カーテンロッド curtain rod; **~-rēru** カーテンレール curtain rail: **shawā-~** シャワーカーテン shower curtain
kātoriji *n* カートリッジ cartridge: **inku-~** インクカートリッジ ink cartridge
Katoríkku *n* カトリック Catholic
kátsu *n* カツ a Japanese "cutlet" (*fried in deep fat*): **ton-~** 豚カツ・トンカツ pork cutlet; **katsu-don** *n* カツ丼 a bowl of rice with sliced pork cutlet on top
katsudō *n* 活動 action, activity, movement
katsugimásu, katsúgu *v* 担ぎます, 担ぐ carries on shoulders
katsuji *n* 活字 movable type: **~ ni shimásu** 活字にします prints, is in print
katsuo *n* カツオ・鰹 bonito: **~-bushi** カツオ[鰹]節 a dried bonito fish
katsura *n* かつら・カツラ a wig
kátsute *adv* かつて at one time, formerly
katsuyaku *n* 活躍 activity
...-kátta *v* …かった : [ADJECTIVE] **-kátta (desu)** …かった(です) was …
...-káttara *v* …かったら: [ADJECTIVE] **káttara** …かったら if/when it is
...-káttari *v* …かったり: [ADJECTIVE] **káttari** …かったり being representatively/sometimes/alternately: **…-ku nákattari** …くなかったり (is…) off and on, sometimes is … and sometimes isn't
katte *n* 勝手 kitchen; **katte-dō′gu** *n* 勝手道具 kitchen utensils; **kátte-guchi** *n* 勝手口 kitchen door, back door

katte *adj, adv* ~ **(na/ni)** 勝手(な/に) selfish(ly), as one wishes
kaunserā *n* カウンセラー counselor
kauntā *n* カウンター counter
kawá *n* 川 river
kawá *n* 河 big river
kawá *n* 皮・革 skin; leather; (*tree*) bark; crust
kawai-garimásu, kawai-gáru *v* かわいがり[可愛がり]ます, かわいがる・可愛がる treats with affection, loves (*children, pets, etc.*)
kawaíi *adj* かわいい・可愛い cute, lovable, darling (= **kawairashíi** かわいらしい・可愛らしい)
kawai-sō´ (na) *adj* かわいそう(な) pitiful, poor
kawakashimásu, kawakásu *v* 乾かします, 乾かす dries it (out)
kawakimásu, kawáku *v* 乾きます, 乾く gets dry
kawakimásu, kawáku *v* 渇きます, 渇く: **nodo ga** ~ のどが渇きます gets thirsty
kawara *n* 瓦 tile: **~-buki (no)** 瓦ぶき(の) tile-roofed
kawari *n* 変わり change (*in health*)
kawari *n* 代わり substitute: **... no ~ ni** ... の代わりに instead of
kawari *n* かわり a second helping (*usually of rice*): **~-jiyū (desu)** おかわり自由(です) has free refills
kawarimásu, kawaru *v* 変わります, 変わる: **(... ni)** ~ (...に)変わります it changes (into...)
kawarimásu, kawaru *v* 代わります, 代わる: **(... ni)** ~ (...に)代わります it takes the place (*of ...*)
kawaru-gáwaru *adv* 代わる代わる・かわるがわる alternately
kawase *n* 為替 a money order: **~-rēto** 為替レート currency exchange rates
kayaku *n* 火薬 gunpowder
Kayō´(bi) *n* 火曜(日) Tuesday
kayoi 通い *adj* ~ **(no)** 通い(の) commuting, live-out (help): ~ **no o-tetsudai(-san)** 通いのお手伝い(さん) a day helper
kayoimásu, kayou *v* 通います, 通う commutes, goes back and forth, goes (regularly)
kayu *n* 粥・かゆ rice gruel, porridge
kayúi *adj* 痒い itchy
kázan *n* 火山 volcano: **~-bai** 火山灰 volcanic ash
kazari 飾り *n* = **~-mono** 飾り物 ornament, decoration
kazarimásu, kazaru *v* 飾ります, 飾る decorates
kazari-mono *n* 飾り物 ornament, decoration
kaze *n* 風 wind
kaze *n* かぜ・カゼ・風邪 a cold: ~ **o hikimásu** かぜをひきます catches (a) cold
kaze-gúsuri *n* かぜ薬・風邪薬 medicine for colds
kazoe-kirenai *adj* 数え切れない countless, innumerable
kazoemásu, kazoéru *v* 数えます, 数える counts

kázoku *n* 家族 family: **~-omoi no (hito)** 家族思いの(人) family-minded (*person*)
kázu *n* 数 number
kazu no ko *n* カズノコ・数の子 herring roe
ke *n* 毛 hair; wool; feathers
...-ke *suffix* …家 (*name of certain*) clan, family: **Suzuki-~** 鈴木家 Suzuki family
kē´buru *n* ケーブル cable: **~-kā** ケーブルカー cable car: **~-terebi** ケーブルテレビ cable TV
kecháppu *n* ケチャップ ketchup
kéchi (na) *adj* けち(な) stingy, miser
kéchinbō, kéchinbo *n* けちん坊, けちんぼ stingy person, skinflint, miser
kedamono *n* けだもの・ケダモノ・獣 animal; beast (= **kemono**)
kédo *conj* けど [INFORMAL] though, but (= [FORMAL] **kéredo (-mo)** けれど(も) however, though, but)
kegá *n* けが・ケガ・怪我 injury, mishap: **~ o shimás<u>u</u>** 怪我をします gets hurt; **~ o sasemás<u>u</u>** 怪我をさせます injures (someone)
ke-gawa *n* 毛皮 fur
kéi *n* 刑 (*criminal*) sentence
...-kei *suffix* …系 **1.** type, model: **dō-~-shoku** 同系色 similar color **2.** of …ancestry: **~-zu** 系図 genealogy, a family tree (= **kakei-zu** 家系図)
keiba *n* 競馬 horse racing/race; keiba-jō *n* 競馬場 racetrack
keibetsu *n* 軽蔑 contempt, despising
kéibi *n* 警備 [BOOKISH] security; keibi-in *n* 警備員 security guard
keiei *n* 経営 management, operation
keiéi-sha *n* 経営者 manager, operator, proprietor
keigo *n* 敬語 honorific (*word*): **~ o tsukaimás<u>u</u>** 敬語を使います uses honorific words
keihin *n* 景品 [BOOKISH] giveaway
keihō *n* 警報 alarm, alert, warning
keiji *n* 繋辞 [BOOKISH] copula, (*grammar term*) link
kéiji *n* 刑事 (*police*) detective
keiji *n* 掲示 bulletin; keiji-ban *n* 掲示板 bulletin board
kéijō *n* 形状 geometry
keika *n* 経過 course (*of time*), progress, development
keikai *n* 警戒 [BOOKISH] vigilance, watch, guard; warning, caution
keikaku *n* 計画 plan, scheme, program, project (= **puran** プラン): **(… no) ~ o tatemás<u>u</u>** (…の)計画を立てます = **(…o) ~ shimás<u>u</u>** (…を)計画します plans
keikan *n* 警官 [BOOKISH] policeman, (*police*) officer (= **keisatsu-kan** 警察官): **~-tai** 警官隊 a contingent of policemen
keiken *n* 経験 experience; shokumu-keiken *n* 職務経験 job experience
keiki *n* 景気 business conditions, prosperity, boom: **~-taisaku**

景気対策 economy-boosting measure(s)
kéiki *n* 契機 [BOOKISH] opportunity
kéiki *n* 刑期 prison term
kei(ryō)ki *n* 計(量)器 meter (*device*)
kéiko *n* 稽古 exercise, practice, drill
keikō *n* 傾向 [BOOKISH] tendency, trend
keikō *n* 経口 [BOOKISH] oral: **~-hinínyaku** 経口避妊薬 oral contraceptive (= **piru** ピル)
keikoku *n* 警告 [BOOKISH] warning: **~-hyōji** 警告表示 alarm display
keikō-tō *n* 蛍光灯 fluorescent light
keimú-sho *n* 刑務所 jail, prison
keireki *n* 経歴 [BOOKISH] career (*history*)
keirin *n* 競輪 [BOOKISH] bicycle race: **~-jō** 競輪場 bicycle race-track
keirō *n* 敬老 [BOOKISH] respect for the aged; **Keirō-no-hí** *n* 敬老の日 Respect-for-the-Aged Day (*Third Monday of September*)
keiryaku *n* 計略 [BOOKISH] plot, scheme, trick, strategy
keiryō-kappu *n* 計量カップ measuring cup
keisan *n* 計算 calculation, computation
keisán-ki *n* 計算機 calculator
keisatsu *n* 警察 police: **~-shó** 警察署 police station; **~-kan** 警察官 policeman, (police) officer
keishịki *n* 形式 form, formality
keishoku *n* 軽食 snack, light foods
keisotsu (na) *adj* 軽率(な) hasty, rash
keitai *n* 形態 pattern, shape
keitai **1.** *adj* 携帯 portable **2.** *n* 携帯 cell-phone, mobile (tele)phone (= **keitai-denwa** 携帯電話)
keitai-denwa *n* 携帯電話 cell-phone, mobile (tele)phone
keiteki *n* 警笛 horn (*of car*) (= **kuráku-shon** クラクション)
keito *n* 毛糸 wool; yarn: **~-dama** 毛糸玉 ball of wool/yarn
keiyaku *n* 契約 contract, agreement; **keiyaku-sho** *n* 契約書 (*written*) contract
keiyō´shi *n* 形容詞 adjective
... kéiyu (de/no) *adv, adj* …経由(で/の) by (*way of*) ..., via ...: **~-bin** 経由便 indirect flight
kéizai *n* 経済 economics, finance; **keizái-gaku** *n* 経済学 (*science of*) economics; **keizai-teki (na)** *adj* 経済的(な) economical
Keizai-Sangyō-shō *n* 経済産業省 Ministry of Economy, Trade and Industry (METI)
kḗki *n* ケーキ cake
kekka *n* 結果 result, effect; as a result (*consequence*): **gen'in to ~** 原因と結果 cause and effect
kekkaku *n* 結核 tuberculosis
kekkan *n* 欠陥 [BOOKISH] defect, deficiency
kekkan *n* 血管 blood vessel
kekkō *n* 欠航 [BOOKISH] cancelled flight; "flight cancelled"

kékkō (na) *adj* 結構(な) **1.** splendid, excellent **2.** fairly well; enough: **Kékkō desu** 結構です. No, thank you.

kekkon *n* 結婚 marriage (= **konin** 婚姻): **(... to) ~ shimásu** (...と) 結婚します marries; kekkón-shiki *n* 結婚式 wedding

kekkyokú *n, adv* 結局 after all, in the long run

kemono *n* けもの・ケモノ・獣 = **kedamono** けだもの・ケダモノ・獣 (*animal; beast*)

kemúi, kemutai *adj* 煙い, 煙たい smoky

kemuri *n* 煙 smoke

kemushi *n* ケムシ・毛虫 caterpillar

kén *n* 県 a Japanese prefecture (*like a state*), **...´-ken** ...県: **Chiba´-ken** 千葉県 Chiba prefecture

kén *n* 剣 (*double-edged*) sword

...´-ken *suffix* ...軒 (*counts houses, small buildings and shops*)

...´-ken *suffix* ...券 ticket: **nyūjō-~** 入場券 admission ticket

kenbái-ki *n* 券売機 ticket vending machine

kenbi-kyō *n* 顕微鏡 microscope

kenbutsu *n* 見物 sightseeing; kenbutsu-nin *n* 見物人 bystander

kénchi *n* 見地 viewpoint

kenchiku *n* 建築 [BOOKISH] construction; architecture; kenchiku-ka *n* 建築家 architect

kénchō *n* 県庁 the prefectural government (office)

kéndō *n* 剣道 the art of fencing (*with bamboo swords*)

ken'etsu *n* 検閲 censor(ship)

kengaku *n* 見学 study by observation, field study/trip/work

kénji *n* 検事 (*public*) prosecutor

kenjū *n* 拳銃 pistol

kenka *n* けんか・喧嘩 quarrel, argument

kenkō *n* 健康 health: **~-shókuhin** 健康食品 health food(s); **~-hoken** 健康保険 health insurance; kenkō (na) *adj* 健康(な) healthy

kenkyo (na) *adj* 謙虚(な) humble (*modest*)

kenkyū *n* 研究 research, study; kenkyū-jo *n* 研究所 research institute, laboratory

kenmei (na) *adj* 賢明(な) wise

kénpō *n* 憲法 constitution: **Kenpō-kinénbi** 憲法記念日 Constitution (Memorial) Day (*3 May*)

kénri *n* 権利 right (*privilege*); kenrí-kin *n* 権利金 "key money" (*to obtain rental lease*)

kenryoku *n* 権力 power, authority

kénsa *n* 検査 inspection, examination, check-up, test

kensatsu *n* 検札 [BOOKISH] ticket examining (*on board*)

kensetsu *n* 建設 construction (*work*) (*building*)

kenshō *n* 検証 vertification

kentō *n* 拳闘 boxing (*martial art*)

kentō´ *n* 見当 aim; direction; estimate, guess: **~ ga tsukimásu** 見当がつきます gets a rough

idea (*of it*): **~ o tsukemásu** 見当をつけます makes a guess, takes aim
kentō *n* 検討 examination, inspection
...-kéntō *suffix* …見当 roughly, about, approximately
ken'yaku *n* 倹約 economy, thrift, economizing: **~ (na)** 倹約(な) thrifty, frugal
kénzan *n* 剣山 a frog (*pinholder*) for flowers
ke-orimono *n* 毛織物 woolen goods
kéredo (-mo) *conj* けれど(も) however, though, but
kerimásu, kéru *v* 蹴ります, 蹴る kicks
késa *n, adv* 今朝 this morning
keshi 消し *adj* **tsuyakeshi (no)** つや消し matted; **keshi-gomu** *n* 消しゴム (*rubber*) eraser
keshi-in *n* 消印 cancellation mark/stamp
késhiki *n* 景色 scenery, view
keshimásu, kesu *v* 消します, 消す extinguishes, puts out; turns off; expunges, erases, deletes
keshō *n* 化粧(**o-keshō** お化粧) cosmetics, make-up; **keshō-hin** *n* 化粧品 cosmetics; **keshō´-shitsu** *n* 化粧室 restroom, bathroom, toilet, lounge
kessaku *n* 傑作 masterpiece
kessan *n* 決算 settling accounts
kesseki *n* 欠席 absence (*from school, work*); **kessékí-sha** *n* 欠席者 absentee
kesshin *n* 決心 determination, resolve: **(... shiyō to) ~ shimásu** (. . . しようと)決心します resolves (*to do*)
kesshite *adv* 決して [+ NEGATIVE] never
kesshō *n* 決勝 finals, title match: **jun-~** 準決勝 semifinals
kḗsu *n* ケース case (*a particular instance*): **~-bai-~** ケースバイケース case by case; case (*container*)
keta *n* けた・ケタ・桁 **1.** (*cross*) beam, girder **2.** abacus rod, (*numerical*) column
ketsu *n* **1.** けつ・尻 buttock **2.** けつ the tail end, the last (*bottom*) (= **shiri** しり・尻)
ketsuatsu *n* 血圧 blood pressure; **ketsuatsu-kei** *n* 血圧計 blood-pressure gauge; sphygmomanometer
ketsúeki *n* 血液 blood
ketsumatsu *n* 結末 outcome
ketsuron *n* 結論 conclusion: **~ to shite** 結論として in conclusion
kettei *n* 決定 determination, decision
kettén *n* 欠点 flaw, defect, shortcoming
kewashíi *adj* 険しい steep, precipitous; severe
kezurimásu, kezuru *v* 削ります, 削る sharpens, shaves
ki *n* 気 spirit; feeling; mind, heart; **ki (ga)** *adv* 気(が): **~ mijikái** 気が短い is impatient: **~ omoi** 気が重い is depressed; **~ tsukimásu**

気が付きます comes to one's senses; ki ni *adj* 気に: **~ irimásu** 気に入ります appeals to one, is pleasing; **(... ga) ~ narimásu** (...が)気になります worries (*one*); **... suru ~ ni narimásu** ...する気にになります gets in the mood (*to do*); ki o *adv* 気を: **~ tsukemásu** 気を付けます (is) careful

ki *n* 木 tree; wood

kibarashi *n* 気晴らし diversion, refresh

kiben *n* 詭弁 sophistry

kibishíi *adj* 厳しい strict, severe

kibō *n* 希望 hope; kibō'-sha *n* 希望者 candidate, applicant

kíbun *n* 気分 feeling, mood

kichaimásu *v* [INFORMAL] 来ちゃいます = **kite-shimaimásu** 来てしまいます (comes)

kíchi *n* 基地 military base

kíchi *n* 機知 wit

ki-chigái (no) *adj* 気違い(の) mad, insane

kichín-to *adv* きちんと punctually; precisely; neat(ly)

kíchō *n* 記帳 [BOOKISH] registration (*at hotel, etc.*)

kichō' *n* 機長 captain (*of an airplane*)

kichō (na) *adj* 貴重(な) valuable; kichō-hin *n* 貴重品 valuables

kichō'men (na) *adj* 几帳面(な) meticulous, precise, particular

kidate-no/ga-yoi *adj* 気立ての/が良い good-natured

kído *n* 木戸 entrance gate, wicket

kídoairaku *n* [BOOKISH] 喜怒哀楽 emotions, delight, anger, sorrow and pleasure

kidorimásu, kidoru *v* 気取ります, 気取る・気どる puts on airs: **kidotte imásu** 気取っています, **kidotta ...** 気取った... affected, stuck-up

kiemásu, kieru *v* 消えます, 消える is extinguished, goes out; fades, vanishes

kigae *n* 着替え a change of clothing

kigaemásu, kigáeru *v* 着替えます, 着替える changes (*clothes*) [*newer form of* **ki-kaemásu** 着替えます]

kigaru (na) *adj* 気軽(な) casual, lighthearted

kígeki *n* 喜劇 comedy

kigen *n* 機嫌 (*state of*) health, mood: **~ ga íi** 機嫌がいい cheerful; **~ ga warúi** 機嫌が悪い unhappy, moody → **go-kigen** ご機嫌 [HONORIFIC]

kígen *n* 期限 term, period; deadline

kígen *n* 起源 origin

kigō *n* 記号 sign, mark, symbol

kígu *n* 器具 implement, fixture, apparatus

kígyō *n* 企業 company, business concern; "the office" (= **kaisha** 会社)

kihon *n* 基本 basis, foundation

kíi *n* キー key: (*computer*)

kiibōdo キーボード keyboard

kiiro (no) *adj* 黄色(の) = **kiiroi** 黄色い yellow
kí-ito *n* 生糸 raw silk
kiji *n* キジ・雉 pheasant
kíji *n* 記事 article, news item, piece, write-up: **shinbun-~** 新聞記事 newspaper article
kiji *n* 生地 cloth material, fabric
kíjitsu *n* [BOOKISH 期日 appointed day; deadline
kijun *n* [BOOKISH] 基準 basis, standard
kíkai *n* 機会 chance, opportunity, occasion
kíkai *n* 機械 machine, machinery, instrument: **~-teki (na)** 機械的(な) mechanical
kikai *n* 器械 instrument
kịkai (na) *adj* 奇怪(な) mysterious, strange
kịkaku *n* 企画 plan(ning), project: **~-bu** 企画部 planning department
kịkaku *n* 規格 norm, standard: **~-ka** 規格化 standardization
kịkán *n* 期間 term, period
kịkán (no) *adj* 季刊(の) quarterly: **kikán-shi** 季刊誌 a quarterly
kịkán *n* [BOOKISH] 機関 engine; instrument; agency, activity, organization; **kinyū-~** 金融機関 financial institution
kịkasemásụ, kikaseru *v* 聞かせます, 聞かせる lets someone hear, tells someone (*a story*); reads (*someone a book*); reasons with (*a child*)
kịken *n* 危険 danger, peril: **~ (na)** 危険(な) dangerous (= **abunaí** 危ない)
kịken *n* 棄権 abstention
kịkí *n* 危機 crisis, critical moment, emergency
kiki-ashi *n* 利き足 stronger leg
kịkimásụ, kịku *v* 聞きます, 聞く listens, hears; obeys; asks
kịkimásụ, kịku *v* 効きます, 効く takes effect, is effective, works
kịki-me *n* 効き目 effect (*effectiveness*) (= **kōyō** 効用, **kōnō** 効能): **~ ga arimásu** 効き目があります is effective
kịki-te *n* 聞き手 hearer, listener
kiki-ude *n* 利き腕 stronger hand: **migi-kiki** 右利き right-hander(s): **hidari-kiki** 左利き left-hander(s)
kịkkake *n* きっかけ opportunity, occasion
kịkkari *adj* きっかり exactly, just
kikō *n* 気候 climate
kikō *n* [BOOKISH] 機構 system, organization, structure: **kokusai-~** 国際機構 international organization
kikō *n* [BOOKISH] 紀行 travel
kikō *n* [BOOKISH] 寄稿 contribution: **~-kiji** 寄稿記事 contributed article
kikō *n* [BOOKISH] 奇行 one's eccentricity
kịkoemásụ, kikoeru *v* 聞こえます, 聞こえる can hear; is heard
kịkoku *n* 帰国 returning to one's country (Japan); **kikoku-shíjo** *n* 帰国子女 returnees

kikú *n* キク・菊 chrysanthemum
ki-kúrage *n* 木くらげ・キクラゲ・木耳 tree-ears (*an edible fungus*)
kikyū *n* 気球 balloon: **netsu-~** 熱気球 hot-air balloon
kimae ga íi *adj* 気前がいい generous
kimagure *adj* 気まぐれ fickle, easy to change one's mood
kimari *n* 決まり rule; settlement, arrangement; order; regulation
kimarimásu, kimaru *v* 決まります, 決まる is settled, is arranged
kimásu, kiru *v* 着ます, 着る wears
kimásu, kúru *v* 来ます, 来る comes
kimé *n* きめ[木目・肌理] **1.** grain, texture **2.** smooth (*human skin*) **3.** care: **~-komakai** きめ細かい, **~-komayaka (na)** きめ細やか(な) meticulous, attentiveness (*attentive*), tender
kimemásu, kimeru *v* 決めます, 決める settles, arranges, decides
kimi *n* 君・きみ you [*familiar*]
kimi *n* 黄身 yolk (*of egg*)
kimí *n* 気味 feeling, sensation: **~ ga warúi** 気味が悪い nervous, apprehensive, weird (*feeling*)
kimídori (iro) *n* 黄緑(色) yellowish green (color)
Kimigayo *n* 君が代 national anthem of Japan
kimó *n* きも[肝・胆] **1.** liver **2.** guts, courage, pluck: **~-dameshi** 肝試し test of courage
kimochi *n* 気持ち feeling, sensation: **~ ga íi** 気持ちがいい it feels good, is comfortable; **~ ga warúi** 気持ちが悪い is uncomfortable, is feeling bad/unwell
ki-mono *n* 着物 clothes; a (*Japanese*) kimono
ki-músume *n* 生娘 virgin (*female*), green girl
ki-muzukashíi *n* 気難しい fussy, difficult (*person*)
kímyō (na) *adj* 奇妙(な) strange, peculiar
kín *n* 金 gold: **~-ka** 金貨 gold coin
-kin *suffix* 金 money: **shikin** 資金 fund, capital: **shikí-~** 敷金 security deposit (*for rental*)
kínai *adv* 機内 on a plane: **~-shoku** 機内食 airplane meal
kínako *n* きな粉[黄な粉] soybean meal/flour
kinben (na) *adj* 勤勉(な) industrious, hardworking, diligent
kinchō *n* 緊張 strain, tension: **~ shite imásu** 緊張しています is tense
kinen *n* 記念 commemoration; kinen-hin *n* 記念品 souvenir
kin'en *n* 禁煙 smoking prohibited, no smoking: **~-sha** 禁煙車 no(n)-smoking car
kinénbi *n* 記念日 anniversary
kingaku *n* 金額 amount (*of money*)
kingan (no) *adj* 近眼(の) near-sighted, shortsighted, myopic
kíngyo *n* 金魚 goldfish
kiníine *n* キニーネ quinine
kin-iro (no) *adj* 金色(の) gold (color), golden

kin-jimásu, kin-jiru *v* 禁じます, 禁じる forbids, prohibits
kínjo *n* 近所 neighborhood, vicinity
kinkán *n* キンカン・金柑 kumquat
kinki-chihō *n* 近畿地方 the Kinki area of Japan (*Osaka, Hyōgo, Kyōto, Shiga, Nara prefectures*)
kínko *n* 金庫 safe (*strongbox*), (*small*) cash box
kinkyū *n* [BOOKISH] 緊急 urgency, emergency; ~ **na** 緊急な urgent, critical
kinmákie *n* [BOOKISH] 金蒔絵 gold lacquer
kínmu *n* 勤務 duty, service, work; **kinmú-saki** *n* 勤務先 place of work/ employment
kínniku *n* 筋肉 muscle: **~-tsū** 筋肉痛 muscular pain, myalgia
kinō´ *n, adv* きのう・昨日 yesterday
kínō *n* 機能 function
ki-no-dókú na *adj* 気の毒な pitiful, pitiable
kínoko *n* キノコ・茸 mushroom
kí-no-mi *n* 木の実 nuts, tree produce (*nuts, fruits, berries*)
kinō´ no ban *n* きのう[昨日]の晩 last night
kinpatsu (no) *adj* 金髪(の) blond
kinpira *n* キンピラ・きんぴら・金平 fried burdock root and carrot strips served cold
Kinrō-kánsha no hí *n* 勤労感謝の日 Labor Thanksgiving Day (23 November)
kínryoku *n* 筋力 muscle (*power*)
kinshi *n* 禁止 prohibition, ban
kinshi *n* 近視 = **kingan** 近眼 (near-sighted)
kintámá *n* 金玉 testicle(s) [INFORMAL]
kínu *n* 絹 silk
Kin'yō´(bi) *n* 金曜(日) Friday
kinyū *n* 記入 entry, filling in of forms
kin'yū *n* 金融 finance: **~-shíjō** 金融市場 the money market
kínzoku *n* 金属 metal
kioku *n* 記憶 memory: **kiokúryoku** 記憶力 memory (*capacity*), retentiveness
kippári (to) *adv* きっぱり(と) definitely, firmly, flatly
kippu *n* 切符 ticket: **~-úriba** 切符売り場 ticket office
kirai (na) *adj* 嫌い(な) disliked
kiraku (na) *adj* 気楽(な) carefree, comfortable; easygoing
kirashimásu, kirásu *v* 切らします, 切らす exhausts the supply of, runs out of: **... o kiráshite imásu** ...を切らしています is out of ...; **shibiré o ~** しびれを切らします loses patience
kiré *v* きれ・切れ a piece, a cut (*of cloth*)
kírei (na) *adj* きれい[綺麗](な) pretty; clean; neat, tidy; nice (-looking), attractive
kiremásu, kiréru *v* 切れます, 切れる **1.** can cut; cuts (*well*) **2.** runs out **3.** breaks (off)
kire-mé *n* 切れ目 a gap, a break, a pause
kirénai *v* 切れない dull(-edged), blunt

kiri *n* 霧 fog, mist: ~ **ga fukái (koi)** 霧が深い(濃い) is foggy

kíri *n* 錐 a hole-punch, an awl

kirí *n* きり end; limit; ~ **ga nai** きりがない endless, no limit (*no boundary*)

kiri-kabu *n* 切り株 (*tree*) stump

kirimásu, kíru *v* 切ります, 切る cuts; cuts off, disconnects; hangs up (*phone*)

kirinuki *n* 切り抜き clipping (*from newspaper, etc.*)

kirisame *n* 霧雨 drizzle

Kirisuto *n* キリスト Christ; Kirisuto-kyō *n* キリスト教 Christianity

kiritsu *n* 規律 discipline

kíro *n* キロ **1.** kilogram **2.** kilometer **3.** kilowatt **4.** kiloliter

kiroku *n* 記録 (*historic*) record; **shin-~** 新記録 a new record (*an event*)

kíryō *n* 器量 personal appearance, looks; ability

kisaku (na) *adj* 気さく(な) not put on airs

kisen *n* 汽船 steamship

kisen *n* [BOOKISH] 貴賎 rank

kisétsu *n* 季節 season: **~-fū** 季節風 seasonal wind

kishá *n* 汽車 (*non-electric/steam*) train

kishá *n* 記者 = **shinbun-~** 新聞記者 newspaper reporter, journalist

kishí *n* 岸 shore, bank

kishi-men *n* きしめん long thin udon

kishitsu *n* 気質 temperament

kishō *n* 気象 weather: **~-dai** 気象台 weather observatory

kishúkúsha *n* 寄宿舎 dormitory; boarding house

kisó *n* 基礎 base, foundation

kisoimásu, kisóu *v* 競います, 競う competes, vies

kisóku *n* 規則 rule, regulation

kissa-ten *n* 喫茶店 a tearoom, a coffee house, a café

kisu *n* キス kiss

kisu *n* キス・鱚 sillago (fish)

kita *n* 北 north: **~-guchi** 北口 the north exit/entrance; Kita-Ámerika *n* 北アメリカ North America; Kita-Chōsén *n* 北朝鮮 North Korea; kita-yori *adj* 北寄り northerly: ~ **no kaze** 北寄りの風 northerly wind

kitaemásu, kitaéru *v* 鍛えます, 鍛える forges, tempers; drills, disciplines

kitai *n* 期待 expectation

kitai *n* 気体 vapor, a gas

kitaku *n* 帰宅 returning home

kitanái *adj* 汚い dirty; untidy, messy

kite *v* 着て: **kite-ikimásu/kimásu** 着ていきます/きます wears it there/here → **kimásu** 着ます

kitei *n* [BOOKISH] 規定 regulation, rule, stipulation: ~ **no …** 規定の … regular, stipulated, compulsory

kiteki *n* 汽笛 whistle (*steam*)

kiten *n* 機転 wit: ~ **no kiku** 機転の利く quick-witted

kitsuen *n* 喫煙 smoking; kitsuén-sha *n* 喫煙者 smoker; kitsuén-shitsu(/-

seki) *n* 喫煙室(/席) smoking room (*area/zone/seat*)

kitsúi *adj* きつい **1.** tight: **suke-jūru ga ~ (desu)** スケジュールがきつい(です) (*one's*) schedule is tight; **uesuto ga ~ (desu)** ウエストがきつい(です) is tight in the waist **2.** severe, hard, strict: **~ seikaku** きつい性格 strict character

kitsune *n* キツネ・狐 fox

kitte *n* 切手 (*postage*) stamp: **~-chō** 切手帳 stamp album

kítto *adv* きっと surely, doubtless, no doubt, undoubtedly

kiwá *n* 際 brink, edge

kiwadói *adj* 際どい delicate, dangerous, ticklish

kiwamarimásu, kiwamáru *v* 極まります, 極まる comes to an end; gets carried to extremes

kiwamemásu, kiwaméru *v* 極めます, 極める carries to extremes

kiwamemásu, kiwaméru *v* 究めます, 究める investigates thoroughly

kiwámete *adv* 極めて extremely

kiyase *adj* 着やせ looking thinner in clothes

kíyō (na) *adj* 器用(な) skillful, nimble, clever

kizamimásu, kizamu *v* 刻みます, 刻む chops fine; carves, engraves; notches, nicks

kizashi *n* 兆し sign(s), symptom(s), hint(s), indication(s), omen(s)

kizu *n* きず・傷・疵・瑕 wound; scratch, crack, flaw, blemish; fault, defect

kizu-ato *n* 傷跡 scar

ki-zúkai *n* 気遣い anxiety, concern, worry, care (= **hairyo** 配慮, **kokoro-kubari** 心配り)

ki-zukaimásu, ki-zukáu *v* 気遣います, 気遣う is anxious/worried about, is concerned over

ki-zukimásu, ki-zúku *v* 気付きます, 気付く notices

ki-zukimásu, ki-zúku *v* 築きます, 築く builds it

kizu-tsukemásu, kizu-tsukéru *v* 傷つけます, 傷つける wounds, injures, damages

kizu-tsukimásu, kizu-tsúku *v* 傷つきます, 傷つく gets wounded, injured, damaged

ko *n* 子 child (= (*person*) **kodomo** 子供)

ko *n* 仔 child (*animals in particular*): **ko-néko** 仔猫 kitten, **ko-inu** 仔犬 puppy, **ko-buta** 仔豚 piglet

kó, koná *n* 粉 flour

ko-... *prefix* 小… little…, small…: **~-bako** 小箱 small box

...´-ko *suffix* …個 (*counts small objects*)

...´-ko *suffix* …湖 Lake…

kō *adv* こう (**kō´** こう + [PARTICLE], **kō´désu** こうです) this way, so, like this

kō´ *n* 香 incense: **~ o takimásu** 香を焚きます burns incense (*in a temple, before the memorial tablet of the deceased, etc.*)

kō-... *prefix* 高… high…:

~-kétsúatsu 高血圧 high blood pressure

...´-kō *suffix* …港 port (*of* …): **Kōbé-~** 神戸港 the port of Kobe

...´-kō *suffix* …校 school, branch (*school*); [BOOKISH] counter for schools

kōbá, kōjō *n* 工場 factory, plant

kobamimásu, kobámu *v* 拒みます, 拒む refuses, rejects; opposes, resists

kóban *n* 小判 Japanese old coins made of gold (*Edo period*)

kōban *n* 交番 police box

kobanashi *n* 小話 anecdote

kobaruto *n* コバルト cobalt: **~-iro** コバルト色, **~-burū** コバルトブルー cobalt blue

Kōbe *n* 神戸 Kobe; **Kōbé-Eki** 神戸駅 Kobe Station

kobito *n* 小人 dwarf

koboremásu, koboréru *v* こぼれます, こぼれる it spills

koboshimásu, kobósu *v* こぼします, こぼす spills it: **guchi o ~** 愚痴をこぼします grumbles, complains

kobú *n* こぶ・瘤 swelling, lump, hump: **rakuda no ~** ラクダのこぶ hump(s) on a camel

kó-bun *n* 子分 henchman, subordinate, follower

kobune *n* 小舟 small boat

kobura *n* コブラ cobra

kobushi *n* こぶし・拳 fist (= **nigiri-~** 握り拳)

ko-buta *n* 子豚・仔豚 piglet(s), little pig(s)

kōbutsu *n* 好物 favorite (*food/drink*)

kōcha *n* 紅茶 (black/red) tea

kō´chi *n* コーチ coach (*sports*)

kochira *pron* こちら **1.** this one (*of two*) **2.** here, this way **3.** I/me, we/us

kochira-gawa *n* こちら側 this/my/our side

kochō *n* [BOOKISH] 誇張 exaggeration

kōchō *n* 校長 principal/head of a school (*elementary school, junior/senior high school*)

kōchō (na) *adj* [BOOKISH] 好調(な) satisfactory, favorable, in a good condition: **~ na dedashi/suberidashi/sutāto** 好調な出だし/滑り出し/スタート flying start, good start

kódai *n* 古代 ancient times: **~ no** 古代の ancient: **~-iseki** 古代遺跡 ancient monument(s)

ko-dakara *n* 子宝 child(ren): **~ ni megumaremásu** 子宝に恵まれます is blessed with child(ren), has a baby/babies

kodama *n* こだま echo

kōdan *n* 公団 public corporation

kōdan *n* 講壇 lecture platform

kodō *n* 鼓動 heartbeat, pulse: **shinzō no ~** 心臓の鼓動 beat of the heart

kō´do *n* コード **1.** (*electricity*) cord **2.** code

kō´do *n* 高度 high degree, altitude

kōdō *n* 公道 highway

kōdō *n* 行動 action, behavior

kōdō *n* 講堂 public (*lecture*) hall, auditorium
kodoku *n* 孤独 loneliness
kodomo *n* 子供 child (= **ko** 子): **~-tachi** 子供たち[達] children; **~-no-hí** こどもの日 Children's Day (*5 May*); **~ no koro** 子供の頃 one's early years
kóe *n* 声 voice; cry: **~ o dáshite** 声を出して aloud, out loud
koeda *n* 小枝 twig
koemásu, koeru *v* 超[越]えます, 超[越]える crosses (*a height, an obstacle*) → **koshimásu, kosu** 超[越]します, 超[越]す
koemásu, koéru *v* 肥えます, 肥える gets fat (= **futorimásu** 太ります)
kōen *n* 公園 public park
kōen *n* [BOOKISH] 講演 lecture, speech, talk
kōen *n* [BOOKISH] 後援 support, backing
koeru... *adj* 超える: **o ~ ...** (を)超える… over…, more than… (*people, country, money, temperature, etc.*); **(sen)-nin o ~ hito** (千)人を超える人 over/more than (one thousand) people
kōfuku *n* 幸福 happiness: **~ (na)** 幸福(な) happy
kōfuku *n* 降伏 surrender
kōfun *n* 興奮 excitement: **~ shite imásu** 興奮しています is excited
kōgai *n* 公害 (*environmental*) pollution
kōgai *n* 郊外 suburbs, suburbia
kōgaku *n* 工学 engineering
kōgaku-shin *n* 向学心 desire to learn: **~ ni moeteimásu** 向学心に燃えています has a strong desire to learn
kogan *n* [BOOKISH] 湖岸 lakeshore
kōgan *n* 睾丸 testicle(s) [FORMAL]
kōgan *n* 紅顔 peaches and cream, rosy, fresh face (*of young man*)
kōgan *n* [BOOKISH] 厚顔 impudence: **~-muchi (no)** 厚顔無恥(の) impudent and shameless
kōgan-zai *n* 抗がん剤 anticancer drug
kogashimásu, kogásu *v* 焦がします, 焦がす scorches it
kogata (no) *adj* 小型(の) small-size (*model*)
kōgeki *n* 攻撃 attack
kogemásu, kogéru *v* 焦げます, 焦げる gets scorched/burned
kō´gi *n* 講義 lecture
kō´gí *n* 抗議 protest
kogimásu, kógu *v* 漕ぎます, 漕ぐ rows (*a boat*)
kogítte *n* 小切手 (*bank*) check
kōgo *n* 口語 spoken language, colloquial (*word*): **~-teki (na)** 口語的(な) colloquial
kogoe *n* 小声 low voice, whisper
Kōgō´(-sama) *n* 皇后(様) the Empress
kogoto *n* 小言 scolding, complaint
kō´gyō *n* 工業 industry
kohada *n* コハダ shad
kōhai *n* 後輩 one's junior (*colleague, fellow student*)
kohaku *n* コハク・琥珀 **1. = kon-iro**

コハク・琥珀(色) amber (*color*) **2.** taffeta elastic webbing **3. ~(san)** コハク・琥珀(酸) succinic acid

kohan *n* [BOOKISH] 湖畔 lakeside

kōhei (na) *adj* 公平(な) fair, impartial

kōhii *n* コーヒー coffee: **~-jáwan/-káppu** コーヒー茶碗/カップ coffee cup; **~-ten/-ya** コーヒー店/屋 coffee shop/house (= **kissaten** 喫茶店)

ko-hịtsúji *n* 小羊・子羊 lamb, small sheep

kōhyō *n* [BOOKISH] 好評 favorable criticism

kói *n* 請い・乞い request (= **tanomí** 頼み)

kói *n* コイ・鯉 carp (*fish*)

kói *n* 恋 love (*affair*), romance

kói (no) *adj* 故意(の) deliberate; **~ ni** 故意に deliberately

kói *n* 濃い deep (*color*), strong (*coffee, tea, taste*), well saturated

kō´i *n* [BOOKISH] 好意・厚意 goodwill, favor: **~ o misemásu** 好意を見せます does a favor

kō´i *n* 行為 act, deed; behavior

koibito *n* 恋人 sweetheart, lover, boyfriend/girlfriend

kóin *n* コイン coin: **~-rókkā** コインロッカー coin locker

kōin *n* 工員 factory worker

koi-nóbori *n* コイ[鯉]のぼり carp streamers (*for Children's Day (5 May)*)

ko-inu *n* 小犬・子犬・仔犬 puppy/puppies, small dog(s)

koiru *n* コイル coil

koitsu *n* こいつ this damn one: **~-ra** こいつら these damn ones

kóji *n* 孤児 orphan: **~-in** 孤児院 orphanage

kō´ji *n* 工事 construction work

kojikí *n* こじき・乞食 beggar

kójin *n* 個人 an individual; **kojin-teki (na)** *n* 個人的(な) individual, personal: **~-teki (na) iken** 個人的(な)意見 personal opinion

kojiremás̱u, kojiréru *v* こじれます, こじれる gets complicated, twisted, entangled; (*illness*) worsens

kōjitsu *n* 口実 excuse, pretext

kojō (de/no) *adv, adj* 湖上(で/の) on the lake (*surface*)

kojō *n* 古城 old castle

kōjō´ *n* 工場 factory, plant

kōjyutsu *n* 口述 dictation

kōjyutsu (no) *adj* 後述(の) after-mentioned

kokan *n* [BOOKISH] 股間 between the legs: **~-setsu** 股関節 hip joint

kō´ka *n* 効果 effect: **hiyō-~** 費用効果 cost effect

kō´ka *n* 硬貨 coin

kō´ka *n* 高価 high price: **~ (na) …** 高価(な) . . . expensive … (= **takai** 高い)

kō´kai *n* 航海 voyage

kō´kai *n* 後悔 regret

kōkai (no) *adj* 公開(の) open to the public, open, public: **eiga no ~** 映画の公開 movie release

kokáin *n* コカイン cocaine

kōkan *n* 交換 exchange; **meishi-~** 名刺交換 exchanging business

cards; **~-ryūgakusei** *n* 交換留学生 exchange student
kōkan-shinkei *n* 交感神経 sympathetic nerve
kōkán-shu *n* 交換手 operator
kōkatsu (na) *adj* 狡猾(な) sly
koké *n* 苔 moss
koké *n* こけ foolishness, a fool: **~ ni saremás<u>u</u>** こけにされます gets trashed
kō-kéiki *n* 好景気 prosperity, good business conditions
kō-ki *n* [BOOKISH] 好機 (*favorable*) opportunity, chance, occasion
kō-ki *n* [BOOKISH] 香気 aroma
kō-ki *n* 後期 the latter period
kō-ki *n* 後記 afterword, postscript (= **ato-gaki** 後書き): **henshū-~** 編集後記 editor's postscript
kō-kí (shin) *n* 好奇(心) curiosity, inquisitiveness
kō-kíatsu *n* 高気圧 high (*barometric*) pressure
kókka *n* 国家 nation
kokkai *n* 国会 assembly, parliament, congress, Diet (= **gikai** 議会)
kokkei (na) *adj* こっけい[滑稽](な) amusing, funny
kokki *n* 国旗 national flag
kokkō *n* 国交 diplomatic relations
kókku (-san) *n* コック(さん) cook, chef
kokkyō *n* 国境 border (*of country*)
koko *pron* ここ here, this place
kō-kō *n* 高校 senior high school
kókóa *n* ココア cocoa
kōkoku *n* 広告 advertisement
kókóná(t)tsu *n* ココナ(ッ)ツ coconut (= **koko-yashi no mi** ココヤシの実)
kokonoka *n* 九日 nine days; the 9th day (*of month*)
kokónotsu *n* 九つ nine; nine years old (= **kyūsai** 九歳)
kokóro *n* 心 mind, heart, spirit, feeling: **~ kara (no)** 心からの) heart-felt, sincere; **kokoro-atari** *n* 心当たり idea; **kokoro-bosói** *adj* 心細い lonely; **kokoro-kubari** *n* 心配り concern, care (= **hairyo** 配慮, **ki-zúkai** 気遣い)
kokoromi *n* 試み trial, attempt, test
kokoromimás<u>u</u>, kokoromíru *v* 試みます, 試みる tries, attempts, tests
kokoro-mochi *n* 心持ち feelings, spirit, mood
kokorozashi *n* 志 **1.** mind; intention; purpose **2.** ambition, hope **3.** goodwill, kindness; gift
kokorozashimás<u>u</u>, kokorozásu *v* 志します, 志す sets one's mind
kokoro-zuke *n* 心付け tip, gratuity (= **chippu** チップ)
kokoro-zuyói *adj* 心強い encouraging, heartening: **~ sonzai** 心強い存在 dependable person
kōkō´-sei *n* 高校生 (*senior*) high-school student: **joshi/danshi ~** 女子/男子高生 high-school girl/boy
...´-koku *suffix* …国 **1.** (*name of certain*) country: **Bei-koku** 米国 America (= **Amerika** アメリカ America, U.S.(A.), **Chū´-goku**

中国 China, **Nihón-koku** 日本国 Japan (= **Nihón, Nippón** 日本)
2. koku-... 国... national, state
kokuban *n* 黒板 blackboard: **~-keshi** 黒板消し, **~-fuki** 黒板拭き eraser
kōkū-bin *n* 航空便 = **kōkū-yū´bin** 航空郵便 airmail
kokubō *n* 国防 national defense
kokudō *n* 国道 highway
Kokudo-Kōtsū-shō *n* 国土交通省 Ministry of Land, Infrastructure, Transport and Tourism (MLIT)
kōkū-gáisha *n* 航空会社 airline company
kokujin *n* 黒人 black people, Afro-American
kokumin *n* 国民 a people, a nation; national(s), citizen(s)
kokúmotsu *n* 穀物 grain (*cereal*)
kokúnai (no) *adj* 国内(の) internal, domestic, inland
kokuritsu (-) *adj* 国立 national, government-established: **~-toshokan** 国立図書館 national library: **~-daigaku** 国立大学 national university
kokúrui *n* 穀類 cereal(s), grain
kokusai *n* 国際: **~-dénwa** 国際電話 international phone call
Kokusai-réngō *n* 国際連合 United Nations
kokusan (no) *adj* 国産(の) domestic(ally) made, made in Japan: **~-hin** 国産品 domestic product: **~-sha** 国産車 domestic car
kokuseki *n* 国籍 nationality
kōkū-shókan *n* 航空書簡 aerogram
kōkyo *n* 皇居 palace (*in Tokyo*); the Imperial Palace
kókyō *n* 故郷 hometown, birthplace (= **furusato** ふるさと)
kōkyō (no) *adj* 公共(の) public: **~-ba** 公共の場 public area
kōkyō-ryō´kin *n* 公共料金 utility bills/charges
kokyū *n* 呼吸 respiration, breathing
kōkyū (na) *adj* 高級(な) high-class/grade, high-ranking; fancy: **~-hin** 高級品 fancy goods
kóma *n* こま・コマ・独楽 a toy top: **~-máwashi** 独楽回し top-spinning
komakái *adj* 細かい **1.** fine, small **2.** detailed, exact **3.** thrifty **4.** small (*change*): **komakakú shimásu** 細かくします cashes it into smaller bills/coins
koma-mono *n* 小間物 notions, haberdashery, dime-store goods
komarasemásu, komaraséru *v* 困らせます, 困らせる bothers, embarrasses
komarimásu, komáru *v* 困ります, 困る gets perplexed, embarrassed, troubled; is at a loss; is in need: **komáru tokoró** 困るところ trouble (*difficulty*)
komāsharu *n* コマーシャル commercial (*message*) (= **shiiému** シーエム): **terebi-~** テレビコマーシャル TV commercial
komayaka (na) *adj* こま[細・濃]や

か(な) meticulous, attentive, tender: **~ na aijō** 細やかな愛情 tender love: **(kime-)~ na shidō** (きめ)細やかな指導 detailed instruction

komé *n* コメ・米 rice (*hulled, uncooked*); **komé-ya** *n* 米屋 rice dealer/store

komemásu, koméru *v* 込めます, 込める includes

komichi *n* 小道 path, lane

komi-itta *v* 込み入った complicated, intricate (*situation, subject*)

komimásu, kómu *v* 込み[混み]ます, 込む・混む gets crowded; **kónde-imásu** 混んでいます is crowded

kōmin *n* 公民 citizen, civilian

kōmoku *n* 項目 item: **(nyūryoku) hissu-~** (入力)必須項目 mandatory field(s)

kómon *n* [BOOKISH] 顧問 consultant, adviser

kōmon *n* 校門 school gate

kōmon *n* 肛門 anus

komórí *n* 子守, 子守り babysitter: **~-uta** 子守歌[唄] lullaby, cradle song

kō´mori *n* コウモリ bat (*flying mammal*); **kōmori-gása** *n* こうもり[コウモリ]傘 umbrella (*black, cloth umbrella often used by males in Japan*)

komúgi *n* 小麦 wheat: **~-ko** 小麦粉 wheat flour

kōmú-in *n* 公務員 government worker/employee, official

kōmurimásu, kōmúru *v* 被ります, 被る sustains, suffers, incurs (*unfair treatment, tribulation*): **dai-songai o ~** 大損害を被ります suffers a serious loss

kón *n* 紺 = **~-iro** 紺色 (dark blue)

koná *n* 粉 powder; flour; **kona-gona** *n* 粉々 in very small pieces; **kona-gúsuri** *n* 粉薬 powdered medicine

kō´nai *n* 構内 campus

konaidá *adv* こないだ, **kono-aidá** この間 the other day, a while ago, lately

konashimásu, konasu *v* こなします, こなす **1.** powders; digests **2.** (ful)fills, manages (*to do it*): **chūmon o ~** 注文をこなします fills an order

kónban *n* 今晩 tonight: **Konban wa** こんばんは Good evening.

konbini(-ensu sutoā) *n* コンビニ(エンスストアー) convenience store

konbō *n* [BOOKISH] 棍棒 club, billy-club, bludgeon

kónbu *n* コンブ・昆布 kelp (*a kind of seaweed*)

konchū *n* 昆虫 insect

kondate *n* [BOOKISH] 献立 menu

kóndo *n, adv* 今度 this time; next

kondō´mu *n* コンドーム condom

kóne *n* コネ connection, "pull": **(hito ni) ~ o tsukemásu** (人に)コネを付けます establishes a connection (*with a person*)

ko-néko *n* 小猫・子猫・仔猫 kitten(s), small cat(s)

konekutā *n* コネクター connector

kongan *n* [BOOKISH] 懇願 entreaty

kongari yakimásu̲ (yaku) *v* こんがり焼きます(焼く) bakes/toasts/roasts/grills/sunburns until a beautiful brown

kongetsu *n* 今月 this month

kongō´-seki *n* [BOOKISH] 金剛石 diamond

kongo (wa) *adv* 今後(は) from now on, in the future

koni (na/ni) *adj, adv* 懇意(な/に) friendly, close, intimate: **... to ~ ni shiteimásu̲** ...と懇意にしています is very intimate with...

konin *n* 婚姻 marriage (= **kekkon** 結婚): **~-todoke** 婚姻届 marriage notification

kōnin (no) *adj* 公認(の) authorized, certified: **~-kaikéishi** 公認会計士 certified public accountant (CPA), chartered accountant

kon (iro) *n* 紺(色) dark blue

konkai *n, adv* 今回 this time

konkan *n* 根幹 [BOOKISH] basis, foundation

konki *n* 根気 [BOOKISH] patience: **~ ga iru shigoto** 根気がいる仕事 work which requires patience

konki *n* 婚期 [BOOKISH] marriageable age: **~ o nogasu** 婚期を逃す is past marriageable age

konkurabe *n* 根比べ waiting game, endurance contest

konkuríito *n* コンクリート concrete (*cement*)

konkū´ru *n* コンクール prize contest, prize competition (= **konpe** コンペ)

kónkyo *n* 根拠 [BOOKISH] basis, grounds, authority, evidence: **~-chi** 根拠地 base, home ground

konkyū *n* 困窮 [BOOKISH] poverty: **~ shite imásu** 困窮しています is in poverty, is in financial difficulties

konna ... *adj* こんな... such as, this kind of: **~ ni** こんなに to this extent, this much

kónnan *n* 困難 difficulty, trouble, hardship; **kónnan (na)** *adj* 困難(な) difficult

Konnichi wa *interj* こんにちは Good afternoon; Hello!

konnyákú *n* コンニャク devil's-tongue root made into gelatin

kono... *adj* この... this ..., these...; **kono-aidá** *adv* この間 the other day, a while ago, lately (= **konaidá** こないだ); **kono-goro** *adv* この頃 recently (= **chiká goro** 近頃, **saikin** 最近); **kono-máe (no)...** *adj* この前(の)... the last...; **kono-tsúgi** *n* この次 next time (= **jikai** 次回)

kōnō *n* 効能 effect (*effectiveness*) (= **kōyō** 効用, **kiki-me** 効き目)

kónomi *n* 好み liking, taste: **~ no ...** 好みの... that one likes, that is to one's taste/liking, favorite ...: **~ no taipu** 好みのタイプ one's type

konomimásu̲, konómu *v* 好みます, 好む likes, is fond of, prefers

kónpasu *n* コンパス compass (*for drafting*)

konpe *n* コンペ prize competition, prize contest
konpon *n* 根本 [BOOKISH] foundation, basis: **~-teki (na)** 根本的(な) fundamental, basic
konpyū´ta *n* コンピュータ computer
konran *n* 混乱 [BOOKISH] mess (*disorder*), confusion, jumble
kónro *n* コンロ stove (*portable cooking*)
konsárutanto *n* コンサルタント consultant: **keiei-~** 経営コンサルタント management consultant
konseki *n* 痕跡 [BOOKISH] trace, mark, vestige (= **áto** 跡): **~ o nokoshimás<u>u</u>** 痕跡を残します leaves a mark
kónsénto *n* コンセント **1.** (*light*) plug, (*electricity*) outlet: **~ ni tsunagimás<u>u</u>** コンセントにつなぎます plugs in **2.** consent: **infōmudo-~** インフォームド・コンセント informed consent
konshū *n* 今週 this week
kōn-sutāchi *n* コーンスターチ cornstarch
konták<u>u</u>to *n* コンタクト = **~-rénzu** コンタクトレンズ contact lenses
kónténa *n* コンテナ container (*for transporting goods*)
kóntes<u>u</u>to *n* コンテスト contest
kón'ya *n* 今夜 tonight
kon'yaku *n* 婚約 engagement (*to be married*): **~-yubiwa** 婚約指輪 engagement ring
kon'yoku *n* 混浴 (*hot springs*) mixed bathing
kónzatsu *n* 混雑 jam, congestion: **~ shitei más<u>u</u>** 混雑しています is crowded
kópii *n* コピー copy (*photocopy*)
koppamijin-ni-narimás<u>u</u> (náru) *v* 木っ端微塵になります(なる) is smashed to pieces
koppu *n* コップ a glass, a cup
kōra *n* コウラ・甲羅 shell (*of tortoise, etc.*)
kō´ra *n* コーラ cola
koraemás<u>u</u>, koráéru *v* 堪えます, 堪える **1.** stands, bears **2.** controls, restrains, represses
kōran *n* コーラン the Koran, the Quran
koramu *n* コラム column, boxed article(s) (= **kakomi-kiji** 囲み記事)
kōrasemásu, kōraseru *v* 凍らせます, 凍らせる freezes it
kō´rasu *n* コーラス chorus, choir
kore *pron* これ this one: **~ kara** これから from now on; **~ kara to i<u>u</u>/y<u>ū</u> …** これという/ゆう… specific, particular
koréra (no) *adj* これら(の) these (*things, matters, etc.*)
kórera *n* コレラ cholera
korí 凝り *n* stiffness, hardening: **káta-(no)-~** 肩(の)こり a stiff shoulder
kōri *n* 氷 ice : **kaki-gōri** かき氷 shaved ice (*eaten with syrup*)
kōri/kóri *n* 行李 wicker trunk
korimás<u>u</u>, kóru *v* 凝ります, 凝る **1.** gets engrossed/absorbed (*in*) **2.** (*shoulder*) gets stiff

korimásu, koriru *v* 懲ります, 懲りる learns a lesson from one's failure

kōrimásu, kōru *v* 凍ります, 凍る it freezes

kōritsu (no) *adj* 公立(の) public, municipal, prefectural

kōritsu *n* 効率 efficiency: **~-teki na** 効率的な efficient: **gyōmu no ~ka** 業務の効率化 streamlining

...koro *suffix* 頃 (*at that*) time, (*at*) about (*a time*), occasion (= **... góro (ni)** ...頃(に) (*at*) about (*a time*)): **ano-~ (wa)** あの頃(は) (*at*) that time, then, (*in*) those days (= **tō´ji (wa)** 当時(は)

koroai *n* 頃合い suitable time: **(sorosoro) ~ desu** (そろそろ)頃合いです It's (about) time to...

korobimásu, korobu *v* 転びます, 転ぶ falls down, tumbles

korogarimásu, korogaru *v* 転がります, 転がる it rolls, tumbles

korogashimásu, korogasu *v* 転がします, 転がす rolls it

koroshimásu, korosu *v* 殺します, 殺す kills

Korukata *n* コルカタ Kolkata (*Calcutta*)

kóruku *n* コルク = **~-sen** コルク栓 cork; korukú-nuki *n* コルク抜き corkscrew

kō´ryo *n* 考慮 consideration, reflection, thought; **~ o ni iremásu** 考慮に入れます takes into consideration/account

kō´ryō´ *n* 香料 spice

koryōrí-ya *n* 小料理屋 small traditional Japanese restaurant

kōryū *n* 交流 **1.** AC (alternating current) **2. ~ shimásu** 交流します exchanges, interchanges

kósa *n* 濃さ strength (*of saturation*), deepness (*of color*)

kosaemásu, kosaeru *v* こさえます, こさえる = **koshiraemásu** こしらえます makes, concocts

kōsai *n* 交際 social relations, company, association: **~-hi** 交際費 an expense account

ko-saji *n* 小さじ teaspoon

kōsaku shimásu (suru) *v* 工作します(する) **1.** builds **2.** handcrafts

kosame *n* 小雨 light rain, drizzle

kōsan *n* 降参 surrender

kōsa-ten *n* 交差点 an intersection (*of streets*), a crossing

kosei *n* 個性 individuality, character, personality: **~-teki** 個性的 unique (= **yuniiku** ユニーク): **~-yutaka** 個性豊か has a very distinctive personality

kōsei *n* 構成 constitution, construction, composition

kōsei *n* 更正 reclamation, reformation

kōsei *n* 更生 revival, reformation; regeneration, rehabilitation: **hikōshōnen no ~** 非行少年の更生 rehabilitation of juvenile delinquents

kōsei *n* 公正 impartiality; kōsei na 公正(な) *adj* impartial, fair

kōsei *n* 校正 proofreading; kōsei-

sha, kōsei-gakari *n* 校正者, 校正係 proofreader
kōsei-bússhitsu *n* 抗生物資 antibiotic(s)
Kōsei-Rōdō-shō *n* 厚生労働省 Ministry of Health, Labor and Welfare
koseki *n* 戸籍 family register: **~-tōhon** 戸籍謄本 full copy of one's family register: **~-shōhon** 戸籍写本 abstract of one's family register
kōsen *n* 光線 ray, beam (*of light*), light
kōsha *n* 後者 the latter
kōsha *n* 校舎 school-house
koshi *n* 腰 loin, hip, lower part of back; koshi-káké *n* 腰掛け seat, chair, bench (= **isu** いす・椅子); koshi -no-kubire *n* 腰のくびれ waist (= **uesuto** ウエスト)
kō´shi *n* 講師 instructor(s), lecturer(s)
Kōshi *n* 孔子 Confucius
koshi̱-kakemásu̱, koshi-kakéru *v* 腰掛けます, 腰掛ける sits down
koshimásu̱, kosu *v* 越します・越す goes/runs over, goes across, moves house (= **hikkoshimásu** 引っ越します)
koshimásu̱, kosu *v* 超します, 超す goes/runs over (= **chō´ka shimásu** 超過します, **ō´bā shimásu** オーバーします); exceeds: **do o ~** 度を超します goes too far
koshimásu, kosu *v* 漉します, 漉す filters/strains it
kōshin *n* 行進 march(ing)
kōshin *n* 更新 renewal, update
kōshin shimásu (suru) *v* 行進します(する) marches
kōshin shimásu (suru) *v* 更新します(する) renews, updates (*a contract, website, etc.*)
koshiraemásu̱, koshiraeru *v* 拵えます, 拵える makes, concocts
kosho *n* 古書 **1.** old book(s), antique book(s) **2.** secondhand book(s) **(= furu-hon** 古本)
koshō *n* 故障 **1.** breakdown, something is wrong **2.** hindrance
koshō´ *n* コショウ・胡椒 pepper
koshō *n* 呼称 appellation, name
kōshō *n* 交渉 negotiations
kōshoku (na) *adj* 好色(な) erotic; lecherous: **~-kan** 好色漢 lecher
kōshū *n* 公衆 the public, the masses: **~-dénwa** 公衆電話 public telephone; kōshū no *adj* 公衆の public
kōshū(kai) *n* 講習(会) lecture class, course (*not regular classes in school*)
... kóso (masani) *adv* …こそ(まさに) precisely, exactly, just; certainly, really → **másu-ni** まさに・正に: **kare-~** 彼こそ he is truly
kōsō (no) *adj* 高層(の) high-rise: **~-bíru** 高層ビル high-rise building, skyscraper
kōsoku *n* 高速 [BOOKISH] high speed: **~-dō´ro** 高速道路 expressway, freeway
kossetsu *n* 骨折 bone fracture
kossori (to) *adv* こっそり(と) secretly, sneakily, on the sly

kōsu *n* コース course; (*traffic, swim*) lane; a set series of chef's choices, a set meal
kosuchūmu *n* コスチューム costume (= **kasō** 仮装)
kōsui *n* 香水 perfume: **~ no kaori** 香水の香り fragrance of perfume
kosupure *n* コスプレ cosplay
kosurimásu, kosúru *v* 擦ります, 擦る rubs, scrapes
kotáé *n* 答(え) an answer, reply, response (= **henjí** 返事, **hentō** 返答)
kotáé *n* 応え a response, an answer (= **henjí** 返事, **hentō** 返答, **ōtō** 応答) (= → **tegótae** 手応え)
kotaemásu, kotáéru *v* 答えます, 答える answers
kotaemásu, kotáéru *v* 応えます, 応える responds, lives up to, meets: **kitai ni ~** 期待に応えます lives up to one's expectations: **yōbō ni ~** 要望に応えます meets one's request
kotai *n* 固体 a solid
kōtai *n* 交替 alternation
Kōtáishi *n* 皇太子, **~-sama** 皇太子さま the Crown Prince; **Kōtáishi-hi** *n* 皇太子妃 the Crown Princess
kōtaku *n* 光沢 luster, gloss, sheen: **~ ga arimásu** 光沢があります lustrous, glossy, shiny
kotatsu *n* こたつ (**o-kóta** おこた) traditional quilt-covered heating arrangement (*foot warmer*)
kotchí *pron* こっち → **kochira** こちら
kotei *n* 固定 fixation
kōtei *n* 校庭 school grounds
kōtei *n* 肯定 affirmation
kōtei *n* 皇帝 emperor: **Rōma-~** ローマ皇帝 Roman emperor
kōtei *n* 工程 [BOOKISH] process, progress: **seisaku-~** 製作工程 process for forming: **sagyō-~** 作業工程 working process
kotēji *n* コテージ cottage
koten *n* 古典 classic work (*literature, art, etc.*) (= **kurashikku** クラシック): **~-ongaku** 古典音楽 classical music
koten *n* 個展 private exhibition
kotesaki de gomakashimásu (gomakasu) *v* 小手先でごまかします (ごまかす) uses cheap tricks
kote-shirabe (ni) *adv* 小手調べ(に) (*for*) a trial, (*for*) practice
kōtetsu *n* 鋼鉄 [BOOKISH] steel (= **suchiiru** スチール)
kotó *n* こと・事 thing, matter; fact; words, sentence; case, circumstance, happening; experience: **... suru ~ ga arimásu** ...することがあります does/do it sometimes, has something to do; **... suru ~ wa arimasén** ...することはありません never does it; **... shita ~ ga arimásu** ...したことがあります has done it before; **... (suru/shinai) ~ wa arimasén** ...(する/しない)ことはありません it isn't that one (does/doesn't, will/won't do it); **... (suru) ~ ni shimásu** ...(する)ことにします

decides to (*do it*)

kóto *n* 琴 Japanese harp; koto-ji *n* 琴柱 [BOOKISH] the bridges on a Japanese harp

kóto *n* 古都 [BOOKISH] ancient capital

kṓ'to *n* コート **1.** coat **2.** (*sports*) court: **tenisu-~** テニスコート tennis court

kotō *n* 孤島 [BOOKISH] solitary island

kotobá *n* 言葉 **1.** word, words; sentence (*spoken*); remark **2.** speech **3.** language (= **gengo** 言語); **o-kotoba o kaesu yō desu ga…** お言葉を返すようですが … I hate to (*don't mean to*) contradict you, but…

kōtō-gákkō *n* 高等学校 = **kōkō** 高校 high school: **~ no séito** 高等学校の生徒 (= **kōkō´-sei** 高校生) high-school student

kotogara *n* 事柄 [BOOKISH] affair, matter (= **kotó** こと・事)

kotonarimásu, kotonáru *v* 異なります, 異なる is different, differs

kóto-ni *adv* ことに・殊に **1.** especially (= **tóku-ni** 特に) **2.** [+ NEGATIVE] less likely **3.** moreover, what is more

kōtō (no) *adj* 口頭(の) oral, verbal: **kōtō-shímon** 口頭試問 oral examination

ko-tori *n* 小鳥 small bird

kotosara *adv* ことさら particularly

kotoshi *n* 今年 this year

kototarimásu, kototariru *v* 事足ります, 事足りる suffices, is enough: **… to ie ba ~** … と言えば事足ります suffice to say that …

kotowárí *n* 断り refusal; notice, warning; permission: **~ mo náku** 断りもなく without notice/permission/leave

kotowarimásu, kotowáru *v* 断ります, 断る **1.** refuses, declines, begs off **2.** makes excuses **3.** gives notice **4.** dismisses, lays off

kotowaza *n* ことわざ・諺 proverb(s)

kotozuké, kotozute *n* 言付け, 言づて a message (*for someone*) (= **mésseji** メッセージ)

kotsú *n* こつ[コツ] knack, trick, tip

kōtsū *n* 交通 traffic, transportation; communication(s): **~-hyō´shiki** 交通標識 traffic signs; **~-shíngō** 交通信号 traffic signal(s)

kotsuban *n* 骨盤 pelvis

kotsubu *n* 小粒 small grain

kō-tsugō *n* 好都合 (*convenience*) expediency

kōtsūjūtai *n* traffic jam 交通渋滞

kotsúzui *n* 骨髄 bone marrow

kottō´-hin *n* 骨董品 curios, antiques

kotton *n* コットン cotton

kōun *n* 幸運 good fortune

ko-uri *n* 小売り retail; kouri-gyō *n* 小売業 retail business; kouri-ten *n* 小売店 retail store, retailer

kowagari *n* 怖[恐]がり a coward (= **okubyō-monó** 臆病者):

kowagarimásu 怖[恐]がります fears, takes flight, is afraid

kowái *adj* こわい・怖[恐]い is afraid; frightful; terrific

kowairo *n* 声色 **1.** tone of voice **2.** impersonation: **~ o tsukaimásu** 声色を使います impersonates

kowane *n* 声音 tone of voice (= **kowairo** 声色)

kowaremásu, kowaréru *v* 壊れます, ~ 壊れる it breaks/smashes

kowaremono *n* こわれ物 fragile (*article*): **kowaremono-chū´i** こわれ物注意 Handle With Care

koware-yasúi *adj* 壊れやすい fragile, easily broken, breakable

kowashimásu, kowásu *v* 壊します, 壊す breaks/smashes it, destroys: **kuruma o ~** 車を壊します wrecks a car; **karada o ~** 体をこわします ruins one's health

koya *n* 小屋 hut, shed, cabin

kōya *n* 荒野 [BOOKISH] wild land, wilderness

kōyaku *n* 公約 (*public*) pledge; **kōyaku-sū** *n* 公約数 common factor

koyama *n* 小山 hill

koyō *n* 雇用 [BOOKISH] employment (*hiring*): **~-keiyakusho** 雇用契約書 employment agreement

kōyō *n* 紅葉 red leaves

kōyō *n* 効用 effect (*effectiveness*) (= **kiki-me** 効き目, **kōnō** 効能): **~ ga arimásu** 効用があります is effective

kōyō (no) *adj* 公用(の) official: **~-go** 公用語 official language

koyomí *n* 暦 calendar

kōyu *n* 香油 balm

kōyu *n* 鉱油 mineral oil

koyū (no) *adj* 固有(の) characteristic

kōyū *n* 交友 companion, friend(s)

kōyū *n* 交遊 social relations, company, association (= **kōsai** 交際)

kō yū (iu) ... *adj* こうゆう(いう)… this kind/sort of ..., such ...

kōza *n* 口座 an account: **ginkō-~** 銀行口座 bank account

kō´zan *n* 鉱山 a mine

kō´zan *n* 高山 high mountain

ko-zara *n* 小皿 saucer

kōzen (no/to) *adj, adv* 公然(の/と) open(ly), public(ly)

ko-zeni *n* 小銭 small change, coins

kozō´ *n* 小僧 **1.** young monk **2.** = **~-san** 小僧さん kid

kōzō *n* 構造 structure, makeup, organization

kōzu *n* 構図 (*picture*) composition

kózuchi *n* 小槌 a small hammer

kozue *n* 梢 treetop

kōzui *n* 洪水 flood: **~ ga okorimásu** 洪水が起こります floods

kózukai *n* 小使い janitor, custodian; attendant; servant

kózukai *n* 小遣い pin money, pocket money

kozútsumi *n* 小包 package, parcel

kú *n* 九 nine (= **kyū** 九)

kú *n* 句 phrase

kú *n* 区, ...´**-ku** ...区 **1.** a ward (*in a city*) (→ **ku-yákusho** 区役所): **Tōkyō nijūsan-~** 東京23 区 twenty-three wards of Tokyo **2.** zone (= **kúiki** 区域); **ku-yákusho** *n* 区役所 ward office

...-ku *suffix* …く: [ADJECTIVE] ... being, so as to be, …-ly

kū´ *v* 食う (VULGAR FORM *of* eats, bites *used mainly by males*) = **kuimásu** 食います (eats, bites) (POLITE FORM **tabemásu** 食べます)

kubarimásu, kubáru *v* 配ります, 配る distributes, allots; deals (*cards*)

kúbetsu *n* 区別 difference, differentiation; discrimination

kubi *n* 首 neck: ~ **ni shimásu** 首にします fires, lays off; **~-kázari** 首飾り necklace; **kubi-wa** *n* 首輪 (*dog*) collar

kubire *n* くびれ neck (*of a bottle*), constricted place, waist

kubomi *n* くぼみ・窪み hollow, dent, depression

kuchi *n* 口 **1.** mouth: ~ **(kará) no** 口(から)の oral **2.** words, speech: ~ **o hasamu** 口をはさむ interrupt **3.** entrance; hole, opening, slot **4.** cork, stopper **5.** job opening; **kuchi-beni** *n* 口紅 lipstick; ~ **o fukimásu** 口笛を吹きます whistles; **kuchi-génka** *n* 口げんか[喧嘩] argument; **kuchi-komi** *n* 口コミ word of mouth

kuchibiru *n* 唇 lip

kuchimásu, kuchiru *v* 朽ちます, 朽ちる rots, decays

kúda *n* 管 pipe, rube

kudakemásu, kudakéru *v* 砕けます, 砕ける **1.** it breaks, smashes, crumbles **2.** can break it

kudakimásu, kudáku *v* 砕きます, 砕く breaks it, smashes it, crumbles it

kudámono *n* 果物 fruit: **~-ya** 果物屋 fruit store/shop

kudari *n* 下り descent; outbound (*from Tokyo*), the down train

kudarimásu, kudaru *v* 下ります, 下る comes/goes down, descends; falls, drops

kudasái *v* 下さい give; (**shite** ~ して下さい) please (do) [IMPERATIVE of **kudasáru** 下さる = **kudasaimásu** 下さいます]

kudasaimásu, kudasáru *v* 下さいます, 下さる gives (*he/she to you, you to me*); does as a favor (*he/she for you, you for me*), kindly (*does*)

kudashi *n* 下し: **~-gúsuri** 下し薬 a purgative, a laxative

kudói *adj* くどい **1.** long-winded, dull **2.** thick, greasy

kufū *n* 工夫 device, scheme, idea, invention, artifice, ingenuity: ~ **(o kora-)shimásu** 工夫(を凝ら)します schemes, contrives

kūfuku (no) *adj* 空腹(の) hungry

Kú-gatsu *n* 九月・9月 September

kugi *n* 釘 nail, peg

kugiri *n* 区切り punctuation; **kugirimásu** 区切ります divides

kūgun *n* 空軍 air force: **~-kíchi** 空軍基地 air base

kugurimásu, kuguru *v* 潜ります, 潜る passes under

kūhaku *n* 空白 a blank (*space*)

kúi *n* 杭 post, stake, pile

kuichigai *n* 食い違い discrepancy

kúiki *n* 区域 zone

kuimásu, kuu´ *v* 食います, 食う eats (*inelegant*) (= **tabemásu** 食べます)

kúi-shínbō (na) *adj* 食いしん坊(な) glutton(ous); greedy

kujaku *n* クジャク・孔雀 peacock

kúji *n* くじ・クジ a lot (*in a lottery*) (= **takara-~** 宝くじ)

kujikemásu, kujikéru *v* 挫けます, 挫ける **1. ashí ga ~** 足が挫けます gets a sprained ankle **2. ki ga ~** 気が挫けます gets disheartened, discouraged **3.** (*a plan*) gets frustrated

kujikimásu, kujíku *v* 挫きます, 挫く **1.** sprains: **ashí o ~** 足を挫きます sprains an ankle **2. ki o ~** 気を挫きます disheartens, discourages **3.** frustrates (*a plan*)

kujira *n* クジラ・鯨 whale

kujō *n* 苦情 complaint: **~ o iu/yū** 苦情を言う complains

kūkan *n* 空間 space

kuki *n* 茎 stalk, stem

kū´ki *n* 空気 air

kūkō *n* 空港 airport

kúmá *n* クマ・熊 bear (*animal*)

kumade *n* 熊手 rake

kumí *n* 組 a set, suit, pack; a class, band, company

kumiai *n* 組合 association, guild, union: **rōdō-~** 労働組合 (labor) union

kumi-awase *n* 組み合わせ assortment, mixture

kumi-awasemásu, kumi-awaseru *v* 組み合わせます, 組み合わせる combines, puts together, teams them up

kumimásu, kumu *v* 汲みます, 汲む scoops, draws, ladles; considers, sympathizes

kumimásu, kúmu *v* 組みます, 組む braids; assembles, sets up, puts together; folds (*arms*), clasps (*hands*), crosses (*legs*); teams up (*with*)

kumi-tate *n* 組み立て structure, setup, makeup, organization, framework

kumi-tatemásu, kumi-tateru *v* 組み立てます, 組み立てる sets up, organizes; assembles, puts together

kúmo *n* 雲 cloud: **~-gakure** 雲隠れ disappearing, dropping out of sight

kúmo *n* クモ・蜘蛛 spider

kúmo no su *n* クモ[蜘蛛]の巣 spiderweb, cobweb (= **kúmo no íto** クモ[蜘蛛]の糸 spider threads

kumori 曇り *n* cloudy weather

kumorimásu, kumóru *v* 曇ります, 曇る gets cloudy: **kumótte imásu** 曇っています is cloudy

... kun *suffix* …君 (*mostly attached to one's junior's or boys' names* INFORMAL)

kuni *n* 国 **1.** country, nation: **~ no** 国の national, state, government **2.** native place, home area

kúnren *n* 訓練 training, drill

kurá *n* 鞍 saddle

kurá *n* 倉・蔵 warehouse, storeroom (*storehouse*), cellar, godown

kū´rā *n* クーラー air conditioner

kurabemásu, kuraberu *v* 比べます・較べます, 比べる・較べる compares, contrasts

kúrabu *n* クラブ club (*group; card suit*); (*golf*) club: ~ **katsudō** クラブ活動 club activities

kurage *n* クラゲ jellyfish

kurai *n* 位 grade, rank

kurai *adj* 暗い dark, gloomy; dim (*light*)

... kúrai *suffix* …くらい・位 = **... gúrai** …ぐらい・位 (about; (*an amount*); at least)

kurákkā *n* クラッカー crackers

kurashikku *n* クラシック classic (= **koten** 古典)

kurashimásu, kurasu *v* 暮らします, 暮らす lives, gets by; makes a living

kúrasu *n* クラス class (*group*)

kurátchi *n* クラッチ clutch (*of car*): **~-pédaru** クラッチペダル clutch pedal

kure *v* 暮れ the dark; the end of the year: ~ **no** 暮れの year-end

kurejitto-kā´do *n* クレジットカード credit card

kuremásu, kureru *v* くれます, くれる gives (*to me/us; he to you*): **shite** ~ してくれます does as a favor (*for me/us; he for you*)

kuremásu, kureru *v* 暮れます, 暮れる: **hi ga** ~ 日が暮れます it gets dark

kurē´n *n* クレーン crane (*machine*)

kurí *n* 栗 chestnut

kuríimu *n* クリーム cream

kuríiníngu *n* クリーニング cleaning: **~-ya** クリーニング屋 (*dry*) cleaner(s); laundry

kuri-kaeshimásu, kiri-kaesu *v* 繰り返します, 繰り返す repeats

kuríppu *n* クリップ clip

Kurísúmasu *n* クリスマス Christmas

kúro (no) *adj* 黒(の) black; **kuro-bíiru** *n* 黒ビール black beer; **kuró-i** *adj* 黒い black (= **kúro (no)** 黒(の))

kúrō *n* 苦労 difficulties, hardships

kurō´ku *n* クローク cloakroom, check room

kúrō´to *n* 玄人 expert, professional

kuruimásu, kuru'u´ *v* 狂います, 狂う gets warped; gets out of order: **ki ga** ~ 気が狂います goes mad (*insane*)

kuruma *n* 車 car; taxi; vehicle, (*hand*) cart (= **jidō´-sha** 自動車)

kurumá-ebi *n* 車エビ[海老] prawn, jumbo shrimp

kurumi *n* クルミ・胡桃 walnut; nut

kurushíi *adj* 苦しい painful; hard; heavy

kurushimemásu, kurushiméru *v* 苦しめます, 苦しめる afflicts, pains, distresses, embarrasses

kurushimí *n* 苦しみ affliction, agony, suffering, distress

kurushimimásu, kurushímu *v* 苦しみます, 苦しむ suffers; gets afflicted/distressed/embarrassed

kusá *n* 草 grass

kusái *adj* 臭い smelly, stinking; fishy, questionable

kusari *n* 鎖 chain

kusarimásu, kusáru *v* 腐ります, 腐る goes bad, rots, decays, spoils, sours: **kusátte imásu** 腐っています is spoiled/rotten

kusé *n* 癖・くせ a (*bad*) habit, a quirk

kūsha *n* 空車 vacant car, "(taxi) available"

kushámi *n* くしゃみ a sneeze

kushí *n* くし・櫛 a comb

kushí *n* 串 a skewer, a spit

kūsho *n* 空所 a blank (*space*)

kusó *n* くそ・クソ・糞 dung, excrement, feces

kūsō *n* 空想 fantasy

kusugurimásu, kusuguru *v* くすぐります, くすぐる tickles

kusuguttai *adj* くすぐったい ticklish

kusuri *n* 薬 medicine, drug: **~-ya (san)** 薬屋(さん) drugstore; druggist

kutakuta, kuttakuta *adj* くたくた, くったくた dead tired, utterly exhausted

...-kutatte ... *suffix, conj* くたって even being ... (= **...-kute mo ...** くても)

...-kute *suffix, conj* ...くて is and (*also/so*)

kutsú *n* 靴・クツ shoes; kutsú-himo *n* 靴ひも shoelace; kutsú-shita *n* 靴下・くつ下 socks, stockings; kutsú-ya *n* 靴屋 shoe shop/store; kutsu-zoko *n* 靴底 shoe sole

kutsurogimásu, kutsurógu *v* くつろぎます, くつろぐ relaxes, gets comfortable

kúttsukimású, kuttsúku *v* くっつきます,くっつく sticks to

kuwa *n* くわ・鍬 hoe

kúwa *n* クワ・桑 mulberry

kuwadate 企て *n* plan, attempt, undertaking

kuwadatemásu, kuwadatéru *v* 企てます, 企てる plans, attempts, undertakes

kuwaemásu, kuwaeru *v* 加えます, 加える adds (*on*); imposes

kuwasemásu, kuwaséru *v* 食わせます, 食わせる feeds (POLITE FORM **tabesasemasu** 食べさせます)

kuwashíi *adj* 詳しい detailed, exact: (**... ni ~** ...に詳しい) is knowledgeable (about ...), is well versed (in ...); **~ kotó** 詳しい事 details; **kuwáshiku** 詳しく in detail

kuyamimásu, kuyamu *v* 悔やみます, 悔やむ regrets

kuyashíi *adj* 悔しい humiliating, mortifying, vexatious

kuzu (mono) *n* くず[クズ](物) waste, scum, mud, trash, rags, scrap, junk (= **kásu** かす・滓); kuzú-kago *n* くずかご wastebasket; kuzú-mono *n* くず物 waste, trash

kúzu *n* クズ・葛 arrowroot; kuzu-ko *n* 葛粉 powdered arrowroot

kuzuremásu, kuzuréru *v* 崩れます, 崩れる it crumbles, breaks (down); (*weather*) deteriorates

kuzushimás<u>u</u>, kuzús<u>u</u> *v* 崩します, 崩す **1.** cashes, changes, breaks (*into small money*) **2.** breaks it down, demolishes **3.** writes (*a character*) in cursive style
kyábarē *n* キャバレー cabaret, night club
kyábetsu *n* キャベツ cabbage
kyaburétā *n* キャブレター carburetor
kyaku *n* 客 visitor, guest, company; customer (= **o-~-sámá** お客様 [HONORIFIC]); **kyaku-ma** *n* 客間 [BOOKISH] guest room; **kyak<u>u</u>-sha** *n* 客車 [BOOKISH] (*railroad*) passenger car, coach
kyánbasu *n* キャンバス canvas
kyándii, kyándē *n* キャンディ, キャンデー candy (= **ame** アメ・飴)
kyánpasu *n* キャンパス campus
kyánpu *n* キャンプ camp(ing)
kyánseru *n* キャンセル cancellation
kyáppu *n* キャップ cap (*of a pen*)
kyáp<u>u</u>ten *n* キャプテン captain
kyarameru *n* キャラメル caramel
kyátsu *n* きゃつ・彼奴 [INFORMAL] that damn one; **~-ra** きゃつ[彼奴]ら those damn ones (= **aitsu** あいつ; **aitsu-ra** あいつら)
kyā *interj* きゃー・キャー: **kyā(t)-to sakebimásu** きゃー(っ)[キャー(ッ)]と叫びます screams
kyṓ *n* 今日・きょう today
kyṓ (no miyako) *n* 京(の都) Kyoto (= **Kyṓto** 京都)
...-kyō *n* …教 (*name of*) religion: **Kirisuto-~** キリスト教 Christianity; **Isuramu-~** イスラム教 Islam (= **kaikyō** 回教); **Buk-~** 仏教 Buddhism
kyōbai *n* 競売 [BOOKISH] auction (= **ōkushon** オークション)
kyōchō *n* 強調 emphasis
kyodai (na) *adj* 巨大(な) huge
kyṓdai (-shimai) *n* 兄弟(姉妹) brothers and/or sisters; brother; sister
kyōdan *n* 教壇 [BOOKISH] platform, pulpit: **~ ni tachimásu** 教壇に立ちます **1.** teaches at school **2.** stands on a platform
kyōdan *n* 凶弾 [BOOKISH] bullet (*of assassin, etc.*): **~ ni taoremásu** 凶弾に倒れます is shot to death (*by an assassin, etc.*)
kyōdan *n* 教団 [BOOKISH] religious organization
kyōdō *n* 共同 union, cooperation, joint (*activity*): **~-seikatsu** 共同生活 living together, living with others
kyōdō *n* 協同 cooperation: **~-kumiai** 協同組合 cooperative association (→ **seikatsu-~-kumiai, seikyō** 生活協同組合, 生協)
kyṓfu *n* 恐怖 [BOOKISH] fear, terror
kyōgeki *n* 京劇 classic Chinese pantomime/opera
kyōgén *n* 狂言 traditional Noh farce
kyṓgi *n* 協議 conference, discussion
kyṓgi *n* 競技 (*athletic*) game, match, contest, (*game*) event; **kyōgi-jō** *n* 競技場 stadium

kyōhan(sha) *n* 共犯(者) accomplice
kyóhi *n* 拒否 refusal, rejection, veto (= **kyozetsu** 拒絶)
kyōiku *n* 教育 education: ~ **o ukemásu** 教育を受けます gets an education
kyōin *n* 教員 [BOOKISH] teacher
kyojin *n* 巨人 giant (*person*)
kyōju *n* 教授 professor: **daigaku-~** 大学教授 university professor
kyojū *n* 居住 [BOOKISH] residency: **~-sha** 居住者 a resident: **~-chi** 居住地 residence (*location*), address (= **jūsho** 住所)
kyóka *n* 許可 permit, permission: **~-sho** 許可証 permit (*card*)
kyōkai *n* 教会 church
kyōkai *n* 協会 society, association
kyōkai *n* 境界 border (*of district, etc.*)
kyōká-sho *n* 教科書 text(book)
kyōki *n* 凶器 [BOOKISH] lethal weapon
kyōki *n* 狂気 [BOOKISH] insanity, madness, lunacy
kyōki *n* 驚喜 [BOOKISH] amazement and gladness
kyokō *n* 虚構 [BOOKISH] fabrication, fiction: ~ **no sekai** 虚構の世界 imaginary world
kyōkō *n* 強行 forcing: **~-toppa** 強行突破 bulldozing one's way through: **~-saiketsu** 強行採決 railroading
kyóku *n* 局, **...´-kyoku** ...局 office, bureau, station: **terebi-~** テレビ局 TV station
kyokuba *n* 曲馬 horseback stunts: **~-dan** 曲馬団 circus (= **sā´kasu** サーカス)
kyokugei *n* 曲芸 acrobat, acrobatics (= **akurobátto** アクロバット): **~-shi** 曲芸師 an acrobat, a stunt performer
kyokugen *n* 極限 [BOOKISH] limit: **~-jōtai** 極限状態 extreme situation, ultimate state
kyōkun *n* 教訓 lesson, teaching, moral
kyokután (na) *adj* 極端(な) extreme
Kyokutō *n* 極東 Far East
kyōkyū *n* 供給 supply(ing), provision: **juyō to** ~ 需要と供給 supply and demand (= **jukyū** 需給)
kyō´mí *n* 興味 interest (*pleasure*): **~-bukái** 興味深い interesting
kyónen *n* 去年 last year
kyóri *n* 距離 distance
kyōryoku *n* 協力 cooperation
kyōryoku (na) *adj* 強力(な) strong, powerful
Kyōsan-shúgi *n* 共産主義 Communism
kyō´shi *n* 教師 teacher, instructor, tutor: **katei-~** 家庭教師 home tutor
kyōshitsu *n* 教室 classroom
kyōshoku *n* 教職 teaching profession: ~ **ni tsukimásu** 教職に就きます becomes a teacher
kyōshuku shimásu (suru) *v* 恐縮します(する) [HONORIFIC] **1.** feels grateful/obliged/ashamed: **waza-waza okoshi itadakimashite ~**

desu わざわざお越しいただきまして恐縮です Thank you very much for taking the trouble to come. **2.** feels sorry/ashamed: **taihen ~ desuga...** 大変恐縮ですが... I am very sorry, but...

kyōsō *n* 競争 competition, rivalry, contest, race; kyōsō-áite *n* 競争相手 competitor

kyōson, kyōzon *n* 共存 [BOOKISH] coexistence: **minzoku ~** 民族共存 ethnic coexistence

kyōten *n* 経典 **1.** sutra (*Buddhist scripture*) (= **o-kyō** お経) **2.** religious text, sacred scripture

Kyō'to *n* 京都 Kyoto; **Kyōtó-Eki** 京都駅 Kyoto Station

kyōtsū (no) *adj* 共通(の) common, general

kyōyo *n* 供与 grant, allowance

kyōyō (no) *adj* 共用(の) for common use, for public use

kyōyō *n* 教養 culture, education, refinement: **~ no nai** 教養のない uneducated, uncultivated

kyōyō *n* 強要 [BOOKISH] forcing

kyōzai *n* 教材 teaching materials

kyozetsu *n* 拒絶 [BOOKISH] refusal, rejection, veto (= **kyóhi** 拒否)

kyū *n* 灸・きゅう (**o-kyō** お灸) moxibustion

kyū *n* 急 crisis, emergency, danger: **~ (na)** 急(な) sudden; urgent; precipitous, steep: **~ na (o-) shirase/renraku** 急な(お)知らせ/連絡 short notice; **~ ni** 急に suddenly (= **totsuzen** 突然); kyū-byō *n* 急病 sudden illness; kyū-kō *n* 急行 express (*train, etc.*); kyū-shi *n* 急死 sudden death; kyū-yō *n* 急用 urgent business

kyū' *n* 級 class, grade

kyū' *n* 九・9 nine (= **kú** 九・9); kyū-banmé *n* 九番目 ninth; kyū'-dai *n* 九台 nine (*machines, vehicles*); kyū'-do *n* 九度 nine degrees; nine times (= **kyū'-kái** 九回); kyū'-hén *n* 九遍 nine times; kyū'-hon *n* 九本 nine (*pencils/bottles, long things*); kyū-kai *n* 九階 nine floors/stories, ninth floor; kyū'-ko *n* 九個 nine pieces (*small objects*) (= **kokonotsu** 九つ); kyū'-kái *n* 九回 nine times (= **kyū'-do** 九度); kyū'-mai *n* 九枚 nine sheets (*flat things*); kyū'-satsu *n* 九冊 nine copies (*books, magazines*); kyū'-tō *n* 九頭 nine (*horses/oxen, large animals*); kyū'-wa *n* 九羽 nine (*birds, rabbits*)

kyū'(-) *prefix* 旧... ... old

kyūden *n* 宮殿 palace

kyū'dō *n* 弓道 (*the traditional art of*) archery (= **kyū'jutsu** 弓術)

kyū'-hyaku *n* 九百・900 nine hundred

kyū'ji *n* 給仕 waiter/waitress, steward, attendant, factotum

kyūjin *n* 求人 job offer(s)

kyūjitsu *n* 休日 day off, holiday

kyū'jo *n* 救助 rescue, relief: **~-tai** 救助隊 rescue party/team

kyūjō *n* 球場 ball park, (*baseball*) stadium (= **yakyū-jō** 野球場)

kyū´-jū *n* 九十・90 ninety
kyūka *n* 休暇 vacation, furlough
kyūkei *n* 休憩 rest, recess, break; kyūkéi-shitsu *n* 休憩室 lounge (*room*), break room
kyūkon *n* 求婚 marriage proposal
kyū´kutsu (na) *adj* 窮屈(な) constrained, uncomfortable
kyūkyū (no) *adj* 救急(の) for emergencies; kyūkyū´-bako *n* 救急箱 first-aid kit; kyūkyū-chiryō shitsu 救急治療室 emergency room, ER; kyūkyū´-sha *n* 救急車 ambulance
kyū-mán *n* 九万・90,000 ninety thousand
kyū´ri *n* キュウリ・胡瓜 cucumber
kyū´ryō *n* 給料 salary, pay (= **sárarii** サラリー, **kyū´yo** 給与); kyūryō´-bi 給料日 payday
kyūseishu *n* 救世主 Savior
kyū-sén *n* 九千・9,000 nine thousand
kyūshi *n* 休止 pause; kyūshi-kigō 休止記号 breath mark
kyūsho *n* 急所 jugular (*vein*)
kyūshoku (katsudō) *n* 求職(活動) job hunting, seeking employment
kyūshoku *n* 休職 leave of absence from work
kyūshoku *n* 給食 school lunch
Kyū´shū-chihō *n* 九州地方 the Kyushu area of Japan (*Fukuoka, Saga, Nagasaki, Kumamoto, Miyazaki, Kagoshima, Ōita prefectures*)
kyūsu *n* きゅうす・急須 teapot
kyūtei *n* 宮廷 (*imperial/royal*) court
Kyū-yaku seisho *n* 旧約聖書 the Old Testament
kyū´yo *n* 給与 allowance, grant, compensation, salary (= **sárarii** サラリー, **kyū´ryō** 給料): **~-meisai (sho)** 給与明細書 pay slip
kyūyō *n* 休養 rest

M

ma *n* 間 **1.** room; space (*available*) **2.** time, interval; (= **hima** 暇) leisure: **ma ni aimás<u>u</u>** 間に合います → **ma-ni-aimás<u>u</u>** 間に合います
ma... *prefix* 真... mid..., right..., very...; ma-fuyu *n* 真冬 midwinter; ma-hiru *n* 真昼 midday; ma-kká (na) *adj* 真っ赤(な) crimson, deep red: **~ ni narimás<u>u</u>** 真っ赤になります turns red, flushes deeply; ma-kkúro (na) *adj* 真っ黒(な) jet black: **~ ni narimás<u>u</u>** 真っ黒になります turns to a deep black; ma-natsu *n* 真夏 midsummer; ma-yónaka *n* 真夜中 midnight; ma-ssáka-sama (ni) *adj* 真っ逆さま(に) head over heels; ma-ssúgu (na) *adj* 真っ直ぐ(な) straight
mā´ まあ *interj* **1.** oh well; I should say; perhaps, I guess **2.** dear me! (*mostly female*); good heavens/grief!

ma-bátaki *n* 瞬き wink(ing), blink(ing)

mabayui *adj* 眩い [BOOKISH] dazzling, glaring

māburu *n* マーブル marble

mabushíi *adj* 眩しい dazzling, glaring (= **mabayui** 眩い)

mábuta *n* まぶた・瞼 eyelid

macchi *n* マッチ match

machí *n* 町・街 town, city: **~ no** 町の local (→ **chō´chō** 町長)

māchi *n* マーチ march

machi-awasemásu, machi-awaseru *v* 待ち合わせます, 待ち合わせる makes an appointment

machibuse *n* 待ち伏せ ambush

machidōshíi *adj* 待ち遠しい long awaited; waiting for a long time

machigáe *n* 間違え = **machigái** 間違い (mistake, error) → **machigaemásu** 間違えます

machigaemásu, machigáéru *v* 間違えます, 間違える mistakes

machigái *n* 間違い mistake, error (= **misu** ミス, **erā** エラー)

machigaimásu, machigáu *v* 間違います, 間違う is mistaken, is wrong, is in error

machigátta *adj* 間違った wrong (*mistaken*)

machimásu, mátsu *v* 待ちます, 待つ waits for, expects, anticipates

máchínē *n* マチネー matinee

máda *adv* まだ **1.** (not) yet [+ NEGATIVE verb] **2.** still (*to be*)

madara *n* 斑 spots, speckles: **~ no** 斑の spotted

...máde *suffix, conj* …まで (*all the way*) to, till, until

... máde ni *suffix, conj* …までに by, no later than, before (*it gets to be time*)

... máde ni wa *suffix, conj* …までには by … at the latest

mádo *n* 窓 window; **mado-gárasu** *n* 窓ガラス windowpane; **madó-guchi** *n* 窓口 window (*opening*), wicket

maekagami *n* 前屈み leaning forward: **~ ni narimásu** 前屈みになります leans forward

mae-mótte *adv* 前もって (*in*) ad-vance (*beforehand*)

mae-muki (no) *adj* 前向き(の) **1.** far-sighted (*forward-looking*) **2.** positive, constructive, affirmative: **~ (na) shikō** 前向き(な)思考 positive thinking

máe (ni) *adv* 前(に) front; in front of; before, ago: **suru ~ ni** する前に before doing

maeoki *n* 前置き introduction

maeuri *n* 前売り advanced sale: **~-ken** 前売り券 advanced-sale ticket

mafurā *n* マフラー muffler, scarf

mafia *n* マフィア Mafia

mafin *n* マフィン muffin

magao *n* 真顔 serious/earnest/sober/conscientious/honest look (*on one's face*) (= **majime na kao** 真面目な顔, **shinken na kao** 真剣な顔)

magari 曲がり *n* a curve, a bend: **heso-~** へそ曲がり perverted person; **~-kado** 曲がり角 street corner

magari *n* 間借り renting a room; magari-nin *n* 間借り人 tenant (*of apartment, room*)

magarimásu, magaru *v* 曲がります, 曲がる **1.** turns, goes around **2.** it bends, curves

māgarin *n* マーガリン margarine

magemásu, mageru *v* 曲げます, 曲げる bends it, curves it

magiremásu, magiréru *v* 紛れます, 紛れる: (**... ni** ~ ...に紛れる) gets distracted (by ...); gets confused (with ...), gets mixed up (*with*)

... mágiwa (ni/de) *suffix, adv* ...間際 (に/で) just before ..., right on the brink of (when) ...

magó *n* 孫 grandchild: **o-~-san** お孫さん (*your/someone else's*) grandchild

magó *n* 馬子 a packhorse driver

magokoro *n* 真心 sincerity: **~ o komete hanashimásu** 真心を込めて話します talks sincerely

magure (atari) *n* まぐれ(当たり) fluke, (*dumb/good*) luck, accident, fortuity (= **gūzen** 偶然): **~ de kachimásu** まぐれで勝ちます wins by a fluke

maguro *n* マグロ・鮪 tuna

magusa *n* まぐさ[秣・馬草] hay

máhi *n* マヒ・麻痺 paralysis

mahō´ *n* 魔法 magic; mahō´-bin *n* 魔法瓶[びん・ビン] vacuum/thermos bottle

mai *n* 舞 (*Japanese*) dance: **~ o maimásu** 舞を舞います dances

mai-... *prefix* 毎... each, every; mai-asa *n, adv* 毎朝 every morning; mai-ban *n, adv* 毎晩 every night; mai-do *n, adv* 毎度 every time; mai-getsu, mai-tsuki *n, adv* 毎月 every month; mai-kai *n, adv* 毎回 every time, each time; mai-nen, mai-toshi *n, adv* 毎年 every year; mái-nichi *n, adv* 毎日 every day; all the time: **~ no** 毎日の daily; **~ no yō´ni** 毎日のように almost everyday; mai-shū *n, adv* 毎週 every week: **~ no** 毎週の weekly; mai-toshi → mai-nen; mai-tsuki → mai-getsu; mai-yo *n, adv* 毎夜 every night (= **mai-ban** 毎晩)

...´-mai *suffix* ...枚 (*counts flat things*)

máigo *n* 迷子 a lost child

mai-hōmu *n* マイホーム owned house, one's house and home; mai-hōmu-shugi(-sha) *n* マイホーム主義(者) family-centred person (= **kazoku-omoi no hito** 家族思いの人)

mainasu *n* マイナス less (*minus*); a minus, a disadvantage

mairimáshita *v* 参りました, [INFORMAL] **máitta** 参った You've got me!; gives up, goes down

mairimásu, máiru *v* 参ります, 参る **1.** [HUMBLE] I come/go **2.** [HUMBLE] visits, calls on **3.** is defeated, loses (= **kōsan** 降参) **4.** is floored, stumped

maisō *n* 埋葬 burial

mājan *n* マージャン・麻雀 mah-

jong: **~-ya** マージャン[麻雀]屋 mahjong parlor
majime (na) *adj* 真面目(な) serious, earnest, sober, conscientious, honest
mājin *n* マージン margin
majinai *n* まじない・呪い **1.** charm **2.** curse **3.** spell, magic, incantation; majinai-shi *n* まじない[呪い]師 witch doctor
majirimásu, majíru *v* 混じります, 混じる it mixes (*with*)
majiwarimásu, majiwáru *v* 交わります, 交わる associates with
majo *n* 魔女 witch
makasemásu, makaséru *v* 任せます, 任せる entrusts with
makashimásu, makasu *v* 負かします, 負かす defeats
make 負け *n* defeat, loss
makemásu, makeru *v* 負けます, 負ける loses, is defeated; comes down on the price; is inferior
makétto *n* マーケット market
maki *n* 薪 firewood
maki *n* **1.** 巻き a roll; a volume **2.** (**…-maki** …巻き) a bolt (*of cloth*)
makimásu, maku *v* 巻きます, 巻く rolls up; winds; wraps; maki-tábako *n* 巻きタバコ cigarette(s)
makimásu, máku *v* 蒔きます, 蒔く sows (*seed*); maki-e *n* 蒔(き)絵 raised lacquer
makoto (no) *adj* 誠[真]まこと(の) sincere; faithful; true; genuine (= **honto (no), hontō (no)** 本当(の)): **~ ni** 誠[真]に sincerely
makú *n* 幕 (*stage*) curtain; (*play*) act
maku ai *n* 幕間 intermission (*between acts*)
makunóuchi *n* 幕の内 a riceball lunch(box)
mákura *n* まくら・マクラ・枕 pillow
mama *n* ママ **1.** (*baby talk*) mommy, mom (= **kā-chan** 母ちゃん) **2.** hostess (*in a bar, etc.*)
mama-... *prefix* まま[継]… step; mama-chichi *n* まま[継]父 stepfather; mama-haha *n* まま[継]母 stepmother; mama-ko *n* まま[継]子 stepchild
mā-mā *adj, adv* まあまあ (just) so-so, not bad
... mamá (de/no) *suffix, adv, adj* … まま(で/の) intact, untouched/undisturbed: **sono ~ de** そのままで just as it is/was
mamé *n* マメ・豆 bean(s)
mamé *n* まめ blister
mame (na) *adj* まめ(な) diligent/dedicated (*person*)
mame (ni) *adv* まめ(に) often, frequently: **heya o ~ ni sōji shimásu** 部屋をまめに掃除します cleans the room often
ma-mó-naku *adv* 間もなく soon, before long, shortly
mamorimásu, mamóru *v* 守ります, 守る defends, protects, guards
mán *n* 万 ten thousand 10,000
man(-) ... *prefix* 満… fully …; man-chō *n* 満潮 high tide; man-getsu *n*

満月 full moon; man'-in *n* 満員 full (*of people*); man-jō-icchi *n* 満場一致 unanimous (*agreement*); man-men *n* 満面 the whole face: **tokui ~ des<u>u</u>** 得意満面です is proud as a peacock, is in triumph; man-pai *adj* 満杯 is filled: **yoyaku ga ~-pai des<u>u</u>** 予約が満杯です is fully booked; man-puku *n*, *v* 満腹 full stomach; man-rui *n* 満塁 (*baseball*) with the bases loaded: **~ hōmuran** 満塁ホームラン a grand slam; man-ten *n* 満点 perfect score; man-ten *n* 満天 the whole sky

manabimás<u>u</u>, manabu *v* 学びます, 学ぶ learns, studies

manaitá *n* まな板 chopping board (*for cooking*)

manazashi *n* 眼差し a look in one's eyes: **yasashii ~** 優しい眼差し gentle look in one's eyes: **utagai no ~** 疑いの眼差し a suspicious look in one's eyes

manbiki *n* 万引き shoplifting, shoplifter

manbyō *n* 万病 all kinds of disease

mane *n* 真似 imitation, mimicry

mánē´jā *n* マネージャー manager

manekimás<u>u</u>, manéku *v* 招きます, 招く invites

manekin *n* マネキン mannequin

manekineko *n* 招き猫 beckoning cat

manemás<u>u</u>, maneru *v* 真似ます, 真似る imitates

manga *n* マンガ・漫画 cartoon, comics, manga: **~-kissa** マンガ[漫画]喫茶 manga cafe

manhōru *n* マンホール manhole

ma-ni-aimás<u>u</u>, ma-ni-áu *v* 間に合います, 間に合う: **... ni ma-ni-aimás<u>u</u>** ...に間に合います is in time (*for* ...); **ma-ni-aimasén** 間に合いません arrives too late (*for* ...), misses (*the train/bus/plane*)

ma-ni-awase *v* 間に合わせ make-shift

ma-ni-awasemás<u>u</u>, ma-ni-awaséru *v* 間に合わせます, 間に合わせる: **... de ma-ni-awasemás<u>u</u>** ...で間に合わせます makes do (*with* ...)

mán'ichi *n* 万一 **= mán ga ichi** 万が一 if by any chance

manjū´ *n* 饅頭 a steamed bun stuffed with ground pork

manmosu *n* マンモス mammoth: **~ no kiba** マンモスの牙 mammoth tusks

mannén-h<u>i</u>tsu *n* 万年筆 fountain pen

manneri(zumu) *n* マンネリ(ズム) mannerism

manpokei *n* 万歩計 pedometer

mánshon *n* マンション a luxury apartment (*house*)

mánto *n* マント cloak

mantora *n* マントラ mantra: **~ o tonaemás<u>u</u>** マントラを唱えます chants mantra

mantsūman *adv* マンツーマン one-to-one, one-on-one: **~ ressun o ukemás<u>u</u>** マンツーマンレッスンを受けます has one-to-one lesson(s)

manugare[manukare]más<u>u</u>, manugareru (manukaréru) *v* まぬがれ[まぬか

れ]ます・免れます, まぬがれる [まぬかれる]・免れる escapes from, is exempt from, avoids: **shi o manugaremás<u>u</u>** 死を免れます escapes death

manzái *n* 漫才 cross-talk comedy: **~ konbi** 漫才コンビ a comic duo

mánzoku (na) *adj* 満足(な) satisfactory: **(... de) ~ shimás<u>u</u>** ...(で)満足します is satisfied/contented (*with* ...)

marason *n* マラソン jog(ging); marathon

maré (na) *adj* 稀(な) rare, infrequent: **~ ni** 稀に rarely

Marēshia *n* マレーシア Malaysia; Marēshia-jin *n* マレーシア人 a Malaysian; Marēshia-go *n* マレーシア語 Bahasa Malaysia (*language*)

mari *n* まり・マリ・鞠 ball, (*Japanese*) *temari* ball

marine *n* マリネ marinade

marifana *n* マリファナ marijuana

maru *n* 丸・まる circle, ring; zero

maru(-) ... *prefix* 丸・まる ... fully, whole...; maru-anki *n* 丸暗記 rote learning; maru-utsushi *n* 丸写し copying entirely; maru-yaki *n* 丸焼き whole roast; maru-yake *n* 丸焼け total loss (*by fire*)

maru de *adj* まるで **1.** completely [+ NEGATIVE]: **Nihon to ~ chigau/kotonaru bunka** 日本とまるで違う/異なる文化 quite different culture from Japanese **2. maru de ...no yō (na)** まるで...のよう(な) as if: **maru de kodomo no yō (na)** まるで子供のよう(な) just like a child

marui *adj* 丸い round

maru ku *adv* 丸く roundly: **me o ~ ku shimás<u>u</u>** 目を丸くします (*with*) wide eyes; **se o ~ ku shimás<u>u</u>** 背を丸くします hunches up

maruta *n* 丸太 log

másaka まさか **1.** *adv* **~ ...dewa nai (des<u>u</u>) yo ne?** まさか...ではない(です)よね? Don't tell me that... **2.** *interj* no kidding!; impossible!

mása-ni *adv* まさに exactly, just; certainly, really

masarimás<u>u</u>, masáru *v* 勝ります, 勝る surpasses, is superior

masatsu *n* まさつ・摩擦 friction: **karada o ~** 体を摩擦します rubs (oneself) down

mashi 増し *n* an increase; a surcharge

mashimás<u>u</u>, masu *v* 増します, 増す increases, raises, swells

mashumaro *n* マシュマロ marshmallow

massā'ji *n* マッサージ massage: **~-shi** マッサージ師 masseur

massatsu *n* 抹殺 [BOOKISH] elimination, murder, killing

masshurūmu *n* マッシュルーム mushroom

masú *n* マス・鱒 trout

mas<u>u</u>-komi *n* マスコミ mass communication (*media*)

masukotto *n* マスコット mascot

másuku *n* マスク mask (= **kamen** 仮面)
masú-masu *adv* 益々 more and more, increasingly
masutādo *n* マスタード mustard (= **karashi** カラシ・芥子)
masuto *n* マスト mast
matá *conj, prep* また・又 again; moreover: ~ **dō´zo** またどうぞ Please (*come, etc.*) again.
matá *n* 股 crotch, groin
máta *conj* また・又 and also/ another/more (= **... mo ~** ... もまた)
matagarimásu, matagáru *v* 跨がります, 跨がる: **... ni ~** ...に跨がります straddles, sits astride, mounts, rides; stretches/extends over, spans
matagimásu, matágu *v* 跨ぎます, 跨ぐ strides over
matátakí *n* 瞬き blink(ing) → **matátakímásu** 瞬きます blinks
mátá-wa *conj* または・又は or, or else, on the other hand; also; and/or
matcha *n* 抹茶 powdered green tea (*for tea ceremony*)
mátchi *n* マッチ match(es) (*for fire*); matchí-bako *n* マッチ箱 matchbox
mato *n* 的 target, aim
matomarimásu, matomaru *v* まとまります, まとまる is settled, arranged, finished
matomemásu, matomeru *v* まとめます, まとめる settles, arranges, finishes
mátsu *n* マツ・松 pine tree (= **~-no-kí** 松の木)
matsuba-zúe *n* 松葉杖 crutch(es)
mátsuge *n* まつげ・睫(毛) eyelash(es)
matsuri *n* 祭り festival
matsutake *n* マツタケ・松茸 a kind of mushroom (*thumb-shaped*)
matsu-yani *n* 松脂 pine resin
mattaku *adv* 全く quite, completely, exactly (= **zenzen** 全然): **~ no** 全くの perfect
mátto *n* マット mat
mawari *n* 周り: **(... no) ~ (ni/no)** (...の) 周り (に/の) around ...
mawari... *prefix* 回り... revolving ..., rotating...; mawari-butai *n* 回り舞台 revolving stage; mawari-kaidan *n* 回り階段 spiral stairway; mawarí-michi *n* 回り道 detour
mawari-kudoi *adj* 回りくどい roundabout
mawarimásu, mawaru *v* 周ります, 周る goes around
mawarimásu, mawaru *v* 回ります, 回る turns, revolves, circulates, rotates
mawashi *n* 回し sumo wrestler's belt (*loincloth*)
mawashimásu, mawasu *v* 回します 回す turns it around, passes it around, circulates it
mawata *n* 真綿 floss silk
mayaku *n* 麻薬 narcotic(s), dope (= **kusuri** クスリ・薬, **yaku** ヤク・薬, **yakubutsu** 薬物)
mayoimásu, mayóu *v* 迷います, 迷う gets lost; gets perplexed

mayonēzu *n* マヨネーズ mayonnaise
máyu *n* 眉 eyebrow(s)
máyu *n* マユ・繭 cocoon
mazarimásu, mazáru *v* 混ざります, 混ざる it mixes
mazemásu, mazéru *v* 混ぜます, 混ぜる mixes it
mázu *adv* まず first of all, before anything else (= **saisho (ni)** 最初(に), **hajime (ni)** 初め(に))
mázu *adv* まず perhaps, nearly
mazúi *adj* 不味い untasty, bad-tasting
mazúi *adj* **1.** まずい poor, awkward **2.** inadvisable **3.** ugly
mazushíi *adj* 貧しい poor (*needy*)
mé *n* 目 eye: **taihen na ~ ni aimásu** 大変な目にあいます (*has/undergoes*) a hard experience
mé *n* 芽 bud
...-me *interj* …め・奴 [*deprecates people*] damn (*fool*) …: **baka-~** ばかめ・馬鹿め damn (*fool*) idiot
...-mé *suffix* …目 [NUMERAL] -th: **itsutsu-~** 五つ目 fifth
méate *n* 目当て a guide (*for the eye*); aim
mechamecha *adj* めちゃめちゃ・目茶目茶 in pieces, all confused, in disorder: **~ ni shimásu** めちゃめちゃにします ruins, upsets, messes up
medachimásu, medátsu *v* 目立ちます, 目立つ stands out, becomes conspicuous
medama-yaki *n* 目玉焼き fried egg(s)
medarisuto *n* メダリスト medalist
medaru *n* メダル medal
medátta ... *v* 目立った… outstanding, conspicuous → **medachimásu** 目立ちます
medátte *adv* 目立って outstandingly, conspicuously: **medátte imásu** 目立っています is outstanding, conspicuous → **medachimásu** 目立ちます
medetái *adj* めでたい **1.** happy (*events*), matter for congratulation **2.** = **o-medetái** おめでたい simple-minded, optimistic; idiot
médo *n* 針孔 the eye of a needle
médo *n* 目処 aim (= **méate** 目当て)
mēdo *n* メード maid
megabaito *n* メガバイト megabyte (MB)
megakemásu, megakéru *v* 目掛けます, 目掛ける aims at: **... o megákete** …を目がけて (*aiming*) at, (*going*) toward
mégane *n* メガネ・眼鏡 (*eye*) glasses: **~ o kakemásu** メガネ[眼鏡]を掛けます puts on (*wears*) glasses
megumaremásu, megumareru *v* 恵まれます, 恵まれる gets blessed: **... ni megumárete imásu** …に恵まれています is blessed with …
megumi *n* 恵み blessing, mercy, charity
megumimásu, megumu *v* 恵みます, 恵む blesses with, gives mercifully (*in charity*)

megurimásu, meguru *v* 巡ります, 巡る centers on, surrounds, concerns

me-gúsuri *n* 目薬・眼薬 eye lotion, eye drops

méi *n* 姪 = **meikko** 姪っ子 niece

...´-mei *suffix* ...名 (*counts people*) [BOOKISH] (= **...-nin** ...人): **ichí-~** 一名 one person

meibo *n* 名簿 list (*catalog*) of names, directory, register, roll

méibutsu *n* 名物 a local specialty, a special attraction, a famous product

méigo-san *n* 姪御さん (*your*) niece

meihaku (na) *adj* 明白(な) clear, obvious, explicit

mei-jimásu, mei-jiru *v* 命じます, 命じる commands; appoints, nominates, orders

meijín *n* 名人 expert

meimon (no) *adj* 名門(の) distinguished: **~-(gak-)kō** 名門(学)校 distinguished school

meirei *n* 命令 order, command

meiro *n* 迷路 labyrinth, maze

mé-isha *n* 目・眼医者 eye doctor, oculist

meishi *n* 名刺 business card, calling card, name card; **meishí-ire** *n* 名刺入れ business card case

meishi *n* 名詞 noun

meisho *n* 名所 famous place: **kankō-~** 観光名所 famous sightseeing spot

méiwaku *n* 迷惑 trouble, bother, nuisance: **~ na** 迷惑な troublesome; **(... ni) (go-)~ o kakemásu** (...に)(ご)迷惑をかけます causes (*one*) trouble

meiwaku-mēru *n* 迷惑メール e-mail spam, junk mail

méiyo *n* 名誉 prestige, honor, glory

mē´kā *n* メーカー maker, manufacturer

me-kákushi *n* 目隠し a blindfold

mekata *n* 目方 weight

me-kyábetsu *n* 芽キャベツ Brussels sprouts

mēkyáppu *n* メーキャップ makeup

mémo *n* メモ memo(-randum), note; **memo-chō** *n* メモ帳 note pad, tablet

memorii *n* メモリー (*computer*) memory (= **yōryō** 容量): **~ ga tarinai** メモリーが足りない runs out of memory

men *n* 面 **1.** mask **2.** face, front **3.** surface (= **hyōmén** 表面)

mén *n* 綿 cotton; **mén-bō** *n* 綿棒 cotton swab

mén *n* めん・麺 noodles

ménbā *n* メンバー member

mendō *n* 面倒 trouble, bother, nuisance; **mendō na** 面倒な bothersome

mendori *n* メンドリ hen

menjō´ *n* 免状 license; diploma

menkai *n* 面会 interview, meeting (= **intabyū** インタビュー)

ménkyo(-sho) *n* 免許(証) **1.** driver's license **2.** license, permit

ménseki *n* 面積 area

mentenansu *n* メンテナンス maintenance
ményū *n* メニュー menu
menzei (no) *adj* 免税(の) tax-free/-exempt: **~-hin** 免税品 tax-free goods
mērā *n* メーラー mailer (*computer*)
merii gō rando *n* メリーゴーランド merry-go-round
merodii *n* メロディー melody
méron *n* メロン melon
mēru *n* メール e-mail: **~ bokkusu** メールボックス e-mail box
meshí *n* 飯 cooked rice; a meal
meshiagarimásu, meshiagaru *v* 召し上がります, 召し上がる [HONORIFIC] eats; drinks
meshí-bitsu *n* めしびつ・飯櫃 rice bucket/tub
meshimásu, mésu *v* 召します, 召す [*in* FORMAL SPEECH *can replace such verbs as* **kimásu** 着ます (*wears*), **tabemásu** 食べます (*eats*), **nomimasu** 飲みます (*drinks*), **(kaze o) hikimásu** (風邪を)ひきます (*catches cold*), *etc., that involve the body*]
meshitá (no) *adj* 目下(の) inferior (*in status/rank/age*)
meshi-tsúkai *n* 召し使い servant
méssēji *n* メッセージ message
mesú *n* 雌・メス female animal
mesu *n* メス surgeon's knife
mētā *n* メーター meter (*device*)
mētoru *n* メートル meter(s) (*of length*)
mé-tsuki *n* 目付き a look (*in one's eye*): **~ ga/no warui** 目付きが/の悪い has evil eyes
métta (na) *adj* 滅多(な) reckless, rash
métta (ni) *adv* 滅多(に) [+ NEGATIVE verb] seldom: **~ ni nakimasen** 滅多に泣きません rarely cries
meue (no) *n* 目上(の) superior (*in status/rank/age*)
meushi *n* 雌牛 cow
me-yaní *n* 目やに matter (*gum, mucus*) from the eye
meyásu *n* 目安 **1.** a standard **2.** guide; aim
mezamashi (dokei) *n* 目覚まし(時計) alarm clock
mezamemásu, mezaméru *v* 目覚めます, 目覚める awake
mezashimásu, mezásu *v* 目指します, 目指す heads for (*a destination*)
mezurashíi *adj* 珍しい rare, uncommon, novel, curious, unusual, unexpected (*but welcome*)
mezuráshiku *adv* 珍しく unusually
mi *n* 実 **1.** fruit **2.** nut: **~ ga tawawani/takusan natteiru ki** 実がたわわに/たくさんなっている木 trees laden with fruit
mi... *prefix* 未. . . un…; **mi-chi (no)** *adj* 未知(の) unknown; **mi-hakken (no)** *adj* 未発見(の) undiscovered; **mi-hattatsu (no)/mi-kaihatsu (no)** *adj* 未発達(の)/未開発(の) undeveloped; **mi-kaiketsu (no)** *adj* 未解決(の) unsolved; **mi-kai (no)** *adj* 未開(の) uncultivated, wild; **mi-kakunin (no)** *adj* 未確認(の)

unidentified, unconfirmed; mi-kon (no) *adj* 未婚(の) unmarried: **~ no haha** 未婚の母 unmarried mother; mi-shō (no) *adj* 未詳(の) [BOOKISH] unknown: **sakusha-~** 作者未詳 unknown author; mi-zō (no) *adj* 未曾有(の) [BOOKISH] unprecedented, unheard-of

mi *n* 身 body; mi ni amarimásu (amaru) *v* 身に余ります(余る): **~ kōei desu** 身に余る光栄です It is an undeserved honor; mi ni shimimásu (shimiru) *v* 身に染みます(染みる), **mi ni shimimashita (shimita)** 身に染みました(染みた) ① It went to my heart. ② pierces one's body: **samusa ga ~** 寒さが身に染みます The cold pierced me.; mi ni tsukemásu (tsukeru) *v* 身につけます(つける) ① wears, puts on ② learns, acquires; mi ni tsumasaremásu (tsumasareru) *v* 身につまされます(つまされる) hits close to home, feels deeply, sympathizes deeply; mi no okiba ga arimasen (nai) *v* 身の置き場がありません(ない) There is no place to be/go.; mi o hikimásu (hiku) *v* 身を引きます(引く) ① retires ② recedes, stands down, backs off; mi o iremásu (ireru) *v* 身を入れます(入れる) puts oneself; mi o ko(na) ni shite hatarakimásu (hataraku) *v* 身を粉にして働きます(働く) works hard, sweats one's guts out; mi o makasemásu (makaseru) *v* 身を任せます(任せる) surrenders oneself 身をゆだねます); mi o tatemásu (tateru) *v* 身を立てます(立てる) establishes oneself (as…), makes a career; mi o yudanemásu (yudaneru) *v* 身をゆだねます(ゆだねる) surrenders oneself (= **mi o makasemásu (makaseru)** 身を任せます(任せる))

mibō´-jin *n* 未亡人 widow

míbun *n* 身分 social standing: **~-shōmei-sho** 身分証明書 ID card (*driver's license, insurance card, student ID card, alien registration card, etc.*)

míburi *n* 身振り gesture, movement (= **jesuchā** ジェスチャー)

michi *n* 道 **1.** way, path: **ikiru ~** 生きる道 the way to live: **kami no ~** 神の道 path of God **2.** street, road; michi-bata *n* 道端 wayside, roadside; michi-jun *n* 道順 the way, the route (*on the road*); michi-zure *n* 道連れ travelling companion, fellow traveler

michibikimás<u>u</u>, michibíku *v* 導きます, 導く leads, guides

michimás<u>u</u>, michíru *v* 満ちます, 満ちる gets complete, full

midaré *n* 乱れ disorder, messiness: **kami no ~ o naoshimás<u>u</u>** 髪の乱れを直します fixes one's messy hair

midaremás<u>u</u>, midaréru *v* 乱れます, 乱れる gets disturbed, disordered

midashi *n* 見出し **1.** heading, caption, headline **2.** a dictionary

entry; a headword **3.** contents, index, title
midashimásu̲, midásu *v* 乱します, 乱す throws into disorder, upsets, disturbs
mídori (no) *adj* 緑(の) green: **~-iro** 緑色 green color
mié *n* 見栄 show, display; (*dramatic*) pose: **~-ppari** 見栄っぱり a show-off: **~ o harimásu̲** 見栄を張ります shows off, puts on air
miemásu̲, miéru *v* 見えます, 見える **1.** is visible, can be seen **2.** appears; shows up, comes **3.** seems
migakimásu̲, migaku *v* 磨きます, 磨く polishes, shines
migara *n* 身柄: **~ no kōsoku** 身柄の拘束 custody
migi *n* 右 right (*not left*); **migi-ashi** *n* 右足 right leg/foot; **migi-dónari** *n* 右隣り next on the right; **migi-kiki (no)** *adj* 右利き(の) right-handed; **migi-máwari (ni)** *adv* 右回り(に) clockwise; **migi-te** *n* 右手 right hand
mígoto (na) *adj* 見事(な) splendid, admirable, beautiful
migurushíi *adj* 見苦しい unseemly, unsightly
mí-hako *n* 三箱 three boxfuls
mihon *n* 見本 **1.** a sample **2.** model, example
mii-hā´ *n* ミーハー lowbrow person
miíra *n* ミイラ mummy
mii´tingu *n* ミーティング meeting, conference [FORMAL] (= [BOOKISH] **káigi** 会議)
miitobōru *n* ミートボール meatball
mijikái *adj* 短い short (*not long*); brief
mijíkáku̲ *adv* 短く briefly, short
mijitaku *n* 身支度 dressing oneself
mikagé-ishi *n* 御影石 granite
mikake *n* 見かけ appearance
mikake *n* 見掛け outward appearance: **~ wa** 見掛けは outwardly, seemingly
mikaku *n* 味覚 sense of taste
míkan *n* ミカン・蜜柑 tangerine, mandarin (*orange*)
mikata *n* 味方 friend), accomplice, supporter, side: **...no ~ ni tsukimásu̲** ...の味方につきます takes sides with...
mi-kátá *n* 見方 a viewpoint: **...no ~ o kaemásu̲** ...の見方を変えます changes one's viewpoint: **~ ni yotte (wa)** 見方によって(は) in a way
mikazuki *n* 三日月 crescent (*moon*)
míki *n* 幹 trunk (*of tree*)
míki *n* 神酒 saké offered to the gods
míki̲sā *n* ミキサー blender
mikka *n* 三日 three days; 3rd day (*of month*)
mikomi *n* 見込み **1.** promise, hope **2.** outlook, expectation **3.** view, opinion
mikoshi̲ *n* 見越し forethought
mikoshi *n* おみこし・御輿 portable shrine (*for festival parades*)
mikuji *n* みくじ・神籤 written fortune
mimai *n* 見舞い a visit (*of solicitude*): **~-kyaku** 見舞い客 visitor

... míman *suffix* …未満 less than, below (*a quantity, an age*)
mimásu̲, míru *v* 見ます, 見る sees, looks, watches; tries doing
mimí *n* 耳 ear: **~ ga tōi** 耳が遠い is hard of hearing
mimi-kázari *n* 耳飾り earring
mimiuchi̲ *n* 耳打ち whisper(ing)
mimoto *n* 身元 one's identity: **~ fumei no shitai** 身元不明の死体 unidentified body
minami *n* 南 south: **~-guchi** 南口 the south exit/entrance; **~-yori (no kaze)** 南寄り(の風) southerly (wind)
Minami-Ámerika *n* 南アメリカ South America
mi-naraimásu̲, mi-narau *v* 見習います, 見習う follows (*learns from*) the example of
miná-san, mina-sama *n* 皆さん, 皆様 you all, everybody; (*you*) ladies and gentlemen
minato *n* 港 port
mine *n* 峰 peak, summit
mineraru-wōtā *n* ミネラルウォーター mineral water
mingei(-hin) *n* 民芸(品) folkcraft
mí ni-... *prefix, v* 見に. . . : **mí ni iku** 見に行く [goes] to see
minikúi *adj* 醜い ugly
mini-sukāto *n* ミニスカート mini-skirt
minkan (no) *adj* 民間(の) civil(ian), private (*non-government*)
mi(n)ná *n* み(ん)な・皆 everybody, all; everything, all, completely (= **zénbu** 全部) : **~ de** み(ん)なで・皆で altogether
minori *n* 実り crop, harvest
minorimásu̲, minóru *v* 実ります, 実る bears fruit; ripens
minoshirokin *n* 身代金 ransom
mi-no-take *n* 身の丈 **1.** one's height **2.** one's condition: **~ ni atta seikatsu o shimásu̲** 身の丈にあった生活をします lives within one's income
mi-no-ue *n* 身の上 one's station in life: **~-banashi** 身の上話 one's life story: **~-sōdan ran** 身の上相談欄 personal-advice column
minshū *n* 民衆 the masses, the people
minshúku *n* 民宿 bed and break-fast (B&B), family inn, hostelry,
minshu-shúgi *n* 民主主義 democ-racy
minto *n* ミント mint
min'yō *n* 民謡 folk song, ballad
mínzoku *n* 民族 (*human*) race
mioboe *n* 見覚え recognition
mi-okurimásu̲, mi-okuru *v* 見送ります, 見送る sees (*them*) off
miomo *n* 身重 pregnant female
mírai *n* 未来 future
mirin *n* ミリン・味醂 sweet rice wine (*for cooking*)
mirú-gai *n* ミルガイ・みる貝 surf clam, geoduck
míruku *n* ミルク milk (= **gyūnyū** 牛乳): **~-sḗki** ミルクセーキ milk-shake
miryoku *n* 魅力 charm (*attraction*);

miryoku-teki (na) *adj* 魅力的(な) charming
mísa *n* ミサ (*Catholic*) mass
misairu *n* ミサイル missile
misakai-nai/naku *adj, adv* 見境ない/なく indiscriminate(ly)
misaki *n* 岬 cape, headland
misao *n* 操 chastity
mise *n* 店 store, shop
mise-kake (no) *adj* 見せかけ(の) sham, make-believe, pretend(ed)
misemásu, miséru *v* 見せます, 見せる shows
mise-mónó *n* 見せ物 show, exhibition, exhibit
mishō (no) *adj* 実生(の) seedling
míso *n* 味噌 (*fermented*) **1.** bean paste (→ **miso-shíru** 味噌汁) **2.** child who is considered to be immature (*while playing, etc.*)
misogi *n* 禊 purification
misoji *n* みそじ・三十路 thirty years old
misoka *n* 晦日 last day of month
misoppa *n* 味噌っ歯 decayed tooth
misora *n* 身空 oneself, one's station in life: **wakai ~ de...** 若い身空で... ...at such a young age
miso-shíru *n* 味噌汁 soup seasoned with *miso*, *miso* soup
missetsu (na) *adj* 密接(な) thick, dense; close, intimate
misu *n* 御簾 bamboo blind
mísu *n* ミス miss, mistake
... mítai desu ...みたいです (= ... **no yō´desu (/da, na, de, ni)** ...の様です(/だ, な, で ,に) seems/looks (like); [NOUN] **~ desu** みたいです, [NOUN] **datta ~ desu** だったみたいです; verb-**(r)u/-tai ~ desu** -う(る)/たみたいです, [ADJECTIVE]**-i/ -katta ~ desu** い/かったみたいです
mitake *n* 身丈 **1.** total length of garment **2.** one's height **3.** one's situation
mitama *n* 御霊 [HONORIFIC] departed soul
mitame *n* 見た目 physical appearance
mitashimásu, mitásu *v* 満たします, 満たす fills up, satisfies
mitate *n* 見立て diagnosis, selection: **isha no ~** 医者の見立て doctor's opinion: **fuku no ~** 服の見立て choosing clothes (*for someone*)
mitei *n* 未定 to be determined
mitomemásu, mitomeru *v* 認めます, 認める recognizes, acknowledges, admits
mitorimásu, mitoru *v* 看取ります, 看取る **1.** cares for the sick, nurses **2.** attends to someone on his/her deathbed
mitorizu *n* 見取り図 blueprint, sketch
mitōshi *n* 見通し prospect, outlook
mikoshi 見越し forethought
mítsú *n* 三つ = **mittsú** 三つ (*three*)
mítsu *n* ミツ・蜜 honey; mitsú-bachi *n* ミツバチ・蜜蜂 (honey-)bee
mitsugo *n* 三つ子 **1.** triplets **2.** three year-old (child)

mitsukarimásu, mitsukaru *v* 見つかります, 見つかる is found, discovered; it turns up

mitsukemásu, mitsukeru *v* 見つけます, 見つける finds, discovers

mi-tsumemásu, mi-tsumeru *v* 見つめます, 見つめる gazes at, stares at

mi-tsumori *n* 見積もり an estimate

mi-tsumorimásu, mi-tsumóru *v* 見積もります, 見積もる estimates, rates

mítsu (na) *adj* 密(な) dense, thick

mitsurin *n* 密林 jungle

mitsuyu *n* 密輸 smuggling

mittsú *n* 三つ three; three years old (= **san-sai** 三歳): **mittsu-mé** 三つ目 third

mittsū *n* 密通 adultery, intrigue

miuchi *n* 身内 family, close relatives and close friends

miugoki *n, v* 身動き [(usually) +NEGATIVE] **1.** moving oneself: **man'indensha de ~ (ga) toremasen** 満員電車で身動き(が)とれません is stuck on a packed train **2.** acts freely: **shigoto ga isogashikute ~ (ga) toremasen** 仕事が忙しくて身動き(が)とれません is tied up with busy work

mi-ukemásu, mi-ukéru *v* 見受けます, 見受ける observes, happens to see; appears (*to be*)

mi-wakemásu, mi-wakéru *v* 見分けます, 見分ける discriminates, distinguishes

miwaku *n* 魅惑 [BOOKISH] enchantment; **miwaku teki (na)** *adj* 魅惑的(な) enchanting

miya *n* 宮 **1. o-miya** お宮 Shinto shrine **2.** prince, princess

miyage *n* 土産 souvenir

miyako *n* 都 capital city

miyori *n* 身寄り relatives: **~ no nai kodomo** 身寄りのない子供 child who has no relatives (*to rely on*): **no nai otoshiyori/kōrei-sha tachi** 身寄りのないお年寄り/高齢者たち old people who have no (*supportive*) relatives

mizo *n* 溝 drain, ditch, gutter

mizoochi *n* 鳩尾 pit of the stomach

mizore *n* 霙 sleet

mizu *n* 水 (*not hot*) water: **tsumetai ~** 冷たい水 cold water: **nurui ~** ぬるい水 lukewarm water; **mizu-búsoku** *n* 水不足 water shortage; **mizu-gi** *n* 水着 swim suit, bathing suit; **mizu-taki** *n* 水炊き chicken, bean curd, etc., dipped into hot broth till ready to eat; **mizu-wari** *n* 水割り (*highball of*) whisky and water

mizū'mi *n* 湖 lake

mo *n* 喪 mourning: **~ ni fukushimásu** 喪に服します mourns (*the passing*)

... mo *suffix, prep* …も too, also, even; (*not*)… either/even; indeed; number **mo** も [+ NEGATIVE] not even (*so much as*), [+ AFFIRMATIVE] as many/much as, all of

... mo ... mo *conj* …も…も both …and …; [+ NEGATIVE] neither … nor …

mō´ *adv* もう already; now: ~ **súgu** もうすぐ right away
mō *adj* もう more; (*not*) … any more: ~ **hitóri** もう一人 another (*one more*) person; ~ **hitótsu** もう一つ another, one more, the other one; ~ **ichi-dó/ík-kái** もう一度/一回 one more time, again; ~ **sukóshi** もう少し (a bit) more
mochi *n* 餅 rice cake
mochi-agemásu, mochi-agéru *v* 持ち上げます, 持ち上げる lifts
mochi-awase *n* 持ち合わせ what is on hand (*in stock*)
mochi-awasemásu, mochi-awaséru *v* 持ち合わせます, 持ち合わせる has on hand (*in stock*)
mochiba *n* 持ち場 one's post of duty
mochi-gome *n* もち米 glutinous rice
mochiimásu, mochiíru *v* 用います, 用いる uses
mochimásu, mótsu *v* 持ちます, 持つ has, holds, carries; it lasts
mochí-mono *n* 持ち物 **1.** belongings **2.** what to bring: **"~: hikki yōgu"** 「持ち物: 筆記用具」"what to bring: writing instrument"
mochí-nushi *n* 持ち主 owner
mochíron *adv* もちろん of course, certainly
mōchō *n* 盲腸 appendix; mōchō´(-en) *n* 盲腸(炎) appendicitis
mōchū *n* 喪中 mourning period
modemu *n* モデム modem
moderu *n* モデル model
mōdō-ken *n* 盲導犬 seeing-eye dog
modorimásu, modóru *v* 戻ります, 戻る goes back, returns, reverts
modoshimásu, modósu *v* 戻します, 戻す **1.** vomits **2.** sends back, returns
moegara *n* 燃え殻 cinder(s)
moemásu, moeru *v* 燃えます, 燃える (*fire*) burns
mō´fu *n* 毛布 blanket
mōfuku *n* 喪服 mourning dress
mogi *n* 模擬 imitation; mogi-shiken *n* 模擬試験 trial test, mock examination
mogura *n* モグラ・土竜 a mole (*rodent*)
mogurí *n* 潜り diving; a diver
mogurimásu, mogúru *v* 潜ります, 潜る dives (*under*); gets into (*bed*); goes under(ground)
mohan *n* 模範 model, pattern, example (= **mihon** 見本, **tehon** 手本: **~ o shimeshimásu** 模範を示します gives an example; mohan-sei *n* 模範生 model student; mohan-kaitō *n* 模範解答 model answers
mohaya *adv* もはや [+ NEGATIVE verb] no longer
móji *n* 文字 letter, character, writing: **ō-~** 大文字 capital letter, upper-case letter: **ko-~** 小文字 lower-case letter; moji-dōri *adv* 文字どおり literally
mōjín *n* 盲人 blind person
mōkarimásu, mōkáru *v* 儲かります, 儲かる is profitable, it makes money

mokei *n* 模型 model, mold (= **moderu** モデル); mokei-hikōki *n* 模型飛行機 model airplane; mokei-jidōsha *n* 模型自動車 model car

mōkemásu, mōkéru *v* 儲けます, 儲ける makes money, profits

mōkemásu, mōkéru *v* 設けます, 設ける prepares, sets up

Mṓko *n* 蒙古 Mongolia (= **mongoru** モンゴル): **Mōko-jin** 蒙古人 a Mongolian

mokugeki *n* 目撃 witness; mokugeki-sha *n* 目撃者 a witness, an eye-witness

mokuhan (-ga) *n* 木版(画) wood-block print

mokuhyō *n* 目標 target, goal: **~ o/wa takaku mote!** 目標を/は高く持て! Shoot for the moon!

mokuji *n* 目次 (*table of*) contents

mokuroku *n* 目録 catalog, list, table, inventory

Mokusei *n* 木星 Jupiter

mokusō *n* 黙想 meditation

mokután *n* 木炭 charcoal

mokuteki *n* 目的 aim, objective, purpose, end, goal (= **nerai** 狙い, **mato** 的, **mokuhyō** 目標): **~ no tame ni (wa) shudan o erabimasen** 目的のために(は)手段を選びません uses any trick to achieve one's ends; mokutekí-chi *n* 目的地 destination, goal: **~ ni (tadori-)tsukimásu** 目的地に辿り着きます arrives at one's destination; mokuteki-go *n* 目的語 (*grammar*) object

mokutō *n* 黙祷 silent prayer: **giseisha ni ippun-kan/sanpun-kan no ~ o sasagemásu** 犠牲者に1分間/3分間の黙祷を捧げます offers a one-minute/three-minutes silent prayer for the victims

Mokuyṓ(bi) *n* 木曜(日) Thursday

mokuyoku *n* 沐浴 bathing, washing oneself (*to clean*)

mokuzai *n* 木材 wood

mokuzen (no) *adj* 目前(の) immediate: **~ no rieki** 目前の利益 immediate advantage

mome-goto *n* 揉め事 discord, tiff, trouble: **o okoshimásu** 揉め事を起こします causes troubles

momemásu, momeru *v* 揉めます, 揉める **1.** is in discord/trouble: **ki ga ~** 気が揉めます feels uneasy/troubled **2.** can massage (*rub with both hands*)

momen *n* 木綿 cotton

momi *n* もみ・籾 unhulled rice

mómi *n* モミ fir

mómiji *n* モミジ・紅葉 **1.** maple **2.** autumn leaves

momimásu, momu *v* 揉みます, 揉む massages, rubs with both hands

momo *n* モモ・桃 peach

mómo *n* 股 thigh

momohiki *n* 股引き longjohns; drawers (= **zubón-shita** ズボン下)

momo-iro (no) *adj* 桃色(の) pink, rosy: **~ hada** 桃色の肌 pink skin

... món ... *interj* もん (*mostly female; informal, baby talk*) because (= **... monó...** もの):

(*baby talk or female*) **datte sō da ~ (monó)** だってそうだもん(もの)

món *n* 紋 family crest

món *n* 門 gate; **món-ban/mon-ei** *n* 門番/門衛 gatekeeper, watchman, guard, porter; **mon-gen** *n* 門限 curfew

Monbu-Kagaku-daijin *n* 文部科学大臣 Minister of Education, Culture, Sports, Science and Technology

Monbú-Kagaku-shō *n* 文部科学省 Ministry of Education, Culture, Sports, Science and Technology (MEXT)

mondai *n* 問題 **1.** question, topic, subject, exercise: **~ ni naránai** 問題にならない unimportant **2.** problem, issue, trouble (= **toraburu** トラブル)

mongái-kan *n* 門外漢 outsider, nonspecialist, layman: **keizai (ni kanshite) wa ~ desu** 経済(に関して)は門外漢です is a layman in economics

Mongoru *n* モンゴル Mongolia (= **mōko** 蒙古); **Mongoru-jin** *n* モンゴル人 a Mongolian; **Mongoru-go** *n* モンゴル語 Mongolian (*language*)

mónku *n* 文句 **1.** phrase: **utai-~** 謳い文句 a motto, catchphrase, slogan: **odoshi-~** 脅し文句 threatening words **2.** complaint: **~ no tsukeyō ga arimasen** 文句のつけようがありません is perfect

monó *n* 物 thing, object, article, something, stuff

...mono *suffix* . . . もの **… shita ~/món desu** …したもの/もんです used to do

monó *n* 者 person, fellow [BOOKISH] (= **hito** 人)

monogátari *n* 物語 tale, legend

monógoto *n* 物事 things, everything

monohoshisō (na/ni) *adj, adv* 物欲しそう(な/に) wistful(ly)

monomane *n* ものまね・物真似 mimic(ry), impersonation

mono-óboe *n* 物覚え memory: **~ ga ii** 物覚えがいい is quick to learn (= **nomikomi ga hayai** のみ込みが早い): **~ ga warui** 物覚えが悪い is slow to learn

mono-óki *n* 物置き shed (*storehouse*)

monorē´ru *n* モノレール monorail

monorōgu *n* モノローグ soliloquy, monologue (= **dokuhaku** 独白)

monosashi *n* 物差し ruler (*foot rule*); measure; criterion

mono-sugói *adj* 物凄い terrible, awesome

mono-súgóku *adv* 物凄く terribly, extremely

monózukí (na) *adj* 物好き(な) curious, inquisitive

monshō *n* 紋章 family crest

moppara *adv* 専ら principally, chiefly

móppu *n* モップ mop

moraimásu, morau *v* もらいます, もらう receives, gets; has someone do it

mō´ra shimásu (suru) *v* 網羅します(する) includes, comprises,

covers (*all*): ~ **shita ...** 網羅した… exhaustive, complete

morashimásu, morásu *v* 漏らします, 漏らす lets leak; reveals

moremásu, moréru *v* 漏れます, 漏れる leaks out; is omitted; it leaks

mori *n* 森 woods, forest

morimásu, moru *v* 盛ります, 盛る heaps/piles it up

morimásu, móru *v* 漏ります, 漏る it leaks

morói *adj* もろい・脆い brittle, frail

morote *n* もろて・諸手 both hands: ~ **o agete sansei shimásu** 諸手を挙げて賛成します totally agrees

morotomo *n* もろとも together [BOOKISH]: **shinaba ~** 死なばもろとも go to the grave together

mō′ru *n* モール braid

moruhine *n* モルヒネ morphine

móshi (... shitára) *conj* もし(…したら) if, perchance

mō′shi-agemásu, mō′shi-agéru *v* 申し上げます, 申し上げる [HUMBLE] I say

mōshi-de *n* 申し出 proposal, offer; report, application, claim

mōshi-demásu, mōshi-déru *v* 申し出ます, 申し出る proposes, offers; reports, applies for, claims

mōshi-ire *n* 申し入れ (*public*) proposal, offering

mōshi-iremásu, mōshi-iréru *v* 申し入れます, 申し入れる (*publicly*) proposes, offers

moshi-ka-shitara *adv* もしかしたら, **moshi-ka-suru to** もしかすると perhaps

mōshi-komi *n* 申し込み application; reservation, subscription; proposal, offer

mōshi-komimásu, mōshi-kómu *v* 申し込みます, 申し込む applies; reserves, subscribes; proposes, offers

mōshikomí-sha *n* 申し込み者・申込者 applicant

mōshimásu, mō′su *v* 申します, 申す [HUMBLE] **1.** I say (= **mōshi-agemásu** 申し上げます) **2.** I humbly do (= **itashimásu** 致します)

móshi-moshi! *interj* もしもし! hello! hey! say there! (*on the phone*)

mō′shitate *n* 申し立て statement, testimony, allegation

mō′shi-wake *n* 申し訳 excuse: [FORMAL] ~ **arimasén/gozaimasén** 申し訳ありません/ございません I am very sorry.

mō′shon *n* モーション motion; sexual overture, pass: **... ni ~ o kakemásu** …にモーションをかけます makes a pass at, makes eyes at

Mosukuwa *n* モスクワ Moscow

mō′tā *n* モーター motor; **mōtā-bōto** *n* モーターボート motorboat

motaremásu, motaréru *v* もたれます, もたれる: **(... ni) ~** (…に)もたれます leans (*against* ...)

motasemásu, motaséru *v* 持たせます,

持たせる lets one have, provides (*one with*), gives

motemásu, motéru *v* 持てます, 持てる **1.** is popular, well-liked **2.** can hold

motenashi *n* もてなし hospitality

mōteru *n* モーテル motel

motó *n* 元・本 origin, source; cause (*of an effect*)

motó *n* 下 (*at the*) foot (*of*), under

...-moto *suffix* …元 the source of an activity: **shuppan-~** 出版元 the publisher(s); **hanbai-~** 販売元 sales agency

móto (no) *adj* 元(の) former, earlier, original: **móto kara** 元から from the beginning, always, all along

motomemásu, motoméru *v* 求めます, 求める **1.** wants, looks for **2.** asks for, demands **3.** buys, gets

motomoto *adv* 元々 from the start, originally; by nature, naturally: **…-témo ~ désu** … ても元々です is no worse off even if …, it will do no harm to …

móto wa *adv* 元は originally; earlier, before

mótó-yori *adv* もとより from the beginning; by nature

motozukimásu, motozúku *v* 基づきます, 基づく is based on; conforms to

motsuré *n* もつれ tangle, entanglement; complications

motsuremásu, motsureru *v* もつれます, もつれる gets entangled/complicated: **shitá ga ~** 舌がもつれます lisps

mottai-nái *adj* もったいない **1.** undeserving **2.** wasteful

motte ikimásu (iku) *v* 持って行きます(行く) takes, carries; brings (*to you, there*)

mótte imásu (iru) *v* 持っています(いる) has, holds, owns, possesses

motte itte *v* 持って行って taking it: **~ kudasái** 持って行って下さい please take it with you

motte kimásu (kúru) *v* 持って来ます(来る) brings (*to me, here*)

motte-kói (no) *adj* もってこい(の) most desirable, ideal; just the thing/ticket

mótto *adv* もっと more, still more; longer, further: **~ íi** もっといい better; **~ warúi** もっと悪い worse; **~ takusán** もっとたくさん lots more; **~ saki (ni)** もっと先(に) further

móttomo *adv, conj* もっとも **1.** indeed, of course **2.** but, however, to be sure

móttómo *adv* 最も most; exceedingly

móya *n* もや・靄 mist, haze

moyashi *n* モヤシ bean sprouts

moyō *n* 模様 pattern, design

moyōshimásu, moyō´su *v* 催します, 催す holds/gives (*an event*); feels

mozaiku *n* モザイク mosaic

mozō *n* 模造 imitation; **mozō-hin** *n* 模造品 imitation products

mu... *prefix* 無… un-, without…, …less; **mu-bō (na)** *adj* 無謀(な)

reckless; mu-chákuriku (no) *adj* 無着陸(の) non-stop (flight); mú-cha (na) *adj* 無茶(な) unreasonable; reckless; disorderly; mú-chi *n* 無知 ignorance; mu-dan (de) *adj* 無断(で) without notice, without permission; mu-ími (na) *adj* 無意味(な) meaningless; mu-íshiki (no/na) *adj* 無意識(の/な) unconscious, involuntary; mu-jō´ken (no) *adj* 無条件(の) unconditional: ~ **no ai** 無条件の愛 unconditional love; mu-jō (na) *adj* 無情(な) heartless, unfeeling; mu-kánkaku (na) *adj* 無感覚(な) numb; mu-kánkei (no/na) *adj* 無関係(の/な): **... to mukánkei** ...と無関係(の/な) unrelated (*unconnected, irrelevant*) to ...; mu-kidō (no) *adj* 無軌道(の) reckless, trackless; mu-kigen (no/ni) *adj, adv* 無期限(の/に) indefinite(ly); mu-kimei (no) *adj* 無記名(の) unsigned, unregistered; mu-kō (no/na) *adj* 無効(の/な) invalid (*not valid*), null; mu-sékinin (na) *adj* 無責任(な) irresponsible; mu-shoku (no) *adj* 無色(の) colorless(ness); mu-teki *n* 無敵 invincibility, too strong to have as rival: **tenka-~** 天下無敵 having no rival in the world; mu-tón-chaku/-jaku (na) *adj* 無頓着/無自覚(な) careless; mú-yō (no) *adj* 無用(の) unnecessary; useless; having no business; mú-zai (no) *adj* 無罪(の) innocent, not guilty; muzō´sa (na) *adj* 無造作(な) effortless, easy

múchi *n* 鞭 a whip

muchū *n* 夢中 trance, ecstasy: **... ni ~ ni narimásu** ...に夢中になります gets entranced with (*engrossed in*) ...

muda-bánashi *n* 無駄話 idle talk, hot air, bull

muda (na) *adj* 無駄(な) futile, no good, wasteful; useless: **muda-ashi** 無駄足 fool's errand

muda-zúkai *n* 無駄使い extravagance, waste

múgi *n* 麦 wheat, barley

mugi-wara *n* 麦わら straw

mugói *adj* むごい cruel, brutal

muika *n* 六日 six days; the 6th day (*of month*): **~-mé** 六日目 the 6th day

mujun *n* 矛盾 inconsistency, contradiction

mukade *n* ムカデ・百足 centipede

mukae 迎え *n* a welcome

mukaemásu, mukaeru *v* 迎えます, 迎える meets; welcomes; invites

mukai-kaze *n* 向かい風 headwind

mukaimásu, mukau *v* 向かいます, 向かう: **... ni ~** ...に向かいます opposes; heads for

múkamuka shimásu *v* むかむか[ムカムカ]します is queasy, feels nauseated

mukashi *n* 昔 long (time) ago; ancient days; mukashi no *adj* 昔の ancient, old(-en); mukashi-bánashi *n* 昔話 legend; folk tale; mukashi kará no *adj* 昔からの old (*from way back*)

mukemásu̱, mukeru *v* 向けます, 向ける turns (*one's face/eyes/attention to*), directs/points it (*at*)

...-muke (no) *suffix, adj* …向け(の) (*bound/intended*) for …: **kazoku-~ (no)** 家族向け(の) for family

mukimásu̱, muku *v* 向きます, 向く faces

mukimásu̱, muku *v* 剥きます,剥く (**… no kawá o ~** … の皮を剥きます) skins, pares, peels

...-muki (no) *suffix, adj* …向き(の) facing; (*suitable*) for …

múko *n* 婿 son-in-law; bridegroom

mukō *prep, adv* 向こう **1.** beyond; across the way, over there: **~ no** 向こうの opposite, facing **2.** → mukō-gawa *n* 向こう側 the other side/party, the opposite side; mukō′-mizu (na) *adj* 向こう見ず(な) reckless, rash

mukuimásu̱, mukuíru *v* 報います, 報いる [BOOKISH] repays; compensates

mumei (no) *adj* 無名(の) nameless, anonymous; obscure

munashii *adj* 空しい・虚しい empty; futile, in vain

muné *n* 胸 **1.** chest, breast **2.** heart, mind

muné *n* 旨 gist, intent, effect

muné *n* 棟 ridge (*of roof*)

murá *n* 村 village: **~-bito, ~ no hito** 村人, 村の人 village people: **~ hachibu** 村八分 ostracism

muragarimásu̱, muragáru *v* 群がります, 群がる they flock/throng together

murásaki *n* **1. murásaki (no)** 紫(の) purple **2.** 紫 soy sauce

muré *n* 群れ group, throng, flock

múri 1. *n* 無理 strain, (*undue*) force: **~ (o) shimásu̱** 無理(を)します overdoes, overworks, forces oneself **2. ~ na** 無理な unreasonable, forced; violent; overdoing; (over-)demanding; muri mo arimasen (nai) *v* 無理もありません(ない) no wonder; múri wa nái *adj* 無理はない it is no wonder that…; muriyari *adv* 無理矢理 forcibly

muryō (no) *adj* 無料(の) free of charge: **~-chū′shajō** 無料駐車場 free parking

musen *n* 無線 radio; wireless; musen-ran *n* 無線 LAN wireless LAN, Wi-Fi (*computer*)

mushi *n* ムシ・虫 insect, bug; moth; worm: **~ no iki** 虫の息 breathing faintly, being at death's door; mushi-megane *n* 虫眼鏡 magnifying glass; mushi-yoke *n* 虫よけ insect repellent; mothballs

mushi *n* 無視 neglect, ignorance

mushi-atsúi *adj* 蒸し暑い muggy, close, sultry, humid

mushi-ba *n* 虫歯 decayed tooth

mushimásu̱, músu *v* 蒸します, 蒸す steams it; is sultry, humid

mushí-mono *n* 蒸し物 steamed foods

múshiro *adv* むしろ rather; preferably

múshi shimásu̱ (suru) *v* 無視します(する) ignores, neglects, disregards

musō *n* 夢想 dream, imagination; musō-ka *n* 夢想家 dreamer
musubi *n* むすび riceball
musubimásu̱, musubu *v* 結びます, 結ぶ ties, ties up: **nékutai o ~** ネクタイを結びます wears a tie
musu̱ko *n* 息子 son: **~-san** 息子さん (*your/someone else's*) son
musume *n* 娘 daughter; girl: **~-san** 娘さん (*your/someone else's*) daughter, lady
musū´ (no) *adj* 無数(の) countless, innumerable
mutsu *n* ムツ big eye fish
mutsu̱kashii, muzukashii *adj* 難しい hard, difficult
muttsú *n* 六つ・6つ six (= **rok-ko** 6個); six years old (= **roku-sai** 六歳)
múyami (ni) *adv* 無闇(に) recklessly; indiscriminately; immoderately
múzumuzu suru *adj* むずむずする itchy, crawly, creepy
myakú *n* 脈: **myaku̱haku** 脈拍 pulse: **~ o hakarimásu̱** 脈を計ります checks one's pulse (rate)
myō... *prefix* 明. . . tomorrow…; myō´-ban *n, adv* 明晩 [BOOKISH] tomorrow night; myō-chō *n, adv* 明朝 [BOOKISH] tomorrow morning; myō-gó-nichi *n, adv* 明後日 [BOOKISH] day after tomorrow (= **asatte** あさって・明後日); myō´-nichi *n, adv* 明日 tomorrow (= **ashi̱ta, asu** 明日)
myōga *n* ミョウガ・茗荷 Japanese ginger (*buds*)
myō´ji, miyoji *n* 名字・苗字 family name [*as written*] (= **sei** 姓)
myō´(na) *adj* 妙(な) strange, queer, wondrous
myūjikaru *n* ミュージカル musical (*show*)

N

n´ ("un") *n* ん(うん) uh-huh, yeah [INFORMAL] (= **hai** はい [FORMAL])
n¯´ ("ūn") *n* んー(うーん) hmm, well, let's see
...´n ... *suffix* …ん… = **…´no …** …の…: **…´n desu̱ (da)** …んです(だ) it's that …
na *n* 名 name (= **namae** 名前); na bakari (no) *adj* 名ばかり(の) nominal; na-dakái *adj* 名高い famous; na-fuda *n* 名札 name plate/tag; dog tag; na no aru *adj* 名のある famous; na no tōtta *adj* 名の通った well-known; na o nokoshimásu̱ (nokosu) *v* 名を残します, 残す earns one's place; na wa tai o arawasu 名は体を表す please show your name
ná *n* 菜 greens, vegetables
... na! *interj* …な! Don't … !
... ná/nā´ *interj* …な/なあ (*usually male*) = **... né/nē´** …ね/ねえ (*female*) isn't it, don't you think/agree

nábe *n* 鍋 **1.** pan, pot **2.** food cooked and served in a pan
nadamemásu, nadaméru *v* 宥めます, 宥める soothes, pacifies
nadare *n* 雪崩 avalanche; snowslide
nademásu, nadéru *v* 撫でます, 撫でる strokes, smooths, pats, pets
... nádo *suffix* …など・等 and so forth/on, and what-not, and the like
náe *n* 苗 seedling: **~-doko** 苗床 seedbed
naemásu, naéru *v* 萎えます, 萎える droops, withers
naemásu, naéru *v* なえます, なえる can twist it (*into a rope*)
nafutarin *n* ナフタリン mothballs
naga-... *prefix* 長. . . long; naga-chōba *n* 長丁場 [BOOKISH] time-consuming: **~-chōba no shigoto** 長丁場の仕事 time-consuming work; naga-gutsu *n* 長靴 boots; naga-iki *n* 長生き longevity, long life; naga-sode *n* 長袖 long sleeves, long-sleeved garment; naga-yu *n* 長湯 a long bath
nagái *adj* 長い long
nagaku *adv* 長く long
nagamé *n* 眺め view, scenery
nagamemásu, nagaméru *v* 眺めます, 眺める gazes/stares at, views
... (-)nágara *suffix, adv* …ながら while (*during/although*)
nagaré *n* 流れ a stream, a flow; nagare-sagyō *n* 流れ作業 assembly line; nagare-zu *n* 流れ図 flow chart
nagaré-boshi *n* 流れ星 shooting star
nagaremásu, nagaréru *v* 流れます, 流れる flows
nágasa *n* 長さ length
Nagásaki *n* 長崎 Nagasaki; **~-shi** 長崎市 Nagasaki City
nagashí *n* 流し kitchen sink
nagashimásu, nagásu *v* 流します, 流す lets it flow, washes away
naga(t)tarashii *n* 長(っ)たらしい [IN NEGATIVE SENSE] lengthy, tedious: **~ enzetsu** 長たらしい演説 lengthy speech
naga-ya *n* 長屋 tenement house
nage-ire *v* 投げ入れ a flower arrangement (*in a tall vase*)
nagekimásu, nagéku *v* 嘆きます, 嘆く grieves, weeps, moans, laments
nagemásu, nagéru *v* 投げます, 投げる throws
nage-nawa *n* 投げ縄 lasso
nagisa *n* なぎさ・渚 water's edge, beach, shore
nagori *n* 名残 traces, remains, remnant
nagurimásu, nagúru *v* 殴ります, 殴る knocks, beats, strikes
nagusame *n* 慰め comfort, consolation
nagusamemásu, nagusaméru *v* 慰めます, 慰める comforts, consoles
nagusami *n* 慰み amusement, entertainment
nái *v* ない = **arimasén** ありません (there is no …, lacks, has no …)
nai-... *prefix* 内. . . within, in(-side), inner, internal; nái-bu (no) *adj* 内部(の) internal; naibu-kokuhatsu *n*

内部告発 exposing from within, whistle-blowing; nái-chi *n* 内地 inside the country; nai-en (no) *adj* 内縁(の) common-law: **~ no otto/tsuma** 内縁の夫/妻 common-law husband/wife; nai-fuku *n* 内服 taking medicine orally; nai-jō *n* 内情 internal affairs; nai-ju *n* 内需 domestic demand; nai-ka *n* 内科 internal medicine; nai-mitsu (no) *adj* 内密(の) confidential, secret, private [FORMAL]: **~ (no) jōhō** 内密(の)情報 confidential information; nai-ran *n* 内乱 civil strife; nai-riku *n* 内陸 inland; nai-shin *n* 内心 ① (*one's*) thoughts in mind: **~ kowai** 内心怖い is scared deep down ② inner center (*not outer center*); nai-shin *n* 内診 ① internal examination (*gynecology*) ② medical examination by a doctor at home; nai-shukketsu *n* 内出血 internal bleeding; nai-tei *n* 内偵 [BOOKISH] secret investigation; nai-teki (na) *adj* 内的(な) internal; nai-zō *n* 内臓 internal organs

...´-nai *suffix* …内 within, in(side) (→ **kanai** 家内, **kokúnai (no)** 国内(の), **kō´nai** 構内)

...-náide *suffix, adv* …ないで not [do] but instead, without [do]ing → **shináide** しないで

náifu *n* ナイフ knife

náigai *n* 内外 **1.** inside and out **2.** home and abroad

...-náigai *suffix* …内外 approximately: **senen-~** 千円内外 approximately 1,000 yen

Naijeria *n* ナイジェリア Nigeria; Naijeria-jin *n* ナイジェリア人 a Nigerian

naiji *n* 内示 unofficial announcement (*in office*)

náikaku *n* 内閣 a government cabinet: **~-sōridaijin** 内閣総理大臣 prime minister

naimásu, náu *v* ないます, なう twists (*into a rope*)

náiron *n* ナイロン nylon

... náishi ... *conj* …ないし… [BOOKISH] **1.** and/or (= **mátáwa** または・又は) **2.** from … to … = **…kara…máde** …から…まで

naishó (no) *adj* 内緒・内証(の) confidential, secret, private [INFORMAL]: **~ no hanashí** 内緒[内証]の話, **~-bánashi** 内緒[内証]話 a private talk

náitā *n* ナイター night game (*of baseball*)

naitei *n* 内定 unofficial decision, informal appointment, unofficial job offer

naiyō *n* 内容 contents

náka *n, prep* 中 inside; **… no ~ de/ni** …の中で/に in …; naka-darumi *n* 中だるみ slump; naká-mi *n* 中身・中味 contents; naka-niwa *n* 中庭 courtyard; naka-yubi *n* 中指 middle finger

náka *n* 仲 relations, terms (*between people*); **(… to) ~ ga íi** (…と)仲がいい is on good terms (with

…); ~ **tagai** 仲違い discord; naka-dachí *n* 仲立ち go-between, intermediary; naká-gai *n* 仲買 broker; naka-má *n* 仲間 friend, pal, companion

nakabá *n* 半ば middle: **kokorozashi-~ de** 志半ばで without fulfilling one's ambition

nakanaka *adv* なかなか extremely, very (*long, hard, bad, etc.*), more than one might expect

nákattara *v* なかったら if/when there isn't/we don't; unless there is (we have)

...-nákattara *suffix, v* …なかったら if/when one doesn't; unless one does

nákattari *v* なかったり sometimes/alternately there isn't (*we don't have*)

...-nákattari (shimásu) *suffix, v* …なかったり(します) sometimes/alternately does not do

nakemásu, nakeru *v* 泣けます, 泣ける can cry

náki ... *prefix, adj* なき… [LITERARY] = **nái …** ない… (lacking, nonexistent)

náki ... *prefix, adj* 亡き… [LITERARY] = **nái …** ない… (deceased): **íma wa ~ …** 今は亡き… the late …: **~ sofu** 亡き祖父 one's dead grandfather; naki-gara *n* 亡骸 [BOOKISH] corpse

nakimásu, naku *v* 泣きます, 泣く weeps; cries; naki-dokoro *n* 泣きどころ[所] Achilles' heel; naki-goe *n* 泣き声 cry, sob (*of person*); naki-goto *n* 泣き言 complaining

nakimásu, naku *v* 鳴きます, 鳴く makes an animal sound; naki-goe *n* 鳴き声 chirp, song, chirping (*of animals, birds, insects, etc*)

nakō´do *n* 仲人 go-between (*matchmaker*)

náku *v* なく so that there isn't any (*we don't have any*); there not being; without

...-naku (narimásu) *suffix, v* …なく(なります) (*gets*) so that one doesn't do (= **…-nai yō´ni (narimásu)**…ないように(なります))

naku-narimásu, naku-naru *v* 亡くなります, 亡くなる dies; gets lost

naku-narimásu, naku-naru *v* なくなります, なくなる vanishes (*from existence*)

nakushimásu, nakusu *v* なくします, なくす loses

...-nákute mo *suffix, v* …なくても even not doing, even if one does not do; **shinákute mo íi** しなくてもいい need not do

...-nákute wa *suffix, v* …なくては not doing, if one does not do; **shinákute wa ikemasén** しなくてはいけません must (*ought to*) do

náma *adj, n* 生 **1. ~ (no/de)** 生(の/で) raw, uncooked, fresh **2.** (= **~-bíiru** 生ビール) draft beer; nama-chūkei *n* 生中継 live coverage; nama-gomi *n* 生ごみ garbage (*kitchen waste*); nama-gusái *adj* 生臭い fishy(-smelling);

nama-henji *n* 生返事 half-hearted reply; nama-hōsō *n* 生放送 live program, live broadcast; nama-yake (no) *adj* 生焼け(の) rare (*little cooked*), underdone

namae *n* 名前 name (= **shimei** 氏名, **seimei** 姓名)

namaiki (na) *adj* 生意気(な) impertinent

namakemásu, namakéru *v* 怠けます, 怠ける idles, is lazy

namake-mono *n* 怠け者 lazy (*person*)

namari *n* ナマリ・鉛 lead (*metal*)

namarí *n* なまり・訛り dialect, accent (= **hōgen** 方言)

namarimásu, namaru *v* 鈍ります, 鈍る **1.** becomes rusty, gets dull: **hōchō ga ~** 包丁が鈍ります a kitchen knife gets dull **2.** becomes weak (*one's body part*)

namazu *n* ナマズ・鯰 catfish

namemásu, naméru *v* なめます, なめる licks, tastes

naméraka (na) *adj* なめらか(な) smooth

namí *n* 波 wave; nami-norí *n* 波乗り surfing

námida *n* 涙 tear (*in eye*): **~-me** 涙目 teary eyes: **~-moroi** 涙もろい easily moved to tears

namiki *n* 並木 row of trees: **~-michi** 並木道 tree-lined road, tree-lined street

nami (no) *adj* 並(の) ordinary, common, average, regular

nán *n* ナン bread

nán *n* 何 (*before* **d**, **t**, **n**) = **náni** 何 what

nán-... *prefix* 何… how many …: **nán** [COUNTER **ka**] **(no…)** 何 [COUNTER か] (の…) a number (of …); nán-ba 何羽 how many (*birds, rabbits*); nan-bai 何倍 how many times (*doubled*); nán-bai 何杯 how many cupfuls; nán-ban 何番 what number; nán-bén 何遍 how many times; nán-biki 何匹 how many (*fishes/bugs, small animals*); nán-bon 何本 how many (*pencils/bottles, long objects*); nán-byaku 何百 how many hundreds; nán-dai 何台 how many (*machines, vehicles*); nán-do 何度 how many times; nan-gai/-kai *n* 何階/階 how many floors/stories; what (number) floor; nán-gatsu 何月 what month; nán-gen 何軒 how many (*buildings, shops, houses…*); nán-ji 何時 what time; nan-kágetsu 何か月 how many months; nán-kai 何回 how many times; nan-kai/-gai 何階 what floor; nán-ko 何個 how many (*piece(s); small object(s)*); nán-mai 何枚 how many (*flat thing(s)*); nán-mán 何万 how many tens of thousands; nán-nen 何年 what year; how many years; nán-nichi 何日 what day (*of the month*); how many days; nán-nin 何人 how many people; nán-paku 何泊 how many nights; nán-pun 何分 how many minutes; nán-sai 何歳 how (*many years*) old; nán-satsu 何冊 how many copies (*books, magazines*); nán-tō 何頭 how many (*large animals*); nan-yō'bi 何曜日 what day (*of the week*); nán-zoku/-soku 何足 how many pairs (*of footwear such as shoes, socks, etc.*)

nan-... *prefix* 南...south (= **minami no...** 南の...); Nan-bei *n* 南米 = **Minami-Ámerika** 南アメリカ South America; nán-boku *n* 南北 north and south; nán-bu *n* 南部 the south, the southern part; nan-kyoku *n* 南極 South Pole; nan-sei *n* 南西 southwest; nan-tō *n* 南東 southeast

nan-... *prefix* 難...difficult, tough; nan-gi *n* 難儀 difficulty, suffering, trouble [BOOKISH]; nan-ido *n* 難易度 difficulty level; nán-ji *n* 難事 difficulty; nan-kan *n* 難関 difficulty, obstacle, challenge; nan-min *n* 難民 refugee; nan-zan *n* 難産 difficult delivery

nan-... *prefix* 軟...soft, weak, mild; nan-jaku *adj* 軟弱 [BOOKISH] weak, soft, flaccid [IN NEGATIVE SENSE]: ~ **na karada** 軟弱な体 weak body; nan-kin *n* 軟禁 [BOOKISH] house arrest; nan-sui *n* 軟水 soft water (*not hard water*)

nána *n* 七・7 seven; naná-do *n* 七度 ① seven degrees ② seven times; naná-hén *n* 七遍 seven times; nana-kai *n* 七階 seven floors/stories, seventh floor; naná-kái *n* 七回 seven times; naná-mei *n* 七名 [BOOKISH] seven people; naná-nen *n* 七年 the year 7; naná-nin *n* 七人 → naná-mei; naná-satsu *n* 七冊 seven copies (*books, magazines*); naná-hyaku *n* 七百・700 seven hundred; naná-jū *n* 七十・70 seventy; nana-mán *n* 七万・70,000 seventy thousand; nana-sén *n* 七千・7,000 seven thousand; naná-tsu *n* 七つ・7つ seven, seven years old (= **nana-sai** 七歳); **nanatsu-mé** 七つ目 seventh

naname (no/ni) *adj, adv* 斜め(の/に) aslant, oblique(ly), diagonal(ly)

nánbā *n* ナンバー (*car*) license plate

nán-da-i *interj* 何だい what is it (= **nán desu ka** 何ですか)

nán-de-mo *adv* 何でも whatever it may be, anything (at all), everything

... nán desu (da, de) *suffix, v* ...なんです(だ, で) it's that it is ...

náni *n* 何 what: ~ **(ga/o) ...-témo** 何(が/を) ...ても whatever

náni-... *prefix* 何...what ..., which ...; nani-go 何語 what language; nani-iro 何色 what color; naní-jin 何人 what nationality

nanibun *adv* 何分 anyway, anyhow

nanige-nái *adj* 何気ない casual

náni ka *n* 何か something, anything

nani mo *adv* 何も [+ NEGATIVE] nothing, (not) anything

náninani *n* 何々 something or other, so-and-so, what's-it(s-name)

náni-shiro *adv* 何しろ after all

náni yori *adv* 何より than what: ~ **mo** 何よりも more than anything
nánji *pron* 汝 [BOOKISH] thou
... nánka *suffix* …なんか and so forth/on, and what-not; the likes of
nankō *n* 軟膏 [BOOKISH] ointment
nankō *n* 難航 **1.** rough sailing **2.** rough passage
nan-nára *conj* 何なら if you prefer, if you like, if you don't mind; if you don't want to
nan ni mo *adv* 何にも [EMPHATIC] → **nani mo** 何も
nán ni mo *adv* 何にも (= **nán no ... ní mo** 何の …にも [+ NEGATIVE] not to/for/at anything
nán no *adj* 何の what (*kind of*); of what
nanoka *n* 七日 seven days; the 7th day (*of month*)
... ná no ni *conj* …なのに in spite of its being …, despite that it is …
nanpa *n* 難破 shipwreck
nán-rá ka no ... *adj* 何らかの… some
nán-ra (no) ... *adj* 何ら(の)… [+ NEGATIVE] not any, not in any way
nán to ... *conj* 何と … with what, what and … ; (*saying/thinking/meaning*) what
nán to itté mo *adv* 何と言っても eventually, come what may
nán to ka shite *adv* 何とかして by some means (*or other*), somehow or other
nan to mo *adv* 何とも [+ NEGATIVE] nothing (at all), not … at all
nán to shitémo *adv* 何としても inevitably; at any cost
náo *adv* 尚 still more; moreover: ~ **íí** 尚いい still better
naorimásu, naóru *v* 直ります, 直る is righted, fixed, repaired, improves
naorimásu, naóru *v* 治ります, 治る is cured, gets well, recovers, improves
nao-sara *adv* 尚更 all the more, still more
naoshí *v* 直し mending, repair(ing), correcting, correction
naoshimásu, naósu *v* 直します, 直す **1.** makes it right, corrects, repairs, mends, fixes, alters, improves it **2.** [INFINITIVE +] does it over (*and better*), re-does it
naoshimásu, naósu *v* 治します, 治す cures it
náppa *n* 菜っ葉 greens, vegetables; rape (*plant*)
nápukin *n* ナプキン **1.** napkin **2.** sanitary pad
... nára *conj* …なら, … ~ **ba** …ならば if it be, provided it is [NEGATIVE **... ja nákereba/nákerya** … じゃなければ/なけりゃ]; [VERB]-**ru/-ta nára** る/たなら, [ADJECTIVE]-**i/katta nára** い/かったなら if (it be a matter of) …
narabemásu, naraberu *v* 並べます, 並べる arranges, lines them up
narabi *v* 並び row (*line*)
narabimásu, narabu *v* 並びます, 並ぶ they line up, arrange themselves

naraigoto *n* 習い事 culture lesson(s)

naraimásu̱, naráu *v* 習います, 習う learns

naraimásu̱, naráu *v* 習います, 習う learns

naraku *n* 奈落 hell: **~ no soko e tsukiotosaremáshita** 奈落の底へ突き落とされました was thrown into the abyss of despair

narashimásu̱, narasu *v* 鳴らします, 鳴らす sounds, rings it

narashimásu̱, narásu *v* 均します, 均す smooths, averages

narashimásu̱, narásu *v* 馴らします, 馴らす domesticates, tames

narazumono *n* ならず者 rogue, vagabond

naremásu̱, naréru *v* 慣れます, 慣れる (**... ni ~** ...に慣れます) gets used to

naremásu̱, naréru *v* 馴れます, 馴れる (= **... ni ~** ...に馴れます) grows familiar with

narenareshii *adj* 馴れ馴れしい too friendly, overly familiar

narēshon *n* ナレーション narration

naresome *n* 馴れ初め the thing which brought man and woman (*lovers*) together, trigger of love

narí *n* なり・形 form; personal appearance

narikin *n* 成金 nouveau riche

narimásu̱, náru *v* なります, なる becomes, gets to be; is done; amounts to, is; [HONORIFIC] **o-nari ni ~** おなりになります, **... ni** ([ADJECTIVE]**-ku**) **~** ...に (...く) なります gets so it is ..., gets to be ..., turns into ... **... suru kotó ni ~** ...する事になります it gets arranged/decided to (do) ...

narimásu̱, naru *v* 鳴ります, 鳴る it sounds, rings

narimono iri (de) *adv* 鳴り物入り (で) with a fanfare

nariyuki *v* 成り行き process, development, course; result: **~ o mimásu̱** 成り行きを見ます watches how things develop (*turn out*)

naru-beku ... *adv* なるべく... as ... as possible

naru-hodo *interj* なるほど I see; quite so; you are so right; how true

nasaimásu̱, nasáru *v* なさいます, なさる (*someone honored*) does

násake *n* 情け affection, feeling, tenderness, compassion, sympathy

nasake-nái *adj* 情けない wretched, miserable; shameful

nashí *n* ナシ・梨 pear

náshi *v* なし [LITERARY] = **nái** ない (= **arimasén** ありません) (there is no ..., lacks, has no ...)

nashimásu̱, násu *v* 成します, 成す achieves, forms, does

... náshi ni *suffix, prep, adv* ...なしに = **... ga náku(te)** ...がなく (て) without, lacking, not having

násu *n* ナス[茄子・茄], **násubi** なすび eggplant

nata *n* なた・鉈 hatches

natsú *n* 夏 summer

natsukashíi *adj* 懐かしい dear (*dearly remembered*), good old, nostalgic
natsume *n* ナツメ・棗 date (*fruit*)
natsu-míkan *n* 夏ミカン・夏蜜柑 Japanese grapefruit (*pomelo*)
natsu-yásumi *n* 夏休み summer vacation/holiday
nattō´ *n* ナットウ・納豆 fermented soy beans
nattoku *n* 納得 understanding, compliance, assent; **(… o) ~ shimásu** (…を)納得します gets persuaded/convinced (*of* …), assents/ consents to, complies with; **(… o) ~ sasemásu** (…を)納得させます persuades/convinces one (*of* …)
náttsu *n* ナッツ nuts
nawá *n* 縄 rope, cord
nawabari *n* 縄張り one's territory: **~-arasoi** 縄張り争い territorial fight
naya *n* 納屋 barn, shed
nayamí *n* 悩み suffering, distress, torment
nayamimásu, nayámu *v* 悩みます, 悩む suffers
nayonayo (shita) *adj* なよなよ(した) wishy-washy, weedy [IN NEGATIVE SENSE]
náze *adv* なぜ・何故 why: **~ ka to iu to** …なぜかと言うと … the reason is that …
nazo *n* 謎 riddle, mystery; **nazo-nazo** *n* なぞなぞ riddle (*game*)
nazukemásu, nazukéru *v* 名付けます, 名付ける names, dubs
…´n desu (da) *suffix, v* …んです(だ) it's that …: **… né/nē´** *interj* …ね/ねぇ (*mostly female*) isn't it, don't you think/agree
ne *n* 音 (= **otó** 音) sound: **suzu no ~** 鈴の音 bell jingles; **ne o agemásu** *v* 音を上げます gives up
ne *n* 値 (= **nedan** 値段) price: **~ ga takái** 値が高い is expensive; **ne-age** *n* 値上げ price rise; raising the cost; **ne-biki** *n* 値引き discount (*of price*); **ne-dan** *n* 値段 price
ne *n* 根 **1.** root (= **nekko** 根っこ); **~ mo ha mo nai uwasa** 根も葉もないうわさ groundless rumor **2.** cause (= **kongen** 根源) **3.** one's nature: **~ wa yasashii-hito desu** 根は優しい人です is basically a gentle person, is a kind person deep down; **ne-hori ha-hori** *adv* 根掘り葉掘り about every detail: **~ kikaremásu/shitsumon saremásu** 根掘り葉掘り聞[訊]かれます/質問されます is questioned about every detail
ne *n* 寝 (= **nemuri** 眠り) sleep(ing); **ne-búsoku** *n* 寝不足 having not enough sleep; **ne-isu** *n* 寝椅子 couch, lounge (*chair*); **ne-maki** *n* 寝巻き pajamas
nébaneba shimásu (suru) *v* ねばねばします(する) is sticky
nebarí *n* 粘り stickiness: **~-zuyoi** 粘り強い persevering: **nebarímásu** 粘ります hangs on
nechigaemásu, nechigaeru *v* 寝違え

ます, 寝違える gets a crick in one's neck (*while sleeping*)

nechiketto *n* ネチケット netiquette (*comes from* network + etiquette)

nechizun *n* ネチズン netizen (*comes from* network + citizen)

negái *v* 願い a request

negaimásu, negáu *v* 願います, 願う asks for, requests, begs

négi *n* ネギ・葱 onion (*green*)

neiro *n* 音色 (*sound*) tone

néji *n* ねじ・ネジ screw; neji-máwashi *n* ねじ回し screw-driver

nejirimásu, nejíru *v* ねじります, ねじる twists

nekashimásu, nekasu *v* 寝かします, 寝かす puts to bed/sleep; lays it on its side

nekki *n* 熱気 **1.** hot air **2.** air of excitement, fever **3.** fever

nékkuresu *n* ネックレス necklace

nekkyō *n* 熱狂 enthusiasm

néko *n* ネコ・猫 cat

nékutai *n* ネクタイ necktie: **~ o musubimásu** ネクタイを結びます puts on (*wears*) a necktie

nemásu, neru *v* 寝ます, 寝る goes to bed, lies down, sleeps

ne-motó *n* 根元 (*the part*) near the root, the base (*of a tree*)

nemui *adj* 眠い sleepy

nemuri *n* 眠り sleep(ing)

nemurimásu, nemuru *v* 眠ります, 眠る sleeps

nén *n* 年 year

nén-... *prefix* 年... yearly, annual; nén-do *n* 年度 year period, fiscal year; nen-kan (no) *adj* 年間(の) for a year; annual: **~-kōsuiryō** 年間降水量 annual rainfall: **~-shotoku** 年間所得 annual income; nen-kan *n* 年鑑 yearbook, almanac; nen-kan (no) *adj* 年刊(の) annual (*publication*); nen-matsu *n* 年末 the end of the year: **~-nenshi kyūka** 年末年始休暇 year-end and New Year's day holidays; nen-pō *n* 年俸 annual salary; nen-ri *n* 年利 annual interest; nen-shi *n* 年始 New Year's day

nén *n* **1.** 念 sense, feeling; desire; caution, care, attention; **~ no tamé (ni)** 念のため(に) to make sure, just in case, to be on the safe side; **(... ni) ~ o iremásu** (...に)念を入れます pays attention (to ...), is careful (*of/about* ...), **~ o oshimásu** 念を押します double-checks

nén-... *prefix* 年... **2.** age; nen-chō(-sha) *n* 年長(者) one's senior; nen-pai(-sha) *n* 年配[年輩](者) the elderly, middle-aged person; nen-shō (-sha) *n* 年少(者) young person, one's junior

nen-... *prefix* 粘... sticky; nen-chaku-tē´pu *n* 粘着テープ adhesive tape; nén-do *n* 粘土 clay

nengá *n* 年賀 New Year's greetings: **~ ni ikimasu** 年賀に行きます makes a New Year's call/visit; nengá-hágaki *n* 年賀葉書 a New Year greeting postcard

nengan *n* 念願 desire: **~ ga kanaimásu** 念願が叶います (*one's*) dream/wish has come true

nengáppi *n* 年月日 date (*year/month/day*) (→ **seinen-gáppi** 生年月日)

nenki *n* 年季 one's term of service: **~ no haitta** 年季の入った seasoned, experienced

nenkin *n* 年金 pension: **kōsei-~** 厚生年金 employee pension; **kojin-~ hoken** 個人年金保険 individual annuity insurance

nenryō´ *n* 燃料 fuel: **~-tanku** 燃料タンク fuel tank

nenshō *n* 燃焼 combustion

nenza *n* 捻挫 sprain

neon *n* ネオン **1.** neon **2.** neon sign

Nepāru *n* ネパール Nepal; **Nepāru-go** *n* ネパール語 Nepalese (*language*); **Nepāru-jin** *n* ネパール人 a Nepalese

neppū *n* 熱風 hot wind

nerai *n* 狙い an aim, object; idea, intention, what one is driving at

neraimásu, nerau *v* 狙います, 狙う aims at, watches for, seeks

neri-hamígaki *v* 練り歯磨き toothpaste (= **hamigaki-ko** 歯磨き粉)

nerí-kó *n* 練り粉 dough

nerimásu, néru *v* 練ります, 練る kneads; drills, trains

nē´-san *n* 姉さん(**o-né´-san** お姉さん) older sister; Miss!; Waitress!

nes-shimásu, nes-suru *v* 熱します, 熱する **1.** gets hot, gets excited **2.** heats it, warms it

nésshín (na) *adj* 熱心(な) enthusiastic; **nésshín ni** *adv* 熱心に enthusiastically

netamashíi *adj* 妬ましい envious; enviable

netamimásu, netámu *v* 妬みます, 妬む envies

netsú *n* **1.** 熱 fever **2. o-nétsu** お熱 heat; **netsu-ben** *n* 熱弁 passionate speech; **netsu-bō** *n* 熱望 ambition (*hope*)

nettai (-chi´hō´) *n* 熱帯(地方) tro-pic(s): **~-kikō** 熱帯気候 tropical climate; **~-shokubutsu** 熱帯植物 tropical plant

netto *n* ネット **1.** net **2.** network **3.** the Net (= **intānetto** インターネット); **netto-bukku** *n* ネットブック netbook (*computer*); **netto-ginkō** *n* ネット銀行 online bank; **netto-kafe** *n* ネットカフェ Internet café; **netto-ōkushon** *n* ネット・オークション online auction; **netto-sāfin** *n* ネットサーフィン net surfing; **netto-tsūhan** *n* ネット通販 online shopping, Internet shopping (= **intānetto tsūhan** インターネット通販)

nettō *n* 熱湯 boiling water: **~ de yakedo o shimásu** 熱湯で火傷をします is scalded with boiling water

netto-wāku *n* ネットワーク network; **netto(wāku)-shimin** *n* ネット(ワーク)市民 netizen (= **nechizun** ネチズン)

neuchi *n* 値打ち value, worth

nezumi *n* ネズミ・鼠 mouse, rat

nezumi-iro (no) *adj* ネズミ色(の) gray

nezumí-tori *n* ネズミ捕り[取り] mousetrap
ní *n* 荷 **1.** load **2.** burden (= **nímotsu** 荷物; ni-zúkuri *n* 荷造り packing
ní *n* 二・2 two; ni bai *n* 二倍 twice (*double*); ni-banmé (no) *adj* 二番目(の) second; ní dai *n* 二台 two (*machines, vehicles*); ni dó *n* 二度 two times, twice; ni do *n* 二度 two degrees (*temperature*); ni fun *n* 二分 two minutes; ní hai *n* 二杯 two cupfuls; ni hén *n* 二遍 two times (= **ni dó** 二度, **ni kái** 二回); ní hon *n* 二本 two (*pencils/ bottles, long objects*); ni kai *n* 二階 second floor; upstairs; ni kái *n* 二回 two times; ní ken *n* 二軒 two buildings; ní ko *n* 二個 two pieces (*small objects*); ní mai *n* 二枚 two sheets (*flat things*); ní-mei *n* 二名 [BOOKISH] = **futarí** 二人・ふたり two people; ní-nen *n* 二年 the year 2; ní-sai *n* 二歳 two years old (= **futatsu** ふたつ); ní satsu *n* 二冊 two copies (*books, magazines*); ní-wa *n* 二羽 two (*birds, rabbits*)
... **ni** (ʹ) particle …に **1.** to/for (*a person*) **2.** at/in (*a place*), at (*a time*) **3.** (= **… é** …へ) to (*a place*) **4.** as, so as to be, (*turns/ makes*) into being, being
ni-aimásu, ni-áu *v* 似合います, 似合う: **… ni ni-aimásu**…に似合います is becoming (*to*), suits
nia misu *n* ニアミス near miss
nibúi *adj* 鈍い dull, blunt
Nichi-... *prefix* 日…, **…-~** …日 Japan(ese), **~-Ei** 日英 Japanese-English, **Ei-~** 英日 English-Japanese
...-nichi *suffix* …日 day (*counts/ names days*)
nichi-botsu *n* 日没 sunset (*time of sunset*)
Nichiyōʹ(-bi) *n* 日曜(日) Sunday
Nichiyō-hin(-ten) *n* 日用品(店) grocery (*store*); houseware (*store*)
niemásu, nieru *v* 煮えます, 煮える it boils, it cooks
nigái *adj* 苦い bitter, wry: **~ kōhii** 苦いコーヒー bitter coffee; **~ keiken** 苦い経験 bitter experience; **~-warai** 苦笑い bitter smile, wry smile
nigaoe *n* 似顔絵 portrait
nigashimásu, nigásu *v* 逃がします, 逃がす turns loose; lets one get away, lets it slip away
nigate *adj* 苦手 (*thing, person, etc.,*) which is not one's cup of tea: **~ na supōtsu** 苦手なスポーツ sport which one is not good at
Ni-gatsú *n* 二月・2月 February
nigemásu, nigéru *v* 逃げます, 逃げる runs away, escapes, flees
nigirimásu, nigiru *v* 握ります, 握る grasps, grips, clutches
nigiri-meshi *n* 握り飯 riceball (= **o-nígiri** おにぎり)
nigirí-zushi *n* にぎり[握り]寿司 sushi hand-packed into small balls (*as traditional in Tokyo*)

nigíyaka (na) *adj* にぎやか・賑やか(な) merry, bustling, lively, flourishing, busy (*place, atmosphere, person, etc.*): **~ na tōri** 賑やかな通り busy street

nigorimásu, nigóru *v* 濁ります, 濁る gets muddy

Nihón *n* 日本 Japan (= **Nippón** 日本, **Nihón-koku** 日本国); Nihon-fū *n* 日本風 Japanese style; Nihon-ga *n* 日本画 Japanese-style painting; Nihon-ginkō *n* 日本銀行 Bank of Japan; Nihon-go *n* 日本語 Japanese (*language/word*); Nihon-jín *n* 日本人 a Japanese; Nihon-ryōri *n* 日本料理 Japanese cuisine; Nihon-sei *n* 日本製 made in Japan

ni-hyakú *n* 二百 200 two hundred

níi-san *n* 兄さん (**o-níi-san** お兄さん) older brother

niji *n* 虹 rainbow

ni-jū *n* 二重 double, duplicate; nijū-nábe *n* 二重鍋 double boiler; nijū-ago *n* 二重あご[顎] double chin

ní-jū *n* 二十・20 twenty: **~-yokka** 二十四日 24 days, 24th day (*of month*); **~-banmé** 二十番目 20th

nijús-sai *n* 二十歳 20 years old (= **hátachi** 二十歳・はたち)

nikawa *n* にかわ・膠 glue

ni-kayoimásu, ni-kayóu *v* 似通います, 似通う **... ni/to ~** ...に/と似通います closely resembles

Nikei (no) *adj* 日系(の) (*of*) Japanese ancestry

níkibi *n* にきび pimple

níkki *n* にっき, **níkkei** にっけい・肉桂 cinnamon

nikki *n* 日記 (*private*) diary

níkkō *n* 日光 sunshine; **Níkkō** 日光 Nikko (*place*); nikkō-yoku *n* 日光浴 sun bathing

nikkyū *n* 日給 daily wage

nikochin *n* ニコチン nicotine

nikomi *n* 煮込み stew (*food*): **~-udon** 煮込みうどん stew with Udon (*Japanese wheat noodle*)

níkoniko *adj* にこにこ smiling: **~ shi(tei)másu** にこにこし(てい)ます smiles

nikú *n* 肉 meat; niku-dángo *n* 肉団子 Chinese meat-balls; nikú-ya *n* 肉屋 butcher (shop)

nikú *n* **1.** 肉 (**o-níku** お肉) meat **2.** flesh (= **nikutai** 肉体); niku-sei *n* 肉声 natural voice (*without a microphone, etc.*); niku-shoku (dōbutsu) *n* 肉食(動物) carnivore; niku-tai *n* 肉体 body; niku-yoku *n* 肉欲 sexual desire

nikúi *adj* 憎い hateful

...nikúi *suffix* ...にくい・難い (**...shi-~** ...しにくい) hard, difficult (*to do*)

nikumimásu, nikúmu *v* 憎みます, 憎む hates, detests

nikushin *n* 肉親 blood relative

níkuzure *n* 荷崩れ cargo shifting

nikuzure *n* 煮崩れ breaking up while boiling/cooking (*fishes, potatoes, etc.*)

nimásu, niru *v* 似ます, 似る resembles

nimásu, niru *v* 煮ます, 煮る boils,

cooks

... -ní mo *suffix* …にも also (*even*) at/in, to, as

ni-mono *n* 煮物 boiled foods

nímotsu *n* 荷物 **1.** baggage **2.** load

...(´) -nin *suffix* …人 person, people; **yo-~** 四人 four people

ninaimásu, ninau *v* 担います, 担う carries on shoulders

ninchi *n* 認知 [BOOKISH] **1.** recognition, acknowledgment **2.** affiliation: **~ sareteinai kodomo** 認知されていない子供 child who is not affiliated by his/her parent (*usually father*)

ningen *n* 人間 human being (= **hito** 人)

ningyo *n* 人魚 mermaid

ningyō *n* 人形 doll; ningyō-shíbai *n* 人形芝居 puppet show; ningyō-tsukai *n* 人形使い puppeteer

nini *n* 任意 [BOOKISH] option

nínja *n* 忍者 a master of stealth, Ninja

ninjin *n* ニンジン・人参 carrot

nínjō *n* 人情 human nature, human feelings, warmheartedness: **~-ka** 人情家 sympathetic person: **giri to ~** 義理と人情 duty and sympathy

nínjutsu *n* 忍術 the art of stealth

ninka *n* 認可 [BOOKISH] permission

ninki *n* 人気 popularity: **~ ga arimásu** 人気があります is popular

ninki *n* 任期 (*one's*) term, term of office: **~ o tsutomemásu** 任期を務めます serves one's term

...-ninmae *suffix* …人前 (*counts portions*)

ninmei *n* 任命 appointment

ninmu *n* 任務 duty, assignment, task, mission: **~ o hatashimásu** 任務を果たします accomplishes one's errand

ninniku *n* ニンニク・大蒜 garlic

ninpu *n* 妊婦 pregnant woman

ninpu *n* 人夫 [BOOKISH] laborer

ninshiki *n* 認識 [BOOKISH] awareness, recognition

ninshin *n* 妊娠 pregnancy: **~ shite imásu** 妊娠しています is pregnant; ninshin-chū´zetsu *n* 妊娠中絶 abortion

ninshō *n* 認証 certification

ninsō *n* 人相 looks, facial features

nintai *n* 忍耐 endurance; nintai-ryoku 忍耐力 ability to be patient

nínzū *n* 人数 number of people; population (= **jinkō** 人口)

niō dachi *n* 仁王立ち standing firm with one's feet set apart (*like two Deva Kings stone statue*)

niói *adj* 臭い・匂い a smell; **(... no) ~ ga shimásu** (…の)臭い[匂い]がします it smells (of …)

nioimásu, nióu *v* 臭います・匂います, 臭う・匂う it smells, is fragrant

Nippon *n* 日本 = **Nihón(-koku)** 日本(国) Japan

nirá *n* ニラ a leek; a green onion

niramimásu, nirámu *v* 睨みます, 睨む glares, stares

níre *n* ニレ・楡 yew (*tree*)

ní-san (no) *adj* 二, 三(の) two or three …

ní-sei *n* 二世 second generation (*Japanese emigrant*); … the Second

nisemásu, niseru *v* 似せます, 似せる imitates, copies; counterfeits (*money*), forges (*a document, a signature*)

nise (no) *adj* にせ・偽(の) false, phony, fake, imitation; nise-mono *n* 偽物・にせもの a fake, an imitation; a forgery; nise-satsu *n* 偽札・贋札・にせ札 counterfeit bill (*currency*)

nishi *n* 西 west: **~-guchi** 西口 the west exit/entrance; nishi-káigan *n* 西海岸 west coast

níshiki *n* 錦 brocade

nishime *n* 煮しめ boiled fish and vegetables

níshin *n* ニシン・鰊 herring

nishoku-tsuki (no) *adj* 二食付き(の) with two meals incuded

nisshi *n* 日誌 diary, journal (*of business, nursing, etc.*); **kango-~** 看護日誌 nurse's daily record

nissū´ *n* 日数 the number of days

nísu *n* ニス = **wánisu** ワニス varnish

... ní te *particle* …にて [LITERARY] = **... de** …で (at; …)

ni-tō (no) *adj* 二等(の) second class; **nitō´-shō** 二等賞 the second prize

nittei *n* 日程 schedule, program, itinerary

niwa *n* 庭 garden

... níwa *suffix, prep, conj* …には to; at/in; as

níwaka (no/ni) *adj, adv* にわか(の/に) sudden(ly), unexpected(ly)

niwatori *n* ニワトリ・鶏 chicken

n´n *interj* んん **1. "un-un"** (うんうん) huh-uh, uh-uh **2. "u-un"** (ううん) nope

nó *n* 野 field (*dry*)

no-... *prefix* 野. . . wild; nó-bana *n* 野花 wildflower; no-usagi *n* 野ウサギ・野兎 wild rabbit

...´no *suffix* …の **1.** the one/time/place that; (= **hitó** 人, **monó** 物, **tokí** 時, **tokoró** 所) **2.** the (*specific*) act/fact of … (*cf.* **kotó** 事) **3.** which/that is … (→ **désu** です, **dá** だ, **na** な)

nō *n* 脳 brain: **dai-~** 大脳 cerebrum: **shō~** 小脳 cerebellum; nō-míso *n* 脳みそ・脳味噌 brain [INFORMAL]

nō´ *n* 能 **1.** ability (= **nōryoku** 能力, **sainō** 才能) **2. o-nō** お能 Noh (*Japanese classical theater*) (→ **nō-men** 能面)

nō-... *prefix* 農. . . farming, agriculture; nō´-chi *n* 農地 farm land; nō´-gyō *n* 農業 agriculture, farming; nō-jō´ *n* 農場 farm; nō-min *n* 農民 farmers

nobashimásu, nobásu *v* 伸ばします, 伸ばす extends (*lengthens, stretches, deters*) it

nobashimásu, nobásu *v* 延ばします, 延ばす prolongs

nobemásu, nobéru *v* 述べます, 述べる tells, relates
nobimásu, nobíru *v* 伸びます, 伸びる it extends, reaches; it spreads
nobori *n* 上り inbound (*to Tokyo*), the up train
noborimásu, noboru *v* 登ります, 登る climbs
noborimásu, noboru *v* 上ります, 上る goes up
noborimásu, noboru *v* 昇ります, 昇る rises: **hi ga ~** 日が昇ります the sun rises
nóbu *n* ノブ knob: **doa-~** ドアノブ door knob
nochi *n* のち・後: **~-hodo** のちほど・後程 later (= **áto (de)** あと・後(で))
nódo *n* のど・喉 throat: **~ ga kawakimáshita** のどが渇きました is thirsty
nō´do *n* 濃度 density, thick (*liquid*), concentration; **kō-~ (no) kōhii** 高濃度(の)コーヒー[珈琲] strong coffee
nódoka (na) *adj* のどか(な) tranquil, peaceful, quiet, calm
nó-hara *n* 野原 field
nó-juku *n* 野宿 rough sleeping
nokemásu, nokeru *v* 退けます, 退ける removes; omits
noki *n* 軒 eaves
nokimásu, noku *v* 退きます, 退く gets out of the way
nókku shimásu (suru) *v* ノックします(する) knocks (*on door*)
nokogírí *v* のこぎり・鋸 a saw (*tool*)
nōkō (na) *adj* 濃厚(な) thick, rich, dense, passionate: **~ na miruku** 濃厚なミルク rich milk: **~ na kisu** 濃厚なキス passionate kiss
nokorí *n* 残り the rest, the remainder, what is left, the leftover; nokori-bi *n* 残り火 embers; nokori-monó *n* 残り物 leftovers, remains, leavings
nokorimásu, nokóru *v* 残ります, 残る remains, is left behind/over
nokoshimásu, nokósu *v* 残します, 残す leaves behind/over
nō-men *n* 能面 mask (*Noh drama*)
nomí *n* ノミ・蚤 flea
nómi *n* ノミ・鑿 chisel
...nómi *suffix, adj* ...のみ (= **... daké** ...だけ) only
nomi-komimásu, nomi-komu *v* 飲み込みます, 飲み込む swallows (*ingests*)
nomimásu, nómu *v* 飲みます, 飲む drinks; smokes; takes (*medicine*); nomi-kai *n* 飲み会 drinking party; nomí-mizu *n* 飲み水 drinking water; nomí-mono *n* 飲み物 beverage, refreshments; nomí-ya *n* 飲み屋 tavern, neighborhood bar
nonbē, nonbei *n* 飲兵衛・呑兵衛, のんべい a heavy drinker [INFORMAL]
nonbiri *adj* のんびり easy, leisurely: **~ ya** のんびり屋 happy-go-lucky person: **ie de ~ shimásu** 家でのんびりします relaxes at home
non-fikushon *n* ノンフィクション nonfiction

nónki (na) *adj* のん気[呑気](な) easygoing, happy-go-lucky, carefree

nonoshirimásu, nonoshíru *v* 罵ります, 罵る reviles, abuses, swears at, curses

non-sumōkā *n* ノンスモーカー non-smoker

nosutarujia *n* ノスタルジア nostalgia

noren *n* のれん・暖簾 shop curtain; credit: **~ o oroshimásu** 暖簾を下ろします closes down one's store; **~ o wakemásu** 暖簾を分けます lets the employee use the same shop name to open his/her own shop

norí *n* ノリ・海苔 seaweed (*green*); nori-maki *n* のり[海苔]巻き sushi rice in a seaweed roll

norí *n* のり・糊 paste; starch

nori-kaemásu, nori-káéru *v* 乗り換えます,乗り換える changes (*vehicles*)

norimásu, noru *v* 乗ります, 乗る gets aboard, rides; is carried; nori-ba *n* 乗り場 boarding area/ place; platform (*at station*); taxi station; bus stop; nori-kae *n* 乗り換え change, transfer (*of vehicle*); nori-mono *n* 乗(り)物 vehicle

Nōrin-Suisan-shō *n* 農林水産省 Ministry of Agriculture, Forestry and Fisheries of Japan (MAFF)

nōritsu *n* 能率 efficiency

norói *n* 呪い a curse

norói *n* のろい slow, dull, sluggish [INFORMAL]

noroimásu, noróu *v* 呪います, 呪う curses, utters a curse

noronoro *adv* のろのろ slowly, sluggishly: **~ unten** のろのろ運転 driving slowly

noruma *n* ノルマ norm, quota: **~ o tasseishimásu** ノルマを達成します achieves one's quota

nō'ryoku *n* 能力 ability (= **nō** 能, **sainō** 才能)

nosemásu, noseru *v* 乗せます, 乗せる loads, puts aboard, ships

nosemásu, noseru *v* 載せます, 載せる publishes (*in book, magazine, etc.*), posts (*an article, etc.*)

nōshuku *n* 濃縮 [BOOKISH] concentration (of liquid or air)

noten (de/no) *adv, adj* 野天(で/の) outdoors: **~-búro** 野天風呂 outdoor bath

nōtenki (na) *adj* 能天気(な) happy-go-lucky, easy, optimistic (person)

nō'to *n* ノート notebook

nottóri *n* 乗っ取り hijack; nottori-han *n* 乗っ取り犯 hijacker; nottori-jíken *n* 乗っ取り事件 a hijacking; (*illegal*) takeover, seizure

nottorimásu, nottóru *v* 乗っ取ります, 乗っ取る hijacks; (*illegally*) takes over, seizes

noyama *n* 野山 fields and mountains

nōzei *n* 納税 payment of taxes

nozokimásu, nozoku *v* 覗きます, 覗く peeks/peeps at; nozokí-ana *n* のぞき[覗き]穴 peephole; nozoki-ya *n* のぞき[覗き]屋 peeping Tom

nozokimásu, nozoku *v* 除きます, 除く eliminates, removes; omits

nozomashíi *adj* 望ましい desirable, welcome

nozomi *n* 望み a desire; a hope, an expectation

nozomimásu, nozomu *v* 望みます, 望む desires, looks to, hopes for

nozomimásu, nozomu *v* 臨みます, 臨む [BOOKISH] looks out on

nū´do *n* ヌード a nude

nugemásu, nugéru *v* 脱げます, 脱げる **1.** it slips/comes off **2.** can take it off

nugimásu, núgu *v* 脱ぎます, 脱ぐ takes off (*clothes, shoes*)

nuguimásu, nuguu´ *v* 拭います, 拭う wipes it away

nuigurumi *n* 縫い包み stuffed toy

nuimásu, nuu´ *v* 縫います, 縫う sews; núi-bari *n* 縫い針 sewing needle; nui-mé *n* 縫い目 seam

nukashimásu, nukasu *v* 抜かします, 抜かす skips, leaves out

nukemásu, nukeru *v* 抜けます, 抜ける comes off; escapes; is omitted; nuke-ana *n* 抜け穴 ① passage which allows one to go through ② escape route ③ loophole

...-nuki (de/no) *suffix, adj, adv* …抜き(で/の) without (*omitting*)

nukimásu, nuku *v* 抜きます, 抜く uncorks; removes; omits; surpasses; selects; nuki-ashi (sashiashi) (de) *adv* 抜き足(差し足)(で) stealthily, on tiptoe; nuki-uchi *n* 抜き打ち (*test, inspection, etc.,*) without notice: **~-kensa** 抜き打ち検査 surprise inspection

numá *n* 沼 pond: **~-chi** 沼地 swamp, marsh

nuno *n* 布 cloth: **~-ji** 布地 fabric

nurashimásu, nurasu *v* 濡らします, 濡らす wets, dampens

nure-ginu *v* 濡れ衣 false accusation

nuremásu, nureru *v* 濡れます, 濡れる gets wet, damp; **nurete imásu** 濡れています is wet

nuri 塗り *n* lacquer, varnish, painting

nuri-kaemásu, nuri-káeru *v* 塗り替えます, 塗り替える repaints

nurimásu, nuru *v* 塗ります, 塗る lacquers, paints, varnishes, stains; (*butter*) spreads; nuri-gúsuri *n* 塗り薬 ointment [INFORMAL]

nurúi *adj* ぬるい・温い lukewarm, tepid

nushi *n* 主 master, owner (= **aruji** 主)

nusumí *n* 盗み theft

nusumimásu, nusúmu *v* 盗みます, 盗む steals, swipes, robs, rips off

... nya/nyā´ ... *suffix* にゃ/にゃあ [INFORMAL] = **... ní wa ...** には

nyō *n* 尿 [BOOKISH] urine, urinating (= **shíkko** しっこ, **o-shíkko** おしっこ)

nyō´bō, nyō´bo *n* 女房 my wife

nyū... *prefix* 入... entering; nyū-en *n* 入園 entering a kindergarten/nursery; nyū-gaku *n* 入学 admission to a school, entering a school; **nyū(gaku)-shi(ken)** 入(学)試(験) entrance exam; **~-shiki** 入学式 school entrance ceremony; nyū-in *n* 入院 entering a hospital, hospital admission; nyū-jō *n* 入場 admission (*to a place*): **~-ken** 入場券 admission ticket, platform (*non-passenger*) ticket; **~-ryō** 入場料 admission fee; nyū-ka *n* 入荷 arrival (*of goods*)(*in shop, market, etc.*); nyū-kai *n* 入会 admission to an association; nyū-koku *n* 入国 entering a country; immigration: **~ kanri-kyoku** 入国管理局 Immigration Bureau of Japan; nyū-kyo *n* 入居 moving into an apartment; **~-sha** 入居者 tenant, resident (*of an apartment*); nyū-seki *n* 入籍 registering one's marriage; nyū-sen *n* 入選 winning a prize; nyū-sha *n* 入社 entering (*joining*) a company: **~-shikén** 入社試験 employment selection exam; nyū-yoku *n* 入浴 bath, taking a bath

nyūbai *n* 入梅 the rainy season (*in Japan*) (= **tsuyu** 梅雨)

nyū-eki *n* 乳液 **1.** latex **2.** milky lotion, milky liquid (*cosmetic*)

nyū-gan *n* 乳がん・乳癌 breast cancer

nyū-gyū *n* 乳牛 dairy cattle

nyū-inryō *n* 乳飲料 milk beverage

nyū-ji *n* 乳児 infant

Nyūjiirándo *n* ニュージーランド New Zealand; **~-jin** ニュージーランド人 a New Zealander

nyūnen (na/ni) *adj, adv* 入念(な/に) careful(ly): **~ ni shirabemásu** 入念に調べます searches carefully

nyū-seihin *n* 乳製品 foods made from milk (*butter, cheese, etc.*)

nyūshō *n* 入賞 winning a prize: **~-sha** 入賞者 a prizewinner

nyū´su *n* ニュース news: **~-bangumi** ニュース番組 news program: **~-kyasutā** ニュースキャスター newscaster

nyū´toraru *n* ニュートラル neutral (*gear*): **(gia o) ~ ni iremásu** (ギアを)ニュートラルに入れます shifts the gear into neutral

Nyūyō´ku *n* ニューヨーク New York

nyūyō (na) *adj* 入用(な) necessary, needed

O

ó *n* 尾 = **shippó** しっぽ・尻尾 tail

ó *n* 緒 = **hanao** 鼻緒 thong, strap

o- *prefix* お・御 [HONORIFIC] (personalizing): "your" or "that important thing"; o-aiso *n* おあいそ・お愛想, **o-aisō** お愛想 ① compliment, flattery (= **aiso** 愛想) ② **o-aiso** おあいそ (*restaurant*) bill, check; o-bā´-san *n* おばあさん・お祖母さん grandmother (*family*) (= **bā-san** ばあさん, **obā-chan** おばあちゃん, **só-bo** 祖母); o-bā´-san *n* おばあさん・お婆さん (*not relative*) old lady/

woman (= **bā-san** ばあさん, **obā-chan** おばあちゃん); o-bon *n* お盆 tray (= **bon** 盆, **torei** トレイ); O-bón *n* お盆 the Bon Festival (*Buddhist All Saints Day*) (= **Bon** 盆); o-bō-san *n* お坊さん Buddhist monk (= **bō-san** 坊さん); o-cha *n* お茶 Japanese green tea; the tea ceremony (= **cha** 茶); o-hachi *n* お鉢 rice bucket/tub (= **hachi** 鉢); o-hana *n* お花 ① flower (= **hana** 花) ② flower arrangement; o-hana *n* お鼻 nose (= **hana** 鼻); o-hima *n* お暇 (*your*) spare time, free time (= **hima** 暇); o-kane *n* お金 money (= **kane** 金); o-kéiko (goto) *n* お稽古(ごと) practice (*artistic*) (= **kéiko** 稽古); o-ikura (désu ka) おいくら(ですか) How much is this? (= **ikura (désu ka)** いくら(ですか)); o-ikutsu (désu ka) おいくつ(ですか) How old (*are you*)? (= **ikutsu (désu ka)** いくつ(ですか)); o-iwai *n* お祝い celebration (= **iwai** 祝い); o-jama *n* お邪魔 (= **jama** 邪魔); **O-jama shimáshita** お邪魔しました. Excuse me for having interrupted/bothered you; o-jíi-san *n* おじいさん・祖父さん grandfather (*family*) (=**jii-san** じいさん・祖父さん, **ojii-chan** おじいちゃん); o-jíi-san *n* おじいさん・お爺さん (*not relative*) old (gentle-)man (=**jii-san** じいさん・爺さん, **ojii-chan** おじいちゃん); o-kā´-san *n* お母さん・おかあさん mother [FORMAL] (= **kā´san** 母さん・かあさん; o-káshi *n* お菓子 confections, sweets, pastry, candy, cakes, cookies, biscuits (= **kashi** 菓子); o-kawari *n* お変わり change (*in health*): ~ **arimasénka.** お変わりありませんか。Is everything all right? (*greeting*) (= **kawari** 変わり); o-ko-san *n* お子さん (*your/someone else's*) child (= **ko** 子); o-kyaku(-san/-sámá) *n* お客(さん/様) visitor; customer, patron (= **kyaku** 客); o-kyō *n* お経 sutra (*Buddhist scripture*) (= **kyō** 経); o-matsuri *n* お祭り festival (= **matsuri** 祭り); o-múko-san *n* お婿さん (*your/someone else's*) son-in-law; bridegroom (= **muko** 婿); o-negai *n* お願い favor (*requested*), request (= **negai** 願い); o-nē´-san *n* お姉さん older sister (= **nē´-san** 姉さん, **ane** 姉, **aneki** 姉貴); o-níi-san *n* お兄さん older brother (= **níi-san** 兄さん, **ani** 兄, **aniki** 兄貴); o-rei *n* お礼 an acknowledgment, a thank-you, a present (*of appreciation*) (= **rei** 礼); o-sake *n* お酒 saké (*Japanese rice wine*); liquor (= **sake** 酒); o-saki ni *adv* お先に Excuse me for going first; ~ **ni shitsúrei shimásu** お先に失礼します Excuse me for being the first to leave; o-séwa *n* お世話 care, assistance, help (= **sewá** 世話) (→ **o-sewa-sama** お世話様); o-shirase *n* お知らせ report, notice, information (= **shirase** 知らせ);

O-shōgatsu *n* お正月 New Year; January (= **Shōgatsu** 正月); o-sōshiki *n* お葬式 funeral (= **sōshiki** 葬式); o-sumō-san *n* お相撲さん sumo wrestler (= **sumō** 相撲, **rikishi** 力士); o-súshi *n* お寿司・お鮨 = **súshi** すし・寿司・鮨 sushi; o-témae *n* お点前 tea ceremony procedures (= **temae** 点前); o-ténki *n* お天気 ① weather (= **ténki** 天気) ② fair weather; o-tera *n* お寺 Buddhist temple (= **tera** 寺); o-tō´-san *n* お父さん・おとうさん father (= **tō´san** 父さん・とうさん, **oyaji** 親父); o-toshi *n* お年・お歳・(*your/someone else's*) age (= **toshi** 年・歳); o-tsuri *n* おつり・お釣り change (*money returned*) (= **tsuri** つり・釣り); o-yakusho *n* お役所 government office (= **yakusho** 役所); o-yasumi *n* お休み rest; holiday; recess; time off (= **yasumí** 休み[INFORMAL], **kyūka** 休暇 [FORMAL]); o-yome-san *n* お嫁さん (*your/someone else's*) bride (= **yome** 嫁); o-zōni *n* お雑煮 rice cakes boiled with vegetables (*eaten as New Year's soup*) (= **zōni** 雑煮)

... o …を particle: marks direct object (*gets what, loves whom*) or path traversed (*goes through/along where, using what path*)

ō´ *n* 王, **ō-sama** 王様 king; ō-chō *n* 王朝 royal dynasty; ō-hi *n* 王妃 queen; ō-i keishō *n* 王位継承 succession to the throne; ō-ja *n* 王者 ① king ② champion: **sekai** ~ 世界王者 world champion ③ ruler; ō-ji (-sama) *n* 王子(様) prince; ō-jo (-sama) *n* 王女(様) princess; ō-kan *n* 王冠 ① crown ② (**bin no** ~ 瓶の王冠) bottle cap; ō-koku *n* 王国 kingdom; ō-sama *n* 王様 king; ō-shitsu *n* 王室 royal family

ō-... *prefix* 大… big, great; ō-áme *n* 大雨 heavy rain; ō-buroshiki *n* 大風呂敷 very large square wrapping cloth; ō-dáiko *n* 大太鼓 large drum; ō-dō´ri 大通り main street, avenue; ō-fúbuki *n* 大吹雪 blizzard; ō-gata *n* 大型 large-size (*model*); ō-gesa (na) *adj* おおげさ[大袈裟](な) exaggerated; ō-hiroma *n* 大広間 great hall; ō-kaze *n* 大風 strong wind; ō´-mízú *n* 大水 flood (= **kōzui** 洪水); ō-moji *n* 大文字 capital letter; ō-mono *n* 大物 a big shot; ō-ótoko *n* 大男 a giant of a man, big man; ō-sáwagi *n* 大騒ぎ fuss, disturbance; ō-sōji *n* 大掃除 great cleaning; ō-uridashi *n* 大売出し big sale; ō-yasu-uri *n* 大安売り special bargain sale; ō-yukí *n* 大雪 heavy snow; ō-zúmō *n* 大相撲 a grand sumo tournament; an exciting match

oashisu *n* オアシス oasis

o-azuke *interj* お預け Wait! (*training one's dog*)

ō´bā *n* オーバー overcoat, (top) coat

o-báke *n* お化け・おばけ ghost, monster

ōbako *n* オオバコ (*plant*) plantain

ōbā(-kōto) *n* オーバー(コート) overcoat

ō´bā (na) *adj* オーバー(な) exaggerated, over(ly), too much

oba(-san) *n* おば[叔母](さん) aunt (*younger sister of father or mother*) (= **oba-chan** おば[叔母]ちゃん)

oba(-san) *n* おば[伯母](さん) aunt (*older sister of father or mother*) (= **oba-chan** おば[伯母]ちゃん)

oba(-san) *n* おば[小母]さん (*not relative*) lady, woman (*middle-aged*) (= **oba-chan** おばちゃん)

Ōbei *n* 欧米 Europe and America

obekka *n* おべっか flattery

óbi *n* 帯 girdle, sash, belt, (*Japanese*) obi

ōbii *n* オービー・OB **1.** (*abbreviation for the word "old boy"*) male graduate, alumnus **2.** (*abbreviation for the word "out of bounds"*) OB (*golf*)

obi-jō (no) *adj* 帯状(の) belt(-like), a narrow strip (*of*)

obitadashii *adj* おびただしい a great number of, immense, tremendous

ōbō (na) *adj* 横暴(な) high-handed, tyrannical

obóé *n* 覚え memory; consciousness; oboe-gaki *n* 覚(え)書(き) memo(-randum), note

oboemásu̱, oboéru *v* 覚えます, 覚える remembers, keeps in mind; learns

oboko (-músume) *n* おぼこ(娘) virgin (*female*)

oboremásu̱, oboreru *v* 溺れます, 溺れる drowns

ō´bo shimásu̱ (suru) *v* 応募します(する) applies

obuimásu̱, obú *v* 負ぶいます, 負ぶう carries on one's back (= **seoimásu̱, shoimásu** 背負います)

ōbun *n* オーブン oven

oburāto *n* オブラート wafer paper

obutsu *n* 汚物 dirt

ōchaku (na) *adj* 横着(な) lazy: ~ **na taido** 横着な態度 lazy attitude

ochi *n* 落ち **1.** omission, lack: **te-~** 手落ち oversight **2.** punch line **3.** the end, the result

ochimásu̱, ochíru *v* 落ちます, 落ちる falls, drops; is omitted; fails; is inferior; óchi-ba *n* 落ち葉 fallen leaves

ochi̱-tsuite 落ち着いて **1.** *adv* calmly **2.** *v* calm down!: **~ kudasai** 落ち着いて下さい Please calm down.

ochi-tsu̱ki *n* 落ち着き: **~ ga aru (nai)** 落ち着きがある(ない) is calm; is restless

ochi-tsu̱kimásu̱, ochi-tsu̱ku *v* 落ち着きます, 落ち着く calms down, keeps cool, settles down, relaxes

o-chóko *n* おちょこ saké cup

o-chūgen *n* お中元 midyear present, summer gift

o-daiji ni *interj* お大事に: **(dōzo) ~ ni (shitekudasai)!** (どうぞ)お大事に(して下さい)! (*Please*) take care of yourself!

ōdāmeido *n* オーダーメイド made-to-order: **~ (no)** オーダーメイド(の) custom-made
ōdan *n* 黄疸 (*medical*) jaundice
ōdan *n* 横断 crossing, going across, intersecting: **~-hodō** 横断歩道 pedestrian crossing
odatemásu, odateru *v* おだてます, おだてる coaxes
odáyaka (na) *adj* 穏やか(な) quiet, calm, peaceful, gentle; moderate
odéko *n* おでこ forehead (= **hitai** 額)
o-dén *n* おでん assorted boiled foods (*Japanese hot pot*)
ōdio *n* オーディオ audio: **~-mania** オーディオマニア audiophile, audio nut
ōdishon *n* オーディション audition
odokashimásu, odokasu *v* 脅かします, 脅かす threatens
odori *n* 踊り dance, dancing
odorimásu, odoru *v* 踊ります, 踊る dances
odorokashimásu, odorokásu *v* 驚かします, 驚かす surprises, scares, astonishes
odorokimásu, odoróku *v* 驚きます, 驚く is surprised, astonished
odoshimásu, odosu *v* 脅します, 脅す threatens
oemásu, oeru *v* 終えます, 終える ends it, finishes, completes
ōen *n* 応援 help, assistance; cheering for; support; **ōen-dan** *n* 応援団 cheering party
ōeru *n* オーエル office lady
oetsu *n* 嗚咽 sobbing
ofisu *n* オフィス office
ōfuku *n* 往復 round trip; **ōfuku-kíppu** *n* 往復切符 round-trip ticket:
ofukuro *n* おふくろ・お袋 (*familiar, usually male*) (= **okā´-san** お母さん・おかあさん) **1.** my mother **2. ofukuro-san** お袋さん (*your/someone else's*) mother
ofureko (no) *adj* オフレコ(の) off the record
ofu-shiizun *n* オフシーズン off season (= **kansanki** 閑散期)
ogakuzu *n* おが屑 sawdust
ogamimásu, ogámu *v* 拝みます, 拝む worships, looks at with respect
ōganikku (no) *adj* オーガニック(の) organic (= **yūki** 有機)
ogawa *n* 小川 brook, stream
ógi *n* オギ・荻 a reed
ōgí *n* 扇 a folding fan
oginái *n* 補い supplement
oginaimásu, oginau *v* 補います, 補う completes; complements, makes good, makes up for
ōgon *n* 黄金 gold (= **kin** 金)
ogorimásu, ogoru *v* 驕ります, 驕る is extravagant
ogorimásu, ogoru *v* 奢ります, 奢る treats (*pays the bill*)
ohako *n* おはこ・十八番 one's hobby; one's "thing", specialty, (*favorite*) trick
O-hayō (gozaimásu) *interj* おはよう(ございます) Good morning!
ōhei *n* 横柄 arrogance (= **gōman** 傲慢・ごうまん): **~ na taido** 横

柄な態度 insolence

o-hína sama *n* おひな[雛]様 (*Dolls Festival*) dolls

o-hi-sama *n* お日様 sun (*baby talk*)

o-hitáshi *n* お浸し boiled greens (*usually spinach, served cold with seasoning*)

o-hitsu *n* お櫃・おひつ rice tub/bucket

o-híya *n* お冷や cold water

Ohōtsuku-kai *n* オホーツク海 Sea of Okhotsk

oi *n* 甥 nephew; **oi-go-san** *n* 甥御さん (*your/someone else's*) nephew; **oi-kko** *n* 甥っ子 nephew (= **oi** 甥)

ói *interj* おい hey! (*mostly male, very informal*)

ō'i *adj* 多い many, numerous; lots; **ō'ku** *adv* 多く a lot of, many

oide *interj* おいで Come! (*training one's dog, etc.*)

oide (ni narimásu) *v* おいで(になります) = **irasshaimásu** いらっしゃいます [HONORIFIC] **1.** comes **2.** goes **3.** is, stays

oi-kakemásu, oi-kakéru *v* 追い掛けます, 追い掛ける chases

oi-koshimásu, oi-kósu *v* 追い越します, 追い越す (*overtakes and*) passes

oimásu, ou *v* 追います, 追う chases, pursues; **oi-kaze** *n* 追い風 tail wind; **oi-koshi** *n* 追い越し Passing: ~ **kinshi** 追い越し禁止 No Passing: ~ **shasen** 追い越し車線 passing line

oimásu, ou *v* 負います, 負う carries on one's back

oimásu, oiru *v* 老います, 老いる grows old

ōimásu, oou', ōu' *v* 覆います, 覆う covers, shields

ōin *n* 押韻 [BOOKISH] rhyme (= **in** 韻)

ōin *n* 押印 [BOOKISH] putting one's seal

ōi ni *adv* おおいに・大いに very, greatly (= **hijō ni** 非常に, **totemo** とても)

óiru *n* オイル oil (*for car engine*)

oishii *adj* おいしい・美味しい tasty, nice, delicious, yummy (= **umai** うま[旨・美味]い)

oishisō *adj* おいしそう looks tasty/nice/delicious/yummy (= **umasō** うま[旨・美味]そう)

oisoreto *adj* おいそれと [(*usually*) + NEGATIVE verb] easily, quickly

oitachi *n* 生い立ち (*one's*) personal history

o-itoma *n* お暇 leave-taking, farewell: ~ **(ita-)shimásu** お暇(致)します I will take my leave.

oi-tsukimásu, oi-tsukú *v* 追い付きます, 追い付く (**... ni** ...に) catches up (*with*), overtakes

o-jigi *n* お辞儀 a polite bow: ~ **o shimásu** お辞儀をします bows

ōjii *n* オージー (*abbreviation for the word "old girl"*) female graduate, alumna

ō-jimásu, ō-jiru *v* 応じます, 応じる responds (*to*), accedes (*to*), complies (*with*)

ōji (-sama) *n* 皇子(様) emperor's son
oji (-san) *n* おじ[叔父](さん) uncle (*younger brother of father or mother*) (= **oji-chan** おじ[叔父]ちゃん)
oji (-san) *n* おじ[伯父](さん) uncle (*older brother of father or mother*) (= **oji-chan** おじ[伯父]ちゃん)
oji (-san) *n* おじ[小父]さん (*not relative*) (gentle) man, (*middle-aged*) man (= **oji-chan** おじちゃん)
ojoku *n* 汚辱 disgrace, shame, scandal
ōjo (-sama) *n* 皇女(様) emperor's daughter
ojō-san *n* お嬢さん a young lady; (*your/someone else's*) daughter; Miss
o-jū´ *n* お重 = **jūbako** 重箱 (nested boxes; picnic boxes)
oka *n* 丘 hill
oka *n* 陸 dry land
okabu *n* お株 = **ohako** おはこ・十八番 (specialty, habit)
O-kaeri nasái! *interj* お帰りなさい! Welcome back!
okage *n* おかげ・お蔭・お陰; **... no ~ de** ...のおかげ[お蔭・お陰]で thanks to ...
okage-sama (de) おかげさま(で) thanks to your solicitude; thank you (*I'm very well* or *it's going very nicely*)
ōkakumaku *n* 横隔膜 diaphragm
O-kamai náku *interj* お構いなく. Don't go to any trouble.
okámi *n* 御上・お上 the authorities, the government
okámi *n* おかみ・女将 = **~-san** おかみ[女将]さん landlady; married woman, (*your/someone else's*) wife (= **oku-san/sama** 奥さん/様)
ō´kami *n* オオカミ・狼 wolf
o-kara *n* オカラ bean-curd lees
ōkare sukunakare *adv* 多かれ少なかれ more or less
okaruto *n* オカルト occult: **~-eiga** オカルト映画 occult film(s)
okashíi *adj* おかしい, **~ na (...)** おかしな(...) **1.** amusing, funny **2.** strange, peculiar, queer
okashimásu, okásu *v* 犯します, 犯す commits, perpetrates; violates
okashimásu, okásu *v* 侵します, 侵す encroaches upon, invades
okashimásu, okásu *v* 冒します, 冒す braves; attacks
ōkata *adv* おおかた・大方 **1.** for the most part **2.** probably
o-káwari *n* お代わり a second helping (*usually of rice*)
o-kazari *n* お飾り (→ **kazari** 飾り) **1.** decorations and/or offerings to the gods and Buddha **2.** New Year's decorations **3.** mere figurehead
okazu *n* おかず main/side dish (*to go with the rice*)
óke *n* 桶 tub, wooden bucket: **furo-~** 風呂桶 bathtub: **kan-~** 棺桶

coffin [INFORMAL] (= **hitsugi** 棺)
ōkē *n* オーケー okay, ok
ōkesutora *n* オーケストラ orchestra
oki *n* 沖 offshore, offing; **oki-ba** *n* 置き場 a place (*to put something*); **oki-miyage** *n* 置き土産 keepsake, parting present/gift; **oki-mono** *n* 置き物 ornament; bric-a-brac; **oki-tegami** *n* 置き手紙 letter/note left behind
ō-kii *adj* 大きい big, large; loud (= **ō´ki na** 大きな); **ō´-kiku** *adv* 大きく greatly, much, loudly; so as to be big/loud: **~ nái (arimasén)** 大きくない(ありません) small, modest; **ō-ki (na)** *adj* 大き(な) big, great
okimásu̱, oku *v* 置きます, 置く puts (*aside*), places, sets, lays; **shi̱te ~** して置きます does for later, does for now (*for the time being*)
okimásu̱, okíru *v* 起きます, 起きる gets up; arises
okina *n* 翁 old man,
o-ki-ni-iri *n* お気に入り favorite: **kono pēji o ~ ni tsuikashimásu̱** このページをお気に入りに追加します bookmarks this page (as a favorite) (*web browser*)
ōki̱sa *n* 大きさ size (= **saizu** サイズ)
okite *n* 掟 law, rule, regulation: **~ o mamorimásu (yaburimásu)** observes (breaks) a rule 掟を守ります(破ります)
okiwasuréru *v* 置き忘れる forgets
okkochimásu̱, okkochíru *v* 落っこちます, 落っこちる falls
okkū (na) *adj* 億劫(な) troublesome, bothersome
ōkō (suru) *adj* 横行(する) rampant
okonai 行い *n* act(ion), deed, conduct: **higoro no ~** 日ごろの行い daily behavior
okonaimásu̱, okonau *v* 行います, 行う acts, does, carries out, performs
okonomi-yaki *n* お好み焼き seasoned pancake
okorí *v* 起こり origin, source, beginning: **koto no ~ (wa)...** 事の起こり(は)... it happened because..., it started like this...
okorí *n* おこり ague, the shakes
okorimásu̱, okóru *v* 起こります, 起こる happens, occurs, arises; springs from
okorimásu̱, okóru *v* 興ります, 興る starts; prospers; rises
okorimásu̱, okóru *v* 怒ります, 怒る gets mad/angry
okoshimásu̱, okósu *v* 起こします, 起こす raises; establishes; gets a person up, rouses
okoshimásu̱, okósu *v* 興します, 興す gives rise to, brings about
okotarimásu̱, okotaru *v* 怠ります, 怠る neglects, shirks; is lazy about
óku *n* 億 a hundred million: **~-man chōja** 億万長者 a billionaire
óku *n* 奥 the back or inside part; **óku-ba** *n* 奥歯 back tooth
oku-... *prefix* 屋... house, roof; **oku-gai (no/de)** *adj*, *adv* 屋外(の/で) outdoor(s), outside; **oku-jō (no/**

de) *adj, adv* 屋上(の/で) on the roof(top), rooftop floor

ō'ku 多く **1.** *n* a lot, for the most part **2.** *adv* mostly

okubi *n* おくび belch

okubyō' *n* 臆病 cowardice: **~ (na)** 臆病(な) cowardly, timid; **~-monó** 臆病者 a coward (= **kowagari** 怖[恐]がり

okure *n* 後れ a lag: **~ o torimásu** 後れを取ります falls behind, gets defeated

okuremásu, okureru *v* 遅れます, 遅れる is late, gets delayed; lags, falls behind; runs late

okurimásu, okuru *v* 送ります, 送る sends; sees a person off; spends (*time*)

okurimásu, okuru *v* 贈ります, 贈る presents, awards; **okuri-mono** *n* 贈り物 gift, present

óku-san/-sama *n* 奥さん/様 (*your/someone else's*) wife; lady, Madam

okusoku *n* 憶測 guess

ō-kyū *n* 応急 emergency; **ōkyū-shochi** *n* 応急処置 first aid; **ōkyū-sochi** *n* 応急措置 emergency measure

okuyami *n* お悔やみ condolences

O-machidō-sama déshita *interj* お待ちどうさまでした. Thank you for waiting. (*at restaurant, etc.*)

omae *pron* お前 (*mostly male. familiar or rude*) you

omake *n* おまけ extra, bonus, premium: **~ ni** おまけに to boot, in addition

o-mamori *n* お守り amulet, charm, good-luck piece

O-matase (ita)shimáshita *interj* お待たせ(致)しました. Sorry to have made you wait.

omáwari (-san) *n* お巡り(さん)・おまわり(さん) policeman, (*police*) officer

o-me *n* お目eyes: **~ ni kakarimásu** お目にかかります I meet/see you; **~ ni kakemásu** お目にかけます I show it to you

ō-medama o kuimásu (kū) *v* 大目玉を食います(食う) gets severely scolded, gets it in the neck

omedeta *n* おめでた blessed event (*pregnancy, childbirth, marriage, etc.*)

o-medetō (gozaimásu) *interj* おめでとう(ございます) congratulations: **akemáshite ~** 明けましておめでとう(ございます) Happy New Year!

omei *n* 汚名 disgrace

ōme ni mimásu (miru) *v* 大目に見ます(見る) overlooks (= **minogashimásu** 見逃します): **(dōka) ōme ni mitekudasai** (どうか)大目に見て下さい Please give me a break.

o-meshi ni narimásu (náru) *v* お召しになります(なる) [HONORIFIC] **1.** wears **2.** buys **3.** invites **4. kaze o ~** 風邪をお召しになります catches a cold

o-mi- *prefix* おみ (*for a few words*) **= o-** お・御 [HONORIFIC]; **o-mi-ki** *n* 御神酒 saké offered to the gods

(= **miki** 神酒); o-míkoshi *n* お神輿 portable shrine (= **mikoshi** 神輿)
ō-mísoka *n* 大晦日 last day of year; New Year's eve
o-miya *n* お宮 shrine (*Shinto shrine*)
o-miyage *n* おみやげ・お土産, **o-míya** おみや (*baby talk*) gift, present (*as souvenir*) (= **miyage** みやげ)
omo-... *prefix* 面... face; omo-naga (na/no) *adj* 面長(な/の) long-faced; ...(na) omo-mochi *suffix*, *n* ...(な) 面持ち a look on one's face: **fuan na** ~ 不安な面持ち a worried look on one's face: **kinchō no** ~ 緊張の面持ち a nervous look on one's face; omo-yatsure *n* 面やつれ drawn and haggard face (*due to worry and/or illness*)
omócha *n* おもちゃ・オモチャ・玩具 toy
omoemás<u>u</u>, omoéru *v* 思えます, 思える **1.** can think **2.** = **omowa-remás<u>u</u>** 思われます (is thought)
omoi *adj* 重い heavy; grave, serious; important
omói *n* 思い thought, idea; feeling, mind, heart; desire, will
omoi-dashimás<u>u</u>, omoi-dásu *v* 思い出します, 思い出す remembers, recalls; omoide *n* 思い出 memory (*a recollection*)
omoigakénai *v* 思いがけない unexpected, surprising
omoimás<u>u</u>, omóu *v* 思います, 思う thinks, feels
omomuki *n* 趣 **1.** taste, flavor **2.** atmosphere, air **3.** circumstance, contents **4.** condition
omoya *n* 母屋 main building/house
omoi-yari *n* おもいやり consideration (*being kind*), solicitude
ómo (na) *adj* 主(な) principal, main: **ómo ni** 主に mainly
omo-ni *n* 重荷 burden (*on one's mind*)
omosa *n* 重さ weight
omoshi *n* 重し a weight (*object*)
omoshirói *adj* おもしろい・面白い interesting, pleasant, amusing, funny
omoté *n* 表 front (*side*), surface, outer side/surface; omote-dōri *n* 表通り main street; omote-muki (no/wa) *adj*, *adv* 表向き(の/は) ostensible (*ostensibly*), on the surface, official(ly)
omowánu ... *adj* 思わぬ...; unexpected, unanticipated
omowaremás<u>u</u>, omowaréru *v* 思われます, 思われる is thought; seems, appears
omowasemás<u>u</u>, omowaséru *v* 思わせます, 思わせる reminds one of, makes one think of
ōmu *n* オウム・鸚鵡 parrot
ō-mugi *n* オオムギ・大麦 barley
omunibasu *n* オムニバス omnibus
omu-ráisu *n* オムライス omelet wrapped around rice
omuretsu *n* オムレツ omelet
omútsu *n* おむつ diapers
on *n* 音 sound; pronunciation; on-kyō *n* 音響 sound: **~-kōka** 音響

効果 sound effect; on-pa *n* 音波 sound wave; on-ritsu *n* 音律 rhythm; on-ryō *n* 音量 sound volume: **~ o agete (sagete) kudasai** 音量を上げて(下げて)下さい Please turn up (down) the volume; on-setsu *n* 音節 syllable; on-yomi *n* 音読み Chinese reading of kanji/ Chinese character in Japanese

on- *prefix* 御 (*for a few words*) = **o-** お・御 [HONORIFIC]: **on-sha** 御社 (*letter*) (your) good self, your esteemed institution/organization; **on-zōshi** 御曹司/御曹子 scion; ... **on-chū** ... 御中 (*letter*) Dear ...; **on-rei mōshiagemasu** 御礼申し上げます Thank you ... for ...

ón *n* 恩(**go-ón** ご恩) obligation; kindness:; **go-ón wa isshō wasuremasen** ご恩は一生忘れません I will never forget your kindness.; on-gaeshi *n* 恩返し returning the favour, repaying the favour; on-jin *n* 恩人 benefactor: **inochi no ~** 命の恩人 person to whom one owes his/her life; ón ni kimásu, ón ni kiru *v* 恩に着ます, 恩に着る I appreciate it. I am deeply grateful.; ón ni kisemásu, ón ni kiseru *v* 恩に着せます, 恩に着せる emphasizes the favor one has done: **on-kisegamashii** 恩着せがましい condescending, patronizing; on-shi *n* 恩師 former teacher

ōnā *n* オーナー owner

onaji (...) *adj* 同じ(...) the same (...): **~ yō´ (na)** 同じよう(な) alike, similar

o-naka *n* お腹 stomach: **~ ga sukimáshita** おなかがすきました is hungry

onanii *n* オナニー masturbation (= **jii** 自慰)

onara *n* おなら flatulence, fart

ónbu shimásu (suru) *v* おんぶします(する) carries baby on back; rides on back

onchū *n* 御中 [HONORIFIC] Messrs. (*on envelope*)

óndo *n* 温度 temperature; **~-kei** 温度計 thermometer

ondori *n* オンドリ・雄鶏 rooster

ōnetsu-byō *n* 黄熱病 (*medical*) yellow fever

óngaku *n* 音楽 music; ongak(u)-ka *n* 音楽家 musician; ongák(u)-kai *n* 音楽会 concert

oní *n* 鬼 **1.** demon, devil, ogre **2.** cruel, cold, and/or heartless person **3.** fiend, person who devotes all his/her energy: **shigoto no ~** 仕事の鬼 a workaholic; oní-baba *n* 鬼婆 hag; oní-gokko *n* 鬼ごっこ tag (*child game*)

onkei *n* 恩恵 favor

onná *n* 女, **~ no hitó/katá** 女の人/方 woman, female; **~ no kyō´dai** 女のきょうだい sister(s) (= **shímai** 姉妹); onna-gata *n* 女形, **oyáma** おやま・女形 female impersonator (in *Kabuki*); onna-mono *n* 女物 women's wear; onná-no-ko *n* 女の子 girl (=

joshi 女子); onna-shújin *n* 女主人 hostess; onna-yu *n* 女湯 women's (*section of the*) bath
óno *n* 斧 ax, hatchet
onóono *adj* 各々・おのおの each, respectively, severally: ~ **no** 各々の respective
onore *n* おのれ self [BOOKISH]
onozukara *adv* 自ずから automatically, spontaneously
onparēdo *n* オンパレード on pa-rade, succession
onrain *n* オンライン online; onrain ōkushon *n* オンライン・オークション online auction; onrain gēmu *n* オンラインゲーム online game (*Internet*); onrain tsūhan saito *n* オンライン通販サイト online shopping site
onryō *n* 怨霊 vengeful ghost/spirit
onsen *n* 温泉 hot spring; spa: **~-ryokan** 温泉旅館 Japanese inn and hot-spring
onshin̲ *n* 音信 contact, news: ~ **futsū desu̲** 音信不通です is out of contact, lost touch with
onshi̲tsu *n* 温室 greenhouse
onsui *n* 温水 warm water
onwa *n* 温和 **1.** mild, moderate (*climate*) **2.** gentle, quiet, calm and peaceful person
on za rokku *n* オンザロック on the rocks (whiskey, etc.)
onzōshi *n* 御曹司 son of a noble/distinguished family
opekku *n* オペック Organization of Petroleum Exporting Countries, OPEC
ópera *n* オペラ opera
óppai *n* おっぱい (= **(o-)chichí** (お)乳 (*baby talk, slang*) breast; milk (= **chíbusa, nyūbō** 乳房)
ō'pun *n* オープン open; ō'pun na *adj* オープンな open, candid
ōra *n* オーラ aura: ~ **ga arimásu** オーラがあります has radiance
ōrai *n* 往来 traffic; communication; thoroughfare
ō'rai *n* オーライ "all right, OK", (*all clear, go ahead*)
ōraka (na) *adj* おおらか(な) generous, big-hearted, easygoing: **~ na seikaku** おおらかな性格 generous personality
Oranda *n* オランダ Holland; (= **Oranda no** オランダの) Dutch
ore *pron* おれ・俺 (*male, unrefined*) I/me
oremásu̲, oréru *v* 折れます, 折れる **1.** it breaks; it folds **2.** can break/fold/bend it
orénji *n* オレンジ orange; orenji-jū'sú *n* オレンジジュース orange juice/drink
oresen-gurafu *n* 折れ線グラフ line graph
ori *n* おり・澱 dregs, sediment
orí *n* 檻 cage; jail
orí *n* 折 time, occasion
orientēshon *n* オリエンテーション orientation
orígami *n* おりがみ・折り紙 paper-folding (art)
oríibu *n* オリーブ olive; oriibu-yu/-

oiru オリーブ油/オイル olive oil
orimásu, óru *v* 居ります, 居る [DEFERENTIAL/HUMBLE] is, stays (= **imásu** 居ます, **iru** 居る)
orimásu, óru *v* 折ります, 折る breaks (*folds, bends*) it; ori-mé *n* 折り目 fold, crease, pleat
orimásu, óru *v* 織ります, 織る weaves it; ori-mono *n* 織物 cloth, textile, fabric
orimásu, oríru *v* 下ります, 下りる goes down
orimásu, oríru *v* 降ります, 降りる gets down, gets off (*a ship/ plane*), gets out (*of a car*)
ori-tatamimásu, ori-tatamu *v* 折り畳みます, 折り畳む folds up
óroka *adj* 愚か [BOOKISH] foolish (= **baka na** 馬鹿な)
ōrora *n* オーロラ aurora
oroshí *v* おろし **1.** a grater (= **~-gane** おろし金) **2.** (*something*) grated: **daikon-~** 大根おろ] grated radish
oroshimásu, orósu *v* 下ろします, 下ろす takes down, lowers; unloads; invests; **yokin o ~** 預金を下ろします withdraws (*deposited money*)
oroshimásu, orósu *v* 降ろします, 降ろす lets one off (*a ship/plane*), drops off (*from a car*), lets out (*of a car*)
oroshimásu, orósu *v* 堕ろします, 堕ろす aborts, has an abortion
óroshí (no/de) *adj, adv* 卸(の/で) wholesale
oroshi-uri *n* 卸し売り (*selling*) wholesale
ōrudo misu *n* オールドミス old maid, spinster
orugōru *n* オルゴール music box
ōru maitii *adj* オールマイティ almighty **1.** the ace of spades (*card game*) **2.** all-around (= **zennō** 全能)
ōru-naito *adj* オールナイト all-night (= **shūya** 終夜): **~ kōgyō** オールナイト興行 all-night show
ōryō *n* 横領 embezzlement
osaemásu, osáéru *v* 押さえます, 押さえる represses; covers; holds
osaemásu, osáéru *v* 抑えます, 抑える controls, restrains
Ōsaka *n* 大阪 Osaka; Ōsaká-Eki *n* 大阪駅 Osaka Station; Ōsaká-jin *n* 大阪人 an Osakan
osamarimásu, osamáru *v* 収まります, 収まる gets reaped (*collected, brought in*)
osamarimásu, osamáru *v* 納まります, 納まる is paid
osamarimásu, osamáru *v* 治まります, 治まる settles (*down/in*)
o-samemásu, osaméru *v* 収め[納め]ます, 収め[納め]る reaps, harvests, collects; gets; finishes
o-samemásu, osaméru *v* 納めます, 納める pays (*tax, premium, etc.*)
o-samemásu, osaméru *v* 治めます, 治める governs; pacifies
o-san *n* お産 childbirth (= **shussan** 出産)
osanái *adj* 幼い infant(ile), very

young; childish, green (*inexperienced*)

o-san shimásu (suru) *v* お産します(する) gives birth to (= **shussan shimásu (suru)** 出産します(する))

osarai *n* おさらい review [INFORMAL] (= **fukushū** 復習)

o-séchi *n* おせち・お節 a season; a festival; **osechi-ryō´ri** *n* おせち料理 festival cookery (*for New Year's*)

o-seibo *n* お歳暮 year-end present, winter gift

o-seji *n* お世辞・おせじ compliment, flattery: **o-~ o iimásu̲** お世辞を言います pays compliments, flatters

o-sékkai *n* お節介 meddling: **o-~ o yakimásu̲** お節介を焼きます meddles; **~ (na)** お節介(な) meddlesome

osen *n* 汚染 [BOOKISH] contamination, pollution

ōsen *n* 応戦 fighting back

o-sewa-sama お世話様 (*thank you for*) your help/attention

oshaberi *n* おしゃべり chatter-box, gossip

osháburi *n* おしゃぶり teething ring, pacifier

osháre *n* おしゃれ・お洒落 dandy: **~ na hi̲to** おしゃれな人 fancy dresser

oshi *n* おし・唖 a (deaf-)mute

o-shíbori *n* おしぼり damp hand-towel

oshie *n* 教え instruction, teaching(s)

oshiego *n* 教え子 a student (*of a teacher's*)

oshiemásu̲, oshieru *v* 教えます, 教える teaches, shows, tells, informs

oshii *adj* 惜しい **1.** regrettable **2.** precious

ōshii *adj* 雄々しい manly, manful, brave, strong (*not feminine or sissy*)

oshi-ire *n* 押し入れ (*traditional Japanese*) closet, cupboard

o-shimai *n* おしまい the end (*baby talk*) (= **owari** 終わり)

oshimásu̲, osu *v* 押します, 押す pushes, presses (*on*)

oshíme *n* おしめ diapers

ōshin *n* 往診 house call

o-shinko *n* おしんこ・お新香 radish (etc.) pickles

oshiroi *n* おしろい・白粉 face powder

oshi̲tsu̲kémásu̲, oshi̲tsu̲kéru *v* 押し付けます, 押し付ける pushes, presses; intrudes

oshiuri *n* 押し売り **1.** high-pressure selling: **shinsetsu no ~** 親切の押し売り unwelcome kindness **2.** a high-pressure salesman

oshí-zushi *n* 押し鮨 sushi rice and marinated fish pressed in squarish molds (*Osaka style*)

ōshoku jinshu *n* 黄色人種 Asians, Mongoloid

oshō (-san) *n* 和尚(さん) Buddhist priest

Ō´shū *n* 欧州 Europe (= **Yōróppa** ヨーロッパ)

osoi *adj* 遅い late; slow
osóimásu, osou *v* 襲います, 襲う attacks, assaults; strikes, hits
osokare hayakare *adv* 遅かれ早かれ sooner or later
osoku *adv* 遅く late; slow: **osóku-tomo** 遅くとも at the latest
o-sómatsu-sama *interj* お粗末さま Please excuse the poor fare (*reply to* **gochisō-sama** ごちそうさま)
osóraku *adv* おそらく・恐らく probably, maybe, possibly
osoré *n* 恐れ fear
osóreirimásu *v* 恐れ入ります **1.** excuse me **2.** thank you
osoremásu, osoréru *v* 恐れます, 恐れる fears
osoroshii *adj* 恐ろしい fearful, dreadful, awful, terrible, horrible
osoróshiku *adv* 恐ろしく terribly
osowarimásu, osowaru *v* 教わります, 教わる is taught, studies, learns
osshaimásu, ossh//aru *v* おっしゃいます, おっしゃる (*someone honored*) says; is called
osú *n* 雄・オス male animal; **… no ~** …の雄 a he-… (→ **o-ushi** 雄牛)
osui *n* 汚水 sewage
osui-dame *n* 汚水溜め cesspool
ōsuji *n* 大筋 outline
Ōsutorária *n* オーストラリア Australia; **Ōsutorariá-jin** *n* オーストラリア人 an Australian
Ōsutoria *n* オーストリア Austria; **Ōsutoriá-jin** *n* オーストリア人 an Austrian
o-suwari *interj* お座り Sit! (*training one's dog*)
otafukukaze *n* おたふく風邪 mumps
o-tagai (no) *adj* お互い(の) mutual, reciprocal: **~ (ni)** お互い(に) mutually, reciprocally
otamajakushi *n* オタマジャクシ tadpole
o-taku *n* お宅 [INFORMAL] your house; you; **o-taku no** *pron* お宅の your, yours
ó-te *interj* お手 Give me your paw! Shake hands! (*training one's dog*)
o-teage *n* お手上げ giving up
o-teárai *n* お手洗い washroom, toilet, restroom
o-témae *n* お手前 prowess, skill, ability
o-tenba *n* お転婆 tomboy
o-ténto-sama *n* おてんとさま・お天道さま the sun (= **táiyō** 太陽)
otétsudai (-san) *n* お手伝い(さん) maid(-servant), (*household*) helper
otó *n* 音 sound, noise: **~ ga shimásu** 音がします it makes a noise, there is a noise
ōtō *n* 応答 reply, response, answer; **shitsugi-ōtō** *n* 質疑応答 questions and answers
ōtóbai *n* オートバイ motorcycle
otokó *n* 男 = **~ no hitó/katá** 男の人/方 man, male, boy; **~ no kyō´dai** 男の兄弟 brother(s); **otoko-gokoro** *n* 男心 man's heart;

otoko-mono *n* 男物 menswear; otokó-no-ko *n* 男の子 boy (= **danshi** 男子); otoko-yámome *n* 男やもめ widower; otoko-yu *n* 男湯 men's (*section of the*) bath

ōtokuchū´ru *n* オートクチュール haute couture, high fashion

o-tokui (-san) *n* お得意(さん) good customer(s), regular customer(s)

otome *n* 乙女 **1.** (*young*) girl, lady **2.** maiden, virgin: **urawakaki ~** [BOOKISH] うら若き乙女 young maiden

o-tómo shimásu (suru) *v* お伴します(する) (*I will*) accompany (you)

otona *n* 大人・おとな adult

otonashíi *adj* おとなしい gentle, well-behaved

otonáshiku *adv* おとなしく gently

otori *n* おとり・囮 decoy; lure

otoroemásu, otoróéru *v* 衰えます, 衰える declines, fades, grows weak

otóru *adj* 劣る is inferior, worse, weak, poor (= **ototta** 劣った)

otoshi-dama *n* お年玉 money given as a New Year's gift

otoshimásu, otósu *v* 落とします, 落とす drops; omits

otoshimono *n* 落とし物 lost, dropped things

otoshi-támago *n* 落とし卵 poached eggs

otōtó *n* 弟 younger brother: **otōto-san** 弟さん (*your/someone else's*) younger brother

ototói *n* おととい・一昨日 day before yesterday

otótoshi *n* おととし・一昨年 year before last

ōtotsu *n* おうとつ・凹凸 unevenness, bump (= **dekoboko** でこぼこ・凸凹)

O-tsukare-sama (déshita) *interj* お疲れ様(でした). You did good work (*today, at the end of a project, etc.*); You must be weary (*tired, exhausted*). (→ **Go-kúrō-sama (deshita).** ご苦労様(でした).)

otsu (na) *adj* おつ[乙](な) chic, stylish

otto *n* 夫 (*my*) husband

ototta *adj* 劣った is inferior, worse, weak, poor (= **otoru** 劣る)

o-ushi *n* 雄牛 bull, ox

o-úsu *n* お薄 light green tea (*tea-ceremony*) (= **usu-cha** 薄茶)

o-wakare *n* お別れ parting, farewell (= **wakaré** 別れ)

owaremásu, owareru *v* 追われます, 追われる gets chased

owari *n* 終わり the end: **~ no ...** 終わりの... the last, final; **~ no nai** 終わりのない endless

owarimásu, owaru *v* 終わります, 終わる it ends; ends it

oyá *n* 親 parent; oya-baka *n* 親ばか[馬鹿] doting parent(s); oya-fukō *n* 親不幸 unfilial behavior, unfilial child; oya-go-san *n* 親御さん (*your/someone else's*) parent (= **goryōshin** ご両親); oya-ji *n* 親父 (*familiar, usually male*) (= **(o-)tō´-san** お父さん・

おとうさん) my father: **oyaji-san** 親父さん (*your/someone else's*) father; óya-ko *n* 親子 parent and child; oya-kōkō *n* 親孝行 filial piety (*honoring one's parents*); oya-moto *n* 親元 (*one's*) parent's home; oya-shirazu *n* 親知らず wisdom tooth

Oya *interj* おや Gee whiz! I say! How (a)bout that!; **Oya mā!** おやまあ good heavens; óyaoya *interj* おやおや Dear dear!, Oh dear.

óyá-bun *n* 親分 boss, ringleader, chief

ōyake (no/ni) *adj, adv* 公(の/に) public(ly), open(ly), official(ly)

óyáma *n* おやま・女形 female impersonator (of **Kabuki**) (= **onnagata** 女形)

ō'ya (-san) *n* 大家(さん) landlord

O-yasumi nasái *interj* おやすみなさい. Good night.

o-yátsu *n* おやつ snacks, sweets (*for mid-afternoon*) (→ **sánji no oyatsu** 三時のおやつ)

oya-yubi *n* 親指 thumb

ōyō *n* 応用 application, putting to use

ōyō (na) *adj* 鷹揚(な) easygoing: **~ na taido** 鷹揚な態度 generous attitude

óyobi *prep* および and (*also*) (= **to** と)

oyobimásu, oyobu *v* およびます, およぶ reaches, extends to, equals

oyogí *n* 泳ぎ swimming

oyogimásu, oyógu *v* 泳ぎます, 泳ぐ swims

oyoso (no) *adj* およそ(の) about, roughly

ōzáppa (na) *adj* おおざっぱ(な) rough

ōzéi *n* 大勢 large crowd, throng: **~ de** 大勢で in large numbers (= **takusan (no)** たくさん(の)); ōzéi no *adj* 大勢の many

ō'-zeki *n* 大関 champion sumo wrestler

o-zon *n* オゾン ozone

ō-zume *n* 大詰め ending: **~ o mukaemásu** 大詰めを迎えます is/will be in the final stage/phase

P

pachinko *n* パチンコ pinball (*machine*): **~-ya** パチンコ屋 pachinko parlor

pái *n* パイ pie

pái *n* パイ・ぱい・牌 a mahjong tile

paináppuru *n* パイナップル pineapple

páipu *n* パイプ pipe; cigarette holder

pairótto *n* パイロット pilot

pajama *n* パジャマ pajamas (= **nemaki** 寝巻き)

pākingu *n* パーキング parking (= **chūsha-jō** 駐車場)

pakkēji *n* パッケージ package

...-paku *suffix* …泊: **ip-paku** 一泊 one night's lodging/stay → **...-haku** …泊

pāma *n* パーマ permanent wave

pán *n* パン bread: **shoku-~** 食パン loaf of bread, sandwich loaf: **~-kēki** パンケーキ pancake; **pan-kó** *n* パン粉 ① bread crumbs ② bread flour; **pan-kúzu** *n* パンくず (*bread*) crumbs; **pán-ya** *n* パン屋 ① bakeshop, bakery ② baker

pánda *n* パンダ panda

pánfu (rétto) *n* パンフ(レット) pamphlet, brochure

pánikku *n* パニック panic; **panikuru** *v* パニくる [INFORMAL] gets panicky

panku *n* パンク puncture, blowout: **taiya ga ~ shimásu** タイヤがパンクします gets a flat tire

pánku *n* パンク punk: **~ rokku** パンクロック punk rock, punk music

pansuto *n* パンスト panty hose

pántaron *n* パンタロン (*women's*) slacks, pantaloons

pántii *n* パンティー underwear for ladies (*panties*)

pántsu *n* パンツ underwear (*underpants*); slacks, pants

papa *n* パパ (*baby talk*) daddy, dad (= **(o-)tō-chan** (お)父ちゃん)

parashūto *n* パラシュート parachute

Pári *n* パリ Paris

paripari (no) *adj* ぱりぱり(の) crisp; first-rate

pāsénto *n* パーセント percent

paso-kon *n* パソコン personal computer

pásu *n* パス pass(ing); **~ shimásu** パスします passes (*an exam*) (= **gōkaku shimásu** 合格します)

pasupṓto *n* パスポート passport

patā́n *n* パターン pattern

pā́tii *n* パーティー party: **hōmu-~** ホームパーティ house party

patokā *n* パトカー patrol car, police car

pātonā *n* パートナー partner

patoron *n* パトロン patron

pāto(taimu) *n* パート(タイム) part-time work

pázuru *n* パズル puzzle: **jigusō-~** ジグソーパズル jigsaw puzzle

pedaru *n* ペダル pedal: **jidensha/jitensha no ~** 自転車のペダル bicycle pedal

pēji *n* ページ・頁 page

Pékin *n* ペキン・北京 Beijing

pén *n* ペン pen

...-pén *suffix* …遍 = **...-hén** …遍 (*counts times*)

pénchi *n* ペンチ pliers, pincers

péndanto *n* ペンダント pendant

penki *n* ペンキ paint; **(... ni) ~ o nurimásu** (…に)ペンキを塗ります paints; **penki-ya** *n* ペンキ屋 painter (*housepainter*)

pénshon *n* ペンション pension (*small hotel, lodge, inn, etc.*)

perapera *adj, adv* ぺらぺら・ペラペラ fluent(ly) (= **ryūchō** 流暢)

péten *n* ペテン fraud (= **sagi** 詐欺, **ikasama** いかさま): **~-shi** ペテ

ン師 swindler (= **sagi-shi** 詐欺師, **ikasama-shi** いかさま師)
pétto *n* ペット pet
piano *n* ピアノ piano: **gurando-~** グランドピアノ grand piano
píiman *n* ピーマン green bell pepper: **aka-~** 赤ピーマン red bell pepper
piínát(t)su *n* ピーナ(ッ)ツ peanut(s)
pikápika (no) *adj* ピカピカ(の) flashing, glittering
píkuníkku *n* ピクニック picnic
pín *n* ピン pin (*for hair*)
pínchi *n* ピンチ pinch (= **kiki** 危機): **~ ni ochiirimásu** ピンチに陥ります gets in a pinch
pínku *adj* ピンク pink: **~-iro** ピンク色 pink color (= **momo-iro** 桃色)
pinsétto *n* ピンセット tweezers
pin (to) *adv* ぴん(と) (*stretched*) taut: **~ to kimásu** ぴんと来ます hits home with one, comes home to one, appeals to one
pinto *n* ピント focus (= **shōten** 焦点); pin-boke *n* ピンぼけ out-of-focus
piramíddo *n* ピラミッド pyramid
pisutoru *n* ピストル revolver, pistol
pittári *adv* ぴったり exactly, perfectly, closely; just right
píza *n* ピザ pizza
póchi, pótsu *n* ぽち, ぽつ a dot
pokétto *n* ポケット pocket
pomā'do *n* ポマード pomade, hair oil
ponbiki *n* ぽん引き a pimp
póndo *n* ポンド pound (*weight or money*)
pónpu *n* ポンプ pump
pónsu, ponzú *n* ポン酢 juice of bitter orange
poppukōn *n* ポップコーン popcorn
poppusu *n* ポップス pops, popular music
pori(-) *n, prefix* ポリ poly(ethylene); plastic; pori-búkuro *n* ポリ袋 (*plastic*) bag
póruno *n* ポルノ pornography; **~-éiga** ポルノ映画 a porno film
pósuto *n* ポスト mail box
pō'tā *n* ポーター porter
potā'ju *n* ポタージュ potage, thick Western soup
pótéto *n* ポテト potato
pótto *n* ポット pot
púragu *n* プラグ (*electric*) outlet, plug
púran *n* プラン plan: **~ o tatemásu** プランを立てます makes a plan
puranetariúmu *n* プラネタリウム planetarium
purásuchíkku *n* プラスチック plastic(s)
puratto-hōmu *n* プラットホーム (*station*) platform
purehabu-jūtaku *n* プレハブ住宅 prefabricated house
purei-gáido *n* プレイガイド a "Play Guide" theater ticket agency
purézento *n* プレゼント present, gift
púrín *n* プリン a small custard; crème brûlée
puríntā *n* プリンター printer

purinto *n* プリント printing, printout, printed matter (= **insatsú** 印刷); purinto auto *n* プリントアウト printing, printout (= **insatsú-butsu** 印刷物)
púro *n* プロ pro(-fessional)
purogurámā *n* プログラマー programmer
purogúramu *n* プログラム program
puro-resu *n* プロレス professional wrestling
pū́ru *n* プール **1.** swimming pool **2.** motor pool, parking lot
pusshúhon *n* プッシュホン touch-tone telephone

R

...´-ra *suffix* …ら and others (= **nado** など･等); all of
rabel *n* ラベル label
rábo *n* ラボ lab (= laboratory)
rágubii *n* ラグビー rugby
rai-... *prefix* 来… **1.** next **2.** coming; rái-getsu *n, adv* 来月 next month; rai-nen *n, adv* 来年 next year; rai-se *n* 来世 afterlife, next life; rai-shū *n, adv* 来週 next week; rai-kyaku *n* 来客 guest, caller, visitor, company
raibaru *n* ライバル rival
raifurú-jū *n* ライフル銃 rifle
ráimu *n* ライム lime (*fruit*)
raion *n* ライオン lion
ráisensu *n* ライセンス license, permit
ráisu *n* ライス rice (*served on plate*)
raitā *n* ライター **1.** lighter (*cigarette*) **2.** writer (*professional*)
ráiu *n* 雷雨 [BOOKISH] thunderstorm
rajiḗtā *n* ラジエーター radiator (*car*)
rájio *n* ラジオ radio: **~-bangumi** ラジオ番組 radio program
rakétto *n* ラケット racket
rakkan *n* 楽観 optimism; rakkan-teki (na) *adj* 楽観的(な) optimistic
rakú *adj* 楽 **1.** comfort (= **anraku** 安楽); rakú (na) *adj* 楽(な) comfortable; **2.** easy (= **kantan** 簡単, **yasashii** やさしい[易しい])
rakuda *n* ラクダ camel
rakudai *n* 落第 [BOOKISH] failure (*in a test*)
rakuen *n* 楽園 paradise: **chijō no ~** 地上の楽園 earthly paradise
rakugo *n* 落語 (*traditional Japanese*) comic storytelling: **~-ka** 落語家 a comic storyteller
rā́men *n* ラーメン Chinese noodles (*in broth*)
ramune *n* ラムネ lemon soda
rán *n* ラン・蘭 orchid
rán *n* 欄 column, field: **nyūryoku ~** 入力欄 entry field
rán *n* 乱 disturbance; war
ranbō *n* 乱暴 violence, outrage;

ranbō (na) *adj* 乱暴(な) violent, wild, rough, disorderly

ránchi *n* ランチ **1.** lunch **2.** launch (*boat*); ranchi-sā´bisu *n* ランチサービス special lunch, a luncheon special

randóseru *n* ランドセル knapsack for elementary school children

ranma *n* らんま・欄間 transom window

ranningu *n* ランニング running

ránpu *n* ランプ **1.** lamp **2.** ramp

rappa *n* ラッパ trumpet, bugle

... rashíi *suffix, adj* …らしい (*seems*) like, apparent, seems to be

rashinban *n* 羅針盤 compass (*for directions*)

rasshu-áwā *n* ラッシュアワー rush hour

ratai (no) *adj* 裸体(の) nude (= **nūdo (no)** ヌード(の)): **~-ga** 裸体画 a nude (*picture*)

Raten-go *n* ラテン語 Latin (*language*)

réa *n* レア rare (*beef*)

rébā *n* レバー **1.** liver (*to eat*) **2.** lever

régyurā *n* レギュラー regular

rei *n* 礼 **1.** thanks, gift **2.** remuneration, reward, fee (= **sharei** 謝礼); rei-kin *n* 礼金 "thank-you money" (*to obtain rental*)

réi *n* 礼 **1.** greeting **2.** bow (= **o-jigi** お辞儀); rei-gí *n* 礼儀 courtesy, etiquette; **~-tadashíi** 礼儀正しい polite; rei-hai *n* 礼拝 worship

réi *n* 零・0 zero; réi-ji *n* 零時・0時 zero o'clock, twelve o'clock

réi *n* 例: **zen~** 前例 precedent; **ichi-~** 一例 example; **~ no …** 例の… the… in question, the said …; the usual/customary …; rei-gai *n* 例外 exception (*to the rule*)

reibō *n* 冷房 air conditioning

reinkō´to *n* レインコート raincoat

reisei (na) *adj* 冷静(な) calm, cool, composed

reishō *n* 冷笑 sneer, scoff

reitō *n* 冷凍 freezing: **~-ko** 冷凍庫 freezer; reitō-shokuhin *n* 冷凍食品 frozen food

reizō´ko *n* 冷蔵庫 refrigerator, icebox

réjā *n* レジャー leisure, recreation: **~-shisetsu** レジャー施設 leisure facilities

réji *n* レジ cashier; checkout counter

rekishi *n* 歴史 history: **~-teki (na)** 歴史的(な) historical; rekishi-ka *n* 歴史家 historian

rékkā *n* レッカー, **~´-sha** レッカー車 wrecker (*tow truck*)

rekō´do *n* レコード a record (*phonograph*)

rekuriē´shon *n* レクリエーション recreation

rémon *n* レモン lemon; **~tii** レモンティー tea with a slice of lemon

ren'ai *n* 恋愛 love: **~-kánkei** 恋愛関係 a love affair; **~-kékkon** 恋愛結婚 a love marriage

rénchi *n* レンチ wrench

renchū, renjū *n* 連中 gang, crowd, clique

rénga *n* レンガ・煉瓦 brick
rengō *n* 連合 union, alliance, Allied; **~´-koku** 連合国 the Allies
rénji *n* レンジ cooking stove, kitchen range; **denshi-~** 電子レンジ microwave oven
renmei *n* 連盟 union, federation
rennyū *n* 練乳 condensed milk
renraku *n* 連絡 connection, liaison; relevance; **renraku-saki** *n* 連絡先 address of contact
renshū *n* 練習 training, practice, drill
rentákā´ *n* レンタカー rental car
rentogen *n* レントゲン, **~-sen** レントゲン線 X-ray
renzoku *n* 連続 continuity; series: **~ terebi dorama** 連続テレビドラマ serial TV drama
rénzu *n* レンズ lens; **kontaku̱to-~** コンタクトレンズ contact lens
repō´to *n* レポート report
rḗsā *n* レーサー racing driver
resépu̱shon *n* レセプション a reception
reshiíto *n* レシート receipt
ressha *n* 列車 a train; **~-jíko** 列車事故 train accident/wreck
réssun *n* レッスン lesson: **piano (no) ~** ピアノ(の)レッスン piano lesson
rḗsu *n* レース **1.** lace: **~ no kāten** レースのカーテン lace curtain **2.** race: **~-jō** レース場 racetracks
resu̱kyū-tai *n* レスキュー隊 rescue team (= **kyūjo-tai** 救助隊)
résuringu *n* レスリング wrestling
résu̱toran *n* レストラン restaurant: **famirii-~** ファミリーレストラン family restaurant
rétasu *n* レタス lettuce
rétsu *n* 列 row, line; queue
retteru *n* レッテル label
rettō *n* 列島, **…-réttō** …列島 archipelago, chain of islands
rí *n* 利 advantage, profit, interest
ríbon *n* リボン ribbon: **~-musubi** リボン結び ribbon-tie
ríeki *n* 利益 benefit, advantage, profit
rihabiri *n* リハビリ rehabilitation: **~-chiryō** リハビリ治療 rehabilitation treatment
rihā´saru *n* リハーサル rehearsal
rihatsu *n* 理髪 haircut(ting); **rihátsu-ten** *n* 理髪店 barbershop
riídā *n* リーダー leader
ríka *n* 理科 science
ríkai *n* 理解 [BOOKISH] understanding, comprehension; **rikái-ryoku** *n* 理解力 comprehension (*ability*)
rikon *n* 離婚 divorce
rikō (na) *adj* 利口(な) clever, sharp, smart, intelligent: **~ ni** *adv* 利口に cleverly
riku (chi) *n* 陸(地) land, dry land
rikúgun *n* 陸軍 army
riku̱tsu *n* 理屈 reason, argument: **he-~** へ理屈 quibble [IN NEGATIVE SENSE]
rimokon *n* リモコン remote control: **terebi no ~** テレビのリモコン TV remote control
rín *n* スズ・鈴 a bell, a doorbell

(= **beru** ベル); suzu-mushi *n* スズムシ・鈴虫 bell cricket

ringo *n* リンゴ apple

rinji (no) *adj* 臨時(の) [BOOKISH] extraordinary, special; temporary: **~-nyūsu** 臨時ニュース irregular/special news: **~ no shigoto** 臨時の仕事 temporary work

rínki-ōhen (ni) *adv* 臨機応変(に) depending on the time and situation, on a case-by-case basis: **~ ni taiōshimás<u>u</u>** 臨機応変に対応します responds flexibly

rinneru *n* リンネル linen

rínri *n* 倫理 ethics: **kigyō-~** 企業倫理 corporate ethics

rippa (na) *adj* 立派(な) splendid, admirable, excellent, great

rireki *n* 履歴 a history, a record, **~-sho** 履歴書 one's personal history, career summary

ririku *n* 離陸 take-off (*plane*)

ríron *n* 理論 theory

ríshi *n* 利子 interest (*on money*)

risō *n* 理想 an ideal: **~-teki (na)** 理想的(な) ideal

risoku *n* 利息 interest (*on money*) (= **rishi** 利子)

rísu *n* リス squirrel

rís<u>u</u>to *n* リスト list

rítsu *n* 率 **1.** rate, proportion; average **2.** a cut, a percentage

rittai *n* 立体 solid; 3-D: **~-kyō** 立体鏡 stereoscope: **~-chūshajō** 立体駐車場 multi-story parking garage

rittoru *n* リットル liter(s)

riyō *n* 利用 use, utilization

riyū *n* 理由 reason, cause, grounds; **... to iu ~ de ...** という理由で for the reason that ...

rizaya *n* 利ざや margin

rízumu *n* リズム rhythm

ro *n* 炉 furnace

... ro (yo) *interj* ...ろ(よ) [*eastern Japan*] = **... yo** ...よ (IMPERATIVE of **...i-** ...い and **... e-** ...え verb stems)

rō-... *prefix* 老... old (*not young*); rō-jin *n* 老人 old person; rō-nen *n* 老年 old age

rō´ *n* ろう・蝋 wax; beeswax

róba *n* ロバ donkey

róbii *n* ロビー lobby

róddo *n* ロッド rod (*curtain, etc.*)

rōdō *n* 労働 labor; **~´-sha** 労働者 worker, laborer

rōdo-shō´ *n* ロードショー roadshow attraction, first-run movie

rōgoku *n* 牢獄 jail

rōhi *n* 浪費 [BOOKISH] extravagance

róji *n* 路地 alley

rōka *n* 廊下 passage(way), corridor

rō´karu (na) *adj* ローカル(な) local

rokétto *n* ロケット rocket

rok-k... *prefix* 六... ・6 six; rok-kái *n* 六回 six times; rók-kai *n* 六階 sixth floor, six stories; rók-ko *n* 六個 six pieces (*small objects*)

rókkā *n* ロッカー locker

rókku *n* ロック rock, rock'n'roll (*music*)

rokú- *n* 六・6 six; roku-banme (no) *adj* 六番目(の) sixth; rokú-dai *n*

六台 six (*machines, vehicles*); rokú-dó *n* 六度 six times (= **rok-kái** 六回); rokú-mai *n* 六枚 six sheets (*flat things*); rokú-mei *n* 六名 six people (= **rokú-nin** 六人); rokú-satsú *n* 六冊 six copies (*books, magazines*)
rokuga *n* 録画 recording (*video*)
Roku-gatsú *n* 六月・6月 June
rokuon *n* 録音 recording (*sound*)
rokuro *n* ろくろ potter's wheel
Rō´ma *n* ローマ Rome
rōmá-ji *n* ローマ字 romanization, Latin letters
rómansu *n* ロマンス romance, love affair: **~-shōsetsu** ロマンス小説 romance novel
rón *n* 論 argument, discussion; treatise; theory; ron-bun *n* 論文 treatise; essay; **gakui ~** 学位論文 dissertation, thesis
Róndon *n* ロンドン London
rōnin *n* 浪人 **1.** an unemployed samurai **2.** a student between schools **3.** a man without a job
ron-jimásu, ron-jiru *v* 論じます, 論じる discusses, argues, debates
rónri *n* 論理 logic; **~-teki (na)** 論理的(な) logical
ronsō *n* 論争 controversy, dispute, argument, debate, discussion
rop-p... *prefix* 六…・6... six; rop-pai *n* 六杯 six cupfuls; rop-pén *n* 六遍 six times (= **rok-kái** 六回, **rokú-dó** 六度); róp-pon *n* 六本 six (*long objects*)
rō´pu *n* ロープ rope
rō´rā *n* ローラー roller; **~ sukē´to** ローラースケート roller-skates/skating
rōru-pan *n* ロールパン roll: **batā-rō´ru** バターロール (*butter*) roll
rosen *n* 路線 (*bus, train*) route
Roshia *n* ロシア Russia; **Roshia-go** ロシア語 Russian (*language*); **Roshiá-jin** ロシア人 a Russian
rōsókú *n* ろうそく candle
rō´suto *n* ロースト roast; **~ bíifu/chíkin** ローストビーフ/チキン roast beef/chicken
rō´tarii *n* ロータリー traffic circle, rotary
rō´to *n* ろうと・漏斗 funnel
...´-rui *suffix* …類 kinds, (*different*) species of …; dō-rui *n* 同類 same kind; shin-rui *n* 親類 kindred, relative; shu-rui *n* 種類 kind, variety; jin-rui *n* 人類 humankind; honyū-rui *n* 哺乳類 mammal (*class*)
rui-... *prefix* 類... similar …; rui-ji *n* 類似 resemblance, similarity; analogy; rui-(gi)go *n* 類(義)語 synonym
ruiseki *n* 累積 [BOOKISH] accumulation: **~-kosuto** 累積コスト accumulated costs; **~-chi** 累積値 accumulation value; **~-ritsu** 累積率 cumulative percentage
rūmu-sā´bisu *n* ルームサービス room service (*at hotel, etc.*)
rū´ru *n* ルール rule
rúsu (no) *adj* 留守(の) absent, away from home; rusu-ban *n* 留守番 caretaking/caretaker; some-

one to take care of the house in one's absence; rusu-ban-denwa *n* 留守番電話 answering machine

ryaku (-go) *n* 略(語) abbreviation

ryakushimásu, ryakúsú *v* 略します, 略す abbreviates, shortens; omits

ryo... *prefix* 旅… travel…; ryo-kaku *n* 旅客 = **ryokyaku** 旅客 (traveler, passenger); ryo-kan *n* 旅館 inn (*traditional*); ryo-ken *n* 旅券 passport (= **pasupōto** パスポート); ryo-kō *n* 旅行 travel, trip; ryo-kō-gaisha *n* 旅行会社 travel agency; ryo-kyaku *n* 旅客 traveler, passenger

ryō´ *n* 猟 hunting (*as sport*); ryō´-shi *n* 猟師 hunter

ryō´ *n* 漁 fishing (*as sport*); ryō´-shi *n* 漁師 fisherman

ryō´ *n* 寮 dormitory, boarding house: **gakusei-~** 学生寮 student dormitory: **dokushin-~** 独身寮 dormitory for singles

ryō´ *n* 陵 mound, mausoleum

ryō´ *n* 領 territory; ryō´-chi *n* 領地 territory: **sen-~** 占領地 occupied territory; ryō´-do *n* 領土 territory, domain

ryō´ *n* 量 quantity, volume

ryō-... *prefix* 両 … both; ryō-gawa *n* 両側 both sides; ryō-hō´ *n, adv* 両方 both; ryō-mén *n* 両面 both sides/directions: **~-kopii** 両面コピー two-sided copy; ryō´-shin *n* 両親 (*both*) parents

...´-ryō *suffix* …料 fee, charge: **nyūjō-~** 入場料 admission fee: **haikan-~** 拝観料 admission fee (*for temple, etc.*): **isha-~** 慰謝料 consolation money, palimony

ryōgae *n* 両替 money exchange/changing

ryō´ji *n* 領事 consul; ryōji-kan *n* 領事館 consulate

ryōkai shimásu (suru) *v* 了解します(する) consents, understands [FORMAL]

ryō´kin *n* 料金 fee, charge, fare, rate; ryō´kin-jo *n* 料金所 tollgate

ryōkō *n* 良好 good [BOOKISH]: **kenkō-~** 健康良好 good health (*mentioned on resume/application, etc.*): **seiseki-~** 成績良好 good record/achievement (*at school, in office, etc.*): **gyōseki-~** 業績良好 good business performance

ryoku-cha *n* 緑茶 green tea

ryō´ri *n* 料理 cooking; ryōrí-nin *n* 料理人 cook; ryōrí-ya *n* 料理屋 a restaurant

ryōshiki *n* 良識 good sense, common sense

ryō´shin *n* 良心 conscience; **~-teki (na)** 良心的(な) conscientious: **~ no kashaku** 良心の呵責 remorse of conscience

ryū´ *n* 竜・龍 dragon

ryūchi *n* 留置 custody: **~-jō** 留置場 detention house

ryū´chō (na) *adj* 流暢(な) fluent [FORMAL] (= [INFORMAL] **perapera** ぺらぺら・ペラペラ)

ryūgaku *n* 留学 studying abroad;

ryūgaku-sei *n* 留学生 foreign student(s)
ryúkku, ryukkusákku *n* リュック, リュックサック knapsack
ryūkō *n* 流行 popularity, vogue, fashion, trend; ryūkō (no) *adj* 流行(の) fashionable
Ryūkyū´ *n* 琉球 the Ryukyu (*Okinawa, etc.*): **Ryūkyū-rettō** 琉球列島, **Ryōkyū-shotō** 琉球諸島 Ryukyu Islands
ryūtsū *n* 流通 circulation, distribution: **~-sentā** 流通センター distribution center: **~-kosuto** 流通コスト distribution cost
ryū´zan *n* 流産 miscarriage

S

sa *n* 差 difference, discrepancy (= **sai** 差異・差違, **chigai** 違い)
...-sa *suffix*…さ …ness (*abstract noun formed from an adjective*)
sā´ *interj* さあ well; come on; let me see
saba *n* サバ・鯖 mackerel
sābā *n* サーバー (*computer*) server
sabaku *n* 砂漠 desert
sábetsu *n* 差別 discrimination; jinshu-sabetsu *n* 人種差別 racial discrimination; sabetsu-yōgo *n* 差別用語 discriminatory words
sabí *n* さび・サビ・錆 rust
sabimásu, sabíru *v* 錆びます, 錆びる it rusts
sabínai *adj* 錆びない rustproof
sabishíi *adj* 寂しい・淋しい lonely
sā´bisu *n* サービス **1.** service: **~-ryō** サービス料 service charge, cover charge: **~-seishin** サービス精神 spirit of good service **2.** free (*as part of the service*): **~-zangyō** サービス残業 unpaid overtime **3.** service (*games*) (= **sābu** サーブ)
sā´bisu-eria *n* サービスエリア **1.** service area (*tennis court, etc.*) **2.** coverage **3.** highway service area
saborimásu, sabóru *v* サボります, サボる loafs, skives (*on the job*); cuts class, plays hookey
sabotāju *n* サボタージュ sabotage
saboten *n* サボテン cactus
sābu *n* サーブ serve (*games*)
sāchi raito *n* サーチライト searchlight
sadamarimásu, sadamáru *v* 定まります, 定まる is settled, fixed
sadamemásu, sadaméru *v* 定めます, 定める settles it, fixes it
sadisuto *n* サディスト sadist
sadizumu *n* サディズム sadism
sádo *n* サド **1.** sadist **2.** sadism
sádō *n* 茶道 tea ceremony
sádō *n* 作動 [BOOKISH] operation (*of machine*)
sāfā *n* サーファー surfer, surfrider
safaia *n* サファイア sapphire
sāfin *n* サーフィン surfing, surfriding

sagaku *n* 差額 the difference (*in price*), the balance
sagan *n* 砂岩 sandstone
sagan *n* 左岸 left bank
sagarimásu, sagáru *v* 下がります, 下がる it hangs down; goes down
sagashimásu, sagasu *v* 探します, 探す looks/hunts for something/someone one wants: **shoku-sagashi** 職探し looking/hunting for a job: **shakuya-sagashi** 借家探し looking/hunting for a house for rent
sagashimásu, sagasu *v* 捜します, 捜す searches for a missing person/thing: **maigo-sagashi** 迷子捜し searching for one's lost child
sagemásu, sagéru *v* さげます・下げます, さげる・下げる hangs it, lowers it, brings it down, clears from the table
sagemásu, sagéru *v* 提げます, 提げる carries (*dangling from hand*)
sagí *n* サギ・鷺 heron
sági *n* 詐欺・サギ fraud
sagurimásu, saguru *v* 探ります, 探る gropes
ságyō *n* 作業 **1.** work (*commonly physical labor*): **josetsu-~** 除雪作業 removing the snow: **nō-~** 農作業 agricultural work: **~-in** 作業員 laborer **2.** operations: **~-jikan** 作業時間 working hours
sáhō *n* 作法 manners, etiquette
sai *n* 菜 side dish (*to go with the rice*) (= **okazu** おかず, **fukushoku(-butsu)** 副食(物))
sái *n* 妻 (*my*) wife: **ryōsai kenbo** 良妻賢母 a good wife and wise mother; **sai-shi** *n* 妻子 wife and child(ren)
sái *n* 差異・差違 [BOOKISH] difference (= **chigai** 違い, **sa** 差)
sái *n* 才 talent, ability: **ta-~ na** 多才な multi-talented
...´-sai *suffix*…歳・才 years of age: **nijús-~** 二十歳[才] = **hátachi** 二十歳・はたち twenty years old, 20
(...-)sái *n* (…)際 time, occasion: **kono-~** この際 on this occasion: **kinkyū no ~** 緊急の際 in case of emergency; **sái-shite** *conj* 際して: **... ni ~** …に際して on the occasion of, at the time of, when, in case of
sai- ... *prefix* 再… re- (*doing*); **sai-gen** *n* 再現 reappearance; **sai-hakkō** *n* 再発行 reissue; **sai-kai** *n* 再開 resuming, restarting; **sai-kai** *n* 再会 meeting again; **sai-kákunin** *n* 再確認 reconfirmation; **sai-kentō** *n* 再検討 review; **sai-kō** *n* 再考 reconsideration; **sai-kon** *n* 再婚 remarriage; **sai-nyū´koku** *n* 再入国 reentry (*into the country*); **sai-sei** *n* 再生 reproduction, playback: **~-botan** 再生ボタン play button: **~-shi** 再生紙 recycled paper; **sai-shikén** *n* 再試験 makeup exam (= **tsuishi (-ken)** 追試(験))
sai- ... *prefix* 最… the most; **sai-ai (no)** 最愛(の) one's beloved: **~ no tsuma** 最愛の妻 one's dear wife; **sai-aku (no)** 最悪(の) the

worst: ~ **no jitai** 最悪の事態 worst-case scenario; sái-chū *n* 最中 midst (= **chū**… 中…); sai-dai (no) *adj* 最大(の) the largest, the most, the greatest: **saidai-kōyakusū** 最大公約数 the greatest common divisor (GCD); sai-dai-gén (no) *adj* 最大限(の) maximal, maximum, utmost; sái-go (no) *adj* 最後(の) last, final: ~ **no bansan** 最後の晩餐 Last Supper: **~-tsūchō** 最後通牒 ultimatum (= **~-tsūkoku** 最後通告); sai-jō (no) *adj* 最上(の) best, highest, topmost: **~-kai** 最上階 the top floor; sai-kai *n* 最下位 last place (*position, rank, etc.*); sai-ryō (no) *adj* 最良(の) the best: ~ **no saku** 最良の策 the best policy; sai-shin (no) *adj* 最新(の) newest, up-to-date; sai-sho *adv* 最初 the very beginning, the outset (= **hajime** 初め): ~ **no** 最初の… the first …; sai-shō (no) *adj* 最小(の) smallest: **~-gén (-do)** 最小限(度) the minimum (degree); sai-shō (no) *adj* 最少(の) least, minimal, minimum; sai-shū (no) *adj* 最終(の) final, the very end (*last*): **~-ban** 最終版 final version: ~ **densha** 最終電車 the last train (= **shūden** 終電); sai-tei (no) *adj* 最低(の) lowest, worst, bottom(most); minimum; sai-zen *n* 最善 the best; one's best/utmost (= **besuto** ベスト)

saibai *n* 栽培 cultivation

sáiban *n* 裁判 trial; saibán-kan *n* 裁判官 judge; saiban-shó *n* 裁判所 court

sabun *n* 差分 difference

sáidā *n* サイダー (*fizzy lemon*) soda: **~-sui** サイダー水 soda water

saidan *n* 祭壇 altar

saidan *n* 裁断 **1.** judgment: ~ **o kudashimásu** 裁断を下します passes judgment **2.** cutting (*paper, cloth, etc.*)

saido-burē'ki *n* サイドブレーキ handbrake

sáiensu *n* サイエンス science (= **kagaku** 科学)

saifu *n* 財布 purse, wallet

saigai *n* 災害 disaster: **shizen-~** 自然災害 natural disaster

sai-getsu *n* 歳月 years, time

saigishin *n* 猜疑心 suspicion: ~ **ga tsuyoi** 猜疑心が強い is very suspicious

saihō *n* 裁縫 sewing: **~-dōgu** 裁縫道具 sewing set

saiken *n* 債券 bond (*debenture*)

saikin *n* 細菌 germ: **~-gaku** 細菌学 bacteriology

saikin *adv* 最近 recently, lately

saikóro *n* さいころ・サイコロ dice, a die (= **sai** さい・采・賽): **sai(kóro) o furimásu** サイ(コロ)を振ります throws a dice

saikú *n* 細工 work(manship), handiwork, ware(s)

saikuringu *n* サイクリング cycling (*by bicycle*)

saikuru *n* サイクル cycle (= **shūki** 周期)

saikutsu *n* 採掘 mining, digging
saimu *n* 債務 [BOOKISH] debt
sáin *n* サイン **1.** signature (= **shomei** 署名) **2.** autograph **3.** sign (= **aizu** 合図, **angō** 暗号, **kigō** 記号)
sainán *n* 災難 calamity, disaster: **~-yoke** 災難除け charm against evil; **~ ni aimásu** 災難に遭います has a disaster
sáinō *n* 才能 talent, ability
sainyū *n* 歳入 annual revenue (*of government, local public organization, etc.*)
sáiren *n* サイレン siren (*sound*); sairen-sā *n* サイレンサー silencer (*gun*)
saisan *n* 採算 profit: **~ ga toremásu** 採算が取れます pays, is profitable
saisan *adv* [BOOKISH] 再三 many times, repeatedly
saisén *n* さい銭・賽銭 money offering (*at a shrine*); **~-bako** さい銭箱・賽銭箱 offering box
saishin (no) *adj* 細心(の) careful: **~ chūi o hara(tte) kudasai** 細心の注意を払(って)下さい please pay close attention
saishokú-shugi-sha *n* 菜食主義者 vegetarian (= **bejitarian** ベジタリアン)
saishū *n* 採集 collection, picking and gathering (*as specimen, data, etc.*): **konchū-~** 昆虫採集 insect collecting
saisoku *n* 催促 reminding someone, urging (= **tokusoku** 督促): **~-jō** 催促状 a reminder
saiten *n* 祭典 **1.** festival **2.** extravaganza
saiten *n* 採点 rating, grading, marking
saiwai *n* 幸い **1.** *n* happiness (= **kōfuku** 幸福, **shiawase** 幸せ・しあわせ): **fukō-chū no ~** 不幸中の幸い is lucky it wasn't worse **2.** *adv* fortunately
saiyō *n* 採用 employment, adoption
sáizu *n* サイズ size (= **ōkisa** 大きさ)
sájí *n* さじ・サジ・匙 spoon (= **supūn** スプーン); sájí-kagen *n* さじ[匙]加減 ① prescription ② allowance ③ consideration; saji o nagemásu (nageru) *v* 匙を投げます(投げる) gives up (*not to literally mean, "throw a spoon"*)
saká *n* 坂 hill, slope
saka-... *prefix* 酒. . . *drinking*; saka-bá *n* 酒場 bar/pub (*for drinking*) (= **izakaya** 居酒屋, **bā** バー, **pabu** パブ); saka-ya *n* 酒屋 liquor shop; saka-mori *n* 酒盛(り) drinking party (= **enkai** 宴会)
sakaemásu, sakáéru *v* 栄えます, 栄える thrives, flourishes, prospers
sakái *n* 境 boundary, border
sakan (na) *adj* 盛ん(な) lively, flourishing, prosperous; splendid, vigorous
sakana *n* 魚 fish; sakaná-tsuri *n* 魚釣り fishing (*as sport*); sakana-ya *n* 魚屋 fish dealer/market
sakana *n* 肴 **1.** appetizers to go with drinks (= **(o-)tsumami** おつ

まみ) **2.** interesting story to add to the fun with drinks
sakanoborimásu, sakanobóru *v* 遡ります・溯ります, 遡る・溯る: **… ni ~** …に遡り[溯り]ます goes against (*the stream*), goes upstream; goes back (*in time*) to; **sore o … ni ~** それを…に遡り[溯り]ます traces it back to …
sakaraimásu, sakaráu *v* 逆らいます, 逆らう: **… ni ~** …に逆らいます defies, opposes, contradicts, acts contrary to
sakari *n* 盛り prime: **~ no tsuita neko** 盛りのついた猫 cat on heat; sakari-ba *n* 盛り場 downtown area (= **hanka-gai** 繁華街)
sakasa(ma) (no/ni) *adj, adv* 逆さ(ま)(の/に) upside down
sā́kasu *n* サーカス circus
sakazukí *n* 杯 saké cup (= **choko** ちょこ(**o-choko** おちょこ)): **fūfu no ~ o kawashimásu** 夫婦の杯を交わします exchanges nuptial cups
sake *n* 酒(**o-sake** お酒) **1.** saké (*Japanese rice wine*) **2.** alcoholic drinks
sáke *n* サケ・鮭 salmon
sakebimásu, sakébu *v* 叫びます, 叫ぶ cries out, shouts
sakemásu, sakéru *v* 避けます, 避ける avoids
sakemásu, sakéru *v* 裂けます, 裂ける **1.** it splits, it tears **2.** can split/tear it
sakeraremásu, sakeraréru *v* 避けられます, 避けられる **1.** is avoided **2.** can avoid
saki *n, adv* 先 **1.** front; future; ahead; first (*ahead of others*); **kono ~** この先 ahead of here **2.** point, tip **3.** address, destination; saki-gake *n* 先駆け pioneer, forerunner, lead; saki-iki, sakiyuki *n* 先行き prospect, future, outlook: **sakiyuki wa akarui desu** 先行きは明るいです has a bright future; saki-hodo 先程 [BOOKISH] a little while ago (= **sakki** さっき)
sakimásu, saku *v* 咲きます, 咲く blooms, blossoms
sakimásu, sáku *v* 裂きます, 裂く splits it; tears it
sakin *n* 砂金 gold dust
sákka *n* 作家 writer (*novelist, etc.*): **joryū-~** 女流作家 a woman writer
sákkā *n* サッカー soccer: **~-senshu** サッカー選手 soccer player (*professional*)
sakkaku *n* 錯覚 illusion: **me no ~** 目の錯覚 optical illusion
sákki *adv* さっき a little while ago [INFORMAL]
sakkin *n* 殺菌 sterilization: **~-kōka** 殺菌効果 antiseptic effect
sákku *n* サック **1.** sack, case **2.** → **kondṓmu** コンドーム
sakkusu *n* サックス saxophone (= **sakusofōn** サクソフォーン)
sakkyoku *n* 作曲 music composition; sakkyoku-ka *n* 作曲家 musical composer
sakoku *n* 鎖国 national isolation

sakotsu *n* 鎖骨 collarbone

saku *n* 柵 fence

saku-..., saki-... *prefix* 昨. . . last; sakú-ban *n, adv* 昨晩 [BOOKISH] last night (= **kinō no yoru/ban** 昨日の夜/晩); saku-jitsu *n, adv* 昨日 [BOOKISH] yesterday (= **kinō** 昨日); saku-nen *n, adv* 昨年 [BOOKISH] last year (= **kyonen** 去年); saki-ototói *n, adv* さきおととい・一昨々日 [BOOKISH] three days ago (= **mikka mae** 三日前)

sakubun *n* 作文 writing a composition (*a theme*)

sakuga *n* 作画 **1.** drawing a picture **2.** taking a photograph

sakugen *n* 削減 cut, reduction: **kosuto-~** コスト削減 cost reduction; **jin'in-~** 人員削減 head-count reduction

sakuhin *n* 作品 a work (*of literature or art*): **geijutsu-~** 芸術作品 a work of art: **bungaku-~** 文学作品 a literary work

sakuin *n* 索引 index

sakui-teki *adj* 作為的 intentional

sakumotsu *n* 作物 **1.** crops **2.** a piece of work (= **sakubutsu** 作物, **sakuhin** 作品)

sakura *n* 桜・サクラ cherry tree: **~ no haná** 桜の花 cherry blossoms: **~-mochi** 桜餅 rice cake with bean paste wrapped in a cherry leaf (*Japanese cakes/sweets*)

sakuranbo *n* サクランボ・桜ん坊・桜桃 cherry

saku(ryaku) *n* 策(略) plot (= **kōryaku** 攻略); saku-shi *n* 策士 plotter

sakusen *n* 作戦 tactics

sakusha *n* 作者 author (= **chosha** 著者)

sakushi *n* 作詞 writing the lyrics: **~-ka** 作詞家 songwriter

sakushu *n* 搾取 [BOOKISH] exploitation: **~ saremásu** 搾取されます be exploited

sakusofōn *n* サクソフォーン saxophone (= **sakkusu** サックス)

sakusō(shita) *adj* 錯綜(した) complicated and intricated: **sakusō-shita jōhō** 錯綜した情報 entangled information

sakyū *n* 砂丘 sand dune: **Tottori-sakyū** 鳥取砂丘 Tottori sand dune

... (-)sama *suffix* …様・さま [HONORIFIC] = **... (-)san** …さん Mr., Ms., Mrs., Miss

samatagemásu, samatagéru *v* 妨げます, 妨げる obstructs, hinders

samayoimásu, samayóu *v* 彷徨います, 彷徨う wanders about

samáza ma (na/no) *adj* 様々(な/の) diverse, all kinds of

same *n* サメ・鮫 shark

samemásu, saméru *v* 覚めます, 覚める wakes up, comes to one's senses

samemásu, saméru *v* 冷めます, 冷める gets cold, cools off

samemásu, saméru *v* 褪めます, 褪める it fades, loses color

samitto *n* サミット summit (*conference*)

sá-mo nákereba *conj* さもなければ [BOOKISH] otherwise (= **sa-mo**

nakuba さもなくば)
samúi *adj* 寒い cold (*air temperature*), chilly
samuke *n* 寒気 chill, rigor (= **okan** 悪寒): ~ **ga shimásu** 寒気がします feels a chill
samurai *n* サムライ・侍 samurai (*Japanese warrior*) (= **bushi** 武士)
san *n* 酸 **1.** acid **2.** sour taste: **~-mi** 酸味 sour taste, sour flavor (= **suppai aji** 酸っぱい味)
san(...) *n*, *prefix* 三・3(. . .) three (, tri-. . .); sán-ba *n* 三羽 three (*birds*, *rabbits*); san-bai *adj* 三倍 triple; sán-bai *n* 三杯 three glassfuls; san-banmé *n* 三番目 third; sán-bén *n* 三遍 three times; sán-biki *n* 三匹 three (*fishes/bugs*, *small animals*); sán-bon *n* 三本 three (*pencils/bottles*, *long objects*); sán-dó *n* 三度 ① three times (= **san-kai** 三回) ② three degrees; san-gai *n* 三階 three floors/stories; third floor; san-gánichi *n* 三が日 the first three days of the New Year; sán-gen *n* 三軒 three buildings/houses; sán-ji *n* 三時 three o'clock; sán-kái *n* 三回 three times (= **san-do** 三度); **san kai-mé** 三回目 the third time; san-kyaku *n* 三脚 tripod (stand): **ninin-~** 二人三脚 ① three-legged race (*on field day, etc.*) ② cooperating with singleness of purpose; sán-mai *n* 三枚 three sheets (*flat things*); sán-mei *n* 三名 [BOOKISH] three people (= **sannín** 三人); san-nen *n* 三年 the year 3; **san nén-kan** 三年間 three years; **san nén-sei** 三年生 third-year student, junior; san-nín *n* 三人 three people (= **sen mei** 三名); san-pai *n* 三拝 [HUMBLE] bowing three times, bowing several times; san-paku *n* 三泊 three night's lodging: **san-paku-yokka** 三泊四日 four days three nights (*tour, etc.*); sán-pun *n* 三分 three minutes; sán-sai *n* 三歳 three years old (= **mittsu** 三つ); sán-satsu *n* 三冊 three (*books, magazines, etc.*); sán-sei *n* 三世 third generation (*of emigrant Japanese*); . . . the Third; san-shi-... *n* 三, 四 = **san-yo(n)-**. . . three or four; sán-shoku *n* 三食 three meals; sán-tō *n* 三頭 three (*horses/oxen, large animals*); san-tō *n* 三等 third class; san-yo(m/n)- *n* 三, 四 = **san-shi-. . .** three or four: **san yon-bai** 三, 四倍 three or four times as much: **san yon-do** 三, 四度 3–4 times: **san yon-man** 三, 四万 thirty or forty thousand: **sanyo-nín** 三, 四人 3–4 people: **sanyo-ninmae** 三, 四人前 3–4 servings; sán-zoku/-soku *n* 三足 three pairs (*of footwear*)
sán *n* 酸 acid; san-sei *n* 酸性 acidity: **~sei-u** 酸性雨 acid rain
... (-) san . . . さん Mr., Ms., Mrs., Miss (= . . . (-) **sama** . . . 様・さま)
...´-san, -´zan . . . 山 (*name of certain*) mountain: **Fuji-san** 富士山 Mt. Fuji: **Eberesuto (-san)** エベレスト(山) Mt. Everest

san-... *prefix* 山... mountain; **san-myaku** *n* 山脈 mountain range: **Arupusu-~** アルプス山脈 Alps (*range*); **san-chō** *n* 山頂 mountain top

sanba *n* サンバ samba

sanba *n* 産婆 midwife

sanbashi *n* 桟橋 pier

sanbi *n* 賛美 admiration, worship: **~-ka** 賛美歌 hymn (= **sei-ka** 聖歌, **san-ka** 賛歌)

sanbun *n* 散文 prose: **~-shi** 散文詩 prose poem

sanbutsu *n* 産物 product, produce; fruit, outcome

sánchi *n* 産地 home (*of a product/ crop*)

sandan-jū *n* 散弾銃 shotgun

sandaru *n* サンダル sandal

san-dii kē´ *n* 3DK three rooms and "DK" (*dining kitchen = eat-in kitchen*)

...-sándo *suffix* ...サンド sandwich (→ **sandoítchi** サンドイッチ): **tsuna-~** ツナサンド tuna-fish sandwich: **tamago-~** タマゴ[卵]サンド egg sandwich

sandō *n* 参道 approach to a shrine; **omote-~** 表参道 main road to a shrine

sandō *n* 賛同 approval, support

sandoítchi *n* サンドイッチ sandwich

sandopē´pā *n* サンド・ペーパー sandpaper

Sanfuranshísu̱ko *n* サンフランシスコ San Francisco

Sán-gatsu *n* 三月・3月 March

sangi-in *n* 参議院 House of Councilors (= **san-in** 参院): **~-senkyo** 参議院選挙 House of Councilors' election

sángo *n* サンゴ・珊瑚 coral; **sango-shō** *n* サンゴ[珊瑚]礁 coral reef

sangurasu *n* サングラス sunglasses

sangyō *n* 産業 industry: **sābisu-~** サービス産業 service industry

sánji *n* 賛辞 [BOOKISH] praise, compliment (= **home-kotoba** 褒め[誉め]言葉): **~ o okurimásu̱** 賛辞を送ります compliments

sanka *n* 賛歌 [BOOKISH] hymn (= **sanbi-ka** 賛美歌, **sei-ka** 聖歌)

sanka *n* 傘下 [BOOKISH] under the umbrella: **~-kigyō** 傘下企業 affiliated enterprise: **~ ni hairimásu̱** 傘下に入ります comes under the umbrella

sanka *n* 参加 participation; **sanká-sha** *n* 参加者 participant

sánkan *n* 参観 [HUMBLE] one's visiting: **jugyō-~-bi** 授業参観日 open school day

sánkaku *n* 三角 triangle: **~-kankei** 三角関係 a love triangle

sankē *n* 3K (*apartment of three rooms plus kitchen*)

sanke-zukimásu̱, sanke-zuku *v* 産気づきます, 産気づく goes into labor

sankō *n* 参考 reference (= **sanshō** 参照): **~-(to-)sho** 参考(図)書 reference book: **gakushū-sankōsho** 学習参考書 study-aid book

sanmon *n* 山門 temple gate

sanpatsu *n* 散髪・さんぱつ haircut; sanpatsu-ya *n* 散髪屋 barber(shop)
sanpo *n* 散歩 a walk, a stroll
sanpuru *n* サンプル sample
sanretsu *n* 参列 presence
sanrín-sha *n* 三輪車 tricycle
sansei *n* 賛成 approval, support (= **sandō** 賛同)
sansei *n* 参政 participation in government: **~-ken** 参政権 political suffrage
sanshō *n* サンショウ・山椒 Japanese pepper (*mild*)
sanshō *n* 参照 reference (= **sankō** 参考)
sánso *n* 酸素 oxygen: **~-masuku** 酸素マスク oxygen mask
sansū *n* 算数 (*elementary school*) arithmetic, calculation (= **keisan** 計算), mathematics (= **sūgaku** 数学)
santora *n* サントラ sound track
saó *n* さお・竿・棹 pole, rod
sapō´tā *n* サポーター jockstrap, (*athletic*) supporter
sappári *adv* さっぱり [+ NEGATIVE verb] not at all: **~ wakarimasen** さっぱり分かりません I have no idea.
sappári-shita *adj* さっぱりした clean, fresh; frank: **~-shita aji** さっぱりした味 plain taste, lightly seasoned (*food*)
sappūkei na *adj* 殺風景な (*looks*) bare, bleak: **~ niwa** 殺風景な庭 a bleak garden
sara *n* 皿 plate, dish; saucer; ash-tray; sara-arai-ki *n* 皿洗い機 dish-washer
sarabureddo *n* サラブレッド **1.** thoroughbred **2.** blue blood
sárada *n* サラダ salad
sarái-... *prefix* 再来... ... after next; sarái-getsu *adv* 再来月 [BOOKISH] month after next (= **nikagetsu-go** 二ヵ月後); sarai-nen *adv* 再来年 [BOOKISH] year after next (= **ni nen-go** 二年後)
sára-ni *adv* 更に anew; (*some*) more; further
sárarii *n* サラリー salary (= **kyū´yo** 給与); sararii-man *n* サラリーマン salaried man, company employee
sarashimásu, sarasu *v* 晒します・曝します, 晒す・曝す **1.** exposes: **fūu ni ~** 風雨にさらし[晒し・曝し]ます exposes it to wind and rain **2.** bleaches: **nuno o ~** 布をさらし[晒し]ます bleaches cloth **3.** dries under the sun: **hi ni ~** 日にさらし[晒し]ます dries it in the sun **4.** reveals: **haji o ~** ~恥をさらし[晒し・曝し]ます brings disgrace on oneself
saremásu, sareru *v* されます, される **1.** has it done to one (*unwantedly*) **2.** is done; **hakai ~** 破壊されます is destroyed **3.** [HONORIFIC] = **nasaimásu** なさいます
sarimásu, sáru *v* 去ります, 去る leaves, goes away; removes it
sāroin *n* サーロイン sirloin: **~-sutēki** サーロイン・ステーキ sirloin steak

sáru *v* 去る **1.** → **sarimásu̲** 去ります **2.** [+ DATE] last …, most recent, (*past day*) of this month
sáru *n* サル・猿 monkey
sarumata *n* サルマタ・猿股 loincloth
sasa *n* ササ・笹 bamboo grass: ~ **no ha** 笹の葉 bamboo leaf
sasáé *n* 支え a support, a prop
sasaemásu̲, sasaeru *v* 支えます, 支える supports, props (*up*)
sásai (na) *adj* 些細(な) petty, trifling, trivial, not a big deal at all (= **torunitarinai** 取るに足りない): ~ **na-mondai** 些細な問題 minor problem: ~ **na-chigai** 些細な違い slight difference
sasáyaka (na) *adj* ささやか(な small (*-scale*), petty: ~ **na pātii** ささやかなパーティ little party: ~ **na okurimono** ささやかな贈り物 modest gift
sasayakí *n* 囁き a whisper, murmur: **~-goe** 囁き声 whispery voice
sasayakimásu̲, sasayáku *v* 囁きます, 囁く whispers
sashi-agemásu̲, sashi-ageru *v* 差し上げます, 差し上げる [HUMBLE/DEFERENTIAL] presents, give (*I give you, you give them*); holds up
sashidegamashii *adj* 差し出がましい officious
sashidéguchi *n* 差し出口 uncalled-for remark; **… no hanashí ni ~ o shimásu̲** …の話に差し出口をします interrupts
sashi̲-e *n* 挿絵 illustration (*of book, newspaper, magazine, etc.*)
sashi̲-komi *n* 差(し)込み plug outlet (*electricity outlet*) (= **sashikomi-guchi** 差(し)込み口)
sashi̲-komimásu̲, sashi-komu *v* 差(し)込みます, 差し込む inserts
sashimásu̲, sásu *v* 指します, 指す points to, indicates
sashimásu̲, sásu *v* 差します, 差す holds (*umbrella*)
sashimásu̲, sásu *v* 刺します, 刺す stabs, stings
sashimí *n* 刺身・さしみ sliced raw fish
sashi̲tsu̲kae *n* 差し支え・さしつかえ **1.** hindrance, impediment **2.** previous appointment/engagement
sáshizu *n* 指図 directions, instructions, a command
sashō *n* 査証 [BOOKISH] visa (= **bíza** ビザ): **nyūkoku-~** 入国査証 an entry visa
sashō *n* 詐称 [BOOKISH] false statement; **nenrei-~** 年齢詐称 false statement of one's age; **mibun-~** 身分詐称 false statement of one's status
sasoi *n* 誘い invitation; temptation
sasoimásu̲, sasou *v* 誘います, 誘う invites; tempts
sásshi, sásshu *n* サッシ, サッシュ sash (*window sash*)
sásshi *n* 冊子 brochure; **shō-sasshi** *n* 小冊子 pamphlet, brochure
sas-shi *n* 察し conjecture, guess; perception, understanding; sympathy: ~ **ga tsu̲kimásu̲** 察し

がつきます perceives, guesses (*correctly*); **o-~ no tōri** お察しの通り as you have surmised
sas-shinásu, sas-suru *v* 察します, 察する perceives, understands; conjectures, guesses; sympathizes
sassokú *adv* 早速 at once, right away, promptly, immediately: ~ **(no)** 早速(の) immediate, prompt
sasuga *adv* さすが: ~ **(ni)** さすが(に) as we might expect, indeed
sasupendā *n* サスペンダー suspender **1.** galluses (= **zubon-tsuri** ズボンつり) **2.** garter
sasupensu *n* サスペンス suspense: **~-eiga** サスペンス映画 suspense film
sátá *n* 沙汰 [BOOKISH] message; command; affair
satchū-zai *n* 殺虫剤 insecticide
sá-te *interj* さて well now/then, and now/then, as to the matter at hand
satei *n* 査定 assessment (*to decide the rank, salary, etc.*): **~-gaku** 査定額 assessed value
sáten *n* サテン satin
saten *n* 茶店 café (= **kissaten** 喫茶店)
sato *n* 里 **1.** village **2.** hometown (= **furusato** ふるさと・故郷, **kokyō** 故郷): **o-sato** お里 one's origin, upbringing; sato-oya *n* 里親 foster parent; sato-gaeri *n* 里帰り goes home (*to see one's parent(s)*)
satō´ *n* 砂糖・サトウ sugar
satori *n* 悟り enlightenment
satorimásu, satóru *v* 悟ります, 悟る realizes (*comprehends*)
satsu *n* 札 folding money, currency bill/note; satsu-iré *n* 札入れ billfold, wallet (= **saifu** 財布); satsu-taba *n* 札束 a roll/wad of (currency) bills
...-satsú *suffix* ...冊 copy (*counts books, magazines*)
...-satsu *suffix* ...札 (currency) bill; **hyakudorú-~ ní-mai** 百ドル札二枚 two $100 bills
satsuei *n* 撮影 shooting a film, filming, taking a photograph: **~-jo** 撮影所 studio (= **sutajio** スタジオ)
satsujin *n* 殺人 murder: **~-jiken** 殺人事件 murder case
Satsumá-age *n* さつま[薩摩]揚げ deep-fried fish cake
Satsuma-imo *n* さつま[薩摩]芋・サツマイモ sweet potato
Saujiarabia *n* サウジアラビア Saudi Arabia; Saujiarabia-jin *n* サウジアラビア人 a Saudi Arabian
sauna *n* サウナ steam bath (*in sports center, health spa, etc.*)
saundo *n* サウンド sound (= **oto** 音, **onkyō** 音響); saundo-efekuto *n* サウンド・エフェクト sound effect; saundo-sukōpu *n* サウンドスケープ soundscape; saundo-torakku *n* サウンド・トラック sound track (= **santora** サントラ)
sawagashíi *adj* 騒がしい boisterous, noisy: **~-pātii** 騒がしいパーティ

noisy party: **~-basho** 騒がしい場所 noisy place

sáwagi *n* 騒ぎ **1.** clamor, noise (*boisterous*) **2.** unrest, disturbance, tumult, strife; riot (= **sōdō** 騒動)

sawagimásu, sawágu *v* 騒ぎます, 騒ぐ makes lots of noise, clamors

sawara *n* サワラ・鰆 mackerel

sawarimásu, sawaru *v* 触ります, 触る touches

sawáyaka (na) *adj* さわやか(な)・爽やか(な) refreshing, bracing; fluent

sáya *n* サヤ・莢 sheath, pod: **~-endō** サヤエンドウ・さやえんどう podded pea: **~-ingen** サヤインゲン・さやいんげん French bean

sayonára, sayōnára *interj* さよなら, さようなら good-bye (= [INFORMAL] **baibai** バイバイ)

sáyori *n* サヨリ halfbeak (*fish*)

sáyū *n* 左右 right and left: **zengo-~** 前後左右 left to right, back and forth

sázae *n* サザエ・栄螺 wreath shell, turban shell, turbo

sé *n* 背 **1.** height, stature (= **sei** せい・背, **se-take** 背丈, **shinchō** 身長): **~ ga takái/hikúi** 背が高い/低い is tall/short **2.** back (*of body*) (= **senaka** 背中); **se-biro** *n* 背広 (*man's*) business suit, lounge suit; **se-bone** *n* 背骨 backbone, spine; **séi** *n* せい・背 height, stature: **~-kurabe** 背比べ comparing heights with someone; **se-naka** *n* 背中 back of body; **se-nobi** *n* 背伸び ① standing on tiptoe ② trying to do more than one is able to do; **se-suji** *n* 背筋 the muscles along the spine; **se-take** *n* 背丈 height, stature: **~ o hakarimásu** 背丈を測ります measures one's height

segare *n* 倅 **1.** [HUMBLE] my son **2.** [IN rather NEGATIVE SENSE] child/young person

sehyō *n* 世評 one's reputation (= **~ no hyōka** 世間の評価)

séi (-) *n* 性 nature; sex; gender; **sei-betsu** *n* 性別 gender; **sei-byō** *n* 性病 venereal disease; **sei-kō** *n* 性交 [BOOKISH] (*sexual*) intercourse (= **sékkusu** セックス); **sei-teki (na)** *adj* 性的(な) sexual

séi *n* 姓 family name, last name; **séi-mei** *n* 姓名 (*one's*) full name (= **shi-mei** 氏名)

sei-... *prefix* 聖. . . sacred, holy; **sei-chi** *n* 聖地 holy place; **sei-bo** *n* 聖母 the Holy Mother; **sei-dō** *n* 聖堂 sacred building (*temple, church, mosque, etc.*): **dai-~** 大聖堂 cathedral; **sei-iki** *n* 聖域 sanctuary; **séi-ka** *n* 聖歌 hymn; **Séi-sho** *n* 聖書 Bible (= **Baiburu** バイブル, **Shin-yaku seisho** 新約聖書, **Kyū-yaku seisho** 旧約聖書)

séi-... *prefix* 西. . . west, western; **séi-bu** *n* 西部 the west, the western part; **sei-hō** *n* 西方 (the) west (*general direction/area*); **sei-nan**

n 西南 southwest; sei-reki *n* 西暦 the Western (*Christian*) calendar: ~ **...´-nen** 西暦 …年 the year … A.D.; Séi-yō *n* 西洋 the West, Europe and Americas (= **ōbei-shokoku** 欧米諸国): **~-fū (no)** 西洋風(の) Western-style

sei-... *prefix* 声… voice, vocal; sei-gaku *n* 声楽 vocal music; sei-iki *n* 声域 range of voice; sei-tai *n* 声帯 vocal cords; sei-yū *n* 声優 voice actor

sei(-) n, *prefix* 生(…) life (= **seimei** 生命, **ínochi** 命); sei-katsu *n* 生活 life, (*daily*) living, livelihood; **nichijo-~** 日常生活 daily life; **~-hi** 生活費 living costs; sei-kei *n* 生計 livelihood, the way of (*earning*) one's living: **... to shite ~ o tate(tei)másu** …として生計を立て(てい)ます earns one's living as ...; séi-mei *n* 生命 life (= **ínochi** 命, **sei** 生): **~-rinri** 生命倫理 bioethics; séi-shi *n* 生死 life and death

... séi *suffix*…せい [IN NEGATIVE SENSE] cause, effect, influence, fault: **... no ~ de** …のせいで because of …, due to …: **... ~ ka** …せいか perhaps because of …

...´-sei *suffix* …生 student: **shōgaku-~** 小学生 elementary school student: **chūgaku-~** 中学生 junior high school student: **kōkō´-~** 高校生 high school student: **daigaku-~** 大学生 college/university student: **daigaku-in-~** 大学院生 grad(-uate) student

...´-sei *suffix* …製 made in …, made of …: **nihon-~** 日本製 made in Japan (= **meido in japan** メイド・イン・ジャパン): **bei-koku-~** 米国製 made in U.S.A.: **gaikoku-~** 外国製 foreign-made

...´-sei *suffix* …星 (*name of certain, kinds of*) star: **waku-~** 惑星 planet: **kō-~** 恒星 fixed star

séibun *n* 成分 ingredient, component: **arukōru-~** アルコール成分 alcohol component

séibutsu *n* 生物 a living thing, a creature (= **ikimono** 生き物); seibutsú-gaku *n* 生物学 biology; seibutsu-gáku-sha *n* 生物学者 biologist

seibutsu *n* 静物 [BOOKISH] still object: **~-ga** 静物画 still-life painting

seichō *n* 成長 growth: **kodomo(-tachi) no ~** 子供(たち)の成長 child(-ren)'s growth: **kōdo-keizai-~** 高度経済成長 high economic growth

seidō *n* 青銅 bronze

seieki *n* 精液 semen

séifu *n* 政府 government

seifuku *n* 制服 uniform (*of school, office, etc.*)

seigén *n* 制限 limit, restriction; seigen-jikan *n* 制限時間 time limit

seihin *n* 製品 product, manufactured goods

seii *n* 誠意 sincerity (= **magokoro** 真心): **~ o komete hanashimásu**

誠意を込めて話します talks sincerely

eiji *n* 政治 politics: **~-ka** 政治家 politician: **kokusai-~** 国際政治 international politics

eijin *n* 成人 adult : **~ no hí** 成人の日 Coming-of-Age Day (*honoring 20-year-olds*) on 2nd Monday of January

eijitsu (na) *adj* 誠実(な) sincere

eijuku *n* 成熟 ripening, maturing

éika *n* 成果 [BOOKISH] good result, outcome (= **yoi kekka** 良い結果)

éika *n* 正価 net price

eikaku *n* 性格 character (*personal traits*)

eikaku (na) *adj* 正確(な) exact, accurate, correct

eikaku (na) *adj* 精確(な) minute, correct and precise

eiketsu (na) *adj* 清潔(な) **1.** clean **2.** pure

éiki *n* 世紀 century: **rai-~** 来世紀 next century

eikō *n* 成功 success

eikyū *n* 請求 claim, demand, request; seikyū-sho *n* 請求書 bill

eimitsu (na) *adj* 精密(な) precise, detailed, minute, thorough, accurate

eimon *n* 正門 the front (*main*) gate

einen *n* 青年 young person, youth, adolescent; seinén-ki *n* 青年期 (*one's*) youth; adolescence

einen-gáppi *n* 生年月日 date of birth

éiri *n* 生理 physiology: **~-teki na** 生理的な physiological; seiri-gaku *n* 生理学 physiology

séiri *n* 整理 adjustment, arrangement; seiri-seiton *n* 整理整頓 keeping everything in order

seiritsu *n* 成立 formation, finalization, conclusion: **kōshō-~** 交渉成立 completion of the deal

Seiron *n* セイロン Ceylon (= **Suri-ránka** スリランカ Sri Lanka)

seiryō *n* 清涼 [BOOKISH] refreshing: **~ (inryō-)sui** 清涼(飲料)水 refreshing drink

séiryoku *n* 勢力 power, energy; influence (= **iryoku** 威力)

seisaku *n* 政策 (*political*) policy

seisaku *n* 制作・製作 manufacture, production

seisan *n* 生産 production, manufacture

seisan *n* 清算 clearance, liquidation

seiseki *n* 成績 results, marks, grades, record: **~-hyō** 成績表 report card

seishi *n* 静止 stillness: **~-ga(zō)** 静止画(像) still image (*photo, etc.*)

seishiki (no/na) *adj* 正式(の/な) formal, official

séishin *n* 精神 soul, mind, spirit, psyche: **~ (no)** 精神(の) mental

seishitsu *n* 性質 character (*of things*), quality, disposition, nature

seisho *n* 聖書 Bible

seishoku *n* 生殖 reproduction, procreation; seishoku-ki *n* 生殖期 reproductive period

seishún *n* 青春 adolescence

seisō *n* 清掃 cleaning (= **sōji** 掃除); seisō-in *n* 清掃員 cleaner (person)
séito *n* 生徒 pupil, student
seitō *n* 政党 political party
seitō *n* 正当 [BOOKISH] propriety, validity, reasonableness: ~ **na riyū** 正当な理由 good/fair reason
seitō *n* 正統 legitimacy, orthodoxy
seiyu *n* 製油 oil manufacturing; seiyu-gaisha *n* 製油会社 oil manufacturing company
seiza *n* 星座 constellation
seiza *n* 静座 sitting quietly, meditation
séizei *adv* せいぜい at most, at best
seizō *n* 製造 production, manufacture: ~-**moto** 製造元 maker (*manufacturer*)
seizon *n* 生存 existence, surviving; seizon-ritsu *n* 生存率 survival rate
seizu *n* 製図 drafting a (*technical*) drawing: **kenchiku-~** 建築製図 architectural drafting
seizui *n* 精髄 [BOOKISH] essence
seji *n* 世辞 (**o-seji** お世辞) compliment, flattery
sékái *n* 世界 world; ~-**jū** 世界中 throughout the world, worldwide; ~-**teki (na)** 世界的(な) worldwide, international
séken *n* 世間 the public, people, the world, society (= **shakai** 社会, **yo-no-naka** 世の中); seken-bánashi *n* 世間話 chat(-ting); seken-tei *n* 世間体 appearances, reputation, decency: ~ **o kinishimásu** 世間体を気にします cares about appearances, cares what people (may) think
sekí *n* せき・咳 cough: ~-**dome shiroppu** せき止めシロップ cough syrup
séki *n* 籍 **1.** (*one's*) family register (= **koseki** 戸籍) **2.** membership: **sakkā-bu ni ~ o okimásu** サッカー部に籍を置きます is a member of the football club
séki *n* 席 seat, (*assigned*) place; sekí-ryō *n* 席料 cover charge
seki-... *prefix* 赤... red; seki-han *n* 赤飯 rice boiled with red beans (*commonly for celebration dinner*); Seki-jū'ji *n* 赤十字 Red Cross
...-seki *suffix* ...隻 (*counts ships/vessels; commonly replaced by* **...-sō** ...艘)
Seki-dō *n* 赤道 equator
sekigaisen *n* 赤外線 infrared rays
sekinin *n* 責任 responsibility, obligation; ~-**sha** 責任者 responsible person
sékiri *n* 赤痢 dysentery
sekitán *n* 石炭 coal
sekitatemásu, sekitateru *v* 急き立てます, 急き立てる urges
sekitóri *n* 関取 (*ranking*) sumo wrestler
sekiyu *n* 石油 petroleum, oil, kerosene: ~-**sutō'bu** 石油ストーブ kerosene heater
sékkai *n* 石灰 lime (*mineral*)
sekkakú *adv* せっかく [+ NEGATIVE verb] with much effort/devotion (*but*); on purpose, taking the

trouble: ~ **desu̲ ga ...** せっかくですが ... It is kind of you (*to ask*), but ...

sekkei *n* 設計 designing, planning (*of machine, etc.*); shekkei-sha *n* 設計者 designer (*of machine, etc.*); shekkei-zu *n* 設計図 draft, blueprint

sekken *n* 石けん・石鹸 soap

sekkin *n* 接近 approach(ing): **~-sen** 接近戦 close game, close contest: **... ni ~ o hakarimásu̲ ...** に接近を図ります seeks access to ...; **... ni ~ shimásu̲** ...に接近します approaches, draws near

sekkō *n* 石こう・石膏 plaster

sekkú *n* 節句; **Tángo no ~** 端午の節句 Boys Festival (5 May)

sékku̲su *n* セックス sex

sekkyō´ *n* 説教 sermon

sekkyoku-teki (na) *adj* 積極的(な) positive, energetic, vigorous

semái *adj* 狭い **1.** narrow, tight, small (*space*): **~-heya** 狭い部屋 small room; **~-michi** 狭い道 narrow street, path **2.** narrow, limited: **shiya ga ~** 視野が狭い has a narrow outlook **3.** narrow, little, small (*mind*) (= **kyōryō** 狭量): **ryōken ga ~** 了見が狭い is narrow-minded

sememásu̲, seméru *v* 攻めます, 攻める attacks, assaults

sememásu̲, seméru *v* 責めます, 責める censures, reproaches, criticizes

semento *n* セメント cement

sémete *adv* せめて at least; at most

semi *n* セミ・蝉 cicada, locust

seminā *n* セミナー seminar, workshop

sén *n* 千 1,000 (= **is-sén** 一千・1,000) thousand; sén-ba *n* 千羽 1,000 (*birds, rabbits*); sen-bai *n* 千倍 a thousand-fold, 1,000 times as much; sén-bai *n* 千杯 1,000 cupfuls; sén-biki *n* 千匹 1,000 (*fishes/bugs, small animals*); sén-bon *n* 千本 1,000 (*pencils/bottles, long objects*); sen-en *n* 千円 a thousand yen; sén-zoku *n* 千足 1,000 pairs of footwear

sén *n* 線 **1.** line (= **shasen** 斜線): **kyoku-~** 曲線 curved line: **choku-~** 直線 straight line **2.** outline **3.** electron beam (→ **āsu-sen** アース線) **4.** (*name of electric train line*): **(jē āru) Yama no te-sen** (JR)山手線 JR Yamanote Line

sén *n* 栓 plug, cork, stopper

sen-... *prefix* 船... ship; sénchō *n* 船長 captain (*of ship*); sen'in *n* 船員 ship's crew (*member*), sailor

(...´-) sen *suffix* (...) 船 (*name of certain*) ship

sen-.../...-sen *prefix, suffix* 戦.../...戦 war; sen-go *adv* [BOOKISH] 戦後 postwar, after/since the war; sén-ji *adv* [BOOKISH] 戦時 wartime; sen-sō *n* 戦争 war; sen-tō *n* [BOOKISH] 戦闘 battle; sen-zen (no) *adj* [BOOKISH] 戦前(の) prewar, before the war; shū-sen *n*

[BOOKISH] 終戦 the end of a war
sen-... *prefix* 先… last, previous, before, former; sen-datté *adv* 先立って a few days ago, recently; sén-getsu *n, adv* 先月 last month; sen-jin *n* 先人 ① ancestor ② forerunner; sen-jitsu *n, adv* 先日 the other day; sen-ku-sha *n* 先駆者 pioneer, a forerunner; sen-nyū-kan *n* 先入観 preconceived idea, prejudice; sen-rei *n* 先例 precedent, prior example; sen-sén-getsu *n* [BOOKISH] 先々月 month before last, two months ago; sen'-yaku *n* 先約 previous appointment/engagement; sén-zo *n* 先祖 ancestor
sen-... *prefix* 先… lead, head, front, top; sen-tan *n* 先端 ① tip, (*pointed*) end ② forefront: **~-gijutsu** 先端技術 high-technology; sen-tō *n* 先頭 lead, head, front, top: **~ ni tachimás<u>u</u>** 先頭に立ちます takes the lead, takes the initiative
sénbei *n* せんべい・煎餅 rice crackers
(...-) sénchi (…)センチ, **~mē´toru** センチメートル centimeter
senchiméntaru (na) *adj* センチメンタル(な) sentimental
senden *n* 宣伝 propaganda, publicity: **~-kōkoku** 宣伝広告 promo
sén'i *n* 繊維 fiber
sén'i *n* 遷移 [BOOKISH] **1.** transition **2.** succession
sénkō *n* 線香 incense, joss stick: **katori-~** 蚊取り線香 mosquito coil: **~-hanabi** 線香花火 Japanese sparkler
senkō *n* 専攻 major (*study*)
sénkyo *n* 選挙 election: **~-ken** 選挙権 right to vote: **~-undō** 選挙運動 election campaign
senkyō´ *n* 宣教 mission work; senkyō´shi *n* 宣教師 missionary
senmen *n* 洗面 washing one's face; senmen-jó *n* 洗面所 lavatory (*to wash up at/in*), bathroom
senmon *n* 専門 specialty, major (*line/field/study*): **~-(yō)go** 専門(用)語 technical term, jargon; **~-ka** 専門家 specialist; **~-i** 専門医 (*medical*) specialist
senpai *n* 先輩 one's senior (*colleague, fellow student*)
senpō *n* 先方 the other side (*party*)
senpū´ *n* 旋風 [BOOKISH] whirlwind
senpū´-ki *n* 扇風機 electric fan
senritsu *n* 旋律 melody
senritsu *n* 戦慄 [BOOKISH] shudder of horror, shiver of horror
sénro *n* 線路 railroad track/line
senryō *n* 占領 military occupation
sensai (na) *adj* 繊細(な) delicate, sensitive
sensaku *n* 詮索 prying, inquiry; sensaku-zuki (na) *adj* 詮索好き(な) nosy
senséi *n* 先生 teacher; doctor; maestro, master (*artisan/artist*) (= **kyōshi** 教師)
sensei *n* 宣誓 [BOOKISH] oath
sensē´shon *n* センセーション a

sensation (*excitement*): **~ o makio-koshimásu** センセーションを巻き起こします makes a splash, causes/creates a sensation

sénshu *n* 選手 athlete; player: **orinpikku--** オリンピック選手 an Olympic athlete: **~-ken** 選手権 championship, title

sensu *n* 扇子 (*Japanese*) fan (*folding*)

sénsu *n* センス sense: **~ ga ii** センスがいい has good taste: **~ ga warui** センスが悪い has poor taste: **yūmoa no ~** ユーモアのセンス sense of humor

sensui *n* 潜水 submerging, diving; sensui-kan *n* 潜水艦 submarine

sentaku *n* 洗濯 laundry, washing (= **~-mono** 洗濯物・洗たくもの); sentákú-ki *n* 洗濯機 washer; sentaku-mono-ire *n* 洗濯物入れ clothesbag (*for laundry*)

sentaku *n* 選択 selection, choice

séntensu *n* センテンス sentence (*linguistic*) (= **bun** 文)

(...-) sénto *suffix* (...)セント cent(s)

séntō *n* 銭湯 public bath

seoimásu, seou *v* 背負います, 背負う carries on the back

seppuku *n* 切腹 *harakiri* (self-disembowelment)

seppun *n* 接吻 [BOOKISH] kiss

serí *n* 競り auction

serí *n* せり・芹 Japanese parsley

serifu *n* せりふ・台詞 one's lines (*in a play*), dialogue

sérohan *n* セロハン cellophane: **~tēpu** セロ(ハン)・テープ cellophane tape, scotch tape

séron *n* 世論 public opinion

sérori *n* セロリ celery

sḗru *n* セール sale: **bāgen-~** バーゲン・セール bargain sale

sessen *n* 接線 tangent line

sessen *n* 接戦 close game, close contest

sésse-to *adv* せっせと diligently, hard (*laboriously*); frequently, often

ses-shimásu *v* 接します, **ses-suru** 接する; **(... ni) ~** (...に)接します **1.** comes in contact (*with*), borders (*on*), is adjacent/contiguous (*to*) **2.** encounters, meets, receives, treats, handles

sesshoku *n* 接触 contact, touch

sesshoku *n* 節食 abstemious diet

sesshō *n* 折衝 negotiation

sḗtā *n* セーター sweater

setai *n* 世帯 a household

setchaku-zai *n* 接着剤 glue, adhesive

setogiwa *n* 瀬戸際 the last moment: **... no ~ ni arimásu** . . . の瀬戸際にあります is on the verge of ...

setomono *n* 瀬戸物 porcelain, china(ware)

Seto-náikai *n* 瀬戸内海 the Inland Sea

sétsu *n* 節 occasion (*time or event*)

sétsu *n* 説 theory

sétsubi *n* 設備 equipment, facilities, accommodations

setsubi-go/-ji *n* 接尾語/辞 suffix

setsudan *n* 切断 [BOOKISH] cutting, cutoff

setsudo *n* 節度 moderation: **~ no aru** 節度のある moderate: **~ o mamorimásu** 節度を守ります is moderate

sétsuei *n* 設営 construction, setting up: **tento (no) ~** テント(の)設営 setting up the tent

setsugen *n* 節減 reduction: **keihi-~** 経費節減 reducing the cost; **denryoku-~** 電力節減 energy conservation

setsugō *n* 接合 connection, conjugation, joining

setsujitsu (na/ni) *adj, adv* 切実(な/に) urgent, serious, keenly, earnestly: **~ na mondai** 切実な問題 serious problem; **~ na yōkyū** 切実な要求 a crying need, pressing need

setsumei *n* 説明 explanation, description; setsumei-shó *n* 説明書 written explanation, instructions, manual

sétsuna *n* 刹那 [BOOKISH] moment, instant (= **shunkan** 瞬間)

setsuritsu *n* 設立 establishment, foundation: **hōjin-~** 法人設立 incorporation; **~-tōki** 設立登記 organizing registration

setsuzókú *n* 接続 connection: **densha no ~** 電車の接続 train connections; setsuzókú-shi *n* 接続詞 a conjunction

séttai *n* 接待 business entertainment

séttei *n* 設定 setup, setting

sétto *n* セット **1.** set (*hair, etc.*) **2.** a set meal

settō *n* 窃盗 theft: **settō-~** 窃盗犯 a thief

settō-go/-ji *n* 接頭語/辞 prefix

settoku *v* 説得 persuasion

sewá *n* 世話 **1.** care, trouble, assistance, help; **(…no) ~ ni narimásu** (…の)世話になります becomes obliged (*to one for help*) → **o-sewa-sama** お世話さま **2.** meddling, minding other people's business

sewashii *adj* 忙しい = **~-nái** 忙しない busy, hectic

sezu *v* せず not doing (= **sezu ni** せずに, **shináide** しないで)

sha-.../...-sha *prefix, suffix* 社.../...社 company; sha-chō *n* 社長 president of a company; shá-in *n* 社員 employee (*of a company*)

sha-... *prefix* 車... vehicle; sha-dō *n* 車道 road(way), drive(way), street; sha-rin *n* 車輪 wheel

...-sha *suffix* ...車 (*name of certain*) vehicle

...´-sha …者 person

shaberimásu, shabéru *v* 喋ります, 喋る [INFORMAL]speak/talk: **o-shaberi himásu** お喋りします chatters

sháberu *n* シャベル shovel

shabon *n* シャボン soap; shabon-dama *n* シャボン玉 soap bubble

shabu-shabu *n* しゃぶしゃぶ beef slices dipped in hot broth till ready to eat

shadan *n* 遮断 interruption

shagamimásu, shagamu *v* しゃがみ

ます, しゃがむ squats, crouches on heels

shagare-goe *n* 嗄れ声 hoarse voice

shageki *n* 射撃 shooting (*firing a rifle, shotgun, etc*)

shajitsu *n* 写実 [BOOKISH] drawing/writing realistically: **~-teki (na)** 写実的(な) realistic

Sháka *n* シャカ・釈迦 Buddha (*Sakyamuni*)

shákai *n* 社会 society: **~ no** 社会の social; **shakai-kágaku** *n* 社会科学 social science(s); **shakai no mado** *n* 社会の窓 one's fly; **shakai no shukuzu** *n* 社会の縮図 society in miniature; **shakai-shúgi** *n* 社会主義 socialism

sháke *n* シャケ・鮭 salmon

shakkín *n* 借金 debt

shákkuri *n* しゃっくり hiccup

sháko *n* シャコ squilla, mantis shrimp

shakō *n* 社交 social intercourse, socializing

shakuhachi *n* 尺八 vertical bamboo flute

shakunetsu *adj* 灼熱 **1.** burning: **~ no taiyō** 灼熱の太陽 scorching sun **2.** passionate: **~ no koi** 灼熱の恋 passionate love

shaku ni sawarimásu (sawaru) *v* 癪に障ります(障る) takes offense, gets irritated/provoked; **... ga shaku ni ~** ...が癪に障ります is offensive, irritating, provoking

shákushi *n* 杓子 ladle (*large wooden*); **shákushi-jōgi** *n* 杓子定規 formalism: **~ ni yarimásu** 杓子定規にやります goes by the book

shamisen *n* 三味線 a three-stringed banjo

Shánhái *n* シャンハイ・上海 Shanghai

shanpán, shanpén *n* シャンパン, シャンペン champagne

shánpū *n* シャンプー shampoo

share *n* しゃれ・洒落 pun

sharei (kin) *n* 謝礼(金) remuneration, reward, fee

shasei *n* 写生 sketching, sketch

shashin *n* 写真 photo, picture: **~-chō** 写真帳 photo album: **~-ka** 写真家 photographer

shátsu *n* シャツ undershirt

sháttā *n* シャッター shutter (*camera, etc.*): **~ o kirimásu** シャッターを切ります releases the shutter

sháwā *n* シャワー shower (*bath*)

shi *n* 詩 poetry, poem, verse; **shijin** *n* 詩人 poet

... shi *suffix* ...し and, and so, what with (*the fact that*) ...

shí *n* 死 death; **shi-in** *n* 死因 cause of death; **shi-nin** *n* 死人 dead person

shí *n* 四 four (**= yón** 四); **shi-go-...** *prefix, adj* 四,五... four or five ...; **shi-jū** *n* 四重 quadruplex: **shi-jū-sō** 四重奏 quartet (*musical instruments, two violins, viola, cello, etc.*): **gengaku-~-kyoku/dan** 弦楽四重奏曲/団 string quartet

shí *n* 市 city (**= tóshi** 都市); **shi-chō´**

n 市長 mayor; shí-min *n* 市民 citizen, civilian (= **kōmin** 公民); shí-nai *n* 市内 within the city; shí-ritsu (no) *adj* 市立(の) municipal; shi-yákusho *n* 市役所 city office, city hall

shiage *n* 仕上げ the finish(*ing touch*)

shiagemásu *v* 仕上げます, **shiagéru** 仕上げる finishes up

shiai *n* 試合 match, contest, meet, tournament

shiasátte *n, adv* しあさって・明々後日 three days from now

shiawase *n* 幸せ・しあわせ happiness; shiawase (na) *adj* 幸せ(な) happy

shiba *n* 芝 turf, lawn; shiba-fu *n* 芝生 lawn, grass; shiba-karí-ki *n* 芝刈り機 lawn mower

Shíba *n* 芝 Shiba; **Shiba-Kō´en** 芝公園 Shiba Park

shibai *n* 芝居 **1.** a play (*drama*) **2.** acting, pretense, fake: **~ o uchimásu** 芝居を打ちます puts on an act

shibáraku *adv* しばらく (*for*) a while: **~ shite** しばらくして after a while

shibarimásu, shibáru *v* 縛ります, 縛る ties up

shíba shíba *adv* しばしば often, repeatedly

Shiberia *n* シベリア Siberia

shibin *n* しびん bedpan (*urinal*)

shibiré *n* しびれ・痺れ numbness: **~ o kirashimásu** しびれを切らします loses patience

shibiremásu, shibiréru *v* 痺れます, 痺れる gets numb, (*a leg, etc.*) goes to sleep

shibō *n* 脂肪 fat (*lard, blubber*)

shibō *n* 志望 a desire, a wish: **haiyū-~** 俳優志望 a would-be actor: **daiichi-~ no daigaku** 第一志望の大学 one's first choice college/university

shiborimásu, shibóru *v* 絞ります, 絞る wrings (*out*), squeezes, strains (*through cloth*)

shibu *n* 支部 branch office

shibúi *adj* 渋い **1.** taste, astringent (*tea*), bitter (*wine*) rough **2.** (*face*) wry, sour: **~ kao o shimásu** 渋い顔をします makes a wry face **3.** appearance cool (*sedate, sober, elegant, tasteful*); shibui iroi *n* 渋い色 elegant color

Shibuya *n* 渋谷 Shibuya; **Shibuyá-Eki** 渋谷駅 Shibuya Station

shichí *n* 七・7 seven (= **nána** 七・7); Shichi-go-san *n* 七五三 the "seven-five-three" day when children of those ages visit shrines (*15 November*)

shichí *n* 質 a pawn (*something pawned*); shichí-ya *n* 質屋 pawnbroker, pawnshop

Shichi-gatsú *n* 七月・7月 July

shichi-jū *n* 七十・70 seventy (= **naná-jū** 七十・70)

shichimen-chō *n* シチメンチョウ・七面鳥 turkey

shichū´ *n* シチュー stew

shidai *n* 次第・しだい **1.** circumstances **2.** *suffix* ([NOUN, VERB] -i い) ~ **desu** 次第です it depends on …; ([VERB] **-i** い) **-shidai** 次第 as soon as …

shidashi-ya *n* 仕出し屋 caterer, catering shop

shidō *n* 指導 guidance, direction, leadership, counsel(ing), coaching; shidō-sha *n* 指導者 guide, director, leader, coach

shifuku *n* 私服 plain clothes; civilian clothes

shígā *n* シガー cigar

shi-gachi (na) *suffix, adj* しがち(な) apt to do, tends to

shígarétto *n* シガレット cigarette(s)

Shi-gatsú *n* 四月・4月 April

shigeki *n* 刺激 stimulation

shigerimásu, shigéru *v* 茂ります, 茂る it grows thick(ly)/luxuriant(ly)

shígoku *adv* 至極 extremely

shigoto *n* 仕事 job, work, task, undertaking, business; operation: ~ **ni ikimásu** 仕事に行きます goes to work

shigure *n* 時雨 an on-and-off drizzle (*in early winter*)

shihái, shíhai *n* 支配 management, control; shihái-nin *n* 支配人 manager; shihái-sha *n* 支配者 ruler

shihanki *n* 四半期 quarter (*year*): **dai ni-~** 第二四半期 the second (*business*) quarter (*of a company*)

shiharai *n* 支払い, payment, disbursement

shíhei *n* 紙幣 paper money, currency (*bill*) (= **(o-)satsu** (お)札)

shihō' (-happō) *n* 四方(八方) all sides/directions

shihon (kin) *n* 資本(金) capital, funds: **~-ka** 資本家 capitalist

shiiému *n* シーエム・CM TV commercial

shiin *n* 子音 consonant

shíin *n* シーン scene

shíitake *n* シイタケ・椎茸, shiitake mushrooms: **hoshi-~** 干し椎茸 dried shiitake mushrooms

shíite *adv* 強いて forcibly: **shíite sasemásu** 強いてさせます forces one to do

shíito *n* シート **1.** sheets; **biniiru** ~ ビニール・シート vinyl sheet **2.** seat; **~-béruto** シート・ベルト seatbelt

shíitsu *n* シーツ sheet (*for bed*)

shíizun *n* シーズン **1.** the season (= **kisetsu** 季節) **2.** high season; **yakyū (no)** ~ 野球(の)シーズン baseball season

shíji *n* 支持 [BOOKISH] support, maintenance

shíji *n* 指示 [BOOKISH] indication, instruction, directions

shíji *n* 私事 [BOOKISH] **1.** personal matter **2.** privacy

shijō *n* 市場 market

shi-jū *n* 四十・40 forty (= **yón-jū** 四十・40)

shíjū *adv* 始終 all the time

shika *n* シカ・鹿 deer

shiká *n* 歯科 dentistry; shiká-i *n* 歯科医 dentist (= **há-isha** 歯医者)

...shika *conj* ... しか [+ NEGATIVE] (nothing) but, except for; (= **...daké** ...だけ [+ POSITIVE]) only, just

shikake *n* 仕掛け device (*gadget*)

shikaku *n* 資格 qualification(s), competency; **zairyū ~** 在留資格 status of residence

shikakúi *adj* 四角い square

shiká-mo *adv* しかも moreover; and yet

shikarimásu, shikaru *v* 叱ります, 叱る scolds

shikáshi *conj* しかし [BOOKISH] but, however (= **demo** でも, **keredo(mo)** けれど(も))

shi-kata *n* 仕方 way (*of doing*), manner, method, means: **~ ga arimasén** 仕方がありません there's nothing I/we can do about it, can't be helped

shikén *n* 試験 [BOOKISH] examination, test, trial, experiment; **shiken-jó** *n* 試験所 (*testing*) laboratory; **shiken-jō** *n* 試験場 exam room/place

shikí *n* 式 ceremony

shiki *n* 指揮 **1.** command **2.** conducting (*orchestra*); **shikí-sha** *n* 指揮者 conductor (*orchestra*)

shikibetsu *n* 識別 discrimination

shikí-kin *n* 敷金 security deposit (*for rental*)

shikimásu, shiku *v* 敷きます, 敷く spreads (*a quilt, etc.*); **shiki-búton** *n* 敷布団 bottom quilt; **shiki-fu** *n* 敷布 (bed)sheet (= **shíitsu** シーツ)

shikín *n* 資金 fund, capital

shikiri *n* 仕切り partition

shikiri ni *adv* しきりに incessantly; intently, hard

shikkári *adv* しっかり firmly, resolutely

shikke, shikki *n* 湿気 dampness, humidity

shikki *n* 湿気 → **shikke** 湿気

shikki *n* 漆器 lacquer(ware)

shíkko *n* しっこ (*slang/baby talk*) urine, urinating (= **nyō** 尿)

shikō *n* 嗜好・し好 liking, fancy, taste; **...ni ~ ga arimásu** ...に嗜好があります has a taste/liking for...; **shikō-hin** *n* 嗜好品・し好品 articles of taste, amenities of life

Shikóku *n* 四国 Shikoku

shikyō-hin *n* 試供品 tester, free sample (*for customers*) (→ **sanpuru** サンプル)

shikyū *adv* 至急 urgently: **~ (no)** 至急(の) urgent

shima *n* 島 island

shima *n* 縞 stripes: **~-moyō** 縞模様 stripe pattern

shimai *n* 終い・仕舞(い) the end: **~ (no)** しまい(の) the final/last

shimaimásu, shimau *v* しまいます, しまう puts away, finishes; **shite shimau** してしまう finishes doing, ends up by doing (*after all*), does anyway, does it all

shimarimásu, shimáru *v* 閉まります, 閉まる it shuts, closes, locks

shimarimásu, shimáru *v* 締まります, 締まる gets steady, braces oneself

shimarimásu, shimáru *v* 締まります, 締まる gets thrifty, frugal

shimásu, suru *v* します, する does (it); it happens; wears; ... ni ([ADJECTIVE] **-ku**) shimásu ...に...(く)します makes it so that (*it is*), makes it into; decides on (= **... ni kimemásu** ...に決めます); ... (shiyō) to shimásu ...(しよう)とします goes (*tries, is about*) to do; ... (suru) koto ni shimásu ...(する)事にします decides to (do); ... to shite(´ mo) ... として(も) (*even*) as a ...

shímatsu *n* 始末 managing, dealing with; outcome, upshot, climax

shimátta *interj* しまった! Damn!, Good heavens

shimauma *n* シマウマ zebra

shime-gane *n* 締め金 buckle

shimei *n* 使命 mission: **~-kan** 使命感 sense of mission

shi-mei *n* 氏名 (*one's*) full name (= **sei-mei** 姓名)

shimei *n* 指名 designation; shimei-tsū´wa *n* 指名通話 person-to-person call; shimei-tehai *n* 指名手配 listing a person (*criminal*) on the wanted list

shimekiri *n* 締め切り・〆切 **1.** closing **2.** "Closed", deadline: **~ kígen/kíjitsu** 締め切り期限/期日 deadline, due date

shimemásu, shiméru *v* 閉めます, 閉める shuts (*closes, locks*) it

shimemásu, shiméru *v* 締めます, 締める **1.** ties, fastens, tightens it (*necktie, belt, kimono sash, seat-belt, etc.*) **2.** tightens up on: **neji o ~** ネジを締めます tightens up a screw **3.** economizes on **4. ki o hiki-~** 気を引き締めます braces oneself

shimeppói *adj* 湿っぽい damp; humid

shimerasemásu, shimerasu *v* 湿らせます, 湿らす moistens/dampens it, wets it

shimerimásu, shimeru *v* 湿ります, 湿る gets damp

shimeshimásu, shimésu *v* 示します, 示す shows, indicates

shimi *n* 染み・しみ stain, blot, blotch, spot

shimijími (to) *adv* しみじみ(と) deeply (*feels*), fully (*appreciates*)

shimimásu, shimiru *v* 染みます, 染みる penetrates, soaks

shimimásu, shimiru *v* 沁みます, 沁みる smarts, is stimulated (*body*), is deeply moved (*heart*): **honemi ni ~** 骨身に沁みます touches one to the quick: **hito no nasake ga mi ni ~** 人の情けが身に沁みます deeply appreciates people's thoughtfulness

shimó *n* 霜・しも frost: **~ ga orimásu** 霜が降ります frosts

shí mo *suffix* しも [+ NEGATIVE verb] **~ shimasén** しもしません nor do, not do either/even

shimon *n* 指紋 fingerprint

shimon *n* 諮問 [BOOKISH] inquiry

shimon *n* 試問 [BOOKISH] questioning, interviewing, examination;

kōtō-~ 口頭試問 oral examination
shín *n* 芯 core, pith, heart: **ringo no ~**リンゴ[林檎]の芯 apple core
shín-... *prefix* 心. . . heart, spirit; shín-chū *n* 心中 in one's heart; shin-pai *n* 心配 worry, uneasiness, concern, anxiety, fear: **~ (na)** 心配(な) uneasy; shín-ri *n* 心理 psychology, mentality; shin-rí-gaku *n* 心理学 (*science/study of*) psychology; **~-sha** 心理学者 psychologist; shín-soko *n* 心底 (*at*) the bottom of one's heart; shin-zō *n* 心臓 heart (*organ*)
shín-... *prefix* 新… … new; shin-geki *n* 新劇 modern drama; shín-nen *n* 新年 new year: **Shín-nen akemashite omedetō (gozaimásu)** 新年明けましておめでとう(ございます)! Happy New Year!; shin-sen (na) *adj* 新鮮(な) fresh; Shin-yaku Seisho *n* 新約聖書 the New Testament
shin-... *prefix* 神… god, deity; shin-den *n* 神殿 the sanctuary of a shrine; shín-dō *n* 神童 child prodigy; shín-pu *n* 神父 priest (*Christian*), Father, Reverend; Shín-tō, Shín-dō *n* 神道 Shinto(ism); shin-wa *n* 神話 myth, mythology
shina *n* 品 **1.** articles, goods (= **shinamono** 品物) **2.** quality; shina-mono *n* 品物 goods, articles (= **shina** 品)
shi-nagara しながら while doing
shináide *v* しないで not doing it, instead of doing it: **~ imásu** しないでいます keeps on not doing it; **~ okimásu** しないでおきます neglects to do it, leaves it undone; **~ mimásu** しないでみます tries not doing it; **~ sumimásu** しないで済みます needs not do it, doesn't have to do it
shinákute mo *v* しなくても even not doing it; **~ íi desu** しなくてもいいです gets by without doing it, doesn't have to do it
shi-naoshimásu, shi-naósu *v* し直します, し直す redoes it, fixes/improves it
Shínbashi *n* 新橋 Shinbashi
shínbō *n* 辛抱 [BOOKISH] endurance, patience, forbearance
shinbun *n* 新聞 newspaper; **~-úriba** 新聞売り場 newsstand; shinbun-dai *n* 新聞代 newspaper bill; shinbún-sha *n* 新聞社 newspaper company
shinchō *n* 身長 height, stature (= **sé** 背, **séi** せい・背, **setake** 背丈): **~ o hakarimásu** 身長を測ります measures one's height
shinchū *n* 真鍮 brass
shindai *n* 寝台 bed, berth, bunk; **~-ken** 寝台券 berth ticket
shindō *n* 振動 vibration: **hageshii ~** 激しい振動 thumping vibration
Shinetsu-chihō *n* 信越地方 the Shinetsu area of Japan (*Niigata, Nagano prefectures*)
shingō *n* 信号 signal: **~-ki** 信号機 traffic light: **~-mushi** 信号無視 running a red light: **ao-~** 青信号

green light: **aka-~** 赤信号 red light

shíngu *n* 寝具 bedding

shínguru *n* シングル **1.** single (*room*) **2.** single, unmarried (= **dokushin** 独身), bachelor

shinimásu, shinu *v* 死にます, 死ぬ dies (= **nakunarimásu** 亡くなります, **o-nakunari ni narimásu** [HONORIFIC] お亡くなりになります (*for human*))

shínjá *n* 信者 a believer; **Kirisuto-kyō (no)** ~ キリスト教(の)信者 a Christian

shin-jimásu, shin-jíru *v* 信じます, 信じる believes in, trusts

shínjitsu *n* 真実 truth (= **hontō no koto** 本当のこと, **makoto** 誠・真)

shinju *n* 真珠 pearl; **Shinjú-wan** 真珠湾 Pearl Harbor

shinjū *n* 心中 double suicide, lovers' suicide

Shinjuku *n* 新宿 Shinjuku; **Shinjukú-Eki** 新宿駅 Shinjuku Station

shinkánsen *n* 新幹線 bullet train (*line*), Shinkansen

shínkei *n* 神経 nerve: **~ ni sawa-rimásu** 神経に障ります gets on one's nerves; shinkéi-shitsu (na) *adj* 神経質(な) nervous

shinkoku (na) *adj* 深刻(な) serious, grave

shinobimásu, shinóbu *v* 忍びます, 忍ぶ bears, puts up with

shínpi *n* 神秘 mystery; **shinpi-teki (na)** 神秘的(な) mysterious, esoteric, miraculous

shínpo *n* 進歩 progress

shínpuru (na) *adj* シンプル(な) simple

shinrai *n* 信頼 trust, confidence, reliance; shinrai-sei *n* 信頼性 reliability: **~ ga takái** 信頼性が高い highly reliable

shínri *n* 真理 truth, veritas: **fuhen no ~** 不変の真理 eternal truth, everlasting truth

shinrui *n* 親類 a relative (= **shinseki** 親戚, **shinzoku** 親族)

shinryaku *n* 侵略 invasion, aggression

shinsatsu *n* 診察 medical examination

shinsei *n* 申請 application (*for a permit*); shinsei-nin *n* 申請人 an applicant; shinsei-shó *n* 申請書 application form (*for a permit*)

shinseki *n* 親戚 a relative

shínsetsu *n* 親切 kindness, goodwill, favor; shínsetsu na *adj* 親切な kind, cordial

shínshi *n* 紳士 gentleman

shinshitsu *n* 寝室 bedroom

shíntai (no) *adj* 身体(の) physical; **~-kénsa** 身体検査 physical exam; **~-shōgáisha** 身体障害者 handicapped person

shín'ya n, *adv* 深夜 late at night

shin'yō *n* 信用 trust, confidence; credit

shinzoku *n* 親族 relatives

shió *n* 潮 tide

shió *n* 塩 salt; shio-karái *adj* 塩辛い salty (= **shoppai** しょっぱい)

shion *n* 子音 consonant
shiori *n* しおり bookmark (*a thin marker made of paper, card, etc.*)
shippai *n* 失敗 failure, blunder, defeat
shippó *n* しっぽ・尻尾 tail
shira-... *prefix* 白. . . white; **shira-gá** *n* 白髪 gray hair; **shira-su** *n* シラス・白子 baby sardines
shirabemásu, shirabéru *v* 調べます, 調べる investigates, examines, checks
shirafu (no) *adj* しらふ(の) (*undrunk*) sober
shirami *n* シラミ louse, lice
shiraremásu, shirareru *v* 知られます, 知られる gets (*widely*) known; becomes famous
shirase *n* 知らせ (= **o-shirase** お知らせ) report, notice, information
shirasemásu, shiraseru *v* 知らせます, 知らせる announces (*informs of*), lets one know, notifies
shiréi *n* 司令 command (*in army, etc.*); **shiréi-bu** *n* 司令部 headquarters
shiréi *n* 指令 command; **shiréi-kan** *n* 指令官 commander
shiremásu, shireru *v* 知れます, 知れる gets known; is identified; becomes clear/evident
shirí *n* 尻 butt(ock), hip, bottom, seat
shiriai *n* 知り合い acquaintance
shirimásu, shiru *v* 知ります, 知る acquaints oneself with, finds out, learns; **shitte imásu** 知っています knows
shiri-tai *v* 知りたい curious about, want(ing) to know
shíritsu (no) *adj* 私立(の) (= **watakushí-ritsu** 私立) privately established entity/organization
shirizokimásu, shirizóku *v* 退きます, 退く retreats, withdraws, retires
shiro *n* 城 castle
shíro *n* 白 white: **~-kuma** 白熊・シロクマ white bear, polar bear; **shíró-mi** *n* 白身 white (*of an egg*), albumen; white meat; **shiró-i** *adj* 白い white
shiróppu *n* シロップ syrup
shírō'to *n* 素人 an amateur, a novice
shíru *n* 汁 juice, gravy; broth, soup
shirushi *n* 印・徴 indication, token, sign, symptom; effect(iveness)
shíryo *n* 思慮 [BOOKISH] consideration, thought(-fulness)
shíryō *n* 資料 materials; data
shíryoku *n* 視力 vision, eyesight, visual acuity
shisei *n* 姿勢 posture; attitude
shisetsu (no) *adj* 私設(の) private
shísetsu *n* 施設 facility, institution, establishment, installation
shíshi *n* シシ・獅子 lion (= **raion** ライオン)
shishu *n* 刺繍 embroidery
shishún-ki *n* 思春期 adolescence
shisō *n* 思想 thought, concept
shíson *n* 子孫 descendants; posterity
...-shi-sō (na) *suffix, adj* しそう(な)

likely/about to do it: **~ mo nái** しそうもない unlikely to do it

shísso (na) *adj* 質素(な) simple, plain, frugal, rustic

shi-sugimásu, shi-sugíru *v* し過ぎます, し過ぎる over(does)

shita(-...) *n, prefix* 下(...) below, under, bottom, lower; (= **toshi-shita** 年下) younger, youngest; shita-baki *n* 下履き (*outdoor*) shoes; shita-gi *n* 下着 underwear; shita-machi *n* 下町 downtown

shitá *n* 舌 tongue

shitagaimásu, shitagau *v* 従います, 従う: **...ni ~** ...に従います conforms to ..., accords with ...

shi-tagarimásu, shi-tagáru *v* したがります, したがる wants (*is eager*) to do

shitagatte *adv, conj* 従って accordingly, therefore; **... ni ~** ...に従って according to ..., in conformity with/to ...

shi-tagátte *v* したがって → **shi-tagarimásu** したがります [INFINITIVE]

shi-tai *v* したい wants to do it

shitaku *n* 支度 preparation, arrangement

shitára *v* したら if/when one does it

shitári (... shimásu) *v* したり (...します) does/is such things as; sometimes does/is; does/is intermittently (*off and on*)

shitashíi *adj* 親しい intimate, familiar

shitate-ya *n* 仕立屋 tailor

shitátte *v* したって = **shitémo** しても even doing, even if it does

shite *v* して doing; does and; **~-kara** してから (next) after doing; **~moíi** してもいい may do it, it is OK to do it; **~ wa ikemasén/ikenai/ damé** してはいけません/いけない/だめ mustn't do it, don't do it!

shitei *n* 指定 designation, appointment; shitéi-seki *n* 指定席 reserved seat(s)

shiteki shimásu (suru) *v* 指摘します(する) indicates, points out

shiten *n* 支店 branch shop

shitetsu *n* 私鉄 private railroad

shitsu *n* 質 quality, nature

...´-shitsu *suffix* ...室 (*name of certain*) room

shitsū *n* 歯痛 toothache (= **ha-ita** 歯痛)

shitsubō *n* 失望 disappointment

shitsúdo *n* 湿度 humidity

shitsugyō *n* 失業 unemployment; **~-sha** 失業者 unemployed person

shitsuke *n* しつけ・躾 training (*of children, ...*), discipline, upbringing

shi-tsuke *n* 仕付け basting, tacking (*with thread*); **~-íto** 仕付け糸 basting/tacking thread

shitsukemásu, shitsukéru *v* しつけ[躾け]ます, しつけ[躾け]る trains (*children, ...*), disciplines, brings up

shi-tsukemásu, shi-tsukéru *v* 仕付けます, 仕付ける bastes, tacks (*with thread*)

shitsumon *n* 質問 question

shi̱tsúrei *n* 失礼 discourtesy; **Shi̱tsúrei desu ga ...** 失礼ですが... Excuse me for asking, but ...; shi̱tsúrei (na) *adj* 失礼(な) impolite

shi̱tsuren *n* 失恋 disappointment in love

shi̱tsu̱teki (na) *adj* 質的(な) qualitative

shi̱tto *n* 嫉妬 jealousy: ~ **bukai hito** 嫉妬深い人 jealous person

shiwa *n* しわ・シワ・皺 wrinkle, crease: ~ **ga dekimásu̱** しわができます it wrinkles (= ~ **ni narimásu̱** しわになります)

shiwaza *n* 仕業 act, deed

shi-yasúi *v* しやすい **1.** easy to do **2.** likely to do it, tends to do it

shi-yō *n* 仕様 method, means, way (= **shi̱-kata** 仕方); (*for products, etc.*) specifications: ~ **ga nái** しようがない hopeless, beyond remedy

shiyō *n* 使用 use, employment; shiyō-chū 使用中 in use, occupied (*toilet, etc.*); shiyō-nin *n* 使用人 servant; shi̱yō′-sha *n* 使用者 user

shiyō *n* 私用 private use/business: ~ **no** 私用の private

shizen *n* 自然 nature: ~ **(no)** 自然(の) natural; ~ **(na)** 自然(な) natural, spontaneous

shízuka (na) *adj* 静か(な) quiet, still

shizumemásu̱, shizuméru *v* 静めます・鎮めます, 静める・鎮める soothes, quiets, calms, pacifies, suppresses

shizumemásu̱, shizumeru *v* 沈めます, 沈める sinks it

shizumimásu̱, shizumu *v* 沈みます, 沈む it sinks

sho- *prep* 諸 [*makes definite plurals of certain nouns*]; **~-ji** 諸事 all matters; everything; **~-tō** 諸島 (*a group of*) islands; an archipelago

shō′ *n* 性 nature, disposition, quality

shō′ *n* 賞 prize, reward; shō′-batsu *n* 賞罰 rewards and punishments; shō-hin *n* 賞品 prize (*object*); shō-kin *n* 賞金 prize money; reward; shō′-yo *n* 賞与 bonus; **~-kin** 賞与金 bonus money

shō-... *prefix* 商. . . sales, business; shō′-bai *n* 商売 trade, business; shō′-gyō *n* 商業 commerce, trade, business; shō′-hin *n* 商品 goods, merchandise, (*sales*) product; shō′-nin *n* 商人 merchant, trader

...′-shō *suffix* ...商 dealer (*seller of* ...): **gyō-~** 行商 peddling

...′-shō *suffix* ...省 **1.** (*name of certain*) Ministry **2.** (*name of certain*) province (*China*)

shōátsú-ki *n* 昇圧機 booster (*of current*)

sho′-batsu *n* 処罰 punishments

shōbén *n* 小便 urine, urinating (*very informal. mostly male*)

shōbō *n* 消防 fire fighting; **~′-sha** 消防車 fire engine; **~′-shi** 消防士 fire fighter

shō′bu *n* 勝負 match, contest

shóbun *n* 処分 [BOOKISH] disposition, abolition

sho'chi *n* 処置 [BOOKISH] dealing with

shōchi *n* 承知 agreement, understanding; **Shōchi shimáshita** 承知しました [HUMBLE] I understand (*and consent*). (*on business e-mail, etc.*) Yes, sir/ma'am.

shochō *n* 所長 institute director

shōchō *n* 象徴 symbol

shōchū' *n* 焼酎 distilled liquor made from yams or rice

shō'dai *n* 招待 = **shō'tai** 招待 invitation

shōdaku *n* 承諾 [BOOKISH] consent, acceptance

shodō *n* 書道 calligraphy (= **shūji** 習字)

shōdokú-yaku/-zai *n* 消毒薬/剤 disinfectant

shō-fuda *n* 正札 price tag

shōga *n* ショウガ・生姜 ginger

shōgai *n* 障害 impediment, obstacle, hindrance; **~-sha** 障害者 handicapped person

shō'gai *n* 生涯 life(long), for all of one's life (time)

shōgakkō *n* 小学校 primary (*elementary*) school → **gakkō** *n* 学校

shōgáku-sei *n* 小学生 primary school student

shō ga nai *adj* [INFORMAL] しょうがない = **shi-yō ga nái** しようがない hopeless, beyond remedy

Shōgatsú *n* 正月 January; New Year

shōgi *n* 将棋 (*Japanese*) chess

shō'go *n* 正午 noon (*exactly*)

shōhi *n* 消費 consumption; **~-sha** 消費者 consumer; **shōhi-zei** *n* 消費税 consumption tax

shohō *n* 処方 prescription, prescribing; **shohō-sen** *n* 処方箋 prescription (slip)

shō'i *n* 少尉 2nd lieutenant; ensign

shoimásu, shou *v* [INFORMAL] しょい[背負い]ます, しょう・背負う [INFORMAL] carries on the back, shoulders it

shōji *n* 障子 translucent sliding panel/door

shōjíkí (na) *adj* 正直(な) honest: **~ni** 正直に honestly

shō-jimásu, shō-jiru *v* 生じます, 生じる **1.** produces, comes about, occurs **2.** arises, happens

shōjin-ryō'ri *n* 精進料理 vegetarian cuisine

shójo *n* 処女 virgin (*female*)

shō'jo *n* 少女 young girl (= **onna no ko** 女の子)

shōjū *n* 小銃 rifle

shōka *n* 消化 digestion; **shōka-fúryō** *n* 消化不良 indigestion

shōkai *n* 紹介 introduction (*of a person*)

shōká-ki *n* 消火器 fire extinguisher

shōka-sen *n* 消火栓 fireplug, hydrant

shōken *n* 証券 security (*stock, bond*)

shóki *n* 書記 secretary

shoki *n* 初期 [BOOKISH] beginning; **shoki-settei** *n* 初期設定 default (*setting*)

shōki (no) *adj* 正気(の) sober, sane; in one's right mind
shōkin *n* 正金 hard cash
shōkin *n* 償金 → **baishō-kin** 賠償金 (*indemnity, reparation*)
shokken *n* 食券 meal ticket
shokki *n* 食器 tableware (*dish, plate, chopsticks, etc.*); **~-dana** 食器棚 dish rack; **~-tódana** 食器戸棚 cupboard
shokkō *n* 職工 factory worker; workman (= **kōin** 工員)
shókku *n* ショック shock
shōko *n* 証拠 proof, evidence, witness
shō´kō *n* 将校 military officer
shoku *n* 職 office, occupation; shokú-gyō *n* 職業 occupation, vocation, job, profession; shoku-reki *n* 職歴 professional experience
shoku *n* (**...´-shoku** ...食) food; (*counts meals*); shoku-dō *n* 食堂 dining room; restaurant; shoku-dō´-sha *n* 食堂車 dining car, diner; shoku-go (ni) *adv* 食後(に) after a meal (= **shokuji no áto de** 食事の後で); shoku-hin *n* 食品 foodstuffs, groceries; shoku-ji *n* 食事 a meal; eating, having a meal; shoku (-ji) tsuki (no) *n* 食(事)付き(の) with meals (*included*); shokú-motsu *n* 食物 food(s); shoku-ryō-hin *n* 食料品 foodstuffs, groceries; shoku-taku *n* 食卓 dinner table; shoku-yoku *n* 食欲 appetite; shoku-zen *n* 食膳 (*low*) individual meal table; shoku-zen (ni) *adv* [BOOKISH] 食前(に) before a meal (= **shokuji no máe ni** 食事の前に)
shokúbutsu *n* 植物 (*botanical*) plant; **~-en** 植物園 botanical garden
shokumín-chi *n* 植民地 colony
shōkyoku-teki (na) *adj* 消極的(な) negative; conservative
shōkyū *n* 昇給 rise in pay
shōkyū *n* 昇級 promotion
shomei *n* 署名 signature
shōmei *n* 証明 proof, verification, attestation, certification; shōmei-shó *n* 証明書 certificate; note of authentication
shōmei *n* 照明 lighting, illumination: **~-kígu** 照明器具 lighting fixtures
shōmén *n* 正面 the face (*front side*)
shomotsu *n* 書物 [BOOKISH] book (= **hón** 本)
shōmyō´ *n* 声明 chanting of Buddhist scriptures
shōnen *n* 少年 boy, lad, youngster (= **otoko no ko** 男の子)
shō´ni *n* 小児 infant, child; shōni-ka *n* 小児科 pediatrics; pediatrician
shōnin *n* 証人 a witness
shoppái *adj* [INFORMAL] しょっぱい [INFORMAL] salty
shóppingu *n* ショッピング shopping (= **kaimono** 買い物)
shō´rai *n, adv* 将来 future (= **yukusue** 行く末, **mirai** 未来)
shōrei *n* 奨励 encouragement, promotion
shóri *n* 処理 managing, disposing of, transacting, dealing with;

shori-jō *n* 処理場 [sewage] treatment plant
shō´ri *n* 勝利 victory; shōrí-sha *n* 勝利者 winner, victor
shorui *n* 書類 form, document, paper(s), writing
shōryaku *n* 省略 abbreviation, omission (= **ryaku** 略)
shōsa *n* 少佐 major; lieutenant commander
shosai *n* 書斎 a study, library (*room*)
shōsai *n* 詳細 [BOOKISH] details
shóseki *n* 書籍 books, publications (= **hón** 本)
shōsetsu *n* 小説 fiction, a novel
shō´shō *adv* 少々 a little [DEFERENTIAL] (= **chótto** ちょっと)
shō´shō *n* 少将 major general; rear admiral
shōshū *n* 召集・招集 conscription, (*military*) draft
shōsoku *n* 消息 news, word (*from/of…*) (= **nyūsu** ニュース)
shotái *n* 所帯・世帯 a household; housekeeping
shō´tai *n* 招待 invitation; shōtái-jō *n* 招待状 invitation (card)
shótchū *adv* [INFORMAL] しょっちゅう all the time
shoten *n* 書店 bookshop
shō´ten *n* 焦点 focus, focal point
shō´to *n* ショート a short (*circuit*); short story; shortstop
shotoku *n* 所得 income; **~-zei** 所得税 income tax
shōtotsu *n* 衝突 collision
Shōwa-jidai *n* 昭和時代 Showa Period (*1926–1989*)
shoyū (no) *adj* 所有(の) possessed, owned, belonging; one's own; shoyū-butsu/-hin *n* 所有物/品 belongings, possessions; shoyū´-sha *n* 所有者 (*legal*) owner
shōyu *n* しょうゆ・醤油 soya sauce
shozai *n* 所在 whereabouts
shōzō *n* 肖像 portrait; shōzō-ga *n* 肖像画 portrait (*drawing and/or painting*)
shu *n* 朱 vermilion; shu-niku *n* 朱肉 red ink pad
shū´, …´-shū *n, suffix* 州, …州 (*name of certain*) state (*U.S., Australia*); province (*Canada*); county (*Britain*)
shū´, …´-shū *n, suffix* 週, …週 (= **shūkan** 週間) week; shū-matsu *n* 週末 weekend; shū-kan *n* 週間 week
shūbun *n* 秋分 autumnal equinox: **~-no-hí** 秋分の日 Autumnal Equinox Day
shuchō *n* 主張 assertion, claim
shūchū *n* 集中 concentration
shúdan *n* 手段 ways, means, measures (= **hōhō** 方法): **saigo no ~** 最後の手段 last resort
shūdan *n* 集団 group, collective body: **~-seikatsu** 集団生活 group living, communal living: **bo-~** 母集団 a population
shūden *n* 終電 the last train (= **~ densha** 最終電車)
shūdō´-in *n* 修道院 convent

shúfu *n* 主婦 housewife
shúfu *n* 首府 → **shutó** 首都
shūgeki *n* 襲撃 attack, charge, raid, attack
shúgi *n* 主義 principle, doctrine, -ism
shūgi-in *n* 衆議院 House of Representatives
shúgo *n* 主語 subject (*of a sentence*)
shūgō *n* 集合 assembly, gathering
shugyō *n* 修行・修業 (*getting one's*) training, ascetic practices, meditation
shūgyō *n* 就業 starting one's work(-day); **shūgyō'-jíkan** *n* 就業時間 working hours
shū'ha *n* 宗派 sect
shūhen *adj* 周辺 circumference, environs, surroundings (= **shūi** 周囲): **tóshi no ~** 都市の周辺 outskirts (*of city*); **~ no ...** 周辺の... the surrounding ...
shū'i *n* 周囲 circumference; surroundings (= **shūhen** 周辺)
shuin *n* 手淫 [BOOKISH] masturbation
shūji *n* 習字 calligraphy (*handwriting*) practice
shújin *n* 主人 **1.** husband; **go-~** ご主人 your husband **2.** master, owner, landlord, boss, host
shúju (no) *adj* 種々(の) all kinds of (= **samazama (na)** 様々(な), **iroiro (na)** 色々(な), **iron na** いろんな)
shújutsu *n* 手術 surgical operation, surgery
shūkaku *n* 収穫 harvest, crop
shukan *n* 主観 subjectivity: **~-teki (na)** 主観的(な) subjective
shūkan *n* 習慣 custom, practice, habit (= **kuse** 癖)
shū'ki *n* 秋期 autumn (*period/term*)
shū'ki *n* 周期 cycle (*length*)
shū'ki *n* 臭気 bad smell, stink (= **akushū** 悪臭); **shūki-dome** *n* 臭気止め deodorant (*household, etc.*)
shukkin *n* 出勤 office attendance
shuku-choku *n* 宿直 night duty
shukudai *n* 宿題 **1.** homework (*at school*): **natsu-yásumi no ~** 夏休みの宿題 summer homework **2.** unsolved problem
shukuga *n* 祝賀 congratulation: **~-kai** 祝賀会 a celebration
shukujitsu *n* 祝日 national holiday
shū-kuríimu *n* シュークリーム a cream puff, an éclair
shuku-saijitsu *n* 祝祭日 → **shukujitsu** 祝日
shukuten *n* 祝典 celebration ceremony
shū'kyō *n* 宗教 religion
shūmai *n* シューマイ pork meatballs steamed in thin pastry
shúmi *n* 趣味 taste, interest, liking, hobby (= **hobii** ホビー)
shumoku *n* 種目 **1.** item: **eigyō-~** 営業種目 item of business **2.** (*competition*) event: **rikujo kyōgi-~** 陸上競技種目 events in athletics (*track and field*)
shunbun *n* 春分 vernal equinox: **~-no-hí** 春分の日 Vernal Equinox Day

shunkan *n* 瞬間 a moment, an instant: **tsugi no ~** 次の瞬間 next moment
shūnyū *n* 収入 earnings, income: **~-ínshi** 収入印紙 tax (*revenue*) stamp (= **inshi** 印紙)
shuppan *n* 出版 publishing; **shuppán-butsu** *n* 出版物 publication(s); **shuppán-sha** *n* 出版社 publishing company
shuppatsu *n* 出発 departure; **~-ten** 出発点 point of departure
shuppin *n* 出品 exhibit(ing): **~-sha** 出品者 exhibitor
shū´ri *n* 修理 repair; **shūrí-kō** *n* 修理工 repairman, mechanic
shūrō *n* 就労 [BOOKISH] work (*for company, etc.*)
shúrui *n* 種類 type, sort, kind, variety
shū´shi *n* 修士 master's degree: **~-gō** 修士号 master's degree
shūshi *n* 終止 [BOOKISH] ending (= **oshimai** おしまい); **shūshí-fu** *n* 終止符 [BOOKISH] period, full stop (*punctuation*)
shū´shin *n* 修身 ethics, morals
shū´shin *n* 終身 all one's life (= **isshō(-gai)** 一生(涯), **shōgai** 生涯, **shūsei** 終生); **shū´shin-kei** *n* 終身刑 life imprisonment; **shū´shin-koyō** *n* 終身雇用 lifetime employment
shushō *n* 首相 prime minister
shūshoku *n* 就職 getting a job, finding employment
shūshū *n* 収集 **1.** collecting (*trash, etc.*): **gomi-shū-~** ゴミ収集車 garbage truck **2.** collection (*as one's hobby, for research, etc.*)
shussei *n* 出生 [BOOKISH] birth (= **umare** 生まれ): **~-chi** 出生地 (*one's*) birthplace
shusseki *n* 出席 attendance, presence (= **sanka** 参加)
shusshin *n* 出身 alumnus (*of* …); coming (*from* …): **~-chi** 出身地 (*one's*) hometown
shúsu *n* 繻子 satin
shutchō *n* 出張 business trip
shūten *n* 終点 terminus, end of the line, last stop, destination
shutó *n* 首都 capital city; **shutó-ken** *n* 首都圏 Tokyo metropolitan area → **kantō-chihō** 関東地方
shūtome *n* 姑 common spoken term for one's mother-in-low
shuyō (na) *adj* 主要(な) leading, chief; **~-tóshi** 主要都市 major city
shūzen *n* 修繕 [BOOKISH] repair
si... → **shi...**
sō´ *n* 僧 Buddhist priest (= **sōryo** 僧侶, **obō-san** お坊さん)
sō´ *interj* そう [hearsay]: **... (suru, shita; dá, dátta), sō´ (desu, da/na, de, ni)** …(する, した; だ, だった), そう(です, だ/な, で, に) it is reported (*said/written*) that, I hear that, they say that …
...-sō *suffix* …そう, **...-sō´** …そう: **shisō (désu, dá/na, dé, ní)** しそう(です,だ/な, で, に) looking (*as though*), about to (*happen*); will at any moment; **abuna-~ (désu, ni**

miemásu̲) 危なそう(です, に見えます) looks dangerous, **jōbu-~ níwa miemasén** 丈夫そうには見えません doesn't look sturdy

...-sō *suffix* …艘 (*counts ships/ boats; commonly replaced by* **...-seki** …隻)

sóba *n* そば・側 near/close(-by), (be-)side

sóba *n* そば・ソバ・蕎麦 buckwheat noodles; **sobá-ya** *n* そば[蕎麦]屋 Japanese noodle shop

sōbetsu *n* 送別 farewell; send-off; **~-kai** 送別会 farewell party (*reception*)

sobiemásu̲, sobiéru *v* そびえます, そびえる rises, looms

sóbo *n* 祖母 grandmother [FORMAL] (= **obā´-san** おばあさん・お祖母さん, **obā-chan** おばあちゃん)

soboku na *adj* 素朴な simple, naive

soboro *n* そぼろ・ソボロ parched minced fish; fish meal

sō´chi *n* 装置 equipment, apparatus

sochira *pron* そちら **1.** there, that way **2.** that one (*of two*) **3.** you; sochira-gawa *n* そちら側 your side

sō´dā *n* ソーダー soda water

sō da *v* そうだ = **sō´ desu̲** そうです that's right, yes

sodachí *n* 育ち growing up, one's early years: **~ ga yoi/warui** お育ちが良い/悪い well-bred/ill-bred

sodachimásu̲, sodátsu *v* 育ちます, 育つ grows up, is raised (reared)

sōdai na *adj* 壮大な magnificent, grand

sōdan *n* 相談 talk, conference (*personal*), consultation, advice: **~-aite** 相談相手 someone to turn to for advice

sodatemásu̲, sodatéru *v* 育てます, 育てる raises, rears, educates

sodate-no-oyá *n* 育ての親 a foster parent

sode *n* 袖・そで sleeve (→ **naga-sode** 長袖)

sō´ (desu̲) *v* そう(です) That's right, yes; Sō´desu̲ ka. そうですか. **1.** Oh? How interesting! **2.** Is that right/so?; Sō´desu̲ ne. そうですね. Well, now; Let me see.

sō´dō *n* 騒動 unrest, disturbance, tumult, strife; riot: **oie-~** お家騒動 family trouble

soemásu̲, soeru *v* 添えます, 添える adds, throws in extra, attaches

sófu *n* 祖父 grandfather [FORMAL] (= **ojii´-san** おじいさん・お祖父さん, **ojii-chan** おじいちゃん)

sofu̲to(wéa) *n* ソフト(ウェア) (*computer*) software

sōgan-kyō *n* 双眼鏡 binoculars

sōgi-ya *n* 葬儀屋 undertaker (*funeral director*)

sōgō *n* 総合 synthesis; sōgō-teki (na) *adj* 総合的(な) composite, comprehensive, overall, synthesized

so´go no *adj* 相互の mutual, reciprocal; so´go ni *adv* 相互に mutually, reciprocally (= **otagai ni** お互いに)

sōi *n* 相違[相異] discrepancy, difference: ... **ni ~ nai** ... に相違

[相異]ない must be ...

soimásu, sou *v* 沿います, 沿う runs along, follows

soitsu *pron* そいつ that damn one; **~-ra** そいつら those damn ones

sō´ ja nái to *adv* [INFORMAL] そうじゃないと = **sō de naito** そうでないと, **sō´ ja nákereba** そうじゃなければ= **sō de nakereba** そうでなければ otherwise

sōji *n* 掃除 cleaning, sweeping (= ~ 清掃): **nenmatsu no ōsōji** 年末の大掃除 year-end cleaning; **sōjíki** *n* 掃除機 a sweeper

sōjū *n* 操縦 handling, operation

sōkei *n* 総計 [BOOKISH] the grand total (= **gōkei** 合計)

sokétto *n* ソケット socket, plug

sōkin *n* 送金 remittance

sokki *n* 速記 shorthand

sokkō-jó *n* 測候所 weather observatory/station

sokkúri *adj* そっくり entirety, completely: **~ (no)** そっくり(の) just like

sókkusu *n* ソックス anklets, socks

soko *pron* そこ there, that place

soko *n* 底 bottom: **umi no ~** 海の底 bottom of the ocean (= **kaitei** 海底); **kokoro no ~** 心の底 bottom of one's heart; **soko-mame** *n* 底まめ bunion, corn, blister

sō´ko *n* 倉庫 warehouse

sókoku *n* 祖国 homeland, mother country (= **bokoku** 母国)

sokonaimásu, sokonáu *v* 損ないます, 損なう harms, injures, hurts; [VERBS INFINITIVE +] fails in doing; **yari-~** やり損ないます botches, misses

...-sokú *suffix* ...足 (*counts pairs of footwear*)

sókudo *n* 速度 speed (= **supiido** スピード); **"Sókudo otóse"** 速度落とせ Reduce Speed.

sokutatsu *n* 速達 special delivery, express

sómatsu na *adj* 粗末な crude, coarse; **o-sómatsu-sama** お粗末さま Please excuse the poor fare (*reply to* **gochisō-sama** ご馳走さま・ごちそうさま)

somemásu, someru *v* 染めます, 染める dyes

sō´men *n* そうめん・素麺 thin white wheat-flour noodles

somukimásu, somúku *v* 背きます, 背く; **(... ni) ~** (...に)背きます disobeys, goes against, violates; rebels, revolts

Sōmu-shō *n* 総務省 Ministry of Internal Affairs and Communications (MIC)

són *n* 損 damage, loss; disadvantage: **~-toku kanjō** 損得勘定 profit-and-loss arithmetic: **son'eki-keisan-sho** 損益計算書 profit and loss statement (P/L)

sonáé *n* 備え preparations, provisions; defenses

sonaemásu, sonáéru *v* 備えます, 備える prepares, fixes, installs, furnishes; possesses

sōnan *n* 遭難 disaster, accident,

shipwreck, train wreck
songai *n* 損害 damage, harm, loss
sonkei *n* 尊敬 respect, esteem: **~-suru-hito** 尊敬する人 someone that one respects
sonna ... *adj* [INFORMAL] そんな… such (a) ..., that kind of ...: **~ ni** そんなに to that extent, that much, so (very/much)
sonnára *adv* [INFORMAL] そんなら then, in that case ([FORMAL] **sore nára** それなら)
sono ... *adj* その … that; **~ áto** その後, **~-go** その後 since then; sonó-hoka *n* その他[外] and others; sonó-ta *n* その他 [BOOKISH] and others (= **sonó-hoka** その他[外]); sono-tókí *n, adv* その時 at that time; sono-uchi *adv* そのうち soon, before long, sometime in the future; sono-ue′ ni *adv* そのうえに moreover, also, besides; sono-koro (wa) *adv* その頃(は) (*at*) that time, then, (*in*) those days; sore jíshin/jítai *n* それ自身/自体 itself ... sono-mónó *adv* …そのもの (*in*) itself, the very ...
són-shimásu, són-suru *v* 損します, 損する = **són o suru** 損をする loses, suffers a loss
sonshitsu *n* 損失 a loss (= **son** 損, **rosu** ロス)
sonzai *n* 存在 existence; being/ person (*in existence*), personage, figure
sō-on *n* 騒音 noise
sóppa *n* 反っ歯 bucktooth
sóra *n* 空 sky
sóra de *adv* そらで by heart, from memory
sorashimásu, sorásu *v* 逸らします, 逸らす **1.** dodges, turns aside **2.** warps it
sore *pron* それ that one, it; sore dátte *adv, conj* [INFORMAL] それだって = **sore démo** それでも still, yet, even so; sore de *conj* それで and (*then/so/also*); sore démo *conj* それでも still, yet, even so; sore hodo *conj* それほど to that extent, so; sore kara *conj* それから and (*then*); after that, since then; sore máde *conj* それまで until then; sore náno ni *conj* それなのに nevertheless, nonetheless, and yet; sore nára *conj* それなら then, in that case; sore ni *conj* それに on top of that, moreover, in addition, plus; soré-ra *pron* それら those, they/them
sore dé wa *conj* それでは, [INFORMAL] **sore ja/jā** それじゃ/じゃあ well, well now/then; in that event: **~ shitsúrei shimásu** それでは失礼します excuse me but I'll be on my way; good-bye
soremásu, soréru *v* 逸れます, 逸れる deviates, strays, digresses
sore-tómo *conj* それとも or else
sore wa sore wa *interj* それはそれは My my! My goodness!
sorézóre *adv* それぞれ respectively, severally (= **onoono** おのおの・各々)
sorí *n* そり・反り a warp, curve, bend

sorí *n* そり・剃り shaving
sóri *n* そり・ソリ sled
sōri-dáijin *n* 総理大臣 prime minister
sorimásu, sóru *v* 剃ります, 剃る shaves
sorimásu, sóru *v* 反ります, 反る bends (*back*), warps
sōritsu *n* 創立 establishment
soroban *n* そろばん・算盤 abacus, counting beads
soróe 揃え *n* an array
soroemásu, soroéru *v* 揃えます, 揃える puts in order; collects; completes a set
sorói *n* 揃い *n* a set (of ...)
sōron *n* 争論 quarrel, dispute
sōron *n* 総論 general remarks, outline, introduction
sórosoro *adv* そろそろ (*leave*) before long, it is about time to
sō´(ryo) *n* 僧(侶) Buddhist priest
sō-ryō´ji *n* 総領事 consul general
sō´sa *n* 操作 operation, handling
sōsaku *n* 創作 creation
sōsaku *n* 捜索 search, investigation: **~-negai** 捜索願(い) an application to the police to search for (*a missing person*); **kataku-~** 家宅捜索 house search; **~-tai** 捜索隊 search party
sō´sē´ji *n* ソーセージ sausage
sósen *n* 祖先 ancestor (= **senzo** 先祖)
sóshiki *n* 組織 system, structure, setup, organization
sōshiki *n* 葬式 funeral
soshite *conj* そして, **sōshite** そうして and then
soshō *n* 訴訟 lawsuit
sōshoku *n* 装飾 ornament, decoration
sosogimásu, sosogu *v* 注ぎます, 注ぐ pours (*into*)
sō´su *n* ソース sauce, gravy
sotchí *pron* [INFORMAL] そっち = **sochira** そちら (there, that way; that one (*of two*); you)
sotchoku (na) *adj* 率直(な) frank
sóto *n* 外 outside, outdoors
sōtō (na) *adv, adj* 相当(な) **1.** quite, rather, fairly **2.** suitable, proper
soto-bori *n* 外堀 outer moat
soto-gawa *n* 外側 the outside: **~ (no)** 外側(の) external
sotsugyō *n* 卒業 graduation; sotsugyō´-sei *n* 卒業生 a graduate; sotsugyō´-shiki *n* 卒業式 commencement, graduation ceremony
Sóuru *n* ソウル Seoul
sō yū (sō iu)... *adj* [INFORMAL] そうゆう(そういう) ...that kind/sort of ...; such ... (= **sonna** そんな)
sōzō *n* 想像 imagination
sōzōshii *adj* 騒々しい noisy
su *n* 巣 nest
sú *n* 酢 vinegar; sú-no-mono *n* 酢の物 vinegared dishes; sú-buta *n* 酢豚 sweet and sour pork
sū´ *n* 数 number (= **kázu** 数); sū-gaku *n* 数学 mathematics (= **sansū** 算数); **~-sha** 数学者 mathematician; ū-ji *n* 数字 numeral, figure (= **kazu** 数)
sū´-... *prefix* 数... several; sū´-jitsu

n, adv 数日 several days; sū´-nen *n, adv* 数年 several years; sū´-nin *n* 数人 several people
subarashíi *adj* すばらしい・素晴しい wonderful, splendid; **subaráshiku** すばらしく・素晴らしく splendidly
subekkói *adj* すべっこい [INFORMAL] slippery, slick, smooth
suberí-dai *n* すべり台・滑り台 a slippery slide
suberimásu, subéru *v* 滑ります, 滑る slides, slips, skates
sube-sube (no) *adj* すべすべ(の) [INFORMAL] smooth, slippery
súbete n, *adv* すべて all
suchuwā´desu *n* スチュワーデス stewardess
suchuwā´do *n* スチュワード steward
sudare *n* すだれ・簾 curtain (*bamboo*)
sude *n* 素手 bare hands
súde ni *adv* すでに・既に already (**= mō´** もう)
sue *n* **1.** 末 end, close **2.** 末 future (**= shōrai** 将来): **… no yuku-~** . . . の行く末 one's future: **yuku-~ wa** 行く末は in the future
suemásu, sueru *v* 据えます, 据える sets it up
suemásu, sueru *v* 吸えます, 吸える can sip (*suck, smoke*)
suemásu, suéru *v* すえます, すえる it spoils, goes bad
súgata *n* 姿 form, figure, shape: **hare-~** 晴れ姿 one in his/her Sunday best
sugi *n* 杉 cryptomeria, Japanese cedar
...-sugi *suffix* …過ぎ past (*the hour*)
sugimásu, sugíru *v* 過ぎます, 過ぎる passes, exceeds; **(shi-)sugimásu** (し)過ぎます overdoes: *adj* ... **sugimásu** . . . 過ぎます is overly/excessively/too
sugói *adj* すごい・凄い **1.** swell, wonderful, marvelous, terrific **2.** fierce, dreadful, ghastly, weird, uncanny
súgóku *adv* すごく・凄く awfully, terribly
sugoshimásu, sugósu *v* 過ごします, 過ごす passes (*time*)
súgu (ni) *adv* すぐ(に) at once, right away, immediately; in a minute; directly, right (*there*)
sugureteimásu, suguréru *v* 優れています, 優れている excels: **(… ni/yóri) ~** (…に/より)優れています surpasses, is superior (*to*): is excellent; **sugúreta …** 優れた… excellent …
súgu sóba (ni) *adv* すぐそば(に) right near (at hand)
suichoku (no) *adj* 垂直(の) vertical; perpendicular
suidō *n* 水道 water system, water service, running water; plumbing; suidō-kan *n* 水道管 water pipe; suidō´-kyoku *n* 水道局 the Waterworks Bureau; municipal water service (*headquarters*); suidō-ya (san) *n* 水道屋(さん) plumber

suiei *n* 水泳 swimming; **~-jō** 水泳場 swimming pool; **suiéi-gí** *n* 水泳着 swimsuit (= **mizuki** 水着)
súifu *n* 水夫 seaman, sailor
súihei *n* 水兵 navy enlisted person, sailor, seaman
suihei (no) *adj* 水平(の) horizontal, level: **~-sen** 水平線 (*sea*) horizon
suii *n* 水位 water level
suijun *n* 水準 **1.** water level **2.** standard
suika *n* スイカ・西瓜 watermelon
Sui, Kin, Chi, Ka, Moku, Do, Ten, Kai 水金地火木土天海 (= 水星、金星、地球、火星、木星、土星、天王星、海王星) Mercury, Venus, Earth, Mars, Jupiter, Saturn, Uranus, Neptune (*eight planets in the solar system*)
suimásu, sū *v* 吸います, 吸う sips, sucks, smokes, breathes in
suimasén *interj* すいません. [INFORMAL] **1.** Excuse me. Sorry. **2.** Thank you. (= **sumimasén** すみません)
suimin *n* 睡眠 sleep; **~-zai** 睡眠剤, **~-yaku** 睡眠薬 sleeping pill(s)
sui-mono *n* 吸い物 clear soup
sui-sei *adj* 水性 water-based: **~-inku** 水性インク water based ink: **~-toryō** 水性塗料 water based paint
sui-sei *adj* 水生 aquatic: **~-dōbutsu** 水生動物 aquatic animal
Sui-sei *n* 彗星 comet: **Harē-~** ハレー彗星 Halley's comet
Sui-sei *n* 水星 Mercury
suisen *n* 水洗 flushing: **~-tóire** 水洗トイレ flush toilet
suisen *n* 推薦 recommendation; **suisen-jō** *n* 推薦状 letter of recommendation
súiso *n* 水素 hydrogen
suisō *n* 水槽 water tank
suisoku *n* 推測 conjecture, guess, surmisal, supposition
Súisu *n* スイス Switzerland; **Suisú-jin** *n* スイス人 a Swiss
suítchi *n* スイッチ switch; ignition switch: **~ o iremásu** スイッチを入れます turns/switches it on, turns on the ignition
suitei *n* 推定 inference, presumption, estimation
suitō-gákari *n* 出納係 cashier
suitorí-gami *n* 吸い取り紙 blotter
Suiyō´(bi) *n* 水曜(日) Wednesday
suizókukan *n* 水族館 aquarium
súji *n* 筋 tendon, muscle, fiber, line: **ao-~ o tatete okorimásu** 青筋を立てて怒ります turns purple with rage
...súji *suffix* . . . 筋 plot: **arasuji** あらすじ summary, outline, synopsis
sukā´fu *n* スカーフ scarf; (*military*) sash
sukā´to *n* スカート skirt
sukébē (na) *adj* 助平(な)・すけべえ(な)・スケベ(な) lecherous; lewd
sukē´to *n* スケート skate(s); skating: **~-bōdo** スケートボード skate board: **~-gutsu** スケート靴

(*a pair of*) skates

suki *n* すき・透き crack; opening; opportunity (= **suki-ma** すき間・透き間・隙間)

sukí (na) *adj* 好き(な) one's favorite

sukídesu, sukida *v* 好きです, 好きだ likes

sukíi *n* スキー ski, skiing

suki-ma *n* すき間・透き間・隙間 crack; opening; opportunity

sukimásu, suku *v* 空きます, 空く gets empty/clear

sukimásu, suku *v* 鋤きます, 鋤く plows

sukimásu, suku *v* すき[梳き]ます, すく・梳く combs

sukimásu, súku *v* 好きます, 好く → **sukídesu, sukida** 好きです, 好きだ

sukimu-míruku *n* スキムミルク skim milk

sukiyaki *n* すき焼き・すきやき thin-sliced beef cooked in an iron pan (*with leeks, mushrooms, bean curd, etc.*)

sukkári *adv* すっかり completely, all

sukóshi *adv* 少し a little, a bit: ~ **(no)** 少し(の) some, a few; some-what; ~ **mo** 少しも [+ NEGATIVE] not in the least; **~-zútsu** 少しずつ bit by bit, a little at a time, gradually

sukuimásu, sukū *v* 救います, 救う helps, rescues, saves

sukuimásu, sukū *v* すく[掬い]います, すくう・掬う scoops

sukunái *adj* 少ない few, meager, scarce, little

sukúnáku *adv* 少なく (*so as to be*) few, little

sukúnáku-tomo *adv* 少なくとも at (*the*) least

sukuranburu-éggu *n* スクランブルエッグ scrambled eggs

sukuríin *n* スクリーン (*movie*) screen

sukuwatto *n* スクワット squat (*bending and stretching exercises, power lifting, etc.*)

sukyándaru *n* スキャンダル scandal

súmái *n* 住まい residence

sumánai, sumimasén *v, interj* すまない, すみません **1.** it never ends **2.** Thank you **3.** Excuse me **4.** I apologize (for what I did).

sumasemásu, sumaséru *v* 済ませます, 済ませる finishes, concludes it

sumashimásu, sumásu *v* 済まします, 済ます **1.** finishes, concludes it **2.** puts up with (*things as they are*)

sumā'to (na) *adj* スマート(な) smart, stylish, fashionable

sumātofon *n* スマートフォン smartphone (*multifunctional mobile phone*)

súmi *n* 隅 an inside corner

sumí *n* 炭 charcoal

sumí *n* 墨 India ink, ink stick; **sumí-e** *n* 墨絵 Indian ink painting

sumimasén *v* すみません **1.** Excuse me. **2.** Sorry. **3.** Thank you.

sumimásu, súmu *v* 済みます, 済む comes to an end
sumimásu, súmu *v* 住みます, 住む lives, takes up residence, resides
sumire *n* スミレ・菫 violet
sumō *n* 相撲・すもう Japanese wrestling, sumo
sumomo *n* スモモ・李 plum
sumō´-tóri *n* 相撲取り a sumo wrestler
...-sún *suffix* ...寸 inch (*Japanese*)
suna *n* 砂 sand; suna-búkuro *n* 砂袋 sandbag
sunákku *n* スナック **1.** a snackshop **2.** an after-hours bar **3.** refreshment; sunakkú-gashi *n* スナック菓子 munch, snack
súnao (na) *adj* 素直(な) docile, gentle, obedient, submissive, meek
sunáwachi *adv* すなわち・即ち namely, to wit; that is to say; in other words
suné *n* すね・臑・脛 shin, leg
sunpō *n* 寸法 measurements
sū´pā(mā´ketto) *n* スーパー(マーケット) supermarket
supái *n* スパイ spy; supai-wea *n* スパイウェア spyware (*computer*)
supaisu *n* スパイス spice
supamu-mēru *n* スパムメール (= **meiwaku-mēru** 迷惑メール), spam mail, e-mail spam (*Internet*)
supána *n* スパナ wrench
supein *n* スペイン Spain; Supein-go *n* スペイン語 Spanish (*language*); Supeín-jín *n* スペイン人 Spaniard, a Spanish person
supéru *n* スペル spell (= **tsuzuri** つづり・綴り)
supēsu *n* スペース **1.** space (= **kūkan** 空間) **2.** blank (= **kūhaku** 空白)
supíido *n* スピード speed: **kokusai -~-yūbin** 国際スピード郵便 EMS (*Express Mail Service*)
supíikā *n* スピーカー (loud)speaker
suponji *n* スポンジ sponge; swab: **~-kēki** スポンジケーキ sponge cake
suponsā *n* スポンサー **1.** sponsor **2.** patron
supō´tsu *n* スポーツ sport(s), athletics (= **undō** 運動)
suppái *adj* すっぱい[酸っぱい] sour, acid: **~-aji** すっぱい[酸っぱい]味 sour flavor, sour taste (= **san-mi** 酸味)
suppon *n* すっぽん・スッポン snapping turtle
supponpon *n* すっぽんぽん (INFORMAL, *slang*) full monty, complete nudity
sū´pu *n* スープ soup
supū´n *n* スプーン spoon
surákkusu *n* スラックス slacks
suremásu, suréru *v* 擦れます, 擦れる **1.** it rubs/grazes **2.** can rub/graze
súri *n* すり・スリ・掏り pick-pocket
suríbachi *n* すり鉢 earthenware mortar with wooden pestle
surii *n* スリー three

surimásu̱, súru *v* 擦ります, 擦る rubs

surimásu̱, súru *v* 摺り[擂り]ます, 摺る[擂る] files; grinds

surimásu̱, súru *v* 刷ります, 刷る prints

surimásu̱, súru *v* すります, する picks one's pocket

suríppa *n* スリッパ slippers

suríppu *n* スリップ slip(ping); **"Surippu-jíko ō´shi"** スリップ事故多し Slippery (*Area*)

Suriránka *n* スリランカ Sri Lanka

súriru *n* スリル thrill

surō´gan *n* スローガン slogan

surō´ (na) *adj* スロー(な) slow

surō´pu *n* スロープ ramp

surudói *adj* 鋭い sharp, acute

surume *n* スルメ dried cuttlefish

sushi *n* すし・スシ・寿司・鮨 sushi (*rice seasoned with sweetened vinegar with raw fish*)

su̱shí-ya *n* 寿司[鮨]屋 a sushi bar

su̱so *n* すそ・裾 hem

sú̱su *n* すす・煤 soot

su̱sumemásu̱, su̱sumeru *v* 進めます, 進める furthers, advances

su̱sumemásu̱, su̱sumeru *v* 勧めます, 勧める encourages, recommends, advises, counsels; persuades, urges

su̱sumimásu̱, susumu *v* 進みます, 進む goes forward, progresses; goes too fast, gets ahead

su̱tā *n* スター star (*actor*)

su̱tajio *n* スタジオ studio

su̱tando *n* スタンド **1.** stand (*for selling things*) **2.** (= **denki̱** ~ 電気スタンド) desk/floor lamp

su̱te *v* 捨て → **su̱temásu̱**; **su̱te-ba** *n* 捨て場 dump site (= **gomi-~** ごみ捨て場); **su̱te-mi (de)** *adv* 捨て身(で) in desperation

su̱teki (na) *adj* すてき[素敵](な) fine, splendid, swell

su̱tē´ki *n* ステーキ (*beef*) steak: **~-sando** ステーキサンド steak sandwich

su̱tékki *n* ステッキ walking stick, cane

su̱temásu̱, su̱teru *v* 捨てます, 捨てる throws away, abandons, dumps

su̱tereo *n* ステレオ stereo (*sound/player*)

su̱tēshon *n* ステーション railroad station (= **eki** 駅)

su̱tó *n* スト = **su̱toráiki** ストライキ strike (*job action*)

su̱tō´bu *n* ストーブ stove, heater

su̱tōkā *n* ストーカー stalker

su̱toráiku *n* ストライク strike (*baseball*)

su̱tóresu *n* ストレス stress, tension: **~-kaishō** ストレス解消 stress relieving, stress release

su̱toretchi *n* ストレッチ stretch (*exercises*)

su̱toríppu *n* ストリップ striptease, strip show, burlesque

su̱tórō *n* ストロー straw (*to drink with*)

sū´tsu *n* スーツ suit

sūtsu̱kē´su *n* スーツケース suitcase

suwaremásu̱, suwareru *v* 座れます,

座れる can sit; seats are available

suwarikomi(-súto) *n* 座り込み(スト) sit-in (*strike*)

suwarimásu, suwaru *v* 座ります, 座る sits (*especially Japanese style*)

suzu *n* スズ・鈴 little bells

súzu *n* スズ・錫 tin

suzuki *n* スズキ・鱸 sea bass

suzume *n* スズメ・雀 sparrow

suzumé-bachi *n* スズメバチ・スズメ蜂 hornet

suzurí *n* すずり・硯 inkstone: **~-bako** すずり[硯]箱 inkstone case

suzushíi *adj* 涼しい cool

sy... → **sh...**

T

tá *n* た・他 = **hoka** 他, **sono-ta, sono-hoka** その他 other(s); **ta-hō´** *n* 他方 a different direction, an-other place: **~ de wa** 他方では on the other hand; **tá (ni)** *adv* 他(に) to/for/as others, additionally (= **hoka (ni)** 他[外](に)); **ta-nin** *n* 他人 outsider, stranger; others (*people*); **tá (no)** *adj* 他(の) = **hoka (no)** 他[外](の) other; **tá-sha** *n* 他社 other companies; **tá-sha** *n* 他者 [BOOKISH] others (*people*) (= **ta-nin** 他人)

tá *n* 田 rice field (= **tanbo** 田んぼ); **ta-nbo** *n* 田んぼ rice field [INFORMAL]; **ta-ué** *n* 田植え rice planting

...-ta *v* ...た = **...-máshita** ...ました did

tába *n* 束 bundle, bunch: **satsu-~** 札束 bundle of bills

tabako *n* タバコ・煙草 tobacco; cigarettes (= **shigaretto** シガレット); **tabakó-ire** *n* タバコ[煙草]入れ cigarette case

tā´ban *n* ターバン turban

tabemásu, tabéru *v* 食べます, 食べる eats (= **shokuji o shimásu** 食事をします)

tabé-mónó *n* 食べ物 food (= **shoku-motsu** 食物)

tabesasemásu, tabesaséru *v* 食べさせます, 食べさせる feeds

tábi *n* たび・タビ・足袋 split-toe socks

tabí *n* 旅 journey (= **ryokō** 旅行)

tabí *n* 度・たび time, occasion; **... ~ (ni)** ...度[たび](に) every time that ...

tabitabi *adv* たびたび・度々 often (= **shibashiba** しばしば, **nando-mo** 何度も)

tabō (na) *adj* 多忙(な) [BOOKISH] busy (= **isogashíi** 忙しい)

tábu *n* タブ a tab

tabū *n* タブー taboo (= **kinki** 禁忌, **go-hatto** ご法度)

tábun *adv* たぶん・多分 probably, likely; perhaps, maybe (**~ ... deshō´** たぶん ...でしょう, **~ ... ká mo shiremasén** たぶん ...か

も知れません)

tabun (ni) *adv* 多分(に) [BOOKISH] a lot, much

taburetto *n* タブレット **1.** tablet **2.** Tablet PC

taburoido *n* タブロイド tabloid

táchi *n* たち・質 nature, disposition

...´-tachi *suffix* ...達・たち [*animate plural*]; and others: **watashi-~** わたし達[私達] we: **anata-~** あなた達 you (*people*): **kimi-~** 君たち[達] you guys

tachi-agarimásu, tachi-agaru *v* 立ち上がります, 立ち上がる rises, stands up

tachi-bá *n* 立場 viewpoint, standpoint, situation

tachi-domarimásu, tachi-domaru *v* 立ち止まります, 立ち止まる comes to a stand

"Tachiiri kinshi" *n* 立ち入り禁止. No Trespassing. Off Limits.

tachimachi *adv* たちまち immediately, instantly

tachimásu, tátsu *v* 立ちます, 立つ stands (up); **tachi-bánashi** *n* 立ち話 (*wayside*) a stand for talking/chatting; **tachi-mi** *n* 立ち見 a stand for watching: **~-seki** 立ち見席 the gallery, standing room

tachimásu, tátsu *v* 発ちます, 発つ leaves (*for a far place*) (= **shuppatsu shimásu** 出発します)

tachimásu, tátsu *v* 経ちます, 経つ elapses

tachimásu, tátsu *v* 断ちます, 断つ [BOOKISH] cuts off

táda *n* ただ free, gratis, no fee/charge (= **muryō** 無料)

tádachi ni *adv* ただちに [BOOKISH] immediately

tadáima *adv* ただいま just now; in a minute (= **tatta-íma** たった今);

Tadaima *interj* ただいま I'm back!, I'm home! (*said on returning to one's residence*)

táda (no) *adj* ただ(の) **1.** only, just **2.** ordinary

tádashi *conj* 但し provided

tadashii *adj* 正しい right; correct; **tadáshiku** 正しく rightly, correctly

tadotadoshii *adj* たどたどしい halting, not smooth

taema-náku *adv* 絶え間なく continuously, without interruption

taemásu, taéru *v* 堪えます, 堪える bears, puts up with

taemásu, taéru *v* 絶えます, 絶える ceases

táezu *adv* 絶えず continuously, without interruption (= **taema-náku** 絶え間なく)

tagá *n* たが a barrel hoop

tagai (no) *adj* 互い(の) mutual, reciprocal, for each other

tagai (ni) *adv* 互い(に) mutually, reciprocally, with each other

tagaku *n* 多額 large sum

...-tagarimásu, -tagaru *suffix, v* ...たがります, ...たがる wants to ..., is eager to ...

tagayashimásu, tagayásu *v* 耕します, 耕す plows

tāgetto *n* ターゲット object, target

agu-bōto *n* タグボート tug boat
ái *n* タイ・鯛 sea bream, red snapper
Tái *n* タイ Thailand; Tai-go *n* タイ語 Thai (*language*); Tai-jin *n* タイ人 a Thai
ái *n* 体 form
ai-... *prep* 対…, **…´-tai** …対 versus, towards, against; **rokú-~ yón** 六対四, 6対4 4 to 6 (*score*)
ai-... *prefix* 退. . . leaving, retire; tai-gaku *n* 退学 ① leaving school: **chūto-~-sha** 中途退学者 a drop-out ② expulsion from school (= **~-shobun** 退学(処分)); tai-i *n* 退位 abdication; tai-in *n* 退院 leaving the hospital; tai-shoku *n* 退職 retirement: **~-kin** 退職金 retirement allowance: **~-nenkin** 退職年金 (*retirement*) pension
tai-... *prefix* 大. . . great, large; tai-bō, tai-mō *n* 大望 ambition, great willingness (= **taishi** 大志); tai-ryō *n* 大量 large quantity: **~-seisan** 大量生産 mass production; tai-sa *n* 大佐 (*army*) colonel; (= **daisa** 大佐) (*navy*) captain; tái-sa *n* 大差 [BOOKISH] a great difference: ~ **de kachimásu** 大差で勝ちます wins by a wide margin; tai-sen *n* 大戦 a great war, a world war: **dai-ichi-ji sekai-~** 第一次世界大戦 World War I; tai-shi *n* 大志 ambition (= **taibō, taimō** 大望); tái-shō *n* 大将 (*general*) admiral: **o-yama no ~** お山の大将 king of the mountain; tai-shoku *n* 大食 gluttony (= **ōgui** 大食い); tái-sō *adj, adv* たいそう・大層 [BOOKISH] very: ~ **(na)** たいそう(な) a great many/much
...-tái *suffix* . . . 帯 belt; zone: **anet-~** 亜熱帯 subtropical zone: **anzen chi-~** 安全地帯 safety zone: **kiken chi-~** 危険地帯 danger zone
...-tai *suffix v* …たい wants to, is eager to; tabe-tai *suffix v* 食べたい wants to eat; shi-tai *suffix v* したい: **shi~ hōdai ni shimásu** したい放題にします does whatever one feels like doing [IN NEGATIVE SENSE]
taibō (no) *adj* 待望(の) long-awaited
taichō *n* 体調 (*physical condition*) tone (= **guai** 具合): ~ **ga ii/yoi** 体調がいい/良い is in good health condition; ~ **ga warui** 体調が悪い is in poor health condition
taidan *n* 対談 [BOOKISH] conversation between two people, dialogue; **~-bangumi** 対談番組 TV talk show
táido *n* 態度 attitude, disposition, behavior: ~ **ga ōkii** 態度が大きい acts big; **kudaketa ~** くだけた態度 friendly attitude
taifū´ *n* 台風 typhoon
taigai *adv* 大概・たいがい **1.** in general; for the most part; practically (= **taitei** たいてい・大抵) **2.** probably, like(ly), like as not
taigū *n* 待遇 **1.** treatment, reception **2.** pay, working conditions **3.** official position, post

taihai-teki (na) *adj* 退廃的(な) decadent

Taihéiyō *n* 太平洋 Pacific Ocean (→ **taiyō** 大洋) **Taiheiyō-sensō** *n* 太平洋戦争 Pacific War

taihen *adv* たいへん・大変 **1.** very, exceedingly, terribly, enormously (= **hijō ni** 非常に): **Taihen osewa ni narimáshita.** 大変お世話になりました I owe you a lot., Thank you so much for everything you have done for me. **2.** laboriously, seriously, disastrously: **sorewa (hontō ni) ~ desu ne** それは(本当に)大変ですね It must be (*really*) hard for you.

taihen (na) *adj* たいへん[大変](な) **1.** exceeding, enormous: **~ na bijin desu** 大変な美人です is very beautiful **2.** serious, disastrous, tough, terrible, difficult: **~ na shigoto desu** 大変な仕事です is tough work

taihi *n* 対比 [BOOKISH] contrast, comparison

táiho *n* 逮捕 arrest(ing)

taihō *n* 大砲 cannon

táii *n* 大尉 captain (*army*); lieutenant (*navy*) (= **dáii** 大尉)

taii *n* 大意 [BOOKISH] outline, summary, drift: **~ o tsukamimásu** 大意をつかみます catches the drift

taii *n* 体位 body position, posture (= **shisei** 姿勢)

tái(i)ku *n* 体育 physical education, athletics; **tai(i)kú-kan** *n* 体育館 gymnasium

taiji *n* 胎児 fetus, unborn baby, embryo

taiji *n* 退治 extermination: **oni-~** 鬼退治 demon extermination

taijū *n* 体重 body weight: **shinchō to ~** 身長と体重 height and weight: **~-kei** 体重計 scales

táika *n* 大家 authority

táika *n* 対価 compensation, consideration

táika *n* 退化 degeneration

taikai *n* 大会 mass meeting; convention, conference; tournament: **sekai-senshuken-~** 世界選手権大会 world championships

taikái *n* 大海 ocean, high sea (= **taiyō** 大洋)

taikaku *n* 体格 body build, physique

taikei *n* 体系 a system

taiken *n* 体験 personal experience

taiko *n* 太鼓 (*Japanese*) drum

taikō *n* 対抗 confrontation, opposition; **... ni ~ shite** …に対抗して in opposition to, against, in rivalry with

taikutsu (na) *adj* 退屈(な) boring, dull

taiman (na) *adj* 怠慢(な) negligent, careless, neglectful

táimatsu *n* たいまつ・松明 torch

taimen *n* 対面 interview

taimen *n* 体面 one's dignity, sense of honor, "face": **~ o tamochimásu** 体面を保ちます keeps up appearances

taiō *n* 対応 **1.** correspondence, handling **2.** equivalent (= **sōō** 相

応): **(… ni) ~ shimásu** (…に)対応します is equivalent (*to*)

ion *n* 体温 body temperature; **~-kei** 体温計 (*clinical*) thermometer

aipo *n* タイポ typo, typing error

áipu *n* タイプ **1.** type, style (= **kata** 型): **atarashii ~** 新しいタイプ new type (= **shin-gata** 新型) **2.** one's type **3.** typewriting, typewriter

aipuráitā *n* タイプライター typewriter

airagemásu, tairageru *v* 平らげます, 平らげる [INFORMAL] eats up

aira-gi *n* タイラギ pin/razor/fan shell (*a kind of scallop*)

aira (na) *adj* 平ら(な) even, flat, smooth

airiku *n* 大陸 continent: **~ (no)** 大陸(の) continental

airitsu *n* 対立 confrontation, opposition, antagonism

áiru *n* タイル tile (*floor, wall*) (*made of plastic, etc.*)

airyoku *n* 体力 stamina: **~ ga arimásu** 体力があります has stamina

aisei *n* 体制 system: **seiji-~** 政治体制 political system: **kyōiku-~** 教育体制 education system

aisei *n* 体勢 posture (= **shisei** 姿勢): **~ o kuzushimásu** 体勢を崩します loses one's balance

aisei *n* 耐性 tolerance: **yakubutsu-~** 薬物耐性 drug resistance

aisei *n* 大勢 general situation

taisei *n* 態勢 preparedness: **~ ga totonoimásu** 態勢が整います is ready

Taiséiyō *n* 大西洋 Atlantic Ocean (→ **taiyō** 大洋)

taisen *n* 対戦 match, competition: **~-aite** 対戦相手 one's opponent

taisetsu (na) *adj* 大切(な) **1.** important: **~ na shorui** 大切な書類 important documents **2.** valuable, precious: **~ na omoide** 大切な思い出 precious memories

taisetsu-ni-shimásu (suru) *v* 大切にします(する) cherishes, treats carefully, gives importance (= **daiji-ni-shimásu** 大事にします): **kazoku o ~** 家族を大切にします gives importance to family

táishaku *n* 貸借 debit and credit, lending and borrowing; **táishaku-taishō hyō** *n* 貸借対照表 balance sheet (B/S)

táishi *n* 大使 ambassador; **taishí-kan** *n* 大使館 embassy

tai-shimásu, tai-súru *v* 対します, 対する: **(… ni) ~** (…に)対します confronts, opposes; **… ni tái-shite** …に対して ① against; toward; as against, as compared with, in contrast to ② with respect to, in regard to

tái-shita … *adj* たいした・大した… important; serious; immense

taishitsu *n* 体質 (*physical*) constitution

taisho *n* 対処 handling of matters

taishō *n* 対象 object, target

taishō *n* 対照 contrast: **hikaku-~** 比較対照 comparison and contrast (→ táishaku-taishō-hyō 貸借対照表)

taishō *n* 対称 symmetry: **sayū-~** 左右対称 bilateral symmetry: **... to ~ o nashimásu** ... と対称をなします is symmetrical to ...

Táishō-jidai *n* 大正時代 Taisho Period (*1912–1926*)

taishū *n* 体臭 body odor (BO)

taishū *n* 大衆 the general public, the masses: **~ (no)** 大衆(の) popular, mass

taisō *n* 体操 calisthenics, physical exercises

taitei *adv* たいてい・大抵 usually: **~ no ...** たいていの ... the usual ..., most ...

taitō (no) *adj* 対等(の) equal, equivalent

táitoru *n* タイトル **1.** title (= **hyōdai** 表題) **2.** title, championship: **~-matchi** タイトルマッチ title match **3.** caption, subtitle (= **jimaku** 字幕)

taiwa *n* 対話 conversation, dialogue

Taiwán *n* 台湾 Taiwan; **Taiwan-jín** 台湾人 a Taiwanese

taiya *n* タイヤ a tire: **kuruma no ~** 車のタイヤ car tires

taiyō *n* 大洋 ocean: **go-~** 五大洋 five oceans (*Pacific Ocean, Indian Ocean, Atlantic Ocean, Arctic Ocean, Antarctic Ocean*)

taiyō *n* 大要 summary (= **gaiyō** 概要, **yōyaku** 要約, **samarii** サマリー)

táiyō *n* 太陽 **1.** sun **2.** joy to someone; taiyō-enerugii *n* 太陽エネルギー solar energy; taiyō-kei *n* 太陽系 solar system; táiyō-kōsen 太陽光線; táiyō no hikari 太陽の光 sunshine

taiyō-nensū *n* 耐用年数 lifespan of a thing, expected lifetime

taiyō-sei *n* 耐用性 durability

taizai *n* 滞在 a stay (*away from home*), a sojourn: **~-saki** 滞在先 place of sojourn

taka *n* タカ・鷹 hawk; taka no tsume *n* タカノツメ・鷹の爪 red pepper

táká *n* 高 quantity: **~ ga shiretei-másu** 高が知れています is limited, not amount to a hill of beans

takaga *adj* たかが no(thing) more than

takái *adj* 高い high, tall; costly, expensive; loud

takará *n* 宝 a treasure (= **takara-mono** 宝物); takará-kuji *n* 宝くじ lottery; takara-mono *n* 宝物 a treasure

tákasa *n* 高さ height (= **kōdo** 高度)

take *n* 竹 bamboo; take-fū'rin *n* 竹風鈴 bamboo wind-chimes

take *n* タケ・茸 (*compounds/dialect*) mushroom (= **kínoko** キノコ)

taki *n* 滝 waterfall

takigi *n* たきぎ・薪 firewood, fuel

takimásu, taku *v* 焚きます, 焚く makes a fire; taki-bi *n* 焚き火 bonfire; taki-tsuke *n* 焚き付け kindling

akimásu, taku *v* 炊きます, 炊く cooks; burns it; takikomi-góhan *n* 炊き込みご飯 a rice dish with seasonal ingredients added

akishiido *n* タキシード tuxedo

akkuru *n* タックル tackle

áko *n* タコ octopus; tako-yaki *n* たこ焼き griddled dumplings with octopus bits inside

áko *n* 凧・たこ kite; takó-ágé *n* 凧揚げ kite-flying

áko *n* たこ callus, corn

akokuseki (no) *adj* 多国籍(の) multinational: **~-kigyō** 多国籍企業 multinational company

aku *n* 宅 **1.** my house **2.** (*your/someone else's*) house (**= o-taku** お宅) **3.** [HUMBLE] my husband; tak-kyū-bin *n* 宅急便 express delivery service; taku-hai-bin *n* 宅配便 delivery service

aku *n* 卓 table, desk; tak-kyū *n* 卓球 table tennis; taku-jō *n, adv* 卓上 on one's table/desk

akúan, takúwan *n* たくあん, たくわん yellow pickles made from sliced daikon

takumashii *adj* たくましい・逞しい **1.** strong, robust (*body*) **2.** strong (*will*)

takumi *n* 巧み skill; takumi na *adj* 巧み(な) skillful; takumi ni *adv* 巧みに skillfully

takurami *n* 企み plan, scheme, plot

takuramimásu, takurámu *v* 企みます, 企む plans, schemes, plots

takuránde *adv* 企んで **1.** intentionally, on purpose, with forethought **2. (… to takuránde)** …と企んで in collusion/cahoots with …

takusán (no) *adj* たくさん[沢山](の) lots (*of*), much/many, a lot (*of*)

tákushii *n* タクシー taxi: **~ (no) untenshu** タクシー(の)運転手 taxi driver: **~-dai** タクシー代 taxi fare

takuwae *n* 蓄え savings, a reserve, a stock (**= chochiku** 貯蓄)

takuwaemásu, takuwaéru *v* 蓄えます, 蓄える saves up, hoards

takúwan *n* たくわん, **takuan** たくあん yellow pickles made from sliced daikon

tamá *n* **1.** 玉 **1.** ball: **keito no ~** 毛糸の玉 ball of wool: **pachinko no ~** パチンコの玉 pachinko ball **2.** round thing: **~ no ase** 玉の汗 beads of sweat **3.** testicle(s) **4.** precious and/or lovely thing: **~ no yō na akanbō/aka-chan** 玉のような赤ん坊/赤ちゃん sweetest baby

tamá *n* 玉・珠 jewel; bead; drop: **ryū no ~** 竜[龍]の玉 dragon ball

tamá *n* 球 **1.** globe (**= chikyū** 地球) **2.** (*light*) bulb (**= denkyū** 電球)

tamá *n* 弾 bullet (**= dangan** 弾丸): **pisutoru no ~** ピストルの弾 pistol bullet

tamágo *n* 卵・玉子・タマゴ egg: **~ no kara** 卵の殻 eggshell

tama-négi *n* タマネギ・玉葱 onion (*round bulb*)

tama (no/ni) *adj*, *adv* たま(の/に) occasional(ly), infrequent(ly), now and then, once in a while
tamari *n* 溜まり・たまり → **tamari-ba** たまり場
tamari-ba *n* たまり場 a gathering place (*hangout, haunt*)
tamarimásu, tamaru *v* 溜まります, 溜まる it accumulates
tamarimásu, tamaru *v* 貯まります, 貯まる it saves (*money*)
támashii *n* 魂 soul
tamatama たまたま occasionally
tamá-tsukí *n* 玉突き billiards; **tamá-tsukí jiko** *n* 玉突き事故 pileup
... tanbí (ni) *suffix*, *adv* [INFORMAL] …たんび(に), **tabí (ni)** 度・たび(に) every time that …
... tamé *suffix* …為・ため **1.** for the sake (*good, benefit*) of **2.** for the purpose of **3.** because (*of*), due to
tameiki *n* ため息 sigh
tamemásu, tameru *v* 溜めます, 溜める amasses/accumulates
tamemásu, tameru *v* 貯めます, 貯める saves (*money*)
tameraimásu, tameráu *v* ためらいます, ためらう hesitates
tameshí *n* 試し trial, test, experiment: **~ ni** 試しに as a trial/test
tameshimásu, tamésu *v* 試します, 試す tries, attempts, experiments with
tāminaru *n* ターミナル terminal: **narita-kūkō dai-ichi-~ kita/minami wingu** 成田空港第1ターミナル北/南ウィング Narita Airport Terminal 1 North/South Wing
ta-minzoku (no) *adj* 多民族(の) multiracial: **~-kokka** 多民族国家 multiracial country
tamochimásu, tamótsu *v* 保ちます, 保つ keeps, preserves, maintains
tamotó *n* たもと・袂 sleeve; edge end
tamushi *n* 田虫 ringworm; athlete's foot
...´-tan *suffix* …反 bolt (*of cloth*)
tana *n* 棚 shelf, rack; **tana-age** *n* 棚上げ shelving: **mondai o ~ shimásu** 問題を棚上げします shelves the issue; **tana kara bota-mochi** *n* 棚からぼた餅 windfall; **tana-oroshi** *n* 棚卸し stocktaking
Tanabata *n* 七夕・たなばた the Festival of the Weaver Star (*7 July*)
tandoku *n* 単独 alone (= **tanshin** 単身): **~-kōdō** 単独行動 independent action
táne *n* 種 **1.** seed **2.** source, cause **3.** material **4.** secret, trick to it **5. hanashi no ~** 話の種 subject, topic
tango *n* 単語 word(s), vocabulary
tango *n* タンゴ tango (*music*); **Tángo no sekku** *n* 端午の節句 Boys' Festival (5 May)
tani, tani-ma *n* 谷, 谷間 valley
tán'i *n* 単位 unit
tanitsu-minzoku *n* 単一民族 single race
tanjō´bi *n* 誕生日 birthday: 誕生日パーティ birthday party

tanjun (na) *adj* 単純(な) simple; simplehearted, simpleminded (*not complicated*): **~-ka** 単純化 simplification: **~-meikai** 単純明快 simple and clear

tánka *n* 短歌 31-syllable poem (*traditional Japanese poem*)

tánka *n* 担架 stretcher, litter: **~ de hakobaremásu** 担架で運ばれます is carried on a stretcher

tánka *n* 単価 unit cost, unit price

tánka *n* 啖呵 [BOOKISH] caustic words (*during a quarrel*)

tanki *n* 短期 short period; **tanki-dáigaku** *n* 短期大学 junior college, two-year college

tankō *n* 炭鉱 coal mine

tanmatsu *n* 端末 computer terminal

tanmono *n* 反物 draperies, dry goods

tán naru ... *adj* 単なる... only, mere [BOOKISH] = **táda no** ただの

tán ni *adv* 単に: **~ ... dake/nomi** 単に...だけ/のみ only, merely (= **táda** ただ)

tannin *n* 担任 (*teacher*) in charge

tanomí *n* 頼み a request: **~ no tsuna** 頼みの綱 one's one and only hope, lifesaver

tanomimásu, tanómu *v* 頼みます, 頼む **1.** requests, begs **2.** relies upon, entrusts with **3.** hires, engages (*a professional*)

tanoshíi *adj* 楽しい pleasant, enjoyable

tanoshími *n* 楽しみ a pleasure, an enjoyment; **... (surú no) o ~ ni shimásu** ...(するの)を楽しみにします ① takes pleasure in (*doing*) ② looks foward to …ing

tanoshimimásu, tanoshímu *v* 楽しみます楽しむ enjoys, takes pleasure in

tanpakú-shitsu *n* 蛋白質・たんぱく質 protein

tanpen-shōsetsu *n* 短編小説 short story (*novel*)

tánpo *n* 担保 mortgage, pledge (= **teitō** 抵当): **butteki-~** 物的担保 collateral on property: **jinteki-~** 人的担保 guarantee: **~-bukken** 担保物件 collateral

tánpon *n* タンポン tampon

tánpopo *n* タンポポ・たんぽぽ dandelion

tansan *n* 炭酸 carbonic acid; **tansán-sui** *n* 炭酸水 soda water

tanseki *n* 胆石 gall stone

tanshi *n* 端子 a terminal (*electronics*)

tanshin *n* 単身 [BOOKISH] alone (= **tandoku** 単独); **tanshin-funin** *n* 単身赴任 job transfer away from one's home

tánsho *n* 短所 shortcoming, fault, weak point: **~ to chōsho** 短所と長所 weak and strong points

tansu *n* たんす・タンス・箪笥 chest of drawers

tantei *n* 探偵 detective: **~-shōsetsu** 探偵小説 detective fiction: **shiritsu-~** 私立探偵 private eye

tantō *n* 担当 responsibility, charge; **tantō´-sha** *n* 担当者 person in charge, responsible person (→ **tannin** 担任)

tantō-chokunyū (na) *adj* 単刀直入(な) point-blank: ~ **ni iu to** *adv* 単刀直入に言うと put bluntly

tánuki *n* タヌキ・狸 **1.** raccoon-dog (*not* badger **anaguma** 穴熊) **2.** sly person

tánzén *n* 丹前 padded bathrobe

taoremásu, taoréru *v* 倒れます, 倒れる falls down, tumbles, collapses

táoru *n* タオル towel

taoshimásu, taósu *v* 倒します, 倒す knocks down, overthrows

tapesutorii *n* タペストリー tapestry

tappú-dansu *n* タップダンス tap dance

tappúri *adv* たっぷり fully, more than enough

tára *n* タラ・鱈 cod (*fish*)

...-tára *suffix, conj* ...たら if, when

tarafuku *adv* たらふく [INFORMAL] (*eat, drink*) one's fill

tarai *n* たらい tub, basin; tarai-mawashi ni saremásu *n* たらい回しにされます is shifted from one section to another

tarako *n* タラコ・鱈子 cod roe

taráppu *n* タラップ gangway

tarashimásu, tarásu *v* 垂らします, 垂らす dangles, drops, spills

tarashimásu, tarásu *v* たらします, たらす = **tarashi-komimásu** たらし込みます, **tarashi-komu** たらし込む seduces; wheedles

taré *n* たれ・タレ gravy, (*cooking*) sauce

taremásu, taréru *v* 垂れます, 垂れる hangs down, dangles; drips

tarento *n* タレント a TV personality, (*person of*) talent

...tári (shimásu/desu) ...たり(します/です) doing representatively/sometimes/alternately: **tári ...-nákáttari** ...たり...なかったり doing off and on, sometimes does and sometimes doesn't

tarimásu, tariru *v* 足ります, 足りる is enough/sufficient, suffices

taru *n* たる・樽 barrel, keg, cask

taru *v* 足る [*dialect, literary*] → **tarimásu** 足ります (is enough/sufficient, suffices)

tāru *n* タール tar: **kōru-~** コール・タール coal tar: **sekiyu-~** 石油タール petroleum tar

tarumimásu, tarumu *v* 弛みます, 弛む gets slack (*loose*), relaxed

taryō *n* 多量 large quantity

táshika *adv* 確か if I remember rightly, probably; táshika ni *adj* 確かに for sure, surely, undoubtedly; indeed; táshika na *adv* 確かな safe, sure, certain

tashikamemásu, tashikaméru *v* 確かめます, 確かめる makes sure, ascertains

tashimásu, tasu *v* 足します, 足す **1.** adds; **ní ni san o ~** 二に三を足します adds three to two, adds three and two **2. yō o ~** 用を足します does one's business, relieves oneself, goes to the bathroom

tashō *adj* 多少 **1.** (*large and/or small*) number, quantity, amount **2. ~ (no)** 多少(の) more or less; somewhat; some

tasogare *n* たそがれ・黄昏 twilight (= **yūgure** 夕暮れ)

tassha (na) *adj* 達者(な) healthy; skillful, expert, good at

tas-shimásu, tas-suru *v* 達します, 達する accomplishes; reaches

tasū´ *n* 多数 large number; majority

tasukarimásu, tasukáru *v* 助かります, 助かる is saved; is relieved

tasukemásu, tasukéru *v* 助けます, 助ける **1.** helps **2.** saves

tatakaimásu, tatakau *v* 戦います, 戦う fights; makes war/game: **teki to ~** 敵と戦います battles an enemy

tatakaimásu, tatakau *v* 闘います, 闘う struggle, fights (*with, against*): **byōki to ~** 病気と闘います fights the disease

tatakí *n* **1.** 叩き pounding; bashing; mincing; **Nihon-~** 日本叩き Japan-bashing **2.** たたき concrete/cement floor

tatakimásu, tatáku *v* 叩きます, 叩く strikes, hits, knocks; pounds (*fish/meat to tenderize or mince it*), minces; **té o ~** 手を叩きます claps

tatami *n* 畳 floor mat(ting), matted floor

tatamimásu, tatamu *v* 畳みます, 畳む folds up

tátchi *n* タッチ touch; **~ no sa de** タッチの差で by the turn of a hair

tate *n* 縦 length, height, longitudine; **tate-gaki** *n* 縦書き vertical writing; **tate-ito** *n* 縦糸 warp (*vertical threads*); **táte no** 縦の *adj* vertical; **táte ni** 縦に *adv* vertically, lengthwise

...-tate (no) *adj* …たて(の) fresh from …

taté-fuda *n* 立(て)札 signboard

tatekaemás<u>u</u>, tatekaeru 建(て)替えます, 建(て)替える rebuilds: **tate-kae** *n* 建(て)替え reconstruction, rebuilding

tatekaemásu, tatekaeru 立(て)替えます, 立(て)替える pays for someone; **tatekae** *n* 立(て)替え paying for someone; **tatekae-kin** *n* 立(て)替え金 advance money

tatémae *n* 建て前 principle, policy

tate-mashi *n* 建て増し house addition/extension, annex

tatemás<u>u</u>, tatéru *v* 建てます, 建てる erects, builds, raises; sets up, establishes

taté-móno *n* 建物 building

tatoé *conj* たとえ even if

tatóe 例え・たとえ *n* example, instance; simile, analogy

tatóeba *adv* 例えば・たとえば for example, for instance

tatoemás<u>u</u>, tatoéru *v* 例えます・喩えます, 例える・喩える gives an example, compares (*draws a simile to*)

tatsu *n* 竜・龍 dragon (= **doragon** ドラゴン)
tatsu no otoshigo *n* タツノオトシゴ・竜の落とし子 sea horse (= **umi-uma, kaiba** 海馬)
tatta *adv* たった just, merely, only
tatta-íma *n, adv* たった今 just now; in (*just*) a minute
tawā *n* タワー tower, pagoda (= **tō** 塔); **Tōkyō-~** 東京タワー Tokyo Tower
tawará *n* たわら・俵 straw bag; bale
tawashi *n* たわし scrub(bing) brush; swab
tayasúku *adv* たやすく easily
táyori 頼り *n* reliance: **~ nai** 頼りない undependable, unreliable
táyori *n* 便り communication, correspondence, a letter, word (*from someone*), news; **kaze no ~** 風の便り a little bird, rumor
tayorimásu, tayóru *v* 頼ります, 頼る relies on, depends on
tayō-sei *n* 多様性 diversity: **seibutsu-~ no hozen** 生物多様性の保全 biodiversity conservatory
tazuna *n* 手綱 reins: **~ o shimemásu** 手綱を締めます tightens the reins
tazunemásu, tazunéru *v* **1.** 尋ねます, 尋ねる asks (*a question*) **2.** 尋ねます, 尋ねる looks for
tazunemásu, tazunéru *v* 訪ねます, 訪ねる visits
té *n* 手 **1.** hand, arm **2.** trick, move **3.** kind **4.** person **5.** help: **té ni** 手に; **sore ga ~ ni hairimásu** それが手に入ります = **sore o ~ ni iremásu** それを手に入れます obtains, gets it; **te-árai** *n* 手洗い ① hand wash ② **o-teárai** お手洗い washroom, rest room, toilet (**toire** トイレ); **té-ate** *n* 手当て treatment; reparation, provision; **té-ate** *n* 手当 allowance; **te-búkuro** *n* 手袋 gloves; **te-dori** *n* 手取り take-home pay; **te-gákari** *n* 手掛かり a hold, a place to hold on; a clue; **te-gami** *n* 手紙 letter (= **shokan** 書簡 [BOOKISH]); **te-gata** *n* 手形 a note, a bill: **yakusoku-~** 約束手形 promissory note; **te-gókoro** *n* 手心 discretion; **te-gótae** *n* 手応え response, effect; **té-guchi** *n* 手口 way (*of doing bad things*), trick; **té-hái** *n* 手配 (*setting up*) a search for a criminal, a dragnet; **té-hazu** *n* 手はず・手筈 arrangements; **te-hón** *n* 手本 model, pattern; **té-kubi** *n* 手首 wrist; **té-mane** *n* 手まね・手真似 gesture with hand(s); **té-mari** *n* 手まり・手毬 (*decorated small*) handball; **te-nímotsu** *n* 手荷物 hand luggage; **té-nó-hira** *n* 手のひら・掌 palm (*of hand*); **te-ori (no)** *adj* 手織り(の) handweaving; **te-sage** *n* 手提げ・手さげ handbag; **te-sei (no)** *adj* 手製(の) homemade, handcrafted; **te-záiku** *n* 手細工 handiwork; **te-zawari** *n* 手ざわり texture, touch, hand feeling; **te-zúkuri (no)** *adj* 手作り(の) homemade, made by hand

..-te *suffix* …て (*does/did*) and, and then, and so; doing; [+ AUXILIARY] (→ **shite** して)

tēburu *n* テーブル table; **~-kake** テーブル掛け tablecloth

tei-... *prefix* 定… fixed, appointed, set; tei-ka *n* 定価 the set price, fixed price; téiki (no) *adj* 定期(の) ① fixed, regular, periodic, scheduled ② → tei-kí-ken 定期券; tei-kí-ken *n* 定期券 pass (*commuter ticket*), season ticket: **teiki-yokin** 定期預金 time deposit; tei-shoku *n* 定食 a set meal; a complete meal

tei-... *prefix* 低… low; tei-ka *n* 低下 fall, drop, decline, descent; tei-kétsúatsu *n* 低血圧 low blood pressure; tei-kíatsu *n* 低気圧 low (*barometric*) pressure; tei-soku *n* 低速 low speed

tei-... *prefix* 停… stop; tei-den *n* 停電 power failure/outage; tei-ryū *n* 停留 stop, stopping; tei-sha *n* 停車 stopping (*of a vehicle*); tei-shi *n* 停止 suspension, interruption; **ichiji-~** 一時停止 pause, suspension

teian *n* 提案 proposal, suggestion

teibō *n* 堤防 dike, embankment

téido *n* 程度 degree, extent, level

teikei *n* 提携 [BOOKISH] cooperation, affiliation

teikō *n* 抵抗 resistance

téikoku *n* 帝国 empire; teikoku-shúgi *n* 帝国主義 imperialism

téinei (na) *adj* ていねい[丁寧](な) polite; careful

te-iré *n* 手入れ repair; upkeep, care

teisai *n* 体裁 appearance, get-up, form, format, layout

teisetsu (na) *adj* 貞節(な) chaste, principled: **~ na tsuma** 貞節な妻 faithful wife

téishu *n* 亭主 **1.** host (*at Japanese tea ceremony*) **2.** landlord **3.** (*my*) husband

teitō *n* 抵当 mortgage, pledge (= **tanpo** 担保)

téjina *n* 手品 jugglery, magic (*tricks*); tejiná-shi *n* 手品師 juggler, magician

tejun *n* 手順 order, procedure, program

...-té kara *suffix* …てから after (do)ing, after one does/did, does/did and then (*next*)

teki *n* 敵 **1.** enemy, foe **2.** opponent; **kō-~-shu** 好敵手 rival

...-teki *suffix* …滴 a drop

...-teki (na) *suffix, adj* 的(な) …ic, …ical, …al, …ly: **chi~ (na)** 知的(な) intellectual: **shi~ (na)** 私的(な) private, personal (= **kojin~ (na)** 個人的(な): **shi-~ (na)** 詩的(な) poetic; -teki ni …的に …ically, …ally: **kanjō-~ narimásu** 感情的になります gets emotional: **kiseki~ tasukarimashita** 奇跡的に助かりました miraculously survived

tékido *n* 適度 [BOOKISH] moderation: **~ na/no** 適度な/の reasonable, moderate: **~ na undō** 適度な運動 moderate exercise

tékigi *adv* 適宜 [BOOKISH] suitably, fitly, properly (= **tekitō** (ni) 適当(に)): ~ **(no)** 適宜の suitable, fit, proper

tekikaku (na) *adj* 適格(な) qualified, eligible: ~**-sha** 適格者 qualified person

tekikaku (na/ni) *adj*, *adv* 的確・適確(な/に) precise(ly), accurate(ly), exact(ly): ~ **na handan** 的確[適確]な判断 accurate judgement

teki-nin *n* 適任 qualified person (= **tekikaku-sha** 適格者)

tekisetsu (na) *adj* 適切(な) to the point, appropriate

teki-shimásu, teki-su *v* 適します, 適す is suitable, qualified

tékísuto *n* テキスト **1.** textbook (= **kyōka-sho** 教科書) **2.** original text

tekitō (na) *adj* 適当(な) **1.** suitable, proper **2.** irresponsible, haphazard, random, half-hearted: ~ **na henji** 適当な返事 vague answer

tekitō (ni) *adv* 適当(に) **1.** suitably, properly (= **tekigi** 適宜) **2.** irresponsibly, haphazardly, randomly, half-heartedly: ~ **ni erabimásu** 適当に選びます chooses randomly: ~ **ni kikinagashimásu** 適当に聞き流します pretends to listen

tekk(-...) *n*, *prefix* 鉄(...) iron, steel; tek-ki *n* 鉄器, ~**-rui** 鉄器類 hardware (items); tek-kyō *n* 鉄橋 iron bridge

teko *n* てこ・挺・挺子 lever

...-te kudasái *interj* ...て下さい please (*do*)

temá *n* 手間 time and effort (*taken up*); one's trouble

tē ma *n* テーマ theme, topic (= **shudai** 主題): ~**-songu** テーマソング theme song (= **shudai-ka** 主題歌)

temae *n* **1.** 手前・てまえ this side (of ...); I/me **2.** 手前 prowess, skill, ability

temae *n* 点前 tea ceremony procedures

temáwari *n* 手回り personal effects; luggage

...-témo *suffix* ...ても even doing/being, even if (*one does/is*); **shitémo íi** してもいい it is OK to do, one may do

ten *n* 点 point, dot, spot; score (*points*); ten-sū́ *n* 点数 score, points

tén *n* 天 **1.** sky **2.** heaven (= **tengoku** 天国); tén-goku *n* 天国 paradise, heaven; ten-jō *n* 天井 ceiling; tén-ki *n* 天気 ① weather; ~**-yóhō** 天気予報 weather forecast ② fair weather; ten-kō *n* 天候 weather; ten-mon (no) *n* 天文(の) astronomical: **ten-mongaku** 天文学 astronomy; tén-shi *n* 天使 angel

tén *n* テン ten; **besutó-**~ ベストテン the best ten

ten-.../...-ten *prefix*, *suffix* 天.../...天 → ten-pura 天ぷら・天麩羅; ten-don *n* 天丼 a bowl of rice with tenpura shrimp on top; ten-pura *n* テンプラ・天ぷら・天麩羅 tenpura, food fried in batter, especially shrimp

ten-.../...-ten prefix, *suffix* 店.../...店 shop; ten'-in *n* 店員 shop clerk, salesclerk, salesperson; ten-po *n* 店舗 [BOOKISH] store, shop (= **mise** 店 (**o-mise** お店)); ten-shu *n* 店主 shopkeeper

tenbō *n* 展望 **1.** looking over, a view **2.** prospecting, prospects; tenbō-dai *n* 展望台 (*sightseeing*) observatory

tengu *n* テング・天狗 **1.** a long-nosed goblin **2.** conceited person

ténisu *n* テニス tennis: **~-kōto** テニスコート tennis court: **~-shūzu** テニスシューズ tennis shoes

tenjí *n* 展示 exhibit; tenjí-kai *n* 展示会 exhibition

ten-jimásu, ten-jiru *v* 転じます, 転じる [BOOKISH] changes, shifts; gets transferred; ten-kin *n* 転勤 job transfer (= **tennin** 転任); ten-kō *n* 転校 school transfer; ten-nin *n* 転任 job transfer

tennen *n* 天然 nature (= **shizen** 自然); tennen-boke *n* 天然ボケ goofy, dopey by nature [IN POSITIVE SENSE]; tennen-gasu *n* 天然ガス natural gas; tennen (no) *adj* 天然(の) natural; tennen-tō *n* 天然痘 smallpox

Tennō´ *n* 天皇 the Emperor; **Tennō-héika** 天皇陛下 His Majesty the Emperor; Tennō-tanjō´bi *n* 天皇誕生日 the Emperor's Birthday (*national holiday in Japan*)

tenōru *n* テノール tenor; tenōru-kashu *n* テノール歌手 a tenor (*singer*)

ténpi *n* 天火 oven

tenpo *n* テンポ tempo

tenrán-kai *n* 展覧会 exhibition (= **tenji-kai** 展示会)

tensai *n* 天才 genius

ténsei *n* 天性 disposition, temperament

ténto *n* テント tent

tepp-... *prefix* 鉄... iron, steel; tep-pan *n* 鉄板 iron plate: **teppan-yaki** 鉄板焼き sliced meat, etc. grilled at table; tep-pō *n* 鉄砲 gun, rifle: **mizu-deppō** 水鉄砲 squirt gun, water pistol

teppén *n* てっぺん top, highest part [INFORMAL] (= **chōjō** 頂上)

tē´pu *n* テープ tape; **sero(han)-~** セロ(ハン)テープ scotch tape; **~-rekō´dā** テープレコーダー tape recorder

terá *n* 寺 Buddhist temple (= **jiin** 寺院)

terashi-awasémásu, terashi-awaséru *v* 照らし合わせます, 照らし合わせる collates

terashimásu, terásu *v* 照らします, 照らす illuminates, lights it up, shines on; compares, collates, checks; **... ni teráshite** ...に照らして in the light of..., in view of ...

térasu *n* テラス terrace, balcony

térebi *n* テレビ television; terebi-bangumi *n* テレビ番組 TV show; terebi-denwa *n* テレビ電話 videophone; terebi-gēmu *n* テレビゲーム video game
terehonkādo *n* テレホンカード telephone card
teremásu, teréru *v* 照れます, 照れる feels embarrassed, awkward, flustered
terepashii *n* テレパシー telepathy
terimásu, téru *v* 照ります, 照る it shines
teriyaki *n* 照り焼き (*fish, chicken, etc.*) broiled with soy sauce and sweeteners
tero (risuto) *n* テロ(リスト) terrorism, terrorist
tesū´ *n* 手数 [BOOKISH] trouble (*taken up*), time and effort (= **tema** 手間): **o-~ okakeshite sumimasen** お手数おかけしてすみません I'm sorry for bothering you.; tesū´-ryō *n* 手数料 handling/service charge
tésuto *n* テスト test [INFORMAL] (= **shiken** 試験)
tetsu *n* 鉄 iron, steel; tetsu-bō *n* 鉄棒 ① horizontal bar ② iron bar; tetsu-dō *n* 鉄道 railroad, railway
tetsudái *n* 手伝い = **o-tétsudai** お手伝い assistance, help
tetsudaimásu, tetsudáu *v* 手伝います, 手伝う helps
tetsúgaku *n* 哲学 philosophy; **~-sha** 哲学者 philosopher
tetsuya *n* 徹夜 staying up all night
te-tsúzuki *n* 手続き formalities, procedure (= **tejun** 手順)
tettei-teki (na/ni) *adj, adv* 徹底的(な/に) thorough(ly)
ti... → **chi...**
tii-kappu *n* ティーカップ Western-style tea cup
tisshu(-pē´pā) *n* ティッシュ(ペーパー) tissue(s)
to *n* 戸 door; to-dana *n* 戸棚 cupboard, enclosed shelves
to *n* 都 **1.** capital (= **shu-to** 首都) **2.** Tokyo (= **Tōkyō-to** 東京都); to-chi-ji *n* 都知事 Governor of Tokyo; to-ei *n* 都営 Toei, metropolitan (*run by Tokyo*), metro; **~-sen** 都営線 (subway) Toei Line; to-kai *n* 都会 city, town; **~-jin** 都会人 city dweller, urbanite; to-min *n* 都民 Tokyoite; tó-nai *n, adv* 都内 within the metropolis (of Tokyo); tó-shi *n* 都市 city; **toshi (no)** 都市(の) urban
... to *prep* …と with [CONCATENATES A NOUN]: **... ~ issho ni** …と一緒に ... with (someone)
... to ... *conj* …と and [CONCATENATES A NOUN]: **anata ~ watashi** あなたと私 you and I
... to *suffix* …と (*said/thought/seemed*) that …; "…" (*quote-*) unquote: **kare wa ... ~ itta** 彼は…と言った he said that ...; ... to iu *suffix* …という which says; which is (*called*), called; which is (*in effect*); to iú no wa ... *suffix*

というのは… What that means (*What that amounts to*) is that …
... to *suffix* …と **1. (su)-ru ~** (す)ると when(ever), if; …and thereupon, …whereupon: **moshikasuru ~** もしかすると perhaps, possibly **2. (shi)-nai ~** (し)ないと unless
tō´ *n* 十 ten (= **jū** 十)
tō´ *n* 籐 rattan, cane
tō´ *n* 塔 tower, pagoda (= **tawā** タワー); **Efferu-tō** エッフェル塔 Eiffel Tower
tō´-... *prefix* 東... east, eastern; tō´-bu *n* 東部 the east, the eastern part; tō-hō *n* 東方 the east; tō-nan *n* 東南 southeast: **~-ajia** 東南アジア Southeast Asia; tō-zai *n* 東西 east and west, the East and the West
...´-tō *suffix* …頭 (*counts large animals*) head [**go-tō** 五頭 *unaccented* (five heads)]
...-tō *suffix* …等 class
Tō´a *n* 東亜 = **Higashi-Ájia** 東アジア
tobaku *n* 賭博 [BOOKISH] gambling
tō´ban *n* 当番 person on duty
tobashimásu, tobasu *v* 飛ばします, 飛ばす lets fly; skips, omits; hurries
tobi-dashimásu, tobi-dásu *v* 跳び出します・跳び出す jumps out
tobi-dashimásu, tobi-dásu *v* 飛び出します, 飛び出す runs/bursts out; it sticks out, protrudes; **uchi o ~** 家を飛び出します runs away (*from home*) (= **iede shimásu** 家出します)
tobimásu, tobu *v* 跳びます, 跳ぶ jumps
tobimásu, tobu *v* 飛びます, 飛ぶ flies
tobira *n* 扉 **1.** a door wing, a door of a gate **2.** title page
toboshíi *adj* 乏しい scarce, meager, scanty
tōbun *n* 糖分 [BOOKISH] sugar content
tōbun *n* 等分 dividing equally
tōbun *n* 当分 for the time being
tōchaku *n* 到着 arrival
tochi *n* 土地 ground, earth, soil; a piece of land
tochū (de/no) *adv, adj* 途中(で/の) on the way; **~-gesha** 途中下車 stopover (*train*)
tōdai *n* 燈台 lighthouse
Tō-dai *n* 東大 Tokyo University (= **Tōkyō-Dáigaku** 東京大学)
todoké *n* 届け notification, notice, report
todokemásu, todokéru *v* 届けます, 届ける **1.** delivers **2.** reports it (*to*), notifies
todoke-saki *n* 届け先 address (*for delivery*)
todokimásu, todóku *v* 届きます, 届く reaches; arrives; gets delivered
todomarimásu, todomáru *v* とどまります, とどまる it stops; it remains
todomemásu, todómeru *v* とどめます, とどめる stops it
todorokimásu, todoróku *v* 轟きます, 轟く [BOOKISH] roars, rumbles

tōfú *n* 豆腐 bean curd
togamé *n* とがめ [BOOKISH] rebuke, censure, blame
togamemásu̱, togaméru *v* とがめます, とがめる [BOOKISH] blames, rebukes, reproves, finds fault with: **ki ga ~** 気がとがめます suffers from a guilty conscience
togarasemásu̱, togaráseru *v* とがらせ[尖らせ]ます, とがらせる・尖らせる sharpens, points
togarimásu̱, togáru *v* とがります・尖ります, とがる・尖る gets sharp (*pointed*)
togé *n* とげ・刺・棘 thorn
tōgé *n* 峠 mountain pass
tōgei *n* 陶芸 ceramic art, ceramics
togemásu̱, togéru *v* 遂げます, 遂げる achieves, accomplishes
togimásu̱, tógu *v* 研ぎます, 研ぐ sharpens, grinds, polishes
tōhenboku *n* 唐変木 damned fool
tōhoku-chi̱hō 東北地方 the Tōhoku area of Japan (*Aomori, Iwate, Miyagi, Akita, Yamagata, Fukushima prefectures*)
tōhon *n* 謄本 full copy: **koseki-~** 戸籍謄本 full copy of one's family register
tōhyō *n* 投票 ballot, vote
tói *n* とい・樋 drain pipe, gutter
tōi *adj* 遠い **1.** far-off, distant **2. mimí ga ~** 耳が遠い is hard of hearing
toiawase *n* 問い合わせ inquiry
toimásu̱, tóu *v* 問います, 問う inquires
tóire *n* トイレ toilet, bathroom; tóiretto-pḗ′pā *n* トイレットペーパー toilet paper
tōitsu *n* 統一 unification, standardization
tōji *n* 冬至 winter solstice
tōji *n* 湯治 hot-spring cure: **~-ba** 湯治場 spa
tō′ji (wa) *adv* 当時(は) (*at*) that time, then, (*in*) those days (= **anokoro (wa)** あの頃(は), **sonokoro (wa)** その頃(は))
tojimásu̱, tojíru *v* 閉じます, 閉じる closes (*a book, door wings, …*)
tōjitsu *n* 当日 the day in question, that very day, on the day
tōjō *n* 搭乗 boarding a plane: **~-chū** 搭乗中 (*in the midst of*) boarding; tōjō′-ken *n* 搭乗券 boarding pass
tōjō *n* 登場 entry upon the stage
... tóka …とか or something (*like it*)
tōka *n* 十日 **1.** 10th day (*of a month*) **2.** (*for*) ten days (= **tōkakan** 十日間)
tokage *n* トカゲ・蜥蜴 lizard
tokai *n* 都会 city: **dai-~** 大都会 metropolis (= **tóshi** 都市)
tōkai-chi̱hō *n* 東海地方 the Tōkai area of Japan (*Mie, Aichi, Gifu, Shizuoka prefectures*)
tokaku (... shimásu̱) *adv* とかく(…します) apt/liable (*to do*): **~ no uwasa** とかくの噂 unsavory rumors
tokashimásu̱, tokásu *v* 溶かします, 溶かす melts/thaws/dissolves it

tokashimásu̲, tokásu *v* とかし[梳かし]ます, とかす・梳かす combs

tokei *n* 時計 time piece; clock; watch

tōkei *n* 統計 statistics

tokemásu̲, tokéru *v* 溶けます, 溶ける it melts/thaws/dissolves

tokemásu̲, tokéru *v* 解けます, 解ける comes undone; gets solved

tokí *n* 時 time

tóki *n* トキ・朱鷺・鴇 crested ibis (*bird*)

tṓki *n* 陶器 pottery, ceramics, china → **jíki** 磁器

tṓki *n* 登記 registration

tṓki *n* 冬期 winter (*period/term*): **~-orinpikku** 冬季オリンピック Winter Olympics

tṓki *n* 投機 speculation: **~ shimásu̲** 投機します speculates

tṓki *n* 投棄 dumping, abandonment

tokidoki 時々・ときどき sometimes

tokimásu̲, tóku *v* 解きます, 解く undoes, unties; solves

tokimásu̲, tóku *v* 説きます, 説く explains, persuades, preaches

tokimásu̲, tóku *v* とき[梳き]ます, とく・梳く comb

tóki ni *adv* …時に at the time that …, when …

tokí ni *adv* ときに・時に by the way, incidentally; sometimes

tokkakari *n* 取っ掛かり a hold, a place to hold on; a clue (= **tega-kari** 手掛かり)

tokkan kōji *n* 突貫工事 eleventh-hour job

tokki *n* 突起 projection, protuberance

tokki *n* 特記 special mention: **~-jikō** 特記事項 special comments, special instruction: **~-nai kagiri** 特記ない限り unless specified otherwise

tokku (ni) *adv* とっく(に) long before (= **tokku no mukashi (ni)** とっくの昔(に))

tokkumiaimásu̲, tokkumiau *v* 取っ組み合います, 取っ組み合う grapple

tokkuri *n* とっくり・徳利 saké bottle/pitcher, ceramic decanter for serving saké

tokkyo *n* 特許 patent

tokkyū *n* 特急 special express (*train*); **~´-ken** 特急券 special-express ticket

tokkyū *n* 特級 special class; (*best*) quality

toko *n* 床 (**o-toko** お床) bed: **~ ni tsu̲kimásu̲** 床に就きます takes to one's bed, goes to bed

... tokó *suffix* …とこ [INFORMAL] place (= **... tokoró** …所)

tokonoma *n* 床の間 alcove in Japanese room

tokoro, ... tokoró *suffix* 所, …所 **1.** place **2.** address

tokoro, ... tokoró ところ, …ところ circumstance, time: **shi̲ta ~ desu̲** したところです has just done it; **shi̲te iru ~ desu̲** しているところです is (*in the midst of*) doing it; **suru ~ desu̲** するところです is about to do it

tokoró-de *conj* ところで by the way; well now

tokoro-dókoro *n, adv* ところどころ various places, here and there

tokoró-ga *conj* ところが but, however

... tokoró ga *suffix, conj* …ところが however

tokoro-gaki *n* 所書き [BOOKISH] address (*written*) (= **atesaki** 宛先, **jū´sho** 住所)

tokoroten *n* ところてん seaweed gelatin strips served cold in a tangy soy sauce

toko-ya *n* 床屋 barber(shop)

toku-... *prefix* 特… special (= **tokubetsu** 特別); **toku-betsu (no)** *adj* 特別(の) special, particular, extra: ~ **ni** 特別に especially; **toku-chō** *n* 特徴 special feature/quality, (*a distinguishing*) characteristic

toku *n* 徳 virtue

toku *n* 得 profit, advantage, gain

tōkú *adv* 遠く **1.** the distance, far off **2.** so as to be far/distant → **tōi** 遠い

tokuhon *n* 読本 reader, reading book

tokúi *n* 得意 **1.** pride; forte, strong point: ~ **(na)** 得意(な) favorite, proud, exultant **2. o-~** お得意 (regular) customer, patron **3.** prosperity

tokúi (na/no) *adj* 特異(な/の) unique, peculiar

tóku (ni) *adv* 特(に) in particular, especially

toku-nítō *n* 特二等 special second class

tokushoku *n* 特色 special feature, characteristic

tokushu (na) *adj* 特殊(な) special, particular

tokuten *n* 得点 points obtained, score (= **sukoa** スコア)

tokuyū (no) *adj* 特有(の) special, particular

Tōkyō *n* 東京 Tokyo; **Tōkyō´-Dáigaku** *n* 東京大学 Tokyo University (= **Tō-dai** 東大); **Tōkyō´-Eki** *n* 東京駅 Tokyo Station

tō´kyoku *n* 当局 the authorities

tomari *n* 泊まり staying overnight; night duty

tomarimásu, tomaru *v* 止まります・止まる it stops

tomarimásu, tomaru *v* 泊まります, 泊まる stays overnight

tōmáwari *n* 遠回り detour

tōmáwashi *n* 遠回し oblique statement

tōmei (na) *adj* 透明(な) clear, transparent

tomemásu, tomeru *v* 止めます, 止める stops it

tomemásu, tomeru *v* 泊めます, 泊める puts one up overnight

tomemásu, tomeru *v* 留めます, 留める fastens (*firmly attaches*); **tomebári** *n* 留め針 pin

tōmen *adv* 当面 for now; **tōmen (no)** *adj* 当面(の) immediate, present; ~ **no mondai** 当面の問題 immediate problem

tómi *n* 富 wealth, fortune, riches, abundance

tomimásu, tómu *v* 富みます, 富む is rich; abounds

tōmin *n* 冬眠 hibernation

tómo *n* 友 [BOOKISH] friend (= **yūjin** 友人); tomodachi *n* 友達 friend

tómo *n* 伴 one's companion, company (= **dōhan-sha** 同伴者)

... tó-mo! *interj* …とも! : **ii tó mo** いいとも Of course!

tó-mo-kaku *adv* ともかく anyway, anyhow, at any rate

tomonaimásu, tomonáu *v* 伴います, 伴う; **... ni ~** …に伴います accompanies

tomo ni *adv* 共に together (= **issho ni** 一緒に)

tō-mórokoshi *n* トウモロコシ corn (*on the cob*); **~-ko** とうもろこし粉 cornstarch

tomoshimásu, tomósu *v* 灯します, 灯す burns (*a light*)

tonaemásu, tonáéru *v* 唱えます, 唱える advocates; shouts; recites; calls; claims

tōnan *n* 盗難 [BOOKISH] (*suffering*) theft

tonari *n* 隣 next-door, neighbor(ing)

tonbo *n* トンボ・蜻蛉 dragonfly

tonda *adj* とんだ outrageous, terrible, shocking

tónde *v* 富んで: ~ **imásu** 富んでいます is rich, abundant → **tomimásu** 富みます

tonde-mo arimasén *adj* とんでもありません Oh, no. No way.

tonde-mo nái *adj* とんでもない outrageous, terrible, shocking

tó-ni-kaku とにかく anyway, anyhow

ton-katsu *n* 豚カツ・トンカツ pork cutlet

tónma *n* とんま・トンマ・頓馬 idiot, fool

tonma *n* とんま dullness, fool, idiot, boob

tonneru *n* トンネル tunnel

ton-ya *n* 問屋 wholesale store

tōnyō-byō *n* 糖尿病 diabetes

tōnyū *n* 豆乳 soybean milk

tōnyū *n* 投入 [BOOKISH] **1.** a throw (*into*) **2.** investment, investing

toppatsu *n* 突発 [BOOKISH] outbreak: **~-jiko** 突発事故 sudden accident; **~-jiken** 突発事件 unforeseen accident; bombshell

toppu *n* トップ top

tora *n* トラ・虎 tiger

toraberāzu chekku *n* トラベラーズチェック traveler's check

toraburu *n* トラブル trouble: **~-mēkā** トラブルメーカー troublemaker

Tora-doshi *n* 寅年 year of the Tiger

toraemásu, toráéru *v* 捕らえます, 捕らえる catches, seizes, captures, arrests

toraiaru *n* トライアル trial: **~-koyō** トライアル雇用 trial employment

torákku *n* トラック **1.** truck **2.** track (*for running*)

torakutā *n* トラクター tractor

toránku *n* トランク (*clothes/car*) trunk

toránkusu *n* トランクス trunks
toranpétto *n* トランペット trumpet
toranporin *n* トランポリン trampoline
toránpu *n* トランプ playing cards
toranshiibā *n* トランシーバー transceiver, walkie-talkie
torei *n* トレイ tray
toremásu, toréru *v* 取れます, 取れる **1.** (*button, etc.*) comes off **2.** can take
torēnā *n* トレーナー sweatshirt
torendo *n* トレンド trend (*fashion, etc.*) (= **keikō** 傾向)
torēningu *n* トレーニング training (*exercise, etc.*) workout: **~-uea** トレーニングウエア training wear: **~-jimu** トレーニングジム training gym
torēshingu-pē'pā *n* トレーシングペーパー tracing paper
tori *n* トリ・鳥 bird; tori-kago *n* トリカゴ・鳥籠 bird cage; tori-i *n* 鳥居 the gate to a Shinto shrine
tori *n* トリ・鶏 chicken; tori-niku *n* トリニク・鶏肉 chicken meat
tori-... *prefix* 取り … [verb PREFIX]: takes and …
tōrí *n* 通り street, avenue; passage (= **michi** 道)
tō'ri *n* とおり・通り way (of doing), manner: **... no ~ ni** …のとおりに like … (= **(no) yō ni** (の)よう[様]に)
tori-agemásu, tori-ageru *v* 取り上げます, 取り上げる takes up; takes away
tori-atsukai *n* 取り扱い treatment, management, transaction
tori-atsukaimásu, tori-atsukau *v* 取り扱います, 取り扱う handles, deals with, manages
tori-awase *n* 取り合わせ assortment
tori-bun *n* 取(り)分 share
tórí-hiki *n* 取り引き・取引 transaction, deal, business, trade
tori-kae *n* 取り替え change, replacement
tori-kaemásu, tori-kaeru *v* 取り替えます, 取り替える replaces it
tori-keshi *n* 取り消し cancellation, revocation; deletion, erasure
tori-keshimásu, tori-kesu *v* 取り消します, 取り消す cancels, revokes; deletes, erases
toriko *n* とりこ・虜 **1.** captive, prisoner (= **horyo** 捕虜) **2.** person who is crazy about something/someone; **koi no ~** 恋の虜 captive of love
tori-kumi *n* 取り組み・取組み wrestling match/bout/program
torimásu, tóru *v* 取ります, 取る **1.** takes; takes away, removes **2.** passes (*the salt, sugar, etc.*) **3.** takes (*a course*)
torimásu, tóru *v* 撮ります, 撮る takes (*a picture*)
tōrimásu, tō'ru *v* 通ります, 通る passes by, passes through
tōrimásu, tō'ru *v* 透ります, 透る penetrates
tōri-michi *n* 通り道 passage(way) (= **tsūro** 通路)

torishimari *n* **1.** 取り締まり・取締り control, management, supervision **2.** 取締 managing director
tori-shimarimásu, tori-shimaru *v* 取り締まります, 取り締まる controls, manages, supervises, directs
toritsugi **1.** 取り次ぎ・取次ぎ answering the door **2.** 取次 an usher; an agency
toriwake *adv* とりわけ especially, in particular
tóro *n* とろ・トロ fatty tuna
torō *n* 徒労 vain effort
tōrō *n* 灯籠 a stone lantern: **~ nagashi** 灯籠流し floating lanterns on a river
tōroku *n* 登録 registration
tō´ron *n* 討論 [BOOKISH] debate, discussion, dispute
tororo *n* トロロ・とろろ grated yam; **~-kónbu** とろろ昆布 kelp flakes
Tóruko *n* トルコ Turkey
toryō *n* 塗料 coating compositions (*paint, Japanese lacquer, varnish, etc.*)
tōsaku *n* 倒錯 [BOOKISH] perversion: **seiteki-~** 性的倒錯 paraphilia
tōsaku *n* 盗作 plagiarism
tōsan *n* 倒産 bankruptcy
tōsan *n* 父さん (*mostly male*) dad (= **oyaji** 親父, **tō-chan** 父ちゃん)
tōsei *n* 統制 control (*of prices, etc.*)
tōsenbo, tōsenbō *n* 通せんぼ・通せん坊 blocking a person's way
toshí *n* 年 **1.** year **2.** 年・歳 (お年・お歳) age: **~ o torimásu** 年を取ります gets old; **toshi-ake** *n* 年明け new year; **toshi-koshi soba** *n* 年越しそば[蕎麦] buckwheat noodles eaten traditionally on New Year's Eve; **toshi-go** *n* 年子 child born within a year of another; **toshi-kakkō** *n* 年格好 one's age (= **toshi-goro** 年頃): **~ ga rokujū kurai no dansei** 年格好が60くらいの男性 a man of about 60; **toshi-ma** *n* 年増 middle-aged woman; **toshi-shita (no)** *adj* 年下(の) younger, junior; **toshi-ue (no)** *n* 年上(の) older, senior; **toshi-yóri** *n* 年寄り an old person (= **kōrei-sha** 高齢者)
tóshi *n* 都市 city: **dai-~** 大都市 big city, metropolis (= **tokai** 都会)
tōshí (no) *adj* 通し(の) direct, through (*to destination*): **~ de ikimásu** 通しで行きます goes direct (*through to destination*); **~-gíppu** 通し切符 a through ticket; **~-bangō** 通し番号 serial number
tōshi *n* 投資 investment, investing
tōshi *n* 凍死 freezing to death, frost-killing
tō´shi *n* 闘志 [BOOKISH] fighting spirit
tōshimásu, tō´su *v* 通します, 通す lets through/in, admits; shows in; pierces
tōshimásu, tō´su *v* 透します, 透す penetrates
tōshin-dai *n* 等身大 life size
tōshin (jisatsu) *n* 投身(自殺) committing suicide by throwing

oneself (*into water, off the platform, etc.*)
tósho *n* 図書 library (*book collection*): **~-gákari** 図書係 the librarian (*in charge*), (*book*) custodian; **toshó-kan** *n* 図書館 library (*building*); **~-in** 図書館員 librarian; **toshó-shitsu** *n* 図書室 library (*book room*)
tō´sho (wa) *adv* 当初(は) [BOOKISH] at first, initially, originally (= **saisho (wa)** 最初(は), **hajime** (wa) 初め(は))
tōshu *n* 党首 party leader
tōshu *n* 投手 a pitcher (*baseball, etc.*)
tōshū *n* 踏襲 following predecessor's way
tóso *n* とそ・屠蘇 spiced saké drunk at New Year's
tōsō *n* 闘争 fight, labor struggle
tōsō *n* 逃走 [BOOKISH] escape
tossa no *adj* とっさの prompt; **tossa ni** *adv* とっさに in an instant, promptly, immediately
tō´sutā *n* トースター toaster
tō´suto *n* トースト toast
... totan ni …途端に (*at*) the instant/moment that …
tōtei *adv* 到底 [+ NEGATIVE VERB] absolutely (not)
tō´te mo *adv* 問うても even inquiring
totemo *adj* とても very [INFORMAL] (= **tottemo** とっても, **taihen** 大変)
tō´tō *adv* とうとう at last, finally (= **tsuini** ついに)
totonoemásu, totonóéru *v* 整えます, 整える regulates, adjusts; prepares
totonoimásu, totonóu *v* 整います, 整う is in order; is ready
totsuzen *adv* 突然 suddenly, abruptly (= **kyū ni** 急に): **~ no** 突然の sudden, abrupt
totté *n* 取っ手・把手 a handle, knob
tótte *v* とって: **...ni ~** (…に)とって (*with reference*) to, for
tottemo *adj* とっても terribly, extremely, completely (= **totemo** とても)
tótte okimásu (oku) *v* 取っておきます(おく) puts aside, reserves, holds
tōwaku *n* 当惑 embarrassment, puzzlement (= **konwaku** 困惑)
tōza *n* 当座, **~-yókin** 当座預金 current deposit, checking account; **tōza no** *adj* 当座(の) [BOOKISH] temporary
tózan *n* 登山 mountain-climbing (= **yama-nobori** 山登り); **tozán-sha** *n* 登山者 mountain-climber
tōzen *adv* 当然 naturally, surely; **~ no** 当然の) proper, deserved
tōzoku *n* 盗賊 burglar
tsū *n* 通 **1.** an authority, an expert **2.** (*counts letter*): **ít-~** 一通 one letter
tsúā *n* ツアー tour **1.** group tour **2.** short trip (= **shō-ryokō** 小旅行)
tsúbá *n* つば・唾 spit, saliva
tsúba *n* つば・鍔 sword-guard
tsubakí *n* つばき・唾 = **tsúbá** つば・唾 (spit)

tsubame *n* ツバメ・燕 swallow (*bird*)
tsubasa *n* つばさ・翼 wing
tsubo *n* つぼ・壷・壺 jar, crock
tsubo *n* 坪 *tsubo* (6 sq. ft.)
tsubomarimásu, tsubomaru *v* つぼまります, つぼまる it puckers up; gets puckered up, is shut; it narrows
tsubomemásu, tsubomeru *v* つぼめます, つぼめる puckers it; shuts it; narrows it
tsubomi *n* つぼみ・蕾 flower bud
tsúbu *n* 粒 grain
tsuburemásu, tsubureru *v* 潰れます, 潰れる it collapses/smashes
tsuburimásu, tsuburu *v* つぶります, つぶる: **mé o ~** 目をつぶります shuts/closes one's eyes
tsubushimásu, tsubusu *v* 潰します, 潰す smashes (*crushes, squeezes*) it
tsubuyakimásu, tsubuyaku *v* つぶやきます, つぶやく murmur; **(tsuittā de) ~** (ツイッターで)つぶやくtweet (*Internet*)
tsuchí *n* 土 earth, ground
tsuchí *n* 槌 hammer
tsūchi *n* 通知 report, notice, notification
tsūchō *n* 通帳 passbook, bankbook: **yokin-~** 預金通帳 deposit book: **chokin-~** 貯金通帳 savings book
tsúe *n* 杖 cane, walking stick
tsūgaku *n* 通学 commuting to school; **tsūgaku-ro** *n* 通学路 school route
tsuge *n* つげ・ツゲ・柘植 boxwood
tsuge 告げ revelation, divine message
tsuge-guchi (ya) *n* 告げ口(屋) (tattle)tale
tsugemásu, tsugeru *v* 告げます, 告げる tells, informs
tsugemásu, tsugeru *v* 注げます, 注げる can pour
tsugemásu, tsugeru *v* 継げます, 継げる can inherit
tsugemásu, tsugeru *v* 接げます, 接げる can join it
tsugi *n* 継ぎ patch; **(... ni) ~ o atemásu** (...に)継ぎを当てます patches it
tsugí *n* 次 next, the following; **~ no** 次の the next one
tsugimásu, tsugu *v* 注ぎます, 注ぐ pours it
tsugimásu, tsugu *v* 継ぎます, 継ぐ inherits, succeeds to
tsugimásu, tsugu *v* 接ぎます, 接ぐ joins it, grafts, glues
tsugi-me *n* 継ぎ目 joint, seam
tsugi-me *n* 接ぎ目 joint, seam
tsugitashi-kō´do *n* 継ぎ足しコード extension cord
tsugí-tsugi (ni) *adv* 次々(に) one after another
tsugō *n* 都合 circumstances, convenience, opportunity: **~ ga íi/warúi** 都合がいい/悪い (it is) convenient/inconvenient; **~ no yoi** 都合のよい expedient: **go-~ shugi** ご都合主義 expediency, opportunism

tsui *n* 対 a pair: **~ ni narimásu** 対になります becomes/makes/forms a pair

tsúi *adv* つい **1.** unintentionally, inadvertently **2.** just (*now*): **~ imashígata** つい今しがた just now; **~ saki-hodo** つい先程 [BOOKISH] just a little while ago

tsúide *adv* 次いで next, in succession, subsequently; **... ni ~** ...に次いで following ..., next after/to ... (*in importance*)

tsuide *n* ついで opportunity, occasion, convenience: **~ no setsu/sai/toki ni** ついでの節/際/時に at your/one's convenience; **~ ga arimásu** ついでがあります has occasion to....

... tsuide (ni) *suffix* ...ついで(に) on the occasion of/that ..., incidentally to ...; while ...; along the way

tsuihō *n* 追放 purge, banishment, exile

tsúin *n* ツイン, **~-rū´mu** ツインルーム twin(-bed)room; **tsuin-béddo** *n* ツインベッド twin beds

tsúi ni *adv* ついに at last, finally (= **tōtō** とうとう)

tsuiraku *n* 墜落 (*plane*) crash

tsui-shi(kén) *n* 追試(験) makeup exam (= **sai-shi(ken)** 再試(験))

tsuitachí *n* 一日 first day of a month

tsuitate *n* 衝立 partition

tsúite *suffix* ついて **... ni ~ (no)** ...について(の) about, concerning; **... ni ~ (wa)** ...について(は) as far as ... is concerned

tsuittā *n* ツイッター Twitter (*Internet*)

tsuji *n* 辻 crossroads; road(side), street: **yotsu-~** 四つ辻 crossroad (= **jūji-ro** 十字路)

tsū-ji *n* 通じ **1.** bowel movement **2.** effect

tsū-jimásu, tsū-jiru *v* 通じます, 通じる gets through, communicates; transmits; is understood; is well versed in; one's bowels move; **(... o) tsū-ji te** (...を)通じて through (*the medium of*)

tsūjín *n* 通人 an expert, an authority; a man of the world

tsūjō *adv* 通常 usually, ordinarily (= **futsū** 普通, **taitei** たいてい・大抵)

tsūjō (no) *adj* 通常(の) usual, ordinary

tsuká *n* 塚 mound

tsuká *n* つか・柄 hilt

tsūka *n* 通貨 currency (*money*) (= **kahei** 貨幣)

tsukáé *n* つかえ obstruction

tsukaemásu, tsukáéru *v* つかえます, つかえる **1.** gets clogged up, obstructed, busy: **nodo ga ~** 喉がつかえます has difficulty in swallowing **2.** feels stuffed up (*physically*) **3.** feels a pressure on one's chest (*mentally*)

tsukai *n* 使い **1.** message, errand **2.** messenger

tsukai-hashiri, tsukai-bashiri *n* 使い走り, **tukai-ppashiri** 使いっ走り errand runner

tsukaimásu, tsukau *v* 使います, 使う uses; spends; employs; handles

tsukamaemásu, tsukamaeru *v* 捕まえます, 捕まえる catches, seizes, arrests

tsukamimásu, tsukámu *v* つかみます, つかむ seizes, grasps, clutches

tsuké *n* 付け bill, account: ~ **de kaimásu** 付けで買います buys it on credit

tsukeawase *n* 付け合わせ garnish, relish

tsukemásu, tsukeru *v* 漬けます, 漬ける pickles; soaks

tsuke-mono *n* 漬物 Japanese pickles

tsukí *n* 月 moon; month; tsukí-hi *n* 月日 time (*days and years*); tsuki-mí *n* 月見 moon viewing; tsukí-yo *n* 月夜 moonlight (*night*)

...-tsuki (no) …付き(の) with (… attached)

tsuki-ai 付き合い *n* お付き合い association, social company, friendship (= **kōsai** 交際)

tsuki-aimásu, tsuki-áu *v* 付き合います, 付き合う: **... to ~** …と付き合います associates (*with*), enjoys the company of, goes out (*with one's lover*)

tsuki-atari 突き当たり *n* the end of a street/corridor

tsuki-atarimásu, tsuki-atáru *v* 突き当たります, 突き当たる runs into; comes to the end of (*a street*)

tsuki-dashimásu, tsuki-dásu *v* 突き出します, 突き出す makes it protrude, sticks it out

tsuki-demásu, tsuki-déru *v* 突き出ます, 突き出る protrudes, sticks out

tsukimásu, tsuku *v* 突きます, 突く stabs, thrusts, pokes, pushes

tsukimásu, tsúku *v* 付きます, 付く **1.** comes in contact **2.** sticks to; joins; follows; touches

tsukimásu, tsúku *v* 着きます, 着く arrives (= **tōchaku shimásu, tōchaku suru** 到着します, 到着する)

tsukimásu, tsúku *v* 点きます, 点く burns, is turned (*on*), is lit

tsukimásu, tsukíru *v* 尽きます, 尽きる comes to an end, runs out

tsūkin *n* 通勤 commuting to work; **~-jíkan** 通勤時間 commuting time

tsūkō *n* 通行 passing, passage, transit: **~-dome** 通行止め closed to traffic, No Passage; **~-nin** 通行人 passer-by

Tsukúba *n* つくば・筑波 Tsukuba

tsukuda-ni *n* ツクダニ・佃煮 conserves boiled down from fish or seaweed

tsukue *n* 机 desk (= **desuku** デスク)

tsukurí 作り **1.** *n* makeup, toilette **2.** *n* artistically arranged slices of raw fish

tsukúri-banashi *n* 作り話 (*stories*) fiction

tsukurimásu, tsukúru *v* 作ります, ~作る makes, creates, produces, manufactures, prepares (*fixes*) (*small or intangible things*);

jikan o ~ 時間を作ります makes (*sets aside*) time, sets up a time

tsukurimásu, tsukúru *v* 造ります, 造る makes, forms, creates, grows, manufactures, builds (*big things*)

tsukuroimásu, tsukuróu *v* 繕います, 繕う mends, repairs

tsukushimásu, tsukúsu *v* 尽くします, 尽くす exhausts, runs out of; exerts oneself, strives

tsúma *n* 妻 wife **1.** my wife (= **kanai** 家内) **2.** (*your/someone else's*) wife (= **oku-san** 奥さん)

tsumá *n* つま・褄 skirt (*of Kimono*)

tsumá *n* ツマ sashimi garnishings

tsumami 摘み・つまみ **1.** *n* a knob; a pinch **2.** *n* = **tsumamimono** つまみ物, **o-tsúmami** おつまみ things to nibble on while drinking (= **sakana** さかな・肴)

tsumamimásu, tsumamu *v* 摘みます, 摘む pinches, picks; summarizes

tsumaránai *adj* つまらない worthless, no good, boring, trivial

tsúmari *adv* つまり after all; in short (= **kekkyoku (no tokoro)** 結局(のところ), **yōsuruni** 要するに)

tsumarimásu, tsumáru *v* 詰まります, 詰まる is clogged up, choked; is stuck; is shortened; is crammed

tsumáru tokoro つまるところ = **tsúmari** つまり (after all)

tsumasaki *n* つま先・爪先 toe, toe tip(s)

tsumashíi *adj* つましい・倹しい is thrifty, frugal

tsuma-yōji *n* つまようじ・爪楊枝 toothpick

tsuma-zukimásu, tsuma-zuku *v* つまずきます, つまずく stumbles

tsume *n* 爪 **1.** claw (= **kagizume** 鉤爪) (→ **taka-no-tsume** 鷹の爪): **tora no ~** トラ[虎]の爪 tiger's claw **3.** hoof; **tsume-kíri** *n* 爪切り nail clippers; **tsume-yásuri** *n* 爪やすり nail file, emery board

tsumemásu, tsuméru *v* 詰めます, 詰める **1.** stuffs, crams **2.** cans

tsumetai *adj* 冷たい cold (*to the touch*)

tsúmi *n* 罪 crime, sin, guilt, fault; **~-bukai** 罪深い sinful

tsumi-(i)re *n* つみれ (つみいれ) fishballs (*for soup*)

tsumimásu, tsumu *v* 積みます, 積む piles it up, accumulates it; deposits; loads

tsumimásu, tsumu *v* 摘みます, 摘む gathers, plucks, clips, picks

tsumitate-kin *n* 積立金 reserve fund: = **~-chókin** 積立貯金 installment savings

...-tsumori . . . つもり intention, plan, (*what one has in*) mind, purpose, expectation

...-tsumori (de)wa/ja... . . . つもり(で)は/じゃ [+ NEGATIVE verb] didn't/don't mean to, had/have no intention of: **kau-tsumori wa arimasen** 買うつもりはありません I have no intention of buying: **sumimasen, ki o warukusaseru-tsumori wa nakattandesu** すみ

ません、気を悪くさせるつもりはなかったんです Sorry, I didn't mean to offend you.

tsumují-kazé *n* つむじ風・旋風 whirlwind

tsuná *n* 綱 rope, cord, cable; tsuna watari *n* 綱渡り walking a tightrope, balancing act

tsúna *n* ツナ tuna(fish) (*canned*); tsuna-sándo *n* ツナサンド tuna-fish sandwich

tsunagari つながり・繋がり *n* connection, relation

tsunagarimásu, tsunagaru *v* つながります, つながる is connected, linked

tsunagi つなぎ *n* a link, a connection

tsunagimásu, tsunagu *v* つなぎます, つなぐ connects, links, ties

tsunami *n* 津波 tsunami

tsúne (no) *adj* 常(の) usual, ordinary

tsunerimásu, tsunéru *v* つねります, つねる pinches

tsunézune *n* つねづね・常々 all the time, usually (= **fudan** 普段, **itsumo** いつも)

tsunó *n* 角 horn (*of an animal*): **sai no ~** サイの角 rhinoceros horn

tsū-píisu *n* ツーピース a two-piece woman's suit

tsurá *n* 面・つら (*slipshod Japanese*) **1.** face (= **kao** 顔) **2.** surface, appearance: **uwat-~ dake de handan shimásu** 上っ面だけで判断します judges only by appearances

tsurai *adj* つらい・辛い painful, cruel, hard

tsuranukimásu, tsuranuku *v* 貫きます, 貫く **1.** goes through, penetrates (= **kantsū shimásu** 貫通します, **kantsū suru** 貫通する): **dangan ga karada o tsuranukimashita** 弾丸が体を貫きました the bullet went through the body **2.** accomplishes: **shinnen o ~** 信念を貫きます has the courage of one's convictions

tsurara *n* ツララ・氷柱 icicle

tsure 連れ *n* company, companion

tsurimásu, tsureru *v* 連れます, 連れる brings along, is accompanied by (*brings/takes one along*)

tsurenái *adj* つれない coldhearted, cruel

tsuri *n* つり・釣り fishing; **tsuri-sen** つり銭 (*small*) change

tsuri 釣り *n* fishing: **sakana-~** 魚釣り fishing: **ippon-zuri** 一本釣り single hook fishing; tsuri-bari *n* 釣り針 fishhook; tsuri-dōgu *n* 釣り道具 fishing gear; tsuri-zao *n* 釣り竿 fishing rod

tsuri *n* つり・吊り hanging (*things*), hanging tool: **kubi-~ jisatsu** 首吊り自殺 suicide by hanging: **zubon-~** ズボンつり[吊り] suspender, galluses; tsuri-bashi *n* つり[吊り]橋 suspension bridge; tsuri-gane *n* つり[吊り]鐘 big bell (*temple, etc.*)

tsuriai *n* 釣(り)合い・つりあい balance, equilibrium, symmetry

tsurimásu, tsuru *v* 吊ります, 吊る hangs it (*by a line*), suspends, strings up

tsurimásu, tsuru *v* 釣ります, 釣る fishes

tsū´ro *n* 通路 **1.** passage(way) (= **tōri-michi** 通り道) **2.** aisle (= **rōka** 廊下) **3.** thoroughfare

tsurú *n* ツル・蔓 vine; earpieces of a glass frame

tsurú *n* つる・弦 string (*of bow or violin*)

tsurú *n* つる・鉉 handle

tsúru *n* ツル・鶴 crane (*bird*)

tsurugí *n* 剣・つるぎ sword

tsūshin *n* 通信 **1.** correspondence: **~-kōza** 通信講座 correspondence course: **~-hanbai** 通信販売 mail order **2.** report, news: **gakkyū~** 学級通信 class report/news **3.** communications: **~-shudan** 通信手段 means of communication

tsutá *n* ツタ・蔦 ivy

tsutaé *n* 伝え → **dengon** 伝言, **messēji** メッセージ

tsutaemásu, tsutaeru *v* 伝えます, 伝える passes it on to someone else; reports, communicates; transmits; hands down

tsutanai *adj* つたない・拙い halting, unskillful, poor (= **heta** 下手)

tsutawarimásu, tsutawaru *v* 伝わります, 伝わる is passed on; is reported, communicated; is transmitted; is handed down

tsuto *n* つと・苞 straw wrapping, straw-wrapped package

tsuto *adv* つと [BOOKISH] quickly

tsutomé *n* 勤め [BOOKISH] work(ing), job (*post*); tsutome-nin *n* 勤め人 office worker; tsutome-saki *n* 勤め先 place of employment, one's office

tsutomé *n* 務め duty, role

tsutomemásu, tsutoméru *v* 勤めます, 勤める [BOOKISH] is employed, works; works as; **ginkō´-in o ~** 銀行員を勤め[務め]ます works as a bank clerk

tsutomemásu, tsutoméru *v* 努めます, 努める [BOOKISH] exerts oneself, strives, endeavors

tsutsu *n* 筒 cylinder, pipe (= **kuda** 管, **kan** 管)

...´tsútsu *suffix* …つつ [LITERARY] **1.** = **…-nágara** …ながら (while doing) **2. … (shi)~ arimásu** …(し)つつあります is about to … (= **…-te imásu** …ています)

tsutsúji *n* ツツジ azalea

tsutsumí *n* 包み package, bundle: **~-gami** 包み紙 package paper (= **hōsō-shi** 包装紙)

tsutsumí *n* 堤 **1.** dike, bank, em--bankment **2.** reservoir (= **chosui-chi** 貯水池)

tsutsumimásu, tsutsúmu *v* 包みます, 包む wraps it up

tsutsushimi *n* 慎み prudence, discretion

tsutsushimimásu, tsutsushimu *v* 慎みます, 慎む is discreet, is careful; refrains from: **kotoba o ~** 言葉を慎みます is careful about how one speaks and behaves

tsutsushimimásu, tsutsushimu *v* 謹みます, 謹む is humble, is reverent

tsu(t)tsukimásu, tsu(t)tsúku *v* つ(っ)つきます, つ(っ)つく pecks at [INFORMAL]

tsuya *n* ツヤ・艶 gloss, shine, luster (= **gurosu** グロス, **kōtaku** 光沢); tsuya-keshi *n* ツヤ[艶]消し matte

tsuya *n* 通夜 (*funeral*)-wake, all-night vigil over a body

tsū´yaku *n* 通訳 interpreter; interpreting: **~-sha** 通訳者 an interpreter

tsuyo-bi *n* 強火 high flame

tsūyō shimásu (suru) *v* 通用します(する) **1.** is used commonly **2.** is accepted among people, is valid: **sekai dewa tsūyō shimasén** 世界では通用しません is not accepted in the world

tsuyói *adj* 強い strong; **tsúyosa** 強さ strength

tsuyu *n* つゆ・梅雨 rainy season (*in Japan*)

tsúyu *n* 露 dew

tsúyu *n* つゆ・汁 (**o-tsúyu** おつゆ) light (*clear*) soup

tsuzukemásu, tsuzukeru *v* 続けます, 続ける continues it, goes on (*with it*)

tsuzukete 続けて *adv* continuously, in succession, going on (*to the next*)

tsuzuki *n* 続き continuation, sequel, series

tsuzukimásu, tsuzuku *v* 続きます, 続く it continues (*will continue*); adjoins

tsuzuku *n* 続く To Be Continued

tsuzumarimásu, tsuzumáru *v* つづまります, つづまる [BOOKISH] it shrinks, gets shortened

tsuzumí *n* 鼓・つづみ drum (*hour-glass-shaped*)

tsuzure *n* 綴れ **1.** rags **2.** hand-woven brocade

tsuzuri *n* 綴り・つづり **1.** spelling **2.** binding, bound (*sewn*) pages

tsuzurimásu, tsuzuru *v* 綴ります, 綴る **1.** spells **2.** composes, writes **3.** patches; binds; sews (*together/up*)

tu... → **tsu...**

ty... → **ch...**

U

u *n* ウ・鵜 cormorant (*fishing bird*); u-kai *n* 鵜飼い cormorant fishing

uba *n* 乳母 nanny (*who cares for baby/babies in a household*); uba-guruma *n* 乳母車 baby carriage

ubaimásu, ubáu *v* 奪います, 奪う seizes, robs, plunders

uchi *n* うち・家 **1.** ~ おうち[お家] house, home; family: ~ **no**

náka de/ni うち[家]の中で/に indoors **2. ... uchí,** ... **uchi (no)** うち(の) [INFORMAL] we/us; I/me; our, my: **~ no kazoku** うちの家族 my family

uchi *n* 内: **... no ~ (de) ...** の内(で) inside; among

uchi *n* うち: **...-(shi)nai ~ ni ...** (し)ないうちに before it happens (*while it has not yet happened*)

uchi-... *prefix* 内... inside, inner; uchi-bori *n* 内堀 inner moat; uchi-gawa *n* 内側 the inside; uchi-ki (na) *adj* 内気(な) shy [IN POSITIVE SENSE]: **~ na seikaku** 内気な性格 shy disposition; uchi-wa *n* 内輪 ① the family circle; the inside: **~ no hanashi** 内輪の話 private matter, family affair ② **uchiwa (na)** 内輪(な) moderate, modest, conservative; uchi-wake *n* 内訳 breakdown, particulars, details: **shishutsu no ~** 支出の内訳 breakdown of expenditures

uchi-age *n* 打ち上げ **1.** launch (*rocket*) **2.** close (*performance, project, etc.*)

uchi-akemásu, uchi-akeru *v* 打ち明けます, 打ち明ける confesses, frankly reveals, confides

uchi-awase *n* 打ち合わせ・打合せ consultation, meeting (*in the office, etc. by appointment*) (**= kaigi** 会議, **miitingu** ミーティング)

uchi-awasemásu, uchi-awaséru *v* 打ち合わせます, 打ち合わせる holds a meeting/consultation

uchi-keshi *n* 打ち消し denial; negation, negative

uchi-keshimásu, uchi-kesu *v* 打ち消します, 打ち消す denies (*a rumor, etc.*), takes back a remark

uchi-koroshimásu, uchi-korósu *v* 撃ち殺します, 撃ち殺す shoots to death

uchimásu, útsu *v* 打ちます, 打つ hits, strikes, hammers; sends a telegram; uchí-mí *n* 打ち身 bruise

uchimásu, útsu *v* 撃ちます, 撃つ fires, shoots (*a gun*)

uchíwa *n* うちわ・団扇 (*Japanese*) a flat fan

uchōten *n* 有頂天 rapturous delight, being beside oneself with joy, being in seventh heaven, being overjoyed: **~ ni narimásu** 有頂天になります goes into raptures

úchū *n* 宇宙 universe, (*outer*) space; uchū-fuku *n* 宇宙服 space-suit; uchū-hikō-shi *n* 宇宙飛行士 astronaut

udé *n* 腕 **1.** arm **2.** special skill; ude-dókei *n* 腕時計 wristwatch; ude-gumi *n* 腕組み folding one's arms; ude-jiman (no) *adj* 腕自慢(の) proud of one's skill; ude-kiki (no) *adj* 腕利き(の) skilled, competent, able; ude-maé *n* 腕前 prowess, skill, ability

údo *n* ウド・独活 Japanese celery

udon *n* うどん Japanese wheat-flour noodles: **~-ya** うどん屋 Japanese noodle shop

ue *n* 上 **1.** ...**ué** ...上 above,

upper part, surface, top: **... no ~ (de/ni/no)** ...の上(で/に/の) on, on top of **2. ué** 上 (= **toshi-~** 年上) older, oldest

ue *v* 飢え hunger, starvation

uédingu-... *prefix* ウエディング... wedding; uédingu-doresu *n* ウエディングドレス wedding dress (= **hanayome-ishō** 花嫁衣裳); uédingu-pātii *n* ウエディングパーティ wedding party; uédingu-ringu *n* ウエディングリング wedding ring

uehāsu *n* ウエハース wafer

ueki *n* 植木 garden/potted plant; ueki-ya *n* 植木屋 gardener

uemásu, ueru *v* 植えます, 植える plants, grows plant

uemásu, uéru *v* 飢えます, 飢える starves (*hungers*)

Ueno *n* 上野 **Ueno**; **Uenó-Eki** 上野駅 Ueno Station; **Ueno-Kō´en** 上野公園 Ueno Park

uérudan *n* ウエルダン well-done (*beef*)

uésuto *n* ウエスト waist (= **koshi** 腰); **~-pōchi** ウエストポーチ belt bag

uē´tā *n* ウエーター waiter

uē´toresu *n* ウエートレス waitress

ugai *n* うがい a gargle; ugai (o) shimásu (suru) *v* うがい(を)します(する) gargles

ugokashimásu, ugokásu *v* 動かします, 動かす moves it

ugokí *n* 動き movement, motion; trend

ugokimásu, ugóku *v* 動きます, 動く one/it moves

uindo-burē´kā *n* ウインドブレーカー windbreaker

uindō shoppingu *n* ウィンドウショッピング window shopping

uínku *n* ウインク wink(ing)

uirusu *n* ウイルス virus; **~-taisaku-sofuto** ウイルス対策ソフト antivirus software

uísúkii *n* ウイスキー, **wísukii** ウィスキー whisky

úji *n* 氏 clan, family; family name (= **sei** 姓)

uji (mushi) *n* ウジ(ムシ)・蛆(虫) maggot

ukabimásu, ukabu *v* 浮かびます, 浮かぶ floats

ukagai *n* 伺い visit; inquiry, consultation

ukagaimásu, ukagau *v* 伺います, 伺う [HUMBLE] I visit (*you*); I inquire; I hear

ukagaimásu, ukagau *v* 窺います, 窺う keeps a watchful eye on (*the situation*); (**kikái/chansu o ~** 機会/チャンスを窺います) watches for (*an opportunity*)

ukai *n* 迂回・う回 detour

ukárimásu, ukáru *v* 受かります, 受かる passes, succeeds

ukatsu *n* うかつ・迂闊 carelessness, inattentiveness, thoughtlessness: **~ ni mo** うかつ[迂闊]にも carelessly, inattentively, thoughtlessly

uke-iremásu, uké-ireru *v* 受け入れます, 受け入れる accepts

ukemásu, ukéru *v* 受けます, 受ける accepts; receives; takes; gets; suffers, incurs

ukemi *n* 受身 **1.** passive voice **2.** passive (*attitude*)

uke-mochimásu, uke-mótsu *v* 受け持ちます, 受け持つ takes/accepts/has charge of

uke-oi *n* 請負・請け負い a contract (*to undertake work*); ukeoi-gyōsha *n* 請(け)負(い)業者 contractor; ukeoi-shigoto *n* 請(け)負(い)仕事 contract work

uke-oimásu, uke-óu *v* 請け負います, 請け負う contracts (*to undertake work*)

ukeoi-nin *n* 請負人 contractor

uketamawarimásu, uketamawáru *v* 承ります, 承る I (*humbly*) hear/listen/consent

uke-torimásu, uke-toru *v* 受け取ります, 受け取る accepts, receives, takes; takes it (= understand it)

uketsugimásu, uketsugu *v* 受け継ぎます, 受け継ぐ succeeds to

uke-tsuke *n* 受付 acceptance; information desk; receptionist

uke-tsukemásu, uke-tsukéru *v* 受け付けます, 受け付ける accepts, receives

uke-uri *n* 受け売り borrowing someone else's ideas

uké-zara *n* 受け皿 saucer (for cup)

uki *n* 雨季・雨期 rainy season

ukiashi dachimásu (dátsu) *v* 浮き足立ちます (立つ) is wavering, is ready to run away

uki-bori *n* 浮き彫り relief (*sculpture consisting of shapes carved on a surface*) (= **reriifu** レリーフ): **shinjutsu o ~ ni shimásu** 真実を浮き彫りにします call attention to the fact that ...

ukimásu, uku *v* 浮きます, 浮く floats

ukiwa *n* 浮き輪 inner tube (*swimming*)

ukiyo *n* 浮世 [BOOKISH] this fleeting world, transient world; ukiyo-e *n* 浮世絵 Japanese woodblock prints

ukkári *adv* うっかり absentmindedly (= **tsui** つい)

umá *n* ウマ・馬 horse

uma ga aimásu (au) *v* ウマ[馬]が合います(合う) gets on well, gets along well

umái *adj* うまい・旨い・美味い (*commonly male*) tasty, delicious (= **oishii** 美味しい)

umái *adj* うまい・上手い **1.** skillful, good (= **jōzu** 上手) **2.** successful, profitable

úmaku *adv* うまく・旨く・美味く so as to be tasty

úmaku *adv* うまく・上手く **1.** skillfully **2.** successfully

ūman ribu *n* ウーマンリブ women's liberation

umare 生まれ・産まれ *n* birth

umaremásu, umareru *v* 生まれ[産まれ]ます, 生まれ[産まれ]る is born

ume *n* ウメ・梅 Japanese apricot ("plum"); ume-boshi *n* 梅干し

pickled plum/apricot; ume-shu *n* 梅酒 apricot wine

umekí *n* うめき・呻き a groan

umekimásu, uméku *v* うめきます・呻きます, うめく・呻く groans

umemásu, umeru *v* 埋めます, 埋める buries (= **uzumemásu** うずめます・埋めます)

umí *n* うみ・膿 pus

úmi *n* 海 sea; umibe *n* 海辺 (sea-)shore, seaside; umi ni sen-nen yama ni sen-nen 海に千年山に千年 ① knowing every trick in the book ② a sly old fox (= **umi-sen yama-sen** 海千山千); umi no hi *n* 海の日 Marine day, Ocean Day (*3rd Monday of July*)

umimásu, umu *v* 生みます・産みます, 生む・産む gives birth to, bears

umimásu, úmu *v* 膿みます, 膿む festers

umō *n* 羽毛 feather

úmu *n* 有無 existence (*or non-existence*): **~ o iwasazu** 有無を言わさず forcibly (= **muriyari** 無理やり)

ún *n* 運 fate, luck (→ **fu-un (na)** 不運(な), **kōun** 幸運); ún ga ii *adj* 運がいい lucky; ún ga warui *adj* 運が悪い unlucky; ún-mei *n* 運命 destiny, fate: **~ no akai-ito** 運命の赤い糸 red string of fate, red thread of destiny; ún-waruku *adv* 運悪く unluckily; ún-yoku *adv* 運良く luckily (= **saiwai** 幸い)

ún *interj* うん = *n* ん [INFORMAL] yeah, yes

unagashimásu, unagásu *v* 促します, 促す stimulates, urges (*on*)

unagi *n* ウナギ・鰻 eel; una-don *n* うな丼 a bowl of rice topped with broiled eel; unagi nobori *n* うなぎ登り[上り]・鰻登り[上り] rising rapidly and steadily (*prices, etc.*)

unarí *n* 唸り・うなり a roar; a growl a groan

unarimásu, unáru *v* 唸ります, 唸る roars; growls; (= **umekimásu** うめきます・呻きます) groans

unazukimásu *v* うなずきます・頷きます, **unazuku** うなずく・頷く nods

únchin *n* 運賃 fare (*transportation*)

undō *n* 運動 **1.** movement: **shakai-~** 社会運動 social movement: **sen-kyo-~** 選挙運動 election campaign **2.** exercise; sports; athletics; **~-senshu** 運動選手 athlete

únga *n* 運河 canal

úni *n* ウニ・雲丹 sea urchin (*roe*)

unpan *n* 運搬 transport(-ation) (*of goods and/or people*)

unsō *n* 運送 transport(-ation) (*of goods*) (= **unpan** 運搬); unsō-gyō-sha 運送業者 *n* transportation company; unsō-ya *n* 運送屋 express/forwarding agent; (*house*) mover (= **hikkoshi-ya** 引っ越し屋)

unten *n* 運転 operation, operating; untén-menkyo (-shō) *n* 運転免許(証) driver's license; untén-shu *n* 運転手 driver

unto *adv* うんと much, a good deal, greatly

unubore ga tsuyói *adj* うぬぼれが強い vain, conceited

"un-un" *interj* うんうん = **n´n** んん

unyu *n* 運輸 transport(ation) (*of goods*) (= **unsō** 運送)

unzári shimásu̲ (suru) *v* うんざりします(する) gets bored, gets sick and tired

uo *n* ウオ・魚 fish (= **sakana** サカナ・魚)

uo no me *n* うおのめ・魚の目 foot corn

uppun *n* うっぷん・鬱憤 frustration, pent-up anger, pent-up discontent: **~ o harashimásu̲** うっぷんを晴らします vents one's anger

urá *n* 裏 reverse (*side*), back; lining; what's behind it; the alley; urá *n* 裏 sole (*of foot*): **ashi no ~** 足の裏 sole of foot; ura-dō´ri *n* 裏通り back street, alley; ura-gáeshi (no) *adj* 裏返し(の) inside-out; ura-gáeshimásu̲, ura-gáesu *v* 裏返します, 裏返す turns over; turns inside out; ura-guchi *n* 裏口 back door; ura-me ni demásu̲/deru *v* 裏目に出ます/出る backfires, turns out badly; ura-mon *n* 裏門 back gate; ura-omote no aru hito *n* 裏表のある人 two-faced person

urá *n* 浦 bay

urabon *n* うら[盂蘭]盆 the Bon Festival (= **o-bón** お盆)

ura-girí *n* 裏切り a double-cross, betrayal, treachery

ura-girimásu̲, ura-gíru *v* 裏切ります, 裏切る betrays, double-crosses

uramí *n* 恨み grudge, resentment, ill will, enmity; urami o kaimásu̲ (kau) *v* 恨みを買います(買う) incurs someone's enmity

uramimásu̲, urámu *v* 恨みます, 恨む begrudges, resents

uranái *n* 占い fortune-telling; **~-shi** 占い師 fortune-teller

urayamashíi *adj* 羨ましい・うらやましい enviable; envious

urayamimásu̲, urayámu *v* 羨みます・うらやみます, 羨む・うらやむ envies

ure-ku̲chi *n* 売れ口 sales outlet

uremásu̲, ureru *v* 売れます, 売れる **1.** it sells, is in demand; thrives; is popular **2.** can sell

ureshíi *adj* うれしい・嬉しい glad, delightful, pleasant, wonderful, happy

úri *n* ウリ・瓜 fruit of the gourd family; úri futatsu *n* ウリ[瓜]二つ like two peas in a pod (*not to literally mean, "two melons"*) (= **sokkuri** そっくり)

uri *v* 売り sale; uri-ba *n* 売り場 (*shop*) counter, stand; shop, store; uri-dashi *n* 売り出し (*special*) sale; **uri-dashimásu̲** 売り出します puts on sale/market; launches; uri-kire *n, adj* 売り切れ sellout; sold out; uri-ko *n* 売り子 sales clerk; shop-girl; uri-mono *n* 売り物 sales goods/

item, (*something*) for sale; uri-nushi *n* 売り主 seller; uri-te *n* 売り手 seller (= **uri-nushi** 売り主)

ri-kiremásu, uri-kiréru *v* 売り切れます, 売り切れる sells out, runs out of

rimásu, uru *v* 売ります, 売る sells

roko *n* ウロコ・鱗 scales (*on a fish*)

rotsukimásu, urotsuku *v* うろつきます, うろつく hangs around

'ru *n* ウール wool

rū'-doshi *n* うるう[閏]年 leap year

rume (-íwashi) *n* ウルメ(イワシ)・潤目(鰯) large (*and usually dried*) sardine

rusái *adj* うるさい annoying, noisy (= **sawagashii** 騒がしい)

rushi *n* ウルシ・漆 lacquer; **~-nuri no utsuwa** 漆塗りの器 lacquerware (= **shikki** 漆器)

ruwashii *adj* うるわしい・麗しい [BOOKISH] **1.** beautiful **2.** heart-warming

sa-barashi *n* 憂さ晴らし distraction (*from emotional pain, suffering, etc.*), diversion, break, something to cheer one up

sagi *n* ウサギ・兎 rabbit, hare

san kusai *adj* うさんくさい・胡散臭い fishy, suspicious-looking

setsu shimásu (suru) *v* 右折します(する) turns right

shi *n* ウシ・牛 ox, oxen; cow, cattle

shinaimásu, ushinau *v* 失います, 失う loses

ushiro *n* 後ろ behind; (*in*) back

úso *n* うそ・嘘 lie, false(hood), fib; usó-tsuki *n* うそつき・嘘つき liar

úsu *n* うす・臼 (*utensil*) mortar

usu-cha *n* 薄茶 weak powdered tea (= **o-úsu** お薄)

usui *adj* 薄い thin

utá *n* 歌 **1.** song **2.** (*Japanese*) 31-syllable poem

utá *n* 詩 modern poem

utagai *adj* 疑い a doubt: **~ náku** 疑いなく undoubtedly, doubtless

utagaimásu, utagau *v* 疑います, 疑う doubts

utagawashíi *v* 疑わしい doubtful

utai *n* 謡 [BOOKISH] chanting a Noh libretto

utaimásu, utau *v* 歌います, 歌う sings; recites, chants

utaimásu, utau *v* うたい[謳い]ます, うたう・謳う expressly states; extols

uten *n* 雨天 [BOOKISH] rainy weather: **~-kekkō** 雨天決行 rain or shine: **~-chūshi** 雨天中止 Canceled in case of rain.

utói *adj* うとい・疎い; **... ni ~** …に疎い[うとい] out of touch with …, not abreast of …

útouto *adv* うとうと drowsing (off) (= **utsura utsura** うつらうつら)

utsubuse *n* うつぶせ・俯せ lying on one's stomach

utsukushíi *adj* 美しい beautiful

utsumukemásu, utsumukeru *v* うつむ

けます, うつむける; **kao o ~** 顔をうつむけます turns one's face down

utsumukimásu, utsumúku *v* うつむきます, うつむく lowers one's eyes, hangs one's head

utsurí *n* 映り reflection, picture quality; (*a becoming*) match

utsurimásu, utsúru *v* 移ります, 移る **1.** one/it moves, shifts **2.** changes **3.** moves house/residence (= **hikkoshimásu** 引越します, **hikkosu** 引越す)

utsurimásu, utsúru *v* 映ります, る映 is reflected; can be seen (*through*); is becoming

utsurimásu, utsúru *v* 写ります, 写る comes out (*photograph*)

utsuro (na) *adj* うつろ・虚ろ(な) hollow, empty, vacant: **~ na hyōjō´ o mísete** うつろ[虚ろ]な表情を見せて with a blank look

utsushimásu, utsúsú *v* 移します, 移す moves/transfers it

utsushimásu, utsúsú *v* うつします, うつす infects, gives another person a disease (*illness*)

utsushimásu, utsúsú *v* 写します, 写す copies; takes a picture of; projects a picture

utsushimásu, utsúsú *v* 映します, 映す reflects, mirrors

utsutsu o nukashimásu (nukasu) *v* うつつを抜かします (抜かす) is engrossed, is addicted

utsuwa *n* 器 **1.** receptacle, utensil, container **2.** tool **3.** ability, personality: **~ ga/no ōkii hito** 器が/の大きい人 person of high caliber

uttae *n* 訴え complaint, lawsuit

uttaemásu, uttaéru *v* 訴えます, 訴える accuses, sues: **kujō o ~** 苦情を訴えます complains

uttetsuke (no) *adj* うってつけ(の) the most suitable; just right, just the …, just the one/ticket

uttóri (to) *adv* うっとり(と) absorbed, fascinated

uttōshii *adj* うっとうしい gloomy, dismal, dreary: **~ tenki** うっとうしい天気 gloomy weather

uwabaki *n* 上履き・上ばき indoor footwear (*slippers, etc.*): **~ jisan** 上履き持参 Bring your indoor shoes.

uwabe *n* 上辺・うわべ **1.** surface (= **hyōmen** 表面) **2.** outer appearances (= **gaikan** 外観): **~ o tsukuroimásu** うわべをつくろい[繕い]ます puts up a front

uwagaki *n* 上書き **1.** address (*written on envelope, etc.*) **2.** overwriting: **~-hozon** 上書き保存 overwrite save: **~-mōdo** 上書きモード overwrite mode

uwagi *n* 上着 coat, jacket, blouse

uwagoto *n* うわごと・うわ言 raving, delirium

uwaki *adj* 浮気 **1. ~ (na)** 浮気(な) fickle **2. ~ (o) shimásu** 浮気(を)します is unfaithful, has an (*extramarital*) affair

uwa-mawarimásu, uwa-mawaru *v* 上回ります, 上回る exceeds

uwasa *n* うわさ・噂 rumor, gossip
uyamai *n* 敬い reverence, respect
uyamaimásu, uyamáu *v* 敬います, 敬う reveres, respects
uyamuya *n* うやむや obscurity, vagueness
uyamuya ni shimásu (suru) *v* うやむやにします (する) is wishy-washy, obscures the issue
uyoku *n* 右翼 (*political party*) the right wing, rightists
úzu *n* 渦, **uzú-maki** 渦巻き whirlpool; (uzu-maki) rōru-kēki *n* (渦巻き)ロールケーキ swiss roll; uzu-shio *n* 渦潮 whirling current
uzumarimásu, uzumaru *v* うずまります・埋まります, うずまる・埋まる gets buried
uzumemásu, uzumeru *v* うずめます・埋めます, うずめる・埋める buries
uzura *n* ウズラ・鶉 quail: **~ no tamago** ウズラ[鶉]の卵 quail egg

W

wá *n* 輪 circle; wheel; link; ring; loop; wa-gomu *n* 輪ゴム rubber band; wak-ka *n* 輪っか・わっか [INFORMAL] circle; wheel; link; ring; loop (= **wa** 輪)
wa *n* 和 **1.** peace (= **hei-wa** 平和, **wa-hei** 和平) **2.** harmony (= **chō-wa** 調和, **kyō-wa** 協和); wa-hei kōshō *n* 和平交渉 [BOOKISH] peace negotiations; wa-hei jōyaku *n* 和平条約 [BOOKISH] peace treaty
wa-... *prefix* 和 ... Japanese ...; wa-ei *n* 和英 Japanese-English (= **nichi-ei** 日英); **waei-jíten** 和英辞典 Japanese-English dictionary; wa-fū *n* 和風 [BOOKISH] Japanese style; wa-fuku *n* 和服 Japanese traditional clothes; kimono; wa-gáshi *n* 和菓子 Japanese cakes/sweets; wa-sei-eigo *n* 和製英語 "Made in Japan" English, Japanese English; wá-shi *n* 和紙 Japanese paper; wa-shitsu *n* 和室 Japanese-style room; wa-shoku *n* 和食 Japanese food; wa-yaku *n* 和訳 translation into Japanese
...-wa *suffix* ... 羽 (*counts birds, rabbits*)
... wa particle ...は as for ..., speaking of ..., let's talk about (*change the subject to*) ...; ..., guess what —; if it be (= **...déwa** ... では = **... nára** ... なら)
... wa *interj* ...わ (*mostly female*) indeed, you see
wā *interj* わあ (*female or children*) Wow!; Gee!; Gosh!
wabí *n* わび・侘び a liking for simple things; simple tastes
wabi *n* 詫び **o-wabi** お詫び apology
wabimásu, wabiru *v* 詫びます, 詫びる [BOOKISH] apologize

wabishíi *v* わびしい・侘しい miserable; lonely

wa-chū *n* 話中 [BOOKISH] busy (*on the phone*) (= **hanashi-chū** 話し中): **~-on** 話中音 busy tone

wa-dachi *n* わだち・ワダチ・轍 (*wheel*) ruts

wadai *n* 話題 topic of conversation, subject (*of talk*)

wá-ga ... *adj* 我が・わが… [BOOKISH] my, our: **~ kuni** 我が国・わが国 our (*this*) country (*commonly Japan*)

wá-ga-hai *pron* 我(が)輩・吾(が)輩 [BOOKISH] (*archaic or obsolete. male*) I/me; waga-mámá (na) *adj* わがまま・我が侭(な) selfish

wágon (sha) *n* ワゴン(車) station wagon

wai-fai *n* ワイ・ファイ (= **musen-ran** 無線LAN) Wi-Fi, wireless LAN (*computer*)

wáin *n* ワイン wine: **aka-~** 赤ワイン red wine: **shiro-~** 白ワイン white wine: **~-gurasu** ワイングラス wine glass

wáipā *n* ワイパー windshield wiper

wáiro *n* わいろ・賄賂 bribe(ry); graft

waisetsu *n* わいせつ obscenity

wai-shatsu *n* Yシャツ shirt

wakai *n* 和解 reconciliation

wakái *adj* 若い young; waka-ba *n* 若葉 young leaves: **Wakaba-māku** 若葉マーク Wakaba mark (*a mark displayed on the windshield to indicate brand new driver*); waka-mono *n* 若者 young person, youth; waka-te *n* 若手 young person

wakame *n* ワカメ・若布 a kind of seaweed

wakaré *n* 別れ parting, farewell

wakaré *n* 分かれ branch(ing), fork(ing), division

wakáre *n* 別れ breakup; farewell; leave

wakaremás<u>u</u>, wakaréru *v* 別れます, 別れる they part, separate

wakaremás<u>u</u>, wakaréru *v* 分かれます 分かれる it branches off, splits

wakareme *n* 分かれ目 turning point

wakarí *n* 分かり comprehension (= **nomikomi** 呑み込み): **~ ga hayái** 分かりが早い quick-witted **(mono)~ ga warúi** (もの)分かりが悪い dull(-witted), stupid

Wakarimáshi<u>t</u>a *v* 分かりました. **1.** Yes, I see. **2.** Yes, I will (*comply with your request*).

wakarimás<u>u</u>, wakáru *v* 分かります, 分かる it is clear (*understood*); understands; finds out; has good sense

wakashimás<u>u</u>, wakasu *v* 沸かします, 沸かす boils it

wáke *n* わけ・訳 **1.** reason (= **riyū** 理由) **2.** meaning (= **imi** 意味), content (= **naiyō** 内容) **3.** case, circumstance (= **jijō** 事情)

wakemae *n* 分け前 share, portion

wakemás<u>u</u>, wakéru *v* 分けます, 分ける divides (*splits, distributes*) it; separates them

wake-mé *n* 分け目 dividing line, part(ing) (*in hair*)

wáke arimasén (nái) *v* 訳ありません(ない) is no problem, is easy

wáke-nai *v* 訳ない・わけない easy, simple, ready; **wake-naku** 訳なく・わけなく easily, simply, readily, with no problem

wakí *n* わき・脇 side; **waki-bara** *n* わき腹・脇腹 flank; **waki-mi** *n* わき見・脇見 looking off; **~-unten** 脇見運転 inattentive driving; **waki-michi** *n* わき道・脇道 side road

wakí *n* わき・腋 side of the body; **waki-ga** *n* わきが・腋臭 armpit smell, body odor; **waki-nó-shita** *n* わき[脇・腋]の下 ① armpit ② under one's arms

waki aiai *n* 和気あいあい in happy harmony

wakimásu, waku *v* 沸きます, 沸く it boils: **o-yu ga ~** お湯が沸きます the water boils (→ **o-yu o waka-shimásu** お湯を沸かします, **o-yu ga wakimáshita** お湯が沸きました)

wakimásu, waku *v* 湧きます, 湧く it gushes, springs forth: **kibō ga wakimáshita** 希望が湧きました I was given hope., I got hope.

wakú *n* 枠 **1.** frame, framework (= **~-gumi** 枠組) **2.** reel, limit, a confine; **waku-gumi** *n* 枠組 ① frame, framework (= **waku** 枠) ② outline

wákuchin *n* ワクチン vaccine

wakusei *n* 惑星 planet

waku-waku shimásu (suru) *v* わくわくします(する) is thrilled, is excited

wamekimásu, waméku *v* わめきます・喚きます, わめく・喚く yells

wan *n* 碗 bowl: **chawan** 茶碗 rice-bowl: **cha-wan-mushi** 茶碗蒸し pot-steamed hotchpotch

wán *n* 湾 bay, gulf: **Tōkyō-~** 東京湾 Tokyo Bay; **wan-gan** *n* 湾岸 gulf coast

wán *n* ワン one; **wán-man** *n* ワンマン ① one-man, operator-only (*bus*); **~-shō´** ワンマンショー one-man show, solo performance ② dictator: **~-keiei** ワンマン経営 Caesar management; **wan-píisu** *n* ワンピース (*one-piece*) dress

wána *n* わな・ワナ・罠 trap; lasso: **~ ni kakarimásu** わな[罠]にかかります gets trapped/snared

wáni *n* ワニ crocodile, alligator

waní-ashi (no) *adj* わに足(の) bowlegged

wánisu *n* ワニス varnish

wanpaku *n* わんぱく・腕白 rudeness: **~-kozō** わんぱく[腕白]小僧 brat, mischievous boy

wanpaku (na) *adj* 腕白・わんぱく(な) naughty, mischievous (*commonly used for children*) (= **yancha (na)** やんちゃ(な))

wánryoku *n* 腕力 [BOOKISH] arm strength, physical force, physical strength

wán-wan *interj* ワンワン bow-wow! (*bark*)

wappu *n* 割賦 allotment, installment

wā-puro *n* ワープロ word processor
wára *n* ワラ・藁 rice straw
warabanshi *n* わら半紙 coarse paper, rough paper
warabe *n* わらべ・童 [BOOKISH] child(ren) (= **jidō** 児童): **~-uta** わらべ歌・童歌 Japanese traditional children's song
warabi *n* ワラビ bracken
warai わらい・嗤い *n* ridicule, sneer, mockery
waraimásu, warau *v* 笑います, 笑う laughs; laughs at; smiles
waraimásu, warau *v* わらい[嗤い]ます, わらう・嗤う ridicules, sneers, mocks
wáre *pron* 我 [BOOKISH] **1.** oneself **2.** I/me (= **wata(ku)shi** わた(く)し・私); ware ni kaerimásu (kaeru) *v* 我に返ります (返る) comes to oneself; ware omou, yue ni ware ari 我思う、ゆえに我あり (*famous saying*) I think, therefore I am.; ware o wasuremásu (wasureru) *v* 我を忘れます(忘れる) ① is hooked on, is carried away ② is stunned; ware-ware *pron* 我々・われわれ [BOOKISH] we; us
waremásu, wareru *v* 割れます, 割れる **1.** it cracks, it splits **2.** can divide/break/dilute it; ware-me *n* 割れ目 crack, crevice, gap; ware-mono *n* 割れ物 fragile
wari *n* 割 **1.** (**…-wari** …割) tens of percent; percentage; **sán-~** 三割 = **sanjup-pāsénto** 30パーセント・30% thirty percent **2.** profit (ability): **~ ni aimasén** 割に合いません it doesn't pay (off); wari-ai *n* 割合 rate, percentage: **~ (ni)** 割合(に) comparatively, relatively
wariate *n* 割り当て quota, allotment
waribashi *n* 割り箸 throwaway chopsticks
wari-biki *n* 割引 discount
wari-kan *n* 割り勘 splitting the bill; (*going*) Dutch treat
warikómimásu, warikómu *v* 割り込みます, 割り込む cuts in (*into*), breaks in; breezes in
wari-mae *n* 割り前 share, portion
warimásu, waru *v* 割ります, 割る divides/splits it, breaks it, dilutes it
wari (ni) *adv* わり(に)・割(に) relatively, comparatively
warízan *n* 割り算 division
warú *n* 悪 bad, evil (= **aku** 悪); warú-i *adj* 悪い ① bad, poor; wrong; vicious ② at fault; Warú-i! *interj* 悪い! Sorry.; warú-fuzake *n* 悪ふざけ practical joke; warú-gashikoi *adj* 悪賢い sly, cunning, crafty, wily (*person*) (= **zuru-gashikoi** ずる賢い, **kōkatsu (na)** 狡猾(な)); warú-gi *n* 悪気 evil intent, malice (= **akui** 悪意); warú-jie *n* 悪知恵 cunning, craft; warú-kuchi/-guchi *n* 悪口 (*verbal*) abuse, slander; waru-mono *n* 悪者 bad guy/fellow, villain, scoundrel: **~ atsukai** 悪者扱い demonize; warú-yoi *n* 悪酔い getting sick from drink

warutsu *n* ワルツ waltz
wásabi *n* ワサビ・山葵 horseradish
washi *n* ワシ・鷲 eagle
washi *pron* わし (*archaic old male*) I/me (= **wata(ku)shi** わた(く)し・私)
Washínton *n* ワシントン Washington
wasuremásu, wasureru *v* 忘れます, 忘れる forgets; **wasure-mono** *n* 忘れ物 ① leaving something behind ② a thing left behind (*forgetfully*); **wasurenái de** *v* 忘れないで: **~ de (… shite) kudasái** 忘れないで(…して)下さい don't forget (*to do* …); **wasurep-pói** *adj* 忘れっぽい forgetful
watá *n* 綿 cotton; **watá-ame** *n* 綿アメ cotton candy (= **wata-gashi** 綿菓子); **wata-bokori** *n* 綿ぼこり dustball; **watá-gashi** *n* 綿菓子 cotton candy; **wata-ge** *n* 綿毛 fluff, cotton fiber; **wata-íré** *n* 綿入れ (*cotton-*) padded garment
watá *n* 腸 guts, intestines
watakushi *pron* わたくし・私 [BOOKISH], **watashi** わたし・私 [HUMBLE] I/me; **~-tachi** わたくし[私]達, **watáshí-táchi** わたし[私]達 we/us; **watakushí-ritsu (no)** *adj* 私立(の) private(-ly established); **~ (no) gakkō** 私立(の)学校 private school; **watakushí-shōsetsu** *n* 私小説 I-Novel (*a novel writing about oneself*) (= **shi-shōsetsu** 私小説)
watari *v* 渡り crossing, ferry (*place*): **~ o tsukemásu** 渡りをつけます forms an understanding with, gets in touch with; **~ ni fúne** 渡りに舟 a timely rescue, a convenient escape/excuse
watarimásu, wataru *v* 渡ります, 渡る crosses over
watashi *pron* 私・わたし = [BOOKISH] **watakushi** 私・わたくし I/me
watashi-búne *n* 渡し舟 ferryboat
watashimásu, watasu *v* 渡します, 渡す hands it over; ferries
watáshí-táchi *pron* わたし[私]達 we, us (= **watakushí-tachi** わたくし[私]達)
watto *n* ワット watt
waza *n* 業 trick, feat
waza *n* 技 skill, technique, art (= **gijutsu** 技術)
wáza-to *adv* わざと deliberately, on purpose, intentionally
wazawai *n* 災い misfortune, mishap, disaster (= **sainan** 災難)
wázawaza *adv* わざわざ expressly, especially; purposely
wazuka *adj* わずか a few, a little (= **sukoshi** 少し)
wazurai *n* 煩い・わずらい [BOOKISH] trouble, worry
wazurai *n* 患い [BOOKISH] illness (= **byōki** 病気)
wazuraimásu, wazurau *v* 煩います, 煩う worries about, is troubled by
wazuraimásu, wazurau *v* 患います, 患う has trouble with (*one's eyes*), suffers from (*an ailment*)
wazurawashii *adj* 煩わしい troublesome; complicated
web *n* ウェブ World Wide Web,

Internet; websaito *n* ウェブサイト website

weburogu *n* ウェブログ(= **burogu** ブログ) weblog, blog (*Internet*)

wísukii *n* ウィスキー whisky

witto *n* ウィット wit

Y

yá *n* 矢 arrow; ya-jirushi *n* 矢印 arrow sign (*such as* "→", "←", "↑", "↓")

ya-..., ...-ya *prefix, suffix* 夜. . . , . . . 夜 night (= **ban** 晩): **shū-~** 終夜 all night; yá-gu *n* 夜具 [BOOKISH] bedclothes; top quilt; yá-kan *n* 夜間 [BOOKISH] (*at*) night; ya-kei *n* 夜景 night view; ya-kō-ressha *n* 夜行列車 night train

ya-... *prefix* 野. . . wild, field; ya-chō *n* 野鳥 wild bird; ya-ei *n* 野営 camp, bivouac; yá-gai *n* 野外 outdoors, in the field: **~-katsudō** 野外活動 outdoor activity; ya-jū *n* 野獣 [BOOKISH] wild beast; ya-ken *n* 野犬 wild dog; ya-sei (no) *adj* 野性(の) wild, not cultivated; ya-sen *n* 野戦 open battle: **~-byōin** 野戦病院 field hospital

... ya ... *conj* …や … and … and … (*choosing typical items*)

... ya *interj* …や [INFORMAL] **1.** = **…i ya** …いや = **… i wa** …いは **2.** = **…e ba** …えば (if)

... -ya *suffix* …屋 (*name of certain*) shop, shopkeeper, dealer; house (→ (o-)sobá-~(お)蕎麦屋: **rāmen-~** ラーメン屋 Ramen shop: **karē-~** カレー屋 curry shop

yā´ *interj* やあ hi! hello! (*mostly male.* VERY INFORMAL. *Cannot be used to address a superior*)

yabái *adj* やばい **1.** (*mostly male, very informal*) dangerous (*will get you into trouble*) **2.** (*mostly young people.* SLANG) awesome

yaban (na) *adj* 野蛮(な) barbarous, barbarian, savage: **~-jín** 野蛮人 a barbarian, a savage

yabō *n* 野望 ambition [IN NEGATIVE SENSE] (= **yashin** 野心) (= **taishi** 大志, **taibō** 大望 [IN NEGATIVE SENSE])

yábo (na) *adj* 野暮(な) [INFORMAL] rustic, inelegant; **~-yō** 野暮用 small errand to run

yabu *n* ヤブ・薮 bush, thicket; yabu-hebi *n* やぶ蛇 boomerang (*something injures the originator*), waking a sleeping giant; yabu-isha *n* ヤブ[藪]医者 quack doctor

yabukemásu, yabukéru *v* 破けます, 破ける **1.** it tears, bursts; is frustrated **2.** can tear/burst it (= **yaburemásu** 破れます)

yabukimásu, yabúku *v* 破きます, 破く tears (*bursts*) it; frustrates; violates; defeats

yabure-kabure *n* やぶれ[破れ]かぶれ desperation (= **jibōjiki** 自暴自棄)
yaburemásu, yaburéru *v* 破れます, 破れる **1.** it tears, bursts; is frustrated **2.** can tear/burst it
yaburemásu, yaburéru *v* 敗れます, 敗れる loses
yaburimásu, yabúru *v* 破ります, 破る tears (*bursts*) it; frustrates; violates; defeats
yabusaka de (wa) arimasen (nai) *v* やぶさかで(は)ありません (ない) is willing to do
yá-chin *n* 家賃 house rent
yádo, yado-ya *n* 宿, 宿屋 inn
yagate *adv* やがて before long; in time (= **mamonaku** まもなく)
yági *n* ヤギ・山羊 goat
yahári *adv* やはり also; either; after all; just we/I thought! (= **yappari** やっぱり)
yaiba *n* やいば・刃 blade; sword
yáji *n* やじ・野次 heckling
yajiuma *n* やじうま・野次馬 rubbernecker: **~-konjō** やじうま根性 extreme curiosity
yakamashíi *adj* やかましい [INFORMAL], boisterous, clamorous, noisy; annoying; overly strict, demanding [IN NEGATIVE SENSE]
yakan *n* やかん teakettle
yáke *n* やけ・自棄 desperation(= **jibō-jiki** 自暴自棄): **~ ni** やけに excessively, unbearably, terribly
yakedo *n* やけど・火傷 burn, scald (*on the skin*) (= **nesshō** 熱傷)
yakemásu, yakeru *v* 焼けます, 焼ける **1.** it burns; it is baked **2.** can burn it
yakemásu, yakeru *v* 妬けます, 妬ける is jealous, envies
yaki 焼き *n* baking, burning, broiling; tempering; exposure
yaki-... *prefix* 焼き... roast: **(ishi-)~imo** (石)焼き芋 (stone-)baked yam; yakí-guri *n* 焼き栗 roasted chestnuts; yaki-gushi *n* 焼き串 skewer, spit; yaki-meshi *n* 焼き飯 fried rice; yaki-móchi *n* やきもち・焼き餅 jealousy; yakí-mochi *n* やきもち・焼き餅 toasted rice-cake; yaki-mono *n* 焼き物 ① pottery ② broiled food/dishes; yaki-niku *n* 焼き肉・焼肉 grilled slices of meat; yaki-soba *n* 焼きそば・やきそば chow mein; fried Chinese noodle; yaki-tori *n* 焼き鳥・やきとり chicken shishkebab (*skewers*)
...-yaki *suffix* ...焼 (*ceramic*) ware from ...; **Imari-~** 伊万里焼 Imari (*ware*)
yakimásu, yaku *v* 焼きます, 焼く burns/broils it, bakes (*roasts, toasts*) it
yakimásu, yaku *v* 妬きます, 妬く is jealous, envies
yákkai *n* 厄介・やっかい trouble, bother (= **meiwaku** 迷惑: **~ (na)** 厄介・やっかい(な) troublesome, annoying
yakko *n* やっこ・奴 **1.** servant, slave **2.** [IN NEGATIVE SENSE] (*undesirable*) person/one: **~-san**

やっこ[奴]さん that guy, he/him **3.** = **~-dō'fu** やっこ[奴]豆腐 (*par-boiled*) tofu (*bean-curd cubes*); **hiya-~** 冷や奴 cold tofu

yakkyoku *n* 薬局 pharmacy, drug-store

yaku *n* ヤク yak (*animal*)

yakú *n* 訳 translation, translated word (→ **honyaku** 翻訳, **tsūyaku** 通訳)

yáku(...) *adj* 約(...) approximately, about ... (= **oyoso** およそ, **daitai** 大体)

yaku *n* 役 **1.** (*cast of*) players **2.** part, role, duty; yaku-mé *n* 役目 duty, function; yaku-sha *n* 役者 actor (= **haiyū** 俳優), actress (= **joyū** 女優); yaku-wari *n* 役割 role, part (= **yakume** 役目)

yaku-... 役... service (*government, official*), use; o-yaku ni tatezu (ni) sumimasen お役に立てず(に)すみません [HUMBLE] I am sorry for not being able to help you.; yaku-nin *n* 役人 public servant, government official (= **kōmuin** 公務員); yaku-sho *n* 役所 government office (→ shi-yakusho 市役所, **ku-yakusho** 区役所)

yaku *n* 薬 drug (→ **kusuri** 薬)

...-yaku, yaku-... *suffix, prefix* ... -薬, 薬... medicines, drugs; yaku-hin 薬品 drugs; chemicals; yaku-mi *n* 薬味 ① spice, condiment ② drug ingredient; yaku-sō 薬草 medicinal herb; yaku-zai *n* 薬剤 [BOOKISH] pharmaceuticals, medicines (= **kusuri** 薬): **yakuzai-shi** 薬剤師 pharmacist

yaku-dachimásu, yaku-dátsu *v* 役立ちます, 役立つ serves a purpose, is useful

yakú-datemásu, yakú-datéru *v* 役立てます, 役立てる puts it to use

yakú ni tatemásu (tatéru) *v* 役に立てます(立てる) puts it to use (= **yakú-datemásu** 役立てます)

yakushimásu, yakúsú *v* 訳します, 訳す translates

yakusoku *n* 約束 promise, agreement, appointment, engagement, date, commitment; yakusoku-goto *n* 約束事 a promise

yákuza *n* やくざ gangster, hoodlum; yákuza (na) *adj* やくざ(な) no-good, worthless; **~ na kagyō** やくざな稼業 improper work; coarse

yakyū *n* 野球 baseball; yakyū-jō *n* 野球場 ball park, (*baseball*) stadium

yamá *n* 山 **1.** mountain **2.** heap, pile, bunch: **shorui no ~** 書類の山 pile of documents **3.** speculation, venture **4.** → yamá(-ba) 山(場); yama-arashi *n* ヤマアラシ・山荒 porcupine; yama-arashi *n* 山嵐 mountain storm; yama-aruki *n* 山歩き trekking (= **haikingu** ハイキング); yamá(-ba) *n* 山(場) climax; yama-biko *n* やまびこ・山彦 echo (= **kodama** こだま・木霊); yama-buki *n* ヤマブキ・山吹 Japanese rose: **~-iro** 山吹色

bright yellow; yama-goya *n* 山小屋 cabin, mountain lodge; yama-imo *n* ヤマイモ・山芋 yam; yama-neko *n* ヤマネコ・山猫 wild cat; yama-nóbori *n* 山登り mountain-climbing (= **tozan** 登山); yama no fumoto *n* 山のふもと[麓] the base of a mountain; yama-otoko *n* 山男 ① mountaineer ② woodsman ③ monster living in the heart of a mountain; yama-suso *n* 山裾 the base of a mountain

yama-shi *n* 山師 speculator

yamashii *adj* やましい ashamed of oneself; has guilty feelings

yama-te *n* 山手, **yama-no-te** 山手・山の手 uptown; the bluff: **Yama-no-te-sen** 山の手線 Yamanote Line

Yámato *n* 大和 Japan (*an ancient name*); yamato-kotoba *n* 大和言葉 words of Japanese origin, native Japanese words (= **wago** 和語); yamato-nadeshiko *n* ヤマトナデシコ・大和撫子 ① dianthus (*flower*) ② beautiful and modest Japanese woman

yamemásu, yameru *v* 止めます, 止める stops it; abolishes, abstains from, gives up

yamemásu, yameru *v* 辞めます, 辞める resigns, quits

yamí *n* 闇 **1.** darkness (= **kurayamí** 暗闇) **2.** disorder **3.** black market **4.** anything illicit, the dark; yamí-ichí(ba) *n* 闇市(場) black market; yamí-kumo (ni) *adv* 闇雲(に) at random, in a blind way; yamí-sōba *n* 闇相場 black-market price

yamimásu, yamu *v* 止みます, 止む it stops

yamome *n* やもめ widow

yámori *n* ヤモリ・守宮 gecko

yanagi *n* ヤナギ・柳 willow

yancha (na) *adj* やんちゃ(な) naughty, mischievous (*commonly used for boys*) (= **wanpaku (na)** 腕白・わんぱく(な))

yáne *n* 屋根 roof

yaní *n* やに・脂 resin, gum → **meyaní** 目やに・目脂

yánushi *n* 家主 landlord, landlady (= **ōya(-san)** 大家(さん))

yaochō *n* 八百長 fixed game

yaoya *n* 八百屋 greengrocer, vegetable market

yappári *adv* やっぱり [INFORMAL] also; either; as I thought (= **yahári** やはり)

yarakashimásu, yarakasu *v* やらかします, やらかす [INFORMAL][IN NEGATIVE SENSE] does it [*demeans the object*] (= **shimásu** します); **héma o ~** へまをやらかします makes a damn mess of it

yari *n* やり・槍 spear

yari-kata *n* やり方 way, method, process, manner

yarimásu, yaru *v* やります, やる does

yarimásu, yaru *v* やり[遣り]ます, やる・遣る **1.** gives **2.** sends: **tegami o ~** 手紙をやります send a letter **3. íp-pai ~** 一杯やります

has a drink **4.** has sex

yari-naoshimásu *v* やり直します, やり直す redoes it, does it over (*again*)

yari-sokonaimásu, yari-sokonáu *v* やり損ないます, やり損なう misses, botches

yarō´ *n* 野郎 (very INFORMAL) scoundrel, so-and-so

yasai *n* 野菜 vegetables

yasashii *adj* 優しい・やさしい gentle; kind, generous (= **shinsetsu** 親切)

yasashii *adj* 易しい・やさしい easy, simple

yasashiku *adv* 優しく・やさしく gently; politely

yase-gaman *n* やせ[痩せ]我慢 playing the martyr

yasemásu, yaseru *v* 痩せます, 痩せる gets thin; **yasete imásu** 痩せています is thin

yáshi *n* ヤシ・椰子 (*coconut*) palm

yáshin *n* 野心 ambition [IN NEGATIVE SENSE] (= **yabō** 野望; **taishi** 大志, **taibō** 大望)

yashinaimásu, yashinau *v* 養います, 養う brings up, rears; fosters; nourishes

...´-yasu, yasu-... *suffix, prefix* …安, 安… cheap(er/lower) by …; **hyakuén-~** 百円安 down/off by ¥100; yasúi *adj* 安い cheap, low(-priced); yasu-mono *n* 安物 cheap stuff; yasu-ne *n* 安値 low price; yasu-ukeai *n* 安請け合い easy promise; yasu-uri *n* 安売り bargain

yasude *n* ヤスデ millipede (*animal*)

yasúi *adj* やすい・易い (= **shi-yasúi** しやすい) easy (*to do*)

yasúi *adj* やすい (= **shi-yasúi** しやすい) likely/apt to (*do*), tends to

yasumemásu, yasuméru *v* 休めます, 休める **1.** rest/relax it, let it rest; ease it **2.** can rest

yasumí *n* 休み **1.** rest (= [BOOKISH] **kyūkei** 休憩) **2.** break, pause (= **teishi** 停止, **chūdan** 中断) **3.** recess (= **kyūkei jikan** 休憩時間) **4.** time off, vacation, holiday (= **kyūka** 休暇)

yasumimásu, yasúmu *v* 休みます, 休む rests, relaxes, takes time off; stays away (from school); goes to bed, sleeps

yasuraka (na/ni) *adj, adv* 安らか(な/に) peaceful(ly)

yasuri *n* やすり file, rasp; yasurí-gami *n* やすり紙 sandpaper (= **kami-yásuri** 紙やすり)

yatai *n* 屋台 street stall; stand

yatara *adv* やたら: **~ na** やたらな indiscriminate, reckless, random: **~ ni** やたらに indiscriminately, randomly, recklessly, blindly, unduly

yatō *n* 野党 opposition party

yatói 雇い *n* employment

yatoimásu, yatóu *v* 雇います, 雇う employs, hires

yatsú *n* 八つ eight (= **yattsú** 八つ); yatsuatari *n* 八つ当たり・やつあたり taking out on

yátsu *n* やつ・奴 [INFORMAL] **1.** guy, fellow, wretch, [IN NEGATIVE SENSE] (*undesirable*) person/one (**= aitsu** あいつ) **2.** (*undesirable*) thing/one **3.** he/him

yattekimásu, yattekúru *v* やってきます, やってくる comes, comes along

yatto *adv* やっと at last; barely, with difficulty

yattoko *n* やっとこ pincers, pliers

yattsú *n* 八つ eight; eight years old

yawarakái *adj* 軟らかい・柔らかい soft, mild

yáya *adj* やや a little, slightly: **~ átte** ややあって after a little while

yaya(k)koshíi *adj* やや(っ)こしい complicated; puzzling; tangled; troublesome

ye... → **e...**

yó *n* 世 the world at large, the public; yó-ron *n* 世論 public opinion

yó *n* 代 the age, the times; one's lifetime

yó *n* 夜 night (**= yóru** 夜); yo-aké *n* 夜明け dawn; yo-fúkáshi *n* 夜更かし staying up late; yo-máwari *n* 夜回り night watchman; yo-naká *n* 夜中 middle of the night; yóru *n* 夜 night

yo-... *prefix* 四 four; yó-ji *n* 四時 four o'clock; yo-jō´-han *n* 四畳半 four-and-a-half mat area, a small Japanese room; yo-ban, yón-ban *n* 四番 number four; yo-nen *n* 四年 ① fourth year ② four years (**= yonén-kan** 四年間); yon-én-sei 四年生 ① fourth-year student (*at elementary school*) ② senior (*at university/college*); yo-nín *n* 四人 four people

... yo *interj* …よ **1.** indeed, mind you, I tell/warn/alert you **2.** (*reinforces* IMPERATIVE)

yō´ *n* 要 gist (**= yō´shi** 要旨, **yōryō´** 要領)

yō´ *n* 用 **1.** business; errand (**= yōji** 用事) **2.** use, service **3.** going to the bathroom; yō-ji *n* 用事 business, errand; yō-ken *n* 用件 business (*something to tell, something to do*); yō-mú-in *n* 用務員 custodian, janitor, servant (*in the school, office, etc.*); yō-táshí *n* 用足し business, errand

yō-... *prefix* 洋… Western; yō-fuku *n* 洋服 (Western-style) clothes, a suit, a dress (**= fuku** 服): **(yō-) fuku-ya** (洋)服屋 tailor, clothing shop; **~-burashi** 洋服ブラシ clothbrush; **~-dansu** 洋服ダンス wardrobe; yō-ga *n* 洋画 ① foreign movie ② Western-style painting; yō-gaku *n* 洋楽 Western-style music; yō-gáshi *n* 洋菓子 western cakes/sweets; yō-hin *n* 洋品 haberdashery; yō-ma *n* 洋間 Western-style room; yō-sai *n* 洋裁 dressmaking; yō-shi *n* 洋紙 Western paper; yō-shoku *n* 洋食 foreign (*Western*) food; yō-shu *n* 洋酒 liquor (*Western*)

yō-... *prefix* 養… foster, protection; yō-fubo *n* 養父母 adoptive parents; yō´-jo *n* 養女 adopted daughter; **(... o) ~ ni shimásu** (...を)養女にします adopts (*a girl*); yō-shi *n* 養子 adopted child; yō-iku *n* 養育 [BOOKISH] ① bringing up children, education; **~-hi** 養育費 expense of bringing up children ② protection (*of old people, orphan children, sick people, etc.*); **~-in** 養育院 asylum; yō-rōin *n* 養老院 old people's home (= **rōjin hōmu** 老人ホーム)

yóbi *n* 予備 preparation: **~ (no)** 予備(の) reserve, spare; yobi-kō *n* 予備校 prep school, cram school; yobi-sénkyo *n* 予備選挙 a primary election

yobimásu, yobu *v* 呼びます, 呼ぶ **1.** calls; names; summons **2.** invites

yobō *n* 予防 precaution, prevention; yobō-sesshu *n* 予防接種 = **yobō-chū´sha** 予防注射 inoculation, vaccination (*injection*)

yōbō *n* 要望 strong desire

yōbō *n* 容貌 facial appearance

yobun (no/ni) *adj, adv* 余分(の/に) extra, excess

yōbun *n* 養分 nutrient substance (= **eiyōbun** 栄養分)

yóchi *n* 余地 [BOOKISH] room, space, margin, leeway: **(mattaku) utagai no ~ ga arimasen** (まったく)疑いの余地がありません There is no doubt about it (at all).

yóchi *n* 予知 prediction; yochi-nōryoku 予知能力 ability to foresee the future

yōchi (na) *adj* 幼稚(な) childish: **~ na kangae** 幼稚な考え childish idea; yōchí-en *n* 幼稚園 kindergarten

yodare *n* よだれ drool: **~ ga déru** よだれが出る drool comes out

yōdai *n* 容態・容体・様態 health condition (*commonly of patient*) (= **yōtai** 容態, **byōjō** 病状)

yō´do *n* ヨード iodine

yōeki *n* 溶液 liquid solution

yōen *adj* 妖艶 seductive beauty, fascinatingly elegant, bewitching (= **adeyaka** あでやか・艶やか)

yoga *n* ヨガ yoga

yō´gan *n* 溶岩 lava

yogen *n* 予言 prediction; **nosutoradamusu no dai-~** ノストラダムスの大予言 the great prophecies of Nostradamus

yōgí-sha *n* 容疑者 a suspect

yogo *n* 予後 prognosis: **~-furyō** 予後不良 poor prognosis: **~-ryōkō** 予後良好 good prognosis

yōgo *n* 擁護 [BOOKISH] protection, support; **jinken-~** 人権擁護 protection of human rights; **dōbutsu-~-dantai** 動物擁護団体 animal protection association

... yōgo *suffix* ...用語 (*special*) term (*technical word, etc.*): **kō-yōgo** 公用語 national language: **senmon-~** 専門用語 technical term: **sabetsu-~** 差別用語 discriminatory words

yogore *n* 汚れ dirt, smudge, blot, blotch

yogoremásu, yogoreru *v* 汚れます, 汚れる gets soiled, smudged; **yogorete imásu** 汚れています is dirty

yogoshimásu, yogosu *v* 汚します, 汚す soils, dirties, stains

yō´gu *n* 用具 tools, implements, instruments, kit; **~-bako** 用具箱 tool box

yōguruto *n* ヨーグルト yogurt

yoha *n* 余波 after-effect (*of typhoon, etc.*), aftermath

yohaku *n* 余白 margin, blank (*space*)

yōhin *n* 用品 = **…-yō´hin** …用品 utensils, appliances, supplies, necessities; **nichi-~** 日用品 daily necessities; **jimu-~** 事務用品 office supplies

yohō *n* 予報 forecast, prediction; **tenki-~** 天気予報 weather forcecast

yohodo *adv* よほど・余程 considerably, a good deal (= **yoppodo** よっぽど); **~ no koto ga nai kagiri** よほどのことがない限り unless something really important comes up

yoi *n* 宵 [BOOKISH] early part of the night, just after nightfall

yói *adj* 良い・よい (= **íi** いい) good [NEGATIVE] **yóku arimasén** 良くありません; (past) **yókatta desu** 良かったです was good

yoi *n* 酔い **1.** intoxication, drunkenness **2.** motion sickness (*seasick, carsick, airsick, etc.*); **kuruma-~** 車酔い car sickness; **norimono-~** 乗り物酔い travel sickness

yō´i *n* 用意 preparation; caution (= **junbi** 準備); **… no ~ o shimásu** …の用意をします prepares for …

yoimásu, yóu *v* 酔います, 酔う gets drunk; gets seasick, carsick, airsick

yoisho *interj* よいしょ upsy-daisy!, alley-oop!, heave-ho!

yōji *n* 楊枝・ようじ toothpick (= **tsuma-~** つまようじ・爪楊枝)

yō´ji *n* 幼児 [BOOKISH] infant

yō´ji *n* 幼時 [BOOKISH] childhood: **~-taiken** 幼時体験 childhood experiences

yō´jin *n* 用心 precaution, caution, care; **"hi no yō´jin"** 「火の用心」 "Be careful of fire!"; **yōjin-bō** *n* 用心棒 bodyguard; **yōjin-bukái** *adj* 用心深い cautious, careful (= **shinchō** 慎重)

yoka *n* 余暇 [BOOKISH] spare time (= **hima (na jikan)** 暇(な時間))

yōka *n* 八日 **1.** 8th day (*of a month*) **2.** (*for*) eight days (= **yōka-kan** 八日間)

yokan *n* 予感 premonition, foreboding: **~ ga shimásu** 予感がします has a feeling that something (bad/unpleasant) is about to come

yō´kan *n* ヨウカン・羊羹 sweet bars of bean paste and agar-agar flavored with chestnut, plum, etc.

yokei (na) *adj* 余計(な) superfluous, unnecessary, uncalled-for: **~ ni** 余計に unnecessarily

yokemásu, yokéru *v* 避けます, 避ける avoids, keeps away from

yoken *n* 予見 prediction (= **yochi** 予知)

yoki *n* 予期 expectation, anticipation

yōki *n* 容器 container, receptacle

yōki *n* 陽気 **1.** weather **2.** cheerfulness, brightness, liveliness; yōki (na) *adj* 陽気な cheerful, bright, lively

yokin *n* 預金 deposit (*of money*); yokin-kō´za *n* 預金口座 bank account; yokin-tsū´chō *n* 預金通帳 bankbook

yokka *n* 四日 **1.** 4th day (*of a month*) **2.** (*for*) four days (= **~-kan** 四日間)

yokkyū *n* 欲求 greed; desire, want (= **yoku** 欲, **yokubō** 欲望, **negai** 願い): **sandai-~** 三大欲求 three basic desires (*food, sex and sleep*) (*also known as part of the four Primitive Fountains: Food, Sleep, and Sex*); yokkyū-fuman *n* 欲求不満 frustration

yoko *n* 横 **1.** side (= **soba** 側, **waki** 脇) **2.** the width (= **haba** 幅) **3.** sideways **4.** sidewise; yoko-chō *n* 横町 sidestreets, alley; yoko-ito *n* 横糸 woof (*horizontal threads*)

yoko-girimásu, yoko-gíru *v* 横切ります, 横切る crosses, cuts across, intersects, passes

Yokohama *n* 横浜 Yokohama; **Yokohamá-kō** *n* 横浜港 the port of Yokohama

yokoku *n* 予告 advance notice; **eiga no ~-hen** 映画の予告編 movie trailer

yoko ni narimásu (náru) *v* 横になります(なる) lies down (= **yokotawárimásu** 横たわります)

yoko ni shimásu (suru) *v* 横にします(する) lays down (= **yokotaemásu** 横たえます)

yokoshimásu, yokósu *v* 寄越します, 寄越す sends (*here*), hands over to me

Yō´koso. *interj* ようこそ Welcome!; **Nihon e ~** 日本へようこそ Welcome to Japan!

yokozuna *n* 横綱 grand champion sumo wrestler

yokú *n* 欲 greed; desire, want (= **yokubō** 欲望); yokubō *n* 欲望 greed; desire, want (= **yoku** 欲)

... yoku *suffix* …欲 desire: **shoku-~** 食欲 food appetite, desire for food or drink: **sei-~** 性欲 sexual desire: **suimin-~** 睡眠欲 desire to sleep (→ **sandai-yokkyū** 三大欲求)

yóku *adv* 良く・よく well, better; **hayaku ~ narimasuyōni** 早く良くなりますように Hope you feel better soon. (*to a sick person*); Yóku irasshaimáshita. *interj* よくいらっしゃいました. Welcome! (= **Yōkoso (irasshaimashita)** ようこそ(いらっしゃいました))

yóku *adv* よく lots, much, thoroughly; carefully; **~ yonde kudasai** よく読んで下さい Please read it carefully.

yóku *adv* よく lots, often, frequently

yóku (-) ... *prefix* 翌… the next (*day*, *night*, *month*, *year;* date); yoku-ban *n* 翌晩 [BOOKISH] the following/next night; yoku-getsu *n* 翌月 [BOOKISH] the following/next month; yoku-jitsu *n* 翌日 [BOOKISH] the following/next day; yoku-shū *n* 翌週 [BOOKISH] the following/next week; yoku-toshi *n* 翌年 [BOOKISH] the following/next year

yokubárí *n* 欲張り a greedy person

yokubarimásu, yokubáru *v* 欲張ります, 欲張る is greedy

yoku (-) ... *prefix* 浴… bath (→ **yukata** 浴衣); yoku-jō *n* 浴場 [BOOKISH] bathhouse; **kōshū-~** 公衆浴場 public bath; yoku-shitsu *n* 浴室 bathroom

yōkyū *n* 要求 requirement, demand, claim, request (= **yōsei** 要請)

yome *n* 嫁 **1.** daughter-in-law **2.** bride (= **o-yome-san** お嫁さん) **3. yome-san** 嫁さん [INFORMAL] (*my*) wife (= **óku-san** 奥さん)

yomi *n* 読み **1.** reading **2.** expectation, forecast **3.** pronunciation; **on-~** 音読み Chinese pronunciation of Kanji/Chinese characters; **kun-~** 訓読み Japanese pronunciation of Kanji/Chinese characters

yomi-kata *n* 読み方 **1.** how to read **2.** how to pronounce the Kanji/Chinese characters

yomimásu, yómu *v* 読みます, 読む **1.** reads **2.** reads out, pronounces **3.** foresees, guesses

yōmō *n* 羊毛 wool

yón *n* 四・4 four; yon-bai *n* 四倍 four-fold, four times as much; yon-banmé (no), yo-banmé (no) *adj* 四番目(の) fourth; yón-ban, yo-ban *n* 四番 number four; yón-dai *n* 四台 four (*machines*, *vehicles*); yón-do *n* 四度 four degrees; four times (= **yón-kái** 四回, **yón-hén** 四遍); yon-do-mé *n* 四度目 the fourth time; yón-fun, yón-pun *n* 四分 four minutes; yón-hai *n* 四杯 four cupfuls; yón-hén *n* 四遍 four times; yón-hiki *n* 四匹 four (*fishes/bugs*, *small animals*); yón-hon *n* 四本 four (*pencils/bottles*, *long objects*); yon-kágetsu *n* 四か月 four months; yon-kai *n* 四階 four floors/stories; fourth floor; yón-kái *n* 四回 four times; yón-mai *n* 四枚 four sheets (*flat things*, *papers*, *dishes*, *etc.*); yon-méi *n* 四名 four people (*also* **yo-mei** 四名, **yo-nín** 四人); yón-pun *n* 四分 four minutes (*also* **yón-fun** 四分); yón-satsu *n* 四冊 four copies (*books*, *magazines*); yón-tō *n* 四頭 four (*horses/oxen*, *large animals*); yón-wa *n* 四羽 four (*birds*, *rabbits*) (*also* **yón-ba** 四羽)

... yō´ (na) *suffix*, *adj* …よう[様](な) seem(ing) to be: **yō ni** …よう[様]に (*so as to be*) like …;

suru ~ iimásu するよう[様]に言います tells one to do it

yondokoro-nai *adj* よんどころない inevitable

yōniku *n* 羊肉 [BOOKISH] lamb (*meat, includes mutton*)

yón-jū *n* 四十・40 forty

...-yō (no) *adj* …用(の) for the use of …

yopparai *n* 酔っ払い drunk (*person*)

yopparaimásu, yopparau *v* 酔っ払います, 酔っ払う gets drunk

yoppodo *adv* よっぽど considerably, a good deal (= **yohodo** よほど・余程)

yori-... *adj* より… [+ADJECTIVE] more …, …-er [BOOKISH]

... yóri *conj* …より **1.** (*more/rather/other*) than … **2.** from, out of; since

yoridori-midori *n* よりどりみどり・選り取り見取り choosing whichever one likes

yorigónomi *n* より好み・選り好み choosiness

yorimásu, yoru *v* 寄ります, 寄る drops in; approaches, comes near; meets

yorimásu, yoru *v* 拠ります, 拠る relies on; **… ni yotte** …によって, **… ni yoru to** …によると, **… ni yoréba** …によれば according to …

yorimásu, yóru *v* 撚ります, 撚る twists, twines (= **nejirimasu** 捻ります, **nejiru** 捻る)

yoroi *n* 鎧 armor

yoroi-do *n* よろい戸・鎧戸 shutter (*house*)

yorokobi 喜び *n* joy

yorokobimásu, yorokóbu *v* 喜びます, 喜ぶ is glad, happy, delighted; rejoices

yoro-mekí *n* よろめき an (*extra-marital*) affair

yoro-mekimásu, yoro-méku *v* よろめきます, よろめく totters, falters, staggers; has an (*extra-marital*) affair

Yōróppa *n* ヨーロッパ Europe (= **Ōshū** 欧州)

yoroshii *adj* よろしい・宜しい very well; satisfactory

yoroshikáttara *adv* よろしかったら if you don't mind; if you like

yoroshiku *n* よろしく・宜しく **1. (… ni) ~ (itte kudasái/o-tsutae kudasái)** (…に)よろしく(言って下さい/お伝え下さい) Give my regards to … **2. → yoroshii** よろしい・宜しい **3. Dō´zo yoroshiku.** どうぞよろしく. How do you do?; Please favor (*my request, me, mine*).

yóroyoro (to) *adj, adv* よろよろ(と) tottering, faltering, staggering; having an affair

yoru *v* **… ni ~ to** …によると according to …

yōryō *n* 要領 **1.** gist: **~ o enai kaitō** 要領を得ない回答 pointless answer, unclear answer **2.** knack: **~ ga ii** 要領がいい is efficient (person)

yōsai *n* 要塞 fortress (*military facility*)
yosan *n* 予算 budget
yōsan *n* 養蚕 raising silkworms, silk farming, sericulture
yose *n* 寄席 vaudeville (*theater*)
yōseki *n* 容積 volume of a container
yosemásu, yoseru *v* 寄せます, 寄せる **1.** lets approach, brings near **2.** collects, gathers **3.** adds **4.** sends
yosen *n* 予選 preliminary; primary
yose-nabe *n* 寄せ鍋 chowder
yose-nami 寄せ波 surf
yóshi *n* 由 reason; meaning; circumstance; means
Yóshi! *interj* よし! OK; very well
yō´shi *n* 用紙 forms, blanks, papers: **genkō-~** 原稿用紙 manuscript paper used for writing Japanese vertically (*commonly one page of 400-characters or 200-characters*): **ankēto-~** アンケート用紙 questionnaire
yō´-shi *n* 要旨 summary, abstract (*gist*) (= **shu-shi** 主旨)
yoshimásu, yósu *v* 止します, 止す stops doing it (= **yamemásu** 止めます)
yō-shimásu, yō-súru *v* 要します, 要する needs, requires, takes, costs; summarizes, sums it up
yōshoku *n* 養殖 raising, farming, culture: **~-shínju** 養殖真珠 cultured pearls
yoshū *n* 予習 preparatory study
yosó *n* よそ・余所 somewhere else; alien, strange: **~ no hitó** よその人 outsider, stranger; yoso-mono *n* よそ者・余所者 outsider, stranger
yosō *n* 予想 expectation, presumption; **~ íjō** 予想以上 above/beyond expectations
yō´so *n* 要素 element
yosoku *n* 予測 forecast, prediction, estimate
yōsu *n* 様子・ようす circumstances; aspect; appearance, look
yōsui *n* 用水 diversion of water, service water, irrigation water; yōsui-ro *n* 用水路 irrigation canal
yō-súru ni *v* 要するに in summary, to sum it up, in short; in effect, what it amounts to (*boils down to*) is ...; after all
yotamono *n* よた者・与太者 hoodlum
yotei *n* 予定 expectation, plan
yōtén *n* 要点 gist, point
yotō *n* 与党 ruling party
yotsu-kado *n* 四つ角 intersection (*of two streets*), crossroads
yotto *n* ヨット yacht
yottsú *n* 四つ four
yowái *adj* 弱い weak; frail; poor at (*math, etc.*); **sake ni ~** 酒に弱い easily intoxicated; yowa-mi *n* 弱み weakness, weak point; yowa-mushi *n* 弱虫 a cream puff, wimp
yowasemásu, yowaséru *v* 酔わせます, 酔わせる gets one drunk, lets one get drunk
yoyaku *n* 予約 reservation, subscription, booking, appointment

yōyaku *adv* ようやく finally, at last; barely

yōyaku *n* 要約 a summary

yoyū *n* 余裕 room, leeway, margin, excess, surplus

yú *n* 湯 hot water, warm water: **o-~ o wakashimásu** お湯を沸かします boils water; yu-ge *n* 湯気 steam; yu-nomi *n* 湯飲み, **~-jáwan** 湯飲み茶碗 Japanese teacup; yu-wá-kashi *n* 湯沸かし teakettle, boiler (*for heating water*); yu-zámashi *n* 湯冷まし cooled boiled water

yú *n* 湯 bath: **otoko-~** 男湯 men's section of a bathhouse: **on'na-~** 女湯 women's section of a bath-house; yú-bune *n* 湯船 bathtub; yu-zame *n* 湯冷め feeling chilly after taking a bath

yū *n* ゆう・言う [INFORMAL] = **iu** 言う, **iimásu** 言います (says)

yū *n* 結う = **yuu** 結う, **yuimásu** 結います does up one's hair

yū *n* 優 excellent: (*grade*) **yū, ryō, ka, fuka** 優、良、可、不可 Excellent, Good, Poor, Failing; yū'-retsu *n* 優劣 relative merits (*superiority or inferiority*); yū-ryō (na) *adj* 優良な superior; yū-shō *n* 優勝 (*winning*) the victory/championship; **~-sha** 優勝者 the winner, victor; yū-shū (na) *adj* 優秀な excellent, superior; yū-tō-sei *n* 優等生 model student

yū *n* 夕 evening (= **yū-gata** 夕方); yū-bé *n* 夕べ evening; yū-dachi *n* 夕立 a sudden shower during afternoon or evening; yū-gata *n* 夕方 evening; yū-giri *n* 夕霧 evening mist; yū-gure *n* 夕暮れ twilight; **~-doki** 夕暮れ時 evening during the twilight hours; yū-han *n* 夕飯 [INFORMAL] = **yū-meshi** 夕飯 supper, dinner (= **yū-shoku** 夕食); yū-hi *n* 夕日・夕陽 setting sun; yū-kaze *n* 夕風 evening breeze; yū-meshi *n* 夕飯 (*commonly male. Very informal*) → yū-han 夕飯; yū-moya *n* 夕もや・夕靄 evening fog; yū-shoku *n* 夕食 evening meal (*supper, dinner*) (= **yū-han, yū-meshi** 夕飯)

yū-... *prefix* 友... friend; yū-jin *n* 友人 [BOOKISH] friend (= **tomo** 友, **tomo-dachi** 友だち・友達); yū-jō *n* 友情 friendship; yū-kō *n* 友好 [BOOKISH] (*official*) friendship, friendly relationship (*among countries, etc.*)

yū-be *n* ゆうべ・昨夜 last night (= **kinō no ban/yoru** 昨日の晩/夜, **saku-ban/ya** 昨夜/晩)

yūben *n* 雄弁 eloquence: ~ **(na)** 雄弁(な) eloquent; yūben-ka *n* 雄弁家 eloquent speaker

yubí *n* 指 **1.** finger (= **te no yubí** 手の指) **2.** toe (= **ashi no yubí** 足の指); yubi-núkí *n* 指貫き thimble; yubl-saki *n* 指先 fingertip; yubi-sashimásu, yubi-sasu *v* 指差します, 指差す points (*commonly indicates something with an extended index finger*); yubi-wa *n* 指輪 ring

yūbin *n* 郵便 mail: **~-chókin** 郵便貯金 postal savings; **~-ká wase** 郵便為替 (*postal*) money order; **~-uke** 郵便受け mailbox; **yūbín-bako** *n* 郵便箱 mailbox; **yūbín-bángō** *n* 郵便番号 zip code; ZIP Code; **yūbín-butsu** *n* 郵便物 mail; **yūbín-kyoku** *n* 郵便局 post office; **yūbín-posuto** *n* 郵便ポスト Red post box; **yūbín-ya (san)** *n* 郵便屋(さん) mail carrier, postman

yū´bi (na) *adj* 優美(な) elegant, graceful

yūbō (na) *adj* 有望(な) promising (= **zento ~ (na)** 前途有望(な)): **~ (na) senshu** 有望(な)選手 promising player

yudan *n* 油断 negligence, carelessness, sloppiness

yudanemásu, yudanéru *v* 委ねます, 委ねる entrusts, commits

Yudayá-jin *n* ユダヤ人 Jew; **~-kyō** ユダヤ教 Judaism

yudemásu, yudéru *v* 茹でます, 茹でる boils (*food*)

yude-támago *n* ゆで卵・茹で卵 boiled egg

yué *n* 故・ゆえ [BOOKISH] reason, grounds; **... ~ ni** ...故に・ゆえに for the reason that ..., because ...

yūenchi *n* 遊園地 amusement park

yū´fuku (na) *adj* 裕福(な) rich, wealthy

yūfō *n* ユーフォー・UFO unidentified flying object (= **mikakunin hikō-buttai** 未確認飛行物体)

yū´ga (na) *adj* 優雅(な) elegant, refined

yugamemásu, yugameru *v* 歪めます, 歪める distorts, warps

yugami *n* 歪み distortion, warp

yūga-tō *n* 誘蛾灯 light trap

yūgi *n* 遊戯 playgame: **~-shitsu** 遊戯室 playroom

yūhei *n* 幽閉 confinement

yūhodō *n* 遊歩道 promenade

yuigon *n* 遺言 **1.** leaving a will **2.** a will, testament (= **~-jō** 遺言状, **~-sho** 遺言書)

yúiitsu (no) *adj* 唯一(の) [BOOKISH] the only (= **tada hitotsu no** ただひとつの・唯一つの)

yuimásu, yū (yuu) *v* 結います, 結う does up one's hair

yūjū-fudan *n* 優柔不断 indecisiveness

yuka *n* 床 floor: **~-ita** 床板 floor board

yúkai (na) *adj* 愉快(な) merry, happy, gay; funny, droll

yūkai *n* 誘拐 kidnap(ping); **yūkai-han** *n* 誘拐犯 kidnapper

yūkaku *n* 遊郭 red-light district

yūkan (na) *adj* 勇敢(な) brave

yūkari *n* ユーカリ eucalyptus

yukata *n* 浴衣・ゆかた (*light*) bathrobe

yuketsu *n* 輸血 blood transfusion

yukí *n* 雪 snow: **~ ga furimásu** 雪が降ります it snows; **yuki-dama** *n* 雪玉 snowball; **yuki-daruma** *n* 雪だるま snowman; **yuki-doke** *n* 雪解け ① melting snow ② thaw (*reduction or easing in tension* *or hostility*); yuki-gassen *n* 雪合戦 snowball fight; yuki-nádare *n* 雪なだれ snowslide, avalanche (= **nadare** 雪崩・なだれ); yuki-onna *n* 雪女 snow woman (*spirit of snow*); yuki-otoko *n* 雪男 yeti

yū´ki *n* 勇気 courage

yū´ki (no) *adj* 有機(の) organic: **~-yasai** 有機野菜 organic vegetables: **~-kagaku** 有機化学 organic chemistry

yukkúri *adv* ゆっくり **1.** slowly **2.** at ease; **Go-yukkúri.** ごゆっくり. Take it easy. Don't feel you have to rush.

yūkō (na) *adj* 有効(な) effective, valid; yūkō-kigen *n* 有効期限 expiration date (*except food.*)(= **shōmi-kigen** 賞味期限)

yukue-fumei *n* 行方不明 missing (*person, pet, etc.*): **~-sha** 行方不明者 a missing person

yumé *n* 夢 dream **1.** succession of images during sleep **2.** aspiration, wish; **~ ga kanaimashita** 夢が叶いました (*My*) dream came true!

yūmei (na) *adj* 有名(な) famous, well-known

yumí *n* 弓 bow (*for archery or violin*); yumi-gata *n* 弓形 curve, arch, bow

yū´moa *n* ユーモア humor, wit

yunifōmu *n* ユニフォーム uniform (*of athlete, etc.*)

yuniiku *n* ユニーク unique (= **kosei-teki** 個性的, **dokutoku** 独特)

yunikōdo *n* ユニコード unicode

yunikōn *n* ユニコーン unicorn (= **ikkaku-jū** 一角獣)

yūnō (na) *adj* 有能(な) capable, efficient

yunyū *n* 輸入 import(ing); yunyū-hin *n* 輸入品 imported goods; yunyū´-zei *n* 輸入税 (*import*) duty

yūran *n* 遊覧 excursion

yūrashia *n* ユーラシア Eurasia

yure 揺れ *n* tremor, shock

yū´rei *n* 幽霊 Japanese ghost (*commonly lacks legs and feet*) (= **bō-rei** 亡霊)

yuremásu, yureru *v* 揺れます, 揺れる it shakes, sways, swings, rocks, rolls

yuri *n* ユリ・百合 lily

yuri-kago *n* 揺りかご・揺り籠 cradle; yuri-kago kara hakaba made 揺りかご[揺り籠]から墓場まで (*slogan*) from the cradle to the grave

yū´ri (na) *adj* 有利(な) profitable, advantageous

yurúi *adj* 緩い・ゆるい loose, slack; lenient; slow

yurushí *n* 許し permission

yurushimásu, yurúsu *v* 許します, 許す allows, lets; pardons, forgives

yūryō *n* 有料 pay (*not free*), charge, fee: **~-chū´shajō** 有料駐車場 paid parking

yūryoku (na) *adj* 有力(な) strong, powerful, influential

yusaburimásu, yusaburu *v* 揺さぶります, 揺さぶる shakes (*sways, swings, rocks, shocks*) it

yūsen *n* 優先 priority: **~-jun'i** 優先順位 order of priority
yūsha *n* 勇者 brave man (→ **yūkan** 勇敢)
yūshi̱ *n* 融資 financing (*of bank, etc.*)
yūshi̱ *n* 有志 volunteer, supporter, interested person
yūshi̱-téssen *n* 有刺鉄線 barbed wire
yushu̱tsu *n* 輸出 export(ing); yushutsu-hin *n* 輸出品 export goods; yushutsu-zei *n* 輸出税 (*export*) duty
yūshoku-jinshu *n* 有色人種 colored races
yusō *n* 輸送 transport(ation)
yūsō *n* 郵送 mailing; yūsō′-ryō *n* 郵送料 postage
yusuburimásu̱, yusuburu *v* 揺すぶります, 揺すぶる shakes (*sways, swings, rocks*) it
yusugimásu̱, yusugu *v* ゆすぎます, ゆすぐ rinses (= **su̱sugu** すすぐ)
yūsu-hósu̱teru *n* ユースホステル youth hostel
yusuri *n* ゆすり・強請り blackmail, extortion
yusurimásu̱, yusuru *v* 揺すります, 揺する shakes (*sways, swings, rocks*) it
yusurimásu̱, yusuru *v* 強請ります, 強請る blackmails, extorts
yútaka (na) *adj* 豊か(な) abundant, plentiful; wealthy (= **hōfu (na)** 豊富(な))
yū-tā′n *n* ユー[U]ターン U-turn
Yuta-shū *n* ユタ州 Utah
yutori *adj* ゆとり leeway, breadth of mind, space; **~-kyōiku** ゆとり教育 less strenuous education (*primary education with reduced hours and/or content of the curriculum*)
yūutsu (na) *adj* 憂うつ・憂鬱(な) melancholy, gloom
yūwaku *n* 誘惑 temptation; seduction
yūzai (no) *adj* 有罪(の) guilty
yúzu *n* ユズ・柚子 citron
yūzū *n* 融通 **1.** financing **2.** adaptability, versatility; yūzū no/ga kiku *adv* 融通の/がきく adaptable, versatile
yuzurimásu̱, yuzuru *v* 譲ります, 譲る gives up; gives in; yields; cedes; is inferior

Z

zá *n* 座 **1.** theater (→ **kabuki-za** 歌舞伎座) **2.** seat; za-búton *n* 座布団 Japanese flat square cushion to sit on; za-dan *n* 座談 [BOOKISH] chat; **~-kai** 座談会 round-table discussion; za-isu *n* 座椅子 backrest (= *legless chair*); za-kyō *n* 座興 entertainment (*at drinking party, etc.*); za-seki *n* 座席 seat: **~-bángō** 座席番号 seat number; za-shiki̱ *n* 座敷 ① tatami room, drawing room ② tatami-floored seating area in Japanese-style restaurant; za-zen *n* 座禅 meditation (*Zen*)

za-... *prefix* 雑… miscellaneous; zak-ka *n* 雑貨 miscellaneous goods, sundries: **~-ten** 雑貨店 variety shop; za-tsuon *n* 雑音 noise(s), static, miscellaneous sounds; zas-shi *n* 雑誌 magazine, periodical, miscellaneous articles; zatsudan *n* 雑談 (*miscellaneous*) chat; zat-ta (na) *adj* 雑多(な) sundry, miscellaneous

zái *n* 材 (= **zaimoku** 材木) lumber; (= **zairyō** 材料) material; zai-moku *n* 材木 lumber, wood; zai-ryō´ *n* 材料 raw material(s), ingredient(s): **sūpu no ~** スープの材料 ingredients for the soup

zái *n* 財 (= **záisan** 財産) wealth; zai-batsu *n* 財閥 a big financial group; zai-dan *n* 財団 a foundation; zai-gen *n* 財源 financial resources; zai-hō *n* 財宝 riches (*money, jewels, etc.*), treasures; zai-kai *n* 財界 financial circles; zai-ryoku *n* 財力 financial power, economic power; zái-san *n* 財産 one's property, wealth, fortune; zai-sei *n* 財政 finance

zai-... *prefix n* 在… (*resident*) in; zai-gaku(-chū) *adv* 在学(中) in school; in college; at university: **~-shōmeisho** 在学証明書 certificate of enrollment; zai-ryū *n* 在留 [BOOKISH] residing, residence: **~-shíkaku** 在留資格 status of residence; zai-seki(-chū) *adv* 在籍(中) ① in school; in college; at university (= **zai-gaku(-chū)** 在学(中)) ② in association: **~-sha** 在籍者 registered person; zai-taku *n* 在宅 [BOOKISH] being at home; **~-kinmu** 在宅勤務 working at home

zai-... *prefix* 罪… sin, crime; zái-aku *n* 罪悪 sin: **~-kan** 罪悪感 feeling/sense of guilt; zai-nin *n* 罪人 criminal

zaiko *n* 在庫 inventory; zaiko-hyō *n* 在庫表 inventory list; zaiko-shobun sēru *n* 在庫処分セール clearance sale

Zaimu-shō *n* 財務省 Ministry of Finance

záiru *n* ザイル a mountain-climbing rope

zamā´-miro *interj* ざまあ見ろ (*mostly male, very informal*) It serves you/them right!

zandaka *n* 残高 (*remaining money*) balance: **(ginkō)yokin-~**(銀行)預金残高 bank balance

zangai *n* 残骸 **1.** wreck(age) which does not preserve its original shape **2.** thrown corpse which does not preserve its original shape

zángé *n* 懺悔 confession (*of sins*)

zangyaku (na) *adj* 残虐(な) merciless and cruel/brutal (*to animals, people*), atrocious; **~-kō´i** 残虐行為 an atrocity

zangyō *n* 残業 overtime (*work*)
zankoku (na) *adj* 残酷(な) cruel to, brutal to, harsh towards (*animals, people*): **~ na shiuchi** 残酷な仕打ち cruel treatment
zannén (na) *adj* 残念(な) regrettable, disappointed; too bad, a pity; **~-nagara** 残念ながら regrettably (= **ikan-nagara** 遺憾ながら [BOOKISH])
zannin (na) *adj* 残忍(な) brutal, cruel (= **zankoku (na)** 残酷(な)): **~ na hito** 残忍な人 cruel person
zara ni *adv* ざらに found everywhere, very common
zárazara (shita) *adj* ざらざら(した) rough(-textured)
zarigani *n* ザリガニ crawfish
zarú *n* ざる・ザル a bamboo sieve/colander
zāsai *n* ザーサイ Chinese pickles
zasetsu *n* 挫折 falling by the wayside, frustration, setback, fail; **~-kan** 挫折感 feeling of frustration, sense of failure; **~ shimásu** 挫折します gets frustrated, falls by the wayside, fails
zatsu (na) *adj* 雑(な) coarse, crude
zatto *adv* ざっと roughly; briefly
... ze *interj* …ぜ (*mostly male.* VERY INFORMAL) indeed, I tell you
zé-hi *adv* ぜひ・是非 **1.** without fail, for sure: **2.** [BOOKISH] right and wrong, pros and cons; **shikei (seido) no ~** 死刑(制度)の是非 pros and cons of the death penalty
zéi *n* 税 tax (= **~-kin** 税金); **shōhi-~** 消費税 consumption tax; **shotoku-~** 所得税 income tax; **jūmin-~** 住民税 resident tax; **zei-kan** *n* 税関 customs, custom house; **zei-kin** *n* 税金 tax (= **zei** 税); **zei-mu sho** *n* 税務署 tax office
zeitákú *n* ぜいたく・贅沢 luxury, extravagance: **~ (na)** ぜいたく・贅沢(な) luxurious; **zeitaku-hin** *n* ぜいたく[贅沢]品 luxury (goods), luxuries
zékken *n* ゼッケン an athlete's number: **~ o tsukemásu** ゼッケンを付けます attaches/assigns a number (*to an athlete*)
zekkō (no) *adj* 絶好(の) best; **~-chō** 絶好調 best condition
zémi *n* ゼミ, **zeminā´ru** ゼミナール seminar
zén *n* 善 goodness; **~-aku** 善悪 good and evil, right and wrong; **zén'-i** *n* 善意 goodwill; **zén-sho** *n* 善処 [BOOKISH]: **~ shimásu** 善処します "I will do my best" (*about the matter*) = Don't expect me to do anything.
Zén *n* 禅 Zen (Buddhism)
zen *n* 膳 (**o-zen** お膳, **gó-zen** 御膳) (*traditional individual low*) meal table, dining tray
zén-... *prefix* 全… all, total, whole, complete, the whole; **zén-bu** *adv* 全部 everything, completely: **~ de** 全部で altogether; **zen'-in** *n* 全員 everyone; **zén-koku (no)** *adj* 全国(の) nation-wide; **zen-men** *n* 全面 the entire surface; **zen-metsu** *n* 全

滅 annihilation; zen-shin *n* 全身 the whole body, body as a whole; zen-tai *n* 全体 the whole, entirety: **~ no** 全体の entire, whole; **~ ni** 全体に wholly, generally; zén-tai *adv* 全体 originally, primarily (= **gánrai** 元来); zen-zen *adv* 全然・ぜんぜん ① [+ NEGATIVE verb] (not) at all, (not) ever ② [INFORMAL] completely, utterly, entirely, altogether

zén-... *prefix* 前…[BOOKISH] former, earlier (= **máe no ...** 前の…); zen-chō *n* 前兆 omen, sign; zén-go *n* 前後 ① before and after; ahead and behind; back and forth ② sequence, order; ...-zén-go *suffix* …前後 approximately, around, about (= **teido** 程度); zen-han *n* 前半 the first half; zen-men *n* 前面 the front side; zen-rei *n* 前例 precedent, prior example; zén-sha *n* 前者 the former; zen-shin *n* 前進 advance; zen-tei *n* 前提 premise; zén-to *n* 前途 the future, prospects; zén'-ya *n* 前夜 the night before

zenmai *n* ぜんまい・ゼンマイ **1.** a spring, hairspring, clock-spring **2.** royal fern, osmund

zensoku *n* ぜんそく・喘息 asthma

zeppeki *n* 絶壁 precipice

zérii *n* ゼリー jelly

zéro *n* ゼロ zero

zetsubō *n* 絶望 despair

zetsuen shimásu *v* 絶縁します insulates

zettai (no) *adv* 絶対(の) absolute: **zettai ni** 絶対に totally, absolutely

zi... → **j...**

... zo *interj* …ぞ (*mostly male.* VERY INFORMAL) indeed, I tell you

zō *n* 像 **1.** statue (= **chō-~** 彫像) **2.** image: **terebi ei-~** テレビ映像 images on TV screen: **ga-~** 画像 picture, image **3.** portrait (= **shō-~** 肖像)

zō *n* ゾウ・象 elephant

zō-... *prefix* 増… increase; zō-dai *n* 増大 enlargement, increase; zō´-ho *n* 増補 supplement; zō-ka *n* 増加 increase, growth; zō-ryō *n* 増量 increase (*quantity*); zō-satsu *n* 増刷 reprint (*publishing*); zō-shin *n* 増進 promotion, betterment, increase

zōgan *n* 象眼 inlaid work; damascene

zōka *n* 造花 artificial flower

zōkei *n* 造詣 profound knowledge (*of academics, arts, technologies, etc.*): **~ ga fukai** 造詣が深い is well versed

zōkin *n* ぞうきん・雑巾 rag, dustcloth

zoku *n* 賊 robber, bandit, thief

...´-zoku *suffix* …族 (*name of certain*) tribe/gang/group of …; the …s

zokugo *n* 俗語 slang

zoku (na) *adj* 俗(な) common, vulgar; popular

zoku-shimás<u>u</u>, zoku-súru *v* 属します, 属する belongs

zokú zoku *adv* ぞくぞく・続々 one right after another, in rapid succession
zóku zoku shimásu (suru) *v* ぞくぞくします(する) **1.** is thrilled with excitement **2.** shivers with chill
zonbún (ni) *adv* 存分(に) as much as one likes
zóngai *adv* 存外 beyond expectations
zōni *n* 雑煮・ぞうに rice cakes boiled with vegetables (*eaten as New Year's soup*)
zon-jiagemásu, zon-jiageru *v* 存じあげます, 存じあげる [HUMBLE] thinks, feels; knows
zon-jimásu, zon-jíru *v* 存じます, 存じる [HUMBLE/DEFERENTIAL] thinks, feels; knows
zonzái (na) *adj* ぞんざい(な) slovenly, rough, carelessly, sloppy
zōri *n* 草履 straw sandals
zórozoro *adv* ぞろぞろ in streams/crowds, in large numbers
zōsen *n* 造船 shipbuilding; zōsen-jó *n* 造船所 shipyard
zōsho *n* 蔵書 book collection, library
zōsui *n* 雑炊 rice boiled in a soup
zō-tei *n* 贈呈 [HUMBLE] presentation: ~ **shimásu** 贈呈します presents
zotto *adv* ぞっと with a shudder/shiver
zu *n* 図 picture, drawing, chart, map, diagram, figure: ~ **ni norimásu** 図に乗ります pushes a good thing too far, takes advantage of a person; zu-an *n* 図案 sketch, design; zu-hyō *n* 図表 chart, diagram (= **chāto** チャート); zu-kai *n* 図解 illustration, diagram
...-zu *suffix* …ず, **…-zu ni** …ずに = **…-nái de** …ないで (not doing, instead of doing)
zubari *adv* ずばり [INFORMAL] frankly: ~ **iimásu** ずばり言います comes directly to the point
zubón *n* ズボン trousers, pants, slacks; zubon-shita *n* ズボン下 underpants, shorts; zubon-tsuri *n* ズボン吊り suspenders
zubutoi *adv* 図太い thick-skinned, impudent: ~ **shinkei** 図太い神経 nerves of steel
zúibun *adv* ずいぶん・随分 **1.** fairly, rather **2.** very, quite, extremely (= **kanari** かなり)
zuihitsu *n* 随筆 essays
zúii (no) *adj* 随意(の) voluntary, optional (= **nin'i (no)** 任意(の))
zúiji *adv* 随時 as needed, at anytime as one likes
-zuke *suffix* 付け dated
...-zuki *suffix* …好き a lover of …, a great … fan
zúkku *n* ズック canvas; duck (*fabric*)
...-zúkuri *suffix* …造り made of …
zūmu *n* ズーム zoom (*camera*)
zúnō *n* 頭脳 [BOOKISH] brains, head, intellect (= **atama** 頭)
zurashimásu, zurasu *v* ずらします, ずらす shifts

zuré *n* ずれ discrepancy, lag, gap
zuremásu, zuréru *v* ずれます, ずれる slips out of place, gets loose
zurō´su *n* ズロース panties; drawers
zúru *n* ずる cheating; **zuru-gashikoi** *adj* ずる賢い cunning, wily; **zurúi** *adj* ずるい sly, cunning, tricky; **zuru-yásumi** *n* ずる休み skipping (*school*); truancy
zusan (na) *adj* ずさん(な) sloppy, slipshod, careless, slovenly
...´zútsu *suffix* …ずつ (*of/for*) each, apiece, at a time
zutsū *n* 頭痛 headache: ~ **no táne** 頭痛の種 one's biggest headache
zutto *adv* ずっと **1.** directly **2.** by far, much (*more*): ~ **máe** ずっと前 way back (*before*), a long time ago **3.** all the way through, all the time
zūzūshíi *adj* ずうずうしい・図々しい brazen, shameless, impudent (= **atsukamashii** 厚かましい)
zy... → **j...**

PART II

ENGLISH – JAPANESE

A

a, an → one (*but usually omitted in Japanese*)
abacus *n* soroban そろばん
abandon *v* sutemásu 捨てます
abase *v* otoshimásu 落とします
abate *v* **1.** (*lose steam*) osamarimásu 治まります, yawaragimásu 和らぎます **2.** herashimásu 減らします **3.** (*exclude*) haijo shimásu 排除します; (*resolve*) mukō ni shimásu 無効にします
abbreviate *v* ryakushimásu 略します
abdicate *v* **1.** shirizokimásu 退きます, jinin shimásu 辞任します **2.** ~ *the throne* taii shimásu 退位します
abdomen *n* onaka おなか・お腹, fukubu 腹部, hara 腹
abduct *v* yūkai shimásu 誘拐します
aberration *n* dassen 脱線, itsudatsu 逸脱, seishin ijō 精神異常
abet *v* keshikakemásu けしかけます
abeyance *n* ichiji teishi 一時停止, horyū 保留
abhor *v* (*dislike intensely*) nikumimásu 憎みます, (*not favored*) kiraimásu 嫌います
abide *v* **1.** (*stay*) nokórimásu 残ります, todomarimásu 留まります **2.** (*dwell*) sumimásu 住みます **3.** (*suffer*) gaman shimásu 我慢します, ...ni taemásu ... に耐えます
ability *n* **1.** (*skill*) nōryoku 能力, udemae 腕前, (o-)témae (お)手前; (*stuff*) kíryō 器量, utsuwa 器・うつわ **2.** (*function*) hataraki 働き; (*proficiency*) jitsuryoku 実力 **3.** (*talent*) sái(nō) 才(能)
abject *adj* mijime (na) 惨め(な), hisán (na) 悲惨(な)
ablaze *adj* **1.** (*shiny*) kagayaiteiru 輝いている **2.** (*burning*) moeteiru 燃えている
able → can
abnormal *adj* (*abnormality*) ijō (na) 異常(な)
aboard *v* *gets* ~ norimásu 乗ります
abode *n* ie 家, jūkyo 住居, jūtaku 住宅
abolish *v* (*demolish*) haishi shimásu 廃止します, yamemásu 止めます
aborigine *n* aborijini アボリジニ, aborijinii アボリジニー, genjūmin 原住民, senjūmin 先住民
abort *v* chūshi shimásu 中止します
abortion *n* datai 堕胎, ninshin chū´zetsu 妊娠中絶
abound *v* tomimásu 富みます
about *prep* **1.** (*an amount*) yáku ... 約..., ... gúrai ...位, ... hodo ...程, ...-zéngo... 前後, ...-kéntō ...見当 **2.** (*a time*) ... góro (ni) ... 頃(に) **3.** (*concerning*) ... ni tsúite (no) ... について(の)
above *prep* ... (no) úé (ni) ... (の)上(に)
abrade *v* **1.** (*to wear down*) suri-

hera shimásu すり減らします, (*to be worn away*) mamō sasemásu 磨耗させます **2.** (*chafe*) iraira sasemasu イライラさせます

breast *adv* yokó ni narande 横に並んで; ***not ~ of*** ...ni utói ...に疎い・うとい

bridge *v* (*shorten*) tanshuku shimásu 短縮します, yōyaku shimásu 要約します; (*abate*) hera shimásu 減らします

broad *adv* gaikoku (de) 外国(で), káigai (de) 海外(で); study abroad *n* ryūgaku 留学

brupt *adj* totsuzen (no) 突然(の)

bscond *v* nigemásu 逃げます

bsence *n* kesseki (no) 欠席(の), (*from home*) rúsu (no) 留守(の)

bsent *v* kesseki shimásu̱ 欠席します

bsolute *adv* zettai (no) 絶対(の)

bsolutely *adv* zettai ni 絶対に, honto (hontō) ni 本当・ほんと(ほんとう)に; ***~ cannot*** tōtei 到底 + [NAGATIVE]

bsorbed *adj* (*fascinated*) uttóri (to) うっとり(と); ***gets ~ in*** ... ni korimásu̱ ...に凝ります

bsorption *n* kyūshū 吸収

bstain *v* **1.** (*stops*) yamemásu̱ やめます・止めます, (*refrains from*) tsutsushimimasu 慎みます; ***~ from*** ... o yamemásu̱ ... をやめます, tachimásu̱ 断ちます **2.** ***(does not vote)*** kíken shimásu̱ 棄権します

bstinence *n* jisei 自制, sessei 節制, kinshu 禁酒

abstract *adj* chūshō-teki (na) 抽象的(な)

absurd *adj* baka-rashíi ばからしい

abundance *n* tómi 富

abundant *adj* yútaka (na) 豊か(な)

abuse 1. *n* warú-ku̱chi/-guchi 悪口 **2.** → **scold, mistreat**

abusive *adj* ranbō (*na*) 乱暴(な), kuchigitanai 口汚い, warui 悪い

abysmal *adj* hidói ひどい・酷い, sokonuke (no) 底抜けの, hakarishirenai 計り知れない

abyss *n* chi no soko 地の底, shin'en 深遠, naraku 奈落, donzoko どん底

AC, alternating current *n* kōryū 交流

academic *adj* akádemikku アカデミック, gakumon 学問

academy *n* gakkō´ 学校

accede *v* tsugimásu 継ぎます, dōi shimásu 同意します; accede to *v* ... ni ō-jimásu̱ ...に応じます

accelerate *v* kasóku shimásu 加速します

accent *n* áku̱sento アクセント

accept *v* **1.** ukemásu̱ 受けます, uke-torimásu̱ 受け取ります, uke-tsu̱kemásu̱ 受け付けます **2.** (*consents*) shōdaku shimásu̱ 承諾します; ***~ a bill (of payment)*** tegata o hi̱ki-ukemásu̱ 手形を引き受けます

acceptance *n* **1.** shōdaku 承諾 **2.** (*resignation*) akirame 諦め

access; ***seeks ~ to*** ... ni sekkin o hakarimásu̱ ...に接近を図ります

accessory *n* (*clothing* ~; *belt, handbag, etc.*) akusesarii アクセサリー

accident *n* **1.** jíko 事故, dekígoto 出来事 **2.** (*disaster*) sōnan 遭難

accidentally *adv* gūzen ni 偶然に, hyótto ひょっと

acclaim **1.** *n* shōsan 称賛 **2.** *v* shōsan shimásu 称賛します

accommodate *v* shukuhaku sasemásu 宿泊させます, tekiō shimásu 適応します

accommodation *n* (*place to stay*) shukuhaku shisetsu 宿泊施設; (*facilities*) sétsubi 設備

accompany *v* **1. ~ ... to** issho ni ikimásu (...と)一緒に行きます; ...ni tomonaimásu ...に伴います **2. is accompanied by** (= *brings along*) ... o tsuremásu ... を連れます

accomplice *n* kyōhansha 共犯者, ichimi 一味

accomplish *v* **1.** (shite) shimaimásu (して) しまいます; hatashimásu 果たします; togemásu 遂げます **2.** (*attains*) ...ni tas-shimásu ...に達します(達する, 達して); ... ga kanaimásu ... がかないます

accordance *n* itchi 一致; **in ~ with** ... ni ō-jite ...に応じて; ... ni shitagátte ...にしたがって・従って

according (to) *adj* **1.** (*relying on*) ... ni yoru to ...によると, ... no hanashíde (wa) ...の話で(は) **2.** (*in conformity with*) ... ni shitagatte ...に従って

accost *v* kóe o kakemásu 声をかけます, hanashikakemásu 話しかけます

account *n* **1.** (*bill*) kanjō´ 勘定 **2.** (*credit*) tsuké つけ **3.** (*bank* ~) kōza 口座, yokin 預金; **on account of** ... no séi de ... のせいで → **because** → **sake** (*for the*); **takes into account** kō´ryo ni iremásu 考慮に入れます

accountant *n* kaikei(-gákari) 会計(係), kaikéi-shi 会計士

accounts *n* (o-)kaikei (お)会計

accumulate *v* **1.** (*it ~s*) tsumorimásu 積もります, tamarimásu たまります; tsumemásu つめます; atsumarimásu 集まります **2.** (*~s it*) tsumimásu 積みます, tamemásu ためます; atsumemásu 集めます

accurate *adj* seikaku (na) 正確(な)

accuse *v* uttaemásu 訴えます; (*criticizes*) hínan shimásu 非難します

accustom *v* **~ oneself to** ... ni naremásu ... に慣れます

ache **1.** *v* (*it aches*) itamimásu 痛みます **2.** *n* (*an ache*) itamí 痛み

achieve → **accomplish**

achievement *n* (*work*) hataraki 働き

acid **1.** *n* sán 酸 **2.** *adj* suppái 酸っぱい

acknowledge *v* mitomemásu 認めます

acoustic *n* **1.** akō´sutíkku (gakki) アコースティック(楽器) **2.** onkyō 音響

acquaint *v* **~ oneself with** (... o)

shirimásu (...を) 知ります; *is acquainted with* ... o shitte imásu ... を知っています

acquaintance *n* shiriai 知り合い, chijin 知人

acquiesce *v* fukujū shimásu 服従します

acquire → **get**

acquit *v* shakuhō´ shimásu 釈放します, kaihō shimásu 解放します, muzai ni shimásu 無罪にします

acre *n* ēkā エーカー

acrobat *n* akurobátto アクロバット, kyokugei 曲芸

acronym *n* kashira moji 頭文字

across *prep, adv* ... (no) mukō(ni) ...(の)向こう(に), múkō 向こう; **across the way** mukō 向こう, mukō-gawa 向こう側; *cuts ~* yoko-giri-másu 横切ります

act *n* **1.** → **do** **2.** (*deed*) shiwaza しわざ・仕業, okonai 行い, kō´i 行為 **3.** (*of play*) makú 幕; dán 段 **4.** hōritsu 法律

acting **1.** *n* (*play acting*) éngi 演技 **2.** → **temporary**; *~ as agent* daikō 代行

action *n* **1.** katsudō 活動 **2.** (*conduct*) okonai 行い; (*behavior*) kōdō 行動 → **activity**

active *adj* kappatsu (na) 活発(な); *is ~* katsuyaku shimásu 活躍します

activity *n* **1.** katsudō 活動, katsuyaku 活躍 **2.** (*work*) hataraki 働き **3.** (*agency*) kikán 機関 → **exercise** → **movement**

actor *n* yakusha 役者, haiyū 俳優

actress *n* joyū 女優

actual *adj* jissai (no) 実際(の); *~ conditions* genjitsu 現実

actually *adv* jitsú wa 実は, jitsu ní 実に

acupuncture *n* hári はり・鍼

acute *adj* **1.** (*sharp*) surudói 鋭い **2.** (*severe*) hageshíi 激しい **3.** (*sudden*) kyūsei (no) 急性(の)

adamant *adj* katái かたい・硬い・固い, gánko (na) 頑固(な), dánko (to shita) 断固(とした)

adapt *v* tekigō´ sasemásu 適合させます

adaptability *n* yūzū 融通; *is adaptable* yūzū ga kikimásu 融通がききます

adapter *n* adáputā´ アダプター

add *v* kuwaemásu 加えます; (*supplements it with*) soemásu 添えます; yosemásu 寄せます

addict *n* jōyō´-sha 常用者, chūdoku (-sha) 中毒(者), izón-sha 依存者

addition *n* tsuiká 追加, tenká 添加; *in ~ to* ...no hoka (ni) ...の他(に), [BOOKISH]... no tá (ni) ...の他(に)

address **1.** *n* jūsho 住所, (...) saki (...)先, (*house number*) banchi 番地, (*written*) tokoro-gaki 所書き, adoresu アドレス; **contact address** *n* renraku-saki 連絡先; **e-mail address** *n* mēru ádoresu (meru-ado) メールアドレス(メルアド) **2.** *n* enzetsu 演説 **3.** *v* torikumimásu 取り組みます

adequate *adj* ...-no tame (ni) ...の

ため(に)

adhere *v* kuttsukimásu くっつきます; fucháku shimásu 付着します

adjacent *adj* **1.** → **next** **2.** *is ~ to* ...ni ses-shimásu̱ ...に接します

adjective *n* keiyō´shi 形容詞

adjoining → **next**

adjust *v* totonoemásu̱ 整えます chōsei/séiri/kagen shimásu̱ 調整/整理/加減します

adjustment *n* chōsei 調整, séiri 整理, kagen 加減, chōsetsu 調節

administration *n* **1.** (*of government*) gyōsei 行政 **2.** (*of business*) keiei 経営, kánri 管理

admirable *adj* mígoto (na) 見事(な), rippa (na) 立派(な)

admiral *n* táishō 大将

admire *v* kanshin shimásu̱ 感心します, homemásu̱ 褒めます, akogaremásu̱ あこがれ[憧れ]ます

admission *n* (*to hospital*) nyūin 入院; (*to school*) nyūgaku 入学; (*to a place*) nyūjō 入場; admission fee *n* nyūjō´-ryō 入場料

admit *v* **1.** (*lets in*) iremásu̱ 入れます, tōshimásu̱ 通します **2.** (*acknowledges*) mitomemásu̱ 認めます; (*confesses*) uchi-akemásu̱ 打ち明けます

admonish *v* chūkoku shimásu 忠告します, chūi shimásu 注意します, kankoku shimásu 勧告します

adolescent *n* seinen 青年

adopt *v* (*a boy*) yōshi ni shimásu̱ 養子にします; (*a girl*) yō´jo ni shimásu̱ 養女にします

adorable *adj* kawaíi かわいい・可愛い, kawairashíi かわいらしい・可愛らしい, airashíi 愛らしい

adore *v* akogaremásu̱ あこがれ[憧れ]ます

adult *n* otona おとな・大人, seijin 成人

adultery *n* kantsū 姦通, furin 不倫

advance **1.** *n* zenshin 前進 **2.** *n in ~* sono máe ni その前に; (*beforehand*) mae motte 前もって, jizen ni 事前に **3.** *v* (*goes ahead*) su̱sumimásu̱ 進みます; (*~s it*) su̱sumemásu̱ 進めます, (*lends money*) yūzū shimásu̱ 融通します

advantage *n* **1.** (o-)toku (お)得, (*benefit*) ríeki 利益; *takes ~ of ...* o riyō shimásu̱ ...を利用します **2.** (*merit*) chō´sho 長所

advent *n* shutsugen 出現, tōrai 到来, kirisuto no kōrin キリストの降臨

adventure *n* bōken 冒険

adverb *n* fu̱ku̱shi 副詞

adversary *n* (o-)aite (お)相手

adverse *adj* fúri (na) 不利(な), gyakkyō (no) 逆境(の)

advertisement, ad *n* kōkoku 広告

advice *n* **1.** adobáisu アドバイス, chūkoku 忠告 **2.** (*consultation*) sōdan 相談

adviser *n* (*consultant*) komon 顧問, sōdan aite 相談相手

advocate *v* tonaemásu̱ 唱えます

aerobics *n* earobíku̱su エアロビクス

aesthetic *adj* bi-teki (na) 美的な

afar *adv* tōku (ni) 遠く(に), enpō 遠方; ***from*** ~ tōku kara 遠くから

affable *adj* áiso/áisō ga íi あいそ/あいそう[愛想]がいい, hitozuki no suru 人好きのする, shitashimiyasui 親しみやすい

affair *n* **1.** kotó 事, kotogara 事柄, jíken 事件, shigoto 仕事 **2.** (*love* ~) (*extramarital*) uwaki 浮気

affect → **influence**

affection *n* nasake 情け (o-)násake (お)情け, aijō 愛情

affiliate **1.** *v* kamei shimásu 加盟します **2.** *n* ko-gaisha 子会社, shiten 支店

affirmation *n* kōtei 肯定

affix *v* setsuji 接辞, tenkábutsu 添加物

affliction *n* kurushimi 苦しみ

afford *v* (jūbun na) (o-)kane ga arimásu (十分な)(お)金があります; yoyū ga arimásu 余裕があります

affront **1.** *v* bujoku shimásu 侮辱します **2.** *n* bujoku 侮辱

Afghanistan *n* Afuganísutan アフガニスタン

afloat *adj, adv* ukan da/de 浮かんだ/で; **afloat cargo** *n* okini 沖荷

afraid; ***is*** ~ ***of*** ... (...ga) kowái desu (...が)怖いです, (...o) kowagarimásu (...を)怖がります

Africa *n* Afurika アフリカ

after **1.** *prep* ... kará ...から, ... (no) áto de ...(の)後で **2.** *adv* ... shita ato ni/de ...した後に/で; **after a long time** *adv* (*of absence*) hisashi-buri ni 久しぶりに; **after a while** *adv* shibáraku shite しばらくして; **after all** *adv* kekkyokú 結局; yappári やっぱり, yappáshi やっぱし; tsúmari つまり; **After you!** *interj* Dōzo o-saki ni どうぞお先に

afternoon *n, adv* hirú kara 昼から, gógo 午後

aftertaste *n* ató-aji 後味; ***leaves a bad*** ~ atóaji ga warúi 後味が悪い

after(ward) *adv* ato 後

afterwards *adv* áto de 後で

again *adv* mō ichi-dó もう一度, mō ik-kái もう一回; matá また・又; aratámete 改めて, kurikaeshimásu (ga) 繰り返します(が)

against *prep* **1.** (*in contrast to*) ...ni táishite ...に対して; (*contrary to*) ...ni hán-shite ...に反して **2.** (*running into*) ... ni butsukatte ...にぶつかって **3.** (*leaning on*) ...ni motárete (no) ...にもたれて(の)

age **1.** *n* toshí とし・年・歳, nenrei 年齢; ***your*** ~ (o-)toshi (お)年, [BOOKISH] nenrei 年齢 **2.** *n* (*era*) jidai 時代 **3.** *v* (*gets old*) toshí o torimásu 年を取ります, fukemásu 老けます

agency *n* **1.** dairi 代理, dairí-ten 代理店 **2.** (*organization*) kikán 機関

aggression *n* shinryaku 侵略

agile *adj* kibin (na) 機敏(な), binshō (na) 敏捷(な), subayái すばやい・素早い

agitation *n* **1.** dōyō 動揺 **2.** kōfun 興奮

ago *adv* ...máe ni ...前に; ***a little while ~*** (tsui) sákki (つい)さっき, (tsui) saki-hodo (つい)先程

agony *n* kurushimi 苦しみ, kutsū 苦痛

agrarian *adj* nōgyō (no) 農業(の), nōmin (no) 農民(の)

agree *v* **1.** (*approves*) sansei shimásu 賛成します; (*concurs*) dōi shimásu 同意します **2.** (*promises*) yakusoku shimásu 約束します **3.** (*accords with*) ... ni kanaimásu ...にかないます, ... to itchi shimásu ...と一致します; ***~ with*** (*in harmony*) ... to chōwa shimásu ...と調和します

agreement *n* **1.** (*promise*) yakusoku 約束; (*contract*) keiyaku 契約; (*treaty*) jōyaku 条約 **2.** (*understanding*) shōchi 承知; (*consensus*) itchi 一致, dōi 同意, gō´i 合意

agriculture *n* nō´gyō 農業

ahead *adv* (o-)saki (ni) (お)先(に); ***gets ~*** susumimásu 進みます

AI *abbrev* (= *artificial intelligence*) E-ai AI, jinkōchinō 人工知能

aid → **help**

AIDS *n* éizu エイズ, AIDS

aikido *n* aikídō 合気道

ailing *adj* byōki de 病気で, byōki ryōyōchū (no) 病気療養中(の)

aim *n* **1.** nerai 狙い, méate 目当て; kentō´ 見当; (*target*) mato 的; ***takes ~*** kentō´ o tsukemásu 見当をつけます **2.** (*goal*) mokuteki 目的; (*direction*) hōshin 方針

aimless *adj* mokuteki ga/no nái 目的が/のない

air **1.** *n* kū´ki 空気 **2.** *n* (*manner*) furí ふり; (*appearance*) fū´ 風 **3.** *n* (*tune*) fushí 節 **4.** *v* ***~s it*** (*dry*) hoshimásu 干します

air base *n* kūgun kíchi 空軍基地

air conditioner, air conditioning *n* kū´rā クーラー, eakon エアコン, reibō (sō´chi) 冷房(装置)

aircraft *n* hikōki 飛行機; **aircraft carrier** *n* kōkū bokan 航空母艦

airline *n* (*company*) kōkū-gáisha 航空会社

airplane *n* hikō´-ki 飛行機

airport *n* kūkō 空港, hikōjō 飛行場

airsick(ness) *n* hikō-yoi 飛行酔い

airy *adj* **1.** kaze tōshi no yoi 風通しのよい **2.** keikai (na) 軽快(な) **3.** keihaku (na) 軽薄(な)

aisle *n* tsū´ro 通路

ajar *adj* **1.** sukoshi hiráite 少し開いて **2.** chōwa shinái (de) 調和しない(で)

alarm *n* keihō (sō´chi) 警報(装置)

alarm clock *n* arāmu アラーム, mezamashi(-dókei) 目覚し(時計)

alas *prep* áa ああ, āá あーあ

album *n* (*photograph*) arubamu アルバム; (*stamp*) kitte-chō 切手帳

alcoholic *n* arukōru chūdoku-sha アルコール中毒者

alert *n* (*alarm*) keihō 警報, arāto アラート

alias *n* gimei 偽名, betsumei 別名, tsūshō 通称

alibi *n* aribái アリバイ

alien *n* **1.** yosó (no) よそ(の) **2.** (*an alien*) → **foreigner** **3.** uchūjin 宇宙人, éirian エイリアン

alienate *v* sogai shimásu 疎外します, tōzakemásu 遠ざけます, sodéni shimásu そでにします

align *v* seiretsu shimásu 整列します, narabimásu 並びます

alike *adj* onaji (yō´na) 同じ(ような), nitéiru 似ている

alimony *n* bekkyo téate 別居手当, rikon téate 離婚手当

alive *adj* **1.** ***is ~*** íkite imásu 生きています **2.** ***keeps it ~*** ikashimásu 生かします

all *pron* **1.** minna みんな・皆, zen'in 全員; ***~ (concerned/ present)*** ichidō 一同 **2.** zénbu 全部, súbete 全て・すべて; (*everything*) íssái 一切, arayúru あらゆる; ***not at ~*** どういたしまして **3.** (*completely*) sukkári すっかり; **all along** *adv* (*from the beginning*) móto kara 元から; **all kinds of** *adj* samazama (na) さまざま(な)・様々(な), iroiro (na/ no) いろいろ・色々(な/の), shúshu (no) 種々(の); **all over** *adv* ① (*everywhere*) hōbō ほうぼう・方々; ...-jū ...中 ② (*finished*) → **end**; **all of a sudden** *adv* totsuzen (ni) 突然(に), fuini 不意に, ikinari いきなり; **all the more** *adv* issō いっそう・一層, nao-sara なおさら・尚更

allay *v* shizumemásu 静めます, yawáragemásu 和らげます

allege *v* **1.** shuchō shimásu 主張します **2.** mōshitatemásu 申し立てます

allergy *n* arérúgii アレルギー

alleviate *v* **1.** yawáragemásu 和らげます **2.** shizumemásu 静めます **3.** kanwa shimásu 緩和します

alley *n* róji 路地; (*back street*) urá 裏, ura-dō´ri 裏通り; (*side street*) yokochō 横町[横丁]

alliance *n* rengō 連合

alligator *n* wáni ワニ

allocate *v* wariatemásu 割り当てます, haibun shimásu 配分します

allot *v* kubarimásu 配ります

allotment *n* wariate 割り当て; (*share*) buntan 分担

allow *v*. **1.** (*permits*) yurushimásu 許します **2.** → **give**

allowance *n* (o-)téate (お)手当; (*grant*) kyō´yo 供与

alloy *n* gōkin 合金

all right *adj* (*OK*) daijōbu (na) 大丈夫(な); (*permissible*) íi いい・良い, yoroshii よろしい

allude *v* honomeka shimásu ほのめかします, anji shimásu 暗示します

allure *n* miryoku 魅力, miwaku 魅惑

ally *n* dāmeikoku 同盟国

almost *adv* hotóndo ほとんど・殆ど; daitai 大体; **almost all, almost all**

the time *n* hotóndo ほとんど・殆ど
alms *n* hodokoshi (mono) 施し(もの)
aloft *adv*, *adj* kūchū ni/de 空中に/で, takaitokoro ni/de 高いところに/で
alone *adv* hitóri (de) 一人[独り]で・ひとり(で); (*leave alone*) *let* ~ hotte/hōtte okimásu 放っておきます
along **1.** *prep*, *adv* ...ni sotte ...に沿って; (*somewhere*) ...no doko ka (de) ...のどこか(で) **2.** *adv* ***brings/takes*** **~** jisan shimásu 持参します; ... o tsurete ikimásu ...を連れて行きます
aloof *adj* takabisha (na) 高飛車(な), otákaku tomatta お高くとまった
aloud *adv* kóe o/ni dáshite 声を/に出して
alphabet (ABC) *n* arufabetto アルファベット, ē bii shíi エービーシー
Alps *n* arupusu アルプス
already *adv* mō´もう, súde-ni すでに・既に
also *conj* **1.** ...mo ... も,, mátá また **2.** [INFORMAL] yappári やっぱり, [BOOKISH] yahári やはり,
altar *n* saidan 祭壇
alter *v* **1.** (*clothing*) naoshimásu 直します **2.** aratamemásu 改めます, kaemásu 変えます
alternate; *v* **~ *(with)*** kōtai shimásu 交代[交替]します
alternative *adj*, *n* ... (no) hō´ (ga) ...(の)方(が)
although *conj* ... no ni ...のに, ... daga ... だが, ... towaie ... とはいえ
altitude *n* kō´do 高度
altogether *adv* **1.** zénbu de 全部で minná de みんなで・皆で **2.** (*completely*) mattakú まったく・全く
alumni *n* sotsugyōsei 卒業生; alumni association *n* dōsō-kai 同窓会
always *adv* ítsu-mo いつも, (*usually*) fúdan ふだん・普段; as always *n* aikawarazu 相変わらず
am → **is**
a.m. *adv* (*morning*) gozen 午前
amalgamate *v* **1.** gappei shimásu 合併します, heigō shimásu 併合します **2.** yūgō shimásu 融合します, mazemásu 混ぜます
amass *v* tamemásu ため[貯め・溜め]ます
amateur *n* amachua アマチュア; (*novice*) shírō´to しろうと・素人
amazement *n* odoroki おどろき・驚き, kyōtan 驚嘆
ambassador *n* táishi 大使
ambition *n* (*hope*) netsubō 熱望, yashin 野心; (*energetic spirit*) háki 覇気
ambivalent *adj* kokoro ga fuántei (na) 心が不安定(な), ánbibarensu (no) アンビバレンス(の), kattō-teki (na) 葛藤的な
ambulance *n* kyūkyū-sha 救急車
ambush **1.** *n* machibuse 待ち伏せ, harikomi 張り込み, fuiuchi 不意打ち, kishū kōgeki 奇襲攻撃 **2.** *v* machibuse shimásu 待ち伏せします, kishū kōgeki o kakemásu

奇襲攻撃をかけます
amenable *adj* jūjun (na) 従順(な), sunao (na) 素直(な)
amend *v* shūsei shimásu̲ 修正します, kaisei shimásu̲ 改正します
amenity *n* **1.** kokochiyosa 心地よさ, kaiteki-sa/sei 快適さ/性 **2.** reigi 礼儀 **3.** benri na shisetsu 便利な施設
America *n* Amerika アメリカ, Beikoku 米国
American *n* Ameriká-jin アメリカ人
amiable *adj* shakō-teki (na) 社交的(な), hitozukiai no yoi 人付き合いのよい, hitoatari no yoi 人当たりのよい
amiss *adv* machigatte 間違って, futekitō ni 不適当に
ammunition *n* **1.** dan'yaku 弾薬, buki 武器 **2.** kōgeki shudan 攻撃手段, bōei shudan 防衛手段
amnesia *n* kioku sōshitsu 記憶喪失, kenbō-shō 健忘症
amnesty *n* onsha 恩赦
among *prep* ... no náka/uchí (ni) ... の中/内(に)
amoral *adj* dōtoku kannen no nai 道徳観念のない
amorous *adj* **1.** iroppoi 色っぽい, namámekashii なまめかしい **2.** kōshoku (na) 好色(な)
amount **1.** *n* (*sum*) gáku 額, kingaku 金額 **2.** *n* (*large and/or small*) ~ tashō 多少 **3.** *v* ~ *to* (*how much*) (o-)ikura ni narimásu̲ (お)いくらになります
ample *adj* **1.** *n* hiroi 広い, kōdai na 広大な **2.** futotta 太った **3.** jūbun (na) じゅうぶん(な)・十分(な) → **enough**
amuse *v* warawasemásu 笑わせます, tanoshimasemásu̲ 楽しませます
amusement *n* **1.** asobi 遊び **2.** nagusami 慰み, goraku 娯楽; amusement park *n* 遊園地
amusing *adj* omoshirói おもしろい・面白い; (*funny*) okashíi おかしい, kokkei (na) こっけい・滑稽(な)
an → **a**
anal *adj* kōmon no 肛門の
analogy *n* **1.** tatoe 例え・たとえ・喩え **2.** ruiji 類似
analysis *n* bunseki 分析
ancestor *n* sósen 祖先, sénzo 先祖
anchor *n* ikari いかり・錨・碇; anchor man *n* nyūsu kyásutā ニュースキャスター
ancient *adj* mukashi no 昔の, kodai no 古代の; ancient times kodai 古代
and *conj* ... (*including each item*) ... to ...と; (*choosing typical items*) ...ya ...や; and also ... oyobi ...および・及び; and now/then sá-te さて/それから; and/or mátá-wa または・又は, ...ya ...や; and others ... -ra... ら;... nádo ...など・等; sonó-hoka その他・そのほか, [BOOKISH] sonó-ta その他; and yet sore démo それでも, shi̲ká-mo しかも, sore náno ni それなのに
Android (phones) *n* Andoroido (Oesu) アンドロイド (OS)

anemia *n* hinketsu(-shō) 貧血(症)
anesthetic *n* másui(-yaku/zai) 麻酔(薬/剤)
anew *adv* atarásh_iku 新しく, aratámete 改めて, sára-ni さらに・更に
angel *n* ténshi 天使, enjeru エンジェル
anger *n* ikari 怒り
angle *n* **1.** kákudo 角度, kakú 角 **2.** (*viewpoint*) kénchi 見地
angry; *gets* ~ okorimásu_ 怒ります, hará o tatemásu_ 腹を立てます, atáma ni kimásu_ 頭にきます
animal *n* dōbutsu 動物, ikímono 生き物
animation *n* **1.** animé アニメ, animēshon アニメーション, dōga 動画 **2.** kakki 活気
ankle *n* ashí-kúbi 足首
annex *n* **1.** (*building*) bekkan 別館 **2.** (*addition*) tate-mashi 建て増し
annihilation *n* zenmetsu 全滅
anniversary *n* (*day*) kinén-bi 記念日
annotation *n* chū 注
announce *v* **1.** (*inform*) shirasemásu_ 知らせます **2.** (*publish*) happyō shimásu_ 発表します **3.** (*wedding, etc.*) hírō shimásu_ 披露します
announcer *n* anaúnsā アナウンサー
annoyance *n* (*trouble*) méiwaku 迷惑
annoying *adj* urusái うるさい, yakamashíi やかましい, méiwaku (na) 迷惑(な), wazurawashíi わずらわしい
annual **1.** *adj* ichinen (no) 一年(の) **2.** *n* nenkan 年刊, nenpo 年報
annuity *n* nenkin 年金
annul *v* haishi shimásu 廃止します mukō ni shimásu_ 無効にします
anonymous *adj* mumei (no) 無名(の)
another *pron* mō h_itótsu もう一つ, mō ichi-... もう一...; another person mō h_itóri もう一人; another place yoso よそ; another time (*some other time*) ítsu-ka いつか, izure いずれ
answer **1.** *n* (*an* ~) kotáé 答え, kaitō 解答, (*a reply*) (o-)henji (お)返事, [BOOKISH] hentō 返答 **2.** *v* (~*s it*) kotaemásu_ 答えます, kaitō shimásu_ 解答します
ant *n* ari アリ・蟻
antagonism *n* tekii 敵意, tairitsu 対立, hánkan 反感, kikkō 拮抗
Antarctica *n* nánkyoku (tairiku) 南極(大陸)
antenna *n* antena アンテナ
antibiotic(s) *n* kōsei bússh_itsu 抗性物質
antic(s) *n* kokkei na shigusa こっけいな・滑稽なしぐさ・仕草, odoketa shigusa おどけたしぐさ・仕草, fuzaketa taido ふざけた態度
anticipate *v* machimásu_ 待ちます, k_itai shimásu_ 期待します; (*presume*) yosō shimásu_ 予想します
antidote *n* **1.** gedókuzai 解毒剤, dok(u)-késhí 毒消し **2.** bōei shudan 防衛手段
antipathy *n* hankan 反感, ken'o

嫌悪, fuítchi 不一致, tairitsu 対立
antique *n* jidai-mono 時代物; (*curio*) kottō-hin 骨董品
antiquity *n* ōmukashi 大昔
antiseptic *n* bōfu-zai 防腐剤
antler *n* edazunó 枝角, tsunó 角
antonym *n* hantai-go 反対語
anus *n* kōmon 肛門
anxiety *n* ki-zúkái 気遣い, shinpai 心配 → **worry**
anxious *adj* ***gets*** ~ harahara shimás<u>u</u> はらはらします
any *adj* ... ka ...か, ... mo ...も (*but often omitted*) → **anything**
anybody *pron* h<u>i</u>to 人, dáre ka 誰か; (*not anyody*) dare mo 誰も; **anybody (at all)** dare de mo 誰でも
anyhow *adv* **1.** (*nevertheless*) tónikaku とにかく; (*anyway*) tómokaku ともかく, nanibun なにぶん, nánishiro なにしろ **2.** (*at all*) dō de mo どうでも
anyone → **anybody**
anyplace → **anywhere**
anything *pron* **1.** (*something*) náni ka 何か (*but often omitted*); (*not anything*) nani mo 何も **2.** (*at all*) nan de mo 何でも
any time *adv* itsu de mo いつでも
anyway *adv* → **anyhow**
anywhere *adv* (*somewhere*) dóko ka (...) どこか(...); ~ ***(at all)*** doko de mo どこでも; ***not*** ~ → **nowhere**
apart; *adv* ***lives*** ~ bekkyo shimás<u>u</u> 別居します; ***takes it*** ~ barashimás<u>u</u> ばらします
apartment (house) *n* apāto アパート, (*luxury*) mánshon マンション; **apartment complex** *n* danchi 団地
apathetic *adj* mukándō (no) 無感動(の), mukánjō (no) 無感情(の), mukánshin (no) 無関心(の)
apathy *n* mukándō 無感動, mukánjō 無感情, mukánshin 無関心
ape *n* **1.** sáru サル・猿 **2.** noróma na hito のろまな人
apiece *adv* (onóono/sorezore) ...zútsu (おのおの/それぞれ) ...ずつ
apologize *v* owabishimásu おわび[お詫び]します, ayamarimás<u>u</u> 謝ります
apology *n* (o-)wabi (お)わび・(お)詫び, ayamári 謝り
appall *v* zotto shimás<u>u</u> ぞっとします, gakuzen to shimás<u>u</u> がくぜん・愕然とします
apparatus *n* sō´chi 装置; kígu 器具
apparel *n* (i)fuku (衣)服; **apparel industry** *n* apareru gyōkai アパレル業界
apparent(ly) *adv* ... rashíi ...らしい
apparition *n* **1.** yūrei 幽霊, bōrei 亡霊 **2.** shutsu-gen 出現
appeal *v* (*appeal to one*) pin to kimás<u>u</u> ぴんときます, ki ni irimás<u>u</u> 気に入ります
appear *v* **1.** (*looks, seems*) miemás<u>u</u> 見えます **2.** (*shows up*) demás<u>u</u> 出ます, arawaremás<u>u</u> 現れます; (*occurs*) hassei shimás<u>u</u> 発生します; ~ ***on stage*** bútai

ni demásu 舞台に出ます, tōjō shimásu 登場します

appearance *n* **1.** yōsu 様子・ようす, ...sama ...様 **2.** gaiken 外見; (*outer appearances*) uwabe うわべ・上辺, omoté 表 **3.** (*get-up, form*) teisai 体裁; (*shape*) kakkō かっこう・格好・恰好

appease *v* nadámemásu なだめます, yawaragemásu 和らげます, iyashimásu いやし・癒します

append *v* fuka shimásu 付加します, tsuketashimásu 付け足します, soemásu 添えます

appendicitis *n* mōchō-en 盲腸炎, chūsui-en 虫垂炎

appetite *n* shokuyoku 食欲

appetizers *n* zensai 前菜

appetizing *adj* oishisō (na) おいしそう(な)

applaud *v* hákushu shimásu 拍手します, hákushu o okurimásu 拍手を送ります

apple *n* ringo りんご・リンゴ

appliances *n* (katei) yō´gu (家庭)用具, katei yō´hin 家庭用品

applicant *n* mōshikomí-sha 申し込み者, kibō-sha 希望者

application *n* **1.** (*for a job, etc.*) mōshi-komi 申し込み, gánsho 願書; (*claim*) mōshi-de 申し出; (*for a permit*) shinsei-sho 申請書 **2.** (*putting to use*) ōyō 応用, jitsuyō 実用; (*for computer*) sofutowea ソフトウェア

apply *v* **1.** (*it applies*) atarimásu 当たります; (*accordingly*) jun-jimásu 準じます **2.** (*applies it*) atemásu 当てます, tsukemásu 付けます; ōyō shimásu 応用します **3.** (*applies for*) mōshi-komi-másu 申し込みます; (*claims*) mōshi-demásu 申し出ます

appoint *v* (*nominates*) mei-jimásu 命じます; (*designates*) shitei shimásu 指定します

appointment *n* yakusoku 約束; (*to see doctor, ...*) yoyaku 予約

apportion *v* ... o wariatemásu ... を割り当てます, ... o bunpai shimásu ... を分配します

appraise *v* hyōka shimásu 評価します, kantei shimásu 鑑定します

appreciation *n* kánsha 感謝, hyōka 評価

apprehend *v* **1.** ríkai shimásu 理解します, sasshimásu 察します **2.** tsukamaemásu 捕まえます, taiho shimásu 逮捕します

apprehensive *adj* kimí ga warúi 気味が悪い

apprentice *n* deshí 弟子

approach *v* (...ni) chika-zukimásu (...に)近付きます, yorimásu 寄ります; sekkin shimásu 接近します

appropriate **1.** *adj* (*suitable*) tekisetsu (na) 適切(な), tekitō (na) 適当(な) **2.** *v* (*sets aside* (*for*)) atemásu 当てます **3.** *v* → **seize**

approval *n* dōi 同意

approve *v* sansei shimásu 賛成します

approximate **1.** *adj* daitai (no) 大

体(の), gaisan (no) 概算(の), chikái 近い **2.** *v* chikazukimásu 近づきます, chikazukemásu 近づけます

approximately *adv* daitai 大体; yáku ... 約...; ... gúrai ...位; ...-zéngo ...前後; ... -kéntō ...見当; ...-náigai (de) ...内外(で)

April *n* Shi-gatsú 四月・4月

apt; *adj* **~ to (do)** (shi-)yasúi (し)やすい・易い; tokaku (...shimásu) とかく(...します); ete-shite (... shimásu) 得てして(します)

aptitude *n* keikō 傾向, sáinō 才能, rikairyoku 理解力

aquarium *n* suizóku-kan 水族館

Arab, Arabian *n, adj* Árabu (no) アラブ(の), (*person*) Arabú-jin (no) アラブ人(の)

arbitrary *adj* nin-i (no) 任意の, dokudan-teki (na) 独断的(な), kimáma (na) 気まま(な)

arc *n* (en)ko (円)弧

arch *n* yumi-gata 弓形, āchi(-gata) アーチ(形)

archaeologist *n* kōko gákusha 考古学者

archaic *adj* sutáreta 廃れた

archery *n* (*the traditional art*) kyūdō 弓道, kyūjutsu 弓術

archipelago *n* rettō 列島

architecture *n* kenchiku 建築

Arctic *n* Hokkyoku 北極

ardent *adj* nesshin (na) 熱心(な), netsuretsu(teki) (na) 熱烈(的)(な)

ardor *n* netsui 熱意, jōnetsu 情熱, nesshin 熱心, ikigomi 意気込み

arduous *adj* kónnan (na) 困難(な)

arid *adj* kánsō shita/shiteiru 乾燥した/している, fumō no/na 不毛の/に

are → **is**

area *n* **1.** ménseki 面積 **2.** (*district*) chihō 地方, chiiki 地域, eria エリア, chitai 地帯 → **place** → **vicinity**

argue *v* kenka shimásu けんか[喧嘩]します; (*discusses, debates*) ron-jimásu 論じます

argument *n* **1.** kenka けんか・喧嘩, kuchi-génka 口げんか・口喧嘩 **2.** (*discussion*) rón 論, ronsō 論争 **3.** (*logic*) rikutsu 理屈

arise *v* okimásu 起きます; (*happens*) shō-jimásu 生じます

arm *n* udé 腕

armor *n* yoroi よろい・鎧

armpit *n* waki nó shita 腋の下・わきの下

arms *n* heiki 兵器, buki 武器

army *n* gúntai 軍隊; (*vs. navy*) rikú-gun 陸軍

aroma *n* ároma アロマ, (yoi) kaori (よい)香り, hōkō 芳香

around **1.** *adv* (... no) mawari ni (...の)周りに; ***goes ~*** (... o) mawarimásu (...を)回ります **2.** → **about, approximately**

arouse *v* shigeki shimásu 刺激します, kōfun shimásu 興奮します

arrange *v* **1.** (*lines them up*) narabemásu 並べます; ***~ themselves*** narabimásu 並びます **2.** (*decides, sets*) kimemásu 決めます, (*a meeting/consultation*) uchi-awa-

semásu 打ち合わせます
arranged *v* **1.** ***gets ~*** (*is put together*) matomarimásu まとまります, (*as a set/array*) soroimásu 揃います; (*gets decided/set*) kimarimásu 決まります **2.** ***it has been ~ that ...*** kotó ni natte (i)másu ...ことになって(い)ます
arrangement *n* **1.** (*settlement*) kimari 決まり; (*adjustment*) séiri 整理 **2.** ***arrangements*** (*preparations*) júnbi 準備, shitaku 支度・仕度; (*plans*) téhazu 手はず・手筈;
flower arrangement *n* ikébana
array *n* soróé 揃え
arrears *n* tainō(kin) 滞納(金)
arrest *v* toraemásu 捕えます, tsukamaemásu 捕まえます, táiho shimásu 逮捕します
arrive (at) *v* **1.** (... ni) tsukimásu (...に)着きます, tōchaku shimásu 到着します, itarimásu 至ります **2.** (*is delivered*) todokimásu 届きます
arrogant *adj* gōman (na) 傲慢(な)
arrow *n* yá 矢; (*sign*) ya-jírushi 矢印
art *n* bíjutsu 美術, geijutsu 芸術
artery *n* **1.** dōmyaku 動脈 **2.** kansen dōro 幹線道路
artful *adj* kōmyō (na) 巧妙(な), kōkatsu (na) 狡猾(な)
arthritis *n* kansetsu-en 関節炎
article *n* (*thing*) monó 物, (*goods*) shina(-mono) 品(物); (*writeup*) kíji 記事; ronbun 論文
articulate **1.** *adj* hakkírishita はっきりした, meikai (na) 明快(な) **2.** *v* hakkíri iimásu はっきり言います
artificial *adj* jinkō (no) 人工(の), jinkō-teki (na) 人工的(な)
artillery *n* taihō 大砲, buki 武器
artisan *n* shokunin 職人
artist *n* geijutsu-ka 芸術家; (*painter*) gaka 画家
as *conj* **1.** (*like*) ... (no) yō´ (ni) ... (の)よう(に) **2.** (*so as to be*) ...ni..に **3.** (*in the role of*) ... to shite ... として; as far as ... is concerned ... ni kákete wa ... にかけては; …ni kan-shite wa… に関しては; as for ... wa ...は; as much as ... gúrai ...位; ...hodo ...程・ほど; as much as possible dekiru-dake 出来るだけ・できるだけ; as regards ... ni kákete wa ...にかけては; ... ni kánshite ...に関して; ni tsúite …について
Asakusa *n* Asakusa 浅草
ascent *n* jōshō 上昇, agáru koto 上がること
ascertain *v* tashikamemásu 確かめます
ashamed *adj* hazukashíi 恥ずかしい; (*guilty feeling*) yamashíi やましい; ***is ~*** of hajimásu 恥ます
ash(es) *n* hai 灰
ashore *adv* kishi (ni) (mukatte) 岸(に)(向かって), riku (ni) (mukatte) 陸(に)(向かって)
ashtray *n* hai-zara 灰皿
Asian **1.** *adj* Ajia (no) アジア(の)

2. *n* (*person*) Ajiá-jin アジア人

ask *v* **1.** (*a favor of a person*) (... ni ...o) tanomimásu (...に...を)頼みます, negaimásu 願います; (*requires*) motomemásu 求めます **2.** (~ *a person a question*) (... ni) kikimásu (...に) 聞きます, tazunemásu 尋ねます, ukagaimásu 伺います

aslant *adv*, *adj* naname (no/ni) 斜め(の/に)

asleep *adv*, *adj* nemutte (iru) 眠って(いる)

aspect *n* **1.** yōsu 様子 **2.** (*grammatical*) ásupékuto アスペクト, (soku/kyoku) men (側/局)面

asphyxiate *v* chissoku shimásu 窒息します

aspiration *n* ganbō 願望, yashin 野心, akogare 憧れ

aspire → **hope**

aspirin *n* asupirin アスピリン

ass **1.** *n* róba ろば・ロバ **2.** *n* gankomono 頑固者; báka ばか **3.** *n* (o-)shíri (お)しり・(お)尻

assail *v* kōgeki shimásu 攻撃します, hínan shimásu 非難します

assault *v* osóimásu 襲います → **attack**

assemble *v* **1.** (*they collect*) atsumarimásu 集まります, shūgō shimásu 集合します; (*collects them*) atsumemásu 集めます **2.** (*fits parts together to make a whole*) kumi-awasemásu 組(み)合せます, kumi-tatemásu 組(み)立てます

assembly *n* **1.** (*gathering*) shūgō 集合 **2.** (*parliament*) kokkai 国会

assent *v* nattoku shimásu 納得します → **consent**

assert *v* shuchō shimásu 主張します

assimilate *v* dōka shimásu 同化します; kyūshū shimásu 吸収します

assist *v* ōen shimásu 応援します; tasukemásu 助けます → **help**

assistance *n* (o-)séwa (お)世話; (o-)tétsudai (お)手伝い; hójo 補助; ōen 応援

assistant *n* joshu 助手, ashísutanto アシスタント

associate with ...to tsuki-aimásu ...と付き合います; ...to majiwarimásu ...と交わります

association *n* **1.** kyōkai 協会; (*academic*) gakkai 学会; (*guild, union*) kumiai 組合 **2.** (*social company*) (o-)tsukíai (お)付き合い

assortment *n* kumi-awase 組み合わせ, tori-awase 取り合わせ

asterisk *n* hoshi-jírushi 星印; asutarisuku アスタリスク

asthma *n* zensoku 喘息

astonished; *adj gets* ~ odorokimásu 驚きます

astringent *adj* shibúi 渋い

astronomy *n* tenmón-gaku 天文学

asylum *n* hinán-jo 避難所, seishin byōin 精神病院

at *prep* ... de...で; (*being located at*) ... ni ...に; **at any rate** tómokaku ともかく; **at best** séizei せいぜい;

at last iyoiyo いよいよ, yōyaku ようやく, tsúi-ni ついに; (*after difficulty*) yatto やっと; at least sukúnáku-tomo 少なくとも, sémete せめて

athlete *n* (undō) sénshu (運動)選手

athletics *n* undō 運動, supōʼtsu スポーツ; (*physical education*) tai(i)ku 体育・たいく

Atlantic Ocean *n* Taiséiyō 大西洋

atmosphere *n* fun'íki 雰囲気

atom *n* génshi 原子

atomic *adj* genshí (-ryoku no) 原子力(の); atomic energy *n* genshí-ryoku 原子力

atrocious *adj* (*brutal*) zangyaku (na) 残虐(な)

attach 1. *v* (*sticks on*) tsukemásu 付けます 2. (*adds*) soemásu 添えます; attached file *n* tenpu fáiru 添付ファイル

attachment *n* fuzoku 付属・附属, fuzoku-hin 付属品・附属品

attack 1. *n* (*an ~*) kōgeki 攻撃, shūgeki 襲撃 2. *v* (*makes an ~*) osóimásu 襲います; sememásu 攻めます

attain → **reach** → **accomplish**

attempt 1. *n* tameshí 試し, kokoromi 試み; (*plot, scheme*) kuwadate 企て 2. *v* (*~s it*) tameshimásu 試します, kokoromimásu 試みます; kuwadatemásu 企てます

attend *v* demásu 出ます; shusseki shimásu 出席します

attendance *n* shusseki 出席; office attendance *n* shukkin 出勤

attendant *n* (*in charge*) kákari 係, kakarí-in 係員, ... -gákari ...係

attention *n* 1. chūʼi 注意, chūmoku 注目 2. omoiyari 思いやり

attitude *n* táido 態度, shisei 姿勢

attorney *n* bengóshi 弁護士

attract *v* hikimásu 引きます; (*charming*) miryoku ga arimásu 魅力があります

attraction *n* atorakushon アトラクション

attractive *adj* (*nice-looking*) kírei (na) きれい・綺麗(な); (*charming*) miryoku-teki (na) 魅力的(な)

auction *n* serí 競り・セリ, kyōbai 競売, ōkushon オークション

audience *n* chōshū 聴衆, kankyaku 観客

audio *n, adj* onsei (no) 音声(の), ōdio オーディオ

audition *n* ōdishon オーディション, shínsa 審査

auditorium *n* kaidō 会堂, kōdō 講堂

aunt *n* (*father's or mather's elder sister*) obá(-san) 伯母(さん); (*father's or mather's younger sister*) obá(-san) 叔母(さん); (*in general*) obá(-san) おば(さん)

auspicious *adj* (o-)medetái (お)めでたい・(お)目出度い

Australia *n* ōsutorária オーストラリア

authentic *adj* kakujitsu (na) 確実(な), honmono (nó) 本物(の), shōshinshōmei (no) 正真正銘(の)

author *n* chó-sha 著者, sáku-sha 作者→ **writer**

authority *n* **1.** (*expert*) táika 大家, tsū´ 通 **2.** (*power*) ken'i 権威 **3.** (*basis*) kónkyo 根拠; the authorities tōkyoku 当局, okámi お上

automatic *adj* jidō-teki (na) 自動的(な)

automation *n* ōtomēshon オートメーション, jidō (ka) 自動(化)

automobile *n* jidō-sha 自動車, kuruma 車

autumn *n* áki 秋; autumn period/term shū´ki 秋期

autumnal equinox *n* shūbun 秋分; Autumnal Equinox Day Shūbun-no-hí 秋分の日

available *adj* (*things*) riyō dekiru 利用できる, (*person*) áiteiru 空いている; ***seats are ~*** suwaremásu̲ 座れます

avalanche *n* nadare なだれ・雪崩; (*snowslide*) yuki-nádare 雪なだれ

avenue *n* tōrí 通り, ōdō´ri 大通り, kaidō 街道; michi 道

average **1.** *n* (*on the ~*) heikin 平均; average age heikin nenrei 平均年令; (*life span, lifetime*) heikin jumyō 平均寿命 **2.** *adj* (*ordinary*) nami (no) 並(の), heibon (na) 平凡(な)

avert *v* **1.** sakemásu̲ 避けます **2.** me o sorashimásu̲ 目をそらします

aviation *n* kōkū (ki) 航空(機)

avoid *v* sakemásu̲ さけます・避けます, yokemásu̲ よけます・避けます

awake *v* (*comes ~*) mezamemásu̲, 目覚めます; ***is ~*** (*not asleep*) nemurimasén 眠りません

award **1.** *n* shō 賞 **2.** *v* (*gives*) (shō o) júyo shimásu̲ (賞を)授与します; okurimásu̲ 贈ります

away *adj* tōku (ni) 遠く(に); away from home rúsu (no) 留守(の); right away súgu すぐ

awesome *adj* (mono)sugói (もの)すごい・(物)凄い, subárashíi すばらしい・素晴らしい

awful *adj* osoroshíi 恐ろしい, hidói ひどい

awkward *adj* mazúi まずい, giko-chinai ぎこちない, buzama (na) ぶざま(な)

awning *n* hi-ōí 日覆い, hiyoke 日よけ, tenmaku 天幕

ax *n* ono おの・オノ・斧

axis, axle *n* jikú 軸

B

babble *n* o-shaberi おしゃべり

baby *n* áka-chan 赤ちゃん, akan-bo 赤ん坊・赤んぼ babysitter *n* bebii shi̲ttā ベビーシッター, (*professional*) komóri 子守

bachelor *n* doku̲shin dansei 独身

男性, hitori mónó ひとり者・独り者

back 1. *adv* (*behind*) ... no ushiro (de/ni) ... の後ろ(で/に) 2. *n* (*of body*) senaka 背中, (*lower part*) koshi 腰 → **support**

back; *go* ~ modorimásu 戻ります; (*to one's usual place*) kaerimásu 帰ります

backdate *v* hizuke o sakanoborasemásu 日付をさかのぼらせます

back down *v* 1. (*retreats*) kōtai shimásu 後退します 2. (*withdraws*) hiki sagarimásu 引き下がります

backfire *n* ura-me ni demásu 裏目に出ます

background *n* 1. haikei 背景, bákku バック 2. (*one's origin, education, etc.*) keireki 経歴 3. (*circumstances of the event, information*) yobi chishiki 予備知識, bákku gura(u)ndo バックグラ(ウ)ンド

backhanded *adj* 1. (*sports*) bakku hando (no) バックハンド(の) 2. (*ambiguous meaning*) aimai (na) あいまい(な)・曖昧(な) 3. (*roundabout, indirect*) mawarikudoi 回りくどい

backlash *n* handō 反動, hanpatsu 反発

backlog *n* 1. (*reserve*) bichiku 備蓄 2. (*stock*) zaiko 在庫 3. (*work*) yarinokoshi no shigoto やり残しの仕事

back-order *n* toriyose chūmon 取り寄せ注文

backpack *n* ryukku-sakku リュックサック

backside *n* 1. ushiro 後ろ, [BOOKISH] kōhō 後方 2. (*buttock*) shiri 尻 (o-shiri お尻)

backstage *adj, adv* butai ura (no/de) 舞台裏(の/で), gakuya (no/de) 楽屋(の/で)

backstroke *n* seoyogi 背泳ぎ

backup *n* 1. (*computer*) bákku appu バックアップ 2. yobi 予備, hikae 控え

backwards *adv* (*contrariwise*) gyaku (ni) 逆(に); ***move*** ~ bákku shimásu バックします, ushiro e/ni sagarimásu 後ろに下がります

backwater *n* 1. (*stagnant place*) teitai chi 停滞地 2. (*stagnant state*) teitai 停滞 3. (*held water*) yodonda mizu よどんだ水

backyard *n* ura-niwa 裏庭

bacon *n* bē´kon ベーコン

bacteria *n* bakuteria バクテリア, saikin 細菌

bad *adj* 1. warúi 悪い, damé (na) だめ・駄目(な); furyō (na) 不良(な); (*inept*) hetá (na) へた・下手(な) 2. fu- 不～; **bad guy** furyō 不良, warumono 悪者, **bad temper** *n* tanki 短気

bad; ***goes*** ~ (*rots, sours*) kusarimásu 腐ります; ***too*** ~ (*regrettable*) zannen (na) 残念(な)

badge *n* bajji バッジ

badger *n* anaguma アナグマ・穴熊

badminton *n* badominton バドミントン

bag *n* **1.** fukuró 袋; (*paper*) kami-búkuro 紙袋 **2.** → **suitcase 3.** → **handbag; purse**
baggage *n* (o-)ní-motsu (お)荷物
baggy *adj* dabudabu (no) だぶだぶ(の)
bailiff *n* teiri 廷吏・ていり
bait *n* esa えさ・餌
bake *v* **1.** yakimásu 焼きます **2.** ***gets baked*** yakemásu 焼けます
baker, bakery, bakeshop *n* pán-ya パン屋, bēkarii ベーカリー
balance *n* **1.** (*equilibrium*) tsuriai 釣り合い, baransu バランス **2.** (*remaining money*) zandaka 残高
balcony *n* barukonii バルコニー
bald **1.** *adj* hágeta ... はげた[禿げた]... **2.** *v* (*gets* ~) hagemásu はげます・禿げます; (*is* ~) hágete imásu はげて[禿げて]います
bale *n* tawará 俵
ball *n* **1.** tamá 玉; (*traditional Japanese handball*) mari まり・鞠, temari てまり・手鞠 **2.** (*sports*) bṓru ボール; ***basket*** **~** basuketto bōru バスケットボール **3.** kyū 球; **ball park** *n* yakyū-jō 野球場, kyūjō 球場
ballad *n* (*Japanese traditional music*) min'yō 民謡
ballerina *n* (*female ballet dancer*) bareriina バレリーナ
ballet *n* bárē バレエ; **ballet dancer** *n* barē dansā バレエダンサー, (*female dancer*) bareriina バレリーナ
balloon *n* **1.** fūsen 風船 **2.** (*hot-air* ~) (netsu)kikyū (熱)気球 **3.** (*toy* ~) fūsen-dama 風船玉 **4.** (*water* ~) mizu-fūsen 水風船
ballot *n* tōhyō 投票; **ballot paper** *n* tōhyō yōshi 投票用紙
ballpoint pen *n* bōru-pen ボールペン
balm *n* kōyu 香油
bamboo *n* take 竹; **bamboo blind** *n* (*Japanese traditional*) misu みす・御簾, sudare すだれ・簾 → **blind**; **bamboo wind-chimes** *n* take-fūrin 竹風鈴
ban **1.** *n* kinshi 禁止 **2.** **~*s it*** *v* kinshi shimásu 禁止します
banana *n* banana バナナ; **~ *shake*** banana sheiku バナナシェイク
band *n* **1.** (*group*) kumí 組 **2.** (*of musicians*) (*Western style*) gakudan 楽団, bando バンド **3.** (*Japanese style*) (o)-hayashi おはやし・(お)囃し **4.** (*watch-band, etc.*) (tokei) bando (時計)バンド **5.** beruto ベルト
bandage *n* hōtai 包帯
bandit *n* zoku 賊
bang *n* (*sound*) ban バン, batan バタン
bangle *n* **1.** (*wristlet*) ude wa 腕輪 **2.** kazari 飾り
banish *v* tsuihō shimásu 追放します
banister *n* tesuri 手すり
banjo *n* banjo バンジョー; ***three stringed*** **~** shamisen しゃみせん・三味線

bank *n* **1.** ginkō 銀行 **2.** (*special storage place*) banku バンク **3.** (~ *of a river or lake*) kishí 岸; bank account *n* ginkō-kóza 銀行口座, yokin-kóza 預金口座; blood bank *n* ketsueki banku 血液バンク
bankruptcy *n* hasan 破産
banner *n* **1.** (*flag*) hata 旗 **2.** (*motto, slogan, etc.*) hyōshiki 標識 **3.** (*hanging cloth or curtain* over *a street, entrance, etc.*) taremaku 垂れ幕 **4.** (*advertising*) banā (kōkoku) バナー（広告）
banquet *n* enkai 宴会
baptism *n* senrei 洗礼
bar *n* **1.** (*for drinking*) saka-ba 酒場, (*Western style*) bā バー, (*neighborhood pub*) nomí-ya 飲み屋, (*after-hours*) sunákku スナック **2.** bō 棒; a bar of soap *n* sekken ík-ko せっけん［石鹸］一個
barbarian *n* yaban-jín 野蛮人
barbecue *n* bābekyū バーベキュー
barber(*shop*) *n* tokoya 床屋, rihá-tsú-ten 理髪店, sanpatsu-ya 散髪屋
bare 1. *adj* (*scarce*) toboshii 乏しい **2.** (*mere*) honno wazuka (no) ほんのわずか(の) **3.** → **naked 4.** → **reveal**; barefoot *adj* hadashi (no) はだし・裸足(の/で); *adv* hadashi (de) はだし・裸足(で); barely *adv* karōjite かろうじて・辛うじて, nantoka なんとか, girigiri ぎりぎり
bargain *n* (*a real find*) horidashi mono 堀出し物, bāgen バーゲン
barge *n* hashike はしけ
bark 1. *n* (*of tree*) kí no kawá 木の皮, [BOOKISH] juhi 樹皮 **2.** *v* (*a dog ~s*) hoemásu 吠えます
barley *n* ō-mugi 大麦
barn *n* naya 納屋
barometer *n* **1.** (*indicator*) baro-mētā バロメーター **2.** (*for atmospheric pressure*) kiatsu-kei 気圧計
barracks *n* **1.** héisha 兵舎 **2.** ba-rakku バラック
barracuda *n* kamásu カマス
barrage *n* shūchū hōka 集中砲火
barrel *n* taru 樽
barren *adj* **1.** (*land*) yaseta やせた, fumō (na/no) 不毛(な/の) **2.** (*sterile*) funin (no) 不妊(の)
barricade *n* barikēdo バリケード
barrier *n* **1.** (*fence*) saku 柵 **2.** (*obstacle*) shōgai-butsu 障害(物) **3.** (*limit*) genkai 限界 **4.** (*limit* or *boundary*) genkai 限界, kyōkai 境界
barrow *n* (*wheel~*) teoshi-guruma 手押し車
barter *n* butsubutsu kōkan 物々交換
base *n* **1.** (*military, etc.*) kichí 基地; military base *n* gunji-kichi 軍事基地 **2.** (*of a tree*) ne-motó 根元 **3.** (*foundation*) kiso 基礎
baseball *n* yakyū 野球, bēsubō´ru ベースボール; baseball stadium *n* yakyū-jō 野球場, kyūjō 球場
basement *n* (*floor*) chikai 地階;

(*room*) chi̲ká (-shi̲tsu) 地下(室)

bash *v* tatakimás**u̲** 叩きます

bashful → shy

bashing *n* tatakí 叩き, basshingu バッシング

basic *adj* ki̲hon-teki (na) 基本的(な), konpon-teki (na) 根本的(な)

basin *n* **1.** (*for washing face*) senmén-ki 洗面器 **2.** tarai たらい **3.** hachí 鉢 **4.** (*flat land surrounded by higher land*) bonchi 盆地; **Kyoto basin** *n* Kyōto bonchi 京都盆地

basis *n* **1.** ki̲hon 基本, konpon 根本, kijun 基準, ki̲so 基礎 **2.** (*grounds*) kónkyo 根拠

basket *n* kago かご・籠, basu̲ketto バスケット

basketball *n* basu̲ketto bōru バスケット・ボール, basu̲ke バスケ

bass *n* **1.** (*sea bass*) suzuki スズキ **2.** (*music*) basu バス, bēsu ベース

baste **1.** *v* (*sewing*) *~ with thread* shi-tsu̲kemásu̲ 仕付けます **2.** *v* (*cooking*) tare o kakemásu̲ タレをかけます

bat *n* **1.** kō´mori コウモリ **2.** (*baseball*) bátto バット

bath *n* (o-)fúro (お)風呂, yokujō 浴場; **bathrobe** *n* basurōbu バスローブ; **bathroom** *n* ① (*for bathing*) (o-)furoba (お)風呂場, yoku-jō/shi̲tsu 浴場/室 ② (*toilet*) tóire トイレ, keshō´-shi̲tsu 化粧室, (o-)teárai (お)手洗い, (o-)benjó (お)便所; **public bath** *n* séntō 銭湯, kōshū yokujō 公衆浴場

baton **1.** (*sports, such as race and rhythmic gymnastics*) baton バトン **2.** (*music*) shiki-bō 指揮棒

battalion *n* (*military*) daitai 大隊

batter *n* (*baseball*) battā バッター, dásha 打者

battery *n* denchi 電池, bátterii バッテリー

battle **1.** *n* tatakai 戦い, arasoi 争い, [BOOKISH] sentō 戦闘 **2.** *v* tatakaimásu̲ 戦います

bay *n* wán 湾, urá 浦

be → is → go → come

beach *n* hama 浜, bíichi ビーチ; (*seashore*) kaigan 海岸

bead *n* **1.** tamá 玉, biizu ビーズ; ***(prayer) ~s*** juzú じゅず・数珠 **2.** ***counting ~s*** **→ abacus**

beagle *n* (*dog*) biiguru-ken ビーグル犬

beak *n* kuchibashi くちばし

beam *n* **1.** (*cross~*) keta けた・桁; ***under the ~*** keta-shi̲ta 桁下・けた下 **2.** (*~ of light*) kōsen 光線

bean *n* mamé マメ・豆; (*soy beans*) daizu ダイズ・大豆

bean curd *n* (o-)tōfu (お)豆腐; (*pot-boiled squares*) yu-dō´fu 湯豆腐; (*deep-fried*) aburá-age 油揚げ

bean jam/paste *n* (*sweet*) án(ko) アン(コ)・餡(こ); (*fermented*) míso みそ・味噌 (o-)míso (お)みそ・(お)味噌

bear **1.** *n* (*animal*) kúmá 熊 **2.** *v* (*puts up with*) shinobimásu̲

忍びます, taemásu 耐えます, shínbō shimásu 辛抱します **3.** → **carry** **4.** → **give birth to** **5.** ~*s fruit* minorimásu 実ります; **bear up** (*stands firm*) ganbarimásu がんばり[頑張り]ます

beard *n* hige ひげ・鬚

bearings; *n one's* ~ hōgaku 方角

beat *v* **1.** (*hits*) nagurimásu なぐり[殴り]ます; (*slaps*) hatakimásu はたきます・叩きます **2.** (*defeats*) makashimásu 負かします **3.** (*heart throbs*) dókidoki shimásu どきどきします; ~ ***around the bush*** (*is non-committal*) hanashí o bokashimásu 話をぼかします

beautiful *adj* utsukushíi 美しい, kírei (na) きれい・綺麗(な)

beauty *n* **1.** [BOOKISH] bi 美, utsukushí-sa 美しさ **2.** (*beautiful woman*) bi-jin 美人, bi-jo 美女

beauty parlor *n* biyō´in 美容院

beaver *n* biibā ビーバー

because *conj* ... kara ...から, ... tame ... ため・為, ... mono ... もの, ... no de ... ので, [BOOKISH] ... yúé ni ... ゆえに・故に; ***perhaps*** ~ ***of*** ... (no) séi ka ... (の)せいか

become *v* (... ni, ... -ku) narimásu (... に, ... く)なります

bed *n* toko 床; (*Western*) béddo (bétto) ベッド(ベット), shindai 寝台; ***goes to*** ~ nemásu 寝ます, yasumimásu, 休みます; **bed-and-breakfast** *n* minshuku 民宿; **bedclothes, bedding** *n* shíngu 寝具, yágu 夜具; (*Japanese quilt*) 布団 (o)-futón (お)布団; **bedroom** *n* shinshitsu 寝室

bedlam *n* **1.** sawagi 騒ぎ; sōran 騒乱 **2.** (*confusion*) konran 混乱

bedraggled *adj* **1.** (*limp and wet*) hikizutte nurashita 引きずって濡らした **2.** (*limp and soiled*) hiki-zutte yogoshita 引きずって汚した

bee *n* hachi 蜂・ハチ; **beehive** *n* mitsubachi no subako ミツバチ[蜜蜂]の巣箱

beef *n* gyūniku 牛肉, biifu ビーフ; **beef slices dipped in hot broth** shabu-shabu しゃぶしゃぶ・シャブシャブ

beefsteak *n* sutēki ステーキ

been → **is** → **go** → **come**

beep *n* **1.** (*sound*) bii-tto iu oto ビーッという音 **2.** (*answering machine*) pii-tto iu oto ピーッという音 **3.** yobidashi-on 呼び出し音

beer *n* bíiru ビール; **draft beer** *n* nama-bíiru 生ビール, náma 生

beet *n* bíito ビート

beetle *n* (*insect*) kabutomushi カブトムシ; **black beetle** *n* gokiburi ゴキブリ

before *adv* (... no) máe (ni) (...の)前(に); ~ ***it happens*** (shi-) nai uchí (ni) (し)ないうち(に); **before a meal** *n, adv* taberu mae (ni) 食べる前(に), [BOOKISH] shokuzen (ni) 食前(に); **before long** *adv* ma-mó-naku まもなく・間もなく, sórosoro そろそろ; (*eventually*) yagate やがて

beg *v* tanomimásu 頼みます, negaimásu 願います; **I beg your pardon, but ...** *interj* shitsúrei desu ga ... 失礼ですが...

beggar *n* kojikí こじき・乞食

begin *v* (*it ~s*) hajimarimásu 始まります; (*~s it*) hajimemásu 始めます

beginning *n* hajime 初め, (*outset*) saisho 最初, [INFORMAL] shoppána しょっぱな・初っぱな, hajimari 始まり

begrudge *v* uramimásu 恨みます (恨む, 恨んで); (*be jealous of another's good fortune, etc.*) hito no kōun o netamimásu 人の幸運をねたみます

behalf *n* **1.** (*support*) shiji 支持 **2.** (*benefit*) rieki 利益; ***in/on ~ of*** ... (... no) tamé (... の)ため・為 **3.** (*representative*) ***in/on ~ of ...*** [INFORMAL] (... no) kawari (ni) ...の代わり(に), (... no) dairi (de) ...の代理(で)

behavior *n* **1.** (*actions*) kōdō 行動 **2.** (*act*) kōi 行為 **3.** (*deportment*) furumai ふるまい・振る舞い **4.** (*manners*) (o-)gyōgi (お)行儀 **5.** (*attitude*) táido 態度

behind **1.** *prep* (... no) ushiro (de/ni) (... の)後ろ(で/に); (*the other side*) urá 裏 **2.** ***falls/gets ~*** okuremásu 遅れます; ***leaves ~*** nokoshimásu 残します, (*forgets*) wasuremono o shimásu 忘れ物をします

beige *n* bēju ベージュ

Beijing *n* pekin 北京

being **1.** *n* (*in existence*; *person*) sonzai 存在; ***human ~*** ningen 人間 **2.** *n* (*creature*) ikimono 生き物 **3.** → **is** **4.** *v* ***comes into ~*** seiritsu shimásu 成立します

belch *n*, *v* geppu (o shimásu) げっぷ(をします)

Belgium *n* berugii ベルギー

believe *v* **1.** ~ (*in*) (... o) shinjimásu (... を)信じます **2.** → **think**

bell *n* **1.** (*large*) kane 鐘 **2.** (*small*) rín/suzu 鈴 **3.** (*doorbell*) béru ベル, yobi-rin 呼び鈴 **4.** (*temple ~*) tsurigane 釣り鐘

belly *n* hará 腹; fuku-bu 腹部; onaka お腹

belong (*to*) *v* (... ni) zokushimásu (... に)属します

belongings *n* mochímono 持ち物

beloved *n* **1.** (*person or pet*) itoshii いとしい・愛しい, saiai (no) 最愛(の) **2.** (*thing*) aiyō (no) 愛用(の) **3.** (*thing* or *place*) okiniiri (no) お気に入りの, daisuki (na) 大好き(な); **beloved daughter** mana-musume 愛娘

below *prep, adv* (... no) shitá (ni) (... の) 下(に); (*less than*) ... íka (... no) ... 以下(... の), ... míman (... no) ... 未満(... の)

belt *n* **1.** beruto ベルト, óbi 帯 **2.** (*sumo wrestler's*) mawashi まわし・回し **3.** (*zone*) (chi)tai 地帯; **belt line** *n* kanjō-sen 環状線

bemused *adj* **1.** (*confused*) konwa-kushita 困惑した, tōwakushita

当惑した **2.** (*lost in thought*) mono-omoi ni fuketta 物思いにふけった

bench *n* benchi ベンチ

bend *v* **1.** (*it ~s*) oremásu 折れます, (*curves*) magarimásu 曲がります, (*warps*) sorimásu 反ります **2.** (*~s it*) orimásu 折ります, magemásu 曲げます, sorashimásu 反らします; **bend backward** *v* karada o sorashimásu 体を反らします; **bend down/ over** *v* kagamimásu 屈みます; **bend forward** *v* mae-kagami ni narimásu 前屈みになります

beneath → **below**

benefactor *n* onjin 恩人

benefit *n* ríeki 利益; (... no) tamé (... の)為

benign **1.** *n* (*pathology*) ryōsei 良性 **2.** *adj* (*gracious*) shinsetsu (na) 親切(な)

Berlin *n* Berurín ベルリン

berth *n* shindai 寝台; **berth ticket** *n* shindái-ken 寝台券

beset (*stricken*); ***gets ~*** (*by illness*) yararemásu やられます

beside *prep, adv* (*next to*) ... no sóba (de/ni) ... のそば(で/に), ... no tonari (de/ni) ...の隣り(で/に)

besides *prep, adv* (*in addition to*) sono úé (ni) その上(に), (sono) hoka (ni) (その)他(に)

best *adj* **1.** ichiban íi 一番いい[良い, 善い]; sairyō (no) 最良(の) **2.** (*highest*) saikō (no) 最高(の) **3.** (*top-class*) jōtō (no) 上等(の) **4.** (*special-quality*) tokkyū (no) 特級(の), zekkō (no) 絶好(の); **at best** *adv* séizei せいぜい; **the best, one's best** *n* saizen 最善; **ten best** *n* besutó-ten ベストテン

bet **1.** *n* (*act of betting*) kake 賭け **2.** *n* (*money*) kake-kin 賭け金 **3.** *v* kakemásu 賭けます, kaké o shimásu 賭をします

betray *v* ura-girimásu 裏切ります; **betrayal** *n* ura-giri 裏切り

betrothal *n* konyaku 婚約; **betrothed** *n* konyaku-sha 婚約者

better *adj* **1.** mótto íi/yoi もっといい/良い, (...) yóri íi/yoi (...)よりいい/良い **2.** (*preferable*) ... (no hṓ) ga íi/yoi ...(の方)がいい/良い

between *prep, adv* (... no) aida (ni) (... の)間(に); ...-kan (...)...間

beverage *n* nomí-mono 飲み物

beware *v* chūi shimásu 注意します; **(Please) beware** ki o tsukete (kudasai) 気をつけて(ください)

beyond *prep, adv* (... no) mukō (ni) (... の)向こう(に); ***~ expectations*** zongai 存外; **beyond remedy** shō (shi-yō) ga nái しょう(しよう・仕様)がない

bias *n* (*prejudice*) henken 偏見, sennyū-kan 先入観

Bible *n* Séisho 聖書, Báiburu バイブル

bibliography *n* tosho mokuroku 図書目録, bunken mokuroku 文献目録

bicycle *n* jitén-sha, jidén-sha 自転

車; bicycle shop *n* jitensha-ya, jidensha-ya 自転車屋

bid **1.** *v* (*to offer*) nyūsatsu shimásu 入札します **2.** *v* (*to command*) meirei shimásu 命令します **3.** *v* (*to express*) ii másu 言います **4.** *n* nyūsatsu 入札

big *adj* **1.** ōkíi 大きい, [INFORMAL] dekai (dekkai) でかい(でっかい) **2.** (*spacious*) hirói 広い; big brother áni 兄, (o-)níi-san (お)兄さん; big sister ane 姉, (o-)nē´-san (お)姉さん

bike *n* **1.** → **bicycle** **2.** (*motorbike*) baiku バイク, ōtobai オートバイ

bilingual *n, adj* bairingaru (no) バイリンガル(の)

bill *n* **1.** (*to pay*) (o-)kanjō (お)勘定; denpyō 伝票, o-aiso お愛想・おあいそ; daikin 代金, ...-dai ... 代; (*account*) tsuké つけ; separate bill/charge (*restaurant*) betsu-ryōkin 別料金; (*Dutch treat*) warikan 割り勘 **2.** (*bank bill, promissory note*) tegata 手形 **3.** (*currency note*) (o-)satsu (お)札 **4.** (*handbill*) bira びら・ビラ

billiards *n* biriyādo ビリヤード

billion *n* jū´-oku 十億 (*U.S.*); chō´ 兆, ít-chō 一兆 (*Britain*)

bin *n* ***trash*** ~ gomi-bako ゴミ箱

bind *v* **1.** (*pages, sheets*) tsuzuri-másu 綴ります **2.** → **tie**

binge *n* donchan-sawagi どんちゃん騒ぎ

bingo *n* (*game*) bingo ビンゴ

binoculars *n* sōgan-kyō 双眼鏡

biography *n* denki 伝記

biological *adj* seibutsugaku-teki (na) 生物学的(な)

biology *n* seibutsú-gaku 生物学

biotechnology *n* baio(-tekunorojii) バイオ(テクノロジー), seibutsu kōgaku 生物工学

bird *n* tori 鳥; bird-watching *n* bādo uotchingu バードウオッチング; yachō-kansatsu 野鳥観察

birth *n* **1.** (*being born*) umare 生まれ, [BOOKISH] shussei 出生 **2.** (*origin*) tanjō 誕生; ***give ~ to ...*** o umimásu ... を生みます, o-san shimásu お産します; birthstone *n* tanjō´seki 誕生石

birthday *n* (o)-tanjō´bi (お)誕生日; bāsudē バースデー, birthday cake *n* (o-)tanjō´bi kēki (お)誕生日ケーキ; bāsudē kēki バースデーケーキ, birthday card *n* (o-)tanjō´bi kādo (お)誕生日カード; bāsudē kādo バースデーカード

birthplace *n* kókyō 故郷, furusato 故郷・ふるさと

biscuit *n* (*cookie*) bisuketto ビスケット

bisexual *n* (*ambisexual*) bai-sekushuaru バイセクシュアル, ryōseiai-sha 両性愛者

bit *n* (*a little*) sukóshi 少し; [INFORMAL] chótto ちょっと

bitch *n* **1.** (*female dog*) mesu-inu 雌犬 **2.** (*malicious and lewd woman*) abazure あばずれ

bitcoin *n* (*cybercurrency and*

worldwide payment system) bittokoin ビットコイン

bite **1.** *v* kamimás<u>u</u> かみます・噛みます, kami-ts<u>u</u>kimás<u>u</u> かみつきます・噛みつきます **2.** *n* ***one ~*** hitó-k<u>u</u>chi ひとくち・一口 **3.** *n* (*hurt*) sashikizu 刺傷

bitter *adj* **1.** (*taste, hard to bear, painful*) nigái 苦い **2.** (*awful*) hidói ひどい・酷い; **bitter experience** nigai keiken 苦い経験

black *adj* kurói 黒い; kúro (no) 黒(の); ***jet ~*** makkúro (na) 真っ黒(な); **black box** *n* burakku bokkusu ブラックボックス; **black market** *n* yami-ichi 闇市, yamí-íchiba 闇市場

blackboard *n* kokuban 黒板

black-hearted *adj* hara gurói 腹黒い

blackmail *n* yusuri ゆすり, kyōkatsu 恐喝

bladder *n* bōkō 膀胱

blade *n* **1.** (*razor*) (kamisórí no) há (かみそりの) 刃 **2.** (*sword*) yaiba やいば・刃 **3.** (*leaf*) ha 葉 **4.** (*on ice skate*) burēdo ブレード

blame **1.** *n* (*censure*) (o-)togame (お)とがめ, hínan 非難 **2.** *v* (*rebukes one*) togamemás<u>u</u> とがめます, hínan shimás<u>u</u> 非難します **3.** → **responsibility**

bland *adj* **1.** (*tasteless*) aji ga usui 味が薄い **2.** (*gentle*) odayaka (na) 穏やか(な) **3.** (*insipid*) tsumaranai つまらない

blank **1.** *n* (*space*) kūsho 空所, yohaku 余白 **2.** *n* (*form*) yōshi 用紙 **3.** *adj* hak<u>u</u>shi (no) 白紙(の) **4.** *adj* (*expression*) utsuro (na) うつろ(な)・空ろ(な)・虚ろ(な); ***with a ~ look*** utsuro na hyōjō o mísete うつろな[虚ろな]表情を見せて

blanket *n* mō´fu 毛布

blast-off *n* hassha 発射

bleach *n* hyōhaku-zai 漂白剤

bleak *adj* **1.** (*hopeless*) kibō no nai 希望のない; ***~ future*** kurai shōrai 暗い将来 **2.** (*desolate*) wabishii わびしい, sappūkei (na) 殺風景(な) **3.** (*cold*) samui 寒い

bleed *v* chi ga demás<u>u</u> 血が出ます, shukketsu shimás<u>u</u> 出血します

blemish *n* **1.** (*scar*) kizu 傷 **2.** (*defect*) ketten 欠点

blend *n* burendo ブレンド, kongō 混合

blender *n* mík<u>i</u>sā ミキサー

bless *v* **1.** ***~ with*** ... o megumimás<u>u</u> ... を恵みます **2.** ***gets blessed with*** ...ni megumaremás<u>u</u> ...に恵まれます

blessed *adj* **1.** megumareta 恵まれた, shukufuku sareta 祝福された **2.** (*holy*) shinsei (na) 神聖(な), seinaru 聖なる; **blessing** *n* megumi 恵み, shukufuku 祝福

blind *n* **1.** (*person*) mōjin 盲人 **2.** (*sun-shade*) hi-ō´í 日覆い, hi-yoke 日よけ, buraindo ブラインド → **bamboo blind**

blink *v* ma-tátaki/ma-bátaki shimás<u>u</u> またたき/まばたき/瞬きします

blister *n* mizu-búkure 水膨れ; (*corn*) mamé まめ, soko mame 底まめ

blizzard *n* (mō-/ō-) fúbuki (猛/大) 吹雪

bloc *n* ken 圏, burokku ブロック

block **1.** *n* (*city block*) *The closest equivalent is* chōme 丁目, *a square of several blocks. For distances, use ...* -chō ... 町 **2.** *n* **~ *of wood*** kakuzai 角材 **3.** *n* (*toy*) tsumiki 積み木, burokku ブロック **4.** *v* (*clogs, impedes*) fusagimásu ふさぎます, burokku shimásu ブロックします; **blocked (off)** *v* ***the road is ~*** dō´ro ga fusagátte imásu 道路がふさがっています

blockade **1.** *n* fūsa 封鎖 **2.** *v* fūsa shimásu 封鎖します

blond *adj* kinpatsu (no) 金髪(の), burondo (no) ブロンド(の)

blood *n* chi 血, [BOOKISH] ketsu-eki 血液; **blood type** *n* ketsueki-gata 血液型

blood pressure *n* ketsuatsu 血圧; ***takes one's ~*** ketsuatsu o hakari-másu 血圧を計ります

bloom *v* sakimásu 咲きます

blossom → **bloom** → **flower**

blot, blotch *n* shimi しみ・染み, yogore 汚れ

blotter *n* suitorí-gami 吸い取り紙

blouse *n* (*woman's, child's*) buráusu ブラウス

blow *v* fukimásu 吹きます; ***~ one's nose*** hana o kamimásu 鼻をかみます

blowfish *n* fúgu フグ・河豚

blowup *n* bakuhatsu 爆発, bakuha 爆破

bludgeon *n* konbō 棍棒・こん棒

blue *adj* **1.** áói 青い; áo (no) 青(の) **2.** (*feel ~*) burū ブルー, yūutsu 憂うつ; **blue-collar worker** *n* burū karā ブルーカラー; nikutai rōdō-sha 肉体労働者

blunder *n* shippai 失敗; chónbo ちょんぼ; (*faux pas*) bu-sáhō 不作法・無作法

blunt *adj* (*dull-edged*) kirénai 切れない; (*dull-pointed*) nibúi 鈍い; (*curt*) bu-áisō (na) 無愛想(な), bukkírábō (na) ぶっきらぼう(な)

blush *v* kao ga akaku narimásu 顔が赤くなります, [BOOKISH] sekimen shimásu 赤面します

board **1.** *n* (*plank*) íta 板 **2.** *n* (*meals*) (o-)shokuji (お)食事 **3.** *v* (*gets on a train/bus*) jōsha shimásu 乗車します, (*a plane*) tōjō shimásu 搭乗します

boarding pass *n* tōjō´-ken 搭乗券, bōdingu-pasu/kādo ボーディングパス/カード

boast *v* jiman shimásu 自慢します

boat *n* fúne 舟・船; (*small*) kobune 小舟・小船, bō´to ボート; **boat race** *n* bōto-rēsu ボートレース

body *n* **1.** karada 体・身体; ***whole ~*** zenshin 全身; ***~ temperature*** taion 体温; ***~ weight*** taijū 体重 **2.** (*collective body, group*) shūdan 集団; **bodybuilding** *n* bodii-biru ボ

ディビル; **bodyguard** *n* bodii-gādo ボディガード, goei 護衛

bog down, gets bogged down *v* iki-zumarimásu 行き詰まります

bohemian *n* bohemian ボヘミアン

boil *v* **1.** ***~s water*** o-yu o waka-shimásu お湯を沸かします; ***water ~s*** o-yu ga wakimásu お湯が沸きます **2.** ***~s*** (*food*) nimásu 煮ます, yudemásu ゆでます・茹でます; (*soup, rice*) takimásu 炊きます **3.** ***it ~s*** niemásu 煮えます

boil *n* (*on skin*) hare-mono はれもの, dekí-mónó できもの(o-déki おでき); **boiled eggs** *n* yude-támago ゆで卵 煮魚; **boiled water** *n* o-yu お湯, (*cooled for drinking*) yu-zámashi 湯冷まし

boiler *n* bóirā ボイラー; (*hot-water maker*) yu-wakashiki 湯沸かし器; (*pot*) kama かま・釜, nábe 鍋

boisterous *adj* yakamashíi やかましい, sawagashíi 騒がしい

bold *adj* daitán (na) 大胆(な), yūkan (na) 勇敢(な)

bolt *n* (*of door*) kannuki かんぬき・閂; (*of nut and bolt*) boruto ボルト; (*of cloth*) ... -maki ... 巻き, -tan 反

bomb **1.** *n* (*explosive device*) bakudan 爆弾 **2.** *n* (*bombing*) bakugeki 爆撃 **3.** *v* (*~s it*) bakugeki shimásu 爆撃します; **bomber** *n* bakugékí-ki 爆撃機; **bombshell** *n* bakudan 爆弾

Bon; *the Bon Festival* (o-)bón (お)盆, urabon うら盆

bond *n* (*debenture*) saiken 債券

bone *n* honé 骨

bonfire *n* taki-bi たき火

bonito *n* katsuo カツオ・鰹; (*dried*) katsuo-bushi かつお節・鰹節

bonnet → **hat** → (*car*) **hood**

bonus *n* **1.** (*wage*) bō´nasu ボーナス, shō´yo 賞与 **2.** (*extra*) omake おまけ

boo-hoo *interj* (*sound of crying*) **1.** ēn ēn エーンエーン(*mostly children's crying*), wān wān ワーンワーン (*louder*) **2.** ōi ōi オーイオーイ

book **1.** *n* hón 本, [BOOKISH] shómotsu 書物; (*publications*) shoseki 書籍 **2.** *n* ~ ***of*** (*commuting*) ***tickets*** kaisū-ken 回数券 **3.** ***~s*** *v* (*reserves*) yoyaku shimásu 予約します; **bookcase** *n* hónbako 本箱; **book up** *v* ***gets booked*** fusa-garimásu ふさがります; **bookfair** *n* bukku-fea ブックフェア; **booking** *n* ① yoyaku 予約 ② bóki 簿記

boom *n* **1.** (*prosperity*) (niwaka) keiki (にわか)景気; keiki (ga ii) 景気(がいい) **2.** (*fad*) bū´mu ブーム **3.** (*sound*) dón ドン

boomerang *n* bumeran ブーメラン

booster *n* (*of current*) shōátsú-ki 昇圧器

booth *n* **1.** (*selling things*) baiten 売店 **2.** (*in a tavern, etc.*) bók-kusu-seki ボックス席 **3.** (*tele-*

phone) denwa bókkusu 電話ボックス **4.** (*office*) būsu ブース

boot(s) *n* naga-gutsu 長靴, būtsu ブーツ, (*rubber*) gomu-naga ゴム長

border 1. *n* (*boundary*) sakái 境; (*of a district, etc.*) kyōkai 境界; (*of a country*) kokkyō 国境; (*edging*) herí へり・縁 **2. *~s on*** *v* ... ni ses-shimásu ... に接します, rinsetsu shimásu 隣接します

boring *adj* (*dull*) taikutsu (na) 退屈(な), tsumaránai つまらない

born 1. *gets ~* *v* umaremásu 生まれます **2. *~ in/of*** *adj* ... no de/umare ... の出/生まれ, ... -úmare (no) ... 生まれ(の)

borrow (*from* ...) *v* (... ni) karimásu (... に)借ります

bosom *n* futokoro 懐・ふところ

boss *n* **1.** shújin 主人 **2.** (*head of company*) shachō 社長 **3.** (*a leader*) jōshi 上司 **4.** (*ring-leader*) óyá-bun 親分, bosu ボス

Boston *n* bosuton ボストン

botch *v* yari-sokonaimásu やり損ないます

both 1. *pron* ryōhō 両方 **2.** *adj* ryōhō no 両方の **3.** *adv* dochira mo どちらも; ***~ ... and ...*** ... mo ... mo ... も ... も; **both directions/sides** *n* ryōmen 両面, ryō-gawa 両側

bother *n* mendō´ 面倒, méiwaku 迷惑; (*intrusion*) jama じゃま・邪魔; (*care*) (o)-séwa (お)世話, o-sewa-sama お世話様, (go-) yákkai (ご)やっかい・(ご)厄介) → **worry**; ***~ a person*** hito no jama o shimásu 人のじゃま[邪魔]をします

bothersome *adj* mendō-kusái 面倒くさい[臭い], yákkai (na) やっかい・厄介(な); jama (na) じゃま・邪魔(な)

bottle *n* **1.** bín 瓶 **2.** (*a bottle of liquor*) ***a ~ of whiskey*** wisukii-botoru (ippon) ウィスキーボトル(一本); ***a ~ of beer*** bíiru íp-pon ビール一本; **bottle opener** *n* sen-nuki 栓抜き

bottom *n* soko 底; (*underneath*) shita 下, ... shitá ... 下; (*buttock*) (o-)shiri (お)尻; **bottoms up** *n* (*toast*) kanpai 乾杯

bounce *v* hazumimásu 弾みます

bound 1. *v* → **bind**; ***~ pages*** tsuzuri 綴り **2.** → **jump**; **bound for** ... -iki (no) ... 行き(の); **bound to** (*do*) *v* kitto ...(suru) deshō きっと...(するでしょう

boundary *n* sakái 境

bouquet *n* haná-tába 花束

boutique *n* butikku ブティック

bow *n* (*archery or violin*) yumí 弓; (*shape*) yumi-gata 弓形; (*of ribbon*) chō-músubi ちょう結び・蝶結び

bow 1. *n* (*of head, etc.*) o-jigi おじぎ・お辞儀 **2.** *v* o-jigi o shimásu おじぎ・お辞儀をします

bowel *n* chō 腸; ***bowels*** naizō 内臓, ***~ movement*** (o-)tsū´-ji (お)通じ, ***has a ~ movement*** tsū-ji ga arimásu 通じがあります

bowl *n* (o-)wan (お)碗; (*ricebowl*) (o-)cháwan (お)茶碗; (*basin, pot*) hachí 鉢

bowl(ful) *n* ...-hai ... 杯 (**1:** íp-pai 一杯, **2:** ní-hai 二杯, **3:** sánbai 三杯)

bowling *n* bōringu ボウリング; ~ ***competition*** bōringu-taikai ボウリング大会, ~ ***ball*** bōringu (no) bōru ボウリング(の)ボール

box *n* hako 箱, ~ ***lunch*** (o-)bentō (お)弁当, (*sold at station*) eki-ben 駅弁

boxer *n* bokusā ボクサー

boxing *n* kentō 拳闘, bók<u>u</u>shingu ボクシング

box office *n* **1.** (*ticket office*) chiketto-uriba チケット売り場 **2.** (*receipts from a play, film, etc.*) kōgyō-shūnyū 興行収入, bokkusu-ofisu ボックスオフィス

boy *n* **1.** otokó-no-ko 男の子, shōnen 少年, bō´ya 坊や, bótchan 坊ちゃん **2.** (*waiter*) bōi ボーイ; **boyfriend** *n* bōi-furéndo ボーイフレンド; káre-shi 彼氏; **Boys' Festival** (*5 May*) *n* Tángo no sekku 端午の節句

boycott *n* boikotto ボイコット

bra *n* bura ブラ → **brassiére**

bracelet *n* ude-wa 腕輪, buresuretto ブレスレット

bracket *n* kakko 括弧; ***square*** ~ (*such as* "[]") kaku-kakko 角括弧

brag *v* hóra o f<u>u</u>kimás<u>u</u> ほらを吹きます

braid *v* amimás<u>u</u> 編みます

brain(s) *n* nō(-míso) 脳(みそ), zunō 頭脳, atamá 頭 (= **head**); **brainstorming** *n* burein sutōmingu ブレインストーミング

brake *n* burē´ki ブレーキ

branch *n* **1.** (*of tree*) eda 枝 **2.** (*of store*) sh<u>i</u>ten 支店 **3.** (*of rail line*) sh<u>i</u>sen 支線 **4.** (*of school*) bún-kō 分校 **5.** (*of office*) bu 部; **branch off** *v* ***it ~es off*** wakaremás<u>u</u> 分かれます

brand *n* burando ブランド, meigara 銘柄, shōhyō 商標; ***famous ~ goods*** yūmei burando-hin 有名ブランド品

brandy *n* burandē ブランデー

brass *n* shinchū 真ちゅう・真鍮

brassiére *n* burájā ブラジャー

brave *adj* yūkan (na) 勇敢(な), tsuyói 強い

bravo *interj* burabō ブラボー

brazier *n* híbachi 火鉢

Brazil *n* Burajiru ブラジル

bread *n* pán パン, shoku-pan 食パン; **bread crumbs** *n* pan-kó パン粉, pan-kúzu パンくず[屑]

breadth *n* haba 幅

break *n* **1.** (*rift or pause*) kire-mé 切れ目 **2.** (*rest*) (o-)yasumi (お)休み, kyūkei 休憩

break *v* **1.** ***it ~s*** *v* kowaremásu 壊れます, (*in two*) oremás<u>u</u> 折れます, (*it splits*) waremás<u>u</u> 割れます, (*it smashes*) kudakemás<u>u</u> 砕けます **2.** ***~s it*** *v* kowashimás<u>u</u> 壊します, (*in two*) orimás<u>u</u> 折り

ます, (*splits*) warimásu 割ります, (*smashes it*) kudakimásu 砕きます; ~ *in* wari-kómimásu 割り込みます; break down ① *it ~s down* (*crumbles*) kuzuremásu 崩れます, (*stops working*) koshō shimásu 故障します ② *~s* (*demolishes*) *it down* kuzushimásu 崩します; break off (*ends it*) kirimásu 切ります; (*it ends*) kiremásu 切れます

breakdown *n* **1.** (*crash*) koshō 故障 **2.** (*item by item*) meisai 明細, uchiwake 内訳

breakfast *n* chōshoku 朝食, asa-góhan 朝ご飯

bream *n* ***sea bream*** tái タイ・鯛

breast *n* (*chest*) muné 胸; (*woman's*) chichí 乳, chibusa 乳房, (*baby talk, slang*) óppai おっぱい; ~ ***cancer*** nyū-gan 乳がん・乳癌

breath *n* íki 息; ***a ~*** hitó-iki 一息; ***draws/takes one's last ~*** íki o hiki-torimásu 息を引き取ります

breathe *v* íki o shimásu 息をします; kokyū shimásu 呼吸します; ***~ a sigh of relief*** hóttó shimásu ほっとします

breed *n* **1.** (*species of plant, etc.*) hinshu 品種 **2.** (*kind*) shurui 種類 **3.** (*lineage*) kettō 血統

breeze *n* (soyó-)kaze (そよ)風; ***shoots the ~*** daberimásu だべります

brewery *n* jōzō-sho 醸造所

bribe(ry) *n* wáiro わいろ・賄賂

brick *n* rénga レンガ・煉瓦

bride *n* haná-yome(-san) 花嫁(さん), (o-)yome(-san) (お)嫁(さん)

bridegroom *n* hana-múko(-san) 花婿(さん), (o-)múko(-san) (お)婿(さん)

bridge *n* **1.** hashí 橋; (*steel*) tekkyō 鉄橋; ***the ~s on a Japanese harp*** koto-ji 琴柱 **2.** (*card*) burijji ブリッジ

bridle *n* baroku 馬勒

brief *adj* (*short*) mijikái 短い; (*simple*) kantan (na) 簡単(な)

briefcase *n* kaban かばん・鞄, buriifu kēsu ブリーフケース

briefing *n* jōkyō setsumei 状況説明

briefly *adj* (*in brief*) zatto ざっと

bright *adj* **1.** akarui 明るい **2.** (*sunny*) hogáraka (na) 朗らか(な) **3.** (*colorful*) hanáyaka (na) 華やか(な) **4.** (*gaudy*) hadé (na) はで・派手(な) **5.** (*of spirit*) yōki (na) 陽気(な)

brilliant *adj* subarashii すばらしい・素晴らしい, sugoi すごい・凄い

brim *n* fuchi ふち・縁, heri へり・縁

brine *n* shiomizu 塩水

bring *v* (*a thing*) motte/tótte kimásu 持って/取って来ます; ***~ along*** (*a person*) tsurete kimásu 連れて来ます; bring about *v* okoshimásu 起こします; bring close/near *v* chika-zukemásu 近付けます, yosemásu 寄せます; bring up *v* (*rears*) sodatemásu 育てます; yashinaimásu 養います; yōiku shimásu 養育します;

(*trains*) shitsukemásu しつけます
brink *n* kiwá 際
Britain → **England**
British → **English**
brittle *adj* morói もろい・脆い
broad *adj* hirói 広い
broadband *n, adj* burōdo-bando ブロードバンド
broadcast **1.** *n* hōsō 放送 **2.** *v* hōsō shimásu 放送します
broad-minded *n* kanyō (na) 寛容(な)
brocade *n* níshiki 錦
broccoli *n* burokkorii ブロッコリー
brochure *n* panfuretto パンフレット, katarogu カタログ
broil *v* yakimásu 焼きます
broke *adj* (*without money*) kinketsu 金欠
broken *adj* (*not working*) damé desu (da/na, de, ni) だめ[駄目]です(だ/な, で, に); koshō shita 故障した
brokenhearted; ***gets*** ~ shitsuren shimásu 失恋します
broker *n* burōkā ブローカー, nakagai 仲買い, nakadachí 仲立ち
brokerage *n* (*commission*) tesūryō 手数料, komisshon コミッション
bronze *n* seidō 青銅, buronzu ブロンズ
brooch *n* burōchi ブローチ
brook *n* ogawa 小川
broom *n* hōki ほうき・箒
broth *n* sūpu スープ
brother *n* (otoko) kyō´dai (男)兄弟; (*older*) (o-)níi-san (お)兄さん, áni 兄; (*younger*) otōtó 弟, (*your younger brother*) otōto-san 弟さん; brother-in-law *n* gíri no áni/otōtó (kyō´dai) 義理の兄/弟(兄弟); brothers and sisters *n* kyō´dai 兄弟, (*female sisters*) shimai 姉妹
brought up; ***gets*** ~ (*is reared*) sodachimásu 育ちます
brow *n* **1.** (*eyebrow*) máyu 眉 **2.** (*forehead*) hitai 額
brown *adj* cha-iro (no/i) 茶色(の/い)
bruise *n* uchímí 打ち身, dabokushō 打撲傷
brush **1.** *n* búrashi ブラシ, haké はけ・刷毛; (*for writing or painting*) fude 筆 **2.** *v* ***~es aside*** haraimásu 払います; brush up *n* burasshu appu ブラッシュアップ
brutal *adj* mugói むごい, zankoku (na) 残酷(な), zangyaku (na) 残虐(な), zannin (na) 残忍(な)
brutality *n* mugósa むごさ, zankoku 残酷, zangyaku 残虐
bubble *n* awá 泡, abukú あぶく; (*soap*) shabon-dama シャボン玉; bubble gum *n* fūsen-gámu 風船ガム
bucket *n* **1.** baketsu バケツ **2.** (*rice*) (o-)hachi (お)鉢, (o-)hitsu (お)ひつ・お櫃, meshi-bitsu 飯びつ・飯櫃
buckle *n* shime-gane 締め金, bákkuru バックル
buckwheat *n* soba そば・蕎麦
bud *n* **1.** (*of leaf*) mé 芽 **2.** (*of flower*) tsubomi つぼみ・蕾
Buddha *n* Hotoke(-sámá) 仏(様),

(*Sakyamuni*) Shaka 釈迦 = O-shakasama お釈迦様; (*statue of Buddha*) Butsu-zō 仏像

uddhism *n* Bukkyō 仏教

uddhist *n* Bukkyō-to 仏教徒; **Buddhist priest** *n* (o-)bō-san (お)坊さん, sō´ryo 僧侶, [INFORMAL] bō´zu 坊主; **Buddhist temple** *n* (o-)terá (お)寺

udget *n* yosan 予算

ug *n* mushi 虫・ムシ

ug *n* (*in computer*) bagu バグ

ugle *n* rappa ラッパ

uild *v* (*erects*) tatemásu 建てます, ki-zukimásu 築きます; (*creates*) tsukurimásu 造ります; kōsaku shimásu 工作します; ***body*** ~ taikaku 体格; **builder** *n* (*person*) kenchiku-sha 建築者; kenchiku-gyōsha 建築業者; **building** *n* taté-mono 建物, bíru ビル

ulb *n* tamá 玉; ***light*** ~ denkyū 電球

ulge *n* fukurami ふくらみ・膨らみ

ulk *n* ōkisa 大きさ, kasá かさ

ull *n* **1.** (*bullshit*) baka/muda-bánashi ばか/無駄話, (*bragging*) hóra ほら・ホラ **2.** o-ushi 雄牛

ulldozer *n* burudózā ブルドーザー

ullet *n* tamá 弾, [BOOKISH] dangan 弾丸

ulletin *n* keiji 掲示

ullet train *n* shinkánsen 新幹線

ullfight(ing) *n* tōgyū 闘牛

ully *n* (*children*) ijimekko いじめっ子

bump *n* **1.** (*swelling*) kobú こぶ・瘤; ***(with)*** ***~s*** bótsubotsu (ga dekite) ぼつぼつ(ができて) **2.** (*in road*) dekoboko でこぼこ・凸凹; **bump into** *v* ... ni butsukari-másu ... にぶつかります; (*happens to meet*) de-aimásu 出会います

bun *n* (*steamed*) manjū まんじゅう; (*beanjam-stuffed*) an-man あんまん

bunch *n* **1.** (*cluster*) fusá 房 **2.** (*pile*) yamá 山 **3.** (*bundle*) tába 束 **4.** (*group*) muré 群れ

bundle *n* tsutsumí 包み; (*bunch*) tába 束

bungalow *n* (*cottage*) bangarō バンガロー

bungle **1.** *n* héma へま **2.** *v* héma o shimásu へまをします

bunk *n* (*bed*) shindai 寝台

bunny *n* (*rabbit*) usagi (chan) ウサギ(ちゃん)

burden *n* ní 荷, (*on one's mind*) omo-ni 重荷

bureau *n* **1.** (*department*) kyóku 局, ...-kyoku ... 局 **2.** (*chest*) tansu たんす・箪笥

bureaucracy *n* kanryō-seido 官僚制度

burglar *n* dorobō 泥棒・どろぼう

burial *n* maisō 埋葬

burn **1.** *v* (*it ~s*) yakemásu 焼けます; (*fire ~s*) moemásu 燃えます **2.** *v* (*~s it*) yakimásu 焼きます; (*~s a fire*; *wood*, *coal*) takimásu 焚きます, (*~s a light*) tomoshimásu ともし[点し]ます **3.** *n* (*on the skin*) yakedo やけど・火傷

burp *n* geppu (o shimásu) げっぷ(をします)

burst *v* (*it bursts*) yaburemásu 破れます, (*explodes*) bakuhatsu shimásu 爆発します; (*~s it*) yaburimásu 破ります; ***~ out*** tobi-dashimásu 飛び出します

bury *v* uzumemásu うずめます・埋めます, umemásu 埋めます; ***gets buried*** uzumarimásu うずまります・埋まります, umarimásu 埋まります

bus *n* básu バス; **bus stop** *n* teiryū-jo 停留所; básu nori-ba バス乗り場

bush *n* [BOOKISH] kanboku 潅木・灌木, shigemi 茂み

Bushido *n* bushi-dō 武士道

business *n* **1.** (*job*) (o-)shígoto (お)仕事, bijinesu ビジネス **2.** (*line of ~*) shō´bai 商売 **3.** (*office work*) jímu 事務 **4.** (*transaction*) tóri-hiki 取り引き・取引 **5.** (*errand*) yōji 用事, (go-)yō´ (ご)用, yō-táshí 用足し **6.** (*enterprise*) jígyō 事業, jitsu-gyo 実業 **7.** (*commerce*) shō´gyō 商業; **business hours** *n* eigyō-jíkan 営業時間; **businessman** *n* jitsugyō-ka 実業家, bijinesu-man ビジネスマン

bust → **burst**

bustling *adj* nigíyaka (na) にぎやか・賑やか(な)

busy *adj* isogashíi いそがしい・忙しい, sewashíi せわしい・忙しい, sewashí nai せわしない; [BOOKISH] tabō (na) 多忙(な)

but *conj* **1.** [BOOKISH] shikáshi しかし, tokoró-ga ところが **2.** démo でも

butcher (*shop*) *n* nikú-ya 肉屋

butt **1.** *n* (*cigarette, cigar*) suigara 吸いがら **2.** → **buttock**

butter *n* bátā バター, báta バタ

butterfly *n* chō´ ちょう・蝶, chōchō ちょうちょう・蝶々, chōcho ちょうちょ

buttock *n* shirí 尻 (o-shiri お尻), (*mostly male* [VERY INFORMAL]) ketsu けつ・尻・穴

button **1.** *n* botan ボタン **2.** *v* (*~s it*) ... no botan o kakemásu ... のボタンをかけます

buxom *n* (*full-bosomed*) hōman na mune (no) 豊満な胸の, fukuyoka (na) ふくよか(な)

buy *v* kaimásu 買います; motomemásu 求めます; ***~ up*** kai-torimásu 買い取ります

buyer *n* **1.** kai-te 買い手 **2.** (*professional*) báiyā バイヤー

buzz *n* **1.** (*phone call*) denwa no yobidashi-on 電話の呼び出し音 **2.** (*rumor*) uwasa 噂・うわさ **3.** (*humming sound of insect*) (mushi no) haoto (虫の)羽音

buzzer *n* búzā ブザー

by *prep* (*no later than*) ... máde ni ... までに; (*means of*) ... de ... で; **by and by** → **soon**; **by ... at the**

latest *adv* ... máde ni wa ... までには; **by chance** *adv* hyótto suruto ひょっと(すると), gūzen (ni) 偶然(に), futo ふと; **by far** *adv* zutto ずっと; háruka (ni) はるか(に)

ye (-bye) → good-bye

bygone *n* kako no koto 過去のこと, sugita koto 過ぎたこと

bylaw *n* kisoku 規則

bypass *n* (*highway*, *surgery*) baipasu バイパス

bystander *n* kenbutsu-nin 見物人

byte *n* (*computer*) baito バイト

C

ab → taxi

abaret *n* kyábarē キャバレー

abin *n* koya 小屋; (*mountain lodge*) yama-goya 山小屋

abinet *n* (*government*) náikaku 内閣

able *n* tsuná 綱, kē´buru ケーブル

able car *n* kēburú-kā´ ケーブルカー

able television *n* kēburú-terebi ケーブルテレビ, yūsen-terebi 有線テレビ

ache *n* (*computer*) kyasshu キャッシュ

actus *n* saboten サボテン

adet *n* shikan kōho sei 士官候補生

adge *v* nedarimásu ねだります; takarimásu たかります

afe *n* (*coffee shop*) kissa-ten 喫茶店, kafe カフェ

afeteria *n* kafeteria カフェテリア, shokudō 食堂

affeine *n* kafein カフェイン

age *n* **1.** (*for bird*) kago かご・籠, tori-kago 鳥かご・鳥籠 **2.** (*for animal*) orí おり・檻

cahoots; *in ~ with* ... to takurände ... と企[たくら]んで

Cairo *n* kairo カイロ

cajole *v* odatemásu おだてます; kangen de damashimásu 甘言でだまします・騙します

cake 1. *n* kē´ki ケーキ; (*sponge-cake*) kasutera カステラ **2.** *n* (o-) káshi (お)菓子; (*Japanese*) wa-gáshi 和菓子 **3.** *n* (*rice cake*) mochi もち・餅

calamity *n* sainán 災難, wazawai 災い

calcium *n* karushium カルシウム

calculate *v* keisan shimásu 計算します

calculator *n* keisán-ki 計算機; ***desk ~*** dentaku 電卓

calendar *n* koyomí 暦; karéndā カレンダー

calf *n* **1.** (*young cow*) ko-ushi 子牛 **2.** (*leg below the knee*) fukurahagi ふくらはぎ

caliber *n* **1.** (*bore caliber*) kōkei 口径 **2.** (*ability*) sainō 才能

calisthenics *n* biyō taisō 美容体操,

jūnan taisō 柔軟体操

call **1.** *n* (*phone call*) denwa 電話 **2.** *n* (*visit*) hōmon 訪問; (*of solicitude*) (o-)mimai (お)見舞 **3.** *v* yobimásu 呼びます; (*phone*) denwa o shimásu 電話をします **4.** *v* (*call on*) → **visit**; call to mind → **recall**; call center *n* kōru sentā コールセンター

called; ***is called ...*** to iimásu ... と言います

caller *n* (*visitor*) raikyaku 来客

calligraphy *n* shodō 書道; (*hand-writing practice*) (o-)shūji (お)習字

calling *n* **1.** (*vocation*) shokugyō 職業 **2.** (*summons*) shōshū 召集

callous *adj* **1.** (*having calluses*) táko no dekita たこのできた **2.** (*insensitive, unfeeling*) mu-shinkei (na) 無神経(な), mu-kan-kaku (na) 無感覚(な) **3.** (*unsympathetic*) mu-jō (na) 無情(な)

callus *n* táko たこ

calm *adj* (*quiet*) shízuka (na) 静か・しずか(な), odáyaka (na) 穏やか・おやだや(な), reisei (na) 冷静(な); nódoka (na) のどか(な); ***~s down*** (*regains composure*) ochitsukimásu 落ち着きます

calorie *n* karorii カロリー

Cambodia *n* kanbojia カンボジア

camcorder *n* bideo kámera ビデオカメラ

came → **come**

camel *n* rakuda ラクダ

cameo *n* kameo カメオ

camera *n* kámera カメラ, shashín ki 写真機

camouflage *n* kamufurāju カムフラージュ

camp **1.** *n* kyánpu キャンプ; (*bivouac*) yaei 野営 **2.** *v* kyánpu (o) shimásu キャンプ(を)します

campaign *n* kyanpēn キャンペーン, undō 運動

camper *n* **1.** (*a person who camps*) kyanpu (o) suru hito キャンプ(を)する人 **2.** (*vehicle*) kyanpin gukā キャンピングカー, kyanpā キャンパー

campsite *n* kyanpu-jō キャンプ場 yaei-chi 野営地

campus *n* kyánpasu キャンパス, (*within the university*) daigakú-kōnai 大学構内; kōtei 校庭

can **1.** *n* (*tin can*) kán 缶・かん **2.** ***~s it*** *v* (kán ni) tsumemásu (缶に)詰めます; canned beer *n* kan bíiru 缶ビール

can *modal v* (*can do it*) (... ga) dekimásu (... が)出来ます・できます, (suru) kotó ga dekimásu (する)事[こと]が出来ます・できます; (... ga) kanaimásu (... が)叶います; can see (... ga) miemásu (... が)見えます; can hear (... ga) kikoemásu (... が)聞こえます

Canada *n* Kánada カナダ

canal *n* únga 運河

canary *n* kanari(y)a カナリア[ヤ]

cancel *v* tori-keshimásu 取り消し

ます; keshimásu 消します
cancellation *n* tori-keshi 取り消し; kyánseru キャンセル; **cancellation mark/stamp** *n* keshi-in 消印
cancer *n* gán がん・癌; (*lung*) haigan 肺がん・肺癌
candid *adj* sotchoku (na) 率直(な)
candidate *n* kōhó-sha 候補者
candle *n* rōsókú ろうそく, kyándoru キャンドル
candor *n* socchoku (sa) 率直(さ)
candy *n* kyándii キャンディー, ame アメ・飴; **candy store** *n* (o-)kashí-ya (お)菓子屋
cane *n* (*walking stick*) sutékki ステッキ; (*staff*) tsúe 杖
canine *n* **1.** (*dog*) inu 犬 **2.** (~ *teeth*) kenshi 犬歯
canister *n* yōki 容器, kan 缶
cannibal *n* kanibaru カニバル, hitokui 人食い
cannon *n* taihō 大砲
cannot *modal v* [NEGATIVE] dekimasén でき[出来]ません; (shi-)kiremasén (し)切れません; ~ ***stand it*** gáman dekimasén がまん[我慢]でき[出来]ません, tamarimasén たまりません
canoe *n* kanū カヌー
canon *n* (*music*) kanon カノン
canopy *n* tengai 天蓋・てんがい
cantaloupe *n* kantarōpu meron カンタロープ・メロン
canteen *n* shokudō 食堂
canvas *n* kyanbasu キャンバス; **canvas shoes** *n* (*sneakers*) suniikā スニーカー
canyon *n* kyōkoku 峡谷・きょうこく
cap *n* **1.** → **hat** **2.** (*of a pen*) kyáppu キャップ **3.** (*of a bottle*) kyáppu キャップ, ōkan 王冠 **4.** (*of a mushroom*) kása かさ・笠
capability *n* **1.** (*ability*) nōryoku 能力 **2.** (*possibility*) kanō-sei 可能性 **3.** (*potential*) shōrai-sei 将来性
capable *adj* nōryoku ga aru 能力がある; yūnō (na) 有能(な)
capacity *n* kyapa(sitii) キャパ(シティー) **1.** (*ability*) nōryoku 能力 **2.** (*volume*) yōseki 容積
cape *n* **1.** (*promontory*) misaki 岬 **2.** (*sleeveless garment*) kēpu ケープ
capital *n* **1.** (*city*) shutó 首都 **2.** (*money*) shihon 資本
capitalize *v* **1.** (*write or print in capital letters*) ōmoji de kakimásu 大文字で書きます **2.** (*supply with capital*) shusshi shimásu 出資します
capitulate *v* kōfuku shimásu 降伏します, kōsan shimásu 降参します
capsize *v* tenpuku shimásu 転覆します, tenpuku sasemásu 転覆させます
capsule *n* kápuseru カプセル
captain *n* (*army*) táii 大尉; (*navy*) taisa 大佐; (*airplane*) kichō´ 機長; (*ship*) sénchō 船長
caption *n* kyapushon キャプション **1.** (*situation*) midashi 見出し

2. (*text of a speech of movie, etc*) jimaku 字幕 3. (*explanation*) setsumei bun 説明文
captivate *v* miwaku shimásu 魅惑します
captive *n* horyo 捕虜
capture *v* toraemásu 捕らえます
car *n* kuruma 車, jidō-sha 自動車; **car park** *n* chūsha-jō 駐車場
car-sharing *n* kā shearingu カーシェアリング
carat *n* karatto カラット
caravan *n* 1. taishō 隊商, kyaraban キャラバン 2. (*large vehicle*) kyaraban-kā キャラバンカー, kanpingu-kā キャンピングカー
carbon *n* tanso 炭素; **carbon dioxide** *n* ni-sanka-tanso 二酸化炭素
carburetor *n* kyaburétā キャブレター
carcass *n* shitai 死体, shigai 死骸
card *n* 1. fuda 札, kā´do カード; (*playing card*) toránpu (ichí-mai) トランプ(一枚) 2. (*calling card, name card*) meishi 名刺 3. (*postcard*) (o-)hágaki (お)はがき・(お)葉書; ***New Year's ~*** nengajō 年賀状
cardboard *n* bōru-gami ボール紙; (*corrugated*) danbō´ru 段ボール
cardiac 1. *n* (*medicine*) kyōshin-zai 強心剤 2. *adj* shizō (no) 心臓(の)
cardigan *n* kādigan カーディガン
care *n* (*caution*) yōjin 用心, nén 念; (*upkeep*) te-iré 手入れ; ***take ~ of*** (*a person*) ... no (o)sewá o shimásu ... の(お)世話をします, ... no mendō o mimásu ... の面倒を見ます; (*a matter*) ... o shóri shimásu ... を処理します; **care for** *v* → **like, love, want** → **look after**
career *n* (*occupation*) shokúgyō 職業; kyaria キャリア; (*history*) rireki 履歴
carefree *adj* kiraku (na) 気楽(な), nónki (na) のんき・呑気(な)
careful *adj* chūibukai 注意深い; ***is ~*** ki o tsukemásu 気を付けます; nén o iremásu 念を入れます
careless *adj* mutón-chaku/-jaku (na) 無頓着(な), zonzái (na) ぞんざい(な), taiman (na) 怠慢(な), fuchū´i (na) 不注意(な)
caress *n, v* aibu/hōyō (shimásu) 愛撫/抱擁(します)
caretaker 1. *n* (*custodian*) kanri-nin 管理人 2. (*caregiver*) kaigo-nin 介護人, sewa-nin 世話人
carnival *n* kānibaru カーニバル, shaniku-sai 謝肉祭
carp *n* (*fish*) kói コイ・鯉; **carp streamers** *n* (*for the Boys' Festival*) koi-nóbori こいのぼり・鯉のぼり
carpenter *n* dáiku 大工
carpet *n* jū´tan じゅうたん・絨毯, kā´pétto カーペット
carriage *n* 1. (*four-wheeled horse-drawn passenger*) basha 馬車 2. (*transporting*) unpan 運搬 3. (*movable part of a machine*) (kikai no) kadōbu (機械の)可動部 4. (*bearing*) mi no konashi 身のこなし

carrier *n* **1.** (*transportation*) yusō 輸送, unsō 運送 **2.** (*of disease*) hokin-sha 保菌者, hoin-sha 保因者 **3.** (*mail* ~) yūbin haitatsu-nin 郵便配達人 **4.** (*newspaper* ~) shinbun haitatsu-nin 新聞配達人 **5.** (*aircraft* ~) kōkū bokan 航空母艦, kūbo 空母

carrot *n* ninjin ニンジン・人参

carry *v* **1.** motte/tótte ikimásu 持って/取っていきます; (*loads aboard*) nosemásu 載せます; (*conveys*) hakobimásu 運びます **2.** (*dangling from the hand*) sagemásu 提げます; (*piggyback*) oimásu 負います, obuimásu おぶ[負ぶ]います; **carry out** (*performs*) okonaimásu 行います; (*brings about*) genjitsu-ka shimásu 現実化します

carsick; *gets* ~ (kuruma ni) yoimásu (車に)酔います

cart *n* teoshi-gúruma 手押し車, daisha 台車

carton → **box**

cartoon *n* manga 漫画・マンガ・まんが

cartridge *n* **1.** (*ink* ~) kātorijji カートリッジ **2.** (~ *in gun*) danyaku-tō 弾薬筒

carve *v* (*inscribe*) kizamimásu 刻みます, horimásu 彫ります

carving *n* horí-mónó 彫り物, (*sculpture*) chōkoku 彫刻; **carving knife** *n* nikukiri-bō´chō 肉切り包丁; chōkokutō 彫刻刀

cascade *n* (*small waterfall*) chiisana taki 小さな滝

case *n* **1.** (*situation*) ba(w)ai 場合, ... wáke... 訳・わけ, (*event*) ... dán ... 段; (*matter*) kotó 事・こと, jiken 事件, (*particular instance*) kḗ´su ケース **2.** (*box*) hako 箱; **in this case** kono ba(w)ai この場合; **in that case** sorenára それなら; (sore) déwa (それ)では, ja じゃ, jā じゃあ; **in case of** ... ni sái-shite... に際して; ... no bāi/tokí ni... の場合/時に

cash **1.** *n* (*money*) genkín 現金; *petty* ~ koguchi genkin 小口現金 **2.** *n* shōkin 賞金; **cashbook** *n* genkin-suitō-chō 現金出納帳; **cash card** *n* kyasshu-kādo キャッシュカード **3.** *v* (*a check*) genkín ni kaemásu 現金にかえます·換えます, genkín ni shimásu 現金にします **4.** *v* (*into smaller bills/coins*) komakáku shimásu 細かくします, kuzushimásu くずします・崩します

cashier *n* suitō-gákari 出納係, réji-gákari レジ係

casino *n* kajino カジノ

cask *n* taru たる・樽

casket *n* **1.** (*coffin*) hitsugi 棺・ひつぎ **2.** (*jewel box*) hōseki-bako 宝石箱

casserole *n* mushiyaki nabe 蒸し焼きなべ

cassette *n* kasetto (tēpu) カセット(テープ)

cast **1.** *n* (*throwing*) hito nage 一投げ **2.** *n* (*selecting actors,* *selected actors*) kyasuto キャスト, haiyaku 配役 **3.** *v* (*throw*) nagemásu̲ 投げます **4.** *v* (*select actors*) kyasutingu shimásu̲ キャスティングします, haiyaku o kimemásu̲ 配役を決めます

castaway *n* **1.** (*shipwrecked person*) hyōryū-sha 漂流者 **2.** (*outcast*) misuterareta hito 見捨てられた人

caste *n* kāsuto カースト

castle *n* (o-)shiro (お)城; (*name of certain*) ...-jō ... 城

castrate *n* kyosei-sha 去勢者

casual *adj* nanige-nái 何気ない; kigaru (na) 気軽(な); kajuaru (na) カジュアル(な); **casual sex** *n* yukizuri no sekkusu 行きずりのセックス

casualty *n* (*injury, damage*) higai 被害; (*victim*) higái-sha 被害者

cat *n* néko 猫・ネコ

catalog *n* katarogu カタログ; mokuroku 目録; (*directory*) meibo 名簿

catalyst *n* shokubai 触媒

catapult *n* (*airplane*) funsha-ki 噴射機, kataparuto カタパルト

cataract *n* **1.** (*large waterfall*) ookina taki 大きな滝 **2.** (*ophthalmology*) hakunai-shō 白内障

catastrophe *n* dai-sanji 大惨事, dai-saigai 大災害

catch **1.** *v* (*seizes*) tsu̲kamaemásu̲ 捕まえます; torimásu̲ 取ります; (*attracts*) hi̲kimásu̲ 引きます **2.** *v* (*a disease*) (byōki ni) kakarimásu̲ (病気に)かかります **3.** *n* ***a good ~*** 獲物・えもの **4.** *n* (*trap*) wana わな・ワナ **5.** *n* (*clasp*) tomegane 留め金; **catch a cold** kaze o hi̲kimásu̲ かぜ[風邪]をひきます; **catch-phrase** kyacchi furēzu キャッチフレーズ; **catch up** (*with*) (... ni) oi-tsukimásu̲ (...に)追いつきます

category *n* kategorii カテゴリー

catering *n* (*meal delivery*) demae 出前, kētaringu ケータリング

caterpillar *n* kemushi 毛虫・ケムシ

cathedral *n* dai-seidō 大聖堂

Catholic *n* Katoríkku (kyō) カトリック(教), (*person*) Katoríkku kyōto カトリック教徒

cattle *n* (*bulls and cows*) ushi 牛・ウシ

caucus *n* tōin shūkai 党員集会

cauldron *n* kama かま・釜

cauliflower *n* karifurawā カリフラワー

cause *n* (*of an effect*) gen'in 原因, moto 元; (*negative effect*) ... séi ... せい; (*source*) táne 種; (*reason*) wáke 訳, riyū 理由; (*purpose, benefit*) tame ため・為; **cause** (*one*) **concern/worry** (... ni) shinpai o kakemásu̲ (...に)心配をかけます; **cause** (*one*) **trouble** (... ni) méiwaku o kakemásu̲ (... に)迷惑をかけます

caustic **1.** *n* fushoku-zai 腐食剤 **2.** *adj* fushoku-sei (no) 腐食性(の)

caution **1.** *n* yōjin 用心; (*precaution*) yō'i 用意, nén 念; ***as*** (*a* *word of*) ~ nen no tamé (ni) 念のため[為](に) **2.** *v* (*warns*) keikai shimásu̲ 警戒します

autious *adj* yōjin-bukái 用心深い

avalry *n* **1.** (*horsemen*) kihei-tai 騎兵隊 **2.** (*military*) kikō-butai 機甲部隊

ave *n* hora-ana 洞穴・ほら穴, hórá 洞・ほら; ... -dō ... 洞

avern *n* dai-dōkutsu 大洞窟

aviar *n* (*roe*) kábia キャビア

avity *n* **1.** (*hole*) ana 穴 **2.** (*hollow area*) kūdō 空洞 **3.** (*tooth* ~) mushiba 虫歯

ease *v* yamimásu̲ やみます·止みます, taemásu̲ 絶えます

easefire *n* teisen 停戦

easeless *adj* taemanai 絶え間ない

edar; *cryptomeria, Japanese ~* *n* sugi 杉・スギ

ede *v* yuzurimásu̲ 譲ります

eiling *n* tenjō 天井

eleb, celebrity *n* serebu セレブ, yūmei-jin 有名人

elebrate *v* iwaimásu̲ 祝います

elebration *n* (*party*) (o-)iwai (お)祝い

elery *n* sérori セロリ; ***Japanese ~*** údo ウド・独活

elestial *adj* ten (no) 天(の), tentai (no) 天体(の)

elibate **1.** *n* (*single person/ people*) dokushin-sha 独身者 **2.** *adj* dokushin (no) 独身(の)

ell *n* **1.** (*biology*) saibō 細胞 **2.** (*prison*) dokubō 独房, rōya 牢屋

ellar *n* (*storehouse*) kurá 倉・蔵; (*basement*) chi̲ká-shi̲tsu 地下室

cello *n* chéro チェロ

cellophane *n* sérohan セロハン

Celt *n* **1.** (*a Celt*) keruto-jin ケルト人 **2.** (*ethnic*) keruto-zoku ケルト族

cement *n* semento セメント; **cement floor** *n* tatakí たたき

cemetery *n* haka-bá 墓場, bóchi 墓地

cenotaph *n* (senbotsu-sha) kinen-hi (戦没者)記念碑

censor **1.** *n* ken'etsu-kan 検閲官 **2.** *v* ken'etsu shimásu̲ 検閲します

censure **1.** *n* (*blame*) hínan 非難 **2.** *v* (*blames one*) hínan shimásu̲ 非難します, sememásu̲ 責めます

census *n* kokusei-chōsa 国勢調査

cent *n* sénto セント; ***percent*** pāsénto パーセント

centennial *n* hyakushūnen 百周年

center *n* mannaka 真ん中・まんなか, chūō 中央, chūshin 中心; (*institution*) séntā センター

centigrade *n* sésshi 摂氏, seshi セ氏; ... -do ... 度

centimeter *n* sénchi センチ, senchi-mē´toru センチメートル

centipede *n* mukade ムカデ・百足

central *adj* mannaka no 真ん中の・まんなかの, chūshin no 中心の, chūō no 中央の; **Central America** *n* chūbei 中米, chūō-amerika 中央アメリカ; **central office** *n* hónbu 本部

century *n* séiki 世紀

ceramics *n* seramikku セラミック; (*ceramic art*) tōgei 陶芸; (*ceramic*

ware) tō´ki 陶器; (*pottery*) yaki-mono 焼き物
cereal *n* kokúmotsu 穀物, kokúrui 穀類; siriaru シリアル
cerebral *adj* nō (no) 脳(の)
ceremony *n* shikí 式, gíshiki 儀式; ***wedding*** ~ kekkon-shiki 結婚式
certain *adj* táshika (na) 確か・たしか(な); kakujitsu (na) 確実(な)
certainly *adv* mochíron もちろん・勿論; táshika ni 確かに; mása-ni まさに
certificate *n* shōmei-sho 証明書
certification *n* shōmei 証明
certified *adj* kōnin (no) 公認(の); **certified public accountant (CPA)** *n* kōnin-kaikéishi 公認会計士
cervical *adj* shikyū-keibu (no) 子宮頚部(の)・子宮けい部(の)
cesarean *n* teiō-sekkai 帝王切開
cesspool *n* osui-dame 汚水溜め・汚水だめ, gesui-dame 下水溜め・下水だめ
Ceylon *n* Seiron セイロン = ***Sri Lanka*** Suriránka スリランカ
chafe *v* surimukimásu すりむきます
chaff *n* momigara もみ殻・もみがら
chagrin *n* kuyashisa 悔しさ・くやしさ
chain *n* kusari 鎖・くさり, chēn チェーン; (*linked*) ***in a*** ~ tsunagatte つながって; **chain smoker** *n* chēn sumōkā チェーンスモーカー; **chain store** *n* chēn-ten チェーン店, chēn sutoa チェーンストア
chair *n* isu 椅子・イス, koshi-káke 腰掛け
chalet *n* sharē シャレー, sansō 山荘
chalk *n* chō´ku チョーク
challenge 1. *n* chárenji チャレンジ, chōsen 挑戦 **2.** *v* (*tries*) idomimásu 挑みます, chárenji shimásu チャレンジします; (*tests*) tameshimásu 試します; **challenger** *n* charenjā チャレンジャー, chōsen-sha 挑戦者
chamber 1. *n* (*room*) heya 部屋 **2.** *n* (*meeting hall*) kaigi-shitsu 会議室 **3.** *n* (*compartment in a firearm*) yakushitsu 薬室 **4.** *n* (*palace room*) ō-shitsu 王室 **5.** *n* (*legislative hall*) giin 議院 **6.** *v* (*enclose bullets*) tama o komemásu 弾をこめます
chameleon *n* kamereon カメレオン
champagne *n* shanpán シャンパン, shanpén シャンペン
champion *n* yūshō-sha 優勝者, chanpion チャンピオン; (*sumo wrestler*) ō´-zeki 大関; ***grand ~ sumo wrestler*** yokozuna 横綱; **championship** *n* senshu-ken 選手権
chance *n* **1.** (*opportunity*) kikái 機会, chánsu チャンス **2.** (*impulse*) hazumi 弾み → **by chance**
chancellor *n* (*minister*) daijin 大臣
change 1. *n* (*small money*) kozeni 小銭, komakái (o)kane 細かい(お)金 **2.** *n* (*money returned*) o-tsuri お釣り・おつり, tsuri-sen 釣り銭 **3.** *n* hénka 変化; (*in health*) o-kawari お変わり;

(*abnormality*) ijō 異常 **4.** *v it ~s* kawarimásu 変わります; hénka shimásu 変化します; utsurimásu 移ります **5.** *v ~s it* kaemásu 変えます; aratamemásu 改めます **6.** *v* (*clothes*) kigaemásu 着替えます **7.** *v* (*train, bus, plane*) nori-kaemásu 乗り換えます; for a change *adj* kibun-tenkan (ni) 気分転換(に), ikinuki (ni) 息抜き(に)

changeable *n* kōi-shitsu 更衣室

channel *n* **1.** (*for radio or television*) channeru チャンネル **2.** kaikyō 海峡; suiro 水路

chant *v* utaimásu 歌い[謡い]ます

chaos *n* kaosu カオス, muchitsujo 無秩序, konton 混沌

chap *n* **1.** (*crack*) hibi ひび **2.** (*capped skin*) akagire あかぎれ **3.** (*fellow*) yatsu やつ

chapel *n* chaperu チャペル, reihaidō 礼拝堂

chapter *n* (*book*) shō 章, chaputā チャプター

char *v* **1.** ***become charred*** kogemásu 焦げます **2.** *~s it* kogashimásu 焦がします

character *n* **1.** (*quality*) seishitsu 性質 **2.** (*personal traits*) seikaku 性格, kosei 個性 **3.** (*written*) jí 字, móji 文字; ***Chinese ~*** kanji 漢字 **4.** (*part or role in a play or film*) kyarakuta キャラクタ, kyarakutā キャラクター

characteristic **1.** *n* (*an earmark*) tokushoku 特色, (*a distinguishing ~*) tokuchō 特徴 **2.** *adj* (*typical*) daihyō-teki (na) 代表的(な); (*specific*) koyū (no) 固有(の), tokuchō-teki (na) 特徴的(な)

charade *n* misekake 見せかけ

charcoal *n* sumí 炭・スミ, mokután 木炭

charge **1.** *n* (*fee*) ryōkin 料金, daikin 代金, (*with fee*) yūryō (no) 有料(の; ***no ~*** muryō (no) 無料(の), [INFORMAL] tada (no) ただ(の); **2.** *n* ***in ~*** (*teacher*) tannin 担任; tantō 担当; ***takes/accepts*** (*is in*) ***~ of*** ... o tannin/tantō shimásu ... を担任/担当します, uke-mochimásu 受け持ちます **3.** *n* (*an attack*) shūgeki 襲撃 **4.** *v* seikyū shimásu 請求します **5.** *v* (*attacks*) shūgeki shimásu 襲撃します **6.** *v* (*fill or furnish rechargeable public transport card*) chāji shimásu チャージします, (*cellphone*) jūden shimásu 充電します

charitable *adj* jizen (no) 慈善(の)

charity *n* hodokoshi 施し, jizen 慈善, charitii チャリティー; (*mercy*) megumi 恵み; charity concert *n* charitii konsāto チャリティーコンサート

charm **1.** *v* (…o) uttori-sasemásu うっとりさせます **2.** *n* (*good-luck piece*) o-mamori お守り; (*attraction*) miryoku 魅力

chart *n* zuhyō 図表, zu 図, chāto チャート

charter *n* tokkyo jō 特許状, chātā

チャーター

chase *v* oi-kakemásu 追いかけます, oimásu 追います, [FORMAL] tsuisekishimásu 追跡します

chaste *adj* teisetsu (na) 貞節(な), junsui (na) 純粋(な)

chastise *v* korashimemásu 懲らしめます

chat **1.** *n* oshaberi おしゃべり・お喋り, sekenbánashi 世間話, muda-banashi 無駄話, zatsudan 雑談 **2.** *v* oshaberi o shimásu おしゃべり・お喋りをします

chatter *v* shaberimásu しゃべります・喋ります

chauffeur *n* okakae unténshu お抱え運転手

chauvinism *n* **1.** (*aggressive patriotism*) kyōshin-teki aikokushin 狂信的愛国心 **2.** (*sexism*) seisabetsu shugi 性差別主義

cheap *adj* yasúi 安い

cheat *v* (*deceives*) damashimásu だまします・騙します, gomakashimásu ごまかします; (*dissembles, shirks, tricks*) zúru o shimásu ずる[ズル]をします; (*on one's spouse*) futei o hatarakimásu 不貞をはたらきます

check **1.** *n* (*bank*) kogítte 小切手, chékku チェック **2.** *n* (*chit*) fuda 札 **3.** *n* (*pays money at the restaurant*)(o-)kanjō (お)勘定, denpyō 伝票, (o-)aisó, (o-)aisō (お)あいそ(う)・(お)愛想 **4.** *v* ~ *it* (*baggage*) azukemásu 預けます **5.** (*investigates*) shirabemásu 調べます, chékku shimásu チェックします; (*inspects*) kénsa shimásu 検査します, (*compares*) terashimásu 照らします; check in (*registers*) chekkúin shimásu チェックインします; check out (*of hotel*) chekkuáuto shimásu チェックアウトします

checkpoint kenmon-jo 検問所

check-up *n* **1.** kénsa 検査 **2.** (*medical checkup*) kenkō shindan 健康診断

cheek *n* hō´ 頬・ほお, hoho 頬・ほほ

cheeky *adj* namaiki (na) 生意気(な)

cheer *n* ōen 応援; ~ *for* ōenshimásu 応援します

cheerful *adj* (*in a good mood*) kigen ga íi 機嫌がいい, (*full of energy*) genki ga ii 元気がいい, (*merry, blitheful*) hogáraka (na) 朗らか・ほがらか(な)

cheerleader *n* (*female*) chia gāru チアガール

Cheers *interj* **1.** (*See you later*) mata (ne) また(ね) **2.** (*toast*) kanpai! 乾杯!

cheese *n* chíizu チーズ

chef *n* shefu シェフ, ryōri chō 料理長, (*chef of Japanese food*) itamae(-san) 板前(さん)

chemicals *n* kagaku-séihin 化学製品; (*pharmaceuticals*) yakuhin 薬品, kagaku-yakuhin 化学薬品

chemistry *n* kágaku 化学, bakegaku 化学

chemotherapy *n* kagaku ryōhō 化学療法
cherish *v* daijí ni shimásu 大事にします, [FORMAL] chō´hō shimásu 重宝します, chōhō-garimásu 重宝がります
cherry *n* (*tree*) sakura no ki 桜の木; (*fruit*) sakuranbo サクランボ・桜んぼ
cherry blossoms *n* sakura (no haná) 桜(の花)
chess *n* **1.** chesu チェス **2.** (*Japanese chess*) shōgi 将棋
chest *n* **1.** (*of body*) muné 胸 **2.** (*box*) hako 箱; (*drawers*) tansu たんす・タンス
chestnut *n* kurí 栗・クリ
chew *v* kamimásu 噛みます・かみます; ~ ***the fat*** (*idly talk*) daberimásu だべります・駄弁ります
chic *adj* shikku (na) シック(な), iki (na) 粋(な), jōhin (na) 上品(な)
chicken *n* tori 鶏・トリ, niwatori 鶏・ニワトリ; ***skewered grilled*** ~ yaki-tori 焼き鳥・やきとり
chide *v* (*rebukes*) tashinamemásu たしなめます, shikarimásu 叱ります
chief **1.** *n* (*head*) chō 長, chōkan 長官, chiifu チーフ, (*ringleader*) óyá-bun 親分 **2.** *adj* (*main*) shuyō (na) 主要(な), ómo na 主な, hon-... 本...
child *n* kodomo 子供・こども・子ども, ko 子, (*elementary school student*) jídō 児童; ***your*** ~ o-ko-san/sama お子さん/さま・様
childish *adj* osanái 幼い; yōchi (na) 幼稚(な); kodomoppoi 子供っぽい
childlike *adj* kodomo rashii 子供らしい; junshin (na) 純真(な)
children *n* kodomó-tachi 子供たち; ***Children's Day*** (*5 May*) Kodomo no hí こどもの日・子供の日
chili *n* chiri チリ; **chili pepper** *n* chiri peppā チリペッパー, tōgarashi トウガラシ・唐辛子
chill *v* ~ ***it*** hiyashimásu 冷やします
chilly *adj* samúi 寒い, hieru 冷える
chime *n* chaimu チャイム
chimney *n* entotsu 煙突・えんとつ
chimpanzee *n* chinpanjii チンパンジー
chin *n* agó あご・顎
China *n* Chū´goku 中国
Chinatown *n* Chaina taun チャイナタウン
china(ware) *n* (*porcelain*) setomono 瀬戸物
Chinese *n* (*language*) Chugoku-go 中国語; (*person*) Chugokú-jin 中国人
Chinese; **Chinese cabbage** *n* (*bok choi*) hakusai 白菜・ハクサイ; **Chinese character** *n* kanji 漢字, jí 字; **Chinese cooking** *n* chūka-ryō´ri 中華料理; **Chinese noodles** *n* (*with soup*) rā´men ラーメン, chūka-

men 中華麺

chip *n* (*of wood*) kóppá 木っ端; (*crack*) kizu 傷; (*electronic engineering*) chippu チップ

chips *n* (*potato chip*) poteto chippusu ポテトチップス

chirp *n* saezuri さえずり

chisel *n* nómi ノミ

chlorine *n* énso 塩素

chocolate *n* choko(rē´to) チョコ(レート); **chocolate bar** *n* ita-choko 板チョコ

choice *n* (*selection*) sentaku 選択

choir *n* **1.** (*chorus group*) gasshō-dan 合唱団 **2.** (*chorus group in church*) seika-tai 聖歌隊

choke *v* **1.** (*he ~s*) íki ga tsumarimásu̲ 息がつまります·詰まります **2.** (*~s him*) ... no íki o tomemásu̲ ... の息を止めます

cholera *n* kórera コレラ

cholesterol *n* koresuterōru コレステロール

choose *v* **1.** [INFORMAL] erabimásu̲ えらびます·選びます; [FORMAL] sentaku shimásu̲ 選択します **2.** (*decides on*) ... ni shimásu̲ ... にします

choosy *adj* yorigónomi ga hageshíi より好みがはげしい·激しい, yorigónomi o shimásu̲ より好みをします

chop 1. *v* (*chops it*) kizamimásu̲ 刻みます; (*fire wood*) (takigi o) warimásu̲ 薪を割ります **2.** *n* (*signature seal*) hankó はんこ, hán はん・判

chopsticks *n* (o-)háshi (お)はし·(お)箸

chord *n* **1.** (*music*) waon 和音; (*guitar chord*) kōdo コード **2.** (*emotion*) kokoro no kinsen 心の琴線

chore *n* zatsuyō 雑用

choreography *n* furitsuke 振り付け

chorus *n* kō´rasu コーラス, (*music sang by a group*) gasshō-kyoku 合唱曲, (*group of singers*) gasshō-dan 合唱団

Christ *n* Kirisu̲to キリスト

Christian 1. *adj* Kirisu̲to-kyō no ... キリスト教の... **2.** *n* (Kirisu̲to-kyō no) shínjá (キリスト教の)信者

Christianity *n* Kirisu̲to-kyō キリスト教

Christmas *n* Kurísúmasu クリスマス; **Christmas Eve** *n* kurisumasu ibu クリスマスイブ

chronic *adj* mansei (no) 慢性(の)

chronological *adj* nendai-jun (no) 年代順(の)

chrysanthemum *n* ki̲kú 菊・キク; (*tasty leaves*) ***garland*** ~ shungiku 春菊・シュンギク

chubby *adj* fukkurashita ふっくらした, futome (no) 太めの

chuck *v* **1.** (*throws*) nagemásu̲ 投げます **2.** (*tosses*) hōrimásu̲ 放ります

church *n* kyōkai 教会

cigar *n* shígā シガー, ha-maki 葉巻; **cigar shop/store** *n* tabako-ya たばこ屋

cigarette *n* tabako たばこ・タバコ・煙草, maki-tábako 巻きたばこ, shígarétto シガレット; **cigarette/cigar butt** *n* suigara 吸い殻; **cigarette lighter** *n* raitā ライター

cinder(s) *n* moegara 燃えがら

cinema → movies

cinnamon *n* shinamon シナモン

cipher *n* **1.** (*zero*) zero ゼロ・零 **2.** (*secret code*) angō 暗号

circle 1. *n* maru 丸, én 円, (*ring*) wá 輪, (*orbit*) kidō 軌道 **2.** *v* maru/en de kakomimásu 丸/円で囲みます

circular *adj* kanjō (no) 環状(の)

circulate *v* (*it ~s*) mawarimásu 回ります; (*~s it*) mawashimásu 回します

circumference *n* shū´i 周囲, shūhen 周辺, enshū 円周

circumstance *n* **1.** ba(w)ai 場合; kotó 事・こと, ... wáke ... 訳・わけ, ... tokoró ... 所・ところ **2.** jijō 事情, jōtai 状態, jōkyō 状況; yóshi 由・よし, ... shidai... 次第・しだい **3.** yōsu 様子・ようす **4.** (*convenience*) tsugō 都合 (go-tsugō ご都合)

circus *n* sā´kasu サーカス

cistern *n* suisō 水槽, chosui tanku 貯水タンク

citation *n* inyō bun 引用文

cite *v* **1.** (*quotes*) inyō shimásu 引用します **2.** (*refers*) genkyū shimásu 言及します

citizen *n* shímin 市民; (*national*) kokumin 国民

citizenship *n* shimin-ken 市民権

citrus *n* kankitsu-rui かんきつ類・柑橘類・カンキツ類

city 1. *n* shí 市, (*town*) machí 町, (*metropolis*) tóshi 都市, tokai 都会 (*dweller*) tokái-jin 都会人; **city council** *n* shi-gikai 市議会 **2.** *adj* (*within the city*) shí-nai (no) 市内(の)

civilian *n* minkan no hito 民間の人, minkan-jin 民間人

civilization *n* bummei 文明, (*culture*) búnka 文化

claim 1. *n* (*demands*) yōkyū/seikyū 要求/請求 **2.** *v* (*maintains*) shuchō shimásu 主張します, tonaemásu 唱えます

clamber *v* yojinoborimásu よじ登ります

clamor 1. *n* (*a ~*) sáwagi 騒ぎ, kensō 喧騒; **2.** *v* (*makes a ~*) sawagimásu 騒ぎます・さわぎます

clamorous *adj* sōzōshii 騒々しい

clamp 1. *n* (*metal piece for fastening*) tomegane 留め金 **2.** *v* (*fastens or fixes*) koteishimásu 固定します

clan *n* ichizoku 一族, ikka 一家

clandestine *adj* himitsu (no) 秘密(の)

clang 1. *n* gachan ガチャン **2.** *v* (*rings loudly*) (gachan to) narashimásu (ガチャンと)鳴らします **3.** *v* (*sounds*) narimásu 鳴ります

clap (*one's hands*) *v* té o tatakimásu 手を叩きます, hákushu shimásu 拍手します

clarification *n* setsumei 説明

clarify *v* **1.** (*makes clear*) akiraka ni shimásu あきらか[明らか]にします **2.** (*becomes clear*) akiraka ni narimásu あきらか[明らか]になります, hakkiri shimásu はっきりします

clarity *n* **1.** (*transparency*) tōmei do 透明度 **2.** seichō sa 清澄さ **3.** meiryō sa 明瞭さ

clasp (*one's hands*) *v* (té o) kumimásu (手を)組みます

class *n* **1.** kúrasu クラス, kyū´ 級, (*in school*) gakkyū 学級; **class instruction** *n* ① júgyō 授業, kōshū 講習 ② kaikyū 階級; **classmate** *n* dōkyū´-sei 同級生, (*former classmate*) dōkí-sei 同期生; **classroom** *n* kyōshitsu 教室

classic *n* kurashikku クラシック, koten 古典

classical *adj* koten (no) 古典(の); **classical music** *n* kurashikku ongaku クラシック音楽, koten ongaku 古典音楽

clatter *v* gátagata shimásu がたがたします

claw *n* tsume 爪・ツメ

clay *n* néndo 粘土

clean **1.** *adj* kírei (na) きれい[綺麗](な), seiketsu (na) 清潔(な); (*fresh*) sappári shita さっぱりした **2.** *~s it* (*up*) *v* kírei ni shimásu きれい[綺麗]にします, (*tidies*) katazukemásu 片付けます・かたづけます, (*sweeps*) sōji shimásu 掃除します

clear **1.** *adj* (*bright*) akarui 明るい; (*sunny*) hárete imásu 晴れています, harete ... 晴れた ...; (*transparent*) tōmei (na) 透明(な) **2.** *adj* (*evident*) akíraka (na) 明らか(な), (*obvious, explicit*) meihaku (na) 明白(な); (*understood*) wakátte imásu 分かっています, wakátta 分かった... **3.** *adj* (*easy to see*) miyasúi 見やすい; (*easy to understand*) wakari-yasúi 分かりやすい **4.** *adj* (*unimpeded*) jama ga nái じゃま[邪魔]がない **5.** *v* (*takes away from the table*) sagemásu 下げます **6.** *gets ~* (*empty*) sukimásu すきます・空きます **7.** *becomes ~* (*evident*) shiremásu 知れます

clerk *n* (*in shop*) ten'in 店員; (*in office*) jimú-in 事務員; (*in bank*) ginkō´-in 銀行員

clever *adj* rikō (na) 利口・りこう(な); (*nimble with fingers*) kíyō (na) 器用(な); (*skilled*) jōzú (na) じょうず・上手(な)

cliff *n* gake がけ・崖

climate *n* kikō 気候

climax *n* yamá 山, chō´ten 頂点; (*upshot*) ketsumatsu 結末; shímatsu 始末

climb *v* noborimásu 登ります

cling *v* kuttsukimásu くっつきます, shigamitsukimásu しがみつきます

clinic *n* byōin 病院

clip **1.** ***clips it*** *v* tsumimásu 摘みます; kirimásu 切ります **2.** *n* kuríppu クリップ → **paperclip**

clique *n* renchū/renjū 連中, habatsu 派閥

cloak *n* mánto マント; **cloakroom** *n* kurō´ku クローク, (tenimotsu) azukarijo (手荷物)預かり所

clock *n* tokei 時計; ***around the ~*** nijūyojikan 24時間, ichinichi-jū 一日中

clockwise *adv* migi-máwari (ni) 右回り(に)

clogged; ***gets ~ (up)*** fusagarimásu ふさがります

clogs **1.** *n* (*wooden shoes*) getá げた・下駄 **2.** *v* (*it ~s up, gets clogged*) tsumarimásu 詰まります, tsukaemásu つかえます

close **1.** *v* **~*s it*** (*shuts*) shimemásu 閉めます, (*a book, etc.*) tojimásu 閉じます; ***~ one's eyes*** mé o tsuburimásu 目をつぶります・瞑ります; (*obstructs*) fusagimásu ふさぎます; (*ends*) owarimásu 終わります **2.** ***it ~s*** shimarimásu 閉まります → **end** **3.** *adj* (*near*) chikái 近い; ***~ by*** (o-)soba (no) (お)そば(の) **4.** *adj* (*humid*) mushi-atsúi 蒸し暑い **5.** *n* (*the end*) owari 終わり, sue 末, matsu 末

closet *n* (*Japanese*) oshi-ire 押し入れ, nándo 納戸; (*Western*) kurōzetto クローゼット

clot **1.** *n* (*a ~*) katamari 固まり・塊・かたまり **2.** *v* (*it ~s*) katamarimásu 固まります

cloth *n* ori-mono 織物, kíji 生地, nuno 布; (*a piece of*) kiré 切れ, nuno-gire 布切れ; (*traditional wrapper*) furoshiki ふろしき・風呂敷

clothes *n* fukú 服, fukusō 服装

cloud *n* kúmo 雲

cloudy; ***gets ~*** kumorimásu 曇ります・くもります; ***~ weather*** kumorí 曇り・くもり

clover *n* kurōba¯ クローバー; ***four-leaf ~*** yotsuba no kurōbā 四つ葉のクローバー

cloves *n* chō´ji 丁字・チョウジ, kurōbu クローブ

clown *n* dōke-shi 道化師

club *n* **1.** (*group; card suit*) kúrabu クラブ **2.** (*stick*) konbō 棍棒・こん棒; (*golf*) (gorufu) kurabu (ゴルフ)クラブ

clue *n* tegákari 手掛かり, itóguchi 糸口

clump *n* katamari 塊・かたまり

clumsy *adj* hetá (na) へた[下手]な, bu-kíyō (na) 不器用(な); gikochi-nái ぎこちない

cluster → **bunch**

clutch **1.** *v* (*grasps*) nigirimásu 握ります, tsukamimásu つかみます **2.** *n* (*of car*) kurátchi クラッチ, (*pedal*) kuratchí-pédaru クラッチペダル

coach **1.** *v* (*~es them*) shidō shimásu 指導します **2.** *n* (*director*) shidō´-sha 指導者; (*sports*) kō´chi コーチ **3.** *n* (*railroad*) kyakusha 客車; coach station *n* (*depot*) basu no hatchaku-jō バスの発着場

coal *n* sekitán 石炭; coal mine *n* tankō 炭鉱

coarse *adj* arai 粗い[荒い]; sómatsu (na) 粗末(な)

coast *n* engan 沿岸, kaigan 海岸

coat *n* uwagi 上着, kō´to コート; (*overcoat*) gaitō 外套, ō´bā オーバー; (*traditional Japanese*) haori 羽織

coax *v* odatemásu おだてます

cocaine *n* kokáin コカイン

cock *n* ondori オンドリ・雄鶏

cockpit *n* kokkupitto コックピット, sōjū-seki 操縦席, sōjū-shitsu 操縦室

cockroach *n* gokiburi ゴキブリ

cocktail (party) *n* kákuteru (pātii) カクテル(パーティー)

cocky *adj* unuboreta うぬぼれた, namaiki (na) 生意気(な)

cocoa *n* kókóa ココア

coconut *n* kókonáttsu ココナッツ; coconut palm *n* yáshi ヤシ・椰子

cocoon *n* máyu マユ・繭

C.O.D. (*collect on delivery*) → **collect** (*on delivery*)

code *n* kō´do コード; (*secret*) angō 暗号

co-ed *n* jo (-shi) gákusei 女(子)学生

coeducation *n* dánjo kyōgaku 男女共学

co-existence *n* kyōson 共存, kyōzon 共存

coffee *n* kōhíi コーヒー

coffee shop/house *n* kōhii-ten コーヒー店, kissa-ten 喫茶店

coffin *n* hitsugi 棺・ひつぎ

cog *n* (*wheel*) ha-gúruma 歯車

coherent *adj* (shubi) ikkan shita 首尾一貫した

cohesion *n* danketsu 団結, ketsugō 結合

coil *n* koiru コイル

coin *n* kō´ka 硬貨, kóin コイン; (*brass or copper*) dō´ka 銅貨; ***tosses a*** ~ kōka/koin o nagete ura-omote de kimemásu 硬貨/コインを投げて裏表で決めます

coincidence *n* gūzen 偶然

coincidental *adj* gūzen itchi shita 偶然一致した

cola *n* kō´ra コーラ

colander *n* mizu-kírí 水切り; (*bamboo*) zarú ざる

cold **1.** *adj* samúi 寒い; (*to touch*) tsumetái 冷たい; ***gets*** ~ sámuku/tsumetáku narimásu 寒く/冷たくなります; samemásu 冷めます; hiemásu 冷えます **2.** *n* kaze かぜ[風邪]; ***catches a*** ~ kaze o hikimásu かぜ[風邪]をひきます; cold medicine *n* kaze-gúsuri かぜ[風邪]薬

coldness *n* tsumetasa 冷たさ, samusa 寒さ

cold water *n* mizu 水, (o-)híya (お)冷や

coleslaw *n* kōru-surō コールスロー, kyabetsu-sárada キャベツサラダ

colic *n* sentsū 疝痛

collaborate *v* **1.** (*cooperates*) kyōryoku shimásu 協力します **2.** (*works collaboratively*) kyōdōsagyō shimásu 共同作業します

collapse *v* taoremásu 倒れます; (*gets smashed*) tsuburemásu つぶれます・潰れます

collar *n* **1.** (*of coat*) kárā カラー, erí えり・襟 **2.** (*of dog*) kubi-wa 首輪

collate *v* (*compares*) terashimásu 照らします, terashi-awasémásu 照らし合わせます

colleague *n* **1.** (*professional ~*) (shokuba no) dōryō (職場の) 同僚 **2.** (*academic ~*) gakuyū 学友

collect *v* **1.~*s them*** atsumemásu 集めます, yosemásu 寄せます・よせます, (*completes a set*) soroemásu 揃えます・そろえます; (*gathers up*) shūshū shimásu 収集します; (*reaps, brings in*) osamemásu 納めます, (*levies taxes etc,*) chōshū shimásu 徴収します; ~ ***tickets*** shūsatsu shimásu 集札します **2. *they ~*** (*come together*) atsumarimásu 集まります; collect call *n* korekuto kōru コレクトコール

collect (*on delivery*), **C.O.D.** *adv* daikin hiki-kae (de) 代金引き換え(で), dai-biki (de) 代引き(で), chakubarai (de) 着払い(で)

collection *n* **1.** (*of books*) zōsho 蔵書, korekushon コレクション **2.** (*of taxes etc.*) chōshū 徴収

collector *n* shūshū-ka 収集家

college *n* daigaku 大学; karejji カレッジ; college student *n* daigákusei 大学生

collide *v* shōtotsu shimásu 衝突します

colloquial **1.** *n* (*language, word*) kōgo 口語 **2.** *adj* kōgo-teki (na) 口語的(な)

collusion; ***in ~ with*** ... to takuránde ... と企んで

colony *n* shokumín-chi 植民地

color *n* iró 色, kárā カラー

color-blind *adj* **1.** (*ophthalmology*) shikikaku ijō (no) 色覚異常(の) **2.** *(nonracialism)* jinshusabetsu o shinai 人種差別をしない

colorful *adj* (*bright*) hanáyaka (na) 華やか(な), karafuru (na) カラフル(な)

colossal *adj* kyodai (na) 巨大(な)

colt *n* (*young male horse*) osu no ko-uma 雄の子馬

column **1.** *n* rán 欄, koramu コラム; (*page ~*) dán 段; (*numerical ~*) keta けた・桁 **2.** → **pillar**

coma *n* konsui 昏睡

comb **1.** *n* kushí くし・櫛 **2.** *v* (*the hair*) kamí o sukimásu 髪をすきます, tokimásu ときます・梳きます, tokashimásu とかします・梳かします

combat *n* sentō 戦闘

combination *n* **1.** kumi-awase 組み合わせ, konbinēshon コンビネーション **2.** (*union*) gappei 合併, gōdō 合同

combine 1. *v* (*combines them*) kumi-awasemásu 組み合わせます, awasemásu 合わせます; (*dually serves as*) kanemásu 兼ねます 2. *v* (*they unite*) gappei/gōdō shimásu 合併/合同します

combustion *n* 1. (*burning*) nenshō 燃焼 2. (*oxidation*) sanka 酸化 3. (*tumult*) sawagi 騒ぎ・さわぎ

come *v* kimásu 来ます; (*I/we come to you*) ikimásu 行きます; come about shō-jimásu 生じます; genjitsu-ka shimásu 現実化します; come along yatte-kimásu やってきます; come back itte kimásu 行ってきます; kaerimásu 帰ります(帰る, 帰って); come down kudarimásu 下ります・おります; (*on the price*) makemásu 負けます; come in hairimásu 入ります, háitte kimásu 入ってきます; come near yorimásu 寄ります・よります, chika-zukimásu 近づきます; come off (*button, etc.*) toremásu 取れます・とれます; nukemásu 抜けます; hazuremásu 外れます・はずれます; come on, ...! (*urging an invitation*) sā´ さあ, hora ほら; come out demásu 出ます, déte kimásu 出てきます; (*appears*) arawaremásu 現れます; come to an end sumimásu 済みます・すみます, owarimásu 終わります, tsukimásu 尽きます・つきます; come what may nán to itté mo なんと言っても

comedy *n* kígeki 喜劇, komedii コメディ

comely *n* 1. (*appearance*) yōshi no ii 容姿のいい, kiryō no yoi 器量の良い 2. (*attractive*) miryoku-teki (na) 魅力的(な)

comet *n* hōkí-boshi ほうき星, suisei 彗星・すい星

comfort 1. *n* anraku 安楽, kiraku 気楽 2. *n* (*consolation*) nagusame 慰め, ian 慰安 3. *v* (*consoles*) nagusamemásu 慰めます

comfortable 1. *adj* rakú (na) 楽(な), anraku (na) 安楽(な), kiraku (na) 気楽(な); kaiteki (na) 快適(な), kimochi ga íi 気持ちがいい 2. → **relax** 3. *adj* (*easy to wear*) ki-yasúi 着やすい, (*easy to sit on*) suwariyasúi 座りやすい・すわりやすい

comforter *n* (*down quilt*) hane-buton 羽布団

comic; comic book *n* manga (-bon) 漫画(本); komikku コミック; comics *n* manga 漫画・まんが

comical *adj* hyōkín (na) ひょうきん(な) → **funny**

Coming-of-Age Day (*2nd Monday of January*) *n* Seijin no hí 成人の日

comma *n* konma コンマ

command 1. *n* (*order, instructions*) meirei 命令; (*historic term*) sátá さた・沙汰 2. *v* (*orders a person*) ... ni ii-tsukemásu ... に言い付けます, mei-jimásu 命じます 3. *v* (*leads*) hikiimásu 率います

commander *n* shiréi-kan 司令官;

(*navy*) chūsa 中佐

commemorate *v* kinen shimásu̲ 記念します

commencement *n* (*ceremony*) sotsugyō´-shi̲ki 卒業式

commend *v* (*praises*) homemásu̲ ほめます・褒めます

comment **1.** *n* (*explanation*) kaisetsu 解説 **2.** *n* (*critique, opinion*) hyōron 評論 **3.** *n* komento コメント → **remark** **4.** *~s on v* (*explains*) kaisetsu shimásu̲ 解説します; (*criticizes*) hyōron shimásu̲ 評論します

commentary *n* **1.** (*interpretation*) kaisétsu 解説 **2.** (*explanatory note*) chūshaku 注釈 **3.** (*records*) kiroku 記録 **4.** (*on-the-spot broadcasting*) jikkyō hōsō 実況放送

commerce *n* shō´gyō 商業; (*trade*) bōeki 貿易

commercial (*message*) *n* komāsharu コマーシャル, shiiému (*CM*) シーエム

commission **1.** *n* (*handling charge*) tesū-ryō 手数料; (*brokerage fee*) sáya さや **2.** *v* (*~s ... to do it*) (sore o ... ni) irai shimásu̲ (それを... に)依頼します

commit *v* **1.** (*entrusts*) yudanemásu̲ ゆだねます・委ねます **2.** (*perpetrates*) okashimásu̲ 犯します; hatarakimásu̲ 働きます

commitment *n* **1.** (*promise*) yakusoku 約束 **2.** (*duty*) gimu 義務 **3.** (*responsibility*) sekinin 責任

committee *n* iín-kai 委員会; committee member(s) *n* íin 委員

commodity *n* shōhin 商品

common *adj* fu̲tsū (no) 普通(の); kyōtsū (no) 共通(の); (*average*) nami (no) 並(の); (*vulgar, popular*) zoku (na) 俗(な); ***very ~*** (*is prevalent*) hayari (no) はやり・流行(の)

commoner *n* shomin 庶民, ippanjin 一般人

common sense *n* (ippan) jōshi̲ki 一般常識

commonwealth *n* renpō 連邦

commotion *n* **1.** (*tumult*) sawagi 騒ぎ **2.** (*agitation*) dōyō 動揺 **3.** (*chaos*) konran 混乱

commune **1.** *v* danwa shimásu̲ 談話します **2.** *n* chihō jichitai 地方自治体

communicate *v* tsu̲taemásu̲ 伝えます; tsūjimásu̲ 通じます

communication *n* (*traffic*) kōtsū 交通, ōrai 往来; (*message, news*) táyori 便り, tsūshin 通信

Communist *n* kyōsan shugí-sha 共産主義者

community *n* komyuniti コミュニティ, komyunitii コミュニティー, (*society*) shákai 社会

commute *v* kayoimásu̲ 通います; ***~ to work*** tsūkin shimásu̲ 通勤します

commuter *n* **1.** (*to work*) tsūkinsha 通勤者 **2.** (*goes to school*) tsūgaku-sha 通学者

companion *n* nakamá 仲間; (o-)

tsure (お)連れ, (o-)tómo (お)供, tomodachi 友達; (o-)aite (お)相手

company *n* (*firm*) kaisha 会社, ... -sha ... 社; (*within the office/ company*) shánai (no) 社内(の); (*group*) kumí 組; (*social*) tsuki-ai 付き合い・つきあい, kōsai 交際; (*guests*) raikyaku 来客, (o-)kyaku (お)客, o-kyaku-san/sámá お客さん/さま・様; **keep one company** ... to tsuki-aimásu ... と付き合います・つきあいます

compare *v* kurabemásu 比べます, hikaku shimásu 比較します; taishō/taihi shimásu 対照/対比します; (*collates*) terashimásu 照らします; ***as compared with*** ... ni tái-shite ... に対して

comparison *n* hikaku 比較; taishō 対照, taihi 対比

compass *n* (*for directions*) rashinban 羅針盤; (*for drafting*) konpasu コンパス

compassion *n* (o-)násake (お)情け

compatibility *n* aishō´ 相性

compensate *v* mukuimásu 報います; (*indemnifies*) hoshō shimásu 補償します; (*certify*) hoshō shimásu 保証します

compensation *n* (*indemnity money*) hoshō-kin 補償金, benshō 弁償, baishō 賠償

compete *v* kisoimásu 競います, kyōsō shimásu 競争します

competency *n* (*qualification*) shikaku 資格

competition *n* kyōsō 競争

competitive *adj* **1.** (*fiercely-~*) kyōsō no hageshii 競争の激しい **2.** (*strong desire to compete*) kyōsō-shin no tsuyoi 競争心の強い

competitor *n* kyōsō-áite 競争相手

complain *v* (*gives utterance*) fuhei/mónku o iimásu 不平/文句を言います; (guchi o) koboshimásu (ぐち・愚痴を)こぼします; (*mutters to oneself*) butsu-butsu iimásu ぶつぶつ言います; kujō o iimásu 苦情を言います; (*makes a formal accusation*) uttaemásu 訴えます

complaint *n* fuhei 不平, mónku 文句, kujō 苦情, (o-)kógoto (お)小言, guchi ぐち・愚痴; (*lawsuit*) uttae 訴え

complement *n* hosoku 補足, hojū 補充

complete 1. *becomes ~* *v* (*full*) michimásu 満ちます **2. *~s it*** *v* kansei shimásu 完成します; (*a set*) soroemásu 揃えます **3.** oginaimásu 補います

complete *adj* (*exhaustive*) mō´ra shita ... 網羅した...

completely *adv* mattakú 全く・まったく, to(t)temo と(っ)ても, sukkári すっかり, sokkúri そっくり; (+ [NAGATIVE]) zenzen 全然; (*all*) zénbu 全部・ぜんぶ, minná みんな・皆

complex *n* konpurekkusu コンプレックス, rettō-kan 劣等感

complexion *n* kao-iro 顔色

complicated *adj* fukuzatsu (na) 複雑(な), komi-itta 込み入った・こみいった, yaya(k)koshíi やや(っ)こしい, wazurawashii 煩わしい; ***gets ~*** kojiremásu こじれます, motsuremásu もつれます

complications *n* (*details*) ikisatsu いきさつ・経緯; (*entanglements*) motsure もつれ

compliment *n* seji 世辞, o-seji お世辞, home-kotoba ほめ言葉

comply; ~ *with* *v* ... ni ō-jimásu ... に応じます; ... o nattoku shimásu ... を納得します

component *n* séibun 成分

compose *v* (*writes*) tsuzurimásu 綴ります・つづります, tsukurimásu 作ります

composed *adj* (*unruffled*) heiki (na) 平気(な); reisei (na) 冷静(な)

composite *adj* sōgō-teki (na) 総合的(な)

composition *n* (*writing*) sakubun 作文; (*constituency*) kōsei 構成

comprehend → **understand** → **include** → **comprise** → **consist of**

comprehension *n* rikai 理解

comprehensive *adj* (*composite*) sōgō-teki (na) 総合的(な)

compress *v* **1.** (*constricts*) asshuku shimásu 圧縮します **2.** (*presses*) appaku shimásu 圧迫します **3.** (*shortens*) tanshuku shimásu 短縮します

comprise *v* (*includes all items*) mō´ra shimásu 網羅します

compromise **1.** *n* (*gives in*) dakyō 妥協 **2.** *v* dakyō shimásu 妥協します

compulsion *n* **1.** (*psychology*) shōdō kyōhaku 衝動強迫 **2.** (*forcing*) kyōsei 強制

compulsive *adj* **1.** (*psychology*) kyōhaku kan'nen no aru 強迫観念のある, osaerarenai 抑えられない **2.** (*very interesting or compelling*) hito (no kokoro) o hikitsukeru 人(の心)を引きつける

compulsory *adj* **1.** (*stipulated*) kitei (no) 規定(の) **2.** (*obligatory*) gimu-teki (na) 義務的(な) **3.** (*required*) hissu (no) 必須(の); **compulsory education** *n* gimu-kyō´iku 義務教育

computation *n* keisan 計算

compute *v* keisan shimásu 計算します

computer *n* konpyū´ta コンピュータ, konpyū´tā コンピューター

computer science *n* konpyū´ta-ka/konpyū´tā saiensu コンピュータ/コンピューター・サイエンス, jōhō kagaku 情報科学, jōhō kōgaku 情報工学

comrade *n* (...) dō´shi (...)同志, (...) nakama (...)仲間

con *n* sagi 詐欺; **con man** *n* sagi-shi 詐欺師・サギ師, peten-shi ペテン師

conceal → **hide** → **cover up**

conceit *n* [INFORMAL] unubore うぬぼれ, [FORMAL] kadai hyōka 過大評価

concentrate *v* shūchū shimásu̱ 集中します

concept *n* gáinen 概念, shi̱sō 思想

conception *n* **1.** (*concept*) gáinen 概念, shi̱sō 思想 **2.** (*fertilization*) jusei 受精 **3.** (*inception of pregnancy*) jutai 受胎, kainin 懐妊

concern **1.** *n* (*relevance*) kankei 関係, (*interest*) kanshin 関心; (*worry*) shinpai 心配; (*business*) kaisha 会社 **2.** *v* (*relates to*) ... ni kanshimásu̱ ... に関します

concerning *prep* ... ni kán-shi̱te ... に関して, ... o megutte ... を巡って

concert *n* ongák(u) -kai 音楽会, ensō´-kai 演奏会, consāto コンサート

concession *n* **1.** (*compromise*) jōho 譲歩 **2.** (*right*) tokken 特権

conciliate *v* nadamemásu̱ なだめます; wakai sasemásu̱ 和解させます; chōtei shimásu̱ 調停します

concise *adj* kanketsu (na) 簡潔(な)

conclude *v* (*brings to an end*) sumashimásu̱ 済まします; (*ends a discussion*) ketsuron shimásu̱ 結論します; (*finalizes*) seiritsu shimásu̱ 成立します

conclusion *n* **1.** (*of discussion*) ketsuron 結論; ***in*** **~** ketsuron to shi̱te 結論として **2.** (*finalization*) seiritsu 成立

concoct *v* koshiraemásu̱ こしらえます, tsukuriagemásu̱ 作り上げます

concrete **1.** *n* (*cement*) konkuríito コンクリート **2.** *adj* (*not abstract*) gutai-teki(na) 具体的(な)

concubine *n* o-mekake(-san) お妾(さん), nígō(-san) 二号(さん)

concur *v* (*agrees*) dōi shimásu̱ 同意します, (*coincides*) itchi shimásu̱ 一致します

concurrent *adj* (*occurring at the same time*) dōji ni okoru 同時に起こる

concussion *n* (*brain*) nō-shintō 脳しんとう

condemn *v* hinan shimásu̱ 非難します

condense *v* **1.** (*concentrates*) gyōshuku shimásu̱ 凝縮します, nōshuku shimásu̱ 濃縮します **2.** (*liquefies*) ekika shimásu̱ 液化します **3.** (*summarizes*) yōyaku shimásu̱ 要約します

condition *n* (*state*) ari-sama 有様・ありさま, jōtai 状態, jijō 事情, jissai 実際, guai 具合, chōshi 調子; (*stipulation*) jōken 条件

condolence *n* okuyami お悔やみ

condom *n* kondōmu コンドーム

condominium *n* kondominiamu コンドミニアム

condone *v* mokunin shimásu̱ 黙認します

conduct **1.** *n* (*behavior*) okonai 行い・おこない **2.** *v* michibimásu̱ 導きます, shi̱ki shimásu̱ 指揮します

conductor *n* (*train*) shashō(-san) 車掌(さん); (*orchestra*) shi̱kí̱-sha 指揮者

cone *n* ensui(-kei) 円錐(形), kōn コーン

confectionery *n* (o-)kashí-ya (お)菓子屋

confederacy *n* rengō 連合, dōmei (koku) 同盟(国)

confer *v* **1.** hanashi-aimásu 話し合います **2.** → **grant**

conference *n* (*personal*) sōdan 相談; [FORMAL] káigí 会議, taikai 大会; (*discussion*) kyō´gí 協議, (*negotiation*) hanashi-ai 話し合い

confess *v* **1.** hákujō shimásu 白状します, jihaku shimásu 自白します, kokuhaku shimásu 告白します **2.** (*frankly reveals*) uchi-akemásu 打ち明けます

confession *n* hákujō 白状; (*of sins*) zángé ざんげ・懺悔

confidence *n* shin'yō 信用, shinrai 信頼, tánomi 頼み; (*self-~*) jishin 自信; (*secure feeling*) anshin 安心

confidential *adj* naisho (no) 内緒(の)

confirm *v* (*a reservation*) (yoyaku o) kakunin shimásu (予約を)確認します

conflict *n* tatakai 戦い

confluence *n* gōryū 合流

conform (*with/to*) *v* ... ni shitagaimásu ... に従います, ... ni motozukimásu ... に基づきます

confront *v* ... ni tai-shimásu ... に対します; ... to tairitsu shimásu ... と対立します; (*opposes*) ... ni taikō shimásu ... に対抗します

confrontation *n* taikō 対抗

confound *v* **1.** kondō shimásu 混同します **2.** (*perplexes*) konwaku sasemásu 困惑させます

Confucius *n* Kōshi 孔子

confused; ***gets*** ~ komarimásu 困ります・こまります, (*flustered*) awatemásu 慌てます・あわてます; (*messy, disorderly*) mecha-mecha めちゃめちゃ

confusion *n* (*disorder*) konran 混乱, kónzatsu 混雑

congenial *adj* aishō´ ga(/no) íi 相性が(/の)いい

congested *n* (*traffic*) jūtai-jō´kyō 渋滞状況; ***is*** ~ jūtai shite imásu 渋滞しています

conglomerate *n* konguromaritto コングロマリット, fukugō-kigyō 複合企業

congratulate *n* (o-)iwai shimásu (お)祝いします

congratulation *n* shukuga 祝賀, o-iwai お祝い; ***Congratulations!*** O-medetō gozaimásu. おめでとうございます

congregate *v* shūgō shimásu 集合します

congress → **Diet; conference**

conjecture **1.** *n* suisoku 推測, (o-) sasshi (お)察し **2.** *v* (*guesses, supposes*) sas-shimásu 察します

conjugal *adj* fūfu (no) 夫婦(の), kon'in (no) 婚姻(の)

conjunction *n* setsuzókú-shi 接続詞

connect (*with*) *v* (... to) tsunagimásu (... と)つなぎます; ... to

renraku shimásu ... と連絡します; tsū-jimásu 通じます
connection *n* renraku 連絡; (*relevance*) kankei 関係; (*relation*) tsunagari つながり; (*link*) tsunagi つなぎ
conscience *n* ryō´shin 良心
conscientious *adj* majime (na) まじめ・真面目(な); ryōshin-teki (na) 良心的(な)
consciousness *n* íshiki 意識, obóé 覚え; ***loses*** ~ íshiki o ushi-naimásu 意識を失います
conscription *n* (*for military service*) shōshū 召集・招集
consent *v* shōchi/shōdaku/dōi shimásu 承知/承諾/同意します, nattoku shimásu 納得します
consequence → result
conservative *adj* hoshu-teki (na) 保守的(な); shōkyoku-teki (na) 消極的(な); (*moderate*) uchiwa (na) 内輪(な)
conserve **1.** *v* (*saves*) setsuyaku shimásu 節約します **2.** *n* (*fruit jam*) jamu ジャム
consider *v* kangaemásu 考えます; (*takes into account*) kō´ryo ni iremásu 考慮に入れます
considerable *adj* sōtō (na) 相当(な), yohodo (no) 余程(の), yoppodo (no)よっぽど(の)
consist; ~ ***of*** ...kara nátte imásu ...から成っています
consolation *n* nagusame 慰め・なぐさめ, ian 慰安
conspicuous *adj* ichijirushíi 著しい・いちじるしい; medátta ... 目立った..., medátte imásu 目立っています
constant *adj* chakujitsu (na) 着実(な); fuhen (no) 不変の
constantly → always
constipation *n* benpi 便秘
constitute *v* kōsei shimásu 構成します
constitution *n* **1.** (*basic laws*) kénpō 憲法; ***Constitution (Memorial) Day*** (*3 May*) Kenpō-kinénbi 憲法記念日 **2.** (*physical*) taishitsu 体質 **3.** (*composition*) kōsei 構成
construct → build
construction *n* (*work*) kō´ji 工事; ***under*** ~ kōji-chū 工事中; (*building*) kensetsu 建設
construe *v* káishaku shimásu 解釈します
consul *n* ryō´ji 領事; **consul general** *n* sō-ryō´ji 総領事
consulate *n* ryōjí-kan 領事館
consult *v* (*a person*) ... to sōdan shimásu ... と相談します
consultant *n* kómon 顧問 , kon-sárutanto コンサルタント
consumer *n* shōhí-sha 消費者
consumption *n* shōhi 消費; **consumption tax** *n* (*duty*) shōhi-zei 消費税
contact **1.** *n* sesshoku 接触; ***comes in*** ~ (*with ...*) (... ni) furemásu (...に)触れます, ses-shimásu 接します, sesshoku shimásu 接触します **2.** *v* (~*s a person*) ... to

renraku shimásu と連絡します, ... ni aimásu ... に会います
contact lenses *n* kontakuto-rénzu コンタクトレンズ, kontákuto コンタクト
contagious disease *n* densenbyō 伝染病
contain *v* ... ga háitte imásu ... が入っています; ... o fukumimásu ... を含みます
container *n* ire-mono 入れ物, yō´ki 容器; (*box*) hako 箱; (*for transporting goods*) kónténa コンテナ
contamination *n* osen 汚染
contempt *n* keibetsu 軽蔑
contented *adj* ... de mánzoku shimásu ... で満足します; osamarimásu 治まります
contents *n* nakámi 中身, naiyō 内容; (*table of ~s*) mokuji 目次, midashi 見出し
contest *n* konkū´ru コンクール, kóntesuto コンテスト; (*competition*) kyōsō 競争; (*sports*) kyō´gi 競技
continent *n* tairiku 大陸
continuation *n* tsuzuki 続き
continue *v* (*it ~s*) tsuzukimásu 続きます; (*~s it*) tsuzukemásu 続けます
contraceptive *n* **1.** hinín-yaku 避妊薬, (*pills*) keikō-hinín-yaku 経口避妊薬 **2.** (*device*) hinín-gu 避妊具; (*condom*) kondō´mu コンドーム
contract **1.** *n* (*an agreement*) keiyaku 契約 **2.** *v* (*agrees to undertake work*) ukeoimásu 請け負います
contractor *n* ukeoí-nin 請け負い人
contradict *v* ... ni sakaraimásu ... に逆らいます → **deny**
contradiction *n* (*inconsistency*) mujun 矛盾
contrary *adj* hantai (no) 反対(の); gyaku (no) 逆(の); ***acts ~ to*** (*goes against*) ... ni han-shimásu ... に反します, ... ni sakaraimásu ... に逆らいます
contrast **1.** *n* taishō/taihi 対照/対比 **2.** *v* (*compares*) kurabemásu 比べます; ***in ~ to/with*** ... ni tái-shite ... に対して, ... ni hán-shite ... に反して
control **1.** *n* shíhai 支配, kánri 管理; (*of prices, etc.*) tōsei 統制 **2.** *v* (*supervises it*) tori-shimarimásu 取り締まります; (*restrains*) osaemásu 抑えます; (*operates equipment*) sōjū shimásu 操縦します
controversy *n* ronsō 論争
convenience *n* (go-)tsugō (ご)都合, tsuide ついでに; ***at your ~*** tsuide no sai ついでの際, tsuide no tokí ni ついでの時に
convenience store *n* konbini コンビニ
convenient *adj* bénri (na) 便利(な), bén ga íi 便がいい; chō´hō (na) 重宝(な); (*easy to arrange*) tsugō ga íi 都合がいい
convent *n* shūdō´-in 修道院
convention → **conference, meeting**
conventional *adj* heibon (na) 平凡(な)
conversation *n* (*ordinary*) hanashí

話, danwa 談話; (*in language class, etc.*) kaiwa 会話
conversion *n* henkan 変換; **~ key** henkan-kíi 変換キー
convert *v* hiki-kaemásu 引き変えます
convey *v* hakobimásu 運びます
cook 1. *n* ryōri-nin 料理人, kók-ku(-san) コック(さん), (*Japanese chef*) itamae 板前 2. *v* (*~s it*) ryóˊri shimásu 料理します, 3. *v* (*it boils*) niemásu 煮えます
cool 1. *adj* suzushíi 涼しい; (*calm*) reisei (na) 冷静(な); (*unperturbed*) heiki (na) 平気(な) 2. *v* **it ~s off/ down** samemásu 冷めます, hie-másu 冷えます; (*~s it*) hiyashi-másu 冷やします
cooperation *n* kyōryoku 協力; (*joint activity*) kyōdō 共同
copy 1. *n* (*of a book*) ... -bu ... 部, ichí-bu 一部 2. *n* (*photocopy*) kópii コピー 3. *n* (*reproduction*) fukusha 複写, fukusei 複製 4. *v* (*copies it*) utsushimásu 写します, fukusha/fukusei shimásu 複写/複製します; (*imitates*) nisemásu 似せます; (*makes a ~*) kópii o torimásu, コピーをとります
cord *n* himo ひも・ヒモ・紐, nawá なわ・縄, kōˊdo コード
cordial *adj* shínsetsu (na) 親切(な), kokoro no komotta 心のこもった
core *n* shín しん・心・芯
cork *n* kóruku コルク, sén 栓, korukú-sen コルク栓
cormorant *n* u ウ・鵜; **cormorant fishing** *n* ukai 鵜飼い
corn *n* 1. (*maize*) tō-mórokoshi トウモロコシ, kōn コーン 2. (*on skin*) uonome 魚の目; (*callus*) táko たこ, (*bunion*) mamé まめ; soko-mame 底まめ
corner *n* (*outside*) kádo 角; (*inside*) súmi 隅
corporation *n* 1. (*joint-stock corporation*) kabushiki-gáisha 株式会社 2. (*incorporated association*) shadan 社団 3. (*public corporation*) kōdan 公団
corps *n* gundan 軍団; ***Peace Corps*** heiwa-bútai 平和部隊
corpse *n* shitai 死体, nakigara なきがら・亡骸, shigai 死骸
correct 1. *adj* tadashíi 正しい 2. *v* atarimásu 当たります; (*~s it*) naoshimásu 直します, aratame-másu 改めます
correspond (*to ...*) *v* (... ni) taiō shimásu (...に)対応します
correspondence *n* (*messages*) tsūshin 通信; (*equivalence*) taiō 対応
corridor *n* rōka 廊下
cosmetics *n* (o-)keshō (お)化粧, keshō-hin 化粧品
cost 1. *n* (*expense*) híyō 費用 2. *v* **it ~s** (*how much*) (íkura) shimásu (いくら)します; (*requires*) yō-shimásu 要します; **at any cost** nán to shité mo 何としても, náni ga nánde mo 何が何でも

costly → **expensive**
costume *n* fu̲ku̲sō 服装
cotton *n* wata 綿, momen 木綿, kotton コットン
couch *n* ne-isu 寝椅子, naga-isu 長椅子
cough *v* sekí o shimásu̲ 咳をします
could → **can; maybe**
counsel **1.** *n* (*guide, coach*) shidōsha 指導者 **2.** *v* (*~s them*) shidō shimásu̲ 指導します
count *v* kazoemásu̲ 数えます
counter *n* (*shop* ~) uri-ba 売り場
counterclockwise *adj* hidari-máwari (ni) 左回り(に)
counterfeit **1.** *adj* nise (no) 偽(の) **2.** *v* nisemásu̲ 似せます; **counterfeit bill** *n* (*currency*) nisesatsu 偽札・にせ札・贋札
country *n* **1.** kuni 国;... -koku ... 国 **2.** (*countryside*) inaka いなか・田舎; (*outdoors*) yagai 野外
county *n* gún 郡 (*U.S.*); shū́ 州 (*Britain*)
couple → **two; a couple** *n* (*husband and wife*) fū́fu 夫婦
courage *n* yū́ki 勇気
course *n* kṓsu コース; (*in school*) kamoku 科目; (*of action*) hōshin 方針; (*of time*) keika 経過; (*development*) nariyuki 成り行き・なりゆき; ***in the ~ ... of*** (*during*) ...-chu (ni) 中(に)
court *n* **1.** (*of law*) saiban-sho 裁判所, hōtei 法廷 **2.** (*sports*) kōto コート **3.** (*imperial/royal*) kyūtei 宮廷; **court dances and music** *n* búgaku 舞楽
courtesy *n* reigí 礼儀
cousin *n* itóko いとこ・従兄弟・従姉妹
cover *n* (*lid*) fu̲ta ふた・蓋; kabā カバー; (*book, magazine, etc.*) hyōshí 表紙
cover *v* **1.** (*~s it*) ōimásu̲ 覆[おお]います; (*includes all items*) mṓra shimásu̲ 網羅します **2.** ***~s up*** (*conceals*) fu̲semásu̲ 伏せます
cow *n* ushi 牛・ウシ
coward *n* okubyō-mono 臆病[憶病・おくびょう]者
crab *n* kani カニ・蟹
crack **1.** *n* su̲ki (-ma) 透き(間); (*wide*) ware-me 割れ目; (*fine*) hibí ひび・ヒビ; (*flaw*) kizu 傷 **2.** ***it ~s*** *v* waremásu̲ 割れます
cradle *n* yuri-kago ゆりかご・揺り籠
crag *n* iwá 岩
cram; ***~s it in*** *v* tsumemásu̲ 詰めます; ***it is crammed in*** tsumarimásu̲ 詰まります
cram school *n* júku 塾
cramp *n* **1.** (*leg*) tsuru つる **2.** (*stomach*) ikeiren 胃痙攣・胃けいれん
crane *n* **1.** (*bird*) tsúru ツル・鶴 **2.** (*machine*) kurḗn クレーン
crash *n* (*plane*) tsuiraku 墜落; (*collision*) shōtotsu 衝突
crass *adj* egetsunái えげつない
crate *n* wakú 枠, hako 箱

crater *n* funka -kō 噴火口
crawl *v* haimásu はいます・這います
crazy *adj* **1.** ki-chigái (no) 気違い・きちがい(の) **2.** ***is ~ about*** ... ni muchū désu ... に夢中です
cream *n* kuríimu クリーム; **cream puff** *n* shū-kurímu シュークリーム
crease *n* **1.** shiwa しわ・皺 **2.** (*pleat*) orimé 折り目
create *v* tsukurimásu 造[創]ります
creator *n* (*god*) sōzō-shu 創造主, (*artists*) kurieitā クリエイター
creature *n* séibutsu 生物, kuriichā クリーチャー
credit *n* **1.** shin'yō 信用 **2.** (*one's ~*) noren のれん・暖簾 **3.** (*on ~*) kaké 掛け; ***buys it on ~*** (*on one's account*) tsuké de kaimásu つけで買います; **credit sales** *n* kakeuri 掛け売り, uri-kake 売り掛け
creed *n* shinjō 信条
creek *n* ogawa 小川
creep **1.** *v* haimásu はい[這い]ます; (*baby*) hai hai shimásu はいはいします **2.** ***that ~*** *n* aitsu あいつ
cremation *n* kasō 火葬, shōkyaku 焼却
crematorium *n* kasō-ba 火葬場
crest; ***family ~*** *n* monshō 紋章, món 紋, kamon 家紋
crevice *n* ware-me 割れ目
crew *n* (*member*) norikumí-in 乗組員, (*of ship*) sen'in 船員
crime *n* tsúmi 罪, hanzai 犯罪
criminal *n* (*culprit*) hánnin 犯人
crimson *adj* makká (na) 真っ赤・まっか(な)
cripple *n* shintai shōgaisha 身体障害者
crisis *n* (*critical moment*) kíkí 危機
crisp *adj* paripari (no) パリパリ・ぱりぱり(の)
criterion *n* (*standard of judgment*) monosáshí ものさし・物差し・物指し, kijun 基準
critic *n* hihyō-ka 批評家, (*judge*) hihán-sha 批判者; (*commentator*) hyōron-ka 評論家
critical *adj* (*judgmental*) hihan-teki (na) 批判的(な); (*urgent*) kinkyū (na) 緊急(な); **critical moment** *n* kíkí 危機
criticize *v* hihyō shimásu 批評します; (*judges*) hihan shimásu 批判します; (*comments on*) hyōron shimásu 評論します; (*censures*) sememásu 責めます
crocodile *n* wáni ワニ・鰐
crony *n* nakama 仲間
crop *n* (*harvest*) minori 実り, shūkaku 収穫
cross **1.** *n* (*symbol*) júji 十字; (*wooden*) jūji-ka 十字架 **2.** *n* ("×") bátsu ばつ (*vs.* maru 丸 "○")
cross *v* **1.** (*goes across*) watarimásu 渡ります, yoko-girimásu 横切ります; (*goes over a height*) koemásu 越えます **2.** (*~es one's*

legs) ashí o kumimás<u>u</u> 脚を組みます

crossing *n* (*street intersection*) kōsa-ten 交差点

crouch *v* shagamimás<u>u</u> しゃがみます; (*so as not to be seen*) mi o f<u>u</u>semás<u>u</u> 身を伏せます

crow *n* kárasu カラス・烏・鴉

crowd *n* gunshū 群衆, renjū/renchū 連中; ***in crowds*** zórozoro ぞろぞろ

crowded; *gets ~* komimás<u>u</u> こみます・混みます

crowdfunding *n* (*raising money from people via the Internet*) kuraudo fandingu クラウドファンディング

crown *n* ōkan 王冠

Crown Prince *n* Kōtáishi 皇太子, Kōtáishi-sama 皇太子様; ***Crown Princess*** Kōtáishi-hi 皇太子妃

crude *adj* sómatsu (na) 粗末(な), zatsu (na) 雑(な)

cruel *adj* mugói むごい, tsurai つらい・辛い, hakujō (na) 薄情(な), zankoku (na) 残酷(な), zangyaku (na) 残虐(な)

cruise *n* kurūzu クルーズ, funatabi 船旅

crumble *v* (*it ~s*) kudakemás<u>u</u> 砕けます; (*~s it*) kudakimás<u>u</u> 砕きます

crush *v* (*~es it*) tsubushimás<u>u</u> つぶします・潰します; (*it gets crushed*) tsuburemás<u>u</u> つぶれます・潰れます

crust *n* kawá 皮

crutch *n* matsuba-zúe 松葉杖

cry *v* nakimás<u>u</u> 泣きます; (*cries out*) sakebimás<u>u</u> 叫びます

crystal *n* suishō 水晶, kesshō 結晶, kurisutaru クリスタル

cub *n* ko 子

cube *n* rippō (-tai) 立方(体)

cuckoo *n* kákkō カッコウ; (*little*) hototógisu ホトトギス

cucumber *n* kyū́ri キュウリ; (*sushi-bar term*) kappa カッパ

cuff *n* káf<u>u</u>su カフス

culprit *n* hánnin 犯人

cult *n* karuto カルト

cultivate *v* tagayashimás<u>u</u> 耕します

cultural shock *n* karuchā-shokku カルチャーショック

culture *n* (*refinement*) kyōyō 教養; (*farming*) yōshok<u>u</u> 養殖; (*civilization*) búnka 文化; ***Culture Day*** (*3 November*) Búnka no hí 文化の日; **culture center** *n* karuchā sentā カルチャーセンター

cunning *adj* zurúi ずるい

cup *n* (o-)cháwan (お)茶碗, koppu コップ, (*with handle*) káppu カップ; (*cupful*) ... -hai ... 杯

cupboard *n* (*enclosed shelves*) todana 戸棚; (*closet*) oshi-ire 押し入れ

curb 1. *n* (*of road*) hodṓ no fuchí 歩道の縁・ふち **2.** *v* yokusei 抑制します **3.** *v* (*restrains*) yokusei shimás<u>u</u> 抑制します

cure *v* naoshimás<u>u</u> 治します

curios *n* kottō-hin 骨董品 → **antique**
curiosity *n* kōkíshin 好奇心
curious *adj* (*inquisitive*) monózukí (na) 物好き(な); (*novel*) mezurashíi 珍しい・めずらしい
currant *n* rēzun レーズン; hoshibudō 干しブドウ
currency *n* (*bill/note*) (o-)satsu (お)札; shihei 紙幣
current 1. *adj* (*present*) génzai no ... 現在の..., gén (-) ... 現...; current address *n* gen-jū´sho 現住所 2. *n* (*tide*) chōryū 潮流; current affairs *n* jiji(mondai) 時事(問題) 3. *n* (*electrical*) denryū 電流
curriculum *n* karikyuramu カリキュラム
curriculum vitae *n* rirekisho 履歴書
curry *n* karē カレー; (*with rice*) karē-ráisu カレーライス
curse 1. *n* noroi のろい・呪い 2. *v* (*utters a ~*) noroimásu のろい[呪い]ます, (*reviles*) nonoshirimásu ののしります・罵る
cursor *n* (*computer*) kāsoru カーソル
cursory *adj* 1. (*hasty*) isogi (no) 急ぎ(の) 2. (*superficial*) hyōmen-teki (na) 表面的(な) 3. (*perfunctory*) ozanari (na) おざなり(な)
curt *adj* bu-áisō (na) 無愛想(な), bukkírábō (na) ぶっきらぼう(な)
curtail *v* herashimásu 減らします
curtain *n* kā´ten カーテン; (*bamboo*) sudare すだれ; (*stage*) makú 幕
curve 1. *n* magari 曲がり; (*road*) kābu カーブ; (*bend*) sorí そり・反り, (*arch*) yumi-gata 弓形 **2.** *it ~s* *v* magarimásu 曲がります **3.** *~s it* *v* magemásu 曲げます
cushion *n* (*seat*) zabúton 座布団; (*spread*) shiki-mono 敷物; kusshon クッション
custodian *n* 1. (*janitor*) kózukai 小使い, yōmu-in 用務員 2. (*administrator*) kanri-nin 管理人
custody *n* (*child custody*) yōiku-ken 養育権
custom *n* 1. shūkan 習慣 2. (*tradition*) dentō 伝統
customary *adj* jū´rai (no) 従来(の)
customer *n* (o-)kyaku (お)客, o-kyaku-sámá お客様; (*patron*) otokui お得意, tokui-saki 得意先; customer service *n* kasutamā sābisu カスタマーサービス
customs *n* (*place*) zeikan 税関; (*tariff*) kanzei 関税, zéi 税; customs duty *n* kanzei 関税
cut 1. *v* kirimásu 切ります; (*mows*) karimásu 刈ります; (*it ~s well*) kiremásu 切れます 2. *n* (*of cloth*) kata 型; (*share*) wake-mae 分け前; (*percentage*) rítsu 率; cuts the price *v* makemásu 負けます; cut across *v* yoko-girimásu 横切ります; cut back *v* sakugenshimásu 削減します; cut class *v* saborimásu さぼります; cut down *v* (*lessens*) herashimásu 減らします; (*reduces*) chijimemásu ちぢめます・縮めます; (*dilutes*)

warimásu 割ります; cut off *v* ki--rimásu 切ります; tachimásu 裁ちます・断ちます・絶ちます

cute *adj* kawaíi かわいい・可愛い, kawairashíi かわいらしい・可愛らしい

cuticle *n* **1.** (*nail*) amakawa 甘皮 **2.** (*hair*) kyutikuru キューティクル **3.** kuchikura クチクラ

cutlery *n* **1.** (*cutting instruments*) há-mono 刃物 **2.** (*tableware*) shokki-rui 食器類

cutlet *n* kátsu(retsu) カツ(レツ); **pork cutlet** *n* tonkatsu 豚カツ・とんかつ・トンカツ

cuttlefish *n* (*squid*) ika イカ

cyberattack/digital attack *n* saibā kōgeki サイバー攻撃

cybercrime *n* saibā hanzai サイバー犯罪

cyberspace *n* saibā-supēsu サイバースペース

cycle *n* (*circulation*) junkan 循環, saikuru サイクル

cyclone *n* saikuron サイクロン, teikiatsu 低気圧

cylinder *n* tsutsu 筒, shirindā シリンダー

cymbal *n* shinbaru シンバル

cynical *adj* hiniku (na) 皮肉(な), shinikaru (na) シニカル(な)

Cyprus *n* kipurosu キプロス

cyst *n* nōhō 嚢胞・のうほう; nōshu 脳腫・のうしゅ

Czechoslovakia *n* chekosurobakia チェコスロバキア

D

dab *n* hitonuri ひと塗り・ひとぬり

daddy, dad *n* papa パパ

dagger *n* tanken 短剣

daily *n* **1.** *n* (*newspaper*) nikkan(-shi) 日刊(紙) **2.** *adj* (*everyday*) mainichi(no) 毎日(の)

dainty *adj* **1.** (*delicate beauty*) yūbi (na) 優美(な), **2.** *n* (*something delicious*) oishii-mono おいしいもの・美味しいもの

dairy *n* (*milk shop*) *n* gyūnyū-ya 牛乳屋

dam *n* dámu ダム

damage **1.** *n* songai 損害; són 損・そん, gái 害, higai 被害・ひがい, damēji ダメージ **2.** *~s it* *v* itamemásu 傷めます, arashimásu 荒らします・あらします; sokonaimásu そこないます・損ないます

Damn! *interj* Shimátta! しまった！

damn (*fool*) *n* …-me …め; *~ idiot* baka-me ばかめ

damp **1.** *adj* shimeppoi 湿っぽい・しめっぽい; **2.** *gets ~ v* shimerimás 湿ります・しめります, nuremásu ぬれます・濡れます

dampness *n* shikki 湿気, shikke 湿気・しっけ

dance **1.** *n* odori 踊り・おどり,

dansu ダンス **2.** *~s v* odorimásu 踊ります・おどります

dancer *n* (*Japanese-style*) odori-te 踊り手; (*Western-style*) dansā ダンサー

dandruff *n* fuke ふけ

Dane *n* (*people*) dēn-zoku デーン族, denmāku no minzoku デンマークの民族

danger *n* kiken 危険・キケン; (*crisis*) kyū 急; (*fear/worry lest …*) … osoré/shinpai …恐れ・おそれ/心配

dangerous *adj* abunai 危ない・あぶない, kiken (na) 危険(な); yabái やばい; (*delicate, ticklish*) kiwadói きわどい

dangle *v* (*dangles it*) sagemásu 下げます, tarashimásu 垂らします; (*it dangles*) taremásu 垂れます

Danish *n* **1.** (*language*) denmāku-go デンマーク語; (*person*) denmāku-jin デンマーク人 **2.** (*pastry*) denishu デニッシュ

dare (*to do*) *v* áete (shimásu) あえて(します)

dark **1.** *adj* kurai 暗い; (*color*) kói [COLOR NAME] (no) 濃い・こい [COLOR NAME] (の) **2.** *the ~ n* higure 日暮れ, yamí 闇; *it gets ~* hi ga kuremásu 日が暮れます

darkness *n* (kura-)yami (暗)闇・(暗)やみ

darling *adj* kawaíi かわいい・可愛い, kawairashíi かわいらしい・可愛らしい

darts *n* dātsu ダーツ

dashboard *n* dasshu-bōdo ダッシュボード

data *n* dēˊta データ, shiryō 資料

database *n* dētabēsu データベース

date *n* **1.** (*of month*) hizuke 日付(け)・日づけ; (*complete*) nen-gáppi 年月日; *~ of birth* seinen-gáppi 生年月日 **2.** (*engagement*) (o-)yakusoku (お)約束・(お)やくそく **3.** (*a couple*) dēto (shimásu) デート(します)

date *n* (*fruit*) natsume なつめ

daughter *n* musume(-san) 娘・むすめ(さん); (*your*) ojōˊ san お嬢さん; *eldest ~* chōjo 長女

dawn *n* yoaké 夜明け・夜あけ, akegata 明け方・あけがた

day *n* hi 日, …hí …日; (*daytime*) (o-)híru・(お)ひる・お昼, hirumá 昼間・ひるま; *the ~ in question, that very ~* tōˊjitsu 当日; (*fixed*) hinichi 日にち・ひにち; **day after tomorrow** *n* asátte あさって・明後日, myōˊgo-nichi 明後日; **day before last/yesterday** *n* ototói おととい・一昨日, issakú-jitsu 一昨日; **day off** *n* yasumí (no hí) 休み・やすみ(の日), kyūka 休暇

daydream **1.** *n* kūsōˊ 空想, haku-chūmu 白昼夢 **2.** *v* bon'yári shimásu ぼんやりします

daylight *n* nitchū 日中, hiru no hikari 昼の光

days *n 1 day* ichi-nichí 一日, *2 days* futsuka 二日, *3 days* mikka 三日, *4 days* yokka 四日, *5 days* itsuka 五日, *6 days* muika 六日,

7 days nanoka 七日, *8 days* yōˊka 八日, *9 days* kokonoka 九日, *10 days* tōˊka 十日, *14 days* jú-yokka 十四日, *24 days* ní-jū yokka 二十四日; (*others* …-nichi … 日)

dazed; ***gets ~*** bōˊtto shimásu ぼうっとします, madoimásu 惑います・まどいます

dazzling *adj* mabushíi まぶしい・眩しい, mabayui まばゆい・眩い

DC, direct current *n* chokuryū 直流

dead **1.** *adj* shinda …死んだ…; ***is ~*** shinde imásu 死んでいます **2.** ***~ person*** *n* nakunatta hitó 亡くなった人, shinda hitó 死んだ人, shinin 死人

deaden *v* **1.** (*becomes dead*) shinimásu 死にます **2.** (*makes less sensitive*) mu-kankaku ni shimásu 無感覚にします **3.** (*weakens*) yowamarimásu 弱まります

deadline *n* shimekiri 締め切り・〆切(り)・しめきり, (saishū-) kígen (最終)期限, kíjitsu 期日

deaf **1.** *n* (*person*) mimí no kikoe-nai hito 耳の聞こえない人; ***is ~*** mimí ga fú-jiyū desu 耳が不自由です **2.** *adj* mimí no kikoenai 耳の聞こえない, mimí ga fujiyū na 耳が不自由な

deafness *n* nanchō 難聴

deal **1.** *n* (*transaction*) torí-hiki 取引 **2.** *v* (*cards*) kubarimásu 配ります; ***a good/great ~*** → **lots, much**; **deal in** (*sells*) urimásu 売ります, hanbai shimásu 販売します; **deal with** tori-atsukaimásu 取り扱います; (*treats a person*) ashiraimásu あしらいます; (*copes*) shóri/shóbun/shóchi shimásu 処理/処分/処置します

dealer *n* kouriten 小売店, (*retail outlet*) hanbái-ten 販売店, diirā ディーラー

dean *n* gakubu-chō 学部長

dear *adj* **1.** (*beloved*) itoshíi いとしい・愛しい, natsukashíi 懐かしい・なつかしい **2.** (*precious*) taisetsu (na) 大切(な); ***Dear dear!*** *interj* Oyaoya! おやおや!; ***Dear me!*** *interj* (*feminine*) Mā! まあ! **3.** → **expensive**

dearly *adv* hijō (ni) 非常(に), kokoro-kara 心から

death *n* shí 死

debacle *n* hōkai 崩壊, dōraku 道楽

debatable *adj* giron no yochi ga aru 議論の余地がある

debate **1.** *n* tōˊron 討論, ronsōˊ 論争 **2.** ***~s it*** *v* ron-jimásu 論じます

debauchery *n* hōtō 放蕩

debit *n* fusai 負債, (*bookkeeping*) karikata 借方

debris *n* zangai 残骸・残がい

debt *n* shakkín 借金

debug *n* debaggu デバッグ

debut *n* debyū デビュー

decade *n* jū nen-kan 十年間・10年間

decadence *n* taihai 退廃

decaffeinated *adj* kafein nuki (no) カフェイン抜き(の)

decay **1.** *v* kuchimásu 朽ちます; kusarimásu 腐ります・くさります **2.** *n* [BOOKISH] fuhai 腐敗

deceased *n* ***the ~*** kojin 故人

deceive → **cheat**

deceit *n* **1.** (*lie*) itsuwari 偽り・いつわり **2.** (*fraud*) sagi 詐欺・サギ

deception *n* (*cheat*) gomakashi ごまかし, (*fraud*) sagi 詐欺・サギ

December *n* Jūni-gatsú 十二月・12月

decency *n* reigi 礼儀

decent *adj* (*respectable*) jō´hin (na) 上品(な), rippa (na) 立派・りっぱ(な)

decide *v* kimemásu 決めます・きめます; kettei shimásu 決定します

decision *n* kettei 決定

deck *n* **1.** (*of ship*) kanpan 甲板, dékki デッキ **2.** → **pack** (*of cards*)

decline *v* **1.** (*refuses*) kotowarimásu 断わります・ことわります, jitai shimásu 辞退します **2.** (*it fades*) otoroemásu 衰えます

decode *v* kaidoku shimásu 解読します

decompose *v* (*rots*) fuhai shimásu 腐敗します

decor *n* sōshoku (hin) 装飾(品)

decorate *v* kazarimásu 飾ります・かざります

decoration *n* kazari(-mono) 飾り・かざり(物), sō´shoku 装飾, dekorēshon デコレーション

decorator *n* sōshoku-sha 装飾者

decoy *n* otori おとり

decrease **1.** *v* (*it ~s*) herimásu 減ります, genshō shimásu 減少します; (*~s it*) herashimásu 減らします・へらします **2.** *n* genshō 減少

decrepit *adj* **1.** (*infirm*) rōsui shita 老衰した **2.** (*dilapidated*) rōkyūka shita 老朽化した

dedicate *v* sasagemásu 捧げます

deduct *v* hikimásu 引きます・ひきます

deed *n* (*act*) shiwaza 仕業・しわざ, kō´i 行為, okonai 行い

deep *adj* **1.** fukái 深い・ふかい **2.** (*saturated color*) kói 濃い・こい; ***~ red*** makká (na) 真っ赤・まっか(な)

deer *n* shika 鹿・シカ

deface *v* gaikan o sokonaimásu 外観を損ないます

defamation *n* chūshō 中傷; (*~ of character*) meiyo-kison 名誉棄損

default *n* deforuto デフォルト, shoki-settei 初期設定

defeat **1.** *n* make 負け・まけ, shippai 失敗・しっぱい **2.** *v* (*~s*) makashimásu 負かします・まかします, yaburimásu 破ります・やぶります; (*is defeated*) makemásu 負けます・まけます, mairimásu 参ります・まいります

defecate *v* daibén o shimásu 大便をします

defect *n* ketten 欠点, kizu 傷・きず

defend *v* mamorimásu 守ります・まもります; kabaimásu 庇います・かばいます

defendant *n* hikoku(-nin) 被告(人)

defense *n* (*military*) bōei 防衛, (*sport*) bōgyo 防御, difensu ディフェンス

defer *v* nobashimásu̲ 延ばします・のばします

deference *n* **1.** (*obedience*) fukujū 服従 **2.** (*respect*) keii 敬意

defiant *adj* hankō-teki (na) 反抗的(な)

deficiency *n* fu̲soku 不足・ふそく, ketsubō 欠乏, kekkan 欠陥

deficit (*figures*) *n* aka-ji 赤字

defile *v* yogoshimásu̲ 汚します

define *v* teigi shimásu̲ 定義します

definite *adj* (*certain amount of*) ittei (no) 一定(の)

deformity *n* kikei 奇形

defy *v* …ni sakaraimásu̲ …に逆らいます

degenerate *adj* daraku shiteiru 堕落している, daraku shita 堕落した

degrade *v* (*to lower in dignity*) otoshimemásu̲ 貶めます・おとしめます

degree *n* **1.** (*extent*) téido 程度・ていど, dó 度, kagen 加減; … **2.** ***degrees*** (*temperature*) …-do …度; (*higher learning*) gákúi 学位

dehydrate *v* dassui-jōtai ni narimásu̲ 脱水状態になります

deity *n* shinsei 神性, kami 神

dejection *n* rakutan 落胆, iki shōchin 意気消沈

delay *v* (*~s it*) okurasemásu̲ 遅らせます・おくらせます; (*gets delayed*) okuremásu̲ 遅れます・おくれます

delegate **1.** *n* (*representative*) daihyō 代表 **2.** *n* (*alternate*) dairi (-nin) 代理(人) **3.** *v* (*commits to another*) inin shimásu̲ 委任します

delete *v* tori-keshimásu̲ 取り消します・とりけします

deliberate *adj* (*intentional*) kói (no) 故意(の); (*careful*) shinchō´ (na) 慎重・しんちょう(な)

delicate *adj* (*fine*) bimyō´ (na) 微妙(な); (*risky*) kiwadói きわどい・際どい

delicious *adj* oishii おいしい・美味しい, [INFORMAL] umái/nmái うまい・んまい

delight **1.** *adj* ***is delighted*** yorokobimásu̲ 喜びます・よろこびます; ***with great ~*** ō´-yórokobi (de) 大喜び(で) **2.** *n* yorokobi 喜び, tanoshimi 楽しみ

delinquent *n* (*juvenile ~*) hikō shōnen shōjo 非行少年少女, furyō 不良

delirium *n* (*pathology*) seishin sakuran 精神錯乱, (*excitement*) kōfun 興奮

deliver *v* todokemásu̲ 届けます・とどけます

delivery *n* **1.** haitatsu 配達, deribarii デリバリー; ***restaurant ~*** (*service/person*) demae 出前 **2.** (*giving birth*) shussan 出産

delta *n* (*plain*) sankaku-su 三角州

deluge *n* (*great flood*) dai-kōzui 大洪水, (*downpour*) gōu 豪雨
delusion *n* sakkaku 錯覚
deluxe *adj* jō´ 上, jō´tō´ (no) 上等(の), gō´ka (na) 豪華(な); **deluxe edition** *n* gōka-ban 豪華版
demand **1.** *n* yō´kyū/seikyū (shimás<u>u</u>) 要求/請求(します) **2.** *v* motomemás<u>u</u> 求めます; ***is in ~*** (*sells*) uremás<u>u</u> 売れます
democratic *adj* minshu-shúgi (no) 民主主義(の), minshu-teki (na) 民主的(な)
demolish *v* kuzushimás<u>u</u> 崩します・くずします; hakai shimás<u>u</u> 破壊します・はかいします
demon *n* akuma 悪魔, dēmon デーモン
denial *n* uchi-keshi 打ち消し・打ちけし, h<u>i</u>tei 否定
denim *n* denimu デニム
denomination → **sect**
dense *adj* kói 濃い, mítsu (na) 密(な), missetsu (na) 密接(な)
dent *n* kubomi 窪み・くぼみ
dentist *n* há-isha 歯医者
denture *n* ireba 入れ歯
deny *v* uchi-keshimás<u>u</u> 打ち消します・うちけします, h<u>i</u>tei shimás<u>u</u> 否定します
deodorant *n* (*personal*) shō´shū-zai 消臭剤
department *n* (*university, hospital*) ká 科; (*company, office*) bumon 部門, bu 部, ka 課
department store *n* depā´to デパート, hyakká-ten 百貨店
departure *n* sh<u>u</u>ppatsu 出発; [TIME/PLACE] ... hátsu (no ...) ...発(の...); **point of departure** *n* sh<u>u</u>ppátsú-ten 出発点; **departure time** *n* sh<u>u</u>ppátsú-jikoku 出発時刻
depend; *v* **~s on** (... ni) tayorimás<u>u</u> (...に)頼ります, izon shimás<u>u</u> 依存します; ***it ~s*** (*on* ...) (... ni) yorimás<u>u</u> (...に)よります
dependent *n* fuyō-kazoku 扶養家族
deposit **1.** *v* azukemás<u>u</u> 預けます・あずけます; (*money*) yokin/chokin shimás<u>u</u> 預金/貯金します; tsumimás<u>u</u> 積みます・つみます **2.** → **downpayment**
depot *n* **1.** (*railroad station*) *eki* 駅 **2.** (*bus station*) basu hatchaku-jō バス発着場 **3.** (*warehouse*) sōko 倉庫
depressed *adj* **1.** (*feeling*) ki ga omoi 気が重[おも]い **2.** ***gets ~*** hekomimás<u>u</u> へこみます
depression *n* (*hard times*) f<u>u</u>kéiki 不景気; (*hollow*) kubomi くぼみ・窪み
depth *n* f<u>u</u>kása 深さ; (*of color*) kósa 濃さ
derision *n* azakeri あざけり, reishō 冷笑
descend *v* kudarimás<u>u</u> 下ります
descendant *n* sh<u>i</u>son 子孫
descent *n* **1.** (*going down*) kudari 下り・くだり **2.** (*family line*) kakei 家系
describe *v* (*pictures it*) byōsha shimás<u>u</u> 描写します, (*elaborates*)

(no kotó) o kuwáshiku iimásu ... (のこと[事])を詳しく言います; (*explains it*) setsumei shimásu 説明します → **relate**

description *n* setsumei 説明

desert *n* sabaku 砂漠・さばく

design **1.** *n* (*sketch*) zuan 図案; dezain デザイン **2.** *v* (*plans it*) hakarimásu 図ります・はかります; dezain shimásu デザインします

designate *v* atemásu 当てます・あてます; shitei shimásu 指定します

desirable *adj* nozomashii 望ましい・のぞましい, hoshíi 欲しい・ほしい; ***most ~*** (*ideal*) motte-kói (no) もってこい(の)

desire **1.** *n* nozomi 望み, omói 思い, nén 念; (*hope*) kibō 希望 **2.** ***~s it*** *v* (... ga) hoshíi (...が) 欲しい; (*wants to do*) (shi-) tái desu (し)たいです; (*hopes for*) nozomimásu 望みます

desk *n* tsukue 机・つくえ, taku 卓; (*desk-top*) takujō´ 卓上

despair *n* zetsubō´ 絶望, yáke やけ

desperate *adj* hisshi (no) 必死(の)

desperately *adv* (*hard*) isshō´-kénmei (ni) 一生懸命(に)

despise *v* keibetsu shimásu 軽蔑します

despite (*that*) *prep* ...ni mo kakawarazu ...にもかかわらず・にも関わらず

dessert *n* dezā´to デザート

destination *n* iki sakí 行き先, mokutekí chi 目的地; (*last stop*) shūten 終点

destiny *n* únmei 運命

destroy *v* kowashimásu 壊します; hakai shimásu 破壊します; horoboshimásu 滅ぼします

detach *v* hanashimásu 離します・はなします

detailed *adj* kuwashíi 詳しい・くわしい; bisai (na) 微細(な); (*machine, etc.*) seimitsu (na) 精密・せいみつ(な)

details *n* kuwashíi koto 詳しいこと, shō´sai 詳細; (*complexities*) ikisatsu いきさつ・経緯

detect → **discover** → **discern**

detective *n* **1.** (*consulting ~*) tantei 探偵 **2.** (*police*) kéiji 刑事 **3.** (*investigator*) sōsa-kan 捜査官

deteriorate *v* (*weather*) kuzuremásu 崩れます

determination *n* (*decision*) kettei 決定; (*resolve*) késshín 決心

detest *v* nikumimásu 憎みます・にくみます

detour *n* mawari-michi 回り道・まわり道, ukai 迂回・うかい, tō´máwari 遠回り・遠まわり

devastate *v* arashimásu 荒らします

develop *v* (*it unfolds*) hattatsu/hatten shimásu 発達/発展します

developing nation *n* hatten tojō´-koku 発展途上国, kōshinkoku 後進国

development *n* hattatsu 発達, hatten 発展, kaihatsu 開発, (*process*) nariyuki 成り行き・な

りゆき, (*course*) keika 経過
device *n* (*gadget*) shikake 仕掛け・しかけ; (*scheme*) kufū 工夫
devil *n* (ogre) oní 鬼・オニ, (*Satan*) ákuma 悪魔・アクマ
dew *n* tsúyu 露・つゆ
diabetes *n* tō´nyō´-byō´ 糖尿病
diagonal *adj* nanáme (no) 斜め・ななめ(の)
diagram *n* zu 図, zuhyō´ 図表, zukai 図解
dial *n* (*telephone*) daiyaru ダイヤル
dialect *n* hō´gén 方言; (*regional accent*) namarí なまり
dialogue *n* (*conversation*) taiwa 対話, kaiwa 会話
diameter *n* chokkei 直径
diamond *n* daiya ダイヤ, daiyamóndo ダイヤモンド, kongō´-seki 金剛石・こんごうせき
diapers *n* oshíme おしめ, omútsu おむつ
diarrhea *n* geri 下痢・げり
diary *n* nikki 日記, daiarii ダイアリー
dice *n* saikóro さいころ・サイコロ
dictation *n* kakítori 書き取り・かきとり, dikutēshon ディクテーション
dictator *n* dokusái-sha 独裁者, wánman ワンマン
dictionary *n* jibikí 字引(き), jishó 辞書・じしょ, jiten 辞典・じてん
did *v* shimáshita しました
die *v* shinimásu 死にます, nakunarimásu 亡くなります; íki o híki-torimásu 息を引き取ります
diesel *n* diizeru ディーゼル
diet *n* kitéi-shoku 規定食, daiettoshoku ダイエット食; daietto (shimásu) ダイエット(します)
Diet *n* (*parliament*) kokkai 国会, gikai 議会; (*building*) (kokkai) giji-dō´ (国会)議事堂
differ *v* kotonarimásu 異なります; **~ *in opinion*** íken ga chigaimásu 意見が違います
difference *n* chigai 違い, sō´i 相違, sa 差・さ, sái 差異; (*a big difference*) táisa 大差・たいさ; ***it makes no ~*** kamaimasén 構いません・かまいません
different *adj* ***is ~*** chigaimásu 違います・ちがいます; kotonarimásu 異なります・ことなります; ***a ~ direction*** tahō´ 他方; ***~ opinion/ view*** iron 異論
difficult *adj* muzukashii 難しい・むずかしい; kónnan (na) 困難(な); (*hard to do*) shi-nikúi しにくい, shi-gatai しがたい・し難い; (*requires much effort*) honé ga oremásu 骨が折れます
difficulty *n* kónnan 困難; (*hardship*) kurō´ 苦労; (*problem*) mondai 問題; (*nuisance*) mendō´ 面倒・めんどう; ***with ~*** yatto やっと
diffusion *n* fukyu´ 普及
dig *v* horimásu 掘ります
digestion *n* shō´ka 消化
digit *n* **1.** (*Arabic figures*) (arabia) sūji (アラビア)数字 **2.** (*digit number*) ketasū 桁数 **3.** (*finger*

or toe) yubi 指

digital *n* dejitaru デジタル

dignity *n* **1.** (*nobility*) hin(-sei) 品(性), kihin 気品 **2.** (*respect and honor*) songen 尊厳; ***death with ~*** songen-shi 尊厳死

digress *v* soremásu それます・逸れます

dike *n* (*levee*) tsutsumí 堤・つつみ, teibō´ 堤防・ていぼう

dilemma *n* tō´waku 当惑, jirenma ジレンマ

diligent *adj* kinben (na) 勤勉(な), mame (na) まめ(な)

dilute **1.** *v* (*~s it*) (mizu de) warimásu (水で)割ります, usumemásu 薄めます **2.** *adj* (*~ acid*) nōdo ga usui 濃度が薄い

dim **1.** *adj* (*faint*) kásuka (na) かすか・微か(な), (*dark*) kurai 暗い・くらい **2.** *v* (*gets ~, hazy*) kasumimásu かすみます・霞みます

dimple *n* ékubo えくぼ

din *n* sōon 騒音

dine *v* shokuji (o) shimásu 食事(を)します

dinner *n* (*meal*) shokuji 食事, góhan ご飯・ごはん, (*supper*) ban góhan 晩ご飯・晩ごはん

dinosaur *n* kyōryū 恐竜

diploma *n* **1.** menjō´ 免状 **2.** (*graduation ~*) sotsugyō-shōsho 卒業証書

diplomacy *n* gaikō´ 外交

diplomat *n* (*diplomatic official*) gaikō´-kan 外交官; (*diplomatic person*) gaikō´-ka 外交家

diplomatic *adj* gaikō´-teki (na) 外交的(な); gaikō´ (no) 外交(の);

diplomatic relations *n* gaikō´ 外交

direct **1.** *adj* chokusetsu (no) 直接(の); ***goes ~*** (*through to destination*) chokusetsu ikimásu 直接行きます **2.** *v* (*tells the way*) (michi o) oshiemásu (道を)教えます **3.** *v* (*guides, coaches*) shidō´ shimásu 指導します; (*a film*) kantoku shimasu 監督します

direction *n* **1.** hō´kō´ 方向; kentō´ 見当; hō´mén 方面; … (no) hō´ …(の)方; hō´gaku 方角 **2.** ***directions*** (*instructions*) shíji 指示, oshie 教え; ***gives ~*** (*to a destination*) michi o oshiemásu 道を教えます

directly *adv* chokusetsu (ni) 直接(に), zutto ずっと, jika-ni じかに・直に, (*immediately*) sugu すぐ, (*shortly*) ma-mó-naku 間もなく・まもなく

director *n* **1.** (*coach*) shidō´-sha 指導者 **2.** (*of a film*) kantoku 監督, direkutā ディレクター

directory *n* (*telephone*) denwa-chō´ 電話帳; (*list of names*) meibo 名簿

dirt *n* yogore 汚れ・よごれ; (*filth*) doró 泥・ドロ; (*grime*) aká あか・垢; (*soil*) tsuchí 土

dirty **1.** *adj* kitanái 汚い・きたない, fuketsu (na) 不潔(な) **2.** *adj* (*~-minded*) gehin (na) 下品(な);

étchi (na) エッチ(な) **3.** *v gets ~* yogoremásu 汚れます・よごれます **4.** *v dirties it* yogoshimásu 汚します・よごします

disability *n* shintai-shōgai 身体障害

disadvantage *n* són 損・そん, fúri 不利; (*shortcoming*) ketten 欠点, mainasu マイナス, tánsho 短所

disagreement *n* fu-itchi 不一致

disappointment *n* shitsubō´ 失望, kitai hazure 期待はずれ, rakutan 落胆; (*in love*) shitsuren 失恋

disapprobation *n* fu-sansei 不賛成

disapproval *n* **1.** (*disfavor*) fu-sansei 不賛成, (*nonrecognition*) fu-shōnin 不承認 **2.** (*accusation*) hinan 非難

disaster *n* sō´nan 遭難・そうなん, sainán 災難・さいなん; *has a ~* sō´nan shimásu 遭難します・そうなんします

disastrous *adj* taihen (na) 大変・たいへん(な)

discard *v* sutemásu 捨てます

discern *v* **1.** (*discriminates*) shikibetsu shimásu 識別します **2.** → **see**

discharge *v* (*from employment*) káiko shimásu 解雇します

disciple *n* deshí 弟子・でし

discipline **1.** *n* kiritsu 規律, chitsujo 秩序; shitsuke しつけ **2.** *v* (*drills, trains*) kitaemásu 鍛えます・きたえます, (*brings up children, …*) shitsukemásu しつけます

disclose *v* (*public*) kōkai shimásu 公開します; abakimásu 暴きます・あばきます; *is disclosed* barémásu ばれます

disco *n* disuko ディスコ

discomfort *n* fukai(-kan) 不快(感)

disconnect *v* hazushimásu 外します・はずします, hanashimásu 離します・はなします, kirimásu 切ります・きります

discontented *adj* fuman (na) 不満・ふまん(な)

discount *n* wari-biki 割引・わりびき, ne-biki 値引き・ねびき

discourage *v* ki o kujikimásu 気をくじきます; *gets discouraged* ki ga kujikemásu 気がくじけます

discourtesy *n* búrei 無礼, shitsúrei 失礼

discover *v* **1.** (*finds*) mitsukemásu 見つけます・みつけます, hakken shimásu 発見します → **find out** **2.** *is discovered* barémásu ばれます; abakaremásu 暴かれます・あばかれます

discrepancy *n* chigai 違い・ちがい, sa 差・さ, sō´i 相違, kuichigai 食い違い・くいちがい; (*gap*) zuré ずれ

discretion *n* tsutsushimi 慎み・つつしみ, funbetsu 分別

discriminate *v* (*distinguishes them*) mi-wakemásu 見分けます, shikibetsu shimásu 識別します

discrimination *n* sábetsu 差別・さべつ; kúbetsu 区別・くべつ; (*distinguishing*) shikibetsu 識別

discuss *v* (*talks it over*) hanashi-aimásu 話し合います・はなしあいます, sō´dan shimásu 相談

します; (*debates, argues*) ronjimásu 論じます

discussion *n* hanashi-ai 話し合い・はなしあい; hanashí 話・はなし; kyō´gí 協議; (*argument*) rón 論, (*debate*) tō´ron 討論, ronsō´ 論争

disease *n* byō´ki 病気

disembark *v* jō´riku shimásu 上陸します

disgrace *n* hají 恥・はじ; chijoku 恥辱, ojoku 汚辱

disgraceful *adj* hazukashíi 恥ずかしい・はずかしい

disgusted; *gets* ~ akiremásu 呆れます・あきれます; iyá ni narimásu 嫌になります・いやになります

dish *n* (o-)sara (お)皿・(お)さら; shokki 食器

dishearten → discourage

dishonest *adj* fu-seijitsu (na/no) 不誠実(な/の), fu-shōjiki (na/no) 不正直(な/の), fusei (na/no) 不正(な/の)

disinfectant *n* shō´dokú-yaku/zai 消毒薬/剤

dislike *v* … ga kirai désu …が嫌いです・…がきらいです, …o iya-garimásu …を嫌がります・…をいやがります

dismal *adj* (*gloomy*) uttō´shíi うっとうしい

dismissal *n* (*from employment*) káiko 解雇; (*of servant*) hima 暇・ひま

disobedient *adj* hankō-teki (na) 反抗的(な)

disobey *v* … ni somukimásu …に背きます・…にそむきます

disorder *n* konran 混乱, kónzatsu 混雑, midaré 乱れ・みだれ, yamí 闇; ***in*** ~ mechamecha めちゃめちゃ

disorderly *adj* ranbō´ (na) 乱暴・らんぼう(な)

dispensary *n* yakkyoku 薬局

disperse *v* (*they scatter*) chirimásu 散ります・ちります

display → show

displeased *adj* fu-kigen (na) 不機嫌・ふきげん(な)

dispose *v* shímatsu shimásu 始末します; shóri shimásu 処理します

disposition *n* **1.** seishitsu 性質; (*nature*) táchi たち・質, shō´ 性; (*temperament*) ténsei 天性; (*attitude*) táido 態度 **2.** (*dealing with*) shóri 処理, shóchi 処置

dispute *n* arasoi 争い・あらそい, tō´ron 討論, sō´ron 争論

dissatisfied *adj* fuman (na) 不満・ふまん(な)

dissertation *n* ronbun 論文

dissipation *n* dō´raku 道楽

dissolve *v* (*~s it*) tokashimásu 溶かします・とかします; (*it ~s*) tokemásu 溶けます・とけます

distance *n* kyóri 距離・きょり

distant *adj* (*far*) tō´i 遠い・とおい, háruka (na) はるか・遥か(な); ***gets*** ~ hedatarimásu 隔たります・へだたります

distinct *adj* hakkíri to shimásu は

っきりとします

distinctly *adv* hakkíri はっきり

distinguish *v* (*discriminates*) mi-wakemásu 見分けます, shikibetsu shimásu 識別します

distort *v* yugamemásu ゆがめます・歪めます

distortion *n* yugami ゆがみ・歪み

distract *v* ki o chirashimásu 気を散らします

distress **1.** *n* nayamí 悩み・なやみ, kurushimi 苦しみ・くるしみ **2.** *v* (*afflicts*) kurushimemásu 苦しめます・くるしめます; ***gets distressed*** kurushimimásu 苦しみます・くるしみます

distribute *v* kubarimásu 配ります・くばります; wakemásu 分けます・わけます

distribution *n* ryūtsū 流通

district *n* chihō´ 地方; hō´mén 方面, ...-hō´men ...方面

disturb *v* (... no) jama o shimásu (...の)じゃま[邪魔]をします

disturbance *n* (*intrusion*) (o-)jama (お)じゃま・邪魔; (*unrest*) sō´dō´ 騒動; (*strife*) arasoi 争い, rán 乱

disused *adj* fuyō´ (no) 不要(の)

ditch **1.** *n* mizo 溝; horí 堀 **2.** *v* mizo o horimásu 溝を掘ります

dive (*under*) *v* mogurimásu 潜ります・もぐります, tobikomimásu 飛び込みます・とびこみます, daibingu shimásu ダイビングします

diver *n* daibā´ ダイバー; (*woman pearl diver*) áma 海女・あま

diverse *adj* sama zama (na) さまざま・様々(な)

divide *v* (*~s it*) warimásu 割ります・わります, wakemásu 分けます・わけます; (*it ~s*) waremásu 割れます・われます; wakaremásu 分かれます・わかれます; *~ **roughly*** (*into main categories*) taibetsu shimásu 大別します

division *n* bú 部; (*army*) shídan 師団; (*branching*) wakaré 分かれ; (*math calculation*) warízan 割り算

divorce **1.** *n* rikon 離婚 **2.** *v* rikon shimásu 離婚します

dizzy *adj* **1.** me ga mararu 目が回る; ***feel ~*** memai ga shimásu めまいがします **2.** bakageta ばかげた

do *v* shimásu します; yarimásu やります; nashimásu なします; (*performs*) okonaimásu 行います; ~ it (*deprecating object*) yarakashimásu やらかします; *~ **it over*** (*again*) yari-naoshimásu やり直します・やりなおします

docile *adj* súnao (na) すなお・素直(な)

dock *n* dókku ドック, ganpeki 岸壁・がんぺき

doctor *n* **1.** (*physician*) (o-)isha(-san) (お)医者(さん), senséi 先生 **2.** (*Ph.D.*) hákase 博士・はかせ

document *n* shorui 書類, bunsho 文書, bunken 文献

documentary *n* dokyumentarii ドキュメンタリー

dodge *v* (*turns it aside*) sorashi-másu そらします・逸らします

does → **do; doesn't** → **don't**

dog *n* inú 犬・イヌ; **dog tag** *n* (*dog license*) inú no kansatsu 犬の鑑札

doll *n* (o-)ningyō´・(お)にんぎょう(お)人形; ***festival doll*** hina-níngyō´ひな人形・雛人形

dollar *n* dóru ドル

dolphin *n* iruka イルカ

domestic *adj* (*not foreign*) kokúnai (no) 国内(の); (*domestically made*) kokusan (no) 国産(の); **domestic help** *n* otetsudai(-san) お手伝い(さん), kaji-tetsudai 家事手伝い

domino *n* domino ドミノ

done *v* (*ready*) dekimáshita 出来ました・できました, dékite imásu 出来ています・できています; (*finished*) (shi-)te shimaimáshita (し)てしまいました; **well-done** *adj* yóku yaketa 良[よ]く焼けた, (*beef*) wérudan ウェルダン

donkey *n* róba ロバ

don't *v* shimasén しません; **don't (do it)!** *interj* (shité wa) damé desu/da (しては)だめです/だ, ikemasén いけません; (shi-)náide kudasai (し)ないで下[くだ]さい; ***Don't worry about it.*** Go-shinpai náku. ご心配なく・ごしんぱいなく.

door *n* to 戸, dóa ドア; (*hinged*) hiraki-do 開き戸・ひらき戸; (*opaque sliding*) fusuma ふすま・襖; ***~ wing, ~ of a gate*** tobira 扉・とびら

dope *n* (*narcotic*) mayaku 麻薬

dormitory *n* kishúkusha 寄宿舎, ryō´ 寮

dose *n* ikkai-ryō 一回量, ikkai-bun 一回分

dot *n* ten 点・てん, chóbo ちょぼ, póchi ぽち, pótsu ぽつ; (*with*) ***dots*** bótsu botsu ぼつぼつ

double 1. *adj* bai (no) 倍(の), (*two-layer*) ni-jū (no) 二重(の); **double bed** *n* daburu-béddo ダブルベッド; **double boiler** *n* nijū-nábe 二重鍋・二重なべ; **doubles** *n* (*tennis*) dáburusu ダブルス; **2. ~s it** *v* (…o) bai ni shimásu (…を)倍にします

double-check *v* nén o oshimásu 念を押します; saíkakunin shimásu 再確認します

double-cross 1. *n* (*treachery*) uragiri 裏切り・うらぎり **2.** *v* ura-girimásu 裏切ります

double-decker *n* nikaidate basu 二階建てバス

doubt 1. *n* gimon 疑問, utagai 疑い・うたがい, fushin 不審 **2.** *v* (*~s it*) utagaimásu 疑います, fushin ni omoimásu 不審に思います

dough *n* pan-kiji パン生地

dove *n* háto 鳩・ハト

down *prep, adv* shita e 下へ; ***down*** (*lower in price by*) ***¥100*** hyaku én-yasu 百円安; **get down** orimásu 下ります・降ります・おります; **go down** kudarimásu 下ります・くだります, sagarimásu 下

ります・さがります; hang down taremásu 垂れます・たれます, sagemásu 下げます; lie down nemásu 寝ます・ねます; take down oroshimásu 下ろします・おろします

download *v* (*computer*) ~ ***the file*** (fairu o) daunrōdo shimásu (ファイルを)ダウンロードします

downpayment *n* atama-kin 頭金

downpour *n* gō´u 豪雨, doshaburi 土砂降り; ***local*** ~ shūchū-gō´u 集中豪雨

doze *v* úto uto shimásu うとうと・ウトウトします

dozen *n* (ichi-) dā´su (一)ダース, jū-ní 十二・12

Dr.… *n* (*physician*) … senséi …先生

draft **1.** *n* (*rough*) shitagaki 下書き, dorafuto ドラフト; (*military conscription*) shō´shū (shimásu) 召集(します) **2.** *n* (*beer*) náma 生, nama bíiru 生ビール **3.** *n* (*call-up*) shō´shū/chōhē (shimásu) 召集/徴兵(します)

drag *v* hipparimásu 引っ張ります・ひっぱります, hikimásu 引きます・ひきます, hikizurimásu 引きずります

dragon *n* ryū 竜・龍・りゅう, tatsu 竜・たつ, doragon ドラゴン

drain **1.** *n* (*kitchen*) gesui 下水; (*ditch*) mizo 溝 **2.** ***it ~s off*** *v* hakemásu はけます; ***it ~s well*** (mizu) haké ga íi désu (水)はけがいいです

drama *n* engeki 演劇, géki 劇, dorama ドラマ

dramatic *adj* géki-teki (na) 劇的(な)

drapes *n* kā´ten カーテン

draw **1.** *v* (*a picture*) egakimásu 描きます **2.** *v* (*pulls*) hikimásu 引きます・ひきます; ~ ***out*** hikidashimásu 引き出します・ひきだします; ~ ***an underline*** kasen o hikimásu 下線を引きます **3.** *v* (*water etc.*) kumimásu 汲みます・くみます **4.** *v* ***~s apart*** hikiwakemásu 引き分けます・ひきわけます **5.** *n* (*game*) hikiwake 引き分け・ひきわけ

drawer *n* (*of desk, etc.*) hiki-dashi 引き出し・ひきだし

drawing *n* (*diagram*) zu 図; (*picture*) é 絵

draw near → **approach**

dread *v* osoremásu 恐れます・おそれます

dreadful *adj* osoroshíi 恐ろしい・おそろしい, sugói すごい・凄い, hidoi ひどい・酷い

dream *n* yumé (o mimásu) 夢・ユメ(をみます)

dreary *adj* uttō´shíi うっとうしい

dregs *n* kásu かす; ori おり

dress **1.** *n* ki-mono 着物; yō´-fuku 洋服, fukú 服, tukusō 服装, (*woman's*) wanpíisu ワンピース, dóresu ドレス **2.** *v* (*wears*) fukú o kimásu 服を着ます

dressmaker *n* yō´sai-shi 洋裁師, doresu-mē´kā ドレスメーカー

dried 1. *adj* hoshí-… 干し…; ~ ***persimmons*** hoshí-gaki 干し柿・ホシガキ 2. → **dry**

drill 1. *n* (*tool*) kíri きり・錐 2. *n* (*practice*) doriru ドリル, (o-) kéi ko (お)けいこ・稽古; (*study*) renshū 練習; (*training*) kúnren 訓練 3. *v* (*trains*) nerimásu̲ 練ります・ねります, kúnren shimásu̲ 訓練します, (*disciplines*) ki̲tae-másu̲ 鍛えます・きたえます

drink 1. *n* (*beverage*) nomí-mono 飲み物・のみもの; ***one*** ~ hi̲tó-ku̲chi 一口; ***has a*** ~ íp-pai nomi-másu̲/yarimásu̲ 一杯飲[の]みます/やります 2. *v* nomimásu̲ 飲みます・のみます

drip *v* taremásu̲ 垂れます・たれます

drive 1. *v* (*a car*) unten shimásu̲ 運転します, doraibu shimásu̲ ドライブします 2. *n* (*what one is driving at*) iitai-koto 言いたい事, nerai ねらい・狙い

driver *n* untén-shu 運転手, doraibā ドライバー

driveway *n* shadō´ 車道

drizzle *n* kosame 小雨; (*on-and-off*) shigure 時雨・しぐれ

droll *adj* yúkai (na) 愉快・ゆかい(な) → **funny**

drool *v* ***is drooling*** yodare ga deteimásu̲ よだれが出ています

droop *v* naemásu̲ 萎えます・なえます

drop 1. *v* (~*s it*) otoshimásu̲ 落とします・おとします, (*lets it fall, spills*) tarashimásu̲ 垂らします・たらします 2. *v* (*it* ~*s*) ochimásu̲ 落ちます・おちます 3. *n* (*a* ~) tsúbu 粒, tamá 玉; (*counting*) …-teki …滴; **drop in** *v* yorimásu̲ 寄ります・よります; **drop off** *v* (*a person from a vehicle*) oroshimásu̲ 降ろします・おろします

drown *v* obore-jini shimásu̲ おぼれ死にします

drowsy *adj* nemui 眠い; darui ダルい

drudge *v* ákuseku hatarakimásu̲ あくせく働きます・はたらきます

drug *n* (*for patient*) (o-)ku̲súri (お)薬, (*chemical substances*) yaku̲hin 薬品

drug addict *n* mayaku-chūdoku-sha 麻薬中毒者

drum *n* (*Japanese-style*) taiko 太鼓・たいこ, (*large*) ō´-dáiko 大太鼓; (*Western-style*) doramu ドラム

drunk; ***gets*** ~ yopparaimásu̲ 酔[よ]っぱらいます・酔っ払います; yoimásu̲ 酔います・よいます

dry *v* (*it dries*) kawakimásu̲ 乾きます・かわきます, kansō shimásu̲ 乾燥します; (*dries it*) kawakashimásu̲ 乾かします・かわかします

duck *n* (*wild*) kámo カモ・鴨, (*tame*) ahiru アヒル

dude *n* mekashiya めかし屋; yatsu やつ・奴

due 1. ***dues*** *n* kaihi 会費, ryōkin

料金 **2.** *adj* (*payment*) kijitsu no 期日(の)

dull *adj* nibúi 鈍い・にぶい, norói のろい; (*uninteresting*) taikutsu (na) 退屈・たいくつ(な), (*long-winded*) kudói くどい; (*dull-witted*) wakarí ga warúi 分かりが悪い

dumb *adj* **1.** (*stupid*) baka (na) ばか・馬鹿(な) **2.** (*unable to speak*) kuchi no kikenai 口の利けない

dump *v* (*discards*) sutemásu 捨てます・すてます

dumpling *n* (o-)dango (お)団子; (*large stuffed bun*) manjū まんじゅう・饅頭; (*small meat-stuffed crescent*) gyōˊza ギョウザ・餃子

dune *n* sakyū 砂丘・さきゅう

dung *n* kusó クソ・糞, fún フン・糞 → **excrement**

dupe *n* kámo カモ

duplicate *n, adj* **1.** (*double*) ni-jū (no) 二重(の) **2.** → **copy**

during *prep* (...) no aida (ni) (...)の間(に); ...-chū (ni) ...中(に)

dust **1.** *n* (*in air*) hokori ホコリ・埃; (*on floor, etc.*) chiri チリ・塵; (*in house*) gomí ごみ **2.** *v* (*~s it*) hatakimásu はたきます

Dutch **1.** *adj* Oranda no オランダの **2.** *n* (*language*) Oranda-go オランダ語 **3.** *n* (*person*) Orandá-jin オランダ人

Dutch treat *n* wari-kan 割り勘・ワリカン

duty *n* **1.** (*obligation*) gímu 義務 **2.** (*function*) (o-)yakume (お)役目, (o-)yaku (お)役, honbun 本分; (*job, post*) (o-)tsutome (お)務め; (*work, service*) kínmu 勤務; ***the person on ~*** (o-)tōˊban (お)当番 **3.** (*import tax*) kanzei 関税, yunyū-zei 輸入税 **4.** → **off duty**

dwindle *v* herimásu 減ります・へります, sukúnáku narimásu 少なくなります・すくなくなります

dye (*it*) *v* somemásu 染めます・そめます

dysentery *n* sékiri 赤痢・セキリ

E

each *pron* [NUMBER, QUANTITY +] ...zútsu ...ずつ; (*every*) mai-...毎..., káku(-) ... 各..., ... goto (ni) ...毎・ごと(に)

each other *pron* o-tagai (ni) お互い・おたがい(に); [VERB-i] -aimásu [VERB-い]合います・あいます

eager *adj* nésshín (na) 熱心・ねっしん(な), setsubō shiteiru 切望している; ***~ to*** (*do*) zé-hi ... (shi-)tai ぜひ[是非]...(し)たい

eagerness *n* netsui 熱意, netsuretsu 熱烈, nesshin 熱心

eagle *n* washi ワシ・鷲

ear *n* mimí 耳・みみ; **earache** *n* mimi no itamí 耳の痛み・みみのいたみ; **ear pad** *n* mimiate 耳あて・耳当て

earlier *adj* (*former*) máe no … 前の…・まえの…; [BOOKISH] zén(-) … 前…・まえ…

early **1.** *adj* hayái 早い・はやい **2.** *adv* háyaku 早く・はやく; (*ahead of time*) hayame (ni) 早め・はやめ(に); ***one's ~ years*** kodomo no koro 子供の頃・こどものころ

earn *v* kasegimásu̲ 稼ぎます・かせぎます

earnest *adj* majime (na) まじめ・真面目(な), (*serious*) honki (no) 本気(の)

earnings *n* (*income*) shūnyū 収入, shotoku 所得

earpiece *n* (*of glass frame*) (megane no) tsurú (めがねの)つる; (*telephone*) juwá-ki 受話器

earring *n* íyaringu イヤリング, mimi-kázari 耳飾り・みみかざり

earshot *n* mimi no todoku kyori 耳の届[とど]く距離, kikoeru kyori 聞こえる距離

earth *n* **1.** tsu̲chí 土, tochi 土地 **2.** ***the Earth*** chi̲kyū 地球; **what on earth** *adv* ittai-zentai 一体全体

earthenware *n* doki 土器; **earthenware pan** *n* hōrókú ほうろく・焙烙; tōki 陶器

earthquake *n* jishin 地震

earthworm *n* mimizu ミミズ

ease **1.** *n* (*comfort*) rakú 楽・らく; **at ease** jiyū (ni) 自由・じゆう(に), yukkúri ゆっくり **2.** ***~s it*** *v* yasumemásu̲ 休めます・やすめます

easily *adv* tayásu̲ku たやすく, wáke-naku わけなく, kantan (ni) 簡単・かんたん(に), muzō´sa (ni) 無造作(に); assári (to) あっさり(と); **easily broken** koware-yasúi 壊れやすい・こわれやすい

east *n* higashi 東・ひがし, tō-… 東…; (*the east*) tōhō 東方, (*the eastern part*) tō´bu 東部

Easter *n* iisutā イースター, fukkatsu-sai 復活祭; **Easter holidays** *n* fukkatsu-sai no kyūka 復活祭の休暇

easy *adj* **1.** yasashii やさしい・易しい, tayasúi たやすい, wákenai わけない, kantan 簡単・かんたん, muzō´sa (na) 無造作(な); ***~ (to do)*** (shi-) yasúi (し)やすい; ***~ to understand*** wakari-yasúi 分かりやすい **2.** → **comfortable**

easygoing *adj* nónki (na) のん気・呑気(な), kiraku (na) 気楽・きらく(な)

eat *v* tabemásu̲ 食べます・たべます; (*has a meal*) shokuji shimásu̲ 食事します; **eat out** *v* gaishoku shimásu̲ 外食します

eat-in kitchen *n* dii-kē´ (DK) ディーケー, dainingu-ki̲tchin ダイニングキッチン

eaves *n* noki 軒・のき, hisashi ひさし

ebb **1.** *n* hiki-shio 引き潮, kanchō 干潮 **2.** *v* otoroemásu̲ 衰えま

す; **ebb and flow** *n* ① (*tide*) shio no michi-hiki 潮の満ち引き ② (*life*) (eiko) seisui (栄枯)盛衰

eccentric *n* **1.** fūgawari na hito 風変わりな人, ekisentorikku エキセントリック **2.** (*freak*) hen-jin 変人, ki-jin 奇人

echo **1.** *n* hibikí 響き, kodama こだま, hankyō 反響, ekō エコー **2.** *v* (*it ~es*) hibikimásu 響きます・ひびきます

éclair *n* ekurea エクレア

eclipse *n* **1.** (*sun*) nisshoku 日食 **2.** (*moon*) gesshoku 月食

ecologically friendly car *n* eko-kā エコカー

ecology *n* seitai-gaku 生態学, ekorojii エコロジー, seitai-kankyō 生態環境

e-commerce *n* denshi shō-torihiki 電子商取引, ii komāsu e-コマース

economic *adj* keizai-gaku (no) 経済学(の), keizai (no) 経済(の)

economical *adj* keizai-teki (na) 経済的(な); toku (na) (お)徳・とく(な)

economics *n* kéizai 経済; (*science/study*) keizái-gaku 経済学

economy *n* **1.** (*saving*) setsuyaku 節約・せつやく **2.** (*economics*) keizai 経済; **economy class** *n* ekonomii-kurasu エコノミークラス; **~-class syndrome** ekonomii-kurasu shōkō-gun エコノミークラス症候群

ecstasy *n* **1.** (*sexual ~, name of drug*) ekusutashii エクスタシー **2.** kōkotsu 恍惚; ***in an ~ of*** muga-muchū (de) 無我夢中(で)

ecumenical *n* **1.** (*general*) fuhen-teki (na) 普遍的(な) **2.** (*~ movement*) kyōkai itchi undō (no) 教会一致運動(の)

eczema *n* shisshin 湿疹・しっしん

edge *n* fuchí ふち・縁, hashi 端・はし, hashikko/hajikko 端っこ・はしっこ/はじっこ, háta 端・はた, ejji エッジ; (*of knife*) ha 刃, ha-saki 刃先

edgy *adj* irairashita イライラした・苛々した

edible **1.** *n* shokuryō-hin 食料品 **2.** *adj* shokuyō (no) 食用(の)

edict *n* **1.** (*government decree*) seirei 政令 **2.** (*act*) hōrei 法令 **3.** (*command*) meirei 命令

edifice **1.** *n* (*large building*) dai-kenzōbutsu 大建造物, kyodai-kenchiku 巨大建築 **2.** (*complex system/organization*) te no konda taikei/soshiki 手の込んだ体系/組織

edition *n* ban 版

editor *n* henshū-chō 編集長, editā エディター

editorial *n* shasetsu 社説

educate *v* (*rears*) sodatemásu 育てます・そだてます → **teach**

education *n* kyōiku 教育; (*learning*) gakúmon 学問, (*culture*) kyōyō 教養; (*bringing up*) yōiku 養育

eel *n* unagi ウナギ・鰻; (*conger eel*) anago アナゴ・穴子

effect *n* (*result*) kekka 結果; (*cause*)

… (no) séi …(の)せい; (*effectiveness*) ki̲ki-me 効き目, shirushi しるし, kōka 効果; (*gist*) muné 旨・むね; in effect yō-súru ni 要するに・ようするに; has/takes effect ki̲kimásu̲ 効きます・ききます; side/after-effect *n* fu̲kú-sayō 副作用

effective *adj* yūkō (na) 有効・ゆうこう(な), kōka-teki (na) 効果的(な)

efficiency *n* nōritsu 能率; kōritsu 効率

efficient *adj* nōritsu-teki (na) 能率的・のうりつてき(な), kōritsu teki (na) 効率的・こうりつてき(な)

effort *n*・(お)ほねおり(o-)hone ori(お)骨折り, dóryoku 努力・どりょく; (go-)kúrō (ご)苦労・(お)くろう; makes an effort do-ryoku shimásu̲ 努力します・どりょくします

effortless *adj* muzō´sa (na) 無造作・むぞうさ(な)

e.g. *adv* tatoeba 例えば・たとえば

egg *n* tamago 卵・玉子・タマゴ

eggplant *n* násu ナス・茄子, násubi ナスビ

ego *n* jíga 自我, ego エゴ

egoism *n* (*selfishness*) riko-shugi 利己主義, wagamama わがまま・我(が)侭

Egypt *n* Ejiputo エジプト

eight *n* hachí 八・8, yattsú 八つ・やっつ; (*8-oared racing boat*) éito/ē´to エイト/エート; ***eight days*** yōka 八日

eighteen *n* jū-hachí 十八・18

eighth *adj* hachi-banmé (no) 八番目(の), yattsu-mé (no) 八つ目(の); the eighth day *n* yōka-mé 八日目, (*the day of the month*) yōka 八日

either one *adv* dochira demo どちらでも

eke *v* yarikuri shimásu̲ やりくりします, maniawasemásu̲ 間に合わせます・まにあわせます

elaborate **1.** *adj* (*complex*) fuku-zatsu (na) 複雑(な) **2.** (*diligent*) kinben (na) 勤勉(な) **3.** kuwa-shiku setsumei shimásu̲ 詳しく説明します

elapse *v* tachimásu̲ 経ちます・たちます, hemásu̲ 経ます・へます, keika shimásu̲ 経過します

elastic *n* (*material*) → **rubber**; elastic band *n* wagomu 輪ゴム・わゴム

elation *n* jōkigen 上機嫌, ōyorokobi 大喜び

elbow *n* hijí 肘・肱・ひじ

elect *v* erabimásu̲ 選びます・えらびます

election *n* sénkyo 選挙

electric *adj* dénki (no) 電気・でんき(の)

electric; electric appliances *n* kaden 家電, denki-kígu 電気器具, denka-seihin 電化製品; electric car *n* denki jidōsha 電気自動車 (also *electrified train, electric train*); electric heater *n* denki-su̲tō´bu 電気ストーブ

electricity *n* dénki 電気・でんき
electron *n* dénshi 電子
electronic *adj* dénshi (no) 電子(の); electronic account settlement *n* denshi-kessai 電子決済
elegant *adj* fū´ryū (na) 風流・ふうりゅう(な), yū´bi (na) 優美・ゆうび(な), yū´ga (na) 優雅・ゆうが(な)
elementary school *n* (*primary school*) shōgákkō 小学校; elementary school student *n* shōgáku-sei 小学生
elephant *n* zō 象・ゾウ
elevator *n* erebē´tā´ エレベーター
eleven *n* jū ichí 十一・11
eliminate *v* habukimás<u>u</u> 省きます・はぶきます, nozokimás<u>u</u> 除[のぞ]きます; háijo shimás<u>u</u> 排除[はうじょ]します
elite **1.** *n* eriito エリート **2.** *adj* ichiryū (no) 一流(の)
else *adv* hoka (no/ni) 他・ほか(の/に); or else mátá-wa または・又は, sore-tómo それとも, aruiwa 或いは・あるいは; somewhere else (dokoka) yosó (no/ni) (どこか)よそ(の/に), (dokoka) betsu no basho (no/ni) (どこか)別の場所・べつのばしょ(の/に)
email *n* mēru メール
embankment *n* teibō 堤防・ていぼう, ts<u>u</u>tsumí 堤・つつみ
embarrass *v* komarasemás<u>u</u> 困らせます・こまらせます, kurushimemás<u>u</u> 苦しめます・くるしめます; **~ *oneself*** hají o kakimás<u>u</u> 恥をかきます
embarrassed; **1.** ***gets*** **~** komarimás<u>u</u> 困ります・こまります; kurushimimás<u>u</u> 苦しみます・くるしみます **2.** ***feels*** **~** teremás<u>u</u> 照れます・てれます, kimari ga warúi (des<u>u</u>) きまりが悪い・きまりがわるい(です) **3.** ***is*** **~** (*ashamed, shy*) hazukashíi 恥ずかしい・はずかしい
embassy *n* taishí-kan 大使館
emblem *n* kishō 記章; (*symbol*) shōchō 象徴, hyōshō 表象
emerge *v* demás<u>u</u> 出ます・でます, arawaremás<u>u</u> 現れます・あらわれます; emergence (*appearance*) *n* sh<u>u</u>tsugen 出現
emergency *n* hijō (jitai) 非常(事態), kinkyū (jitai) 緊急(事態), (*temporary*) rinji 臨時・りんじ; (*crisis*) kí<u>k</u>i 危機; emergency brake *n* hijō-burē´ki 非常ブレーキ
emigrant *n* imin 移民, ijū-sha 移住者
Emoticon *n* (*computer*) kaomoji 顔文字, emōtikon エモーティコン
emotion *n* kanjō 感情・かんじょう; (*feeling*) kandō 感動・かんどう, kangeki 感激・かんげき
Emperor *n* **1.** (*Japanese*) Tennō 天皇; ***His Majesty the*** **~** Tennō-héika 天皇陛下 **2.** kōtei 皇帝
emphasis *n* kyōchō 強調
empire *n* téikoku 帝国
employ *v* **1.** ts<u>u</u>kaimás<u>u</u> 使います・つかいます, yatoimás<u>u</u> 雇います・やといます **2.** ***is employed*** ts<u>u</u>tómete imás<u>u</u> 勤めていま

す・つとめています; yatówarete imás<u>u</u> 雇われています・やとわれています

employee *n* jūgyō-in 従業員; (*of a company*) sha-in 社員, kaishá-in 会社員

employer *n* koyō-sha 雇用者, koyō-nushi 雇用主

employment *n* (*use*) shiyō 使用; (*hiring*) koyō 雇用, yatói 雇い・やとい; (*job*) (o-)ts<u>u</u>tome (お)勤め(お)つとめ; **place of employment** *n* ts<u>u</u>tome-saki 勤め先

empty **1.** *adj* kara (no) 空・から(の), karappo (no) 空っぽ・からっぽ(の); (*with nothing in it*) nani mo háitte inai … 何も入っていない…・なにもはいっていない…; (*hollow*) utsuro (na) 虚ろ・うつろ(な); (*is vacant*) aite imás<u>u</u> 空いています・あいています(いる, いて) **2.** *adj* aki-…空[あ]き…; **empty house** *n* aki-ya 空[あ]き家 **3.** ***gets emptied*** *v* akimás<u>u</u> 空きます・あきます, s<u>u</u>kimás<u>u</u> すきます・空きます **4.** ***empties it*** *v* akemás<u>u</u> 空けます・あけます; (*gives a toast*) kanpai shimás<u>u</u> 乾杯します・かんぱいします

enclose *v* (*in envelope*) dōfū shimás<u>u</u> 同封します

encompass *v* fukumimásu 含みます・ふくみます, kakomimás<u>u</u> 囲みます

encounter *v* … ni de-aimás<u>u</u> …に出会います・…にであいます, sōgū shimás<u>u</u> 遭遇します

encourage *v* s<u>u</u>sumemás<u>u</u> 勧めます・すすめます hagemashimás<u>u</u> 励まします・はげまします

encouragement *n* shōrei 奨励

encyclopedia *n* hyakka-jíten 百科事典

end **1.** *n* (*the ending*) owari 終わり・おわり, o-shimai おしまい, kirí 切り・きり; (*close*) sue 末・すえ; (*purpose*) mok<u>u</u>teki 目的; **end of the year** *n* (toshi no) kure (年の)暮れ・くれ, nenmatsu 年末 **2.** *v* (*it ~s, ~s it*) owarimásu 終わります・おわります; (*comes to an ~*) sumimás<u>u</u> 済みます・すみます, (*runs out*) tskimás<u>u</u> 尽きます・つきます

endeavor *v* ts<u>u</u>tomemás<u>u</u> 努めます・つとめます, dóryoku shimás<u>u</u> 努力します・どりょくします

ending *n* owari 終わり, ketsumatsu 結末; **ending address** *n* shūryō adoresu 終了アドレス; **happy ending** *n* happii endo ハッピーエンド

endless *adj* (*no limit*) owari no nai 終わりのない・おわりのない, kirí ga nai 切りがない・きりがない; (*forever*) eien (no) 永遠(の)

endorse → **sign** → **support**

endurance *n* (*patience*) shínbō 辛抱・しんぼう

endure *v* (*puts up with*) shínbō shimás<u>u</u> 辛抱します

enemy *n* teki 敵

energetic *adj* génki (na) 元気・げんき(な), enerugísshu (na) エネ

ルギッシュ(な); (*vigorous*) sekkyoku-teki (na) 積極的(な)

energy *n* **1.** ikiói 勢い・いきおい **2.** enérúgii エネルギー **3.** (*pep*) génki 元気(o-génki お元気)

engage *v* **1.** (*hires a professional*) tanomimásu̲ 頼みます・たのみます **2.** *~s in* (*an activity*) ...ni jū´ji shimásu̲ ...に従事します **3.** *gets engaged* (*booked up, occupied*) fu̲sagarimásu̲ ふさがります

engaged *adj* (*to be married*) kon'yaku shi̲te imásu̲ 婚約しています

engagement *n* (*date*) yaku̲soku 約束・やくそく

engine *n* ki̲kan 機関, (*automobile*) énjin エンジン; *the ~ starts* énjin ga kakarimásu̲ エンジンがかかります

engineering *n* kōgaku 工学

England *n* Igirisu イギリス, Eikoku 英国

English *n* (*language*) Eigo 英語; (*person*) Igirisú-jin イギリス人; **English translation** *n* eiyaku 英訳

engrave *v* chōkoku shimásu̲ 彫刻します, kizamimásu̲ 刻みます・きざみます

engrossed; *gets ~ in* ... ni muchū ni narimásu̲ ...に夢中になります; ...ni korimásu̲ ...に凝ります・...にこります

enjoy *v* tanoshimimásu̲ 楽しみます・たのしみます; enjói shimásu̲ エンジョイします; *~ the company of* ... to tsu̲ki-aimásu̲ ...と付き合います・...とつきあいます

enjoyable *adj* tanoshíi 楽しい・たのしい

enjoyment *n* tanoshimi 楽しみ・たのしみ, enjói エンジョイ

enlargement *n* zōdai 増大

enlightenment *n* satori 悟り・さとり

enliven; *~ with* kakki-zukemásu̲ 活気づけます・かっきづけます; nigiyaka ni shimásu̲ にぎやかにします

enormous *adj* bakudai (na) 莫大・ばくだい(な); taihen (na) 大変・たいへん(な)

enough *adj* **1.** jūbún (na) 十分・じゅうぶん(な); tappúri たっぷり; kékkō 結構・けっこう **2.** *is ~* tarimásu̲ 足ります・たります

enquiry *n* shitumon 質問, toiawase 問い合わせ

enroll (*in school*) *v* nyūgaku shimásu̲ 入学します

entangled; *gets ~* kojiremásu̲ こじれます, motsuremásu̲ もつれます

enter *v* ... (no naka) ni hairimásu̲ ... (の中[なか])に入ります; (*appears on stage*) tōjō shimásu̲ 登場します

enterprise *n* jígyō 事業

entertain *v* (*with food*) gochisō shimásu̲ ごちそう[ご馳走]します

entertainer *n* geinō´-jin 芸能人

enthusiastic *adj* nésshín (na) 熱心・ねっしん(な)

entire *adj* zentai (no) 全体・ぜんたい(の); **entire surface** zenmen 全面

entirety *n* zenzen 全然・ぜんぜん; sokkúri そっくり → **all** → **completely**

entrance *n* iriguchi 入(り)口・いりぐち, toguchi 戸口; (*front entry*) génkan 玄関; **entrance exam** *n* (*school*) nyūgaku shikén 入学試験; (*company*) nyūsha-shikén 入社試験; **entrance gate** ① (*wicket*) madoguchi 窓口 ② (*station*) kaisatsuguchi 改札口

entranced; ***gets ~ with*** … ni muchū ni narimásu …に夢中になります

entrust (*one with it*) *v* (sore o …ni) azukemásu (それを…に)預けます・あずけます; yudanemásu 委ねます・ゆだねます; makasemásu 任せます・まかせます; tanomimásu 頼みます・たのみます; irai shimásu 依頼します

entry *n* **1.** (*head word of dictionary*), midashi-go 見出し語・見だし語 **2.** (*~ upon the stage*) tōjō 登場 **3.** sanka 参加 **4.** (*registration*) tōroku 登録 **5.** (*computer*) nyūryoku 入力

envelope *n* fūtō 封筒・ふうとう

enviable/envious *adj* netamashíi ねたましい・妬ましい, urayamashíi うらやましい・羨ましい

environment *n* kankyō 環境・かんきょう; **environmental pollution** *n* kankyō-osen 環境汚染

envy *v* urayamimásu うらやみ[羨み]ます, netamimásu ねたみ[妬み]ます

epidemic *n* ryūkō-byō 流行病; densenbyō 伝染病

episode *n* (*story*) episōdo エピソード, sōwa 挿話

equal *adj* **1.** byōdō (na) 平等(な); (*on an ~ level*) taitō (no) 対等(の); (*equivalent to*) … to hitoshíi …と等しい **2.** (*extends to*) … ni oyobimásu …に及び[およ]ます

equality *n* byōdō 平等

equation *n* (*~ form*) hōtei-shiki 方程式

equator *n* sekidō 赤道

equilibrium *n* tsuriai 釣り合い・つりあい

equipment *n* (*apparatus*) sō´chi 装置, kiki 機器, (*facilities*) sétsubi 設備

equivalent *adj* taitō (no) 対等(の); ***~ to …*** to hitoshíi …と等しい・…とひとしい; … ni sōtō shimásu …に相当します

era *n* jidai 時代; …-jídai …時代

erase *v* keshimásu 消します・けします, tori-keshimásu 取り消します・とりけします

erect *v* tatemásu 立てます・たてます, (*builds*) tatemásu 建てます

erotic *adj* iroppói 色っぽい・いろっぽい, kōshoku (na) 好色(な)

err *v* ayamarimásu 誤ります・あやまります

errand *n* yōji 用事・ようじ, tsukai 使い, yō-táshí 用足し; **errand runner** *n* tsukai bashiri (tsukai-ppashiri) 使い走り

error *n* machigai 間違い・まちが

い, ayamári 誤り・あやまり, erā エラー; *is in* ~ machigaemásu 間違えます・まちがえます

eruption *n* funka 噴火; (*skin* ~) hasshin 発疹・はっしん; hosshin 発疹・ほっしん; fukidemono 吹き出物

escalator *n* esukarē´tā エスカレーター

escape *v* nigemásu 逃げます・にげます; nukemásu 抜けます・ぬけます; **a convenient escape** watari ni fúne 渡りに舟・わたりに舟

especially *adv* tokubetsu (ni) 特別(に)・とくべつ(に), kóto(-ni) こと(に)・殊(に); toriwake とりわけ; sekkakú せっかく

essay *n* zuihitsu 随筆, essē エッセー, sakubun 作文; shōron 小論

essential *adj* (*necessary*) hitsuyō (na) 必要・ひつよう(な)

essentials *n* (*supplies*) hitsuju-hin 必需品; *daily* ~ seikatsu hitsuju-hin 生活必需品

establish *v* tatemásu 建てます; okoshimásu 起こします・おこします

esteem *n* sonkei 尊敬・そんけい

estimate 1. *n* (*an* ~) mitsumori 見積もり・みつもり, kentō´ 見当, suitei 推定, (*forecast*) yosoku 予測 2. *v* (~*s it*) mi-tsumorimásu 見積もります・みつもります, (*makes a guess*) kentō´ o tsukemásu 見当をつけます, (*infers*) suitei shimásu 推定します, (*forecasts*) yosoku shimásu 予測します

estrange *v* *gets estranged* hedatarimásu 隔たります・へだたります

estranged *adj* utói うとい・疎い

eternal *adj* eien (no) 永遠・えいえん(の)

eternity *n* eien 永遠・えいえん, eikyū 永久

Ethernet *n* Ēsanetto イーサネット

ethics *n* rínri 倫理, dōtoku 道徳

ethnic *n* minzoku 民族

etiquette *n* reigí 礼儀, echikétto エチケット

euro *n* yūro ユーロ

Europe *n* Yōróppa ヨーロッパ, Ō´shū 欧州; **Europe and America** *n* Ō-Bei 欧米, Séiyō 西洋

evacuate *v* (*to flee*) hinan shimásu 避難します, (*gets repatriated*) hiki-agemásu 引き揚げます・ひきあげます

evaluation score *n* hyōten 評点

even 1. *adj* (*smooth, flat*) taira (na) 平ら・たいら(な) 2. *adj* dōtō (no) 同等(の); … **to** hitoshíi …と等しい; kinitsu na 均一な 3. *adj* gokaku no 互角の 4. *adv* … mo …も; … (de) sae (で)さえ; ~ *doing adv* (*if it does*) (shi-)té mo/(shi-) tátte (し)ても/(し)たって; **even so** (sore) démo (それ)でも

evening *n* ban 晩・ばん, yūgata 夕方・ゆうがた, yoi 宵・よい; **evening at school** *n* hōkago 放課後

event *n* kotó 事・こと; (*incident*)

jíken 事件; (*case*) dán 段; (*ceremony*) gyō´jí 行事, ibento イベント; (*game*) kyō´gí (shumoku) 競技(種目)

eventually *adv* (*come what may*) nán to itté mo 何[なん]と言っても; (*in due time*) sono uchi ni そのうちに; saishū-teki ni(wa) 最終的に(は) → **at last**

ever **1.** *adv* (*always*) ítsu-mo いつも; ***as ~*** aikawarazu 相変わらず・あいかわらず **2.** *adv* (*once*) ítsu-ka いつか, … kotó ga arimásu 事[こと]があります; ever since *adv* … írai …以来・いらい

every ... *adj* dóno … démo どの…でも; … goto (ni) … ごと・毎(に), mai-… 毎…; arayuru あらゆる; every day *adv*, *n* máinichi 毎日・まいにち, higoto (ni) 日毎(に), híbi 日々; ***almost ~ day*** máinichi no yō´ni 毎日のように; every month *adv*, *n* mai-tsuki 毎月, maigetsu 毎月; every morning *adv*, *n* mái-asa 毎朝; every night *adv*, *n* mai-ban 毎晩, mai-yo 毎夜; every station *n* kaku-eki 各駅; every time *adv*, *n* maido 毎度; ***~ that*** … tabí(ni) …度(に); every week *adv*, *n* maishū 毎週

everybody *pron* mi(n)ná み(ん)な・皆, miná-san 皆さん・みなさん; dare demo 誰でも・だれでも (= **everyone**)

everyday... *adj* (*daily*) máinichi no … 毎日の…; (*usual*) fúdan no … 普段の…・ふだんの…

everyday clothes *n* fudán-gí 普段着・ふだん着

everyone *pron* zen'in 全員

everyplace → **everywhere**

everything *pron* minná みんな・皆, zénbu 全部・ぜんぶ, nan demo 何でも・なんでも, íssái 一切; monógoto 物事

everywhere *adv* doko demo どこでも, dóko ni mo どこにも, hō´bō 方々・ほうぼう

evidence *n* shōko 証拠; (*basis*) kónkyo 根拠・こんきょ

evil *n* **1.** → **bad** **2.** (*a devil*) ákú 悪; evil spirit *n* ákuma 悪魔・アクマ

e-wallet *n* denshi-saifu 電子財布

exact *adj* (*detailed*) kuwashíi 詳しい・くわしい, komakái 細かい・こまかい; (*correct*) seikaku (na) 正確・せいかく(な)

exactly *adv* chōdo ちょうど, pit-tári ぴったり, hakkíri はっきり; másani まさに・正に; … daké… だけ

exaggerate *v* kochō shimásu 誇張します

examination *n* **1.** (*test*) shikén 試験 **2.** (*inquiry*) chō´sa 調査 **3.** (*inspection*) kénsa 検査, (*medical*) shinsatsu 診察

examine *v* **1.** (*investigates*) shirabemásu 調べます・しらべます **2.** kentō shimásu 検討します・けんとうします **3.** (*medically*) mimásu 診ます・みます, shinsatsu shimásu 診察します・しん

さつします **4. ~ *tickets*** kaisatsu shimásu 改札します; (*aboard*) kensatsu shimásu 検札します

example *n* réi 例, ichi-rei 一例, tatoe 例え・たとえ, tatoi 例い・たとい; ***follows*** (*learns from*) ***the ~ of …*** o mi-naraimásu …を見習います; for example → **e.g.**

excavate *v* horimásu 掘ります

exceed *v* sugimásu 過ぎます, chōka shimásu 超過します

exceedingly *adv* móttómo 最も・もっとも, góku ごく・極, taihen 大変・たいへん, hijō ni 非常に・ひじょうに

excel *v* sugúrete imásu 優れています・すぐれています

excellent *adj* sugúreta 優れた・すぐれた, yūshū (na) 優秀(な); kékkō (na) 結構・けっこう(な)

except (*for*) *prep* …no hoka…の他, …ígai …以外・…いがい

exception *n* reigai 例外; ***without ~*** (*all*) íssái 一切・いっさい

excess *n* chōka 超過, kajō 過剰; (*leeway, margin*) yoyū 余裕・よゆう; ***is in ~*** amarimásu 余ります・あまります

excessive *adj* yokei (na) 余計・よけい(な), hōgai (na) 法外(な); (*extreme*) kageki (na) 過激(な), kyokután na 極端(な)

exchange *v* (tori-)kaemásu (取り)替えます・かえます, hiki-kaemásu 引き換えます・ひきかえます, kōkan shimásu 交換します

exchange rate *n* kawase rēto 為替レート

excitement *n* kōfun 興奮

exciting *adj* wakuwaku saseru ワクワクさせる, kōfun saseru 興奮させる, kōfun suru 興奮する

exclude *v* háijo shimásu 排除します

exclusion *n* háijo 排除

excrement *n* daibén 大便, kusó 糞・クソ

excursion *n* ensoku 遠足・えんそく, yūran 遊覧

excuse *n* ii-wake 言い訳・いいわけ, mōshiwake 申し訳・申しわけ; (*pretext*) kōjitsu 口実; makes excuses (*apologizes*) ii-wake o shimásu 言い訳をします; (*declines*) kotowarimásu 断ります・ことわります

Excuse me. Sumimasén すみません; Osóre-irimásu. 恐れ入ります・おそれいります; Dō´mo. どうも; Gomen nasái. ごめんなさい; Shitsúrei shimásu. 失礼します.; Excuse me but I'll be on my way. Sore déwa shitsúrei (ita)shimásu. それでは失礼(いた)します.

exempt *v* ***is ~ from*** … o manukaremásu …を免れます・まぬかれます; tax-exempt *adj* menzei (no) 免税(の)

exercise **1.** *n* (*physical*) undō 運動, (*calisthenics*) taisō 体操; (*study*) renshū 練習・れんしゅう, (*practice*) dóríru ドリル, (o-)keiko (お)稽古お・(お)けいこ **2.** *v* undō shimásu 運動します

exert *v* (*~s oneself*) tsutomemásu

努めます・つとめます; tsukushimásu 尽くします・つくします

exhaust 1. *n* haiki 排気; (*fumes*) haiki-gásu 排気ガス 2. *~s it v* tsukai-hatashimásu 使い果たします・使いはたします; (*runs out of*) kirashimásu 切らします・きらします

exhibit 1. *n* tenji(-kai) 展示(会), tenrán-kai 展覧会 2. *v ~s it* misemásu 見せます・みせます; shuppin shimásu 出品します

exhibition *n* tenjí-kai 展示会, tenrán-kai 展覧会, hakuránkai 博覧会

exhibitor *n* shuppín-sha 出品者

exist *v* sonzai shimásu 存在します

existence *n* (*survives or does not survive*) sonzai 存在, seizon 生存; (or *exists or does not exist*) úmu 有無

exit 1. *n* dé-guchi 出口; ***north/ south/ east/west ~*** kita/minami/ higashi/nishi-guchi 北/南/東/西口 2. *v* taijō shimásu 退場します

exorbitant *adj* hogai (na) 法外(な)

expand *v* hirogarimásu 広がります・ひろがります; bōchō shimásu 膨脹します

expect *v* (*awaits*) mátte imásu 待っています・まっています, kitai shimásu 期待します; (*anticipates*) yosō shimásu 予想します; **expect to** (*do*) ... (suru) tsumori dé su ... (する)つもりです

expectation *n* mikomi 見込み・みこみ, tsumori つもり, ate 当て・あて, yosō 予想・よそう, yotei 予定・よてい; kitai 期待・きたい; ...hazu ...はず

expedient *adj* tsugō no yoi 都合のよい

expense *n* híyō 費用, kei-hi 経費; ...-hi ...費

expensive *adj* (ne ga) takái (値が)高い

experience 1. *n* keiken 経験・けいけん, (*personal*) taiken 体験・たいけん; (*a sometime happening*) ...kotó ...事・こと; (*professional*) shokureki 職歴 2. *v* (*~s, undergoes*) keiken shimásu 経験します, ...mé ni aimásu ...目にあいます

experiment 1. *n* jikken (o shimásu) 実験・じっけん(をします); (*test*) shikén 試験, tameshí 試し 2. *v ~s with* ... o tameshimásu, ...を試します・...をためします

expert 1. *adj* jōzú (na) じょうず・上手(な), tassha (na) 達者(な) 2. *n* meijín 名人, tsū 通, tsūjin 通人, (*veteran*) kúrō´to くろうと・玄人, beteran ベテラン, (*specialist*) senmon-ka 専門家

expire *v* (*contract, rights, etc.*) shikkō shimásu 失効します

explain *v* setsumei shimásu 説明します・せつめいします; tokimásu 説きます; káishaku shimásu 解釈します・かいしゃくします

explanation *n* setsumei 説明・せつめい; (*interpretation*) kái-shaku 解釈; (*excuse*) ii-wake 言い訳・いいわけ

explicit *adj* meihaku (na) 明白(な)
explode *v* bakuhatsu shimásu 爆発します
exploit **1.** *n* tegara 手柄 **2.** *v* riyō shimásu 利用します
explosion *n* bakuhatsu 爆発
export **1.** *n* (*exporting*) yushutsu 輸出 **2.** *v* **~s it** yushutsu shimásu 輸出します; **export goods** *n* yushutsu-hin 輸出品
exposition *n* **1.** (*a fair*) hakurán-kai 博覧会 **2.** (*explanation*) káishaku 解釈
express **1.** *n* (*train, bus*) kyūkō 急行 **2.** *v* (*puts into words*) ii-arawashimásu 言い表します・言いあらわします; **express train** *n* kyūkō-ressha 急行列車
expression *n* (*way of saying*) iikata 言い方・言いかた, (*phrase*) hyōgen 表現・ひょうげん; (*on face*) hyōjō 表情・ひょうじょう, kao 顔・かお
extend *v* **1.** (*~s it*) nobashimásu 延ばします・のばします, enchō shimásu 延長します **2.** (*it ~s*) nobimásu 伸びます・のびます, (*reaches*) oyobimásu 及びます・およびます
extension *n* (*cord*) enchō-kō´do 延長コード; (*phone line, inside*) naisen 内線, (*outside*) gaisen 外線
extent *n* kágirí 限り・かぎり; hodo 程・ほど; teido 程度; kagen 加減; ***to what ~*** dónna ni どんなに
exterior *n* gáibu 外部, gaimen 外面
external *adj* soto-gawa (no) 外側(の); gáibu/gaimen (no) 外部/外面(の); gai-... 外...
extinguish *v* keshimásu 消します・けします; ***gets extinguished*** kiemásu 消えます・きえます
extol *v* homemásu 褒めます・ほめます
extortion *n* yusuri ゆすり
extra **1.** *n* (*actor/actress*) ekisutora エキストラ **2.** *n* (*bonus*) omake おまけ **3.** *adj* yobun (no/ni) 余分・よぶん(に/の); (*special*) tokubetsu (no) 特別・とくべつ(の); **extra charge** *n* betsu-ryō´kin 別料金
extract *n* ekisu エキス
extraordinary *adj* rinji (no) 臨時(の); namihazureta 並外れた・並はずれた
extravagant *adj* zeitákú (na) ぜいたく・贅沢(な); ogorimásu おごります・驕ります
extreme *adj* kyokután (na) 極端(な); (*radical*) kageki (na) 過激(な)
extremely *adv* hijō (ni) 非常・ひじょう(に), hanahada 甚だ・はなはだ, góku ごく・極, shigoku しごく, kyokután (ni) 極端・きょくたん(に), to(t)temo と(っ)ても, monosúgóku 物凄く・ものすごく, zúibun 随分・ずいぶん; (*more than one might expect*) nakanaka なかなか
eye *n* **1.** mé 目[眼] **2.** (*detective*) tantei 探偵; (*of a needle*) médo めど; ***(with) wide ~s*** me o maruku shimásu 目を丸くします; **public**

eye *n* seken no me 世間の目
eyeglasses *n* mégane 眼鏡・めがね・メガネ; ***puts on*** (*wears*) ~ mégane o kakemásu 眼鏡・メガネをかけます
eyesight *n* shíryoku 視力

F

fable *n* gūwa 寓話
fabric *n* ori-mono 織物・おりもの, kíji 生地・きじ
fabulous *adj* subarashii すばらしい・素晴らしい, wakuwaku suru ワクワクする
face 1. *n* kao 顔・かお, tsurá つら・面; (*one's honor*) taimen 体面 **2.** *n* (*front*) shō´men 正面 **3.** *v* (*~s it*) mukimásu 向きます・むきます **4.** *v* atarimásu 当たります・あたります; **face towel** *n* fēsu taoru フェースタオル
Facebook *n* (*Internet*) feisu bukku フェイスブック
facial *adj* kao (no) 顔(の)
facilities *n* shisetsu 施設・しせつ, sétsubi 設備; bén 便・びん
facsimile *n* fakushimiri ファクシミリ, fákkusu ファックス → **fax**
fact *n* kotó 事・こと, jíjitsu 事実・じじつ; ***in*** ~ jitsú wa 実は・じつは, jissai (wa) 実際・じっさい(な)
factory *n* kō´ba/kō´jō´ 工場
fad *n* ichiji-teki ryūkō 一時的流行
fade *v* **1.** samemásu さめます, asemásu あせます・褪せます **2.** (*grows weak*) otoroemásu 衰えます・おとろえます **3.** (*vanishes*) kiemásu 消えます・きえます;
fade-out *n* fēdo auto フェードアウト
fail *v* **1.** shippai shimásu 失敗します **2.** (*exam*) ochimásu 落ちます・おちます, rakudai shimásu 落第します **3.** (*is wide off the mark*) hazuremásu 外れます・はずれます **4.** (*engine etc. breaks down*) koshō´ shimásu 故障します
failure *n* **1.** shippai 失敗・しっぱい **2.** (*exam*) rakudai 落第, fugō´kaku 不合格; **power failure** *n* teiden 停電
faint 1. *adj* (*dim*) kásuka (na) かすか[微か](な) **2.** *v* (*loses consciousness*) ki o ushinaimásu 気を失い[うしない]ます
fair *n* (*market*) íchi 市, íchi-bá 市場・いちば, (*temple festival*) én-nichi 縁日・えんにち
fair *adj* (*just, impartial*) kō´hei (na) 公平(な); (*sunny*) hárete imásu 晴れています・はれています; ~ ***weather*** haré 晴れ・はれ, (o-)ténki (お)天気・てんき
fairly *adv* (*rather*) kánari かなり, sō´tō´ 相当・そうとう, zúibun 随分・ずいぶん
fairy tale *n* dōwa 童話, otogibánashi おとぎ話
faithful *adj* seijitsu (na) 誠実(な),

chūjitsu (na) 忠実(な), makoto (no) 誠・まこと(の)

fake **1.** *adj* nise (no) 偽・にせ(の), inchiki (na) いんちき・インチキ(な) **2.** *n* (*thing*) nise-mono 偽物・にせもの, inchiki いんちき・インチキ, feiku フェイク

falcon *n* taka タカ・鷹, hayabusa ハヤブサ・隼

fall **1.** *n* (*autumn*) áki 秋 **2.** *v* (*it falls*) ochimásu 落ちます・おちます, okkochimásu 落っこちます・おっこちます **3.** *v* (*falls and scatters*) chirimásu, 散ります・ちります; **fall behind** okuremásu 遅れます・おくれます; okure o torimásu 後れを取ります・おくれをとります; **fall down** taoremásu 倒れます・たおれます, korobimásu 転びます・ころびます

fallacy *n* goshin 誤信

falls *n* taki 滝・たき (= **waterfalls**)

false *adj* (*falsehood*) úso (no) うそ・嘘・ウソ(の); (*fake*) nise (no) 偽・にせ(の), (*artificial*) jinzō´ (no) 人造(の); **false alarm** *n* go-keihō 誤警報

falsehood *n* úso うそ・嘘・ウソ, itsuwari 偽り・いつわり

falter *v* yoro-mekimásu よろめきます, yóro-yoro shimásu よろよろします

fame *n* **1.** (*reputation*) hyō´ban 評判 **2.** → **honor**

familiar *adj* shitashíi 親しい・したしい → **know**

family *n* uchi 家・うち, … (o-)uchi (お)家; kázoku 家族・かぞく, (*household*) 家庭; (*clan*) úji 氏・うじ, …-ke …家

family inn *n* minshuku 民宿・みんしゅく

family name *n* (*surname*) sei 姓, , (*as written*) myō´ji, miyoji 名字・苗字, úji 氏, kámei 家名

famine *n* ue 飢え, kikin 飢饉・ききん

famous *adj* yūmei (na) 有名・ゆうめい(な), na-dakái 名高い, hyoban (no) 評判・ひょうばん(の); **gets** ~ shiraremásu 知られます・しられます, yūmei ni na--rimásu 有名になります

fan *n* **1.** ō´gí 扇・おうぎ; (*electric*) senpū´-ki 扇風機・せんぷうき **2.** (*enthusiast*) fán ファン; **baseball fan** *n* yakyū-fan 野球ファン・やきゅうファン

fancy *adj* (*high-grade*) kō´kyū (no) 高級(の); **fancy goods** *n* kō´kyū-hin 高級品

fanfare *n* fanfāre ファンファーレ

fang *n* kiba 牙・キバ

fantastic *n* subarashii 素晴らしい

fantasy *n* (*imaginary*) kūsō 空想, fantajii ファンタジー

FAQ *abbrev* (= *frequently asked questions*) yoku aru shitsumon よくある質問, efu ei-kyū/feiku FAQ

far *adj* tō´i 遠い・とおい, háruka (na) はるかな・遥か(な); háruka (ni) はるかに・遥か(に); **how far** donogurai/donokurai どの位,

dóko made どこまで; as far as it goes ichiō´ 一応; by far zutto ずっと, háruka (ni) はるか・遥か(に)

fare *n* (*fee*) ryō´kin 料金, (*transportation*) únchin 運賃

Far East *n* kyokutō´ 極東

farewell *n* (o-)wakare (お)別れ・(お)わかれ; **farewell party** *n* sō´bé-tsukai 送別れ会, o-wakare-kai お別れ会

farm *n* nō´jō´ 農場

farmer *n* nō´ka 農家, nō´min 農民

far-off *adj* tō´i 遠い・とおい, háruka (na) はるか・遥か(な)

farsighted *adj* enshi (no) 遠視(の); (*forward-looking*) mae-muki (no) 前向き・前むき(の); senken no mei (no/ga aru) 先見の明(の/がある)

fart *n* onara (o shimásu) おなら(をします); [IMPOLITE] hé (o hiri-másu) へ・屁(をひります)

fascinated *adj* uttóri (to) うっとり(と)

fascist *n* fashisuto ファシスト

fashion 1. *n* (*way*) ryūkō´ 流行, hayari はやり[流行り], fásshon ファッション; (…) fū (…)風・ふう 2. ***is in ~*** hayarimásu はやり[流行り]ます

fashionable *adj* hayari (no) はやり[流行り](の), ryūkō´ (no) 流行(の); haikara (na) ハイカラ(な), sumā´to (na) スマート(な)

fast *adj* háyaku 速く・はやく; hayái 速い・はやい; (*clock runs fast*) susunde imásu 進んでいます・すすんでいます

fasten *v* 1. (*firmly attaches*) tome-másu 留めます・とめます 2. (*tightens, secures*) shimemásu 締めます・しめます

fastener *n* fasunā ファスナー, chakku チャック

fast food *n* fāsuto fūdo ファーストフード

fastidious → **choosy**

fat 1. *n* (*grease*) abura あぶら・脂, (*lard, blubber*) shibō´ 脂肪・しぼう 2. ***gets ~*** *v* futorimásu 太ります・ふとります, koemásu 肥えます・こえます 3. *adj* (*plump*) futói 太い・ふとい, futotta 太った・ふとった

fate *n* ún 運, únmei 運命・うんめい, shukumei 宿命

father *n* otō´san お父さん・おとうさん, chichí 父, chichi oya 父親・ちちおや

Father *n* (*Reverend*) …shínpu(-san) …神父(さん)

fatigue *n* hirō 疲労

fatty *adj* abrakkói 脂っこい・あぶらっこい; ~ ***tuna*** tóro とろ・トロ

faucet *n* jaguchi 蛇口・じゃぐち

fault 1. *n* (*defect*) kizu きず; (*shortcoming*) tánsho 短所; (*guilt*) tsúmi 罪・つみ; (*cause*) …séi …せい 2. ***at ~*** warúi 悪い・わるい 3. ***finds ~ with*** toga-memásu とがめ[咎め]ます

favor 1. *n* (*kindness*) (go-)shínsetsu (ご)親切,・(ご)しんせつ (*good-will*) kō´i 好意・こうい; (*request*) o-nagai お願い・おねがい **2.** ***does a ~*** kō´i o misemásu̲ 好意を見せます[みせます]; ***does me/us the ~ of …ing*** …te kudasaimásu̲/kuremásu̲ …て下さいます・…てくださいます/くれます **3. *~s*** *v* (*a choice*) … (no) hō´ga íi to omoimásu̲ …(の)方がいいと思います・…(の)ほうがいいとおもいます

favorite *adj* dái-su̲ki (na) 大好き・だいすき(な), (ichiban) su̲kí (na) (一番)好き(な); o-kiniiri (no) お気に入り・おきにいり

favoritism *n* ekohiiki えこひいき

fax *n* fákku̲su ファックス

fear 1. *n* (*a fear*) osoré 恐れ・おそれ, kyō´fu 恐怖・きょうふ; shinpai 心配・しんぱい **2. *~s it*** *v* osoremásu̲ 恐れます・おそれます; kowagarimásu̲ 怖がります・こわがります; (*worries about*) shinpai shimásu̲ 心配します・しんぱいします

fearful *adj* osoroshíi 恐ろしい・おそろしい

feat *n* waza 業・わざ; (*deed*) shiwaza 仕業・しわざ

feather *n* hane 羽, umō´ 羽毛・うもう; ke 毛

feature *n* tokuchō 特徴

February *n* Ni-gatsú 二月・2月

feces *n* ku̲só くそ・糞, fún ふん・糞; bén 便, daibén 大便

federation *n* renmei 連盟

fee *n* ryō´kin 料金; …-ryō´ …料; (*reward*) sharei 謝礼, rei 礼; ***membership ~*** kaihi 会費

feeble → **weak**

feed *v* tabesasemásu̲ 食べさせます・たべさせます

feel 1. *v* (*by touch*) sawarimásu̲ さわり[触り]ます **2.** (*by emotion*) kan-jimásu̲ 感じます・かんじます **3.** (*thinks*) omoimásu̲ 思います・おもいます **4.** zon-jimásu̲ 存じます・ぞんじます; zon-jiagemásu̲ 存じあげます・ぞんじあげます **5.** (*body reaction*) moyō´shimásu̲ 催します・もよおします

feeling *n* kimochi 気持ち・きもち, kanji 感じ・かんじ, ki 気・き, nén 念・ねん; (*sense*) kimí 気味・きみ; kokóro 心・こころ, omói 思い・おもい; (*mood*) kokoro-mochi 心持ち・こころもち, kíbun 気分・きぶん; (*one's view*) íkō´ 意向; (*health*) (karada no) guai (体[からだ]の)具合・ぐあい; (*compassion*) (o-)násake (お)情け・(な)さけ, nínjō´ 人情・にんじょう

fellow *n* (*person*) hi̲to 人・ひと, … hi̲tó …人; monó 者, yátsu やつ・奴; (*comrade*) fellow … … dō´shi …同志; (*man*) otoko 男

female *n* onná (no hi̲to) 女・おんな(の人[ひと]), josei 女性; ***female …*** (*animal*) mesu no … メスの…

fence *n* kakíne 垣根・かきね, (*wall*) hei 塀・へい

fencing *n* fenshingu フェンシン

グ; ***the art of Japanese ~*** (*with bamboo swords*) kéndō´ 剣道・ケンドウ

ermented *adj* 発酵した; **fermented bean paste** míso みそ・ミソ・味噌 (o-míso おみそ・お味噌)

ern *n* shída しだ・シダ

erry (*them over*) *v* watashimás<u>u</u> 渡します・わたします

ester *v* umimás<u>u</u> うみます・膿みます

estival *n* (o-)matsuri (お)祭り・(お)まつり

eudal (*period, system*) *adj* hō´ken (-jídai/-séido) no 封建(時代/制度)の; **feudal lord** *n* (o-)daimyō´ (お)大名

ever *n* (o-)nétsu (お)熱; fiibā フィーバー; ***became feverish*** fiibā shimás<u>u</u> フィーバーします

ew *adj* s<u>u</u>kóshi (no) 少し・すこし(の); s<u>u</u>kunái 少ない・すくない; **a few** wazuka わずか; s<u>u</u>koshi 少し→ **several**

ewer *adj* (yori) s<u>u</u>kunái (より)少ない・すくない

ib *n* (*lie*) úso うそ・嘘

iber *n* sén'i 繊維・せんい; (*line*) súji 筋・すじ

ickle *adj* uwaki (na) 浮気・うわき(な)

iction *n* shō´setsu 小説, ts<u>u</u>kuribanashi 作り話・つくりばなし, fikushon フィクション; **science fiction** *n* saiensu fikushon サイエンスフィクション

ief *n* ryōchi 領地

field *n* (*dry*) hatake 畑・はたけ; nóhara 野原・のはら, hárappa 原っぱ・はらっぱ; (*rice paddy*) tá 田・た, tanbo 田んぼ・たんぼ; (*specialty*) senmon 専門・せんもん; **field day** *n* ① (*military*) yagai-enshū-bi 野外演習日 ② (*athletic festival*) undō-kai 運動会

fierce *adj* hageshíi 激しい・はげしい, sugói すごい・凄い

fifth *adj* go-banmé (no) 五番目(の), its<u>u</u>tsu-mé (no) 五つ目・いつつめ(の); **the fifth day** its<u>u</u>ka-me 五日目, (*of the month*) its<u>u</u>ka 五日

fig *n* ichíjiku いちじく・イチジク

fight *v* tatakaimás<u>u</u> 戦います・たたかいます → **argue**

figure → **count; number; think; shape; body; being, person; diagram**

file *n* **1.** (*nail ~, etc.*) yasuri やすり **2.** (*computer*) fairu ファイル **3.** → **folder** **4.** *v* (*grinds*) surimás<u>u</u> すります **5.** *v* (*submits*) teishutsu shimás<u>u</u> 提出します; ***~ income tax*** kakutei o shinkoku shimás<u>u</u> 確定申告をします **6.** *v* (*stores document*) shorui o tojimás<u>u</u> 書類を綴じます

filet *n* (*of pork etc.*) hire ヒレ

Filipino *n* (*language*) Firipin-go フィリピン語; (*person*) Firipin-jin フィリピン人

fill *v* **1.** ippai ni shimás<u>u</u> 一杯にします・いっぱいにします; mitashimás<u>u</u> 満たします・み

たします; ~*s the tank*, ~*s it up* man-tan ni shimásu̲ 満タンにします **2.** (*fulfills*) konashimásu̲ こなします, ~ *an order* chūmon o konashimásu̲ 注文をこなします **3.** ~*s in* (*details*) kaki-iremásu̲ 書き入れます・かきいれます, kinyū shimásu̲ 記入します

film *n* f(u)irumu フィルム(フイルム); (*movie*) eiga 映画

filter 1. *n* f(u)írutā フィルター(フイルター) **2.** *v* (~*s it*) koshimásu̲ こします

filthy → **dirty**

fin *n* hire ひれ・ヒレ

final *adj* saigo (no) 最後・さいご(の), saishū (no) 最終(の)

finalization *n* seiritsu 成立

finance 1. *n* kin'yū 金融; kéizai 経済; zaisei 財政 **2.** ~*s it v* yūzū shimásu̲ 融通します

find 1. *v* mitsu̲kemásu̲ 見つけます・みつけます **2.** *n* (*bargain*) horidashi-mono 掘り出し物・ほりだしもの; find fault with togamemásu̲ とがめ[咎め]ます; find out (*hears*) (... ga) mimí ni hairimásu̲ (...が)耳に入ります・(...が)みみにはいります; (... ga) wakarimásu̲ (...が)分かります・(...が)わかります

fine 1. *adj* (*small/detailed*) komakái 細かい・こまかい, (*minute*) bisai (na) 微細・びさい(な), (*delicate*) bimyō´ (na) 微妙・びみょう(な) **2.** → **OK, good, splendid, fair 3.** *n* (*penalty*) bakkin 罰金・ばっきん

finger *n* yubí 指・ゆび

fingerprint *n* shimon 指紋・しもん

finish 1. *n* → **end 2.** *v* (*finishes ... ing*) ...te shimaimásu̲ ...てしまいます

Finland *n* Finrando フィンランド

fire 1. *n* hí 火, (*accidental*) káji 火事・かじ, kasai 火災; (*bonfire*) takibi たき火・たきび **2.** *v* (*lays off, disemploys*) kubi ni shimásu̲ 首にします・くびにします, kotowarimásu̲ 断ります・ことわります, káiko shimásu̲ 解雇します・かいこします; ***got fired*** kubi ni narimáshi̲ta 首になりました・くびになりました; fire alarm *n* kasai-kéihō´ 火災警報; (*device*) kasai-hō´chi̲ki 火災報知器; fire engine *n* shō´bō´-sha 消防車; fire fighter, fireman *n* shō´bō´-shi 消防士

fireworks *n* hána-bi 花火・はなび

firm 1. *adj* jō´bu (na) 丈夫・じょうぶ(な); (*hard*) katai 固い・硬い・堅い・かたい **2.** *n* (*business*) → **company**

firmly *adv* kataku 固く・硬く・堅く・かたく; (*securely*) chanto ちゃんと; (*resolutely*) shi̲kkári しっかり

first *adj* hajime (no) 初め・はじめ(の), saisho (no) 最初・さいしょ(の), hatsu (no) 初・はつ(の); (*number one*) ichí-ban (no) 一番・いちばん(の); first aid *n* ō´kyū-téate 応急手当; first class *adj* ik-kyū 一級; (*ticket, seat*) it-tō´ 一等; (*hotel, school*) ichiryū (no) 一流・いちりゅう(の); first day of the month *n* tsuitachí 一日・ついたち; first day of the year *n* ganjitsu 元日, gantan 元旦・がんたん; first time *adj* hajímete (no) 初めて・はじめて(の)

irst-rate *adj* ichiryū (no) 一流・いちりゅう(の); jō´tō (no) 上等・じょうとう(の)

ish **1.** *n* (o-)sakana (お)さかな・(お)魚, uo 魚; ***sliced raw ~*** sashimi 刺身・さしみ **2.** *v* (*angles*) tsurimásu 釣ります・つります; fishballs *n* (*for soup*) tsumire つみれ・ツミレ; fish dealer/market *n* sakana-ya 魚屋・さかな屋

isherman *n* ryō´shi 漁師, gyo´fu 魚夫

ishing *n* (*as sport*) (sakaná-) tsuri (魚)釣り・つり, ryō´ 漁・りょう; (*business*) gyogyō´ 漁業

ishy *adj* (*questionable*) kusái 臭い・くさい; ***~-smelling*** namagusái 生臭い・なまぐさい

ist *n* kobushi こぶし・拳, genkotsu げんこつ・拳骨, genko げんこ

it **1.** *adj* (*suitable*) tekigi (no) 適宜・てきぎ(の); ***~s … nicely***… ni yóku aimásu …に良く合います・…によくあいます **2.** *v* ***~s it to …*** ni ate-hamemásu …に当てはめます・…にあてはめます **3.** *n* (*a good ~*) saizu ga atteiru サイズが合っている

five *n* gó 五・5; itsútsu 五つ・いつつ; fáibu ファイブ

fix **1.** *v* (*repairs*) naoshimásu 直します・なおします; (*makes*) tsukurimásu 作ります・つくります; (*prepares*) sonaemásu 備えます・そなえます; (*settles*) sadamemásu 定めます・さだめます **2.** *n* (*plight*) hamé 羽目・はめ, kukyō 苦境

fixed *adj* (*settled*) ittei (no) 一定・いってい(の); (*periodic*) téiki (no) 定期・ていき(の); tei-…定…

fixture *n* kígu 器具

flag *n* hatá 旗・はた; (*national*) kokki 国旗

flame *n* honō´ 炎・ほのお

flap **1.** *n* (*of envelope, etc.*) futa ふた・蓋, furappu フラップ **2.** *v* ***~s the wings*** habatakimásu 羽ばたきます

flare *n* hatsuen-tō 発炎筒, furea フレア

flashlight *n* kaichū-déntō´ 懐中電灯, dentō´ 電灯

flashy *adj* hadé (na) 派手・はで(な)

flask *n* furasuko フラスコ

flat **1.** *n* heimén 平面 **2.** *n* (*apartment*) furátto フラット, apāto アパート **3.** *adj* taira (na) 平ら・たいら(な), hiratai 平たい・ひらたい; (*flavorless*) ajikenái 味気ない; flat land *n* heichi 平地; flat rate *n* kin'itsu-ryōkin 均一料金

flatter *v* o-seji o iimásu お世辞を

言います・おせじをいいます; goma o surimás<u>u</u> ごま[胡麻・ゴマ]をすります

flatulate *v* → **fart**

flatulence *n* onara おなら・オナラ, hé へ・屁

flavor **1.** *n* aji 味・あじ, fū´mí 風味; (*seasoning*) chō´mi 調味, kagen 加減 **2.** *v* (*seasons it*) … ni aji o ts<u>u</u>kemás<u>u</u> …に味を付け[つけ]ます; **flavor sprinkles** (*to top rice*) *n* furikake ふりかけ・フリカケ

flaw *n* kizu 傷・きず, (*defect*) ketten 欠点

flee *v* nigemás<u>u</u> 逃げます・にげます

fleet *n* (*fleet of ships*) kantai 艦隊

fleeting *adj* (*transitory*) hakánai はかない・儚い

flesh *n* nik<u>u</u>tai 肉体

flicker *n* chiratsuki ちらつき; chika-chikashita hikari チカチカした光

flies → **fly**

flight (*number* …) *n* …-bin …便

flight attendant *n* kyak<u>u</u>sh<u>i</u>tsu jō´-muin 客室乗務員, furaito-aten-danto フライト・アテンダント

float **1.** *v* (*it floats*) ukabimás<u>u</u> 浮かびます・うかびます, ukimás<u>u</u>, 浮きます・うきます; (*~s it*) ukabemás<u>u</u> 浮かべます・うかべます **2.** *n* (*swimming ~*) ukiwa 浮き輪

flock **1.** *n* muré 群れ・むれ **2.** *v* ***they ~ together*** muragarimás<u>u</u> 群がります

flood **1.** *n* kō´zui 洪水, ō´mízú 大水 **2.** *v* hanran shimás<u>u</u> 氾濫します・はんらんします

floor *n* yuka 床, furoa フロア; (*story*) (-)kai 階; ***mezzanine ~*** chū-ní-kai 中二階; **floor lamp** *n* (denki) s<u>u</u>tándo (電気)スタンド; **floor mat(ting)** *n* tatami 畳・タタミ

floppy *n* furoppii (disuku) フロッピー・ディスク, FD

florist *n* haná-ya 花屋

flounder *n* hirame ひらめ・ヒラメ

flour *n* koná 粉・こな, kó 粉; (*wheat*) komugi-ko 小麦粉, meriken-ko メリケン粉

flourish *v* sakaemás<u>u</u> 栄えます・さかえます

flow **1.** ***it ~s*** *v* nagaremás<u>u</u> 流れます・ながれます **2.** ***~s it*** *v* naga-shimás<u>u</u> 流します・ながします **3.** *n* (*outflow*) de 出, nagaré 流れ・ながれ

flower **1.** *n* (o-)hana (お)花・(お)はな **2.** *v* (*blooms*) (hana ga) sakimás<u>u</u> (花が)咲きます; **flower arrangement** *n* (*arranging*) o-hana お花, ikébana 生け花・いけばな, kadō 華道; **flowerpot** *n* uekí-bachi 植木鉢・うえき鉢; **flower shop** → **florist**; **flower viewing** *n* (o-)hanami (お)花見・(お)はなみ

flu *n* infuruénza インフルエンザ

fluent *adj* ryū´chō´ (na) 流ちょう[流暢](な); (*can speak it fluently*) jiyū (/ryū´chō´) ni hanasemás<u>u</u> 自由(/流暢)に話せます

luent(ly) *adj* (*adv*) (*speaking*) perapera (to) ぺらぺら・ペラペラ(と); (*writing*) surasura (to) すらすら(と)

lush **1.** *n* (*the ~ on one's face*) sekimen (shimásu) 赤面(します) **2.** *v* (*~s the toilet*) (toire o) nagashimásu (トイレを)流します・ながします; **flush toilet** *n* suisentóire 水洗トイレ

lustered; ***gets*** ~ awatemásu あわてます・慌てます; ***feels*** ~ teremásu 照れます・てれます; ***a person easily*** ~ awate-mono あわて者・慌て者

flutter; ***one's heart ~s*** dókidoki shimásu どきどき[ドキドキ]します

fly **1.** *n* (*insect*) hae 蝿・ハエ **2.** *v* (*moves in air*) tobimásu 飛びます・とびます; (*flies it*) tobashimásu 飛ばします・とばします, ***flies a kite*** táko o agemásu 凧を揚げます・たこをあげます; (*pilots*) sō´jū shimásu 操縦します; (*goes by plane*) hikō´-ki de ikimásu 飛行機で行きます・ひこうきでいきます

foam → bubble

focus **1.** *n* (*camera*) pinto ピント; (*focal point*) shō´ten 焦点; ***out-of-~*** pinboke ピンぼけ **2.** *v* shōten o awasemásu 焦点を合わせます; shūchū-sasemasu 集中させます

fodder *n* shiryō 飼料

fog *n* kiri 霧・きり

fold **1.** *n* ori-mé 折り目 **2.** *v* (*~s it*) orimásu 折ります・おります, (*~s it up*) tatamimásu 畳みます・たたみます; (*it ~s*) oremásu 折れます; ***~s one's arms*** udé o kumimásu 腕を組みます

folder *n* **1.** ***file*** ~ kami-básami 紙挟み, fairu ファイル **2.** (*computer*) foruda フォルダ, forudā フォルダー

folk *adj* minkan no 民間の; **folkcraft** *n* mingei 民芸, mingei-hin 民芸品; **folk dance** *n* fōku dansu フォークダンス, minyō-buyō 民謡舞踊;

folks → people; parents; family

follow *v* (*follows it*) … no áto o tsukemásu …のあとをつけます; (*adheres to*) … ni tsukimásu … に付きます・… につきます; (*conforms to*) … ni shitagaimásu … に従います・… にしたがいます; (*runs along*) … ni soimásu …に沿います・…にそいます; ***~ the example of*** ... o mi-naraimásu …を見習います

follower *n* (*adherent*) shijisha 支持者

following **1.** *adj* tsugí (no) 次・つぎ(の), ika (no) 以下(の), kaki (no) 下記(の) **2.** *n* (*a following*) fan ファン

folly *n* gukō 愚行, orokasa 愚かさ・おろかさ

fond of → like

fondness *n* konomi 好み

food *n* **1.** tabe-mónó 食べ物・たべもの, góhan 御飯・ごはん, shokúmotsu 食物; (*meal*) shoku

食, (*Western*) yō´-shoku 洋食; (*Japanese*) wa-shoku 和食 **2.** *n* (*stuff*) → **groceries**; food poisoning shoku-chūdoku 食中毒, shoku-atari 食あたり

fool 1. *n* báka ばか・馬鹿, tónma とんま・頓馬; fool around *v* fuza-kemásu ふざけます **2.** *~s (someone) v* karakaimásu からかいます

foolish *adj* baka-rashíi ばか[馬鹿]らしい, báka (na) ばか[馬鹿](な)

foot *n* ashí 足; (*of a mountain*) fumotó ふもと・麓

football *n* (*American*) (amerikan) futto-bōru (アメリカン) フットボール, amefuto アメフト

footlight *n* futto-raito フットライト, kyakkō 脚光

footnote *n* kyakuchū 脚注

footprint *n* ashi-áto 足跡

footwear *n* hakimono 履物・はきもの

for *prep* … (no) tamé (ni)…(の)ため(に); … ni (wa) … に(は); … ni tótte … にとって; …no… … の… ; (*for the use of*) …-yō´ (no) …用(の); (*suitable for*) …-muki (no) …向き・…むき(の); do it for me/us, they do it for you … -te kuremásu…てくれます; do it for you/them, you do it for them … -te agemásu …てあげます; for a long time *adv* (*now*) zutto máe kara ずっと前から; for a while *adv* shibáraku しばらく; hitómazu ひとまず; for example, for instance *adv* tatóeba 例えば・たとえば; for sure *adv* kanarazu 必ず・かならず, zéhi 是非・ぜひ, táshikani 確かに・たしかに; for the first time *adv* hajímete 初めて・はじめて; for the most part *adv* taigai 大概・たいがい, ō´kata おおかた・大方; for the reason that ... *adv* to iu riyū de … という理由で, …yué ni …故に・ゆえに; for the time being *adv* tō´bun 当分, hitómazu ひとまず

forbearance *n* shínbō´ しんぼう・辛抱

forbid *v* kin-jimásu 禁じます・きんじます

force 1. *n* (*power*) jitsuryoku 実力 **2.** *v ~s one* (*to do*) múri ni sase-másu 無理に

forceps *n* pinsetto ピンセット

ford *n* asase 浅瀬

foreboding *n* yokan 予感・よかん

forecast 1. *n* yohō´ 予報, yosoku 予測; *weather ~* tenki-yóhō´ 天気予報 **2.** *~s it v* (*predicts, estimates it*) yosoku shimásu 予測します

forehead *n* hitai 額・ひたい, odéko おでこ

foreign *adj* gaikoku (no) 外国(の), gai-… 外…, (*Western*) yō´… 洋…; foreign language *n* gaikoku-go 外国語; foreign policy *n* gaikō-seisaku 外交政策; foreign student(s) *n* ryūgaku-sei 留学生

foreigner *n* gaijin 外人, gaikokújin 外国人

forest *n* mori 森・もり, (*grove*)

hayashi 林・はやし

forever *adv* ítsu mo いつも, eien ni 永遠に・えいえんに, eikyū ni 永久に・えいきゅうに

foreword *n* jobun 序文, mae-gaki 前書き

forge *v* **1.** (*a signature, document, etc.*) nisemásu̲ 似せます・にせます **2.** (*tempers metal*) ki̲taemásu̲ 鍛えます・きたえます

forgery *n* (*making a fake copy*) gizō´ 偽造; (*a fake*) nise-mono 偽物・にせもの

forget *v* wasuremásu̲ 忘れます・わすれます; ***don't ~ to do it*** wasurenáide shi̲te kudasai 忘れないでして下さい・わすれないでください

forgive *v* yurushimásu̲ 許します・ゆるします

forgiveness *n* yurushi 許し

fork *n* **1.** fō´ku フォーク **2.** (*forking, branching*) wakare 分かれ・わかれ, matá 又・叉, futa-matá 二叉[股]; **fork out money (for ...)** (... ni) okane o dashimasu (...に)お金を出します

forklift *n* fōku rifuto フォークリフト

form **1.** *n* katachi 形, (*pattern*) katá 型, (*figure*) (o-)súgata お姿・(お)すがた, kakkō´ 格好・恰好・かっこう; (o-)nári (お)なり, (*style*) tái 体; (*appearance*) teisai 体裁; (*blank paper*) yō´shi 用紙; (*document*) shorui 書類 **2.** *v* (*creates it*) nashimásu̲ 成します・なします, tsu̲kurimásu̲ 作ります・つくります

formal *adj* seishi̲ki (na/no) 正式・せいしき(な/の); fōmaru (na) フォーマル(な); keishi̲ki̲teki (na) 形式的(な)

formality *n* keishi̲ki̲teki 形式的

format **1.** *n* (*book, magazine*) teisai 体裁, hankei 版型; (*data*) fō´matto フォーマット **2.** *v* (*~s a disk*) (disuku o) fōmatto(-ka) shimásu̲ (ディスクを)フォーマット(化)します

former *adj* máe (no) 前・まえ(の); móto (no) もと[元](の); [BOOKISH] zén… 前…; ***the ~*** zénsha 前者

formerly *adv* móto wa もと[元]は; kátsu̲te かつて

fortnight *n* ni-shūkan 2週間・二週間

fortunate *adj* saiwai (na) 幸い・さいわい(な)

fortune *n* (*property*) zaisan 財産; (*luck*) ún 運, únmei 運命・うんめい; (*good luck*) saiwai 幸い・さいわい, shiawase 幸せ・しあわせ; (*written*) (o-)mikuji (お)みくじ; **fortune-telling** *n* uranai 占い・うらない

forty *n* yón jū 四十・40, shi-jū 四十

forward **1.** *adv* (*ahead*) máe e/ni 前[まえ]へ/に; ***goes ~*** su̲sumimásu̲ 進みます・すすみます **2.** *adj* (*pushy*) bu-énryo (na) 無遠慮・ぶえんりょ(な)

forwarding *adj* tensō (no) 転送(の),

unsō (no) 運送(の); forwarding agency *n* unsō-gyōsha 運送業者

foster *v* yashinaimásu 養います・やしないます; foster child *n* sodate-go 育て子, sato-go 里子; foster parent *n* sodate no oyá 育ての親・そだての親, sato-oya 里親

foul *n, v* hansoku (shimásu) 反則(します) → dirty

found 1. → find; *gets* ~ mitsukarimásu 見つかります・みつかります 2. → establish

foundation *n* (*base*) kisó 基礎・きそ, (*basis*) konpon 根本, kihon 基本・きほん; (*non-profit organization*) zaidan 財団

fountain *n* funsui 噴水

fountain pen *n* mannén-hitsu 万年筆

four *n* yón 四・4, shí 四・4, yottsú 四つ・よっつ; ***number*** ~ yoban (*also* yónban) 四番

four or five *n* shi-go-... 四, 五...

fourteen *n* jū́-yón, jū-shí 十四・14

fourteenth *adj* jūyo(m) -banmé (no) 十四番目(の); ***the ~ day*** jūyokka-mé 十四日目, (*of the month*) jū́-yokka 十四日

fourth *adj* yo-banmé (no) (*also* yonbanmé) 四番目(の), yottsumé (no) 四つ目(の)

fowl *n* kakin 家禽・かきん

fox *n* kitsune きつね・キツネ・狐

fraction *n* 1. ichibu 一部 2. (*mathematics*) bunsū 分数

fragile *adj* koware-yasúi 壊れやすい・こわれやすい

fragrance *n* kaori 香り・かおり

fragrant *adj* kaorimásu 香ります・かおります

frail *adj* morói もろい・脆い; yowái 弱い・よわい

frame *n* wakú 枠, fuchí ふち・縁, kamachí かまち・框; (*of picture*) gaku-buchi 額縁; (*of glasses*) mégane no fuchí 眼鏡の縁・メガネのふち

framework *n* kumi-tate 組み立て・くみたて, honegumi 骨組み, furēmu wāku フレームワーク

France *n* Furansu フランス

frank *adj* sotchoku (na) 率直(な), assárishita... あっさりした...; (*unreserved*) enryo ga/no nái 遠慮が/のない, enryo shinai 遠慮しない・えんりょしない

frankly *adv* sotchoku ni 率直に, assári (to) あっさり(と); (*unreservedly*) enryo shináide 遠慮しないで; zubari ずばり

frantically *adv* chi-mánako ni nátte 血眼になって・ちまなこになって

fraud *n* sági 詐欺・サギ, inchiki いんちき

freak *n* hen-jin 変人

freckle *n* sobakasu そばかす

free *adj* (*gratis*) táda (no) ただ(の); (*no fee/ charge*) muryṓ (no) 無料(の); (*unrestrained*) jiyū (na) 自由・じゆう(な); (*unoccupied*) hima (na) 暇・ひま(な); ***sets ~*** (*releases*) hanashimásu 放します・はなします → liberate; free-of-charge, FOC *adj* muryō no 無料の; free parking

muryō-chūshajō 無料駐車場
freedom *n* jiyū´ 自由・じゆう
freelance, freelancing *n* (*work*) jiyū´-gyō´ 自由業
freeze *v* (*it ~s*) kō´rimásu 凍ります・こおります; (*~s it*) kō´rasemásu 凍らせます・こおらせます, reitō shimásu 冷凍します; Freeze! Ugokuna! 動くな！
freezer *n* reitōko 冷凍庫
French *n* (*language*) Furansu-go フランス語; (*person*) Furansújin フランス人
frequently → often
fresh *adj* atarashíi 新しい・あたらしい, shinsen (na) 新鮮・しんせん(な); *~ from …* …-tate (no) …たて(の), …-ágari (no) …上がり・…あがり(の)
freshman *n* **1.** (*first year grade*) ichinén-sei 一年生 **2.** (*new student*) shinnyu-sei 新入生
friction *n* masatsu 摩擦・まさつ
Friday *n* Kin'yōbi 金曜日; Friday prayers *n* kinyō-reihai 金曜礼拝
friend *n* (o-)tomodachi (お)友達・(お)ともだち; furendo フレンド; tómó 友・とも; yūjin 友人, (*pal*) (o-)nakama (お)仲間; aibō 相棒・あいぼう; best friend *n* ichiban no shinyū 一番の親友; muni no tomodachi 無二の友達
friendly *adj* yūkō-teki (na) 友好的(な)
friendship *n* (*keeping company*) (o-)tsukíai (お)付き合い・(お)つきあい
frightened → afraid
frightful *adj* kowái 怖い・こわい
frizzy *adj* chijireta 縮れた・ちぢれた; *~ hair* chijireta kami(no ke) 縮れた[ちぢれた]髪(の毛)
frock *n* doresu ドレス
frog *n* kaeru かえる・蛙・カエル
from *prep* … kara …から; *~ now on* kore kara これから, kongo 今後・こんご; *~ … to …* …kara …máde …から…まで
front **1.** *n* máe 前・まえ, (*ahead*) saki 先・さき; zenpō´ 前方; (*side*) omoté 表・おもて **2.** *adj* (*surface*) shō´mén (no) 正面(の), zenmen (no) 前面(の); front gate/entrance *n* seimon 正門, omotemon 表門; front desk *n* furonto フロント
frontier *n* (*international border*) kokkyō 国境
frost *n* shimó 霜・しも
frostbite *n* tōshō 凍傷, shimo-yake 霜焼け・しもやけ
frown *v* **1.** nigái/shibui kao o shimásu 苦い/渋い顔[にがい/しぶいかお]をします, kao o shikamemásu 顔をしかめます **2.** *n* jūmen 渋面, shibui kao 渋い面
frozen; *is ~* kō´tte imásu 凍っています・こおっています; frozen food *n* reitō-shokuhin 冷凍食品
frugal *adj* tsumashíi つましい, ken'yaku (na) 倹約(な), shísso (na) 質素・しっそ(な)
fruit *n* kudámono くだもの・果物; kí-no mi 木の実・きのみ,

mi 実・ミ; fruit juice *n* kajū 果汁, furūtsu jūsu フルーツジュース; fruit market/shop *n* kudamónó-ya くだもの屋・果物屋

fruitful *adj* minori no ōi 実りの多い, yūeki (na) 有益(な)

frustrate *v* yaburimásu 破ります・やぶります, zasetsu sasemásu 挫折させます・ざせつさせます; (*a plan*) kujikimásu くじきます・挫きます

frustrated; *gets* ~ yaburemásu 破れます・やぶれます, zasetsu shimásu 挫折します・ざせつします; (*a plan*) kujikemásu くじけます・挫けます

frustration *n* zasetsu 挫折・ざせつ; (*feeling of* ~) zasetsú-kan 挫折感・ざせつかん

fry *v* agemásu 揚げます・あげます; (*pan fries, sautés*) itamemásu 炒めます・いためます

ftp *n* (*file transfer protocol*) efu-tii-pii, ftp エフ・ティー・ピー

fuel *n* nenryō´ 燃料; (*firewood*) taki-gi たきぎ・薪; (*gasoline*) gasorin ガソリン; fuel tank *n* nenryō´-tanku 燃料タンク

fugitive *n* tōbō-sha 逃亡者

Fujiyama *n* Fúji (-san) 富士(山)

fulfill *v* konashimásu こなします → **accomplish**

full *adj* ippai (no) いっぱい[一杯](の); (*of people*) man'in (no) 満員(の); *gets* ~ michimásu 満ちます・みちます; full coverage insurance *n* zengaku-hoken 全額保険; full moon *n* mangetsu 満月; full name *n* furu nēmu フルネーム, shimei 氏名; full stop *n* (*period*) shūshí-fu 終止符, piriodo ピリオド

fully *adv* tappúri たっぷり; mán(-) … 満… maru(-) … まる…

fun *n* omoshirói (kotó) おもしろい[面白い]こと; asobi 遊び・あそび

function *n* **1.** (o-)yakume (お)役目; hataraki 働き・はたらき; kinō 機能 **2.** (*mathematics*) kansū 関数; (*function as…*) …to shite kinō shimásu …として機能します

fund *n* shikín 資金, (*capital*) shihon 資本

fundamentally *adv* konpon-teki (ni) 根本的(に), kihon-teki (ni) 基本的(に)

funeral *n* (o-)sō´shiki (お)葬式・そうしき; funeral home *n* (o-) sō´shiki-jō (お)葬式場, sō´gi-jō (お)葬儀場

funfair *n* yūen-chi 遊園地

fun-loving *adj* omoshiroi-koto zuki (no) 面白いこと好き(の), tanoshii-koto ga suki (na) 楽しいことが好き(な)

funnel *n* jō´go じょうご, [BOOKISH] rō´to ろうと・漏斗

funny *adj* okashíi おかしい, okáshi na おかしな; (*comical*) kokkei (na) こっけい・滑稽(な), hyōkín (na) ひょうきん(な), (*droll*) yúkai (na) 愉快・ゆかい(な), (*strange*) hén (na) 変・へん(な)

ur *n* ke-gawa 毛皮

urious *adj* gekido-shita 激怒した

urnace *n* ro 炉; kamado かまど; danbō´ (sō´chi) 暖房(装置)

urnish *v* (*provides*) sonaemásu̲ 備えます・そなえます

urniture *n* kágu 家具; furniture store *n* kagú-ya 家具屋

urry *adj* kegawa no yō (na) 毛皮のよう(な)

urther **1.** *adv* (*more*) mótto saki (ni) もっと先(に), (*elsewhere*) hoka no basho (de) 他の場所(で) **2.** (*advances it*) *v* mótto su̲su-memásu̲ 進めます・すすめます

fuse *n* hyū´zu ヒューズ

fuss *n* (ō´-)sáwagi (大)騒ぎ・(お)さわぎ

futile *adj* muda (na) 無駄・むだ(な), munashii 空しい・虚しい・むなしい

futon *n* futon ふとん・布団

future *n* shō´rai 将来, mírai 未来・みらい, (o-)saki (お)先・(お)さき; zénto 前途, sue 末; in the near future chi̲kái uchí (ni) 近いうち・ちかいうち(に)

G

gabble *v* pechakucha shaberimásu̲ ぺちゃくちゃ[ペチャクチャ]喋ります[しゃべります]

gaffe *n* bu-sáhō 無作法・不作法・ぶさほう

gaiety *n* o-matsuri sawagi お祭り騒ぎ

gain **1.** *n* (o-)toku (お)得・とく, (*income*) shotoku (お)所得 **2.** *v* → **get**

gait *n* aruki-kata 歩き方

gale *n* bōfú 暴風

gall bladder *n* (*medical*) tannō 胆嚢・胆のう

gallery *n* gyararii ギャラリー, garō 画廊

gallop **1.** *n* gyaroppu ギャロップ **2.** *v* kakemásu̲ 駆けます・かけます

gambling *n* kaké(-goto) 賭け事, tobaku とばく・賭博, baku̲chi ばくち・博奕

game *n* **1.** asobi 遊び・あそび, gē´mu ゲーム; ***card*** ~ toranpu トランプ **2.** (*athletic*) kyōgi 競技

gang *n* renchū/renjū 連中, nakama 仲間

gap *n* su̲ki-ma すき間・隙間, su̲ki すき・隙; ware-me 割れ目・われめ, kire-mé 切れ目・きれめ; zuré ずれ, gyáppu ギャップ

garage *n* gárē´ji ガレージ, sháko 車庫

garbage *n* gomí ごみ・ゴミ, (*kitchen waste*) nama-gomi 生ごみ; garbage collector *n* gomí-ya (san) ごみ屋(さん)

garden *n* niwa 庭・にわ

gardener *n* ueki-ya 植木屋, niwa-shi 庭師・にわし
gargle *v* ugai shimásu うがいします
garlic *n* ninniku にんにく・ニンニク・大蒜, gērikku ガーリック
garnishings *n* (*to go with sashimi*) tsumá つま・ツマ, tsukeawase つけ合わせ
garter *n* gā´tā ガーター
gas *n* **1.** (*natural*) gásu ガス **2.** (*a gas, vapor*) kitai 気体 **3.** (*gasoline*) gasorin ガソリン; **gas bill** *n* gasú-dai ガス代; **gas meter** *n* gasu-mētē ガスメーター
gasp *v* aegimásu あえぎ[喘ぎ]ます
gate *n* món 門・もん, (*gateway*) deiriguchi 出入り口; (*of shrine*) torii 鳥居; (*front*) omote-mon 表門, (*back*) uramon 裏門, (*main [front]*) seimon 正門; (*at airport terminal*) gē´to ゲート
gatekeeper *n* mónban 門番
gather **1.** *v* (*they ~*) atsumarimásu 集まります・あつまります, (*to make a set*) soroimásu 揃います・そろいます, (*congregate*) shūgō shimásu 集合します; (*~s them*) atsumemásu 集めます・あつめます, yosemásu 寄せます・よせます **2.** *v* (*plucks, clips*) tsumimásu 摘みます・つみます **3.** *n* (*pleat*) hida ひだ, gyazā ギャザー
gathering *n* shūgō 集合; **gathering place** *n* tamari-ba たまり場
gaudy *adj* hadé (na) はで・派手(な)
gauze *n* gā´ze ガーゼ
gave → **give**
gaze *v* mi-tsumemásu 見つめます・みつめます, nagamemásu 眺めます・ながめます
gay *adj* **1.** akarui 明るい・あかるい, yúkai (na) 愉快・ゆかい(な) **2.** (*homosexual*) hómo (no) ホモ(の), gei (no) ゲイ(の)
gear *n* gí(y)a ギア[ギヤ], hagúruma 歯車・はぐるま; **gear box** *n* gí(y)a bokkusu ギア[ギヤ]ボックス, hensoku-sōchi 変速装置
Gee! *interj* wā! わあ!, ā! ああ!, sugoi! すごい!
geisha *n* geisha 芸者
gel *n* geru ゲル, jeru ジェル
gem *n* hōseki 宝石; **gem dealer** *n* hōsekí-shō 宝石商
gender *n* séi 性
gene *n* idenshi 遺伝子
general **1.** *adj* (*over all*) ippan (no) 一般(の); (*common*) kyōtsū (no) 共通(の) **2.** *n* (*army*) táishō 大将; **in general** daitai 大体・だいたい, taigai 大概・たいがい, ippan ni 一般に, futsū 普通 (= **generally**); **the general public** taishū 大衆
generally *adv* ippanteki ni 一般的に, zentai ni 全体に; daitai 大体・だいたい, taigai 大概・たいがい
generation *n* sedai 世代, dōjidai 同時代; **generations after generations, for generations** dáidai 代々
generator *n* hatsudén-ki 発電機
generous *adj* kimae ga íi 気前がい

い, kandai (na) 寛大・かんだい(な)
genius *n* tensai 天才
gentle *adj* yasashii 優しい・やさしい, (*well-behaved*) otonashíi おとなしい, (*docile*) súnao (na) すなお[素直](な); (*calm*) odáyaka (na) 穏やか・おだやか(な)
gentleman *n* dánsei 男性, shínshi 紳士・しんし; (*middle-aged man*) ojisan おじさん, (*old man*) ojíisan おじいさん
gently *adv* yasashi̲ku 優しく・やさしく, otonáshi̲ku おとなしく
gents' *n* dansei-yō toire 男性用トイレ
genuine *adj* hontō (no) 本当・ほんとう(の), honmono (no) 本物・ほんもの(の), makoto (no) 真・まこと(の)
geographical *adj* chiri-teki (na) 地理的(な), chiri-jō (no) 地理上(の)
geography *n* chíri 地理; (*study/science*) chirí-gaku 地理学
geology *n* (*of a place*) chi̲shi̲tsu 地質; (*study/science*) chi̲shi̲tsú-gaku 地質学
germ *n* saikin 細菌, baikin ばい菌・バイキン
Germany *n* Dóitsu ドイツ
gesture *n* miburi 身振り・みぶり; jesuchā ジェスチャー, (*hand gesture*) temane 手まね, (*motion*) dōsa 動作
get *v* (*receives*) moraimásu̲ もらいます・貰います; **get (*someone*) to do it** *v* ① (hi̲to ni) shi̲te moraimásu̲ (人に)してもらいます ② [BOOKISH] emásu̲ 得ます・えます; **get caught (in) between** *v* hasamarimásu̲ 挟まります・はさまります; **get down** *v* (*descends*) orimásu̲ 降ります・おります; (*crouches*) mi o fu̲semásu̲ 身を伏せます; **get in** *v* (*enters*) hairimásu̲ 入ります・はいります; (*puts it in*) iremásu̲ 入れます・いれます; **get into** *v* (*a vehicle*) (… ni) norimásu̲ (…に)乗ります・のります; **get off** *v* (*gets down*) orimásu̲ 降ります・おります; **get out** *v* (*leaves*) demásu̲ 出ます・でます; (*gets it out*) dashimásu̲ 出します; **get out of the way** *v* dokimásu̲ どきます, nokimásu̲ の[退]きます; **get to be** → **become**
Getting off! *interj* Orimásu̲! 降ります!
geyser *n* kankessen 間欠泉, kanketsu-onsen 間欠温泉
Ghana *n* Gēna ガーナ
ghastly *adj* sugói すごい・凄い; *adv* sugóku warúi すごく[凄く]悪い[わるい]
ghetto *n* gettō ゲットー
ghost *n* yū´rei 幽霊・ゆうれい, gōsuto ゴースト; (*goblin*) obáke お化け・オバケ, bake-mónó 化け物・ばけもの
giant *n* kyojin 巨人, ōótoko 大男
gibberish *n* chinpunkanpun no/na hanashi ちんぷんかんぷんの/な

話; detarame でたらめ

gift *n* purezento プレゼント gifuto ギフト → **present**; **gift shop** *n* miyagemono-ya みやげ[土産]物屋

gigabyte, GB *n* (*computer*) giga-baito ギガ・バイト

gigantic *adj* **1.** (*vast amounts of*) bōdai (na) 膨大・ぼうだい(な) **2.** kyodai (na) 巨大(な)

gill *n* era エラ・えら

gilt *n* kinpaku 金ぱく・金箔, kinmekki 金メッキ

gimmick *n* gimikku ギミック, shikake 仕掛け

gin *n* jin ジン

ginger *n* shōga しょうが・ショウガ・生姜; **pickled ginger** *n* s<u>u</u>shō´ga 酢しょうが, gári がり・ガリ

gingko *n* (*tree*) ichō いちょう・イチョウ・銀杏; **gingko nuts** *n* gin-nán ぎんなん・ギンナン・銀杏

giraffe *n* kirin キリン

girder *n* keta けた・ケタ・桁; ***under the ~*** keta-sh<u>i</u>ta けた下・桁下

girl *n* musume(-san) 娘(さん); onná-no-ko 女の子; jóshi 女子

giro system *n* furikae-seido 振替制度

girth *n* shūi 周囲

gist *n* muné 旨; yō 要, yō´shi 要旨, shushi 主旨, yōten 要点, yōryō´ 要領, kosshi 骨子

give *v* **1.** (*they to you/me, you to me*) kuremás<u>u</u> くれます, kudasai-más<u>u</u> 下さいます・くださいます **2.** (*I to you/them, you to them, they to them*) agemás<u>u</u> あげます, yarimás<u>u</u> やります **3.** (*provides*) ataemás<u>u</u> 与えます・あたえます, motasemás<u>u</u> 持たせます・もたせます; ***~ mercifully*** (*in charity*) megumimás<u>u</u> 恵みます **4.** (*entrusts temporarily*) azukemás<u>u</u> 預けます・あずけます; **give birth to ...** *v* o umimás<u>u</u> ...を生み[産み]ます; **give in/up** *v* (*cedes, concedes*) yuzurimás<u>u</u> 譲ります・ゆずります; **give up (on) ...** *v* o akiramemás<u>u</u> ...を諦めます

glacial *adj* hyōga-ki (no) 氷河[ヒョウガ]期(の); **glacial age** *n* hyōga-ki 氷河[ヒョウガ]期

glacier *n* hyōga 氷河・ヒョウガ

glad *adj* ureshíi うれしい・嬉しい; ***is ~*** yorokobimás<u>u</u> 喜びます・よろこびます; **glad to ...** *v* yorokon-de ... o shimás<u>u</u> 喜んで...をします

glamor *n* guramē グラマー

glamorous *adj* miryoku-teki (na) 魅力的(な), miwaku-teki (na) 魅惑的(な)

gland *n* sen 腺・せん

glare *v* ... o niramimás<u>u</u> ...をにらみ[睨み]ます

glass *n* (*the substance*) garasu ガラス; (*the container*) koppu コップ, gúrasu グラス

glass, glassful ...-hai ...杯

glasses *n* mégane めがね・メガネ・眼鏡

glazier *n* garasu-ya ガラス屋

gleam, glitter *v* kagayakimás<u>u</u> 輝き

ます・かがやきます; glittering *adj* pikápika/kirakira kagayaku ぴかぴか・ピカピカ/きらきら・キラキラ輝く

glen *n* tani-ma 谷間

glider *n* guraidē グライダー

glimmer *n* (*light*) kasuka na hikari かすかな光・微かな光

globe *n* (*shape*) tamá 球; (*map*) chikyū´-gi 地球儀

gloom *n* (*depression*) yūutsu 憂うつ[鬱]・ゆううつ

gloomy *adj* uttōshíi うっとうしい, kurai 暗い・くらい, yūutsu (na) 憂うつ[鬱]・ゆううつ(な), inki (na) 陰気(な)

glorious *adj* hanáyaka (na) 華やか・はなやか(な)

glory *n* méiyo 名誉

gloss *n* **1.** (*shine*) tsuya つや・ツヤ・艶 **2.** (*lipstick*) gurosu グロス

glove *n* tebúkuro 手袋・てぶくろ; gúrabu グラブ, gúrōbu グローブ

glow **1.** *v* hikarimásu 光ります・ひかります **2.** *n* (*shine*) kagayaki 輝き, (~ *of sunset*) yūyake 夕焼け

glue **1.** *n* setchakuzai 接着剤, nori のり・ノリ, nikawa にかわ・ニカワ・膠 **2.** *v* (~*s it*) setchakuzai de tsukemásu 接着剤で付けます[つけます], tsugimásu 接ぎます

glut *n* kajō 過剰

glutton *n* kúi-shínbō 食いしん坊・くいしんぼう, taishoku-ka 大食家

gluttony *n* ōgui 大食い

gnarl *n* fushí 節

gnaw *v* kajirimásu かじります・齧ります

go *v* ikimásu 行きます; go against ... *v* ni somukimásu ...に背きます; ...ni han-shimásu ...に反します; go around *v* (*a curve*) magarimásu 曲がります・まがります; (*revolves*) mawarimásu 回ります・まわります; go back *v* modorimásu 戻ります・もどります, kaerimásu 帰ります・かえります; go back *v* (*in time*) to ... ni sakanoborimásu ... にさかのぼります・遡ります; go back and forth *v* ittari kitari shimásu 行ったり来たりします kayoimásu 通います・かよいます; go down *v* orimásu 下ります・おります; kudarimásu 下ります・くだります; sagarimásu 下がります・さがります; (*on the price*) makemásu 負けます・まけます; (*dwindles*) herimásu 減ります・へります; go forward *v* susumimásu 進みます・すすみます; go home *v* kaerimásu 帰ります・かえります; go in *v* hairimásu 入ります・はいります, háitte ikimásu 入って行きます・はいっていきます; go out *v* demásu 出ます・でます, déte ikimásu 出て行きます・でていきます; (*of the house*) dekakemásu 出かけ[掛け]ます・でかけます, gaishutsu shimásu 外出します; (*appears*) arawaremásu 現れます・あらわれます; (*lights, fire, etc.*)

kiemásu 消えます・きえます; go over *v* (*exceeds*) sugimásu 過ぎます・すぎます, chōka shimásu 超過します; koshimásu 超[越]します; (*revises*) fukushū shimásu 復習します; go to *v* (*reaches*) itarimásu 至ります・いたります; go to bed *v* yasumimásu 休みます・やすみます, nemásu 寝ます・ねます; go too far *v* (*to excess*) do o koshimásu 度を超します・度をこします; go too fast *v* (*clock*) susumimásu 進みます・すすみます; go to the end of *v* (*a street*) tsuki-atarimásu 突き当たります・つきあたります; go to work *v* (*start work*) shigoto ni ikimásu 仕事に行きます, shūrō shimásu 就労します; go up *v* agarimásu 上がります・あがります, noborimásu 上ります・のぼります

Go *n* (*board game*) gó 碁・ご, ígo 囲碁・いご

goal *n* mokuteki 目的, ate 当て; (*destination*) mokutekí-chi 目的地; (*sports*) gō´ru ゴール

goalkeeper *n* gōru kiipā ゴールキーパー

goat *n* yági やぎ・ヤギ・山羊

goblin *n* (*long-nosed*) tengu 天狗・てんぐ・テング

God, gods *n* kámi(-sama) 神(様)・かみ(さま)

godchild *n* nazuke-go 名付け子

goddaughter *n* nazuke-musume 名付け娘・なづけむすめ

goddess *n* megami 女神

godfather *n* nazuke-oya 名付け親・なづけ親

godmother *n* nazuke-oya 名付け親・なづけ親

godown *n* (*storeroom*) kurá 蔵・倉・くら

godson *n* nazuke-go 名付け子・なづけ子, nazuke-musuko 名付け息子・なづけむすこ

goggle *n* gōguru ゴーグル

gold *n* kín 金, gōrudo ゴールド

golden *adj* (*color*) kin-iro (no) 金色(の)

goldfish *n* kíngyo 金魚・キンギョ

goldsmith *n* kin-zaiku shokunin 金細工職人

golf *n* górufu ゴルフ; golf ball *n* gorufu-bōru ゴルフボール

gondola *n* gondora ゴンドラ

gong *n* gongu ゴング, dora どら

gone → **go**; *v* *is* ~ itte imásu 行っています

gonorrhea *n* rinbyō りん病・淋病

good *adj* íi いい・良い・好い・善い, yói 良い・好い・善い・よい; good at (… ga) umái (…が)うまい, jōzú (na) じょうず[上手](な); a good deal *adv* yohodo よほど・余程, yoppodo よっぽど; unto うんと; takusán (no) たくさん・沢山(の); for the good of … *adv* no tamé ni …のため[為]に; Good afternoon. *interj* konnichi wa. こんにちは・今日は.; good-bye *interj* sayonara さよなら, sayōnára さようなら; Good evening. *interj* konban wa. こんばんは・今晩は.; Good morning. *interj* O-hayō (gozaimásu). おはよう[お早う]ございます.; Good night. *interj* O-yasumi nasái. おやすみ[お休み]なさい.; no good furyō (no) 不良(の)

good-hearted *adj* shinsetsu (na) 親切・しんせつ(な), omoiyari no aru 思いやりのある, yasashii 優しい・やさしい

good heavens/grief *interj* shimatta しまった, oya-mā おやまあ, (*feminine*) mā まあ

good-natured *adj* kidate no yoi 気立ての良い・きだてのよい

goodness *n* zén 善

goods *n* shina(mono) 品(物); (*merchandise*) shōhin 商品

goodwill *n* kō´i 好意, kokorozashi 志・こころざし, shínsetsu 親切・しんせつ, zén'i 善意

goof 1. *n* (*blunder*) hema へま・ヘマ, doji どじ・ドジ, chónbo ちょんぼ・チョンボ 2. *v* ~ (*up*) hema o shimásu へま(を)します

Google *n* (*Internet search engine*) gūguru グーグル

goose *n* gachō がちょう・ガチョウ・鵞鳥

gorgeous *adj* gōka (na) 豪華(な); rippa (na) 立派・りっぱ(な); hanáyaka (na) 華やか・はなやか(な)

Gosh! *interj* wā わあ

gossip *n* 1. uwasa うわさ・噂; muda-/baka-bánashi 無駄/ばか話 2. (*a* ~) osháberi おしゃべり

gourd *n* hyōtán ひょうたん・ヒョウタン・瓢箪; sponge gourd *n* hechima へちま・ヘチマ・糸瓜

gourmet *n, adj* gurume (no) グルメ(の), shokutsū (no) 食通(の), bishokuka (no) 美食家(の)

govern *v* osamemásu 治めます・おさめます

government *n* séifu 政府; (*cabinet*) náikaku 内閣; (*nation*) kuni (no) 国(の), (*national*) kokuritsu (no) 国立(の); (*the authorities*) tō´kyoku 当局, okámi お上; government official *n* yakunin 役人; government worker/employee *n* kōmú-in 公務員

governor *n* chíji 知事

gown *n* gaun ガウン

grab → **seize**

graceful *adj* yū´bi (na) 優美(な)

grade 1. *n* (*value, quality*) tōkyū 等級, (*class*) kyú 級, gakkyu 学級; (*step*) dán 段; (*evaluation score*) hyōten 評点, hyō´ka 評価; (*academic record*) seiseki 成績 2. *v* (*to ~ a test paper*) saitenshi-másu 採点します, seiseki o tsuke-másu 成績をつけます

grade school *n* shōgakkō 小学校; grade school children *n* shōgaku-sei 小学生

gradually *adv* dandan だんだん, jojo ni 徐々に, sukoshízútsu 少しずつ・すこしずつ, sórosoro (to) そろそろ(と); (*finally*) yōyaku ようやく

graduate 1. *v* sotsugyō shimásu 卒業します; ~ ***from*** (daigaku o) demásu (大学を)出ます 2. *n* sotsugyō´-sei 卒業生; **graduate student** *n* daigakuín-sei 大学院生

graft 1. *n* (*bribery*) wáiro 賄賂・わいろ・ワイロ, oshoku 汚職 2. *n* tsugiki 接ぎ木 3. *v* (*attaches*) tsugimásu 接ぎます・つぎます

grain *n* 1. tsúbu 粒 2. (*cereal*) kokúmotsu 穀物, kokúrui 穀類 3. (*texture*) kimé きめ・木目・肌理

gram *n* gúramu グラム

grammar *n* bunpō 文法, guramā グラマー

grand *adj* subarashíi すばらしい・素晴らしい, erái 偉い・えらい, sōdai (na) 壮大(な)

grandchild *n* magó 孫(o-mago-san お孫さん)

grandfather *n* ojíi-san おじいさん・お祖父さん, sófu 祖父

grandmother *n* obā´-san おばあさん・お祖母さん, sóbo 祖母

grandson *n* mago (musuko) 孫(息子)

granite *n* kakō´-gan かこう岩・花崗岩・カコウガン, mikagé-ishi みかげ石・御影石・ミカゲイシ

grant 1. *n* hojokin 補助金, joseikin 助成金 2. *v* (~*s it*) ataemásu 与えます・あたえます

grapes *n* budō ぶどう・ブドウ・葡萄

graph *n* grafu グラフ

grasp *v* tsukamimásu つかみます・掴みます; nigirimásu 握ります

grass *n* kusá 草・くさ; (*lawn*) shibafu 芝生・しばふ

grassland *n* sōgen 草原・そうげん

grated *v* suri-oroshita すりおろした; **grated radish** *n* daikon-óroshi 大根おろし[下ろし]・ダイコンオロシ

grateful *adj* arigatái ありがたい・有り難い; **I am grateful** arigatáku zon-jimásu ありがたく存じます; **feels grateful/obliged** kyōshuku shimásu 恐縮します

grater *n* oroshí-gane 下ろし金

gratification *n* manzoku 満足

gratis → **free**

gratitude *n* kansha 感謝・かんしゃ

gratuity *n* kokoro-zuke 心付け・こころづけ

grave *n* (*tomb*) (o-)haka (お)墓・(お)はか; **graveyard** *n* haka-bá 墓場, bóchi 墓地

grave *adj* (*serious*) omoi 重い・おもい, shinkoku (na) 深刻・しんこく(な)

gravy *n* taré たれ; (o-)sō´su (お)ソース; niku-jū/jíru 肉汁

gray *adj* hai-iro (no) 灰色(の), nezumi-iro (no) ねずみ色(の); gurē´ no グレーの

graze *v* kasurimásu かすります・掠ります; kasumemásu かすめます・掠めます

grease *n* abura 脂・油・アブラ

greasy *adj* aburakkói 脂っこい・あぶらっこい; kudói くどい

great *adj* (*superior*) idai (na) 偉大(な), erái 偉い・えらい; ōki (na)

大き(な)・おおきな, dai- 大… → **big** → **good** → **grand**; a great difference taisa 大差; a great many táisō (na) たいそう・大層(な)

Great Britain *n* Eikoku 英国, igirisu イギリス

Greece *n* Gírisha ギリシャ

greedy *adj* yokubárí (na) 欲張り・よくばり(な), kúi-shínbō (na) 食いしん坊・くいしんぼう(な); yokubarimásu 欲張ります・よくばります; ***a ~ person*** yokubárí 欲張り・よくばり

green *adj* **1.** mídori (no) 緑(の), aói 青い・あおい; guríin (no) グリーン(の) **2.** (*inexperienced*) osanái 幼い・おさない

Green Car *n* (*deluxe coach*) guriín-sha グリーン車

green onion *n* nira にら・ニラ・韮; naga-nagi 長ねぎ[葱]・ナガネギ, négi ねぎ・ネギ・葱; (*chives, scallion*) asátsuki あさつき・アサツキ・浅葱

greens *n* náppa 菜っ葉・ナッパ, ná 菜・ナ; (*boiled greens served cold with seasoning*) o-hitáshi おひたし・オヒタシ

green tea *n* (o-)cha (お)茶

greet *v* (*welcomes, receives*) áisatsu (o) shimásu あいさつ・挨拶(を)します; de-mukaemásu 出迎えます

greeting *n* áisatsu あいさつ・挨拶; réi 礼

grenade *n* shuryūdan 手榴弾

grief *n* nagekí 嘆き・なげき, kana-shimi 悲しみ

grievance *n* fuhei 不平, fuman 不満

grieve *v* nagekimásu 嘆きます・なげきます; kokóro o itamemásu 心を痛めます

grill *v* yakimásu 焼きます・やきます, aburimásu あぶります・炙ります

grime *n* yogore 汚れ

grin **1.** *n* (hanikanda) egao はにかんだ笑顔 **2.** *v* (nit-to, niyat-to) waraimásu (にっと/にやっと)笑います

grind *v* surimásu すります; (*into powder*) hikimásu ひきます → **sharpen** → **polish**

grip *v* nigirimásu 握ります・にぎります

gripe **1.** *n* (*complaint*) guchi ぐち・愚痴 **2.** *v* (*complains*) → **grumble**

groan **1.** *n* (*a ~*) umekí うめき・呻き **2.** *v* (*~s*) umekimásu うめきます・呻きます; fuman o iimásu 不満を言います

groceries *n* shokuryō-hin 食料品, shokuhin 食品

groin *n* matá 股・また

groom *n* hanamuko 花婿・はなむこ, shinrō 新郎

groove *n* mizo 溝

grope *v* sagurimásu 探ります・さぐります; groper *n* (*molester*) chikan 痴漢・チカン

gross *adj* (*crass*) egetsunai えげつない; (*rude*) gehin (na) 下品(な)

grotesque *n* gurotesuku グロテスク
grotto *n* dōkutsu 洞窟・洞くつ
ground **1.** *n* (*land*) tochi 土地・とち, jí 地, (*earth*) tsuchí 土・つち; (*surface*) jímen 地面・じめん, (*playground*) guraundo グラウンド **2.** *n* (*basecoat*) shitanuri 下塗り **3.** *adj* hiita 挽いた **4.** *v* (*to be grounded*) ... o gaishutsu kinshi ni shimásu ...を外出禁止にします; **ground meat** *n* hiki-niku 挽き肉・ヒキニク
grounds *n* (*reason*) riyū 理由・りゆう, yué 故・ゆえ
group *n* gurū´pu グループ, dantai 団体; shūdan 集団; (*class*) kúrasu クラス; (*throng, flock*) muré 群れ
grove *n* hayashi 林・はやし
grow *v* **1.** (*it ~s*) seichō shimásu 成長します; (*gets big*) ō´kiku/ō´ku narimásu 大きく[おおきく]/多く[おおく]なります; (*increases*) fuemásu 増えます・ふえます; (*appears*) hassei shimásu 発生します; (*develops*) hatten shimásu 発展します **2.** (*~s it*) (*a plant*) uemásu 植えます・うえます, (*a crop*) tsukurimásu 作ります・つくります **3.** (*becomes*) (… ni, …-ku) narimásu (…に, …く) なります; **grow late** *v* (yó ga) fukemásu (夜が)更けます・ふけます; **grow up** *v* sodachimásu 育ちます・そだちます; seichō shimásu 成長します
grower *n* saibai-sha 栽培者, shiiku-sha 飼育者
growl **1.** *n* (*a ~*) unarí (goe) うなり・唸り(声) **2.** *v* (*~s*) unarimásu うなり[唸り]ます
growth *n* seichō 成長; (*increase*) zōka 増加; (*development*) hatten 発展
grudge *n* uramí 恨み・うらみ
gruel *n* (*rice*) (o-)kayu (お)かゆ[粥]
grumble *v* boyakimásu ぼやきます, gúzuguzu shimásu ぐずぐずします, (guchi o) koboshimásu (愚痴を)こぼします
grumbling *n* fuhei 不平・ふへい
guarantee *n, v* hoshō (shimásu) 保証(します); **letter of guarantee** *n* hoshō-sho 保証書
guard **1.** *n* bán 番, gādo-man ガードマン, (*gate keeper*) mónban 門番, shuei 守衛; (*vigilance*) keikai 警戒 **2.** *v* **~s** ***it*** mamorimásu 守ります, keibi shimásu 警備します; ***~s against*** … o keikai shimásu …を警戒します; **guard dog** *n banken* 番犬
guardian *n* hogo-sha 保護者, kōken-nin 後見人; **guardian angel** *n* shugo-tenshi 守護天使
guess **1.** *n* (*conjecture*) sasshi 察し・さっし, (*estimate*) suisoku 推測, kentō 見当 **2.** *v* (*~es*) sasshimásu 察します・さっします, suisoku shimásu 推測します, kentō o tsukemásu 見当をつけます; (*correctly*) sasshi ga tsukimásu 察しがつきます・さっし

がつきます, atemásu 当てます・あてます

guest *n* (o-)kyaku (お)客・(お)きゃく, okyaku-san/-sámá お客[きゃく]さん/様・さま; (*caller*) raikyaku 来客; **guest of honor** *n* shuhin 主賓[ひん], kihin 貴賓[ひん]

guidance *n* annai 案内; (*direction, counseling*) shidō 指導

guide 1. *n* (*person*) annai-gákari 案内係, annai-nin 案内人, annái-sha 案内者, gáido ガイド; (*coach, counsel*) shidō´-sha 指導者; (*book*) annai-sho 案内書, gaido bukku ガイドブック **2.** *v* (*~s them*) annái shimásu 案内します, michibikimásu 導きます・みちびきます; (*directs, counsels*) shidō shimásu 指導します

guild *n* (*union*) kumiai 組合, girudo ギルド

guilt *n* tsúmi 罪・つみ; ***feeling/sense of ~*** záiaku-kan 罪悪感

guilty *adj* yūzai (no) 有罪(の)

guitar *n* gitā ギター

gulf *n* wán 湾・ワン

gullet *n* shokudō 食道

gullible *adj* baka-shō´jiki (na) ばか正直(な)

gully *n* kyōkoku 峡谷

gulp 1. *n* ikki ni nomu 一気に飲む, hitoiki de nomu 一息で飲む **2.** ***~s down*** *v* gutto/gabugabu nomimásu ぐっと/がぶがぶ飲みます

gum *n* (*chewing*) (chūin) gámu (チューイン)ガム

gun *n* jū´ 銃, teppō 鉄砲・てっぽう

gunfire *n* happō 発砲

gunpowder *n* kayaku 火薬

gunshot → **gunfire**

gush *v* hotobashirimásu ほとばしります, wakimásu わき[湧き・涌き]ます

guts *n* harawata はらわた・腸・腑, watá わた・腸 → **courage**

gutter *n* mizo 溝; (*ditch*) dobu どぶ; (*drain pipe*) tói 樋・とい

guy *n* yátsu やつ・奴; ***that*** ~ aitsu あいつ, (*polite*) sono/ano hitó その/あの人

gymnasium, gym *n* tai(í)kú-kan 体育館, jímu ジム

gymnastics *n* taisō 体操・たいそう

gynecologist *n* fujin-ka 婦人科

gypsy *n* jipushii ジプシー

H

haberdashery *n* (*notions*) komamono 小間物, yōhin 洋品

habit *n* shūkan 習慣; (*bad ~*) kusé 癖・くせ

habitat *n* seisoku-chi 生息地; sumika 住処・すみか

habitation *n* kyojū-chi 居住地; sumai 住まい・すまい

habitual *adj* shūkan (no) 習慣(の); itsumono いつもの

hack *n* hakkingu ハッキング, (*computer*) hakkā ハッカー
had → **have; *gets* ~ *(by ...)*** *v* (... ni) yararemás<u>u</u> (...に)やられます
hag *n* (oni) baba (鬼)ばば
haggard *adj* yatsureta やつれた, yatsureteiru やつれている
haggle *n* ii-arasoi 言い争い, ronsō 論争
hail **1.** *n* arare/hyō´ **2.** *v* arare/hyō´ ga furimás<u>u</u> あられ・アラレ/ひょう・ヒョウが降ります
hailstone → **hail**
hair *n* (*on head*) kamí 髪・かみ, kamí no ke 髪の毛・かみのけ; (*general*) ke 毛; **hair spray** *n* hea supurē ヘアスプレー
hairdresser → **beauty parlor** → **barber**(*shop*)
hairy *adj* kebukai 毛深い
hale *adj* genki ga yoi 元気が良い・げんきがよい, genki (na) 元気・げんき(な)
half *n* hanbún 半分・はんぶん; ***~ a ...*** han-... 半..., ...no hanbún ...の半分; ***and a ~*** ...- hán ...半; ***the first ~*** zenhan 前半; **half a day** *n* han-nichí 半日; **half a month** *n* han-ts<u>u</u>kí 半月
half brother *n* **1.** (*different mother*) ibo kyōdai 異母兄弟 **2.** (*different father*) ifu kyōdai 異父兄弟
half-cooked *adj* (*meat*) nama-nie (no) 生煮え(の)
half-done *adj* (*meat*) han'yake (no) 半焼け(の), namayake (no) 生焼け(の)
halfhearted *adj* ii-kagen (na) いい加減・いいかげん(な)
half price *n* hangaku 半額; ***half-price*** hangaku (no) 半額(の)
half sister *n* **1.** (*different mother*) ibo shimai 異母姉妹 **2.** (*different father*) ifu shimai 異父姉妹
halfway *adj* tochū (no) 途中(の)
hall *n* (*building*) kaikan 会館; (*lecture hall*) kōdō 講堂, hōru ホール; (*entrance*) génkan 玄関
hallucination *n* genkaku 幻覚
halt → **stop**
ham *n* hámu ハム; **ham sandwich** *n* hamu sándo ハムサンド
hamburger *n* (*sandwich*) hanbā´gā ハンバーガー; (*ground beef*) hanbā´gu ハンバーグ
hamlet *n* chiisai mura 小さい村
hammer **1.** *n* kanazuchi かなづち・金槌, hánmā/hánma ハンマー/ハンマ, ts<u>u</u>chí 槌・つち, (*small*) kózuchi 小槌; **claw hammer** *n* kuginuki 釘抜き・くぎぬき **2.** *v* (*hits*) uchimás<u>u</u> 打ちます・うちます
hamper *n* (*basket*) kago かご・カゴ
hamster *n* hamusutā ハムスター
hand *n* té 手; (*of clock*) hári 針・はり; ***has on ~*** (*in stock*) mochi-awasemás<u>u</u> 持ち合わせます・もちあわせます; **hand down** *v* ts<u>u</u>taemás<u>u</u> 伝えます・つたえます; **hand over** *v* watashimás<u>u</u> 渡します・わたします; (*to me*) yoko-shimás<u>u</u> よこします; **hand up** *v* kōsan shimás<u>u</u> 降参します;

Hands up! te o agero! 手を挙げろ！
handbag *n* hando bággu (hando bákku) ハンドバッグ(ハンドバック), tesage 手提げ・手さげ
handball *n* hando bōru ハンドボール
handbill *n* bira びら・ビラ
handbook *n* hando bukku ハンドブック, tebiki-sho 手引(き)書
handbrake *n* saido burē´ki サイドブレーキ
handcuff *n* te jō 手錠
handful *n* shōryō 少量, hito-nigiri 一握り・ひとにぎり
handicapped *adj* (*physically*) karada ga fú-jiyū (na) 体が不自由(な); **handicapped person** *n* (shintai) shōgái-sha (身体)障害者
handicraft *n* shukōgei-hin 手工芸品
handiwork *n* te-záiku 手細工, saiku 細工, te-shigoto 手仕事
handkerchief *n* hankachi ハンカチ
handle 1. *n* totté 取っ手・とって, handoru ハンドル, tsurú つる・ツル・鉉, é 柄 **2.** *v* tori-atsukaimásu 取り扱います・とりあつかいます; (*copes with it*) shóri shimásu 処理します; (*uses a tool*) tsukaimásu 使います・つかいます; (*controls, operates*) sōjū shimásu 操縦します; (*receives*) …ni ses-shimásu …に接します → **sell** → **touch**
Handle With Care Kowaremono chū´i こわれ物注意・コワレモノ注意
hand luggage *n* te-nímotsu 手荷物
handshake *n* ákushu 握手・あくしゅ
handsome *n* hansamu ハンサム, nimai-me 二枚目
handwriting *n* te-gaki 手書き, niku-hitsu 肉筆
handy *adj* bénri (na) 便利・べんり(な)
handyman *n* (*or his shop*) benri-ya 便利屋・べんり屋
hang *v* **1.** *it ~s* kakarimásu 掛かります・かかります **2.** *~s it* kakemásu 掛けます・かけます, (*suspends it*) tsurimásu 吊ります・つります **3.** *~s one's head* utsumukimásu うつむきます・俯きます; **hang down** *v* ① *it ~s down* taremásu 垂れます・たれます; sagarimásu 下がります・さがります; bura-sagarimásu ぶら下がります ② *~s it down* sagemásu 下げます・さげます; bura-sagemásu ぶら下げます; **hang in there** *v* ganbarimásu がんばり[頑張り]ます; **hang up** *v* (*phone*) (denwa o) kirimásu (電話を)切ります・きります
hang gliding *n* hangu-guraidā-nori ハンググライダー乗り
hangout *n* tamari-ba 溜まり場・たまり場
hangover *n* futsuka-yoi 二日酔い
haphazard *adj* ii-kagen (na) いい加減・いいかげん(な)
happen *v* okorimásu 起こります・おこります; *~ to see/observe* mi-ukemásu 見受けます・みうけま

す; ~ *to see/meet* de-aimásu 出会います・であいます

happiness *n* kōfuku 幸福, shiawase 幸せ・しあわせ

happy *adj* ureshíi うれしい・嬉しい, yúkai (na) 愉快・ゆかい(な), kōfuku (na) 幸福(な), shiawase (na) 幸せ・しあわせ(な); (*cheerful*) yōki (na) 陽気(な); (*is delighted*) yorokobimásu 喜びます・よろこびます → **lucky**

Happy New Year *interj* Shínnen/ Akemáshite o-medetō gozaimásu. 新年/あけ[明け]まして おめでとうございます.

harbor → **port**

hard *adj* **1.** katai 固い・硬い・堅い・かたい; (*difficult*) muzukashii 難しい・むずかしい, (*hard to do*) shi-nikúi しにくい; (*onerous*) kurushíi 苦しい・くるしい; (*cruelly, terribly*) hídoku ひどく **2.** (*working* ~) yóku 良く・よく; (*laboriously*) ákuseku あくせく, sésse-to せっせと; (*intently*) shikiri ni しきりに **3.** *adv* (*zealously*) nésshín ni 熱心に; (*seriously*) majime ni まじめ[真面目]に

harden *v* **1.** *it ~s* katamarimásu 固まります・かたまります **2.** *~s it* katamemásu 固めます・かためます

hard disk *n* hādo disuku ハードディスク

hardly *adv* hotóndo ほとんど・殆ど + [NEGATIVE]

hardness *n* katasa 硬さ・かたさ

hard of hearing *adj* mimí ga tōi 耳が遠い・耳がとおい

hardship *n* kónnan 困難, kúrō 苦労

hardware *n* **1.** kanamono 金物; (*items*) tekki 鉄器, tekkí-rui 鉄器類; (*store*) kanamono-ya 金物屋 → **houseware**; (*machine*) kikai setsubi 機械設備 **2.** (*computer*) hādowéa ハードウェア

hardworking *adj* kinben (na) 勤勉(な)

hare *n* usagi うさぎ・ウサギ・兎

harm **1.** *n* gái 害, songai 損害 **2.** *~s it* *v* sokonaimásu 損ないます・そこないます; *without ~* (*incident*) buji (ni) 無事・ぶじ(に); *no ~* ...shite mo mondai nai ...しても問題ない

harmony *n* chōwa 調和; *is in ~ with* ... to chōwa shimásu ...と調和します

harp *n* (*Japanese*) (o-)kóto (お)琴; (*Western*) hā´pu ハープ

harpoon *n* mori 銛・モリ

harsh *adj* (*cruel*) zankoku (na) 残酷(な)

harvest **1.** *n* minori 実り・みのり, shūkaku 収穫 **2.** *v* (*~s it*) osamemásu 収めます・おさめます, shūkaku shimásu 収穫します

has → **have**

hashtag (#) *n* hasshutagu ハッシュタグ

haste *n* isogí 急ぎ・いそぎ

hasten → **hurry**

hasty *adj* (*hurried*) isogí no 急ぎの; (*rash*) keisotsu (na) 軽率(な)

hat *n* bōshi 帽子; ***bamboo ~*** kása 笠・カサ
hate *v* (… ga) iyádesu (…が) 嫌です; (… o) nikumimásu (…を) 憎みます・にくみます
haughty *adj* gōman (na) 傲慢(な); ***is/acts ~*** ibarimásu 威張ります・いばります
haul *n* (*goods in transit*) yusō-hin 輸送品
haunch *n* den-bu 臀部・でんぶ, koshi 腰・こし
have *v* (…ga) arimásu (…が) あります, (…o) mótte imásu (…を) 持っています・もっています; (*keeps, retains*) kakaemásu 抱えます・かかえます; **have someone do it** *v* (hito ni sore o) sasemásu (人にそれを) させます, (*as a favor*) shite moraimásu してもらいます; **have it done** *v* (*by someone to another*) (hito ni sore o) saremásu (人にそれを) されます; **have no ...** *v* (…ga) arimasén (…が) ありません
have to → **must**
Hawaii *n* Háwai ハワイ
hawk *n* taka たか・タカ・鷹
hay *n* magusa まぐさ・秣, hoshi-gusa 干し草・ホシグサ
hazard *n* hazādo ハザード, (*danger*) kiken 危険・キケン
haze *n* móya もや・靄, (*mist*) kasumi かすみ・霞
hazy; ***gets ~*** kasumimásu かすみます・霞みます
he *n* káre 彼・かれ, anó-hito あの人 (*but use name, title, or role; often omitted*); (*that guy*) yátsu やつ・奴, yakko san やっこさん
he-... (*animal*) … no osú …の雄・…のオス
head *n* atamá 頭・あたま; (*brains*) zunō 頭脳; (*leader*) kashirá 頭, chō´ 長, (*of a school*) kōchō 校長; **head for ...** *v* ni mukaimásu …に向かいます・…にむかいます; … o mezashimásu …を目指します・をめざします; **head over heels** *adv* massáka-sama ni まっさかさまに・真っ逆さまに
headache *n* zutsū 頭痛; ***have a ~*** zutsū ga shimásu 頭痛がします, atamá ga itái 頭が痛い
heading *n* (*caption*) midashi 見出し・みだし, (*title*) taitoru タイトル
headlight(s) *n* heddo ráito ヘッドライト, zenshōtō 前照灯
headline *n* midashi 見出し・みだし, heddo rain ヘッドライン
head office *n* honten 本店, (*corporate headquarter*) honsha 本社
headquarters *n* hónbu 本部; (*building; military*) shiréi-bu 指令(司令)部; (*corporate ~*) honsha 本社
heady *adj* sēkyū (na) 性急(な)
heal *v* iyashimásu 癒します・いやします
health *n* kenkō 健康, (*one's ~*) karada 体・身体・からだ; (*state of one's ~*) (go-)kigen (ご)機嫌, o-kagen お加減・おかげん; (*hygiene, sanitation*) eisei 衛生;

health service *n* (*hospital*) byōin 病院; health insurance *n* kenkō hoken 健康保険

healthy *adj* kenkō (na) 健康・けんこう(な), génki (na) 元気・げんき(な), tassha (na) 達者(な), mame (na) まめ(な); (*sturdy*) jōbu (na) 丈夫・じょうぶ(な)

heap **1.** *n* yamá 山・やま **2.** *~s it up* *v* morimásu 盛ります

hear *v* kikimásu 聞きます・ききます

hearsay *n* (*rumor*) uwasa うわさ・噂

hearse *n* reikyū-sha 霊柩車

heart *n* shinzō 心臓; (*as seat of emotions*) (o-)kokoro (お)心・(お)こころ; (*core, spirit*) shín 芯・シン; (*mind*) muné 胸, omói 思い; (*spirit*) ki 気; by heart *adv* (*from memory*) sóra de 空で・そらで; heartache *n* shintsū 心痛; heart attack *n* shinzō mahi 心臓麻痺, shinzō hossa 心臓発作

heartening *adj* kokoro-zuyoi 心強い・こころづよい

heartfelt *adj* kokóro kara (no) 心から・こころから(の)

heartless *adj* mujō (na) 無情(な), hakujō (na) 薄情(な)

heat **1.** *n* átsu-sa 熱さ・暑さ・あつさ, netsú 熱 **2.** *~s it* *v* átsuku shimásu 熱くします, nesshimásu 熱します → **warm it up** **3.** *it ~s up* *v* átsuku narimásu 熱く[暑く・あつく]なります, nesshimásu 熱します

heater *n* sutōˊbu ストーブ, híitā ヒーター, kanetsú-ki 加熱器

heating *n* (*of room, etc.*) danbō 暖房; heating saké *n* (o-)kan (お)燗, kán-zake 燗酒・かん酒

heatstroke *n* nissha-byō 日射病, nessha-byō 熱射病

heat wave *n* neppa 熱波

heaven *n* tén 天・てん; (*sky*) sóra 空・そら; (*paradise*) téngoku 天国・てんごく

heavy *n* omoi 重い・おもい; (*onerous*) kurushíi 苦しい・くるしい; heavy rain *n* ō-áme 大雨; (*torrential downpour*) gōˊu 豪雨; heavy snow *n* ō-yuki 大雪; heavy tax *n* jū-zei 重税; heavy work (load) *n* tsurai shigoto つらい仕事

hedge *n* ikegaki 生け垣・いけがき

heed *n* chūi 注意

heel *n* kakato かかと・踵

height *n* takasa 高さ; (*stature*) séi 背・せい (= sé 背)

heir *n* sōzoku-nin 相続人

helicopter *n* herikoputā ヘリコプター

hell *n* jigokú 地獄・じごく

hello **1.** (*on phone*) móshi moshi もしもし **2.** (*saying at door*) [FORMAL] Gomen kudasái ごめん下さい. [CASUAL] konnichi wa こんにちは **3.** (*on encounter*) ā ああ + [NAME] *and/or* [TITLE]; yā やあ; gokigen yō ごきげんよう

help **1.** *n* (*assistance*) tetsudái 手伝い・てつだい; (*good offices*) assen あっせん・斡旋, sewá 世話; (*aid*) énjo 援助, hójo 補助;

(*support*) ōen 応援; ***with the ~ of …*** no assen/sewá de …の あっせん/世話で **2.** *v* (*assists*) tetsudaimás<u>u</u> 手伝います・てつだいます; (*rescues*) tas<u>u</u>kemás<u>u</u> 助けます・たすけます; (*saves*) s<u>u</u>kuimás<u>u</u> 救います; (*supports*) ōen shimás<u>u</u> 応援します

helper *n* joshu 助手; ***household ~*** o-tétsudai(-san) お手伝い・おてつだい(さん)

hemorrhoids *n* ji 痔・ぢ

hen *n* mendori 雌鳥・メンドリ

hepatitis *n* kan'en 肝炎

her → **she; herself** → **oneself**

herb *n* k<u>u</u>sá 草・クサ; yak<u>u</u>sō 薬草・ヤクソウ, hāˊbu ハーブ

herd *n* mure 群れ

here *n* koko ここ; kochira こちら, kotchí こっち; ***is ~*** k<u>i</u>téimás<u>u</u> 来ています

hero *n* eiyū 英雄, hiirō ヒーロー

heroine *n* eiyū 英雄, hiroin ヒロイン

herpes *n* hōshin 疱疹, hérupesu ヘルペス

hers (*belonging to her*) → **she**

hesitate *v* tameraimás<u>u</u> ためらいます・躊躇います; chūcho shimás<u>u</u> ちゅうちょ[躊躇]します; enryo shimás<u>u</u> 遠慮します・えんりょします

hey! *interj* (*masculine*) ói! おい!, tchotto! ちょっと!, (*feminine*) nē! ねえ!, ano né! あのね!

hi! *interj* (*masculine*) yá やあ! → **hello** → **hey**

hiccup *n* shákkuri しゃっくり

hide 1. *v* (*~s it*) kak<u>u</u>shimás<u>u</u> 隠します・かくします; (*it ~s*) kakuremás<u>u</u> 隠れます・かくれます **2.** *n* (*skin of an animal*) kawa 皮, híkaku 皮革, (*skin of a human*) hifu 皮膚

high *adj* takái 高い・たかい; kō-… 高…; ***highest*** (*maximum, top*) saikō (no) 最高(の), saijō (no) 最上(の); ***higher by ¥100*** hyakuén-daka 百円高; high (barometric) pressure *n* kō-kíatsu 高気圧; high blood pressure *n* kō-kétsúatsu 高血圧

high-class *adj* (*high-grade/-ranking*) kōkyū (na) 高級(な), haikurasu (no) ハイクラス(の)

high degree *n* kōˊdo 高度

highest *adj/adv* ichiban takái 一番高い, saikō (no) 最高(の); ichiban ue 一番上, saijō (no) 最上(の)

highhanded *adj* gōin (na) 強引(な)

highland *n* kōchi 高地

highlight *n* midokoro 見所, medama 目玉, hairaito ハイライト

highly *adv* ōi ni おおいに, hijō ni 非常に・ひじょうに, kiwamete 極めて

highrise *adj* kōsō (no) 高層(の); high-rise (office) building *n* kōsō ofisubiru 高層(オフィス)ビル

high school *n* kōtō-gákkō 高等学校, kō-kō 高校; high school student *n* kōkōˊ-sei 高校生

high speed *adj* kōsoku 高速

highway *n* kaidō 街道, kokudō 国道, kōdō 公道; (*expressway*) kōsoku-dōro 高速道路

hijack 1. *v* (*airplane*) nottorimásu 乗っ取ります 2. *n* haijakku ハイジャック

hike, hiking *n* háikíngu (o shimásu) ハイキング(をします)

hilarious *adj* yukai (na) 愉快(な)

hill *n* (*slope*) saká 坂; (*small mountain*) oka 丘・おか, koyama 小山

hilt *n* tsuká 塚・つか

him → **he; himself** → **oneself**

hind *adj* ushiro (no) 後ろの・うしろの; **hind leg** *n* ato-ashi 後肢, ushiro ashi 後ろ肢・うしろあし

hinder *v* samatagemásu 妨げます・さまたげます

hinge 1. *n* chō-tsúgai ちょうつがい・蝶番 2. *v* **~s on** ... ni sayū-saremásu ...に左右されます; **hinged door** *n* hirakí-do 開き戸

hint 1. *n* hínto ヒント, honome-kashí ほのめかし, anji 暗示, tega-kari 手掛かり 2. *v* (*~s it*) hono-mekashimásu ほのめかします, anji shimásu 暗示します

hip 1. *n* (*buttock*) (o-)shiri (お)尻・(お)しり, (*thigh*) mómo もも・股; (*loins*) koshi 腰・こし, hippu ヒップ 2. *adj* [SLANG] (*cool*) ikashita いかした, iketeru イケてる

hippopotamus *n* kaba かば・カバ・河馬

hiragana *n* hirágáná ひらがな・平仮名

hire *v* yatoimásu 雇います・やといます; (*a professional*) tanomi-másu 頼みます・たのみます

his (*belonging to him*) → **he**

historian *n* rekishi-ka 歴史家

history *n* rekishi 歴史; ***one's personal*** **~** rireki 履歴, keireki 経歴, (*resume*) rirekisho 履歴書

hit 1. *n* híttó ヒット; atari 当たり 2. *v* butsukemásu ぶつけます, uchimásu 打ちます・うちます; (*strike*) tatakimásu 叩きます・たたきます; atemásu 当てます・あてます 3. *v* atarimásu 当たります・あたります; ***gets*** **~** (*robbed, beset, wounded, killed*) yararemásu やられます

hitch 1. *n* (*knot*) musubi-me 結び目・むすび目 2. *n* (*barrier*) shōgai 障害 3. *n, v* (*hitchhike*) hittchi-haiku (shimásu) ヒッチハイク(します)

hoard *v* takuwaemásu 蓄えます・たくわえます, (*buys up*) kaidame shimásu 買いだめします

hoarse *adj* hasukii (na) ハスキー(な); shiwa-gareta しわがれた

hobby *n* shúmi 趣味・しゅみ; hobii ホビー; ohako おはこ・十八番 (= ***hobbyhorse***)

hoe *n* kuwa くわ・クワ・鍬

Hokkaido *n* Hokkáidō 北海道

hold 1. *v* (té ni) mochimásu (手に)持ちます・もちます, mótte imásu 持っています・もっています; (*in arms*) dakimásu 抱きます・だきます, (*under the arm*) kakaemásu 抱えます・か

かえます; (*an open umbrella*) sashimás<u>u</u> 差します・さします; (*keeps in reserve*) tótte okimás<u>u</u> 取って置きます; (*gives an event*) moyōshimás<u>u</u> 催します・もよおします; ~ *in the mouth* (kuchi ni) f<u>u</u>kumimás<u>u</u> (口に)含みます **2.** *n* (*place to hold on*) tegákari 手掛かり; hold back *v* (*hesitates*) (go-)enryo shimás<u>u</u> (ご)遠慮・えんりょします; hold it *v* (sono-mama de) machimás<u>u</u> (そのままで)待ちます, taiki shimás<u>u</u> 待機します; hold it up *v* (*lift*) sashi-agemás<u>u</u> 差し上げます・さしあげます

hole *n* aná 穴・あな; (*opening*) k<u>u</u>chi 口・クチ

holiday *n* yasumí 休み・やすみ, kyūjitsu 休日; (*official*) saijitsu 祭日, shukujitsu 祝日

Holland *n* Oranda オランダ

hollow 1. *adj* (*empty*) utsuro (na) うつろ(な) **2.** *n* (*a dent*) kubomi くぼみ・窪み; *gets ~* hekomimá-s<u>u</u> へこみます・凹みます

holly *n* hiiragi ヒイラギ

holocaust *n* dai-gyakusatsu 大虐殺; ***the Holocaust*** yudaya-jin (no) dai-gyakusatsu ユダヤ人(の)大虐殺

home *n* (o-)uchi (お)家, … uchí …家; (*one's residence*) jitaku 自宅; (*household*) katei 家庭; ***goes ~*** kaerimás<u>u</u> 帰ります・かえります; home and abroad náigai 内外; (one's) home area kuni 国, inaka いなか・田舎 (= **hometown**); one's parent's home jikka 実家

home help *n* hōmu herupā ホームヘルパー

homeland *n* sókoku 祖国, (*motherland*) bókoku 母国

homeless *n* hōmuresu ホームレス, furō´-sha 浮浪者

homemade *adj* tesei (no) 手製(の), tezúkuri (no) 手作り・てづくり(の)

homepage *n* hōmupēji ホームページ

homesick *adj* hōmu sh<u>i</u>kku (no) ホームシック(の)

hometown *n* kókyō 故郷; hōmu taun ホームタウン; (*countryside*) inaka いなか・田舎; (o-)sato (お)里

homicide *n* **1.** (*murder*) satsujin 殺人 **2.** (*killer*) satsujin-han 殺人犯

homosexual 1. *n* hómo ホモ **2.** *adj* dōséi ai (no) 同性愛(の)

honest *adj* shōjíkí (na) 正直・しょうじき(な), katagi (na) 堅気(な); (*proper*) tadashíi 正しい・ただしい; (*earnest*) majime (na) まじめ[真面目](な)

honey 1. *n* mítsu 蜜・ミツ, hachi-mitsu 蜂蜜・ハチミツ **2.** *interj* hanii ハニー

Hong Kong *n* Hónkón ホンコン・香港

Honolulu *n* Honoruru ホノルル

honor *n* méiyo 名誉; (=*"face"*) taimen 体面; (*sense of obligation*) girí 義理

honorable *adj* (*respectable*)

sonkeidekiru 尊敬できる, rippa na 立派な

Honshu *n* Hónshū 本州

hood *n* **1.** (*of car*) bonnétto ボンネット **2.** (*for head*) fūdo フード

hoodlum *n* yotamonoよたもの・与太者; chinpira ちんぴら・チンピラ

hoof *n* hizume ヒヅメ・蹄

hook **1.** *n* kagí カギ・鈎; (*snap*) hókku ホック; ***fishing ~*** tsuribari 釣り針 **2.** *v* (*to ~ a fish*) tsurimásu 釣ります; ***~ up*** setsuzoku shimásu 接続します **3.** *v* (*to hang*) tsurushimásu 吊るします, hikkakémásu 引っ掛けます

hookey; ***plays ~*** saborimásu さぼります, zuru-yásumi shimásu ずる休みします

hoop *n* wa(k-ka) 輪(っか)

hope **1.** *n* nozomi 望み・のぞみ, kibō 希望, (*anticipation*) mikomi 見込み, (*ambition*) kokorozashi 志 **2.** ***~s for*** *v* nozomimásu 望みます・のぞみます, kibō shimásu 希望します; ***I ~ that …*** (da) to íi desu …(だ)といいです

horizon *n* (*sea*) suihei sen 水平線, (*land*) chihei sen 地平線

hormone *n* horumon ホルモン

horn *n* (*of animal*) tsunó 角・ツノ; (*of car*) keiteki 警笛, kurakushon クラクション; (*music*) hórun ホルン

horrible *adj* osoroshíi 恐ろしい・おそろしい

horse *n* umá 馬

horse mackerel *n* áji アジ・鯵

horseradish *n* (seiyō) wásabi (セイヨウ)ワサビ・山葵

hospital *n* byōin 病院; ***~ admission*** nyūin 入院

hospitality *n* o-motenashi おもてなし, kantai 歓待

host *n* shújin 主人, téishu 亭主

hostage *n* (*captive*) hitojichi 人質

hostelry *n* minshuku 民宿

hostess *n* onna shújin 女主人; hósutesu ホステス

hostile *adj* tekii/tekitaishin/hankan o motta 敵意/敵対心/反感を持った

hostility *n* tekii 敵意

hot *adj* **1.** atsúi 熱い・暑い・あつい; (*pungent, spicy*) karai からい・辛い **2.** ***gets ~*** nes-shimásu 熱します・ねっします; **hot air** *n* (*idle talk*) baka-/muda-bánashi ばか/無駄話; **hot blood** *n* tanki 短気; **hot cake** *n* hotto-kēki ホットケーキ, pan-kēki パンケーキ

hotel *n* hóteru ホテル; **hotel bill** *n* hoterú-dai ホテル代

hotline *n* hottorain ホットライン

hot spring *n* onsen 温泉; **hot-spring cure** *n* tōji 湯治

hot water *n* oyu お湯, yú 湯・ゆ, (*burning hot water*) nettō 熱湯

hot-water bottle *n* yu-tánpo 湯たんぽ・ゆたんぽ

hour *n* jikan 時間・じかん

hourglass *n* suna-dokei 砂時計

house *n* (o-)uchi (お)家, … uchí …家, ié 家; taku 宅, …-ya …家;

house addition/extension *n* tatemashi 建て増し; house refuse *n* gomí ごみ・ゴミ; house rent *n* yá-chin 家賃; rental house *n* (~ *for rent or rented* ~) kashi-ya 貸家; your house o-taku お宅

household *n* katei 家庭; shotái 所帯; household budget *n* 家計

housekeeper *n* kaséi-fu 家政婦

houseware *n* (*store*) nichiyōhin-ten 日用品店

housewife *n* shúfu 主婦

housework *n* kaji 家事

how *adv* dō どう, [DEFERENTIAL] ikága いかが・如何; How are you (feeling)? *interj* Go-kigen (wa) ikága desu ka. ご機嫌(は)いかが[如何]ですか. O-génki desu ka. お元気ですか.; how come *adv* dō´-shite どうして; How do you do? *interj* (*on first being introduced*) Hajimemáshite. 初めまして・はじめまして.; how far/long *adv* (*distance*) dono-gurai/kurai どの位・どのくらい; how long *adv* (*time length*) ítsu made いつまで; ítsu kara いつから; how many *adj* íkutsu いくつ; nán-... 何..., íku-... いく・幾...; how much *adj* íkura いくら, dono-gurai どの位, ika-hodo いか程; dónna ni どんなに; how old *adj* íkutsu いくつ; nán-sai 何歳; how true *interj* naru-hodo (sō desu né) なるほど[成る程](そうですね)

however *adv* kéredo (mo) けれど(も), shikáshi しかし, démo でも, dátte だって, tokoróga ところが, tádashi ただし・但し; (*to be sure*) móttómo もっとも

hug *v* daki-shimemásu 抱き締めます・だきしめます

huge *adj* kyodai (na) 巨大(な), bakudai (na) 莫大・ばくだい(な)

huh?! *exclam* hóra! ほら! ; hē へー; ***Interesting, huh?!*** Omoshiroi-desho!? 面白いでしょ!?, (*male*) Omoshiroi-daro!? 面白いだろ!?

hull *n* **1.** (*of grain, etc.*) kawa 皮, kara 殻, (*of strawberry*) heta へた **2.** (*of boat*) sentai 船体

human being *n* ningen 人間; jínrui 人類; humankind → **human being**; human feelings/nature *n* nínjō 人情; human rights *n* jinken 人権

humble *adj* (*modest*) kenkyo (na) 謙虚(な)

humid *adj* (*in summer*) mushi-atsúi 蒸し暑い, (*gets sultry*) mushimásu 蒸します; (*in winter*) shimeppoi 湿っぽい・しめっぽい

humiliating *adj* kuyashíi 悔しい・くやしい

humor *n* yū´moa ユーモア

hundred *n* hyakú 百・100

hungry **1.** *n gets* ~ o-naka ga sukimásu おなかがすきます, hara ga herimásu 腹が減ります・腹がへります **2.** *adj* kūfuku (no) 空腹(の)

hunt *v* kári/ryō´ o shimásu 狩り/猟をします

hunter *n* káriudo 狩人, ryō´-shi 猟

師, hantā ハンター
hurdle *n* (*obstacle*) shōgai(-butsu) 障害物, (*sport*) hādoru ハードル
hurray! *exclam* banzái! 万歳・バンザイ!
hurricane *n* bōfū 暴風, harikēn ハリケーン
hurry *v* isogimásu 急ぎます・いそぎます; tobashimásu 飛ばします・とばします; in a big hurry ō-ísogi (de/no) 大急ぎ(で/の)
hurt **1.** *v it ~s* (*is painful*) *v* itái 痛い・いたい **2.** *v gets ~* kegá o shimásu けが[怪我]をします **3.** *adj* (*injures*) itamemásu 傷めます; (*damages*) sokonaimásu 損ないます・そこないます **4.** *n* kizu 傷, kega けが, kutsū 苦痛
husband *n* otto 夫, shújin 主人; husband and wife *n* fū´fu 夫婦; my husband otto 夫, shújin 主人, taku 宅; your husband go-shújin ご主人
hut *n* koya 小屋・こや
hybrid car *n* eko-kā エコカー
hydrogen *n* súiso 水素
hygiene *n* eisei 衛生

I

I *n* [FORMAL *for male*] watashi わたし・私, [FORMAL] watakushi わたくし・私; (*male*) boku ぼく・僕; (*male, unrefined*) ore おれ・オレ・俺; (*female*) atashi あたし; I see! *interj* naru-hodo なるほど・成る程, wakatta わかった・分かった
ice *n* kōri 氷・こおり
icebox *n* reizō´ko 冷蔵庫, reitō´ko 冷凍庫 → **refrigerator**
ice cream *n* aisu-kuríimu アイスクリーム
icon *n* **1.** (*computer*) aikon アイコン; *~ box* aikon-bokkusu アイコン・ボックス **2.** (*image*) zō 像; icon memory *n* zanzō 残像
idea *n* (thought) kangáe 考え・かんがえ, omóitsuki 思いつき; kokoro atari 心当たり; (*opinion*) íken 意見, (*your opinion*) go-íken ご意見; aidéa アイデア; (*intention, aim*) nerai 狙い → **rough idea**
ideal *adj* risō-teki (na) 理想的(な); (*most desirable*) motte-kói (no) もってこい(の)
identical *adj* hitoshíi 等しい・ひとしい → **same**; identical twins *n* ichiransei-sōsēji 一卵性双生児
identified; *gets ~* shiremásu 知れます
identity card *n* mibun-shōmei-sho 身分証明書, ai dii-kādo IDカード
ideology *n* ideorogii イデオロギー, kannen 観念, shisō 思想, kangae 考え
idiot *n* (*fool*) báka ばか・バカ, manuke 間抜け・まぬけ
idle **1.** *v* (*is lazy*) namakemásu 怠けます・なまけます **2.** *adj* muda (na) 無駄・むだ(な); idle

talk baka/muda-bánashi ばか/無駄話

dleness *n* taida 怠惰, bushō 無精

.e. *adv* sunawachi すなわち, iikaereba 言い換えれば

f *conj* móshi … (shi-) tára もし…(し)たら; … (no) ba(w)ai …(の)場合; if by any chance *conj* mán'ichi 万一; if you prefer/like *conj* nan-nára なんなら; if I remember rightly *conj* táshi̱ka 確か・たしか; if you don't mind *conj* yoroshi̱káttara よろしかったら・宜しかったら; nan-nára なんなら; if you don't want to/if you like *conj* nan-nára なんなら; if there be *conj* áreba あれば, árya ありゃ

gnition *n* tenka 点火; (*car*) ~ *switch* (kuruma no) tenka suítchi (車の)点火スイッチ

gnorance *n* muchi 無知

gnore *v* múshi shimásu̱ 無視します

kebana *n* ikebana 生け花・いけばな

ll → **sick; bad**

llegal *adj* fu̱hō (no) 不法(の), i̱hō (no) 違法(の); illegal work(er) *n* fu̱hō shūrō(-sha) 不法就労(者)

llicit *adj* yamí no 闇の・やみの, fu̱hō (na) 不法(な), mumenkyo (no) 無免許(の),

llness *n* byōki 病気

lluminate *v* terashimásu̱ 照らします・てらします

llumination *n* iruminēshon イルミネーション, shōmei 照明

llustration *n* zukai 図解, irasu̱to (rēshon) イラスト(レーション)

ill-will *n* (*resentment*) uramí 恨み・うらみ, (*hostile feeling*) teki-i 敵意

image *n* (ga)zō (画)像, imēji イメージ, (*video picture*) eizō 映像; (*psychological, social*) imē'ji イメージ

imaginary *adj* kakū (no) 架空(の), sōzōjō (no) 想像上(の)

imagination *n* (*imaginative power*) sōzō-ryoku 想像力, sōzō 想像

imagine *v* sōzō shimásu̱ 想像します → **suppose, think**

imbalance *n* fu-antei 不安定, anbaransu アンバランス

imbecile **1.** *adj* teinō (na) 低脳(な) **2.** *n* teinō na hito 低脳な人

imitate *v* … no mane o shimásu̱ …のまね[真似]をします, …o manemásu̱ …をまね[真似]します, nisemásu̱ 似せます

imitation *n* **1.** (*man-made*) jinzō 人造; (*fake*) nise 偽, mozō-hin 模造品, nise-mono 偽物 **2.** (*mimicry*) mane まね・真似

immediate *adj* tōmen (no) 当面(の), mokuzen (no) 目前(の)

immediately *adv* súgu (ni) すぐ(に), sassokú 早速・さっそく, jiki (ni) じき(に), tádachi-ni 直ちに・ただちに; (*without waiting*) matánaide 待たないで

immense *adj* tái-shi̱ta 大した・たいした; bakudai (na) 莫大・ばくだい(な)

immigrant *n* imin 移民

immigration *n* (*entry*) nyūkoku 入国; immigration office *n* nyūkoku kanri-kyoku 入国管理局
imminent *adj* sashisematta 差し迫った・さしせまった, majika (no) 間近(の)
immorality *n* fu-dō´toku 不道徳
immortal *adj* fu-shi (no) 不死(の); fu-metsu (no) 不滅(の); fu-kyū (no) 不朽(の); immortal soul *n* fu-shi no tamashii 不死の魂; immortal work *n* fu-kyū no meisaku 不朽の名作
immunization *n* yobō-chūsha 予防注射
impartial *adj* kōhei (na) 公平(な); kōsei (na) 公正(な)
impartiality *n* kōsei 公正
impatient *adj* ki ga mijikái 気が短い・気がみじかい
impediment *n* shōgai 障害; (*hindrance*) sashitsukae 差し支え・さしつかえ
imperial *adj* téikoku (no) 帝国(の)
impertinent *adj* namaiki (na) 生意気・なまいき(な)
impetus *n* hazumi 弾み・はずみ
impish *adj* itazura na いたずらな, wanpaku na わんぱくな
implant 1. *n* (*tooth*) sáshi-ba 差し歯, (*medical*) ishoku 移植 2. *v* umekomimásu 埋め込みます, ishoku shimásu 移植します
implement 1. *n* (*tool*) yō´gu 用具; (*apparatus*) kígu 器具 2. *v* (*to carry out*) jik-kō shimásu 実行します
imply *v* 1. fukumimásu 含みます・ふくみます 2. → hint
impolite *adj* búrei (na) 無礼(な), shitsúrei (na) 失礼・しつれい(な)
import *v* yunyū shimásu 輸入します; (*goods*) yunyū-hin 輸入品
importance; *a matter of* ~ dáijí 大事, jū-dái-ji 重大事
important *adj* jūyō (na) 重要(な), taisetsu (na) 大切・たいせつ(な), jūdai (na) 重大(な), (*precious*) daijí (na) 大事(な); tái-shita (kotó) 大した・たいした(事[こと]); omoi 重い・おもい
impose; ~ *it v* kuwaemásu 加えます・くわえます
imposition *n* 1. (*forcible*) kyōsei 強制 2. (*obligation*) gimu 義務
impossible *adj* dekínai 出来ない・できない, fukánō (na) 不可能(な); impossible! *interj* másaka まさか
imposter *n* sagi-shi 詐欺師
impotent *adj* muryoku (na) 無力(な)
impression *n* inshō 印象
impressive *adj* inshō-teki (na) 印象的(な)
imprisonment *n* tōgoku 投獄
improve *v* 1. (*it ~s*) naorimásu 直ります・なおります, yóku narimásu 良くなります・よくなります 2. (*~s it*) naoshimásu 直します・なおします, yóku shimásu 良くします・よくします
impudent *adj* atsukamashii 厚かましい・あつかましい, zūzūshii ず

うずうしい・図々しい
impulse *n* hazumi 弾み・はずみ, shigeki 刺激, shōdō 衝動
impulsive *adj* shōdō-teki (na) 衝動的(な)
impunity *n* buji 無事
in *prep* … de … で, (*located in*) …ni …に; (*inside*) …no náka (de/ni) …の中・…のなか(で/に); (*resident in*) zai- … 在…; **come in** *v* (… ni) háitte kimásu̲ (…に)入って来ます・はいってきます; **go in** *v* (… ni) hairimásu̲ …に入ります, háitte ikimásu̲ 入って行きます
inadvertently *adv* tsúi つい, ukkari うっかり
inadvisable *adj* mazúi まずい
inbound (*to Tokyo*) *adj* nobori (no) 上り(の)
inbox (*for emails*) *n* jushin torē (E-mēru) 受信トレー (Eメール)
incense *n* kō 香・コウ; (o-)sénkō お線香, sénkō 線香・センコウ
inception *n* kaishi 開始, hajimari はじまり・始まり
incessantly *adv* shi̲kiri-ni しきりに
incest *n* kinshin sōkan 近親相姦
incentive *n* dōki 動機
inch *n* (…)ínchi (…)インチ; (*Japanese*) (…-) sún (…)寸
incident *n* jíken 事件, jíhen 事変
incidentally *adv* (*by the way*) sore wa sō´ to それはそうと, tokoró de ところで, chinami ni ちなみ[因み]に, tsuide ni ついでに, tokí ni 時に・ときに
incision *n* sekkai 切開
incite *v* aorimásu̲ あおります, shigeki shimásu̲ 刺激します
inclination *n* katamuki 傾き・かたむき; (*intention*) ikō 意向
include *v* iremásu̲ 入れます・いれます, komemásu̲ 込めます, fu̲kumemásu̲ 含めます・ふくめます; (*covers all items*) mō´ra shimásu̲ 網羅します
income *n* shotoku 所得, shūnyū 収入; **income tax** *n* shotokú-zei 所得税
inconsistent *adj* **is ~** mujun shi̲te imásu̲ 矛盾しています
inconvenience **1.** *n* (*trouble taken*) tesū´ 手数, tékazu 手数, futsugō 不都合 **2.** ... ni meiwaku/tesū o kakemásu̲ ...に迷惑/手数を掛けます
inconvenient *adj* fúben (na) 不便(な); fújiyū (na) 不自由(な)
increase **1.** *v* (*it ~s/~s it*) mashimásu̲ 増します・まします; (*it / they ~(s)*) fuemásu̲ 増えます・ふえます, (*~s it/them*) fuyashimásu̲ 増やします・ふやします **2.** *n* (*an ~*) mashi 増し; zōka 増加, zōdai 増大, zōshin 増進
incur *v* (*unfair treatment, tribulation*) kōmurimásu̲ 被ります・こうむります
indecent *adj* gehín (na) 下品(な); (*obscene*) waisetsu (na) わいせつ・猥褻(な)
indeed *adv* honto ni ほんとに・本当に, hontō ni ほんとうに・本当

に, jitsú ni 実に・じつに, tashika ni 確かに・たしかに; (*of course*) móttomo もっとも・最も; (*as one would expect*) sasuga (ni) さすが(に)

indefinite *adj* futei (no) 不定(の), fumeiryō (na) 不明瞭(な)

indemnity *n* baishō(-kin) 賠償(金), (*indemnity allowance*) hoshōkin 補償金

independent *adj* dokuritsu shita ... 独立した...; *is* ~ dokuritsu shite imásu 独立しています

index *n* sakuin 索引・さくいん, midashi 見出し・みだし

India *n* Índo インド

indicate *v* shimeshimásu 示します・しめします; sashimásu 指します・さします; shiteki shimásu 指摘します, shíji shimásu 指示します

indication *n* shíji 指示, (*token, sign*) shirushi しるし・印

indicator *n* (*car*) uinkā ウインカー

indict *v* kiso shimásu 起訴します

indictment *n* kiso 起訴

indifferent to ... *adj* ni mu-kánshin (no) ... に無関心(の)

indigent *n* (people) hinkon-sha 貧困者

indigestion *n* shōka-fúryō 消化不良

indignant; *adj gets* ~ fungai shimásu 憤慨します, ikidōrimásu 憤ります・いきどおります

indignation *n* fungai 憤慨, ikidōri 憤り・いきどおり

indignity *n* bujoku 侮辱, kutsujoku 屈辱

indirect *adj* kansetsu (no) 間接(の); indirect lighting *n* kansetsu shōmei 間接照明; indirect medical cost *n* kansetsu iryōhi 間接医療費

indiscreet *adj* keisotsu (na) 軽率(な)

indiscriminate *adj* musabetsu (no) 無差別(の), yatara na やたらな, mechakucha (na) めちゃくちゃ・メチャクチャ(な)

indiscriminately *adv* yatara ni やたらに, múyami ni むやみに

indispensable *adj* hissu (no) 必須(の), fukaketsu (no) 不可欠(の)

individual **1.** *adj* kojin-teki (na) 個人的(な) **2.** *n* (*a person*) kójin 個人

individually *adv* betsu betsu ni 別々に

indolence *n* taida 怠惰, namake 怠け・なまけ

Indonesia *n* Indonéshia インドネシア

indoors *adv* uchi (no náka) de/ni 家(の中)で/に

indulgent *adj* kandai (na) 寛大(な), amai 甘い

industrialization *n* kō´gyō-ka 工業化, sangyō-ka 産業化

industrious *adj* kinben (na) 勤勉(な)

industry *n* kō´gyō 工業, sangyō 産業, gyōkai 業界; industry analyst *n* gyōkai anarisuto 業界アナリスト

inept *adj* hetá (na) へた[下手](な)

inequality *n* hu-kōhei 不公平, fu-byōdō 不平等

inertia *n* (*physics*) kansei 慣性, dasei 惰性

inevitable *adj* yondokoro-nái よんどころない・拠ん所無い, shi̲ka-ta-nái 仕方ない・しかたない

inevitably *adv* kanarazu 必ず・かならず; nán to shi̲témo 何としても・なんとしても; iyaō-naku いやおう[否応]なく

inexpensive *adj* yasui 安い

inexperienced *adj* keiken busoku (no) 経験不足(の)

inexpert *adj* hetá (na) へた[下手](な)

infancy *n* (*childhood*) yōnen-ki 幼年期

infant *n* yō´ji 幼児, shō´ni 小児, akanbō 赤ん坊・あかんぼう, aka-chan 赤ちゃん

infantry *n* hohei 歩兵

infection *n* **1.** kansen 感染 **2.** (*infectious disease*) densenbyō 伝染病; virus infection uirusu kansen ウイルス感染

inference *n* suitei 推定

inferior *adj* furyō (no) 不良(の); *is* ~ ochimásu̲ 落ちます・おちます, otorimásu̲ 劣ります・おとります; yuzurimásu̲ 譲ります・ゆずります makemásu̲ 負けます・まけます

inflation *n* infure インフレ

influence *n* (*effect*) eikyō 影響, … séi …せい; (*power*) séiryoku 勢力

influential *adj* yūryoku (na) 有力(な)

influenza → **flu**

inform *v* ki̲kasemásu̲ 聞かせます, shirasemásu̲ 知らせます・しらせます, tsugemásu̲ 告げます・つげます; (*instructs*) oshiemásu̲ 教えます・おしえます; (*tells*) mimí ni iremásu̲ 耳に入れます

informal *adj* hi-kō´shi̲ki (no) 非公式(の)

information *n* jōhō 情報, shirase 知らせ・しらせ; (*reception desk*) uke-tsu̲ke 受付

information desk *n* annai-jo 案内所, furonto フロント

information technology, IT *n* jōhō gijutsu 情報技術, jōhō kōgaku 情報工学, infomēshon tekunorojii インフォメーション・テクノロジー

informer *n* mikkoku-sha 密告者, jōhō-ya 情報屋, jōhō-teikyō-sha 情報提供者

infotainment *n* (*documentary film*) dokyumentarii dorama ドキュメンタリードラマ

infrequent *adj* tama no たまの, mare na まれ[稀]な

infrequently *adv* tama ni たまに, mare ni まれ[稀]に

infringement *n ihan* 違反

infusion *n* chūnyū 注入, yueki 輸液

ingredient *n* (*component*) séibun 成分; (*cooking* ~) shokuzai 食材

inherit *v* (*succeeds to*) tsugimásu̲ 継ぎます

injection *n* chūsha 注射; preventive injection yobō-chu̲sha 予防注射

injure *v* **1.** kega (o) saseru 怪我(を)させる, itamemásu̲ 傷めます; (*damages it*) sokonaimásu̲ 損ないます **2.** *~s it* kizu tsu̲kemásu̲ 傷つけます; kega o sasemásu̲ 怪我をさせます
injury *n* kegá けが・怪我
ink *n* inki インキ, inku インク
inland *adj* (*domestic*) kokúnai (no) 国内(の)
...-in-law *adj* girí no … 義理の…
inlet *n* (*opening*) ku̲chi 口
inn *n* (*Japanese-style*) ryokan 旅館; yado-ya 宿屋, yádo 宿
inner *adj* **1.** (*inside*) naibu no 内部の, uchigawa no 内側の **2.** (*secret*) kakureta 隠れた **3.** (*one's mind*) naimen-teki na 内面的な; **inner moat** *n* uchi-bori 内堀(り)
innocent *adj* (*naive*) mújaki (na) 無邪気(な); múku (na) 無垢(な); (*not guilty*) múzai (no) 無罪(の); **innocent lie** *n* warugi no nai uso 悪気のない嘘[うそ]
innumerable *adj* musū (no) 無数(の), kazoe-kire nai 数え切れない
inoculation *n* yobō-chū´sha 予防注射
inpatient *n* nyūin-kanja 入院患者
inquire *v* toimásu̲ 問います → **ask**
inquiry *n* (o-)toiawase (お)問い合わせ; (o-)ukagai (お)伺い; (*survey*) chō´sa 調査
inquisitive *adj* monózukí (na) 物好き(な)
insane *adj* ki-chigái (no) 気違い(の); *goes ~* ki ga kuruimásu̲ 気が狂います(狂う, 狂って)
insect *n* konchū 昆虫・コンチュウ, (*bug*) mushi 虫・ムシ
insecticide *n* bōchū-zai 防虫剤
insert *v* sashi-komimásu̲ 差し込みます・さしこみます (*puts it between*) hasamimásu̲ 挟みます・はさみます
inside *adj, adv, prep* (… no) náka (de/ni) (…の)中(で/に), …-nai …内; (*among*) (… no) uchí(de/ni) (…の)中(で/に); *the ~* uchigawa 内側, uchiwa 内輪, okunai 屋内; *is ~* háitte imásu̲ 入っています; **inside and out** *adv* ① náigai no 内外の ② nani mo ka mo 何もかも; **inside information** *n* naibu-jōhō 内部情報
insipid *adj* ajike-nái 味気ない
inspect *v* kénsa/kansatsu shimásu̲ 検査/監察します
inspection *n* kénsa 検査, kansatsu 監察
Instagram *n* insutaguramu インスタグラム
install *v* sonaemásu̲ 備えます・そなえます
installation *n* sh̲isetsu 施設
installment(s) *n* kappu/wappu 割賦; (*monthly payments*) geppu 月賦, bunkatsu barai 分割払い; **installment savings** *n* tsumitatekin 積立金
instance *n* (*example*) tatoe 例え・たとえ, tatoi 例い・たとい, réi 例, ichi-rei 一例; **for instance**

tatóeba 例えば・たとえば
instant *n* (*moment*) shunkan 瞬間, sétsuna せつな・刹那; in an instant tachimachi (ni) たちまち(に), súgu すぐ, tossa ni とっさに
instead *adv* (sono) kawari ni (その)代わりに
institute *n* (*research*) kenkyū-jo 研究所; institute director *n* shochō 所長
institution *n* shi̲setsu 施設
instruct → **teach**
instructions *n* (*directions*) sáshizu 指図, shíji 指示; (*written explanation*) setsumei-sho 説明書
instructor *n* **1.** kyōˊshi 教師, senséi 先生 **2.** (*sports*) insutorakutā インストラクター
instrument *n* (*implement*) yōˊgu 用具; (*mechanism*) ki̲kái 機械, ki̲kan 機関; (*musical*) gakki 楽器
insufficiency *n* fu̲soku 不足, … -búsoku …不足
insufficient *adj* tarimasén 足りません・たりません
insulate *v* zetsuen shimásu̲ 絶縁します
insult *n*, *v* bujoku (shimásu̲) 侮辱(します)
insurance *n* hoken 保険
insure (*it*) *v* (… ni) hoken o kakemásu̲ (…に)保険をかけます
intact *adj* sono mamá (de/no) そのまま(で/の), mu-kizu (no) 無傷(の)
integrate *v* ... o matomemásu̲ ...をまとめます, tōitsushimásu̲ 統一します
integrity *n* seijitsu 誠実, shōjiki 正直
intellectual *adj* chi̲teki (na) 知的(な)
intelligence *n* **1.** (*information*) jōhō 情報 **2.** chisei 知性, chinō 知能
intelligent *adj* chi̲teki (na) 知的(な), rikō (na) 利口(な)
intend *v* ~ *(to do)* (suru) tsumori désu̲ (する)つもりです
intention *n* tsumori つもり, íto 意図, íshi 意思; (*aim*) nerai 狙い・ねらい
intentionally *adv* wazato わざと, takuránde 企んで → **[on] purpose**
intercourse *n* (*social*) shakō 社交; (*sexual*) seikō 性交
interest **1.** *n* (*on money*) risoku 利息, ríshi 利子, rí 利; (*pleasure*) kyōˊmí 興味, shúmi 趣味; (*relevance*) kankei 関係, (*concern*) kanshin 関心 **2.** *v* ... no kyōmi o hikimásu̲ ...の興味を引きます
interesting *adj* omoshirói おもしろい・面白い, kyōmi-bukái 興味深い
interfere *v* jama ni narimásu̲ じゃま[邪魔]になります, jama o shimásu̲ じゃま[邪魔]をします, kanshō shimásu̲ 干渉します
interference *n* jama じゃま・邪魔; (*meddling*) kanshō 干渉
interior *n* okunai 屋内, shi̲tsunai 室内; uchigawa 内側; interior decoration interia dezain インテリアデザイン

interjection *n* (*word*) kantō´shi 間投詞
intermediary *n* chūkai-sha 仲介者, shōkai-sha 紹介者
intermission *n* (*between acts*) makuai 幕あい・幕間
internal *adj* **1.** náibu (no) 内部(の), nai-teki (na) 内的(な) **2.** (*to the nation*) kokúnai (no) 国内(の), náichi (no) 内地(の) **3.** (*within the office/company*) shánai (no) 社内(の); **internal evidence** nai-teki shō´ko 内的証拠
international *adj* kokusai-teki (na) 国際的(な); (*worldwide*) sekai-teki (na) 世界的(な)
Internet *n* (*world wide web*) (intā) netto (インター)ネット
interpret *v* tsū´yaku shimásu 通訳します; (*explains, construes*) káishaku shimásu 解釈します
interpretation *n* tsū´yaku 通訳; káishaku 解訳
interrupt *v* (*with a remark*) (…no hanashí ni) kuchi o hasamimásu (…の話に)口をはみます
interruption *n* (*suspension*) teishi 停止; shadan 遮断; (*remark*) sashideguchi 差し出口
intersection (*of streets*) *n* kōsaten 交差点, yotsu-kado 四つ角
interval *n* aida 間・あいだ, ma 間; kankaku 間隔
interview *n* **1.** kaiken 会見 **2.** taimen 体面 **3.** (*meeting with*) menkai 面会 **4.** (*job* ~) mensetsu 面接, intabyū インタビュー; **press interview** *n* kisha kaiken 記者会見
intestines *n* harawata はらわた・腸, watá わた・腸, chō 腸
intimate *adj* shitashíi 親しい・したしい; missetsu (na) 密接(な)
intimidate *v* kowagarasemásu 怖がらせます
intolerable *adj* tamarimasén たまりません, taeraremasén 耐えられません
intoxication *n* yoi 酔い
intramural *adj* kō´nai (no) 校内(の), chō´nai/shinai (no) 町/市内(の)
intricate *adj* (*situation, subject*) komi-itta 込み入った
introduction *n* (go-)shōkai (ご)紹介
intrude *v* (*to force*) oshi-tsukémásu 押し付けます・おしつけます
intuition *n* chokkan 直観・直感
invalid **1.** *adj* (*not valid*) mukō (na) 無効(な) **2.** *n* (*ill person*) byōnin 病人
invasion *n* shinryaku 侵略
invention *n* hatsumei 発明
inventory *n* mokuroku 目録, zaiko 在庫; (~ *list*) zaiko-hyō 在庫表
invest *v* oroshimásu 下ろします・おろします; tōshi shimásu 投資します
investigate *v* shirabemásu 調べます・しらべます; kiwamemásu 究めます; kentō shimásu 検討します
investigation *n* **1.** (*research*) chōsa 調査 **2.** (*study*) kenkyū 研究
invisible *n* (mé ni) miemasén (目

に)見えません

invitation *n* sasoi 誘い, shō´tai 招待; (*card*) shōtái-jō 招待状

invite *v* yobimásu 呼びます・よびます, sasoimásu 誘います・さそいます, manekimásu 招きます・まねきます, shōtai shimásu 招待します, mukaemásu 迎えます・むかえます

involuntary *adj* muíshiki (no/na) 無意識(の/な)

Iran *n* Iran イラン

Iraq *n* Iraku イラク

Ireland *n* Airurándo アイルランド

iris *n* (*eye*) kōsai 虹彩

iron *n* (*metal*) tetsu 鉄・てつ; (*clothes iron*) airon アイロン

ironic *adj* hiniku (na) 皮肉(な)

irregular *adj* fukísóku (na) 不規則(な)

irrelevant to ... *adj* to mu-kánkei (no) ...と無関係(の)

irresponsible *adj* mu-sékinin (na) 無責任(な)

irrigation *n* kangai 灌漑・かんがい

irritate *v* jirashimasu じらします, irairasasemasu イライラさせます; ***gets irritated/is irritating*** shaku ni sawarimásu しゃく[癪]にさわります

is (*am, are, be*); *v* **1.** (*it is*) ... désu です **2.** (*there is; it is there*) arimásu あります **3.** (*person is there*) imásu います

Islam *n* Isuramu-kyō イスラム教, kaikyō 回教

island *n* shimá 島; (*group of*) ***islands*** ...-shótō ...諸島, (*archipelago*) rettō 列島, ...-réttō ...列島

(-)ism *n, suffix* shúgi 主義

isn't (*aren't*) **1.** *v* (*it isn't*) ...ja arimasén ...じゃありません **2.** (*there isn't*) arimasén ありません

isolation *n* koritsu 孤立

Israel *n* Isuraeru イスラエル

Israeli *n* Isuraeru-jin イスラエル人

issue **1.** *n* hakkō(butsu) 発行(物); (*magazine issues*) -gatsu-gō 月号 **2.** *v* (*publishes*) hakkō shimásu 発行します → **put out**

it *pron* sore それ (*but usually omitted*)

italic *n* itarikku(-tai) イタリック(体); shatai 斜体

Italy *n* Itaria イタリア

itch *n* kayúmi かゆみ・痒み

itchy *adj* kayúi かゆい・痒い; múzumuzu suru むずむずする

item *n* **1.** kōmoku 項目 **2.** (*sports*) shumoku 種目 **3.** (*game*) aitemu アイテム

itinerary *n* nittei 日程

its *pron* sore no それの, are no あれの

itself *pron* sore jíshin/jítai それ自身/自体; ... ~ (*as we might expect*) sasuga no ... さすがの...; ***...(in)*** ~ ... sono-mónó ...そのもの, (sore) jítai (それ)自体; ***of/by*** ~ hitori-de ni ひとりでに・独りでに

ivory *n* zōge 象牙・ゾウゲ

J

jab *n* **1.** tsuki 突き **2.** (*boxing*) jabu ジャブ
jacket *n* uwagi 上着, jákétto ジャケット; ***traditional workman's ~*** hantén 半天・ハンテン, happi はっぴ・法被・ハッピ
jail *n* keimú-sho 刑務所, rōgoku 牢獄, rōya 牢屋
jam *n* (*to eat*) jámu ジャム
Jamaica *n* jamaika ジャマイカ
janitor *n* kózukai 小使い, yōmúin 用務員; kanri-nin 管理人
January *n* Ichi-gatsú 一月・1月
Japan *n* Nihón 日本・にほん, Nippón 日本・にっぽん; ***made in ~*** Nihon-sei (no) 日本製(の), meido in japan (no) メイド・イン・ジャパン(の), koku̲san (no) 国産(の)
Japanese **1.** *n* (*language*) Nihon-go 日本語; (*person*) Nihon-jín 日本人 **2.** *adj* (*of Japan*) Nihón no 日本の; wa-… 和;, nichi- 日…; Japanese cuisine *n* Nihon-ryō´ri 日本料理, kappō´ 割烹; kaiseki-ryō´ri 懐石料理; Japanese-English dictionary *n* waei-jíten 和英辞典; Japanese food *n* wa-shoku 和食; Japanese noodles *n* (*wheat-flour*) udon うどん・ウドン; (*buck-wheat-flour*) soba そば(o-soba おそば); Japanese restaurant *n* kappō´ 割烹, (nihon)ryōrí-ya (日本)料理屋
Japanese style *adj* wafū 和風, nihon-fū 日本風; Japanese-style wrestling *n* sumō 相撲・スモウ (= ***Sumo wrestling***)
jar *n* kamé かめ・瓶; tsubo つぼ・壷; (*glass*) garasu-bin ガラス瓶, bín びん・瓶
jargon *n* senmon-go 専門語; tawago-to 戯言・たわごと
jaundice *n* ōdan 黄疸・おうだん
jaunt *n* ensoku 遠足
javelin *n* nage-yari 投げ槍・投げやり
jaw *n* agó あご・顎
jazz *n* jazu ジャズ
jealous *adj* urayamashii 羨ましい・うらやましい; ***gets ~*** (yaki-móchí o) yakimásu̲ (焼きもちを)焼きます, urayamimásu̲ 羨みます・うらやみます
jeans *n* jiinzu ジーンズ, jiipan ジーパン
jeep *n* jiipu ジープ
jeer **1.** *n* hiyakashi 冷やかし **2.** *v* hiyakashimásu̲ 冷やかします
jellyfish *n* kurage くらげ・水母・クラゲ
jeopardy *n* kiki 危機, kiken 危険
jerk; ***with a ~*** gutto ぐっと
jersey *n* jāji ジャージ
Jesus Christ *n* iesu kirisuto イエス・キリスト
jet (*plane*) *n* jettó-ki ジェット機; jet lag *n* jisa-boke 時差ぼけ

jetty *n* bōha-tei 防波堤
Jew *n* Yudayá-jin ユダヤ人
jewel *n* hōseki 宝石, tamá 玉; **jeweler** *n* hōseki-shō 宝石商
job *n* (o-)shígoto (お)仕事, (o-)tsutome (お)勤め, (*place*) tsutome-saki 勤め先; **getting a job** shūshoku 就職; **job hopping** *n* tenshoku 転職
jockey *n kishu* 騎手
jog(ging) *n* jogingu (o shimásu) ジョギング(をします), marason マラソン
join *v* (*joins them together*) awasemásu 合わせます・あわせます, (*grafts, glues*) tsugimásu 接ぎます; (*enters*) …ni hairimásu … に入ります; (*in cooperation*) tsukimásu 付きます・つきます; ~ (*forces*) gōdō shimásu 合同します
joint **1.** *n* fushí 節; (*of two bones*) kansetsu 関節; (*of pipe; seam*) tsugi-me 接ぎ目・つぎめ **2.** *adj* (*combined*) gōdō no … 合同の …; **joint venture, JV** *n* kyōdō/gōben jigyō 共同/合弁事業
joke *n* jōdán 冗談, share しゃれ・洒落
journal *n* **1.** jānaru ジャーナル **2.** (*diary*) nikki 日記 **3.** (*newspaper*) shinbun 新聞 **4.** (*magazine*) zasshi 雑誌
journalist *n* **1.** jānarisuto ジャーナリスト **2.** (*newspaper ~*) shinbun-kishá 新聞記者 **3.** (*reporter*) kishá 記者
journey *n* tabi 旅, ryokō 旅行
jovial *adj* yōki (na) 陽気(な)
joy *n* yorokobi 喜び・よろこび
joyful *adj* ureshii 嬉しい・うれしい, tanoshii 楽しい・たのしい
judge **1.** *n* hánji 判事, saibánkan 裁判官 **2.** *v* (*gives judgment*) hándán shimásu 判断します, (*criticizes*) hihan shimásu 批判します
judgment *n* hándán 判断; (*criticism*) hihan 批判
judicious *adj* kenmei (na) 賢明(な)
judo *n* jū´dō 柔道
jug *n* mizusashi 水差し
juggler *n* **1.** (*magician*) tejiná-shi 手品師 **2.** jagurā ジャグラー
juice *n* jū´su ジュース; shíru 汁; ~ ***of bitter orange*** pónsu ポンス, ponzu ポン酢
juicy *adj* jū´shii (na) ジューシー(な), shiruke no/ga ōi 汁気の/が多い
jujitsu *n* jūjutsu 柔術(= **judo**)
July *n* Shichi-gatsú 七月・7月
jumble *n* gotchamaze ごちゃ混ぜ, yoseatsume 寄せ集め・よせあつめ
jump *v* tobimásu 跳びます・とびます, janpu shimásu ジャンプします; ~***s out*** tobi-dashimásu 飛び出します・とびだします
June *n* Roku-gatsú 六月・6月
jungle *n* mitsurin 密林, jánguru ジャングル
junior *adj* (*younger*) toshi-shita (no) 年下(の); (*colleague, fellow*

student) kōhai 後輩; junior high school *n* chūgákkō 中学校; ~ ***student*** chūgáku-sei 中学生

junk *n* kúzu くず・クズ, kuzu-mono くず物, garakuta がらくた・ガラクタ

junk food *n* janku-fūdo ジャンクフード

junkyard *n* sute-ba 捨て場

jurisdiction *n* shihō-ken 司法権

jury *n* baishin(-in dan) 陪審員団

just **1.** *adv* (*exactly*) chōdo ちょうど・丁度, mása ni まさに・正に; (*only*) …daké …だけ, (*merely*) táda ただ **2.** *adj* (*equal, fair*) tadashii 正しい, kōsei na 公正な; just a moment chótto ちょっと; just now tatta-íma たった今, tadáima ただ今・只今, tsúi imashígata つい今しがた; just right pittári ぴったり; uttetsuke (no) うってつけ(の); just the (*one/thing/ticket, …*) uttetsuke (no) うってつけ(の)

justice *n* **1.** (*rightness*) seigi 正義, seitō-sei 正当性 **2.** (*judiciary*) shihō 司法

juvenile delinquent *n* hikō-shōnen 非行少年, chinpira ちんぴら・チンピラ

K

kangaroo *n* kangarū カンガルー

karate *n* (*weaponless self defense*) karate 空手・カラテ

katakana *n* katákána カタカナ・かたかな・片仮名

kayak *n* kayakku カヤック

keen *adj* nesshin (na) 熱心(な)

keenly *adv* (*feels*) shimijími (to) しみじみ(と)

keep *v* tamochimásu 保ちます・たもちます; (*retains*) kakaemásu 抱えます・かかえます; (*takes in trust*) azukarimásu 預かります・あずかります; (*raises animals*) kaimásu 飼います・かいます; keep away from *v* yokemásu よけます・避けます; keep company with *v* (…o) chika-zukemásu (…を) 近付けます; keep cool *v* (*calms down*) ochi-tsukimásu) 落ち着きます; Keep it up! ganbare! 頑張れ!

keepsake *n* **1.** (*legacy*) katami 形見 **2.** (*remembrance*) kinen no shina 記念の品, kinen-hin 記念品

kelp *n* kónbu 昆布・コンブ

kennel *n* inu-goya 犬小屋

kernel *n* koku-tsubu 穀粒

kerosene *n* tōyu 灯油, sekiyu 石油

ketchup *n* kecháppu ケチャップ

kettle *n* (*teakettle*) yakan やかん・ヤカン・薬缶, yu-wákashi 湯沸かし; (*cauldron*) kama かま・釜

key *n* kagí 鍵, kíi キー

"key money" (*to obtain rental lease*) kenri-kin 権利金

kick *v* kerimásu̲ 蹴ります・けります; **kick out** *v* (*company*) kubi ni shimásu̲ クビにしますし, (*school*) yame/taigaku-sasemásu̲ 辞め/退学させます; **kick the habit** *v* (tabako, sake o) yamemásu̲ (たばこ, 酒を)やめます

kid *n* kodomo 子供・子ども, kozō 小僧・こぞう → **child**; **kid around** fuzakemásu̲ ふざけます; **kids oneself about ...** (*underestimates*) ... o amaku mimásu̲ ...を甘く見ます・...をあまくみます; **no kidding!** másaka まさか, uso (da/darō)! うそ(だ/だろう)!

kidnap *n, v* yūkai (shimásu̲) 誘拐(します); **kidnapping** *n* yūkai 誘拐, rachi 拉致

kidney *n* jinzō 腎臓

kill *v* koroshimásu̲ 殺します; [SLANG] barashimásu̲ ばらします

killed; *gets* ~ korosaremásu̲ 殺されます, yararemásu̲ やられます

killer *n* satsujin-han 殺人犯

kiln *n* kama かま・釜

kilogram *n* kiro(guramu) キロ(グラム)

kilometer *n* kiro(mētoru) キロ(メートル)

kiloliter *n* kiro(rittoru) キロ(リットル)

kilowatt *n* kiro(watto) キロ(ワット)

kimono *n* **1.** (*Japanese attire*) wa-fu̲ku 和服, ki-mono 着物・キモノ **2.** (*light, for summer*) yukata ゆかた・浴衣

kin *n* (*relatives*) shinseki 親戚, ketsuen 血縁

kind **1.** *n* (*variety*) shúrui 種類, té 手; **a kind of ...** no ís-shu ...の一種 (ís-shu no ... 一種の...); **all kinds of** samazama (na) 様々・さまざま(な), iroiro (na/no) 色々・いろいろ(な/の); **kinds of ...-rui** ...類; **2.** *adj* (*nice*) (go-)shínsetsu (na) (ご)親切・しんせつ(な)

kindergarten *n* yōchíen 幼稚園・ようちえん

kindly *adv* atatakáku あたたかく・温かく; (*kindly does*) (shi-)te kuremásu̲ (し)てくれます, kudasaimásu̲ 下さいます・くださいます

kindness *n* (go-)ón (ご)恩・(ご)おん, (o-)kokoro-zashi (お)志・(お)こころざし, (go-)shínsetsu (ご)親切・(ご)しんせつ

king *n* ō 王, ō-sama 王様

kingdom *n* ō-koku 王国

kinsfolk → **kin**

kinship *n* shinzoku 親族

kiosk *n* (*selling things*) baiten 売店, kiosuku キオスク

kiss *n* ki(s)su (shimásu̲) キ(ッ)ス(します); seppun (shimásu̲) 接吻(します)

kit (*of tools*) *n* yō´gu 用具, kitto キット; **~ *bag*** yōgu-búkuro 用具袋

kitchen *n* daidokoro 台所, (o-)katte (お)勝手, (*Western-style*) kitchin キッチン; **kitchen utensils** *n* daidokoro-dō´gu 台所道具

kite *n* táko 凧・たこ・タコ; ***flies***

a ~ táko o agemásu 凧を揚げます・凧をあげます; *~-flying* takó-ágé 凧揚げ・凧あげ
kitten *n* konéko 子猫・コネコ
knack *n* kotsú こつ; yōryō´ 要領
knapsack *n* **1.** ryúkku リュック, ryukkusákku リュックサック **2.** (*elementary school bag*) randóseru ランドセル
knead *v* nerimásu 練ります・ねります
knee *n* hiza ひざ・膝
kneel *v* hizamazukimásu 跪きます・ひざまずきます
knew → **know**
knife *n* **1.** náifu ナイフ **2.** (*kitchen* ~) hōchō 包丁・ホウチョウ, (*butcher* ~) nikukiri-bō´chō 肉切り包丁
knight *n* naito ナイト, kishi 騎士
knit *n* amimásu 編みます・あみます
knob *n* (*bump*) kobú こぶ, (*gnarl*) fushí 節; *door* ~ hiki-te 引き手, totte 取っ手・とって, doa nobu ドアノブ
knock 1. *v* (*hits*) nagurimásu 殴ります・なぐります **2.** *v* (*on door*) (to o) tatakimásu (戸を)叩きます・たたきます, nókku shimásu ノックします **3.** *n* nokku ノック; **knock down** *v* taoshinásu 倒します・たおします; **knockout** *n* (*boxing*) nokkuauto ノックアウト
knot *n* musubi(-me) 結び(目)・むすび(め); (*gnarl*) fushí 節
know *v*… o shitte imásu …を知っています・…をしっています, (*understands*)…ga wakarimásu …が分かります・…がわかります; ***doesn't know*** shirimasen 知りません・しりません, wakarimasén 分かりません・わかりません; **know-it-all** *n* shittakaburi 知ったかぶり; **know-how** *n* nōhau ノウハウ; yarikata やり方
knowledge *n* chíshiki 知識; (*learning, academics*) gakúmon 学問
known; ***gets*** ~ shiremásu 知れます・しれます, (*widely*) shiraremásu 知られます・しられます; **known as …** (*so-called*) iwáyúru … いわゆる
knuckle *n* yubi-kansetsu 指関節; **knuckle down** *v* isshōkenmei yarimásu 一生懸命やります; **knuckle under** *v* kōsan shimásu 降参します
Kobe *n* Kōbe 神戸
Korea *n* **1.** (*South Korea*) Kánkoku 韓国 **2.** (*North Korea*) Kita-chōsen 北朝鮮
Kurile (*Islands*) *n* Chishíma 千島, Chishíma-réttō 千島列島
Kyoto *n* Kyōto 京都
Kyūshu *n* Kyū´shū 九州

L

lab *n* rábo ラボ; (*research*) kenkyūjo 研究所; (*testing*) shiken jo 試験所

label 1. *n* retteru レッテル, (*tag*) fuda 札・ふだ, rabel ラベル **2.** *n* (*record*) rēberu レーベル **3.** *v* raberu o tsukemásu/harimásu ラベルを付けます/貼ります; grade labeling *n* tōkyū hyōji 等級標示

labor *n* rōdō 労働; labor union *n* rōdō kumiai 労働組合

laboratory *n* **1.** (*research room*) kenkyū-shitsu 研究室 **2.** (*experimental* ~) jikken-shitsu 実験室, rabo ラボ

laborer *n* rōdō-sha 労働者

laboriously *adv* ákuseku あくせく

lace *n* rē´su レース, mō´ru モール

lack 1. *n* (*shortage*) fusoku 不足 **2.** *v* (*is not available*) …ga arimasén …がありません

lackluster *adj* **1.** saenai さえない, patto shinai ぱっとしない **2.** (*object*) tsuya no nai つやのない

lacquer 1. *n* urushi 漆・ウルシ, nuri 塗り・ぬり; lacquer ware nurimono 塗り物, shikki 漆器 **2.** *v* (~*s it*) nurimásu 塗ります・ぬります

lad *n* **1.** (*boy*) shōnen 少年 **2.** (*young man*) wakamono 若者, seinen 青年

ladder *n* hashigo はしご・ハシゴ・梯子

laden *adj* tsunda 積んだ

ladle *n* hishaku ひしゃく・柄杓; (*large wooden*) shákushi しゃくし・杓子

lady *n* fujin 婦人, óku-san/-sama 奥[おく]さん/様; (*young*) ojōsan お嬢さん, redii レディ, (*middle-aged*) oba-san おばさん, (*old*) obāsan おばあさん → woman

lag 1. *n* (*a* ~) okure 遅れ・おくれ, [FORMAL] chien 遅延 **2.** *v* (~*s behind*) okuremásu 遅れます・おくれます; time lag *n* jisa 時差

lake *n* mizū´mi 湖・みずうみ, …-ko …湖; lake-side *n* kohan 湖畔; lakeshore *n* kogan 湖岸

lamb *n* ko-hítsúji 子羊・コヒツジ

lame 1. *adj* ashí ga fú-jiyū (na) 足が不自由(な) → **cripple(d) 2.** *n* (*fabric*) rame ラメ

lament *v* nagekimásu 嘆きます・なげきます

lamentation *n* nagekí 嘆き・なげき

lamp *n* ránpu ランプ; akari 明かり・あかり; dentō 電灯・電燈; ***desk/floor*** ~ (denki-)sutándo (電気)スタンド

land 1. *n* riku 陸・りく, oka 丘・おか, jí 地; (*a piece of* ~) tochi 土地 **2.** *v* (*comes ashore*) jōriku shimásu 上陸します; (*from the air*) chakuriku shimásu 着陸します

landing *n* chakuriku 着陸, jōriku 上陸

landlord *n* ō´ya(-san) 大家・おおや(さん), yanushi 家主; (*owner*) ōnā オーナー; (*rental manager*) kanri-nin 管理人

landmark *n* mejirushi 目印

landowner *n* ji-nushi 地主

landscape *n* fū´kei 風景・ふうけい, keshiki 景色

landslide **1.** *n* (*earth slide*) ji-súberi 地滑り・地すべり **2.** *adj* (*overwhelming*) taisa (no) 大差(の), attō-teki (na) 圧倒的(な)

lane *n* (*traffic, swim*) kō´su コース; (*path*) komichi 小道

language *n* **1.** kotobá 言葉・ことば, [FORMAL] géngo 言語; …-go …語; *~ learning* gogaku gakushū語学学習 **2.** (*foreign ~*) gaikoku-go 外国語

lanky *adj* yaseta やせた・痩せた, hosoi 細い・ほそい

lantern *n* (*of paper*) chōchín ちょうちん・提灯; (*traditional night-light*) andon あんどん・行灯

lap *n* hiza ひざ・膝

lapse *n* **1.** (*time ~*) toki no keika 時の経過 **2.** (*small error*) kashitsu 過失, chiisana machigai 小さな間違い・小さなまちがい

laptop *n* rapputoppu (-gata) pasokon ラップトップ(型)パソコン, nōto (-gata) pasokon ノート(型)パソコン

large *adj* ōkíi 大きい・おおきい, ō´ki-na 大きな・おおきな; (*wide, spacious*) hirói 広い・ひろい; **large crowd** *n* ōzéi 大勢; **large number** *n* tasū 多数; **large quantity** *n* taryō 多量, tairyō 大量

last *adj* **1.** (*final*) owari no 終わりの・おわりの, sáigo no 最後の; (*the tail end*) bíri (no) びり(の) **2.** (*the preceding …*) kono máe no この前の, sen-…先…・…さき…, saru 去る (+ DATE); *it ~s* mochimásu 持ちます・もちます; **at last** tō´tō とうとう, yatto (no kotóde) やっと(のことで), iyó-iyo いよいよ, tsúini ついに, yōyaku ようやく

last day (*of month*) *n, adv* getsumatsu 月末, misoka みそか・晦日; (*of year*) ō-mísoka 大みそか・大晦日; ***the Last Day*** saigo no shinpan (no hi) 最後の審判(の日)

last month *n, adv* séngetsu 先月

last night *n, adv* kinō no ban きのう[昨日]の晩, kinō no yoru きのう[昨日]の夜, sakúban 昨晩, yūbé ゆうべ・昨夜

last week *n, adv* senshū 先週

last year *n, adv* kyónen 去年, sakunen 昨年

late **1.** *adj* osoi 遅い・おそい; (*lags, fails to be on time*) okuremás<u>u</u> 遅れます・おくれます; ***is too ~ (for it)*** ma ni aimasén 間に合いません・まにあいません; ***till ~*** osokú made 遅くまで・おそくまで; ***till ~ at night*** yóru osokú made 夜遅くまで, shín'ya made 深夜まで **2.** *adv* osoku 遅く

lately *adv* **1.** (*other day*) kono aidá この間, konaidá こないだ **2.** (*recently*) chikágoro 近頃, saikin 最近

later (*on*) *adv* áto (de) 後・あと(で), áto no … 後の…, [FORMAL] nochihodo 後程・のちほど, [BOOKISH] kō´(-)…後…; ***does for*** ~ (shi-)teokimásu (し)ておきます, (shi-)tokimásu (し)ときます; **See you later.** *interj* Jā mata. じゃあまた, Jāne. じゃあね

latest **1.** *n* saishin (no mono) 最新(の物・もの) **2.** *adj* (*newest*) saishin (no) 最新(の); **at the latest** … máde ni wa …まで[迄]には, osóku tomo 遅くとも・おそくとも

Latin *n* Raten-go ラテン語; ***~ letters*** rōmá-ji ローマ字

latter *adj* áto no … 後の・あとの…, [BOOKISH] kō´(-) … 後…

laugh *v* ***~ at*** (… o) waraimásu (…を)笑います; **loud laugh** (***~ out loud***) ōwarai 大笑, bakushō 爆笑

launch *n* hassha 発射, uchiage 打ち上げ

launder *v* sentaku shimásu 洗濯します

laundry *n* o-séntaku お洗濯; (*a laundry*) sentaku-ya 洗濯屋; (*cleaner*) kuriiningu-ya クリーニング屋

lava *n* yōgan 溶岩

lavatory *n* (*to wash up in*) senmen-jo 洗面所, keshō-shitsu 化粧室 → **bathroom, toilet**

law *n* hōritsu 法律, hō 法; (*rule*) hōsoku 法則; (*science/study*) hōgaku 法学 → **...-in-law**

lawn *n* shiba 芝・しば, shibafu 芝生・しばふ

lawsuit *n* soshō 訴訟; uttae 訴え・うったえ

lawyer *n* bengó-shi 弁護士

lax *adj* yurúi 緩い・ゆるい

laxative *n* gezai 下剤

lay *v* (*puts*) okimásu 置きます・おきます; (*did lie down*) nemáshita 寝ました; **lay aside** *v* sutemásu 捨てます, mizu ni nagashimásu 水に流します; **lay down** *v* yoko ni shimásu 横にします; yokotaemásu 横たえます; **lay off** *v* kaiko shimásu 解雇します

layman *n* mongái-kan 門外漢

lazy *adj* namaketa 怠けた; ***gets ~*** namakemásu 怠けます・なまけます; (*shirks*) okotarimásu 怠ります・おこたります

lead **1.** *n* (*metal*) namari 鉛・なまり **2.** *v* (*guides them*) annái shimásu 案内します, michibikimásu 導きます・みちびきます, riído shimásu リードします; (*coaches them*) shidō shimásu 指導します; (*commands them*) hikiimásu 率います・ひきいます

leader *n* chō 長; (*director, coach*) shidō´-sha 指導者; riídā リーダー; **team leader** *n* han chō 班長, chiimu riídā チームリーダー

leading *adj* (*chief*) shuyō (na) 主要(な), omo (na) 主(な)

leaf *n* happa 葉っぱ・はっぱ, ha 葉・は

leaflet *n* chirashi ちらし・チラシ, bira びら・ビラ

leak *v* **1.** ***it ~s*** morimásu 漏ります・もります, moremásu 漏れます・もれます **2.** ***~s it*** morashimásu 漏らします・もらします

lean **1.** *v* katamuku 傾く; ... o katamukeru 〜を傾ける; ***~ against*** … ni motaremásu …にもたれます; ***~ toward*** … no hō´ni katamukimásu …の方に傾きます; (*to one side*) kata-yorimásu 片寄ります・かたよります; ***~ out of***… ... kara nori-dashimásu … から乗り出します **2.** (*meat/fish*) *adj* akami (no) 赤味(の)

leap → **jump**; **leap year** *n* urū´doshi うるう[閏]年・うるうどし

learn *v* naraimásu 習います・ならいます, manabimásu 学びます; (*finds out*) shirimásu 知ります・しります, (*hears*) … ga mimí ni hairimásu …が耳に入ります

learning *n* gakúmon 学問, gaku 学; (*study of a basic subject*) gakushū 学習

least *adj* (*smallest*) saishō (no) 最小(の); **at least** sukúnáku-tomo 少なくとも・すくなくとも, sémete せめて; (*anyway*) tó-ni-kaku とにかく

leather *n* kawá 皮・革・カワ

leave *v* demásu 出ます・でます; sarimásu 去ります・さります; (*for a far place*) tachimásu 発ちます・たちます; (*to go home*) kaerimásu 帰ります; (*withdraws*) hiki-agemásu 引き揚げます, hiki-torimásu 引き取ります・ひきとります; (*~ one's seat*) seki o hazushimásu 席を外します; **leave it behind** *v* nokoshimásu 残します; (*forgetfully*) wasuremono o shimásu 忘れ物をします, oki-wasurémásu 置き忘れます・おきわすれます; **leave it empty** *v* akemásu 空けます・あけます; **leave it intact** *v* (*untouched*) sono mamá ni shimásu そのままにします ; **leave it undone** *v* shináide okimásu しないでおきます; **leave out** (*skips*) nukashimásu 抜かします・ぬかします

leave-taking *n* itoma 暇・ひま

lecherous *adj* sukébē (na) すけべ(え)な・助平(な)・スケベ(な), kōshoku (na) 好色(な)

lecture *n* kōgi 講義, (*talk*) kōen 講演; ***~ platform*** endan 演壇, kōdan 講壇

lecturer *n* **1.** (*instructor*) kō´shi 講師 **2.** (*public speaker*) kō´en-sha 講演者

leek *n* nira にら・ニラ・韮; négi ねぎ・ネギ・葱

leeway *n* yoyū 余裕, yochi 余地

left **1.** *adj* (*not right*) hidari (no) 左の **2.** → **leave** **3.** → **rest**

leftover *n* nokorí 残り・のこり; (*surplus*) amarí 余り・あまり; ***leftovers*** *n* nokori-mono 残り物

leg *n* ashí 脚・足・あし, (*shin*)

suné すね・脛・臑
legacy *n* isan 遺産
legal *adj* **1.** hōritsu-jō (no) 法律上(の), hōteki (na) 法的(な) **2.** (*lawful*) gōhō (na) 合法(な)
legend *n* mukashi-bánashi 昔話, densetsu 伝説, monogátari 物語
leisure *n* **1.** (*spare time*) hima 暇, ma 間, yoka 余暇 **2.** réjā レジャー
lemon *n* remon レモン; *~ soda* ramune ラムネ
lend *v* kashimás<u>u</u> 貸します・かします; *~s money* (*finances it*) yūzū shimás<u>u</u> 融通します
length *n* nágasa 長さ
lengthen *v* (mótto) nágaku shimás<u>u</u> (もっと)長くします; (*prolongs it*) nobashimás<u>u</u> 伸ばします・のばします; enchō shimás<u>u</u> 延長します
lenient *adj* yurúi ゆるい・緩い; amai 甘い・あまい
lens *n* **1.** rénzu レンズ **2.** (*eye*) suishōtai 水晶体; **eye lens** *n* gan renzu 眼レンズ; **lens eye** *n* suishōtai 水晶体
leopard *n* hyō ひょう・ヒョウ・豹
lesbian *n* rezu(-bian) レズ(ビアン)
less *adj* (yori) s<u>u</u>kunái (より)少ない・すくない; (*minus*) mai-nasu マイナス; **less than** (...) íka (...)以下, ...míman ...未満; **no less than** (...) íjō (...)以上, ... mo no ... もの (*= as many as*)
lessen *v* s<u>u</u>kúnáku/chíisaku shimás<u>u</u> 少なく/小さくします; herashimás<u>u</u> 減らします・へらします
lesson *n* ...-ka ...課, réssun レッスン; *takes ~s (in)* (...o) naraimás<u>u</u> (...を)習います・ならいます
let *v* *~s (one) do it* (... ni sore o) sasemás<u>u</u> (...にそれを)させます, yurushimás<u>u</u> 許します・ゆるします; (*as a favor*) (...ni sore o) sasete (...にそれを)させて + [GIVE]; **let approach** *v* yosemás<u>u</u> 寄せます・よせます; **let fly** *v* tobashimás<u>u</u> 飛ばします・とばします; **let get away** *v* nigashimás<u>u</u> 逃がします・にがします; **let go** *v* (*releases*) hanashimás<u>u</u> 放します・はなします; **let in** *v* (*air, the sun, light*) iremás<u>u</u> 入れます・いれます; **let off/out** *v* (*of a vehicle*) oroshimás<u>u</u> 降ろします・おろします; **let me know** *interj* [FORMAL] O-shirase kudasai お知らせください; Go-renraku kudasai ご連絡ください; **let me see** *interj* (*well now*) sā´さあ; Sō´des<u>u</u> ne. そうですね.
let's (*do it*) (shi-)mashō´(し)ましょう
lethal *adj* chimei-teki (na) 致命的(な)
lethargy *n* mukiryoku 無気力
letter *n* tegami 手紙・てがみ, (*news*) táyori 便り・たより; (*of alphabet*) móji 文字, (*character*) jí 字; *~ of guarantee* hoshō-sho

保証書; letter box *n* yūbin posuto 郵便ポスト; letter paper and envelope *n* retā setto レターセット

lettuce *n* rétasu レタス

level *adj* (*flat*) taira (na) 平ら・たいら(な); (*extent*) téido 程度・ていど; (*standard*; *water level*) suijun 水準, reberu レベル

lever *n* teko てこ・挺子, rébā レバー

levity *n* keisotsu 軽率

levy *v* chōshū shimásu 徴収します

lewd *adj* sukébē (na) すけべ(え)・助平(な)・スケベ(な), midara (na) 淫ら・みだら(な), hiwai (na) 卑猥・ひわい(な)

liaison *n* renraku 連絡

liar *n* usó-tsuki うそ[嘘]つき

liberate *v* kaihō shimásu 解放します; liberation *n* kaihō 解放

librarian *n* tosho-gákari 図書係, toshokán-in 図書館員, shisho 司書

library *n* (*building*) toshó-kan 図書館; (*room*) toshó-shitsu 図書室; (*collection*) zōsho 蔵書; main library *n* chūō-toshokan 中央図書館; National Diet Library *n* kokuritsu kokkai toshokan 国立国会図書館

license *n* ménkyo 免許, ráisensu ライセンス, menkyo-shō/-jō 免許証/状; menjō 免状; ~ *(tag)* kansatsu 鑑札; driver's license *n* unten menkyo(-shō) 運転免許(証), menkyo(-shō) 免許(証); license agreement *n* raisensu keiyaku ライセンス契約

lick *v* namemásu なめます・舐めます

lid *n* futa ふた・蓋

lie **1.** *n* (*falsehood*) úso うそ・嘘, itsuwari 偽り・いつわり; ***a ~ comes to light*** uso ga baremásu うそがばれます **2.** *v* ***~s (down)*** nemásu 寝ます; yoko ni narimásu 横になります; yoko-tawárimásu 横たわります

life *n* ínochi 命, seimei 生命; (*daily living*) seikatsu 生活; (*lifetime*) shō´gai 生涯, isshō 一生, yo 世; (*one's ~*) jínsei 人生; ***brings ~ to*** … o ikashimásu …を生かします

lifeguard *n* raifu gādo ライフガード, kyūjo-in 救助員

life partner *n* (*spouse*) shōgai no hanryo 生涯の伴侶

lifestyle *n* raifu sutairu ライフスタイル, ikikata 生き方

lift **1.** *v* mochi-agemásu 持ち上げます・もちあげます, agemásu 上げます・あげます **2.** → **elevator**

light **1.** *n* hikarí 光・ひかり, akari 明かり・あかり, (*ray*) kōsen 光線; (*electric*) dénki 電気, dentō 電灯; ***in the ~ of*** … ni teráshite …に照らして **2.** ***~s it up*** *v* tera-shimásu 照らします **3.** *adj* (*not heavy*) karui 軽い・かるい; (*bright*) akarui 明るい・あかるい; (*pale*) usui 薄い・うすい; ***light rain*** kosame 小雨・こさめ

lighter *n* (*cigarette*) ráitā ライター

lighthouse *n* tōdai 灯台
lighting *n* (*illumination*) shōmei 照明, raitingu ライティング; ~ *fixtures* shōmei kígu 照明器具
lightning *n* inabíkari 稲光り・イナビカリ, inazuma 稲妻・イナズマ
like 1. *v* (*is fond of*) …ga sukídesu … が好きです, … o konomimásu …を好みます; ***would ~*** → **want, wish 2.** *prep* (*similar*) … no yō´(na) …の様・…のよう(な); (*is similar to*) … ni nite imásu …に似ています; like that *adj* sō (sō´ + [PARTICLE]/désu) そう(そう + [PARTICLE]/です); sonna … そんな…; ā (ā´ + [PARTICLE]/désu) ああ(ああ + [PARTICLE]/です), anna … あんな…; like this *adj* kō (kō´ + [PARTICLE]/désu) こう(こう + [PARTICLE]/です); konna … こんな…
likely 1. *adj* ari-sō´(na) ありそう(な); (shi-) sō´ (na) (し)そう(な) **2.** *adv* (*probably*) tábun たぶん・多分; like(ly) as not *adv* taigai 大概・たいがい; likely to *adv* (*do*) (shi-) yasúi (し)やすい
liking *n* (*a fancy*) shikō 志向, konomí 好み
lime 1. *n* (*fruit*) ráimu ライム **2.** (*mineral*) sékkai 石灰
limit 1. *n* kágirí 限り, seigén 制限; géndo 限度; hodo 程・ほど; hán'i 範囲; rimitto リミット; time limit taimu rimitto タイムリミット, seigen (jikan) 制限(時間) **2.** ***limits*** (*delimits*) ***it*** *v* kagirimásu 限ります・かぎります; (*restricts*) gentei shimásu 限定します, seigén shimásu 制限します
limitation *n* gentei 限定, seigén 制限
line *n* sén 線, rétsu 列, (*of letters*) gyō´ 行; (*plot*) súji 筋; (*in a play*) serifu せりふ・台詞; ***the ~ is busy*** (o-)hanashi chu (お)話し中です・はなしちゅうです; (*of work*) shokúgyō 職業, gyō´業
linen *n* áma 亜麻・アマ, asa 麻・アサ, rinneru リンネル
line up *v* (*they line up*) narabimásu 並びます・ならびます; (*~s them up*) narabemásu 並べます・ならべます
linguistics *n* (*language learning*) gogaku 語学; (*science of language*) gengó-gaku 言語学
lining *n* urá 裏; (*material*) ura-ji 裏地; lining of a sleeve *n* sode ura 袖裏
link 1. *n* wá 輪 **2.** ***~s them*** *v* tsunagimásu つなぎます・繋ぎます
link address *n* (*computer*) rinku adoresu リンクアドレス, rinku saki リンク先
linked; *is ~* (*with* …) (… to) tsunagarimásu (…と)つながります・繋がります
lion *n* raion ライオン, shíshi 獅子・シシ
lip *n* kuchibiru くちびる・唇
liquid *n* eki(-tai) 液(体); mizu 水
liquor *n* (o-)sake (お)酒, (*Western*) yōshu 洋酒; (*distilled from yam or rice*) shōchū´ 焼酎

lisp *v* shi̲ tága motsuremásu̲ 舌がもつれます

list **1.** *n* (*of items*) hyō 表, mokuroku 目録, rísu̲to リスト; (*of names*) meibo 名簿 **2.** *v* (*~s them*) hyō ni shimásu̲ 表にします, (*puts it in a ~*) (rísu̲to ni) iremásu (リストに)入れます

listen *v* ki̲kimásu̲ 聞きます

listener *n* ki̲ki-te 聞き手, risunā リスナー

lit; *is ~* tsúite imásu̲ ついています・点いています

liter *n* rittoru リットル

literary *adj* (*literature*) búngaku (no) 文学(の); (*bookish*) bungoteki (na) 文語的(な)

literature *n* búngaku 文学

litter **1.** *n* (*rubbish*) kúzu くず・屑, kuzu-mono くず物・屑物, garaku̲ta がらくた **2.** *n* (*stretcher*) tánka 担架 **3.** *v* (*to throw ~*) (gomi o) chirakashimásu̲ (ゴミを)散らかします

little *adj* (*in size*) chiisái 小さい, chíisa-na 小さな; chi̲tchái ちっちゃい, chítcha-na ちっちゃな; (*in quantity*) su̲kunái 少ない, su̲kóshi (no) 少し(の); **a little** su̲kóshi 少し, wazuka わずか; (*somewhat*) yáya やや; **a little while ago** saki-hodo 先程, sákki さっき; **little by little** su̲koshí zútsu 少しずつ; sórosoro そろそろ

live **1.** *v* (*resides*) súnde imásu̲ 住んでいます; (*is alive*) íki̲te imásu̲ 生きています; (*gets along*) kurashimásu̲ 暮らします **2.** *adj* (*animal*) ikita 生きた, (*broadcast*) raibu (no) ライブ(の), nama/jikkō hōso (no) 生/実況放送(の)

livelihood *n* seikei 生計

lively *adj* (*cheerful*) yōki (na) 陽気(な), (*peppy*) kappatsu (na) 活発(な), ikiiki (to) shita 生き生き(と)した, génki (na) 元気(な), (*flourishing*) nigíyaka (na) 賑やか・にぎやか(な)

liver *n* kimó 肝, kanzō 肝臓; (*as food*) rébā レバー; **liver transplant** *n* kan(-zō) ishoku 肝(臓)移植

livestock *n* kachiku 家畜

living allowance *n* seikatsu-hi teate 生活費手当(て)

living costs *n* seikatsú-hi 生活費

lizard *n* tokage とかげ・トカゲ・蜥蜴

load **1.** *n* (o-)nímotsu (お)荷物, ní 荷 **2.** *~ it* *v* (*piles it on*) tsumimásu̲ 積みます・つみます, (*puts it aboard*) nosemásu̲ 載せます・のせます

loaf *v* (*around*) búrabura shimásu̲ ぶらぶらします; (*on the job*) saborimásu̲ さぼります・サボります

loaf *n* (*of bread*) katamari 固まり・塊・かたまり, hi̲tó-kátamari 一固まり[塊]・ひとかたまり; **sandwich loaf** *n* shoku-pan 食パン

loan → **lend**

lobby *n* róbii ロビー

lobster *n* ise ebi 伊勢えび[海老・エビ]・イセエビ, robusutā ロブ

スター

local **1.** *adj* chihō´ (no) 地方(の), rō´karu (na) ローカル(な); (*of the city*) machí (no) 町(の), (*within the city*) shínai (no) 市内(の) **2.** *n* jimoto 地元; local paper *n* chihō´-shi 地方紙, chihō´-shinbun 地方新聞; local train *n* kakueki téisha (no ressha) 各駅停車(の列車)

location *n* **1.** íchi 位置, basho 場所 **2.** (*computer*) rokēshon ロケーション **3.** (*shooting place*) roke-chi ロケ地

lock **1.** *n* jō(-mae) 錠(前), kagí 鍵, rokku ロック **2.** *v* *~s* (*a door*) (to ni) kagí o kakemásu (戸に)鍵を掛けます・かぎをかけます; (*shuts it*) shimemásu 閉めます・しめます **3.** *it ~s v* kagí ga ka-karimásu 鍵が掛かります・かぎがかかります, (*it shuts*) shimari-másu 閉まります・しまります

locker *n* rókkā ロッカー; (*coin-operated*) ***baggage ~s*** koin rókkā コインロッカー

lodging *n* (*lodging house*) geshuku (-ya) 下宿(屋)

log *n* maruta 丸太

logic *n* rónri 論理, rikutsu 理屈

login *n* (*computer*) roguin ログイン, setsuzoku 接続

loin(s) *n* koshi 腰

London *n* Róndon ロンドン

loneliness *n* kodoku 孤独・こどく

lonely *adj* hitori (no) ひとり・独り(の), sabishíi 寂しい・淋しい・さびしい, wabishíi わびしい・侘びしい, kokoro-bosói 心細い; feel lonely sabishíi 寂しい・淋しい・さびしい

long **1.** *adj* nagái 長い **2.** *adv* nága-ku 長く **3.** *~s for* *v* machi-koga-remásu 待ち焦がれます・まちこがれます; for a long time *adv* nága-ku 長く・ながく, nagái aida 長い間, (*in the past*) máe kara 前から; after a long time *adv* (*of absence*) hisashi-buri ni 久しぶりに・ひさしぶり; how long (a time) *adv* dono-gurai どの位・どのくらい; long ago *adv* mukashi 昔・むかし; súde-ni 既に・すでに; long and slender/narrow *adj* hosói 細い・ほそい; long awaited *adj* machidōshíi 待ち遠しい

long-distance *adj* chō-kyóri (no) 長距離(の); long distance runner *n* chō-kyori rannā 長距離ランナー

longer *adj* mótto (nágaku) もっと(長く); ***no ~, not any ~*** mō´ もう + [NEGATIVE]

long-range *adj* chō´ki 長期

longsighted → **farsighted**

long-winded *adj* kudó´i くどい

look **1.** *n* (*appearance*) yōsu 様子・ようす; (*personal appearance*) kíryō 器量, kao 顔; (*a ~ in one's eyes*) mé-tsuki 目付き・目つき **2.** ***it ~s like*** *v* (*as though*) … yō´/mítai desu …よう/みたいです; [NOUN] dátta yō´/mítai desu …だったよう/みたいです; [VERB]-(r)u/-ta yō´/mítai desu う[る]/た

よう/みたいです; [ADJECTIVE]-i/-kátta yō´/mítai desu い/かったよう/みたいです **3.** ~ ***(at)*** *v* (... o) mimásu (...を)見ます, **look after** *v* ... no sewá o shimásu ...の世話をします, ... no mendō´ o mimásu ...の面倒を見ます・...のめんどうをみます, (*a matter*) shóri o shimásu 処理をします; (*takes over*) hiki-torimásu 引き取ります; **look around for** *v* (*shop around for*) busshoku shimásu 物色します; **look back** *v* furi-kaeri-másu 振り返ります・ふりかえります; **look down** *v* utsumukimásu うつむきます・俯きます; **look for** ① (*searches*) sagashimásu 捜し[探し]ます; motomemásu 求めます・もとめます, tazunemásu 尋ねます・たずねます ② (*expects*) machimásu 待ちます・まちます; **look out on, look out to** *v* ... o nozomimásu ...を望みます・...をのぞみます; **look up** *v* (*a word*) hikimásu 引きます・ひきます

loom *n* hatá 機

loop *n* **1.** (*ring*) wá 輪 **2.** (*shape*) kanjō 環状; ~ ***line*** kanjō-sen 環状線 **3.** (*computer*) rūpu ループ

loophole *n* (*hole*) aná 穴・アナ

loose 1. *adj* yurúi ゆるい・緩い, bára (de) ばら(で) **2.** ***lets it*** ~ *v* (*releases*) hanashimásu 放します・はなします **3.** ***gets/comes*** ~ *v* zuremásu ずれます, (*slack*) tarumimásu たるみ[弛み]ます

loot *n* ryakudatsu-hin 略奪品

lord *n* (*feudal*) daimyō 大名; ryōshu 領主; go-shujin-sama ご主人様

lorry *n* torakku トラック

lose *v* nakushimásu なくします, ushinaimásu 失います・うしないます; (*gets defeated*) make-másu 負けます・まけます, mairimásu 参ります・まいります; **lose color** *v* (iró ga) samemásu 色がさめます; **lose consciousness** *v* ki/íshiki o ushinaimásu 気/意識を失います; **lose patience** *v* shibiré o kirashimásu しびれを切らします

loss *n* **1.** songai 損害, sonshitsu 損失 **2.** (*defeat*) make 負け shippai 失敗

lost 1. ***it gets*** ~ *v* naku-narimásu なくなります **2.** (*a person*) ***gets*** ~ *v* (michi ni) mayoimásu (道に)迷います・まよいます **3.** *n* (*item*) otoshimono 落とし物

lot 1. *n* (*in a lottery*) kúji くじ・クジ; (*vacant land*) aki-chi 空き地; ***parking*** ~ chūsha-jō 駐車場 **2.** ***a lot, lots*** *adj* (*much/many*) takusán (no) たくさん[沢山](の), ō´i 多い・おおい, ō´ku no 多くの・おおくの; ō´ku 多く・おおく, tábun ni 多分に; yóku よく

lottery *n* takará-kuji 宝くじ・宝クジ, fukubiki 福引(き)

loud *adj* (*noise*) ōkíi 大きい・おおきい, ō´ki-na 大きな・おおきな; ***in a ~ voice*** ō´góe de 大声で, kowadaka (ni) 声高(に); (*color*) hadé(na) はで[派手](な)

oudspeaker *n* kakuséi-ki 拡声器, supíikā スピーカー

ounge *n* **1.** (*break room*) kyūkéi-shitsu 休憩室 **2.** (*in a hotel, etc.*) raunji ラウンジ

ovable *adj* kawaíi かわいい・可愛い, kawairashíi かわいらしい・可愛らしい

ove **1.** *n* kói 恋, ren'ai 恋愛, ái 愛, rabu ラブ; *~ marriage* ren'ai-kékkon 恋愛結婚 **2.** *n* (*tennis*) rabu ラブ; *fifteen ~* fifutiin rabu フィフティーン・ラブ **3.** *v* aishimásu 愛します; kawai-garimásu かわい[可愛]がります → **like**; *falls in ~* (*with*) … ni horemásu …に惚れ[ほれ]ます, kói ni ochimásu 恋に落ちます; **love affair** *n* ren'ai-kánkei 恋愛関係, rómansu ロマンス

ovely *adj* **1.** airashii 愛らしい **2.** (*beautiful*) utsukushii 美しい・うつくしい **3.** (*pretty*) kawaii 可愛い・かわいい

over *n* koibito 恋人, íi-hito いい人; (*devotee of …*) (…no) aikōka (…の)愛好家

ow *adj* (*short*) hikúi 低い; (*cheap*) yasúi 安い; *~ gear* teisoku gí(y)a 低速ギア[ヤ]; **low blood pressure** *n* tei-kétsúatsu 低血圧; **low-wage** *adj* tei-chingin (no) 低賃金(の)

ower **1.** *adj* shita (no) 下(の); *~ (cheaper) by ¥100* hyakuén-yasu 百円安 **2.** *~s it v* sagemásu 下げます・さげます, oroshimásu 下ろします・おろします; *~ one's eyes* mé o fusemásu 目を伏せます, utsumukimásu うつむきます・俯きます

lowest *adj* (*minimum, minimal*) sáika (no) 最下(の), (*bottom*) saitei (no) 最低(の); ***the lowest*** (*degree*) saitei géndo 最低限度

lowly *adj* (*shabby*) iyashii 卑しい・いやしい

loyal *adj* chūjitsu (na) 忠実(な), seijitsu (na) 誠実(な)

luck *n* **1.** ún 運 **2.** (*fate*) únmei 運命 **3.** (*happiness*) shiawase 幸せ・しあわせ; **good luck** ① *interj* ganbatte (kudasai). 頑張って下さい・がんばってください ② *n* kōun 幸運; **bad luck** ① *adj* un ga warui 運が悪い ② *n* aku-un 悪運, fu-un 不運

lucky *adj* ún ga íi 運がいい; shiawase (na) 幸せ・しあわせ(な); (*strikes it lucky*) tsúite imásu ついています; **lucky bag** *n* fuku-bukuro 福袋

luggage *n* (te-)nímotsu (手)荷物, temáwari 手回り, temawari-hin 手回り品

lukewarm *adj* nurúi ぬるい

lumber *n* zaimoku 材木, zái 材

lump *n* katamari 固まり・塊・かたまり

lunch *n* hiru góhan 昼御飯・昼ごはん, chūshoku 昼食, ránchi ランチ; (*box*) bentṓ 弁当

lung cancer *n* hai-gan 肺がん・肺癌

lungs *n* hai 肺

lure **1.** *n* (*decoy*) otori おとり **2.** *n*

(*fishing*) ruā ルアー **3.** *v* obiki-dashimásu おびき出します

lurid *adj* **1.** (*horrible*) zottosuru ぞっとする **2.** (*shocking*) shokkingu (na) ショッキング(な) **3.** (*bright red*) makka (na) 真っ赤(な)

luscious *adj* **1.** (*delicious*) oishii 美味しい・おいしい **2.** (*good smell*) kaori ga/no yoi 香りが/の良い・かおりが/のよい

lush *adj* (midori no) shigetta (緑の)茂った, aoao to shita 青々とした, mizumizushii みずみずしい

luxury, luxurious *adj* zeitákú (na) ぜいたく[贅沢](な); (*deluxe*) gōˊka (na) 豪華(な)

lyrics *n* kashi 歌詞

M

macaroni *n* makaroni マカロニ

machine *n* kikái 機械, mashin マシン

machinery *n* kikái 機械

mackerel *n* saba サバ・鯖; **mackerel pike** *n* sanma サンマ・秋刀魚

mad *adj* (*insane*) ki-chigái (no) 気違い(の); (*goes mad*) ki ga kuruimásu 気が狂います; muchū ni narimásu 夢中になります; ***gets ~*** (*angry*) okorimasu 怒ります

Madam *n* óku-san/-sama 奥さん/様, madamu マダム

made → **make**

made in …-sei; …製; ***~ in Japan*** Nihon-sei (no) 日本製(の), meido in japan メイド・イン・ジャパン

madman *n* kichigai 気違い

madness *n* kyōki 狂気

magazine *n* zasshi 雑誌, magajin マガジン

magic (*tricks*) *n* téjina 手品; majikku マジック

magical *adj* mahō (no) 魔法(の); ***~ world*** mahō no sekai 魔法の世界

magician *n* tejiná-shi 手品師

magistrate *n* hanji 判事

magnet *n* jíshaku 磁石, magunetto マグネット **magnetic** *adj* jíki (no) 磁気(の), jíshaku (no) 磁石(の)

magnificent *adj* subarashíi すばらしい・素晴らしい; sōdai (na) 壮大(な)

magnifying glass *n* rūpe ルーペ, mushi megane 虫メガネ

magnitude *n* magunichūdo マグニチュード

magpie *n* kasasagi カササギ・鵲

mahjong *n* majan マージャン・麻雀; **mahjong parlor** *n* mājan-ya マージャン[麻雀]屋

mahogany *n* mahoganii マホガニー

maid *n* (*servant*) otétsudai(-san) お手伝い(さん), mēˊdo/meido メード/メイド

maiden *n* otome 乙女・おとめ,

(*girl*) shōjo 少女

mail 1. *n* yūbin 郵便 2. *v* (~*s it*) (tegami o) dashimásu (手紙を)出します・だします, yūsō shimásu 郵送します; **mail box** *n* yūbínbako 郵便箱, pósuto ポスト; **mail drop** *n* pósuto ポスト; **mail order** *n* tsūshin hanbai 通信販売

mailman, mail deliverer *n* yūbin-ya (san) 郵便屋(さん)

main *adj* ómo (na) 主(な), shuyō (na) 主要(な); hon-… 本…; **main course** *n* mein kōsu メインコース; **main store** *n* honten 本店

mainland *n* hondo 本土

mainly *adv* ómo ni 主に

mainstream *n* honryū 本流

maintain *v* (*preserves*) hóshu shimásu 保守します; (*supports*) shíji/íji shimásu 支持/維持します; (*insists*) shuchō shimásu 主張します

maintenance *n* (*preservation*) hóshu 保守; (*support*) shíji 支持, (*upkeep*) íji 維持

majesty *n* ō zoku 王族; **Your Majesty** *interj* Heika 陛下

major *n* (*army*) shōsa 少佐; (*line/field/study*) senmon 専門; (*mainstream*) mejā メジャー; (*study*) senkō (shimásu) 専攻(します) → **main** → **big**; **major city** *n* shuyō tóshi 主要都市; **major general** *n* shō´shō 少将

majority *n* dai-búbun 大部分, dai-tasū´ 大多数, (*more than half*) kahansū 過半数

make 1. *v* (*does*) shimásu します; (*creates*) tsukurimásu 作ります, (*concocts*) koshiraemásu こしらえます 2. *n* seizō 製造, (*type*) kata(-shiki) 型(式); **make a fire** *v* (hí o) takimásu (火を)焚きます・たきます; **make a living** *v* kurashimásu 暮らします; **make do** *v* (*with* …) (…de) ma-ni-awasemásu (…で)間に合わせます; **make up for** *v* …o oginaimásu …を補います; **make sure** *v* tashikamemásu 確かめます; **make the most of …** *v* o ikashimásu …を生かします

make-believe *adj* mise-kake (no) 見せかけ・みせかけ(の)

maker *n* (*manufacturer*) mē´kā メーカー, seizō-moto 製造元

makeup *n* keshō´ 化粧, mēkyáppu メーキャップ; (*cosmetics*) keshō hin 化粧品

malady *n* byōki 病気

malaria *n* mararia マラリア

male 1. *n* otokó男, dansei 男性; (*animal*) (…no) osú (…の)雄; ~ ***and female*** dánjo 男女 2. *adj* (*gender*) otokó (no) 男(の), dansei (no) 男性(の); (*animal*) osú (no) 雄(の)

malevolence *n* akui 悪意

malfunction *n* koshō 故障

malice *n* ákúi 悪意

malignant *adj* akushitsu (na) 悪質(な)

mall *n* (shoppingu) mōru (ショッピング)モール

mallet *n* kizuchi 木槌; **mallet of luck**

n uchide no kozuchi 打ち出の小槌
malt *n* bakuga 麦芽; **malt beer** *n* moruto biiru モルトビール
mama *n* mama ママ, o-kāsan おかあさん・お母さん, o-kāchan おかあちゃん・お母ちゃん
mammal *n* honyū-rui 哺乳類, honyū dōbutsu 哺乳動物
mammoth *n* manmosu マンモス
man *n* **1.** (*male*) otokó 男, otoko no hito/katá 男の人/方, dánshi 男子, (*middle-aged*) oji-san おじさん, (*old*) ojíisan おじいさん, (*young*) o-níi-san お兄さん **2.** (*person*) hito 人, … hitó …人
manage *v* (*treats*) tori-atsukaimásu 取り扱います; (*copes with*) shóri shimásu 処理します; (*runs a business*) keiei shimásu 経営します; (*a team*) kantoku shimásu 監督します; **manage to** (*do*) dō´ni ka shimásu どうにかします; konashimásu こなします
manager *n* kanri-nin 管理人, mánē´jā マネージャー; (*sports*) kantoku 監督
Manchuria *n* Mánshū 満州
Mandarin Chinese *n* Mandarin マンダリン, Chūgoku hyōjun-go 中国標準語, pekin-go 北京語
mandatory *adj* kyosei-teki (na) 強制的(な)
mane *n* tategami たてがみ
maneuver *n* sakusen 作戦, enshū 演習
manga *n* (*comic*) manga 漫画・まんが・マンガ
mangle *v* zutazuta ni shimásu ずたずたにします, mechamecha ni shimásu めちゃめちゃにします
mango *n* mangō マンゴー
manhandle *v* teara ni atsukaimásu 手荒に扱います
manhood *n* **1.** (*manly*) otoko rashisa 男らしさ **2.** (*adult male*) seijin danshi 成人男子, seinen dansei 成年男性
maniac *n* maniakku マニアック
manicure *n* manikyua マニキュア
manifest 1. *adj* akiraka (na) 明らか・あきらか(な) **2.** *v* arawaremásu 現れます, (*make it clear*) akiraka ni shimásu 明らかにします
Manila *n* Mánira マニラ
manipulate *v* sōjū shimásu 操縦します, (*a person*) (hito o) ayatsuru (人を)操る・あやつる
mankind *n* jinrui 人類
manly *adj* otokorashii 男らしい
mannequin *n* manekin (ningyō) マネキン(人形)
manner (*of doing*) *n* yari-kata やり方, shi-kata 仕方; furí ふり; (*fashion*) (…) fū (…)風・ふう
manners *n* gyōgi 行儀, sáhō 作法, manā マナー → **etiquette**
manor *n* shōen 荘園
manpower *n* rōdō-ryoku 労働力
mansion *n* daigōtei 大邸宅
mantelpiece *n* rodana 炉棚, danro no mae no tana 暖炉の前の棚
manual *n* manyuaru マニュアル,

tebikisho 手引き書
manufacture *v* seisan/seizō shimásu 生産/製造します, tsukurimásu 作[造]ります・つくります
manuscript *n* genkō 原稿
many *adj* takusán (no) たくさん[沢山](の), ō´ku (no) 多く(の); ***how ~*** íkutsu いくつ, nán-… 何…
map *n* chízu 地図, mappu マップ, (*diagram*) zu 図
marathon *n* marason マラソン; ***~ runner*** marason senshu マラソン選手, marason rannā マラソンランナー; ***~ relay race*** ekiden 駅伝
marbles *n* o-hájiki おはじき, biidama ビー玉
march **1.** *n* kōshin 行進, māchi マーチ **2.** (*music*) kōshin kyoku 行進曲 **3.** *v* kōshin shimásu 行進します
March *n* Sán-gatsu 三月・3月
mare *n* (*horse*) meuma 雌馬
margarine *n* māgarin マーガリン
margin *n* (*white space*) yohaku 余白; (*leeway*) yoyū 余裕, yochi 余地; (*price difference*) rizáya 利鞘・利ざや, mājin マージン
marijuana *n* marifana マリファナ
marina *n* mariina マリーナ
marine(s), Marine Corps *n* kaihei tai 海兵隊
marital *adj* kon'in (no) 婚姻(の)
mark **1.** *n* (*sign*) shirushi 印, kigō 記号, māku マーク, ato 跡 **2.** *n* (*vestige*) konseki 痕跡; ***leaves a ~*** konseki o nokoshimásu 痕跡を残します **3.** *n* (*score point*) ten 点, (*score*) tensū´ 点数; (*school grades*) seiseki 成績 **4.** *v* (*makes a ~ on*) (… ni) shirushi/kigō/ten o tsukemásu (…に)印/記号/点を付けます
market *n* íchi(-bá) 市(場), shijō 市場, mā´kétto マーケット; ***vegetable ~*** seika íchiba 青果市場
marmalade *n* māmarēdo マーマレード
maroon *n* kuri iro 栗色・くり色
marriage *n* kekkon 結婚; ***~ proposal*** endan 縁談
marrow *n* kotsuzui 骨髄
marry *v* (… to) kekkon shimásu (…と)結婚します
Mars *n* kasei 火星
marsh *n* numa (chi) 沼(地)
martial arts *n* bújutsu 武術, búdō 武道; ***~ hall*** dō jō 道場
marvelous *adj* suteki (na) すてき[素敵](な), sugói すごい・凄い
mask *n* men 面, kamen 仮面, másuku マスク; (*Noh drama*) nō-men 能面
mash *v* suritsubushimásu すり潰します・すりつぶします
mason *n* sekkō 石工
masquerade *n* kasō pātii 仮装パーティ, kamen budō kai 仮面舞踏会
mass *n* **1.** (*Buddhist*) hōji 法事, (*Catholic*) mísa ミサ **2.** (*lump*) katamari 固まり・塊; (*people*) taishū 大衆, kōshū 公衆, minshū 民衆; **mass media** *n* マスメディア

massacre 1. *n* daigyakusatsu 大虐殺, minagoroshi 皆殺し 2. *v* gyakusatsu shimásu̲ 虐殺します
massage 1. *n* massā́ji マッサージ, anma あんま・按摩 2. *v* (*rubs with both hands*) momimásu̲ 揉みます・もみます
masseur *n* massājí-shi マッサージ師, anma あんま・按摩
massive *adj* bōdai (na) 膨大(な)
mast *n* hashira 柱, masuto マスト
master *n* 1. (*of house*) shújin 主人, danna-san/-sama 旦那さん/様 2. (*of shop*) masutā マスター, danna 旦那 3. (*owner*) (mochí-)nushi (持ち)主 4. (*college degree*) shū́shi 修士
masturbate *v* jíi/shuin o shimásu̲ 自慰/手淫をします, onanii o shimásu̲ オナニーをします
mat *n* shi̲ki-mono 敷物・しきもの, mátto マット; (*Japanese floor*) tatami 畳・タタミ, (*thin*) gozá ござ・ゴザ
match 1. *n* (*sports*) shiai 試合, kyṓgi 競技; (*contest*) shṓbu 勝負 2. *v* (*~es, equals, is a ~ for*) … ni kanaimásu̲ …にかないます, …to yóku aimásu̲ …とよく合います
matchbox *n* matchí-bako マッチ箱
matchmaker *n* 1. matchí seizō gyō-sha マッチ製造業者 2. nakōdo 仲人・なこうど
mate *n* 1. (*friend*) nakama 仲間, tomodachi 友達・友だち 2. (*spouse*) haigū-sha 配偶者; classmate *n* dōkyū-sei 同級生, kurasu meito クラスメイト
materials *n* zairyṓ 材料, genryṓ 原料, shíryō 資料
mathematics *n* 1. sūgaku 数学; ***mathematician*** sūgáku-sha 数学者 2. (*subject of elementary school*) sansū 算数・さんすう
matinee *n* máchínē マチネー; hiru no bú 昼の部
matter *n* 1. kotó 事・こと, (*problem*) mondai 問題・もんだい 2. (*something that is*) ***the ~*** (*amiss, wrong*) ijō 異常, (*hitch*) komátta kotó 困った事・こまったこと; It doesn't matter. *interj* Kamaimasén 構いません・かまいません.
mattress *n* mattoresu マットレス
mature *v* (*growth, developed*) seijuku shimásu̲ 成熟します
maturity *n* seijuku 成熟
mausoleum *n* (*an Imperial tomb*) ryṓ 陵, (dai)reibyō (大)霊廟
maxim *n* kakugen 格言
maximum *n* saidai-gén 最大限
May *n* Gó-gatsu 五月・5月
may *v* (*perhaps*) …kámo shiremasén …かもしれません; (*it is OK to do*) (shi)-témo íi desu̲ (し)てもいいです
maybe *adv* tábun (… deshṓ) 多分(…でしょう), … kámo shiremasén …かもしれません; hyótto shi̲ta ra/shi̲te/suru to ひょっとしたら/して/すると; arúi-wa あるいは・或いは

mayonnaise *n* mayonēzu マヨネーズ
mayor *n* shichō´ 市長
maze *n* meiro 迷路, meikyū 迷宮
me *pron* watashi わたし・私, watakushi わたくし・私; (*male*) boku ぼく・僕, [*unrefined*] ore おれ・オレ・俺; watashi/ watakushi (o/ni) 私(を/に); (*male*) boku/ore (o/ni) 僕/俺(を/に)
meager *adj* sukunái 少ない, toboshii 乏しい
meal *n* (o-)shokuji (お)食事; (o-)shokuji o shimásu (お)食事をします, góhan ご飯 góhan o tabemásu ご飯を食べます; a set/ complete meal *n* teishoku 定食
mean *v it ~s …* … to iu ími desu …という意味です; … o ími shimásu …を意味します; ***what I ~ is …*** ii-tai kotó wa … 言いたい事は…・いいたいことは…
meaning *n* ími 意味, wáke 訳・わけ; (*significance*) ígi 意義; (*what one wants to say*) ii-tai kotó 言いたい事・いいたいこと
means *n* **1.** shúdan 手段, hōhō 方法, shi-kata 仕方, shi-yō 仕様 **2.** → **mean**; by all means zé-hi 是非・ぜひ; means of transportation *n* kōtsū shudan 交通手段; kōtsū kikan 交通機関; use any means hudan o erabimasen 手段を選びません
meantime *n* aida 間・あいだ; in the meantime *adv* sono aida (ni) そのあいだ・その間(に), sono-uchi (ni) そのうち(に)
meanwhile *adv* sono-uchi (ni) そのうち(に); (*on the other hand*) ippō´ 一方
measles *n* hashika はしか
measure **1.** *n* → (*a*) **means** **2.** *n* (*ruler*) mono-sáshí 物差し, mejā メジャー **3.** *~s it v* hakarimásu 計ります; measuring tape *n* maki-jaku 巻き尺
measurement(s) *n* sunpō 寸法
meat *n* (o-)níku (お)肉・(お)ニク; ***grilled ~*** yaki-niku 焼肉・ヤキニク
mechanic *n* (*car repairman*) shūrí kō 修理工, seibi-shi 整備士; ***automobile ~*** jidōsha seibishi 自動車整備士
medal *n* medaru メダル, kunshō 勲章; ***gold ~*** kin medaru 金メダル
medallion *n* ōgata medaru 大型メダル
meddle *v* o-sékkai o yakimásu おせっかい[お節介]を焼きます
media *n* (masu-)media (マス)メディア → **mass**
mediator *n* assen-sha あっせん・斡旋者; chōtei-sha 調停者; chūsai-nin 仲裁人
medical *adj* igaku no 医学の, naika no 内科の; medical department *n* ígaku bu 医学部, íkyoku 医局; medical examination *n* shinsatsu 診察, kenkō´ shindan 健康診断
medicine *n* **1.** kusuri 薬・くすり, [FORMAL] yakuzai 薬剤 **2.** (*doctoring*) ígaku 医学
meditation *n* mokusō 黙想; meisō 瞑想; meditēshon メディテイシ

ョン; (*ascetic training*) shugyō 修行, gyō´ 行; (*Zen*) zazen 座禅

Mediterranean *n* chichū-kai 地中海

medium **1.** *adj* chūkan (no) 中間(の) **2.** *n* chūkan 中間; baitai 媒体;

medium-size *n* (*model*) chūgata 中型

meek *adj* súnao (na) すなお[素直](な)

meet *v* **1.** (*sees a person*) …ni aimásu̲ …に会います; (*welcomes*) …o mukaemásu̲ …を迎えます, … o de-mukaemásu̲ …を出迎えます (*happens to meet*) de-aimásu̲ 出会います, (*encounters*) ses-shimásu̲ 接します **2.** (*they assemble*) atsumarimásu̲ 集まります, shūgō shimásu̲ 集合します

meeting *n* **1.** kái 会; (*mass ~*) taikai 大会; (*conference*) káigí 会議, miitingu ミーティング **2.** (*interview*) menkai 面会; (*of prospective bride and groom*) miai 見合い **3.** (*by prior arrangement*) uchi-awase 打ち合わせ

megahertz (MHz) *n* megaherutsu メガヘルツ·

melancholy *n, adj* yūutsu (na) 憂うつ・ゆううつ(な), merankorii (na) メランコリー(な)

mellow *v* (*gets ~*) enjuku shimásu̲ 円熟します

melody *n* merodii メロディー, senritsu 旋律

melon *n* méron メロン; úri 瓜・ウリ

melt *v* (*it ~s*) tokemásu̲ 溶けます; (*~s it*) tokashimásu̲ 溶かします

member *n* ménbā メンバー, kai-in 会員; (ichi-)in (一)員

membership *n* ménbā shippu メンバーシップ, kai-in 会員

memo(randum) *n* mémo メモ

memorial *n* kinen hi 記念碑;

memorial service *n* (*remembrance ceremony*) tuitō-shi̲ki 追悼式; (*funeral*) kokubetsu-shi̲ki 告別式; (*100 days after the death*) hyákkanichi 百か日

memorize *v* anki shimásu̲ 暗記します

memory *n* obóe 覚え・おぼえ, monoóboe 物覚え・ものおぼえ, kioku 記憶, (*computer*) memori メモリ, memorii メモリー, (*capacity*) kiokú-ryoku 記憶力; (*a recollection*) omoide 思い出

memory stick *n* memori sutikku メモリスティック

men → **man**

mend *v* *~s it* naoshimásu̲ 直します・なおします, ts̲ukuroimásu̲ 繕います・つくろいます

menstruation *n* gekkei 月経, seiri 生理

mental *adj* séishin (no) 精神(の);

mental disease *n* seishin-byō 精神病, seishin shōgai 精神障害, seishin shikkan 精神疾患

mentality *n* shínri 心理, kangaekata 考え方

mention **1.** *v* … ni furemásu̲ …に触れます; [BOOKISH] …ni genkyū shimásu̲ …に言及します **2.** → **say**; **Don't mention it.** *interj*

Dō´ itashimashite. どういたしまして.

mentor *n* (yoki) jogen-sha (良き)助言者, shidō-sha 指導者, senpai 先輩

menu *n* kondate 献立・こんだて, ményū メニュー

menu bar *n* menyū-bā メニューバー

merchandise *n* shōhin 商品

merchant *n* shō´nin 商人

mercy *n* megumi 恵み・めぐみ; nasake 情け・なさけ

mere *adj* hon no … ほんの…; táda ただ; [BOOKISH] tán naru … 単なる…

merely *adv* táda ただ, tatta たった; [BOOKISH] tán ni 単に

merge *v* (*they unite*) gappei shimásu 合併します; (*they flow together*) gōryū shimásu 合流します

merger *n* gappei 合併; (*confluence*) gōryū 合流

merit *n* (*strong point*) chō´sho 長所

merry *adj* yúkai (na) 愉快・ゆかい(な), (*bustling*) nigíyaka (na) にぎやか[賑やか](な); **Merry Christmas.** ***interj*** Kurísúmásu omedetō クリスマスおめでとう

mess *n* (*disorder*) konran 混乱; (*predicament*) komátta koto 困った事・こまったこと, (*plight*) (kurushíi) hamé (苦しい)羽目; ***makes a damn ~ of it*** héma o yarakashimásu へま[ヘマ]をやらかします

message *n* kotozuke ことづけ・言付け, kotozute ことづて・言伝て, mésséji メッセージ, o-tsuge お告げ; **message board** *n* dengonban 伝言板

messenger *n* tsukai 使い, (*Internet*) messenjā メッセンジャー; **messenger of God** *n* kami no tsukai 神の使い

messiah *n* kyūsei-shu 救世主, meshia メシア

messy *adj* kitanái 汚い・きたない, chirakatte(i)ru 散らかって(い)る

metal *n* kínzoku 金属, metaru メタル; **heavy metal** *n (music)* hebimeta ヘビメタ

meter *n* **1.** (*of length*) mētoru メートル **2.** (*device*) kéiki 計器, mētā メーター

method *n* shi-kata 仕方; shi-yō 仕様, hōhō 方法, … hō´…法

metro(politan) *adj* tokai (no) 都会(の); (*run by Tokyo*) toei 都営

Mexico *n* mekishiko メキシコ

microcomputer *n* maikuro konpyūta/konpyūtā マイクロコンピュータ/コンピューター

microphone *n* maiku マイク, maikurohon マイクロホン

microscope *n* kenbi-kyō 顕微鏡

microwave *n* (*kitchen ~*) denshi renji 電子レンジ

midday *n* mahiru 真昼, shōgo 正午

middle *adj* mannaka (no) 真ん中・まんなか(の), chūkan (no) 中間(の); **the middle of** (*month*) *n* chūjun 中旬, nakaba 半ば・なかば;

middle of the night *n* (ma)yonaka 真夜中
midnight *n* ma-yónaka 真夜中
midst *n* (... no) sáichū (...の) 最中
might 1. *n* → **perhaps 2.** *v* → **power**
mild *adj* yawarakái 柔らかい・やわらかい; (*taste*) maroyaka まろやか; (*moderate*) odayaka (na) 穏やか(な)
mile *n* mairu マイル
military *n, adj* gunrai (no) 軍隊(の), gunjin (no) 軍人(の); military base *n* (gunji) kíchí (軍事)基地; military officer *n* shō´kō 将校; military uniform *n* gunpuku 軍服
milk *n* míruku ミルク, gyūnyū 牛乳; ***mother's*** ~ chichí 乳, bonyū 母乳
millet *n* áwa あわ・アワ・粟
milligram *n* miriguramu ミリグラム
million *n* hyaku mán 百万・1,000,000
millionaire *n* mirionerā ミリオネラー, hyaku man chōja 百万長者
mimic *n* ... no mane (o shimásu) ...のまね[真似](をします)
minced meat *n* hiki-niku 挽き肉・ヒキニク
mind *n* kokóro 心, omói 思い・想い, séishin 精神; muné 旨・むね; ki 気; kokorozashi 志, (*what one has in mind*) tsumori つもり, ikō 意向; bear/keep in mind fuku-mimásu 含みます; oboemásu 覚えます; Do you mind? *interj* Íi desu ka? いいですか?; if you don't mind *adv* nan-nára なんなら, yoroshikáttara よろしく[宜し]かったら; one's right mind *n* shōki 正気; set one's mind *v* kokoro-zashimásu 志します・こころざします
mine *pron* (*my*) wata(ku)shi no わた(く)しの・私の
mine *n* (*coal, etc.*) kō´zan 鉱山
miner *n* tankō sagyōin 炭坑作業員
minimal *adj* (*smallest, least*) saishō no 最小の; (*lowest*) saitei (no) 最低(の), sáika (no) 最下(の)
minimum 1. *n* (*degree*) saishō-gén 最小限 **2.** *adj* → **minimal**; minimum rate *n* saitei chingin 最低賃金; minimum standard of living *n* saitei seikatsu suijun 最低生活水準
minister *n* (*pastor*) bokushi 牧師; (*cabinet*) dáijin 大臣
minus *n* mainasu マイナス
minute *n* ...-fun ...分; in a minute *adv* súgu (ni) すぐ(に); tadáima ただ今・只今・ただいま; minutes after *adv* chokugo (ni) 直後(に)
minute *adj* **1.** (*fine, detailed*) bisai (na) 微細(な), seimitsu (na) 精 **2.** 密(な)
minutes *n* gijiroku 議事録
mirror 1. *n* kagamí 鏡・カガミ **2.** *v* (*reflects it*) utsushimásu 映します; side mirror *n* (*car*) saido mirā サイドミラー; rearview mirror *n* (*car*) bakku mirā バックミラー
miscarriage *n* ryū´zan 流産
miscast *v* haiyaku o ayamarimásu 配役を誤ります・あやまります
miscellaneous *adj* samazama (na) 様々・さまざま(な), zatta (na)

惟多(な); ~ *goods* zakka 雑貨
schief *n* itazura いたずら・悪戯
schievous *adj* wanpaku (na) 腕ヨ・ワンパク(な); ~ *child* itazuakko いたずらっ子
serable *adj* wabishíi わびしい・佗しい; nasake-nái 情けない・なさけない
sfortune *n* fu̲kō´ 不幸, wazawai 災い・わざわい
shap *n* kegá けが・怪我, wazawai 災い・わざわい → **accident**
srepresent *v* gomakashimásu̲ ごまかします・誤魔化します
iss **1.** *n* (*mistake*) mísu ミス **2.** *v* (*goes wide off the mark*) hazuremásu̲ 外れます・はずれます, (*fails*) shippai shimásu̲ 失敗します **3.** *v* (*is not in time for*) …ni) ma ni aimasén (…に)間に合いません・まにあいません **4.** *v* (*yearns for*) …ga natsu̲kashíi …が懐かしい; (*feels lonely without*) …ga inaku̲te/náku̲te sabishíi …がいなくて/なくて寂しい
iss *n*… san … さん, … san no jō´-san … さんのお嬢さん
issing **1.** *n* (*person*) yukue fumei no hito 行方不明の人, yukue fumei-sha 行方不明者 **2.** *adj* yukue fumei (no) 行方不明(の), miataranai 見当たらない, mitsukaranai 見つからない, fusoku shita 不足した
ission *n* (*task*) ninmu 任務, (*operation*) sakusen 作戦, (*Christianity*) fukyō (katsudō) 布教(活動)
missionary *n* senkyō´shi 宣教師
mist *n* kasumi かすみ・霞, kiri きり・霧, móya もや・靄
mistake **1.** *n* machigái 間違い・まちがい, ayamárí 誤り・あやまり, ayamáchí 過ち・あやまち, mísu ミス, misu̲teíku ミステイク **2.** *v* (*makes a* ~) machigaimásu̲ 間違います・まちがいます, ayamarimásu̲ 誤ります・あやまります **3.** ~*s it* *v* machigaemásu̲ 間違えます・まちがえます
mistreat *v* gyaku̲tai shimásu̲ 虐待します
mistress *n* **1.** (*Madam*) óku-san/-sama 奥さん/様 **2.** (*lover*) kánojo 彼女; (*concubine*) mekaké 妾・めかけ, nígō(-san) 二号(さん)
misty; ***gets*** ~ kasumimásu̲ かすみます・霞みます
misunderstand *v* gokai shimásu̲ 誤解します
mix *v* (*mixes it in with*) (… ni sore o) mazemásu̲ (…にそれを)混ぜます・まぜます; (*it mixes*) mazarimásu̲ 混ざります・まざります, majirimásu̲ 混じります・まじります
mixture *n* (*assortment*) kumiawase 組み合わせ・くみあわせ, kongō 混合
moan *v* nagekimásu̲ 嘆きます・なげきます
moat *n* horí 堀
mobile **1.** *n* keitai (denwa) 携帯

(電話) **2.** *adj* mochi-hakoberu 持ち運べる

mobile phone *n* keitai (denwa) 携帯(電話)

model *n* mohan 模範, (o-)tehon (お)手本; (*mold*) mokei 模型; (*type*) katá 型, …-gata …型, …-kei …型; móderu モデル; supermodel *n* sūpā moderu スーパーモデル

moderate 1. *adj* (*reasonable*) tekido (no) 適度(の); (*properly limited/restrained*) odayaka (na) 穏やか・おだやか(な); (*conservative*) hikaeme (na) 控えめ・ひかえめ(な) **2. *~s it*** *v* kagen shimásu 加減します

modern *adj* géndai (no) 現代(の), kindai (no) 近代(の), modan モダン; modern music *n* kindai ongaku 近代音楽; modern state *n* kindai kokka 近代国家

modest *adj* kenkyo (na) 謙虚(な), hikaeme (na) 控え目・ひかえめ(な), uchiki (na) 内気(な); (*small*) ō´kiku nái 大きくない

Mohammed *n* mohameddo モハメッド, muhanmado ムハンマド

moisten *v* shimeshimásu 湿します・しめします

mold 1. *n* (*pattern*) katá 型; (*model*) mokei 模型 **2.** (*growth*) kabi かび・カビ・黴; ***is moldy*** kabi ga háete imásu かびが生えています **3.** *v* (*shapes, forms*) katachi-zukurimásu 形作ります

mole *n* (*on skin*) hokuro ほくろ・ホクロ; (*rodent*) mogura もぐら・モグラ・土竜

molester *n* (*sexual*) chikan 痴漢・ちかん・チカン

moment *n* (*instant*) shunkan 瞬間, sétsuna せつな・刹那; just a mome chótto matte kudasai ちょっと待って下さい; on the spur of the mome tokí no hazumi de 時の弾みで

momentum *n* hazumi 弾み・はずみ

Monday *n* Getsuyō´(-bi) 月曜(日)

money *n* (o-)kane (お)金; (*money given as a New Year's gift*) otoshi-dama お年玉

Mongolia *n* Mongoru モンゴル

monk *n* (*Buddhist*) bō´zu 坊主, obō-san お坊さん; ***young ~*** kozō´ 小僧, kozō-san 小僧さん

monkey *n* sáru 猿・サル (o-saru お猿

monorail *n* monorē´ru モノレール

monster *n* kaibutsu 怪物, kaijū 怪獣, monsutā モンスター

month *n* tsukí 月, …-getsu …月

monthly *adj* maitsuki (no) 毎月(の); ***~ installments/payments*** geppu 月賦; ***~ salary*** gekkyū 月給

monument *n* monyumento モニュメント, kinen hi 記念碑

mood *n* kíbun 気分, kokoro-mochi 心持ち, mūdo ムード; good mood *n* jō-kigen 上機嫌, (go-)kigen (ご)機嫌

moody *adj* kigen ga warúi 機嫌が悪い

moon *n* tsukí 月

moon viewing *n* (o-)tsukimi (お)

目見
op *n* móppu モップ
oral **1.** *n* moraru モラル **2.** *adj* dōtoku-teki (na) 道徳的(な)
orality, morals *n* dōtoku 道徳; *ethics*) shū´shin 修身
ore *adj* mótto もっと, mō ukóshi もう少し, mō もう + NUMBER]; (*some* ~) sára-ni さらに・更に; a little more *adj* mō ukóshi もう少し; a lot more *adj* nótto takusán もっとたくさん 沢山]; all the more ..., still/much ~ ... *dv* issō ...一層・いっそう, nao-ara なおさら・尚更; the more ... he more *adv* ...-suréba suruho-o/dake ...すればする程/だけ... issō ... 一層・いっそう...); more nd more *adv* masú-masu ますます・益々, iyó-iyo いよいよ
oreover *adv* sono ue (ni) その上・そのうえ(に), matá 又・また, áo 尚・なお, shiká-mo しかも, ótoni ことに・殊に
orning *n* ása 朝・あさ, go zen 午前; *this* ~ kesa 今朝; Good morning.)-hayō (gozaimásu). おはよう お早う]ございます.
orning meal *n* chōshoku 朝食, sa-góhan 朝ご飯
orphine *n* moruhine モルヒネ
ortar *n* (*utensil*) úsu うす・臼; uríbachi すり鉢; (*material*) norutaru モルタル, shikkui しっくい・漆喰
oscow *n* Mosukuwa モスクワ
osquito *n* ka 蚊・カ; mosquito net *n* kaya かや・カヤ・蚊帳
most *adj* ichiban 一番, móttómo 最も; most of the ... *adj* ... no daibúbun ...の大部分; at most *adv* ō´kute 多くて, sémete せめて, séizei せいぜい; for the most part *adv* ōkata おおかた, taigai 大概・たいがい, ō´ku 多く; the most *adj* (*largest*) saidai (no) 最大(の); most recent *adj* kono mae/aida (no) この前/間(の); tsui saikin (no) つい最近(の)
mother *n* okā´-san お母さん, háha 母, haha-oya 母親; ofukuro おふくろ・お袋
mother-in-law *n* gíbo 義母; shūtome しゅうとめ・姑, o-shūtome-san お姑さん
motion *n* ugokí 動き・うごき; mō´shon モーション; ~ ***sickness*** norimono-yoi 乗物酔い
motivation, motive *n* dōki 動機; yaruki やる気
motor *n* hatsudō´-ki 発動機, mō´tā モーター → **automobile**
motto *n* hyōgo 標語, mottō モットー
mould → **mold** (*shapes, forms*)
mound *n* tsuká 塚; (*burial*) ryō´ 陵
mount *v* (*ride*) ... ni norimásu ... に乗ります; (*sits astride*) ... ni matagarimásu ...にまたがります・跨ります; (*climb*) ... ni noborimásu ...に登ります
mountain *n* yamá 山; ...-san ...山
Mount Fuji *n* Fúji-san 富士山
mouse *n* **1.** nezumi ねずみ・ネ

ズミ・鼠 **2.** (*computer*) mausu マウス

mouth *n* **1.** (*human*) kuchi 口 **2.** (*river* ~) kakō 河口

mouthful *n* (*one* ~) hitó-kuchi 一口

move **1.** *v* (*it* ~*s*) ugokimásu 動きます; (~*s it*) ugokashimásu 動かします **2.** (~*s residence*) utsurimásu 移ります, (*changes residence*) hikkoshimásu 引っ越します

movement *n* ugokí 動き; katsudō 活動; undō 運動; (*gesture*) miburi みぶり・身振り, dōsa 動作

mover *n* (*household* ~) hikkoshi-ya 引っ越し屋, (hikkoshi no) unsō-ya (引っ越し の)運送屋

movie(s) *n* eiga 映画; movie theater *n* eigá-kan 映画館

moving *n* (*one's household*) hikkoshi 引っ越し; ***moving man*** → **mover**; mover's van *n* hikkoshi torákku 引っ越しトラック

mow *v* karimásu 刈ります

Mr. *n* … san …さん; ***Mrs.*** … san (no óku-san) …さん(の奥さん), ...-fujin ...夫人; ***Mr. and Mrs.*** … fusái … 夫妻; ***Ms.*** … san …さん, …jóshi …女史

much *adj, adv* takusán (no) たくさん[沢山](の), ō´ku (no) 多く・おおく(の), un to うんと; is/has much *adj* … ga ō´i …が多い; not (very) much *adv* anmari あんまり + [NEGATIVE]; how much *adv* íkura いくら・幾ら, dono-gurai どの位・どのくらい; as much as *adv* … gúrai …位, …no yō´ni のように[様]に; much more *adv* mótto takusán もっとたくさん[沢山], zutto ō´ku ずっと多く; (*still more*) issō いっそう・一層 nao-sara なおさら・尚更

mucus *n* (*nasal*) hana (mizu) 鼻(水

mud *n* doró 泥・ドロ

muddy *adj* doro-dárake (no) 泥だらけ(の)

muffin *n* mafin マフィン

muffler *n* mafurā マフラー

mug *n* **1.** (*cup*) magu kappu マグカップ **2.** (*beer* ~) jokki ジョッ

muggy *adj* mushi-atsúi 蒸し暑い

mule *n* (*animal*) raba ラバ・騾馬

multiply *v* **1.** (*grows*) fuemásu 増えます・ふえます **2.** (3 by 5 s ni góo) kakemásu (3に5を)かけます・掛けます **3.** (*increases*) fuyashimásu 増やします

mummy *n* miira ミイラ

municipal *adj* shiritsu (no) 市立(の), kōritsu (no) 公立(の), (*urban*) shínai (no) 市内(の)

murder *n* satsujin 殺人, hitogóroshi 人殺し → **kill**

murmur → **whisper**

muscle *n* kínniku 筋肉, súji 筋; (*power*) kínryoku 筋力, chikará 力

museum *n* hakubútsú-kan 博物館 (*art gallery*) bijútsu-kan 美術館

mushroom *n* kínoko きのこ・キノコ・茸; (*thumb-like*) matsutake 松茸・マツタケ; (*large brown*)

shíitake 椎茸; (*straw*) enokí-dake/-take えのき[榎・エノキ]茸
music *n* óngaku 音楽, myūjikku ミュージック, (*traditional to the imperial court*) gágaku 雅楽
musical instrument *n* gakki 楽器
musician *n* ongaku-ka 音楽家, myūjishan ミュージシャン
muskmelon *n* masuku meron マスクメロン
Muslim *n* isuramu kyōto イスラム教徒, kai kyōto 回教徒
must *auxiliary verb* ~ **do** (shi-) nákereba narimasén (し)なければなりません; ~ ***not*** (*do*) (shi-)té wa ikemasén (し)てはいけません
mustache *n* kuchi hige 口ひげ[髭]
mustard *n* karashi からし・カラシ・芥子, masutādo マスタード
mutt *n* (*dog*) zasshu (ken) 雑種(犬)
mutton *n* maton マトン, hitsuji no niku 羊の肉 → **lamb**
mutual *adj* o-tagai (no) お互い・おたがい(の); [BOOKISH] sō´go (no) 相互(の)
my *pron* wata(ku)shi no わた(く)し[私](の); ~ ***wife*** kánai 家内
myopic *adj* kingan (no) 近眼(の), kinshi (no) 近視(の)
myself *pron* jibun 自分, (watakushi) jíshin (私)自身; **by myself** jibun jíshin de 自分自身で
mysterious *adj* (*strange*) fushigi (na) 不思議(な); (*esoteric*) shinpi-teki (na) 神秘的(な)
mystery *n* nazo 謎・ナゾ, misuterii ミステリー, (*secret*) himitsu 秘密・ヒミツ
myth *adj* shinwa 神話

N

Nagasaki *n* Nagásaki 長崎
nail *n* kugi 釘・くぎ; (*finger, toe*) tsume 爪・ツメ; **nail polish** *n* manikyua (eki) マニキュア(液)
naive *adj* mújaki (na) むじゃき・無邪気(な), soboku (na) 素朴(な), naiibu (na) ナイーブ(な)
naked *adj* hadaka (no) 裸(の) → **nude**
name **1.** *n* (o-)namae (お)名前, na 名 **2.** *v* (*calls*) (...to) yobimásu (...と)呼びます, (*dubs*) nazukemásu 名付けます; (*says the ~ of*) ...no namae o iimásu ...の名前を言います; **list of names** *n* meibo 名簿; **name card** *n* meishi 名刺; **name seal/stamp** *n* ("*chop*") hankó はんこ・判こ・判子
nameless *adj* mumei (no) 無名(の)
namesake *n* dōmei no hito 同名の人
nap *n* hiru-ne (o shimásu) 昼寝(をします); ***takes a ~*** hitó-nemuri 一眠り
napkin *n* nápukín ナプキン, fukín ふきん・布巾
narcotic(s) *n* mayaku 麻薬

narrative *n* monogatari 物語; naratibu ナラティブ

narrator *n* narētā ナレーター; katari-te 語り手

narrow *adj* semái 狭い・せまい; hosói 細い・ほそい; **narrow mind** *n* henkyō na kokoro 偏狭な心; kyōryō na kokoro 狭量な心; **narrow road** *n* hosomichi 細道

nasty *adj* iyá (na) 嫌(な), akuratsu (na) 悪らつ・悪辣(な)

nation *n* (*country*) kuni 国, kókka 国家; (*people*) kokumin 国民

national *adj* kuni (no) 国(の); koku-…国…; kokuritsu (no) 国立(の); kokumin (no) 国民の; nashonaru ナショナル

national defense *n* kokubō 国防

national park *n* kokuritsu kōen 国立公園

nationality *n* kokuseki 国籍

national(s) *n* kokumin 国民

nation-wide *n* zénkokuteki (na/ni) 全国的(な/に)

native *adj* bokoku (no) 母国(の); umaretsuki (no) 生まれつき(の); neitibu ネイティブ; **native land** *n* bokoku 母国; **native language** *n* bokoku-go 母国語

natural *adj* **1.** shizen (no, na) 自然(の, な); tennen (no) 天然(の) **2.** *adj* (*proper, deserved*) tōzen (no) 当然(の) **3.** (*to be expected*) … (suru) monó desu …(する)ものです

natural gas *n* tennen-gásu 天然ガス

naturally *adv* shizen ni 自然に; (*by nature*) motomoto もともと・元々 → **spontaneously** → **of course**

nature *n* **1.** shizen 自然 **2.** seishitsu 性質, shō 性, séi 性; (*quality*) shitsú 質; (*disposition*) táchi 質; ***human*** ~ nínjō 人情 **3.** ***by*** ~ mótó-yori もとより, motomoto もともと・元々

naughty *adj* wanpaku (na) 腕白・わんぱく(な), itazura (na) いたずら・悪戯(な); **naughty child** *n* itazurákko いたずらっ子・悪戯っ子

nausea *n* hakike 吐き気, (*medical term*) oshin 悪心, ōki 嘔気

nauseate *v* ***feels nauseated*** hakiké (o moyōshimásu) 吐き気(を催します) → **queasy**

navel *n* (o-)heso (お)へそ

navigate *v* kōkai shimásu 航海します; annái shimásu 案内します

navy *n* káigun 海軍

near *adj* chikái 近い; *adv* chikaku (ni) 近く(に)

near (by) *adj* sóba (no) そば・側(の); chikáku (no) 近く(の)

nearly *adv* hotóndo ほとんど・殆ど; mázu まず; hóbo ほぼ

nearsighted *adj* (*myopic*) kingan (no) 近眼(の), kinshi (no) 近視(の)

neat *adj* (*tidy*) kichín-to shite imásu きちんとしています; (*attractive*) kírei (na) きれい[綺麗](な)

necessarily *adv* kanarazu 必ず; ***not*** ~ kagirimasen 限りません

necessary *adj* hitsuyō (na) 必要

(な), (*needed*) nyūyō (na) 入用(な); …ga irimásu …が要ります
necessity *n* hitsuyō 必要
neck *n* kubi 首; (*of a bottle*) kubire くびれ
necktie *n* nékutai ネクタイ; ***puts on*** (*wears*) ***a*** ~ nékutai o musubimásu ネクタイを結びます, nékutai o shimásu ネクタイをします
need 1. *v ~s to do* (… ga) irimásu (…が)要ります, (… o) yō-shimásu (…を)要します; (suru) hitsuyō ga arimásu (する)必要があります, (shi)-nákereba narimasén (し)なければなりません; *~s not do* (shi) nákute mo íi desu (し)なくてもいいです **2.** *n* (*necessity*) hitsuyō 必要; (*poverty*) hinkon 貧困, fújiyū 不自由; ***is in*** ~ (*of help*) komarimásu 困ります
needle *n* hári 針; **sewing needle** *n* núibari 縫い針
needy *adj* mazushíi 貧しい, fú-jiyū (na) 不自由(な), hinkon (na) 貧困(な)
negative 1. *adj* shōkyoku-teki (na) 消極的(な), hitei-teki (na) 否定的(な), negatibu (na) ネガティブ(な) **2.** *n* (*film*) nega ネガ
neglect 1. *v* (*disregards*) múshi shimásu 無視します; (*leaves undone*) hōtte okimásu 放っておきます; (*shirks*) okotarimásu 怠ります **2.** *n* ikuji-hōki 育児放棄
negligence *n* taiman 怠慢; (*carelessness*) yudan 油断, fuchūi 不注意
negligible *adj* wazuka (na) わずか(な)
negotiable *adj* kōshō no yochi ga aru 交渉の余地がある
negotiate *v* hanashi-aimásu 話し合います; kōshō 交渉
negotiation *n* hanashi-ai 話し合い, kōshō (shimasu) 交渉(します)
neighborhood *n* (go-)kínjo (ご)近所
neighbor(ing) *adj* tonari (no) 隣り(の)
neither ... nor ... *adv* … mo… mo… も…も + [NEGATIVE]
neither one dóchira (no …) mo どちら(の…)も + [NEGATIVE]
nephew *n* oi おい・甥; ***your*** ~ oigo-san 甥子さん
nerve *n* shínkei 神経; ***gets on one's*** ~***s*** shínkei ni sawarimásu 神経に障ります
nervous *adj* **1.** shinkéi-shitsu (na) 神経質(な) **2.** (*self-conscious*) agarimásu 上がります **3.** (*gets agitated*) dōyō shimásu 動揺します → **flustered 4.** (*feeling apprehensive*) kimí ga warúi 気味が悪い; **nervous breakdown** *n* shinkei suijaku 神経衰弱
nest *n* su 巣
net *n* **1.** ami 網, nétto ネット **2.** = ***Internet*** nettó ネット
Netbook *n* (*computer*) netto-bukku ネットブック
Netherlands *n* Oranda オランダ
Netizen *n* (*internet*) netto-shimin ネット市民 (*from* Internet +

citizen)
net price *n* séika 正価
network *n* **1.** nettowāku ネットワーク, jōhō-mō 情報網 **2.** (*human ~*) jinmyaku 人脈; computer network *n* konpyūta/konpyūtā nettowāku コンピュータ/コンピューターネットワーク
neurotic *adj* noirōze (no) ノイローゼ(の)
neutral(ity) *adj* chūritsu (no) 中立(の), nyūtoraru ニュートラル
never *adv* kesshite 決して + [NEGATIVE]; ***has ~ (done)*** (shi)-ta kotó ga arimasén (し)た事がありません; ***~ (does)*** (su)-ru kotó wa arimasén (す)る事はありません; ***~ mind*** kamaimasén 構いません
nevertheless *adv* sore náno ni それなのに, tó-ni-kaku とにかく
new *adj* atarashíi 新しい; shín(-) … 新…; shínki (no) 新規(の), nyū ニュー; new address *n* ① (*home*) shin-jūsho 新住所 ② (*email*) atarashii adoresu 新しいアドレス; newborn baby *n* shinseiji 新生児; new version *n* atarashii bājon 新しいバージョン, shin bājon 新バージョン; new year *n* shínnen 新年; ***Happy new year.*** (Shínnen/Akemáshite) o-medetō (新年/明けまして)おめでとう.; New Year's (day) *n* ganjitsu 元日, gantan 元旦; O-shōgatsu お正月
newcomer *n* shinjin 新人
newest *adj* saishin (no) 最新(の)
newlyweds *n* shinkon fūfu 新婚夫婦
news *n* nyū´su ニュース, tsūshin 通信; (*newspaper item*) kíji 記事; (*word from*) táyori 便り, shōsoku 消息
newscaster *n* nyūsu kyasutā ニュースキャスター
newsletter *n* nyūsu retā ニュースレター, kaihō 会報
newspaper *n* shinbun 新聞; (*morning*) chōkan 朝刊, (*evening*) yūkan 夕刊; (*company*) shinbún-sha 新聞社
New York *n* Nyūyōku ニューヨーク
New Zealand *n* Nyūjiirándo ニュージーランド
next *adj* (*in time/order*) tsugí (no) 次(の), (*date etc.*) yóku(-) … 翌…; (*the next one*) tsugí 次, tsugí no 次の; (*going on to the ~*) tsuzukete 続けて; ***~ to*** (*in space*), ***~ door to …*** no tonari (no) …の隣り(の); ***~ on the left/right*** hidari-/migi-dónari (no) 左/右隣り(の); ***~ after/to …*** (*in importance*) … ni tsúide (no) …に次いで(の); next day *n, adv* yoku-jitsu 翌日, tsugi no hi 次の日; next evening *n, adv* yokuban 翌晩, tsugi no hi no yo(ru) 次の日の夜; next month *n, adv* ráigetsu 来月; next time *n, adv* kóndo 今度, jikai 次回, kono-tsúgí この次; next week *n, adv* raishū 来週
nibble *v* kajirimásu かじります・齧ります

nice *adj* **1.** ii/yoi いい/良い → **good** **2.** oishii おいしい → **delicious** **3.** kirei (na) きれい(な), utsukushii 美しい, hare (no) 晴れ(の) → **fair** **4.** shinsetsu (na) 親切(な), yasashii やさしい → **kind** **5.** → **delicate**; **nice weather** *n* íi ténki (いい) 天気

nick *v* kizamimásu 刻みます

nickname *n* adana あだ名, aishō 愛称, nikkunēmu ニックネーム

niece *n* méi めい・姪; ***your ~*** mei-go-san めいごさん・姪子さん

night *n* yóru 夜, yó 夜; ban 晩; ***(at) ~*** yakan 夜間, ***late at ~*** yóru osoku 夜遅く, shín'ya 深夜; **night(s) of lodging** …-haku …泊; **night bus** *n* yakō basu 夜行バス; **nightclothes** *n* pajama パジャマ; **nightclub** *n* (*cabaret*) kyábariē キャバレー; naito kurabu ナイトクラブ; **night duty** *n* shukuchoku 宿直; **night shift** *n* yakin 夜勤

nil *n* zero ゼロ

nimble *adj* kíyō (na) 器用(な)

nine *n* kyū 九・9, kú 九・9, kokónotsu 九つ; náin ナイン

ninety *n* kyū´-jū 九十・90, ku-jū´ 九十; ***~ thousand*** kyū-mán 九万・90,000

ninjitsu, ninjutsu *n* nínjutsu 忍術

ninth *adj* kyū-banme (no) 九番目(の)・9番目(の)ku-banmé (no) 九番目(の), kokonotsumé (no) 九つ目(の); ***the ~ day*** koko-noka-mé九日目・9日目, (*of the month*) kokonoka 九日・9日

no *adv* iie いいえ (*or just say the negative verb*); **no charge/fee** *n, adj* múryō (no) 無料(の), tada (no) ただ(の); **no doubt** *adv* (*surely*) kitto きっと; **no good** *adj* tsumaránai つまらない; damé (na) だめ[駄目](な); furyō (na) 不良(な); (*futile*) muda (na) 無駄(な); (*worthless*) yákuza (na) やくざ(な); **no later than** *adj* … máde ni wa …までには; **no need to worry** *interj, adj* daijō´bu (na) 大丈夫(な); shinpai nai/(go-) muyō 心配ない/(ご)無用; **No smoking** kin'en 禁煙; **No, thank you.** *interj* Kékkō desu. 結構です.; **no use** *adj* damé (na) だめ[駄目](な)

noble *adj* kidakai 気高い, kōketsu (na) 高潔(な), sūkō (na) 崇高(な)

nobody *pron* dare mo 誰も + [NEGATIVE]

nod *v* unazukimásu うなずきます・頷きます

Noh *n* (*Japanese classical theater*) nō 能, o-nō お能; ***traditional Noh farce*** kyōgén 狂言

noise *n* otó 音

noisy *adj* yakamashíi やかましい, sōzōshíi 騒々しい, urusai うるさい

nomad *n* yūboku-min 遊牧民

nominal *adj* meimoku-jō (no) 名目上(の)

nominate *v* shimei shimásu 指名します; mei-jimásu 命じます; suisen shimásu 推薦します; nominēto

shimásu ノミネートします
noncommittal *adj* (*beats around the bush*) hanashí o bokashimásu 話をぼかします
none *pron* (*nothing*) nani mo 何も + [NEGATIVE]; (*not even one*) hitotsu mo 一つも + [NEGATIVE], (*person*) hitori mo 一人も + [NEGATIVE]
nonetheless *adv* sore náno ni それなのに
nonsense *n* baka na kotó ばかなこと; baka-bánashi ばか話; detarame でたらめ; tawagoto たわごと・戯言; nansensu ナンセンス
nonsmoker *n* non-sumōkā ノンスモーカー; tabako o suwanai hito たばこ[タバコ・煙草]を吸わない人; hi-kitsuen-sha 非喫煙者
no(n)-smoking *n* kin'én seki 禁煙席
nonspecialist *n* mongái-kan 門外漢
nonstop *adj* (*flight*) mu-chákuriku (no) 無着陸(の)
noodles *n* mén(-rui) めん[麺](類); (o-)sóba (お)そば・蕎麦; (*Japanese wheat-flour*) udon うどん, (*thin*) sōmen そうめん (*chilled*) hiya-múgi 冷や麦・ヒヤムギ; (*Chinese*) rā´men ラーメン; **noodle shop** *n* (o-)sobá-ya (お)そば[蕎麦]屋; udon-ya うどん屋
noon *n* hirú 昼(o-híru お昼); (*exactly noon*) shō´go 正午
nope *adv* (*no*) iya いや
no place → **nowhere**
norm *n* (*standard*) kikaku 規格, hyōjun 標準
normal *adj* hyōjun (no) 標準(の), futsū (no) 普通(の), nōmaru (no) ノーマル(の) → **usual**
north *n* kita 北, hoku-... 北...; (*the* ~) hoppō 北方, (*the northern part*) hókubu 北部; ***~ and south*** nánboku 南北
North America *n* Kita-Ámerika 北アメリカ, Hoku-Bei 北米
North Pole *n* Hokkyoku 北極
North Sea *n* Hokkai 北海
Norway *n* Noruwei ノルウェイ
nose *n* hana 鼻(o-hana お鼻)
not *adv* ***does*** ~ [VERB]-masén ません; ***is*** ~ [ADJECTIVE]-ku arimasén くありません; [NOUN] ja arimasén じゃありません; **not as/so much as ...** *adj*...hodo... ほど・程 + [NEGATIVE]; **not at all** *adv* ① sappári さっぱり; kesshite 決して + [NEGATIVE] ② (*you're welcome*) dō´ itashimashite どういたしまして; **not working properly** *adj* guai ga warúi 具合が悪い; **not yet** *adv* máda まだ + [NEGATIVE]
notch **1.** *v* (*makes a notch*) kizamimásu 刻みます, kizami-me/kirikomi o iremásu 刻み目/切り込みを入れます **2.** *n* kizami-me 刻み目
note *n* (*memorandum*) mémo メモ; chū´ 注; (*reminder*) chū´i 注意; (*promissory note*) tegata 手形
notebook *n* nō´to ノート, nōtobúkku ノートブック

ıothing *pron* nani mo 何も + [NEGATIVE]; ~ ***(at all)*** nan to mo 何とも + [NEGATIVE]; there is nothing like (*better than*) … ni kagirimásu …に限ります

ıotice **1.** *v* … ni ki ga tsukimásu …に気が付きます, kizukimásu 気付きます **2.** *n* (*notification*) shirase 知らせ, todoké 届け, tsūchi 通知; (*reminder*) chū´i 注意; with short notice *adv* kyū na (o-) shirase (de) 急な(お)知らせ(で); totsuzen no shirase (de) 突然の知らせ(で); without notice *adv* mudan de 無断で; kotowárí mo náku 断りもなく

otify *v* shirasemásu 知らせます, (*notifies formally or officially*) tsūchi shimásu 通知します; todokemásu 届けます

otion *n* kangae 考え, iken 意見 → **idea** → **concept**

oun *n* meishi 名詞

ourish *v* yashinaimásu 養います

ourishment *n* eiyō 栄養

ovel **1.** *n* (*fiction*) shōsetsu 小説 **2.** (*curious*) *adj* mezurashíi 珍しい

ovember *n* Jūichi-gatsú 十一月・11月

ow *adv* íma 今, (*already*) mō´ もう; from now on kore kara これから, kongo 今後; just now tadáima ただ今, tsúi imashígata つい今しがた; until now ima-máde 今まで; well now (sore) ja (それ)じゃ, jā´ じゃあ, déwa では, sá-te さて; now and then tama ni たまに

nowhere *adv* doko (de/ni/e) mo どこ(で/に/へ)も + [NEGATIVE]

nuclear *adj* káku (no) 核(の)

nude **1.** *adj* hadaka (no) 裸(の), nūdo (no) ヌード(の); ratai (no) 裸体(の) **2.** *n* nū´do ヌード; (*picture*) ratai-ga 裸体画 → **naked**

nuisance *n* mendō 面倒・めんどう

numb *adj* mu-kánkaku (na) 無感覚(な); ***goes/gets*** ~ shibiremásu しびれます

number *n* kázu 数, sū´ 数, nanbā ナンバー; bán 番, …-ban …番; (*written numeral*) sūji 数字; (*assigned*) bangō´番号; (*large and/or small*) tashō 多少; a number of … íkutsu ka no … いくつかの…, nan-[COUNTER] ka no … 何 [COUNTER] かの…, sū-[COUNTER] no … 数 [COUNTER] の…; in large numbers ōzéi 大勢, dóndon どんどん, zorozoro ぞろぞろ; the number of days nissū´ 日数, hinichi 日にち; the number of people nínzū 人数; the number of times kaisū 回数

number one *adj* ichí-ban (no) 一番(の)

numbness *n* shibiré しびれ

numeral *n* sūji 数字, sū´ 数

numerous → **many**

nun *n* áma 尼

nurse **1.** *n* kangó-fu 看護婦, nāsu ナース **2.** *v* (*~s a patient*) kángo shimásu 看護します

nursery *n* takuji-jo 託児所

nursery school *n* (*pre-kindergarten*) hoikú-en 保育園
nursing (*a patient*) *n* kángo 看護, kanbyō 看病
nutrition *n* eiyō 栄養
nuts *n* náttsu ナッツ, kurumi くるみ・クルミ・胡桃; kí-no-mi 木の実・キノミ (*includes fruits and berries*), mi 実・ミ
nylon *n* náiron ナイロン

O

oak *n* ōku オーク
oar *n* kai 櫂・かい, ōru オール
oasis *n* oashisu オアシス
oat *n* ōto mugi オートムギ, karasu mugi カラスムギ
oath *n* chikai (no kotoba) 誓い(の言葉)
obedient *adj* súnao (na) すなお[素直](な)
obeisance *n* (*salute*) keirei 敬礼
obesity *n* himan 肥満
obey (*a person*) *v* (… ga) yū/iu kotó o kikimásu (…が)言う事を聞きます・いうことをききます
obituary *n* shibō kiji 死亡記事
object **1.** *n* taishō 対象; (*thing*) monó 物; buttai 物体; obujekuto オブジェクト; (*objective, goal*) mokuteki 目的, ate 当て; (*aim*) nerai 狙い **2.** *v* *~s to* (*opposes*) … ni hantai shimásu …に反対します
objective *n* mokuhyō 目標
obligation *n* (*duty*) gímu 義務, (*responsibility*) sekinin 責任; (*sense of ~*) (o-)giri (お)義理; (*for a kindness*) (go-)ón (ご)恩
obliged *adj* **1.** ***becomes ~*** (*to … for help*) (…no) sewá ni narimásu (…の)世話になります **2.** ***feels ~*** (*grateful*) kyōshuku shimásu 恐縮します
oblong *n* **1.** (*box*) chōhō-kei 長方形 **2.** (*oval*) chōdaen-kei 長だ円形・長楕円形
obscene *adj* waisetsu (na) わいせつ(な)
obscure *adj* (*unknown*) fumei (no) 不明(の); (*unrenowned*) mumei (no) 無名(の) → **dark**
observatory *n* (*astronomical*) tenmon-dai 天文台; (*weather station*) sokkō-jo 測候所, kishō-dai 気象台; (*sightseeing*) tenbō-dai 展望台
observe *v* **1.** (*happens to see*) kizukimásu 気付きます・気づきます **2.** (*watches*) kansatsu/kansoku shimásu 観察/観測します; **observe a rule** *v* okite o mamorimásu 掟を守ります
observer *n* kansatsu-sha 観察者; tachiai-nin 立会人
obstacle *n* sashitsukae 差し支え・さしつかえ; (o-)jama (お)じゃま[邪魔]; shōgai 障害

obstruct *v* (*hinders*) samatagemásu 妨げます・さまたげます; ***gets obstructed*** (*clogged*) tsukaemásu つかえます

obtain *v* té ni iremásu 手に入れます → **get**

obvious *adj* meihaku (na) 明白(な), akiraka (na) 明らか・あきらか(な)

occasion *n* (*time*) tokí 時・とき, (*at that time*) koro 頃・ころ; (*event*) sétsu 節, sái 際, orí 折・おり, jísetsu 時節; (*opportunity*) kikái 機会; tsuide ついで; (*circumstance*) ba(w)ai 場合; ***on the ~ of*** … ni sái-shite … に際して

occasional *adj* (*infrequent*) tama no たまの; tokidoki no 時々・ときどきの

occupant *n* kyojū-sha 居住者

occupation *n* (*job*) shokúgyō 職業, shoku 職; (*military*) senryō 占領

occupied *adj* **1.** ***is ~*** (*toilet, etc.*) shiyōchū 使用中 **2.** (*a seat*) (*They're coming!*) Kimásu 来ます **3.** → **busy 4.** ***gets ~*** (*booked up*) fusagarimásu ふさがります

occur *v* okorimásu 起ります, hassei shimásu 発生します; shōjimásu 生じます; genjitsu-ka shimásu 現実化します

occurrence *n* hassei 発生

ocean *n* taiyō 大洋, taikai/daikai 大海

o'clock *adv* …-ji …時 (4 ~ yó-ji 四時)

October *n* Ju-gatsú 十月・10月

octopus *n* táko たこ・タコ・蛸

odd *adj* (*peculiar, strange*) hén (na) 変(な); kawatta 変わった; kawatteiru 変わっている; okashina おかしな

odor → **smell**

of ... *prep* … no …の

of course mochíron もちろん・勿論, muron むろん・無論, mót-tómo もっとも

off; ***time ~*** yasumí 休み; ***day ~*** ofu (no hi) オフ(の日), hiban (no hi) 非番(の日); **~** (*down in price by*) ***¥100*** hyakeún-yasu 百円安

off *adv* ***(turns) ~*** (*light, radio, etc.*) …o keshimásu …を消します; (*button, etc.*) ***comes ~*** toremásu 取れます, (*slips off*) nukemásu 抜けます; ***gets ~*** (*a vehicle*) orimásu 降ります; ***takes ~*** (*clothes, shoes*) nugimásu 脱ぎます; ***does/is ~ and on*** … -tári/-káttari/dáttari shimásu …たり/かったり/だったりします; ***gets ~ the track*** dassen shimásu 脱線します; **off duty** (*taxi*) kaisō(-chū) 回送(中); ***~ taxi*** kaisō´-sha 回送車; **Off Limits** "tachiiri kinshi" "立入り禁止"; **offline** *n* ofu rain オフライン; **off the record** *n* ofureko オフレコ

offend *v* **1.** (*violates*) … ni ihan shimásu …に違反します **2.** fu-yúkai ni shimásu 不愉快にします **3.** → **anger**

offense *n* burei 無礼; ihan 違反

offer **1.** *n* mōshi-komi 申し込み, ofā オファー; (*makes an ~*) mōshidemásu 申し出ます **2.** *v* (*proposes*) teian shimásu 提案します, (*recommends*) susumemásu 勧めます; **job offer** *n* saiyō 採用

offering *n* mōshi-de 申し出, mōshi-komi 申し込み; (*public*) mōshi-ire 申し入れ; o-sonae お供え

office *n* (*business*) jimú-sho 事務所; (*government*) (o-)yakusho (お)役所; (*within the company*) shánai 社内, ofisu オフィス

officer *n* (*military*) shō´kō 将校; ***police ~*** omáwari-san おまわりさん, [FORMAL] keikan 警官

official **1.** *adj* (*public*) ōyake (no) 公(の) **2.** *n* (*a government ~*) kōmu-in 公務員; yakunin 役人

offline *n* ofurain オフライン

often *adv* yóku よく, tabitabi たびたび, hinpan (ni) 頻繁(に), shíba-shiba しばしば, sésse-to せっせと

ogre *n* oní 鬼・オニ

oh *interj* wā わあ; ā´ ああ; ***oh?*** sō´desu ka そうですか, árá あら; ***oh well*** mā´ まあ (*tends to be a female expression*)

oil *n* abura 油, (*petroleum, machine oil*) sekiyu 石油; (*for lubricating cars*) óiru オイル; ***hair ~*** pomā´do ポマード

ointment *n* nuri-gúsuri 塗り薬, nankō 軟膏

O.K. *adv* íi desu いいです; (*I approve*) sansei (désu) 賛成(です); (*safe; functioning*) daijōbu (désu) 大丈夫(です); ōkē (désu) オーケー(です)

Okinawa *n* Okinawa 沖縄; Ryūkyū´ 琉球

old **1.** *adj* (*not new*) furúi 古い, (*from way back*) mukashi karáno 昔からの; kyū´(-) … 旧… **2.** *adj* (*not young*) toshi-tótta 年取った, rō-… 老…; ***gets ~*** toshí o torimásu 年を取ります, fukemásu 老けます **3.** *n* (*old person*) rōjin 老人; **old friend** *n* mukashi kará no tomodachi/yūjin 昔からの友達/友人

older *adj* toshi-ue (no) 年上(の)

older brother *n* áni 兄; (o-)níi-san (お)兄さん

older sister *n* ane 姉; (o-)né-san (お)姉さん

oldest *adj* ichiban (toshi-)ue (no) 一番(年)上(の)

old person *n* (o-)toshiyori (お)年寄り, rōjin 老人; kōrei-sha 高齢者; (*man*) ojíi-san おじいさん, (*woman*) obā´-san おばあさん

omelet *n* omuretsu オムレツ; ***~ wrapped around rice*** omu-ráisu オムライス

omen *n* engi 縁起, zenchō 前兆

omission *n* shōryaku 省略, ryaku 略

omit *v* **1.** otoshimásu 落とします, habukimásu 省きます, nokemásu のけ[除け]ます, nukimásu 抜きます, nozokimásu 除きます;

(*skips*) tobashimásu とばします・飛ばします; (*curtails*) ryakushimásu 略します **2. *gets omitted*** ochimásu 落ちます; nukemásu 抜けます; moremásu 漏れます・もれます

on *prep* **1.** … de …で, (*located*) … ni …に; (*atop*) … no ue (de/ni) …の上(で/に) **2. *has/ puts* ~** (*clothes, etc.*) → **wear 3. *turns* ~** (*light, radio, etc.*) … o tsukemásu …を付けます; on the way tochū 途中; on the whole daitai だいたい・大体

once *adv* ichi-dó 一度・いちど, ik-kái 一回; ichiō 一応・いちおう; (*sometime*) ítsu ka いつか; **~ *did*** shitakotó ga arimásu した事があります・したことがあります; **~ *in a while*** tama ni たまに

one *n* ichí 一; hitótsu 一つ・ひとつ; hito-… 一…, ichi-… 一…; wán ワン; (*person*) (o-)hitori お一人・(お)ひとり, ichí-mei 一名; **~ *of a pair, the other* ~** katáhō 片方, katáppō 片っ方, katáppo 片っぽ・かたっぽ; one after another tsugí-tsugi ni 次々に, zokuzoku 続々, áitsuide 相次いで; one and the same hitótsu 一つ・ひとつ; one by one ichi-ichi 一々

oneself *pron* jibun 自分; wáre 我; **~ *(as we might expect)*** sasuga no … さすがの…; ***talking to* ~** hítori-goto 独り言

one-way *adj* (*ticket*) katamichi(-kíppu) 片道(切符); (*traffic*) ippō-tsū´kō 一方通行

onion *n* (*green*) négi ねぎ・ネギ・葱; (*round bulb*) tama-négi 玉ねぎ[葱]・タマネギ

only *adj* táda … ただ…, tatta … たった…, … daké…だけ, … bákari …ばかり; … ni sugínai …に過ぎない

Ontario *n* Ontario オンタリオ

oops *interj* otto おっと, o' おっ, a' あっ

opaque *adj* futōmei (na) 不透明(な)

opal *n* opāru オパール

open *v* **1. *~s it*** akemásu 開けます, (*~s it up*) hirakimásu 開きます; (*begins it*) hajimemásu 始めます **2. *it ~s*** akimásu 開きます; (*it begins*) hajimarimásu 始まります, (*a place, an event*) ō´pun shimásu オープンします, kaijō shimásu 開場します (*a shop/business*) kaiten shimásu 開店します **3. ~ *to the public*** kōkai (no) 公開(の); ***~s it to the public*** kōkai shimásu 公開します; open door *n* (*admission free*) nyūjō muryō 入場無料; open-minded *adj* ① (*broad-minded*) kokoro no hiroi 心の広い ② (*unprejudiced*) henken no nai 偏見のない; open-mouthed *adj* (*dumbfounded*) azen to shita 唖然とした

opening *n* **1.** (*inlet*) kuchi 口 **2.** (*gap*) suki(-ma) 透き/隙(間) **3.** (*of a place*) kaijō 開場, ō´pun オープン; **~ *ceremony*** kaijō/kaikaishiki 開場/開会式; ~ *time* kaijō-jíkan 開場時間 **4.** (*book*) bōtō 冒頭; job opening *n* shūshoku-guchi 就職口

open(ly) *adv* (*publicly*) kōzen (no/to) 公然(の/と); (*candid*) ō´pun (na/ni) オープン(な/に), sotchoku (na/ni) 率直(な/に)

opera *n* kágeki 歌劇, ópera オペラ

operate *v* (*machinery*) sōjū shimásu 操縦します; (*vehicle*) unten shimásu 運転します; (*machinery*) ugokashimásu 動かします; (*business*) keiei shimásu 経営します(する, して)

operation *n* (*surgical*) shújutsu 手術; (*driving*) unten 運転; (*handling*) sōjū 操縦; (*management*) keiei 経営; (*working*) sagyō 作業, shigoto 仕事

operator *n* **1.** (*telephone*) (denwa) kōkánshu (電話)交換手; operētā オペレーター **2.** (*vehicle*) unténshu 運転手 **3.** (*business*) keiéi-sha 経営者

opinion *n* (go-)íken (ご)意見, kangáe 考え; hyō´ka 評価; (*outlook*) mikomi 見込み, (*observation*) kansoku 観測; ***public*** ~ yóron 世論

opium *n* ahen アヘン・阿片

opponent *n* (*sports*) (o-)aite (お)相手; taikō-sha 対抗者; (*rival*) teki 敵

opportunity *n* kikái 機会; chansu チャンス; (*opening*) suki(-ma) 透き/隙(間); (*opportune time*) jíki 時機, jísetsu 時節

oppose *v* … ni hantai shimásu …に反対します, … o kobamimásu …を拒みます; (*resists*) … ni hankō shimásu …に反抗します; … to tairitsu shimásu …と対立します, …ni taikō shimásu …に対抗します; (*faces*) … ni mukaimásu …に向かいます

opposite *adj* (*facing*) mukō (no) 向こう(の), (o-)múkai (no) (お)向かい(の); (*contrary*) gyaku (no) 逆(の), (*opposing*) hantai (no) 反対(の)

opposition *n* (*resistance*) hankō 反抗; (*confrontation*) taikō 対抗; ***in ~ to*** … ni taikō shite …に対抗して; ~ ***party*** yatō 野党

oppression *n* appaku 圧迫

optimistic *adj* rakkan-teki (na) 楽観的(な)

optional *adj* zuii (no) 随意(の), nin'i (no) 任意(の)

or *conj* … ka …か; mátá-wa または・又は; or else sore-tómo それとも, mátá-wa または・又は, arúiwa あるいは・或いは; or something (*like it*) … tó ka … とか

oral *adj* **1.** kuchi no 口の, kuchi kará no 口からの; keikō(-) 経口; ~ ***contraceptive*** keikōhinín'yaku 経口避妊薬 **2.** (*verbal*) kōtō (no) 口頭(の); ~ ***examination*** kōtō-shímon 口頭試問

orange *n* **1.** orénji オレンジ; (*Mandrain orange, tangerine*) míkan みかん・ミカン・蜜柑; (*bitter*) daidái だいだい・ダイダイ・橙 2. (*color*) 橙黄色・とうこうしょく

orbit *n* kidō 軌道

orchestra *n* ōkesutora オーケストラ

orchid *n* rán 蘭・ラン

order 1. *n* júnjo 順序, jun 順; ***alphabetical*** ~ ē-bii-shii (ABC)-jun エービーシー[ABC]順; (*turn*) junban 順番 2. *n* (*grade, step*) dán 段, dankai 段階 3. *n* (*procedure*) tejun 手順 4. *n* (*rule*) kimari 決まり; chitsujo 秩序 5. *n* (*command*) meirei 命令 6. *v* (*clothes, meal, etc.*) chūmon shimásu 注文します 7. *v* (*a person to do something*) … ni ii-tsukemásu …に言い付けます・言いつけます, meijimásu 命じます; puts in order (*tidies up*) katazukemásu 片付けます; (*arranges as a set*) soroemásu 揃えます・そろえます

ordinary *adj* futsū (no) 普通・ふつう(の), tsūjō (no) 通常(の), tsúne (no) 常(の), fúdan (no) 普段・ふだん(の); táda (no) ただ(の); (*average*) nami (no) 並(の)

organic *adj* ōganikku (no) オーガニック(の), yūki (no) 有機(の)

organization *n* (*setup*) soshiki 組織; (*structure*) kumi-tate 組み立て・くみたて, kōzō 構造; (*group*) dantai 団体

organize *v* (*forms*) kumi-tatemásu 組み立てます・くみたてます; hensei shimásu 編成します

Oriental *adj* Tō´yō (no) 東洋(の)

origin *n* kígen 起源, (*cause*) gen'in 原因, moto 元, okorí 起こり, hassei 発生

originally *adv* móto wa 元は・もとは, motomoto 元々・もともと, hónrai wa 本来は, gánrai wa 元来は; (*in itself*) jitai 自体

ornament *n* kazari(-mono) 飾り(物), sōshoku-hin 装飾品, (*decoration*) sōshoku 装飾

orphan *n* kóji 孤児; orphanage *n* kojí-in 孤児院

Osaka *n* Ōsaka 大阪

other *adj* hoka (no) 他(の), betsu (no) 別(の); [BOOKISH] tá (no) 他(の); ~ ***companies*** tásha 他社; in other words *conj* sunáwachi すなわち・即ち; the other day *adv* kon[o]aidá こないだ[この間]; the other fellow *n* aité (o-)aite (お)相手; the other side *n* senpō 先方; on the other hand tahō de wa 他方では; other than … yóri …より

otherwise *adv* sá-mo nákereba さもなければ, sō´shinai to そうしないと, [INFORMAL] sō´ja nái to そうじゃないと

ouch! *interj* itái! 痛い・いたい!, itáí! 痛(っ)・いた(っ)!

ought to *auxiliary verb* ~ ***(do)*** (shi)-ta hō´ga íi deshō (し)た方がいいでしょう, [BOOKISH] (su)-ru béki desu (す)るべきです

our(s) *pron* watakushí-tachi no (watáshí-táchi no) わたくし[私]達の(わたし[私]達の)

out *adv* sóto e/ni 外へ/に; (*away*

from home) (o-)rúsu (desu) (お)留守(です), gaishutsu-chū (désu) 外出中(です); ***come/go ~*** (... kara) demásu (...から)出ます; ***let ~*** (*of a vehicle*) oroshimásu 降ろします; **out loud** *adv* kóe o dáshite 声を出して; **out of order;** ***gets ~*** kuruimásu 狂います; (*broken machine*) koshō shiteimásu 故障しています; **out of service** *n, adj* kaisō(-chū) 回送(中); ***a car ~*** kaisō-sha 回送車; **out of the way;** ***gets ~*** dokimásu どきます・退く, nokimásu のきます・退きます; **out of touch with ...** *adj* ni utói ...に疎い・うとい

outage *n* (*power ~*) teiden 停電・ていてん

outbound *adj* (*from Tokyo*) kudari 下り

outbox *n* (*e-mail*) sōshin bokkusu 送信ボックス

outbreak *n* toppatsu 突発; hassei 発生

outbuilding *n* hanare 離れ

outburst *n* bakuhatsu 爆発

outcome *n* (*of situation*) ketsumatsu 結末; (*result*) séika 成果; (*product*) sanbutsu 産物; (*medical diagnosis*) tenki 転帰

outdoor(s) *adj* (*adv*) sóto no (/de/ni/e) 外の(/で/に/へ); yagai no (/de) 野外の(/で); autodoa (no) アウトドア(の); okugai no (/de/ni/e) 屋外の(/で/に/へ); ***~ bath*** noten-búro 野天風呂

outer *adj* ***~ appearance*** uwabe うわべ・上辺; ***~ lane/track*** auto-kō´su アウトコース; ***~ space*** úchū 宇宙

outfit *n* ***judo ~*** jūdō´-gi 柔道着; ***karate ~*** karaté-gí 空手着

outflow *n* de 出; ryūshutsu 流出

outing *n* (*picnic etc.*) ensoku 遠足・えんそく

outlet *n* **1.** déguchi 出口; (*for water/emotion/goods*) haké-kuchi/-guchi はけ口; (*sales ~*) ure-kuchi 売れ口; (*store*) chokubái-ten 直売店 **2.** (*electric ~*) kónsénto コンセント; (*plug*) sashi-komi 差し込み・さしこみ, puragu プラグ

outline *n* **1.** (*synopsis*) gaiyō 概要, auto rain アウトライン **2.** (*line*) rinkaku 輪郭

outlook *n* mikomi 見込み・見こみ, mitōshi 見通し

output *n* auto putto アウトプット, seisan 生産, sanshutsu 産出

outrageous *adj* tonde-mo nái とんでもない, tonda とんだ

outset *n* (*beginning*) hána はな・端, saisho 最初, shoppana 初っ端・しょっぱな

outside **1.** *adv* sóto (de/ni) 外(で/に) **2.** *adj* soto-gawa 外側(の), sóto (no) 外(の) **3.** *n* ***the ~*** soto-gawa 外側, hata はた・端, gáibu 外部, gaimen 外面

outskirts *n* (*suburb*) shígai 市外, kōgai 郊外, (tóshi no) shūhen (都市の)周辺

outsourcing *n* autosōshingu アウトソーシング, gyōmu itaku 業務委託, gaichū 外注, gaibu hatchū

外部発注

outspread *adj* hirogatta 広がった

outstanding *adj* medátta 目立った・めだった, kencho (na) 顕著(な), medátte imásu̲ 目立っています・めだっています

outward **1.** *adj* soto (no) 外の, (*ostensible*) mikake jō (no) 見かけ・みかけ上(の), hyōmen jō (no) 表面上(の) **2.** *adv* soto e 外へ

outwitted; *gets* ~ (*tricked*) gomakasaremásu̲ ごまかされます・誤魔化されます

oval **1.** *n* daen(-kei) 楕円(形)・だ円(形) **2.** *adj* daen-kei (no) 楕円[だ円]形(の)

ovation *n* daikassai 大喝采; ***standing* ~** sutandingu obēshon スタンディング・オベーション

ovary *n* ransō 卵巣, (*plant*) shibō 子房

oven *n* ōbun オーブン, témpi 天火, kama かま・窯, kamado かまど・竈

over **1.** *prep* (*above*) … no ue (de/ni) …の上(で/に), … o ōimásu …を覆います; (*more than*) … ijō 以上; ... yori ōku ...より多く; … o sugimásu …を過ぎます; … o koemásu …を超えます **2.** *adj* (*above*)… no ue (no) …の上(の) **3.** *adv* (*above*) ue (ni) 上(に); (*covered*) ichimen (ni) 一面(に); (*finished*) owarimashita 終わりました; (*run over*) kurikae-shimásu 繰り返します; **over there** mukō 向こう, mukai 向かい, sochira/sotchi そちら/そっち, achira/atchi あちら/あっち; (*other side*) mukō gawa ni 向こう側に

overall *adj, adv* (*composite*) sōgō-teki (na/ni) 総合的(な/に), zentai-teki (na/ni) 全体的(な/に)

overcharge *v* **~ (*for*)** fu̲kkakemásu̲ ふっかけます; ***gets ~ed for*** fu̲kka-kelaremásu̲ ふっかけられます

overcoat *n* ō´bā オーバー, kōto コート, gaitō 外套,

overcome *v* uchikachimásu̲ 打ち勝ちます, kokufukushimásu̲ 克服します

overdo *v* **~ (*it*)** múri o shimásu̲ 無理をします, (sore o) múri ni yari-másu̲ (それを)無理にやります

overestimate **1.** *n* kadai hyōka 過大評価 **2.** *v* kadai hyōka shimásu̲ 過大評価します

overemphasize *v* kyōchōshisugi-másu̲ 強調し過ぎます・強調しすぎます

overexposure *n* roshutsu kado 露出過度

overflow *v* afuremásu̲ あふれ[溢れ]ます; hanran shimásu 氾濫します

overheat **1.** *n* kanetsu 過熱, (*engine, etc.*) ōbā hiito オーバーヒート **2.** *v* kanetsu shimásu̲ 過熱します, (*engine, etc.*) ōbā hiito shimásu̲ オーバーヒートします

overlap *v* kasanarimásu 重なります, [INFORMAL] daburimásu̲ だぶります

overly *adv* amari ni mo あまりにも; … -sugimásu …過ぎます; ~ ***strict*** yakamashíi やかましい
over-optimism *n* chō rakkan shugi 超楽観主義, chō rakuten-teki/ka 超楽天的/家
overprice *v* takane o tsukesugimásu 高値を付け過ぎます・つけすぎます
overprint *v* **1.** surikasanemásu 刷り重ねます **2.** surisugimásu 刷り過ぎます
overseas *adj* káigai 海外; ~ ***travel*** kaigai-ryokō 海外旅行
oversee *v* kantoku shimásu 監督します
overshoot *v* ikisugimásu 行き過ぎます
overtake *v* … ni oi-tsukimásu …に追い付きます
overthrow *v* taoshimásu 倒します, hikkuri kaeshimásu ひっくり返します
overtime; ***runs*** ~ jikan ga ō´bā shimásu 時間がオーバーします; ~ ***work*** zangyō 残業
overwork *v* múri o shimásu 無理をします
owe *v* (*borrow money*) (hito ni kane o) karite imásu (人に金を)借りています
owing *adj* ~ ***to*** … (no) séi de… (の)せいで → **because**
owl *n* fukúrō´ ふくろう・フクロウ・梟
own **1.** *v* (*possesses*) mótte imásu 持っています **2.** *adj* (*one's own*) jibun no 自分の, shoyū no 所有の
owner *n* (mochí-)nushi (持ち)主, shoyūsha 所有者; (*master*) shújin 主人, ōnā オーナー; (*landowner*) ji-nushi 地主
ox *n* (*cattle*) ushi 牛・ウシ, (*male*) o-ushi 雄牛
oxygen *n* sánso 酸素
oyster *n* káki かき・カキ・牡蠣, oisutā オイスター
ozone layer *n* ozon sō オゾン層

P

pace *n* pēsu ペース, hochō 歩調; **walking pace** *n* aruku hayasa 歩く速さ, aruku sokudo 歩く速度
Pacific Ocean *n* Taihéiyō 太平洋
pacify *v* shizumemásu 静[鎮]めます; (*soothes*) nadamemásu なだめます・宥めます; (*suppresses an uprising*) osamemásu 収めます
pack **1.** *n* (*of cards*) (toránpu) hitó-kumi (トランプ)一組; (*of cigarettes*) (tabako) hitó-hako (たばこ)一箱 **2.** *v* (*one's bags*) ni-zúkuri o shimásu 荷造りをします **3.** *v* (*wraps it up*) tsutsumimásu 包みます, hōsō shimásu 包装します

package *n* kozútsumi 小包, nimotsu 荷物, pakkēji パッケージ
packed *adj* **1.** (*full*) tsumatte(i)ru 詰まって(い)る, tsumatta 詰まった **2.** (*crowded*) konde(i)ru 混んで(い)る, konda 混んだ; **packed train** *n* man'in densha 満員電車
packet *n* (kogata) hōsō´-butsu (小型)包装物, kozútsumi 小包
pact *n* kyōtei 協定, jōyaku 条約
pad *n* (*note pad*) memo-chō メモ帳; **shoulder pad** *n* kata-ate 肩当て, kata paddo 肩パッド
paddle *n* kai 櫂
paddy *n* suiden 水田
page *n* pēji ページ・頁
pail *n* te-oke 手桶
pain **1.** *n* itamí 痛み; (*suffering*) kurushimi 苦しみ, (*trouble, bother*) mendō 面倒; ***takes (great) ~s*** honé o orimás<u>u</u> 骨を折ります **2.** *v* (*distresses*) kurushimemás<u>u</u> 苦しめます
painful *adj* itái 痛い; kurushíi 苦しい, tsurai 辛い
paint **1.** *n* penki ペンキ, enogu 絵の具, tosō 塗装 **2.** *v* (penki o) nurimás<u>u</u> (ペンキを)塗ります; (*picture*) e o kakimás<u>u</u> 絵を描きます
pair *n* (it-) tsui (一)対; pea ペア; (*of footwear*) is-sokú 一足
pajamas *n* pajama パジャマ; nemaki 寝巻き
Pakistan *n* Pakisutan パキスタン
pal *n* (o-)nakama (お)仲間; **pen pal** *n* pen paru ペンパル, pen furendo ペンフレンド, buntsū nakama 文通仲間, buntsū tomodachi 文通友達
palace *n* (*in Tokyo*) kō´kyo 皇居; (*in Kyoto*) gósho 御所; (*in general*) kyūden 宮殿, paresu パレス
pale *adj* **1.** (*color*) (iro ga) usui (色が)薄い; usui […iro] (no) 薄い[…色](の) **2.** (*face*) (kao ga) aói (顔が)青い, (kao ga) aojiroi (顔が)青白い
Palestine *n* Paresuchina パレスチナ
palm *n* (*tree*) yáshi ヤシ・椰子; (*~ of hand*) té-nó-hira 手のひら・掌
pamper *v* amayakashimás<u>u</u> 甘やかします
pamphlet *n* pánfurétto パンフレット; (*leaflet, handbill*) bira びら・ビラ, chirashi ちらし・チラシ
pan *n* (o-)nabe (お)鍋; ***food cooked and served in a ~*** nabémono 鍋物; nabe-ryōri 鍋料理
pancake *n* pankēki パンケーキ, hottokēki ホットケーキ; ***~ mix*** hottokēki no moto ホットケーキの素
pancreas *n* suizō 膵臓・すい臓
panda *n* panda パンダ
panel *n* paneru パネル; **panel discussion** *n* paneru disukasshon パネルディスカッション; **panel house** *n* baishun yado 売春宿
panic *n* pánikku パニック, [BOOKISH] kyōkō 恐慌
pant *v* (*for breath*) aegimás<u>u</u> あえぎ[喘ぎ]ます
panther *n* hyō 豹・ヒョウ, pyūma

ピューマ

panties *n* pántii パンティー, pántsu パンツ

pantry *n* (*dish cupboard*) shokki(tó)dana 食器(戸)棚; (*room*) shokuryō´-ko 食料庫

pants *n* zubón ズボン, (*slacks*) surákkusu スラックス; (*underpants*) zubon-shita ズボン下; (*women's*) pántaron パンタロン

papa *n* papa パパ, o-tōsan おとうさん・お父さん, o-tōchan おとうちゃん・お父ちゃん

papaya *n* papaiya パパイヤ

paper *n* **1.** kamí 紙; yōshi 用紙, (*squared*) genkōyō´shi 原稿用紙; (*tissues*) chiri-gami ちり紙, tisshu ティッシュ; (*Japanese*) wáshi 和紙; ***colored ~*** irógami 色紙 **2.** (*newspaper*) shinbun 新聞, **3.** (*research report*) happyō 発表 **4.** → **document**; paper bag *n* kamibúkuro 紙袋; paperclip *n* kamibásami 紙挟み, kuríppu クリップ; paperfolding (art) *n* orígami 折り紙・おりがみ; paperweight *n* bunchin 文鎮・ブンチン

Papua New Guinea *n* Papua nyūginia パプアニューギニア

parachute *n* parashūto パラシュート

parade *n* parēdo パレード, gyōretsu 行列, (*march*) kōshin 行進; demo kōshin デモ行進; parade ground *n* eppei-jō 閲兵場

paradise *n* téngoku 天国, gokuraku 極楽, paradaisu パラダイス

paraffin *n* parafin パラフィン

paraglider *n* paraguraidā パラグライダー

paragraph *n* danraku 段落, setsu 節, paragurafu パラグラフ

Paraguay *n* Paraguai パラグアイ

parakeet *n* inko インコ

parallel *n* heikō 並行; parallel lines *n* heikō sen 並行線

paralysis *n* (*medical*) máhi 麻痺

paralytic *n* mahi kanja 麻痺患者

parameter *n* paramēta パラメータ, paramētā パラメーター; hensū 変数

paramount *adj* saikō (no) 最高(の); shijō (no) 至上(の)

paraphrase *n* parafurēzu パラフレーズ

parasite *n* parasaito パラサイト, isōrō 居候, (*worm*) kiseichū 寄生虫

parasol *n* hi-gása 日傘; (*beach umbrella*) parasoru パラソル

parcel *n* kozútsumi 小包, nimotsu 荷物

pardon *v* yurushimásu 許します; Pardon? (*say once more*) [POLITE] Mō ichido osshatte kudasai. もう一度おっしゃって下さい.; (*male*) Nandatte! 何だって!; (*female*) Nandesutte! 何ですって!; Shitsúrei desu ga. 失礼ですが. → **Sorry?, Excuse me.**; Pardon me! Shitsúrei shimásu 失礼します; Sumimasén すみません; Gomennasai. ごめんなさい.

pare *v* (*peels it*) mukimásu むきます・剥きます

parent *n* oyá 親, kata oya 片親, ***your ~*** oyagosan 親御さん; ***one's ~s*** oyátachi 親達, (*father and mother*) ryō´shin 両親, ***your ~s*** go-ryō´shin ご両親; parent and child *n* óyako 親子

parenting *n* ikuji 育児; kosodate 子育て

Paris *n* Pári パリ

parish *n* kyō(-kai) ku 教(会)区

park **1.** *n* kōen 公園; (*parking lot*) chūsha-jō 駐車場 **2.** *v* (*a car*) chūsha shimásu 駐車します

parking *n* chūsha 駐車; free parking *n* muryō chū´shajō 無料駐車場; No parking *n* chūsha kinshi 駐車禁止; paid parking *n* yūryō chūshajō 有料駐車場

parliament → **Diet**

parliamentary *adj* gikai (no) 議会(の)

parlor *n* (*drawing room*) kyakuma 客間; beauty parlor *n* biyōin 美容院, byūtii saron ビューティサロン

parrot *n* ōmu おうむ・オウム・鸚鵡

part *n* **1.** búbun 部分, ichí-bu 一部; (*portion*) bún 分, (*section*) bú 部; ***I for my ~*** watashi wa watashi de わたし[私]はわたし[私]で **2.** (*passage of a text*) … tokoró …所; ***this ~*** koko ここ **3.** (*parting of hair*) wake-me 分け目 **4.** (*role*) yakuwari 役割, yakú 役 **5.** *v* (*to divide*) wakemásu 分けます; (*they separate*) wakaremásu 別れます; ***~ with …*** o hanashimásu …を離します

partial *adj* ichibu (no) 一部(の), ichibubun 一部分

participant *n* sanká-sha 参加者

participate *v* sanka shimásu 参加します

particle *n* **1.** (*auxiliary word*) joshi 助詞 **2.** (*physics*) ryūshi 粒子

particular *adj* **1.** (*especial*) tokubetsu no 特別の; (*separate*) betsu no 別の; (*peculiar, unique*) tókushu na 特殊な, tokuyū no 特有の **2.** (*specific*) áru … ある…, kore to iú/yū … これと言う/ゆう… → **choosy**; in particular *adv* tóku-ni 特に, toriwake とりわけ

particularly *adv* toku ni 特に, tokubetsu ni 特別に, toriwake とりわけ, koto ni 殊に; ***not ~*** betsu ni 別に + [NEGATIVE]

partition *n* shikiri 仕切り, (*computer*) pātishon パーティション

partner *n* aité 相手(o-aite お相手), pātonā パートナー

parts *n* buhin 部品; bubun 部分, pātsu パーツ

part-time *adj* arubáito (no) アルバイト(の), baito (no) バイト(の); pāto taimu (no) パートタイム(の); hi-jōkin (no) 非常勤(の); part-time high school *n* teiji-sei kōkō 定時制高校; part-time job *n* arubáito (no shigoto) アルバイト(の仕事); pāto taimu (no shigoto) パートタイム(の仕事)

party *n* **1.** enkai 宴会, pā´ti パーティ, pā´tii パーティー, …-kai …会 → **reception** **2.** ***political ~***

seitō 政党; birthday party *n* tanjōbi kai 誕生日会, bāsudē pāti/pāti(i) バースデー・パーティ/パーティー; opposition party *n* yatō 野党; year-end party *n* bōnen kai 忘年会; welcome party *n* kangei kai 歓迎会

pass **1.** *n* (*commuter ticket*) teikí-ken 定期券 **2.** *n* (*mountain* ~) tōgé 峠, …-tō´ge …峠 **3.** *n* (*sexual overture*) kudoku 口説く, iiyoru 言い寄る; ***makes a ~ at …*** o kudokimásu …口説きます; nanpa shimásu ナンパします **4.** *v* (*goes past*) …o tōrimásu …を通ります; (*exceeds*) sugimásu 過ぎます; (*hands over*) watashimásu 渡します; (*hands around*) mawashimásu 回します; (*salt, sugar, etc.*) torimásu 取ります **5.** *v* (*exam*) (shikén ni) gōkaku shimásu (試験に)合格します, ukárimásu 受かります, (shikén o) pásu-shimásu (試験を)パスします **6.** *v* (*time ~es*) tachimásu 経ちます, hemásu 経ます, keika shimásu 経過します; (*~es time*) sugoshimásu 過ごします **7.** *v* (*overtakes and ~es a vehicle*) … o oi-koshimásu …を追い越します; ***No passing*** oi-koshi kinshi 追い越し禁止 **8.** *v* ~ ***it on*** tsutaemásu 伝えます; ***is passed on*** tsutawarimásu 伝わります; pass out (*loses consciousness*) íshiki o ushinaimásu 意識を失います

passage *n* tsūkō 通行; (*thoroughfare*) tōrí通り, tsū´ro 通路, (*corridor*) roka 廊下; (*of text*) … tokoró…ところ, issetsu 一節

passenger *n* jōkyaku 乗客, ryokyaku 旅客; ~ ***car*** (*automobile*) jōyōsha 乗用車, (*train*) kyakusha 客車

passion *n* jōnetsu 情熱, gekijō 激情, netchū 熱中

passive *adj* judō-teki (na) 受動的(な), shōkyoku-teki (na) 消極的(な)

passport *n* ryoken 旅券, pasupō´to パスポート

password *n* pasuwādo パスワード

past *adv* (*the* ~) káko 過去; (… ~ *the hour*) …- (fún-) sugi … (分)過ぎ

pasta *n* pasuta パスタ

paste **1.** *n* nori のり・ノリ・糊 **2.** *n* (*pate*) pēsuto ペースト, neri-mono 練り物 **3.** *v* (*~s it*) norízukeshimásu のり付けします

pastime *n* dōrákú 道楽; goraku 娯楽, shúmi 趣味

pastor *n* bokushi 牧師

pastry *n* (o-)káshi (お)菓子, kashi-pan 菓子パン, pesutorii ペストリー, pai kiji パイ生地

pat *v* (karuku) tatakimásu (軽く)叩きます・たたきます

patch **1.** *v* (*~es it*) (… ni) tsugi o atemásu (…に)継ぎを当てます, tsuzurimásu つづり[綴り]ます **2.** *n* (*a* ~) tsugi 継ぎ, patchi パッチ

path *n* komichi 小道, michi 道

patience *n* gáman 我慢, konki 根

気, [BOOKISH] nintai 忍耐, shinbō 辛抱; *loses ~* shibiré o kirashimásu しびれを切らします

patient 1. *adj* (*puts up with it*) gáman shimásu 我慢します; (*has patience*) gaman-zuyói 我慢強い, nintai-zuyói 忍耐強い 2. *n* (*medical*) kanja 患者, (*ill person*) byōnin 病人, byōki no hito 病気の人

patriot *n* aikoku-sha 愛国者

patrol *n* patorōru パトロール; junkai 巡回; **patrolman** *n* junsa 巡査

patron *n* (*customer, client*) tokuisaki 得意, suponsā スポンサー; patoron パトロン

pattern *n* patā´n/patán パターン/パタン, moyō 模様, (o-)tehon (お)手本, katá 型, gara 柄

pauper *n* seikatsuhogo-sha 生活保護者, hinmin 貧民 → **beggar**

pause 1. *n* (*rest*) yasumí 休み; pōzu ポーズ; (*break in talk etc.*) kire-mé 切れ目 2. *v* hitoiki-tsukimásu 一息つきます; tameraimásu ためらいます

pavement *n* (*roadway*) shadō 車道; (*walkway*) hodō 歩道

paw *n* ashi 足; te 手

pawn *n* 1. (*something pawned*) shichí 質 2. (*chess*) pōn ポーン

pay 1. *n* (*one's wage*) kyū´ryō 給料, chingin 賃金 2. *adj* (*not free*) yūryō (no) 有料(の) 3. *v ~s (out)* haraimásu 払います, dashimásu 出します; (*taxes*) osamemásu 納めます; *~ attention to …* ni chū´i o haraimásu …に注意を払います, … ni nén o iremásu …に念を入れます; *~ compliments* o-seiji o iimásu お世辞を言います; *~ one's share* buntan shimásu 分担します; (*profitable*) wari ni aimásu 割に合います; **pay raise** *n* bēsu-appu (béa) ベースアップ(ベア)

payment *n* shiharai 支払い, (*of taxes*) [BOOKISH] nōzei 納税

peace *n* heiwa 平和, heion 平穏, heian 平安; *~ of mind* anshin 安心

peaceful *adj* (*calm*) odáyaka (na) 穏やか(な), nódoka (na) のどか(な)

peach *n* momo もも・モモ・桃

peak *n* itadaki 頂, chōjō´ 頂上; miné 峰; (*highpoint*) chō´tén 頂点

peanuts *n* píinátsu ピーナツ, píináttsu ピーナッツ, rakkasei 落花生,

pear *n* nashí なし・ナシ・梨

pearl *n* shinju 真珠, pāru パール; **pearl diver** *n* (*woman*) áma 海女

Pearl Harbor *n* Shinjú-wan 真珠湾

pebble *n* koishi 小石; jari 砂利

peck *(at) v* (… o) tsu(t)tsukimásu (…を)つ(っ)つきます

peculiar *adj* okashíi おかしい・可笑しい, okashina おかしな・可笑しな, kímyō (na) 奇妙(な), hén (na) 変(な) → **particular**

pedal *n* 1. pédaru ペダル 2. *gas pedal* *n* ákuseru アクセル

pedestrian crossing *n* ōdan hodō 横断歩道

pediatrician *n* shōniká-i 小児科医

peek *v* (… o) nozokimásu (…を)のぞき[覗き]ます

peel **1.** *n* (*rind*) kawá 皮 **2.** *v* **~s** ***it*** …no kawá o mukimásu …の皮をむきます; ***~s it off*** hagimásu はぎ[剥ぎ]ます; ***it ~s off*** hagemásu はげ[剥げ]ます

peep (*at/into*) → **peek**

peg *n* kugi くぎ・釘

pen *n* pén ペン; (*ballpoint*) bōrupen ボールペン; (*fountain*) mannén-hitsu 万年筆

penalty *n* **1.** (*fine*) bakkin 罰金 **2.** batsu 罰; penarutii ペナルティ

pence *n* pensu ペンス

pencil *n* enpitsu 鉛筆

penetrate *v* **1.** tōrimásu 通り[透り]ます, tōshimásu 通し[透し]ます **2.** (*soaks in, permeates*) shimimásu 染みます **3.** minukimásu 見抜きます

penguin *n* pengin ペンギン

peninsula *n* hantō 半島

penis *n* pénisu ペニス, dankon 男根

pension *n* **1.** nenkin 年金, taishoku-nénkin 退職年金 **2.** (*bed & breakfast*) penshon ペンション

people *n* hito 人, … hitó…人; hitó-tachi 人達・人たち; hitóbitto 人々; [COUNTED] …-nin …人, [BOOKISH] …-mei …名

pep *n* génki 元気

pepper *n* (*black*) koshō´ こしょう・コショウ・胡椒

perceive *v* **1.** kizukimasu 気付きます・気づきます **2.** …o rikai shimásu ～を理解します

percent *n* (…-) pāsénto (…)パーセント; ***ten*** **~** ichí-wari 一割, ***one*** **~** ichí-bu 一分

perfect **1.** *adj* kanzen (na) 完全(な), kanpeki (na) 完璧(な), pāfekuto (no/na) パーフェクト(の/な) **2.** *v* **~s** ***it*** kansei sasemásu 完成させます; **perfect circle, perfectly round** manmaru (no) 真ん丸・まんまる(の)

perfectly *adv* kanzen ni 完全に, kanpeki (ni) 完璧(に), pittári ぴったり, pittáshi ぴったし

perform *v* okonaimásu 行います; (*act*) enjimásu 演じます; (*music, etc.*) ensō shimásu 演奏します; ***~ an operation*** shújutsu shimásu 手術します

performance *n* **1.** (*of a task, duty*) jikkō 実行 **2.** (*daytime/evening* ~) (hirú/yóru no) bú (昼/夜の)部 **3.** (*artistic*) éngi 演技, pafōmansu パフォーマンス; (*musical instrument*) ensō 演奏 → **show**

perfume *n* kōsui 香水

perfunctory *adj* ii-kagen (na) いい加減(な)

perhaps *adv* … ká mo shiremasén …かも知れません, … ká mo wakarimasén… かも分かりません, moshi-kasuru to もしかすると, tábun … (deshō) 多分…(でしょう), [BOOKISH] osoraku … (deshō) 恐らく・おそらく …(でしょう)

peril *n* kiken 危険, [BOOKISH]

kiki, 危機
period *n* (*of time*) ki̲kan 期間, (*limit*) kígen 期限; (*era*) jidai 時代, …-jídai …時代; (*punctuation*) shūshí-fū 終止符
perish *v* horobimásu̲ 滅びます
permanent *adj* eien (no) 永遠(の); funen (no) 不変(の); kawaranai 変わらない; **permanent residence** *n* eijū 永住, honseki 本籍; **permanent visa** *n* eijū biza 永住ビザ
permission *n* kyóka 許可, ninka 認可; menkyo 免許, ráisensu ライセンス; ***without*** ~ mudan de 無断で, kotowárí mo náku 断りもなく
permissive *adj* amai 甘い
permit *n* kyoka(-shō) 許可(証), ráisensu ライセンス → **allow** → **permission** → **license**
perpendicular *adj* suichoku (no) 垂直(の)
perpetrate *v* (tsumi o) okashimásu̲ (罪を)犯します
perplexed; ***gets*** ~ komarimásu̲ 困ります; mayoimásu̲ 迷います
persecute *n* hakugai shimásu̲ 迫害します
perseverance *n* gáman 我慢
persist *v* koshitsu shimásu̲ 固執します, jizoku shimásu̲ 持続します
persimmon *n* (*fruit*) kaki 柿・カキ
person *n* hi̲to 人, … hi̲tó …人; (*honored*) …katá …方; … monó …者, …yátsu …やつ・奴; ko 個, te 手; …-jin …人, …-nin …人; …-sha …者; hi̲tóri 一人; (*being*) sonzai 存在 → **people**
personal *adj* kojin-teki (na) 個人的(な); kojin-yō (no) 個人用(の), (*for one's own use*) jibun-yō (no) 自分用(の); shiteki (na) 私的(な); **personal appearance** *n* (mi-)narí (身)なり; kíryō 器量; **personal business** *n* shiyō 私用, shiji 私事; **personal computer** *n* paso-kon パソコン, pii shii PC; **personal experience** *n* taiken 体験, kojin-teki na keiken 個人的な経験; **personal history** *n* rireki 履歴; (*resume*) rireki-sho 履歴書
personality *n* kosei 個性, pāsonaritii パーソナリティ
personnel *n* ~ ***department*** jinji-ka 人事課; ~ ***cost*** jinken-hi 人件費
person-to-person *adj* man tsū man マンツーマン, ittaiichi 一対一; **person-to-person call** *n* shimei-tsū´wa 指名通話
perspire → **sweat**
persuade *v* settoku shimásu̲ 説得します; (… ni sore o) nattoku sasemásu̲(…にそれを)納得させます
persuasion *n* settoku 説得
pertain *v* ~ ***to*** … ni kan-shimásu̲ …に関します
pessimistic *adj* hi̲kan-teki (na) 悲観的(な)
pet **1.** *n* pétto ペット **2.** *v* (*pats, strokes*) nademásu̲ なで[撫で]ます
petrol *n* gasorin ガソリン
petroleum *n* sekiyu 石油
petty *adj* sásai (na) ささい[些細]

な, sasáyaka (na) ささやか(な); *~ cash* koguchi-genkin 小口現金

pharmacy *n* yakkyoku 薬局

pheasant *n* kiji きじ・キジ・雉

phenomenon *n* genshō 現象

Philippines *n* Fírípin フィリピン

philosopher *n* tetsugákú-sha 哲学者

phone *n* denwa 電話; (*cell-phone, mobile-phone*) keitai dénwa 携帯電話 → **telephone;** phone number *n* denwa bangō 電話番号

phony *adj* nise (no) にせ・偽(の)

photo, photograph **1.** *n* shashin 写真; *~ of a wanted criminal* tehaishá-shin 手配写真 **2.** *v* (*takes a ~ of*) … no shashin o torimásu̲ …の写真を撮ります

phrase *n* mónku 文句, kú 句, furēzu フレーズ

physical *adj* karada (no) 体(の), shíntai (no) 身体(の); physical assault *n* bōkō-jiken 暴行事件

physician *n* isha 医者, o-isha(-san) お医者(さん)

physics *n* butsuri-gaku 物理学

pianist *n* (*professional*) pianisuto ピアニスト

piano *n* piano ピアノ; ***plays the ~*** piano o hi̲kimásu̲ ピアノを弾きます

pick *v* **1.** → **choose** **2.** (*plucks*) tsu-mimásu̲ 摘みます; ***~s it up*** … o hiroimásu̲ …を拾います; ***~s one up*** (*by car, etc.*) mukae ni iki-másu̲ 迎えに行きます; tsumami-másu̲ つまみます

pickle *n* tsu̲kemono 漬物・つけもの; o-shinko おしんこ・お新香; (*Chinese*) zāsai ザーサイ; pickled ginger *n* gári ガリ, amazu shō´ga 甘酢しょうが[生姜・ショウガ]

pickpocket *n* súri すり

picnic *n* ensoku 遠足, pi̲kuníkku ピクニック

picture *n* é 絵; (*photo*) shashin 写真; (*diagram, drawing*) zu 図; (*films*) eizō 映像; ***~ postcard*** e-hágaki 絵葉書; ***takes a ~*** sha-shin o torimásu̲ 写真を撮ります; utsu̲shimásu̲ 映します

pie *n* pái パイ

piece *n* (*one*) ~ (ík)-ko (一)個, (hi̲tó)-tsu (一)つ; (*a cut*) (hi̲tó-) kire (一)切; in pieces *adv* bara-bara (ni) ばらばら(に), mecha-mecha めちゃめちゃ・メチャメチャ; into pieces *adv* barabara ni narimásu ばらばらになります

pier *n* sanbashi 桟橋, hato-ba 波止場

pierce *v* tōshimásu̲ 通します

pig *n* buta 豚・ブタ

pile *n* **1.** (*stake*) kúi くい・杭 **2.** (*heap*) (hi̲tó)-yama (一)山

pile *v* **1.** ***~s them up*** kasanemásu̲ 重ねます; ***they ~ up*** kasanari-másu̲ 重なります **2.** ***~s it up*** tsu-mimásu̲ 積みます, morimásu̲ 盛ります

piles → **hemorrhoids**

pill *n* (*medicine*) (o-)ku̲súri (お)薬, (*specifically*) gan'yaku 丸薬; (*contraceptive*) keikō-hinin-yaku

経口避妊薬, piru ピル
pillar *n* hashira 柱
pillow *n* mákura まくら・枕
pilot *n* pairótto パイロット; (*plane captain*) kichō´ 機長
pimple *n* níkibi にきび, dekímónó できもの・出来物, o-déki おでき
pin *n* (*for hair*) (hea-)pín (ヘア)ピン, pin-dome ピン留め; (*for sewing*) hári 針; mushi-pin 虫ピン; **pin money** *n* kózukai 小遣い
pincers *n* yattoko やっとこ
pinch 1. *n* pínchi ピンチ, kiki 危機 2. *v* tsunerimásu つねります, tsumamimásu つまみます
pine *n* (*tree*) mátsu (no kí) 松(の木)
pink *n* (*adj*) momo-iro (no) 桃色(の), pínku (no) ピンク(の)
pinpoint *v* seikaku ni shimeshimásu 正確に示します
pioneer *n* paionia パイオニア, kaitaku-sha 開拓者, senku-sha 先駆者
pipe *n* páipu パイプ; (*tube*) tsutsu 筒, kúda 管
pipeline *n* páipu rain パイプライン; rūto ルート, yusōkanro 輸送管路
pirate *n* kaizoku 海賊; **pirate ship** *n* kaizoku-sen 海賊船
piss *n* shōbén 小便 → **urine; urinate**
pistol *n* pisutoru ピストル, kenjū 拳銃
pitch *n* (*baseball*) tōkyū 投球, (*cricket*) pitchi ピッチ
pitcher *n* tōshu 投手; pitchā ピッチャー; ***water*** **~** mizu-sáshi 水差し; ***saké*** **~** (*decanter*) tokkuri とっくり・トックリ・徳利
pith *n* shín 芯
pitiful, pitiable *adj* kawai-sō´ (na) かわいそう・可哀想(な), (o-)ki no dókú (na) (お)気の毒(な)
pittance *n* shōryō 少量
pity 1. *v* (*pities*) dōjō shimásu 同情します 2. *n* (*it is a ~*) zannen (na) ... 残念(な)..., kinodoku 気の毒, dōjō 同情
pizza *n* píza ピザ
place 1. *n* tokoró 所, basho 場所; (*assigned seat*) (o-)séki (お)席; (*for something*) ba 場, ...-ba ...場; (*to put something*) oki-ba 置き場 2. *v* → **put**; **takes place** → **happen**; **takes the place of** *v* ... ni kawarimásu ...に代わります; **place of employment** *n* tsutome saki 勤め先; [BOOKISH] kinmu saki 勤務先, shoku-ba 職場; **place of residence** *n* kyojū-chi 居住地
plain 1. *adj* (*not gaudy*) jimí (na) 地味(な), (*simple, frugal*) shísso (na) 質素(な) 2. *n* (*flat land*) heiya 平野, heichi 平地
plan 1. *n* keikaku 計画; kikaku 企画; puran プラン; (*schedule*) yotei 予定; (*scheme*) takurami たくらみ・企み; kuwadate 企て; (*intention*) tsumori つもり, íto 意図 2. *v* keikaku shimásu 計画します; kikaku shimásu 企画します; kuwadatemásu 企てます; (*schedule*) yotei shimásu 予定します; (*devises*) takuramimásu たくらみ[企み]ます

plane *n* hikō-ki 飛行機
planet *n* wakusei 惑星
plank *n* íta 板
plant **1.** *n* (*a plant*) shokúbutsu 植物; (*garden/potted*) ueki 植木 **2.** *n* (*factory*) kōjō 工場 **3.** *v* (*~s it*) uemásu 植えます
plaster *n* sekkō 石こう[膏]
plastic *n* purásuchíkku プラスチック; (*polyethylene*) pori(-) ポリ; ~ ***bag*** poribúkuro ポリ袋, biniirubúkuro ビニール袋
plate *n* (o-)sara (お)皿; shokki 食器, purēto プレート
platform *n* **1.** (*at station*) hō′mu ホーム, nori-ba 乗り場; ~ (*non-passenger entry*) ***ticket*** nyūjō′-ken 入場券 **2.** (*lecture ~*) endan 演壇, kōdan 講壇
play *v* asobimásu 遊びます; (*a game*) shimásu します; (*a stringed instrument or piano*) hikimásu 弾きます; (*musical instrument*) ensō shimásu 演奏します; ~ ***it safe*** daijío torimásu 大事をとります
play *n* (*drama*) shibai 芝居, engeki 演劇
player *n* (*sports*) sénshu 選手, (*instrument*) purēyā プレーヤー; CD player *n* shiidii purēyā CDプレーヤー
playground *n* undō-jō 運動場
plaza *n* híró-bá 広場; puraza プラザ
pleasant *adj* tanoshíi 楽しい; omoshirói おもしろい・面白い; ureshíi うれしい・嬉しい; kaiteki (na) 快適(な)
Please ... *interj* Dō′zo ... どうぞ ...; ~ ***do me a favor.*** O-negai shimásu. お願いします.; ...(shi) te kudasái ...(し)て下さい
pleasure *n* (o-)tanoshimi (お)楽しみ
pleat *n* ori-mé 折り目; puriitsu プリーツ
pledge **1.** *n* chikai 誓い **2.** *v* (*swears it*) chikaimásu 誓います → **promise**
plentiful *adj* yútaka (na) 豊か(な)
plenty *n* takusán たくさん・沢山
pliers *n* (*pincers*) pénchi ペンチ, yattoko やっとこ・鋏
plight *n* hamé はめ・羽目
plot *n* (*story line*) súji 筋; (*scheme, trick*) keiryaku 計略, hakarigoto はかりごと・謀, inbō 陰謀
plow **1.** *n* (*a tool*) suki すき・鋤 **2.** *v* (*~s it*) tagayashimásu 耕します, sukimásu すき[鋤き]ます
pluck *v* tsumimásu 摘みます
plug *n* sén 栓; (*electricity*) puragu プラグ, sashikomi 差し込み, kónsénto コンセント
plum *n* **1.** sumomo すもも・スモモ・李 **2.** (*Japanese apricot*) ume 梅・ウメ
plumber *n* suidō-ya (san) 水道屋(さん); (*city water department*) suidō-kyoku 水道局
plump *adj* futói 太い
plunder *v* ubaimásu 奪います, ryakudatsu shimásu 略奪します
plural *n* fukusū 複数

plus *n* purasu プラス
p.m. *adv* (*afternoon*) gógo 午後
pneumonia *n* haien 肺炎
poacher *n* (*person*) [BOOKISH] mitsuryō-sha 密猟者
pocket *n* pokétto ポケット; kaichū (no) 懐中(の)
pocket money *n* kózukai 小遣い・こづかい, (o-)kózukai (お)小遣い
pockmarked face *n* abata-zura あばた面
pod *n* sáya さや・サヤ
podcast *n* (*online broadcasts*) poddokyasuto (rajio-bangumi) ポッドキャスト（ラジオ番組）
podium *n* endan 演壇, shiki dai 指揮台
poem *n* shi 詩, utá 歌 → **verse**
poet *n* shijin 詩人, kajin 歌人
point *n* ten 点, (*score*) tok<u>u</u>ten 得点; (*in a statement*) f<u>u</u>shí 節; (*gist*) yōten 要点; (*tip*, *end*) saki 先; ***to the ~*** tek<u>i</u>setsu (na/ni) 適切(な/に)
point *v* (*puts a ~ on*) togarase-más<u>u</u> とがらせ[尖らせ]ます; ***~ at/to …*** o sashimás<u>u</u> …を指します; ***~ out*** sh<u>i</u>teki shimás<u>u</u> 指摘します; shíji shimás<u>u</u> 指示します
poison *n* dokú 毒, doku-so 毒素
poke *v* ts<u>u</u>kimás<u>u</u> 突きます; ***~s fun at*** karakaimás<u>u</u> からかいます
pole *n* (*rod*) bō 棒, saó さお・竿, pōru ポール; ***telephone/light ~*** denchū 電柱
police *n* keisatsu 警察; ***~ box*** kōban 交番; ***~ station*** keisatsu-sho 警察署; **policeman, police officer** *n* omáwari-san お巡り[おまわり]さん, keikan 警官, [BOOKISH] junsa 巡査
policy *n* hōshin 方針, tatémae 建て前, porishii ポリシー, (*political*) seisaku 政策; ***makes … one's ~*** … o tatémae to shimás<u>u</u> …を建て前とします
polio *n* shōni-máhi 小児麻痺
polish *v* (*shines*) migakimás<u>u</u> 磨きます; (*grinds*) togimás<u>u</u> 研ぎます
polite *adj* (go-)téinei téinei (na) (ご)丁寧(な), (*well-behaved*) otonashíi おとなしい・大人しい, reigi-tadashíi 礼儀正しい
politician *n* seiji-ka 政治家
pollution *n* osen 汚染, kō´gai 公害; **environmental pollution** *n* kankyō-osen 環境汚染
pomelo *n* (*Japanese*) natsu-míkan 夏みかん・夏蜜柑・ナツミカン
pond *n* iké 池
pony *n* ponii ポニー
pool; ***~ pool*** (*parking* (*lot*)) mōtā pū´ru モータープール, chūsha-jō 駐車場; ***swimming ~*** pū´ru プール
poor *adj* (*needy*) bínbō (na) 貧乏(な), mazushíi 貧しい; (*clumsy*) hetá (na) へた[下手](な); (*bad*) warúi 悪い; (*pitiful*) kawaisō (na) かわいそう[可哀相](な)
pop **1.** *n* (*soda water*) sōda ソーダ, jūsu ジュース **2.** *v* (*it ~s*) hajikemás<u>u</u> はじけます **3.** *v* (*~s it*) hajikesasemás<u>u</u> はじけさせます

popular *adj* **1.** ninki (no aru) 人気(のある); taishū (no) 大衆(の); zoku (na) 俗(な); hayari (no) はやり・流行り(の) **2.** ***is*** ~ ninki ga arimásu 人気があります; hayatteimásu はや[流行]っています; ureteimásu 売れています; (*a person is well liked*) motemásu もてます

population *n* jinkō 人口; nínzu 人数, nínzū 人数

porcelain *n* setomono 瀬戸物, jíki 磁器 → **china(ware)**

porch *n* **1.** (*entrance hall*) génkan 玄関, pōchi ポーチ, beranda ベランダ **2.** (*veranda*) engawa 縁側

pork *n* buta-niku 豚肉, pōku ポーク; **pork dumpling** *n* shūmai シューマイ・焼売

pornography *n* póruno ポルノ, ero-hon エロ本; (*traditional*) shunga 春画

porridge *n* (o-)kayu (お)かゆ[粥]

port *n* minato 港

porter *n* pō´tā ポーター; (*redcap*) akabō 赤帽

portion *n* búbun 部分, bún 分, ichí-bu 一部, wari-mae 割り前; (*serving*) …-ninmae …人前

portrait *n* shōzō(-ga) 肖像(画), zō 像

position *n* **1.** íchi 位置, pojishon ポジション **2.** (*status, rank*) chíi 地位 **3.** → **place** → **job**

positive *adj* **1.** sekkyoku-teki (na) 積極的(な), pojitibu ポジティブ **2.** → **sure**; **positive thinking** *n* mae-muki (na) shikō 前向き(な)思考

possess *v* **1.** → **have** → **own** **2.** sonaemásu 備えます

possession *n* (*thing owned*) shoyū-butsu 所有物, shoyū-hin 所有品

possible *adj* kanō (na) 可能(な); ***is*** ~ dekimásu でき[出来]ます, kanaimásu かない[叶い]ます

possibly *adv* hyótto shitára/shite/suru to ひょっとしたら/して/すると; arúi-wa あるいは・或いは

post *n* **1.** yūbin 郵便; ***a*** ~ yūbin-bustu 郵便物; (*mailbox*) yūbin-posuto 郵便ポスト → **mail** **2.** (*pillar*) hashira 柱 **3.** (*duty*) yakú 役, (*job*) shoku 職

postage *n* yūbin-ryō´kin 郵便料金, yūsō´-ryō 郵送料; ~ ***stamp*** kitte 切手, yūbin-kítte/-gítte 郵便切手/切手

postcard *n* (o-)hágaki (お)葉書; (*picture*) e-hágaki 絵葉書

poster *n* posutā ポスター

postman *n* yūbin-ya (san) 郵便屋(さん)

post office *n* yūbín-kyoku 郵便局

postpone *v* enki shimásu 延期します, nobashimásu 延ばします

posture *n* shisei 姿勢

postwar *adj* sengo (no) 戦後(の)

pot *n* **1.** (*piece of pottery*) yaki-mono 焼き物 **2.** (*for cooking*) kama かま・釜; (*pan*) (o-)nabe (お)鍋; (*kettle*) pótto ポット **3.** (*for plants*) hachí 鉢; ***potted plant*** hachiue 鉢植え, hachí-mono 鉢物, ueki 植木

potato *n* pótéto ポテト; (*baked sweet potato*) yaki-imo 焼き芋・ヤキイモ

potential *n* (*possibility*) kanōsei 可能性, (*potentiality*) senzaisei 潜在性; **potential ability** *n* senzai nōryoku 潜在能力

pottery *n* yaki-mono 焼き物, tō´ki 陶器

pouch *n* pōchi ポーチ, fukuro 袋; **pouch of a kangaroo** *n* kangarū no fukuro カンガルーの袋

poultry *n* [BOOKISH] kakin 家禽

pound **1.** *n* (*weight or money*) póndo ポンド **2.** *~s it* *v* tatakimásu 叩きます

pour *v* **1.** tsugimásu つぎ[注ぎ]ます, sosogimásu そそぎ[注ぎ]ます **2.** ~ *on* abisemásu 浴びせます

pout *v* fukuremásu ふくれます

poverty *n* hinkon 貧困, binbō 貧乏

powder *n* koná 粉; funmatsu 粉末; paudā パウダー; (*face*) oshiroi おしろい・白粉; **powder soap** *n* kona sekken 粉石鹸・粉せっけん

power *n* chikará 力, jituryoku 実力; kenryoku 権力; (*person of power*) kenryoku-sha 権力者; (*energy, influence*) séiryoku 勢力; (*electricity*) dénki 電気; **power line** *n* densen 電線

powerful *adj* yūryoku (na) 有力(な); kyōryoku (na) 強力(な); pawafuru (na) パワフル(な)

practical *adj* jitchi (no) 実地(の), jissenteki (na) 実践的(な); jitsuyōteki (na) 実用的(な); **practical use** *n* jitsuyō 実用

practice *n* **1.** (*drill*) renshū 練習; (*artistic*) (o-)kéiko (お)けいこ[稽古] **2.** (*realization*) jikkō 実行, (*reality*) jissai 実際; (*habit*) shūkan 習慣; ***puts to ~*** jisshi shimásu 実施します

praise **1.** *n* (*homage*) home-kótoba ほめ[褒め]言葉, homé ほめ・褒め, [BOOKISH] shōsan 称賛 **2.** *v* (*lauds*) homemásu ほめ[褒め]ます

prank *n* itazura いたずら・悪戯

prawn *n* kurumá-ebi 車えび[海老]・クルマエビ

pray *v* inorimásu 祈ります

preach *v* sekkyō shimásu 説教します, (oshie o) tokimásu (教えを)説きます

preacher *n* (*priest*) bokushi(-san) 牧師(さん)

prearrange *v* uchi-awasemásu 打ち合わせます

precaution *n* (*care*) yō´jin 用心, keikai 警戒, nén 念; (*prevention*) yobō 予防; ***as a ~*** nen no tamé (ni) 念の為(に)

precedent *n* senrei 先例, zenrei 前例, réi 例

precious *adj* taisetsu (na) 大切(な), daijí (na) 大事(な), kichō (na) 貴重(な); oshíi 惜しい

precipice *n* (*cliff*) zeppeki 絶壁; kiki 危機

precipitate *v* (*rains, snows*) furimásu 降ります

precise *adj* seimitsu (na) 精密(な)

predicament *n* kyūchi 窮地, kukyō

苦境

predict *v* yogen shimásu 予言します

prediction *n* (*weather, etc.*) yohō 予報, yogen 予言

preface *n* jobun 序文, maegaki 前書き

prefecture *n* kén 県, …-ken …県; *~ office* kenchō 県庁

prefer *v* … no hō´ ga sukídesu …の方が好きです; … no hō´ o konomimásu …の方を好みます

preferably *adv* isso いっそ, múshiro むしろ

prefix *n* settō-go 接頭語, settō-ji 接頭辞

pregnancy *n* ninshin 妊娠

prehistory *n* senshi jidai 先史時代, [BOOKISH] yūshi izen 有史以前

prejudice *n* henken 偏見, sennyū-kan 先入観, sabetsu 差別

preliminary *n* yosen 予選

prelude *n* (*music*) pureryūdo プレリュード, zensō kyoku 前奏曲, jokyoku 序曲

premature *adj* hayasugiru 早過ぎる, [BOOKISH] jiki shōsō (no) 時期尚早(の); **premature baby** *n* sōzan-ji 早産児, mijuku-ji 未熟児

premeditated *adj* (*not accidental, preplanned*) keikakuteki (ni) 計画的(に); (*intentionally*) koi (ni) 故意(に)

premiere *n* puremia プレミア, (*film*) hatsu kōkai 初公開

premise *n* zentei 前提, katei 仮定

premium *n* puremiamu プレミアム, (*bonus*) [BOOKISH] hōshōkin 報奨金; shōhin 賞品; omake おまけ, keihin 景品

premonition *n* yokan 予感

preparation(s) *n* yō´i 用意, júnbi 準備; shitaku したく・支度; (*anticipatory steps*) yóbi 予備; (*advance study*) yoshū 予習; (*provisions*) sonáé 備え

prep(aratory) school *n* yobi-kō 予備校

prepare *v* **1.** … no yō´i/júnbi o shimásu …の用意/準備をします **2.** (*arranges*) …no shitaku o shimásu …のしたく[支度]をします **3.** (*studies ahead*) yoshū shimásu 予習します **4.** (*readies it*) totonoemásu 整えます **5.** (*makes it*) tsukurimásu 作ります **6.** (*sets up, provides*) mōkemásu 設けます

prescribe *v* **1.** (*~s medicine*) shohō shimásu 処方します **2.** (*stipulates*) kitei shimásu 規定します

prescription *n* shohō 処方; (*~ slip*) shohō-sen 処方せん[箋]

present 1. *adj* (*the ~ time*) génzai (no) 現在(の); íma (no) 今(の); kóndo (no) 今度(の) **2.** *adj* (*in attendance*) shusseki (no) 出席(の) **3.** *n* génzai 現在; íma 今; hon- …本…, kon-… 今…; ***at ~*** íma wa 今は, génzai wa 現在は; ***up to the ~*** imamáde 今まで, koremáde これまで; ***the ~ conditions/state*** genjō 現状

present *n* (*gift*) okuri-mono 贈り物, purézento プレゼント; o-rei

お礼; kokorozashi 志; (*as a souvenir*) (o-)miyage (お)みやげ[土産]

present *v* (*gives*) agemásu あげます, sashi-agemásu 差し上げます; okurimásu 贈ります

preservation *n* [BOOKISH] hozon 保存; hogo 保護; **preservation of environment** *n* kankyō hogo 環境保護, kankyō hozen 環境保全; **wildlife preservation** *n* yasei seibutsu no hogo 野生生物の保護

preservative *n* bōfu-zai 防腐剤; hozon-ryō 保存料

preserve *v* tamochimásu 保ちます, hozon shimásu 保存します; mamorimásu 守ります

president *n* (*of a nation*) daitō´ryō 大統領; (*of a company*) shachō 社長; (*of a university, college, etc.*) gakuchō 学長; (*of a school*) kōchō 校長

press **1.** *v* ~ *(on)* oshimásu 押します; (~ ... (*up*)*on* ...) oshitsukémásu 押し付けます **2.** *v* (*iron*) airon o atemásu アイロンをあてます; (*hug*) daki-shimemásu 抱きしめます **3.** *n* (*printing* ~) insatsu-ki 印刷機; (*publishing*) shuppan-kai 出版界

pressure *n* atsuryoku 圧力; appaku 圧迫; puresshā プレッシャー

prestige *n* méiyo 名誉; meiyo 名誉

presumably *adv* dōmo… rashii どうも…らしい; tabun … da to omou たぶん … だと思う

presume *v* suitei/yosō shimásu 推定/予想します → **think**

presumption *n* suitei 推定, yosō 予想; katei 仮定

pretend *v* … (no) furí o shimásu …(の)ふりをします

pretense *n* furí ふり; misekake 見せかけ

pretext *n* kōjitsu 口実; iiwake 言い訳

pretty **1.** *adj* kírei (na) きれい[綺麗](な), kawaii かわいい → **fairly, rather** **2.** *adv* (*very*) kanari かなり, [BOOKISH] hijō ni 非常に

prevalence *n* fukyū 普及; **prevalence of diseases** *n* byōki no ryūkō 病気の流行; **prevalence of the Internet** *n* intānetto no fukyū インターネットの普及

prevent *v* **1.** (*hinders*) (… no) jama o shimásu (…の)じゃま[邪魔]をします; (*thwarts*) habamimásu 阻みます **2.** (*blocks*) fusegimásu 防ぎます, (*wards off*) yobō shimásu 予防します

prevention *n* yobō 予防, bōshi 防止

preview *n* **1.** shitami 下見 **2.** shisha 試写; **preview room** *n* shisha-shitsu 試写室

previous *adj* máe no 前の; **previous appointment/engagement** sen'yaku 先約; **previous story** *n* (*TV, etc.*) zenkai no (o-)hanashi 前回の(お)話・はなし

previously *adv* izen ni 以前に, maemotte 前もって

prewar *adj* senzen (no) 戦前(の)

prey *n* (*sacrifice*) gisei 犠牲

price *n* (o-)nédan (お)値段, kakaku 価格, ne 値; (*the set/regular/net price*) teika 定価; **price index** *n* bukka-shisū 物価指数; **price tag** *n* shō-fuda 正札, ne fuda 値札

pride *n* hokori 誇り; puraido プライド, (*boast*) jiman 自慢; (*strong point*) tokui 得意

priest *n* (*Christian*) shínpu(-san) 神父(さん), bokushi 牧師; (*Buddhist*) sō´(ryo) 僧侶; (*Shinto*) kánnushi 神主

prim *adj* kichintoshita きちんとした, totonotta 整った

primarily *adv* gánrai 元来, zéntai 全体

primary *adj* daiichi (no) 第一(の); shokyū (no) 初級(の)

prime minister *n* sōri-dáijin 総理大臣, shushō 首相

prince *n* miya(-sama) 宮(様), ōji(-sama) 王子(様), purinsu プリンス; ***Crown*** ~ kōtaishi(-sama) 皇太子(様)

princess *n* (o)híme(-sama) (お)姫(様); ōjo(-sama) 王女(様), purinsesu プリンセス; ***Crown*** ~ kōtaishi-hi 皇太子妃

principal **1.** *n* (*head of a school*) kōchō 校長; shuyaku 主役 **2.** *adj* (*main*) ómo (na) 主(な)

principle *n* (*policy*) hōshin 方針; (*doctrine*) gensoku 原則, shúgi 主義

print *n* (*woodblock*) mokuhan (-ga) 木版(画), hanga 版画; insatsu 印刷

print *v* (*~s it*) insatsu shimásu 印刷します, purinto shimásu プリントします, surimásu 刷ります; (*in ~*) katsuji ni shimásu 活字にします

prior *adj* jizen (no) 事前(の), saki (no) 先(の); **prior arrangement** *n* uchi-awase 打ち合わせ

priority *n* yūsen(-ken) 優先(権); ***first*** ~ sai-yūsen 最優先; ***order of*** ~ yūsen-jun('i) 優先順(位)

prism *n* purizumu プリズム

prison *n* keimusho 刑務所, [BOOKISH] kangoku 監獄 → **jail**

privacy *n* puraibashii プライバシー; shiseikatsu 私生活

private *adj* (*use*) jibun-yō (no) 自分用(の), shiyō (no) 私用(の); (*undisturbed*) jama sarenai じゃま[邪魔]されない; (*confidential*) naishó (no) 内緒(の), (*secret*) himitsu (no) 秘密(の), puraibēto プライベート; (*privately established*) watakushí-ritsu/shiritsu (no) 私立(の), shisetsu (no) 私設(の); **private company** *n* minkan kigyō 民間企業; **private school** *n* shiritsu (gakkō) 私立学校, watakushiritsu 私立・わたくしりつ; **private talk** *n* uchiwa no hanashí 内輪の話, naisho-bánashi 内緒話

privilege *n* tokken 特権, tokuten 特典, kenri 権利

prize **1.** *n* shō´賞, …-shō …賞, (*object*) shōhin 賞品, (*money*) shōkin 賞金; ***grand*** ~ taishō 大賞, guranpuri グランプリ

2. *n* (*reward*) go-hō´bi ごほうび・ご褒美

probably *adv* tábun 多分・たぶん, osóraku 恐らく・おそらく, ōkata おおかた・大方, taigai 大概・たいがい

problem *n* mondai 問題, kadai 課題; difficult problem *n* nanmon 難問

procedure *n* (*formalities*) tetsúzuki 手続き; (*program*) tejun 手順

proceed *v* **1.** susumimasu 進みます **2.** tsuzukemásu 続けます

proceeding *n* gijiroku 議事録; sinkō 進行

process 1. *n* (*method*) yari-kata やり方, hōhō 方法, (*course, stage*) katei 過程, purosesu プロセス; (*development*) nariyuki 成り行き **2.** *v* (*handles*) shóri shimásu 処理します; (*industrially treats*) kakō shimásu 加工します

produce 1. *v* (~*s it*) … ga dekimásu …ができ[出来]ます, … o tsukurimásu …を作ります, … o seizō/seisaku shimásu …を製造/制作します **2.** *v* (*brings it about*) … o shō-jimásu;…を生じます **3.** → **product**

producer *n* seisan-sha 生産者; (*movie, drama, etc.*) seisaku-sha 制作者, enshutsuka 演出家

product *n* (sei)sanbutsu (生)産物; seihin 製品

production *n* (*manufacture*) seisan 生産, seizō 製造; (*movie, drama, etc.*) seisaku 制作, purodakushon プロダクション; production company *n* seisaku-gaisha 制作会社

profession *n* (*vocation*) shokúgyō 職業

professional *n* (*an expert*) kúrō´to くろうと・玄人, púro プロ; professional wrestling *n* puro-resu プロレス

professor *n* kyōju 教授

proficiency *n* jitsuryoku 実力

profile *n* purofiiru プロフィール; (*face in* ~) yokogao 横顔; (*side view*) sokumen (zu) 側面(図)

profit 1. *n* ríeki 利益; (o-)toku (お)得; (*interest*) rí 利 **2.** *v* (*makes a* ~) mōkemásu もうけ[儲け]ます; profit and loss *n* son eki 損益, son toku 損得

profitable *adj* yū´ri (na) 有利(な), toku (na) 得(な); umái うまい; (*pay*) rieki ni naru 利益になる; mōkaru 儲かる

profound *adj* fukai 深い, [BOOKISH] shin'en (na) 深遠(な)

program *n* (*TV, etc.*) bangumi 番組, purogúramu プログラム; (*plan*) keikaku 計画; (*computer* ~) purogramu プログラム, sofuto(wea) ソフト(ウェア)

progress 1. *n* shinkō 進行, shínpo 進歩, shínchoku 進捗; keika 経過 **2.** *v* (*it* ~*es*) susumimásu 進みます, shínpo shimásu 進歩します

prohibition *n* kinshi 禁止

project 1. *v* (*a picture/movie*) utsushimásu 映します; keikaku shimásu 計画します **2.** *n* keikaku 計画, kikaku 企画, purojekuto プロジェクト

projection *n* (*movie*) eishá 映写, tōei 投影

projector *n* (*movie*) eishá-ki 映写機, purojekutā プロジェクター

prolong → **lengthen**

prominent *adj* ichijirushíi 著しい, medatta 目立った・めだった, (*famous*) chomei (na) 著名(な)

promise **1.** *n* (o-)yakusoku (お)約束, yakusoku-goto 約束事; (*outlook*) mikomi 見込み **2.** *v* **~s it** yakusoku shimásu 約束します; ***fulfills a ~*** yakusoku o hatashimásu 約束を果たします

promising *adj* mikomi no aru 見込みのある, shōraisei no aru 将来性のある, kitai dekiru 期待できる, [BOOKISH] yūbō (na) 有望(な), zento yūbō (na) 前途有望(な); promising future *n* akarui mirai 明るい未来; promising job *n* shōraisei no aru shigoto 将来性のある仕事

promotion *n* (*salary rise*) shōkyū 昇給; (*incentive*) shōrei 奨励; (*betterment, increase*) zōshin 増進, hanbai sokushin 販売促進

prompt *adj* sassokú (no) 早速(の), [BOOKISH] jinsoku (na) 迅速(な), (*instant*) tossa (no) とっさ(の); prompt reply *n* jinsoku na hentō 迅速な返答

pronunciation *n* hatsuon 発音; pronunciation symbol *n* hatsuon kigō 発音記号

proofreader *n* kōsei-sha 校正者

prop **1.** *n* (*a support*) sasae 支え **2.** *n* kodōgu 小道具 **3.** *v* **~s it (up)** *v* sasaemásu 支えます

propaganda *n* senden 宣伝, senden katsudō 宣伝活動

propel *v* susumasemásu 進ませます; suishin shimásu 推進します

propeller *n* puropera プロペラ

proper *adj* (*appropriate*) tekitō (na) 適当(な), tekisetsu (na) 適切(な), chanto shita ちゃんとした; (*expected, deserved*) tōzen (no) 当然(の); (*correct*) tadashíi 正しい・ただしい

property *n* (*fortune*) zaisan 財産; shoyū(ken) 所有(権)

proportion *n* rítsu 率; wariai 割合; puropōshon プロポーション

proposal *n* **1.** mōshi-komi 申し込み, mōshi-de 申し出 **2.** (*public*) mōshi-ire 申し入れ **3.** (*suggestion*) kikaku (an) 企画(案), kikaku-sho 企画書, teian-sho 提案書; (*of marriage*) endan 縁談; kyūkon 求婚

propose *v* **1.** teian shimásu 提案します; mōshi-komimásu 申し込みます, mōshi-demásu 申し出ます; (*publicly*) mōshi-iremásu 申し入れます **2.** **~ to** (*marriage*) kyūkon shimásu 求婚します

proprietor *n* keiéi-sha 経営者

prosecutor *n* kénji 検事

prospect(s) *n* (*outlook*) mikomi 見込み, mitōshi 見通し, zénto 前途

prospective *adj* mikomi no aru

見込みのある, kitai sareru 期待される; **prospective customer** *n* mikomi kyaku 見込み客
prosper *v* sakaemásu 栄えます
prosperity *n* keiki 景気; kō-kéiki 好景気
prosperous *adj* sakan (na) 盛ん(な)
prostitute *n* baishún-fu 売春婦
protect *v* mamorimásu 守ります; (*safeguards*) hógo shimásu 保護します; kabaimásu 庇います・かばいます
protection *n* bōei 防衛, bōgyo 防御, purotekushon プロテクション
protein *n* tanpakú-shitsu たんぱく[蛋白]質・タンパク質
protest *n* kō´gí (shimásu) 抗議(します)
protocol *n* purotokoru プロトコル, gaikō girei 外交儀礼
protrude *v* tsuki-demásu 突き出ます, tobi-dashiamásu 跳び[飛び]出します
proud *adj* **1.** tokui (na) 得意(な) **2.** *is ~ of* … o jiman shimásu …を自慢します
prove *v* shōmei shimásu 証明します
proverb *n* kotowaza ことわざ・諺
provide *v* (*provides one with*) motasemásu 持たせます; ataemásu 与えます → **give** → **prepare**; *~ a treat* gochisō shimásu ごちそう[ご馳走]します
province *n* (*of old Japan*) (… no) kuni (…の)国; (*modern prefecture*) kén 県, …-ken …県
provision *n* (*supply*) kyōkyū 供給; (*allowance*) téate 手当; (*stipulation*) jōken 条件; (*preparations*) sonáé 備え
provoke; ***gets provoked*, *is provoking*** shaku ni sawarimásu しゃく[癪]に障ります
prowess *n* (*ability*) udemae 腕前; yūki 勇気
prudence *n* tsutsushimi 慎しみ・つつしみ
psyche *n* séishin 精神
psychiatrist *n* seishin-ka-i 精神科医
psychology *n* shínri 心理; (*science/study*) shinrí-gaku 心理学
pub *n* (*Western-style*) pabu パブ; (*Asian*-style) izakaya 居酒屋
public **1.** *adj* kōshū (no) 公衆(の); kōkai (no) 公開(の); kōkyō (no) 公共(の); (*open*) kōzen (no) 公然(の); (*officially established*) kōritsu (no) 公立(の) **2.** *n* (*society*) yo-nó-naka 世の中, yo 世, séken 世間; **public hall** *n* kaikan 会館; **public holiday** *n* shukujitsu 祝日, saijitsu 祭日
publication *n* shuppan 出版; (*things*) shuppán-butsu 出版物; (*publishing*) hakkō 発行; (*books*) shoseki 書籍
publicity *n* senden 宣伝
publish *v* **1.** arawashimásu 著します, shuppan shimásu 出版します; hakkō shimásu 発行します **2.** (*puts it in a newspaper*) nosemásu 載せます → **announce**

publishing **1.** *n* shuppán-gyō 出版業 **2.** *adj* shuppan (no) 出版(の); publishing company *n* shuppán-sha 出版社; publishing industry *n* shuppán gyōkai 出版業界
pucker *v* ***~s it up*** subomemásu すぼめます; ***it ~s up*** subomarimásu すぼまります
puddle *n* mizutamari 水たまり
puke → **vomit**
pull *v* hipparimásu 引っ張ります, hikimásu 引きます; ***~ out*** hikidashimásu 引き出します; ***~ up*** (*refloats it*) hiki-agemásu 引き上げます; (*stop*) tomemásu 止めます
pull *n* (*connnections*) kone コネ; ***has ~ (with …)*** kao ga kikimásu 顔がききます, kóne ga arimásu コネがあります
pulp *n* (*of paper*) parupu パルプ
pulse *n* myakú 脈, myakuhaku 脈拍
pulverize *v* funmatsu ni shimásu 粉末にします, kona-gona in shimásu こなごなにします
pump *n* pónpu ポンプ
pumpkin *n* kabocha かぼちゃ・カボチャ・南瓜
pun *n* share しゃれ・洒落, dajare だじゃれ・駄洒落, goro-áwase ごろ[語呂]合わせ
punch *n* panchi パンチ
punctual *adj* jikan o mamoru 時間を守る, jikandōri (no) 時間通り(の)
punctuation *n* kugiri 区切り, kutō ten 句読点
puncture *n* (*of tire*) panku パンク
pungent *adj* karái からい・辛い
punish *v* bas-shimásu 罰します, (*~es one's child*) oshioki (o) shimásu お仕置き(を)します
punishment *n* batsu 罰; (*abuse*) gyakutai 虐待, (*physical ~*) táibatsu 体罰, oshioki お仕置き
pupil *n* **1.** (*student*) séito 生徒; (*apprentice, disciple*) deshi 弟子 **2.** (*~ of the eye*) hitomi ひとみ・瞳
puppet *n* ayatsuri ningyō 操り人形; puppet show *n* ningyō-geki 人形劇; (*Japanese traditional*) búnraku 文楽
puppy *n* koinu 小犬・コイヌ
purchase → **buy**
pure *adj* junsui (na) 純粋(な), jún (na) 純(な); (*clean*) seiketsu (na) 清潔(な)
purge *n* tsuihō 追放
purple *adj* murásaki (no) 紫(の)
purpose *n* (*intention*) (o-)tsumori (お)つもり, íto 意図, kokorozashi 志; (*goal*) mokuteki 目的; ***for the ~ of*** … (no) tamé (ni) …(の)ため[為](に); ***on ~*** wáza-to わざと, wázawaza わざわざ, ito-teki ni 意図的に, takuránde たくらんで・企んで; ***serves a ~*** → **useful**
purse *n* saifu 財布, gamaguchi がまぐち
pursue *v* oimásu 追います
pus *n* (*medical*) umí うみ・膿
push **1.** *v* oshimásu 押します; (*thrusts*) tsukimásu 突きます; oshitsukémásu 押し付けます;

~ ***a good thing too far*** zu ni norimásu 図に乗ります **2.** *n* oshi 押し; (*recommendation*) osusume おすすめ・お勧め; (*pressure*) atsuryoku 圧力

pushy *adj* zūzūshíi ずうずうしい・図々しい, bu-énryo (na) 無遠慮(な)

put *v* okimásu 置きます; put aboard nosemásu 載せます; put aside tótte okimásu 取っておきます; put away shimaimásu しまいます; put in iremásu 入れます; ~ ***a call*** denwa o iremásu 電話を入れます; put in order soroemásu 揃えます; (*tidies it up*) katazukemásu 片付けます; put into words ii-arawashimásu 言い表します; put it another way ii-kaemásu 言い換えます; put it together (*assembles it*) kumi-tatemásu 組み立てます; put on (*clothes*) kimasu 着ます; (*footwear*) hakimasu はきます・履きます; (*headwear*) kaburimasu かぶり[被り]ます; (*glasses*) kakemasu かけます・掛けます → **wear**; put on airs kidorimásu 気取ります; put one on top of another kasanemásu 重ねます; put out dashimásu 出します; (*extinguishes*) keshimásu 消します; put pressure on appaku shimásu 圧迫します; put to bed/sleep nekashimásu 寝かします; put together awasemásu 合わせます; (*sets up*) kumimásu 組みます; put someone up overnight tomemásu 泊めます; put up with gáman shimásu 我慢します; shinobimásu 忍びます, taemásu 耐えます, shínbō shimásu 辛抱します

puzzle *n* nazo なぞ・謎, pázuru パズル

pyramid *n* piramíddo ピラミッド

Q

QR code *n* (*quick response code*) kyūāru-kōdo QRコード

quail *n* uzura ウズラ・鶉

qualification(s) *n* (*competency*) shikaku 資格

qualified *adj* tekishita 適した, shikaku ga aru 資格がある

qualify *v* (*suitable*) teki-shimásu 適します

quality *n* shitsu 質, hin 品, hinshitsu 品質; ***best*** ~ tokkyū (no) 特級(の); quality control *n* hinshitsu kanri 品質管理

qualm *n* fuan 不安

quantity *n* ryō 量; táká 多寡; (*large*) taryō 多量; tairyō 大量; (*large and/or small*) tashō 多少

quarrel *n, v* kenka (shimásu) けんか[喧嘩](します), kuchi-genka (shimásu) 口げんか[口喧嘩](します), kōron (shimásu) 口論(します) → **argument** → **dispute**

quarrelsome *adj* **1.** (*inclined to quarrel*) kenka-zuki (no/na) 喧嘩好き(の/な) **2.** (*argumentative*) giron-zuki (no/na) 議論好き(の/な)

quart *n* kuwōto クォート

quarter *n* **1.** yonbun-no-ichi 四分の一・4分の1; (*of a year*) shi̱-hanki 四半期・4半期; (*time*) jūgo-fun 15分 **2.** (*district*) hōmén 方面, …-hō´men …方面

quartet *n* karutetto カルテット; (*music*) shijū-sō kyoku 四重奏曲; (*group*) shijū-sō-dan 四重奏団

quay *n* hato-ba 波止場; futō 埠頭

queasy *adj* **1.** (*feels nauseated*) múkamuka shimásu̱ むかむかします, haki-kéga shimásu̱ 吐き気がします, haki-ké o moyō-shimásu̱ 吐き気を催します **2.** (*feels anxious*) shinpai (na) 心配(な), ochitsukanai 落ち着かない

queen *n* joō 女王, (*card*) kuiin クイーン; **queen-size** *adj* kuiin saizu (no) クイーンサイズ(の)

queer *adj* hén (na) 変(な), okashíi おかしい; (*wondrous*) myō´ (na) 妙(な)

quest *n* tankyū 探求, tansaku 探索, tsuikyū 追求

question *n* shi̱tsumon 質問; (*problem*) mondai 問題; (*doubt, query*) gimon 疑問

questionable *adj* ayashii 怪しい・あやしい, ikagawashíi いかがわしい, utagawashíi 疑わしい; (*fishy*) ku̱sái くさい・臭い

question mark *n* gimón-fu 疑問符

questionnaire *n* ankēto アンケート

queue *n* rétsu 列; ***forms a ~*** rétsu o tsu̱kurimásu̱ 列を作ります

quick *adj* hayái 速い・早い・はやい

quick-witted *adj* kiten no ki̱ku 機転のきく, atama no kaiten no yoi/hayai 頭の回転のよい/早い

quiet **1.** *adj* shízuka (na) 静か・しずか(な), odáyaka (na) 穏やか・おだやか(な), nódoka (na) のどやか(な); ***gets ~*** shizumari-másu̱ 静まります・しずまります **2.** *v* ***~s it, makes it ~*** shizumemásu̱ 静めます・しずめます

quilt *n* (*padded*) fu̱ton ふとん; ***bottom ~*** shi̱ki-búton 敷布団; ***top ~*** kake-búton 掛け布団, yágu 夜具

quinine *n* kiníine キニーネ

quirk *n* ku̱sé 癖・くせ

quit *v* yamemásu̱ やめ[止め, 辞め]ます

quite *adv* sōtō 相当, daibu だいぶ・大分, zúibun ずいぶん・随分; (*completely*) mattakú 全く・まったく → **very** → **almost**; ***~ a …*** chótto shi̱ta … ちょっとした …; ***~ so*** naru-hodo なるほど・成る程

quitter *n* okubyō-mono 臆病者, ikuji nashi 意気地なし

quiver *v* furuemásu̱ 震えます

quiz *n* kuizu クイズ

quota *n* wariate 割り当て, noruma ノルマ

quotation *n* ínyō 引用

quote *v* in'yō shimásu̱ 引用します

R

rabbi *n* rabi ラビ

rabbit *n* usagi ウサギ・兎; **rabbit hole** *n* usagi no suana ウサギ・兎の巣穴

race **1.** *n* kyōsō 競争, rēsu レース; (*bike*) keirin 競輪; (*horse*) keiba 競馬 **2.** *n* (*of people*) jinshu 人種, minzoku 民族; ***the human ~*** jinrui 人類 **3.** *v* kyōsō shimásu 競争します; ***~ the engine*** énjin o fukashimásu エンジンを吹かします; **boat race** *n* kyōtei 競艇; bōto rēsu ボートレース; **race discrimination** *n* jinshu-teki henken 人種的偏見

racial *adj* jinshu (no) 人種(の)

racism *n* jinshu sabetsu 人種差別

rack *n* tana 棚; **coat rack** *n* kōtokake コート掛け; **magazine rack** *n* magajin rakku マガジンラック

racket *n* (*tennis, etc.*) rakétto ラケット

radar *n* rēdā レーダー

radiation *n* hōsha 放射; hōsha-sen 放射線

radical *adj* (*extremist*) kageki (na) 過激(な)

radio *n* rajio ラジオ; **radio program** *n* rajio-bangumi ラジオ番組; **radio cab** *n* musen takushii 無線タクシー

radioactive *adj* hōsha-sei (no) 放射性(の); **radioactive waste** *n* hōsha-sei haikibutsu 放射性廃棄物

radish *n* (*the giant white ~*) daikon 大根

radius *n* hankei 半径

raffle *n* (*lottery*) fukubiki 福引き

raft *n* ikada いかだ・筏

rag *n* bóro ぼろ; kuzu くず・屑; (*dust cloth*) zōkin ぞうきん・雑巾

rage **1.** *v* abaremásu 暴れます, aremásu 荒れます, (*be angry*) ikarimásu 怒ります, (*be furious*) ikarikuruimásu 怒り狂います **2.** *n* (*outrage*) gekido 激怒; (*passion*) jōnetsu 情熱

raid **1.** *n* (*attacking*) shūgeki 襲撃, kōgeki 攻撃; (*bombing*) bakugeki 爆撃 **2.** *v* ***~s it*** shūgekí/kōgekí/bakugekí shimásu 襲撃/攻撃/爆撃します; (*invades, makes a ~ on*) fumi-komimásu 踏み込みます

rail *n* rēru レール

railroad, railway *n* tetsudō 鉄道

rain **1.** *n* áme 雨; ***light ~*** kosame 小雨; ***heavy ~*** ō-ame 大雨, gō´u 豪雨 **2.** *v* (*it ~s*) áme ga furimásu 雨が降ります

rainbow *n* niji 虹; **rainbow colors** *n* niji iro 虹色

raincoat *n* reinkō´to レインコート

rainfall *n* kōu 降雨

rainy season *n* (*in Japan*) tsuyu つゆ・梅雨, nyūbai 入梅, (*outside Japan*) uki 雨季

raise **1.** *v* agemásu あげ[上げ, 挙げ, 揚げ]ます; (*arouses*) okoshimásu 起こします; (*increases*) mashimásu 増します, (*price, wage, fee*) híki-agemásu 引き上げます; (*erects*) tatemásu 立てます **2.** *v* (*fosters, nourishes*) yashinaimásu 養います; (*rears a child*) sodatemásu 育てます; (*keeps animals, etc.*) kaimásu 飼います; ***is raised*** (*reared*) sodachimásu 育ちます **3.** (*collects money*) tsunorimásu 募ります **4.** *n* (*salary increae*) shōkyū 昇給; (*price increase*) neagari 値上り

raisin(s) *n* hoshi-búdō 干しぶどう [葡萄], rēzun レーズン

rake 1. *n* kumade くまで・熊手 **2.** *v* (*~s them up*) kaki-atsumemásu かき集めます

rally *n* shūkai 集会, kaigō 会合

ram *n* rámu ラム, hitsuji 羊・ヒツジ, o-hitsuji 雄羊

ramp *n* surō´pu スロープ, ránpu ランプ

rampage 1. *n* bōryoku 暴力, bōsō 暴走 **2.** *v* abaremásu 暴れます

ranch *n* dai-bokujō 大牧場, dai-nōen 大農園

random *adj* iikagen (na) いいかげん・いい加減(な); detarame (na) でたらめ・出鱈目(な); yatara (na) やたら(な); (*math, computer*) musakui (no) 無作為(の)

range *n* (*kitchen*) kamado かまど・竈, rénji レンジ; (*gas*) gasurénji ガスレンジ; (*mountains*) sanmyaku 山脈; (*scope*) han'i 範囲; age range *n* nenrei haba 年齢幅; firing range *n* shatei 射程

rank 1. *n* kuraiā 位, ...-i ...位; chíi 地位, kaikyū 階級, kaisō 階層, ranku ランク **2.** *v* (*to grade*) chii o shimemásu 地位を占めます; high rank *n* kōkyū 高級; kōi 高位

ransom *n* minoshirokin 身代金

rape 1. *n* (*plant*) náppa 菜っ葉・ナッパ, ná 菜 **2.** *n* (*forcible intercourse*) gōkan 強姦, reipu レイプ **3.** *v* ~*s* gōkan shimásu 強姦します

rapid *adj* subayai 素早い; jinsoku (na) 迅速(な); kyūsoku (na) 急速(な) → **fast**; in rapid succession *adv* zokuzoku ぞくぞく・続々

rapids *n* (*river*) kyūryū 急流

rare *adj* (*infrequent*) mare (na) まれ[稀](な), (*precious, curious*) mezurashíi 珍しい; (*uncooked*) náma no 生の, (*little cooked*) nama-yake (no) 生焼け(の), réa (no) レア(の); rare case *n* mare na kēsu まれな[稀な]ケース

rash 1. *n* (*medical*) hosshin 発疹・ほっしん, hasshin 発疹・はっしん **2.** *adj* (*hasty*) keisotsu (na) 軽率(な), métta (na) めった(な), mukō´-mizu (na) 向こう見ず・むこうみず(な); skin rash *n* (*medical*) hishin 皮疹

rat *n* nezumi ねずみ・ネズミ・鼠; dobu nezumi ドブネズミ・溝鼠

rate 1. *n* (*ratio*) rítsu 率, (*percentage*) wariai 割合; (*charge*) ryōkin 料金 **2.** *v* (*estimates it*) mitsumorimásu 見積ります; admission rate *n* nyūin ritsu 入院率; tax rate *n* zei ritsu 税率

rather *adv* múshiro むしろ; (*preferably*) isso いっそ; (*fairly*) kánari かなり, ii-kagen いい加減 → **pretty, moderate**

ratio *n* ritsu 率, hiritsu 比率, (*percentage*) wariai 割合; birth ratio *n* shussei ritsu 出生率; ratio method *n* hiritsu hō 比率法

ration **1.** *n* haikyū 配給 **2.** *v* (*~s it*) haikyū shimásu 配給します

rational *adj* gōri-teki (na) 合理的(な); risei-teki (*na*) 理性的(な)

rattan *n* tō´ 藤・フジ

rattle *v* gáragara narimásu がらがら鳴ります; (*clatters*) gátagata shimásu がたがたします

ravine *n* kyōkoku 峡谷

raving *n* uwagoto うわごと・うわ言

raw *adj* náma (no, de) 生(の/で); ***sliced ~ fish*** (o-)sashimí (お)刺身刺身)

ray *n* kōsen 光線; a ray of sunlight *n* hizashi 日差し; X-ray *n* ekkusu sen X線, rentogen レントゲン

rayon *n* rēyon レーヨン

razor *n* kamisórí かみそり・剃刀; ***~ blade*** kamisórí no ha かみそりの刃

reach **1.** *v* (*it is delivered*) todokimásu 届きます; (*it extends to*) … ni oyobimásu …に及びます, nobimásu 伸びます; (*arrives at*) …ni tsukimásu …に着きます; (*achieves*) …ni tas-shimásu …に達します **2.** *n* (*within ~*) (te no) todoku hani/kyori (手の)届く範囲/距離

react *v* hannō shimásu 反応します

reaction *n* (*response*) hannō 反応; (*repercussion*) handō 反動; adverse reaction *n* (*medical*) yūgai hannō 有害反応; allergic reaction *n* arerugii hannō アレルギー反応

reactionary *adj* handō-teki (na) 反動的(な)

read *v* yomimásu 読みます; read aloud *v* ondoku shimásu 音読します; read rapidly *v* sokudoku shimásu 速読します; read with pleasure, like to read *v* aidoku shimásu 愛読します; read silently *v* mokudoku shimásu 黙読します; read thoroughly *v* jukudoku shimásu 熟読します

reader *n* (*person*) dokusha 読者; (*book*) tokuhon 読本

readily *adv* (*easily*) wáke-naku 訳なく・わけなく, muzō´sa ni 無造作に

ready **1.** *adj* (yō´i ga) dékíte imásu (用意が)出来ています, dekimáshíta 出来ました; (*is arranged*) totonoimásu 整います **2.** *adj* (*easy*) wáke-nai 訳ない **3.** *v* ***readies it*** (*provides*) sonaemásu 備えます, (*arranges it*) totonoemásu 整えます

ready-made **1.** *n* kiseihin 既製品 **2.** *adj* kisei (hin) (no) 既製(品)(の), dekiai (no) 出来合い(の)

real *adj* **1.** hontō (no) 本当(の); riaru リアル → **genuine; *the ~***

thing honmono 本物 **2.** (*actual*) genjitsu (no) 現実(の); real estate *n* fudōsan 不動産; real income *n* jisshitsu shotoku 実質所得; real world *n* jisshakai 実社会; genjitsu (no) sekai 現実(の)世界

realistic *adj* genjitsu-teki (na) 現実的(な); realistic plan *n* genjitsu-teki na keikaku/puran 現実的な計画/プラン

reality *n* jissai 実際; genjitsu 現実; riaritii リアリティ

realization *n* jikkō 実行; genjitsu-ka 現実化

realize *v* **1.** (*comprehends*) … ga wakarimás<u>u</u> …が分かります, satorimás<u>u</u> 悟ります **2.** (*carries out*) genjitsu-ka shimás<u>u</u> 現実化します **3.** (*notices*) kizuki-más<u>u</u> 気づきます → **accomplish**; ***a desire is realized*** nozomi ga kanaimás<u>u</u> 望みが叶い[かない]ます

really *adv* hontō/honto (ni) 本当/ほんと(に), jitsú (ni) 実(に); ***Really??*** (*No kidding!*) [EXCLAM] másaka まさか

real-time *adv* (*"live" or instanteous*) riaru-taimu (no) リアルタイム(の)

reap *v* osamemás<u>u</u> 収めます, shūkaku shimás<u>u</u> 収穫します

rear **1.** → **back, behind** **2.** → **raise**

reason *n* wáke わけ・訳, riyū 理由; (*what is sensible*) dōrí 道理; (*logic*) rik<u>u</u>tsu 理屈, ronri 論理; (*meaning*) yóshi 由; (*grounds*) yué 故, kónkyo 根拠; ***for the ~ that*** …to iu riyū de …という理由で, …yuéni …故[ゆえ]に; good reason *n* seitō na riyū 正当な理由; without reason *adv* riyū naku 理由なく

reasonable *adj* (*natural, proper*) atarimae (no) 当り前(の); teki-setsu (na) 適切(な); datō (na) 妥当(な); (*rational*) gōri-teki (na) 合理的(な); tegoro (na) 手頃(な); reasonable price *n* tegoro na kakaku 手頃な価格, datō na nedan 妥当な値段

rebate *n* haraimodoshi 払い戻し, ribēto リベート; tax rebate *n* zeikin (no) kanpu 税金(の)還付

rebel **1.** *n* hangyaku-sha 反逆者 **2.** *v* (*against*) … ni somukimás<u>u</u> …に背き[そむき]ます, hangya-ku shimás<u>u</u> 反逆します, hanran o okoshimás<u>u</u> 反乱を起こします

rebellion *n* hangyaku 反逆

rebuke **1.** *n* (o-)togamé (お)とがめ・(お)咎め, hinan 非難, [BOOKISH] shisseki 叱責 **2.** *v* (*blames*) toga-memás<u>u</u> とがめ[咎め]ます

recall **1.** *n* (*of defective products*) rikōru リコール **2.** *v* (*remembers*) omoi-dashimás<u>u</u> 思い出します

receipt *n* uke-tori 受け取り, ryōshū-sho 領収書, juryō´-shō 受領書, reshiito レシート

receive *v* moraimás<u>u</u> もらいます, ukemás<u>u</u> 受けます, uke-torimás<u>u</u> 受け取ります, uke-ts<u>u</u>kemás<u>u</u> 受け付けます; h<u>í</u>ki-torimás<u>u</u> 引き取ります; ses-shimás<u>u</u> 接します

recent *adj* saikin no 最近の, konogoro no この頃の, chíkágoro no 近頃の; **the most recent** *adj* saishin no 最新の
receptacle *n* yō´ki 容器, utsuwa 器
reception *n* resépushon レセプション; uketsuke 受付; **reception room** *n* ōsetsuma 応接間; ōsetsushitsu 応接室
recess *n* yasumí 休み
recession *n* fukéiki 不景気; keiki (no) kōtai 景気(の)後退
recipe *n* reshipi レシピ
reciprocal *adj* o-tagai (no) お互い(の); sō´go (no) 相互(の)
recital *n* risaitaru リサイタル
recite *v* utaimásu 歌います; tonaemásu 唱えます; anshō shimásu 暗唱します
reckless *adj* mubō (na) 無謀(な), múcha (na) むちゃ[無茶](な), mukō´-mizu (na) 向こう見ず・むこうみず(な)
reckon *v* kazoemásu 数えます
reclamation *n* kaikon 開墾
recognition *n* ninshiki 認識
recognize *v* mitomemásu 認めます
recoil *v* atozusarimásu 後ずさります, kōtai shimásu 後退します
recollect *v* omoidashimásu 思い出します
recommend *v* susumemásu 勧め[薦め]ます
recommendation *n* suisen 推薦, (*letter*) suisen-jō 推薦状
recompense *v* benshō shimásu 弁償します
reconcile *v* nakanaori shimásu 仲直りします, [BOOKISH] wakai shimásu 和解します
reconfirm **1.** *n* sai-kákunin 再確認, (flight) rikonfāmu リコンファーム **2.** *v* (*reservations*) (yoyaku o) sai-kákunin shimásu (予約を)再確認します
record **1.** *n* (*phonograph*) rekō´do レコード; (*results, marks*) seiseki 成績; (*historic*) kiroku 記録; ***a new ~*** (*an event*) shin-kiroku 新記録 **2.** *v* **~*s it*** (*sound*) rokuon shimásu 録音します; (*event*) kiroku shimásu 記録します; **birth record** *n* shussei kiroku 出生記録; **death record** *n* shibō kiroku 死亡記録
recorder *n* rokuón-ki 録音機 ; ***tape ~*** tēpu rekōdā テープレコーダー
recover *v* kaifuku shimásu 回復します
recovery *n* kaifuku 回復
recreation *n* goraku 娯楽; ian 慰安; réjā レジャー, rekuriē´shon レクリエーション
recruit **1.** *n* shinnyū-shain 新入社員 **2.** *v* boshū shimásu 募集します; saiyō shimásu 採用します
recruitment *n* boshū 募集; saiyō 採用; rikurūto リクルート
recuperate → **recover**
recuperation → **recovery**
recycle *n, v* risaikuru (shimásu) リサイクル(します); sairiyō (shimásu) 再利用(します)
red *adj* akai 赤い; áka (no) 赤(の);

the ~ (*deficit figures*) aka-ji 赤字; red bean *n* azukíあずき・アズキ・小豆; Red Cross *n* Sekijū´ji 赤十字
redo *v* (*does it over* (*again*)) yari-naoshimásu やり直します
reduce *v* **1.** herashimásu 減らします, (*curtails*) habukimásu 省きます; (*summarizes*) tsuzumemásu つづめます → **lessen** → **lower** → **shorten** **2.** (*loses weight*) yasemásu やせ[痩せ]ます
reed *n* áshi/yóshi アシ/ヨシ・葦
reef *n* anshō 暗礁; coral reef *n* sango-shō サンゴ礁・珊瑚礁
reel **1.** *n* (*spool*) ito maki 糸巻き, riiru リール; (*frame*) waku 枠 **2.** *v* (~*s it*) kurimásu 繰ります **3.** → **stagger**
reentry *n* (*into the country*) sai-nyūkoku 再入国; reentry permit *n* sainyūkoku kyoka 再入国許可
refer *v* ~*s to* … ni furemásu …に触れます; [BOOKISH] … ni genkyū shimásu …に言及します; (*reference*) sanshō shimásu 参照します
referee *n* refurii レフリー, shinpan (-in) 審判(員)
reference *n* sanshō 参照; reference book *n* sankō-sho 参考書
refined *adj* (*genteel*) (o-)jōhín (na) (お)上品(な), yū´ga (na) 優雅(な)
refinery *n* (*oil*) seiyu-sho 製油所
reflect *v* (*mirrors it*) utsushimásu 映します; ***gets reflected*** utsuri-másu 映ります; (*ponders*) hansha shimásu 反射します; ~***s on*** hansei shimásu 反省します
reflection *n* utsurí 写り; hansha 反射; kage 影; (*consideration*) kō´ryo 考慮; hansei 反省
reform *v* (*starts a new life*) kōsei shimásu 更生します
reformation *n* **1.** (*improvement*) kairyō 改良, kaizen 改善 **2.** (*innovation*) kaikaku 改革 **3.** (*remedy*) kōsei 更生
reformatory *n* shōnen-in 少年院
refrain; ~ ***from*** … o enryo shimásu …を遠慮します
refresh *v* sawáyaka na kibun ni shimásu さわやか[爽やか]な気分にします
refreshments *n* (*food*) tabe-mónó 食べ物; (*drink*) nomí-mono 飲み物; (*tea*) o-cha お茶
refrigerator *n* reizō´ko 冷蔵庫
refugee *n* hinán-sha 避難者, nan-min 難民; refugee camp *n* nanmin kyanpu 難民キャンプ
refund **1.** *n* harai-modoshi 払い戻し, henkin 返金 **2.** *v* (~*s it*) harai-modoshimásu 払い戻します, henkin shimásu 返金します; tax refund *n* zeikin (no) kanpu 税金(の)還付
refusal *n* kotowárí 断り; kyóhi 拒否; kyozetsu 拒絶
refuse **1.** *n* (*rubbish*) kuzu くず・屑, gomi ごみ・ゴミ **2.** *v* koto-warimásu 断ります; kyóhí shi-másu 拒否します; jitai shimásu 辞退します; (*rejects it*) kobami-

másu̲ 拒みます

regard **1.** *v* mimásu 見ます; kangaemasu 考えます → **think** **2.** *n* sonkei 尊敬, keii 敬意; ***~s to*** … ni yoroshí̲ku (ittekudasái, o-tsu̲tae kudasái) …によろしく[宜しく](言って下さい, お伝え下さい)

regarding *prep* ***in/with regard to*** … ni tái-shi̲te …に対して, … ni tsúite (no) …について(の)

regardless → **nevertheless**

regeneration *n* kōsei 更生

region *n* chíhō 地方, chíiki 地域

regional *adj* chíhō (no) 地方(の), chíiki (no) 地域(の)

register **1.** *n* (*of names*) meibo 名簿, (*enrollment*) kiroku 記録 **2.** *v* (*checks into hotel*) chekkúín shimásu̲ チェックインします; (*enrolls, signs up*) tōroku shimásu̲ 登録します; ***~ a letter*** tegami o kakí-tome ni shimásu̲ 手紙を書留にします

registration *n* tōroku 登録, tō´ki 登記

regret **1.** *n* kō´kai 後悔 **2.** *v* (*~s it*) kōkai shimásu̲ 後悔します, kuyamimásu̲ 悔やみます

regrettable *adj* oshíi 惜しい, zannén (na) 残念(な), ainiku (na) あいにく(な), ikan (na) 遺憾(な)

regular *adj* (*usual*) fu̲tsū no 普通の, (*ordinary*) nami no 並の, régyurā レギュラー; (*periodic/scheduled*) téiki no 定期の; ***regulars*** (*army*) jōbi-gun 常備軍; regular customer *n* jōren kyaku 常連客, kotei kyaku 固定客, tokuisaki 得意先; regular exam(ination) *n* teiki shiken 定期試験; regular size *n* futsū saizu 普通サイズ

regulation *n* ki̲sóku 規則, ki̲tei 規定; kimari 決まり

rehabilitation *n* rihabiri リハビリ

rehearsal *n* rihāsaru リハーサル

reincarnation *n* umarekawari 生まれ変わり

reign *n* chisei 治世

rein(s) *n* tázuna 手綱・たづな

reject *v* kobamimásu̲ 拒みます; kyóhí shimásu̲ 拒否します

rejection *n* kyozetsu 拒絶; acute rejection *n* (*medical*) kyūsei kyozetsu hannō 急性拒絶反応

rejoice *v* yorokobimásu̲ 喜びます

relate *v* **1.** (*tells*) katarimásu̲ 語ります, nobemásu̲ 述べます **2.** (*is connected/relevant to*) … ni kanshimásu̲ …に関します

relation(ship) *n* kankei 関係; tsunagari つながり; (*between people*) náka 仲, aidagara 間柄

relative **1.** *n* (*person*) shinrui 親類, shinseki 親戚 **2.** *adj* kankei/kanren no aru 関係/関連のある

relax *v* (*looses tension*) tarumimásu̲ たるみ[弛み]ます; (*gets comfortable*) ku̲tsurogimásu̲ くつろぎ[寛ぎ]ます; (*rests oneself*) yasumimásu̲ 休みます, rirakkusu shimásu̲ リラックスします, (*enjoys oneself*) asobimásu̲ 遊びます

release **1.** *n* (*publication*) hatsubai

発売, (*movie*) kōkai 公開; ***press*** ~ puresu ririisu プレスリリース **2.** *v* (*announce*) happyō shimásu 発表します; (*let go*) kahō shimásu 解放します; **release date** *n* hatsubai bi 発売日, kōkai-bi 公開日

relevant *adj* (*related*) kanren/kankei no aru 関連/関係のある; ***is ~ to*** … ni kanren shimásu …に関連します

reliable *adj* (*steady*) te-gatai 手堅い; (*trustworthy*) shinrai dekíru 信頼できる, ***is highly*** ~ shinrai-sei ga takái 信頼性が高い

reliance *n* ate 当て, tánomi 頼み, shinrai 信頼

relief *n* (*rescue*) kyū´jo 救助; (*from worry*) anshin 安心; ***breathes a sigh of*** ~ hóttó shimásu ほっとします

relieve *v* **1.** ***is relieved*** anshin shimásu 安心します; (*gets saved*) tasukarimásu 助かります **2.** ***~s oneself*** (*goes to the bathroom*) yō´o tashimásu 用を足します

religion *n* shū´kyō 宗教, …-kyō …教

relish *n* ***small dish of*** ~ tsukeawase 付け合せ

rely; ***~ on*** … ni tayorimásu …に頼ります, (*requests*) tanomimásu 頼みます, iraishimásu 依頼します

remain *v* (*gets left behind*) nokorimásu 残ります, (*is in excess*) amarimásu 余ります; (*stops*) todomarimásu とどまります; (*stays*) imásu います, (*rather than go*) ikimasén 行きません

remainder *n* (*leftover*) nokorí 残り, (*surplus*) (o-)ámari (お)余り; áto no (mono, hító, …) 後の(物, 人, …)

remains *n* (*what remains*) nokori-mono 残り物; ***the remaining*** … áto/nokori no …後/残りの…

remark **1.** *n* kotobá 言葉, … (yū/iu/itta) kotó… (言う/言った)事; ***uncalled-for*** ~ sashide-guchi 差し出口 **2.** *v* → **say**

remarkable *adj* ijō (na) 異常(な); ichijirushíi 著しい

remember *v* (*recalls*) omoi-dashimásu 思い出します; (*retains in memory*) obóete imásu 覚えています

remind; ***~ one of*** … … o omowasemásu …を思わせます; kizukasemásu 気付かせます

reminder *n* hínto ヒント, chū´i 注意, saisoku-jō 催促状, rimaindā リマインダー

remittance *n* sōkin 送金

remodel *v* kaichiku shimásu 改築します, rifōmu shimásu リフォームします

remote *adj* enkaku-chi 遠隔地; **remote area** *n* hekichi へき地・僻地; **remote control** *n* ① enkaku seigyo 遠隔制御 ② (*TV, etc.*) rimo-kon リモコン,

remove *v* torimásu 取ります, nozokimásu 除きます; sarimásu 去り

ます; háijo shimásu 排除します
remuneration *n* sharei 謝礼; (*salary*) kyūryō 給料
renewal *n* kōshin 更新, rinyūaru リニューアル; **license renewal** *n* menkyo (no) kōshin 免許(の)更新; **renewal fee** *n* kōshin-ryō 更新料
rent **1.** *n* (*cost*) karí-chin 借り賃, (*house*) yá-chin 家賃 **2.** *v* (*~s it out to*) kashimásu 貸します; (*~s it from*) karimásu 借ります
rental *n, adj* chintai (no) 賃貸(の), rentaru (no) レンタル(の); **rental fee** *n* shiyōryō 使用料, rentaru ryōkin レンタル料金; **rental house** *n* kashiya 貸家
renovate *v* **1.** (*repair*) shūri shimásu 修理します **2.** (*rebuild*) rifōmu shimásu リフォームします
reorder **1.** *v* (*adjusts*) séiri shimásu 整理します **2.** *n* sai-chūmon 再注文; tsuika-chūmon 追加注文
reorganization *n* sai-hensei 再編成
reorganize → **reorder**
repair **1.** *n* (*repairing*) naoshí 直し, shū´ri 修理, shūzen 修繕, tsukurói 繕い; (*upkeep, care*) te-iré 手入れ **2.** *v ~s it* naoshimásu 直します; (*mends, patches, sews*) tsukuroimásu 繕います; shū´ri/shūzen shimásu 修理/修繕します; (*it gets repaired*) …ga naorimásu … が直ります, (*gets it repaired*) … o naóshite moraimásu … を直してもらいます
repay *v* (*compensates*) mukuimásu 報います
repeat **1.** *v* mō ichi-do iimásu もう一度言います; kuri-kaeshimásu 繰り返します **2.** *n* ripiito リピート; kurikaeshi 繰り返し; [BOOKISH] hanpuku 反復
repeatedly *adv* (*often*) shíbashiba しばしば; (*ever so many times*) nán-do/-kai mo 何度/回も
repel *v* (*water, etc.*) hajikimásu 弾きます
repercussion *n* handō 反動
repetition *n* kurikaeshi 繰り返し, hanpuku 反復
rephrase *v* ii-kaemásu 言い換えます
replace *v* tori-kaemásu 取り換えます
replacement *n* torikae 取り換え, sashikae 差し替え, [BOOKISH] chikan 置換
replica *n* fukusei (-hin) 複製品, mozō(-hin) 模造品, repurika レプリカ
reply **1.** *n* kaitō 回答 **2.** *v* ***replies to*** kaitō shimásu 回答します
report **1.** *n* (*notice*) (o-)shirase (お)知らせ, tsūchi 通知, (o-)todoke (お)届け; (*announcement*) hōkoku 報告, repō´to レポート; (*message*) dengon 伝言; (*research paper*) happyō 発表; (*claim*) mōshi-de 申し出 **2.** *v* (*announces*) hōkoku shimásu 報告します, (*relays, tells*) tsutaemásu 伝えます, (*is reported*) tsutawarimásu 伝わります,

(*notifies*) todokemás<u>u</u> 届けます; (*presents research*) happyō shimás<u>u</u> 発表します; (*claims*) mōshi-demás<u>u</u> 申し出ます → **inform** → **tell**; ~ ***for work*** sh<u>u</u>kkin shimás<u>u</u> 出勤します; **report card** *n* seisekí-hyō 成績表

reporter *n* ripōtā リポーター, (*news* ~) shinbun-k<u>i</u>shá 新聞記者, (shuzai) k<u>i</u>shá (取材)記者

representative **1.** *n* daihyō 代表, daihyō´-sha 代表者 **2.** *adj* (*typical, model*) daihyō-teki (na) 代表的(な)

reprint *n, v* zōsatsu (shimás<u>u</u>) 増刷(します)

reproach *n, v* hínan (shimás<u>u</u>) 非難(します), sememás<u>u</u> 責めます

reproduce *v* (*replay*) saisei shimás<u>u</u> 再生します; (*replicates/copies it*) fuk<u>u</u>sei/fuk<u>u</u>sha shimás<u>u</u> 複製/複写します

reproduction *n* (*replication*) fuk<u>u</u>sei 複製, (*copy*) fuk<u>u</u>sha 複写; (*replay*) saisei 再生

reputation *n* hyōban 評判

request **1.** *n* negái 願い, tanomí 頼み, irai 依頼, rikuesuto リクエスト; (*a demand*) yōkyū 要求, seikyū 請求; (*requesting*) kói 請い **2.** *v* (*asks a favor*) negaimás<u>u</u> 願います, tanomimás<u>u</u> 頼みます, irai shimás<u>u</u> 依頼します; (*demands*) seikyū shimás<u>u</u> 請求します

require *v* **1.** (*demands*) yōkyū shimás<u>u</u> 要求します **2.** → **need** → **take** (*time/money*) → **stipulate**

requirement *n* yōkyū 要求; (*qualification*) sh<u>i</u>kaku 資格; **admission requirements** *n* nyūgaku shikaku 入学資格; **entry requirements** *n* tōroku hitsuyō jōken 登録必要条件

rescue **1.** *n* kyū´jo 救助 **2.** *v* tas<u>u</u>kemás<u>u</u> 助けます, s<u>u</u>kuimás<u>u</u> 救います; kyū´jo shimás<u>u</u> 救助します

research **1.** *v* kenkyū shimás<u>u</u> 研究します, chōsa shimás<u>u</u> 調査します, risāchi shimás<u>u</u> リサーチします **2.** (*investigation*) *n* chō´sa 調査; **researcher** *n* kenkyū-in 研究員, kenkyū-sha 研究者, chōsa-in 調査員

resemblance *n* ruiji 類似

resemble *v* … ni nite imás<u>u</u> …に似ています, nimás<u>u</u> 似ます; … ni/to ruiji shimás<u>u</u> …に/と類似します; ***closely*** ~ … ni/to nikayoimás<u>u</u> …に/と似通います

resent *v* fungai shimás<u>u</u> 憤慨します; ikidōrimás<u>u</u> 憤ります; uramimás<u>u</u> 恨みます

reservation *n* (*booking*) yoyaku 予約, mōshí-komi 申し込み

reserve *n* **1.** (*reticence*) enryo 遠慮; ***shows*** ~ enryo shimás<u>u</u> 遠慮します **2.** (*spare*) yobi 予備

reserve *adj* (*spare*) yóbi (no) 予備(の); **reserve fund** *n* tsumitate-kin 積立金

reserve *v* (*makes a booking*) yoyaku shimás<u>u</u> 予約します, mōshíkomimás<u>u</u> 申し込みます; (*puts* *aside, holds*) tótte okimás<u>u</u> 取って置きます

reservoir *n* chosúi-chi 貯水池, jōsúi-chi 浄水池

residence *n* **1.** (*place*) (o-)súmai (お)住まい, jū´sho 住所, jūtaku 住宅; ***one's ~ (home)*** jitaku 自宅 **2.** (*residing*) zairyū 在留; ***permanent ~*** honseki 本籍, (*place*) honsékí-chi 本籍地

resident *n* (*person*) kyojū´-sha 居住者, jūmin 住民

resign *v* (*job*) (shigoto o) yamemás<u>u</u> (仕事を)辞めます, jishoku shimás<u>u</u> 辞職します

resigned; ***is ~ to*** … o kákúgo shimás<u>u</u> …を覚悟します, akiramemás<u>u</u> 諦めます

resist *v* … ni hankō/teikō shimás<u>u</u> …に反抗/抵抗します, kobamimás<u>u</u> 拒みます

resistance *n* hankō 反抗, teikō 抵抗

resolutely *adv* shí<u>k</u>kári しっかり

resolve **1.** *n* (*determination*) késshín 決心 **2.** *v* ***~s to do*** (shiyō to) késshín shimás<u>u</u> (しようと)決心します **3.** *v* (*medical*) shōsan shimás<u>u</u> 消散します

resonate *v* kyōmei shimás<u>u</u> 共鳴します

resound *v* (*echo*) hibikimás<u>u</u> 響きます

respect **1.** *n* sonkei 尊敬, uyamai 敬い **2.** *v* sonkei shimás<u>u</u> 尊敬します; uyamaimás<u>u</u> 敬います; ogamimás<u>u</u> 拝みます; ***Respect-for-the-Aged Day*** (*the 3rd Monday of September*) Keirō no hí 敬老の日

respectable *adj* katagi (na) 堅気(な); (*proper*) chanto sh<u>i</u>ta … ちゃんとした…; (*considerable*) chótto shíta … ちょっとした…

respective *adj* sorézore no … それぞれの…, onóono no … 各々[おのおの]の…, kaku … 各...

respiration *n* kokyū 呼吸

respond *v* kotaemás<u>u</u> 答えます; ō-jimás<u>u</u> 応じます

response *n* kotáé 答え, resuponsu レスポンス, resu レス

responsibility *n* sekinin 責任; (*charge*) tantō 担当; (*cause*) gen'in 原因; **sense of responsibility** *n* sekinin-kan 責任感

responsible; ***~ for*** (*is in charge of*) … o tantō sh<u>i</u>te imás<u>u</u> …を担当しています; (*is the cause of*) … no gen'in des<u>u</u> …の原因です; **responsible person** *n* sekinín-sha 責任者; (*the one in charge*) tantō´-sha 担当者

rest **1.** *n* (*a break/pause*) (o-) yasumi (お)休み, kyukei 休憩 **2.** *n* ***the ~*** (*remainder*) nokorí 残り; **3.** *v* (*takes a ~*) yasumimás<u>u</u> 休みます

restaurant *n* rés<u>u</u>toran レストラン; ryōrí-ten/-ya 料理店/屋

restoration *n* kaifuku 回復, fukugen 復元

restrain *v* osaemás<u>u</u> 抑えます; ***properly restrained*** iikagen (na)

いい加減(な)
restrict *v* seigén/gentei shimásu 制限/限定します
restriction *n* seigén 制限, gentei 限定
result *n* kekka 結果; (*outcome*) séika 成果; (*marks, grades*) seiseki 成績; experimental result *n* jikken kekka 実験成果; laboratory results *n* kensa kekka 検査結果
resume **1.** *n* rireki-sho 履歴書 **2.** *v* (*continues*) saikai shimásu 再開します
retail **1.** *n* ko-uri 小売 **2.** *v* (*~s it*) ko-uri shimásu 小売りします; retail price *n* 小売価格
retailer *n* ko-uri gyōsha 小売業者
retain *v* (*keeps it*) kakaemásu 抱えます
reticence *n* (go-)enryo (ご)遠慮
retire *v* **1.** (*from job*) intai/taishoku shimásu 引退/退職します **2.** (*withdraws*) shirizokimásu 退きます, híki-torimásu 引き取ります
retirement *n* intai 引退, taishoku 退職; retirement pension *n* taishoku-nénkin 退職年金
retort **1.** *v* (*refutes*) hanron shimásu 反論する, iikaeshimásu 言い返します **2.** *v* (*revenges*) shikae shimasu 仕返しをします **3.** *n* (*answer back*) iikaeshi 言い返し
retreat **1.** *n* (*escape*) hinan 避難, (*retirement*) intai 引退, (*stay-at-home*) hikikomori 引きこもり **2.** *v* shirizokimásu 退きます
retribution *n* bachí 罰・ばち
return *v* **1.** (*reverses direction*) modorimásu 戻ります; (*goes back/home*) kaerimásu 帰ります; (*comes back to where one is now*) itte kimásu 行って来ます; ~ ***from abroad*** kíkoku shimásu 帰国します **2.** ***~s it*** kaeshimásu 返します; modoshimásu 戻します; (*turns back*) hiki-kaeshimásu 引き返します **3.** *n* (*response*) hentō 返答; (*replacement*) henkyaku 返却; (*restoration*) kaifuku 回復; return trip *n* ōfuku ryokō 往復旅行
reveal *v* morashimásu 漏らします; (*shows*) arawashimásu 現(わ)します; (*makes it public*) akíraka ni shimásu 明らかにします
revelation *n* otsuge お告げ
revenge *v* (… no) fukushū o shimásu (…の)復讐をします
revenue *n* **1.** (*governmental ~*) sainyū 歳入 **2.** (*income*) shūnyū 収入, shūeki 収益
revere *v* uyamaimásu 敬います
reverence *n* sonkei 尊敬, uyami 敬い
Reverend *n* … bokushi …牧師, … shínpu …神父
reverse **1.** *n, adj* hantai (no) 反対(の), gyaku (no) 逆(の); uragawa (no) 裏側(の) **2.** *v* (*turns around*) gyaku [sakasama, hanten, hantai] shimásu 逆[逆さま・反転・反対]にします, uragaeshimásu 裏返します
revert *v* modorimásu 戻ります

review **1.** *n* rebyū レビュー, (*study*) fuku͟shū 復習; (*criticism*) híhyō 批評, (*commentary*) hyōron 評論 **2.** *v* (*studies it*) fuku͟shū shimásu͟ 復習します; (*criticizes it/comments on it*) híhyō/hyōron shimásu͟ 批評/評論します; (*considers it*) kentō shimásu͟ 検討します; movie review *n* eiga hyōron 映画評論

revise *v* kaitei shimásu 改訂します

revision *n* kaitei(-ban) 改訂(版), kōsei 校正

revival *n* (*regeneration*) fukkatsu 復活, saisei 再生, ribaibaru リバイバル → **recover**

revive *v* (*brings back to life*) ikashimásu͟ 生かします

revoke *v* tori-keshimásu͟ 取り消します

revolt **1.** *n* hanran 反乱, hankō 反抗 **2.** *v* somukimásu͟ 背きます; hanran o okoshimásu 反乱を起こします

revolution *n* (*political*) kakumei 革命, reboryūshon レボリューション; (*revolving*) kaiten 回転

revolve *v* mawarimásu͟ 回ります, kaiten shimásu͟ 回転します

reward **1.** *n* shōkin 賞金, shō´yo 賞与; sharei 謝礼; (go-)hō´bi (ご)ほうび・褒美 **2.** *v* **~s for** (...shita) kai ga arimásu (...した)かいがあります; rewards and punishments shōbatsu 賞罰

rewrite; **~ *it*** kakí-naoshimásu͟ 書き直します, kakí-kaemásu͟ 書き換えます

rhythm *n* rízumu リズム

rib *n* rokkotsu ろっ骨・肋骨, abarabone あばら骨・肋骨

ribbon *n* himo ひも・紐, ríbon リボン; ink ribbon *n* inku ríbon インクリボン

rice *n* (o-)kome (お)米; (*cooked*) góhan ご飯, meshí 飯; ***~ boiled in a soup*** 雑炊; ***~ boiled with red beans*** sekíhan 赤飯; rice bowl *n* chawan 茶碗(o-cháwan お茶碗); rice cake *n* (o-)mochi (お)もち・(お)モチ・(お)餅; rice cooker *n* suihanki 炊飯器; rice curry *n* (*rice with curry*) karē-ráisu カレーライス; rice field *n* tá 田, tanbo 田んぼ, suiden 水田; rice wine → **saké**

riceball *n* (o-)músubi (お)むすび・(お)結び; nigiri-meshi にぎり[握り]飯; ***~ lunch(box)*** makunóuchi (bentō) 幕の内(弁当)

rich *adj* (*wealthy*) kanemóchí (no) 金持ち(の), yūfu͟ku (na) 裕福(な), ritchi (na) リッチ(な); (*abundant*) yútaka (na) 豊か(な), hōfu (na) 豊富(な); ***is ~/abundant in*** … ni tomimásu͟ … に富みます; rich person *n* okanemochi お金持ち

rickshaw *n* jinríki͟sha 人力車

riddle *n* nazo 謎, nazonazo なぞなぞ

ride **1.** *n* (*~ a vehicle*) jōsha 乗車, (*driving*) doraibu ドライブ, (*horse riding*) jōba 乗馬 **2.** *v* … ni norimásu͟ …に乗ります, … ni

notte ikimásu̲ …に乗って行きます; (*sits astride*) matagarimásu̲ またがり[跨り]ます; ***gives a ~ to*** … *v* o nosemásu̲ … を乗せます
ridge *n* (*of roof*) mune 棟
ridiculous *adj* bakageta ばかげた, bakabakashii ばかばかしい
rifle *n* shōjū 小銃, raifurú (-jū) ライフル(銃), teppō 鉄砲
right **1.** *adj* (*adv*) (*not left*) migi (no) 右(の) **2.** *adj* (*correct*) tadashíi, íi いい, yóku 良く **3.** *n* (*privilege*) kénri 権利; **just right** *adj* píttári ぴったり; **That's right.** *interj* Sō´ desu̲. そうです., Sonotō´ri desu̲. その通りです.; **right after** *adv* chokugo (ni) 直後(に); **right there** *adv* chōdo (a)soko (ni) ちょうど(あ)そこ(に); **right and wrong** *n* zén-aku 善悪
rigid *adj* katai 堅い・硬い
rim *n* herí へり・縁, fu̲chí ふち・縁
rind *n* kawa 皮
ring **1.** *n* (*on finger*) yubi-wa 指輪, ringu リング; (*circle*) wá 輪, maru 丸・円・まる, en 円・えん; **engagement ring** *n* konyaku yubi-wa 婚約指輪, engēji ringu エンゲージリング; **wedding ring** *n* kekkon yubi-wa 結婚指輪 **2.** *v* (*a bell sounds*) narimásu̲ 鳴ります; (*sounds a bell*) narashimásu̲ 鳴らします
rink *n* aisu sukēto-jō アイススケート場, (rōrā) sukēto-jō (ローラー) スケート場
rinse *v* yusugimásu ゆすぎます; su̲sugimásu すすぎます
riot *n* bōdō 暴動, sōdō 騒動
ripen *v* (*it gets ripe*) juku̲shimásu̲ 熟します, seijuku shimásu̲ 成熟します; minorimásu̲ 実ります
ripped; *gets ~ off* (*overcharged*) boraremásu̲ ぼられます, (*robbed*) yararemásu̲ やられます
rise **1.** *n* (*in price, wage, fee*) hí̲ki-age 引き上げ; ***gives ~ to*** … o okoshimásu̲ …を起こします, shō-jimásu̲ 生じます **2.** *v* (*gets up*) okimásu̲ 起きます; (*goes up*) agarimásu̲ 上がります, (*climbs, sun rises*) noborimásu̲ 登り[昇り]ます; (*stands up*) tachi-agarimásu̲ 立ち上がります; (*looms*) sobiemásu̲ そびえます・聳えます
risk *n* risuku リスク; kiken 危険
risky *adj* risukii (na) リスキー(な); kiken (na) 危険(な)
rival *n* teki 敵; kyōgōsha 競合者, raibaru ライバル
rivalry *n* kyōsō 競争; ***in ~ with*** … ni taikō shi̲te …に対抗して
river *n* kawá 川・河
rivet *n* ribetto リベット; byō 鋲・びょう
road *n* michi 道, dō´ro 道路, (*main road*) kaidō 街道
road rage *n* kōtsūjūtai de no iraira 交通渋滞でのイライラ
roam *v* idō 移動
roar **1.** *n* (*a ~*) unarí うなり・唸り **2.** *v* (*~s*) unarimásu̲ うなり[唸り]ます **3.** *v* (*rumbles*)

todorokimásu とどろき[轟き]ます

roast 1. *n* yaki-… 焼き…, …-yaki …焼き; rō´suto ロースト; *~ beef/chicken* rōsuto-bíifu/-chíkin ローストビーフ/チキン **2.** *v* (*~s it*) yakimásu 焼きます; irimásu いり[炒り]ます

rob *v* (*steals*) nusumimásu 盗みます; (*plunders*) ubaimásu 奪います; (*robs it of …*) kasume-torimásu かすめ取ります; ***gets robbed*** (*hit with a robbery*) (gōtō ni) yararemásu (強盗に)やられます

robber *n* gōtō 強盗, dorobō どろぼう・泥棒; zoku 賊

robot *n* robotto ロボット

rock *n* (*stone*) ishí 石, (*crag*) iwá 岩; (*music*) rókku ロック (also ***rock'n'roll*** rokkun-rōru ロックンロール)

rock *v* (*it ~s*) yuremásu 揺れます

rocket *n* rokétto ロケット

rocky *adj* iwa no ōi 岩の多い

rod *n* saó さお・竿; (*curtain, etc.*) róddo ロッド

roe *n* (*caviar*)*; **salmon** ~* ikura イクラ, (*salmon/trout*) sujikoすじこ・スジコ・筋子, ***cod*** *~* tarákó たらこ・タラコ・鱈子

role *n* yakuwari 役割, yakú 役, o-yakume お役目; (o-)tsutome (お)務め

roll 1. *v* (*it ~s*) korogarimásu 転がります, (*sways*) yuremásu 揺れます; (*~s it*) korogashimásu 転がします; (*~s it up*) makimásu 巻きます **2.** *n* (*bread*) rōru-pan ロールパン, (batā-)rō´ru (バター)ロール **3.** *n* (*a ~ of toilet paper*) (toiretto-pē´pā) hító-maki (トイレットペーパー)一巻; ***~ of*** (*currency*) ***bills*** satsu-taba 札束

romance *n* rómansu ロマンス, ren'ai 恋愛, roman ロマン, rōman 浪漫; **romance novel** *n* romansu shōsetsu ロマンス小説, ren'ai shōsetsu 恋愛小説

Romania *n* Rūmania ルーマニア

romantic *adj* romanchikku (na) ロマンチック(な)

Rome *n* Rō´ma ローマ

roof 1. *n* yáne 屋根; (*rooftop*) okujō 屋上 **2.** *v **~s a house*** uchi no yáne o fukimásu 家の屋根をふき[葺き]ます

rookie *n* **1.** shinjin 新人 **2.** (*game*) shinjin senshu 新人選手, rūkii ルーキー

room *n* **1.** heyá 部屋 (o-heya お部屋), (…-) ma (…)間; …-shítsu …室; (*tatami room*) zashíkí 座敷 (o-zashíki お座敷) **2.** (*extra space*) yochi 余地, (*leeway*) yoyū 余裕; **Japanese-style room** *n* washitsu 和室; **room and board** *n* geshuku 下宿; **roommate** *n* dōshítsú-sha 同室者, rūmu-meito ルームメイト; **room service** *n* rūmu-sā´bisu ルームサービス

root *n* né 根, ***near the ~*** ne-motó 根元; (*cause*) gen'in 原因; **root of all evil** *n* shoaku no kongen 諸

悪の根源

rope *n* nawá 縄・繩・なわ, tsuná 綱・つな; rō´pu ロープ; ***mountain-climbing*** ~ záiru ザイル

rose *n* bara (no haná) ばら[薔薇・バラ](の花)

rosy *adj* barairo (no) ばら色(の)

rot *v* kuchimásu 朽ちます, kusarimásu 腐ります

rotate *v* kaiten shimásu 回転します

rotation *n* kaiten 回転

rough *adj* **1.** (*coarse*; *wild*) arai 荒い[粗い], zatsu-… 雑…; (*in texture*) zárazara (shíta …) ざらざら(した…); (*bumpy*) dekoboko (no) でこぼこ・凸凹(の); (*approximate*) ōyoso (no) おおよそ(の); ōmaka na おおまかな; daitai (no) 大体(の) **2.** ***gets*** ~ aremásu 荒れます; ***gets a ~ idea of it*** kentō´ga tsukimásu 見当がつきます; **rough road** *n* dekoboko (shita) michi でこぼこ(した)道; **rough work** *n* arashigoto 荒仕事

round **1.** *n, adj* enkei (no) 円形(の), wa 輪, marui 丸い; ***~ thing*** tamá 玉・珠; ***make*** ~ maruku shimásu 丸くします **2.** *n* (*game, match*) raundo ラウンド, shiai 試合 **3.** ***~s off*** *v* shishagonyū shimásu 四捨五入します **4.** *adv* (*during*) ... no aida-jū ...の間中; marumeru 丸める; **final round** *n* kesshō-sen 決勝戦; **first-round match** *n* (dai) ikkai-sen 第1回戦, yosen 予選; **round-the-world** *adj* sekai isshū (no) 世界一周の; **round trip (ticket)** *n* ōfuku(-kíppu) 往復(切符)

rouse *v* okoshimásu 起こします

route *n* sén 線; rūto ルート; keiro 経路; (*bus, train*) rosen 路線

routine *n* **1.** nikka 日課 **2.** (*computer*) rūchin ルーチン; **routine work** *n* o-kimari no shigoto お決まりの仕事, kima(riki)tta shigoto 決ま(りき)った仕事; [BOOKISH] nichijō gyōmu 日常業務

row **1.** *n* (*line*) rétsu 列, narabi 並び, (*of trees*) namiki 並木; ***... are in a*** ~ ... narande imásu 並んでいます; (*linked*) ***in a*** ~ tsunagatte つながって **2.** *v* (*a boat*) kogimásu こぎ[漕ぎ]ます **3.** *v* (*to quarrel*) kenka shimásu けんかします, kōron shimásu 口論します; **first row of seats** *n* saizenretsu (no seki) 最前列(の席)

royal *adj* ō (no) 王(の); **royal family** *n* **1.** ōzoku 王族, ōshitsu 王室 **2.** (*Japanese*) kōshitsu 皇室

royalty *n* chosakuken ryō 著作権料, (*on a book*) inzei 印税; **royalty basis** *n* inzei hōshiki 印税方式; **royal blend** *n* roiyaru burendo ロイヤルブレンド

rub **1.** masatsu 摩擦; (*difficulty*) konnan 困難 **2.** *v* (*~s it*) kosurimásu こすります, surimásu 擦ります, masatsu shimásu 摩擦します; (*with both hands*) momimásu もみ[揉み]ます **3.** (*it ~s*) suremásu 擦れます

rubber *n* gómu ゴム; (*condom*)

sákku サック

rubbish *n* gomí ごみ・ゴミ; kúzu くず・屑, kuzu-mono くず物・屑物, garakuta がらくた; **rubbish bin** *n* gomí-bako ごみ・ゴミ箱

rucksack *n* ryukkusakku リュックサック

rudder *n* káji かじ・舵

rude *adj* búrei (na) 無礼(な); buénryo (na) 無遠慮(な)

rudiment *n* (*basic*) kiso 基礎

ruffian *n* abare-mono 暴れ者

rug *n* shíki-mono 敷物, jū´tan じゅうたん・絨毯

rugby *n* ragubii ラグビー

ruin **1.** *~s it v* damé ni shimásu だめ[駄目]にします; arashimásu 荒らします; *~ one's health* karada o kowashimásu 体を壊します・からだをこわします **2.** *goes to ~ v* aremásu 荒れます **3.** *ruins n* iseki 遺跡

rule **1.** *n* (*regulation*) kísóku 規則, kítei 規定; rū´ru ルール; (*law*) hōsoku 法則, hō´ 法 **2.** *v* shihai shimásu 支配します

ruler *n* (*to measure with*) jō´gi 定規, (*foot rule*) monosáshí 物差し

rum *n* ramu-shu ラム酒

rumble *v* todorokimásu とどろき[轟き]ます

rumor *n* uwasa うわさ・噂

run **1.** *n* (*dash*) kyōsō 競走; (*exercise*) ranning ランニング **3.** *v* hashirimásu 走ります, (*gallops*) kakemásu 駆けます; *~s a marathon* marason o shimásu マラソンをします **4.** *v* (*connects*) tsū-jimásu 通じます **5.** *v* (*operates a machine*) unten shimásu 運転します **6.** *v* (*manages, operates a business*) keihei shimásu 経営します; **run along** *v* (*side*) soimásu 沿います; **run away** *v* (*flees*) nigemásu 逃げます, ochimásu 落ちます; (*from home*) (uchi o) tobi-dashimásu (家を)飛び出します, iede shimásu 家出します; **run fast** *v* (*timepiece*) susumimásu 進みます; **run into** *v* ① → **collide** ② → **meet** ③ (*comes to the end of a street*) tsuki-atarimásu 突き当たります; **run out** *v* ① (*dashes out*) tobi-dashimásu 跳び[飛び]出します ② *it ~s out* (*stock is exhausted*) kiremásu 切れます, (*gets used up*) tsukimásu 尽きます ③ *~s out of* … o kirashimásu …を切らします, … o tsukaitsukushimásu …を使い尽くします, tsukai-hatashimásu 使い果たします; (*it sells out*) uri-kiremásu 売り切れます; **run over** *v* ① (*a person*) híkimásu ひきます・轢きます; *gets ~ by* … ni híkaremásu …にひかれ[轢かれ]ます ② → **exceed**; **run overtime** *v* jikan ga ō´bā shimásu 時間がオーバーします, jikan o sugimásu 時間を過ぎます

runner *n* rannā ランナー; sōsha 走者; **long-distance runner** *n* chōkyori rannā 長距離ランナー; chōkyori sōsha 長距離走者

rural *adj* inaka (no) いなか・田舎(の)

rush *v* isogimásu 急ぎます; ō-ísogi de shimásu 大急ぎでします; ***with a ~*** (*suddenly*) dotto どっと; ***feels rushed*** aserimásu 焦ります; **rush hour** *n* rasshu-áwā ラッシュアワー

Russia *n* Róshia ロシア; (*Soviet Union*) Sóren ソ連

rust **1.** *n* sabí さび・錆 **2.** *v* (*it ~s*) sabimásu さびます・錆びます

rustic *adj* inaka (no) 田舎・いなか(の), shisso (na) 質素(な); yábo (na) やぼ[野暮](な)

rustle *n* sarasara/kasakasa to iu oto サラサラ/カサカサという音

rusty *n* sabita さびた・錆びた

rut *n* wa-dachi わだち・轍

ruthless *adj* mujihi (na) 無慈悲(な); reikoku (na) 冷酷(な)

Rwanda *n* Ruwanda ルワンダ

Ryukyu (islands) *n* Ryūkyū´ 琉球 (= Okinawa)

S

Sabbath *n* ansoku-bi 安息日

sabotage *n* bōgai kōsaku 妨害工作, hakai kōsaku 破壊工作, sabotāju サボタージュ

saccharin *n* sakkarin サッカリン

sack **1.** *n* (*bag*) fukuró 袋, (*large bag*) ōkina fukuro 大きな袋 **2.** *n* (*pillage*) ryakudatsu 略奪 **3.** *n* (*dismissal from employment*) kaiko 解雇 **4.** (*bed*) beddo ベッド, shindai 寝台 **5.** *v* kaiko shimásu 解雇します **6.** *v* [INFORMAL] kubi ni shimásu 首にします

sacking *n* (*cloth*) asa nuno 麻布

sacrament *n* seireiten 聖礼典

sacred *adj* **1.** (*holy*) shinsei (na) 神聖(な) **2.** (*religious*) shūkyō-teki (na) 宗教的な, shūkyō (no) 宗教の; **sacred building** *n* sei-dō 聖堂

sacrifice **1.** *n* gisei 犠牲, ikenie 生(け)贄・いけにえ; ***makes a ~ (scapegoat) of*** … o gisei ni shimásu …を犠牲にします; **2.** ***is sacrificed*** *v* gisei ni narimásu を犠牲になります

sad *adj* **1.** kanashii 悲しい・かなしい; ***to be ~*** kanashimimásu 悲しみます・かなしみます **2.** (*regrettable*) zannen (na) 残念(な) **3.** (*miserable*) mijime (na) 惨め・みじめ(な) **4.** (*deplorable*) nagekawashii 嘆かわしい・なげかわしい; **look sad** *v* kanashisō ni miemásu 悲しそうに見えます

saddle **1.** *n* (*for horse*) kurá くら・鞍 **2.** *n* (*of bicycle*) sadoru サドル **3.** *v* owasemásu 負わせます

sadness *n* kanashimi 悲しみ・かなしみ

safari *n* safari サファリ, shuryō (ryokō) 狩猟(旅行), tanken (ryokō) 探検(旅行); **safari park** *n* safari pāku サファリパーク

safe 1. *adj* (*harmproof*) anzen (na) 安全(な); (*reliable*) daijō'bu (na) 大丈夫・だいじょうぶ(な), jōbu (na) 丈夫(な); (*steady*) te-gatai 手堅い; (*certain*) táshika (na) 確か(な); kakujitsu (na) 確実(な) 2. *n* (*strongbox*) kínko 金庫 3. ***to be on the ~ side*** nen no tamé (ni) 念のため[為](に); **safe and sound** *adj* buji (ni) 無事(に)

safeguard 1. *n* (*protection*) hogo 保護 2. *n* (*safety device*) anzen sōchi 安全装置 3. *v* hógo shimásu 保護します

safely *adv* (*harmfree, without incident*) búji (ni) 無事(に); (*for sure*) chanto ちゃんと, táshika (ni) 確かに

safety *n* anzen 安全; **safety belt** *n* anzén beruto 安全ベルト; **safety first** *n* anzen daiichi 安全第一; **safety pin** *n* anzénpín 安全ピン

sag *v* tarumimásu たるみます, tawamimásu たわみます

saga *n* 1. sāga サーガ 2. (*tales of adventure*) bōken monogatari 冒険物語 3. *n* (*tale of heroism*) eiyūden 英雄伝, eiyū monogatari 英雄物語

sage *n* 1. (*wise person*) kenja 賢者, kenjin 賢人 2. (*saint*) seija 聖者, seijin 聖人 → **saint**

Sahara *n* Sahara サハラ; ***~ desert*** Sahara sabaku サハラ砂漠

sail 1. *n* ho 帆 2. *v* (*makes a voyage*) kōkai shimásu 航海します

sailor *n* funánori 船乗り, súifu 水夫, sērā セーラー; (*member of the crew*) sen'in 船員; (*navy enlisted person*) súihei 水兵

saint *n* seija 聖者, seijin 聖人

saké *n* (*rice wine*) (o-)sake (お)酒, Nihon-shu 日本酒; ***sweet ~*** (*for cooking*) mirin みりん・ミリン・味醂; ***~ cup*** (o-)chóko (お)ちょこ, (o-)sakazuki (お)杯; ***~ offered to the gods*** o-miki お神酒・おみき

sake; ***for the ~ of …*** no tamé ni … のため[為]に, ***for the ~ of doing …*** suru tamé ni …するため[為]に

salad *n* sárada サラダ; **fruit salad** *n* furūtsu sarada フルーツサラダ; **salad dressing** *n* sarada (yō) doresshingu サラダ(用)ドレッシング

salaried man *n* sararii man サラリーマン, kaisha-in 会社員, kyūryō-tori 給料取り・給料とり

salary *n* hōkyū 俸給, (o-)kyū'ryō (お)給料, sárarii サラリー; (*monthly*) gekkyū 月給

sale *n* hanbai 販売; hatsubai 発売; (*special*) uridashi 売り出し, (bāgen)seru (バーゲン)セール; ***~ goods/item***, (*something*) ***for ~*** uri-mono 売り物

sales agency *n* hanbai-moto 販売元, hanbai dairi-ten 販売代理店

sales assistant *n* ten'in 店員, uriko 売り子, hanbai-in 販売員

saliva *n* tsúba つば・ツバ・唾, tsubakí つばき・ツバキ・唾, [BOOKISH] daeki 唾液・だえき

salmon *n* sáke さけ・サケ・鮭, sāmon サーモン, sháke シャケ・鮭

salon *n* saron サロン

saloon *n* **1.** (*great hall*) (ō-)hiroma (大)広間 **2.** (*bar*) sakaba 酒場

salt *n* (o-)shío (お)塩・(お)しお; ***table ~*** shokúen 食塩

salty *adj* shio-karái 塩辛い・塩からい, shoppái しょっぱい・塩っぱい

salute 1. *n* keirei 敬礼 **2.** *v* keirei shimásu̲ 敬礼します

salvage *n* hi̲ki-age 引き揚げ

salvation *n* kyūsai 救済; **Salvation Army** *n* kyūsei gun 救世軍

salve *n* **1.** (*ointment*) nankō 軟膏 **2.** (*comfort*) nagusame 慰め・なぐさめ

same 1. *pron* onaji … 同じ…・おなじ…, [BOOKISH] dō´(-) … 同 … **2.** *adj/adv* onaji yō´ (na/ni) 同じ様・おなじよう(な/に); ***one and the ~*** hi̲tótsu 一つ・ひとつ; ***~ period*** dō´ki 同期

sample 1. *n* mihon 見本, sanpuru サンプル **2.** *n* (*free ~*) shikyō-hin 試供品 **3.** *v* (*tries doing*) (shi)-te mimásu̲ (し)てみます

samurai *n* (*Japanese warrior*) samurai 侍・サムライ, búshi 武士・ぶし

sanatorium *n* sanatoriumu サナトリウム; hoyōchi 保養地; ryōyō-jo 療養所

sanctify *v* shinseika shimásu̲ 神聖化します

sanction *n* [BOOKISH] seisai (sochi) 制裁(措置)

sanctuary *n* **1.** sei-iki 聖域 **2.** (*asylum*) hinanjo 避難所 **3.** (*church*) kyōkai 教会

sand *n* suna 砂・すな; ***~ dune*** sakyū 砂丘・さきゅう

sandal *n* sandaru サンダル; (*Japanese traditional style*) ***straw ~s*** zōri 草履

sandwich *n* sandoítchi サンドイッチ; …-sándo …サンド

sandy *adj* suna no 砂の, suna no yō (na) 砂のよう(な)

sane *adj* shōki (no) 正気(の)

San Francisco *n* Sanfuranshísu̲ko サンフランシスコ

sanguine 1. *adj* kaikatsu (na) 快活(な), (*happy-go-lucky*) rakuten-teki (na) 楽天的(な) **2.** (*optimistic*) rakkan-teki (na) 楽観的(な)

sanitary *adj* eisei-teki (na) 衛生的(な), eisei (no) 衛生(の); ***~ napkin*** (seiri-yō) nápu̲kín (生理用)ナプキン

sanitation *n* eisei 衛生, kōshū eisei 公衆衛生

sanity *n* shōki 正気, funbetsu 分別

Santa Claus *n* Santa (kurōsu) サンタ(クロース)

sap *v* yowarasemásu̲ 弱らせます

sapling *n* (*tree*) naegi 苗木

sapphire *n* safaia サファイア

sarcastic *adj* hiniku (na) 皮肉(な), iyami (na) 嫌味・いやみ(な), iyamippoi 嫌味っぽい・いやみっぽい

sardine *n* iwashi いわし・イワシ・鰯; shirasu しらす・シラス・白子
sash *n* (*girdle*) óbi 帯・おび; (*window-sash*) mado-waku 窓枠, sásshi サッシ, sásshu サッシュ
Satan *n* satan サタン, ákuma 悪魔・アクマ
satchel *n* kaban かばん・鞄
sate **1.** *v* → **satiate** **2.** *n* (*skewered food*) satē サテー
satellite *n* eisei 衛星; sateraito サテライト; **satellite transmission** *n* eisei chūkei 衛星中継
satiate *v* (*sate*) tannō sasemásu̱ 堪能させます
satin *n* shúsu しゅす・シュス・繻子, sáten サテン
satire *n* fūshi 風刺
satisfaction *n* manzoku 満足
satisfactory *adj* yoroshii よろしい・宜しい, mánzoku (na) 満足(な), mánzoku dekiru 満足できる, nattoku (no) iku 納得(の)いく
satisfy *v* mánzoku sasemásu̱ 満足させます; (*fulfills*) mitashimásu̱ 満たします
saturate *v* (*soaks*) zubunure ni sasemásu̱ ずぶ濡れにさせます
saturation *n* [BOOKISH] hōwa 飽和; **saturation point** *n* hōwa ten 飽和点
Saturday *n* Doyō´bi 土曜日
sauce *n* sō´su ソース; (*cooking*) taré たれ・タレ; ***soy*** **~** (o-)shōyu (お)しょうゆ[(お)醤油]
saucepan *n* nabe 鍋・ナベ
saucer *n* (o-)kózara (お)小皿, (o-)sara (お)皿; (*for cup*) uké-zara 受け皿; **flying saucer** *n* sora tobu enban 空飛ぶ円盤
Saudi Arabia *n* Saujiarabia サウジアラビア
sauna *n* sauna サウナ
sausage *n* sō´sē´ji ソーセージ
sauté **1.** *n* sotē ソテー **2.** *v* itamemásu̱ 炒めます・いためます
savage **1.** *adj* yaban (na) 野蛮(な) **2.** ***a savage*** *n* yaban-jín 野蛮人
savanna *n* sabanna サバンナ
save *v* **1.** (*saves up, hoards*) takuwaemásu̱ 蓄えます, (*deposits money*) chokin shimásu̱ 貯金します; (*accumulates*) tamemásu̱ ため[溜め]ます **2.** (*curtails, omits*) habukimásu̱ 省きます; (*economizes on*) setsuyaku shimásu̱ 節約します, ken'yaku shimásu̱ 倹約します **3.** → **rescue**
savings *n* takuwae 蓄え・たくわえ; ***installment*** **~** tsumitate-kin 積立金; **savings account** *n* yokin-kō´za 預金口座, tsumitate-chókin 積立貯金; **savings box** *n* chokin-bako 貯金箱
savior *n* **1.** (*one who saves/rescues*) kyūsai-sha 救済者 **2.** (*messiah*) kyūsei-shu 救世主
savor *v* (*tastes*) ajiwaimásu 味わいます; ajiwai-tanoshimimásu 味わい楽しみます
saw **1.** *n* (*tool*) nokogírí のこぎり・鋸 **2.** *v* (*~s it*) nokogírí de hi̱kimásu̱ のこぎり[鋸]で引きます; **sawmill** *n* seizai kōjō 製材工場, seizaisho 製材所

saw *v* (*did see*) mimáshi̲ta 見ました; (*met a person*) … ni aimáshi̲ta …に会いました

saxophone *n* sakkusu サックス; sakusuhōn サクスホーン

say *v* (*that* …) (… to) iimásu̲ (…と)言います; **say it another way** *v* ii-kaemásu̲ 言い換えます・言いかえます; **Say there!** *interj* Móshi-moshi! もしもし!

saying *n* kotowaza ことわざ・諺; kakugen 格言

scab *n* kasabuta かさぶた

scaffold *n* **1.** (*for the execution*) shokei dai 処刑台; shikei dai 死刑台; kōshu dai 絞首台 **2.** (*framework*) ashi ba 足場

scaffold *n* kasabuta かさぶた

scald **1.** *n* (*mark on the skin*) yakedo やけど・火傷 **2.** *v* (*~s*) yakimásu̲ 焼きます, (*gets scalded*) yakemásu̲ 焼けます

scale *n* **1.** (*measurement tool*) sukēru スケール **2.** (*fish*) uroko うろこ・ウロコ・鱗; **scale down** *v* shukushō shimásu̲ 縮小します; **scale up** *v* kakudai shimásu̲ 拡大します

scales *n* (*weighing*) hakarí 秤・はかり

scallop(s) *n* hotaté-gai ほたて[帆立・ホタテ]貝; (*pin/razor/fan shell*) taira-gi たいらぎ

scalp *n* atama no kawa 頭の皮

scalpel *n* (geka-yō) mesu (外科用)メス

scamper *v* awatete hashirimásu̲ 慌てて走ります, isoide hashirimásu̲ 急いで走ります

scan *v* sukyan shimásu̲ スキャンします

scandal *n* su̲kyándaru スキャンダル, [BOOKISH] fu̲shōji 不祥事; (*disgrace*) ojoku 汚辱

Scandinavia *n* Sukanjinabia スカンジナビア

scanner *n* sukyanā スキャナー

scant, scanty *adj* toboshii 乏しい・とぼしい

scapegoat *n* sukēpugōto スケープゴート; migawari 身代わり → **sacrifice**

scar *n* kizu-ato 傷跡

scarce *adj* su̲kunái 少ない・すくない, toboshii 乏しい・とぼしい

scarcity *n* (*shortage*) fu̲soku 不足; (… ga) su̲kunái kotó (…が)少ない事・すくないこと

scare *v* odorokashimásu̲ 驚かします・おどろかします; bikkuri sasemásu̲ びっくりさせます・吃驚させます; harahara sasemásu はらはらさせます

scarf *n* su̲kā´fu スカーフ

scarlet *n, adj* su̲kāretto (no) スカーレット(の), hiiro (no) 緋色(の)

scatter *v* chira(ka)shimásu̲ 散ら(か)します; barabara ni narimásu ばらばらになります

scatterbrain *n* awate-mono 慌て者・あわてもの

scenario *n* shinario シナリオ; kyakuhon 脚本; **scenario writer** *n* shinario raitā シナリオライター; kyakuhon-ka 脚本家

scene *n* (*story, play*) shíin シーン; dán 段; bamen 場面; (*sight*) arisama 有り様・ありさま

scenery *n* késhiki 景色, fū'kei 風景, (*view*) nagamé 眺め・ながめ

scent *n* kaori 香り・かおり, hōkō 芳香

schedule 1. *n* (*plan*) yotei 予定, sukejūru スケジュール **2.** *n* (*timetable*) yotei-hyō 予定表, jikan-hyō 時間表 **3.** *n* (*daily routine*) nittei 日程 **4.** *n* (*train*) daiya ダイヤ; (*train timetable*) jikoku-hyō 時刻表; (*list*) hyō 表 **5.** *v* yotei shimásu̲ 予定します, sukejūru o tatemásu̲ スケジュールを立てます, keikaku shimásu̲ 計画します

scheme 1. *n* (*plan*) keikaku 計画; (*device*) kufū 工夫; (*plot, trick*) keiryaku 計略, hakarigoto はかりごと・謀 **2.** *v* (*plot, plan*) ... no keikaku o tatemásu̲ ...の計画を立てます

scholar *n* gaku̲sha 学者

scholarship *n* shōgaku̲-kin 奨学金; sukarashippu スカラシップ

school *n* (*educational establishment*) gakkō 学校; sukūru スクール; ***primary*** ~ shōgákkō 小学校, ***middle*** (*junior high*) ~ chū-gákkō 中学校; ***high*** ~ kōtō-gákkō 高等学校, kōkō 高校; ***tutoring/cram*** ~ júku 塾; ***in*** ~ zaigaku(-chū) 在学(中); **coed school** *n* kyōgaku 共学; **driving school** *n* (jidōsha) kyōshūjo (自動車)教習所; (jidōsha) kyōshū gakkō (自動車)教習学校; **school activity** *n* kōnai katsudō 校内活動; **school age** *n* gakurei (ki) 学齢(期); shū-gaku nenrei 就学年齢; **school hours** *n* jugyō-jíkan 授業時間; **school textbook** *n* (gakkō no) kyōkasho (学校の)教科書; **school year** *n* gakunen 学年

science *n* kágaku 科学, sáiensu サイエンス, (*study*) gaku 学, ríka 理科

science fiction *n* esu-efu SF (エス・エフ), saiensu fikushon サイエンス・フィクション

scientist *n* kagakú̲sha 科学者, saientisuto サイエンティスト

scissors *n* hasamí はさみ・鋏

scold *v* shi̲karimásu̲ しかり[叱り]ます

scolding *n* kogoto (お)こごと (o-)kógoto (お)小言, o-shi̲kari おしかり[叱り]; (*abuse*) warú-ku̲chi/-guchi 悪口

scoop 1. *n* sukoppu スコップ; [BOOKISH] hi̲shaku ひしゃく・柄杓, (*one scoopful*) hi̲tó-mori 一盛り・ひともり **2.** *v* (*~s it up*) kumimásu̲ くみ[汲み]ます, su̲kuimásu̲ すくいます・掬います

scooter *n* sukūtā スクーター

scope *n* hán'i 範囲

scorch *v* **1.** (*~es it*) kogashimásu̲ 焦がします **2.** (*it gets scorched*) kogemásu̲ 焦げます

score 1. *n* sukoa スコア, (*game*)

toku<u>ten</u> 得点; (~ *points*) tensū 点数; (*musical* ~) gakufu 楽譜 **2.** *v* (*makes a* ~) ten o torimás<u>u</u> 点を取ります・点をとります

scotch *n* (*whisky*) sukotchi スコッチ

scotch tape *n* serohan tēpu セロハンテープ, serotēpu セロテープ

Scotland *n* sukottorando スコットランド

scoundrel *n* akutō 悪党

scramble *v* **1.** (*mixes*) kakimaze-más<u>u</u> かき混ぜます・掻き混ぜます **2.** (*climbs*) hainoborimás<u>u</u> 這い登ります・はいのぼります **3.** (*fights*) ubaiaimás<u>u</u> 奪い合います・奪いあいます; **scrambled eggs** *n* iri-támago いり卵・炒り卵

scrap 1. *n* kúzu くず・屑, danpen 断片, kuzu-mono くず物・屑物; (*refuse*) sukurappu スクラップ **2.** *v* sukurappu ni shimás<u>u</u> スクラップにします; **scrapbook** *n* sukurappu bukku スクラップブック

scrape *v* kosurimás<u>u</u> こすります・擦ります

scratch 1. *v* (*scratches it*) (hi<u>k</u>)ka-kimás<u>u</u> (ひっ)かきます **2.** *n* (*a* ~) hikkaki-kizu 引っかき傷・ひっかき傷

scrawl 1. *n* hashiri-gaki 走り書き, naguri-gaki 殴り書き・なぐり書き **2.** *v* hashirigaki shimás<u>u</u> 走り書きします, nagurigaki shimás<u>u</u> 殴り書きします・なぐり書きします

scrawny *adj* yase(koke)teiru 痩せ(こけ)ている・やせ(こけ)ている, yaseta 痩せた・やせた

scream 1. *v* himei o agemás<u>u</u> 悲鳴を上げます・悲鳴をあげます, sakebimás<u>u</u> 叫びます・さけびます **2.** *n* himei 悲鳴・ひめい

screen 1. *n* (*folding*) byōbu びょうぶ・屏風 **2.** *n* (*TV, computer*) gamen 画面 **3.** *n* (*movie*) s<u>u</u>kurīn スクリーン **4.** *v* (*examines*) kensa shimás<u>u</u> 検査します **5.** *v* (*movie*) ... o jōē shimás<u>u</u> ...を上映します

screenshot *n* (*of webpage, etc.*) sukurīn-shotto スクリーン・ショット

screw 1. *n* néji ねじ・ネジ **2.** *v* (*tightens*) (kataku) shimemás<u>u</u> (堅く)締めます; **screw up** *v* dai-nashi ni shimás<u>u</u> 台無しにします, [INFORMAL] mechamecha ni shimás<u>u</u> めちゃめちゃにします

screwdriver *n* neji-máwashi ねじ回し・ネジまわし

scribble *n* hashirigaki 走り書き, nagurigaki 殴り書き

script *n* kyakuhon 脚本, daihon 台本

scroll *n* maki-mono 巻(き)物・まきもの; (*hanging*) kaké-mono 掛け物, kakéjiku 掛軸, kakéji 掛け字

scuba *n* sukyūba スキューバ; **scuba diving** *n* sukyūba daibingu スキューバダイビング

sculptor *n* chōkoku-ka 彫刻家

scuffle *n* tsukamiai 掴み合い・つかみあい, tokkumiai 取っ組み合い・とっくみあい

scurry *v* (*goes in haste*) awatete ikimásu 慌てて行きます・あわてていきます, (*goes quickly*) isoide ikimásu 急いで行きます・いそいでいきます

sea *n* úmi 海・うみ, ...-kai ...海; ***Inland ~*** Seto-náikai 瀬戸内海, ***~ of Japan*** Nihón-kai 日本海; **sea bass** *n* suzuki すずき・スズキ・鱸; **sea bathing** *n* kaisuiyoku 海水浴; **seafood** *n* gyokairui 魚介類・魚貝類; **sea level** *n* kaibatsu 海抜; **seamail** *n* funabin 船便; **seaman** *n* súifu 水夫; (*navy*) súihei 水兵; **seashore** *n* kaigan 海岸; **seasickness** *n* funayoi 船酔い; **seaweed-gelatin strips** *n* tokoroten ところてん・トコロテン

seal 1. *n* (*for stamping one's name*) hán(kó) はん(こ)・判(子), ín 印 **2.** *n* (*animal*) azárashi あざらし・アザラシ・海豹 ottosei オットセイ **3.** *v* (*~s a letter*) (tegami no) fū´o shimásu (手紙の)封をします, mippū shimásu 密封します, fusagimásu ふさぎます

seam *n* nui-mé 縫い目・ぬいめ, tsugi-me 接ぎ目・つぎめ

seamy *adj* **1.** uramen (no) 裏面(の) **2.** (*unpleasant*) fukai (na) 不快(な)

sear *n* yakekoge 焼け焦げ

search 1. *n* sōsaku 捜索 **2.** *n* (*Internet*) kensaku 検索 **3.** *v* ***~es for*** (*seeks*) ... o sagashinásu ...を探し[捜し]ます・...をさがします; **searching for one's lost child** *n* maigo-sagashi 迷子捜し; **search party** *n* sōsaku-tai 捜索隊

search engine *n* kensaku enjin 検索エンジン

searchlight *n* sāchi raito サーチライト, [BOOKISH] tanshōtō 探照灯

season 1. *n* kisétsu 季節; shíizun シーズン; jíki 時季; jísetsu 時節 **2.** *v* (*flavors it*) ... ni aji o tsukemásu ... ...に味を付けます; **four seasons** *n* shiki 四季; **off-season** *n* shiizun ofu シーズンオフ; **season ticket** *n* teikí-ken 定期券

seasoning *n* (*food*) chō´mi 調味, aji 味・あじ; kagen 加減・かげん

seat *n* (o-)séki (お)席, zaseki 座席, shiito シート, koshi-káké 腰掛け; (*bottom, butt*) (o-)shiri (お)尻; (*taking a seat*) chakuseki 着席

secluded *adj* hotozato-hanareta 人里離れた, kakurisareta 隔離された

seclusion *n* kakuri 隔離

second 1. *adj* ni-banmé (no) 二番目(の), futatsu-mé (no) 二つ目の; ***the ~ day*** futsuka-mé 二日目, (*of the month*) futsuka 二日 **2.** *n* (*of a minute*) -byō 秒; ***one ~*** ichí-byō 一秒; **second floor** *n* ni-kai 二階; **second generation** *n* ní-sei 二世; **second time** *n* nido-mé 二度目, nikai-mé 二回目

secondhand 1. *adj* chūko/chūburu (no) 中古(の), furúi 古い **2.** *n* (*goods*) chūko-hin 中古品; **secondhand shop/store** *n* risaikuru shoppu リサイクル・ショップ

secrecy *n* himitsu 秘密, [BOOKISH] kimitsu 機密; **secrecy agreement** *n* shuhi gimu keiyaku 守秘義務契約

secret **1.** *n* himitsu 秘密, shiiku-retto シークレット **2.** ***n the secret*** (*trick to it*) táne 種 **3.** *adj* (*confidential*) naisho (no) 内緒(の); **secret agent** *n* himitsu kōsaku-in 秘密工作員

secretariat *n* jimu-kyoku 事務局

secretary *n* shóki 書記; (*private*) hishó 秘書; **secretary of foreign affairs** *n* gaimu chōkan 外務長官

secretion *n* bunpi 分泌

sect *n* shūha 宗派, ha 派, habatsu 派閥

section *n* bú 部; ká 課; sekushon セクション, …-ka …課; (*area*) chíkú 地区

sector *n* (*area*) chíkú 地区; sekutā セクター

secure *adj* **1.** ***is*** ~ chanto shite imásu ちゃんとしています **2.** ***feels*** ~ anshin shimásu 安心します **3.** → **get**

security *n* (*stock, bond*) shōken 証券; (*secure feeling*) anshin 安心

sedan *n* sedan セダン

sedative *n* chinsei-zai 鎮静剤; chintsū-zai 鎮痛剤

sedentary *adj* suwarigachi (no/na) 座りがち(の/な)

sediment *n* kásu かす・滓; ori おり・澱; chinden-butsu 沈殿物

sedition *n* sendō 扇動・せんどう

seduce *v* tarashi-komimásu たらし込みます, yūwaku shimásu 誘惑します

seduction *n* yūwaku 誘惑

see *v* **1.** mimásu 見ます **2.** (*meets a person*) … ni aimásu …に会います **3.** (*understands*) wakarimásu 分かります; ***I see!*** Naruhodo! なるほど **4.** ***~s one off*** (mi-)okurimásu (見)送ります

seed *n* táne 種・タネ

seedy *adj* **1.** tane ga ōi 種が多い **2.** misuborashiii みすぼらしい

seek *v* busshoku shimásu 物色します→ **search (for)**

seem *v* (*like*) … to miemásu … と見えます, … (no) yō´desu … (の)よう[様]です, … rashíi desu …らしいです

seemingly *adv* (*outwardly*) mikake wa 見かけは・見掛けは, mi-kake-jō 見かけ上・見掛け上

seep *v* shintō shimásu 浸透します・しんとうします, shimidemásu 染み出ます・しみでます, moremásu 漏れます・もれます

seesaw *n* shiisō シーソー

segment *n* bubun 部分; segumento セグメント

segregate *v* bunri shimásu 分離します・ぶんりします, hanashi-masu 離します

seize *v* tsukamimásu つかみます・掴みます, toraemásu 捕らえます, tsukamaemásu 捕まえ[つかまえ]ます; (*plunders*) ubaimásu 奪います・うばいます; (*illegally takes over*) nottorimásu 乗っ取ります・乗っとります

seizure *n* **1.** (*illegal takeover*) nottorijíken 乗っ取り事件・乗っとり事件 **2.** (*medical*) hossa 発作
seldom *adv* métta ni めった[滅多]に + [NEGATIVE], hotóndo 殆ど・ほとんど + [NEGATIVE]; (*infrequently*) tama ni たまに
select → **choose; selection** → **choice**
selection *n* sentaku 選択; sereku-shon セレクション
self *n* jibun 自分; ji-... 自...; onore 己; jíko 自己; hon-nin 本人; self-assertion *n* jiko shuchō 自己主張; self-centered *adj* jiko chū-shin-teki (na) 自己中心的(な); self-confidence *n* jishin 自信; self-conscious; *feels* ~ agarimásu̲ 上がり[あがり]ます; self-defense *n* jiei 自衛, jiko bōei 自己防衛; self-discipline *n* jiko tanren 自己鍛錬; self-employed *adj* jiei (*no*) 自営(の), jieigyō (*no*) 自営業(の); self-esteem *n* jisonshin 自尊心; self-pity *n* [BOOKISH] jiko renbin 自己憐憫; self-respect *n* [BOOKISH] jison-shin 自尊心; self-satisfaction *n* jiko manzoku 自己満足
selfish *adj* katte (na) 勝手(な), jibun-kátte/-gátte (na) 自分勝手(な), waga-mámá (na) わがまま・我が侭(な)
sell *v* **1.** *~s it* urimásu̲ 売ります **2.** *it ~s* (*well*) (yóku) uremásu̲ (良く)売れます; hakemásu̲ はけます; sell out *v* uri-kiremásu̲ 売り切れます
selfie *n* jidoribō 自撮り棒
seller *n* uri-te 売り手; uri-nushi 売り主; (*dealer*) hanbai-nin 販売人
semen *n* sei eki 精液
semester *n* gakki 学期; semester final examination *n* kimatsu shiken 期末試験
semicircle *n* hanshū 半周
semicolon *n* semikoron セミコロン
semifinal *n* jun-kesshō 準決勝
seminar *n* zémi ゼミ, zeminā́ru ゼミナール, seminā セミナー, kōshūkai 講習会
seminary *n* shingakkō 神学校
senator *n* jōin giin 上院議員
send *v* okurimásu̲ 送ります, yari-másu̲ やります, yosemásu̲ 寄せます; (*a person*) ikasemásu̲ 行かせます
sender *n* **1.** (*mail, etc.*) hassōnin 発送人, okurinushi 送り主 **2.** (*mail, e-mail, etc.*) sashidashinin 差出人, sōshin-sha 送信者
send-off *n* (*farewell*) sōbetsu 送別, ~ ***party*** sōbétsú-kai 送別会
senior *adj* (*older*) toshi-ue (no) 年上(の); (*colleague, fellow student*) senpai 先輩; (*4th-year student*) yonén-sei 四年生; *senior citizen* (o-)toshiyori (お)年寄り, rōjin 老人, kōrei-sha 高齢者, kōrei no hito 高齢の人
sensation *n* (*feeling*) kimochi 気持ち・気持, kimí 気味; (*sense*) kankaku 感覚; (*excitement*) sensḗshon センセーション
sense *n* sénsu センス; ***common ~***

jōshi̲ki 常識; ~ *of honor* taimen 体面, [BOOKISH] renchí-shin 廉恥心; sense of humor *n* yūmoa no sensu ユーモアのセンス
senses; *come to one's ~* (*recovers consciousness*) ki ga tsu̲kimásu̲ 気が付きます, me ga samemásu̲ 目が覚めます
sensibility *n* kankaku 感覚
sensible *adj* gōri-teki (na) 合理的(な), atarimae (no) 当り前(の)
sensitive *adj* **1.** binkan (na) 敏感(な) **2.** (*easily pained*) kizutsukiyasui 傷つきやすい, sensai (na) 繊細(な), derikēto (na) デリケート(な) **3.** (*easily annoyed*) shinkei kabin (no) 神経過敏(の) **4.** (*requiring caution*) chūi ga hitsuyō na 注意が必要な, chūi o haraubeki 注意を払うべき
sensual *adj* kannō-teki (na) 官能的(な)
sentence *n* **1.** (*written*) bún(shō) 文(章); (*spoken*) kotó 事・こと, kotoba 言葉・ことば **2.** (*judicial verdict*) hanketsu 判決
sentiment *n* kanshō 感傷
sentimental *adj* senchiméntaru (na) センチメンタル(な); o-senchi (na) おせんち(な); kanshōteki na 感傷的(な)
sentry *n* mihari 見張り, hoshō 歩哨
Seoul *n* Sóuru ソウル
separate **1.** *adj* (*different*) betsu (no) 別(の); barabara (ni) ばらばら(に) **2.** *v* (*~s them*) wakemásu̲ 分けます; (*gets them apart*) hedatemásu̲ 隔てます・へだてます **3.** *v* (*they ~*) wakaremásu̲ 分かれ[別れ]ます; (*gets distant*) hanaremásu̲ 離れます **4.** *v ~s it* (*from*) … o hanashimásu̲ …を離します
separation *n* bun'ri 分離; bekkyo 別居
September *n* Ku-gatsú 九月・9月
septic *adj* (*medical*) haiketsu-sei (no) 敗血性(の)
sequel *n* tsuzuki 続き・つづき, renzoku 連続
sequence *n* shiikuensu シークエンス, renzoku 連続, (*order*) júnjo 順序, zéngo 前後; in sequence *adv* junban (ni) 順番(に)
serenade *n* serenādo セレナード, sayo-kyoku 小夜曲
serene *adj* odayaka (na) 穏やか(な)・おだやか(な), shizuka (na) 静か・しずか(な)
sergeant *n* **1.** (*army*) gúnsō 軍曹 **2.** (*police*) junsa buchō 巡査部長
serial *n, adj* rensai (no) 連載(の), renzoku (no) 連続の; serial number *n* shiriaru nanbā シリアルナンバー; tōshi bangō 通し番号
series *n* (hi̲tó-)tsuzuki (ひと)続き; renzoku 連続; shiriizu シリーズ; TV series *n* renzoku terebi bangumi 連続テレビ番組
serious *adj* (*character*) majime (na) まじめ[真面目](な); (*in earnest*) honki (no) 本気(の); (*heavy, grave*) omoi 重い, jūdai

(na) 重大(な), shinkoku (na) 深刻(な); taihen (na) 大変(な), tái-shita ... 大した...・たいした...
sermon *n* sekkyō 説教
serpent *n* (*snake*) hebi 蛇・ヘビ
serum *n* kessei 血清
servant *n* meshi-tsukai 召し使い; shiyō-nin 使用人; yōmú-in 用務員, kózukai 小使い
serve **1.** *n* (*games*) sābu サーブ **2.** *v* (*a meal*) dashimásu 出します; *~ the rice wine, pour the saké* (o-)shaku o shimásu (お)酌をします; **serve a purpose** *v* yakúni tachi-másu 役に立ちます, yaku-dachi-másu 役立ちます
server *n* sābā サーバー
service *n* **1.** (*in restaurant, etc.*) sā´bisu サービス **2.** (*maintenance and repair*) afutāsābisu アフターサービス **3.** (*utility*) yakú 役 **4.** (*armed forces*) gúntai 軍隊 **5.** (*duty, work*) kínmu 勤務 **6.** (*games*) sābu サーブ; **service area** *n* sā´bisu eria サービスエリア; **service charge** *n* tesū´-ryō 手数料, sābisu-ryō サービス料
... serving(s) ... -nínmae ...人前
serviette *n* (shokutaku yō) napukin (食卓用)ナプキン
servile *adj* iyashii いやしい・卑しい, hikutsu (na) 卑屈(な), dorei no yō (na) 奴隷のよう(な)
sesame *n* goma ごま・ゴマ・胡麻
session *n* **1.** sesshon セッション **2.** (*court sitting*) kaitei 開廷 **3.** (*assembly*) kai 会, kaigō 会合 **4.** (*meeting*) kaigi 会議
set **1.** *n* (*collection*) kumí 組, hitó-kumi 一組; (*array*) soroi 揃い・そろい; ***makes (up) a ~*** soroimásu 揃い[そろい]ます, ***makes into a ~*** soroemásu 揃え[そろえ]ます **2.** *n* (*hair*) sétto セット **3.** *v ~s it* (*puts it there*) okimásu 置きます **4.** → **sit** → **settle** → **decide**; **set aside** *v* atemásu 当てます・あてます; **set off/out** *v* (*departs*) dekakemásu 出かけます; **set up** *v* tatemásu 立てます; (*provides*) mōkemásu 設けます; (*assembles*) kumi-tatemásu 組み立てます
settle *v* (*decides it*) kimemásu 決めます, (*fixes*) sadamemásu 定めます; (*completes*) matomemásu まとめます; (*disposes of*) shíma-tsu shimásu 始末します; (*solves, resolves*) kaiketsu shimásu 解決します; (*gets relaxed/calm*) ochitsukimásu 落ち着きます; ***~ down/in*** osamarimásu 収[治・納]まります・おさまります
settlement *n* kimari 決まり; (*solution*) kaiketsu 解決
setup *n* **1.** (*organization*) soshiki 組織 **2.** (*arrangement*) settoappu セットアップ, junbi 準備, settei 設定
seven *n* nána 七・7, shichí 七・7, nanátsu 七つ・7つ; sébun セブン
seventeen *n* jū-nána 十七・17, jūshichí 十七・17
seventh *adj* nana-banmé (no) 七

番目(の), nana-tsu-mé (no) 七つ目(の); ***the ~ day*** nanoka-mé 七日目・7日目, (*of the month*) nanoka 七日・7日; ***~ floor*** nana-kai 七階

several *adj* f<u>u</u>tatsú-mi(t)tsu (no) 二つ三つ(の), ní-san (no) 二三(の), jakkan (no) 若干(の); ík<u>u</u>tsu ka (no) いくつか(の); sū-... 数... (***~ days*** sū-jitsu 数日, ***~ people*** sū-nin 数人)

severe *adj* kibishíi 厳しい・きびしい; kitsui きつい; (*terrible*) hidói ひどい・酷い; sibia シビア

sew *v* nuimás<u>u</u> 縫います

sewage *n* gesui 下水, osui 汚水; ***~ treatment plant*** gesui shori-jō 下水処理場

sewer *n* gesui-kan 下水管

sewing *n* saihō 裁縫

sex *n* sei 性, sékk<u>u</u>su セックス; (*the erotic*) iró 色, éro エロ

sexual *adj* sei-teki (na) 性的(な); ***make (a) ~ advance(s)*** kudoki-masu 口説きます

sexual harassment *n* sekuhara セクハラ, sekusharu harasumento セクシャル・ハラスメント

shabby *adj* **1.** (*worn*) tsukaifuru-shita 使い古した **2.** (*wearing worn clothes*) boro (boro no fuku) o kita ぼろ(ぼろの服)を着た, boro (boro no fuku) o kiteiru ぼろ(ぼろの服)を着ている, (minari no) misuborashii 身なりのみすぼらしい **3.** (*unworthy*), (o-)somatsu (na) (お)粗末(な)

shackle **1.** *n* (*fetter*) sokubaku 束縛, ashi kase 足枷・足かせ, kōsoku dōgu 拘束道具 **2.** *v* soku-baku shimás<u>u</u> 束縛します, kōsoku shimás<u>u</u> 拘束します, ashikase o kakemás<u>u</u> 足枷・足かせをかけます

shade *n* káge 陰・かげ; (*of trees*) kí no káge 木の陰, kokage 木陰・こかげ; ***window ~*** (mádo no) hiyoke (窓の)日よけ

shadow *n* káge 影・かげ, shadō シャドー, shadou シャドウ, (*from sunlight*) hi-kage 日影; (*of a person*) káge-bō´shi 影法師

shady *adj* (*fishy*) ayashii 怪しい, ikagawashíi いかがわしい

shaft *n* shafuto シャフト, e 柄

shaggy **1.** *adj* mojamoja (no) もじゃもじゃ(の), kemukujara (no) 毛むくじゃら(の) **2.** *n* (*hairstyle*) shagii シャギー

shake **1.** *v* (*~s it*) furimás<u>u</u> 振ります・ふります; yusaburimasu 揺さぶります; ***~ hands*** ák<u>u</u>shu shi-más<u>u</u> 握手します; ***~ out*** harai-más<u>u</u> 払います **2.** *v* (*it ~s*) furue-más<u>u</u> 震えます, (*sways*) yuremás<u>u</u> 揺れます・ゆれます **3.** *n* (*milk-shake*) (miruku-)sē´ki (ミルク)セーキ; sheiku シェイク

shall **1.** ***Shall I/we do it?*** Shimashō´ ka. しましょうか. **2.** → **will**

shallow *adj* asai 浅い・あさい

sham *adj* mise-kake (no) 見せかけ・みせかけ(の)

shamble *n* yoromeita aruki よろめ

いた歩き

shame *n* hazukashíi (kotó) 恥ずかしい・はずかしい(事・こと), hají 恥・はじ; (*scandal*) ojoku 汚辱

shampoo **1.** *n* shánpū シャンプー **2.** *v* kami o araimásu 髪を洗います

Shanghai *n* Shánhái シャンハイ・上海

shape *n* katachi 形, katá 型; (*figure*) súgata 姿, kakkō かっこう・格好・恰好; (*condition*) guai 具合

share **1.** *n* (*portion*) toribún 取り分, wake-mae 分け前・わけまえ; (*allotment*) buntan 分担 **2.** *v* → **divide** → **Dutch treat** **3.** *v* *~s in, pays/does one's ~* buntan shimásu 分担します

shark *n* same さめ・サメ・鮫, fuka ふか・フカ・鱶, shāku シャーク

sharp *adj* surudói 鋭い・するどい, shāpu (na) シャープ(な); (*clever*) rikō (na) 利口(な); ***gets ~*** (*pointed*) togarimásu 尖り[とがり]ます

sharpen *v* (*pencil*) kezurimásu 削ります, togarashimásu 尖らし[とがらし]ます; (*blade*) togimásu 研ぎます

shave *v* hige o sorimásu ひげを剃ります

shaver *n* (*electric*) denki-kámisori 電気かみそり

shawl *n* shōru ショール

she *pron* káno-jo 彼女, anó-hito あの人, anó-ko あの子 (*but use name, title, or role; often omitted*)

sheaf *n* taba 束・たば

shear *n* ōbasami 大鋏・大ばさみ・オオバサミ

shed *n* naya 納屋; (*storehouse*) mono-ókí 物置; (*hut*) koya 小屋

sheep *n* hitsuji 羊・ヒツジ

sheet *n* (*of paper, glass, etc.*) (ichí)-mai (一)枚; (*bed ~*) shíitsu シーツ, shikifu 敷布

shelf *n* tana 棚; ***enclosed shelves*** to-dana 戸棚; **book shelf** *n* hon-dana 本棚, sho-dana 書棚

shell *n* kara 殻・カラ; (*of shellfish*), kai-gara 貝殻・カイガラ; (*of tortoise etc.*) kōra 甲羅・コウラ

shelter *n* sherutā シェルター, hinanjo 避難所

shepherd *n* hitsujikai 羊飼い

sheriff *n* hoankan 保安官

Shiba *n* Shíba 芝

Shibuya *n* Shibuya 渋谷

shield **1.** *n* táte 盾・たて, shiirudo シールド **2.** *v* (*protects*) hógo shimásu 保護します; (*covers*) ōimásu 覆い[おおい]ます

shift **1.** *v* (*it ~s*) utsurimásu 移ります **2.** *v* (*~s/changes it*) ten-ji-másu 転じます **3.** *v* (*alternates*) kōtai shimásu 交替・交代します **4.** *n* idō 移動 **5.** *n* henka 変化, shifuto シフト; **day shift** *n* nikkin 日勤; **night shift** *n* yakin 夜勤; **shift key** *n* (*keyboard*) shifuto kii シフトキー

Shikoku *n* Shikóku 四国

shilling *n* shiringu シリング

Shimbashi *n* Shínbashi 新橋

shimmer 1. *n* yurameki 揺らめき・ゆらめき 2. *v* yuramekimásu 揺らめきます・ゆらめきます
shin *n* suné すね・脛
shine 1. *n* (*gloss*) tsuya つや・ツヤ・艶 2. *v* (*it ~s*) hikarimásu 光ります, (*gleams*) kagayakimásu 輝きます・かがやきます; (*the sun*) terimásu 照ります; (*polishes it*) migakimásu 磨きます 3. *~s on* (*illuminates*) …o terashimásu …を照らします
shingle *n* íta 板; *~s a roof* íta de yáne o fukimásu 板で屋根をふき[葺き]ます
shingles *n* (taijō-) hō´shin (帯状) 疱疹, herupesu ヘルペス
Shinjuku *n* Shinjuku 新宿
Shinto(ism) *n* Shíntō/Shíndō 神道
ship *n* fúne 船・舟, (*steamship*) kisen 汽船, …-sen …船; **ship's crew** *n* sen'in 船員
shipwreck *n* nanpa 難破・ナンパ, sōnan 遭難
shipyard *n* zōsen-jo 造船所
shirk *v* 1. okotarimásu 怠ります, namakemásu 怠けます 2. nogaremásu 逃れます・のがれます, sakemásu 避けます; **shirk one's job** *v* shigoto o okotarimásu 仕事を怠ります・おこたります; **shirk payment** *v* (shiharai o) fumitaoshimásu 支払いを踏み倒します; **shirk responsibility** *v* sekinin o nogaremásu 責任を逃れます, sekinin o kaihi shimásu 責任を回避します
shirt *n* wai-shatsu Yシャツ; (*undershirt*) shátsu シャツ
shiver 1. *v* zotto shimásu ぞっとします, furuemásu 震えます, ononokimásu 慄きます・おののきます 2. *n with a ~* zotto ぞっと, samuke 寒け
shock *n* shókku ショック, [BOOKISH] shōgeki 衝撃
shoe *n* kutsú 靴・くつ, (*outdoor shoes*) shita-baki 下履き
shogunate *n* bákufu 幕府; bakufu-jídai 幕府時代
shoot *v* 1. (*~s at*) uchimásu 撃ちます 2. (*arrow*) irimásu 射ります 3. (*~s to death*) uchi-koroshimásu 撃ち殺す; **shoot a film** *v* eiga o satsuei shimásu 映画を撮影します; **shoot for the stars** *v* takanozomi o shimásu 高望みをします
shop *n* (*store*) misé 店, uri-ba 売り場, shō´ten 商店, shoppu ショップ; …-ya …屋, …-ten …店
shop *v* (*does the shopping*; *buys*) kaimono shimásu 買い物します; **shop around for** … *v* o busshoku shimásu …を物色します; **shop clerk** *n* ten'in 店員
shoplift *v* kapparaimásu かっぱらいます, manbiki o shimásu 万引き[まんびき]をします
shopping *n* kaimono 買い物, shoppingu ショッピング; **shopping center** *n* shoppingu-séntā ショッピングセンター
shore *n* kishí 岸・きし, [BOOKISH]

kishíbe 岸辺・きしべ; (*seashore*) kaigan 海岸, [BOOKISH] (*seaside*) umibe 海辺・うみべ; [BOOKISH] (*lakeshore*) kogan 湖岸

short *adj* (*not long*) mijikái 短い; (*not tall*) (séga) hikúi (背が)低い; (*deficient*) … ga tarimasén …が足りません; **in short** *adv* tsúmari つまり, yōsúru ni 要するに・ようするに

shortage *n* fusoku 不足; **water shortage** *n* mizu-búsoku 水不足

shortchange *v* tsuri-sen o gomakashimásu 釣(り)銭を誤魔化します・ごまかします, kozeni o gomakashimásu 小銭を誤魔化します・ごまかします

short circuit *n* (*electric*) (denki ga) shō´to (shimásu) ショート(します)

shortcoming *n* tánsho 短所, ketten 欠点

shortcut *n* **1.** chiká-michi 近道 **2.** (*computer*) shōto katto ショートカット

shorten *v* **1. ~s *it*** mijíkáku shimásu 短くします・みじかくします; chijimemásu 縮めます; herashimásu 減らします・へらします; (*abbreviates*) ryakushimásu 略します **2.** mijíkáku narimásu 短くなります・みじかくなります; chiji-márimásu 縮まります

shorthand *n* sokki 速記

short-handed *adj* hitode ga tarinai 人手が足りない, hitode-busoku (no) 人手不足(の)

shortly *adv* ma-mó-naku 間もなく・まもなく, chikáku 近く・ちかく

shorts *n* **1.** (*outerwear*) shōto-pántsu ショートパンツ; tanpan 短パン **2.** (*undershorts*) zubon-shita ズボン下

shortsighted *adj* (*myopic*) kinshi (no) 近視(の), kingan (no) 近眼(の)

short-tempered *adj* tanki (no/na) 短気(の/な)

shot *n* **1.** (*fire*) hassha 発射; happō 発砲 **2.** (*for a goal*) shūto シュート **3.** (*TV scene, film*) katto カット; **big shot** *n* ōmono 大物; ōgosho 大御所; **give it one's best shot** *v* zenryoku o tsukushite (yatte) mimásu 全力を尽くして[つくして](やって)みます; **Good shot!** *interj* Naisu shotto! ナイスショット!; **have a shot at** *v* (*tries*) tameshite mimásu 試してみます

shotgun *n* shotto-gan ショットガン; [BOOKISH] sandan-jū 散弾銃

should → **ought**

shoulder **1.** *n* káta 肩・かた **2.** *v* (*carries on shoulders*) shoimásu しょいます, seoimásu 背負います, hikiukemásu 引き受けます; **over-the-shoulder** *adj* katagoshi (no) 肩ごし・肩越し(の); **shoulder blade** *n* kenkōkotsu 肩甲骨

shout **1.** *v* (*calls out*) sakebimásu 叫びます・さけびます; (*chants*) tonaemásu 唱えます・となえます; (*yells*) donarimásu どなりま

す・怒鳴ります **2.** *n* sakebi-goe 叫び声, ōgoe 大声

shove *n, v* tsuyoku oshimásu 強く押します

shovel *n* sháberu シャベル

show *n* **1.** (*display*) mié 見栄・ミエ **2.** (*an exhibit*) mise-mónó 見せ物, shō ショー **3.** → **movies** → **play**

show *v* **1.** (*displays it*) misemásu 見せます **2.** (*reveals*) arawashimásu 表します; (*indicates*) shimeshimásu 示します **3.** (*tells*) oshiemásu 教えます; **show in** *v* (*ushers*) tōshimásu 通します; annai shimásu 案内します; **show off** *v* jiman shimásu 自慢します; misebirakashimásu 見せびらかします; **show up** *v* arawaremásu 現れます; (*comes*) miemásu 見えます

showcase *n* shō kēsu ショー・ケース, tenji-yō kēsu 展示用ケース

showdown *n* taiketsu 対決, dotanba 土壇場

shower 1. *n* (*bath*) sháwā シャワー; ***sudden*** ~ niwaka-áme にわか雨 **2.** *v* (*takes a* ~) sháwā o abimásu シャワーを浴びます; ~ ***on*** abisemásu 浴びせます

shred *n* kirehashi 切れ端

shredder *n* shureddā シュレッダー

shrew *n* gamigami on'na がみがみ女

shrewd *adj* josai nai 如才ない

shrill *adj* kandakai 甲高い; **shrill voice** *n* kiiroi koe 黄色い声, kandakai koe 甲高い声, kanakiri-goe 金切り声

shrimp *n* ebi えび・エビ

shrine *n* (*Shinto*) (o-)miya (お)宮; jínja 神社, (*large*) jingū´ 神宮

shrink *v* chijimimásu 縮みます, chijimárimásu 縮まります, (*shortens, abridges*) tsuzumarimásu つづまり[約まり]ます

shrivel *v* chijimimásu 縮みます, shioremásu しおれます

shrub *n* kanboku 潅木・かんぼく, yabu やぶ・藪

shudder *v* zotto shinmásu ぞっとします・ゾッとします; ***with a*** ~ zotto ぞっと・ゾッと

shuffle *v* mazemásu 混ぜます; ~ ***the cards*** toránpu o kirimásu トランプを切ります

shut *v* **1.** (~*s it*) shimemásu 閉めます; (*a book, etc.*) tojimásu 閉じます **2.** (*it gets* ~) shimarimásu 閉まります; (*it puckers up*) tsubomarimásu つぼまります; ~ ***one's eyes*** mé o tsuburimásu 目を瞑ります・目をつぶります; ~ ***up*** (*not speak*) damarimásu 黙ります

shutter *n* (*camera, etc.*) sháttā シャッター; (*house or storefront*) yoroi-do よろい[鎧]戸, (*rain* ~*s*) amádo 雨戸・あまど

shy *adj* uchiki (na) 内気(な), shai (na) シャイ(な), hazukashíi 恥ずかしい・はずかしい; ***acts*** ~ hanikamimásu はにかみます, enryo shimásu 遠慮します

shyness *n* (go-)enryo (ご)遠慮

Siberia *n* Shiberia シベリア

sibling *n* (*brother*) kyōdai 兄弟, (*sister*) shimai 姉妹

sick *adj* byōki (no) 病気(の); ***gets ~ and tired*** unzári shimásu うんざりします→ **queasy**

sickly *adj* byōki-gachi (na) 病気がち(な)

sickness *n* byōki 病気

side *n* **1.** yoko 横; -gawa 側 **2.** (*beside, nearby*) sóba そば・側・傍, (*off to the side*) hata 端 **3.** (*of body*) wakí わき・脇; **both sides** ryō-gawa 両側; **that side** achira-gawa あちら側; **(the) left side** hidari-gawa 左側; **(the) right side** migi-gawa 右側; **the other side** mukō-gawa 向こう側・むこうがわ; **this side** (*my/our side*) kochira-gawa こちら側; **one side ... the other side** ippō´... (mō) ippō 一方 ...(もう)一方; (*party*) senpō 先方; **which side** dochira-gawa どちら側; **your side** sochira-gawa そちら側; **sideboard** *n* shokki-tódana 食器戸棚; **side dish** *n* (*to go with the rice*) okazu おかず; **side effect** *n* fukusayō 副作用; **side job, sideline** *n* arubáito アルバイト; **sidestep** *v* sakemás<u>u</u> 避けます, [BOOKISH] kaihi shimás<u>u</u> 回避します; **side street** *n* yokochō 横丁; **sidetracked;** ***gets*** ~ dassen shimás<u>u</u> 脱線します

siege *n* hōi 包囲, hōi kōgeki 包囲攻撃

sieve, sifter *n* furui ふるい・篩, zarú ざる

sight *n* (*scene*) ari-sama ありさま・有り様; (*scenery*) késh<u>i</u>ki 景色; (*eyesight*) shíryoku 視力; ***sees the ~s*** kenbutsu shimás<u>u</u> 見物します

sightseeing *n* kenbutsu 見物, kankō 観光; ~ ***tour*** kankō-tsuā 観光ツアー

sign **1.** *n* (*symptom*) shirushi しるし[徴], chōkō 徴候; (*omen*) zenchō 前兆 **2.** *n* (*signboard*) kanban 看板 **3.** *n* (*marker*) hyōsh<u>i</u>ki 標識 **4.** *n* (*symbol*) kigō 記号 **5.** *v* (*writes one's name*) shomei shimás<u>u</u> 署名します; **signs and symptoms** *n* (*medical*) chōkō to shōjō 徴候と症状

signal *n* shingō 信号, aizu 合図, shigunaru シグナル

signature *n* shomei 署名, sain サイン

significance *n* ígi 意義

signpost *n* dōhyō 道標, dōro (annai) hyōshiki 道路(案内)標識

silencer *n* (*gun*) sairen-sā サイレンサー

silent; ***is*** ~ (*not speak*) damarimás<u>u</u> 黙ります

silhouette *n* shiruetto シルエット

silicon *n* shirikon シリコン

silk *n* kínu 絹・きぬ, shiruku シルク; ***raw*** ~ kí-ito 生糸・きいと

silkworm *n* (o-)káiko (お)蚕・カイコ

sill *n* ***(window/door)*** ~ (mádo/to no) sh<u>i</u>kii (窓/戸の)敷居

silly *adj* bakabakashii ばかばかしい, bakageteiru ばかげている・

馬鹿げている
silver *n* gín 銀・ぎん, shirubā シルバー
similar *adj* onaji yō´ (na) 同じよう[様]な・おなじような, hitoshíi 等しい・ひとしい, nita 似た, ruiji no 類似の
simple *adj* kantan (na) 簡単・かんたん(な), tanjun (na) 単純(な), shínpuru (na) シンプル(な); (*easy*) wáke-nai 訳ない・わけない; (*plain*) assári shita あっさりした; (*tastefully restrained*) shibúi 渋い・しぶい; ~ (*modest*) ***tastes*** wabi わび・侘び
simply *adv* **1.** kantan ni 簡単に・かんたんに; (*easily*) wáke-naku 訳なく・わけなく; assári (to) あっさり(と) **2.** (*merely*) táda ただ, … ni sugimasén …に過ぎません
simultaneous *adj* dōji (no) 同時(の); **simultaneous translation** *n* dōjitsū´-yaku 同時通訳
sin *n* tsúmi 罪; záiaku 罪悪
since **1.** *prep* … kara …から; (sono) áto/go (その)後; ~ ***then*** sono-go その後; (…) írai (…)以来 **2.** *conj* … shite kara …してから **3.** → **because**
sincere *adj* makoto (no) 誠(の), seijitsu (na) 誠実(な); (*heartfelt*) kokóro kara (no) 心から(の)
sincerity *n* seii 誠意, magokoro 真心
sing *v* utaimásu 歌います
singer *n* kashu 歌手, shingā シンガー
single **1.** *adj* (*for one person*) hitóri no 一人[独り]の **2.** *n* (*unmarried*) hitori-mónó 独り者, dokushin 独身; **single (room)** *n* shínguru シングル, shinguru-rū´mu シングルルーム
sink **1.** *n* (*in kitchen*) nagashí 流し **2.** *v* (*it ~s*) shizumimásu 沈みます; (*~s it*) shizumemásu 沈めます
sip *v* suimásu 吸います
sir... …sama …様・さま, …san …さん
siren *n* (*sound*) sairen サイレン
sirloin *n* sāroin サーロイン; **sirloin steak** *n* sāroin-sutēki サーロインステーキ
sister *n* **1.** onna no kyō´dai 女の兄弟; (*older*) ane 姉・あね, (o-)nē´-san (お)姉さん・おねえさん; (*younger*) imōtó 妹・いもうと, (o-)imōto-san 妹さん **2.** (*nun*) sisutā シスター
sit *v* (*especially Japanese-style*) suwarimásu 座ります・すわります, (*on a cushion*) shikimásu 敷きます; (*in chair*) (koshi-)kakemásu (腰)掛けます
site *n* (*building lot*) shiki-chi 敷地; genba 現場; basho 場所
situation *n* jōtai 状態, jōkyō 状況, jítai 事態; (*circumstance*) ba(w)ai 場合; (*stage*) kurai 位; (*location*) íchi 位置
six *n* rokú 六・6, muttsú 六つ; shíkkusu シックス
sixteen *n* jū-rokú 十六・16
sixth *adj* roku-banmé (no) 六番目

(の), muttsu-mé (no) 六つ目(の); ***the ~ day*** muika-mé 六日目, (*of the month*) muika 六日

size *n* ōkisa 大きさ, sáizu サイズ

skate, skating **1.** *n* sukē´to スケート, rōrā sukē´to ローラースケート **2.** *v* sukē´to o shimásu スケートをします; suberimásu 滑ります; **ice skating** *n* aisu sukēto アイススケート; **skateboard** *n* sukēto bōdo スケートボード

sketch *n* shasei 写生; suketchi スケッチ; shitae 下絵

ski, skiing *n* sukíi (o shimásu) スキー(をします); **ski resort** *n* sukii-jō スキー場; sukii rizōto スキー・リゾート

skill *n* udemae 腕前; ginō 技能; sukiru スキル

skillful *adj* jōzú (na) じょうず[上手](な), umái うまい, takumi (na) 巧み(な); (*proficient*) tassha (na) 達者(な); (*nimble*) kíyō (na) 器用(な)

skim *v* (*grazes*) kasumemásu かすめ[掠め]ます; ***~ off*** kasume-tori-másu かすめ[掠め]取ります

skin **1.** *n* hifu 皮膚; (*of animal, potato, …*) kawá 皮 **2.** *v* (*pares/peels it*) mukimásu むきます・剥きます, hagimásu はぎます・剥ぎます; **skin cancer** *n* (*medical*) hihu gan 皮膚がん・皮膚癌

skip *v* (*leaves out*) nukashimásu 抜かします, tobashimásu 飛ばします; **skip school** gakkō o saborimásu 学校をさぼります, zuru-yásumi shimásu ずる休みします

skirt *n* sukā´to スカート

sky *n* sóra 空; (*heaven*) tén 天; (*blue, empty*) aozóra 青空

skydiving *n* sukai daibingu スカイ・ダイビング

Skype *n* sukaipu スカイプ

slack *adj* yurúi 緩い・弛い・ゆるい; ***gets ~*** taruminásu たるみ[弛み]ます

slacks *n* surákkusu スラックス, zubon ズボン

slander **1.** *n* warú-kuchi/-guchi 悪口, [BOOKISH] hibō ひぼう・誹謗 **2.** *v* ... o chūshō shimásu ...を中傷します

slang *n* zokugo 俗語, surangu スラング

slant **1.** *n* katamuki 傾き・かたむき **2.** *v* (*leans*) katamukimásu 傾きます・かたむきます

slap *v* hatakimásu はたき[叩き]ます; hippatakimasu 引っぱたきます; (*one's face*) … no kao o uchimásu …の顔を打ちます, ... ni binta shimasu ビンタします

slash *n* surasshu スラッシュ; shasen 斜線, "/"

slave *n* dorei 奴隷; yakko やっこ・奴

sled *n* sóri そり・ソリ・橇

sleep **1.** *n* (*sleeping*) nemuri 眠り, ne 寝, suimin 睡眠; ***not enough ~*** ne-búsoku 寝不足 **2.** *v* (*sleeps*) nemurimásu 眠ります; yasumimásu 休みます; (*goes to bed*) nemásu 寝ます; (*a*

*leg, etc.) **goes to ~** (gets numb)* shibiremás<u>u</u> しびれます・痺れる; sleep soundly → **sound asleep**
sleepy *adj* nemui 眠い・ねむい
sleet *n* mizore みぞれ
sleeve *n* (o-)sode (お)袖・そで
slender *adj* hosói 細い・ほそい
slice 1. *n* suraisu スライス **2.** *v* → **cut; piece**
slick *adj* subekkói すべっこい・滑っこい
slide 1. *n* suberí-dai すべり台・滑り台, o-súberi お滑り **2.** *v* suberi-más<u>u</u> 滑ります
slider *n* suraidā スライダー
slight *adj* chótto sh<u>i</u>ta … ちょっとした…
slip 1. *n* → **slide 2.** *~ out of ... v* nuke-dashimás<u>u</u> 抜け出します
slippers *n* suríppa スリッパ, uwa-baki うわばき・上履き
slippery *adj* suberi yasui すべりやすい・滑りやすい; subekkói すべっこい・滑っこい; ***Slippery (Area)*** "Surippu-jíko ō´shi" "スリップ事故多し"
slipshod *adj* zusan (na) ずさん[杜撰](な)
slogan *n* surō´gan スローガン, hyōgo 標語
slope *n* saká 坂
sloppy *adj* zonzái (na) ぞんざい(な), zusan (na) ずさん[杜撰](な)
slot *n* k<u>u</u>chi 口, aná 穴
slot machine *n* (*vending machine*) (jidō-)hambái-ki (自動)販売機; (*gambling*) surotto mashiin スロットマシーン
slow *adj* osoi 遅い, surō´ (na) スロー(な); (*sluggish*) norói のろい, yurúi 緩い; (*clock runs ~*) okurete imás<u>u</u> 遅れています; **slow motion** *n* (*film, etc.*) surō mōshon スローモーション
slowly *adv* yukkúri ゆっくり; (*tardily, late*) osoku 遅く・おそく
sluggish *adj* norói のろい
slum *n* suramu(-gai) スラム(街), hinmín-k<u>u</u>tsu/-gai 貧民窟/街
sly *adj* zurúi ずるい
small *adj* (*little*) chiisái/ch<u>i</u>tchái 小さい/ちっちゃい, chíisa-na/ch<u>í</u>tcha-na …小さな/ちっちゃな…; ko-… 小; (*fine*) komakái 細かい; (*~-scale*) sasáyaka (na) ささやか(な)
smallpox *n* (*medical*) tennentō 天然痘・てんねん痘
smart *adj* (*intelligent*) atamá ga íi 頭がいい, rikō (na) 利口(な); (*stylish*) sumā´to (na) スマート(な), iki (na) いき[粋]な
smartphone *n* (*multifunctional mobile phone*) sumātofon スマートフォン
smash *v* **1.** (*breaks it*) kowashi-más<u>u</u> 壊します, kudakimás<u>u</u> 砕きます; (*crushes it*) tsubushi-más<u>u</u> 潰し[つぶし]ます **2.** (*it breaks*) kowaremás<u>u</u> 壊れます, kudakemás<u>u</u> 砕けます; (*it crushes*) tsuburemás<u>u</u> 潰れ[つぶれ]ます
smell 1. *n* (*odor*) niói におい・臭

い・匂い **2.** *v* (*it ~s*) nioimásu においし臭い・匂い]ます, niói ga shimásu におい[臭い・匂い]がします **3.** *v* (*~s it*) kagimásu 嗅ぎます

smelly *adj* kusái 臭い・くさい

smile **1.** *v* níkoniko shimásu にこにこします・ニコニコします; hohoemimásu 微笑みます・ほほえみます **2.** *n* (*smiling face*) e-gao 笑顔; hohoemí 微笑み・ほほえみ; [BOOKISH] bishō 微笑・びしょう

smoke **1.** *v* (*tobacco*), tabako o suimásu たばこを吸います; kitsuen shimásu 喫煙します **2.** *v* ibushimásu いぶし[燻し]ます **3.** *n* kemuri 煙・けむり

smoking *n* kitsuen 喫煙; **smoking prohibited** *n* kin'en 禁煙; **non-smoking seat** *n* kin'en seki 禁煙席

smoky *adj* kemui 煙い・けむい, kemutai 煙たい・けむたい

smooth **1.** *adj* naméraka (na) 滑らか・なめらか(な), sube sube shita, (*flat*) taira (na) 平ら(な), (*slippery*) subekkói 滑っこい・すべっこい **2.** *v* narashimásu ならし[均し]ます; (*pats*) nademásu なで[撫で]ます

smudge *n* yogore 汚れ・よごれ

smuggle *v* mitsuyu shimásu 密輸します

snack *n* keishoku 軽食, karui monó/tabemónó/shokuji 軽い物/食べ物/食事

snake *n* hébi 蛇・ヘビ

snap *v* **1.** (*it ~s*) hajikemásu はじけ[弾け]ます **2.** (*~s it*) hajikimásu はじき[弾き]ます

sneakers *n* suniikā スニーカー, zukkú-gutsu ズック靴

sneeze *n, v* kushámi (o shimásu) くしゃみ(をします)

snore *n, v* ibikí (o kakimásu) いびき・鼾(をかきます)

snow *n* yukí (ga furimásu) 雪(が降ります)

snowstorm *n* fúbuki 吹雪・ふぶき

so *adv* **1.** (*like that*) sō´ そう (sō そう + [VERB]), (*like this*) kō´ こう (kō こう + [VERB]) **2.** (*that much*) sonna ni そんなに, (*this much*) konna ni こんなに, **3.** (*and so*) … kara …から, …-te …て (…-kute …くて, … de… で); dá kara (sa) だから(さ); **so as to be** [NOUN] ni に, [ADJECTIVE]-ku く; … yō ni …よう[様]に; **so to speak** *adv* iwaba いわば・言わば

soak *v* **1.** *~s it* tsukemásu 漬けます **2.** *it ~s* tsukarimásu 漬かります **3.** *it ~s in* shimimásu 染みます

so-and-so *n* **1.** dáredare だれだれ・誰々, dáresore だれそれ・誰それ; yátsu やつ・奴 **2.** náninani なになに・何々

soap *n* sekken 石けん・石鹸, shabon シャボン, sōpu ソープ; **soap bubble** *n* shabon-dama シャボン玉

sober *adj* (*in one's right mind*) shōki (no) 正気(の); (*plain*) jimí (na) 地味(な); (*undrunk*) shirafu

(no) しらふ(の)
soccer *n* sákkā サッカー
sociable *adj* aisó (/aisō´) ga (/no) íi あいそ(う)[愛想]が(/の)いい, shakō-teki (na) 社交的(な)
social *adj* shákai (no) 社会(の); ***~ company*** (o-)tsukíai (お)付き合い, (*~ friendly intercourse/relations*) kōsai 交際; ***~ standing*** míbun 身分, shakai-teki chíi 社会的地位
social science(s) *n* shakai-kágaku 社会科学
society *n* shákai 社会; (*association*) kyōkai 協会, (*scholarly*) gakkai 学会; …-kai …会
socket *n* sokétto ソケット
socks *n* kutsu-shita 靴下
soft *adj* yawarakái 柔らかい・やわらかい, sofuto (na) ソフト(な); ***~ ice cream*** sofuto-kuríimu ソフトクリーム
software *n* sofutowéa ソフトウェア
soil **1.** *n* (*earth*) tsuchí 土, tochi 土地; (*stain*) 汚れ **2.** *v* (*makes it dirty*) yogoshimásu 汚します; (*gets dirty*) yogoremásu 汚れます
soldier *n* heishi 兵士, hei 兵, gunjin 軍人
sole **1.** *n* (*fish*) shita-bírame 舌平目・シタビラメ **2.** *n* (*of foot*) ashi no urá 足の裏 **3.** *adj* → **only** (*one*)
solicitude *n* omoi-yari 思いやり; ***thanks to your ~*** okage-sama de おかげ[お蔭]さまで; ***a visit of ~*** (o-)mimai (お)見舞い
solid **1.** *adj* (*firm*) katai 固い・硬い・堅い・かたい **2.** *n* (*a solid*) kotai 固体, rittai 立体
solstice *n* ***summer ~*** geshi 夏至, ***winter ~*** tōji 冬至
solution *n* kaiketsu (saku) 解決(策)
solve *v* **1.** tokimásu 解きます **2.** kaiketsu shimásu 解決します
Somalia *n* Somaria ソマリア
somber *adj* **1.** inki (na) 陰気(な) **2.** (*color*) kusunda くすんだ
some **1.** *adj* (*pron*) (*a little*) sukóshi 少し (*but often omitted*); (*certain*) nánráka no … 何らかの… (*a certain amount*) íkura ka (no) いくらか・幾らか(の), (*a certain number*) íkutsu ka (no) いくつか・幾つか(の); tashō (no) 多少(の) **2.** *pron* (*particular*) áru …ある…; ***~ people*** áru hito ある人, … hitómo arimásu …人もあります
somebody → **someone**
someday *adv* izure いずれ, ítsu-ka いつか; [BOOKISH] ichijitsú 一日
somehow *adv* dō´ni ka どうにか; (*vaguely*) dō´mo どうも; ***~ or other*** nán to ka shite 何とかして, (*necessarily*) dō-shitemo どうしても
someone *pron* dáre ka 誰か; (…) hito (…)人; ***~ or other*** dáredare だれだれ・誰々, dáresore だれそれ・誰それ
something *pron* náni ka 何か; (…) monó (…)物; something or other náninani なにもの・何々

sometime *adj* ítsu ka いつか; izure いずれ

sometimes *adv* tokidoki 時々, tokí ni 時に; (*occasionally*) tama ni たまに…; … (suru) kotó ga arimásu̲ … (する)事があります

somewhat *adv* su̲kóshi 少し, chótto ちょっと → **somehow**

somewhere *adv* doko ka どこか; somewhere else yosóよそ; somewhere or other dókodoko どこどこ, dókosoko どこそこ

son *n* musu̲ko 息子; (*your son*) bótchan 坊ちゃん; ***eldest ~*** chō´nán 長男

song *n* utá 歌, songu ソング

soon *adv* ma-mó-naku 間もなく・まもなく, mō (súgu) もう(すぐ), jiki ni じき[直]に; as soon as … (suru) to (súgu) (する)と(すぐ); (shi̲te) kara súgu (して)からすぐ

soot *n* sú̲su すす・スス・煤

soothe *v* shizumemásu̲ 静めます・鎮めます, nadamemásu̲ なだめ[宥め]ます

sophisticated *adj* tokaiteki (na) 都会的(な), senrensareta 洗練された

sore **1.** *adj* itái 痛い **2.** *n* (*a ~ spot*) itái tokoró 痛い所, (*from shoe rubbing*) ku̲tsu-zure 靴ずれ → **boil** → **wound**

sorry *adj* (*for you/him*) (o-)ki-no-dókúdesu̲ (お)気の毒です; Sorry! *interj* Sumimasén. すみません., Gomennasai. ごめんなさい.

sort *n* (*kind*) shúruí 種類, ís-shu 一種

soul *n* séishin 精神, támashii 魂・たましい; (*person*) hi̲to 人, ningen 人間; soul mate *n* sōru meito ソールメイト

sound **1.** *n* (*noise*) otó 音; ne 音 **2.** *n* (*audio*) onkyō 音響; saundo サウンド **3.** *v it ~s* narimásu̲ 鳴ります, (*makes an animal ~*) nakimásu̲ 鳴きます **4.** *v ~s it* narashimásu̲ 鳴らします; sound asleep *adj* gussúri ぐっすり, gūgū ぐうぐう; sound out *v* (*a person*) dashin shimásu̲ 打診します; sound wave *n* onpa 音波

soup *n* (*Western-style*) sū´pu スープ; soup pan *n* sūpu nabe スープ鍋; soup stock *n* dashi だし・ダシ

sour **1.** *adj* su̲ppái 酸っぱい・すっぱい **2.** *v it ~s* ku̲sarimásu̲ 腐ります

source *n* moto もと・元; táne 種; okorí 起こり

south *n* minami 南, nan-… 南…; (*the south*) nanpō 南方, (*the southern part*) nánbu 南部

southeast *n* nantō 南東

southwest *n* nansei 南西

souvenir *n* (o-)miyage (お)みやげ[土産], miyage-mono みやげ[土産]物; kinen-hin 記念品

sow **1.** *v* (*seeds*) makimásu̲ まき[蒔き]ます **2.** *n* (*female pig*) mesubuta 雌豚・メスブタ

soybean *n* daizu 大豆・ダイズ; ***fermented ~*** nattō´納豆・ナットウ

soy sauce *n* (o-)shōyu (お)しょうゆ

[醤油・ショウユ]; (*in sushi restaurant*) murásaki 紫・ムラサキ

spa *n* supa スパ; onsen 温泉, tōji-ba 湯治場

space *n* **1.** (*available*) ma 間; (*between*) aida 間; (*inter~*) kūkan 空間, sukima すき間, supēsu スペース; (*outer ~*) úchū 宇宙; (*room, leeway*) yochi 余地 **2. → blank**

Spain *n* Supéin スペイン

span **1.** *n* (*term*) kikan 期間, supan スパン **2.** *v* (*stretches over it*) … ni matagarimásu …に跨がり[またがり]ます

spare **1.** *adj* (*reserve*) yóbi (no) 予備(の) **2.** *n* (*leeway, surplus*) yoyū 余裕; ***~ time*** hima 暇, yoka 余暇 **3. → save**

spark *n* híbana 火花

sparkle *n* kirameki きらめき・煌き, kagayaki 輝き

sparrow *n* suzume 雀・すずめ・スズメ

speak *v* hanashimásu 話します, iimásu 言います

spear *n* yari 槍・ヤリ

special *adj* tokubetsu (no) 特別(の); supesharu (na) スペシャル(な), toku-… 特…; (*peculiar*) tokushu (no) 特殊(の); (*favorite*) tokui (na/no) 得意(な/の); (*emergency*) rinji (no) 臨時(の); **special delivery** *n* sokutatsu 速達; **special feature/quality** *n* tokushoku 特色, tokuchō 特徴・特長; **special offer** *n* tokubetsu hōshi-hin 特別奉仕品

specialist *n* senmon-ka 専門家; (*medical*) senmón-i 専門医

specialty *n* senmon 専門, (*forte*) tokui 得意, (*trick*) ohako おはこ・十八番

species …-rui …類; ***a ~ of*** … no ís-shu …の一種

specific *adj* (*particular*) kore to iu …これという; hakkiri to shita はっきりとした; gutaiteki (na) 具体的(な)

spectator *n* kankyaku 観客

speculation *n* (*venture*) yamá やま, tōki 投機

speech *n* hanashí 話, kotobá 言葉, kuchi 口; (*public*) enzetsu 演説, kōen 講演, supiichi スピーチ

speed *n* háyasa 速さ, sókudo 速度, supíido スピード; (*hourly*) jisoku 時速

spell *v* (jí o) tsuzurimásu (字を)綴り[つづり]ます

spelling *n* tsuzuri 綴り・つづり, supéru スペル; (*way written*) kaki-kátá 書き方, (*letters*) jí 字

spend *v* tsukaimásu 使います, (*pays*) dashimásu 出します; (*uses time*) sugoshimásu 過ごします; okurimásu 送ります

sphere *n* kyū 球, kyūtai 球体

spice *n* kō´(shin)ryō´ 香(辛)料, chōmi(-ryō) 調味(料), supaisu スパイス

spicy *adj* karai からい・辛い, supaishii スパイシー

spider *n* kúmo くも・クモ・蜘蛛

spill *v* (*it ~s*) koboremásu こぼれ

ます・零れます; (*~s it*) koboshimásu こぼします・零します; tarashimásu 垂らします

spine *n* sebone 背骨

spinning *n* bōseki 紡績

spiral *n* rasen 螺旋・らせん

spirit *n* séishin 精神, kokóro 心, támashii 魂, supiritto スピリット; kokoro-mochi 心持ち; ki 気

spit 1. *n* (*spittle*) tsúba つば・ツバ・唾, tsubakí つばき・ツバキ・唾 **2.** *v* (*~s out*) (tsúba o) hakimásu (つばを)吐きます

spite; ***in ~ of …*** (ná) no ni …(な)のに

splendid *adj* rippa (na) 立派・りっぱ(な), subarashíi すばらしい・素晴らしい, suteki (na) すてき・素敵(な), mígoto (na) 見事(な), kékkō (na) 結構(な)

split *v* **1.** (*~s it*) sakimásu 裂きます, warimásu 割ります; (*divides it*) wakemásu 分けます **2.** (*it ~s*) sakemásu 裂けます, waremásu 割れます; (*it separates*) wakaremásu 別れます

spoil *v* **1.** ***~s it*** wáruku (damé ni) shimásu 悪く(駄目に)します; itamemásu 傷めます; ***~ a person's mood*** kíbun o kowashimásu 気分を壊します, kíbun o gaishimásu 気分を害します **2.** ***it gets spoiled*** wáruku narimásu 悪くなります, itamimásu 傷みます **3.** ***it ~s*** (*sours*) kusarimásu 腐ります; (*rots*) itamimásu 傷みます

sponge *n* kaimen 海綿, suponji スポンジ; **sponge gourd** *n* hechima へちま・ヘチマ・糸瓜

spontaneously *adv* hitori-de ni 独りでに・ひとりでに, onozukara 自ずから・おのずから

spoon *n* supū´n スプーン, sájí さじ・サジ・匙

spoonful *n* (hitó)-saji (一)匙・(ひと)さじ

sport(s) *n* supō´tsu スポーツ, undō 運動; ***~ Day*** (*2nd Monday of October*) Taiiku no hí 体育の日

spot *n* **1.** ten 点; (*spotted*) madara (no) まだら[斑](の), (*blot*) shimi 染み・しみ, (*with*) *~s* bótsubotsu ぼつぼつ・ボツボツ **2.** (*place*) basho 場所

sprain *v* (*an ankle*) (ashí o) kujikimásu (足を)挫き[くじき]ます; ***gets a sprained ankle*** ashí ga kujikemásu 足が挫け[くじけ]ます

spread *v* **1.** (*~s it*) hirogemásu 広げます, (*diffuses it*) hiromemásu 広めます; (*~s it out*) nobashimásu 伸ばします, nobemásu 伸べます; (*~s it on*) harimásu 張ります **2.** (*it ~s*) hirogarimásu 広がります; (*it gets diffused*) hiromarimásu 広まります, fukyū shimásu 普及します; (*it ~s out*) nobimásu 伸びます; (*it ~s on*) (batā o) nurimásu (バターを)塗ります

spring 1. *n* (*season*) háru 春; (*device*) bane(-jíkake) ばね・バネ(仕掛け), (*of clock*) zenmai ぜんまい; ***hot ~*** onsen 温泉 **2.** *v* ***~s forth***

(*gushes*) wakimásu わき[湧き]ます **3.** *v* **~*s from*** … kara okorimásu … から起こります
springtime *n* háru 春
sprinkle; ~ ***it*** *v* furi-kakemásu 振りかけます
spy *n* supai スパイ kanbō 間諜
spyware *n* supaiwea スパイウェア
square *n* shikaku 四角; *adj* shikakú (no) 四角(の), shikakúi 四角い; kakú 角; (*plaza*) híró-bá 広場
squash *v* tsuburemásu つぶれます・潰れます
squat **1.** *n* sukuwatto スクワット **2.** *v* shagamimásu しゃがみます
squeeze *adj* tsubushimásu 潰し[つぶし]ます; (~*s out*) shiborimásu 絞ります・しぼります
squid *n* ika いか・イカ・烏賊
squirrel *n* rísu りす・リス・栗鼠
Sri Lanka *n* Suriránka スリランカ
stab *v* (tsuki-)sashimásu (突き)刺します
stable **1.** *adj* anteishita 安定した **2.** *n* uma-goya 馬小屋, kyūsha 厩舎
stadium *n* kyōgi-jō 競技場; ***baseball*** ~ yakyū-jō 野球場, kyūjō 球場
stage *n* bútai 舞台; sutēji ステージ, (*of a process*) dankai 段階
stagger *v* yoro-mekimásu よろめきます
staggering *adj* yóroyoro (no) よろよろ(の), chidori-ashi (no) 千鳥足(の)
stain **1.** *n* shimi 染み・しみ **2.** *v* (*paints it*) nurimásu 塗ります; (*soils it*) yogoshimásu 汚します, (*gets soiled*) yogoremásu 汚れます
stairs, stairway *n* kaidan 階段; (*wooden*) hashigo-dan はしご[梯子]段
stake *n* (*post*) kúi 杭
stale *adj* (*not fresh*) furúi 古い
stamp *n* **1.** (*postal*) kitte 切手; ~ ***album*** kitte-chō 切手帳 **2.** (*seal*) ín 印; (*cancellation mark*) keshi-in 消印 **3.** sutanpu スタンプ
stand **1.** *n* (*sales booth*) uri-ba 売り場, baiten 売店, sutando スタンド; (*food stall*) yatai 屋台 **2.** *v* (~*s up*) tachimásu 立ちます; **~*s it up*** tatemásu 立てます **3.** **~*s it*** *v* (*tolerates*) gáman shimásu 我慢します, koraemásu こらえます, shínbō shimásu 辛抱します; stand against (*opposes*) … ni taikō shimásu …に対抗します; stand firm ganbarimásu がんばり[頑張り]ます; stand out (*prominently*) medachimásu 目立ちます; stand still tachi-domarimásu 立ち止まります
standard **1.** *adj* hyōjun (no) 標準(の); ~ ***Japanese*** hyōjun-go 標準語 **2.** *n* meyasu 目安; kikaku 規格; kijun 基準
standardize *v* tōitsu shimásu 統一します; kikaku-ka shimásu 規格化します
staple *n* (hochikisu no) hári (ホチキスの)針

stapler *n* hóchikisu ホチキス
star *n* hoshi 星; (*symbol*) hoshi-jírushi 星印; (*actor*) sutā´スター, hanágata 花形; **Hollywood star** *n* hariuddo sutā ハリウッド・スター; **star sign** *n* seiza 星座
starch *n* **1.** (*laundry*) norí 糊・のり **2.** (*food*) denpun でんぷん・澱粉; ***potato ~*** katakúríko 片栗粉
stare *v* ***~s (at)*** (... o) jíro-jiro mi--másu (...を)じろじろ見ます; mi-tsumemásu 見詰め[見つめ]ます, nagamemásu 眺めます
start 1. *n* hajimari 始まり; shup-patsu 出発; ***at (from) the ~*** shoppana kara しょっぱなから; ***from the ~*** hajime kara 始めから, hónrai 本来 **2.** *v* (*it ~s*) hajimari-másu 始まります; (*sets out*) demásu 出ます **3.** *v* (*~s it*) haji-memásu 始めます, (*~s doing it*) shi-hajimemásu し始めます; ***it ~s to rain*** áme ga furi-hajimemásu 雨が降り始めます, áme ni nari-másu 雨になります
startle *v* bikkúri sasemásu びっくりさせます・吃驚させます; ***gets startled*** bikkúri shimásu びっくりします・吃驚します
starve *v* uemásu 飢えます
state 1. *n* (*of the U.S.*) shū´ 州, ... -shū ...州; (*status*) bún 分; ***~ of affairs*** jōkyō 状況, jítai 事態 → **condition** → **nation 2.** *v* ***expressly ~s*** utaimásu うたい[謳い]ます → **say**
station *n* **1.** (*rail*) éki 駅・えき; (*box lunches sold at railroad stations*) eki-ben 駅弁 **2.** ***gas station*** gasorin sutándo ガソリンスタンド
stationary *n* (*not moving*) ugokanai 動かない, (*not moving*) henkanai 変化しない
stationery *n* (*letter paper*) binsen 便箋; (*writing supplies*) bunbō´-gu 文房具; (*shop*) bunbōgu-ya 文房具屋
statistics *n* tōkei 統計
statue *n* zō 像, chōzō 彫像, (*bronze*) dōzō 銅像
stature *n* (*height*) séi/sé 背・せ(い)
status *n* bún 分, (*social, personal*) míbun 身分, (*position*) chíi 地位; ***status quo*** genjō 現状
stay 1. *n* (*away from home*) taizai 滞在 **2.** *v* taizai shimásu 滞在します **3.** *v* imásu います **4.** *v* todomarimásu とどまり[止まり・留まり]ます; (*overnight*) toma-rimásu 泊まります; **stay away** *v* (*from school, etc.*) yasumimásu 休みます; (*skips work*) sabori-másu サボります; **stay up all night** *v* tetsuya shimásu 徹夜します; ***~ late*** yofúkáshi (o) shimásu 夜更し(を)します
steadily *adv* jitto じっと; zutto ずっと
steady *adj* katagi (na) 堅気(な), tegatai 手堅い; chakujitsu (na) 着実(な)
steak *n* sutēki ステーキ, (*beef-steak*) biifutēki ビーフ・ステーキ

steal *v* nusumimásu 盗みます, kapparaimásu かっぱらいます
stealth *n* (*espionage*) ***the art of ~*** nínjutsu 忍術; ***a master of ~*** nínja 忍者
steam **1.** *n* jōˊki 蒸気, yúge 湯気 **2.** *v* (*~s food*) fukashimásu ふかします, mushimásu 蒸します
steamed foods *n* mushí-mono 蒸し物
steamship *n* kisen 汽船
steel *n* hagane 鋼・はがね・ハガネ, kōtetsu 鋼鉄, tetsu 鉄
steep *adj* (*precipitous*) kyū (na) 急(な), kewashíi 険しい
stem *n* (*of plant*) kuki 茎・クキ
step **1.** *n* (*stairs*) kaidan 階段, dan 段 **2.** *n* suteppu ステップ **3.** *v* (*walk*) arukimásu 歩きます → **measure** → **stage** **4.** *v* ***~s into/on*** fumi-komimásu 踏み込みます; ***~s on the gas*** ákuseru o fumimásu アクセルを踏みます
stepchild *n* mama-ko まま[継]子
stepfather *n* mama-chichi まま[継]父
stepmother *n* mama-haha まま[継]母
steps → **stairs**
stereo *n* (*sound/player*) sutereo ステレオ
sterilization *n* sakkin 殺菌
stew *n* shichū シチュー
steward *n* bōi ボーイ, kyūˊji 給仕, suchuwādo スチュワード
stewardess *n* suchuwāˊdesu スチュワーデス
stick **1.** *n* (*club*) bō(-kkire) 棒(っ切れ); (*staff*) tsúe 杖, (*cane*) sutékki ステッキ **2.** *n* (*of gum, candy, etc.*) … ichí-mai …一枚, (*of yakitori, etc.*) íp-pon 一本 **3.** *v* (*it ~s to*) … ni kuttsukimásu …にくっつきます **4.** *v* (*~s it on*) tsukemásu 付けます (*pastes it on*) harimásu 貼ります; **stick out** (*~s it out*) tsuki-dashimásu 突き出します → **protrude**
stickiness *n* nebarí 粘り
stiff *adj* **1.** → **hard** **2.** (*shoulder*) ***gets ~*** (katá ga) korimásu 肩が凝ります; ***~ shoulder, stiffness of shoulder*** kata no kori 肩の凝り
still *adv* (*yet*) máda まだ; (*but*) (sore) démo (それ)でも; ***~ better*** issō/náo íi 一層[いっそう]/尚[なお]いい; ***~ more*** mótto もっと; náo 尚・なお; issō 一層・いっそう; **still-life painting** *n* seibutsu ga 静物画
still → **quiet**; *interj* ***~ still!*** (Tatta mama) ugo-kánaide kudasai. (立ったまま)動かないで下さい., Jitto tatteite kudasai. じっと立っていて下さい.
stimulate *v* unagashimásu 促します
stimulation *n* shigeki 刺激
sting **1.** *v* sashimásu 刺します **2.** *n* (*bee's ~*) hari 針
stingy *adj* kéchi (na) けち(な); ***~ person*** kéchinbo けちんぼ, kéchinbō けちんぼう
stipulate *v* kitei shimásu 規定します
stipulation *n* kitei 規定 → **provision** → **condition**

stir *v* **1.** *~s it* kaki-mawashimásu かき回します **2.** *~s up* (*fans, incites*) aorimásu あおり[煽り]ます

stock *n* **1.** (*financial*) kabu 株; (*soup*) dashí だし・ダシ; (*on hand*) zaiko(-hin) 在庫(品), sutokku ストック; mochiawase (no) 持ち合わせ(の) **2.** *has in ~* (*on hand*) zaiko ga arimásu 在庫があります; mochi-awasemásu 持ち合わせます; motte imásu 持っています

stockings *n* kutsu-shita 靴下・くつした

stomach *n* i-búkuro 胃袋, i 胃; (*strictly, belly*) o-naka おなか, hará 腹; ***develops ~ trouble*** o-naka o kowashimásu おなかを壊します

stone *n* ishí 石

stop 1. *v* (*it comes to rest*) tomarimásu 止まります, todomarimásu とどまり[止まり・留まり]ます → **stand still**; (*it ceases*) yamimásu 止みます **2.** *v* (*~s it*) tomemásu 止めます, todomemásu とどめ[止め]ます, yoshimásu よします; (*~s doing*) … o yamemásu …を止めます **3.** *n* (*halting place*) teiryū-jo 停留所; (*end*) owari 終わり; stop up fusagimásu ふさぎます; ***gets stopped up*** fusagarimásu ふさがります

store *n* (*shop*) misé 店; sutoa ストア; storeroom *n* (*storehouse*) kurá 倉・蔵

storm *n* árashi 嵐・あらし, [BOOKISH] bōfū´ 暴風

story *n* **1.** hanashí 話, sutōrii ストーリー **2.** → **floor**

stove *n* sutō´bu ストーブ, (*kitchen*) kamado かまど・竈, kama かま・釜, rénji レンジ; (*portable cooking*) kónro コンロ

straddle *v* … ni matagarimásu …に跨がり[またがり]ます

straight *adj* massúgu (na) まっすぐ・真っ直ぐ(な); straight line *n* chokusen 直線

straighten *v* (*tidies it*) ***~s it up*** katazukemásu 片付けます

strain 1. *n* (*tension*) kinchō 緊張 **2.** *v* (*forces*) múri ni shimásu 無理にします; (*filters*) koshimásu こし[漉し]ます, (*through cloth*) shiborimásu 絞ります・しぼります

strait(s) *n* kaikyō 海峡

strange *adj* hén (na) 変(な), fushigi (na) 不思議(な); (*peculiar*) kímyō (na) 奇妙(な), okashíi おかしい; (*wondrous*) myō´ (na) 妙(な)

stranger *n* (*unknown person*) shiranai hitó 知らない人; (*outsider*) yosó no hitóよその人, tanin 他人

strap *n* himo ひも・紐; (*to hang on to*) tsuri-kawa 吊り革; (*watch-band, etc.*) bando バンド

straw *n* wára わら・ワラ・藁, mugiwara 麦わら[藁]; (*to drink with*) sutórō ストロー

strawberry *n* ichigo いちご・イチゴ・苺

stray **1.** *n* (*child*) maigo; (*animals*) mayoi-inu (-neko) 迷い犬(猫) **2.** *adj* michi ni mayotta 道に迷った, hagureta はぐれた **3.** *v* (*digresses*) soremás<u>u</u> 逸れ[それ]ます

stream *n* nagaré 流れ; ***in ~s*** zoro-zoro ぞろぞろ

streamline *v* (*procedures, …*) gōri-ka shimás<u>u</u> 合理化します

street *n* michi 道, torí 通り, shadō 車道, tsuji 辻; (*on*) ***the ~*** gaitō (de) 街頭(で)

strength *n* tsuyosa 強さ, (*power*) ch<u>i</u>kará 力・ちから; (*real ~*) jitsuryoku 実力; (*of saturation*) kósa 濃さ

strengthen *v* ***~s*** (*it*) tsúyoku shimás<u>u</u> 強くします, katamemás<u>u</u> 固めます

stretch **1.** *v* (*~es it*) nobashimás<u>u</u> 伸ばします; (*it ~es*) nobimás<u>u</u> 伸びます, (*taut*) harimás<u>u</u> 張ります **2.** *n* nobi 伸び, senobi 背伸び; stretch over (*extends over*) … ni ma-tagarimás<u>u</u> …に跨がり[またがり]ます

stretcher *n* tánka 担架

strew *v* chirashimás<u>u</u> 散らします

strict *adj* (*severe*) kibishíi 厳しい, katai 固い・堅い, yakamashíi やかましい; (*precise*) genmitsu (na) 厳密(な); genjū (na) 厳重(な)

strife *n* arasoi 争い, [BOOKISH] sō´dō 騒動

strike **1.** *n* (*job action*) s<u>u</u>tóスト, s<u>u</u>toraiki ストライキ; (*baseball*) s<u>u</u>toráiku ストライク **2.** → **hit**

striking *adj* (*outstanding*) ichiji-rushíi 著しい

string **1.** *n* (*thread*) íto 糸; (*cord*) himo ひも・紐; (*of violin or bow*) tsurú つる・弦 **2.** (*linked*) ***in a ~*** tsunagatte つながって **3.** ***~s up*** *v* (*suspends*) tsurimás<u>u</u> 吊ります

stripe *n* shimá しま・縞, sutoraipu ストライプ; **stripe pattern** *n* shima-moyō 縞模様

striptease *n* s<u>u</u>toríppu ストリップ

strive *v* ts<u>u</u>tomemás<u>u</u> 努めます, dóryoku shimás<u>u</u> 努力します, tsuk<u>u</u>shimás<u>u</u> 尽くします

stroke **1.** *n* (*sounds of bell*) (kane no) hibiki (鐘の)響き **2.** *n* (*sports*) ichida 一打 **3.** *v* nade-más<u>u</u> なで[撫で]ます **4.** *v* (*strikes*) uchimás<u>u</u> 打ちます **5.** *v* (*draws*) kakimás<u>u</u> 描きます; **stroke order** *n* kakijun 書き順

stroll *n, v* sanpo (shimás<u>u</u>) 散歩(します)

strong *adj* tsuyói 強い; (*coffee, etc.*) kói 濃い; (*influential*) yū-ryoku (na) 有力(な)

structure *n* kōzō 構造; (*setup*) kumi-tate 組み立て; (*system*) soshiki 組織

struggle **1.** *n* (*contention*) arasoi 争い **2.** *v* ***~s for*** (*contends*) … o arasoimás<u>u</u> …を争います

stuck; ***gets ~*** (*clogged*) tsumari-más<u>u</u> 詰まります

student *n* gakusei 学生, …-sei …生, (*pupil*) séito 生徒

studio *n* (*private*) atorie アトリエ; (*public*) sutajio スタジオ; **studio apartment** *n* wan-rū´mu ワンルーム

study 1. *n* benkyō 勉強; gakushū 学習; **~ *by observation*, *field* ~** ken-gaku 見学 **2.** *n* (*room*) shosai 書斎 **3.** *v* (*studies it*) benkyō shimásu 勉強します, manabimásu 学びます, (*is tutored/taught*) osowarimásu 教わります **4.** *v* → **research** → **science**

stuff 1. *n* (*thing*) monó 物 **2.** *v* (*crams*) tsumemásu 詰めます

stumble *v* tsuma-zukimásu つまずきます・躓きます

stump *n* (*tree*) kiri-kabu 切り株

stunt *n* kyokugéi 曲芸; ***horseback ~s*** kyokuba 曲馬

stupid *adj* báka (na) ばか・バカ・馬鹿(な)

sturdy *adj* jōbu (na) 丈夫(な)

style *n* **1.** … fū´/…-fū …風; … shiki/ …-shiki …式 **2.** (*form*) tái 態

stylish *adj* sumā´to (na) スマート(な), iki (na) いき[粋](な), otsu (na) 乙(な)

subject *n* (*topic*) mondai 問題, (*of conversation*) wadai 話題; táne 種; (*school*) kamoku 科目

subjective *adj* shukan-teki (na) 主観的な

submarine *n* sensui-kan 潜水艦

submissive *adj* súnao (na) すなお[素直](な)

subordinate *n* búka 部下, (*follower*) kó-bun 子分

subscribe *v* yoyaku shimásu 予約します, mōshi-komimásu 申し込みます

subscription *n* yoyaku 予約

subsequently *adv* tsuide 次いで → **later** → **next**

substance *n* (*material*) busshitsu 物資

substantial *adj* **1.** (*concrete*) gutaiteki (na) 具体的(な) **2.** → **considerable**

substitute *n* kawari 代わり; dai-yōhin 代用品

subtle *adj* wazuka (na) わずか(な), kasuka (na) 微か・かすか(な), (*delicate*) bimyō (na) 微妙(な)

subtract *v* hikimásu 引きます

suburb *n* kō´gai 郊外, shígai 市外, (*outskirts*) basue 場末

subway *n* chiká-tetsu 地下鉄

succeed *v* (*is successful*) seikō shimásu 成功します; ***~s to*** (*takes over for*) uketsugimásu 受け継ぎます, tsugimásu 継ぎます; (*in a projection*) hiki-tsugimásu 引き継ぎます; (*in a test*) ukárimásu 受かります

success *n* seikō 成功; gōkaku 合格; ***making a ~ out of life*** shusse 出世; **success story** *n* seikō-dan 成功談; sakusesu sutōrii サクセス・ストーリー

successful *adj* umái うまい; uma-kuiku うまくいく

such *adj* sonna そんな, sono yō´na そのよう[様]な, sō yū そうゆう; (*like this*) konna こんな, kono yō´na このよう[様]な, kō yū こうゆう

such-and-such a place dókodoko どこどこ, dókosoko どこそこ

suck *v* suimásu 吸います; shaburimásu しゃぶります; **It sucks!** *interj* saitē da 最低だ, hidoi ひどい

sucker *n* (*dupe*) kámo かも・カモ・鴨

sudden *adj* (*unexpected*) totsuzen (no) 突然(の), níwaka にわか; (*urgent*) kyū (na) 急(な); ~ ***shower*** yūdachi 夕立・ゆうだち, niwaka ame にわか雨

suddenly *adv* fui ni 不意に, totsuzen 突然; (*unexpectedly*) níwaka ni にわかに, (*immediately*) tachimachi (ni) たちまち(に); (*urgently*) kyū ni 急に; (*with a sudden start of surprise*) hatto (shite) はっと(して)

sue *v* uttaemásu 訴えます

suffer *v* kurushimimásu 苦しみます, nayamimásu 悩みます, wazuraimásu 煩い[わずらい]ます;(*incurs*) kōmurimásu 被り[こうむり]ます, ukemásu 受けます; **suffer from** ... o wazuraimásu ...を煩い[わずらい]ます → **incur**

suffering *n* kurushimi 苦しみ, (*anguish*) nayamí 悩み

suffice, sufficient *v*, *adj* tarimásu 足ります

suffix *n* setsubi-go/-ji 接尾語/辞

sugar *n* (o-)satō (お)砂糖・(お)サトウ

suggest(ion) → **propose** (*proposal*) → **hint**

suicide *n* jisatsu 自殺; **double suicide** *n* shinjū 心中; **suicidal wishes** *n* ji-satsu ganbō 自殺願望, [BOOKISH] kishi nenryo 希死念慮

suit **1.** *n* (o-)yō´fuku (お)洋服, fukú 服, (*business*) sebiro 背広, sū´tsu スーツ, (*diving suit*) sensui fuku 潜水服, daibingu sūtsu ダイビング・スーツ **2.** *n* (*of playing cards*) kumí 組 **3.** *v* (*matches with*) ...ni aimásu ...に合います; ***~s one's taste*** kuchi ni aimásu 口に合います **4.** *v* (*is becoming to*) ...ni ni-aimásu ...に似合います

suitable *adj* fusawashíi ふさわしい, tekitō (na) 適当(な), tekigi (na) 適宜(な); (*moderate*) kakkō (na) 格好(な); ***is ~*** teki-shimásu 適します

suitcase *n* kaban かばん・鞄, sūtsukē´su スーツケース; (*luggage*) (te-)nímotsu (手)荷物

sulk *v* fukuremásu 膨れます

sultry *adj* (*weather*) mushi-atsúi 蒸し暑い; (*behavior*) jōnetsuteki (na) 情熱的(な); ***gets ~*** mushimásu 蒸します

sum **1.** *n* gáku 額 **2.** ***to ~ it up*** yōsúru ni 要するに

summary *n* taiyō 大要, yōyaku 要約, (*gist*) yō´shi 要旨; gaiyō 概要; ***in ~*** yōsúru ni 要するに・よ

うするに

summer *n* natsú 夏; ~ ***gift*** (o-) chūgen (お)中元; ~ ***period/term*** káki 夏期; ~ ***school*** kaki-kōshū 夏期講習

summit *n* itadaki 頂・いただき, chōjō´ 頂上, mine 峰・みね

summon *v* yobimásu 呼びます

sumo → **wrestling, wrestler**

sun *n* táiyō 太陽・たいよう, hi 日, o-ténto-sama おてんとさま・お天道様

sunbathing *n* (*enjoying the warmth of the sun*) hinata-bókko ひなた[日向]ぼっこ, (*sunbathing, tanning*) nikkōyoku 日光浴

sunburn *n* hiyake 日焼け

Sunday *n* Nichiyō´bi 日曜日

sundry *adj* zatta (na) 雑多(な); ***sundries*** zakka 雑貨

sunglass *n* sangurasu サングラス

sunny *adj* (*room, etc.*) hiatari ga íi 日当りがいい

sunshine *n* hinata ひなた・日向, níkkō 日光, sanshain サンシャイン

super *adj* chō 超, sūpā スーパー; **superman** *n* sū´pāman スーパーマン, chōjin 超人; **supernatural** *n* chō shizen (no) 超自然(の)

superfluous *adj* yokei (na) 余計・よけい(な); (*surplus*) kajō (no) 過剰(の)

superintendent *n* kantoku 監督

superior 1. *adj* yūshū (na) 優秀(な); jōtō (no) 上等(の); ue (no) 上(の), meue (no) 目上(の) **2.** *adj* erái 偉い; masatte iru 勝っている **3.** *n* ***a superior*** menue no hitó 目上の人

supermarket *n* sū´pā スーパー, sū´pā-mā´ketto スーパーマーケット

supervise *v* kantoku shimásu 監督します

supervisor *n* kantoku 監督, sū´pā-baizā スーパーバイザー

supper *n* ban-góhan 晩ご飯, yūshoku 夕食, yū-han 夕飯

supplement *n* hosoku 補足, zōho 増補; (*pills*) sapuriment サプリメント, sapuri サプリ; ***food ~s*** eiyō-hojo-shokuhin 栄養補助食品

supplies *n* ...-yō´hin ...用品, (*necessities*) hitsuju-hin 必需品, (*expendables*) shōmō-hin 消耗品

supply 1. *v* ***supplies it*** kyōkyū shimásu 供給します; hokyū shimásu 補給します → **provide** → **give** → **sell 2.** ***supply(ing)*** *n* kyōkyū 供給; hokyū 補給

support 1. *n* (*approval*) sansei 賛成, sandō 賛同; (*backing, help*) kōen 後援, bákku-appu バックアップ, ōen 応援; (*aid*) énjo 援助, sapōto サポート **2.** *v* (*~s it*) ōen shimásu 応援します, bákku-appu shimásu バックアップします; (*props it*) sasaemásu 支えます; (*endorses*) shíji shimásu 支持します

supporter *n* (*football*) fan ファン

suppose *v* ... to shimásu ...とします; sō omoimásu そう思いま

す → think → imagine

supposition *n* katei 仮定; (*conjecture*) suisoku 推測

suppress *v* appaku shimásu 圧迫します

surcharge *n* tsuika-ryōkin 追加料金

sure *adj* táshika (na) 確か・たしか(な); for sure *adv* kanarazu 必ず・かならず, táshika ni 確かに・たしかに, zé-hi ぜひ・是非; make sure *v* tashikamemásu 確かめます・たしかめます; ***to make sure*** nen no tamé (ni) 念のため[為](に); to be sure *adv* móttómo もっとも → of course

surely *adv* kitto きっと

surf **1.** *n* yoseru-nami 寄せる波 **2.** *v* sā´fin o shimásu サーフィンをします; (*to surf the Internet*) netto sā´fin o shimásu ネットサーフィンをします

surface **1.** *n* mén 面, hyōmén 表面; (*top*) uwabe うわべ・上辺; ***entire*** ~ zenmen 全面 **2.** *v* (*becomes known*) barémásu ばれます

surgeon *n* geká-i 外科医

surgery *n* (*surgical operation*) shújutsu 手術; (*as a medical specialty*) geka 外科

surmise **1.** *n* suisoku 推測 **2.** *v* suisoku shimásu 推測します

surpass *v* suguremásu 優れ[すぐれ]ます, nukimásu 抜きます, masarimásu 勝ります

surplus *n* yoyū 余裕; kajō (no) 過剰(の)

surprised; ***gets*** ~ bikkúri shimásu びっくりします, odorokimásu 驚きます

surrender *n, v* kōfuku/kōsan shimásu 降伏/降参します

surround *v* kakomimásu 囲みます; (*centers on*) megurimásu 巡ります

surrounding **1.** *adj the* ~ … shūhen no … 周辺の… **2.** *adj* (*centering on*) … o megutte …を巡って **3.** ***surroundings*** *n* shū´i 周囲

sushi *n* (o-)súshi (お)すし[寿司・鮨], sushí すし・寿司・鮨

suspect **1.** *v* utagaimásu 疑います **2.** *n* yōgí-sha 容疑者

suspend *v* **1.** (*hangs it*) tsurimásu 吊ります, burasagemásu ぶら下げます **2.** (*stops in the midst*) chūshi shimásu 中止します

suspenders *n* zubón-tsuri ズボンつり, sasupendā サスペンダー

suspense *n* sasupensu サスペンス; suspense film *n* sasupensu eiga サスペンス映画

suspension *n* (*stoppage*) teishi 停止, (*abeyance*) chūshi 中止

suspicious *adj* fushigi (na) 不思議(な), ayashii 怪しい, ikagawashíi いかがわしい

sustain *v* (*incurs*) kōmurimásu 被り[こうむり]ます

sutra *n* (*Buddhist scripture*) o-kyō お経, kyōten 経典

swab *n* (*scrub*) tawashi たわし・タワシ, (*cotton*) watá 綿, (*earpick*) mimikákí 耳かき

swallow **1.** *n* (*bird*) tsubame つばめ・ツバメ・燕 **2.** *v* (*ingests*) nomi-komimásu 飲み込みます

swamp *n* numá 沼

swan *n* hakuchō 白鳥・ハクチョウ

sway *v* **1.** (*it ~s*) yuremásu 揺れます **2.** (*~s it*) yusu-burimásu 揺すぶります, yurimásu 揺ります

swear *v* **1.** (*vows*) chikaimásu 誓います **2.** (*reviles*) nonoshirimásu ののしります・罵ります

sweat *n, v* áse (ga demásu) 汗(が出ます)

sweater *n* sē´tā セーター

sweep *v* sōji shimásu 掃除します; hakimásu 掃きます

sweet *adj* amai 甘い; **sweet and sour** *adj* amazuppai 甘酸っぱい; **sweet roll with beanjam inside** *n* anpan あんパン

sweetheart *n* ii-hito いい人, koibito 恋人

sweet potato *n* satsuma-imo さつま[薩摩]芋・サツマイモ → **potato**

swell *adj* (*splendid*) suteki (na) すてき[素敵](な), (*terrific*) sugói すごい・凄い

swell *v* *~s (up)* haremásu 腫れ[はれ]ます; fukuramimásu 膨らみ[ふくらみ]ます, fukuremásu 膨れ[ふくれ]ます

swelling *n* hare-mono 腫れ物; dekí-mónó できもの・出来物, o-déki おでき; (*bump*) kobú こぶ・瘤

swim **1.** *n* (hitó-)oyogi (ひと)泳ぎ **2.** *v* oyogimásu 泳ぎます; **swim suit** *n* mizu-gi 水着

swimming *n* oyogí 泳ぎ, suiei 水泳, suimingu スイミング; **~ *pool*** pū´ru プール

swing **1.** *v* (*it ~s*) yuremásu 揺れます **2.** *v* (*~s it*) yusuburimásu 揺すぶります, yurimásu 揺ります **3.** *n* (*a ~*) búranko ぶらんこ **4.** ***gets into the ~ of things*** chōshi ni norimásu 調子に乗ります, chōshi ga demásu 調子が出ます

swipe *v* kapparaimásu かっぱらいます; nusumimásu 盗みます

Swiss **1.** *adj* Súisu no スイスの **2.** *n* (*person*) Suisú-jin スイス人

switch *n* suítchi スイッチ

Switzerland *n* Súisu スイス

sword *n* kataná 刀

syllable *n* onsetsu 音節

symbol *n* shinboru シンボル, [BOOKISH] shōchō 象徴; (*mark*) kigō 記号; **symbol of peace** *n* heiwa no shōchō 平和の象徴, heiwa no shinboru 平和のシンボル

symmetry *n* tsuriai 釣り合い・つりあい; taiō 対応

sympathize *v* ***~s with*** … ni dōjō shimásu …に同情します; (*takes into consideration*) … o kumimásu …を汲みます; sasshimásu 察します

sympathy *n* dōjō 同情, kyōkan 共感

symptom *n* (*sign*) shirushi しるし[徴]; shōjō 症状; (*unusual state*) ijō 異常

syndrome *n* (*medical*) shōkōgun

症候群, shindorōmu シンドローム

synthesis *n* sōgō 総合

syphilis *n* (*medical*) baidoku 梅毒

Syria *n* shiria シリア

syringe *n* (*for injections*) chūsháki 注射器; (*for water*) chūsúiki 注水器

syrup *n* shiróppu シロップ

system *n* soshiki 組織, séido 制度, taikei 体系, chitsujo 秩序, shisutemu システム

systematic *adj* kichōmen na きちょうめんな, kisoku-tadashii 規則正しい, tejundōri no 手順通りの

T

tab *n* tsumami つまみ; tábu タブ → **bill**

tabby *n* tora neko トラ猫

table *n* **1.** tēburu テーブル, táku 卓; (*dinner table*) shokutaku 食卓 **2.** (*list*) hyō 表; (*inventory*) mokuroku 目録; **multiplication table** *n* kakezan hyō 掛け算表; **table lamp** *n* denki sutando 電気スタンド; **table of contents, TOC** *n* mokuji 目次; **table salt** *n* shokúen 食塩, shokutakú-en 食卓塩

tablet *n* (*pill*) jōzai 錠剤, taburetto タブレット; (*note pad*) memo-chō メモ帳

taboo *n* tabū タブー; kinki 禁忌

taciturn *adj* mukuchi (na) 無口(な); [BOOKISH] kamoku (na) 寡黙(な)

tack **1.** *n* byō´ びょう・鋲; (*sewing*) shi-tsuke 仕付け **2.** *v* ***~s it on the wall*** … o kabe ni byō´ de tomemásu …を壁にびょう[鋲]で留めます; (*with thread*) shi-tsukemásu 仕付けます

tackle *n* takkuru タックル

tact *n* **1.** kiten 機転, saiki 才気 **2.** kanshoku 感触

tactics *n* (*strategy*) senjutsu 戦術, sakusen 作戦

tadpole *n* otamajakushi オタマジャクシ

tag *n* fuda 札; (*baggage/package ~*) ní-fuda 荷札, tagu タグ; **name tag** *n* na fuda 名札

tail *n* shippó しっぽ・尻尾, ó 尾

tailor *n* shitate-ya 仕立屋, yōfuku-ya 洋服屋

Taiwan *n* Taiwan 台湾; ***a Taiwanese*** Taiwán-jin 台湾人

Tajikistan *n* Tajikisutan タジキスタン

take *v* **1.** torimásu 取ります, totte/motte ikimásu 取って/持って行きます **2.** hipparimásu 引っ張ります **3.** (*requires*) yō-shimásu 要します; (*requires time/money*) (jikan/kane ga) kakarimásu (時間/金が)かかります **4.** (*incurs*) ukemásu 受けます; (*accepts; understands*) uke-torimásu 受け取ります; ***~ it seriously*** honki ni shimásu 本気にします; *~ one's blood pressure* ketsuatsu o hakarimásu 血圧を計ります; take advantage of *v* … o riyō shimásu …を利用します; zu ni norimásu 図に乗ります; take away *v* totte ikimásu 取って行きます; (*confiscates, deprives of*) tori-agemásu 取り上げます; (*clears from table*) sagemásu 下げます; take aim *v* nerai o tsukemásu 狙いをつけます; take apart *v* barashimásu ばらします; take care of *v* ① (*handles*) … o shóri shimásu …を処理します ② (*~ a person*) … no sewá o shimásu … の世話をします, ... no mendō´o mimásu …の面倒をみます; Take care (of yourself). *interj* O-daiji ni! お大事に!; take charge of ... *v* ... o hiki-ukemásu …を引き受けます, tannin/tantō shimásu 担任/担当します; take down *v* oroshimásu 下ろし[降ろし]ます; take effect *v* (*is effective*) kikimásu 効きます; take fright *v* kowagarimásu 怖がり[こわがり]ます; take in(to) *v* iremásu 入れます; take in trust *v* azukarimásu 預かります; Take it easy. *interj* ① Go-yukkúri. ごゆっくり. ② → **good-bye**; take off *v* ① (*removes*) hazushimásu 外します; (*clothes, shoes, etc.*) nugimásu, 脱ぎます ② (*plane*) ririku shimásu 離陸します; take-off *n* (*of a plane*) ririku 離陸; take offense *v* shaku ni sawarimásu しゃく[癪]にさわり[障り]ます; take over *v* hiki-tori/tsugimásu 引き取り/継ぎます; (*illegally seizes*) nottorimásu 乗っ取ります; takeover *n* (*illegal seizure*) nottorijíken 乗っ取り事件; take pains *v* honé o orimásu 骨を折ります; take refuge *v* hínan shimásu 避難します; take responsibility for *v* (*responsibility for situation*) … o hiki-ukemásu …を引き受けます, … no sekinin o tori/oimásu …の責任を取り/負います

takeaway, takeout *n* (*food*) (o-) mochikaeri (お)持ち帰り

tale *n* (o-)hanashí (お)話, monogátari 物語; fairy tale *n* yōsei monogatari 妖精物語, otogi-banashi 御伽噺・おとぎ話; old tale *n* mukashi-banashi 昔話

talent *n* sainō 才能, sái 才; (*personality*) tarento タレント; *~ agency* *n* geinō purodakushon 芸能プロダクション

talisman (*of a shrine*) *n* o-fuda お札, go-fu 護符, o-mamori お守り

talk **1.** *n* hanashí 話; (*conference, discussion*) hanashi-ai 話し合い, (*consultation*) sōdan 相談 → **speech** **2.** *v* (*speaks*) hanashimásu 話します; *~ together* hanashi-aimásu 話し合います; talk back *v* kuchi-gotae o shimásu 口答えをします; talk big *v* (*boost*) hora o fukimásu ほらを吹きます・ふくます

talkative *adj* hanashizuki (na) 話し

好き(な), oshaberi (na) おしゃべり・お喋り(な)

tall *adj* takái 高い; (*of body height*) sé ga takái 背が高い; **tall story** *n* (*unbelivable story*) ほら[法螺]

tambourine *n* tanbarin タンバリン

tame *v* ~ *it* narashimás<u>u</u> 馴らします, kainarashimás<u>u</u> 飼い慣らします

tan *n* hiyake 日焼け; **tanned** *adj* hiyakeshita 日焼けした

tandem *n* tandemu タンデム, futarinori-yō (no) jitensha/jidensha 二人乗り用(の)自転車

tangerine *n* (*Mandarin orange*) míkan みかん・ミカン・蜜柑

tangible *adj* gutai-teki (na) 具体的(な)

tangle *n* (*entanglement*) motsure もつれ・縺れ

tango *n* tango タンゴ

tank *n* tanku タンク

tanker *n* tankā タンカー

Tanzania *n* Tanzania タンザニア

tap **1.** *v* (karuku) tatakimás<u>u</u> (軽く)叩きます・たたきます **2.** *v* tōchō shimás<u>u</u> 盗聴します **3.** *n* jaguchi 蛇口 **4.** *n* (*tap-daicing*) タップダンス; **tap water** *n* suidōsui 水道水

tape *n* tē´pu テープ; himo ひも・紐; **adhesive tape** *n* bansōkō 絆創膏・ばんそうこう; **adhesive cellophane tape** *n* serohan tēpu セロハンテープ

tapestry *n* tapesutorii タペストリー

tar *n* tāru タール

target *n* mato 的, taishō 対象; (*goal*) mok<u>u</u>hyō 目標, tāgetto ターゲット

tariff *n* kanzei 関税

tart *n* (*pie*) taruto タルト; **tart pastry** *n* taruto kiji タルト生地

task *n* shigoto 仕事; tasuku タスク

tassel *n* fusa 房

taste **1.** *n* (*flavor*) aji 味, fūmi 風味; (*has flavor*) aji ga shimás<u>u</u> 味がします **2.** (*liking*) shúmi 趣味; tēsuto テースト, sensu センス, (o-)konomi (お)好み; ***simple*** (*modest*) *~s* wabi わび・侘び; **bitter taste of life** *n* (jinsei no) nigai keiken (人生の)苦い経験; **good taste** *n* yoi shumi 良い趣味, ii sensu いいセンス; **sweet taste** *n* amai aji 甘い味, kanmi 甘味

taste *v* (*~s it*) ajiwaimás<u>u</u> 味わいます, namemás<u>u</u> なめ[舐め]ます; (*tries eating it*) tábete mimás<u>u</u> 食べてみます

tasty *adj* oishii おいしい・美味しい, umái うまい・旨い・美味い, bimi 美味

tatami *n* tatami たたみ・畳

tattoo *n* ire-zumi 入れ墨・刺青

taught → **teach**; **is taught** osowarimás<u>u</u> 教わります

taut; ***stretched*** ~ pin-to hatta ピンと張った

tavern *n* nomí-ya 飲み屋; izaka-ya 居酒屋

tax *n* zéi 税, zeikin 税金; ~ (*revenue*) ***stamp*** shūnyū-ínshi 収

入印紙; consumption tax *n* shōhi zei 消費税; income tax *n* shotoku zei 所得税; national tax *n* koku zei; tax-free *adj* menzei (no) 免税(の); **~ *shop*** menzei-ten 免税店; tax refund *n* zeikin (no) kanpu 税金(の)還付

taxi *n* tákushii タクシー, **~ *stand/ station*** takushii nori-ba タクシー乗り場

tea *n* cha 茶; (*green*) ryoku-cha 緑茶, o-cha お茶; (*black*) kōcha 紅茶, tii ティー; (*powdered green, for tea ceremony*) matcha 抹茶; Japanese tea *n* nihon cha 日本茶; tea bag *n* tii baggu ティーバッグ; teacake *n* (o-)cha-gáshi (お)茶菓子; tea ceremony *n* o-cha お茶, cha-no-yu 茶の湯, sadō 茶道; teacup *n* yunomí 湯飲み; (*also ricebowl*) (o-)cháwan (お)茶碗; teapot *n* do-bin どびん・土瓶, kyūsu きゅうす・急須, cha-bin ちゃびん・茶瓶; tearoom *n* kissa-ten 喫茶店; (*for tea ceremony*) (o-)chashitsu (お)茶室; tea scoop *n* (*for tea ceremony*) chashaku 茶杓; tea party *n* o-chakai お茶会

teach *v* oshiemásu 教えます

teacher *n* senséi 先生; (*school-teacher*) gakkō no senséi 学校の先生, (*instructor*) kyō´shi 教師; head teacher *n* kōchō (sensei) 校長(先生)

teaching *n* kyōju 教授, oshie 教え; ***classroom* ~** júgyō 授業; **~ *hours*** jugyō-jíkan 授業時間; teaching materials *n* kyōzai 教材

team *n* chíimu チーム

team up (*with*) (… to) kumimásu (…と)組みます

teamwork *n* chiimu-wā´ku チームワーク, kyōdō sagyō 共同作業

tear 1. *n* (*in eye*) námida 涙; burst into tears *v* watto nakidashimásu わっと泣き出します; tears of joy *n* ureshinamida 嬉し涙 **2.** *v* (*~s it*) sakimásu 裂きます, yaburimásu 破ります; ***~s into pieces*** chigirimásu 千切ります **3.** *v* (*it ~s*) sakemásu 裂けます, yaburemásu 破れます

tearful *adj* namidagunda 涙ぐんだ; tearful eyes *n* namidagunda me 涙ぐんだ目; tearful farewell *n* namida no wakare 涙の別れ; tearful look *n* nakisō na kao 泣きそうな顔

tease *v* (*pokes fun at*) karakaimásu からかいます; (*torments*) ijimemásu いじめます・苛めます

technical *adj* senmon-teki (na) 専門的(な); tekunikaru (na) テクニカル(な)

technician *n* gijutsu-ka 技術家

technique *n* gíjutsu 技術; waza 技; tekunikku テクニック

teenager *n* tiin eijā ティーンエイジャー; jūdai (no hito) 10代(の人); jūsan sai kara jūkyū sai 13歳から19歳

teeth → **tooth**

Teheran *n* Teheran テヘラン

telecast *n* terebi hōsō テレビ放送

telecommunication *n* (denki) tsūshin

(電気)通信

teleconference *n* denwa kaigi 電話会議; terebi kaigi テレビ会議

telegram *n* denpō (o uchimásu̲) 電報(を打ちます)

telephone 1. *n* = ~ ***call*** denwa 電話; ***mobile ~/cell-phone*** keitai denwa 携帯電話; ***touch-tone ~*** *n* pu̲sshúhon プッシュホン; **telephone card** *n* terehon kādo テレホンカード; **telephone number** *n* denwa-bángō 電話番号; **telephone operator** *n* (denwa-)kōkán-shu (電話)交換手, (denwa) operētā (電話)オペレーター **2.** *v* ~*s* (... ni) denwa o kakemásu̲/shimasu (...に)電話をかけます/します

telescope *n* bōenkyō 望遠鏡

television *n* térebi テレビ, terebíjon テレビジョン

telex *n* terekkusu テレックス

tell *v* **1.** iimásu̲ 言います; (*relates*) nobemásu̲ 述べます; katarimásu̲ 語ります **2.** (*informs one of*) ... no mimí ni iremásu̲ ...耳に入れます, ... ni ki̲kasemásu̲; ...に聞かせます, ... ni tsugemásu̲ ...に告げます **3.** (*instructs*) oshiemásu̲ 教えます; ~ ***on*** (*tattles*) ii-tsu̲kemásu̲ 言い付けます

teller *n* **1.** (*narrator*) hanashite 話し手; katarite 語り手 **2.** (*bank*) (ginkō no) suitō-gakari (銀行の)出納係; **story teller** *n* sutōrii terā ストーリー・テラー

temper 1. *n* (*disposition*) ijí 意地; táchi たち・質, ténsei 天性, táido 態度 **2.** *v* (*forges metal*) kitaemásu̲ 鍛えます; **be in a bad temper** *v* kigen ga warui desu̲ 機嫌が悪いです; **lose one's temper** *v* tanki o okoshimásu̲ 短気を起こします

temperament *n* ténsei 天性; ki̲shi̲tsu 気質

temperature *n* óndo 温度; (*of body*) taion 体温; (*fever*) netsú 熱; (*air*) kion 気温; (*room air*) shitsuon 室温

temple *n* **1.** (*Asian*) (o-)tera (お)寺; ...-ji ...寺 **2.** shinden 神殿 **3.** (*flat part on each side of the head*) komekami こめかみ; **temple bell** *n* tsurigane 釣り鐘; **temple fair** *n* énnichi 縁日

temporal *adj* **1.** ichiji-teki (na) 一時的(な) **2.** sokutō-bu (no) 側頭部(の)

temporary *adj* rinji (no) 臨時(の), tōza (no) 当座(の); (*passing*) ichíji (no) 一時(の), ichiji-teki (na) 一時的(な); (*tentative*) kari (no) 仮(の), ka-... 仮...; **temporary availability** *n* ichiji-teki ni riyō kanō 一時的に利用可能, ichiji-teki ni nyūshu kanō 一時的に入手可能; **temporary ceasefire** *n* ichiji teisen 一時停戦

tempt *v* sasoimásu̲ 誘います

temptation *n* sasoi 誘い, yūwaku 誘惑

tempura *n* tenpura てんぷら・テンプラ・天麩(婦)羅

ten *n* jū́ 十・10, tṓ 十・10; ***ten days*** tōka 十日・10日

tenant *n* (*of apartment, room*) magari-nin 間借人, nyūkyó-sha 入居者, tenanto テナント; **tenant owner** *n* tenanto no ōnā テナントのオーナー

tend (*to do/happen*) *v* yóku ... (shimásu) よく...(します); (shi)-yasúi desu (し)やすいです

tendency *n* keikō 傾向

tender → **gentle, soft** → **hurt**

tenderness *n* nasake 情け

tennis *n* ténisu テニス; **tennis court** *n* tenisu kōto テニスコート

tenor *n* ténā テナー, tenōru テノール

tense *v* (*taut*) hatte imásu 張っています; (*strained*) kinchō shite imásu 緊張しています; (*situation*) kinpaku shimásu 緊迫します

tension *n* kinchō 緊張; tenshon テンション

tent *n* ténto テント

tentative *adj* kari (no) 仮(の)

tenth *adj* jū-banmé (no) 十番目(の), tō-mé (no) 十目(の); ***the ~ day*** tōka-mé 十日目, (*of the month*) tōka 十日・10日; ***~ floor*** juk-kai 十階

ten thousand *n* mán 万・10,000, ichi-mán 一万・10,000

term *n* (*period*) kikán 期間, (*time limit*) kígen 期限; (*of school*) gakki 学期; (*technical word*) senmon-yōgo 専門用語, yōgo 用語; (*stipulation*) jōken 条件

terminal (*place*), **terminus** *n* shūten 終点; hatchaku-chi 発着地; tāminaru ターミナル

terms *n* (*between people*) náka 仲

terrible *adj* (mono-)sugói (もの)すごい・(物)凄い, taihen (na) 大変(な); (*severe*) hidoi ひどい・酷い; (*frightening*) osoroshíi 恐ろしい; (*shocking*) tonde-mo nái とんでもない, tonda とんだ

terribly *adv* súgóku すごく・凄く, mono-súgóku ものすごく・物凄く, taihen 大変; hídoku ひどく・酷く; osoróshiku 恐ろしく; (*unbearably*) yáke ni やけに

terrific *adj* sugói すごい/凄い, kowái こわい・怖い

territory *n* ryō´do 領土, ryō´chi 領地, teritorii テリトリー, nawabari 縄張り

terror *n* kyō´fu 恐怖; **reign of terror** *n* kyō´fu jidai 恐怖時代

terrorism *n* téro テロ

terrorist *n* terorisuto テロリスト

test *n* **1.** shikén 試験, tésuto テスト; (*check of blood, etc.*) kénsa 検査 → **trial** → **experiment** **2.** → **try**; **achievement test** *n* gakuryoku shiken 学力試験; **blood test** *n* ketsueki kensa 血液検査; **DNA test** *n* dii enu ei kantei DNA 鑑定; **eye test** *n* shiryoku kensa 視力検査; **hearing test** *n* ① (*checkup*) chōryoku kensa 聴力検査 ② (*exam*) hiyaringu tesuto ヒヤリング・テスト, kikitori shiken 聞き取り試験; **routine test** *n* (*examination*) teiki shiken 定期試験; **test tube** *n* shiken-kan 試験管

testament *n* (*will*) yuigon 遺言; ***the Old/New* ~** Kyū-/Shin-yaku 旧/新約

testicle(s) *n* kintámá 金玉, (*medical*) kōgan 睾丸

testify *v* shōgen shimásu 証言します

testimony *n* shōgen 証言

Texas *n* Tekisasu テキサス

text **1.** *n* bun 文, (*computer*) tekisuto テキスト **2.** *v* (mēru o) uchimásu (メールを)打ちます

textile *n* ori-mono 織物; textile industry *n* sen'i sangyō 繊維産業, bōseki kōgyō 紡績工業

texture *n* jí 地, ori-ji 織地; kimé きめ・肌理; (*touch*) tezawari 手触り・手ざわり, shitsukan 質感

Thailand *n* Tai タイ

than ... ... yóri ...より

thank *v* o-rei o iimásu お礼を言います; Thank you. *interj* Arígatō gozaimásu. ありがとう[有り難う]ございます; Dō´mo. どうも; Sumimasén すみません; osóreirimásu. 恐れ入ります; Thank you for the hard work. *interj* Go-kúrō-sama (deshita) . ご苦労さま(でした).; Thank you for the treat. *interj* Gochisō-sama (déshita) . ご馳走[ごちそう]さま(でした); thank-you letter *n* o-rei no tegami お礼の手紙, sankyū retā サンキューレター; [BOOKISH] kansha-jō 感謝状, reijō 礼状

thanks *n* (*gratitude*) kansha (no kotobá) 感謝(の言葉); (o-)rei (お)礼; ***~ to your solicitude*** okagesama de お蔭さまで

thanksgiving *n* **1.** (*gratitude*) kansha 感謝 **2.** (*day*) kansha-sai 感謝祭

that *pron* **1.** (*one*) sore それ, soitsu そいつ, (*of two*) sochira/sotchí そちら/そっち; (*over there*; *obvious*) are あれ, (*of two*) achira/atchí あちら/あっち; ***~ damn one*** soitsu そいつ, aitsu あいつ, kyátsu きゃつ; ***to ~ extent*** sonna ni そんなに; anna ni あんなに **2. *that ...*** sono ... その...; ano ... あの...; (*said/thought that*) ... to ...と; (*which/who*) — *not translated*; that is to say *adv* sunáwachi すなわち・即ち; that kind of *adj* sono/ano yō na その/あのよう[様]な, sō/ā yū そう/あゆう, sonna/anna そんな/あんな; that place *pron* ① soko そこ; sochira/sotchí そちら/そっち ② (*over there*, *obvious*) asoko あそこ, asuko あすこ; achira/atchí あちら/あっち; that side *n* achiragawa あちら側; That's right *interj* sō´ (desu) そう(です)

that... **1.** sono ...その...; (*over there*; *obvious*) ano ... あの...; ***said/ thought that*** ... (sono yō ni) itta/ kangaeta, omotta (そのように)言った/考えた・思った **2.** [RELATIVE PRONOUN] = **which..., who...**

thatch *n* káya かや・茅, (*straw*) wára わら・藁, (*grass*) kusá 草

thaw *v* (*it thaws*) tokemásu 解(溶)けます; (*thaws it*) tokashimásu

解(溶)かします

the *article* (*usually not translated*); ano … あの…, hon- 本…

theater *n* (*building*) gekijyō 劇場, za 座; (*drama*) engeki 演劇, (*play*) shibai 芝居, (*traditional*) kabuki 歌舞伎; ***the Kabuki ~*** (*building*) Kabuki-za 歌舞伎座

theft *n* nusumí 盗み, tōnan 盗難

them, they *pron* (*people*) anóhito-tachi あの人達, káre-ra 彼等 (*or name/title/role* + -tachi 達・たち); (*things*) soré-ra それら

theme *n* (*topic*) tē´ma テーマ, shudai 主題; (*composition*) sakubun 作文; **theme song** *n* tēma songu テーマソング; shudai-ka 主題歌

then *adv* (*at that time*) sono tókí その時, tō´ji 当時; (*after that*) sore kara それから; (*in that case*) sore nára それなら; ***and/ well ~*** sá-te さて

theology *n* shingaku 神学

theory *n* riron 理論, rikutsu 理屈, seorii セオリー, …-ron …論

there *adv* soko (ni) そこ(に); (*over ~*) asoko/asuko (ni) あそこ/あすこ(に)

therefore *adv* dákara (sa) だから(さ); (*accordingly*) shitagatte したがって・従って

there is/are … *adv* …ga arimásu … があります; ***~ no …*** … ga (/wa) arimasén …が(/は)ありません

thermal *adj* netsu (no) 熱(の); **thermal energy** *n* netsu enerugii 熱エネルギー

thermometer *n* ondo-kei 温度計; (*body*) taion-kei 体温計

these *pron* … kono … この…; ~ (*ones*) koré-ra これら; ***~ damn ones*** koitsú-ra こいつら

thesis *n* ronbun 論文, gakuirón-bun 学位論文

they → **them**

thick *adj* atsui 厚い, buatsui 分厚い・部厚い, atsubottai 厚ぼったい; (*and round*) futói 太い; (*dense, close*) kói 濃い

thief *n* dorobō どろぼう・泥棒; [BOOKISH] zoku 賊, tōzoku 盗賊; **sneak thief** *n* koso-doro こそどろ・こそ泥; akisu 空き巣

thigh *n* mómo もも・股, futomomo 太股・ふともも

thimble *n* yubi-núkí 指ぬき

thin **1.** *adj* usui 薄い; (*and round*) hosói 細い **2.** ***gets ~*** (*loses weight*) yasemásu やせ[痩せ]ます

thing *n* monó 物, yátsu やつ・奴; (*fact, matter*) kotó 事; ***things*** monógoto 物事; **just the thing** *n, adj* (*ideal*) motte-kói (no) もってこい(の)

think *v* (*that* …) (… to) omoimásu (… と)思います, kangaemásu 考えます

third *adj* sanbanmé (no) 三番目, mittsu-mé (no) 三つ目(の); ***the ~ day*** mikka-mé 三日目, (*of the month*) mikka 三日・3日; ***~ or fourth*** san-yo-banmé (no) 三, 四番目(の); **third class** *adj* san-tō (no)

三等(の); third floor *n* san-gai 三階
thirsty *adj* nódo ga kawaita のど[喉]が渇いた, nódo ga kawaite(i)ru のど[喉]が渇いて(い)る
thirteen *n* jū-san 十三・13
thirty *n* san-jū 三十・30; thirty percent *n* sán-wari 三割, sanjuppāsénto 三十パーセント・30%
this *pron* **1.** (*one*) kore これ, hon-… 本…; (*of two*) kochira/kotchí こちら/こっち; *~ damn one* koitsu こいつ; *to ~ extent* konna ni こんなに **2.** *this …* kono … この…; this afternoon *adv, n* kyṓno gógo 今日の午後; this kind of *adj* kono yṓna このよう[様]な, kō yū こうゆう, konna こんな; this much *adv* konna ni こんなに; this place *pron* koko ここ; kochira/kotchí こちら/こっち; this side *n* kochira-gawa こちら側; *~ of …* no temae …の手前; this time *adv, n* kóndo 今度, íma 今, kono tabí このたび[度]; this way *n* (*like this*) kō こう (kṓこう + [PARTICLE] *or* désu です); (*this direction*) kochira/kotchí こちら/こっち
thorn *n* togé とげ・トゲ・棘
thorny *adj* **1.** togé no ōi とげ[トゲ・棘]の多い **2.** ibara (no) イバラ・茨(の); thorny problem *n* nandai 難題
thorough *adj* tettei-teki (na) 徹底的(な); (*detailed*) seimitsu (na) 精密(な)
thoroughly *adv* tettei-teki ni 徹底的(に)
those → **them**
those ... *pron* sono … その…, ano … あの…; *~* (*ones*) soré-ra それら, aré-ra あれら; *~ damn ones* soitsú-ra そいつら, aitsú-ra あいつら; *~ present* shusséki-sha 出席者; those days *n* tṓji 当時
though *conj* démo でも, kéredo (mo) けれど(も)
thought **1.** *n* kangáe 考え, omói 思い, shikō 思考; shisō 思想; (*fulness*) shíryo 思慮 **2.** → **think**
thousand *n* sén 千・1,000, is-sén 一千・1,000; *a ~ yen* sen-en 千円・1,000円
thread *n* íto 糸
threat *n* odoshi 脅し, [BOOKISH] kyōhaku 脅迫
threaten *v* odo(ka)shimásu 脅(か)します
threatening *adj* kyōhaku-teki (na) 脅迫的(な); threatening call *n* kyōhaku denwa 脅迫電話
three *n* san 三・3, mittsú 三つ; san-… 三…, mi-… 三…; suríi スリー; (*people*) san-nín 三人, [BOOKISH] sánmei 三名
threshold *n* **1.** shikii 敷居 **2.** (*threshold value*) ikichi 閾値
thrifty *adj* tsumashíi つましい・倹しい, ken'yaku (na) 倹約(な), komakái 細かい
thrill **1.** *n* súríru スリル **2.** *adj* (*is thrilled*) waku-waku/zokuzoku shimásu わくわく/ぞくぞくします

thrilling *adj* suriru o kanjisaseru スリルを感じさせる, waku-waku/zokuzoku suru わくわく/ぞくぞくする

thrive *v* sakaemásu 栄えます; uremásu 売れます

throat *n* nódo のど・喉

throb *v* dokidoki shimásu どきどき・ドキドキします

throne *n* ōi 王位, ōza 王座

throng 1. *n* ōzéi 大勢; (*flock*) muré 群れ **2.** ***they ~ together*** *v* muragarimásu 群がります

through 1. *prep* ***putting ~*** … o tō´shite …を通して; ***gets ~*** tsūjimásu 通じます **2.** *prep* (*throughout*) …-jū …じゅう・中; …no aida-jū …の間じゅう[間中]; ***all the way ~*** zutto ずっと **3.** (*by means of*) … de …で, … o tsukatte …を使って **4.** (*extending ~*) … ni kákete …かけて

throughout *prep* (*the entire* [PLACE/TIME]) …-jū …じゅう・中; ***~ the world*** sekai-jū 世界じゅう[中]

throw *v* nagemásu 投げます; ***~ away*** sutemásu 捨てます; ***~ into disorder*** midashimásu 乱します

throw up → **vomit**

thrust *v* tsukimásu 突きます; **thrust stage** *n* haridashi butai 張り出し舞台

thumb *n* oya-yubi 親指

thumb drive *n* (*small computer storage*) samu-doraibu サムドライブ

thumbprint *n* (*when used to stamp a document*) boin 母印・拇印

thunder *n* kaminárí (ga narimásu) 雷(が鳴ります)

thunderstorm *n* ráiu 雷雨

Thursday *n* Mokuyō´bi 木曜日

Tibet *n* Chibetto チベット

tick *n* chekku チェック

tick mark *n* chekku māku チェックマーク, re ten レ点

ticket *n* kippu 切符, chikétto チケット; …-ken …券; ***just the ~*** (*ideal*) motte-kói (no) もってこい(の), (*most suitable*) uttetsuke (no) うってつけ(の); ***admission ~*** nyōjō-ken 入場券; **ticket agency** *n* ***theater ~*** pureigáido プレイガイド (*"Play Guide"*); **ticket book** *n* (*for commuting*) kaisū´-ken 回数券; **ticket vending machine** *n* kenbáiki 券売機; **ticket wicket** *n* kaisatsu-guchi 改札口

tickle *v* kusugurimásu くすぐります

tide *n* shió 潮; chōryū 潮流

tidy 1. *adj* kírei (na) きれい(な) **2.** ***tidies it up*** *v* katazukemásu 片付けます; ***it gets ~*** katazukimásu 片付きます

tie 1. *v* musubimásu 結びます; (*fastens*) tsunagimásu つなぎます **2.** *n* (*necktie*) nékutai ネクタイ; (*game*) hikiwake 引き分け

tiff *n* mome-goto もめ事・揉め事

tiger *n* tora 虎・トラ; taigā タイガー

tight *adj* (*tight-fitting*) kitsui きつい; (*hard*) katai 堅い; (*skimpy*) semái 狭い → **drunk**

tights *n* taitsu タイツ

tile **1.** *n* (*roof*) kawara 瓦; ***~-roofed*** kawara-buki (no) 瓦ぶき・瓦葺き(の) **2.** *n* (*floor, wall*) táiru タイル **3.** *v* ***~s a roof*** kawara de yáne o fuk̲imásu̲ 瓦で屋根をふき[葺き]ます

timber *n* zaimoku 材木

time *n* **1.** tokí 時, … tókí …時, (o-)jíkan (お)時間, jibun 時分; (*specified*) jíkoku 時刻; (*season*) jíki 時期; (*opportunity*) jíki 時機, (*appropriate occasion*) jísetsu 時節; (*interval, time while …*) aida 間 **2.** *n* (*occasion*) tabí たび・度, orí 折, sái 際, tokoró ところ; (*period*) koro 頃; ***at one ~*** kátsu̲te かって, kátte かって; ***for the ~ being*** tōbun 当分, íma no tokoró wa 今のところは; ***is in ~*** (*for …*) (… ni) ma ni aimásu̲ (…に)間に合います; (*the trend of*) ***the times*** (go-)jísei (ご)時世; **in a short time** *adv* mamonaku まもなく, sugu (ni) すぐ(に); **in time** *adv* (*eventually*) yagate やがて; **on time** *adv* jikandōri ni 時間通りに, teikoku ni 定刻に; **this/next time** *adv, n* kóndo 今度; **what time** *adv, n* nán-ji 何時; **time and again** *adv* nando mo 何度も; **time deposit** *n* teiki-yókin 定期預金; **time difference, time-lag** *n* jísa 時差; **time loan** *n* teiki kashitsuke-kin 定期貸付金; **time management** *n* jikan (no) kanri 時間(の)管理; **time off** *n* yasumí 休み; **timepiece** *n* tokei 時計; **timetable** *n* jikoku-hyō 時刻表; (*school*) jikan-wari 時間割(り)

timekeeper *n* (*person*) jikan kiroku-gakari 時間記録係

timer *n* taimā タイマー

timid *adj* (*shy*) uchik̲i (na) 内気(な), (*cowardly*) okubyō (na) 臆病(な); **timid attitude** *n* ozuozu-shita taido おずおずした態度

tin *n* buriki ブリキ, súzu すず・スズ・錫

tinkle *n* chirin chirin (to iu oto) チリンチリン(という音)

tint *n* iroai 色合い

tiny *adj* totemo chiisana とても小さな, chippoke (na) ちっぽけ(な); **tiny tot** *n* chibikko ちびっ子

tip **1.** *n* (*money*) chíppu チップ, kokoro-zuke 心付け, chadai 茶代; (*point*) saki 先 **2.** *v* ***it ~s over*** hik̲kuri-kaerimásu̲ ひっくり返ります, ***~s it over*** hik̲kuri-kaeshimásu̲ ひっくり返します

tire *n* (*of wheel*) taiya タイヤ; **tire chain** *n* taiya chēn タイヤ・チェーン

tired; ***gets ~*** tsu̲karemásu̲ 疲れます, ku̲tabiremásu̲ くたびれます; ***gets ~ of*** … ni akimásu̲ …に飽きます; ***dead ~*** ku(t)taku̲ta く(っ)たくた; hetoheto へとへと

tissue *n* ti̲sshu-pē´pā ティッシュペーパー; hana-gami 鼻紙, chiri-gami ちり紙

title *n* (*of book , article, …*) hyōdai 表題・標題, daimei 題名,

midashi 見出し; (*job* ~) katagaki 肩書; (*of anything, esp. movie, person, athlete*) táitoru タイトル; ~ ***page*** tobira 扉; title match *n* taitoru matchi タイトルマッチ
to *prep* … ni …に, … e …へ
toad *n* hikigaeru ヒキガエル
toast **1.** *n* tō´suto トースト; (*"bottoms up"*) kanpai 乾杯 **2.** *v* (*~s it*) yakimásu 焼きます
toaster *n* tō´sutā トースター
tobacco *n* tabako たばこ・煙草; ~ ***shop*** tabako-ya たばこ屋・煙草屋
today *n* kyō´ 今日; [BOOKISH] honjitsu 本日
toe *n* ashi no yubí 足の指; (*toe-tip*) tsumasaki つま先・爪先
tofu *n* tōfu 豆腐
together *adv* issho ni いっしょ[一緒]に, tomo ni 共に
toilet *n* tóire トイレ, tóirétto トイレット; keshō-shitsu 化粧室, (o-)teárai (お)手洗, benjó 便所
token *n* (*sign, indication*) (o-)shirushi (お)しるし・(お)印・(お)徴
Tokyo *n* Tōkyō 東京; ***the metropolis of Tokyo*** Tōkyō´-to 東京都; Tokyoite *n* Tōkyō´-jin 東京人; tomin 都民
told → **tell**
tolerate *v* gáman shimásu 我慢します, taemásu 耐えます
toll *n* tsūkō-ryō 通行料; (*telephone charge*) tsūwa-ryō 通話料; toll-free *adj* tsūwa-ryō muryō (no) 通話料無料(の); furii daiyaru (no) フリーダイヤル(の); tollgate *n* ryōkin-jo 料金所
tomato *n* tomato トマト
tomb *n* (o-)haka (お)墓, boketsu 墓穴
tombstone *n* boseki 墓石, [BOOKISH] bohi 墓碑
tomcat *n* osu neko 雄猫・オスねこ
tomorrow *n* ashitá あした・明日, asú 明日; [BOOKISH] myō´nichi 明日; tomorrow night ashita no ban あした[明日]の晩; [BOOKISH] myō´ban 明晩
tone *n* (*sound*) neiro 音色, (*voice*) kuchō 口調
tongue *n* shitá 舌; ***barbed/spiteful*** ~ doku-zetsu 毒舌; ox tongue *n* gyūtan 牛タン
tonight *n* kónban 今晩; kón'ya 今夜
tonight's guest *n* kónya no gesuto 今夜のゲスト
tonsil *n* hentō-sen 扁桃腺
too *adv* (*also*) … mo …も; (*overly*) anmari あんまり, amari (ni) あまり(に); ...-sugimásu ...すぎます; too bad zannen (na) 残念(な); (*in commiseration*) ikemasén いけません; too many ō-sugimásu 多すぎます
took → **take**
tool *n* (o-)dōgu (お)道具, yō´gu 用具, utsuwa 器; tsūru ツール; tool box *n* dōgu-bako 道具箱, yōgu-bako 用具箱
toolbar (*computer*) *n* tsūrubā ツールバー

tooth *n* há 歯; ***protruding (buck)*** **~** déppa 出っ歯; **toothache** *n* ha-ita 歯痛; **toothpick** *n* tsuma-yōji つまようじ・爪楊枝, yōji ようじ・楊枝
top **1.** *n* ue 上; (*top side*) jōmen 上面, hyōmen 表面; (*highest part*) teppén てっぺん, (*summit*) chōjō´ 頂上 **2.** *n* (*toy*) kóma こま・独楽; ***~-spinning*** koma-máwashi こま[独楽]回し **3.** *adj* (*topmost, best*) saijō (no) 最上(の), saikō (no) 最高(の); toppu (no) トップ(の)
topic *n* (*of talk*) wadai 話題, topikku トピック; daimoku 題目, (hanashi no) táne (話の)種
tops *adj* (*best*) saikō (no) 最高(の), saijō (no) 最上(の)
torch *n* táimatsu たいまつ・松明 → **flashlight**
tore, torn → **tear**
torment **1.** *n* (*suffering*) nayamí 悩み; (*teasing*) ijime いじめ・苛め **2.** → **tease**
tornado *n* torunēdo トルネード, tatsumaki 竜巻
Toronto *n* Toronto トロント
tortoise *n* káme 亀・カメ
toss → **throw**
total **1.** *adj* zénbu (de/no) 全部(で/の); (*absolute*) zettai (no) 絶対(の) **2.** *n* zén(-) …全; tōtaru トータル, (*sum*) gōkei 合計, (*grand total*) sōkei 総計
totter *v* yoro-mekimásu̱ よろめきます
touch *v* sawarimásu̱ 触ります; … ni (téo) furemásu̱ …に(手を)触れます, …ni tsu̱kimásu̱ …に付きます; atemásu̱ 当てます; (*comes in contact with*) sesshimásu̱ 接します, sesshoku̱ shimásu̱ 接触します; kandō sasemásu̱ 感動させる; ***gets in ~ with*** … to renraku shimásu̱ …と連絡します, … to renraku o torimásu̱ …と連絡を取ります; ***out of ~ with*** … ni utói …に疎い・うとい
tough *adj* katai 固い・堅い → **hard** → **strong**; **tough guy** *n* tafu gai タフガイ
tour *n* ryokō (shimásu̱) 旅行(します); (*sight-seeing*) kankō 観光, tsúā ツアー; (*official, duty*) shu̱tchō 出張
tourist *n* kankō´-kyaku 観光客; tsūrisuto ツーリスト; **tourist lodge** *n* minshu̱ku 民宿
tournament *n* taikai 大会; shiai 試合; senshu̱ken 選手権; tōnamento トーナメント
tow *v* hi̱kimásu̱ 引[曳]きます
toward *prep* … no hō´ e …の方へ; (*towards, confronting*) … ni táishi̱te …に対して, tai-… 対…
towel *n* te-nugui 手拭い・てぬぐい, táoru タオル, fukín 布きん・ふきん
tower *n* tō´ 塔; tawā タワー; **Tokyo Tower** *n* Tōkyō tawā 東京タワー
town *n* machí 町, tokai 都会
toy *n* omócha おもちゃ・オモチャ・玩具

trace *n* (*clue*) tegákari 手掛かり, ate 当て; (*vestige*) konseki 痕跡, ato 跡; **trace it back to** sore o ... ni sakanoborimás<u>u</u> それを...にさかのぼり[遡り]ます

track **1.** *n* (*railtrack*) sénro 線路; (*for running*) torákku トラック; (*remains*) ato 跡; *~ number (six)* (roku)-bansen (六)番線 **2.** *v* (*to go back and investigate*) ato o tsumemás<u>u</u> 跡を付けます, (*to ~ online the transaction of something*) suiseki shimás<u>u</u> 追跡します

tracks *n* ashi ato 足跡

tractor *n* torakutā トラクター

trade **1.** *n* (*international*) bōeki 貿易; (*business*) shō´bai 商売, (*commerce*) shō´gyō 商業; (*transaction*) tóri-h<u>i</u>ki 取り引き **2.** *v* tórí-h<u>i</u>ki shimás<u>u</u> 取り引きします; (*exchanges A for B*) A o B to kōkan shimás<u>u</u> A を B と交換します

trademark *n* shōhyō 商標; torēdo māku トレードマーク

trader *n* shō´nin 商人; bōékí-shō 貿易商

tradition *n* dentō 伝統; (*legend*) densetsu 伝説

traditional *adj* dentō-teki (na) 伝統的(な); (*accustomed*) imamade no 今までの, koremade no これまでの, [BOOKISH] jū´rai (no) 従来(の); **traditional arts** *n* dentō geijutsu 伝統芸術; **traditional lifestyle** *n* dentō-teki na seikatsu yōshiki 伝統的な生活様式

traffic *n* kōtsū 交通; ōrai 往来; **traffic accident** *n* kōtsū jiko 交通事故; **traffic jam** *n* kōtsū-jū´tai 交通渋滞

tragedy *n* hígeki 悲劇

tragic *adj* hígeki-teki (na) 悲劇的(な); h<u>i</u>san (na) 悲惨(な); aénái あえない・敢えない; ***tragically enough*** aénaku mo あえなくも・敢えなくも

trailer *n* (*movie*) yokoku-hen 予告編, (eiga no) torērā (映画の)トレーラー

train **1.** *n* densha 電車; ressha 列車; (*non-electric/steam*) k<u>i</u>shá 汽車; (*train numbers*) ...-gō´sha ...号車 **2.** *v* (*drills*) kúnren shimás<u>u</u> 訓練します, (*practices*) renshū shimásu 練習します; (*brings up children, disciplines*) sh<u>i</u>ts<u>u</u>kemás<u>u</u> しつけ[躾け]ます; **bullet train** *n* shinkansen 新幹線; **local train** *n* kakueki (densha) 各駅(電車); **train wreck** *n* ressha-jíko 列車事故

trainee *n* kenshū-in 研修員, minarai 見習い

trainer *n* torēnā トレーナー

training *n* kúnren 訓練; (*practice*) renshū 練習; (*imparting discipline*) sh<u>i</u>ts<u>u</u>ke しつけ・躾; (*in ascetic practices*) shugyō 修行

tram *n* romen densha 路面電車

trampoline *n* toranporin トランポリン

trance *n* toransu jōtai トランス状態; ***in a ~*** muchū (no/de) 夢中

(の/で)

tranquil *adj* nódoka (na) のどか・長閑(な)

transaction *n* tori-atsu̲kai 取扱い; (*business*) tórí-hi̲ki 取り引き

transfer **1.** *v* (*trains, etc.*) nori-kaemásu̲ 乗り換えます; (*job*) tennin (shimásu̲) 転任(します), ten-jimásu̲ 転じます; (~*s it*) utsu̲shimásu̲ 移します; furi-kaemásu 振替えます **2.** *n* idō 移動, nori-kae 乗り換え

transmigrant *n* imin 移民, ijūsha 移住者

transmission *n* sōshin 送信, dentatsu 伝達, denpa 伝播

transitory *adj* hakanái はかない

translate *v* yaku̲shimásu̲ 訳します, hon'yaku shimásu̲ 翻訳します; (*Japanese into English*) wayaku shimasu 和訳します; **translate freely** *v* iyaku shimásu̲ 意訳します; **translate literally** *v* chokuyaku shimásu̲ 直訳します

translation *n* hon'yaku 翻訳, yakú 訳; **automatic translation** *n* jidō hon'-yaku 自動翻訳; **machine translation** *n* kikai hon'yaku 機械翻訳

translator hon'yákú-sha 翻訳者, yaku-sha 訳者

transmit *v* tsu̲taemásu̲ 伝えます, tsūjimásu̲ 通じます

transparent *adj* tōmei (na) 透明(な)

transport(ation) *n* unsō 運送, unpan 運搬, yusō 輸送; (*traffic*) kōtsū 交通

trap **1.** *n* wána わな・罠 **2.** *v* (~*s it*) wána ni kakemásu̲ わな[罠]にかけます; (*gets trapped*) wána ni kakarimásu̲ わな[罠]にかかります

trash *n* (*scrap, junk*) kuzu くず・屑, gomi ごみ; **trash box** *n* gomi-bako ごみ箱

travel *n* ryokō (shimásu̲) 旅行(します); **travel agency** *n* ryokō dai-riten 旅行代理店; **travel vendor** *n* ryokō-gaisha 旅行会社

tray *n* (o-)bon (お)盆, torei トレイ; (*dining tray, low meal table*) (o-)zen (お)膳 (gó-zen ご膳) → **ash tray**

treachery *n* (*acts of* ~) ura-giri 裏切り, haishin-kōi 背信行為

treasure *n* (o-)takara (お)宝, takara-mono 宝物, [BOOKISH] zaihō 財宝; **national treasure** *n* kokuhō 国宝

treat **1.** *n* gochi̲sō (shimásu̲) ごちそう[ご馳走](します) **2.** *v* (*pays the bill*) ogorimásu̲ おごります; (*medically*) chiryō shimásu̲ 治療します → **handle**

treatise *n* ronbun 論文, rón 論

treatment *n* téate 手当(o-téate お手当); (*handling*) toriatsu̲kai 取り扱い; (*reception*) taigū 待遇; (*medical*) chiryō 治療, ryōhō 療法; **drug treatment** *n* yakubutsu ryōhō 薬物療法

treaty *n* jōyaku 条約

tree *n* kí 木

tremble *v* furuemásu̲ 震えます, yuremásu̲ 揺れます

…*est*)
…eshí 試
…iaru トラ
…aiken-ban
…n トライア

…aku 三角, san-
…kakkei 三角形
…*ent*) toraianguru トラ
…ル; love triangle *n*
…kankei 三角関係

…*e* ~ (*group, gang*) *of …*
…zoku …族

…**k** *n* **1.** (*feat*) waza 業, géi 芸, torikku トリック, ***one's favorite* ~** ohako おはこ・十八番; (*move*) té 手; (*knack*) kotsú こつ・コツ, téguchi 手口; (*plot, scheme*) keiryaku 計略, hakarigoto 謀・はかりごと; ***~ to it*** (*the secret of it*) táne 種 **2. → cheat**

tricky *adj* zurúi ずるい, torikkii トリッキー, bimyō (na) 微妙(な), (*difficult*) muzukashii 難しい; **tricky question** *n* kōmyō na shitsumon 巧妙な質問

trigger *n* hikigane 引き金, kikkake きっかけ; **trigger finger** *n* hitosashi-…人差し指・ひとさし指;
…ppy *adj* kōsen-teki (na) …的(な), (*critic*) arasagashi…sukina あら捜しの好きな

…*n* ryokō 旅行; ***business* ~** shutchō 出張

triple *n* sanbai 三倍; *adj* sanbai (no) 三倍(の); toripuru トリプル; **triple time** *n* sanbyōshi 三拍子

trite *adj* heibon (na) 平凡(な)

trivial *adj* tsumaránai つまらない; chótto shita ちょっとした; sásai (na) ささい[些細](な) **→ unimportant**

trolley *n* torokko トロッコ

troops *n* (*army*) gúntai 軍隊, gún 軍; (*detachment*) bútai 部隊

trophy *n* torofii トロフィー

tropic(s) *n* nettai(-chihō) 熱帯(地方)

tropical *adj* nettai (no) 熱帯(の); toropikaru (na) トロピカル(な); **tropical fruits** *n* toropikaru furūtsu トロピカルフルーツ; **tropical island** *n* nettai no shima 熱帯の島

trouble *n* (*inconvenience*) tékázu 手数, (o-)tesū (お)手数; (*time taken up*) (o-)téma (お)手間; (*nuisance*) (go-)méiwaku (ご)迷惑, (go-)mendō (ご)面倒, toraburu トラブル, (*care*) (o-)séwa (お)世話, o-sewa-sama お世話様; (*bother*) (go-)yákkai (ご)やっかい・厄介; (*difficulty*) kónnan 困難, komáru kotó 困ること; (*ailment*) wazurai 煩い・わずらい, byōki 病気 **→ worry;**

goes to much trouble hone o orimásu 骨を折ります; is troubled by (*an ailment*), has trouble with ... o wazuraimásu ...を煩います

troublesome *adj* yaya(k)koshii やや(っ)こしい; méiwaku (na) 迷惑(な); yákkai (na) やっかい・厄介(な); mendō (na) 面倒(な); wazurawashii 煩わしい; hanzatsu (na) 煩雑(な)

trousers *n* zubón ズボン

trout *n* másu ます・マス・鱒

truck *n* torákku トラック; (*3-wheeled*) ōto-sánrin オート三輪

truck driver *n* torákku (no) untenshu トラック(の)運転手

true *adj* honto/hontō (no) ほんと(う)/本当(の); ***how ~*** naru-hodo なるほど・成る程

truly *adv* honto (hontō) ni ほんと(ほんとう)に・本当に, makoto ni 誠に, jitsúni 実に

trumpet *n* toranpétto トランペット, rappa ラッパ

trunk *n* (*of tree*) miki 幹; (*of elephant*) hana 鼻; (*baggage*; *car ~*) toránku トランク

trunks *n* (*sports*) tanpan 短パン; (*swin*) suiei-pantsu 水泳パンツ

trust 1. *n* tánomi 頼み, irai 依頼; shin'yō 信用, shinrai 信頼, ate 当て; anshin 安心 **2.** *v* (*~s them*) shin'yō shimásu 信用します, shin-jimásu 信じます; ***gives in ~*** azukemásu 預けます; ***takes in ~*** azukarimásu 預かります

truth *n* shinjitsu 真実, honto/hontō no kotó ほん... の事

try *v* **1.** (*attemp*...) ...します; [BOOKIS...] 試みます **2.** (*do*...) másu (し)てみま... (shi)-yō/(ya)-rō to... よう/(や)ろうとし... ganbarimásu がんば... ます; dóryoku shimá... ます

T-shirt *n* tii shatsu Tシ...

tsunami *n* tsunami 津波

tub *n* óke 桶・おけ; (*basi*...) たらい; (*bathtub*) yúbune...

tube *n* kúda 管, kán 管; (*fle*... *squeezable, inflatable*) chū... チューブ; ***test ~*** shikenkan 試...管; ***TV ~*** buraunkan ブラウン...

tuberculosis, TB *n* (hai-)kekkaku (肺)結核, haibyō 肺病

Tuesday *n* Kayō'bi 火曜日

tug; *~ at* hipparimásu 引っ張ります

tugboat *n* hiki-fune 引き船・曳き船; tagu-bōto タグボート

tumble *v* korogarimásu 転がります; taoremásu 倒れます, korobimásu 転びます

tummy *n* onaka おなか; (*baby talk*) ponpon ポンポン

tumult *n* sō'dō 騒動

tuna *n* maguro まぐろ・マグロ・鮪; (*canned tunafish*) tsúna ツナ; fresh slices of raw tuna *n* maguro no sashimi まぐろ[マグロ・鮪]の刺身

tune *n* kyoku 曲; chōshi 調子; tōn トーン, fushí 節

tuner *n* **1.** (*person*) chōritsu-shi 調律師 **2.** (*tool*) chūnā チューナー

tunnel *n* tonneru トンネル

turf *n* shiba 芝・シバ, shibafu 芝生・シバフ

turkey *n* shichimen-chō 七面鳥・シチメンチョウ

Turkey *n* Tóruko トルコ

turn **1.** *n* (*order*) junban 順番; (*spin*) kaiten 回転; (*corner*) magarikado 曲がり角 **2.** *v* (*changes directions*) magarimásu 曲がります; (*goes round*) mawarimásu 回ります(回る, 回って) **3.** *v* (*makes it go round*) mawashimásu 回します; (*directs one's face/eyes/attention to*) … ni mukemásu …に向けます; turn aside (*diverts*) sorashimásu 逸らし[そらし]ます; turn back hiki-kaeshimásu 引き返します; turn inside out ura-gáeshimásu 裏返します; turn into ① (*becomes*) ([NOUN] ni に, [ADJECTIVE]-ku く) narimásu なります ② (*makes it into*) ([NOUN] ni に, [ADJECTIVE]-ku く) shimásu します; turn left/right sasetsu/usetsu shimásu 左折/右折します; turn loose nigashimásu 逃がします; turn off (*light, radio, etc.*) … o keshimásu を消します; *~ the ignition* suítchi o kirimásu スイッチを切ります; turn on (*light, etc.*) … o tsukemásu …を付けます; *~ the ignition* suítchi o iremásu スイッチを入れます; turn over ura-gaeshimasu 裏返します; turn up (*it gets found*) mitsukarimásu 見付かります

turnip *n* kabu かぶ・カブ・蕪, kabura かぶら・カブラ・蕪

turtle *n* káme 亀・カメ; (*snapping*) suppon すっぽん・スッポン

turtleneck *n* tātoru nekku タートルネック

tusk *n* kiba 牙・キバ

tutor *n* kateikyō´shi 家庭教師, chūtā チューター

tuxedo *n* takishiido タキシード

TV *n* térebi テレビ

tweed *n* tsuiido ツイード

tweet **1.** *v* (*Internet*) (tsuittā de) tsubuyaku (ツイッターで)つぶやく **2.** (*bird*) saezurimásu さえずります **3.** (*bird*) (kotori no) saezuri (小鳥の)さえずり

tweezers *n* pinsétto ピンセット

twelve *n* jū-ní 十二・12

twentieth *adj* nijū-banmé (no) 二十番目(の); *the ~ day* hatsukamé 二十日目, (*of the month*) hatsuka 二十日・20日

twenty *n* ní-jū 二十・20, futá-jū 二十; *20 years old* hátachi 二十歳・20歳, níjús-sai 二十歳・20歳

twice *adv* (*two times*) ni-dó 二度, ni-kái 二回; (*double*) ni-bai 二倍

twilight *n* yūgata 夕方; tasogare たそがれ・黄昏

twine 1. *n* → **string** (= *thread, cord*) 2. *v* (*twists*) yorimásu よります・縒ります
twinkle 1. *n* kirameki きらめき・煌き 2. *v* kiramekimásu きらめきます・煌きます, kagayakimásu 輝きます
twins *n* futago 双子・ふたご
twist *v* nejirimásu ねじります・捻ります, hinerimásu ひねります・捻ります, yorimásu よります; ***gets twisted*** (*entangled*) kojiremásu こじれます・拗れます
Twitter *n* (*Internet*) tsuittā ツイッター
two *n* ní 二・2, futatsú 二つ・2つ; futa-... 二..., ni-... 二...; (*people*) futarí 二人, [BOOKISH] ní-mei 二名
type *n* táipu タイプ, (*sort*) shúrui 種類; (*model*) katá 型, ...-gata ...型; (*print*) katsuji 活字; **different type** *n* betsu no taipu 別のタイプ; chigau taipu 違うタイプ, kotonaru shurui 異なる種類
type (*write*) *n* táipu (shimásu) タイプ(します)
typewriter *n* taipuráitā タイプライター, táipu タイプ
typhoon *n* taifū´ 台風
typical *adj* tenkei-teki (na) 典型的(な), daihyō-teki (na) 代表的(な); (*usual*) futsū (no) 普通(の)
typist *n* taipisuto タイピスト
tyrant *n* bōkun 暴君

U

Ueno *n* Ueno 上野; ***Ueno Park*** Ueno-Kō´en 上野公園
ugly *adj* (*look*) minikúi 醜い・みにくい; mazúi まずい
uh *interj* ē-to ええと; ***uh*** ... anō あのう...; ***uh-huh*** *n* ん; ***uh-uh, huh-uh*** nn んん
UK *n* igirisu イギリス, eikoku 英国
ulcer *n* (*gastric*) i-káiyō 胃潰瘍・胃かいよう
ultimate 1. *n* kyūkyoku 究極 2. *adj* kyūkyoku no 究極の
ultrasound *n* 1. chōonpa 超音波 2. (~ *diagnosis*) chōonpa shindan 超音波診断
ultraviolet *n* shigaisen 紫外線, *adj* shigaisen (no) 紫外線(の)
umbrella *n* kása かさ・傘; (*oilpaper*) ban-gasa 番傘, kara-kása 唐傘; (*western-style*) yō-gása 洋傘
umpire *n* shinpan(-in) 審判(員)
unacceptable *adj* mitomerarenai 認められない
unaccountable *adj* setsumei dekinai 説明できない
unanimous *adj* manjō itchi (no/de) 満場一致(の/で), zen'in itchi (no/de) 全員一致(の/で)
unanticipated *adj* omowánu ...思わぬ・おもわぬ...
unapproachable *adj* chikayorigatai

近寄りがたい・近寄り難い, chikazukinikui 近づきにくい
unassuming *adj* kidoranai 気取らない
unavoidable *adj* yamu-o-énai やむを得ない
unbalanced *adj* fuantei (na) 不安定(な), katayotta 偏った, baransu no warui バランスの悪い
unbeatable *adj* muteki (no) 無敵(の)
unbelievable *adj* shinjirarenai 信じられない
unbiased *adj* katayori no nai 偏りのない, sennyū-kan no nai 先入観のない
unbutton *v* … no botan o hazushimásu …のボタンを外します
uncalled-for *adj* yokei (na) 余計・よけい(な)
uncertain *adj* futei (no) 不定(の); ayashii 怪しい・あやしい
unchaste *adj* futei (na) 不貞(な)
uncle *n* oji(-san) おじ[叔父, 伯父](さん)
unclean *adj* fuketsu (na) 不潔(な)
uncomfortable *adj* kimochi ga warúi 気持ちが悪い; (*not feel at home*) igokochi ga warui 居心地が悪い; (*to wear*) kigokochi ga warui 着心地が悪い
uncommon *adj* mezurashíi 珍しい・めずらしい
unconcerned *adj* **1.** → **calm** **2.** ~ *with* … ni mu-kánshin (na) …に無関心(な)
unconnected *adj* … to mukánkei (no) …と無関係(の)
unconscious *adj* íshiki fumei (no) 意識不明(の); (*involuntary*) mu-íshiki (no/na) 無意識(の/な)
uncooked *adj* náma (no) 生(の)
uncork *v* (… no sén o) nukimásu (…の栓を)抜きます; (… no kuchi o) akemásu (…の口を)空けます
uncover *v* bakuro shimásu 曝露します
uncultivated *adj* kyōyō no nai 教養のない; mukyōyō (*no*) 無教養(の); (*wild*) soya (na) 粗野(な)
undecided *adj* (*indefinite*) futei (no) 不定(の)
under *prep, adv* … no shitá (de/ni/no) …の下(で/に/の); (*the tutelage of*) … no motó (de) …の下(で)
undercut *v* **1.** (*cuts under*) shita o kirimásu 下を切ります **2.** (*offers at a lower price*) yasune de urimásu 安値で売ります
underdone *adj* nama-yake (no) 生焼け(の)
underestimate *v* (*kids oneself about*) amaku mimásu 甘く見ます・あまくみます, (*person*) mikubirimásu みくびります, kashōhyōka shimásu 過小評価します
undergo *v* (*experiences*) keiken shimásu 経験します; … mé ni aimásu …目に会います
undergraduate (*student*) *n* daigákusei 大学生
underground **1.** *adj* chiká (no) 地下

(の) 2. → **subway**

underline *n, v* kasen (o hikimásu) 下線(を引きます)

underneath 1. *n* shita 下 2. *prep, adv* shita ni 下に

undershirt *n* shátsu シャツ

understand *v* (… ga) wakarimásu (…が)分かります; (… o) rikai shimásu (…を)理解します

understanding *n* rikai 理解, (*ability*) rikái-ryoku 理解力 → **agreement**

undertake *v* (*plans, attempts, schemes*) kuwadatemásu 企てます

undertaker *n* (*funeral director*) sōgi-ya 葬儀屋

undertaking *n* shigoto 仕事; (*enterprise*) jígyō 事業, kuwada te 企て

undervalue *n* kashōhyōka shimásu 過小評価します

underwater 1. *adj* suichū (no) 水中(の) 2. *adv* suichū de 水中で

underwear *n* shita-gi 下着, hadagí 肌着; (*underpants*) shitabaki 下穿き, pántsu パンツ, (*women's drawers*) zurō´su ズロース, (*panties*) pántii パンティー

underworld *n* 1. (*another world*) anoyo あの世 2. (*gangland*) ankoku-gai 暗黒街

undeserving *adj* mottai-nái もったいない

undisturbed *adj* sono mamá (de/no) そのまま(で/の)

undo *v* hazushimásu 外します; moto ni modoshimásu 元に戻します; (*unties*) hodokimásu ほどきます, tokimásu 解きます

undone; *comes* ~ tokemásu 解けます; ***leaves it* ~** shinái de okimásu しないでおきます

undoubtedly *adv* utagai náku 疑いなく, táshika ni 確かに・たしかに, kitto きっと

undress *v* 1. (*takes off one's clothes*) fuku o nugimásu 服を脱ぎます 2. (*takes off someone's clothes*) fuku o nugasemásu 服を脱がせます

unduly *adv* yatara ni やたらに

uneasy *adj* shinpai (na) 心配(な), fuan (na) 不安(な)

unemployed; ~ *person* shitsugyō-sha 失業者

uneven *adj* dekoboko (no) でこぼこ・凸凹(の)

unexpected *adj* igai (na) 意外(な), omoigakénai 思いがけない; (*sudden*) níwaka (no) にわか(の); (*but welcome*) mezurashíi 珍しい

unexpectedly *adv* igai ni 意外に, futo ふと, (*suddenly*) níwaka ni にわかに

unfair *adj* fu-kōhei (na) 不公平(な); (*unjustified*) futō (na) 不当(な)

unfaithful *adj* (*to her husband*) futei (na) 不貞(な)

unfasten *v* hazushimásu 外します・はずします

unfavorable *adj* fúri (na) 不利(な); (*unlikable*) konomashikunái 好ましくない

unfeeling *adj* hakujō (na) 薄情(な)
unfortunate *adj* (*unlucky*) fu̲kō´ (na) 不幸(な), fu-un (na) 不運(な); (*regrettable, inopportune*) ainiku (na) あいにく(な) → **pitiful**
unfortunately *adv* ainiku あいにく, zannen nagara/desuga 残念ながら/ですが, [BOOKISH] ikan nagara 遺憾ながら
unfriendly *adj* fushinsetsu (na) 不親切(な), buaisō (na) 無愛想(な), sokkenai そっけない
ungrateful *adj* on shirazu (na/no) 恩知らず(な/の), kansha shinai 感謝しない
unhappy *adj* (*gloomy*) inki (na) 陰気(な), (*moody*) kigen ga warúi 機嫌が悪い
unhealthy *adj* **1.** fu-kenkō (na) 不健康(な) **2.** (*bad for one's health*) karada ni warúi 体に悪い **3.** (*sickly*) byōki-gachi (na) 病気がち(な)
unification *n* tōitsu 統一
uniform **1.** *n* seifu̲ku 制服, yunifōmu ユニフォーム; (*military*) gunpu̲ku 軍服; (*school*) gaku̲séi-fu̲ku 学生服 **2.** *adj* (the same) byōdō (na) 平等(な), taitō (no) 対等(の)
unify *v* tōitsu shimásu̲ 統一します
unimportant *adj* (*matter*) mondai ni naránai 問題にならない
unintentionally *adv* tsúi つい, ukkari うっかり, mu-ishiki ni 無意識に, itosezu ni 意図せずに
union *n* (*labor*) kumiai 組合, rōdōkúmiai 労働組合; (*alliance*) rengō 連合, renmei 連盟; (*joint*) kyōdō 共同, (*merger*) gappei 合併, gōdō 合同
unique *adj* yúiitsu (no) 唯一(の); yuniiku (na) ユニーク(な)
unit *n* tán'i 単位; (*military*) bútai 部隊
unite *v* (*they merge*) gappei/gōdō shimásu̲ 合併/合同します; (*combines dual functions as*) ... o kanemásu̲ ...を兼ねます
United Nations *n* Koku̲sai-Réngō 国際連合
United States *n* Amerika(-Gasshū´-koku) アメリカ(合衆国)
universe *n* úchū 宇宙; yunibāsu ユニバース
university *n* daigaku 大学; ***at ~*** zaigaku(-chū) 在学(中)
unjustified *adj* fu̲tō (na) 不当(な)
unkind *adj* fu-shínsetsu (na) 不親切(な) → **mean**
unknown *adj* fumei (no) 不明(の); shiranai 知らない
unless *conj* (shi)-nákereba (し)なければ, (shi)-nai to (し)ないと
unlikely *adj* ari-sō´mo nái ありそうもない; (shi)-sō mo nái (し)そうもない
unload *v* oroshimásu̲ 降ろします
unlock *v* ... no kagí o akemásu̲ ...の鍵を開けます
unlucky *adj* ún ga warúi 運が悪い; (*fails to strike it lucky*) tsúite imasén ついていません
unmarried *adj* hi̲tori-mónó 独り者, doku̲shin 独身

unnatural *adj* fu-shízen (na) 不自然(な)
unnecessary, unneeded *adj* iranai いらない, muyō (na) 無用(な), fuyō (na) 不要(な); (*superfluous*) yokei (na) 余計(な)
unoccupied *adj* (*free of business*) hima (na) 暇(な)
unofficial *adj* hi-kō´shiki (no) 非公式(の)
unpack *v* nimotsu o hodokimásu 荷物を解きます・ほどきます
unpleasant *adj* iyá (na) 嫌(な); fuyúkai (na) 不愉快(な)
unprofitable *adj* wari ga warúi 割が悪い
unqualified *adj* mushikaku (no) 無資格(の); (*unlimited*) mujōken (no) 無条件(の)
unreasonable *adj* múri (na) 無理(な); múcha (na) むちゃ[無茶](な); hidói ひどい
unrelated (*to* …) *adj* (… tó wa) mukánkei (no) (…とは)無関係(の)
unreliable *adj* ayashii 怪しい, detarame (na) でたらめ(な)
unreserved *adj* (*frank*; *rude*) buén-ryo (na) 無遠慮(な)
unrest *n* sō´dō 騒動; fuan 不安; shinpai 心配
unsafe *adj* (*troubled*) bussō´ (na) 物騒(な)
unscrupulous *adj* akuratsu (na) 悪らつ(な)・悪辣(な)
unseemly, unsightly *adj* migurushíi 見苦しい
unskillful *adj* hetá (na) へた[下手](な), mazúi まずい
unsociable *adj* bu-áisō (na) 無愛想(な)
unsophisticated *adj* sekenshirazu (na) 世間知らず(な); mújaki (na) 無邪気・むじゃき(な), soboku (na) 素朴(な)
unsuitable *adj* kakkō ga warúi かっこう・格好[恰好]が悪い
untangle *v* motsure o tokimásu もつれを解きます, kaiketsu shimásu 解決します
untidy *adj* kitanái 汚い; chirakat-te(i)ru 散らかって(い)る
untie *v* tokimásu 解きます, hodo-kimásu ほどきます
until *prep* … máde …まで・迄; ~ *now* ima-made 今まで[迄]
untouched *adj* sono mamá (de/no) そのまま(で/の)
unusual *adj* (*abnormal*) ijō (na) 異常(な); (*extreme*) hijō (na) 非常(な), (*novel*) kawatta 変わった, mezurashí 珍しい
unwell; *feeling* ~ kimochi ga warúi 気持が悪い
unwilling (*to do*) *adj* (shi)-taku arimasén (し)たくありません
unzipped *adj* *comes* ~ (chákku ga) akimásu (チャックが)空きます; *to unzip a file* (*computer*) fairu o kaitō shimásu ファイルを解凍します
up *prep* (… no) úé e (…の)上へ; *up* (*higher by*) *¥100* hyakuén-daka 百円高; **bring up** *v* (*trains*)

shitsukemásu しつけ[躾け]ます; (*rears*) sodatemásu 育てます; **get up** *v* okimásu 起きます; (*gets one up*) okoshimásu 起こします; **go up** *v* agarimásu 上がります, noborimásu 上り[昇り]ます; **make up for** *v* oginaimásu 補います; **up to now** jū´rai 従来, ima-máde 今まで[迄]; **up-to-date** *adj* (*modern*) géndai (no) 現代(の); (*latest*) saishin (no) 最新(の)

upbringing *n* shitsuke しつけ・躾; sodachí 育ち

update 1. *n* kōshin 更新; saishin (-ban) 最新(版) **2.** *v* kōshin shimásu 更新します, saishin(-ban) ni shimásu 最新(版)にします

upfront money *n* atama-kin 頭金

upkeep *n* íji 維持; (*expense*) ijí-hi 維持費; (*care, repair*) te-iré 手入れ

upload *v* (*computer*) appurōdo shimásu アップロードします

upon → **on**

upper *adj* ue (no) 上(の)

upright *adj* katai 堅い → **honest**

uprising *n* bōdō 暴動, hanran 反乱

upset 1. *v* (*it overturns*) hikkuri-kaerimásu ひっくり返ります, (*overturns it*) hikkuri-kaeshimásu ひっくり返します → **spill 2.** *v* (*disturbs*) midashimásu 乱します, (*is disturbed*) midaremásu 乱れます, (*gets nervous*) dōyō shimásu 動揺します **3.** *n* (*stomach* ~) imotare 胃もたれ, muneyake 胸焼け

upshot *n* shímatsu しまつ・始末

upside *n* **1.** jōbu 上部, ue-no-hō 上のほう **2.** riten 利点

upside down *adv* sakasa(ma) (ni) 逆さ(ま)(に), abekobe (ni) あべこべ(に)

upstairs *adv* ni-kai 二階, o-níkai (de/ni, e, no) お二階(で/に, へ, の)

uptown (*Tokyo*) *n* yama-te 山手, yama-no-te 山の手

up until *adv* (...) ízen (...)以前

upwards of (...) íjō (...)以上

urban *adj* toshi (no) 都市(の); shínai (no) 市内(の)

urge *v* (*bustles up*) sekitatemásu せき立てます・急き立てます; susumemásu 勧めます; (*persuades*) unagashimásu 促します

urgency *n* shikyū 至急, kinkyū 緊急

urgent *adj* kyū (na) 急(な), kinkyū (na) 緊急(な), shikyu (no) 至急(の); **urgent business** *n* kyūyō 急用

urinal *n* (*place*) shōben-jo 小便所; (*thing*) shōbén-ki 小便器, (*bedpan*) shibin しびん・し瓶

urinate *v* shōbén shimásu, shonben shimásu 小便します

urine *n* shōbén, shonben 小便, (*medical*) nyō 尿

URL (*website address*) *abbrev* (= *Uniform Resource Locator*) yū-āru-eru ユーアールエル

urn *n* tsubo つぼ・壷

us *pron* watáshí-táchi わたしたち[私達], watakúshí-tachi [私達];

ware ware われわれ・我々

U.S. *n* Amerika アメリカ, Beikoku 米国

usable *adj* shiyō dekiru 使用できる, shiyō kanō (na) 使用可能(な), riyō dekiru 利用できる, riyō kanō (na) 利用可能(な)

usage *n* shiyō 使用, kanyō 慣用

USB *abbrev (= Universal Serial Bus)* yū-esu-bī USB

use **1.** *n* (*utility*) shiyō 使用; (*utilization*) riyō 利用; (*putting to ~*) ōyō 応用 **2.** *n* (*for the ~ of*) …-yō …用 **3.** *n* (*service*) (go-) yō (ご)用, (o-)yaku (お)役 **4.** *v* tsukaimásu 使います, mochiimásu 用います; (*makes ~ of*) riyō shimásu 利用します

used *adj* (*secondhand*) chūko (no) 中古(の), furúi 古い; **used to (do)** (shi)-ta monó/món desu (し)たもの/もんです; ***gets ~ to*** … ni naremásu …に慣れます

useful *adj* yaku ni tatsu 役に立つ; yakudatsu 役立つ, yūyō (na) 有用(な), chō´hō (na) 重宝(な); ***is ~*** yakú ni tachimásu 役に立ちます, yaku-dachimásu 役立ちます; chō´hō shimásu 重宝します

useless *adj* **1.** (*wasteful*) muda (na) 無駄(な) **2.** (*of no use, unworthy*) muyō (no) 無用(の) **3.** (*unworthy, of no value*) fuyō (no) 不用(の)

user *n* shiyō´-sha 使用者; riyō´-sha 利用者; (*computer*) yūza ユーザ, yūzā ユーザー

usher **1.** *n* toritsugi 取り次ぎ・とりつぎ; (*greeter*) annai-gákari 案内係, annai-nin 案内人 **2.** *v* (*~s one*) annái shimásu 案内します

usual *adj* futsū (no) 普通(の), ítsumo (no) いつも(の), heijō (no) 平常(の), fúdan (no) 普段(の); ***as ~*** ítsumo no yō´ni いつものよう[様]に, aikawarazu 相変らず・あいかわらず

usually *adv* (*normally*) futsū (wa) 普通・ふつう(は), tsūjō (wa) 通常(は), (*mostly*) taitei (wa) たいてい・大抵(は), (*daily*) fúdan (wa) 普段・ふだん(は), higoro (wa) 日頃(は), (*always*) ítsumo (wa) いつも(は)

utensil *n* utsuwa 器; …-yōhin …用品

utilities (*bills*) *n* kōkyō-ryō´kin 公共料金

utility *n* jitsuyō 実用

utilization *n* riyō 利用

utilize *v* riyō shimásu 利用します

utmost; ***to the ~*** ákú-made (mo) あくまで(も); ***does one's ~*** saizen o tsukushimásu 最善を尽くします

utter → **speak, say;** ***~ a curse*** noroimásu 呪います

utterly *adv* mattaku 全く・まったく, sukkári すっかり, zenzen 全然・ぜんぜん; ***~ exhausted*** ku(t) takuta く(っ)たくた

U-turn *n* yūtā´n ユーターン・Uターン; ***makes a ~*** yūtā´n shimásu ユーターン・[Uターン]します

V

vacant *adj* **1.** (*open*) aite imásu̲ 空いています **2.** (*hollow*) utsuro (na) うつろ・虚ろ(な); ~ ***car*** (*available taxi*) kūsha 空車; ~ ***lot*** aki-chi 空き地
vacate *v* akemásu̲ 空けます
vacation *n* yasumí 休み, kyūka 休暇, bakēshon バケーション
vaccination *n* waku̲chin sesshu ワクチン接種
vaccine *n* waku̲chin ワクチン
vacuum *v* sōjiki o kakemásu̲ 掃除機をかけます
vacuum cleaner *n* (denki) sōjíki (電気)掃除機
vagabond, vagrant *n* furō´-sha 浮浪者
vagina *n* chitsu 膣
vague *adj* aimai (na) あいまい(な)・曖昧(な); ii-kagen (na) いい加減(な)
vain (*conceited*) *adj* unubore ga tsuyói うぬぼれが強い; **in vain** *adj, adv* munashii 空しい・虚しい・むなしい, muda (na/ni) 無駄(な/に)
Valentine's Day *n* barentain dē バレンタインデー
valiant *adj* yūkan (na) 勇敢(な)
valid *adj* yūkō (na) 有効(な)
valley *n* tani(-ma) 谷(間)
valuable *adj* taisetsu (na) 大切(な), ki̲chō (na) 貴重(な) → **expensive**
valuables *n* ki̲chō-hin 貴重品
value **1.** *n* káchi 価値, neuchi 値打ち **2.** *v* ~*s* (*cherishes*) ***it*** chōhō shimásu̲ 重宝します, chōhō-garimásu̲ 重宝がります
valve *n* bén 弁
van *n* (*car*) raito ban ライトバン
vanish *v* (*from sight*) miénaku narimásu̲ 見えなくなります; (*from existence*) náku narimásu̲ なくなります; (*gets extinguished*) kiemásu̲ 消えます
vanity *n* kyoei-shin 虚栄心, unubore うぬぼれ
vapor *n* kitai 気体 → **steam**
various *adj* iroiro (na/no) いろいろ[色々](な/の), ironna いろんな, samazama (na) さまざま・様々(な); ~ ***places*** tokorodókoro ところどころ・所々
varnish *n* nísu ニス = wánisu (o nurimásu̲) ワニス(を塗ります); nuri 塗り
vase *n* bin 瓶; (*for flowers*) kabin 花瓶, káki 花器
vast *adj* bakudai (na) 莫大(な)
vegetable *n* yasai 野菜; (*greens*) aó-mono 青物, náppa 菜っ葉, ná 菜
vegetarian *n* bejitarian ベジタリアン; saishoku shugi-sha 菜食主義者; ~ ***cuisine*** shōjin-ryō´ri 精進料理
vehicle *n* nori-mono 乗り物, kuruma 車, …-sha …車
vein *n* (*vena*) jōmyaku 静脈

veil *n* bēru ベール
velocity *n* sokudo 速度, hayasa 速さ, supiido スピード
velvet *n* birōdo ビロード, berubetto ベルベット
vending machine *n* hanbái-ki 販売機; *ticket* ~ kenbái-ki 券売機
vendor *n* uriko 売り子 → **seller, dealer**
venereal disease *n* seibyō 性病
Venezuela *n* benezuera ベネズエラ
vengeance *n* fukushū 復讐
ventilation *n* kanki 換気; ~ *system* kanki-sō´chi 換気装置
venture *n* bōken 冒険; tōkiteki jigyō 投機的事業; tōki 投機; (*speculation, wild guess*) yamá やま・山
veranda *n* beranda ベランダ; engawa 縁側
verb *n* dōshi 動詞
verbal *adj* (*spoken*) kōtō (no) 口頭(の)
verification *n* shōmei 証明; kenshō 検証
verify *v* shōmei shimásu 証明します
versatility *n* yūzū 融通; *is versatile* yūzū ga kikimásu 融通がききます
verse *n* shi 詩
versus *prep* tai-... 対...
vertical *adj* táte (no) 縦(の), suichoku (no) 垂直(の)
vertigo *n* memai めまい・眩暈・目眩
very *adv* zúibun ずいぶん・随分, taihen たいへん・大変, totemo とても, hijō ni 非常に, táisō たいそう・大層, góku ごく; amari (ni) あまり(に); ōi-ni 大いに・おおいに; ***the very*** + [NOUN] = ***the*** [NOUN] ***itself*** ... sono-mónó... そのもの; at the very beginning/first saisho (no/ni) 最初(の/に); very well (*satisfactory*) yoroshii よろしい・宜しい; (*OK*) yóshi 良し
vest *n* chokki チョッキ; besuto ベスト
vestige *n* konseki 痕跡
vet *n* jū-i 獣医
veteran **1.** *n* taieki gunjin 退役軍人; **2.** *adj* (*experienced*) beteran (no) ベテラン(の)
veto **1.** *n* kyóhi 拒否 **2.** *v* (*rejects it*) kyóhi shimásu 拒否します
vexatious *adj* haradatashíi 腹立たしい
via ... *prep* kéiyu (de) ...経由(で); ...o tō´tte ...を通って, ... o héte ...を経て
vibrate *v* shindō shimásu 振動します
vibration *n* shindō 振動; (*cell-phone, etc.*) baiburēshon バイブレーション, baibu バイブ
vice *n* warúi shūkan 悪い習慣, akufū 悪風
vice-president *n* (*of company*) fuku-shácho 副社長; (*of nation*) fuku-daitō´ryō 副大統領
vice versa *adv* hantai ni 反対に, gyaku ni 逆に, gyaku mo onaji 逆も同じ, gyaku mo dōyō 逆も同様

vicinity *n* fukín 付近, kínjo 近所, chikáku 近く, … hen …辺

vicious *adj* warúi 悪い, hidói ひどい

victim *n* (*of sacrifice*) giséi-sha 犠牲者, (*of injury*) higái-sha 被害者; ***falls ~ to*** … no gisei ni narimásu …犠牲になります

victor *n* shōrí-sha 勝利者, yūshō-sha 優勝者

victory *n* shōri 勝利, yūshō 優勝; ***wins the ~*** yūshō shimásu 優勝します

video *n* ***~tape*** bideótēpu ビデオテープ

vie → **compete**

view **1.** *n* (*scenery*) nagamé 眺め; ***in ~ of*** … ni teráshite …に照らして, … o kangáete …を考えて **2.** *v* (*gazes at*) nagamemásu 眺めます **3.** → **opinion** → **outlook** → **look**

viewpoint *n* kénchi 見地, mi-kátá 見方, tachi-ba 立場

vigilance *n* keikai 警戒

vigor *n* génki 元気, katsuryoku 活力

vigorous *adj* sakan (na) 盛ん・さかん(な); sekkyoku-teki (na) 積極的(な) → **energetic** → **healthy** → **strong**

villa *n* bessō´ 別荘

village *n* murá 村

villain *n* warumono 悪者; akuto 悪党

vine *n* **1.** tsurú つる・ツル・蔓 **2.** (*grape tree*) budō no ki ブドウ[葡萄]の木

vinegar *n* sú 酢, o-su お酢

vineyard *n* budō-en ブドウ園・葡萄園

vintage **1.** *n* bintēji ビンテージ **2.** *adj* gokujō (no) 極上(の)

violate *v* (*breaks the law*) okashimásu 犯します; yaburimásu 破ります; … ni ihan shimásu …に違反します, … ni somukimásu …に背きます

violation *n* ihan 違反

violence *n* (*brute force*) bōryoku 暴力; **domestic violence** *n* katei-nai bōryoku 家庭内暴力, domesutikku baiorensu ドメスティック・バイオレンス

violent *adj* (*severe*) hageshíi 激しい・はげしい; (*unruly*) ranbō (na) 乱暴(な); múri (na) 無理(な)

violin *n* baiorin バイオリン

virgin *n* (*female*) shójo 処女, bājin バージン, ki-músume 生娘; (*male*) dōtei 童貞

virtue *n* bitoku 美徳 , toku 徳

virus *n* bíirusu ビールス, uirusu ウイルス

visa *n* bíza ビザ, [BOOKISH] sashō 査証

visible *adj* (mé ni) mieru (目に)見える

vision *n* **1.** (*eyesight*) shíryoku 視力 **2.** (*dream*) kūsō 空想 **3.** (*foresight*) bijon ビジョン

visit **1.** *v* hōmon shimásu 訪問します; tazunemásu 訪ねます **2.** *n* hōmon 訪問, (o-)asobi (お)遊び, (o-)ukagai (お)伺い・うかがい; (*of solicitude*) (o-)mimai (お)見

舞い; (*interview*) menkai 面会

visitor *n* o-kyaku (お)客, o-kyaku-san/sámá お客さん/様; raikyaku 来客; (*solicitous*) mimái-kyaku 見舞い客; (*for interview*) menkai-nin 面会人

vitamin(s) *n* bitamin ビタミン; (*pills*) bitamin-zai ビタミン剤

vivid *adj* senmei (na) 鮮明(な); azayaka (*na*) 鮮やか(な); ikiiki to shita 生き生きとした

vixen *n* kuchi urusai onna 口うるさい女

vocabulary *n* kotobá 言葉, gói 語彙, tango 単語

vocal *adj* koe no 声の, ónsei (no) 音声(の)

vocalist *n* vōkaru ヴォーカル, bōkaru ボーカル, (*classical music*) seigaku-ka 声楽家

vocation *n* shokúgyō 職業

vocational *adj* shokugyō (no) 職業(の), shokugyō-jō (no) 職業上(の); **vocational sickness** *n* shokugyō-byō 職業病

vogue *n* ryūkō 流行

voice *n* kóe 声

voice mail *n* boisu mēru ボイスメール

void → **invalid** (= *not valid*)

volcanic ash *n* kazánbai 火山灰

volcano *n* kázan 火山, borukēno ボルケーノ

volleyball *n* barēbō´ru バレーボール

volt *n* boruto ボルト

voltage *n* den'átsú 電圧; **high-voltage cable** *n* kōatsu-sen 高圧線

volume *n* (*book*) hón 本, …-bon …本; (*of a set*) (dái …-) kan (第…)巻; (*quantity*) ryō´ 裏

voluntary *adj* mizukara 自ら・みずから; (*optional*) zuii (no) 随意(の)

volunteer *n* borantia ボランティア

vomit **1.** *n* hédo へど・反吐, (*medical*) ōto 嘔吐 **2.** *v* modoshimásu̲ 戻します **3.** *v* (*throws up*) (hédo o) hakimásu̲ (へどを)吐きます

vote **1.** *n* tōhyō 投票 **2.** *v* tōhyō shimásu̲ 投票します

voter *n* tōhyō-sha 投票者, yūken-sha 有権者

vow → **pledge**

vowel *n* boin 母音, boon 母音

voyage *n* kōkai 航海; ***makes a ~*** kōkai shimásu̲ 航海します

V-shaped *adj* bui-ji gata (no) V字形(の), kusabi gata (no) くさび形(の)

V sign *n* bui sain Vサイン

vulgar *adj* gehín (na) 下品(な); iyashii 卑しい・いやしい; (*mundane*) zoku (na) 俗(な)

vulgarities *n* gehín 下品; zoku 俗; soya 粗野

vulture *n* kondoru コンドル; hagewashi ハゲワシ; hagetaka ハゲタカ

W

wad *n* (chiisana) katamari (小さな・ちいさな)かたまり
waddle *v* yotayota arukimásu̲ よたよた歩きます, yochiyochi arukimásu̲ よちよち歩きます
wade *v* arúite ikimásu̲ 歩いて行きます, (*across*) arúite watarimásu̲ 歩いて渡ります
waffle *n* (*sweet*) waffuru ワッフル
wag *v* yuremásu̲ 揺れます・ゆれます, yureugokimásu̲ 揺れ動きます・ゆれうごきます, (*tail*) furimásu̲ 振ります
wage *n* chíngin 賃金, (*salary*) kyūryō 給料 → **salary**
wagon *n* **1.** ni basha 荷馬車 **2.** (*station* ~) sutēshon wagon ステーションワゴン; wagon-sha ワゴン車
Waikiki *n* Waikiki ワイキキ
waist *n* koshi 腰 (= **loins**), uésu̲to ウエスト; (*specifically*) koshi no kubire 腰のくびれ; kubire くびれ; **waistcoat** *n* besuto ベスト, chokki チョッキ; **waist pocket** *n* waki poketto 脇ポケット
waiter *n* úē´tā ウエーター; ueitā ウエイター; bōi(-san) ボーイ(さん) → **wait person**
wait; *v* **~ *for*...** o machimásu̲ ...を待ちます; Please wait a moment. *interj* [FORMAL] Shōshō omachikudasai. 少々お待ちください., [INFORMAL] Chotto mattekudasai. ちょっと待ってください.; Please wait to be seated. *interj* (*restaurant*) Kakarinomono ga (o-seki ni) go-an'nai suru made omachikudasai. 係りの者が(お席に)ご案内するまでお待ちください.
waiting *n* taiki 待機; **waiting for a long time** *adj* machidōshíi 待ち遠しい; **waiting list** *n* kyanseru machi meibo キャンセル待ち名簿, weitingu risuto ウェイティング・リスト; **waiting room** *n* machiái-shi̲tsu 待合室
wait person *n* kyū´ji 給仕; sekkyaku-gakari 接客係; kakari (no mono) 係(の者)
waitress *n* úē´toresu ウエートレス; ueitoresu ウエイトレス → **wait person**
wake up *v* méga samemásu̲ 目が覚めます・さめます, (*rises*) okimásu̲ 起きます; (*wakes a person up*) ... o okoshimásu̲ ...を起こします
Wales *n* wēruzu ウェールズ, uēruzu ウエールズ
walk **1.** *v* arukimásu̲ 歩きます, arúite ikimásu̲ 歩いて行きます **2.** *v* (*strolls*) sanpo (shimásu̲) 散歩(します); ***goes for a ~*** sanpo ni ikimásu̲ 散歩に行きます **3.** *n* (*way*) hodō 歩道 **4.** *n* (*walking*) hokō 歩行

walking *n* hokō 歩行, wōkingu ウォーキング; **walking shoes** *n* wōkingu shūzu ウォーキングシューズ; **walking stick** *n* (*cane*) sutékki ステッキ, tsúe 杖

Walkman *n* Wōkuman ウォークマン

walkway *n* hodō 歩道

wall *n* (*of house*) kabe 壁; (*around courtyard, etc.*) hei 塀・へい

wallet *n* saifu 財布・さいふ, gamaguchi がま口, (*billfold*) satsu-ire 札入れ

wallpaper *n* kabegami 壁紙

walnut *n* kurumi クルミ・胡桃

waltz *n* warutsu ワルツ

wander *v* (*walks around*) arukimawarimásu 歩き回ります, (*hangs round*) buratsukimásu ぶらつきます, buraburashimásu ぶらぶらします, samayoimásu さまよいます・彷徨います

want *v* **1.** … ga irimásu …が要ります, (*desires something*) hoshigarimásu 欲しがります; … ga hoshíi desu …が欲しいです; (*looks for, seeks to buy*) motomemásu 求めます **2.** *~s to do* (*it*) (…ga) shi-tái desu (…が)したいです, (… o) shi-tagarimásu (…を)したがります; *~s to have* (*it*) *done* (*by…*) (…ni) … o shi-te morai-tái desu (…に)…をしてもらいたいです **3.** → **need, poverty**; **does as one wants** *v* katte ni shimásu 勝手にします

wanted criminal *n* shimei-tehai(nin) 指名手配(人)

war *n* sensō 戦争, rán 乱; *after/since the ~* sengo (no) 戦後(の); (*after*) *the end of the ~* shūsen (-go) 終戦(後); *before the ~* senzen (no) 戦前(の); **a great war** taisen 大戦; *World ~ II* Dái ní-ji Sekai-Táisen 第二次世界大戦

ward *n* (*city district*) kú 区, …-ku …区

wardrobe *n* yōfuku dansu 洋服箪笥・洋服だんす, ishō dansu 衣装箪笥・衣装だんす

ware *n* saiku 細工; (*ceramic ware*) tō´ki 陶器, setomono 瀬戸物, …-yaki …焼き

warehouse *n* sō´ko 倉庫, kurá 倉

warlike *adj* kōsen-teki (na) 好戦的(な)

warm **1.** *v ~s it up v* atatamemásu あたため[温め・暖め]ます, nesshimásu 熱します; *~s the rice wine* (o-)kán o tsukemásu/shimásu (お)燗をつけます/します **2.** *v ~s up* atatamárimásu あたたまり[温まり・暖まり]ます **3.** *adj* atatakai/attakai あたたかい/あったかい・(*not cool*) 暖かい・(*not cold*) 温かい; (*lukewarm liquids*) nurúi ぬるい; (*dedicated*) nessin (na) 熱心(な)

warmhearted *adj* kokoró ga atatakái 心が温かい, atsui 厚い・篤い

warmth *n* (*heat*) átsu-sa 熱さ・暑さ

warn *v* keikoku shimásu 警告します, chūi shimásu 注意します

warning *n* keikoku 警告; (*alert*) keihō 警報; (*notice*) kotowárí 断

り; warning label *n* keikoku hyōji 警告表示, keikoku raberu 警告ラベル

warp **1.** *n* sorí そり・反り **2.** *v* (*it ~s*) sorimásu そり[反り]ます; (*~s it*) sorashimásu そらし[反らし]ます, yugamemásu 歪め[ゆがめ]ます **3.** ***gets warped*** *v* (*distorted*) yugamimásu 歪み[ゆがみ]ます; (*crooked*) kuruimásu 狂います **4.** *n* (*vertical threads*) tate-ito たて糸・縦糸

warranty *n* hoshō(-sho) 保証(書)

warrior *n* **1.** senshi 戦士 **2.** (*Japanese*) samurai 侍・サムライ, búshi 武士・ぶし

warship *n* gunkan 軍艦

wartime *n* sénji(chū) 戦時(中), sensō no toki 戦争の時・とき

was *v* … déshita (… dátta) … でした; arimáshita ありました; imáshita いました → **is**

wash **1.** *v* araimásu 洗います; (*launders*) sentaku shimásu 洗濯します **2.** *n* ***the wash(ing)*** *n* sentaku 洗濯, sentaku-mono 洗濯物; wash basin *n* senmén-ki 洗面器; wash tub *n* sentaku tarai 洗濯たらい

washcloth *n* (*hand towel*) te-nugui 手拭い, (*dishcloth*) fukín ふきん・布巾

washer *n* (*washing machine*) sentákú-ki 洗濯機

washing machine → **washer**

Washington *n* Washínton ワシントン

washout *n* **1.** (*big mistake*) daishippai 大失敗 **2.** (*a failure*) shippai-sha 失敗者

washroom *n* (o-)teárai (お)手洗い, senmen-jo 洗面所

washstand *n* senmen dai 洗面台

wasn't *v*… ja/dewa arimasén deshita … じゃ/ではありませんでした; arimasén deshita ありませんでした; imasén deshita いませんでした → **isn't**

wasp *n* hachi 蜂・ハチ, suzumebachi 雀蜂・スズメバチ

waste **1.** *n* (*trash*) kúzu 屑・くず, kuzu-mono 屑物・くず物; (*extravagance*) mudazukai 無駄遣い, rōhi 浪費 **2.** *v* (*~s it*) muda ni shimásu 無駄にします; (*is extravagant with*) muda-zúkai shimásu 無駄使いします, rōhi shimásu 浪費します **3.** ***falls to ~*** aremásu 荒れます; waste away *v* shōmō shimásu 消耗します; waste of effort *n* mudabone 無駄骨, torō´ 徒労; waste of talent *n* takara no mochigusare 宝の持ち腐れ; waste of time *n* jikan no muda 時間の無駄・むだ; What a waste! *interj* Mottainai! もったいない!

wasteful *adj* mottai-nái もったいない, muda (na) 無駄・むだ(な)

watch **1.** *n* (*timepiece*) tokei 時計 **2.** *v* (*looks at/after*) mimásu 見ます・観ます・みます; (*guards it*) … no bán o shimásu … の番をします **3.** *v* (*observes*) kansatsu shimásu 観察します; night watch (man) yakei (-in) 夜警(員), yakan keibiin 夜間警備員, yo-máwari 夜回り・夜まわり; watch for neraimásu 狙います・ねらいます; ~ *a chance* kikái o ukagaimásu 機会を窺い[うかがい]ます; watch out for (*guards against*) keikai shimásu 警戒します; Watch out! Abunai! 危ない・あぶない!

watcher *n* (*nurse*) kango-nin 看護人; (*observer*) kansatsu-sha 観察者; (*researcher*) kenkyū-sha 研究者; fire-watcher *n* kasai keibiin 火災警備員

watchful; *keeps a ~ eye* (*on the situation*) (jōkyō o) ukagaimásu (状況・情況を)窺い[うかがい]ます

watchman *n* bannín 番人, keibiin 警備員; (*gatekeeper*) mónban 門番 → **night watch(man)**

water *n* mizu 水; ***hot*** ~ o-yu お湯, yú 湯 ; ***drinking*** ~ nomí-mizu 飲み水, o-híya お冷や・おひや; water gate *n* suimon 水門; waterfall *n* taki 滝・たき; waterfront *n* kashi 河岸; watering hole *n* mizu tamari 水溜り・水たまり; water level *n* suii 水位; suijun 水準; water power *n* suiryoku 水力; ~ ***plant*** suiryoku hatsudensho 水力発電所; waterproof *adj* bōsui (no) 防水(の); water service → **waterworks**; water-skiing *n* suijō sukii 水上スキー; waterworks *n* suidō 水道; ~ ***Bureau*** suidō´-kyoku 水道局; ***turn on the*** ~ namida o nagasu 涙を流す (= *to cry, in order to get sympathy*); waterwheel *n* suisha 水車

watchmaker *n* tokei-ya 時計屋

watermelon *n* suika すいか・スイカ・西瓜

wattage *n* watto-ryō ワット量

wave 1. *n* namí 波 **2.** *n* (*permanent*) páma パーマ **3.** *v* (*~s a hand*) té o furimásu 手を振ります

waver *n* yure 揺れ

wax *n* (*bee ~*) mitsurō みつろう・ミツロウ・蜜蝋, rō´ ろう・ロウ・蝋

waxwork *n* rō-zaiku 蝋細工・ろう細工, rō´ ningyō 蝋人形・ろう人形

way *n* michi 道; (*method*) shi-kata 仕方, shi-yō 仕様, yari-kata やり方; (*means*) shúdan 手段; (*manner*) tō´ri 通り, (*fashion*) fū´ 風, (*trick*) téguchi 手口; any way *adv* nanraka no hōhō (de) 何らか[なんらか]の方法で; all the way *adv* (*from far*) harubaru はるばる, tōi tokoro 遠いところ; by way of ... → **via**; by the way *adv*, *conj* ① (*incidentally*) sore wa sō´ to それはそうと, tokoróde ところで, chinami ni ちなみに, tsuide ni ついでに, tokí ni 時に ② *adv* (*way of*) ... o tō´tte ... を通って; (*via*) ... keiyu (de/no) ... 経由(で/の); get in the way *v* (o-)jama ni narimásu (お)じゃま[邪魔]になります, (o-)jama o shimásu (お)じゃま[邪魔]をします; get out of the way dokimásu̲ どきます・退きます, nokimásu̲ のきます・退きます; give way *v* yuzurimásu̲ 譲ります・ゆずります; make way *v* (*goes forward*) zenshin shimásu̲ 前進します; No way! → **no**; on the way tochū (de) 途中(で); way above... *adj* ...o haruka ni koeta ...をはるかに超えた; way ahead *adv* zutto saki (ni) ずっと先(に); way back *adv* (*before*) zutto máe (ni) ずっと前(に), zutto izen (ni) ずっと以前(に), zutto mukashi (ni) ずっと昔(に)

wayside *n* michibata 道端; robō 路傍; gaitō 街頭

we *pron* watáshí-táchi わたしたち・私達, jibun-tachi 自分たち・自分達, [INFORMAL] uchira うちら, [BOOKISH] watakus̲hí-tachi わたくしたち・私達; ware-ware われわれ・我々

weak *adj* **1.** yowái 弱い・よわい; fú-jiyū (na) 不自由(な); (*coffee, etc.*) usui 薄い・うすい **2.** *grows* ~ otoroemásu̲ 衰えます・おとろえます

weak point *n* (*shortcoming*) tánsho 短所; (*weakness*) yowami 弱み・よわみ; jakuten 弱点; yowai tokoro 弱いところ

wealth *n* tómi 富, zaisan 財産, zái 財

wealthy → **rich**

weapon *n* heiki 兵器; buki 武器; kyōki 凶器

wear 1. *n* fuku 服; irui 衣類 **2.** *v* (*on body*) kiteimásu̲ 着ています; (*pants, footwear*) haiteimásu̲ はいています・履いています, (*hat, headwear*) kabutteimásu̲ かぶっています・被っています, (*a pin, ornament, etc.*) ts̲uketeimásu̲ 付けています, (*necktie, belt*) shimeteimásu̲ 締めています, (*on hands, fingers*) hameteimásu̲ はめています

weary 1. *adj* → **tired 2.** *v* ***wearies*** (*of…*) (*be sick of*) (… ni) akimásu̲ (…に)飽きます

weather *n* ténki 天気 (o-ténki お天気); ki̲shō 気象; hiyori 日和

weave *v* orimásu̲ 織ります・おります

weaver *n* (*person*) orite 織り手, (*machine*) hataori 機織り; the Festival of the Weaver Star Tanabata 七夕・たなばた (*7 July*)

web 1. → *n* kúmo no su/ito クもの巣/系 **2.** → **Internet**

wedding *n* kekkon 結婚, wedingu ウェディング, (*ceremony*) kekkón-shi̲ki 結婚式; wedding invitation *n* kekkonshiki (no) shōkai-jō 結婚式(の)紹介状

Wednesday *n* Suiyō´bi 水曜日, Suiyō´ 水曜

weed *n* ku̲sá 草・くさ, zassō 雑草

week *n* shūkan 週間; shū´ 週, …-shū …週; week after next *n, adv* saraishū 再来週; week before last *n, adv* sensén-shū 先々週

weekend *n, adv* shūmatsu 週末

weep *v* nakimásu̲ 泣きます; (*laments*) nagekimásu̲ 嘆きます

・なげきます

weigh **1.** *v it ~s* … (…) no omosa ga … arimásu (…の)重さが…あります **2.** *v ~s it* (…no) omosa o hakarimásu (…の)重さを量ります・おもさをはかります **3.** *n* omosa 重さ, mekata 目方, jūryō 重量; (*of body*) taijū 体重; (*object*) omoshi 重し・おもし

weight/weighing scales *n* hakarí はかり・秤・ハカリ

weird *adj* ayashii 怪しい・あやしい, fushigi (na) 不思議・ふしぎ(な), sugói すごい・凄い; (*feeling*) kimí ga warúi 気味が悪い

welcome **1.** *n* (*greeting*) mukae 迎え・むかえ, kangei 歓迎 **2.** *adj* (*it is ~*) nozomashii 望ましい, arigatái ありがたい・有り難い **3.** *v* (*~s one*) … o mukaemásu … を迎えます・をむかえます, … o de-mukaemásu …を出迎えます・をでむかえます; Welcome! *interj* Yóku irasshaimáshita! よくいらっしゃいました!; Yō´koso! ようこそ!; Irasshaimáse! いらっしゃいませ！; You're welcome! *interj* Dō´ itashimáshite. どういたしまして.; Welcome back/home! *interj* O-kaeri nasái. お帰りなさい.

welfare *n* fukúshi 福祉; *~ policy* fukushi-séisaku 福祉政策

well **1.** *n* (*for water*) ído 井戸 **2.** *adj* (*good, nice*) yóku よく・良く; (*healthy*) génki (na) 元気(な); (*splendid*) rippa (na/ni) 立派(な/に); *gets ~* naorimásu 治り[直り]ます **3.** *adv* (*come on*) sā´ さあ; *~ now/then* (sore) déwa (それ)では, (sore) jā (それ)じゃあ, jā じゃあ, sáte さて; ē-to ええと; tokoró-de ところで; (*let me think*) sō´desu né そうですね; (*maybe*) mā まあ; very well (*satisfactory*) yoroshii よろしい・宜しい

well-behaved *adj* otonashíi おとなしい・大人しい

well-known *adj* yūmei (na) 有名(な), chomei (na) 著明(な)

well-liked; *is ~* motemásu もてます

west *n* nishi 西, sei-… 西…; (*the west*) seihō 西方, (*the western part*) séibu 西部, (*the Occident*) Séiyō 西洋, (*Europe and America*) O-Bei 欧米; ***Western Japan*** Kánsái 関西

western **1.** *adj* nishi (no) 西(の) **2.** *n* seibu-geki 西部劇

wet **1.** *adj* nureta … ぬれた・濡れた (*moist*) shimetta 湿った, shimeppoi 湿っぽい **2.** *it gets ~ v* nuremásu 濡れます **3.** *makes it ~ v* nurashimásu 濡らします, (*dampens it*) shimeshimásu 湿します

whale *n* kujira くじら・クジラ・鯨

wharf *n* hato-ba 波止場

what *pron* náni 何・なに [nán 何 *before* t, d, n]; nán no … 何の…, náni-… 何… [*before any sound*]; (*which*) dóno … どの…; (*in what way*) dō´ どう; what … (*one/fact that*) … (no) monó/

kotó… (の)物/事, …no …の; what color nani-iro 何色, dónna iró どんな色; what day (*of the week*) nan-yō´bi 何曜日; (*of the month*) nán-nichi 何日; whatever nan demo 何でも・なんでも; **what kind of** dono yō´na どのよう[様]な, dō´yū どうゆう, dónna どんな; what language nani-go 何語; what month nán-gatsu 何月; what part ① (*where*) dóko どこ ② (*thing*) dono bubun どの部分; what place dóko どこ; dóchira どちら, dótchi どっち; what sort of → **what kind of**; what time nán-ji 何時; what year nán-nen 何年

wheat *n* komúgi 小麦・コムギ; múgi 麦・ムギ

wheedle *v* tarashi-komimás<u>u</u> たらし込みます

wheel *n* wá 輪, sharin 車輪, hoiiru ホイール; (*steering ~*) handoru ハンドル

wheelchair *n* kuruma isu 車椅子・車いす

when *pron* ítsu いつ; about when itsugoro いつ頃・いつごろ; since when ítsu kara いつから; until when ítsu made いつまで; by when ítsu made ni いつまでに

when ... *adv* (*the time that …*) … (no) tókí… (の)時; (*where upon*) … (suru) to … (する)と, (sh<u>i</u>)-tára … (し)たら, … (sh<u>i</u>)-ta tókí… (し)た時; (*and then*) (shi)-te (し)て, (shi)-tékara (し)てから, (shi)-te sore kara (し)てそれから; (*on the occasion of*) … ni sái-sh<u>i</u>te …に際して

where *pron* dóko どこ; [DEFERENTIAL] dóchira どちら

where ... *adv* (*the place that …*) … (no) tokoró… (の)所; (*and there*) …-te soko (de/ni) …てそこ(で/に)

whereabouts *n* shozai 所在

whereupon 1. *adv* → **when ... 2.** … tokoró ga …ところが

whether *conj* … ka dō´ka …かどうか

which *pron* **1.** (*of two*) dóchira/dótchi no … どちら/どっちの… (*or* … no dóchira/dótchi… のどちら/どっち); (*of more than two*) dóno … どの… (*or* … no dóre …のどれ); which damn (*one*) dóitsu どいつ

which ... 1. → **that ... 2.** (*and that*) (soshite) sore (ga/wa) (そして)それ(が/は)

while ... *conj* (no) aida … (の)間; … (shi)-nagara …(し)ながら; ...-chu (ni) ...中(に); (for) a while *n* shibáraku しばらく; a little while ago sak<u>i</u>hodo 先程, sákki さっき

whip *n, v* múchi (de uchimás<u>u</u>) むち[鞭](で打ちます)

whirlpool *n* uzú-maki 渦巻き・うずまき, úzu 渦・うず

whisky *n* uís<u>ú</u>kíi ウイスキー, wís<u>u</u>kii ウィスキー

whisper 1. *n* (*a ~*) kogoe 小声, sasayaki ささやき・囁き **2.** *v* (*~s it*) sasayakimás<u>u</u> ささやき

[囁き]ます, mimiuchi shimásu 耳打ちします

whistle *n* fue 笛; (*v*) (*with lips*) kuchibue (o fukimásu) 口笛(を吹きます); (*steam*) kiteki 汽笛

white *adj* shirói 白い; shíro (no) 白(の); howáito (no) ホワイト(の); ***snow*** ~ masshíro (na) 真っ白(な); ***the ~ of an egg*** shírómi 白身

who *pron* dáre 誰; [DEFERENTIAL] dónata どなた, dóchira (sama) どちら(様)

who ... 1. → **that ...** 2. (*and he/she/they*) ... (soshite) sonó-hito ga/wa ...(そして)その人が/は

whole *adj* zentai (no) 全体(の); zén(-) ... 全...; ***the ~ thing*** (*all of it*) zénbu 全部; **one's whole life** isshō 一生

wholesale *adj* óroshí (de) 卸し(で); ***selling*** ~ oroshi-uri 卸し売り

wholly *adv* zentai (teki) ni 全体(的)に

whore *n* baishun-fu 売春婦, jorō´ 女郎 → **prostitute**

whose *pron* dáre no 誰の

whose ... 1. → **that ...** 2. (*and his/her/their*) ... (soshite) sonó-hito no ...(そして)その人の

why *adv* dō´shite どうして, náze なぜ, dō´ どう; ***that's*** ~ dákara (sá) だから(さ)

wicket *n* kído 木戸; (*ticket*) kai-satsu-guchi 改札口; (*window*) madó-guchi 窓口, ...-guchi ...口

wide 1. *adj* (haba ga) hirói (幅が) 広い 2. *adj* hiroku 広く; ***widely*** *adv* hiroku 広く

widow *n* mibō´-jin 未亡人, yamome やもめ, goke(-san) 後家(さん)

widower *n* otoko-yámome 男やもめ

width *n* hírosa 広さ, haba 幅; yoko 横; yoko haba 横幅

wife *n* (*your/his wife*) óku-san/-sama 奥さん/様, fujin 夫人; (*my wife*) kánai 家内, sái/tsúma 妻, nyō´bo/nyō´bō 女房; wáifu ワイフ

wild *adj* 1. wairudo ワイルド; (*disorderly*) ranbō (na) 乱暴(な); (*rough*) arai 荒い; (*roughneck*) abare-mono 暴れ者; (*not cultivated*) yasei no 野性の 2. ***gets*** ~ aremásu 荒れます

wildlife *n* yasei dōbutsu 野生動物, yasei seibutsu 野生生物

wild person *n* abare-mono 暴れ者・あばれ者

will *n* (*intention*) íshi 意志, omói 思い; (*testament*) yuigon 遺言; **will be ...** ... désu ...です; **will do** shimásu します

win *v* (*game/war*) ... ni kachimásu ...に勝ちます; (*prize*) jushō shimásu 受賞します, ... o (kachi) torimásu ...を(勝ち)取ります → **victory**

wind 1. *v* magarimásu 曲がります 2. *v* ***~s it*** (*around/up*) makimásu 巻きます; (*reels*) kurimásu 繰ります 3. *n* (*breeze*) kaze 風; ***seasonal*** ~ 季節風; ***strong*** (*heavy*) ~ 強風; **wind up** (*concludes it*) shimemásu 締めます, keri o

tsukemásu けりをつけます; against the wind sakaraimásu 逆らいます
windbreaker *n* (*jacket*) uindo-burēkā ウインドブレーカー, jánpā ジャンパー
window *n* mádo 窓; (*opening, wicket*) madó-guchi 窓口; ***transom*** ~ ranma 欄間
windshield wiper *n* waípā ワイパー
windy *adj* kaze ga tsuyói 風が強い
wine *n* **1.** wáin ワイン, budō´shu ぶどう[葡萄・ブドウ]酒 **2.** → **rice wine, saké**
wing *n* (*of bird or plane*) tsubasa 翼・つばさ; (*of insect*) hane 羽・羽根・翅; (*of door/gate*) tobira 扉・とびら
wink *n* ma-bátaki まばたき・瞬き, uínku/wínku (shimásu) ウインク/ウィンク(します)
winner *n* (*victor*) shōrí-sha 勝利者, yūshō-sha 優勝者; (*awardee*) jushō´sha 受賞者
winter *n* fuyú 冬; ~ ***solstice*** tōji 冬至; winter vacation *n* fuyu yasumi 冬休み, [BOOKISH] tōki kyūka 冬期休暇
wipe *v* fukimásu 拭きます・ふきます; ~ ***away*** nuguimásu 拭います・ぬぐいます
wire *n* harigane 針金・はりがね, (*electric*) densen 電線, (*telephone line*) denwa-sen 電話線 → **telegram**
wisdom *n* chié 知恵・ちえ
wise *adj* kashikói 賢い・かしこい, kenmei (na) 賢明(な)
wish *n* (o-)negai (お)願い, kibō 希望; my best wishes to ... (*please send*) ...ni (dō´zo) yoroshiku ...に(どうぞ)よろしく[宜しく]; wish for ... ga hoshíi desu ...が欲しいです; wish that ... (it does) (shi)-tára íi desu (ga) (し)たらいいです(が); wish to do (shi)-tái desu (し)たいです; wish to have it done (shi)-te morai-tái desu (し)てもらいたいです
wit *n* yū´moa ユーモア, kichi 機知, witto ウィット; to wit sunáwachi すなわち・即ち
with *prep* ... to ...と, to issho ni ... と一緒に; (*by using*) ... de ... で; (*with ... attached/included*) ... ga tsúita ...が付いた, ...-tsuki (no) ...付き(の); ~ ***bath*** furo/basu-tsuki (no) 風呂/バス付き(の); ~ ***difficulty*** yatto やっと; ~ ***forethought*** mitōshite 見通して; ~ ***great delight*** ō-yórokobi de 大喜びで; ~ ***meals*** (*included*) shoku (ji)-tsuki (no) 食(事)付き(の); with respect to ... ni kákete wa ... にかけては; ... ni kán-shite ... に関して
withdraw *v* **1.** (*pulls out*) hiki-agemásu 引き上げます, hiki-torimásu 引き取ります **2.** (*takes out money*) (yokin/okane o) oroshimásu (預金/お金を)下ろします; (yokin/okane o) hiki-dashimásu (預金/お金を)引き出します

wither *v* karemás<u>u</u> 枯れます, naemás<u>u</u> 萎え[なえ]ます

within *prep* (...) ínai (...) 以内; ...-nai ...内; ... no náka (de/ni/no) ...の中(で/に/の); *~ (time)* ...-chu (ni) ...中(に); **within the city** shínai 市内; **within the office/company** shánai (no) 社内(の)

without *prep* (*excluding*) ... no hoka ni ...のほか[他・外]に; (*not having*) ... ga nái to ...がないと, ... ga náku (te) ...がなく(て), ... náshi ni ...なしに; (*omitting*) ...-nuki (de/no) ...抜き(で/の); **without exception** (*all*) reigai náku 例外なく, íssái いっさい・一切; **without fail** zé-hi 是非・ぜひ; **without notice/permission** mudan de 無断で

witness *n* (*in court*) shōnin 証人; shōko 証拠

wolf *n* ōˊkami おおかみ・オオカミ・狼 つけ込みます

woman *n* onná 女, onna no h<u>i</u>tó/katá 女の人/方; josei 女性, jóshi 女子; (*lady*) fujin 婦人; okámi おかみ・お内儀

womanizer *n* onna-tárashi 女たらし

wonder 1. *v* odorokimás<u>u</u> 驚きます; ***I ~*** ... ka shira ... かしら, ... ka ne ...かね 2. *n* odoroki 驚き; fushigi 不思議; ***it is no ~ that ...*** ... no mo múri wa arimasén ... のも無理はありません

wonderful *adj* subarashíi すばらしい・素晴らしい, s<u>u</u>teki (na) すてき・素敵(な), sugói すごい・凄い; (*delightful*) ureshíi うれしい・嬉しい; (*wondrous*) f<u>u</u>shigi (na) 不思議(な), myō (na) 妙(な)

won't do *v* shimasén しません; ***it ~*** ikemasén いけません, damé des<u>u</u> だめです

wood *n* kí 木, mokuzai 木材, (*lumber*) zaimoku 材木

wooden *adj* **1.** mokusei no 木製の **2.** muhyōjō no 無表情の; **wooden stairs** *n* hashigo-dan はしご[梯子]段

woods *n* (*forest*) mori 森・もり

wool *n* ūˊru ウール, ke 毛, keito 毛糸, yōmō 羊毛

woolen goods, woolens *n* keorimono 毛織物

word *n* **1.** kotobá 言葉・ことば, tango 単語; ...-go ...語; (*one's words/speech*) k<u>u</u>chi 口; (*written characters*) jí 字; (*compound ~*) jukugo 熟語 **2.** (*news*) táyori 便り・たより, shōsoku 消息; **in other words** *adv* sunáwachi すなわち・即ち, iikaeruto 言い換えると

work **1.** *n* hataraki 働き・はたらき; (*job*) (o-)shígoto (お)仕事; (*operations*) ságyō 作業; ***place of ~*** kinmú-saki 勤務先; shoku-ba 職場; ***construction ~*** kōˊji 工事; ***~ in progress*** kōji-chū 工事中 **2.** *n a ~* (*of literature or art*) sak<u>u</u>hin 作品 **3.** *n* (*workmanship*) saiku 細工 **4.** *v* (*does ~*) shigoto o shimás<u>u</u> 仕事をします; (*labors*) hatarakimás<u>u</u> 働きます;

kínmu shimásu 勤務します; (*is employed at/by*) … ni tsutómete imásu …に勤めています; (*hires oneself out for pay*) kasegimásu 稼ぎます; ~ *as* (*a* …) (… o) tsutomemásu (…を)務めます **5.** *v* (*it ~s*) (*is effective*) kikimásu 効きます **6.** *v* → **study**

workaholic *n* wākahorikku ワーカホリック; hataraki-sugi (no hito) はたらきすぎ・働き過ぎ(の人); shigoto chūdoku(-sha) 仕事中毒(者)

worker *n* (*laborer*) hiyatoi 日雇い; rodo-sha 労働者; (*workman*) koin 工員, shokko 職工; (*employee, staff*) shain 社員, shokuin 職員

working *n* hataraki 働き; (*duty, job*) (o-)tsutome (お)勤め; (*operating*) unten 運転, ságyō 作業; ~ ***hours*** sagyō-jíkan 作業時間, kinmu-jíkan 勤務時間

world *n* sékái 世界; (*at large*) yo (no naka) 世(の中)・よのなか, (*people*) séken 世間; ~ ***war*** sekai-táisen 世界大戦

World Cup *n* Wārudo kappu ワールドカップ

worldwide *adj* sekai-teki (na) 世界的(な), sekai-jū 世界中

worm *n* mushi 虫・ムシ

worry **1.** *n* shinpai 心配・しんぱい, ki-zúkái 気遣い・気づかい, wa-zurai 煩い・わずらい **2.** ***worries*** (*about* …) *v* (… o) shinpai shimásu (…を)心配します, wazuraimásu 煩い[わずらい]ます; ki-zukaimásu 気遣います・気づかいます; kokoró o itame-másu 心を痛めます; ***Don't ~ about it.*** Goshinpai náku. ご心配なく・ごしんぱいなく, Shinpai shinaide (kudasai). 心配・しんぱいしないで(ください).

worse *adj, adv* mótto warúi もっと悪い; otorimásu 劣ります・おとります; ***is no ~ off even if …*** …-témo motomoto désu …てももともと[元々]です; ***grow ~*** akka shimásu 悪化します

worsen *v* (*illness gets worse*) kojiremásu こじれます; akka shimásu 悪化します

worship **1.** *n* sūhai 崇拝, (*service*) raihai 礼拝 **2.** *v* ogamimásu 拝みます

worst *adj* ichiban warúi 一番悪い; saiaku (no) 最悪(の); (*lowest*) saitei (no) 最低(の)

worth → **value**

worthless *adj* tsumaránai つまらない, yákuza (na) やくざ(な)

would → **perhaps**

would like → **want, wish**

wound **1.** *n* (*injury*) kizu 傷, kegá けが・怪我 **2.** *v* (*gets wounded*) kizu-tsukimásu 傷付きます, yararemásu やられます; (*injures*) kizu-tsukemásu 傷付けます

Wow! *interj* wā! わあ!

wrap *v* tsutsumimásu 包みます, hōsō shimásu 包装します; (*something around it*) makimásu

巻きます

wrapper *n* (*traditional cloth*) furoshi̲ki ふろしき・風呂敷; (*package paper*) hōsōshi 包装紙

wreath *n* (*lei*) hanawa 花輪; ~ ***shell*** sázae さざえ・サザエ・栄螺

wreck **1.** *n* (*accident*) jíko 事故, (*collision*) shōtotsu 衝突; (*ship* ~) nanpa 難破, sōnan 遭難; (*train* ~) ressha-jíko 列車事故, sōnan 遭難; (*the wreckage*) zangai 残骸 **2.** *v* (*ruins it*) kowashimásu̲ 壊します; ***~s a car*** kuruma o kowashimásu̲ 車を壊します

wrestler *n* ***sumo*** ~ sumō´-tóri 相撲取り, o-sumō-san お相撲さん; (*ranking*) seki-tórí 関取; (*champion*) ō´-zeki 大関; (*grand champion*) yokozuna 横綱

wrestling *n* résuringu レスリング; (*professional*) puro-resu プロレス; (*Japanese*) sumō 相撲・スモウ・すもう; **wrestling tournament** *n* basho 場所; ***grand*** ~ ō-zúmō 大相撲

wretched *adj* nasake-nái 情けない・なさけない

wring (*out*) *v* shiborimásu̲ 絞ります

wrinkle **1.** *n* shiwa しわ・シワ・皺 **2.** *v* (*it ~s*) shiwa ga dekimásu̲ しわ[皺]ができます

wrist *n* té-kubi 手首

write *v* kakimásu̲ 書きます; (*composes*) tsu̲kurimásu̲ 作ります, tsuzurimásu̲ 綴ります・つづります; (*publishes*) arawashimásu̲ 著します

writer *n* sakka 作家, chósha 著者; (*the author*) hi̲ssha 筆者

writing *n* (*written characters*) móji 文字, jí 字; shorui 書類; ***~ a composition/theme*** sakubun 作文

wrong **1.** *adj* (*mistaken*) machigátta 間違った・まちがった, (*is in error*) machigaemásu̲ 間違えます・まちがえます; (*different*) chigatta 違った・ちがった; (*wrongful*) warúi 悪い; (*amiss*) (… no) guai ga warúi (…の)具合が悪い; ***something*** ~ ijō 異常 **2.** *n* (*malfunction*) koshō 故障

wry *adj* shibúi 渋い・しぶい, nigái 苦い・にがい; ***~ face*** shibúi/nigái kao 渋い・しぶい/苦い・にがい顔

X

X *n* (*symbol "wrong"*) bátsu ばつ・バツ, battén ばってん・罰点

x-axis *n* ekkusu jiku X軸

X box *n* ekkusu bokkusu エックスボックス

xenophobia *n* (*hatred of foreign people*) gaikoku-jin girai 外国人嫌い

Xerox *v* kopii shimasu̲ コピーします

Xian *v* shiian 西安・シーアン

Xmas *n* (*Christmas*) kurisumásu̲ クリスマスプレゼント; **Xmas gift** *n* (*Christmas*) kurisumasu̲ purezento クリスマスプレゼント

X-rating *n* seijin muke eiga shitei 成人向き映画指定

X-ray **1.** *n* ekkūsu-sen X線, rentogen (shashin) レントゲン(写真) **2.** *v* ekkūsu-sen (de) kensa shimásu̲ X線(で)検査します, rentogen (shashin) o torimásu̲ レントゲン(写真)を撮ります

yacht *n* **1.** (*sailboat*) yotto ヨット **2.** (*motor cruiser*) kurūzā クルーザー; **luxury yacht** *n* gōka kaisoku-sen 豪華快速船

Yahoo! *n* Yahū (kensaku enjin) ヤフー(検索エンジン)

yak *n* (*animal*) yaku ヤク

yam *n* imó イモ・芋 (o-imo お芋), yamu imo ヤムイモ

Yankee *n* Yankii ヤンキー

yap *v* hoemásu̲ 吠えます・ほえます

yard *n* niwa 庭

yarn *n* ito 糸; (*for knitting*) ke-ito 毛糸・けいと

yawn **1.** *n* akubi あくび[欠伸] **2.** *v* akubi o shimásu̲ あくび[欠伸]をします

yeah *interj* ā ああ; un うん

year *n* toshí 年; nén 年, …-nen …年; ***years old …*** -sai …歳; ***1 ~ old*** hi̲tótsu 一つ・ひとつ, ***10 ~s old*** tō´ 十・とお, ***20 ~s old*** hátachi/nijús-sai 二十歳・はたち; **year after next** *n* sarainen 再来年・さ来年; **year before last** *n* otótoshi おととし・一昨年 issakú-nen 一昨年

year-end *adj* kure (no) 暮れ(の), nenmatsu (no) 年末(の); ***~ party*** bōnén-kai 忘年会; ***~ gift*** (o-)seibo (お)歳暮

yearly **1.** *adj* nén ichido (no) 年一度(の), nen ikkai (no) 年1回(の) **2.** *adv* nen (ni) ichido 年(に)一度, maitoshi 毎年, mainen (no) 毎年(の)

yearn; ***~ for*** akogaremásu あこがれ[憧れ]ます

yeast *n* iisuto イースト

yell *v* wamekimásu̲ わめき[喚き]ます, sakebimásu̲ 叫びます・さけびます → **shout**

yellow **1.** *n* kiiro 黄色 **2.** *adj* kiiroi 黄色い; kiiro (no) 黄色(の)

Yemen Arab Republic *n* Iemen arabu kyōwa-koku イエメン・アラブ共和国

yen *n* én 円, …-en …円; **high value of the yen** *n* en-daka 円高; **low value of the yen** *n* en-yasu 円安; **yen credit** *n* enshakkan 円借款

yes *adv* hái はい, ē´ええ; sō´desu そうです; (*or just say the verb*) ***Yes, I see./Yes, I will (comply).*** Wakarimáshita. わかりました.; Yes and no. *interj* Dochiratomo iemasen. どちらとも言えません., Sā dōdeshō. さあどうでしょう.

yesterday *n, adj, adv* kinō´ (no) きのう・昨日(の)

yet *adv* máda まだ, ***and*** ~ sore démo それでも, shiká-mo しかも → **but**

yew *n* ichii いちい・イチイ・櫟

yield 1. *n* (*product; income*) dekiagari 出来上がり・できあがり 2. *v* (*gives in/up*) yuzurimásu 譲ります 3. *v* (*produces*) sanshutsu shimásu 産出します

YMCA *n* Wai emu shii ei YMCA, Kirisuto-kyō seinen-kai キリスト教青年会

yoga *n* yoga ヨガ

yogurt *n* yōguruto ヨーグルト

Yokohama *n* Yokohama 横浜; ***the port of*** ~ Yokohamá-kō 横浜港

yolk *n* (*of egg*) kimi 黄身・キミ

yonder *adv* achira あちら, atchí あっち

you *pron* anáta あなた, ánta あんた (*but use name, title, or role whenever possible*); sochira (sama) そちら(様); o-taku お宅, o-taku sama お宅様; (*intimate*) kimi 君; (*condescending*) omae お前・おまえ; you all miná-san 皆さん・みなさん, anáta-tachi あなた達[たち], anata-gata あなた方

young 1. *adj* wakái 若い・わかい; ***very*** ~ osanái 幼い・おさない; ~ ***boy*** shōnen 少年, ~ ***girl*** shō´jo 少女; ~ ***novelist*** wakate-sákka 若手作家 2. ***the*** ~ → **youth**

younger *adj* toshi-shita (no) 年下(の); ~ ***brother*** otōtó 弟, (*your*) otōto-san 弟さん; ~ ***sister*** imōtó 妹, (*your*) (o-)imōto-san (お)妹さん

youngest *adj* ichiban wakái 一番若い, (toshi-)shita (no) (年)下(の)

young lady *n* ojō´-san お嬢さん; musume(-san) 娘(さん)

young man *n* seinen 青年

young person → **youth**

youngster *n* (*young person*) wakamono 若者

your(s) *pron* anáta-tachi/anata-gata no mono あなた達[たち]/あなた方の物

yourself, yourselves *pron* anáta-jishin あなた自身

youth *n* 1. (*period in life*) wakasa 若さ・わかさ 2. (*young person*) wakamono 若者・わかもの

youth hostel *n* yūsu-hósuteru ユースホステル

YouTube *n* yūtyūbu ユーチューブ

Z

zany *n* dōke-shi 道化師

zap *v* **1.** (*shoots someone dead*) uchikoroshimásu̲ 撃ち殺します **2.** (*defeats*) (uchi) makashimásu̲ (打ち)負かします **3.** (*deletes*) sakujo shimásu̲ 削除します

zapped **1.** *adj* (*dead tired*) tsukare-hateta 疲れ果てた・つかれはてた **2.** *n* (*vigor*) genki 元気, katsu-ryoku 活力

zapper *n* (*remote control*) rimokon リモコン

zeal *n* (*enthusiasm*) netsui 熱意; netsujō 熱情; nesshin 熱心

zebra *n* shimauma シマウマ・縞馬

Zen *n* (*Buddhism*) Zén 禅

Zen Buddhist *n* Zen sō 禅僧

zero *n* réi 零, zéro ゼロ; (*written symbol*) maru 丸

zest *n* **1.** (*enthusiasm*) netsui 熱意 **2.** (*interest*) tsuyoi kyōmi 強い興味 **3.** (*enjoyment*) yorokobi 喜び

ZIP, zip code *n* yūbinbángō 郵便番号

zipped file *n* jippu-fairu ZIPファイル

zipper *n* chákku チャック, jíppā ジッパー; fásunā ファスナー

zinc *n* aen 亜鉛

zodiac *n* (*horoscope*) jūnikyū-zu 十二宮図

zone *n* chi̲tai 地帯, kúiki 区域; zōn ゾーン; tái 帯, …-tai …帯

zoo *n* dōbutsú-en 動物園

zoology *n* dōbutsú-gaku 動物学

zoom *n* kakudai 拡大, (*camera*) zūmu ズーム; **zoom lens** *n* (*camera*) zūmu-renzu ズームレンズ

zucchini *n* (*vegetable*) zukkīni ズッキーニ

zzz *n*, *interj* gūgū グーグー, ぐうぐう

"Books to Span the East and West"

Tuttle Publishing was founded in 1832 in the small New England town of Rutland, Vermont [USA]. Our core values remain as strong today as they were then—to publish best-in-class books which bring people together one page at a time. In 1948, we established a publishing outpost in Japan—and Tuttle is now a leader in publishing English-language books about the arts, languages and cultures of Asia. The world has become a much smaller place today and Asia's economic and cultural influence has grown. Yet the need for meaningful dialogue and information about this diverse region has never been greater. Over the past seven decades, Tuttle has published thousands of books on subjects ranging from martial arts and paper crafts to language learning and literature—and our talented authors, illustrators, designers and photographers have won many prestigious awards. We welcome you to explore the wealth of information available on Asia at **www.tuttlepublishing.com**.